"Following the exposition of biblical theology in the first two volumes of *The Whole Counsel of God*, Dr. Gamble's third volume surveys Christian thought from the classical Greek period to the present day. This important volume accomplishes three major feats. First, the author's study of historical theology and philosophy will serve as a masterful encyclopedic reference work on thinkers from Aristotle to Zwingli and beyond. Second, throughout the book, his interfacing of the traditional loci of systematic theology at various junctures reflecting the time period just studied is ingenious and immensely helpful. And third, his treatment of modern and postmodern thought provides a valuable foundation for philosophical apologetics. For me, this volume is the capstone of the three-volume set and is worth the price of the set all by itself."
—**Joel R. Beeke**, President, Puritan Reformed Theological Seminary

"*The Whole Counsel of God: God's People in the Western World* is a remarkable achievement. Gamble's volume is sweeping, interesting, and, at times, quirky, not unlike the orthodox Protestantism he describes so well. Whether you are an insider or an outsider looking in, Gamble is the place to turn for a serious and accessible account of that tradition."
—**Stephen D. Crocco**, Divinity Librarian, Yale Divinity School

"This volume brings Richard C. Gamble's ambitious integrative theological project—biblical, systematic, and historical—to completion. The coverage is remarkably comprehensive, the judgments careful and well-informed. Seminary students in particular will be well served by a careful reading of this entire project."
—**William B. Evans**, Younts Professor of Bible and Religion, Erskine College

"Dr. Gamble's survey of the development of Latin Christianity will be of great value in college and seminary classes. It completes an ambitious and unique project, providing a synthesis of biblical theology, systematic theology, and church history; it should provide an excellent basis for further detailed study."
—**Robert Letham**, Professor of Systematic and Historical Theology, Union School of Theology

"Richard Gamble's massive project reaches its crescendo in this volume. The prior volumes of the *Whole Counsel of God* engaged the biblical theology of the Old and New Testaments. Professor Gamble herein addresses the variegated expressions of theology developed throughout the centuries of Christianity. This conclusion of his remarkable achievement is a substantial and insightful guide to the contours of the leading ideas and significant persons of Christian thought, providing a starting point for students and a valuable resource for scholars of all theological traditions."

—**Peter A. Lillback**, President, Westminster Theological Seminary

"Dr. Gamble's volumes are a gold mine of biblical, theological, historical, and philosophical data, and this third volume is a rich addition to the other two. Any student who will have the advantage of reading and studying this volume will be well equipped and well prepared for Christian engagement with the world of unbelief. I know of no other single source that effectively vacuum-packs such a wealth of useful material, as well as practical insights. I heartily commend this volume to energetic Christian readers; the time needed to work through it will be worth the lifetime of help that it gives to Christians who hope to thoughtfully understand and challenge unbelief in its many forms."

—**K. Scott Oliphint**, Professor of Apologetics, Westminster Theological Seminary

"Gamble completes in this volume his massive undertaking of weaving together biblical, systematic, and historical theology, focusing here on the history and development of the Christian faith and people in the Western world. He combines the insights of many years of teaching in these disciplines with a pastor's heart that renders this volume not only instructive but also edifying. He writes from a transcendental epistemological perspective (Van Tillian) that recognizes the foundational importance of revelation (special and general) for all knowledge. Certainty is located not in our theoretical constructs but in the precepts of Scripture, in which light all our work is to be undertaken. Gamble seeks to faithfully labor in this light, yielding a tome that integrates our understanding of life and doctrine in the

West, in both Christendom and its aftermath, under the comprehensive lordship of Christ."

—**Alan D. Strange,** Professor of Church History, Mid-America Reformed Seminary

The Whole Counsel of God

Volume 3

GOD'S PEOPLE IN THE
WESTERN WORLD

The Whole Counsel of God

Volume 3

GOD'S PEOPLE IN THE
WESTERN WORLD

Richard C. Gamble

P U B L I S H I N G

P.O. BOX 817 • PHILLIPSBURG • NEW JERSEY 08865-0817

Scripture quotations are from the ESV® Bible (The Holy Bible, English Standard Version®), copyright © 2001 by Crossway, a publishing ministry of Good News Publishers. Used by permission. All rights reserved.

Italics within Scripture quotations indicate emphasis added.

Printed in the United States of America

ISBN: 978-1-59638-182-7 (cloth)

Library of Congress Cataloging-in-Publication Data

Gamble, Richard C.
  The whole counsel of God / Richard C. Gamble.
    p. cm.
  Includes bibliographical references and indexes.
  ISBN 978-0-87552-191-6 (cloth volume 1) ISBN 978-1-59638-181-0 (cloth volume 2) ISBN 978-1-59638-182-7 (cloth volume 3)
  1. BibleTheology. 2. Theology, Doctrinal. 3. Reformed ChurchDoctrines. I. Title.
    BS543.G33 2009
    230'.42dc22
                        2009017106

"I taught you the whole counsel of God and delivered it to you."
Samuel Rutherford letter to parishioner, 1637

Soli Deo Gloria

Contents

CONTENTS

Analytical Outline

Foreword

WHEN THE FIRST VOLUME of Professor Richard Gamble's projected trilogy *The Whole Counsel of God* was published in 2009, most readers would have shared my own twofold reaction.

First, and most importantly, it was impossible not to admire and commend the vision that gave birth to the project. The first volume, with its subtitle, *God's Mighty Acts in the Old Testament*, announced a program whose goal was to set forth the fullness of the Christian faith through the carefully crafted lenses of what we might call *trinoculars*.

Trinocular vision (to continue the coinage) views the faith of the church through three lenses: biblical theology, systematic theology, and historical theology. The genius of this perspective is that, in one sense, it is simply the extension of the prayer of the apostle Paul that the church "may have strength to comprehend with all the saints what is the breadth and length and height and depth, and to know the love of Christ that surpasses knowledge, that you may be filled with all the fullness of God" (Eph. 3:18–19). Even if Paul's focus here is on one particular divine attribute, love, the burden of his prayer applies to all the divine attributes, to all the divine acts, and indeed to all that constitutes our theology.

Intuitively it is this massive apostolic prayer-vision that *The Whole Counsel of God* seeks to answer and fulfill, not least because it is a work that has been pursued in the fullest sense "with all the saints." Hence the first two volumes had their foundation in biblical theology and in the unfolding of the biblical account of the progress of revelation in God's mighty acts in history interpreted by his reliable Word.

But Dr. Gamble was not deceived into thinking that biblical theology as an account of the historical progression of revelation is the omega point of the theological enterprise. Indeed, despite the naive and un-self-critical perspectives of some "biblical" theologians, he recognized that as soon as we move from simply describing the progress of revelation from passage to passage and begin *to collate* and *to compare* and *to draw conclusions*, we have shifted gears from the historically descriptive to the normative by that process of internally coherent and logical deduction that is characteristic of system-thinking. In a word, we have already begun to do *systematic* theology.

What takes place in the hands of the systematic theologian, therefore, is but a development of the process already present in the work of the biblical theologian. The systematician simply extends the process a stage further. He seeks to utilize this biblical theology in a way that is sensitive to it and at the same time completes its trajectory by viewing the whole from the perspective of the completed canon of Scripture. The result is an exposition of the biblical message *as a whole*, in a logical and often topical fashion, and with an eye to communicating this message to the contemporary world. The responsibility to do this is already implicit in the Great Commission of Matthew 28:18–20. That commission, given originally and directly to only eleven men, in itself necessitated both the writing of the New Testament (otherwise, how could eleven men reach all men and women?) and its translation into the languages of the nations (otherwise, how could the message be understood?). But it also necessitated the further task of interpreting and communicating the unchanging gospel to what Tate and Brady called "all the changing scenes of life." Only thus could the theology speak into the life situations of men and women and societies in different times and places.

If one thing is obvious, it is the demands that this task makes on the learning and intellectual facility of anyone who attempts the project. A theologian may have his areas of specialization, but the discipline of systematic theology as a whole calls for the generalist rather than the specialist. The breadth of learning required to expound one topic in a biblical-theological-systematic fashion is considerable; the ability to do this over the entire range of topics in the dogmatic encyclopedia is exceptional.

In volumes 1 and 2 of *The Whole Counsel of God*, Rick Gamble impressively pursued and fulfilled this goal. In and of itself, this would have earned him more plaudits than most of us might dream of amassing in a lifetime. But now in volume 3, as was promised from the beginning, he has gone a third mile.

To "comprehend with all the saints" means doing theology in concert with the church from Adam to the apostle John, from Genesis 1 through Revelation 22. But it also means engaging with the way in which the church of God has received the "*whole* counsel of God." In *written form*, that *whole* has been available to all the saints only since the ink dried on the final benediction of Revelation 22:21. And so to the exposition of biblical theology and the formulation of systematic theology in volumes 1 and 2, Dr. Gamble now comes in this culminating volume to an exposition of historical theology. He thus builds into his project the three lenses—biblical, systematic, historical—that help us to reflect on and to grasp "the breadth and length and height and depth" of the *whole* of "the whole counsel of God." In doing so, he alerts us to the enormous benefits that contemporary Christians have received from two thousand years of reflection on the revelation given to us in Scripture.

A knowledge of the history of theology is a major weakness of, but a great desideratum for, life in the contemporary church. George Santayana's aphorism is perhaps truer of the church today than at any other time since the Reformation, that "those who cannot remember the past are condemned to repeat it"—and, alas, especially its mistakes and missteps. This applies to both our theology and our practice, not least because the two are ultimately inseparable. This third volume, therefore, is not only a wonderful survey of the development of doctrine and the history of theology and theologians, but a work of enormous pastoral and practical usefulness as well as of strictly historical and theological value.

But I mentioned earlier a *twofold* reaction to the original announcement of this trilogy. If the first was *admiration*, the second came in the form of a question mark! Would Dr. Gamble have the fortitude, the perseverance, and the mental and physical energy to complete such a monumental project? One can only assume that the publishers were so keen to publish it that they refrained from asking, "Are you sure that you will live long enough to complete such a prodigious piece of work?" The compilation of the immense bibliography at the end of this volume alone must have constituted a daunting task; how much more the almost one thousand pages and nearly 500,000 words that precede it. One only has to reflect momentarily on the time and effort required to read these volumes, far less research, think through, write, reread, check, and then proofread them, to realize what an achievement in diligence *The Whole Counsel of God* represents.

Now that the trilogy has reached the stage of a foreword being written for it, perhaps one may also be allowed a moment of personal privilege. My friendship with Rick Gamble began in the early 1980s, when we were young colleagues together at Westminster Theological Seminary in Philadelphia. The publication now of his magnum opus reminds me of some words that issued from another friendship forged at the same seminary fifty years earlier. In writing his editorial preface to Professor John Murray's commentary *The Epistle to the Romans*, Ned B. Stonehouse wrote of his "sense of elation" at the publication of his colleague's work and his "enthusiastic appraisal of the author . . . as well as a warm affection for him personally." He also noted, "A measure of restraint must be observed, however, considering especially my intimate relationships with the author over a period of nearly thirty-five years."

I echo these sentiments and hope I act as the mouthpiece for many in expressing a deep sense of gratitude to the author for producing this library of theological learning. It is bound to stimulate, instruct, and challenge a whole range of readers—from Christians who are simply seeking to grow in their understanding of the faith to students and scholars seeking to further hone their theology. And with this sense of gratitude there is a corresponding thankfulness to God for giving Rick Gamble the strength and perseverance that have surely been needed to carry the burden and fulfill the vision that first launched *The Whole Counsel of God*.

Sinclair B. Ferguson
Chancellor's Professor of Systematic Theology
Reformed Theological Seminary

Acknowledgments

JOHN HUGHES AND HIS editors have been very helpful drawing together and working through volumes two and three. Thanks to Hilary Gamble for her cheerful assistance with the bibliography. Much gratitude to Drew Gordon for reading parts of the manuscript. Thanks to teaching assistants Brian Wright, Venketesh Gopalakrishnan, Joseph Dunlap, and Johnathan Kruis. Jack Smith supplied invaluable editorial help. The biggest thanks are extended to my daughter Dr. Whitney Gamble, who read the entire manuscript and made innumerable improvements to it. I am very pleased to say that Whitney Gamble and Jack Smith have now become Whitney and Jack Gamble-Smith. My beloved wife Janice has always done more than her fair share in keeping the house running and has again served me by a final read through the book.

Introduction to *God's People in the Western World*

VOLUMES 1 AND 2 of this series endeavored to present the pearl of great price—the contents of the written Word of God, where God graciously disclosed himself to sinful men and women. The church has been entrusted with a precious gift in the Scriptures, the whole counsel of God.

This third volume traces the church's handling of this priceless pearl through two thousand years of unfolding history. This volume entertains two major goals. First, the hope is that readers will be confident that they have understood the development of theology in its context since the time of the canon's close. Second, with that knowledge, readers should feel equipped to defend and declare this precious theology in the midst of a hostile world.

To aid in the second goal, part of this volume's task is to demonstrate past ways in which theology declined, thereby resulting in a cry of warning to the church not to tread similar paths. All theologians are sinners living in a particular age and era and as thinkers are influenced by their own culture and context. The mark of an excellent theologian is one who can stand, to the best of his or her ability, above culture and judge that culture's thinking based on a biblical philosophy of reality.[1]

The earliest Christian apologists faced the problem of defending Christianity against external attacks while unconsciously operating under many of the same philosophical presuppositions as their opponents. Sadly, this problem is not limited to the early apologists.[2] "The

---

1. See Richard C. Gamble, *The Whole Counsel of God*, vol. 2, *The Full Revelation of God* (Phillipsburg, NJ: P&R Publishing, 2018) (WCG2), 949–80.

2. Cornelius Van Til, *A Christian Theory of Knowledge* (Nutley, NJ: Presbyterian and Reformed, 1969), 85: "The question for them was how thy could protect the deposit of faith against those who were real heretics while they were themselves so largely controlled in their thinking by false modes of thought."

Christian, as did Tertullian," said Van Til, "must contest the very principles of his opponent's position."[3] Proper Christian apologetics will always endeavor to stand above cultural presuppositions.

Contemporary theologians must develop a standard by which to judge past and present thinkers. The task of the theologian is to ascertain the depths of how the thinking and contributions of past theologians have been influenced by their cultural milieus. Did a theologian attempt to baptize paganism and maneuver it into Christian thought? Theologians are given the responsibility not merely to explain the past but also to weigh it on the scales of biblical fidelity. The church would benefit if Christians would remember that it is proper—even necessary—to make value judgments concerning theological faithfulness to the written Word of God. It is this author's hope that the exercise of moving from one generation to the next in an evaluation of past theology will better equip readers to critique their own culture and, more importantly, to present systematic theology in a fashion that is radically and refreshingly biblical.

Bridge Builders and Burners. Theologian Douglas Kelly implements a helpful model in analyzing theological method as it relates to non-Christian philosophy. He separates thinkers into two categories: *bridge builders*—those who in some measure seek to benefit from non-biblical philosophical models—and *bridge burners*—those who reject such non-biblical models.

While bridge builders of the early church affirmed that pagan philosophy was theologically insufficient, they still recognized glimmers of God's truth within these philosophical systems.[4] The early church still admired the thinking of pagans because they believed that even paganism contained the "seed of reason."

Then there were the bridge burners. These apologists presented Christianity as the only true philosophy—one that was set in deep and abiding competition with Greek thought. They viewed Greek speculative thinking as the chief enemy of Christian belief. The two worldviews stood as opposites. This group included men such as Irenaeus. He

3. Cornelius Van Til, as cited by Greg L. Bahnsen, *Van Til's Apologetic: Readings & Analysis* (Phillipsburg, NJ: P&R Publishing, 1998), 730.

4. Douglas F. Kelly, *Systematic Theology*, vol. 1, *The God Who Is the Holy Trinity* (Fearn, Scotland: Mentor, 2008), 188.

articulated the difference between Greek philosophical theories of the logos and the Christian understanding of the Logos by detailing how the philosophical usage had to be modified in the light of Scripture's teaching.[5] In his famous quotations, "What indeed has Athens to do with Jerusalem?" and "Away with all attempts to produce a mottled Christianity of Stoic, Platonic, and Dialectic composition," Tertullian revealed his identity as a bridge burner.[6]

In continuity with the two previous volumes, this third volume includes a study of apologetics and sections of practical application as an integral component of the whole counsel of God. In reference to application, it is the author's deepest prayer that the reader, after having studied these three volumes, will be better equipped to proclaim the holy Word of God.

Biblical Theme. One of the prominent themes of the Bible involves understanding how God has painted the landscape of his developing kingdom throughout human history. The apostle John was pulled into the heavens and there saw a scroll.[7] The scroll was covered in writing both inside and out, but no one could read it. John wept over this sealed treasure. But the Lion of Judah and Lamb of God took and opened the scroll. In that scroll was the unfolding history of Christ's church.[8] It is the intention of this author that readers realize that the history of Christ's church is their history, and that it is brimming with value and insight.

The proper presentation of history, whether focusing on its intellectual or social aspects, requires a specific set of contents. To comprehend the life and contributions of a past theologian, the student must understand the historical, social, and intellectual context of that theologian's time, in addition to the doctrine that he presents.

5. Douglas F. Kelly, *Systematic Theology*, vol. 2, *The Beauty of Christ—A Trinitarian Vision* (Fearn, Scotland: Mentor, 2014), 206.

6. De praescriptione haereticorum 7, as cited by Kelly, *Systematic Theology*, 1:191.

7. Revelation 5:1–5: "Then I saw in the right hand of him who was seated on the throne a scroll written within and on the back, sealed with seven seals. And I saw a strong angel proclaiming with a loud voice, 'Who is worthy to open the scroll and break its seals?' And no one in heaven or on earth or under the earth was able to open the scroll or to look into it, and I began to weep loudly because no one was found worthy to open the scroll or to look into it. And one of the elders said to me, 'Weep no more; behold, the Lion of the tribe of Judah, the Root of David, has conquered, so that he can open the scroll and its seven seals."

8. Thanks to colleague Dr. David Whitla for this insight. See on this theme his inaugural lecture, "Lord of History," in *RPTJ* 6, no. 2 (Spring 2020): 4–9.

Scope of the Volume. The introduction to the first volume, written now more than a decade ago, noted that all books are written within a specific historical, theological, and biographical context. The trajectory of this author's thinking has remained consistent with those first words all those years ago: this volume is written from the perspective of a Reformed Presbyterian minister. My years of teaching historical and systematic theology have concentrated exclusively on the Western church and her rich tradition; thus this book is limited to this perspective by both providence and necessity. The treatment of the Reformation, Scottish Presbyterianism, and twentieth-century American Presbyterianism will be more thorough than other topics if for no other reason than that these are pivotal and cherished sections of the church's story.

Other Texts. There are a number of reliable one-volume church histories.[9] There are also several dependable one-volume historical theologies.[10] John M. Frame wrote an excellent one-volume history of Western philosophy and theology.[11] In terms of historical method or type, his text is strong in intellectual history. It is the hope of this author that this third volume contains all the content and explanations

---

9. Williston Walker's *A History of the Christian Church* (New York: Scribner's Sons, 1959) is the standard. It was revised and expanded in 1985. A more recent and popular text is Diarmaid MacCulloch's *Christianity: The First Three Thousand Years* (New York: Viking, 2010). MacCulloch's work is written from a nonbelieving standpoint. John D. Woodbridge and Frank A. James III, have penned a biblically faithful two-volume work, *Church History* (Grand Rapids: Zondervan, 2013), complete with a video series.

10. A popular text was Geoffrey W. Bromiley, *Historical Theology: An Introduction* (Grand Rapids: Eerdmans, 1978). Much better is the more recent one by Greg R. Allison, *Historical Theology: An Introduction to Christian Doctrine—A Companion to Wayne Grudem's Systematic Theology* (Grand Rapids: Zondervan, 2011). Wayne Grudem and Gregg Allison determined that Grudem's *Systematic Theology* (Grand Rapids, Zondervan: 1994) needed a companion volume of historical theology to parallel and supplement Grudem's work. Allison relied on abundant primary source quotations, sometimes with his own Latin translations, which was a great plus. While the book contains a helpful glossary of major church leaders, however, many names are simply mentioned in the text without giving context or even birth and death dates so as to relate the name and context of the cited theologian. For example, in the medieval section Allison cites William of Anidanis, John of Turecremata, Gerald of Bologna, William of Waterford, and Thomas Netter Waldensis, but the reader does not know when these men lived, what they did, or why they are worth mentioning. A Heinrich Totting von Oyta is cited, but his name, despite being interesting, does not appear in the glossary or even the index. For some strange reason, Allison's text has only three references to Peter Lombard but mentions countless little-known figures of much less importance.

11. John M. Frame, *A History of Western Philosophy and Theology* (Phillipsburg, NJ: P&R Publishing, 2015) (*HWPT*).

found in church histories and historical theologies but also cradles the narrative in its vibrant historical setting.

Historical theology does not develop in a chronological, cultural, or social vacuum. While primary quotations are helpful, they are insufficient. A proper analysis of the development of doctrine requires a more robust presentation, which is the endeavor of this text. This author's goal consisted in being fair and charitable to the topic at hand, but at times this author could not or did not deem it beneficial to restrain his position in the shadows.[12]

The method of *The Whole Counsel of God* volumes 1–3 reflects in some fashion the method of the great Scottish Free Church systematician James Buchanan of Edinburgh. Buchanan's definitive book *Justification* began analysis with the OT, moved to the NT, then to the ancient church and scholastics, proceeded to the Reformation, the Roman church after the Reformation, and then developed the doctrine to his own day.[13] In many ways, this series has been organized according this work and others like it.

The Whole Counsel of God volume 3 endeavors to provide historical and systematic analysis within the doctrine's historical background. For those preparing for ministerial exams, chapters 3, 7, 10, and 15 summarize historical theology in the patristic, medieval, and Reformational periods. Chapter 23 summarizes modern theology.

---

12. For example, Allison acknowledges that the ancient and medieval churches held to infant baptism—but given his own theological commitments he laments their choice.

13. James Buchanan, *The Doctrine of Justification: An Outline of Its History in the Church and of Its Exposition from Scripture* (1984; repr., Edinburgh: Banner of Truth, 1991). Carl R. Trueman wrote a helpful historical background for that work: "A Tract for the Times: James Buchanan's *The Doctrine of Justification in Historical and Theological Context*," in *The Faith Once Delivered*, ed. Anthony Selvagio (Phillipsburg, NJ: P&R Publishing, 2007), 33–42.

Abbreviations

CCSL 50a	Rita Beyers et al., eds., *Corpus Christianorum: Series Latina*, 226 vols. (Turnhout, Belgium: Brepols, 1953–)
CVT	John M. Frame, *Cornelius Van Til: An Analysis of His Thought* (Phillipsburg, NJ: P&R Publishing, 1995)
ECT	Evangelicals and Catholics Together: The Christian Mission in the Third Millennium
ET	English Translation
HWPT	John M. Frame, *A History of Western Philosophy and Theology* (Phillipsburg, NJ: P&R Publishing, 2015)
Institutes	John Calvin, *Institutes of the Christian Religion*, ed. John T. McNeill, trans. Ford Lewis Battles (Philadelphia: Westminster Press, 1960)
IST	Cornelius Van Til, *Introduction to Systematic Theology*, 2nd ed. (Phillipsburg, NJ: P&R Publishing, 2007)
LCC	Library of Christian Classics
LXX	Septuagint
NIV	New International Version
NT	New Testament
OPC	Orthodox Presbyterian Church
OT	Old Testament
RD	Herman Bavinck, *Reformed Dogmatics*, ed. John Bolt, trans. John Vriend (Grand Rapids: Baker Academic, 2006)
RPTJ	*Reformed Presbyterian Theological Journal*
WCF	Westminster Confession of Faith
WCF	*Westminster Confession of Faith* (Atlanta: Committee for Christian Education and Publications, Presbyterian Church in America, 1986); published together with the Westminster Larger Catechism (WLC), the Westminster Shorter Catechism (WSC), and proof texts

WCG1	Richard C. Gamble, *The Whole Counsel of God*, vol. 1, *God's Mighty Acts in the Old Testament* (Phillipsburg, NJ: P&R Publishing, 2009)
WCG2	Richard C. Gamble, *The Whole Counsel of God*, vol. 2, *The Full Revelation of God* (Phillipsburg, NJ: P&R Publishing, 2018)
WCG3	Richard C. Gamble, *The Whole Counsel of God*, vol. 3, *God's People in the Western World* (Phillipsburg, NJ: P&R Publishing, 2021)
WLC	Westminster Larger Catechism
WSC	Westminster Shorter Catechism
WS–C	Westminster Seminary California
WTJ	*Westminster Theological Journal*

PART 1

The Church under the Cross

⚞ 1 ⚟

Philosophical Backgrounds and Persecution of the Church

AT THE END OF the first century, Christianity was a geographically and numerically limited movement. Yet by the year A.D. 350, it had grown from its small beginnings to constitute more than 50 percent of the population. By the time of Emperor Charlemagne's reign in the eighth century, Christianity permeated Western Europe.

Early Christian thought did not develop in a vacuum. Two cultural phenomena in particular heavily shaped and informed the church's nascent theology: Greek philosophy and the reality of persecution. Christian thinkers were steeped in Greek thought, so it is impossible to understand their formulation of theology without at least a cursory examination of pagan philosophy. And while the church battled the encroachment of philosophy, she also faced the terror of the sword at the hands of the authorities. This era was one of heresy and persecution, of abdication and corruption; but in the midst of this darkness, Christ was upholding and maturing his bride, the church.

The reader will be rewarded by a careful examination of this chapter because Greek thought was influential throughout the early church period and into the Middle Ages. Even today, various mutations of ancient philosophical ideas permeate our society. As believers, we are called to be able to give an account for our hope to those around us, so there is great value in deeply studying the history of pagan thought to be the most effective we can be in our calling.

Milesian Thinking

General Characteristics of the Group. Philosophy asks questions about who we are, how we got here, and the nature of the world around us. In general, the Milesian thinkers attempted to find an underlying unity amid the great diversity of life. Their search for unity was a quest for understanding the world, a desire to present a cohesive account of the seeming randomness of life. The question of how human beings understand things forces the philosopher to address the problem of "the one and the many." This question is not limited to ancient Greek thinking—it is just as important today. To understand the entire universe, which is "the many," the philosopher reduces the world's complexity to some type of unity, known as "the one." Earliest Greek philosophical thought conceived some type of "beginning principle" to explain that unity. The task of the beginning principle was to provide an explanation of the efficient cause of all things, and from that principle the notion of "time" could begin. The questions that the earliest thinkers asked were important. They wanted to determine what was fundamental to reality, from where that reality arose, and how the universe arrived at its present state.[1]

Milesian thought was exemplified by Thales, Anaximander, and Anaximenes, three philosophers from the Ionian town of Miletus. They believed that the universe consisted of four elements: earth, air, fire, and water. They wanted to find out which of these four was the most basic, the one element that constituted and explained the universe. They accounted for the reality around them based on the assumption of a single, living, corporeal substance or "stuff." The Milesians argued that this stuff of the universe was everlasting. It had no beginning. The world around them—nature—filled all space. Nature itself, in its vast expanse, was the source of all worlds.

The Milesians used the theory of *hylozoism*, from *hylo*, meaning "matter," and *zoism*, meaning "life," to explain the phenomena of motion by arguing that all matter was alive.[2] With this theory, the

---

1. John M. Frame, *A History of Western Philosophy and Theology* (Phillipsburg, NJ: P&R Publishing, 2015) (*HWPT*), 52.

2. Gordon H. Clark, *Thales to Dewey: A History of Philosophy* (Boston: Houghton Mifflin, 1957), 14. For information on hylozoism, see Eduard Zeller, *Outlines of the History of Greek*

4

Milesians began what we term a scientific rather than religious attitude toward all nature. They interpreted the phenomenon of nature as something that had a natural rather than a supernatural cause. In other words, the Milesians were not satisfied with the notion of a god moving the stars in massive chariots.[3]

Thales (624–546 B.C.).[4] Thales was one of the three main philosophers associated with the Milesian school. He was the first person to predict the solar eclipse that occurred in 585 B.C. While such a prediction is a common practice today, it was quite remarkable for his time. Even more important than the actual prediction was the method Thales used to produce this prediction. Long before Thales's time, data had been gathered concerning the stars and various events related to them. What Thales did was to gather those various pieces of information into an organized system and, based on that system, establish the ability to project laws. Some textbooks call the result of Thales's work the birth of philosophy because he reduced the multiplicity of information into a unity.

Thales applied his method of reducing multiplicity into unity not only to the stars but also to everything in life. He asked whether the vast diversity of life could come from one eternal, elemental "stuff." Thales thought that there was, in fact, an elemental stuff. For him, "the one" of "the one and the many" was water. Thales could understand the whole universe through the lens of this one elemental stuff. He was convinced that the earth floats on top of water. To verify that fact, he thought, all one needed to do was dig a well—eventually the digger would find water.[5] For Thales, the air was evaporated water, and the earth was hardened water.[6]

While water may be a naive choice for the one unifying principle, that choice is understandable based on Thales's limited information.

Philosophy (New York: Meridian Books, 1960), 43. See also Francis Nigel Lee, *A Christian Introduction to the History of Philosophy* (Nutley, NJ: Craig Press, 1969), 74. This theory "regarded all living beings as having evolved from lifeless being, and even attempted to reduce all being to one materialistic essence in which the Greek matter motive dominated the Greek form motive."

3. See Seymour G. Martin, *A History of Philosophy* (New York: Appleton-Century-Crofts, 1941), 12–14.

4. See G. S. Kirk and J. E. Raven, *The Presocratic Philosophers* (Cambridge: Cambridge University Press, 1963), 74–98.

5. Zeller, *Outlines of the History of Greek Philosophy*, 42.

6. Lee, *Christian Introduction to Philosophy*, 74.

Before quantum theory, chemists taught that ninety-four elements made up the entire world. Now students are told that the universe is composed of some type of energy or field of force. We now know that water is not the correct answer to the question of what makes the universe—but is a more modern concept of *energy* necessarily a better option?

Thales's notion was not far off from reality. In fact, the human body is made up mostly of water. Specifically, "life" is found in the liquid blood of humanity. There is also more water covering the earth than there is land. And a relationship between water and fire is found in lightning storms. By means of evaporation, water can transform into air. Furthermore, water is "alive" and can animate all things. So for Thales, all things were alive because they were animated by water—even things that we would today call inanimate.[7]

While based on experience in some sense, Thales's proposal that water was the basic element of the universe went beyond sensory experience alone. His theory represented an example of extreme rationalism, a use of reason that exceeded its limits. It can thus legitimately be criticized from within: for instance, if all is water, then are the gods water? If even the gods are water, they must be controlled by water and thus not truly be gods. Is the human mind also water?[8]

Anaximander (610–545 B.C.).[9] Philosophy is a record of the next generation of thinkers' interacting with their predecessors. Anaximander, one of Thales's followers, was unsatisfied with Thales's explanation that water was the single element or material cause of the universe. Water could not provide the answer to the question of the one and the many for one simple reason: water extinguishes fire and cannot possibly create it.

To improve on the thinking of his teacher, Anaximander posited an element that he called the *boundless*, also known as the *unlimited* or the *infinite*, as the single source.[10] This element perhaps meant

---

7. Clark, *Thales to Dewey*, 9; Cornelius Van Til, *A Survey of Christian Epistemology* (Nutley, NJ: Presbyterian and Reformed, 1977), 25.

8. *HWPT*, 54.

9. Kirk and Raven, *Presocratic Philosophers*, 99–142.

10. Clark, *Thales to Dewey*, 11: "To him water seemed to be on a level with earth, air, and fire: these are all the results of natural processes, the developed things and not the source from which things come. The source cannot be any one of them, but must somehow contain them or at least contain the qualities from which they can be developed."

"unlimited space" or some infinite quality that had no beginning or end. The boundless had no qualitatives, such as wetness or heat, but it contained all the basic qualities.

Ultimately Thales was wrong, according to Anaximander, and for one simple reason—Thales was incoherent. Thales's propositions did not "stick together"—he admitted that all consisted of water but also acknowledged the existence of fire, water's antithesis. For Anaximander, the proof for truth was systematic coherence or internal coherence.[11]

Yet despite this incoherence, Anaximander's own system could not prove that it was impossible for all to come from water because no necessarily evident deduction demonstrates that water is *not* the source of all things. So it was left to Anaximander's follower Anaximenes to improve on his theory about how to answer the problem of the one and the many.

Anaximenes (d. 528 B.C.).[12] Anaximenes thought it was unreasonable to assert some type of unperceived "boundless." He was convinced that there had to be an empirical or seeable substance. If the substance was not water, why should it not be air?[13] If someone dies, it is not because water has left him, but rather because air has left him; a person can have water in him, but if he does not have breath, he is dead. Anaximenes was convinced that there was a connection between temperature and a body's density, and he was the first to posit that the moon derived its light from the sun.[14]

Criticism of the Milesians. The Milesian school held to the philosophical presupposition that the source and origin for all reality was some type of corporeal or physical unity, whether water or the boundless. Later philosophy would assert the idea of an incorporeal unity to explain the origin of all things. Yet positing either an incorporeal unity or a corporeal unity excludes the idea of a creating God. Of course, Thales and his followers talked about "gods," but we do not

---

11. Edward J. Carnell, *An Introduction to Christian Apologetics* (Grand Rapids: Eerdmans, 1948), 107.

12. Kirk and Raven, *Presocratic Philosophers*, 143–62; Lee, *Christian Introduction to Philosophy*, 74: "Anaximenes, however, was a partial universalist (who distinguished a human microcosm as well as a cosmic macrocosm); and Anaximander was in fact an objectivist (who sought the cosmic laws objectively outside the things subjected to those laws)."

13. Clark, *Thales to Dewey*, 12.

14. Zeller, *Outlines*, 46.

see evidence of interaction between the Milesian understanding of the origin of the universe and the Hebraic and biblical notion of an almighty, personal God's creation of the universe.

Inherent in the Milesian conception, and necessary to it, was an inability to account for the peculiarities of the world around us. The Milesians made sense of "being" in their abstract yet somehow corporeal universal notion that could not be further divided for comprehension.[15]

Their concept of the origin of all things was intellectually possible, for they thought of it! Nevertheless, there can be no *proof* for the actual existence of such a universal concept. No one can actually know, or demonstrate to someone else, that there is any type of "primordial origin."

There is an important and fundamental error in their conception. While philosophers may have conceived such an eternal mover or ultimate being, their notion confused the relationship between the thought or conception of the "stuff" and the "being" of that stuff. In other words, thinking about something does not mean that it exists. For example, one can read about unicorns in a novel and, while reading the book, can see the unicorns running and jumping with the mind's eye. Yet unicorns do not exist in reality.[16] More specifically, differentiating between what can be conceived in the mind and the physical reality of that notion is proved from the study of geometry, which was beginning at that time.[17]

Philosophical presuppositions are foundational to all thinking, and the early Greeks' attempt to explain the world's origin, based on their false premise of a corporeal universal—one thing—was inherently doomed to failure. It could not adequately explain the world around them. Through time, thinkers realized the inadequacy of Milesian

15. Herman Bavinck, *The Philosophy of Revelation* (Grand Rapids: Eerdmans, 1953), 41–42: "all the peculiarities which actuality presents to our view have been eliminated, and nothing is left except the notion of universal, abstract being, which is not capable of any further definition."

16. Wouldn't it be wonderful if by imagining we had money in the bank, that conception became reality?

17. Bavinck, *Philosophy of Revelation*, 41–42: "In geometry points are conceived as occupying no space, but it does not follow that such points can exist anywhere objectively in the real world. Real space and real time are always finite, but this does not prevent the attribution to them in thought of infinite extension and duration."

thought and attempted to tackle the big philosophical questions of being and existence in their own way.

THE ELEATICS AND HERACLITUS

Xenophanes of Colophon (d. 475 B.C.). Born before 590 B.C., Xenophanes was a contemporary of the mathematician Pythagoras.[18] While some historians dismiss him as more a poet than a philosopher, he wrestled with the philosophical problems of the one and the many, the nature of being and becoming, and rest and motion.[19]

Xenophanes contributed to what we would now term a philosophy of religion.[20] He attacked the Greek poets' propensity to anthropomorphize the gods. The Greek poets ascribed to the gods all mortal sins, such as lying and stealing, and fashioned the gods after their own image.[21] Xenophanes, on the other hand, understood "god" to be an unchangeable being bearing no resemblance to human nature. Xenophanes's one god was his universal, unchanging unity that made sense of the plurality of the world. And for him, there was an inseparable connection between this unchangeable being and the world around us. This thinking made him one of the earliest pantheists.[22]

Xenophanes was important because he gave abstract thinking preference to unreliable sensory experience. He was one of the earliest persons to argue that one could not have certain knowledge about anything, only true belief, which must be supported by reason and conviction.[23] His views comprised an important precursor to modern ideas of skepticism and agnosticism.

Heraclitus (ca. 530–472 B.C.).[24] Moving away geographically but not far in terms of ideas or time is Heraclitus, who lived in Ephesus. Because he saw philosophy as a distinct discipline, some say that he

18. Kirk and Raven, *Presocratic Philosophers*, 163–81.
19. Martin, *History of Philosophy*, 18, 20. Xenophanes noted that the black-skinned god of the Africans and the white-skinned god of the Thracians indicated that the "true god" must be quite different. See also Lee, *Christian Introduction to Philosophy*, 76.
20. Zeller, *Outlines*, 59.
21. Martin, *History of Philosophy*, 19.
22. But from monism, how can a person account for multiplicity?
23. Zeller, *Outlines*, 59–60.
24. Ibid., 60; Martin, *History of Philosophy*, 31; Clark, *Thales to Dewey*, 17.

was the first philosopher.[25] Heraclitus wrote a work titled *Concerning Nature*, from which fragments are found in other writers. Like Xenophanes, he was critical of contemporary polytheism.

Heraclitus's philosophical starting point was the observation of nature. He thought that nature was a uniform whole that neither came into being nor would ever pass away. He rejected water, as well as air, as the one basic reality. He identified fire as the basic material stuff of the universe, the single original element.[26] Perhaps he chose fire because it was the swiftest of the elements and could help him explain the origin of motion and change.[27] Heraclitus held that motion was necessary for the world itself, and fire, since it is necessarily dynamic, was the embodiment of motion.[28] When fire stops changing, it stops being fire.

Heraclitus held that all things in the world change constantly.[29] There was, according to him, a repeating cosmic cycle. Everything, everywhere, must change—he even believed that a new sun was created every day.[30] For him, if something appeared to be permanent, that appearance was merely an illusion.

One of his most famous statements was, "You cannot step twice into the same river." On a first hearing, the phrase does not seem to make sense—we normally think of a river as something that remains, something that does not change. If you fish, perhaps you enjoy a fishing hole that your father showed you and his father showed him. The river is the "same" for you as it was for your grandfather decades ago. But Heraclitus was correct when he said that the river had changed. The water in which your grandfather fished is no longer there. Furthermore, you are a different person when you step into the river for a second time. You are, at the very least, older than you were even moments ago.

When analyzing Heraclitus's views, one discovers an epistemological problem with his claim that everything is in flux. If everything

---

25. Martin, *History of Philosophy*, 31.
26. Ibid., 35–37.
27. Clark, *Thales to Dewey*, 17.
28. Martin, *History of Philosophy*, 36. It is the very "incarnation" of change.
29. Zeller, *Outlines*, 61. See also Martin, *History of Philosophy*, 33–35.
30. Martin, *History of Philosophy*, 33; J. N. D. Kelly, *Early Christian Doctrines* (London: Black, 1977), 121: Heraclitus's universal monad "comprised in itself mutually contradictory qualities, being at once divisible and indivisible, created and uncreated, mortal and immortal."

changes, then how can something receive a name? For example, if there were an animal standing in front of me, it could be named a "lion." But if that (hypothetical) animal is changing, then it is no longer a lion today in the same sense that it was a lion yesterday. Since the lion that is in front of me today will not be the same lion tomorrow, how can people know the nature of "lionness"? What will "it" change into tomorrow? Will the lion stop being carnivorous and suddenly want to eat a peanut-butter-and-jelly sandwich? Ultimately with this type of thinking, nothing can be named or truly known.

When a person says that something exists, that person usually thinks the existent object is real and is not in a great state of change. Modeling clay can be manipulated into different shapes, but throughout the process the various shapes remain clay. If the clay itself changed when it was molded into various shapes—for instance, from clay to glass to water to gold—and it continued to change constantly, we would not say that the material is clay.

What kind of material constantly changes? The answer is that it must be nothing—it cannot be real. If all things are always changing, and thus unreal, there is nothing to be known, nothing to be named.

Heraclitus was aware of his massive epistemological problem and attempted to solve it. He saw the conflict of opposite forces swirling about the world—forces such as life and death, hot and cold—as working in some type of balance. It was clearly an uneven balance, he thought, for if it were perfectly even, then everything in the visible world would be "frozen."[31]

According to Heraclitus, for a person to possess knowledge, knowledge must somehow be correlated to the immutable or unchanging. But if everything is constantly changing, what is immutable? The answer is change itself. Change is the one thing, or law, that does not change. The constant is the uneven flow of change. This flow is best exemplified in the patterns of day and night, the four seasons, and human waking and sleeping.

To use another example, Heraclitus might say that the cup of coffee on your desk is different now from what it was when you started to read about Heraclitus. It has been in flux. But it did not turn into

31. Martin, *History of Philosophy*, 37.

prune juice. It is still coffee, although now it is cold because it took you so long to read through this section on Heraclitus. Your coffee's reduction in temperature is part of the nature of the change. It is in flux, but there are boundaries beyond which the coffee will not change.

Heraclitus's law of "imperfect balance" has been called by later philosophers the "doctrine of nature's rhythm."[32] This statement is the first articulation of what today we call a *natural law*.[33] Heraclitus considered this constant, uneven change in the world to be both natural and just.[34] He confirmed the presence and fusion of opposites as "normal."[35] In a sense, the normal was paradoxical. There was an identity of opposites.[36]

As believers thinking through Heraclitus's teaching, we know that God, the possessor of all wisdom, had Adam name the animals. God himself guaranteed that the apex of his creation had epistemological certainty, not flux. To have knowledge—and this is perhaps the most important aspect of Western philosophical thought for the Christian—it must be a correlate of the immutable or unchanging.

Parmenides (540–470 B.C.).[37] Parmenides is considered by many historians to be the greatest thinker before Socrates. Most of his work dates to around 475 B.C.[38] He was convinced that there was a unity within the universe. If the world is rational, there should be a rational explanation of it.

The views of Parmenides represented an antithesis to Heraclitus's philosophy, and he criticized previous philosophers for what he believed were their nonsensical ideas.[39] He asserted that Thales's notion that

32. Ibid., 38–39. Martin speculates that Heraclitus held to a rhythm that included many worlds.

33. Ibid., 39.

34. Ibid., 40–41.

35. Although not given by Heraclitus, an example of this type of strife could be the interaction between a horse and rider. The rider wants to harness the horse's power. He wants to control the horse's strength for his own needs. Yet the horse yearns to be free. This situation is one of "natural" conflict. In time, however, the horse learns that the rider will give him a sweet apple after riding, and it is "worth" it to the horse to give up his freedom temporarily.

36. Ibid., 42: "This fusion of opposites is the deepest paradox of the conception of Nature as a process. Heraclitus . . . at least made this notable advance in perceiving that the real import of change lies in this paradox of the identity of opposites."

37. Ibid., 46–51.

38. Clark, *Thales to Dewey*, 26.

39. Zeller, *Outlines*, 65. Parmenides stood against Heraclitus's notion of eternal flux (see Lee, *Christian Introduction to Philosophy*, 76).

the principal substance was water and Heraclitus's thought that the principal element was fire were both wrong. Water and fire cancel each other out; they cannot coexist, so both Thales and Heraclitus were misguided.

Parmenides simply denied the existence of change.[40] Change cannot be real—it must be an illusion. Something cannot change from being to nonbeing; therefore, nonbeing does not exist. But Parmenides's worldview is also removed from common sense.

Concluding that the world of flux was illusory, Parmenides turned to a different philosophical starting point. For him, only that which is eternal and changeless, that is, the realm of coherent truth, is what is truly real.

Parmenides was convinced that polytheism was intellectually stupid. Basically, Greek polytheists thought of their gods as powerful human beings who were born and who could die. Parmenides said that anyone who asserted that the gods were born must necessarily claim that they will die. And to assert that the gods were born is to assert that there was a time when the gods did not exist.[41]

The notions of change or becoming that were so important to earlier thinkers were to him a mere illusion.[42] Being could not have had a beginning, for being was unchangeable, immovable, and indestructible. If at any time it was nonbeing, then it necessarily had a beginning. Being was timeless, simple, and perfect. It was identical with thought.[43]

For Parmenides, this being was an infinitely extended sphere, a solid, impenetrable atom. Parmenides's concept of being as one and infinite, a sphere, would be picked up by later thinkers and called the One with a capital O. In the Christian period, the One will be postulated as an alternative to our God.

---

40. John M. Frame, "Greeks Bearing Gifts," in *Revolutions in Worldview: Understanding the Flow of Western Thought*, ed. W. Andrew Hoffecker (Phillipsburg, NJ: P&R Publishing, 2007), 10.

41. See Reginald E. Allen, ed., *Greek Philosophy, Thales to Aristotle* (New York: Free Press, 1991).

42. Clark, *Thales to Dewey*, 26; Zeller, *Outlines*, 65.

43. Cornelius Van Til, *Who Do You Say That I Am?* (Nutley, NJ: Presbyterian and Reformed, 1975), 68: "All reality was one changeless block of being, he had committed his individuality to a similar complete fusion with fate, and when Heraclitus had alleged all to be flux, he had consigned his individuality to a similarly total blending with chance."

Atomists. Some Greek thinkers went beyond the early arguments of the pre-Socratics. They did not hold to one fundamental element of the universe; instead, they thought it was composed of many elements. The atomists (adherents of atomism) held that the universe consisted of countless numbers of indivisible and constantly moving atoms. But these atoms were not the cause of motion.[44]

Epicurus (341–270 B.C.) held that the atoms had weight and fell in a cosmic parallel line "down."[45] Sometimes in their descent they would swerve, however. That swerving caused objects to form. That the atoms in the human body also sometimes swerved accounted for human free choice. The indeterminacy of the atoms was then supposedly the basis for human moral responsibility.[46]

Epicurus is known for his innovations in ethics. He connected moral responsibility with human freedom from causal compulsion. While this idea is philosophically respectable, the random swerving of atoms in a person's body certainly does not make that person's acts morally responsible. In fact, it should be argued that since the person does not cause the atoms to swerve, he should not be considered responsible for the consequences of the swerving.

Epicurus is better known for his ethic that people should avoid pain and seek the absence of pain, called *pleasure*. This philosophy is called *hedonism*. The most pleasurable life, he thought, is that of quiet contemplation.

PYTHAGORAS AND THE PYTHAGOREANS[47]

This important philosophical school located in southern Italy represented a change in Greek thinking.[48] The Pythagoreans were dualists instead of monists and were scientific but had religious interests as

---

44. Frame, "Greeks Bearing Gifts," 12, 14.

45. *WCG* 2:952–54, 975–76, 980, 1010.

46. *HWPT*, 57–58.

47. P. Merlan, "Greek Philosophy from Plato to Plotinus," in *The Cambridge History of Later Greek and Early Medieval Philosophy*, ed. A. H. Armstrong (Cambridge: Cambridge University Press, 1967), 84–106. Besides the authentic writings of Moderatus, Nicomachus, and Numenius, the Pythagorean corpus includes anonymous and spurious works. See also Frame, "Greeks Bearing Gifts," 14.

48. Zeller, *Outlines*, 47.

well. The technical term *philosophy*, as a longing for wisdom, seems to have been first used by this group.[49]

Pythagoras of Croton (572–500 B.C.). Pythagoras was a historical contemporary of Anaximenes.[50] While we do not know much about him, we can surmise that he landed in about 530 B.C. in western Greece and founded his school in southern Italy—at Croton, which was already well known for its medical learning. We know three things about Pythagoras: he held to the transmigration of souls, or reincarnation, he pursued science, and he founded a society that had ethical and religious principles.[51]

The School and Its Teachers. Members of Pythagoras's group were perhaps influenced by the poet Homer and the mystery religions or Orphic teaching.[52] They wanted to enter the divine state of bliss.[53] To accomplish their goal, they followed a strict code of morality that denied any excess and sensuality. They did not eat meat, and they promoted the study of music and medicine.[54] Supposedly, medicine purged the body and music purged the soul.[55] They invented number theory and the study of geometry because math, for them, was the ultimate reality. Pythagoras himself developed what is known as the Pythagorean Theorem.[56] For the Pythagoreans, mathematics became the key to cosmology itself.[57] In the end, the Pythagoreans were persecuted for their beliefs and expelled from Italy.[58]

---

49. Martin, *History of Philosophy*, 23–24: thinkers in this school embodied the "Pythagorean envisagement of the 'lover of wisdom' as a 'spectator' at the game of life, whose very contemplative detachment from the active struggle liberates and purifies his soul." This statement is similar to what Aristotle will say later.

50. Zeller, *Outlines*, 47. Even though two biographies were written about him and Aristotle wrote *On the Pythagoreans*, the best sources of information probably come from his critics Xenophanes and Heraclitus.

51. Martin, *History of Philosophy*, 20.

52. Ibid., 21. They agreed with the Orphics that the soul is in a "prison house" when located in the body. Frame, "Greeks Bearing Gifts," 14: "our souls are divine because they are rational; so salvation comes through knowledge."

53. Clark, *Thales to Dewey*, 22.

54. Zeller, *Outlines*, 49.

55. Martin, *History of Philosophy*, 22: "The most effective means of purifying man's soul is the cultivation and exercise of the intellect in the pursuit of knowledge and science."

56. The square of the hypotenuse of a right triangle is equal to the sum of the squares of the other two sides.

57. Clark, *Thales to Dewey*, 24.

58. Martin, *History of Philosophy*, 29.

Conclusion. Concluding our analysis of earliest Greek thought, we see that Greek isolation from the God of the Bible led the Greeks to promote an understanding of the world that contained no reference to a creator in their cosmology, morality, or ethics. They had no notion of reducing the vast complexity of the universe to an almighty and personal God's creative act.[59] The concept of a sovereign *ex nihilo* ("out of nothing") creation was simply foreign to them. They had never thought of such an idea. A proper system of ethics requires a vertical referent, a divine lawgiver, but earliest Greek ethical thought demonstrated its sad isolation from biblical thinking.[60] We will now turn our attention to some well-known names in Greek thinking.

SOCRATES OF ATHENS (469–399 B.C.) AND THE SOPHISTS

A hallmark of a great philosopher is the challenging of epistemological assumptions of the day. Such intellectual challenging produces shifts in patterns of thought. Socrates was one of those great philosophers.[61] But he did more than simply challenge the past—he provided paths to the future that anticipated many of the great forthcoming movements.[62]

Starting Point. The ancient temple of Apollo in Delphi has an inscription that reads, "Know Thyself." Socrates understood that admonition as an instruction to know the nature of the inner self. He thought that an unexamined life is not worth living and that when someone carefully examines himself, he finds that his own nature provides his guide for morality and so that he knows right from wrong. The knowledge of the self is, for Socrates, true wisdom.

Socrates took as his philosophical starting point his own perceived epistemological inabilities. He professed that he knew little, and his claim actually made him wiser than those who thought that they knew

59. Clark, *Thales to Dewey*, 14.
60. Martin, *History of Philosophy*, 80; Clark, *Thales to Dewey*, 57.
61. See A. E. Taylor, *Socrates* (New York: Appleton, 1933).
62. Greg L. Bahnsen, "The Reformation of Christian Apologetics," in *Foundations of Christian Scholarship*, ed. Gary North (Vallecito, CA: Ross House, 1979), 195. Socrates is credited with foreshadowing the spirit of the Renaissance, Kant's emphasis on epistemic subjectivity, the modern spirit of autonomy, idealism, pragmatism, existentialism, and even linguistic analysis!

16

a lot![63] Specifically, Socrates held that the human intellect was virtuous and that, in fact, no man knowingly does evil.[64] His method was to convince his interlocutor that though he thought he knew something, he did not. Socrates's mission was to convince people of their ignorance and to show that knowledge was possible. His notion of philosophy was the common search for an ideal of knowledge that had not yet been attained. We can summarize his philosophical contributions as promoting an attitude of mind or humility and the assumption that no one does wrong willingly—or stated another way, vice comes from ignorance.[65]

Socrates wanted to present a religious apologetic because he thought of himself as divinely commissioned to raise questions and challenge the philosophers in Athens. In fact, Socrates literally based his life on this supposedly divine commission by choosing to drink the cup of death instead of enduring exile.[66] Philosophy for him was not an academic pursuit but much more—it was a way of life, even a means of salvation for the purified soul from perpetual reincarnations.[67]

Philosophical Method. When Socrates wanted to define an idea or a principle, for example, the concept of *virtue*, he would gather as much information on the topic as was then possible. One of the ways in which he assembled his information was through a question-and-answer style of inquiry, which supposedly helped the inquirer gain clear thinking. When a person comes to know something, thought Socrates, he is in fact simply recollecting something that he knew previously.[68] Eventually his approach became known as the Socratic method.

Socrates also used induction and general definition. By using induction, he moved from the many to the one. He also tried to see general principles that stemmed from the many. In other words, he believed the

---

63. Lee, *Christian Introduction to Philosophy*, 82.

64. Bahnsen, "Reformation of Christian Apologetics," 198.

65. Frame, "Greeks Bearing Gifts," 16–17. Socrates refuted the rationalism of the Sophists or showed that it is self-refuting.

66. See Socrates's *Apology* 30a, as cited by Bahnsen, "Reformation of Christian Apologetics," 196.

67. Bahnsen, "Reformation of Christian Apologetics," 197–200; 198: "All of life and every thought had to be brought under obedience to the lordship of man's reason."

68. Ibid., 199.

use of induction led to providing a general or single definition.[69] The general definition was the "form" of something—its essential nature.[70]

Nous as Foundational for Knowledge. At the root of the world was what Socrates termed a *nous*. The philosopher's task is to contemplate this *nous*, or "knowledge." When the philosopher could somehow "capture" this true *nous*, a divine power from the *nous* would come within the thinker, enlighten his human soul, and keep it from evil.[71] Thus there is a spark of divine wisdom in each mind or soul.[72] In other words, Socrates believed that the temporal was mixed with the eternal in man himself.[73]

He was convinced that sensory perception is an inadequate source of knowledge. Sensory perception is in flux, as Heraclitus had earlier taught. Thus to know something combines the static, which is human judgment, and the changing, which is sensory perception. Also, true knowledge, according to Socrates, requires the knower to give the grounds for the answer. Mere opinion, without knowing the grounds for the opinion, is not knowledge.[74] Perhaps at this point a Christian student could object that being forced to take tests is a syncretistic accommodation to foreign philosophy!

Sophists. Sweeping changes confronted Greek culture in the fifth century B.C.[75] There were conflicts within Greece and hostility against the Persians. King Cyrus the Great led his powerful Persian Empire and was succeeded by King Darius. Athens aided the Greek cities in Asia Minor when they revolted, unsuccessfully, against Darius. Darius then determined to punish Athens, and as the story goes, the Greeks around Athens rallied together and defeated the Persians. That victory was good for Athens, but the city-states that supported Athens now found themselves under strenuous Athenian power. Those oppressed by Athens appealed to Sparta, Athens's enemy, for aid against Athens. A long struggle ensued—the Peloponnesian War, which ended with

69. Frame, "Greeks Bearing Gifts," 17.
70. Bahnsen, "Reformation of Christian Apologetics," 199.
71. Lee, *Christian Introduction to Philosophy*, 82–83.
72. Bahnsen, "Reformation of Christian Apologetics," 197.
73. Ibid., 198. This view is the beginning of the religion of "immanent reason."
74. Ibid., 199–200.
75. Thomas H. Greer, *A Brief History of the Western World*, 4th ed. (New York: Harcourt Brace Jovanovich, 1982), 39.

Athens's defeat in 404 B.C. This conflict brought social, political, and economic disruption and drove philosophical thought into creative directions. Philosophers were no longer solely concerned with the structure of the natural world but turned their attention to human nature and society.[76]

One of the important changes in Greek society concerned the nature and theory of law. Law seemed to change rapidly and almost arbitrarily with the rotation of forceful leaders and the shifting desires of an evolving society. Philosophers noticed this phenomenon and began to ask, "If law is arbitrary, then why does it need to be obeyed?" and "Are laws sacred and immovable, or simply grounded in the whims of society and rulers?" In this crisis, a group of educators established themselves in Greece to meet the needs of the time. They were called the Sophists, from the Greek word meaning "wisdom," because they considered themselves to be wise men. These educators taught in a manner that was much different from that of earlier teachers—and they instructed in a "new virtue." That new virtue stressed social effectiveness and an integrated personality.[77] They saw that life was to be lived and that philosophers and thinkers had to be "practical" people.

Protagoras, a contemporary of Socrates, was a Sophist who was famous for holding that "man is the measure of all things."[78] By this statement, Protagoras apparently meant that the only standard or criterion for truth is the perception(s) of each individual.[79]

PLATO OF ATHENS (427–347 B.C.)

Plato was a student of Socrates, and he critiqued the Sophists.[80] Philosophers quip that the history of philosophy is a series of footnotes

---

76. Clark, *Thales to Dewey*, 46–48; Frame, "Greeks Bearing Gifts," 15.

77. That statement is also a nice way of saying that they taught their students all the dirty political tricks that were necessary for them to survive in politics during those trying days.

78. Lee, *Christian Introduction to Philosophy*, 80. This phrase means that man is not a cold, bare intellect but has an active, living will. Life is a matter of willing a goal, and wisdom is measured by the standard of success. See also Clark, *Thales to Dewey*, 49.

79. Carnell, *Christian Apologetics*, 35: "For Protagoras, then, knowledge *is* sensation."

80. *CVT*, 234: "Plato was able to show that their skepticism was itself a dogmatic assertion, offered as a sure, universal truth. Others, like Parmenides, sought to understand everything in terms of timeless logic, but he needed to resort to mythology to explain the 'illusions' that did

to Plato. He and Aristotle are counted as the two greatest minds in Western philosophical history.[81]

Two Worlds. Plato knew that the world of senses and feelings can deceive a person. Our eyes can be deceived by an illusion, and our heart can be broken when we wrongly think that someone loves us who does not. Thus what is truly real is that which does not fool us. This "real" world is the world of ideas. The world of sense is real, but it is not the *most* real world. The world of ideas cannot be known by the senses; it must be known through contemplation by the mind.

One of Plato's writings was titled *Symposium*. In this dialogue, a certain woman was permitted to come back to the earth from the world of Hades because of deeds she performed. From this story, it would seem that eternal life on earth is one of the highest rewards one could receive. But although eternal life on earth, according to the Greek mind, would be the best imaginable fate for the average person, apparently there was an even higher reality—immortality itself.

In *Symposium*, there even appears to be a type of person or a group of persons who were in their own nature immortal. Of course for Plato, the philosophers are those special people. For them, living a life continually on the earth would be no reward at all, but rather a punishment. Even while they live on the earth, they have their eyes held high to the beauty of beauty itself. The philosopher desires to be united with the beauty and truth he sees while he is on the earth, though he does not see them as clearly as he could.

Plato's great philosophical contribution was teaching that two very different worlds exist.[82] Thereby, he was able to unite some of Parmenides's thinking, namely, that being is changeless, and Heraclitus's notion that elements are in constant change.[83]

---

not cohere with his rationalistic worldview. The irrationalistic Sophists were also rationalists; the rationalistic Parmenides was also an irrationalist."

81. Frame, "Greeks Bearing Gifts," in *"Revolutions in Worldview: Understanding the Flow of Western Thought*, ed. W. Andrew Hoffecker (Phillipsburg, NJ: P&R Publishing, 2007), 18.

82. Martin noted that the theory of forms is also integral to understanding certain conceptions in the writings of both Augustine and Aquinas. See Martin, *History of Philosophy*, 106.

83. Douglas F. Kelly, *Systematic Theology*, vol. 1, *The God Who Is the Holy Trinity* (Fearn, Scotland: Mentor, 2008), 38–39: Plato attempted "to establish a realist epistemology (i.e., how knowing is related to being). Against the nominalistic (i.e., 'names' or words do not take one to objective reality) Sophists and against the relativism that ensues from the constant 'flux' of Heraclitus." See also Frame, "Greeks Bearing Gifts," 18.

One of Plato's two worlds is that in which objects can be seen, smelled, and tasted. Plato described that world or reality as the "sensible" world, the "changeable" world, the "material" world, or the "visible" world. If you and I were to take a walk in a colorful, fragrant rose garden, we would behold beauty. But Plato's idea of beauty has a referent beyond this part or piece of beauty, namely, the *idea* of beauty. The rose and its beauty are concrete abstractions of this real beauty and not nearly as beautiful as beauty itself. The rose is just a shadow of the real beauty.

A major characteristic of the visible world is that it is in a state of becoming. Since the world is becoming, following earlier Greek thought, it was considered to be nonbeing and not strictly knowable.[84] This present, sensible world is an imperfect copy of yet another world.

The second sphere is one that cannot be seen. This world is the real world, not the earth where we live. This other world is invisible, in contrast to the material world. The invisible world is a place of pure ideas, known as *forms*. This world contains the prototypes of the objects seen in the sensible world and is called "the ideal sphere," "the intelligible world," "the invisible world," "the world of forms," "the world of pure ideas," and "the form world."[85] Perhaps Plato borrowed parts of this notion from Pythagorean thinking.[86] While this form world is invisible, it can nevertheless somehow be known. To know this place is the philosophical goal of all human life.

Sadly, according to Plato, most people wrongly think that the changeable or sensible world is the real world. But instead, it is the place of nonbeing, the world of becoming. The sensible world is modeled on the form world, and the forms make it possible to know their visible imitation.[87]

84. Frame, "Greeks Bearing Gifts," 20.
85. Merlan, "Greek Philosophy," 20: "When Plato says that the ideas are truly being, he always implies that they are changeless (unmoved)."
86. The *Euthyphro* was the first dialogue in which the Greek words *idea* and *eidos* (both meaning "to see") appear. Geometric *pattern*, or *figure*, was apparently an important concept in the origin of these words. David Ross (*Plato's Theory of Ideas* [Oxford: Clarendon, 1951], 14) says that there are differing judgments on the subject. The words mean "visible form" to C. M. Gillespie, and according to H. C. Belding, "as a principle of Plato's metaphysic they are a fusion of Socrates's construction concerning moral values with the Pythagorean teaching of number patterns."
87. Frame, "Greeks Bearing Gifts," 19.

Creation by the Artificer. In the *Timaeus*, Plato proposed that a semipowerful god, called the *artificer* or *demiurge*, decided to create a world.[88] This god, using a model of animated being found in preexisting chaos, formed the realm of existing matter into particular instances of the eternal prototypes.[89] From looking at animated being, the artificer made an image of it; the image was then called *space* or the *receptacle*. For this created world to be both intelligent and animated, it required a cosmic soul—it needed a soul simply to exist. The artificer built the world from the preexisting chaos and then apparently wrapped the cosmic soul around it.[90] Plato's creative proposal was an advance over the thoughts of previous philosophers.[91]

World of Forms as Answer to "One and Many" Problem. Plato wrote a number of early dialogues, each one of which asked questions about abstract concepts—for example, about temperance, courage, piety, and beauty.[92] Plato thought that the questions about the concepts implied that only a single "thing" was represented by each of the abstract qualities or concepts. For example, the many human experiences of the concept of equality must relate to one universal concept.

This single thing that each abstract quality or concept represents was termed the *form* of the thing. The forms are the universal, invisible, unchanging ideas behind the changing realities that exist on earth. The beauty of a rose communicates its beauty whether it is a yellow or a red rose, since it corresponds to the unchanging form of what the essence of beauty is. Plato's forms constituted "the one" in the problem of "the one and the many."[93] There was an ultimate and supreme "Form of the Good," which was the highest form. It was also termed the *nous*, the "mind"—a word that had already been used by Socrates.[94]

---

88. Ibid.: The demiurge "is subordinate to the Forms and limited by the nature of the matter."

89. Greg L. Bahnsen, *Van Til's Apologetic: Readings & Analysis* (Phillipsburg, NJ: Presbyterian and Reformed, 1983), 18n111.

90. Merlan, "Greek Philosophy," 23.

91. Bahnsen, *Van Til's Apologetic*, 18n111.

92. Some of those minor Socratic dialogues are the *Charmides*, *Laches*, and *Hippias Major*. For more information, see A. E. Taylor, *Plato, The Man and His Work* (London: Methuen, 1955), 23–102.

93. Frame, "Greeks Bearing Gifts," 18.

94. Merlan, "Greek Philosophy," 20. There are five fundamental qualities of the ideas: being, movement, rest, identity, and diversity.

Plato's concept of the forms appeared in his later and more famous writing, *Phaedo*. He posed the question, "What put the idea of 'just' or 'equal' in the human mind? When someone picks up two sticks, he observes that the sticks can be equal but are never perfectly equal. The sticks, due to their imperfection, cannot give the examiners the mathematical notion of equality, that is, perfect or absolute equality. Plato therefore proposed that the ideas of "just" and "equal," which were never actually observed in life, were *suggested* to us by the apparent equality of the two sticks. The person knows, by seeing inequality, that a true equality exists in the universal form of equality.

In *Phaedo*, Plato writes Socrates's words and proposes that sensory experience has reminded people of things that were not "sensibly" experienced from the beginning of human life. No one has experienced perfect equality between two supposedly equal sticks; therefore, understanding these abstract concepts must be immediately acquired at birth (the most likely option) or come from before birth. This type of knowledge is actually not something learned at school but is rather a recollection of the notion of equality that arrived in the person's mind before birth.[95] If abstract notions or forms such as equality existed somewhere before a person's birth and the person learned them before birth, then his soul also existed, was intelligent, and was able to learn before his birth.[96]

People recollect the forms in two ways. The first way is by resemblances. A picture of someone is a resemblance of the person photographed. So as one grows and lives life, he or she is reminded of the forms as their resemblances are observed on earth. The second way is by contiguity or the association of an object with the object's owner.[97] For example, when I see a professor's briefcase on a table, I associate that briefcase with the professor.

---

95. *Phaedo* in Plato, *The Trial and Death of Socrates: Being the Euthyphron, Apology, Crito, and Phaedo of Plato*, trans. F. J. Church (London: Macmillan, 1927), 139: "Socrates said: 'It [recollection] cannot have been after we were born men.' Simmias replied, 'No, certainly not.' Socrates asked, 'then it was before?' 'Yes.'"

96. Taylor, *Plato*, 188. Taylor insists that the theory does justice to the dictum that "precepts without concepts are blind, concepts without precepts are empty." Martin, *History of Philosophy*, 102: "The analysis of these physical theories in the *Phaedo* conspires with the refutation of epistemological theories in the *Theatetus* to prove the need of supersensible realities." Some scholars hold that the theory of anamnesis found in *Phaedo* is intimately connected to knowledge of the forms. See Ross, *Plato's Theory*.

97. Ross, *Plato's Theory*, 22.

It is not difficult to be critical of Plato's notion of the world of forms. First, Plato had no ground to say that the form world is more real than the sensible world. He simply assumed that there were degrees of reality. Plato admitted that he could not solve this problem.[98] Second, the forms cannot provide an account for the diversity of qualities in the sensible world. For example, there is no form of imperfection because the forms are, by definition, perfection. Thus the form world cannot account for this experience in the sensible world.[99] Third, the forms themselves require explanation. Neither that which is imperfect or imperfection as a category, nor change, both of which are observable in the visible world, need a rational explanation that is not found in the world of forms. Thus the visible world is somehow unnatural or irrational.[100]

Form of the Good. The "Form of the Good" is represented in Plato's *Symposium* as "the goal of the pilgrimage of the philosophic lover."[101] There is a relationship between the forms and the Form of the Good. Neither the forms in themselves nor knowledge of the forms can be identified with the unique Form of the Good,[102] which is the form that allows the thinker to realize the other forms. The other forms ultimately derive from the Form of the Good.

The Form of the Good is called the "significance of being," which implies that the forms are causally dependent on the Form of the Good. The forms are dependent on the Form of the Good because they are partial expressions of a unity that is found in the total economy of the Form of the Good.[103]

Some scholars say that the relationship between the forms and the Form of the Good is similar to the relationship between the genus and the species. The species come before the genus and are understandable only in reference to the species.[104] The Form of the Good is the

---

98. Frame, "Greeks Bearing Gifts," 23.

99. Ibid., 22.

100. Ibid., 23: "He is rationalistic about the forms and irrationalistic about the sense-world. For him, reason is totally competent to understand the forms but not competent to make sense of the changing world of experience. Yet he tries to analyze the changing world by means of changeless forms—an irrational world by a rationalistic principle."

101. Taylor, *Plato*, 287.

102. Robert E. Cushman, *Therapeia: Plato's Conception of Philosophy* (Chapel Hill: University of North Carolina Press, 1958).

103. Ibid., 152.

104. Ibid.

cause of being in respect to the forms, namely, as the cause of their intelligibility.

One problem with the Form of the Good is that it transcends the empirical world. Thus every predicate concerning the Form of the Good properly belonged to some of its effects, not actually to the Form of the Good. The philosopher could make a connection with the Form of the Good only analogically. That analogy was certainly not an exact duplicate of the Form of the Good itself. Philosophers' knowledge of the details of the universe adds to and enriches their concepts of the source of reality, that is, the Form of the Good, yet they can never comprehend that source itself.[105]

Plato's "god," or demiurge, was the self-moving principle of the universe. Some famous secular philosophers have wrongly identified *Phaedo*'s Form of the Good with the God of Christianity.[106] They have done so because Socrates shows that the distinction between existence and essence falls away in the Form of the Good. In fact, Socrates maintained that the Form of the Good cannot properly be called one of the forms since it transcends even the forms themselves.[107]

Perhaps Socrates and Plato were not fully aware of the significance of their own thought when they spoke of a god or demiurge. This god was on a lower level of reality than the more ultimate Form of the Good. Socrates's and Plato's conception of theism perhaps became necessary because, though they did not explicitly say so, they were still haunted by a feeling that the good was, after all, some type of value or something essential, and it needed an intermediate link to connect it with the hierarchy of realities or existents.[108]

Types of Human Knowing. Plato made a number of assumptions to account for epistemology. He granted that there was a world of

105. Taylor, *Plato*, 354–58.
106. Ibid., 191–92: "The ideal of Socrates (from the *Phaedo*) and the Christian ideal are fundamentally identical." Ibid., 289: "Thus, metaphysically the Form of Good is what Christian philosophy has meant by God, and nothing else."
107. Merlan, "Greek Philosophy," 32–34.
108. Taylor, *Plato*, 289. Others firmly disagree with this position and argue that there is no warrant for identifying the demiurge with any of the forms. Theism became part of Plato's philosophy at a later period than the time of the composition of the *Republic*. Certainly it depends on what one means by the word *theism*. Merlan ("Greek Philosophy," 32) said: "from the beginning to the end of Plato's literary activity, the world of gods plays a prominent role in very many of his dialogues." Demonology also played an important role (see ibid., 33–35).

ideas, an artificer or demiurge, as well as a time-space "receptacle."[109] He also held that knowledge did not come primarily from the human senses. Knowledge came via the rational ability to go beyond sensory experience and find truth.[110]

According to Plato, there is opinion, and there is knowledge. Opinion has two parts, as does knowledge. Humans have information, which comes from sensory perception and imagination. That information is conjecture because it is the experience of the particulars, which are only partly real because they are necessarily constantly changing. Since time and space are changing, opinions that are based on sensory experience alone are therefore imperfect and do not qualify as true knowledge. Better than conjecture is belief, which distinguishes between the images of the objects and the actual objects.

It is the human soul that enables a person supposedly to know the unseen world of pure ideas. The soul somehow knows that world by remembering it, since the soul existed eternally in the pure world of ideas before it was imprisoned in the human body at birth.[111]

Thus human knowledge is actually remembering what was previously learned in the form world. This epistemological theory supposedly accounts, for example, for how a slave boy with no formal education can know about the complicated nature of a perfect triangle.[112] Such knowledge did not come from the boy's sensory experience or formal education, so it must be prenatal.

True knowledge first consists in understanding, which comes when the thinker sees this world's "things" as instances of general concepts.[113] Pure knowledge can only be of the ideal, the fully real. It is the fourth stage of the intuitive vision of the forms.[114] Such knowledge can be stated without qualification. Those knowable objects, which are real, are stable, universal. They are not known through sensory experience. This type of knowledge is innate, recollected, or intuited from before the soul was imprisoned in the body. The particulars of this sensory

---

109. Carnell, *Christian Apologetics*, 95.
110. Frame, "Greeks Bearing Gifts," 18.
111. Plato's *Theaetetus* discusses epistemology. See Martin, *History of Philosophy*, 98–100.
112. Plato used the slave boy as an illustration in *The Meno* (see Martin, *History of Philosophy*, 81).
113. Frame, "Greeks Bearing Gifts," 20.
114. Ibid.

world participate in the idea of which they are an instance—like different actors participate by playing a role in a stage play. Finally, the notion of heavenly ideas, as propounded by Plato, stands in opposition to the Heraclitean doctrine of universal flux insofar as such ideas are "non-sensible" things not subject to change.[115]

Plato's teaching has an application for apologetics. For Plato, the ever-changing world of Heraclitus produced intellectual terror. Plato sought something stable on which to build his philosophical ideas—if everything was in flux, the only way forward was intellectual suicide, since there could be no certainty of anything. Plato found stability in his understanding of the forms. But Plato hit on something that is true and useful: unless one can find intellectual certainty, there is little hope in life. The Christian apologist can push this point with the unbeliever—does the unbeliever believe that there is something that is absolutely certain in this life? If he answers affirmatively, then the apologist can ask why the unbeliever believes what he believes. What is his intellectual foundation? Maybe he has certainty because of science or because of his parents or simply because he has had a specific experience on which he is basing his thoughts. But none of these answers provides an adequate foundation. Science and parents and experience can be false! If the unbeliever answers that he believes that all is in flux, that there is no certainty, then no language is meaningful. A word could mean one thing at one moment and at the next moment mean something completely opposite.

Body and Soul. Plato's doctrine of the soul set the standard for Greek thought on the matter. Drawing some points from his predecessors Thales and Heraclitus, both of whom held to the high importance of corporeality—they made little distinction between the soul that is in humanity and the soul of the universe. In other words, there is little distinction between the body/soul's relationship to the corporeal universe. In Christian thought, a soul can exist separately from the body—but that idea was not a primary emphasis in Greek thought.

Phaedo forwards a formal argument for the immortality of the soul. The argument runs this way: That which is always in motion

---

115. Ross, *Plato's Theory*, 19. Plato nuanced his view of knowledge when he discussed beautiful objects in the *Phaedrus*. While controlled by the intellect, the passions also contribute (Frame, "Greeks Bearing Gifts," 20). Sadly, the object discussed is the (sexual) beauty of a boy.

is immortal. That which moves itself, the source of all motion, cannot come into being. That source of all motion is imperishable. That which moves itself is immortal—it is the soul. The soul, therefore, is immortal.[116] By being self-moved, the soul is the source of all motion.[117] The human soul, which is the intellect, is the self-mover of man.[118]

In *Phaedo*, Socrates said that one had to be prepared for life after death.[119] There is perhaps a connection, almost a parallel, between this pagan doctrine and the biblical doctrine of heaven and hell. Plato taught that when someone was purified, he was permitted to dwell with god, and if someone was not purified, he must lie in the mire of hell.

Plato believed in the reincarnation of immortal souls that had a prior intelligent existence.[120] Only very few people in society fit this category—primarily the philosophers. For Plato, not every soul is actually immortal. What is immortal is the thing that Plato calls the "all-soul." In comparison to the soul, the body is relatively unimportant.[121] The most important parts of human life are the pursuit of philosophy and the activities of the soul.[122]

Ethical Life. Plato's major interest was not abstract metaphysics or complicated epistemology but rather instruction on how to live well, including his ethics and political theory.[123] Part of the reason for that interest came from Plato's living in a time of political turmoil. He wanted to develop an ideal civil society based on the Socratic principle of inwardness.[124]

---

116. Taylor, *Plato*, 183–85. See Merlan, "Greek Philosophy," 28–29.

117. Merlan, "Greek Philosophy," 25–26.

118. Lee, *Christian Introduction to Philosophy*, 84. Frame ("Greeks Bearing Gifts," 20–21) mentions that Plato divided the soul into the appetitive, the spirited, and the rational.

119. Socrates, *Phaedo*, 150: "True virtue in reality is a kind of purifying from all these things; and temperance and justice and courage and wisdom itself are the purification. Whosoever comes to Hades uninitiated and profane will be in the mire, while he that has been purified and initiated shall dwell with the gods."

120. See Frame, "Greeks Bearing Gifts," 20.

121. Socrates (*Phaedo*, 29) stated: "the soul and the body are united, and nature ordains the one to be a slave and to be ruled, and the other to be a master and to rule."

122. Lee, *Christian Introduction to Philosophy*, 85. Lee criticized Plato's "theology." His god was not the God of the Bible. His god was not even personal. The "other world" was opposed to this (material) world. His views, through his followers Aristotle and Aquinas, "have so often paralyzed some Christians from living lives fully relevant to Christ this side of the grave."

123. Frame, "Greeks Bearing Gifts," 21.

124. Van Til, *Who Do You Say That I Am?*, 67.

His doctrine of the state was connected to his anthropology. He believed that there was a hierarchy of human beings. For example, peasants, he thought, were governed by what he termed the *appetitive soul*, soldiers were governed by the spirited soul, and rulers were governed by the highest soul—the rational soul. Thus the best type of ruler or king would be a "philosopher-king."

The best state would be a totalitarian one, run by philosophers, in which the upper class would share their women communally and the rulers would raise the children. Art would not play an important role because it is necessarily only shadowy conjecture.[125] It is in the political state that humanity supposedly reaches its highest expression. The state is the highest form of human development, and all should be subject to it.[126]

Plato's ethics were founded on an incorrect notion of right and wrong. He argued that wrong is always done out of ignorance. When someone knows what is right, he will do it.[127] If Plato is correct on that point, then the world has been covered in ignorance for millennia!

In summary, Plato was one of the most influential thinkers of all time. His ideas shaped human thought for centuries, and they still do. His forms were an attempt to find unity and meaning in a chaotic world. Many theologians find Plato's philosophy useful and have tried to integrate it with a biblical understanding of the world as they, too, have sought answers to the problem of the one and the many. But as we will continue to see throughout the centuries of church history, attempting to synthesize and integrate a biblical worldview with pagan philosophy will always end up distorting the biblical message.

ARISTOTLE (384–322 B.C.)

Introduction. Plato's philosophy was important for the theological development of the early church until around A.D. 600. Then Aristotle became paramount in the Middle Ages. Aristotle's philosophy is still

---

125. Frame, "Greeks Bearing Gifts," 21.
126. Lee, *Christian Introduction to Philosophy*, 87.
127. Frame, "Greeks Bearing Gifts," 21.

dominant in Catholicism today and in some sectors of Protestant Christianity.

Aristotle was born a physician's son near the border of Macedonia in northern Greece in a city known as Stagira. He made his way to Athens and was a student of Plato at the Academy. Aristotle spent about twenty years there and then with Xenocrates established his own, more scientifically oriented school, the Lyceum. Aristotle was appointed tutor to the son of King Philip of Macedonia—Alexander, who would later conquer the known world and be designated Alexander the Great.

Aristotle apparently agreed with Plato for a time, but there was a clear break between the two great thinkers by the year 353 B.C. Aristotle believed that philosophy's task was to explain the natural world. He viewed Plato's notion of two worlds as an exercise in poetic metaphor. Aristotle rejected the existence of Plato's form world because Plato could not account for the cause of the world of ideas.[128] In contrast, Aristotle asserted that there was no separate world of forms; rather, the form of an object existed in each object.[129]

By rejecting Plato's world of ideas, however, Aristotle encountered a number of his own philosophical problems. One of them was the challenge of changing phenomena. To answer that unsolved problem, one needs to understand how Aristotle viewed the world.

Visible World. Instead of positing two realms, as Plato did, Aristotle argued that the material universe consists of both form and matter.[130] All substances in the universe—the entire known world, all reality—had these separate qualities of form and of matter within them.[131] Aristotle was thus a philosophical dualist.

Aristotle contended that animals possess matter, which is their body, and they possess form, which is their ability to sense and move. The purpose and definition of an object are located in its form. The form is the same in all the species of a given being. Inanimate objects also possess form and matter. Aristotle gave the example of a ship to distinguish between form and matter. When a ship is at anchor, it is

---

128. Lee, *Christian Introduction to Philosophy*, 86; Frame, "Greeks Bearing Gifts," 23.

129. Kelly, *Systematic Theology*, 1:39.

130. One of Aristotle's best-known theories is called *hylomorphism*, from *hyle*, meaning "matter," and *morphé*, meaning "form."

131. Frame, "Greeks Bearing Gifts," 23.

matter. When it is moving, sailing on the water, doing what it was created for, it exhibits its form. The sailing is the form of the ship. Thus Aristotle did not deny Plato's notion of forms altogether, but he disagreed about their location.[132]

The two thinkers also disagreed about the nature of matter. Matter was not necessarily some type of physical stuff. Matter was rather the individuating principle of an object. More precisely, the terms *matter* and *form* relate to the concepts of individual and potential. This potential was Aristotle's idea of the universal. His notion of the universal became a suprapersonal spirit of thought or potential, which he termed the *nous*.

Having learned something about the terms *form, matter, individual,* and *potential,* we can see how individual human beings are also composed of both form and matter. For example, in that they are both men, the essence and specific nature of Plato and Aristotle were the same—therefore, they have the same form. For Aristotle the form is also called the *soul*.

Accordingly, the purpose of human beings is to think, or to express fully their rationality. Hence the form of a man is his thinking, rational soul.[133] The body and soul are not exactly the same for Aristotle. The soul may be defined as the life of an animal or the form or actuality of that body.[134] Simply stated, the body is the organic matter of the person. The organic matter is apparently the instrument through which a part of life or soul expresses itself.[135]

Against Plato's opinion, Aristotle rejected the notion of the pre-existence of the soul.[136] For him, when a person dies, he is simply laid in the grave. His matter has reached its final goal. He will not be reincarnated as another person. Thus he rejected Plato's anthropological dualism, the notion that the body is the "prison house" of the soul. Yet he still held to a distinction between body and soul. He saw duality within overall unity.

---

132. Aristotle's discussion of form and matter will be foundational for the later medieval understanding of the sacraments.

133. Ibid.

134. W. K. C. Guthrie, *The Greek Philosophers from Thales to Aristotle* (New York: Harper & Row, 1975), 144.

135. Ibid., 143.

136. Merlan, "Greek Philosophy," 39.

While Aristotle denied the soul's immortality, he did not want to face annihilation. He believed that the soul was not in its own right a complete substance, but apparently he was not as interested in contemplating another world outside the present one as Plato was. So Aristotle thought that a part of the soul, called the *nous*, or "intellect," was immortal and thus actually divine.[137]

It is the *nous* that activates the form—the rational soul—of a person in his thinking. All humans have the potential to think and contemplate. Yet clearly some people think more than do others. The reason for this difference among people is found in the *nous*. By thinking, a person realizes his potential. Aristotle's *nous*, the highest manifestation of the reasoning faculty, was different from the other vital principles. The *nous* was probably a separate substance capable of survival after the body's demise.

If the *nous* alone was capable of independent existence and therefore imperishable, then certain implications followed. Aristotle, at the end of the *Ethics*, exhorted his readers to the life of pure thought, which resembled the activity of the "prime mover." He argued that the reward after death was the absorption of one's mind into the "incorporeal mind." There was no personal survival of individuals.[138] We need further to investigate Aristotle's notion of the prime or unmoved mover.

Unmoved Mover. Aristotle believed that neither form nor matter ever existed by itself—with one exception. That exception was called the *one* or *pure form* or the *unmoved mover*. The unmoved mover, or first principle, was necessary to Aristotle's universe. Supposedly, it had an ether or an uppermost heaven where this divine changeless being dwelled.[139]

This unmoved mover was also called *intelligence* and was the supreme principle of the universe, or god.[140] An impersonal pure reason, the prime or unmoved mover engaged in eternal thoughts

137. Lee, *Christian Introduction to Philosophy*, 86.
138. Guthrie, *Greek Philosophers*, 87, 95. Frederick C. Copleston, *A History of Philosophy*, vol. 1, *Greece and Rome from the Pre-Socratics to Plotinus* (Garden City, NY: Image Books, 1962), 1:378, comments that given the resurrection of the soul and the close union of the soul and body, the soul's resurrection suggests that the resurrection of the body is demanded by the soul.
139. Merlan, "Greek Philosophy," 40.
140. Ibid., 42–43.

and was pure thought eternally thinking only about itself. The prime mover could be conceptualized as subsistent thought that cogitates on itself.[141]

For Aristotle, the existence of a god or unmoved mover hinged completely on the philosophical problem of the existence of motion. Aristotle was deeply concerned to explain the nature of change or motion. He believed that every movement required something to act on it—an external moving cause or stimulus. Since he presupposed an eternal framework for the universe, he believed the cause of the universe must also be eternal.[142]

The prime mover gives motion to the world by drawing the world to itself, the prime mover.[143] The stars move, as does the world, by their attraction to the changeless changer.[144] Being eternal, the first mover is not restricted to the progression from potency to actuality, nor can it be. The unmoved mover is the pure, actual form that is the origin of motion and proceeds from matter toward form as its goal.[145] The unmoved mover is the final cause of all things.

The unmoved mover has no matter and, as pure act, is the final cause toward which all actualization or potentiality is moving. Aristotle's unmoved mover, or god, was the final step in a chain of reasoning that ended in the conclusion that it is impossibile for anything to be self-moved. *Dynamis* was an important term in this theory; it identified the tendency toward and capacity for change and development in a particular direction.[146]

As a Greek philosopher, Aristotle did not maintain that the first mover was a creator god. There was no logical necessity for the first mover to create the world it acted on. The world had existed from all eternity—it was not created at any time.

The first mover, being immaterial, certainly does not and cannot perform any physical, bodily action; therefore, its operation must be

141. Lee, *Christian Introduction to Philosophy*, 86.

142. Guthrie, *Greek Philosophers*, 132, 138.

143. Frederick C. Copleston, *A History of Philosophy*, vol. 5, *British Philosophy Hobbes to Hume* (Westminster, MD: Newman Press, 1968), 5:314.

144. Merlan, "Greek Philosophy," 39.

145. Herman Dooyeweerd, *A New Critique of Theoretical Thought*, vol. 1, *The Necessary Presuppositions of Philosophy*, trans. David Freeman and William Young (Philadelphia: Presbyterian and Reformed, 1953), 182.

146. Guthrie, *Greek Philosophers*, 135.

entirely spiritual or intellectual.[147] Thus Aristotle's god is cognizant only of himself.[148] He, or it, is intelligence "intelligizing" itself and is pure form.[149] This notion is the opposite of the personal and absolute God of the Bible.[150]

We have briefly investigated Aristotle's notions of the visible world, humans in that world, and the unmoved mover beyond that world. Next we will investigate Aristotle's understanding of how humans comprehend that world.

Epistemology. Aristotle recognized that not all people have the same amount of knowledge. Some people understand things in only a simplistic way, gained through experience, while others know on a higher plane. People with true knowledge know certain universals—for example, that medicine is good for the body—while the simpler person knows only that the medicine he took worked but does not know the general, universal goodness of medicine itself. The person with true knowledge may be likened to an artist, who is aware of universals and so wants to produce beauty.

Aristotle thought that knowledge is derived from sensory experience and further reflection on that experience. The consequences of his epistemology are at least twofold. First, he rejected Plato's notion of innate ideas in that, by definition, an idea from sensory experience is not innate. Second, he rejected any theory of divine illumination. Divine illumination may be equivalent to the natural light of the intellect, and Aristotle rejected the possibility of the intellect's concurring with God.[151] In other words, Aristotle believed that knowledge was possible, and further, that it must be known of the form of the thing, not of its matter.

The true explanation of things was to be sought in their end, that is, in their teleology.[152] In part Aristotle came to this position through his interaction with Empedocles (495–435 B.C.). Empedocles pro-

---

147. Ibid. Guthrie calls immateriality pure actuality or *energia*—"the unimpeded flow of activity made possible once actuality has been acquired."

148. *HWPT*, 48: "But this god did not reveal his thoughts to Aristotle. Rather, it is a hypothesis of Aristotle's own reason and thus an idol."

149. Merlan, "Greek Philosophy," 42–43.

150. Dooyeweerd, *New Critique*, 1:180; *HWPT*, 48.

151. Frederick C. Copleston, *A History of Philosophy*, vol. 2, *Medieval Philosophy Augustine to Scotus* (London: Burns and Oates and Washbourne, 1950), 2:147.

152. Guthrie, *Greek Philosophers*, 126.

pounded a doctrine that denied the existence of final causes in nature, and Aristotle, in opposition, tried to prove the existence of teleology in nature. He thought that each object had potentiality, an actual *telos* or "end." There must be an absolute standard of reference for this *telos*, and that standard was provided by its god.

Logic. Aristotle is perhaps best known for his logic. He was convinced that logic is the foundation on which the principles of all true judgment depend. For Aristotle, logic is not just the formal science of thinking. The laws of logic help the thinker understand the relationship between truth and reality. Truth must be connected to reality, so the laws of logic, because they uncover the relationship between truth and reality, transcend the laws of thought and reflect the laws of reality itself.[153]

It is impossible to be mistaken about the law of contradiction (sometimes called the "law of noncontradiction"). It is not only a law of thought but also of being.[154] The law of contradiction goes something like this: The same attribute cannot attach and not attach to the same thing in the same respect—contrary attributes cannot belong to the same subject at the same time.[155] When we were children, perhaps our mothers asked us whether we ate any of her freshly baked chocolate chip cookies. When with chocolate smeared all over our lips we heartily denied that we had done so, our mothers knew that the law of contradiction was there at work. Either our denial was false, or she did not see the chocolate on our lips. Certainly, both things could not be true at the same time. The law of contradiction is as plain a part of reality as the chocolate on a child's face!

If anyone objected to the law of contradiction and asserted that contrary attributes attach to the same thing, it would be necessary to conclude that we cannot believe what that person says. For example, it is plain that the number "three" cannot be both odd and even. No one can actually think that the number three is both odd and even at the same time, even if he makes the assertion verbally. To make such

153. Clark, *Thales to Dewey*, 97. For the importance of studying logic, see Vern S. Poythress, *Logic: A God-Centered Approach* (Wheaton, IL: Crossway, 2013), 27–28.

154. Poythress (*Logic*, 570–71) rightly reminds us that none of the laws of logic is "basic" in itself or independent of God.

155. Ibid., 62: "something cannot both have a property and not have the same property at the same time and in the same way."

an assertion is to pretend that contrary attributes attach to the same subject or to claim two contrary opinions at the same time.

Comprehending Aristotle is essential to grasping Western thought in general and much of Christian thinking in particular. Aristotle was "rediscovered" during the Middle Ages, and his rules of logic and scientific categorization completely revolutionized not only how people thought about the world but also how theologians conceived the God of the Bible. By the time of the Reformation, using an Aristotelian method was the undisputed way of doing theology. To understand the development of doctrine, we need to know about two more pagan philosophical schools: Stoicism and Gnosticism.

STOICISM AND GNOSTICISM

Stoic World. Stoicism was operative at the time of the NT. The Stoic world comprised a broad conception of matter in which even something intangible, such as virtue or the soul, was material. This philosophy held that the universe is governed by a "world soul" that rules by law.[156]

Stoic thinkers believed they knew about themselves and their world through self-authenticating sensation. The goal of human life, they said, is to live in accord with the world's fixed laws or reason, laws that they could know. Thus the good life is one that follows reason and is lived according to nature and society's universal structures.[157]

The Stoics stood against the Platonic differentiation of a transcendent world of ideas and an ordinary world. For them, all that exists must be material.[158] The universe consists of unformed matter, without quality, that is organized by dynamic reason or a plan, called the *logos*. This logos is material—it is a spirit or fiery vapor. It permeates all reality, and they called it *god* or *providence*—the soul that fills the universe. Since all events happen according to this logos, it is advantageous to submit to it; such submission to the logos's providence is the heart of the Stoic ethic.[159] Ultimately, a conflagration will reabsorb

---

156. WCG2 briefly introduces Stoicism. See *WCG* 2:952n21, 953n29, 954.
157. *WCG* 2:1024.
158. Kelly, *Doctrines*, 17.
159. Ibid., 18.

all the unformed matter into the logos. To put Stoic teaching another way, "the universe is, at bottom, a living fire."[160]

The Soul. Relative to human nature, the human soul was conceived by the Stoics as a portion of the divine fire, which is the logos. It gives the body its form and character. The soul is material and will survive the body, but only until a time when all will be burned up by fire. The soul has an immanent logos, which is internally present reason, and an expressed logos, which reason makes known by means of speech or self-expression.[161]

Gnostic Origins. The final pagan philosophy important for understanding the development of Christian doctrine is Gnosticism. Research concerning Gnosticism's origins has developed over the years. Older scholarship maintained that Gnosticism was a Christian heresy, a Greek mythology mixed with biblical concepts. This view can be traced to the church fathers, who thought that it was the church's arch enemy and worse than Greek philosophy itself.[162]

A change to that opinion came via the famous German church historian Adolf von Harnack in the late nineteenth/early twentieth century. He argued that, in contrast to the gradual erosion of orthodoxy by Greek thinking, Gnosticism achieved an immediate takeover.[163] R. M. Grant claimed that Gnosticism was a Jewish phenomenon that rose out of the Jews' discontent with God, especially after the destruction of Jerusalem in A.D. 70. God had let them down—he is therefore the evil god of Gnosticism.[164] Bultmann argued that Gnosticism began prior to Christ with a group called the "Mandeans of Iran." The Mandeans then influenced Christianity. Some sectors of Christianity were attracted to Gnosticism, while others were repelled.[165] Bultmann theorized that humanity at the time of early Christianity felt an estrangement from the world and was consumed with existential angst. This angst then

160. William Edgar and K. Scott Oliphint, *Christian Apologetics Past and Present: A Primary Source Reader* (Wheaton, IL: Crossway, 2009), 1:39.

161. Stoicism as a philosophy was complex. See Kelly, *Doctrines*, 18–19.

162. Irenaeus, Tertullian, and Hippolytus each mentioned it.

163. Adolf von Harnack, *History of Dogma*, trans. Neil Buchanan (Boston: Little, Brown, 1902), 1:223–66.

164. Robert M. Grant, *Gnosticism and Early Christianity* (New York: Columbia University Press, 1959).

165. Rudolf Bultmann, *Theologie des Neuen Testaments*, 5 Aufl. (Tübingen: Mohr Siebeck, 1965), 162–83.

sparked a desire for the mystic religion of Gnosticism. Bultmann's theory was the standard interpretation in the middle and latter half of the twentieth century, but recently, support for it has eroded even among critical scholars.[166]

Gnostic Themes. Certain themes ran throughout the various gnostic systems.[167] Gnosticism claimed to mediate a *gnosis*, or "knowledge," that would bring salvation. Gnosticism, while demonstrating diversity in detail, affirmed the antithesis of spirit and matter. The supreme deity always remained in the sphere of the spirit, but this deity sent a type of savior or original man who helped obtain release for those who are captive in the sphere of matter. The knowledge that brings salvation is comprehending that deliverance to the realm of the spirit, which comes somehow through this savior.

We see the philosophical schools continuing to develop as we move closer in time to the NT period. For a brief introduction to the philosophical schools of the apostolic age, see WCG2.[168] We will now move from reviewing pagan contemplation to the world of biblically informed thinking.

PHILO (25 B.C.–A.D. 45/50)

Teaching. Philo was a hellenized Jew who maintained that the Greek translation of the OT, the Septuagint, was divinely inspired in its translation and contained the infallibly revealed will of God in the Mosaic law. To interpret the Scriptures, he employed an allegorical method that had been implemented earlier by Greek philosophers. His theological work was a synthesis of the OT and Greek philosophy. He

166. This thesis was originally published by Hans Jonas, *The Gnostic Religion: The Message of the Alien God and the Beginnings of Christianity*, 2nd rev. ed. (Boston: Beacon, 1963); *Gnosis und spätantiker Geist: Erster Teil, Die mythologische Gnosis*, 3rd ed., Forschungen zur Religion und Literatur des Alten und Neuen Testaments 33 (Göttingen: Vandenhoeck & Ruprecht, 1964); and to include for the first time Jonas's discussion of Plotinus, *Gnosis und spätantiker Geist: Zweiter Teil, Von der Mythologie zur mystischen Philosophie: Erste und zweite Hälfte*, 3rd ed., ed. Kurt Rudolph, Forschungen zur Religion und Literatur des Alten und Neuen Testaments 159 (Göttingen: Vandenhoeck & Ruprecht, 1993).

167. See WCG 2:955; Louis Berkhof, *The History of Christian Doctrines* (Carlisle, PA: Banner of Truth, 1969), 45–50, for more information regarding Gnosticism.

168. For the Stoics and Epicurians, see WCG 2:952–54; for modified Platonism, see WCG 2:954–55. For more information on Stoicism's impact on theology, see the analysis in chapter 6.

thought Moses used an outward form of myth, history, and ceremonial law that expressed an inward, spiritual meaning that was in accord with the best Greek theology.[169]

Philo maintained that God is immutable and that humankind's purpose in the universe is at least in part to serve God. The human mind is made in the image of the divine reason or logos and can therefore contemplate reality beyond time and space. General education prepares the mind for the study of philosophy, which also helps in the study of religion. Theology, however, cannot be understood without divine revelation, and that revelation is found in the Scriptures.[170]

God, for Philo, was the God of his father Abraham and a personal God who loves his creatures even though they err. God's thoughts are higher than human thoughts. God's world and all creation are continually dependent on him. But Philo fused his doctrine of God with the theology of Platonism.[171]

One problem of Philo's theology is a problem with language in relation to God. He thought that there was no creaturely language that was adequate to express the transcendent creator's being. Since the material world is not eternal and is therefore dependent, language is also incapable of expressing the eternality of the transcendent creator.[172] Because of God's great transcendence, Philo believed that what he termed the *logos* performed two functions: the logos helps God in creation and helps people's minds to apprehend God. Philo did not hold that the logos is the sole agent of creation—that thought came later. Philo, as a Jew, had to assert that it was God who created, but the logos helped God in that creation.[173]

Influence. Philo never converted to Christianity, yet his teaching was influential in the formation of early Christian theology because he bridged the gap between Greek philosophy and some biblical teachings. For instance, Philo's doctrine of a sovereign creator God is embraced

---

169. Henry Chadwick, "Philo and the Beginnings of Christian Thought," in *The Cambridge History of Later Greek and Early Medieval Philosophy*, ed. A. H. Armstrong (Cambridge: Cambridge University Press, 1970), 137–38.

170. Ibid., 139–40.

171. Cornelius Van Til, *A Christian Theory of Knowledge* (Nutley, NJ: Presbyterian and Reformed, 1969), 73.

172. Chadwick, "Christian Thought," 142.

173. Kelly, *Doctrines*, 10.

in Christianity, and his doctrine of the logos could also be—and was—adapted to apply to Jesus of Nazareth. Philo also conceived a triad of divine beings that could perhaps be interpreted as a trinity. He said that to the contemplative soul, God appears like a triad, which consists of himself with his two chief powers, creative goodness and kingly power, symbolized by the angels. While this thought is far from a mature doctrine of the Trinity, in the pathways of early Christian thought Philo's theory was adapted in part by Christian theologians.[174]

PERSECUTION OF GOD'S PEOPLE

In addition to understanding the various philosophies surrounding the early church, it is essential to grasp the context of persecution in which the postbiblical church grew.

General Characteristics. Christianity was a persecuted religion until the year of A.D. 312.[175] The persecution of Christians came first from the Jews, then from the Gentiles—accounts of which appear as early as the Gospels and Acts. After the close of the biblical canon, persecution continued, though not uninterruptedly, for more than two hundred years. By A.D. 180, Christianity had spread through the countries of the Mediterranean and continued even farther into the provinces.

Classifying and counting the number of organized persecutions proves difficult. Augustine in the *City of God* put the number of persecutions at ten. Lactantius cited six, while other ancient writers have suggested nine. The exact number of them is not important to remember—we need to investigate the various background elements that provide a unified structure to all the persecutions of the ancient church. After we have finished our investigation, we will seek to interpret the causes of these persecutions.[176]

Persecution under the Jews. During the famous Bar Cochba conflict (A.D. 132–135), when Jewish leaders attempted to revolt against

174. Chadwick, "Christian Thought," 145.
175. See Richard C. Gamble, "Christianity from the Early Fathers to Charlemagne," in *Revolutions in Worldview: Understanding the Flow of Western Thought*, ed. W. Andrew Hoffecker (Phillipsburg, NJ: P&R Publishing, 2007), 109–12.
176. Karl Heussi, *Kompendium der Kirchengeschichte* (Tübingen: Mohr Siebeck, 1971), 47.

Rome, the leader of the insurrection forced all Christians either to join him or be murdered. The rebellion failed, and the Roman government nearly destroyed Judaism. The Jewish historian Josephus recounted the horrific loss of Jewish life—he estimated that 1.1 million Jews were killed in the fighting and ninety-seven thousand taken captive, then sold into slavery or put to death for sport in Roman arenas.[177]

Palestinian Jewish Christians abstained from participating in the conflict in obedience to their interpretation of Jesus's words in Luke 21:20–24. They left Judea before the serious fighting began.[178] But their refusal to help in the revolt made them traitors in the eyes of the non-Christian Jews. After the war, the Pharisees placed an official curse on all Christians in the Jewish liturgy, thus making it impossible for Jewish Christians to worship in the synagogue. The Pharisees reestablished their own Sanhedrin and rallied the shattered forces of Judaism around their strict interpretation of the OT and the Mosaic law.

The fall of Jerusalem to Rome also meant that both Jews and Christians lost their spiritual home. Jerusalem ceased to have any importance in the life of the early church for the next three hundred years. This geographical separation of the early Christians from Christianity's Palestinian roots quickened the church's drift away from a Jewish membership to a Gentile one and from a Hebrew and Aramaic mindset to a Greek one.

Persecution under the Roman Government. The Roman state had generally been tolerant of religions; it classified groups as "permitted" or "non-permitted." Once it became clear that Christianity was no longer part of a Jewish sect, it lost permitted status.

The Roman Empire was polytheistic and syncretistic, meaning that Romans worshipped a plethora of Roman gods as well as the gods of other peoples. The worship of many gods was accepted. Most importantly, however, everyone was required to worship the Roman emperor as god and lord.

The persecution of Christians arose because of their exclusive truth claims. Christianity stood against the fundamentally polytheistic aspects of Roman culture and society. Christians claimed that there

---

177. Nicholas R. Needham, *2,000 Years of Christ's Power*, vol. 1, *The Age of the Early Church Fathers* (London: Grace Publications, 1997), 51.

178. Ibid., 52.

was only one true God, and the great Christian confession that there was one Lord, his son Jesus Christ, amounted to a political offense, a treasonable act against the emperor. Governors began to test suspected Christians to see whether they were "true" Romans by demanding that they worship Caesar and proclaim, "Caesar is Lord." Christians would refuse, because for them Jesus is the Lord, not Caesar.[179]

Christians were also perceived by the general Roman public to be killjoys or sticks-in-the-mud. We know this to be the case in part because of the account found in the *Epistle to Diognetus* (ca. A.D. 130), which reports, "the world hates the Christians, though it receives no wrong from them, because they set themselves against its pleasures."[180] Further, in the text from *Octavius*, by Minucius Felix (ca. 180), a pagan disputant complains that Christians abstain from the pleasures of a gentleman[181]—that is, the theater and the gladiatorial games.

The Christians were blamed for their lack of interest in public affairs, for their choice to remain separate from the rest of society and from pagan social duties.[182] Christians were charged with eating human flesh, rumored to be done in the Lord's Supper, and with incestuous relationships, since Christians greeted each other with a holy kiss or married a "sister" in Christ.[183] Their religion as a whole was so unpopular that Tacitus, who died after 117, said that the Christians were a class of people loathed for their vices. In *A Life of Nero*, Suetonius called the religion a new and baneful superstition.[184]

Christians were charged with being atheists, since they worshipped no visible gods. The charge of atheism, however, was not understood then as it is now. Atheism as defined in Roman culture was the indifference of a citizen to his duties, political or social, as well as disloyalty to the state. Emperor Domitian (A.D. 81–96) condemned many Christians to death under the charge of atheism.

179. See Larry W. Hurtado, *Lord Jesus Christ: Devotion to Jesus in Earliest Christianity* (Grand Rapids: Eerdmans, 2005).

180. Clayton N. Jefford, *The Epistle to Diognetus (with the Fragment of Quadratus): Introduction, Text and Commentary* (Oxford: Oxford University Press, 2013), 208.

181. Cornelius Tacitus, *The Annals of Imperial Rome*, trans. and intro. by Michael Grant (Baltimore: Penguin Books, 1959).

182. Louis Duchesne, *Early History of the Christian Church: From Its Foundation to the End of the Fifth Century* (London: John Murray, 1965), 1:146.

183. Edgar and Oliphint, *Christian Apologetics*, 1:37–38.

184. See Seutonius, *Lives of the Twelve Caesars* (Charles River Editors, 2018), Atla Epub.

Christianity was an illegal religion from the time of Emperor Trajan (A.D. 98–117), who first pronounced Christianity forbidden.[185] He prohibited all secret societies or clubs by reviving a law that was already on the books. Trajan's policy regulated the treatment of Christians for more than a century. It was under Emperor Trajan that Ignatius of Antioch was torn to shreds by beasts in Rome.[186]

Under Antonius Pius (A.D. 138–161), Polycarp of Smyrna suffered martyrdom in A.D. 156. The philosopher-ruler Marcus Aurelius (A.D. 161–180) passed a statute that punished those who endeavored to persuade people to fear God. This law was probably aimed at Christianity. Under his rulership, the famous apologist Justin Martyr received his name after being put to death in about A.D. 166. During the reign of Septimus Severus (A.D. 193–211) persecution continued. Clement of Alexandria provides some details of life during his reign: "Many martyrs are daily burned, confined, or beheaded, before our eyes."[187]

Persecution became widespread under emperors Decius (A.D. 250/51) and Diocletian (A.D. 303–313).[188] Decius led the cruelest persecutions yet, and they continued under his successor, Gallus (A.D. 251–253). Emperor Valerian came to power in A.D. 253, and persecution during his reign produced more martyrs than died under any other emperor.[189] The slaughter rested on a series of legal edicts that prohibited all Christian meetings; attendance at such a meeting was punishable by death.[190] During Valerian's reign, Cyprian was martyred.[191]

A period of relative rest followed during the reign of Valerian's son Gallienus (A.D. 260–268). He chose not to enforce his father's edicts, though neither did he give Christianity permitted status. A similar rest from persecution occurred under Emperor Aurelian (A.D. 270–275).[192]

The Diocletian persecution, noted above, exceeded all previous official outbursts in its intensity. Edicts grew progressively worse by ordering the destruction of church buildings, the burning of Bibles,

---

185. Needham, *2,000 Years*, 1:80.
186. Heussi, *Kompendium*, 44.
187. From Clement's *Stromata*, as cited by W. H. C. Frend, *Martyrdom and Persecution in the Early Church* (Grand Rapids: Baker, 1981), 353–55.
188. Needham, *2,000 Years*, 1:144, 149–51.
189. Ibid., 44.
190. Ibid., 45. The earlier persecution edict had been established in A.D. 250.
191. Ibid.
192. Ibid.

and the removal of all Christians from public office and by demanding, on pain of death, that Christians sacrifice to the gods.

Eusebius, the famous church historian, witnessed the persecutions in Egypt and other areas. He related accounts of church buildings torn to the ground, Bibles burned at marketplaces, and the hunting down, capture, and torture of pastors. Death frequently came at the fangs of wild beasts. It was so terrible and bloody that Eusebius reports that even the beasts got tired of their frequent attacks on the innocent Christians. Finally, edicts of toleration were issued in A.D. 311 under Galerius. This development does not end the story of Christian persecution, but it does end the tale of woe suffered by the ancient church.

Analysis of the Persecutions. In general, persecutions of the second century were sporadic and prompted by the mob. The average Roman citizen could not understand and did not like this novel religion, with its supposed barbarian origins and lack of patriotism for the empire—a religion whose gloomy adherents held to a blind and irrational faith. At that time, average Christians appear to have had neither sophisticated culture nor high social standing and were usually economically poor.

In the third century, however, persecution was directed in large measure by the state and was universal. The government had by then come to fear the threat of the church.[193] One of the reasons for this fear was the suspicion that Christianity was an illicit cult or a vulgar innovation whose religious aspect was probably a mere facade concealing something far worse.[194] The Roman government was always suspect of clubs, and Christianity could have appeared to be dangerously antisocial. It was not on the list of approved societies, so the government had to ban it.

For the ancient believer, persecution was an ever-present reality. Believers knew that persecution would occur either in their lifetime or their children's lifetime. Such an understanding of the world would necessarily create a sense of urgency and importance for their profession of faith. Professing Christ was a matter of life and death. While the early church had to discuss what to do with the "lapsed"—those who had capitulated in some way to pagan worship to escape perse-

---

193. B. J. Kidd, *A History of the Christian Church to AD 461* (Oxford: Oxford University Press, 1922), 233.

194. F. F. Bruce, *The Growing Day: The Progress of Christianity from the Fall of Jerusalem to the Accession of Constantine* (Grand Rapids: Eerdmans, 1953), 15.

cution—in general, when Christianity comes with a high price, only the strong in faith are willing to endure. This testing produces a purer Christianity. As believers today, we wonder whether God would give us the strength to withstand under torture. We could ask ourselves what it would be like always to have to worship in secret, or to have all our property confiscated. I wonder whether I could stand to see the persecution of my loved ones or bear the insults that were commonplace for Christians for so many years.

When thinking through how to interpret persecution, it is good to remember that God is in control of all events on earth—his sovereign mercy ordains everything that happens. Further, God's blessing on his people does not always mean that he is going to bless them financially or physically. Early Christians, with few exceptions, were not rich people. Yet God greatly blessed the ancient church.

Despite enduring persecution, Christianity maintained an outward face that critiqued the surrounding pagan culture. One example consists in the church's stance against abortions, which were very common and accepted. Finally, the fact that the church is not suffering persecution in all parts of the world today should result in praise to God in our hearts and prayer that he keeps us faithful.[195] Remembering that persecution was the backdrop of all the theological advances during these centuries, the next chapter will examine the theologians who lived in this context. They are known as the "apostolic fathers" and the "apologists."

KEY TERMS

Milesian thinking
beginning principle
hylozoism
atomists
Pythagoreans
Sophists
world of forms
form and matter

195. See Peter Leithart, *Against Christianity* (Moscow, ID: Canon Press, 2003).

law of contradiction
unmoved mover
Gnosticism
apostolic fathers
apologists

STUDY QUESTIONS

1. What is the proper method for studying the developing doctrine of Christ's church?
2. What are some of the benefits of studying the history of Christ's church?
3. What are some of the main characteristics of Milesian thinking?
4. What is the philosophical question of "the one and the many," and why is knowing it important?
5. What are some of the main lines of Socrates's thinking?
6. What are some of the differences between Plato's two worlds?
7. What are some of the types of human knowing, and why is human knowing important?
8. Why did Aristotle reject Plato's two worlds?
9. Does knowing about persecution in the ancient church make an impact on your thinking about the contemporary church's witness to the world?
10. What were some of the weaknesses of the interpretation of Scripture during this period?

RESOURCES FOR FURTHER STUDY

Coxe, A. Cleveland, ed. *The Ante-Nicene Fathers*. Vol. 1, *The Apostolic Fathers, Justin Martyr, Irenaeus*. Vol. 2, *Fathers of the Second Century: Hermas, Tatian, Athenagoras, Theophilus, and Clement of Alexandria*. Vol. 3, *Latin Christianity: Its Founder, Tertullian I. Apologetic; II. Anti-Marcion; III. Ethical*. Grand Rapids: Eerdmans, 1988. Helpful introductions and complete texts of many of the writings from this time period, despite the translations not being contemporary.

Frame, John M. "Greeks Bearing Gifts." In *Revolutions in Worldview: Understanding the Flow of Western Thought*, edited by W. Andrew Hoffecker,

1–36. Phillipsburg, NJ: P&R Publishing, 2007. An excellent summary of Greek philosophical thought written from a distinctly Christian vantage point by an excellent communicator.

Kelly, J. N. D. *Early Christian Doctrines*. London: Black, 1977. An expertly written textbook that has been the gold standard in patristics for decades.

Needham, Nicholas R. *2,000 Years of Christ's Power*. Vol. 1, *The Age of the Early Church Fathers*. London: Grace Publications, 1997. A very readable text that is accurate and dependable.

Walker, Williston. *A History of the Christian Church*. New York: Scribner's Sons, 1959. A standard college and seminary one-volume textbook that has been revised over the decades since its first publication.

~ 2 ~

The Apostolic Fathers, the Rise of Heresy, and the Apologists

THE AIM OF THE previous chapter was to till the ground with background philosophical material and to offer a brief glance into the early years of church history. This chapter will examine the lives and context of some of Christianity's earliest theologians in preparation for chapter 3, a summary chapter tracing their theology through standard *loci* of systematic theology. One of the best ways to open the thought world of the earliest post-NT era is through the lens of the extant literature. The amount of theological advance made in this era is incredible considering that the writings were from, for example, a man on his way to suffer martyrdom by the teeth and claws of wild beasts! In the light of their circumstances, the writers of this era did not have the leisure to write doctrinal treatises or full systematic theologies.[1] Thus the writings that we do have reflect the most pressing concerns of the church as she confronted impending persecution and the rise of heresy.

APOSTOLIC FATHERS

A group whom we call the *apostolic fathers* composed that first group of writings. They did not use the title for themselves! The term first appeared in the seventeenth century to represent figures and writ-

---

1. See Geoffrey Bromiley, *Historical Theology: An Introduction* (Grand Rapids: Eerdmans, 1978), 3; Richard C. Gamble, "Christianity from the Early Fathers to Charlemagne," in *Revolutions in Worldview: Understanding the Flow of Western Thought*, ed. W. Andrew Hoffecker (Phillipsburg, NJ: P&R Publishing, 2007), 100–101.

ings that emerged in the aftermath of the apostolic witness. We will begin with biographical sketches of some of the most important theologians of the time.

Clement of Rome and *1 Clement*. Clement was supposedly the third successor to the apostle Peter. Although we know little of his early life, he rose to become a prominent bishop in Rome.[2] Approximately at the end of Emperor Domitian's reign (A.D. 81–96), a debate erupted between some members of the church at Corinth and the congregation's leaders. Clement wrote a letter titled *1 Clement*, or *Epistle to the Corinthians*, to admonish the members to submit to their leaders.[3] *1 Clement* is the earliest known Christian writing after the NT.

Clement wrote to settle differences and plead for unity, discipline, and love in the midst of church dissension. The epistle insisted that God had prescribed the time, the place, and the way that he wanted to be worshipped. When believers follow God's law, they do not sin. If they fail to obey, they will be visited by death.[4] Clement also taught that God bestowed authority on the ordained clergy and that this God-given authority made an indelible mark on the minister. The document has rightly been called the birthplace of the Roman Catholic notion of the rights of the church.

2 Clement. This piece of literature is the oldest extant post-NT sermon.[5] It was preached in ca. A.D. 140, perhaps in Corinth or Rome, by an unknown preacher. If the sermon was given in Rome, then perhaps the author was Clement.[6] It is similar in content and style to *The Shepherd of Hermas*, discussed below.[7] The author advised strict

2. Gamble, "Christianity to Charlemagne," 100; Nicholas R. Needham, *2,000 Years of Christ's Power*, vol. 1, *The Age of the Early Church Fathers* (London: Grace Publications, 1997), 58–59.

3. An English translation of the text can be found in A. Cleveland Coxe, ed., *The Ante-Nicene Fathers*, vol. 1, *The Apostolic Fathers, Justin Martyr, Irenaeus* (Grand Rapids: Eerdmans, 1988), 1–23.

4. Ibid., 1:16, 17.

5. See Needham, *2,000 Years*, 1:58–59.

6. Ernst Staehelin, *Die Verkündigung des Reiches Gottes in der Kirche Jesu Christi*, vol. 1, *Von der Zeit der Apostel bis zur Auflösung des Römischen Reiches* (Basel: Reinhardt, 1951), 116. See Karl Heussi, *Kompendium der Kirchengeschichte* (Tübingen: Mohr Siebeck, 1971), 26. Most scholars deny that it was written by Clement. Recent discussion of authorship is found in Christopher Tuckett, ed., *2 Clement: Introduction, Text, and Commentary* (Oxford: Oxford University Press, 2012), 15–17.

7. It expresses both the divinity and humanity of Christ. In *2 Clement* 20, 5, Christ is called the "prince of incorruptibility," the one "through whom God made manifest to us truth and

obedience to the presbyters.[8] The sermon's high doctrine of Scripture is prominent. He introduced a gospel quotation as Scripture, understood the unity of Scripture, saw the NT as Scripture, and equated the written Word of God directly with the God of truth.[9]

Pseudo-Clementines. This Christian "novel," perhaps written before A.D. 150, most probably appeared in the city of Corinth.[10] It consists of twenty homilies or devotionals that narrate the conversion of a man named Clement and the miraculous reunion that he had with his lost family. It also describes various episodes in his accompanying of Peter, including the conflict between Peter and Simon Magus.[11]

Ignatius of Antioch (A.D. 50–108). Ignatius suffered a martyr's death in Rome probably during Emperor Trajan's reign (A.D. 98–117). On the way to his brutal execution, to be eaten alive by beasts, he wrote seven letters.[12] Four of them were written from the city of Smyrna and three while he was in Troas.[13] From Smyrna, he wrote letters to churches in Ephesus, Magnesia, and Tralles exhorting the communities to obedience and thanking them for their faithfulness to him.[14] He also wrote to Christians in Rome imploring them not to attempt to intervene in his behalf to hinder his martyrdom.[15] In additional letters from Troas to the cities of Philadelphia and Smyrna and to the presbyter Polycarp, Ignatius requested that their churches send delegates to congratulate survivors of the persecution.[16] The letter to Polycarp

heavenly life." The church existed before creation. Then she was spiritual and barren. Now she has become flesh. She is the body of Christ. Baptism is called a "seal" that must be kept. See Johannes Quasten, *Patrology* (Utrecht: Spectrum, 1975), 1:55.

8. J. N. D. Kelly, *Early Christian Doctrines* (London: Black, 1977), 35.

9. Bromiley, *Historical Theology*, 9.

10. See Oscar Cullmann, *Le problème littéraire et historique du Roman Pseudo-Clémentin* (Paris: Librarie Félix Alcan, 1930). There has been great scholarly debate concerning when the text was written. The traditional opinion is that it was written in the third or fourth century. But there is a high possibility that it was composed earlier. For more information from a later-date position, see Wilhelm Schneemelcher and R. M. Wilson, *New Testament Apocrypha: Writings Related to the Apostles* (Louisville: Westminster John Knox Press, 1992), 2:483–85.

11. Quasten (*Patrology*, 1:61) says that in the "books of Recognitions" there is a clear statement of the Trinity. But there is a fuzzy conception of God—a combination of pantheism and personal deity. See Heussi, *Kompendium*, 25.

12. See Gamble, "Christianity to Charlemagne," 101–2; Needham, *2,000 Years*, 1:59.

13. Staehelin, *Von der Zeit*, 1:90–93. See Heussi, *Kompendium*, 26.

14. Coxe, *Ante-Nicene Fathers*, 1:43–72.

15. Ibid., 1:73–78.

16. Ibid., 1:79–96.

contains pastoral advice to help Polycarp in his ministry as bishop. Ignatius's letters indicate the strength of ties between churches and a shared consciousness, which led them to seek consensus on matters of great concern.

Papias of Hierapolis (ca. A.D. 60–130). Papias wrote the *Explanation of the Sayings of the Lord* possibly as early as A.D. 95—at the latest, in A.D. 150. What little we know about him comes from the church historian Eusebius, who preserved part of Papias's works but, unfortunately for Papias, called him a "man of very little intelligence."[17] The *Sayings* contain the best statement for the canonicity of the Gospel of Mark.[18]

Polycarp of Smyrna (A.D. 69–155). It is thought that Polycarp sat at the feet of the apostle John.[19] Before suffering martyrdom in A.D. 155 (or 156), he wrote the *Epistle to the Philippians*, a letter of exhortation.[20] Polycarp defended the doctrine of the incarnation and Christ's death on the cross; he also enjoined prayer for the civil authorities.

Polycarp's courage in the face of martyrdom and his refusal to proffer worship to the emperor lent confidence to the church as persecution spread in the second century. It signaled how, from its inception, the good news of the NT emboldened followers to die for their faith.[21]

Epistle of Barnabas (A.D. 96–138).[22] This work, written sometime between A.D. 96 and 138, during Emperor Hadrian's reign, is more like a theological tract than a letter. The author was not the apostle Barnabas but was probably a Gentile convert who wrote from the city of Alexandria with the goal of imparting what he called "perfect knowledge and faith."

The work consists of a theoretical and a practical section. The tract asserts Christ's preexistence and teaches that baptism confers adoption, thus transforming believers into temples of the Holy Spirit. The

17. Ibid., 1:51–58.
18. See Eusebius's *Church History* 3.39.15–16. An English translation is available in Eusebius, *The History of the Church from Christ to Constantine*, trans. G. A. Williamson (New York: Dorset, 1965), 152–53.
19. See Gamble, "Christianity to Charlemagne," 102; Needham, *2,000 Years*, 1:61.
20. Coxe, *Ante-Nicene Fathers*, 1:31–36.
21. Ibid., 1:37–44.
22. See Gamble, "Christianity to Charlemagne," 102–3; Needham, *2,000 Years*, 1:61. There is a German language translation by Hans Windisch, *Handbuch zum Neuen Testament, Ergänzungsband die apostolischen Väter*, vol. 3, *Der Barnabasbrief* (Tübingen: Mohr Siebeck, 1920).

work holds to a Christian obligation to protect the life of the infant, even that of the unborn. The ancient church systematically rescued abandoned children who were left to die at garbage sites.[23]

The author expressed himself with either real or pretended humility, not as one who is a "Teacher" but as one simply from the congregation. Nevertheless, he was certainly a teacher, and his exegetical method set the tone for interpreting Scripture for centuries.

The author thought that the OT is best understood not as straightforward history; rather, it should be interpreted by the use of allegory or typology. Using typology, events in Israelite history became important not for their historicity but for their spiritual or moral meaning. In that way, the OT speaks clearly of that which was to come in the NT.

The epistle probes the celebration of the Sabbath for Christians on Sunday, not Saturday. The author underlined the Ten Commandments' Sabbath command, as well as the covenantal promise that when the Sabbath was embraced in the heart, God's love would be poured out on his people. He also called the Sabbath the beginning of creation.

The author's allegorical elaboration of the completion of creation in six days meant that the Lord would complete the earth's history in six thousand years. Each day of creation stood for one thousand years. When God said at Isaiah 1:13 that he rejected Israel's Sabbaths and new moons, he meant not that the present Sabbath was unwelcome but that a time will come when he will bring all things to rest, and at that time he will create another world. That new world will last for eight days, thus signaling the beginning of perhaps another world. This period of days will be a time of great joy.[24]

Israel's dietary laws prohibited eating pork. The author of *Barnabas* thought that the prohibition should not be taken literally; rather, the commandment forbade too much interaction with men who are, in fact, like pigs.

Finally, the writer viewed Jesus as previewed in the OT. The cross is found both in the outstretched hands of the praying Moses and

23. Coxe, *Ante-Nicene Fathers*, 1:148: "Thou shalt not slay the child by procuring abortion; nor again shalt thou destroy it after it is born." See Michael J. Gorman, *Abortion and the Early Church* (Eugene, OR: Wipf & Stock, 1998).
24. Coxe, *Ante-Nicene Fathers*, 1:146–47.

in the snake that Moses lifted up in the wilderness. He also saw the scapegoat of Leviticus 16:7–10 as picturing the coming Christ. *Barnabas's* allegorizing method gained wide acceptance in the early church and led many Christians to search for hidden meanings in Scripture instead of receiving their literal, historical meaning as the basis for comprehending a given biblical text.

The Shepherd of Hermas (A.D. 96–140). *The Shepherd of Hermas* is a book of revelations supposedly granted to the Roman Christian named Hermas, brother of Pius, a bishop from A.D. 140 to 154.[25] It is difficult to determine the work's date of composition—it was perhaps written in two parts sometime between A.D. 96 and 140. The first section of *The Shepherd* contains four visions, with a transition section leading into a second section containing twelve commands and nine parables. Both sections were supposedly delivered by two heavenly beings: an old woman and a shepherd.[26]

Like the *Epistle of Barnabas*, *The Shepherd of Hermas* depends heavily on the use of allegory. It views the church as a tower made of stones drawn from water. If those stones become damaged, then they can only be cleansed or repaired once. This writing exercised a strong pastoral influence, which led people to postpone baptism for fear of sinning after they had received baptism. *The Shepherd* also held that the Holy Spirit was identified with Christ—there were only two divine persons.[27]

Didache (A.D. 100–150). The full title of this work reads, "The Lord's instruction to the Gentiles through the twelve Apostles." The text was not known to the scholarly world until 1883. While not actually written by the apostles, the document provides a brief summary of early doctrine as well as ethical norms and church practice.[28] Since the work is a compilation, it is difficult to determine a precise date for its composition. Scholars estimate that it was written either in Syria or in Egypt sometime between A.D. 100 and 150.[29]

25. See Gamble, "Christianity to Charlemagne," 103–4; Needham, *2,000 Years*, 1:61.

26. An English text can be found in A. Cleveland Coxe, *The Ante-Nicene Fathers*, vol. 2, *Fathers of the Second Century: Hermas, Tatian, Athenagoras, Theophilus, and Clement of Alexandria* (Grand Rapids: Eerdmans, 1988), 9–55.

27. Staehelin, *Von der Zeit*, 102; Kelly, *Doctrines*, 92.

28. Needham, *2,000 Years*, 1:59.

29. Heussi, *Kompendium*, 26.

The text is divided into two main parts. The first part, chapters 1–10, contains practical advice and liturgical instructions. The first six chapters present for the newly baptized opposing patterns for walking. One pattern is the way of life, summarized by segments from the Ten Commandments, ethical injunctions against magic, omens, abortion and infanticide. The contrasting pattern, the way of death, includes an extended list of sins. Chapters 7–10 propose liturgical suggestions for Christian baptism.[30] The second part, chapters 11–15, contains disciplinary regulations. The last chapter discusses the return of the Lord.

The apostolic fathers present fascinating information on how Christ's fledgling church lived, worshipped, and thought about the Bible and how to apply it to life during those stressful days.

HERETICS

The earliest years of the ancient church witnessed the appearance of those whom we call "heretics," whose ideas differed sharply from both biblical Christianity and from the church's emerging tradition. Three movements posed a significant threat to biblical Christianity in the second century: Marcionism, Montanism, and later Gnosticism.

Marcion (A.D. 110–160).[31] Marcion's father was a bishop from an area near the Black Sea who apparently dismissed his own son from the congregation for espousing false theological positions. Marcion then traveled west and visited Smyrna, where he met the leader Polycarp, then turned to Rome. Marcion exercised influence over the congregation at Rome. Conflict seemed to accompany him, and in July A.D. 144 he was separated from that congregation.

His writing, *Antitheses*, posed an enormous difference between the OT God, conceived as a cruel, ignorant, fickle deity, and the NT God of love, mercy, and forgiveness. Marcion's teaching denied the unity of biblical revelation. In support of his radical dualism, he proposed

---

30. See Thomas O'Lachlan, *The Didache: A Window on the Earliest Christians* (London: SPCK, 2011).

31. See Gamble, "Christianity to Charlemagne," 105; William Edgar and K. Scott Oliphint, *Christian Apologetics Past and Present: A Primary Source Reader* (Wheaton, IL: Crossway, 2009), 86; Needham, *2,000 Years*, 1:97–98; Louis Berkhof, *The History of Christian Doctrines* (Carlisle, PA: Banner of Truth, 1969), 52.

a canon consisting of his own work, the Gospel of Luke expurgated of all passages favorable to the OT, and a similarly altered Pauline corpus. Marcion's teaching was extremely popular and spread rapidly throughout the church. His altered canon forced the church to propose its own list in response. Marcion died about A.D. 160.[32]

Montanus and Montanism. In about the year A.D. 156, a man named Montanus, a converted pagan priest, appeared in the small town of Ardabau in Phrygien. He claimed to have received what he termed "spiritual revelations" from God—not only did God send him revelations, but also God the Father, the Son, and especially the Holy Spirit worked in him and spoke through him.[33] Montanus saw himself as a vehicle of the Holy Spirit either simply supplementing the Holy Spirit's work or, more likely, as the incarnation of the Paraclete.[34] Those divine revelations were sufficiently important that Montanus thought he had to communicate them to the whole church.

Montanus preached the imminent arrival of the heavenly Jerusalem on the earth. Before its coming, there would be a general distribution of and filling with the Holy Spirit. Connected to Montanus's prophetic message was also a supposedly God-given task to prepare the way for this great occurrence. To prepare for the arrival of the heavenly Jerusalem, the church must engage in certain ascetic practices, particularly fasting.

Later Gnosticism. In addition to the teachings of Marcion and Montanus, a third angle of attack against the church came from the developments of later Gnosticism. There were two types of later Gnosticism.[35] The first was Manichaeism, established by Mani (A.D. 210–276), a Persian raised in a Jewish-Christian group. Mani supposedly received revelations that there were two great powers, light and darkness. Jesus's

---

32. Marcion's ideas, rather than being branded as heretical, have wrongly been defended as being an early type of Luther's! See Kurt D. Schmidt, *Grundriss der Kirchengeschichte* (Göttingen: Vandenhoek & Ruprecht, 1963), 69. Schmidt offers a spirited defense of Marcion's teaching and argues that he was imprisoned for the same inner testimony as was the Reformer Martin Luther.

33. See Gamble, "Christianity to Charlemagne," 105–6; Needham, *2,000 Years*, 1:104–11; William Cunningham, *Historical Theology* (Edinburgh: Banner of Truth, 1979), 1:162–63; Kelly, *Doctrines*, 59.

34. Edgar and Oliphint, *Christian Apologetics*, 116. He was joined by two women who, supposedly, were also embodiments of the Spirit.

35. Earlier Gnosticism's origins and themes were presented in the previous chapter.

role was to help people release their souls from their bodies so they could join the light.[36]

The second type of later Gnosticism is represented by Valentinus (A.D. 160) and his disciples. Valentinus was born in Alexandria and worked in Rome; he was a member of the church there. He thought that there was a good god, variously named Unknown Father or Unbegotten. This god had a wife named Silence, and they had paired, divine children called *aeons*. There were thirty such divine couples. Some of them, such as those named Mind and Truth, were stronger than others. All these aeons made up the heavenly realm, or *pleroma*. Outside the *pleroma* two aeons were produced, named Christ and Holy Spirit. Their mission was to rescue the divine child Sophia, which they accomplished, and in thankfulness the aeons of the *pleroma* produced yet one more child, named Jesus. This Jesus was born of a virgin and had to live among humans. He revealed truth to humanity but was still crucified. On the cross, the aeon left his earthly body and he died.[37]

Gnosticism and Montanism mounted a profound threat to Christian belief and practice. The extreme views of these heresies posed a radical alternative to scriptural teaching and the emerging teaching of the church.

APOLOGISTS

In response to some of these heresies, a group arose known as the apologists, writers who defended the faith when Christianity came under attack.[38] While early heresies illustrate the internal threats to Christianity's integrity, opposition arose from various external sources as well. We saw in the previous chapter that the Roman state regarded

---

36. Edgar and Oliphint, *Christian Apologetics*, 84: "Its appeal was to the common notion that there is a struggle between good and evil in the world in which the two often appear equally matched."

37. Ibid., 84–85.

38. Important figures from this time include Quadratus, who presented an apology to Emperor Hadrian in ca. A.D. 125 in which Quadratus presented Jesus's miracles as proof of his being the Savior. See Eusebius, *History of the Church*, 155–56. Also, Aristo of Pella defended Christianity against Judaism in a tract written ca. A.D. 140. We know simply the tract's title, "Discussion between Jason and Papiscus concerning Christ." See Gamble, "Christianity to Charlemagne," 106; Berkhof, *History of Christian Doctrines*, 56–58.

the profession of Christianity as a capital crime. Since the time of Emperor Hadrian, believers wrote letters or tracts defending Christianity against the misunderstandings and slanders of the opposition. The new religion was also viewed in derision by the Roman intellectual elite. The apologists desired to demonstrate that converting to Christianity did not entail committing intellectual suicide.

The apologists presented Christianity as a philosophy of life. It was, in fact, the lone true philosophy, one set in deep and abiding competition with Greek thinking. Some argue that because of that goal, the apologists took on the methods, words, and even perspectives of Hellenistic philosophical thinking. This approach has been called the "hellenization of Christianity."

It is naive to think that the apologists, while historically distant from us today, were somehow vastly inferior in their understanding of the claims of Christ on life as a whole. While Christianity was indeed presented as a philosophy, a number of apologists viewed Greek speculative thinking as the archenemy of Christianity. For them, Christian belief and pagan philosophical theorizing stood as polar opposites. The early apologists' task and challenges were not so dissimilar to those of our own time.[39]

Aristides of Athens (died 134 A.D.) Aristides held the exalted post of philosopher of the city of Athens. He addressed the earliest surviving apology to either Emperor Hadrian, thus dating it to ca. A.D. 125, or more likely to Emperor Antonius Pius, thereby giving it a date of ca. A.D. 140.[40]

Aristides presented Christianity as a philosophy that rises above all others due to its consistency with reason and its answers to the questions that philosophers ask. He criticized polytheism by use of *reductio ad absurdum*. He systematically demonstrated that all other religions worship false deities. And he claimed that he came to this knowledge through contemplation of the world and its existing harmonies.[41]

Aristides described the attributes of the godhead primarily in terms of what God is not; this approach will be called the *via negativa*, mean-

---

39. These issues touch on the question of theological method that is further analyzed in chapter 6 and subsequent chapters.

40. Gamble, "Christianity to Charlemagne," 106–7; Needham, *2,000 Years*, 1:84.

41. Edgar and Oliphint, *Christian Apologetics*, 1:30–33.

ing "negative way." God is not like a man or any part of creation—the Creator always transcends his creation.[42] Aristides described Christ as the Son of God Most High who had come down from heaven and was born of a Hebrew virgin. To accomplish that for which he was incarnated, he was crucified, died, and was buried, but after three days he ascended to heaven.[43]

Justin Martyr (d. A.D. 165). Born in Palestine of pagan parents, Justin was the most important of the apologists. His earlier intellectual pilgrimage included forays into Stoicism, Aristotelianism, Pythagoreanism, Platonism, and several other schools of thought coming in between. Supposedly, while Justin was walking on the shore, an old man convinced him to read the OT prophets and the apostles of Christ. Following Justin's conversion at Ephesus, he defended Christianity for the rest of his life. He founded a school in Rome during the time of Emperor Antonius Pius (A.D. 138–161). In ca. A.D. 165, Justin was beheaded with six of his companions.[44]

Justin authored a number of works. He addressed his *First Apology* (ca. A.D. 150/55) to Emperor Antonius Pius, as did many of the apologists. The first part of this work pointed out the injustice of governmental punishment of believers simply because they were Christians. Since Christianity was not proven to be a crime, the empire was in danger of committing a worse offense than the Athenians did when they killed Socrates. Christians were not atheists; instead, they were the intellectual and spiritual heirs of truth, wherever it is found. Justin's second part of the apology justified Christianity with a positive presentation of its doctrines.[45]

Justin wrote *The Dialogue with Trypho* after *First Apology*. A lengthy work containing 142 chapters, *The Dialogue* is a transcript of a two-day discussion conceivably held at Ephesus with a learned Jew—perhaps the rabbi Tarphon mentioned in the Mishnah. The introduction included a narrative of Justin's conversion. *The Dialogue* is usually divided into three parts: the first section, chapters

---

42. Ibid., 1:30.
43. Ibid., 1:31.
44. Gamble, "Christianity to Charlemagne," 107–8; Bromiley, *Historical Theology*, 13–17; Needham, *2,000 Years*, 1:85–87.
45. Coxe, *Ante-Nicene Fathers*, 1:159–87; Edgar and Oliphint, *Christian Apologetics*, 1:42–63.

9–47, presented the Christian understanding of the OT;[46] the second section, chapters 48–108, defended the deity of Christ;[47] the third section, chapters 109–42, presented Christians as the new Israel.[48] Justin composed other works, including *Against All Heresies*, written against Marcion; *Discourse against the Greeks*; *On the Sovereignty of God*; and *On the Soul*.[49]

Justin's theology placed God at the center of all thought. God was without origin and nameless.[50] Unfortunately, Justin's description of God sounded very similar to Plato's description of the demiurge. His Christology names a "Logos Mediator," with a clear subordination of the Logos to the Father; he referred to Jesus as a teacher. This "Logos Christology" provided a point of contact between pagan philosophy and Christianity. Justin considered Christ to be superior to all philosophers as the incarnate "Reason" or "Logos of God." Using Stoic terminology, Justin argued that the philosophers had only the *logos spermaticos*—an innate idea of the Word—but Christianity had the very Logos himself. He argued that Platonic philosophy had only plagiarized Moses; therefore, those who lived according to reason were genuine believers even though they lived among godless people. But only among Christians has the Logos been fully revealed and thus come to fruition.

Justin's doctrine of humanity was significant for the later development of what will be called Pelagianism and later Arminianism. Marrying Platonic philosophy with Christianity, Justin saw humanity as possessing complete independence, that is, unlimited free will. There was no divine foreordination.

Tatian the Syrian (A.D. 120–180). Coming from the East, Tatian arrived in Rome, where he became a Christian and a student of Justin's. After Justin's death, Tatian returned home. He opposed marriage, drinking wine, and eating meat. His writings include the *Diatessaron*.[51]

---

46. Coxe, *Ante-Nicene Fathers*, 1:194–219.

47. Ibid., 1:219–53.

48. Ibid., 1:253–70.

49. Ibid., 1:271–308.

50. In chapter 6 of his *Second Apology*, Justin says, "But to the Father of all, who is unbegotten, there is no name given"; see Coxe, *Ante-Nicene Fathers*, 1:190.

51. See William L. Petersen, *Tatian's Diatessaron: Its Creation, Dissemination, Significance, and History in Scholarship* (Leiden: Brill, 1994).

Today this work would be called a "harmony of the Gospels," since it takes parts of all four of our canonical gospels and makes them into one story. There are no copies of Tatian's original, and scholars are not certain whether it was written in Greek or Syriac. Tatian's *Address to the Greeks*, written after A.D. 165, was perhaps not really intended to be an apology for Christianity. But whatever its actual purpose, in this work Tatian, unlike his mentor, utterly rejected and sharply criticized Greek cults. Four sections of his *Address*—on cosmology, demonology, a critique of Greek society, and on Christianity's moral value—elevate Christian thinking over against pagan thought.[52]

Melito of Sardis (d. ca. A.D. 170). Very little is known of Melito's life. We know that around A.D. 170 he wrote an apology, parts of which appear in Eusebius's *Church History*. Another work, titled "Homily on the Passion" and discovered only recently, contains the story of the exodus and the Passover, both of which serve as a type of Christ's redemptive work. Melito asserted Christ's divinity, his preexistence, his incarnation, and the doctrine of original sin.[53]

Athenagoras of Athens (A.D. 133–190). Athenagoras is judged to be the most eloquent of the Christian apologists and was kinder than Tatian in his attitude toward Greek culture. In his *Supplication for the Christians*, written ca. A.D. 177, he refuted the three standard legal charges made against Christians: that they were atheistic, cannibalistic, and incestuous.[54]

Athenagoras's *On the Resurrection of the Dead* attempts to prove the doctrine of the resurrection from the viewpoint of reason. He argued that the resurrection of the dead in no way interfered with God's nature; furthermore, it is consistent with the nature of humanity—God created human beings for eternity.

Athenagoras illustrated early delineations of Trinitarian belief among apologists. He carefully avoided subordinationism in his Trinitarian teaching, and he affirmed the deity of the Holy Spirit. He was convinced that true wisdom depended on divine revelation.[55]

---

52. Gamble, "Christianity to Charlemagne," 108.
53. Ibid., 109.
54. See Gamble, "Christianity to Charlemagne," 108; Needham, *2,000 Years*, 1:84. See more on those charges in the section on persecution above. The text is found in Edgar and Oliphint, *Christian Apologetics*, 1:71–82.
55. Edgar and Oliphint (*Christian Apologetics*, 67) say that he had a Greek view of matter.

Theophilus of Antioch (ca. A.D. 180). Theophilus converted to Christianity from a pagan background. His writings include *To Autolycus* (ca. A.D. 180), in which he defended Christianity against the objections of his pagan friend Autolycus. His defense of Scripture stands out as the first postbiblical work to develop the doctrine of the Scripture's inspiration, and it illustrates that the infallibility of Scripture and the continuity of the Old and New Testaments were assumed from the earliest times. Theophilus called Paul's writings and the Gospels the "holy word of God."[56]

Epistle to Diognetus (ca. A.D. 130). This work takes the form of a letter but is an apology addressed to a high-ranking pagan named Diognetus. The apology aggressively attacks paganism by mocking pagan gods as useless and helpless, being made of wood and stone. Scholars are not certain of this work's time of writing, but it was probably composed at the beginning of the third century. We no longer have a manuscript of the letter because the one text of it that had survived (and was housed in a library in Strasbourg, France) was burned in 1870.[57]

Hermias (ca. A.D. 200–600). This work was a satire on pagan philosophy. Based only on internal evidence, scholars estimate its composition sometime between A.D. 200 and 600. The work consists of ten chapters, and the author is unknown.[58]

Irenaeus of Lyons (ca. A.D. 130–202). The most important theologian of the second century was Irenaeus of Lyon.[59] He summed up that era's thought and dominated Christian orthodoxy before Origen. Some call him the founder of Christian theology, since he was the first one to formulate the whole of Christian doctrine in dogmatic terms. Irenaeus was likely born in either Asia Minor or Smyrna and, at least for a time, was a student of Polycarp's. Well-educated in Greek philosophy and poetry,[60] he would eventually move to the prosperous city of Lyons in France. After persecution rolled through Lyons in A.D. 177, Irenaeus was made bishop.

---

56. Gamble, "Christianity to Charlemagne," 109.
57. Bromiley, *Historical Theology*, 10–13; Needham, *2,000 Years*, 1:61–62.
58. For a critical text in French, see R. P. C. Hanson, ed., *Hermias: Satire des philosophes païens*, Sources Chrétiennes 388 (Paris: Les Éditions du Cerf, 1993).
59. Berkhof, *History of Christian Doctrines*, 63.
60. See Gamble, "Christianity to Charlemagne," 112–13; Needham, *2,000 Years*, 1:99.

During the controversy with the Montanists, Irenaeus was sent to Rome to help mediate discussions.[61] Jerome listed Irenaeus as dying a martyr's death, though we cannot be certain about this detail. During his life, Irenaeus pushed forward Christian thought in several key areas. As an apologist, he leveled a devastating attack against Gnosticism. In the process, he defended the authority of the Scriptures and articulated one of the earliest full-orbed theologies to counter false teaching. The writing of Irenaeus is rather difficult to comprehend, but because of his significance in the early church, it is imperative for Christians to know at least something of his thought.[62]

Irenaeus's main work was *Detection and Overthrow of the Pretended but False Gnosis,*[63] which he composed during the time of Emperor Kommodus (A.D. 180–192). In this work, Irenaeus attacked the Valentinians, the Marcionites, and other gnostic schools. He exposed how each of these false schools of thought failed to measure up to the teachings of the apostles. The Gnostics claimed that secret teachings had been handed down by Jesus and his apostles, but Irenaeus opposed this misguided belief. Genuine Christianity appears not in Gnosticism's secret myths or incoherent instruction, but in the rule of truth consistent with the content of the Bible and the tradition upheld by the bishops and presbyters.

Irenaeus exposed Gnosticism's errors by demonstrating the historical veracity of his own teaching. He showed how his teaching derived from Polycarp's and how Polycarp learned directly from the apostle John. Contra the gnostic denigration of the material world, Irenaeus affirmed the biblical God as the Creator and Redeemer of both the material and spiritual worlds.[64]

61. See the brief analysis of Montanism in this chapter.

62. Kelly, *Doctrines,* 88–90, 147–49. For primary texts, see Maurice Wiles and Mark Santer, eds., *Documents in Early Christian Thought* (Cambridge: Cambridge University Press, 1975), 128–32, 183–87, 225.

63. See Coxe, *Ante-Nicene Fathers,* 1:315–567.

64. In *Demonstration of the Apostolic Preaching,* discovered in 1904 and published a few years later, Irenaeus defended Christianity's truth in simpler terms than those found in *Against Heresies.* He first presented the Christian faith as he understood it by dealing with the Trinity (as three divine persons), the creation and fall of humankind, and redemption through the incarnation. The second part demonstrated from the OT that Jesus was the son of David and also the Messiah. Irenaeus ends by saying that Christians should live in godliness.

Irenaeus emerged as the first theologian of stature in the post-apostolic church. His works reveal a thorough, constructive approach to wrestling with the rationality and coherence of the gospel's message. He presented the themes of creation, fall, and redemption, while also refuting beliefs that were antithetical to Scripture. Though some of his ideas and methods of handling Scripture should not be embraced by believers,[65] overall, Irenaeus remained faithful to the teaching of the apostles and defended their teaching with conviction and comprehensiveness against rival systems of thought.

Tertullian (ca. A.D. 155/60–225).[66] Quintus Septimius Florens Tertullian was born to pagan parents in the city of Carthage. He became an accomplished Roman lawyer and was converted to the Christian faith in Rome somewhere between A.D. 193 and 197. After his conversion, Tertullian left Rome to return home, where he pastored a church. Sometime before A.D. 207, he joined the heretical Montanists. As a result of his apparent talent and leadership ability, Tertullian quickly became the head of a sect within Montanism—one fittingly named the "Tertullianists." This group would last until the time of Augustine, some two hundred years later. Tertullian died sometime after A.D. 220.[67]

Augustine aside, Tertullian is considered to have been the most important and original ecclesiastical author of the ancient church in the Latin language.[68] His writings expressed the most comprehensive theological vision in the West. His works reveal a compelling, logical, and zealous legal mind at work. Tertullian's writings can be categorized under several topical headings. The first of these headings might be his apologetic works.[69] Written in A.D. 197, the *Apology* is considered the

65. For example, he appears to embrace an early form of the ransom-to-Satan theory of the atonement that will later be rejected by the church. Irenaeus also saw glimpses of the Trinity in the parable of the good Samaritan. The innkeeper signified the Holy Spirit, and the two *denarii* for his lodging signified the Father and the Son.

66. See Gamble, "Christianity to Charlemagne," 114–16; Needham, *2,000 Years*, 1:126–30; Cornelius Van Til, *A Christian Theory of Knowledge* (Nutley, NJ: Presbyterian and Reformed, 1969), 83–109.

67. Staehelin, *Von der Zeit*, 143; Edgar and Oliphint, *Christian Apologetics*, 115–16.

68. His Latin is extremely difficult; there have been many scholarly studies concerning his style. He used new terms and preferred uncommon forms.

69. Other works include *To the Heathen*, written in A.D. 197, which is similar in content to the *Apology*. *To Scapula* was written in A.D. 212 and consists of five chapters. Scapula was a proconsul of Africa, and Tertullian wrote regarding the persecution. *Scorpiace* was an antidote to the stinging scorpions of Gnosticism, who thought it foolish for Christians to succumb to

most significant of his apologetic works.[70] It is more practical than it is theoretical. He directed it to governors of the Roman provinces to explain how Christians were hated because of their refusal to venerate the gods. He made it apparent that Christians were not enemies of the state. Tertullian also refuted the idea that Christ is a new god; rather, Christianity is divine revelation. Much of Tertullian's work consisted in critiques of paganism.[71] He wrote *Against the Jews* to clarify a dispute between two proselytes. He likely used parts of Justin's *Dialogue with Trypho*.

The breadth of Tertullian's ideas is reflected in the titles, content, and sheer volume of his writings. Hardly a topic within the purview of Christian thinking fails to receive treatment in his works. Written in A.D. 197, *The Testimony of the Soul* contends that the soul inherently knows that there is a God and a life after death.[72]

A number of Tertullian's writings are considered to be controversial.[73] *The Prescription against Heretics* was intended to end controversies between catholic Christians on one hand and heretics on the other. The Latin word *praescriptio*, used in the Latin title, was a term taken from the Roman court of law. The term was used when the defendant objected to the manner in which the plaintiff presented his legal case. This legal objection had to be written out before the case appeared for trial and thus was termed a *prae* (meaning "before") *scribere* (meaning "to write").

The issue in the legal case between Christians and heretics centered on the Scriptures. Tertullian argued that heretics could not even use the Bible (a *praescriptio* against non-Christians' using the Bible) because

---

martyrdom. *On the Flesh of Christ* opposed the docetic denial of Christ's flesh. In *The Resurrection of the Flesh*, Tertullian wrote against those who denied a resurrection.

70. An English translation is found in A. Cleveland Coxe, ed., *The Ante-Nicene Fathers*, vol. 3, *Latin Christianity: Its Founder, Tertullian I. Apologetic; II. Anti-Marcion; III. Ethical* (Grand Rapids: Eerdmans, 1988), 17–60.

71. Edgar and Oliphint, *Christian Apologetics*, 1:117: "Unlike Justin, Tertullian makes no attempt to find a capacity for true religion among pagans. While he acknowledges general revelation, he is sharply critical of those outside the church, even the greatest philosophers."

72. Written between A.D. 210 and 213, it argues that the believer must use God's revelation, not pagan thought, for his information. For the text, see the collection edited by Wiles and Santer, *Documents*, 49.

73. Some other controversial or polemical writings include *Against Marcion*, which gives us the main source of our knowledge of Marcion, and *Against Hermogenes*. Hermogenes was a Gnostic. He also wrote *Against the Valentinians* and *Against Quintilian*.

it was not theirs to use. This work was Tertullian's most valuable controversial one.

Another heading under which Tertullian's writings could be categorized is "moral writings." In his moral writings, Tertullian addressed a multitude of ethical issues.[74] In this genre fit *The Shows*, in which Tertullian condemned Christian participation in public games. In *On the Dress of Women*, he warned women, who are temples of God, not to be dominated by pagan fashion but instead to exude modesty in their dress. He condemned hair dye, cosmetics, and jewelry as diabolical in origin.

In *To His Wife* (A.D. 200–206), Tertullian made suggestions for his wife after his death. He advised her to remain a widow, since he saw no good reasons for remarriage. *Exhortation to Chastity* (A.D. 204–212) was dedicated to a friend who had recently lost his wife. *Concerning the Veiling of Virgins* advocated the practice of veils for virgins because contemporary etiquette required it. *The Crown* (A.D. 211), written about Christians in military service, argued that Christians should not wear crowns.[75] In *Concerning Idolatry*, Tertullian elaborated the same theme as in *The Crown*, but he added to his list of prohibitions that there were to be no artists or professors of literature in the church.

Tertullian also wrote on ecclesiastical topics. In *To the Martyrs*, he encouraged imprisoned Christians to persevere in the faith. *On Baptism* is the only ante-Nicene work on the nature of the sacraments. In twenty chapters, he used the images of Israel's passing through the Red Sea, the water that burst from the rock when Moses struck it, and John the Baptist as prefigures of Christ.[76]

Tertullian's *Concerning Prayer* (A.D. 198–200) is the earliest surviving exposition of the Lord's Prayer. *Concerning Patience* was written between A.D. 200 and 203. In this work he praised patience, while admitting that he had very little of it. *Concerning Repentance* (A.D. 203) debated ecclesiastical reconciliation. Tertullian believed that reconciliation required public confession by the sinner and plain food for the

---

74. Latin titles for the works and one date of composition are: *De spectaculis*; *De culto feminarum*; *De patientia*; *De paenitentia* (A.D. 203); *Ad uxorem*; *De exhortatione castilate*; *De exhortatione castilate*; *De ieiunio adversus psychicos*.

75. For the text see Wiles and Santer, *Documents*, 133.

76. Ibid., 173.

penitent. In *Concerning Flight in Persecution* (A.D. 212), he urged Christians not to flee from persecution. *Fasting* attacked Catholics from a rigorous Montanist perspective. In *Monogamy* (A.D. 217), Tertullian rejected all second marriages. In *On Modesty*, he argued that the power of "the keys" did not reside in Rome or with a particular bishop but were spiritual—that is, tied to apostolic origin.[77]

As a Heretic. Tertullian was a clear and often helpful writer. He helped to articulate the Trinity and to defend the faith against false teaching. Yet he was condemned as a heretic. How can these things be true of the same person? In the ancient church, heresy was a dynamic concept. The definition of heresy shifted with time. What was not considered heretical in one era might be so in the next. And it is only natural that the church was struggling to define the boundaries of orthodoxy. Scripture is the standard by which heretics are measured, but it would take time for the church to determine the precise parameters of Scripture's teaching on complicated theological issues.

If someone's teaching influences the basic doctrine of God and the concomitant teaching regarding Scripture, then there is sufficient ground for the charge of heresy. Charges were leveled against Tertullian from three angles: he was guilty of Trinitarian, ecclesiological, and scriptural fallacies.

Tertullian was accused of Trinitarian error because, as a Montanist, he did not baptize into the three divine persons. Instead, he confused the Father, Son, and Holy Spirit.[78] The Montanists' ecclesiastical error was what they perceived as a developing laxity in church discipline. They substituted a charismatic society for the visible, hierarchical church structure. Thus Tertullian was accused of ecclesiological error. With regard to Scripture, Montanus and his followers believed themselves to be vehicles of a new outpouring of the Holy Spirit. They held that their prophetic oracles were true revelations of the Holy Spirit that were regarded as supplementing the ancient Scriptures. Thus, as a Montanist, Tertullian was also accused of scriptural error. But God in his goodness raised up other theologians who steadily advanced theology.

---

77. See Benjamin B. Warfield, *Studies in Tertullian and Augustine* (Whitefish, MT: Kessinger, 2010), 3–109.

78. Kelly, *Doctrines*, 199–200.

Hippolytus of Rome (A.D. 170–235). Hippolytus may have been born in the East, likely before A.D. 170. He was the last Roman to write in the Greek language and was martyred in the year A.D. 235.[79] Hippolytus disagreed with the bishop of Rome, Callistus, for his tolerance of bishops who had more than one wife, so Hippolytus had himself elected as the new bishop of Rome. The Roman Catholic Church, therefore, refers to Hippolytus as the first anti-pope. This tension between Hippolytus and Callistus remained from A.D. 223 through just months before Hippolytus's death in A.D. 235. As a result of the dispute, Hippolytus had been exiled to Sardinia. Either in Sardinia or just prior to his exile, Hippolytus resigned as bishop of Rome, and in A.D. 235 a man named Anteros was elected the new bishop of Rome, thus ending the so-called *schism*.[80]

Novatian (A.D. 200–258). Novatian is famous for the schism that bears his name. His place of origin is unknown, but around the year A.D. 250 he was one of the leading pastors of the city of Rome. He was secretary of the college of presbyters. Novatian desired to be made the bishop of Rome, but in A.D. 251 a man named Cornelius was chosen instead. As is often the case in church history, personal desires and bruised pride played prominent roles in generating conflict.

Novatian found a way to oppose Cornelius.[81] The controversy concerned the lapsed in the faith. According to the ancient church, the lapsed "owe" Jesus their loyalty but fail to "pay" in times of persecution. Novatian, contrary to his earlier opinion, said that the lapsed—those who denied Christ in times of persecution—should forever be excommunicated from the church. Earlier in his life, Novatian had taught that when a lapsed believer was truly penitent—especially one who was on the verge of death—he should be forgiven. The ground for this position was that God alone knew the nature of the lapsed believer's heart. But Cornelius was unwilling to bar from communion those who were truly penitent, and now Novatian used this opportunity to oppose him.

---

79. Quasten, *Patrology*, 2:163. For a sampling of Hippolytus's contribution to church liturgy, see Needham, *2,000 Years*, 1:72–73.

80. Staehelin, *Von der Zeit*, 155–56. Hippolytus wrote almost as much as did Origen, including antiheretical treatises, commentaries, and a chuch order. For information, see Quasten, *Patrology*, 2:164–98.

81. Quasten, *Patrology*, 2:212–14; Needham, *2,000 Years*, 1:74.

The method of Novatian's ordination to the bishopric is an interesting story, though likely an embellished one. Novatian sought out three bishops (the minimum number necessary for such an ordination) from an obscure region of Italy. These bishops were known for their lack of ability and their simplicity. Supposedly, Novatian had dinner with the three bishops and served them so much wine that they became intoxicated, at which point Novatian forced them to ordain him as bishop. Cyprian and the other North African bishops then opposed his ordination. A council of sixty bishops met in Rome and excommunicated Novatian.

The schism spread from Rome to Spain in the West and to Syria in the East; the disruption lasted for more than a century. Though little is known of Novatian after this time, it is likely that he was killed during the persecution of Gallus or Valerian.[82] His most significant work was titled *De trinitate*, and it will be analyzed in the following doctrinal section.[83]

Cyprian (A.D. 200–258).[84] Thascius Caecilius Cyprian was an African, born most likely in the city of Carthage to an educated and well-to-do pagan family. He achieved great fame as a rhetorician, but he grew disheartened over the immorality that surrounded him and the corruption of the government. Sometime before A.D. 248, Cyprian converted to Christianity and, shortly thereafter, the people elected him as bishop of the city of Carthage.[85] Shortly after his election as bishop, however, the Decian persecution broke out; it compelled every Christian of the empire to make a pagan sacrifice. Cyprian fled the city, supposedly not in fear, and maintained close contact with his congregation. Of no surprise, not all his members looked favorably on his escape from the city. But in A.D. 251 a synod was held that excommunicated his opponents and determined that all the lapsed could be admitted to penance. This penance likely resulted in the lapsed persons' being treated in a similar manner as the catechumen, and on their deathbeds they were permitted full fellowship in the church.[86]

---

82. Heussi, *Kompendium*, 60; see also Schmidt, *Grundriss*, 124.
83. Heussi, *Kompendium*, 54.
84. See Wiles and Santer, *Documents*, 160; Needham, *2,000 Years*, 1:130–35.
85. In North Africa, it appears that the people had very much to say concerning choosing their pastors.
86. Quasten, *Patrology*, 2:340–42.

Life, however, did not get easier for Cyprian. A plague decimated the surrounding area and likely spread throughout the empire. The Christians were blamed for the plague. Cyprian cared for the afflicted—even those who were not in the church.

His last years (from A.D. 255 on) were spent addressing the validity of baptism performed by heretics. Tertullian's view, which was supported by Cyprian and reaffirmed by the synods of Carthage in A.D. 255 and 256, determined that baptisms performed by heretics were invalid. Strangely enough, there was not even time to oppose Cyprian's opinion, for Emperor Valerian issued an edict against Christians. The edict banished Cyprian, then in A.D. 258 had him beheaded near Carthage.[87]

Cyprian's writings were significant. He wrote *On Virgins' Dress* in A.D. 249. In this work he cautioned against what he considered at the time to be uncomely clothing.[88] *On the Unity of the Church* (A.D. 251) addressed problems that arose from the Decian persecution, when many Christians abandoned their faith. After the persecution settled, the church was split over whether or not to receive the lapsed members back into fellowship. Cyprian's position was that there must be a long season of penance, with exceptions granted for those who were near death. Others—in particular a deacon named Feliccissimus—were more moderate in their stance on the reception of lapsed believers.

Christians were (incorrectly) held responsible for the weakening of the Roman state and for all the natural catastrophes that plagued the empire. Demetrian, an influential polemicist, considered Christians to be responsible for the woes of the Roman Empire. So in A.D. 252 Cyprian wrote to him an open letter, titled *To Demetrianus*.[89] His last writing, *On the Lord's Prayer*, was likely a sermon he preached sometime from A.D. 251 to 252.[90]

Lactantius (after A.D. 317). Caecilius Firmianus Lactantius was likely trained in Africa as a rhetorician. Emperor Dicoletian summoned Lactantius to Bithynia, the new eastern capital, to teach Latin

87. Staehelin, *Von der Zeit*, 197; Altaner and Stuiber, *Patrologie*, 172–73; Schmidt, *Grundriss*, 119, 131.

88. Staehelin, *Von der Zeit*, 197; Altaner and Stuiber, *Patrologie*, 176; Quasten, *Patrology*, 2:347.

89. Staehelin, *Von der Zeit*, 201–2; Altaner and Stuiber, *Patrologie*, 174. Altaner and Stuiber charge Jerome with false praise for this document. They say that its contents are "unimportant."

90. Staehelin, *Von der Zeit*, 200; Quasten, *Patrology*, 2:353–55.

rhetoric.[91] Lactantius was not well received by his students and thus had to support himself through writing, though he was permitted to retain his teaching post.[92]

In A.D. 303, the Diocletian persecution forced him to resign his position, since he had apparently become a Christian. Sometime from A.D. 305 to 306, Lactantius fled the city. Though the date of his death is unknown, in A.D. 317 Emperor Constantine summoned him to the city of Trier in France to tutor his eldest son, Crispus. By this time, Lactantius was an old man and poor.[93]

Between A.D. 305 and 310, Lactantius wrote a large work titled *Institutiones divinae*.[94] It was both an apology for (that is, a defense of) Christianity as well as a presentation of the faith's main teachings. He penned some later writings as well.[95]

Lactantius's theology had two peculiarities: he believed that the Holy Spirit is not separate from the Son of God, and he held to a thousand-year reign of Christ upon the earth.[96] This next section will transition to the eastern part of the empire.

EASTERN WRITERS

Clement of Alexandria (A.D. 150–211). Sadly, little is known of the life of the prominent theologian Titus Flavius Clemens. He was born to non-Christian parents, likely in Athens, where he received much of his training. No details of his conversion to Christianity are known except that, when he did become a Christian, he sought out the best tutors in the empire.

He settled upon studying in the famous city of Alexandria and ended up being appointed head of the school in ca. A.D. 200.[97] A few years later, under the persecution of Septimus Severus, he was forced to flee from Egypt and found refuge in Cappadocia. He died in Cap-

---

91. Staehelin (*Von der Zeit*, 214) says that he was called to Nikomedia in northern Asia Minor, where the emperor had his residence.
92. Ibid.
93. Ibid., 215.
94. For an excerpt of this work, see Needham, *2,000 Years*, 1:161–62.
95. Staehelin, *Von der Zeit*, 214; see also Altaner and Stuiber, *Patrologie*, 185.
96. Altaner and Stuiber, *Patrologie*, 185.
97. See Needham, *2,000 Years*, 1:117–18.

padocia sometime between A.D. 211 and 215 without having had the opportunity to return to Egypt.

The verdict of historians is that Clement was neither a creative nor a profound thinker. He read many works, cited more than three hundred and sixty profane writers, and possessed a fair knowledge of the Scriptures, but he never demonstrated brilliance.[98]

Clement's writings include *Warning to the Gentiles*, which is also known as *Exhortation to the Heathen*.[99] In this work, he presented Christ as the true teacher of the new world and offered a critique of the heathen world.

The Teacher is a continuation of the earlier book in three sections. He wrote it with the goal of teaching converted heathens how to live as new Christians. *The Carpet* was a somewhat disorganized presentation of Greek philosophy. He believed that Greek philosophy borrowed much of its wisdom from the Hebrew Bible.

What Kingdom Will Be Saved? demonstrated that even the state could be saved and admitted into the kingdom of heaven. Only the unrepentant sinner is excluded from heaven. The *Stromata* or *Miscellanies* is a collection of Clement's religious and theological thoughts that demonstrate his deep thinking and breadth of philosophical training.[100]

Clement made contributions toward developing a relationship between Christian faith, theology, and philosophy. He opposed those whom he derogatorily termed the *orthodoxists*. The orthodoxists were those who rejected all philosophical thinking and were known for being anti-intellectual.

In contrast, Clement encouraged believers to use Greek philosophy to aid their understanding of Christianity. Clement believed that philosophy was a help to the Christian faith. He never said that Greek philosophy could lead a person to faith, but he believed that it could help make Christianity more attractive to outsiders. He also maintained that faith comes prior to philosophy. And by faith, he meant a general faith that intuits or senses the basic principles of reasoning—a faith

98. See Gamble, "Christianity to Charlemagne," 116–18.

99. See Coxe, *Ante-Nicene Fathers*, 2:171–206.

100. Williston Walker, Richard A. Norris, David W. Lotz, and bRobert T. Handy, *A History of the Christian Church*, 4th ed. (New York: Scribner's Sons, 1985), 73.

that knows the intellectual methods for proper reasoning. He was not referring to a distinctly Christian faith.

Clement taught that thinkers such as Plato and Aristotle had this type of faith. According to Clement, both faith and reason—or Christianity and philosophy—were gifts from the hand of God. Philosophy was God's covenant with the Greeks, just as the Law was God's covenant with the Jews. Clement understood the river of truth to have various tributaries. Thus philosophy—particularly the works of Plato and Aristotle—was given to the Greeks to draw them to Christ. That is not to say, however, that Clement was uncritical of Greek philosophy. He did find fault with the Sophists.

Relative to theology proper, Clement held that God is the most high—that is, God is utterly transcendent. He is beyond being, and it would be improper even to call God *Being*. Clement taught that the believer could not even speak of God, since he has no name and cannot properly be called *Father* or even *Lord*. In Clement's system, it seems that God could be known only through a sort of mystical experience.[101]

Origen (A.D. 185–253). It has been said of Origen that "no man of purer spirit or nobler aims ornaments the history of the ancient church."[102] Origen's theology is so vast and complex that one should be careful not to attempt to attribute any one source as *the* major philosophical or theological influence or all-controlling factor in his theology. Undoubtedly, he was a thinker who was surrounded by structures of thought such as those of Middle Platonism, Philo of Alexandria, and Justin Martyr. But the Platonism of Alexandria was perhaps the ultimate presupposition underlying Origen's theology, and even his biblical exegesis.[103]

Because the church historian Eusebius devoted a large part of his sixth book to Origen, we know many details about his life. Jerome also mentions him in his veritable "Who's Who," his *De viris illustribus*.

In roughly A.D. 185, Origen was born into a Christian family. In A.D. 202, his father suffered martyrdom. To keep her son from follow-

101. Staehelin, *Von der Zeit*, 169–80; Schmidt, *Grundriss*, 101; Altaner and Stuiber, *Patrologie*, 190–96.
102. Walker, *History*, 74.
103. Kelly, *Doctrines*, 71.

ing in his father's footsteps, his mother actually hid Origen's clothes so he could not leave the house. At the age of eighteen, Origen was placed in charge of the catechumen school at Alexandria, which had been largely destroyed due to persecution. Supposedly, he followed an ascetic lifestyle—to such an extent that he emasculated himself in a fervent though misguided attempt at obedience to Matthew 19:20.[104]

Origen taught all the preparatory classes in Alexandria from A.D. 202 to 231. When the work became overly burdensome, he hired an assistant and taught the advanced courses. He attended the lectures of the philosopher Ammonius Saccas, the so-called "founder of Neoplatonism."

When Origen eventually became a well-known theologian, his not being ordained began to cause problems with his bishop. So he was ordained by other bishops—of Jerusalem and Caesarea—which only caused more problems for him. In A.D. 231, a synod excommunicated him, and he left Alexandria. Origen was imprisoned and tortured while working as a teacher in Caesarea during the Decian persecution, and he died in A.D. 253.[105]

Origen was a prolific writer. Jerome estimated that he wrote about two thousand works. Epiphanius of Salamis thought the number was closer to six thousand. But because of Origen's condemnation by the church in the sixth century, the titles of only eight hundred of his works are known today.

Origen had seven or more stenographers writing in his lecture room. His work in textual criticism created what is called the Hexapla—a sixfold Bible. The basis of it was the Hebrew text of the OT, a Hebrew text in Greek letters to aid in pronunciation, Aquila's Greek translation, the LXX, and two more Greek translations. Origen wrote commentaries on every book of the Bible.

The most important of Origen's apologetic works was *Against Celsus*, which he wrote between A.D. 246 and 248. Celsus was an able Platonist philosopher who attempted to "deconvert" Christians. He used Jewish arguments, among others, against Christianity. He saw Christ as a magician and imposter, and he argued for the superior-

104. Gamble, "Christianity to Charlemagne," 118.
105. Staehelin, *Von der Zeit*, 180; Schmidt, *Grundriss*, 101, 106, 161; Altaner and Stuiber, *Patrologie*, 197–208.

ity of Greek thinking. Origen responded by defending the truth and historical reliability of the gospel's claims and contending that these characteristics make the Christian faith superior to Greek philosophical speculation.[106]

Origen's most important theological work is titled *First Principles* (ca. A.D. 220), which many consider to be the first true systematic theology. Sadly, the original Greek text of this work has not been found, but researchers do have access to an early Latin translation of it. In speaking of the importance of *First Principles*, Williston Walker writes that it was "not merely the first great systematic presentation of Christianity, but its thoughts and methods thenceforth controlled Greek dogmatic development."[107]

In general, Origen interpreted Christianity through the lens of Greek philosophical thought. He made Christianity scientific—in the way that word would have been comprehended at the time. Strongly influenced by the philosophies of Stoicism and Neoplatonism,[108] his ideas were condemned in A.D. 553 at the second Council of Constantinople.

Eusebius of Caesarea (A.D. 263–339). Eusebius, known as the father of ecclesiastical history, was bishop of Caesarea in Palestine.[109] It was here that Origen was exiled, and the presbyter Pamphilus expanded Origen's library to establish the school at Caesarea as a significant center of learning. Pamphilus helped to train Eusebius and thus instilled in him an admiration for Origen. In A.D. 324, Eusebius published the significant *History of the Church*; he used Pamphilius's library to

106. Notice how Origen refutes Plato's notion of the highest good in *Contra Celsus*, chapter 5: "Observe now the difference between the fine phrases of Plato respecting 'the chief good'; and the declarations of our prophets regarding the 'light' of the blessed; and notice that the truth as it is contained in Plato concerning this subject did not at all help his readers to attain to a pure worship of God, nor even himself, who could philosophize so grandly about the 'chief good,' whereas the simple language of the holy Scriptures has led to their honest readers being filled with a divine spirit; and this light is nourished within them by the oil, which in a certain parable is said to have preserved the light of the troches of the five wise virgins" (as cited by Edgar and Oliphint, *Christian Apologetics*, 168).

107. Walker, *History*, 75.

108. Origen's younger contemporary, the Neoplatonist Porphyry, commented that "in his conception of God and the world, Origen thought as a Greek and [was] brought under foreign mythical ideas" (as cited by Staehelin, *Von der Zeit*, 181). Walker (*History*, 76) said: "The real world is the spiritual reality behind this temporary, phenomenal, visible world."

109. For excerpts of his *History of the Church*, see Needham, *2,000 Years*, 1:54–57, 114–15, 156, 162–63.

compile the work.[110] At the Council of Antioch, Eusebius was accused of Arianism.[111]

Cyril of Jerusalem (A.D. 315–386). In ca. A.D. 348, Cyril became a bishop. Almost immediately, he came into conflict with the powerful Acacius, metropolitan of Caesarea, who was an Arian. The Arians attacked Cyril, and three times he was ejected from his bishopric.[112] He attended the Council of Constantinople in A.D. 381 and died ca. A.D. 386. His *Catechetical Lectures* were transcripts of lectures delivered to new believers before their baptism. He also wrote a letter to Emperor Constantius and several sermons.[113]

In conclusion, this period was a unique time in the history of the church. In these dark days, Christ's bride lived day and night beneath the shadow of state-sponsored persecution. The church had to battle enemies internally and externally and did not have the leisure to reflect critically on exegetical and theological method. More thorough exegesis and deeper theological reflection would follow in the decades ahead. She was not only persecuted physically but also struggled to steady herself against the weighty intellectual arguments thrust against her. Such a bleak beginning for the early church raises the question of how this teetering group of believers ever survived. But Christ cared for his bride even when it seemed as though all hope had been extinguished. The next chapter will examine these thinkers' theology. But the above survey of the writings from the time of the early church demonstrates that ancient Christianity displayed a dynamic faith and a concern for unity, organization, and the celebration of the sacraments in the midst of defining and fighting heresy. It taught ethical principles that demanded a vital Christian life consistent with biblical teaching.

---

110. Schmidt, *Grundriss*, 18, 187. See Altaner and Stuiber, *Patrologie*, 217–18.

111. G. W. H. Lampe, "Christian Theology in the Patristic Period," in *A History of Christian Doctrine*, ed. Hubert Cunliffe-Jones (1978; repr., New York: T&T Clark, 2006), 91; Kelly, *Doctrines*, 263.

112. He fled to Tarsus at his first deposition in A.D. 357 and returned the next year. He was deposed again in A.D. 360 but returned in A.D. 362 when Julian the Apostate became emperor. His deposition by Emperor Valens in A.D. 367 lasted until the emperor's death in 378. Quasten, *Patrology*, 3:362.

113. Ibid., 3:363–69.

KEY TERMS

subordinationism
typology
apostolic fathers
apologists

STUDY QUESTIONS

1. Why was Tertullian considered a heretic?
2. What differentiates Eastern writers from Western writers?
3. How do you analyze Origen's many accomplishments?

RESOURCES FOR FURTHER STUDY

Coxe, A. Cleveland, ed. *The Ante-Nicene Fathers*. Vol. 1, *The Apostolic Fathers, Justin Martyr, Irenaeus*. Vol. 2, *Fathers of the Second Century: Hermas, Tatian, Athenagoras, Theophilus, and Clement of Alexandria*. Vol. 3, *Latin Christianity: Its Founder, Tertullian I. Apologetic; II. Anti-Marcion; III. Ethical*. Grand Rapids: Eerdmans, 1988. Helpful introductions and complete texts of many of the writings from this time period, despite the translations' not being contemporary.

Edgar, William, and K. Scott Oliphint. *Christian Apologetics Past and Present: A Primary Source Reader*. Vol. 1, *To 1500*. Wheaton, IL: Crossway, 2009. Helpful biographical information on many of the theologians surveyed in this chapter (pages 1–172) with primary texts and annotations on their writings.

Kelly, J. N. D. *Early Christian Creeds*. London: Longman, 1972. A gold standard for patristic research and writing, though Kelly was not evangelical and criticisms of his opinions are found in footnotes throughout patristic analysis.

———. *Early Christian Doctrines*. London: Black, 1977. A gold standard for patristic research and writing, though Kelly was not evangelical and criticisms of his opinions are found in footnotes throughout patristic analysis.

Quasten, Johannes. *Patrology*. 3 vols. Utrecht: Spectrum, 1975. An excellent and reliable multivolume reference.

~ 3 ~

Early Patristic Theology

MOVING FROM THE HISTORICAL and social context of the patristic writers, we will now examine a synthesis of their understanding of the various loci of systematic theology, such as the doctrine of God, Scripture, the church, and the Trinity. Since this chapter analyzes theology in its earliest development, it will cover only select loci. The rise of false teaching that contrasted sharply with biblical truth and practice challenged church leaders to form standards that would oppose fallacious systems of thought and aberrant religious methods. Such antithesis characterizes every age in the ongoing history of the faith.

A CHRISTIAN/PAGAN SYNTHESIS?

A major theme throughout this volume is that admixture or synthesis between Christian thinking and pagan deliberation always enfeebles Christian thought. Christian theology does not need a pagan superstructure to outline or elaborate doctrine. God himself provides all the tools necessary to describe himself.[1] The NT does not mix divine

---

1. William Cunningham, speaking of the earliest church history, said: "we cannot trace the incipient corruption of doctrine wholly at least to the influence of philosophical speculation, or indeed to any one specific cause, except what is in some sense the proximate cause of all error and heresy,—viz., the want of due subjection to the authority of God's word, and of due diligence and impartiality in the use of the right means of attaining to a correct knowledge of its meaning. . . . The danger arises only from giving to philosophy a place and influence to which it has no well-founded claim, and especially from employing it in such a way as implies, or leads to, a casting down of the word of God from the place of authority, which it ought ever to occupy. . . . The evils which literature and science may have inflicted upon the cause of true religion are to be prevented or cured, not by prohibiting or abandoning literary and philosophical pursuits, but by keeping them in their proper place, and especially by steadily and faithfully applying the great

revelation with human cogitation in its theological method. It offers a radically biblical way to present the claims of Christ to unbelievers and a radically biblical way to present Christian theology. In WCG2, the argument was made that Peter was neither capitulating to nor combatting Greek philosophy in 2 Peter 1:5; rather, Peter presented a "massive, complex presentation of a very mature and complete world and life view."[2]

Paul also had a distinct theological and philosophical method in his Areopagus address, recorded in Acts 17:17–34. He recognized two fundamentally conflicting systems of thought. He then pressed the philosophical differences between them.[3] When constructing a theological method, it is important to determine in what places Christian theologians have either knowingly or unwittingly adopted pagan philosophical thinking into their Christian doctrine. All theologians are influenced by their culture. Greek theologians wrote and thought in Greek and not in Latin; therefore, chapter 1 of this volume included an extended discussion of pre-Christian philosophy. "Cultural" or "philosophical" adoption can be quantified by theologians using the same technical philosophical words without changing their pagan philosophical meaning. After traversing patristic *loci*, this chapter will end with an example of how to analyze and critique theological methods using a case study of the early church's interaction with Stoicism.

DOCTRINE OF GOD

Knowability. Arguing from a number of positions, early Christian theologians held that God was knowable. Both Origen and Aristides

---

truths that the Bible is the word of God; that all that it contains is true; that it is the only source whence full and certain knowledge concerning God, concerning man's relation to his Maker, and his duty and destiny, can be derived. So long as these truths are held and *faithfully acted upon*, literature and philosophy will do no harm to religion; and if it be alleged that an addiction to philosophical pursuits has a *tendency* to prejudice men against these truths, or to prevent them from fully following them out, even when they professedly admit them, we must deny that this tendency is inherent, and still more, that it is irresistible, and maintain that the temptation (for it is nothing more) may be, and should be, guarded against" (William Cunningham, *Historical Theology* [Edinburgh: Banner of Truth, 1979], 1:147–48).

2. Richard C. Gamble, *The Whole Counsel of God*, vol. 2, *The Full Revelation of God* (Phillipsburg, NJ: P&R Publishing, 2018) (*WCG2*), 883; also 882–84.

3. *WCG* 2:975–76, 980.

asserted that God could be known through the visible creation. Even though there was plenty of evidence of God through creation, nevertheless, lamented Origen, many sophisticated people thought that nature's power simply came through chance.[4]

Aristides described the godhead's attributes primarily in terms of the *via negativa*. God is not like a man or any part of creation. The creator always transcends his creation. In a similar fashion, Justin Martyr described God as being without origin and nameless. Clement held that God was utterly transcendent, beyond being. In the final analysis, the believer cannot even speak of God since he has no name and cannot properly be called *Father* or even *Lord*. In Clement's system, God can be known only through some type of mystical experience.

Character or Attributes. The earliest writers acknowledged that God was eternal, perfect, self-existent, omnipresent, omnipotent, omniscient, and spiritual.[5] Some attempted to describe these divine attributes. Justin Martyr called the Father the "only unbegotten God."[6] He held that God is omnipresent and omniscient. God is impassible, which means that God does not experience, nor is he affected by, human feelings.

Aristides and Tertullian spoke of God's eternity, perfection, self-existence, spirituality, omnipresence, omniscience, and omnipotence. Melito of Sardis affirmed and explained Justin Martyr's notion that God is the only unbegotten one. That God is unlimited can be taken too far, warned Origen, by reasoning absurd things about him. They affirmed that God is present everywhere and knows everything that occurs. Eusebius held that God was without beginning, the first principle of all things, and an indivisible monad.[7] All the early fathers rejected patripassianism, or the idea that God the Father was crucified or suffered on the cross.[8]

---

4. Greg R. Allison, *Historical Theology: An Introduction to Christian Doctrine—A Companion to Wayne Grudem's Systematic Theology* (Grand Rapids: Zondervan, 2011), 188.

5. Aristides, *The Apology*, in A. Cleveland Coxe, ed., *The Ante-Nicene* Fathers, vol. 10, *The Writings of the Fathers down to A.D. 325* (Grand Rapids: Eerdmans, 1988), 263–64, as cited by Allison, *Historical Theology*, 211.

6. Allison, *Historical Theology*, 212.

7. Thus God alone is ingenerate and without beginning. G. W. H. Lampe, "Christian Theology in the Patristic Period," in *A History of Christian Doctrine*, ed. Hubert Cunliffe-Jones (1978; repr., New York: T&T Clark, 2006), 91.

8. Allison, *Historical Theology*, 213.

Christology. Melito of Sardis, Justin Martyr, and Irenaeus all defended Jesus's full humanity and deity. Both were necessary for salvation.[9] Melito agreed with Justin that the theophanies recorded in the OT, creation itself, and even God's acts in the history of Israel were all to be ascribed to Christ; he identified Christ as the sacrificial lamb of the Passover. He also emphasized Christ's preexistence. If the treatise on the incarnation ascribed to Melito is genuine, then it is certain that he taught Christ's two natures—that Christ was fully God and completely human. This complete humanity and divinity were distinct from each other; they were nearly independent in Melito's theology.[10]

Melito's Christology may be illuminated by exploring the theological context of his day. Melito was striving against Docetism and a form of Ebionism, which taught that Jesus was a mere man on whom the Spirit descended at his baptism. Ebionites denied the incarnation and argued that Jesus was a man in whom God's power worked. This view perhaps explains the reason for Melito's emphasis on Christ's two natures and their near independence.

Irenaeus claimed that sinners need God to work out their salvation. They could not be reconciled to God unless God first came to humanity.[11] Christ was the center of Ignatius's thought.[12] He clearly affirmed both Christ's divinity and humanity, and he maintained Christ's pre-

9. Irenaeus (*Adversus haereses* [Edinburgh: T&T Clark, 1884], III.19.1) said: "For by no other means could we have attained to incorruptibility and immortality, unless we had been united to incorruptibility and immortality. But how could we have been united unless first, incorruptibility and immortality had become that which we also are" (as cited by Douglas F. Kelly, *Systematic Theology*, vol. 2, *The Beauty of Christ—A Trinitarian Vision* [Fearn, Scotland: Mentor, 2014], 184).

Irenaeus, *Adversus haereses*, IV.20.4, as cited by Douglas F. Kelly, *Systematic Theology*, vol. 1, *The God Who Is the Holy Trinity* (Fearn, Scotland: Mentor, 2008), 30, and Allison, *Historical Theology*, 367.

10. Philip Carrington, *The Early Christian Church: The Second Christian Century* (Cambridge: Cambridge University Press, 1957), 2:237: "Christ is the son of God. He is the Word of the Father, begotten before the light, the creator of all things with the Father, the fashioner of men, the all-in-all; he became incarnate in the Virgin's womb; he was born a perfect man that he might save lost mankind and gather together his scattered members."

11. Irenaeus, *Adversus haereses*, IV.20.4, as cited by Kelly, *Systematic Theology*, 1:30, and Allison, *Historical Theology*, 367.

12. Christ is the Father's "thought," he is God incarnate and God revealed as man. See Ignatius's *Epistle to the Ephesians* 3.2; 7.2; 19.3; Jean-Paul Migne, *Patrologiae Cursus Completus: Series Graeca* (Paris: Garnier Fratres, 1857), 5:648, 652, 660.

existence.[13] Ignatius's concept of the Son was as the revelation of the transcendent God.[14]

In the *Epistle of Barnabas*, Christ is the Son of God who took on flesh as a divine revelation. The purpose of Christ's taking on flesh was to reveal God to those who could not look directly at God. *Barnabas* compared the impossibility of looking directly at the sun with the impossibility of seeing God directly. According to this epistle, Christ's coming was necessary to communicate God's revelation to humanity. The *Barnabas* also taught that "let us" in Genesis 1:26 refers to the preexistent Son,[15] and this preexistent Son was conceived as a different hypostasis.[16]

Tertullian inherited a logos Christology from the apologists—he identified the Jesus of history with this Greek philosophical logos. This identification resulted in Christ the Son's being viewed as strongly subordinate to the Father. Even though to some extent Tertullian realized the philosophical problem, he was not able to solve it.[17]

For Eusebius, Christ as the preexistent Logos is the power and wisdom of God, in second place to the Father, who ministers to the Father as he creates all things. Eusebius taught that Christ must create because the Father, who is absolute being, cannot have contact with the contingent created order. He taught that the Father preexisted the Son and begot him by an act of his will.[18] For Eusebius, the phrase "only begotten" meant that the Son did not resemble the creatures he made but the Father who begot him. The Son is also *consubstantial*,

13. Ignatius, *Epistle to the Smyrnaeans* 1.1; Migne, *Patrologiae Graeca*, 5:708. See Hans Lietzmann, *Geschichte der alten Kirche* (Berlin: de Gruyter, 1932), 1:257–59. Wolfson wrongly argues that Ignatius, like Clement, does not recognize that there is a Trinity until Christ's birth. Ignatius thought that Christ's sonship began with the incarnation. Before Christ's birth, there is God and a preexistent Christ who is identified with both the Holy Spirit and the Logos. See H. A. Wolfson, *The Philosophy of the Church Fathers* (Cambridge: Harvard University Press, 1956), 1:184, 186.

14. Ignatius, *Epistle to the Romans* 6.3: "Permit me to be an imitator of the passion of my God"; Lampe, "Christian Theology," 26n6: "Ignatius can speak in terms which could seem extraordinarily paradoxical in the Greek world where the impassibility of the divine was held to be axiomatic truth, of the 'passion of our God.'"

15. Epistle of Barnabas 5; Migne, *Patrologiae Graeca*, 2:736.

16. Lampe, "Christian Theology," 27.

17. Cornelius Van Til, *A Christian Theory of Knowledge* (Nutley, NJ: Presbyterian and Reformed, 1969), 85–87, 88: The Son of God is "made a second in manner of existence—in position not in nature." For more on Tertullian's Christology, see Kelly, *Systematic Theology*, 1:150–52.

18. Lampe, "Christian Theology," 92.

which meant that the Son is *of* the Father, particularly in carrying the image of the godhead. The Son's consubstantiality did not mean that he was part of the Father's nature or substance; therefore the Son, or the Logos, may be called *God*.

In Eusebius's theology, the Son is not of equal divine essence with the Father, for such coexistence with the Father would imply two ingenerate first principles. It was important for Eusebius to hold to the unity of the Father—there could be no diminution of his power or any change in him. The Son is, however, in all points perfectly *similar* to the Father, who begot him.[19]

To Eusebius, the similarity, or consubstantiality, of the Father and the Son meant that the Son is neither part of the Father's nature nor part of his substance. The unity of the Father and the Son consists in their sharing glory; therefore, Eusebius advocated an advanced subordinationism:[20] the Son was not—and cannot be—of the divine essence of the Father but of his "free will." Eusebius refused to concede that Christ is coeternal with the Father.[21]

Origen had postulated that the point of contact between the Word and his flesh was in Jesus's soul. Eusebius rejected this notion and instead maintained that the Word indwelled Christ's flesh like a soul. So when Christ died, the Word left the flesh. But to preserve the Word's transcendence, Eusebius believed that the flesh's experiences did not affect the Word. To recognize the true divinity of the Son meant, for Eusebius, to sacrifice the oneness of the godhead. While this view may sound like Arianism—and Eusebius did in fact defend Arian bishops— some have contested that conclusion.[22] Eusebius also taught that the Holy Spirit was a creation of the Son.

In *Against Heresies*, Irenaeus presented a unique Christology and anthropology. He asserted that Jesus must have lived to be about fifty years old! This teaching, which contradicts the portrait of Christ pre-

19. Ibid., 99.
20. Johannes Quasten, *Patrology* (Utrecht: Spectrum, 1975), 3:342: "the Son of God is not of the essence of the Father but of His free will and the Holy Spirit is not more than a creation of the Son. He remains convinced that to recognize the true divinity of the Son means to sacrifice the oneness of the Godhead."
21. J. N. D. Kelly, *Early Christian Doctrines* (London: Black, 1977), 225–26.
22. Lampe ("Christian Theology," 92) says that he should not be so classified; rather, his Christology is more representative of the theory of the union of the Logos with the flesh.

sented in the Gospels, is a by-product of his theory of recapitulation.[23] Irenaeus developed this theory of recapitulation from a misreading of Ephesians 1:10, which he believed taught that Christ brought redemption by recapitulating all the stages of human life in sinless obedience. If this understanding of Ephesians 1:10 were accurate, Jesus would have needed to have lived more more than merely thirty years.[24]

Holy Spirit. *The Shepherd of Hermas* identifies the Holy Spirit with Christ. They were two divine persons. Eusebius taught that the Holy Spirit was a creation of the Son.

The *Didache*, Justin Martyr, and Tertullian's "rule of faith" all acknowledged that baptism was done in the name of all three persons of the Trinity.[25] Origen and Novatian contrasted the Holy Spirit's earlier work in the OT with his work after Christ's resurrection. They denied that there were two Spirits but underlined that the Holy Spirit's work was contrasting. His new work was closely associated with the Father and the Son. Cyril is particularly important for his development of the doctrine of the Holy Spirit. He affirmed that the Holy Spirit is divine and in union with the Son, the Spirit participates in the godhead of the Father, and he has perfect knowledge of the Father. Cyril never stated that the Holy Spirit was consubstantial with the Father and the Son, yet he believed the Spirit is ever present with the Father and the Son and is glorified with them. The Spirit also has a distinct personality and is attributed with direct personal action.

An early heresy arose concerning the Holy Spirit's work—Montanus claimed to be the Holy Spirit's mouthpiece and thus to speak divine revelation. He apparently claimed to be the Trinity. The church rejected him and his followers.[26]

Creation. As reviewed in previous chapters, pagan philosophy presented various and complex theories of creation. Epicurus saw it as a chance collision of atoms in the limitless void. Gnosticism, connecting back to Plato and Plotinus, posited a demiurge. This notion presupposed that matter was evil or that the supreme deity could not

---

23. Lietzmann, *Geschichte*, 1:259–62; Kelly, *Early Christian Doctrines*, 170.

24. See Irenaeus, *Adversus haeresus* 2.22, as cited by Eusebius, *Church History* 3.25, with Eusebius's Greek text presented in Frederic W. Farrar, *History of Interpretation* (Grand Rapids: Baker, 1961), 176n7.

25. Allison, *Historical Theology*, 432–33.

26. Ibid., 432.

create the world. Emanations projected from the deity and the demi-urge were spiritual enough and natural enough to make the world.

Patristic authors answered the questions of how, when, and why God created the universe. Justin Martyr, Irenaeus, and Origen acknowl-edged the different roles of the persons of the Trinity in creation. Lac-tantius answered the "Why?" question when he said that the world was created for living beings. "How?" was answered by arguing that the world was created *ex nihilo*.[27] This teaching set these theologians in opposition to Plato's notion that matter was eternal. Tatian and Theophilus specifically opposed Plato. Origen, however, had a peculiar interpretation of creation that brought him more in line with Greek thinking: he thought that an invisible creation took place before this heaven and earth existed.

Providence and Evil. Dealing with God's providence and the pres-ence of evil has always perplexed theologians. Tertullian and Clement of Alexandria both spoke of God's permitting evil events rather than his willing them. Origen said that God's providence does not will evil like it does good—it permits evil but wills good. Origen, along with Athenagoras, affirmed human free will. People can do that which pleases God and is worthy of praise. Those who do evil deserve pun-ishment even though their evil acts accord with divine providence.[28]

Spiritual Realm. Origen acknowledged that angels and demons exist but claimed we cannot know much about them. Others, such as Athenagoras and Eusebius, speculated about them. Tertullian knew that angels had wings, even though they were by nature incorporeal. He speculated that their task was to control matter and argued that they have custody of nations and stimulate members of them to seek God.[29]

DOCTRINE OF THE TRINITY[30]

Apostolic Fathers. The ancient church held to both monotheism and trinitarianism. Discussions of the Trinity filled early theologians'

---

27. Irenaeus and Tertullian argued for creation *ex nihilo*; Allison, *Historical Theology*, 257.
28. Ibid., 278–80.
29. Ibid., 299–300.
30. See Louis Berkhof, *The History of Christian Doctrines* (Carlisle, PA: Banner of Truth, 1969), 59–60; Georg Kretschmar, *Studien zur frühchristlichen Trinitätstheologie* (Tübingen:

treatment of prayer, worship, ecclesiology, and apologetics. Earliest Trinitarian analysis touched on economic or functional relationships as well as ontological relationships between members of the Trinity.

While Clement of Rome assumed that Christ existed prior to the incarnation, he did not address the relationship between the three persons.[31] Ignatius wrestled with the nature of the relationship between the Father, Son, and Holy Spirit. The triadic formula appeared three times in his writings.[32] But it is possible that Ignatius did not recognize that there was a true Trinity until Christ's birth. Before then, there was a God and a preexistent Christ, who was identified with both the Holy Spirit and the Logos.[33]

In *The Shepherd of Hermas*, the savior, in reward for his merits, was elevated to be able to be the companion of the Father and the Holy Spirit. Thus Hermas maintained that, analogously to Christ's taking on human nature, he was the adopted Son of God.[34] While *The Shepherd*'s Trinitarian theology is highly interesting, it does not provide solid groundwork for later Trinitarian thought. *The Shepherd* envisions three persons in the Trinity, but a distinction between them comes only after the incarnation. First there is the Father, then a second divine person, identified with the Holy Spirit, who is the divine principle in the incarnate Christ.[35] *The Shepherd*'s theology was a combination of what could be termed *binitarianism* and *adoptionism*, though it attempted to conform to the church's triadic formula.[36]

This brief examination of the apostolic fathers demonstrates that they did not fully understand or clearly elaborate the doctrine of the Trinity. Although Ignatius and Clement enunciated a triadic formula,

---

Mohr Siebeck, 1956); Jean Daniélou, *A History of Early Christian Doctrine before the Council of Nicaea*, vols. 1–3 (Philadelphia: Westminster Press, 1978–1980); George Leonard Prestige, *God in Patristic Thought* (London: SPCK, 1952).

31. Clement of Rome, *Epistle to the Corinthians* 16.2; J. N. D. Kelly, *Doctrines*, 91; Wolfson, *Philosophy*, 1:183–91. Wolfson does not see a concept of the Trinity in Clement before Christ's birth and resurrection.

32. Ignatius, Epistle to the Ephesians 9.1; Epistle to the Magnesians 13.1, 2; Migne, *Patrologiae Graeca*, 5:652.

33. Thus it is also not possible to determine whether he has a doctrine of the generation of the Logos. See Wolfson, *Philosophy*, 1:192.

34. Quasten, *Patrology*, 1:100.

35. *The Shepherd of Hermas*, Similitudes 5.6, 5–7; 9.1.1; Migne, *Patrologiae Graeca*, 2:962, 981–82.

36. Kelly, *Doctrines*, 94.

the relationship between the three persons was not well developed. We may conclude at least that all the apostolic fathers asserted a preexistent Christ who existed with the Father.[37] While such theological imprecision would be insufficient for any ministerial candidate today, this period of the church's history and theology was still primitive and developing.[38]

Apologists. The apologists represent the next stage in the development of Trinitarian doctrine. Their theology is more complex than that developed by their predecessors. At Justin Martyr's time, the threefold name of the Father, Son, and Holy Spirit was already in use for baptisms. Justin related that candidates for baptism received washing with water in the name of the Father and Lord of the universe, and of our Savior Jesus Christ, and the Holy Spirit.

In Justinian theology, the title *Father* means "transcendent God." This God is too transcendent and remote to have direct dealings with the world. He is inexpressible, immovable, and nameless. The words *Father*, *God*, and *Lord* are not real names but simply appellations that are derived from his functions.[39] Justin brought together a Platonic distinction between God in himself and God as he relates to the world, with the biblical distinction between the Father and the Son.

Justin's doctrine of the Father had consequences for his doctrine of the Logos. His understanding of the Logos is important because it created a bridge between Christianity and Greek philosophy. He held that the Logos was divine and performed two functions: he was the Father's agent in ordering and creating the universe, and he was the revealer of truth to men.[40]

Justin described the Logos as God's unique Son. This unique Son emanated and proceeded from the Father. The apologists had already

37. Kelly (ibid., 90) asserts that the apostolic fathers were more witnesses of the faith than interpreters of the faith and "Of a doctrine of the Trinity in the strict sense there is of course no sign" (ibid., 95). Wolfson (*Philosophy*, 1:191) says that the apostolic fathers taught that the Trinity actually began with Christ's birth. Prior to the incarnation, there were two preexistent beings, God the Father and the Holy Spirit, the latter of whom was identified with the preexistent Christ. The term *Logos* was identified with the Holy Spirit.

38. Their theology sounds more like one that is based on the OT alone. The OT clearly identified different persons within the godhead, but a full Trinitarian theology was not yet revealed. See Richard C. Gamble, *The Whole Counsel of God*, vol. 1, *God's Mighty Acts in the Old Testament* (Phillipsburg, NJ: P&R Publishing) (*WCG1*), 633–38.

39. Herman Bavinck, *The Doctrine of God* (Carlisle, PA: Banner of Truth, 1977), 21.

40. Quasten, *Patrology*, 1:209–11.

implemented the Stoic contrast between the *logos endiathetos*, the "uttered word," and the *logos prophorikos*, the "word remaining within." Such a distinction made it possible to differentiate between the pretemporal oneness of Christ with the Father and also his appearance in space and time. For Justin, this emanation of the Logos was purposive, since it was done by the Father's will. Justin employed numerous analogies in attempting to describe the emanation. For example, it is like fire and how a number of torches may be lit from one fire, or like a ray of light to the sun. The purpose of these analogies was to emphasize the fact that the distinction between the Father and the Logos is in number only—there is no division of the *ousia* ("essence") of the Father in the emanation of the Logos. Subordinationism is probably inherent within this doctrine of the Logos. Justin articulated something of a doctrine of the Holy Spirit, but it is difficult to determine exactly what he meant: the prophetic Spirit is categorized as in the "third grade."[41]

Melito of Sardis had difficulty determining the relationship between the members of the Trinity. If, as some scholars think, Melito failed to assert the distinction between the Father and the Son, then we have the beginning of what has been called *modalism*, or "Monarchian Trinitarian theology." This tradition will play an important role as we continue to outline the history of Trinitarian theology.

Tatian, a student of Justin in Rome, presents his readers with a picture of God as without beginning, the source of the universe, and a Spirit who is invisible, intangible, and not extended in matter. Tatian developed Justin's doctrine of the Logos: as in Justinian thought, the Logos was generated as the agent to create and sustain the creation. Yet Tatian defined more carefully the two successive stages of the Logos. While generated, he was considered to be of equal nature with the Father.[42] Tatian implemented Justin's analogy between the generation of the Logos and that of the fire. But some do not see in Tatian's thought an advance over Justin's in distinguishing between the Logos/Son and the Holy Spirit.[43]

---

41. Carrington, *Early Christian Church*, 115. Carrington thinks that Justin's *Apology* I, 6 proves that Justin places angels on the same level as the Holy Spirit. But a careful reading of the passage does not confirm Carrington's conclusion.

42. Prestige, *God in Patristic Thought*, 234.

43. Lampe, "Christian Theology," 37.

Athenagoras of Athens further developed Tatian's ideas and illustrated early delineations of Trinitarian belief among the apologists. Athenagoras has, for his place in history, an ingenious and well-developed definition of the doctrine of the Trinity. This definition of the Trinity is found in *Legatio* 10:

> Who therefore would not be at loss to hear men who speak of God the Father, and God the Son and the Holy Spirit, and show both their power in union and their distinction in order being called atheists?[44]

Athenagoras stressed that the Logos could not be said to have been brought into existence; furthermore, he added that this Logos or Word is the Son of God. God governs and rules the created universe by his Word. But Athenagoras carefully avoided the subordinationism found in the other Greek apologists' views, and he affirmed the deity of the Holy Spirit. The Holy Spirit was viewed as a divine effluence who comes from God, then returns to him.

Theophilus of Antioch followed Tatian and Athenagoras both chronologically and theologically. He was the first theologian to use the Greek term *trias* ("three") for the union of the three persons in God. Nevertheless, he did not advance theologically to the point where this triad will be named the Father, the Son, and the Holy Spirit. For Theopilus, this triad is the Father, the Word, and "Wisdom." God the Father is uncreated, immortal, immutable, and almighty. The Word, or Logos, is seen both as *endiathetos* and *prophorikos*, as well as the agent of creation and God's counselor before creation began. Theophilus believed that God, as *logos endiathetos*, was never deprived of the Logos, but the generation of the Logos was a deliberate act of the Father—the same idea that Justin and Tatian had advanced earlier.

Theophilus's theory of a twofold stage of the Logos became important for Antiochene theology. His attention to the third person of the Trinity was an important development in Trinitarian theology as well—his third person is the wisdom of God. This idea is a peculiarity in patristic thought, in which the majority of Christian writers identify

44. As cited by Quasten, *Patrology*, 1:233.

"Wisdom" with the second person. Theophilus's thinking was later adopted by Irenaeus.[45]

Irenaeus of Lyons (ca. A.D. 130–202). Irenaeus advanced beyond the apologists at two important points of Trinitarian theology. First, he had a much more developed perception of the work of the Trinity, that is, what each member of the Trinity does outside himself. Second, he gave the Holy Spirit a more definite place in the scheme of the Trinity.[46]

The best place to begin Irenaeus's notion of the work of the Trinity, or what is termed the *economic Trinity*, is with the act of creation. Creation is God's work out of nothing. The creator of the world is the one true God, who is also the God of the OT as well as the Father of the Logos. The Son, or Word, is divine and spoke to the OT patriarchs in the theophanies. Irenaeus does not speculate on the manner of the Word's generation, even while he was certain that the Word did not become the Son of God at the time or by virtue of the incarnation. The relationship between the Word and the Father is an eternal one, and it is through the Word that the Father reveals himself. Although Irenaeus did not expressly employ the terminology of Christ's two natures, he maintained that belief: Jesus was not only divine, but he was also human like we are human.

Irenaeus linked the Word and the Spirit as the instruments of creation. While this teaching is clearly biblical, given his philosophical context, Irenaeus was able in this way to bring a transcendent God more closely in touch with his creation than did other early theologians.[47]

The Holy Spirit, besides partaking in creation with the Word, is the divine Wisdom. On the order of the Father, the Spirit also inspired the prophets. Irenaeus's theology does not expressly designate the Holy Spirit as God, but it is indubitable that it ranks the Spirit as divine. While Irenaeus's theology represents a number of advances, his Trinitarian theology still falls short of Nicaea's.[48]

45. Jean Daniélou, *Gospel Message and Hellenistic Culture* (Philadelphia: Westminster Press, 1980), 2:356.

46. Even though the word for Trinity (*trias*) had already appeared in Theophilus, it does not appear in Irenaeus's writings.

47. Lampe, "Christian Theology," 45.

48. Bavinck (*Doctrine of God*, 21) summarizes: He "presents the false and partly Gnostic antithesis between the Father: hidden, invisible, unknowable; and the Son, who revealed him."

Tertullian (ca. A.D. 155/60–225). Tertullian's doctrine of the Trinity represented the apex of the ante-Nicene era—his Trinitarian formulations were implemented at the Council of Nicaea.[49] Tertullian provided the important Trinitarian formula, "one in essence and three in persons"—he was the first theologian to use the Latin term for "Trinity." Because Tertullian's thought is both important and complex, there are different schools of interpreting it.[50]

Tertullian's term for what theologians understand by the doctrine of the Trinity was *economy*.[51] Tertullian held to one God. But this one God was to be comprehended in reference to the divine dispensation or economy. In that economy, there was a Son of the one God, his Word, which proceeded from him through whom all things were made.[52] The Father was the source, and the Holy Spirit proceeded from the Father through the Son.[53] Tertullian taught that the Son or Logos was of the Father's substance.[54] Although the Son was of the same substance, he was nevertheless different from the Father. The differentiation was expressed in the sense of personhood.[55] Thus the Son was distinct from the Father but was not divided from him; he was a second person in addition to the Father.[56] The Holy Spirit was likewise a person and distinct from the Father and from the Son. He was considered a representative, or deputy, of the Son and issued from the Father by way of the Son.[57]

49. Quasten, *Patrology*, 2:285; Lampe, "Christian Theology," 55.

50. Robert A. Markus, in "Trinitarian Theology and the Economy," *Journal of Theological Studies* 9, no. 1 (1958): 89–102, presented the two schools of interpretation. On the one side are Harnack and Loofs. They argued for equating Tertullian with fourth-century economic views of the Trinity. Prestige said that the two are radically different. Markus sided with Prestige. Prestige refused to assimilate Tertullian's view to Marcellus's Trinitarian teaching. To claim that Tertullian's view is radically different from later economic views, however, may be an overstatement.

51. Prestige, *God*, 98.

52. Lampe, "Christian Theology," 55.

53. Tertullian (in *Against Praxeas*, as cited by Joel R. Beeke and Paul M. Smalley, *Reformed Systematic Theology*, vol. 1, *Revelation and God* [Wheaton, IL: Crossway, 2019], 904) stated: "I believe the Spirit to proceed from no other source than from the Father through the Son."

54. In *De pudicitia* 4 he said: "Filium non aliunde deduco, sed do substantia Patris." See J. P. Migne, *Patrologiae Cursus Completus: Series Latina* (Paris: Garnier Fratres, 1857), 2:987.

55. Kelly (*Doctrines*, 115) said "the primary sense of persona was 'mask.'" See also Quasten, *Patrology*, 2:325.

56. Tertullian, *Adversus Praxean* 12, Corpus Scriptorum Ecclesiasticorum Latinorum (Leipzig: Freytag, 1906), 47:232–34.

57. Kelly, *Doctrines*, 112; Prestige, *God*, 99. The Holy Spirit, as well as the Son, was "tam consortibus substantiae patris."

Tertullian advanced the doctrine of the Trinity in that he recognized, at least of the Father and the Son, that they are what we term *persons*. He also attempted to define more precisely the oneness of the divine substance, which nevertheless had three expressions.[58] He grasped an important Trinitarian distinction between *ousia*, "essence," and *prosopon*, "person."[59] Within the godhead there was unity; there was oneness in substance and origin of the three persons. Thus Tertullian demonstrated that the "threeness" of God was compatible with divine unity.[60] When Tertullian used the words *una substantia*, "one substance," he implied not only an equality of substance but also a unity and identity of substance.[61]

Monarchianism. While Tertullian was formulating his understanding of the Trinity, error was already creeping into the church. One example of that error was Monarchianism, which underlined God's unity. Dynamic Monarchianism believed that Jesus was just an ordinary man. While Jesus was powerfully indwelled by the Spirit, he was not God. Theodotus of Rome began this teaching, and Paul of Samosata developed it. Modalistic Monarchianism, also known as modalism or Sabellianism, became widespread in the early church. It was begun by Praxeas of Rome and developed by Noetus of Smyrna, his disciple Callistus, and Sabellius. They held that there is one God who can have three different names but does not have three distinct persons. Modalistic Monarchianism was fairly widespread, and its proponents held to two significant tenets—that God was one, and that Jesus was fully divine. While Christians should reject modalistic Monarchianism, both of these tenets are essential to embrace! Modalistic Monarchians struggled with the teaching that Jesus the Christ was personally distinct from God the Father; to them it seemed to

58. Such a formulation of the Trinity is thought to be subordinationistic. See Quasten, *Patrology*, 2:286; Kelly, *Doctrines*, 113.

59. Michael Horton, *The Christian Faith: A Systematic Theology for Pilgrims on the Way* (Grand Rapids: Zondervan, 2011), 284. Decades after Tertullian's death, Athanasius failed to grasp this important distinction and used the word "*ousia*" to refer to divine essence as well as person.

60. Quasten, *Patrology*, 2:286; Kelly, *Doctrines*, 113. Even Lampe ("Christian Theology," 55) admits that the *Adversus Praxean* is "a real attempt to say something about the relation between the diversity of the Godhead (in respect of its manifestation and operation) and its essential unity."

61. Quasten (*Patrology*, 2:325) cites *De pudicitia* 2. See also Prestige, *God*, 221.

be the heresy of two gods. So modalists refused to acknowledge the distinct persons of the one divine substance. They argued that there was only one God—the Father; therefore, they believed that it was the Father who suffered on the cross. For if Christ suffered, then the Father also must have suffered, since there could be no division within God. Their presupposition concerning God's being led to the erroneous belief that the Father suffered in the crucifixion—a belief that was termed *patripassianism*.[62]

Tertullian wrote against the Monarchians in *Against Praxeas*.[63] Praxeas argued incorrectly that since the Father, Son, and Holy Spirit are merely different modes or manifestations of the one divine being in different eras, it was actually the Father who suffered on the cross. In response, Tertullian spoke of one essence, or substance, and three persons. He also used analogies for this reality—for example, a tree, its root, and its fruit.[64] To express both the oneness and threeness of the godhead, Tertullian coined the Latin term *trinitas*. This writing emerged as a significant work for the doctrine of the Trinity.[65] It was used at the Council of Nicaea, and Augustine later expanded its meaning.

Tertullian was convinced that the Monarchians, already seen since Mileto, inappropriately smashed time and history into deity.[66] The answer to their challenge required a more biblical doctrine of God's being and work.[67] First, God had to be personal while at the same time maintaining an internal unity. Also, God had to be the Creator who was active in time by controlling creation.[68]

Hippolytus of Rome (A.D. 170–235). Hippolytus fought both modalism and Monarchianism in *The Refutation of All Heresies*. Tertullian and Hippolytus had theological agreements as well as dif-

---

62. For more information and greater detail, see Kelly, *Doctrines*, 115–20, and Berkhof, *History of Christian Doctrines*, 77–80.

63. Benjamin B. Warfield, *Studies in Tertullian and Augustine* (Whitefish, MT: Kessinger, 2010), 10–12.

64. Beeke and Smalley, *Reformed Systematic Theology*, 1:904.

65. On his Christology, see Maurice Wiles and Mark Santer, eds., *Documents in Early Christian Thought* (Cambridge: Cambridge University Press, 1975), 44; Warfield, *Studies*, 6–9.

66. Van Til, *Christian Theory of Knowledge*, 86.

67. The modalistic Monarchians adopted a Greek philosophical view of God. For them he was more like Heraclitus's original element of the universe, fire. See the analysis of Heraclitus in chapter 1. Kelly (*Doctrines*, 121) claims that Praxeas used Heraclitus's actual arguments and texts.

68. Van Til, *Christian Theory of Knowledge*, 87.

ferences. They agreed that God, as the "Three," as they were revealed in the economy, were a manifestation of the multiplicity that can be comprehended in the immanent life of the godhead.[69] Hippolytus held that there was always a plurality within the godhead, but Tertullian, while not necessarily disagreeing, was more explicit in asserting that the immanent Word had an otherness or individuality.[70]

Hippolytus stated that the Word was the Son before the incarnation. This claim stood in contradistinction to the earlier apologists, as well as to Tertullian, who dated the Son's generation only from the time of creation. It seems clear that the apologists and Tertullian did not affirm that before creation the Father was the Father of the Son. By the time of Tertullian, however, the significance of the appellation "Father" was at least gradually developing.[71]

Novatian (A.D. 200–258). Novatian is best known for a schism named after him. His *De trinitate*, however, has been highly praised by scholars.[72] His work was meant to be a full exposition of the rule of truth, beginning with God's ineffability and incomprehensibility.[73] But Novatian's thinking represented a step backward in the history of Trinitarian doctrine. He was very concerned not to teach a duality of gods; therefore, he concluded that the Father had bestowed deity upon the Son—a deity, however, that ultimately reverted back to the Father.[74]

With this thinking, Novatian propounded a subordinationistic Christology, perhaps in his attempt to avoid ditheism. Although his Christology was subordinationistic, Novatian perceived the Son as

69. Kelly, *Doctrines*, 110–14.
70. Ibid., 111. Independently of Tertullian, Prestige (*God*, 110) believes that "Hippolytus' main point is that the Father was in the incarnate Son simply and solely because He was in the eternal Son."
71. Kelly, *Doctrines*, 112.
72. Quasten (*Patrology*, 2:217) argues that Novatian's *De trinitate* sums up the doctrine developed by Justin, Theophilus of Antioch, Irenaeus, Hippolytus, and Tertullian: "The treatment of the subject is much more exact and systematic, much more complete and extensive than that of any prior attempt." He adds that the work "brings the development of the Trinitarian doctrine to a certain conclusion for the pre-Augustinian period, and reads like a manual of Western Christology" (ibid., 2:227).
73. Kelly, *Doctrines*, 126; Lampe, "Christian Theology," 62.
74. This notion can connect back to Tertullian's idea to deputize or be representative. When a sheriff deputizes someone, he puts a badge on that person's lapel, and this normal citizen while functioning as a deputy may shoot another person. When the citizen takes the badge off, he cannot perform those actions without incurring punishment. For a time he is deputized, and the power to act as deputy actually reverts back to the sheriff who deputizes him.

both fully man and fully God. Nevertheless, his subordinationism went beyond that of his predecessors, for he viewed the Logos as some type of temporary and passing personal manifestation of the Father. Yet he held that Christ was also preexistent. Accordingly, Novatian did not teach that the generation of the Son occurred simultaneously with creation.[75] For Novatian, the Holy Spirit is not called the *tertia persona* ("third person"), the term Tertullian used. Novatian viewed the Holy Spirit as less than the Son,[76] and he treated the subject of the Spirit in only one book of *De trinitate*.[77] While clearly a man of many talents and learning, Novation held to a poorly defined Trinitiarian theology because he thought as a Christian Stoic.[78]

Clement of Alexandria. Regressing chronologically, we turn to the East and the thought of Clement of Alexandria, who wrote before A.D. 215, primarily to provide a short historical introduction to Origen's teaching on the Trinity.[79] Clement taught that God is the "One." By that phrase, he meant that there were no creaturely analogies for God's being. Whatever human beings call God does not express his being but simply his power.[80] Clement was firmly against adoptionistic teaching. For Clement, Christ was eternal, the perfect image of God the Father and the mediator between God and man. Like Irenaeus, Clement was against the earlier doctrine of *logos prophorikos*. Clement was influenced by what has been called Middle Platonism in his understanding of God. For him, God must be absolutely transcendent; the Word, like the *nous* of Middle Platonism, was a unity and plurality.

---

75. Novatian, *De trinitate* 11; Migne, *Patrologiae Latina*, 3:930; Novatian, *De trinitate* 16; Migne, *Patrologiae Latina*, 3:942. According to Kelly (*Doctrines*, 123, 126), Novatian does not teach the eternal generation of the Son. The charges of ditheism were brought against Hippolytus and Tertullian. (See also Quasten, *Patrology*, 2:228–29.) That is, the Son existed *in substantia* before the foundation of the world. See Novatian, *De trinitate* 16.2; Migne, *Patrologiae Latina*, 3:942.

76. Tertullian, *Adversus Praxean* 11; Migne, *Patrologiae Latina*, 2:189–91; Quasten, *Patrology*, 2:230.

77. Kelly (*Doctrines*, 126) calls Novatian's doctrine of the Holy Spirit rudimentary and goes on to say that "he seems to have no inkling of the Trinitarian nature of the Godhead."

78. Quasten, *Patrology*, 2:216: "His works betray the influence of that philosophy on several occasions."

79. Berkhof, *History of Christian Doctrines*, 70.

80. Bavinck, *Doctrine of God*, 21: "Whenever we eliminate from our thought everything pertaining to the creature, that which remains is not what God is but what he is not. It is not proper to ascribe to him form, movement, place, number, attribute, name, etc."

The Spirit is the power and light issuing from the Word and attracts people to God.[81]

Origen (A.D. 185–253). Origen addressed the Trinity ontologically and used the word *hypostasis* to refer to the persons of God: he is three hypostases who share the same essence. The Trinitarian relationships are eternal; thus the Son's generation from the Father is eternal. The generation demonstrates their unity of nature and substance. The Son is *homoousios*, of the "same nature," with the Father. The Holy Spirit was not made or created but always existed. The Holy Spirit proceeds from the Father from eternity.[82]

Origen's Trinitarian theology began with God the Father as the apex. The Father is immutable, impassible, does not need the world, though he created it, and is beyond space and time. The Father alone is *autotheos*, "God of himself"—that is, God in the strict sense—and *agenetos*, "ingenerate." As an absolute being, the Father is also incomprehensible, as well as being *aplos agathos*, the "primal goodness."[83] In that the Father is perfect goodness and power, it was necessary in Origen's system for the Father to have objects on which to exercise these attributes. A further necessity was that the object of the Father's goodness must also, like the Father, be eternal.

The Son of God mediates between God the Father and the spiritual beings that have been the eternal objects of the Father's goodness. Here, Origen is probably reiterating Philo's understanding of the logos. Origen said the Son takes the position of mediator and high priest between the Creator and his creatures. In terms of this relationship, the Son is the Father's image and has a plurality of aspects that embrace his relationship between the Father and the world.[84] So comprehending the Son's function helps us understand the Son's nature.

The scholarly world is certainly not of one mind on Origen's understanding of the Son's nature. Some hold that for Origen the Son is different in substance from the Father or even separate in person,

---

81. Kelly (*Doctrines*, 9–10) concludes concerning Clement: "Thus we have a Trinity which, though in all its lineaments Platonic, Clement unhesitatingly identifies with Christian Theism" (ibid., 127).

82. Allison, *Historical Theology*, 237–38.

83. Quasten, *Patrology*, 2:75.

84. These aspects, or, *epinoiai*, represent the ideas of Platonism proper.

though they have harmony or identity of will.[85] Others believe that the relationship is even less intimate—that the Son is simply an effulgence of God's glory, not an actual effulgence of God.[86] In this view, the Logos is only a mirror of God the Father; the Son, therefore, is greatly transcended by the Father. Still others assert that for Origen the Father and the Son are actually unified in substance.[87]

In the light of the scholarly disagreements, we can summarize Origen's conception of the Son in relationship to the Father. First, it appears that Origen rejected the notion that the Son or Logos is on an equal level with God the Father.[88] Second, it seems safe to conclude that, because Origen assumed Middle Platonism's axiom of the necessary inferiority of that which is produced to that which produces, Origen was necessarily a subordinationist.[89]

A related question is whether the Son or Logos was a created being. While the answer for twenty-first-century Christians is simple—of course not!—the answer for Origen was not easy. He called the Logos a *created being*—in Greek, a *ktisma*.[90] This Son was generated by the Father's will and is known as the created being Wisdom. For Origen, the Scriptures said that the Lord created Wisdom, then tradition identified Wisdom with the Logos; therefore, the Lord created the Logos.[91]

But Origen does not always use the Greek word *ktisma* to refer to the Son. Somehow for him, this way of thinking does not deny Christ's deity. The church of Origen's day would have condemned such a view. Origen confusedly called the Son both *ktisma* and *genetos* and at the

85. Kelly, *Doctrines*, 129.

86. Prestige (*God*, 133) asserts that in relation to the Father, the Logos is an image of his goodness and an effulgence of his glory, but not an effulgence of God.

87. Quasten, *Patrology*, 2:78.

88. Prestige asserts that there is no distinction between greater or lesser in the divine triad as Origen understands it. He attempts to conform Origen's thought to the idea that the Logos is no less God in that he is not the source of deity.

89. This assumption is not held by all scholars. Robert Letham (*The Holy Trinity: In Scripture, History, Theology, and Worship*, rev. and exp. ed. [Phillipsburg, NJ: P&R Publishing, 2019], 105) holds that the subordination is of glory only. Also, while Origen has "a clear strand of thought in which the Son derives his deity from the Father," still, "there is enough to see Origen's basic orthodoxy."

90. Prestige (*God*, 132–33) argues that the Son was a created being. He maintains that Origen asserted both the individuality of the Son and the necessary separation between the godhead and created reality.

91. Prestige (ibid., 136–37) argues that separating that which is *geneta* from God will, for Origen, leaves both Christ and the Holy Spirit on the same side as human beings.

same time not *genetos*, that is, *agenetos*. The Logos for Origen is unlike all the creatures in that intrinsically he is life in the same sense as is the Father. George Leonard Prestige presupposes that it is logically impossible for the Logos to be both *genetos* and *agenetos* when the two words have opposite meanings. His solution is:

> He is *agenetos* or uncreated because He belongs to the triad of deity, and uncreated life is the substance of His being. On the other hand, He is *genetos* or derivative because He is not Himself the source or origin of that being, but derives it from the Father. The two state-ments are thus not in the least inconsistent.[92]

J. N. D. Kelly says that for Origen the Son is begotten, not created by the Father.[93] If the Son is begotten, the next question is the nature of the Son's begetting. It can safely be asserted that for Origen the Son had no beginning in time. The Son came into being through an act of eternal generation.[94] This act is supratemporal and represents an eternal process within God's eternal being that was actual before creation and in the present moment. This Son who is begotten by eternal generation is also God, yet, in that he is begotten, his deity is derivative and he becomes a second or secondary God. In Origen's thought, the true God is one; therefore, the second God cannot be apart from the first God. Origen's doctrine of the eternal generation of the Son—namely, that each one of the three persons is a distinct hypostasis from eternity—takes his thinking beyond that of Tertullian and Hippolytus, who limited their understanding of God's being to the economy.[95]

Summarizing Origen, we observe that his doctrine of the Logos, as well as of the Spirit, was an advance in Trinitarian speculation. First, Origen's emphasis on the divinity of the Logos was as important as his theory of the second God. Also, granting that Origen views a descending hierarchy in the Trinity, there is in his thought a Holy Spirit who is brought into existence through the Word, is chief in rank of

92. Ibid., 138.

93. Kelly, *Doctrines*, 154–58. Origen's later followers had to deny that the Son was *geneta* because of the Arians' uses of the term.

94. Origen, therefore, cannot simply be placed among the later Arians who maintained that there was a time when the Son was not. See ibid., 128.

95. Ibid., 129.

all beings, beginning with the Father, and comes into being through Christ. The Holy Spirit is on the side of the created beings, as is the Son, but both stand by themselves. Finally, Origen was an extreme subordinationist. If the Son is in some way a creation, he is an eternal creation. Even so, Origen believes he can affirm Christ's deity.

Moving on chronologically, we come to Gregory the Wonder-worker, who was Origen's student and took part in the Council of Antioch (A.D. 265). As bishop of Neocaesarea, he wrote a creed dealing with the doctrine of the Trinity. In it, he maintains that the Son and the Holy Spirit are eternal, that there is a perfect Trinity, and that within that Trinity there is nothing created or at one time nonexistent and then existent.

Further, Dionysius of Alexandria wrote the *Refutation and Apology* ca. A.D. 248. In this writing he defends orthodoxy and states that there was never a time when God was not the Father. From the doctrine of God, we will move next to the church's early doctrine of Scripture.

DOCTRINE OF SCRIPTURE

Canon. The church of the first two centuries had both oral and written apostolic testimony. Written records and unwritten tradition were viewed as fixed and in agreement.[96] Apostolic tradition was public and conformed with Scripture. Heretics, on the other hand, claimed secret knowledge and consented to neither Scripture nor tradition.[97]

Polycarp, who was probably taught by John the apostle, cited Ephesians and described it as Scripture. *Second Clement* equated the authority of the OT books with that of the apostles. The *Epistle of Barnabas* quoted Jesus's words in Matthew as, "it is written." Papias of Hierapolis contains the best statement for the canonicity of Mark's gospel.[98]

Inspiration. *Second Clement* displays a high doctrine of Scripture. The author introduced as Scripture a quotation from the Gospels,

---

96. Ignatius, *To the Smyrnaeans*, as cited by Robert Letham, *Systematic Theology* (Wheaton, IL: Crossway, 2019), 222–23.

97. Allison, *Historical Theology*, 40.

98. See Eusebius, *Church History* 3.39.15–16. An English translation is available in Eusebius, *The History of the Church from Christ to Constantine*, trans. G. A. Williamson (New York: Dorset, 1965), 152–53.

understood the unity of Scripture, saw the NT as Scripture, and equated the written Word of God directly with the God of truth. Theophilus of Antioch stands out as the first postbiblical author to develop the doctrine of Scripture's inspiration and illustrates that the infallibility of Scripture and continuity of the Old and New Testaments were assumed from the earliest times. Theophilus called Paul's writings and the Gospels the "holy word of God."

Authority and Tradition. The earliest church fathers held that Scripture's authority was due to its divine author. God's voice is heard in it. Because it is authoritative, Scripture determines proper belief. Truth is found in Scripture, especially as it is compared with Scripture.

However, heretics also claimed that Scripture was their theological source, so the church referred to its own authority and tradition. The argument against heresy appealed to the church's doctrine as what the church had always believed; the church's authority did not stand in opposition to Scripture's authority. We must be very careful when we read that there were authorities in the ancient church that were considered to be equal to that of Scripture.[99]

There is a passage from Irenaeus's *Against Heresies* that is useful as a test case for interpretation: Irenaeus states that if the apostles had not written the NT, we could have recourse to their churches to ascertain the truth. From that statement, some scholars have wrongly concluded that the church held a canon of truth that was independent of and judged to be above Scripture.[100]

But a closer examination of the passage demonstrates that Irenaeus was not appealing to a rule of faith but to Scripture itself. In fact, Irenaeus was combatting Gnostics, Marcionites, and Valentinians, who

99. For example, Kelly (*Doctrines*, 33) while knowing that both Polycarp and Justin viewed the NT as the foundation of their faith, wrongly asserts: "general probability makes it unlikely that Christian teachers had these books [the OT and the works of the apostles] specifically in mind on the majority of occasions when they referred to the apostolic testimony." His statement here is an unjustifiable assertion of pure opinion. When he advances to the analysis of Irenaeus and Tertullian, Kelly continues to maintain a distinction between "Scripture" and the "church's living tradition." This legitimate distinction for the first century is illegitimate afterwards. Kelly also wrongly asserts that both the Scriptures and the church's unwritten tradition are likewise vehicles of God's revelation (ibid., 39)—another unwarranted assumption that he repeats (ibid., 42) without patristic documentation.

100. See Charles E. Hill, "The Truth above All Demonstration," in *The Enduring Authority of the Christian Scriptures*, ed. D. A. Carson (Grand Rapids: Eerdmans, 2016), 72–74, for a presentation of contemporary scholarship that takes this mistaken position.

proposed a body of truth that subordinated Scripture to their own tradition.[101] Irenaeus constantly appealed to tradition, most often in his defense of the faith against the Gnostics. Though he frequently used the word *tradition*, it is difficult to determine with precision what he meant by it. At times it seems that he was appealing to a shorter form of the Old Roman Creed, which is similar to the later Apostles' Creed (see later section in this chapter), while at other times his appeal to tradition was to the authority of bishops and presbyters. In his desire to ensure the continuation of apostolic truth, Irenaeus especially valued the bishops who could be traced back to the first century.[102] Irenaeus leaned heavily on Scripture in his writings; he quoted or referred to about nine hundred texts of Scripture throughout his works. His exegetical method emphasized two prominent tools: the first was an appeal to Scripture, and the second was his habit of interpreting difficult passages through the lens of easier passages.[103]

In the light of her mandate to combat heresy, the church continued to develop a proper interpretation of the biblical texts. The church maintained that her interpretation stood in unbroken continuity with that of the apostolic churches. Analysis of the relationship between Scripture and tradition in the ancient church must be handled carefully. During the time of the apostolic fathers until about A.D. 95, there was an oral tradition or living liturgy that existed side by side with the apostles' own written testimony.

Irenaeus taught that tradition, held in the church, demonstrated how Scripture was best understood. He identified the transmission of divine truth with episcopal succession. But the bishops who followed the apostles had a derivative witness. Their function was to preserve the

101. See Hill, "The Truth," 74–75, for a closer analysis of Irenaeus's text.

102. Farrar, *History of Interpretation*, 175n3. In addition, some have asserted that Irenaeus is the father of biblical theology because he saw God as actively working in this world. In reaction against Gnosticism, whose god could not get his hands dirty, God not only touches but is also active in the world from the beginning to the consummation revealed by John. Irenaeus also revived hope concerning the kingdom of God. The hope was for a revival of that great kingdom within this sin-filled world. See Ernst Staehelin, *Die Verkündigung des Reiches Gottes in der Kirche Jesu Christi*, vol. 1, *Von der Zeit der Apostel bis zur Auflösung des Römischen Reiches* (Basel: Verlag Friedrich Reinhardt, 1951), 1:128; and William Edgar and K. Scott Oliphint, *Christian Apologetics Past and Present: A Primary Source Reader* (Wheaton, IL: Crossway, 2009), 1:86–87.

103. Farrar, *History of Interpretation*, 175. Explaining difficult passages by those that are easy to understand is found in *Adversus haeresus* 2.10 §2.

integrity and totality of the original apostolic witness. It was Scripture that contained the original kerygma in toto.[104] Irenaeus condemned extrascriptural tradition.[105]

Inerrancy. The ancient-church fathers believed that Scripture's affirmations correspond to reality. Its stories and facts are true. It recounts true stories that are not always favorable. Scripture does not contradict Scripture. Because it cannot contradict itself, easier passages help with understanding the more difficult ones. Because God cannot lie, the Bible communicates without error. The prophets spoke in harmony. Supposed contradictions are more like different perspectives on the same event or teaching.[106]

Clarity or Perspicuity. Since Scripture is clear, the more plain passages interpret the more obscure passages.[107] Clement of Alexandria emphasized Scripture's mysteries. He wrote on the impossibility of expressing God. Scripture was, for him, something like a parable. He saw two types of believers—those who were spiritual and could understand, and those who could not understand.[108] Origen developed this thinking. The Bible was clear on crucial truths and spoke in clear language. There was mystery in the Scriptures, however. Mystery is spiritual truth that is hidden under its words. Its hidden meaning could be probed only by those with the key of knowledge. But no one could fully probe divine mystery.

Biblical Interpretation. Going back in time to Philo, there were three exegetical schools of biblical interpretation. Philo despised the literalists, the first school. The second school, the rationalists, apostatized from Judaism. Philo belonged to the third school and implemented allegorical exegesis.[109]

His "On the Allegories of the Sacred Laws" provides examples of his allegorical method. Concerning the world's creation in six days, Philo said that six is only mentioned because it is a perfect number.

---

104. Heiko Augustinus Oberman, *The Harvest of Medieval Theology: Gabriel Biel and Late Medieval Nominalism* (Cambridge: Harvard University Press, 1963), 367.

105. John D. Woodbridge, *Biblical Authority: A Critique of the Rogers/McKim Proposal* (Grand Rapids: Zondervan, 1982), 32.

106. Allison, *Historical Theology*, 99–102.

107. Ibid., 121–22.

108. Ibid., 122–23.

109. Farrar, *History of Interpretation*, 137.

God did not actually rest on the seventh day, but since he stopped making mortal creatures, he worked on divine beings. To think that God actually planted a garden in paradise is impious, from Philo's vantagepoint. The meaning of that story is that God implants terrestrial virtue in the human race. The tree of life is that most general virtue which some people call goodness. The river that goes forth out of Eden is also generic goodness—its four heads are the cardinal virtues.[110]

Philo interpreted Jacob's arrival at a place where the sun set as, actually, a picture of what happens when one acquires wisdom by training through the divine Word, when sensory experience becomes useless. When Jacob declares that he will pass over the Jordan River with his staff, Philo interprets the word *Jordan* to mean "baseness" and the word *staff* to mean "discipline." The point of the story is that Jacob, by discipline, had risen above baseness.

While this type of allegory may sound strange to contemporary ears, it was a literary methodology implemented during Philo's time, even though it required the abandonment of instructive human history.[111] Philo attempted to support his theory from the Scripture. As an example, he highlighted the statement in Numbers 23:19, "God is not a man," while noting that in Deuteronomy 1:31 the Bible also states, "the Lord your God carried you as a man carries his son." In these two passages, Philo supposedly found two methods of biblical interpretation, the literal and the allegorical.

Philo provided rules for what he deemed proper allegorical interpretation. Some of the rules excluded the possibility of literality. In others, the two senses lived side by side. He thought that the literal sense should be excluded when it contains a contradiction or a statement unworthy of God. The two senses could stand side by side when an expression is repeated, such as the repetition of Abraham's name, or when a superfluous word occurs—for example, in the phrase, "eating you should eat." This last phrase for Philo meant to eat in a proper spirit and with conscious knowledge. He believed that each word could also carry all possible meanings apart from its context;

110. Ibid., 143.
111. Daniélou, *Gospel Message*, 2:197.

for example, "the lip of the Nile" actually means to beware of Pharaoh's speech.[112]

All the apostolic fathers, without exception, proclaimed the words of the Bible to be the very words of the Holy Spirit.[113] That proper doctrine of Scripture did not keep them from some strange hermeneutical methods, however.[114] The apostolic fathers used a modified form of allegorical exegesis that is commonly called *typology*. The words *typology* and *allegory* must be defined carefully.[115] Both the NT writers and the ancient church employed typology. Judaism used midrash in expositing the Scriptures, and this technique included allegory.[116] Allegory comments on a text of Scripture to draw out a deeper meaning and apply it to a contemporary situation. The allegorical method as such was repudiated by church fathers such as Arnobius; yet the apostolic fathers used a form of allegory in that they made the OT speak directly to Christian truth.[117] For instance, the *Epistle of Barnabas* finds something that can be referred to Christ or to Christianity throughout the OT—the letter quotes Isaiah 45:1 as, "The Lord said to my Christ the Lord."[118]

Beginning with Justin Martyr, we see a systematization of the typological method of interpretation. Justin recognized three levels within the OT: the law, wisdom, and Christ as the end of the laws of worship. In the early stages of biblical interpretation, there were few problems with the OT. But the question arose as to how the OT law could be God's revelation. There appeared to be two answers to this question: (1) the NT expanded the teaching of the OT, and (2) the NT replaced the OT. Marcion's answer was the second one, and he reduced the four gospels to only one. Irenaeus, in contrast, insisted on

112. Farrar, *History of Interpretation*, 151.
113. Ibid., 165–71. This is a mechanical view of inspiration. For example, Athenagoras said, "the Spirit uses the writers as a flute player might blow into his flute."
114. The apostolic fathers also implement what we call the apocryphal biblical literature. It is not often implemented, and it is a matter of debate as to whether citations are quoted as Scripture.
115. For more on allegory, see *WCG* 1:528–29. For Paul's use of allegory, see *WCG* 2:91. See also Kelly, *Doctrines*, 70.
116. See *WCG* 2:42–43.
117. Farrar, *History of Interpretation*, 167n1.
118. Ibid., 168. See K. J. Woollcombe, "The Biblical Origins and Patristic Development of Typology," in *Essays on Typology*, ed. G. W. H. Lampe and K. J. Woollcombe (Naperville, IL: Allenson, 1957), 39–75.

four. The necessity of four gospels was then based on the information found in the fourth chapter of Revelation, where the four gospels were represented by four animals.

Justin Martyr maintained as well a mechanical theory of inspiration.[119] He also thought that the OT was mainly for Christians. In every OT theophany, he saw a certain Christophany. Philo probably influenced Justin on these issues.[120] He thought that the OT writers spoke in mysteries, types, and symbols.

From the earliest times, the church has had an unfortunate exegetical tradition of interpreting Scripture without paying attention to the natural sense of the language. For example, the *Epistle of Barnabas* said: "The number of men in Abraham's band that rescued his nephew Lot, namely, 318, signified that our redemption is by the cross of Jesus, since the Greek letter corresponding to 300 is T (Ta), whose form makes it a symbol of the cross, while that corresponding to 10 is I (Iota) and 8 is H (Heta), which are the first two letters of the Greek form of the name Jesus."[121] Clearly, the church would need to make further hermeneutical advances.

The *Epistle of Barnabas* took the position that the OT is best understood by using allegory, or better, typology. When implementing typology, events in Israelite history become important for their spiritual or moral meaning. In that way, the OT speaks clearly of that which was to come in the NT. As mentioned earlier the text viewed the days of creation as meaning that the earth's history would be finished in six thousand years.[122] The prohibition to eat pork actually meant a demand not to interact with unbelievers.

Irenaeus also used this type of interpretation. For example, he maintained that the three persons of the Trinity were found in the parable of the good Samaritan: the innkeeper to whom the Samaritan brought the man signified the Holy Spirit, and the two denarii paid for his lodging signified the Father and the Son. Thus this parable

119. Farrar, *History of Interpretation*, 172–74.
120. Ibid., 174.
121. Philip Edgcumbe Hughes, *Lefèvre: Pioneer of Ecclesiastical Renewal in France* (Grand Rapids: Eerdmans, 1985), 58.
122. Ernst Staehelin, *Die Verkündigung des Reiches Gottes in der Kirche Jesu Christi*, vol. 1, *Von der Zeit der Apostel bis zur Auflösung des Römischen Reiches* (Basel: Verlag Friedrich Reinhardt, 1951), 1:96.

taught that "by the Spirit we receive the image and superscription of the Father and the Son."[123]

By the third century, there were at least two distinct schools of biblical interpretation. The Alexandrian school of interpretation, as represented by Clement and Origen, was a proponent of allegorical interpretation. The Antiochene school, as represented by the Cappadocian fathers, represented a grammatical-historical method of exegesis.

Exegetically, Clement and Origen represented the direct antithesis to the labors of Tertullian and Irenaeus. For example, Clement appealed to the existence of a secret tradition, while Tertullian denied the existence of such a tradition.[124]

Clement did not deny the existence of a literal sense of Scripture, but he taught that this literal sense furnished an only elementary faith.[125] In principle, Clement's interpretation was identical to Philo's. Clement even allegorized the Decalogue and the NT miracles as though they were parables.

Origen's exegetical theories were similar to those of Philo and Clement. Origen, who had a high view of Scripture, embodied a good example that adherence to the doctrine of inerrancy does not ensure proper exegetical methods. Origen associated a literal interpretation of the OT with Judaizing tendencies. He considered a literal reading of Scripture to be fit for simpleminded folk.[126] Normally, he asserted that the literal and allegorical senses of Scripture must both be retained, but at times he disregarded the literal sense as untrue.

Origen's method held that the senses of Scripture were threefold—first, the moral sense. This sense was the application of the text to the soul and appears more in his sermons than in his commentaries.[127] His second sense was the spiritual sense. It was concerned with the impending fulfillment of types and shadows throughout Scripture. And

---

123. As cited by Hughes, *Lefèvre*, 58.
124. Farrar, *History of Interpretation*, 183.
125. Ibid., 186.
126. R. P. C. Hanson, *Allegory and Event: A Study of the Sources and Significance of Origen's Interpretation of Scripture* (Richmond, VA: John Knox Press, 1959), 237.
127. For more information on Origen, see Henri de Lubac, *Geist aus der Geschichte: Das Schriftverständnis des Origines*, trans. Hans Urs von Balthasar (Einsiedeln: Johannes Verlag, 1968). See earlier analysis for Origen's threefold sense of Scripture.

the third sense was the allegorical, which concerned the secret mysteries of God's activities toward men. This three-tiered system allowed
for almost any possible interpretation.[128] Origen's writings are filled
with abuses of Scripture that flowed from this complex approach. For
example, he taught that the word *horse* actually means "voice"; the
word *today* means "the present age"; the word *leaven* means "teaching"; and the word *linen* means "chastity."

Antiochene exegesis, on the other hand, represented the historical-
grammatical method of interpretation.[129] This school of interpretation
was not limited to one city, such as Alexandria, but was a theological
and exegetical tendency. The school began with Diodore of Tarsus,
who then taught Theodore of Mopsuestia and Chrysostom. Diodore
commented on large portions of Scripture and emphasized the literal
sense of the text.[130]

Though Theodore rejected Origen's theories, he gleaned from him
the value of attention to linguistic detail. He was known as the exegete
of the ancient church. Theodore attempted to study each passage as a
whole, not as an isolated series of unrelated texts. He raised questions
concerning church organization, early history, and slaves and women
in the ancient world.[131]

The Cappadocians, while admiring Origen, avoided allegory. Basil
said, "When I hear of grass, I understand it to mean grass, and so
of plants, and fishes, and beasts, and cattle; all of them as they are
spoken of, so I receive."[132]

Chrysostom also interpreted the Bible according to its natural
sense—he saw this literal sense as a helpful guide for moral conduct
and personal instruction. There are very few exegetical errors in his
writings. He tried to elicit, not introduce, a meaning from the scriptural text, and he continued to develop discussions of the literal text
by studying the literary context. For him, Scripture was perspicuous;

128. Williston Walker, *A History of the Christian Church* (New York: Scribner's Sons,
1959), 75.
129. Farrar, *History of Interpretation*, 210: it "possessed a deeper insight into the true
method of exegesis than any which preceeded or succeeded it during a thousand years." For more
information, see Robert Kepple, "An Analysis of Antiochene Exegesis of Galatians 4:24–26,"
Westminster Theological Journal 39, no. 2 (September 1977): 239–49.
130. Farrar, *History of Interpretation*, 212.
131. Ibid., 215. For the text, see Wiles and Santer, *Documents*, 151.
132. Basil, *Hexaemeron* IX.1.

thus the only aids to its interpretation are a willing heart, the guidance of the wise, and the assistance of the Holy Spirit.

HUMANITY

Pre-Fall Image of God. Among early-church theologians there was spirited debate on the origin of the soul. Plato had said that the soul is eternal. The church responded that the soul is immortal but not eternal. Aristotle defined a human being as a rational animal. The church countered by arguing that humans are created in the image of God with reason and free will.

Irenaeus taught that unbelievers, who are still in God's image, are composed of body and soul. Believers, who are in both God's image and likeness, are composed of body, soul, and spirit. Irenaeus is credited with developing the trichotomist view.[133]

Tertullian opposed trichotomy and supported the dichotomist view that men and women are body and soul or spirit. Also, Tertullian supported the traducianist view of the soul's creation, namely, that the soul and body come into being when a baby is conceived. The body and soul are produced simultaneously. In *Treatise on the Soul*, Tertullian argued against the creationist view that God creates a human soul and then joins it to a body—the soul is impressed on the infant after the process of childbirth.[134]

Post-Fall Image of God. The ancient church fathers wrestled with the nature of original sin. Some early patristic writers underlined individual sin rather than corporate identity with Adam. Clement of Alexandria thought that Adam fell by misusing reason and chose not to progress toward perfection. Adam's sin only affected him and was not transmitted to his descendants.[135] Justin Martyr taught an unlimited free will—people are nurtured in sin but individually culpable for their actions. Adam is the ancestor and we are the descendants, yet each person sins individually.

133. For more on trichotomy, see *WCG* 1:244–49; Allison, *Historical Theology*, 322–24.
134. Allison, *Historical Theology*, 324.
135. Ibid., 344.

Tertullian, on the other hand, viewed Adam as the root of all souls. All die in Adam, even those who were never in the garden. People share in his transgression and participate in his death. Human sin is "evil which arises from the soul's corrupt origin."[136] He held that postlapsarian humanity was a dichotomy, a unity in duality of body and soul, with the flesh's functioning as the instrument of sin.[137]

Origen taught that there were preexistent spirits who were all equal and alike. All these spirits, as rational creatures, were endowed with free will. These spirits are in God's image and like God by grace. They are also in a perpetual process of becoming divine. With the fall, however, came diversity among these souls, thus creating angelic hierarchies, people in various spiritual conditions, and evil demons. Each person on earth is caught between a good and an evil spirit and has to learn to discern between them. Because each person still has free will, some people will climb higher back toward God. In Origen's view, angels can become men, as happened in the case of John the Baptist, and demons can also rise to become men.[138]

SOTERIOLOGY

Predestination, Election, and Reprobation. Greek philosophical thinking underlined fatalism and absolute determinism. In response, many in the early church wanted to emphasize free will and self-determination while still trying to hold to God's sovereignty. Theologians in this period saw divine foreknowledge and predestination as intimately linked to human willing.

Justin Martyr and Clement of Alexandria said that some are foreknown by God to believe in him. Predestination, therefore, is based on divine foreknowledge—that is, God knows those who will become righteous. God then passes over those who choose darkness.[139]

Scripture teaches that there is more to predestination than simply God's foreknowledge, but Origen tried to explain away passages that

136. Tertullian, *Treatise on the Soul*, as cited by Allison, *Historical Theology*, 344.
137. Tertullian, *De anima* 9–10, as cited by Letham, *Systematic Theology*, 342–43.
138. Daniélou, *Gospel Message*, 2:416–19.
139. Allison, *Historical Theology*, 454–55. Both Clement of Rome and Clement of Alexandria used the word "elect."

were invoked to support the teaching. Origen ascribed more to God than to humans in salvation, yet he argued that people cooperate in that salvation. He thought that God did not condemn or justify beforehand. The "vessels of honor" mentioned in Romans 9:21 were designated as honorable by a preceding cause. Those causes were people's own responsible and free decisions and actions. For Origen, human free will and self-determination in salvation was very important.[140]

This type of thinking was found in other sources. Ignatius, *The Shepherd of Hermas*, and Clement of Alexandria all saw salvation as a cooperative effort, a synergy including the human desire to do right, with the consequence of God's grace. But that grace was anticipated by divine foreknowledge and was a mixture of human will and God's grace.[141] This period of soteriology should be judged as primitive and falling short of the mark of Scripture.

Justification. The ancient church did not teach justification by works. Clement of Rome and the *Epistle of Barnabas* underlined justification through faith and not through works or wisdom.[142] Also, the *Letter to Diognetus* placed justification in the context of the removal of sin and the gift of Christ's righteousness.[143]

The doctrine was also worked out in a philosophical context heavy in fatalism, however. Contra fatalism, Origen wanted to underline the relationship between justification and free will, or self-determination. Origen restricted the "faith alone" aspect of justification to its beginning.[144]

Regeneration, Conversion, and Calling. The early church focused on regeneration and conversion, with little emphasis on calling. Cyprian and Barnabas underlined that regeneration was God's work. Leaders analyzed the nature and importance of faith, which is a divine gift. Faith is rooted in Christ's words.[145]

---

140. Ibid., 455.

141. Ibid.

142. Clement of Rome, *Epistle to the Corinthians*, as cited by Michael Horton, *Justification*, 2 vols. (Grand Rapids: Zondervan, 2018), 1:75.

143. *Letter to Diognetus* 9.3–5, in Allison, *Historical Theology*, 499: "For what else but his righteousness could have covered our sins? In whom was it possible for us, the lawless and the ungodly, to be justified, except in the Son of God alone? O the sweet exchange, O the incomprehensible work of God, O the unexpected blessings, that the sinfulness of many should be hidden in one righteous man, while the righteousness of one should justify many sinners!"

144. Horton, *Justification*, 1:88.

145. Ibid., 475–76; Allison, *Historical Theology*.

Union with Christ was important to Irenaeus, who asserted the unity of Christians in their being in Christ. This being in Christ is fundamental to Christianity. The believer is to be found in Jesus Christ, and his life in Christ is one of faith and love.

Repentance, according to Tertullian, is a change of mind and not simply a confession of sin. Origen underlined that repentance includes acknowledgment of grievous actions against God together with a change in conduct. Clement of Alexandria said that this repentance is an effect of faith. Unbelievers are addicted to sin and will not forsake it unless they first have faith. Cyprian presented dozens of passages demonstrating that God truly forgives sin when someone repents from the heart.

New birth in Christ produces radical change. A person who has repented and been forgiven should sin no longer. This change of lifestyle was the Holy Spirit's work. A number of early theologians narrated their conversions and testified to amazing changes in people of the church.[146] Conversion was connected to baptism.

Sanctification. Clement of Alexandria provided a detailed list of internal and external attributes that believers were to exemplify.[147] Tertullian provided a similar list and equated those godly characteristics with what it was to be a Christian. Part of the reason for these characteristics was to differentiate believers from unbelievers. Clement argued that certain occupations should be prohibited for members in Christ's church.[148] An exemplary Christian lifestyle was an apologetic tool in that Christian faith issued in truly changed lives. Aristides cited the changed lives of believers as a demonstration of Christianity's superiority over other religions.[149]

---

146. Allison, *Historical Theology*, 476–77.

147. Clement's list, in *Stromata* and *The Instructor*, includes: "discreet laughter, calmness and composure, simplicity and thriftiness, reverence and thankfulness, edifying and chaste conversation, self-discipline, wise servanthood (especially toward the needy and enemies), forgiveness, and Christ-centeredness" (as cited by Allison, *Historical Theology*, 521).

148. Clement includes, for example, "pimps, prostitutes, idol makers, actors or actresses in the theatre, charioteers, duelers, racers, gamblers, Olympic athletes, musicians (specifically, those who played the pipe, lute, or harp at the Olympic games), dance masters, or hucksters" (ibid., 522).

149. Among the many beautiful fruits of a mature Christian walk, Aristides in *Apology* included the following example: "If there is anyone among them who is poor and needy, and if they do not have any extra food, they fast two or three days in order to supply to the needy their lack of food" (ibid.).

Unbelievers countered that Christians were so "holy" that they were of no use in the real world. Tertullian answered that charge and said that Christians have not withdrawn from the world but walk with caution and discipline while they are in the world.

Perseverance and Assurance. Tertullian stood against any believer's presumption that he would persevere to the end, for presumption leads to less apprehension. Less apprehension means less precaution, and less precaution means more risk. On the other hand, if men and women are fearful, then they will be cautious, and that cautiousness leads to salvation. Cyprian took a similar position by praising fear as the keeper of innocence but warning that assurance begets carelessness.[150] Hippolytus held that sins committed after baptism could not be remitted—that is, if someone fell into sin, then no hope remained for salvation. This view led to postponing baptism until the end of life.[151]

Better theologians turned to God's goodness and grace in providing assurance of salvation. Justin testified at his martyrdom that he was confident of God's gift of perseverance. *The Shepherd of Hermas* took this view, as did Cyprian, who marveled at God's mercy in saving and keeping his people.[152]

Atonement Theory. Many early writers held to an idea of an atonement theory. Clement of Rome implemented the notions of substitution and example. The *Letter to Diognetus* rejoiced in the great exchange and ransom. Justin Martyr underlined Christ's taking on our curse. Melito of Sardis elaborated redemption by sacrifice as exemplified by the sacrifice of the ram in place of Isaac.

Irenaeus developed the recapitulation theory of the atonement, which held that all the events of Christ's life summed up fallen humanity. Christ's recapitulation provided a new orientation or example. The first Adam disobeyed, the second Adam reconciled.[153]

---

150. Tertullian, *On the Apparel of Women* 2.2, and Cyprian, *Letter* 1.4, in Allison, *Historical Theology*, 544.

151. Allison says that doing so was a practice and that "some writers issued warnings against returning to sin and evil after committing oneself to Christ through baptism," but he gives no reference other than Hippolytus (ibid., 545).

152. Cyprian, *Treatise 4: On the Lord's Prayer* 12, reads: "we make this supplication in our constant prayers, we ask this day and night, that the sanctification and quickening which is received from the grace of God may be preserved by His protection" (as cited by Allison, *Historical Theology*, 546).

153. Kelly, *Doctrines*, 172–74.

Origen argued that all people illegitimately belong to Satan. Christ's death was a ransom paid to Satan to release people. Satan dictated the terms of salvation. Christ's death was a blow to Satan, who had obtained dominion over the world.[154]

ECCLESIOLOGY

Church Defined. Christ's church is unified. Irenaeus, Hippolytus, and Clement of Alexandria all argued that this unity is an outstanding characteristic of the church.[155] Irenaeus emphasized the unity of Christians in their "being in Christ."[156] This being in Christ is fundamental to Christianity. The believer is to be found in Jesus Christ, and his life in Christ is to be one of faith and love.[157]

Christ's church is also holy. Theophilus described the church as a holy assembly that, in contrast to the sin-tossed world, had the doctrines of truth. But every member of the church then, as now, knew that less-than-holy members exist within the assembly. To address that problem, Justin Martyr proposed differentiating between genuine believers within the congregation and those who are not Christians, even though they profess Christ's teaching with their lips.

The church is also apostolic. Tertullian believed that Christ appointed the preachers of his own day who preached the same truth as the apostles, who received that truth from God himself.[158] Heretics do not follow the apostles' teaching but instead invent other doctrines. An apostolic church adheres to the apostles' teaching found in Scripture. Novatian said that it was God's plan to send apostolic messengers into the whole world—messengers who would speak the truth and instruct all humanity.[159]

154. Ibid., 184–87.
155. Allison, *Historical Theology*, 567.
156. Lietzmann, *Geschichte* 1:263–64.
157. Ignatius, *Epistle to the Ephesians* 9.2; 10; 11.1; 15.3 (as cited in Lietzmann, *Geschichte*, 1:256).
158. Tertullian, *Prescription against Heretics* 21: "our rule is that no others ought to be received as preachers than those whom Christ appointed." Allison (*Historical Theology*, 568–69) writes: "All doctrine which agrees with the apostolic churches—those matrixes and original sources of the faith—must be considered as truth, as undoubtedly containing that which the church received from the apostles, the apostles from Christ, and Christ from God."
159. Novatian, *De trinitate* VIII.42, as cited by Kelly, *Systematic Theology*, 1:24.

Church and State. Even during this period of tremendous persecution, Clement of Alexandria—in *What Kingdom Will Be Saved?*—demonstrated that even the state can be saved. The state was not kept out of the kingdom of heaven.

Baptism. Tertullian's *On Baptism* used the stories of Israel's passing through the Red Sea, the water that came from the rock when Moses struck it, and John's baptizing activities as images that used baptism by water to prefigure Christ.

Origen asserted the existence of a tradition from the apostles to baptize little children—but he objected to it because of children's innocence, and innocent people do not need forgiveness. Yet he also argued that infants who do not commit personal sins are not pure: "because the filth of birth is removed by the sacrament of baptism, for that reason infants, too, are baptized."[160]

Lord's Supper. The Lord's Supper was viewed in symbolic terms. Irenaeus called the Lord's Supper the body and blood of Christ and spoke of the bread and wine and Christ's body and blood as antitypes. Tertullian said that while Jesus's words were symbolic, the bread and wine are not empty symbols, for believers truly feed on the body and blood of Christ.[161] There are benefits to taking the Lord's Supper: it is an antidote to death, and it nourishes and sanctifies believers.

ESCHATOLOGY

Millennium. The early church held to premillennialism and amillennialism.[162] Premillennialism holds that there is to be a thousand-year reign of Christ on the earth immediately after his return. Papias, Justin Martyr, Irenaeus, and Lactantius held to this view.[163] The millennium

---

160. Origen, Homilies on the Gospel of Luke 14.5. See also his Commentary on Romans, 5.9.3, in Allison, *Historical Theology*, 619.

161. Ibid., 639.

162. Justin Martyr (*Dialogue with Trypho* 80), who held to premillennialism, said that "many who belong to the pure and pious faith and are true Christians think otherwise" (as cited by Allison, *Historical Theology*, 686).

163. Allison asserts that the ancient church held firmly to a premillennial dispensational position—probably his own view. In support, he cited Lactantius. But a careful reading of Lactantius does not reveal Allison's unwarranted assertion that he, or any other ancient church father, held to: "Christ will return, Antichrist will be defeated, Christians will be resurrected

was elaborately described as a time of great physical prosperity in which carnivorous beasts would eat hay.[164]

Many in the early church believed that Christ's return was imminent—which is not the same as immediate.[165] It was not far off. There were events that would precede Christ's return. Hippolytus, Justin Martyr, and Irenaeus taught that there would be intense tribulation connected with the presence of the Antichrist, then came judgment and the end of the world. Irenaeus and Tertullian thought that there would be a rapture.[166]

Eternal State. Tertullian expressed a great hope and desire for the eternal state, which would come after the world was destroyed by fire and would usher in Christ's exaltation and the saints' glory. Melito of Sardis agreed that the earth would be destroyed. On the other hand, some ancient church fathers, such as Irenaeus, Origen, and Methodius, held that the heavens and earth would be transformed, not destroyed.[167]

CASE STUDY

Stoicism and the Early Fathers. Stoicism provides a case study for observing how early Christian theologians either did or did not adopt philosophical categories to understand God.[168] There is a significant difference between biblical and Stoic philosophical teaching. WCG2 recounted that Stoicism was materialistic—it taught that everything was made of matter and that this matter was controlled by a world soul who ruled by law and order. Thus the wise life for the Stoic was to live in accord with the world's fixed laws of reason.[169]

---

bodily, these believers will reign with Christ on the earth for one thousand years, unbelievers will be resurrected after the millennium, the final judgment will take place, and God will establish the eternal state of heaven and hell" (Lactantius, *The Divine Institutes*, 7.16; 7.213–14; 7.214, as cited by Allison, *Historical Theology*, 724–25). If there were support for such conjecture somewhere in the vast corpus of patristic writings, Allison should have provided it.

164. Allison, *Historical Theology*, 685–87.

165. For more information on eschatology, see *WCG* 2:652–60.

166. That there is tribulation before Christ's return is called the *posttribulation* position. See Allison, *Historical Theology*, 684–85.

167. Ibid., 725–26.

168. The chapter could examine other philosophical systems as well, but Stoicism is more limited and still proves the point well.

169. *WCG* 2:952–53, 1024. See also chapter 1 of this volume, pages 36–37.

Stoicism's doctrine of the logos, which can mean "word," "reason," or "plan," and the Bible's teaching that God created the world by his Word, or the Logos, became connected early through the influence of Philo. Particularly important was Philo's inconsistent doctrine of the logos, in which he taught that the logos was God's agent in creation and the means by which the mind apprehends God.[170] It was by God's Word that he revealed himself to the prophets.

Stoicism influenced others as well. Some important scholars have attributed to Stoic influence Clement of Rome's notion of a harmony of the world order.[171] Justin Martyr, before his conversion, also studied Stoicism. He said that he rejected Stoicism because it could not explain God's being;[172] nevertheless, Justin's doctrine of the Logos is touted as "a bridge between pagan philosophy and Christianity."[173] He seemed to regard the Logos as the God-man's governing principle.[174] There is mixed judgment concerning Justin's notion of providence as guided by the Logos. Some argue that he developed the idea of human responsibility against the Stoic doctrine of fate.[175] Others assert that the Stoic

170. See chapter 1, page 39. Kelly (*Doctrines*, 10) says: "for the Stoics Logos (which also means reason or plan) was the rational principle immanent in reality, giving form and meaning to it; at the same time reality was comprehensible to men because of the presence of Logos in them. . . . Just as in man there is *logos endiathetos* (i.e. the rational thought in the mind) and also a *logos prophorikos* (i.e. the thought uttered as a word), so the divine logos is first of all the ideas or thoughts of God's mind."

171. Quasten, *Patrology*, 1:47; Kelly, *Doctrines*, 83. Such a world order may have biblical rather than Stoic content.

172. Quasten, *Patrology*, 1:196.

173. Ibid., 1:209. In chapter 1, on page 59 I argued that this "Logos Christology provided a point of contact between pagan philosophy and Christianity. Justin considered Christ to be superior to all philosophers as the incarnate 'Reason' or 'Logos of God.' Using Stoic terminology, Justin argued that the philosophers had only the *logos spermaticos*, while Christianity had the very Logos himself." In chapter 2, on page 87, I elaborated: "The apologists had already implemented the Stoic contrast between the *logos endiathetos*, the 'uttered word,' and the *logos prophorikos*, the 'word remaining within.' Such a distinction made it possible to differentiate between the pretemporal oneness of Christ with the Father and also his appearance in space and time. For Justin, this emanation of the Logos was purposive, since it was done by the Father's will. Justin employed numerous analogies in attempting to describe the emanation. For example, it is like fire and how a number of torches may be lit from one fire, or like a ray of light to the sun. The purpose of these analogies was to emphasize the fact that the distinction between the Father and the Logos is in number only—there is no division of the *ousia* ('essence') of the Father in the emanation of the Logos. Subordinationism is probably inherent within this doctrine of the Logos." This misunderstanding is clearly evident in Justin's work but is not confined to him.

174. Kelly, *Doctrines*, 146.

175. Ibid., 166.

notion of providence as guided by the logos "bore some significance in Justin's *Apology*."[176]

Some have claimed that the Alexandrian exegetical method, using allegory, has Stoic roots. This type of methodology is observed in Clement's *Exhortation* as well as his *The Tutor*.[177] Clement was the one who said that philosophy was to the Greeks as the Law was to Hebrews.[178] He based theology on the Logos as the source of all knowledge.[179]

As observed in previous chapters, Origen's thinking is complex, yet there are clear traces of Stoic philosophy discernable in his theology. For example, Origen used Stoic words and their meanings to explain the nature of the believer's bodily resurrection.[180] More difficult to dissect is Stoic influence on his doctrine of the Trinity. In chapter 2 we examined Origen's assertion that the Trinity is three persons, or three hypostases. *Hypostasis* was a Stoic word for real existence or essence, and Origen retained the Stoic meaning of the term.[181]

Some also claim that Novatian was influenced by Stoic philosophy. This influence, it is asserted, may be seen in his doctrine of God as creator and the beauty and harmony of the world, as well as in his use of Aristotelian syllogism and dialectical method.[182]

Tertullian's understanding and use of Stoicism was complex: on the one hand, he condemned Greek philosophy—Justin had called Socrates a Christian, but Tertullian designated him a corruptor of youth.[183] Tertullian decried the Stoics, who put matter on the same level as the Lord. On the other hand, Tertullian argued that the human soul was corporeal—a common Stoic claim—and positively cited the Stoics in his antagonism against the Platonists.[184] Tertullian was also

---

176. Edgar and Oliphint, *Christian Apologetics*, 39.

177. *The Exhortation* has Stoic literary parallels, while *The Tutor* has Stoic/Christian ethics. See Quasten, *Patrology*, 2:3, 8, 12, 158.

178. Ibid., 2:320.

179. Ibid., 2:75. Yet he also stood against aspects of Stoic doctrine. See chapter 2, page 74: "Like Irenaeus, Clement was against the earlier doctrine of *logos prophorikos*."

180. Kelly, *Doctrines*, 471: "Origen equates [the soul's distinctive form] with the principle of energy which, according to Stoic principles, maintains the body's identity in the flux of ever-changing matter."

181. Ibid., 129.

182. See chapter 1 of *On the Trinity* as cited by Quasten, *Patrology*, 2:217, and *On Shows*, also as cited by Quasten, *Patrology*, 2:223.

183. Quasten, *Patrology*, 2:321.

184. Ibid., 2:276, 287, 289; Kelly, *Doctrines*, 175.

apparently influenced by Stoicism in his doctrine of God and his ethical principles.[185] Tertullian viewed the Holy Spirit with a Stoicism-tinged notion that the Spirit is a highly rarified species of matter.[186]

Lactantius refuted the Stoic notion that God was kind and not angry.[187] He was nevertheless a dualist who posited two principles: a good God and an antigod, the Devil. The soul belongs to God, and the body is from the earth and belongs to the Devil. This strong dualism most likely came from Stoicism.[188]

Analysis and Criteria for Judgment. The question is how to evaluate this brief presentation of Stoic influence on Christian theology. As complex thinkers, all the theologians mentioned were influenced by Stoicism because it simply could not be avoided—it was part of their culture. A claim that an early theologian was "influenced" by Stoicism is neither astounding nor particularly important.

The next level of influence *is* significant, however—namely, the use of a pagan philosophical idea in Christian theological discussion but with modification to the underlying philosophical presuppositions concerning it. For instance, Clement of Rome's discussion of a world harmony may have been expressed through Stoic categories, but he modified the discussion to fit his idea of biblical categories. Similarly, Novatian's thoughts on God as creator were influenced by Stoicism, but he reshaped them as well. Tertullian was influenced in his view of God and the soul, but he also transformed the Stoic meanings into a biblical-philosophical fusion.

The third level of influence is the most serious one. This final level is when a pagan philosophical idea is dragged into biblical reflection and the biblical idea is modified or transformed better to reflect the pagan philosophical concept. Philo, although not a Christian, fits squarely into this third level. He amended the Bible's clear narrative of divine creation *ex nihilo* and used Stoicism's idea of the logos to explain creation. Likewise, Justin Martyr's notion of the Logos as the God-man's governing principle was probably an adaptation of Stoic

185. Quasten, *Patrology*, 2:357.
186. Kelly, *Doctrines*, 114.
187. Quasten, *Patrology*, 2:399. His teacher Arnobius was also apparently influenced by Stoicism. See Quasten, *Patrology*, 2:389.
188. Quasten, *Patrology*, 2:407.

thinking placed into theology. Clement of Alexandria's theology of the Logos as the source of all knowledge was only slightly modified at best. Origen's theology of the believer's bodily resurrection was a conscious use of Stoic thinking placed into Christian theologizing, as was his direct transfer of the Stoic notion of hypostasis to the Trinity. Tertullian's view of the Holy Spirit as a rarified species of matter is Stoic and unbiblical. Lactantius's dualism should also be judged as Stoic and unbiblical.

Conclusion to Part 1. The apostolic fathers serve as a first glimpse of Christian thinking. They demonstrate the second-century concern for order in the church in polity, liturgy, and morality. They commend obedience in contrast to following current pagan fashions. They helped formalize early Christian belief and behavior. But compared with Paul, the apostolic fathers appear more legalistic; they seem not to have fully appropriated the significance of the gospel as one of grace. Their writings provide a bridge between the biblical revelation and the more fully balanced and developed Christianity that would subsequently appear.

Key Terms

  adoptionism
  recapitulation Christology
  Monarchianism
  Antiochene exegesis
  Alexandrian exegesis
  Sabellianism
  trichotomy
  premillennialism

Study Questions

1. Did the apologists view the doctrine of the Trinity the same way that we do today?
2. Do you see a fundamental weakness in Clement of Alexandria's or Origen's doctrine of the Trinity?

3. In what ways did the early church consider God knowable?
4. Why did the early church consider it important to hold to Christ's full deity and humanity?
5. Describe and evaluate the differences between Antiochene and Alexandrian exegesis.
6. Is it important to distinguish between essence and person in God's being? Why or why not?
7. How do you evaluate the bridge builders and bridge burners?
8. What are some important philosophical and cultural influences affecting the church today?
9. What were some of the weaknesses of scriptural interpretation during this period?

RESOURCES FOR FURTHER STUDY

Daniélou, Jean. *A History of Early Christian Doctrine before the Council of Nicaea.* 3 vols. Philadelphia: Westminster Press, 1978–1980. A three-volume work of which the best is the third volume, which describes the origins of Latin Christianity.

Letham, Robert. *The Holy Trinity: In Scripture, History, Theology, and Worship.* Rev. and exp. ed. Phillipsburg, NJ: P&R Publishing, 2019. A recently updated work that is important for reading this chapter and is authored by a deeply learned and solid theologian, all of whose publications are worth reading.

Prestige, G. L. *God in Patristic Thought.* London: SPCK, 1952. Another seminal work focusing only on the doctrine of God.

PART 2

The Church Defines Herself

4

Nicene Age and Creeds

IT IS OFTEN IN the midst of conflict that the church undergoes the greatest season of growth. During the Nicene era, as the church began to splinter and segment over theological disagreements, she was forced to define her role and her doctrine with precision and clarity. This clarity would often come down to a phrase or even a single letter. Church creeds were born out of these seasons of disagreement and division. The word *creed* is not as easy to define as one might think.[1] The term has been defined as a group of declaratory statements "stereotyped in form and officially sanctioned by local church authorities."[2] In the second and third centuries, formal creeds were, at best, seldom used.[3] Creeds were not merely developed to combat heresy—they also served a more positive function, namely, that of expressing publicly the church's reason for being.[4] While today many evangelicals question the usefulness and value of creeds, theologians of the early church knew that they were essential to begin to understand and define clearly some of the complexities of Scripture's teaching. Men and women gave their lives for these truths—and the creeds should be held with a spirit of gratitude and conviction by the church. To understand how some of the most famous creeds came to be, we must first set the theological and political context.

1. See Oscar Cullmann, *The Earliest Christian Confessions*, trans. J. K. S. Reid (London: Lutterworth, 1949).
2. J. N. D. Kelly, *Early Christian Creeds* (London: Longman, 1972), 95.
3. Even from the time of Justin Martyr, however, there was something approaching a settled form of questioning posed to candidates for baptism. These baptismal interrogations functioned as a type of creed. See Karl Heussi, *Kompendium der Kirchengeschichte* (Tübingen: Mohr Siebeck, 1971), 28.
4. Kelly, *Creeds*, 96.

THEOLOGICAL AND POLITICAL CONTEXT OF THE ERA

Theological Context.[5] While on earth, the Lord testified that he and the Father were one, yet Jesus also asked the rich young ruler, "Why do you call me good? No one but my Father is good." Reconciling these two statements of Jesus is not easy. The Bible, however, does not leave the tension there. Jesus could also tell a supposedly unknown, inquisitive sinner perched in a tree that he would dine with him while also claiming that no one but his Father knows the time or the hour of his return.

Verses that recount these words and events, and others like them, reveal an inherent tension in the person of Christ. To put the matter bluntly, the tension in Jesus's earthly ministry is this: the one who transformed jugs of water into wine, who called Lazarus out from his grave, who called Peter to himself as he stood upon the waves—this man could also be nailed to a tree and die the most shameful of deaths at the hand of the ones he came to save. A tension indeed.

Truly, Jesus is the God-man; but the relationship between his deity and humanity is not easily understood.[6] And the resurrection only complicates matters further. After Jesus conquered death, Mary could worship him and cling to his feet. His new body still had the tear marks from the nails—marks that Thomas could see and touch. Jesus could kneel beside a fire and cook fish for his depressed, defeated disciples. Yet this same Jesus could walk through locked doors and suddenly vanish in the midst of conversation. At the end of his time on earth and after being seen by many people, he ascended bodily into heaven and is now seated at the Father's right hand.

These records, along with other passages, have taught the church throughout the ages to cry out in union, "Jesus is God!" The church for the past two thousand years has found comfort in the reality that she has a great high priest who knows and resonates with her weaknesses, because this high priest—*the* High Priest—is truly man. The

5. Louis Berkhof, *The History of Christian Doctrines* (Carlisle, PA: Banner of Truth, 1969), 83–90.

6. For more information on Christ's unipersonality, see Richard C. Gamble, *The Whole Counsel of God*, vol. 2, *The Full Revelation of God* (Phillipsburg, NJ: P&R Publishing, 2018) (WCG2), 424–27.

church therefore confesses that this Jesus of Nazareth, the child of Mary and Joseph, is also Lord.

While the modern church adds its voice to the timeless anthem that Jesus is Lord, the modern world is far different from that of the early followers of Christ. The church's worship today is not hidden away in catacombs. Although persecution of the church continues in many parts of the world today, government officials are no longer using Christians as candles to light their dinner parties. The persecution that marked the fourth century halted when Constantine rescinded anti-Christian decrees and instituted Christianity as the official religion of the empire. All of a sudden, the church was no longer struggling simply to survive. It now had both the time and leisure to reflect and resolve theological dilemmas.

Turning this dilemma to examine it from yet another angle, how has the church synthesized Paul's teaching that Jesus took the form of a servant with the teaching of the Beloved Apostle, who beheld his glory? The church needed to determine how it was possible for the divine and the human to come together in the person of Jesus.

Political Context. These questions were addressed, debated, and resolved in the fourth century from the time of the Council of Nicaea in A.D. 325 to the Council of Constantinople in A.D. 381.[7] During these years, the Emperor Constantine had far different political goals from his predecessor Diocletian's. In A.D. 313, Constantine brought an end to the state-sanctioned persecution of Christians. Unlike Diocletian, Constantine did not see Christianity as an opponent—he saw it as a tool to be leveraged. It is possible that Constantine may have even been a Christian.

Beginning in A.D. 314 to 320, a historico-political theology emerged. Constantine believed that the empire should have one unified church, so he convened a synod with all the church leaders. Constantine set the agenda, led the proceedings, and paid for the travel costs and living expenses of those in attendance. Constantine not only called the meeting but also controlled the outcome of the council.[8] In his "Who's

---

7. For more information, see Richard C. Gamble, "Not One Iota," *Tabletalk Magazine*, August 1, 2004, 11–14.

8. Kurt D. Schmidt, *Grundriss der Kirchengeschichte* (Göttingen: Vandenhoek & Ruprecht, 1963), 91.

Who" (that is, *The History of the Church*), Eusebius recognized the tension between the imperial authority and the religious council, and he made the emperor's claims supreme. Constantine claimed to have the authority to judge and condemn theologians, and his doing so set in place a practice that quickly became a political norm. By A.D. 324, Constantine exercised control over all matters of the church. Historians refer to this development as the rise of the imperial church.[9]

THE ARIAN CONTROVERSY

The primary controversy over which Constantine and subsequent emperors would preside was the Arian controversy. Arius's teachings, based on the theological questions outlined above, caused extreme division, eventually splitting the church. Out of the struggle rose a scripturally faithful and clear answer through the work of the councils of Nicaea and Constantinople. After decades of conflict, the church would be able to understand, define, and teach an orthodox statement concerning Christ's nature and person.

Arius's Theology. A massive number of works have been written on the origins of Arianism. The large amount of material hints at the level of disagreement there has been on the matter. Beginning in the nineteenth century, some believed that Arianism was rooted in Antiochene Judaism, paganism, or Gnosticism.[10] But there are more probable roots—specifically, Arius's relationship to Plato and Origen.[11]

9. Aloys Grillmeier, *Christ in Christian Tradition*, vol. 1, *From the Apostolic Age to Chalcedon (451)*, trans. John Bowden (Atlanta: John Knox Press, 1975), 249–64.

10. Some argued that there was Jewish influence from Antioch on Arius, while others, such as H. M. Gwatkin (*The Arian Controversy* [London: Longmans, Green, 1889]) maintained that Arianism was non-Jewish and had its roots in pagan thought. Hermann Hagemann (*Die Römische Kirche und ihr Einfluß auf Disciplin und Dogma in den ersten drei Jahrhunderten: Nach den Quellen auf's Neue untersucht* [Freiburg im Breisgau: Herder, 1864]) thought that he saw a connection between the thought of Arius concerning the doctrine of God and that of the Gnostics of the same time. Ferdinand Christian Baur's opinion, in *Lehrbuch der Dogmengeschichte* (Tübingen: Verlag und Druck von L. Fr. Fues, 1858), was closer to Gwatkin's.

11. A number of scholarly works have sought to determine Arianism's theological roots. J. L. von Mosheim (*Institutionum historiae ecclesticae antiquae et recentoris libri quatuor* [Helmstedt, 1755]) and Friedrich Loofs (*Leitfaden zum Studium der Dogmengeshichte* [Berlin: de Gruyter, 1959]) saw them in a modified Origenism. R. Seeburg (*Text-Book of the History of Doctrines* [Grand Rapids: Baker, 1977]) saw at least some of the roots of Arius's thought going all the way back to the apologists. Yet closer to Arius was the theology of Paul of Samosata

The most important part of Arius's theology was that God was utterly transcendent and perfect.[12] From this correct notion came Arius's belief that God's unity prohibited distinctions within the divine nature. In addition, Arius taught that divine contact with the world was impossible.[13] The transcendent God, therefore, was ultimately unknowable; his being was hidden from all—even the Son.[14]

Arius's cardinal principle was that all creatures, Christ included, were radically dependent on a creator who related to his creation only by his will and pleasure.[15] Because the Father could have no contact with the world, the Son was the instrument of creation. Since God is the source of all things and cannot, by definition, give his essence to another being, the Son, too, must exist by an act of God's creation.[16] The Son was called into being *ex nihilo*.[17] Thus the Son is a creature with a beginning.[18] Since Jesus was begotten in time, the Arians expressed their position with a simple, poisonous statement: "There was a time when he was not." Essentially, Arianism denied the eternality of the second person of the Trinity.[19]

In addition, Arius taught that the Son has no knowledge of the Father, nor does he participate in the Father's essence. The Son is thus liable to change, even to sin.[20] Arius considered the title *Son of God* to be a courtesy given to Jesus as God's adopted son.[21] Arians believed that the Son was neither truly God nor truly man, for Arius also disregarded the notion that Jesus had a human soul. So Arius

---

and dynamic Monarchianism. Seeburg was quick to point out, however, that Arius developed Paul's teaching so that, "what Paul taught concerning the man Jesus, Arius—and apparently Lucian before him—transferred to a median being, the Logos." In the 1940s, M. Werner (*Die Entstehung des christlichen Dogmas* [Bern/Leipzig: Haupt, 1941; 2. Aufl., 1953]) suggested that the roots of Arianism were to be found in early Christian "Angelchristology."

12. Kelly, *Creeds*, 232; J. N. D. Kelly, *Early Christian Doctrines* (London: Black, 1977), 227.

13. Gwatkin, *Arian Controversy*, 6.

14. Kelly, *Creeds*, 233; Kelly, *Doctrines*, 228.

15. Robert C. Gregg and Dennis E. Groh, *Early Arianism: A View of Salvation* (London: SCM Press, 1981), 5.

16. He was thus a creature or a work of God the Creator who was promoted to being a divine son. See ibid., 2.

17. Kelly, *Creeds*, 232–33; Kelly, *Doctrines*, 227.

18. Heussi, *Kompendium*, 74.

19. Ibid., 75.

20. See Kelly, *Creeds*, 233, and Kelly, *Doctrines*, 228, although scholars have debated whether Arius ever actually made such a claim concerning Christ.

21. Kelly, *Creeds*, 234. Kelly, *Doctrines*, 229.

believed in a Christ who was unable to act as a mediator between God and man.[22]

To Arius, the Holy Spirit's relationship to the Son is akin to the Son's relationship to the Father. This Trinity of Father, Son, and Holy Spirit is composed of persons all, but they are completely *different* persons who share no nature among themselves.[23] This misguided understanding of the Trinity is comparable to a descending series of honor.[24]

Certain scriptural themes were particularly important to Arius. For example, in Jewish synagogues the Hebrew statement "Hear O Israel, the Lord our God, the Lord is One" was memorized and repeated. All Christians should respond, "Amen!" But if the Lord is "One," what should the church think of Jesus? The answer for Arius was simple: at the incarnation, Jesus of Nazareth *became* the God-man. Here as well, Christians should respond in agreement—Jesus did become the God-man two thousand years ago when he was born of the Virgin Mary. But beneath this seemingly orthodox response lay heresy that would splinter the church and demean the person of Christ. Orthodox Christians would affirm that in the small town of Bethlehem Jesus became the God-man, but they would also affirm that the second person of the Trinity existed in full deity before Bethlehem was ever breathed into existence. The preexistence of Christ was the issue for Arius. He stated his position quite clearly: there was a time when Jesus was not the eternal Son of God.

Alexander of Alexandria's Theology. The first phase of the Arian controversy (A.D. 318–325) began in Alexandria and quickly spread outward.[25] While Alexander, bishop of Alexandria, initially held a posture of kind admonition toward Arius's teaching, he would become one of Arius's fiercest opponents. Alexander viewed the Father as the nongenerated one, who is immutable and perpetually in the same mode of existence. The Logos, he believed, is coeternal with the Father, a

22. Gwatkin, *Arian Controversy*, 8. Arius and the orthodox had a different conception of salvation, according to Gregg and Groh (*Early Arianism*, 8): "Salvation, for orthodoxy, is effected by the Son's essential identity with the Father—that which links God and Christ to creation is the divine nature's assumption of flesh. Salvation for Arianism is effected by the Son's identity with the creatures—that which links Christ and creatures to God is conformity of will."
23. Kelly, *Doctrines*, 229n6.
24. Gwatkin, *Arian Controversy*, 7.
25. Arius was probably a student of Lucian of Antioch. See Heussi, *Kompendium*, 74.

distinct hypostasis, generated without beginning, an intermediary between the created order and God, and inseparable from the Father. He is also the only begotten of the Father, as unchangeable and immutable as the Father, and an exact image of the Father.[26] Alexander conceived the Word as a person—as mediator, not creature. Using Origen's conception of eternal generation, Alexander taught that the Son is coeternal. His Sonship is real and not adoptive, which implies that he shares his Father's nature.[27]

Athanasius's Theology. Another fighter in the theological battle for clarity and truth during these decades was Athanasius. He lived in the center of the hurricane of Arianism.[28] Born in A.D. 295, he was of a later and entirely different generation from that of those who had endured persecution under Diocletian.[29] He was trained by Bishop Alexander of Alexandria and attended the Nicene council as an assistant. Eventually he was elevated to the position of metropolitan of Alexandria, the highest bishopric of the East.[30]

Athanasius was one of the most outstanding personalities of ancient church history. He is deemed the father of orthodoxy by the Greek church and is recognized by the Roman church as one of the four great Eastern church fathers.[31] There is a phrase often used to summarize his life: "Athanasius against the world, and the world against Athanasius." He was deposed and banished from the empire five times, for a total of twenty years. During his third exile, while Athanasius was in the Egyptian desert, Emperor Julian the Apostate called for the return of all exiles.

---

26. George Leonard Prestige, *God in Patristic Thought* (London: SPCK, 1952), 12–13. G. W. H. Lampe ("Christian Theology in the Patristic Period," in *A History of Christian Doctrine*, ed. Hubert Cunliffe-Jones [1978; repr., New York: T&T Clark, 2006], 93) asserts that eternal generation had a different meaning for Alexander and Athanasius than it did for Origen. See also Johannes Quasten, *Patrology* (Utrecht: Spectrum, 1975), 3:18–19; Kelly, *Doctrines*, 225. Alexander's understanding of "I and my Father are one" was that Jesus and the Father were not one in nature but actually two hypostases.

27. Kelly, *Doctrines*, 224–25. See Quasten, *Patrology*, 3:18.

28. For more information, see Dietrich Ritschl, *Athanasius: Versuch einer Interpretation* (Zürich: Theologische Studien, 1964).

29. Hans Freiherr von Campenhausen, *Griechische Kirchenväter* (Stuttgart: Kohlhammer, 1977), 72.

30. This area included all of Egypt and Libya. See Heussi, *Kompendium*, 75.

31. Quasten, *Patrology*, 3:20.

Two of Athanasius's apologetic works remain today.[32] He also had to write personal defenses and attacks against the Arians, including: *Orationes contra Arianos, Apologia contra Arianos*, from A.D. 350; *Apologia ad Constantium*, A.D. 356; *Historia Arianorum ad Monachos*; and *De decretis synodi Nicaenae*, A.D. 352. His remaining exegetical work is a commentary on the Psalms in which he used allegory. His final work, both ascetic and practical, was the *Life of St. Anthony*, written ca. A.D. 365.

Athanasius's passion was to vindicate Christ's deity; in his Christology, Athanasius asserted the consubstantiality of the Son with the Father and helped explain the generation of the Logos.[33] The Word of God, or Son, was both divine and eternal. The generation of the Son was an eternal process. The Son is the eternal offspring of the Father and shares the Father's immaterial and indivisible nature. Yet Athanasius held that the Father and Son are distinct.[34]

The identity of substance between the Father and the Son was significant in Athanasius's thinking.[35] He reasoned that if they share the same godhead, then they must also have an identity of substance.[36] This identity of likeness, or substance, is not comparable to that of a man to a man, but it is likeness of nature. The Son is the image of the Father. The identity of substance means that there is an identity of being between the two.[37]

Concerning the begetting or generation of the Son, or Logos, it was not by the Father's will, contra Arius, but instead by his nature.[38]

32. *A Discourse against the Greeks: On the Incarnation of the Divine Word.*

33. Quasten, *Patrology*, 3:66.

34. Kelly, *Doctrines*, 245; Quasten, *Patrology*, 3:69.

35. Athanasius, in *Letter to Epictetus*, says: "That then which was born from Mary was according to the divine Scriptures human by nature, and the body of the Lord was a true one; but it was this, because it was the same as our body, for Mary was our sister inasmuch as we are all from Adam" (as cited by Douglas F. Kelly, *Systematic Theology*, vol. 2, *The Beauty of Christ—A Trinitarian Vision* [Fearn, Scotland: Mentor, 2014], 188).

36. Kelly, *Doctrines*, 239. Yet Kelly (ibid., 245) also says: "Considered as two Persons, therefore, Father and Son are 'alike.'"

37. Lampe, "Christian Theology," 104–5: "The deity of the Father and Son is actually identical. . . . The nature of Father and Son is one; the Son as offspring, is different from the Father: as God he is the same. Father and Son are one in the identity of the one deity; hence whatever is predicated of God is predicated interchangeably of the Father and the Son."

38. Ibid., 105. Kelly, *Doctrines*, 244. While it happens according to the Father's will, it is wrong to regard it as a specific act of volition. If it were such an act (as was taught during the earlier time of the apostolic fathers and apologists), then the Son would be a creature.

Athanasius taught that the begetting should not be interpreted anthro-pomorphically.[39] Yet, unfortunately, he also held that the Logos entered a human body—teaching that might lean toward heretical Docetism. Because of the weakness in his notion of Christ's unipersonality, Atha-nasius held that all human weakness is simply ascribed to the flesh, while the Logos only appropriated this weakness as his own.[40]

Transitioning to theology proper, Athanasius argued that Arian-ism threatened the Christian doctrine of God by presupposing that the divine triad is not eternal.[41] Athanasius held to two emphases: that God is both monad and yet distinct.[42] The Father and Son share the same *ousia* or substance but are still distinguishable.[43] God exists as a triad. The triad shares the same essence, which is indivisible, and has the same activity.[44] The Father eternally begets the Son, and the Son is eternally begotten. The unity of activity permits no subordination.[45]

Athanasius also held that the Holy Spirit is fully divine and con-substantial with the Father and the Son. The Spirit is omnipresent and immutable and bestows life and sanctification. The Holy Spirit is the Spirit of the Son bestowed by the Son to sanctify and enlighten.[46] It was the Spirit who inspired the prophets. The Holy Spirit proceeds from both the Father and the Son.[47]

39. This discussion of "generation" helped clarify that the Greek word *agenetos* should not be used to describe the relationship between the Father and the Son because the generation is eternal. *Agenetos* should be used only in the description of the relation between creatures and God.

40. This part of Athanasius's teaching is under debate. For more information, see Lampe, "Christian Theology," 109, 125. Quasten (*Patrology*, 3:73) says that "in Athanasius' Christol-ogy there is no prominent place for the human soul of Christ."

41. Kelly, *Doctrines*, 233.

42. Ibid., 246. According to Kelly, God is as much monad for Athanasius as for Arius.

43. Lampe, "Christian Theology," 104–5; Kelly, *Doctrines*, 246.

44. Kelly, *Doctrines*, 247: "The distinction between Them is real, and lies in the distinction between the Godhead considered as eternally activating, expressing and begetting Itself, and the selfsame Godhead considered as eternally activated, expressed and begotten."

45. Lampe, "Christian Theology," 104. Quasten, *Patrology*, 3:68: "If the Son says, 'The Father is greater than I,' this means: 'The Father is the origin, the Son the derivation.'"

46. Kelly, *Doctrines*, 257–58. Kelly adds that while he undoubtedly teaches the divinity of the Holy Spirit, he nowhere explicitly calls him "God." See also Lampe, "Christian Theology," 107. His thinking about the Holy Spirit follows general Alexandrian lines. See Quasten, *Patrol-ogy*, 3:76.

47. It must be granted that Athanasius does not explicitly assert the double procession, although Quasten is convinced that he teaches it. See Quasten, *Patrology*, 3:77.

Athanasius opposed the Pneumatomachians. These "Spirit fighters" had reservations concerning the Holy Spirit's divinity.[48] They pointed to the silence of the Bible concerning the divinity of the Holy Spirit and were unable to conceive the godhead as containing more than the Father and the Son. They concluded that the Spirit, then, could be no more divine than were other spirits. The Tropici maintained that the Holy Spirit was just an angel.[49] Athanasius also fought this more local sect.[50]

Athanasius's entire approach to theology was different from and opposed to that of Arius. The primary motive in Athanasius's thinking was neither philosophical nor cosmological speculation but, rather, the conviction of redemption.[51] Athanasius rejected Arius's proposal that the likeness of the Father and the Son was simply one of the will—that is, a likeness comparable to a human being's imitation of a revered teacher. Athanasius also differed from Arius by maintaining the eternal generation of the Son. He used that argument to refute Arius's claim that if the Son is eternal, then he should be termed *brother*, not *Son*, of God.[52]

THE COUNCIL AND CREED OF NICAEA

When Arius was called before a synod of one hundred bishops in A.D. 318, he did not listen to their admonishments—and he was subsequently excommunicated. Nevertheless, Arius continued to write and draw supporters. Thus a new council was needed, and Constantine called the Council of Nicaea in A.D. 325.

Of One Substance? The controversy came down to the difference in one letter—a difference between those who defined the substance of Christ as *homoousios*, "of one substance," and those who defined

---

48. The Macedonians were named after Macedonius, bishop of Constantinople. See Kelly, *Doctrines*, 260.

49. Their name probably comes from the Greek word *tropos*, which means "figure." This method was the one they employed in exegesis. See Kelly, *Doctrines*, 256; Lampe, "Christian Theology," 107.

50. See Kelly, *Doctrines*, 257, 260.

51. Ibid., 243. Athanasius also rejected the idea of the necessity of the Son's mediatorial activity in the work of creation. See Quasten, *Patrology*, 3:67.

52. Lampe, "Christian Theology," 105.

it as *homoiousios*, "of similar substance." The Greek word for "of one substance" (*homoousios*) is the combination of two Greek words: *homo*, which means "the same;" and *ousia*, which means "substance." But *homoi*, in *homoiousios*, means "similar." Is Christ of the same substance as the Father or of similar substance? The difference is as small as one little letter—an *i*—which is inserted into the second position. How important is one letter really? If I evaluate a student's outstanding paper and intend to give an "A" grade but forget one little line in my writing, I would have just given my student an "F." Words, letters, and lines matter. So those who taught that Jesus was *homoousios* meant that Jesus was of the same substance as the Father, but those who taught that he was *homoiousios* meant that Jesus is of a *like* substance as the Father.

In regard to the substance or essence of something, however, that something is either completely of a substance or it is not. For example, one apple can be like another apple. They could be of a different color or taste, but both are still apples. There is room for differences—in sweetness, color, and size—but an apple cannot taste like a ham sandwich and look like an elephant and still be an apple! An apple has to have all the qualities of an apple. Put simply, an apple has to be an apple in its substance or it is not an apple—it is a ham sandwich or an elephant or what have you.

After considerable debate, the theologians at the Council of Nicaea agreed. Regarding the substance of divinity or humanity, there is no *almost* divine or *partly* human. God has to be fully God, and a man has to be fully man. *Homoiousios*—with the *i*—was unanimously rejected. In response, most participants gave up their position that Jesus could be like God in substance and instead affirmed Christ's eternal and preexistent nature—he is of one substance with the Father. Their formulations anathematized Arius and banned him and his teachings from the church and the empire.[53]

The first anti-Arian clause in the creed, reflecting the decision of the bishops, reads, "that is, from the substance of the Father." This clause was a more precise expression of Christ's being begotten from the Father. It excluded the possibility that the Son was, like a creature,

53. Philip Schaff, *History of the Christian Church*, 8 vols. (Grand Rapids: Eerdmans, 1979), 3:618.

created out of nothing. Later, the teaching became even more explicit in the phrase, "of the same substance as the Father."[54] Arius specifically condemned this phrase and argued that it tended toward Manichaeism.

The second specifically anti-Arian phrase in the Nicene Creed is "true God from true God." This phrase explicitly affirms that in whatever way the Father is God, in the same way the Son is God. But Arius did not object to referring to Christ as "true God." The most important phrase of this creed was, "of one substance with the Father." It was orthodoxy's weightiest blow. This phrase, without question, asserted the full deity of the Son.

Two ancillary points relate to the creed's text. First, the phrase "from the substance of the Father" is not found in the Bible. Earlier creeds had attempted to use only explicit scriptural words and statements. Second, the Greek words *hypostasis* and *ousia* were employed equivalently at this time. Later, after the Council of Alexandria in A.D. 362, these terms would be more precisely defined.

Without question, theological progression during this time was immensely significant, but there were also significant practical decisions being made then. The determinations of theologians sitting in ecumenical council are called *canons*. Members of the ecumenical council drew up twenty canons addressing a range of essential practical matters.

One of these practical matters related to when to celebrate Easter. The theologians at the council were convinced that the celebration of Easter should be on the fourteenth day of Nisan—Aviv in the Hebrew calendar. The Quartodecimans, such as Polycarp, celebrated on the fourteenth, no matter which day of the week it fell on. Others argued that while Easter should be structured around the fourteenth, of highest importance was that it was celebrated on a Sunday. Later in the third century, Easter began to be celebrated relative to the solar year. So at this time there were three approaches to the practice of Easter observance. The council decided that Easter should be celebrated on a Sunday, but never at the same time as the feast of the Jews—in other words, not on the fourteenth of Nisan.

Some other canons included clerical discipline. The church adopted the civil divisions of the empire. They required three elders for the

---

54. This phrase was not really new, since it had been used earlier by Theognostus, a theologian of the end of the third century.

performance of an ordination. They dealt with the lapsed and with excommunication. For those who had lapsed from the faith during persecution, the process for reconciliation was for the lapsed to stand among the hearers for two years, participate with the kneelers for another seven years, then pray with those who were going to partake for another two years. Then, and then only, would they be invited to partake of the Lord's Supper. They also ruled against a proposal that required clerical celibacy.

The conclusions of the counsel at Nicaea saved Christian theology from philosophical speculation. But the decisions made there alienated much of Eastern church thought—not only the Arians but followers of Origen as well. The creed and its results were regarded by many as a drastic step.[55] The anathemas leveled against former church members began a new era in the church.[56]

Still, this new theological clarity also brought benefits. There were now grounds for peace within the church. The Nicene Creed was the first formula that could legally claim universal authority. A firm stance had been taken, and the controversy concerning Christ's nature should have ceased.

Later Assemblies. Even after the condemnation of Arianism and the political and theological victories for Athanasius, there were many who remained unconvinced of the church's new doctrinal stance. Between the years A.D. 325 and 361, a number of controversial church assemblies were held in an empire under duress. In A.D. 337 Constantine died, thereby dividing his vast kingdom between his three sons: the eldest, Constantine II, was given Britain, Gaul, and Spain; Constantius II was assigned the East—Asia Minor, Syria, and Egypt; and the youngest son, Constance, received the central sector of the empire, including North Africa. In A.D. 340, Constantine II was murdered, likely by the plotting of his youngest brother.

In the summer of A.D. 341, the so-called Dedication Council convened in Antioch. This council met ten years after Constantine had begun the construction of a church building there—a project that his son Constantius would finish. Ninety-seven eastern bishops assembled at the council for the dedication. While the new building

---

55. Kelly, *Creeds*, 212–29.
56. Ibid., 207.

was an ostensible reason for the gathering, in fact the impetus for the assembly came from an earlier meeting that had been held in Rome. In that earlier Western synod, Athanasius and Marcellus of Ancyra were pronounced guiltless of theological crimes and admitted back into the fellowship of the church.[57]

The creed produced by this Dedication Council was written in an intense scriptural tone. As far as possible, the council attempted to express its doctrine using scriptural language. Though Arianism was excluded by the creed, Arians would likely have found this creed to be, in many ways, inoffensive to their position. For example, the council described the Son as "unalterable" and "unchangeable," words that Arius was willing to accept, based on his own interpretation of them.

In A.D. 350, Emperor Constance was murdered by a man named Magnentius in his attempt to seize power. But in A.D. 353 Magnentius was defeated by Constance's brother, Constantius II. From A.D. 353 until his death in A.D. 361, Constantius II became the sole ruler of the empire, both Eastern and Western. Considering Constantius II's inclination toward Arianism, what followed is no surprise. The anti-Athanasius, or anti-Western, faction of Christianity gained ascendance. The Nicene faith itself came under attack. This time saw a resurgence of Arius's ideas, restated in even more radical terms than before.

The leaders of these extremists were Aetius (A.D. 336) and Eunomius (A.D. 394), who became known as Anomeans. They remained unconvinced of Nicaea's teaching and refused to bow their knees to the notion of a full incarnation of the eternally divine Son of God. So they pulled even further in the opposite direction; they now said that Jesus was *anomoi*, "unlike," the Father in his substance. They taught that the Son was of another essence and was created out of nothing.

In God's providence, there was a counterreaction to this Arian movement. Those who were initially suspicious of the *homoousios* teaching grew increasingly uncomfortable with the more radical Anomeans. Now that the opposition had moved so far in the other direction, it was apparent that their stance had to be rejected. Thus even the proponents of *homoiousios* teaching stood alongside advocates

---

57. Both theologians had been deposed at councils at Tyre (A.D. 335) and Constantinople (A.D. 336).

of the *homoousios* view to fight against this new enemy—those who thought that Jesus was "unlike" the Father in substance.

Athanasius suffered greatly during this time. In A.D. 356 he was violently thrown out of his episcopal chair and was abandoned by the Western bishops because of the political environment. In A.D. 357, the Confession of Sirmium, Yugoslavia, prohibited the use of the terms *homoousios* and *homoiousios* and included a few statements that appeared to cast Christ in a suspiciously subordinationistic role as well.[58] It seemed as though all the work and efforts of Athanasius were for nothing.

In A.D. 359, Emperor Constantius forced every bishop to sign a *homoean* creed, called the Fourth Sirmian. Dissimilar to the terms *homoousios* and *homoiousios*, the term *homoean* meant that Christ and the Father are simply "alike." The Sirmian creed stated that Christ was "*like* the Father Who begat him"—"like in all respects." But the writers avoided the use of technical terms. Both sides could supposedly interpret the term *homoean* in a way that affirmed their stance. The generation of the Son explained in this way would exclude the possibility of Arianism, while the Arians were pleased that with the exclusion of *ousia*, *homoousios* was also excluded, thus meaning that it could not be said that the Son was the same as the Father in substance. And with the signing of that creed, the church of Christ officially adopted the *homoean* view. Then in January of A.D. 360 in Constantinople, the emperor had a new symbol drawn up—one that repudiated all previous creeds! This change ushered in a final, twenty-year struggle.

Apostles' Creed.[59] At this time, the church was using what is known as the Apostles' Creed (abbreviated *T*), a grandchild of the Old Roman Creed (abbreviated *R*).[60] The Latin source of the Apostles' Creed was produced in A.D. 404.[61] There is, however, a nearly identical creed

---

58. For a complete history, see Charles Joseph Hefele, *A History of the Christian Councils* (Edinburgh: T&T Clark, 1862), 2:1–320.

59. Kelly, *Creeds*, 101.

60. Heussi, *Kompendium*, 320.

61. The printed text was *Commentarius in symbolum apostolorum*, by Tyrannius Rufinus. See Kelly, *Creeds*, 101–19. Kelly says that *R* was firmly established by the middle of the third century and had been written by the beginning of the century. It probably originated at the turn of the second century. Against earlier scholarship, Kelly (ibid., 122) maintains that *R* is a conflation, "the result of the welding together of a short Trinitarian formula and of an originally independent Christological summary."

in the Greek language, from Marcellus of Ancyra, dated about sixty years earlier (ca. A.D. 340).[62]

There are approximately eleven variations of *R* in the Textus Receptus of the Apostles' Creed; they were printed in 1568.[63] Luther modified the text of the Apostles' Creed by substituting the word *Christian* for the word *catholic* before *church*.[64]

As early as Augustine (A.D. 354–430), pastors had advised their people to recite the Apostles' Creed daily. By the year A.D. 650, many monasteries recited this creed together each night. The primary role of the Apostles' Creed was to serve as a declaration made at baptism. In the eighth century, it began to function as such in the Latin West.[65]

In A.D. 359, at the fourth formula of Sirmium, the phrase "descent to hell" first appeared in the creed to affirm that Christ died and descended to the underworld.[66] This phrase was prominent initially in the Eastern church's creedal material. The Western church admitted the addition through Eastern influence. The descent of Christ is mentioned by Polycarp, Irenaeus, Tertullian, and others.[67]

THE THIRD PHASE OF THE DEBATE (A.D. 361–381)

Hilary of Poitiers (A.D. 310–367). Hilary of Poitiers was actively involved in the Arian struggle—so much so that he was called the Athanasius of the West.[68] Exiled in A.D. 356 because of his conflict with the Arians, he thoroughly learned their doctrines and wrote the majority of his work *De trinitate* in exile. *De trinitate* was the first systematic refutation of Arianism by a Western theologian.[69] The work was cherished at the time, and it was likely known by Augustine. This

---

62. Heussi, *Kompendium*, 28.

63. Hittorp, a canon of Cologne, compiled *T* in what is called the Ordo Romanus Antiquus.

64. Kelly, *Creeds*, 369.

65. Ibid., 370.

66. See Bo Reicke, *The Disobedient Spirits and Christian Baptism* (New York: AMS Press, 1984).

67. Kelly, *Creeds*, 378.

68. Karl von Hase, *Kirchengeschichte: Lehrbuch, zunächst für academische Vorlesungen* (Leipzig: Breitkopf & Härtel, 1836), 137.

69. C. F. A. Borchardt, *Hilary of Poitiers' Role in the Arian Struggle* (The Hague: Nijhoff, 1966), 187.

work contributed significantly to the development of the doctrine of the Trinity.

Although there may have been a Docetic strain in the thinking of Hilary of Poitiers, he remained well within the bounds of orthodoxy.[70] In his refutation of the Arians, he helped define the distinctions within the godhead, the divinity and eternality of the Son of God, and the unity and equality of the Father and the Son.[71]

Hilary's method in his refutation of the Arians focused on God's infinity. Implementing this particular *Leitmotiv* rather than pushing the standard notion of the ontological equality of God enabled him to be particularly perceptive in combating a conception of God confined to an analogy with finite beings. He said, "The human mind will not understand this, and a comparison taken from human existence will not provide an analogy for the divine existence."[72] Hilary's creative theological work combined with significant political changes.

Politics: New Emperors and Germanic Movement. In A.D. 361, Emperor Constantius II, the ruler of the empire, died. He was succeeded by his cousin Julian, who is known throughout Christian tradition as "Julian the Apostate." Julian was a Neoplatonist and legally a Christian, but in practice Julian was a committed pagan. As such, he wished to reform and revive pagan religion, so he excluded Christians from teaching in imperially supported schools and occupying high imperial offices. Julian also proclaimed religious freedom. Those who had previously been banned and exiled were invited back into the empire.[73] Julian's reign was short lived, however, as he died in A.D. 363.

Then the Arian Emperor Valens (A.D. 364–378) assumed control. Under his rule, the orthodox faced persecution. In A.D. 378, Emperor Valens lost his life and his army at the battle of Adrianople. He faced defeat at the hands of an uncivilized group known as the Visigoths.

70. Borchardt underlines the Docetism; nevertheless, Hilary is rightly considered the first "doctor" of the Western church.

71. These arguments are found through Hilary's *De trinitate* V–XI. See J. P. Migne, *Patrologiae Cursus Completus: Series Latina* (Paris: Garnier Fratres, 1857), 10:130–404.

72. Hilary, *De trinitate* 3, 24, as cited by E. P. Meijering, *Hilary of Poitiers on the Trinity* (Leiden: Brill, 1982), 128; see pages 183–84 for his summary.

73. Julian tolerated the rival factions within Christianity in the hope that they would destroy each other.

Thus began a new crisis in the relationship between the Roman Empire and the Germanic tribes, which had crossed the borders of the Rhine and Danube rivers. In the next two centuries, the Holy Roman Empire was conquered and divided by four groups of Germanic tribes: the Goths, Franks, Vandals, and Lombards.[74]

This history of the barbarian invasions in Rome is complex. The movement of eastern tribes from the mountains of Asia and the pressure on the Germanic tribes to move westward incited conflict between the Germanic tribes and the Roman Empire. By the fourth century, the Franks were living within the confines of the empire in present-day France and Germany. As the barbarians began to serve in the Roman army in greater numbers, interaction between the barbarians and the Roman armies increased. The Germanic tribes also provided outlets for Roman goods, and a slow cultural assimilation ensued.

At this time, the Germanic tribes encountered Christianity. In the fourth century, a man by the name of Ulphila planted the seeds of Christianity among the Germanic tribes. Ulphila was a Goth who had been raised in the church and conducted the first translation of the Scriptures into the Gothic language. This translation is the earliest extant piece of Germanic literature.

An Arian bishop, Ulphila was instrumental in the conversion of the Visigoths. In A.D. 376, the king of the Visigoths led the entire nation into Arianism. By this time, the Visigoths, the Ostrogoths, and the Vandals had, all at different times, encountered and embraced Christianity. The Franks and Saxons in the north, however, were still predominantly pagan.

Through this political and theological turmoil, a new orthodoxy gradually developed. Orthodoxy's eventual victory came through political circumstances. Beginning in A.D. 379, the new emperor, Theodosius the Great, pushed back against Arianism. Theodosius had been raised in theological orthodoxy, and in A.D. 380 he reinstituted the Nicene form of the faith as the law of the empire.[75]

---

74. Jacques Le Goff, *Medieval Civilization 400–1500*, trans. Julia Barrow (Oxford: Blackwell, 1988), 3–36; Nicholas R. Needham, *2,000 Years of Christ's Power*, vol. 1, *The Age of the Early Church Fathers* (London: Grace Publications, 1997), 287–323.

75. Grillmeier, *Apostolic Age*, 249; Heussi, *Kompendium*, 78.

THEOLOGIANS OF THE TIME: CAPPADOCIAN FATHERS, EPIPHANIUS, CHRYSOSTOM, AND JEROME

Theodosius made Gregory of Nazianzus, one of the three Cappadocian fathers, bishop of Constantinople. Through Gregory's influence and the theological precision of the other Cappadocian fathers, Arianism was soon diminished in the city.

The theologians known as the Cappadocian fathers were Basil of Caesarea (A.D. 330–379), Gregory of Nyssa (A.D. 335–394), and Gregory of Nazianzus (A.D. 329–390).[76] Cappadocian theology also includes the less prominent Didymus of Alexandria, Amphil, and Evagrius Ponticus. The Cappadocian fathers would be instrumental in bringing about the final word on the controversy surrounding Christ's nature and relationship to the Father.

Cappadocian Theology. Cappadocian theology is, at least to a limited extent, grounded in the theology of Athanasius. The Cappadocians extended his thought and clarified some of the key theological terms. Beginning with their conception of the godhead, the *ousia*, or existence or essence of the godhead, was not an abstract essence but a concrete reality. They believed in the unity of the divine essence, while also asserting the existence of the three persons. Put simply, the Cappadocian fathers taught that one God exists in three modes of being.[77]

The source of the godhead is the Father—which is to say that he is the source or cause of the other two persons. Within the godhead, as the triad is worshipped, so also is the monad worshipped. Even as the Father is the source of the other two persons, still the distinction of the hypostases does not remove the oneness of the nature of the godhead.

The Cappadocian fathers maintained that the Son was generated from the Father's being and acted as the Creator. Their Trinitarian thinking began by recognizing the Son. The Son makes the Father known in that the hypostasis of the Father is recognizable in the Son. God exists undivided, yet he is divided into persons. He is undivided

---

76. Ernst Staehelin, *Die Verkündigung des Reiches Gottes in der Kirche Jesu Christi*, vol. 1, *Von der Zeit der Apostel bis zur Auflösung des Römischen Reiches* (Basel: Verlag Friedrich Reinhardt, 1951), 251–68.

77. Kelly, *Doctrines*, 264.

in that there is within the three hypostases an identity of nature. They also held that the Holy Spirit was not subordinated to the Father or to the Son and that the Holy Spirit was consubstantial with both the Father and the Son.

The Cappadocians' conception of the unity within the Trinity merits further analysis. Basil introduced the notion of identifying particularities, which are modes of being. A mode of being is also a hypostasis. He differentiated *ousia* and *hypostasis* as universal and particular, respectively. For example, each human being represents the universal man, also known as *ousia*, and different human beings are also recognized by their personal characteristics, also known as *hypostasis*. This distinction is analogous to that of the godhead. For the Cappadocians, the persons of the Trinity were distinguished by their origin and relationship to each other.[78] The hypostases of the godhead are determined by their identifying particularities; for instance, Basil identified God's identifying particularities as "fatherhood," "sonship," and "sanctification." With the clarified definitions of *ousia* and *hypostasis*, the Cappadocians were able to assert that the formula, one ousia and three hypostases, is the only acceptable one.

Basing their understanding of the Trinity on these identifying particularities, the Cappadocians made an important Trinitarian advance. This important advance elicited the disapproval of some: in equating the words *ousia* with universal and *hypostasis* with particular, it sounds as though their understanding could lend itself to a tritheistic interpretation.[79]

Basil was also interested in understanding the Holy Spirit. Early in his theological career, Basil abstained from discussing the doctrine of the Holy Spirit. But later he wrote a new profession of faith in which he claimed that the Holy Spirit was inseparable from the Father and the Son and ought to be given the same worship as the Father and the Son. While Basil never refers to the Holy Spirit as God per se, his work makes clear that he regards the Holy Spirit as God.[80]

78. The statement of Amphilochius of Iconium may thus be explained that the words "Father," "Son," and "Spirit" represent not the being but rather a mode of relation or existence of God.

79. Lampe, "Christian Theology," 113.

80. Kelly, *Doctrines*, 261.

Basil gave many reasons for this claim. He noted the testimony of Scripture to the Spirit's greatness and dignity, the power and vastness of his operation, his association with the Father and the Son in whatever they accomplish, especially in the work of sanctification, and his personal relation to both the Father and the Son. His opponents challenged this assertion, however, by claiming that if the Holy Spirit is *homoousious* with the Father, then he is a second son. In response, Basil asserted that the Holy Spirit is not generated like the Son is, but through the Son the Spirit receives divine qualities from the Father.[81]

Gregory of Nazianzus also contributed to the doctrine of the Holy Spirit. He advanced the definitions submitted by Basil concerning the character of the three persons. For Gregory, the definitions were *agenetos* ("ungeneratedness"), *genesis* ("generatedness"), and *ekporeusis* or *ekpempsis* ("procession"). Thus Gregory maintained that the distinctive characteristic of the Holy Spirit is procession. Contrary to Basil, Gregory of Nazianzus did not hesitate to refer to the Holy Spirit as God. He also asserted that the Holy Spirit is consubstantial with the Father and the Son. Gregory made various scriptural arguments to support his contention that the Holy Spirit is God but also contended that the Holy Spirit discloses his deity as he lives within the believer.

Gregory exercised admirable theological restraint when he submitted that he was content with the scriptural pronouncements concerning the Holy Spirit's procession. He said that it was clear that the Holy Spirit proceeds from the Father, but he conceded that he was unable to explain what that procession actually means.

In response to the charge that the Cappadocians' conception of God could be tritheistic, it should be noted that Gregory of Nazianzus asserted the unity of the godhead. The persons of the godhead are, in essence, indistinguishable. For him, the Son is identical in substance with the Father.

The third Cappadocian father, Gregory of Nyssa, was the theological superior of the other two Cappadocians. On the Trinity, he taught that the Father begets the Son and the Spirit proceeds from the Father. Gregory of Nyssa emphasized their unity in activity: the three persons share a unity of nature from their identity of activity.

---

81. Berkhof, *History of Christian Doctrines*, 87–91.

He thought that the analogy of humankind as unified but diverse broke down in its attempt to explain the Trinity because no part of the godhead acts independently of the other members.[82] The inevitable conclusion concerning Trinitarian speculation is that the distinction between the Father, Son, and Holy Spirit consists in their immanent mutual relations.

His doctrine of the Holy Spirit concluded that there was a shared oneness of nature among all three persons. He explicitly asserted that the Holy Spirit proceeds from the Father and receives from the Son—an assertion of immense significance in later Trinitarian speculation. The Father is the cause of the other two persons. The Son is directly produced by the Father and is thus the only begotten; the Spirit is related to the Son as effect is to cause. In subordination to the Father, who is the fountainhead, the Son of God is the agent of the Spirit's production.[83] In sum, Gregory of Nyssa taught the consubstantiality of the Holy Spirit as well as his procession from the Father. Thus Gregory explained with greater clarity the relationship of the Holy Spirit to the Son.[84]

Other theologians were also instrumental in the fight for doctrinal clarity during this time. Epiphanius of Salamis and John Chrysostom are two such theologians who must be mentioned.

Epiphanius of Salamis (A.D. 310–403) maintained that proof for the Trinity may be found in the baptismal formula, the *Trishagion* ("thrice holy") of the angels, and, of course, the Scriptures themselves. In his work titled *Ancoratus*, Epiphanius affirmed the deity of the Son and the Spirit as well as their consubstantiality with the Father. Concerning their mode of origin, he taught that the Holy Spirit is from both the Father and the Son. He also held that the Holy Spirit is of the same substance as the Father and the Son.

John Chrysostom (A.D. 349–407).[85] John Chrysostom was born into a well-to-do family in the city of Antioch. He received a good education in philosophy and rhetoric. As a young man, he rebelled against earthly wisdom in pursuit of divine wisdom.

82. Kelly, *Doctrines*, 267.
83. Ibid., 263.
84. Quasten, *Patrology*, 3:287.
85. Staehlin, *Von der Zeit*, 296.

He was baptized in A.D. 372 and studied with the bishop of Antioch, known as Meletius the Confessor. For the next eight years, he disciplined himself by adhering to a strict ascetic lifestyle. For the last two years of this season of his life, he lived alone as a monk in the mountains near Antioch. His rigorous asceticism greatly impaired his health.[86]

In A.D. 381 he was made a deacon, and in A.D. 386 he was ordained as a priest or preacher. He preached in the main church of Antioch and gained the reputation of being "golden mouthed." In the year A.D. 397, Emperor Arkadian elevated him to the position of bishop of Constantinople.[87]

His labors in Constantinople were quite difficult, and in all likelihood he was not well-suited for the task. He was not prepared to deal with the political intrigues of the capital, the immorality of the city, or the clergy. Admirably, he was unwilling to make any compromises with any form of corruption. He worked hard to improve social welfare and for the morality of the presbyters. He was very concerned for the sick and poor of the city. While he enjoyed the great honor of a personal relationship with the emperor, nevertheless Chrysostom lived a modest, even simple life. Chrysostom had the golden ware that was used for the Eucharist sold so that the money could be used to help the urban poor.[88]

He stood against the abuses that were occurring in the churches—specifically simony, or the purchase of church office. He longed for a true reformation of the church. The abuses seen in Constantinople are reflective of the tension within the church between the pursuit of worldly wealth and power and the genuine spiritual power of Christianity.

The empress, named Eudoxia, did not like Chrysostom—or many of the other pastors, for that matter.[89] Chrysostom's opponents assembled in A.D. 403 at the Synod of the Oak; the synod declared him

86. Tradition had it that for those two years he never slept lying down but always standing up.

87. It is said that he did not want the position and was compelled by force to take it. See Staehelin, *Von der Zeit*, 297; Berthold Altaner and Alfred Stuiber, *Patrologie: Leben, Schriften und Lehre der Kirchenväter* (Freiburg: Herder, 1978), 322.

88. For more information, see Rudolf Brändle, *John Chrysostom: Bishop, Reformer, Martyr*, trans. John Cawte and Silke Trzcionka (Strathfield, Australia: St Pauls Publications, 2004).

89. Altaner and Stuiber, *Patrologie*, 323. She particularly did not like Flavian, bishop of Alexandria.

deposed, banished for a day, and then recalled. In A.D. 404, however, Chrysostom was banished from both the city and the empire. But the location to which he was banished was not far away, and people from Antioch still came to visit him. So he was then banished to a location that was even farther away, and he died in A.D. 407 en route to his next destination. His years in banishment were spent in immense suffering and abject poverty.[90]

During his lifetime, Chrysostom wrote a vast corpus of literature.[91] He wrote a number of topical sermons and sermons on the OT books of Genesis and Psalms, and the church today still has access to a number of his sermons on the NT.[92]

Besides his sermons and biblical commentaries (see below for the latter), Chrysostom also wrote practical treatises: *On the Priesthood, On Monastic Life, On Virginity and Widowhood, On the Education of Children, On Suffering,* and *Against Pagans and Jews.*

In his exegetical work, in line with Antiochene exegesis, he sought the historical sense of Scripture. More information on Antiochene exegesis will be given at the end of this chapter.[93] It has been argued that because of the high esteem in which Chrysostom was held, his grammatical-historical method prevailed in the church rather than the then-popular allegorical method of interpretation.[94]

Correctly, it has been said that Chrysostom was exegetically the best of all the church fathers.[95] Having Greek as a mother tongue gives one a distinct advantage for understanding the NT! He did not, however, know Hebrew, so he used the LXX as his OT text. Many years

90. Ibid.
91. Ibid. The extant corpus is larger than that of all other Eastern writers.
92. From Matthew, John, Acts, Romans, 1 and 2 Corinthians, Galatians, Ephesians, Philippians, Colossians, 1 and 2 Thessalonians, 1 and 2 Timothy, Titus, and Hebrews.
93. The roots of this method did not begin with Chrysostom but perhaps began earlier with Lucian, who had taught in Antioch since A.D. 260, then died in A.D. 312. Methodius of Olympus was also important, but it was Eusebius of Emesa (who died in A.D. 359), a disciple of Eusebius of Caesarea, under whom Diodore of Tarsus (d. ca. A.D. 394) had been trained and who, in his turn, had been the teacher of Chrysostom and of Theodore of Mopsuestia in Antioch. Diodore even dedicated a special treatise to exegetical issues. See Chrysostomus Baur, *John Chrysostom and His Time,* trans. M. Gonzaga (Westminster, MD: Newman Press, 1959), 1:318.
94. Ibid., 1:319.
95. Altaner and Stuiber, *Patrologie,* 324: "No church father exegeted scripture so solidly and practically as did Chrysostom."

later, the Swiss reformer John Calvin would use many of Chrysostom's exegetical insights.

During Chrysostom's time, it was not unusual for monks or presbyters to memorize large portions of the Bible, and Chrysostom's years as a monk were devoted to meditation on the Scriptures.[96] So his knowledge of Scripture was enormous. Likely, however, his NT did not include 2 Peter, 2 or 3 John, Jude, or Revelation.[97]

Chrysostom possessed a high view of Scripture. He understood the Bible to be the holy and infallible Word of God. He believed that it was God himself who wrote the words of Scripture. Also, he was convinced that the Holy Spirit speaks in Scripture. Chrysostom held that every iota and every syllable of Scripture were given for a purpose.[98] Because of its divine inspiration, Scripture was free from error. Scriptural proofs were therefore surer than arguments from reason.[99]

In regard to anthropology and soteriology, in general Chrysostom lacked some of the precision of Augustine and the Latin West. In his doctrine of original sin, he taught that children were not born in sin but were free from sin. This teaching is similar overall to that of the Cappadocians. The Pelagians and semi-Pelagians would utilize this notion of original sin, although it would be unfair to say that Chrysostom in any way held to Pelagian or semi-Pelagian teaching.[100] He considered original sin to be something of a wound on human nature. Yet he still held that all humankind participated in Adam's sin.

Chrysostom also had an immature soteriology. He viewed Christ's works of redemption as, in some sense, counteracting the work of the Devil. He taught that men in their sin had subjected themselves to the Devil's jurisdiction; therefore the Devil possessed the right to deal as he wished with humanity. Nevertheless, by inciting Judas to hand Christ over to the authorities, the Devil had overstepped, thus bringing condemnation on himself. In Christ's resurrection, the Devil was banished from his own kingdom.

---

96. Baur, *Chrysostom*, 1:316.

97. Ibid., 1:317.

98. Ibid., 1:318: "The inspiration of God extends into the collect thought content of the Holy Scripture, not merely in dogmatic and moral theology, but also in matters of scientific and historical learning, dates, lists of names, forms of salutation, inscriptions, and similar things."

99. Ibid.

100. Altaner and Stuiber, *Patrologie*, 329.

Chrysostom taught that Christ's death was first seen in the sacrifices of the OT. He believed that the efficacy of Christ's sacrifice was sufficient for the entirety of the human race; thus Christ died for all people. So if not all have reached salvation, the blame is not to be attributed to an insufficiency of Christ's sacrifice but to some people's refusal to accept his atoning work on their behalf. This understanding is quite different from Augustine's more proper formulation.

Regarding the Lord's Supper, Chrysostom believed that when believers partake of the table, they are holding the body of Christ in their hands, for Christ is present in the Eucharist. In the Eucharist was the same body that walked the earth. Chrysostom taught that Christ actually drank his own blood when he celebrated the Last Supper. Christ is the actual priest at the altar offering himself to his people.[101]

Jerome (A.D. 347–420), the final theologian we must examine, was still living in Constantinople when the council began in May of A.D. 381. But there was to be another council in Rome, and since Jerome was invited by the bishop of Rome to attend it, he decided to travel back with Paulinus of Antioch and Epiphanius of Salamis. So he did not attend the Council of Constantinople.[102] The exact date of Jerome's birth is unknown, though likely it fell between A.D. 340 and 350. He was born within the confines of the Roman Empire in a province named Dalmatia.[103]

Jerome was raised in a well-to-do household and in the Catholic faith. He was, however, not to receive baptism until much later, since a delay of baptism was the custom at that time—a custom that theologians such as Gregory of Nazianzus, Gregory of Nyssa, and John Chrysostom were combatting. Apart from Augustine, no early Christian author was saturated in the classics to the extent that Jerome was.

Though academically pristine, the moral tenor of Jerome's early life was not without reproach. For the rest of his life, Jerome would carry the sting and remorse of the sins he committed as a young student.[104]

---

101. Ibid.

102. Pierre de Labriolle, *History and Literature of Christianity from Tertullian to Boethius* (New York: Barnes and Noble Books, 1968), 340.

103. Ibid., 335.

104. Ibid., 335–36. His professor of grammar in Rome was the famous Donatus, author of the manuals that were named *Ars Major* and *Ars Minor*, on which grammar was based beyond the ninth century.

Baptized in Rome, he was determined to travel to the East and become an ascetic. His journey eastward was not easy, and a number of his companions died along the way. He fell ill at Antioch and decided to remain there to hear Apollinaris of Laodicea's lectures. Fifty miles from Antioch, Jerome decided to terminate his journey, and from A.D. 375 to 377 he lived in a monastery in the desert.

Life as a monk was not easy. Jerome provided a small, miserable snapshot of his life as a monk—a hideous sac for clothing, a body black with sweat and dust, lying on the dirt, drinking only water, and eating uncooked food. But not even this physical torment could guarantee him liberation from the worst of temptations.[105] He would spend days and nights in fasting but would experience no relief from the cries of his flesh. So he would flee to even more barren terrain. And sometimes, in the midst of his tearful prayers, he would be granted relief.

While in the desert, Jerome began to learn the Hebrew language—and would become one of the finest Hebrew scholars of his day. Anyone who has been privileged to learn Hebrew will enjoy his comments on the experience:

> I set myself to learn the Hebrew alphabet and to study a language of guttural and heavy-breathing words. Such effort as I had expended and many the difficulties I had suffered, how many times in desperation did I not break off from a study which the stubborn desire for knowledge made me resume again afterwards, I alone can testify, I who have toiled so hardly, and with me those who then shared my life. And I render thanks to God for any delicious fruit I now gather from so bitter a sowing.[106]

The peace and quiet that Jerome sought were not to be his in the desert. Doctrinal difficulties began to plague his life—a kind of plague that, sadly, is not limited to the ancient church. A controversy was developing in the city of Antioch concerning the nature of the

---

105. Jerome's description (in *Epistolae* 22.7) was graphic: "I who from fear of Gehenna had condemned myself to such a prison tenanted only by scorpions and wild beasts, often felt myself transported into the midst of girls dancing. I was pale from fasting, and my imagination was boiling over with desire in a frozen body wherein the fire of my passions wrought frenzy" (as cited by de Labriolle, *History and Literature*, 337).

106. Jerome, *Epistolae* 75.12, as cited by de Labriole, *History and Literature*, 338.

Trinity. The various factions sought alliance with Jerome. He was uncertain who was right, so he sought the advice of the bishop of Rome—Damasus. Jerome wrote two letters to him on the matter but received no reply. He began to be treated poorly for not choosing a side. The factions' pretensions to regulate consciences became unbearable to Jerome. He grew dissatisfied with the monks, who, from their sackcloth-and-ashes lifestlye, seemed to believe themselves to be judges of the world. Jerome thought their posture was more fitting for kings than for penitent monks.

Jerome left the desert and returned to Antioch for a short stay. Somehow, he had developed a relationship with Gregory of Nazianzus at Constantinople, where he ended up going. Gregory taught exegesis to Jerome, and Jerome referred to Gregory as his teacher. During this time, Jerome developed an admiration for Origen—a favorable opinion that would not endure.

Eventually, Jerome moved to Rome. Between A.D. 382 and 385 he wrote a number of works. He had already begun writing the biographies of different monks, and the following were later published: *Life of Paul*, *Life of Malchus*, and *Life of Hilarion*. He had also begun his work titled *Chronicle*. Jerome used Eusebius of Caesarea's *Church History* as his model for the *Chronicle*. Inasmuch as his work was destined for the West, he felt he ought to insert a great number of facts dealing with general history, and especially with Roman history and literature. Lastly, and this time without using a guide, he extended his *Chronicle* beyond Eusebius's *Church History* by treating the twentieth year of Constantine down to the year A.D. 378, the date of the death of Emperor Valens.

There are a number of faults in Jerome's work, as it seems that at times he chose events of personal import and considered them to be of great import for the entire church. For example, he emphasized the tale of the murder of a rather obscure monk by the Saracens. Nevertheless, his *Chronicle* is an important and helpful book.[107]

107. De Labriolle, *History and Literature*, 344: ". . . work has rendered great service. To judge of this it is only necessary to examine a modern history of the Church, or even a history of Roman literature. . . . The *Chronicle* has been one of the fundamental books upon which all researches on the past of mankind have been based."

In addition, Jerome translated a number of Origen's writings.[108] Jerome's philosophy of translation was that nonscriptural works should be translated in a readable manner. He opposed slavish literalism, which could make the original text read rather woodenly. But he held that translation of the Scriptures demands more scrupulous literalness because even its word order has symbolic value.

While living in Rome, Jerome did not write much of great import. Only twenty-six of his letters remain from this time. Yet it was while he was in Rome that he began the task that was to fill the next twenty years of his life—the revision and translation of the sacred books of the Bible.[109]

Jerome's method of translation was to take a certain number of Latin versions and the oldest Greek manuscripts he could procure. Where the Greek text disclosed evident misinterpretations in the Latin translations, he corrected them. When the Latin versions offered meanings that were sufficiently divergent, he chose the one that seemed to him to reflect the Greek most closely. At first, most of the theologians, including Augustine, found little to criticize in Jerome's translational work. This calm would not last forever, however.

When the bishop of Rome died, Jerome decided to return eastward. In A.D. 386 he settled in Bethlehem with a few friends and their families. One of these friends was a rich widow named Paula, who from her own fortune built convents—one for men and three for women—and hostels. Paula was head of the women's and Jerome in charge of the men's convents.

Jerome wrote most of his works in Bethlehem. The account of his translations leaves one in awe. For almost fourteen years, he worked on his translation of the OT from Hebrew into Latin—and relied no longer on the earlier Latin translations or the Greek LXX but on the Hebrew alone. His motivation in translation was to take from the Jews, for the last time, the advantage of being able to dive into the depths of the scriptural language while leaving the Christians behind.

108. He was quite fascinated by this scholar's theology and life and translated into Latin fourteen homilies on Ezekiel as well as twenty-five other OT homilies.
109. Ibid., 351: "Pope Damasus . . . therefore begged Jerome to take in hand, not a fresh translation of the New Testament—but a simple revision of the Latin Translations."

Nearly the entirety of Christianity treated this new translation with distrust and hostility. Jerome's great problem was that he considered the LXX as of secondary authority to the Hebrew Scriptures.[110] Theologically, Jerome was correct in this prioritization, but the first Christians were deeply attached to the authority of the LXX. All OT commentaries written prior to Jerome's work were based on the LXX. The LXX was accepted and read in churches and considered to be inspired by the unanimous opinions of the doctors of the church. But because Jerome's translation was properly based on the Hebrew text, it reflected a total recasting of the OT. Thousands of phrases disappeared from it, others were added to it, the order of several books was changed, and a different sense was encountered.[111] As a result, there was an outcry against Jerome.[112]

Jerome, however, was not satisfied to merely translate the Bible—he sought to facilitate biblical understanding by following his translations with commentaries. He completed these exegetical works in Bethlehem. Jerome's exegetical method was not perfect. He acknowledged that his impulsive personality made the meticulous nature of translation and exegesis painful for him. For example, he wrote his commentary on Matthew in two weeks; he finished Ephesians at the rate of one thousand lines per day. At this time, allegorical exegesis was the most popular method of interpretation. It seems that Jerome's intention was to intermix historical and allegorical interpretation, or possibly to overlay one with the other.

In the last years of the fourth century, Origen's renown was still glimmering despite many efforts to quench his influence. In A.D. 374, Epiphanius of Salamis considered it his task to drive all Origenistic thought out of the orthodox church.

Jerome had been influenced and impressed by Origen. In his earlier writings Jerome even referred to Origen as the instructor of the churches from the time of the apostles. The future would tell a different story of Origen, for his opponents would succeed and his theology would

110. Ibid., 357.
111. Ibid.
112. Ibid., 360. Even Augustine did not like the idea of a new translation from the Hebrew. He saw no serious reason to upset so many interests and venerable traditions, and he energetically counseled Jerome to confine himself to giving a good translation of the LXX, which was known everywhere and which the apostles themselves had used.

be labeled unsound and inadvisable. But at this time the controversy surrounding Origen was in its early years. In defense of Origen, his followers pointed to Jerome for validation. Jerome did not approve, and the situation only acquired more enemies for him. In the midst of the conflict, Jerome admitted that he praised Origen's exegesis, not his doctrine; his genius, not his faith; the scholar, not the propagandist. Thus Jerome himself eventually fought against the supporters of Origen. In A.D. 420 in a cell in Bethlehem, Jerome died an old man.

THE CREED AND COUNCIL OF CONSTANTINOPLE (A.D. 381)

Finally in A.D. 381, after the work of many theologians, continual controversy, and empire-wide political and social upheaval, the church was ready for a definitive council that would conclusively cement the church's position that Christ is one with the Father.[113] This time the bishops were called to Constantinople, and one hundred and fifty men gathered there in A.D. 381. None of the bishops was from the West. There is a beauty to be seen in this council—the West had already supported Athanasius, and now the East decided to support orthodoxy. The prominent theologian Gregory of Nazianzus presided, with the emperor in attendance at the initial sessions as well.

The theologians affirmed a full creed, now referred to as the Nicene Creed, though its full title is the *Niceno-Constantinopolitan Creed*.[114] Wisely, the Niceno-Constantinopolitan Creed does not attempt to explain comprehensively the mystery of how Christ can be fully God and fully man. It does establish, however, that believers can reflect theologically between two boundaries—that Christ's divine nature must be full, and that his human nature must be complete. The creed warns against a false relationship between the two natures.

In the incarnation, there was no conversion of God into man. Similarly, there was no conversion of man into God. God as God can-

---

113. Schaff, *History*, 3:650.
114. Earlier scholarship, such as that represented by Philip Schaff (*History*, 3:639), generally assumed that this creed was a reworking of the earlier Nicene Creed with a few additions. Later scholars have argued that the Nicene Creed does not appear to be the basis for the Constantinopolitan. Instead, it was probably composed from an earlier liturgical form. See Kelly, *Creeds*, 296–331.

not be humanized. In the same way, man cannot be deified. Further, after the incarnation the relationship between the human and divine in Christ was never disconnected. Christ was not schizophrenic—he remained one whole person.

There are thus two aspects, or parts, to Christ's unified nature. Yet he had one, undivided self-consciousness. The creed affirmed that even after the incarnation, and for eternity, the distinction between the two aspects of his nature continues. While they are distinct, without confusion or conversion, they are also without separation or division. In terms of Christ's will, the divine will remains divine, and the human will remains human. In Christ the God-man, the two natures have one common life and interpenetrate each other. This relationship is similar to the relationship between the three persons of the Trinity. The Nicene Creed was a truly universal creed and received affirmation in the West and East from the Council of Chalcedon in A.D. 451 onward.[115]

In conclusion, if not for the arduous labors of these fourth-century theologians, the church would be impoverished concerning the glorious doctrine of the person of Jesus Christ. The creed reaffirmed the Nicene Creed and condemned the Eunomians, the Arians or Eudoxians, the semi-Arians or the Pneumatomachians, the Sabellians, the Marcellians, the Photinians, and the Apollinarians. The theological controversy concerning Arianism reached resolution; it was agreed that the Arian party had to be excluded from the empire.

This council also solidified the political notion of a Christian state. The empire had already affirmed Christianity in A.D. 313, and now the state could pass laws against "heretical" Christians because the lines of orthodoxy were drawn. This development would prove to be important in the state's attempts to eliminate Donatism and later Priscillianism.[116]

This chapter has looked with gratitude on the creeds of the early church, as well as on the men who crafted them. The next chapter will examine the life and teaching of one of the greatest theologians with whom the church has ever been gifted—Augustine of Hippo.

115. Grillmeier, *Apostolic Age*, 249.
116. Heussi, *Kompendium*, 78–80.

KEY TERMS

Nicene Creed
Arius's theology
Constantinopolitan Creed
Apostles' Creed
Cappadocian fathers

STUDY QUESTIONS

1. Why do you think that creeds are helpful to the church?
2. Should the government pay for church meetings or persecute heretics?
3. Can you explain the developments from the Nicene Creed to the Council of Constantinople?
4. How did Cappadocian theology advance the doctrine of the Trinity?

RESOURCES FOR FURTHER STUDY

This chapter discusses a number of specialized areas of study, each of which is fascinating in its own right. Creedal development and the function of creeds is essential for understanding theology. The Reformers treasured the Cappadocians and Chrysostom. Understanding the development of exegetical schools helps pastors better preach the gospel.

Brändle, Rudolf. *John Chrysostom: Bishop, Reformer, Martyr*. Translated by John Cawte and Silke Trzcionka. Strathfield, Australia: St Pauls Publications, 2004. A volume by one of my former teachers that underlines the thinking of Chrysostom on social issues in addition to his being well known as a theologian and preacher.

Kelly, J. N. D. *Early Christian Creeds*. London: Longman, 1972. Particularly valuable for the study of the creeds. Compare Kelly's *Early Christian Doctrines*, highlighted in an earlier chapter.

Young, Frances. *From Nicaea to Chalcedon*. Philadelphia: Fortress, 1983. A scholarly but readable introduction to all the theologians involved and one that nestles them in their historical context.

5

Augustine (A.D. 354–430)

AUGUSTINE WAS THE PREEMINENT father of the Western church. Few throughout history rival his influence on it, as well as on philosophy, theology, and the culture at large. His understanding and development of Christian truth, coupled with the breadth of his interests and literary productions, surpass all who preceded him. Regarded by German theologians as the "Faust of Antiquity," Augustine is one of the great doctors of the church.[1] Yet to understand the influence of Augustine, we must start further "upstream" by first acquainting ourselves with several men around him.

MARIUS VICTORINUS (A.D. 290–364)

View of God. Another North African significantly influenced Augustine's Trinitarian conceptions.[2] Victorinus supported the doctrine of the consubstantiality of the Father and the Son.[3]

---

1. Kurt D. Schmidt, *Grundriss der Kirchengeschichte* (Göttingen: Vandenhoek & Ruprecht, 1963), 110.
2. On Augustine and Victorinus, see Reinhold Schmidt, *Marius Victorinus Rhetor und seine Beziehungen zu Augustin* (Kiel: Uebermuth, 1985). Also helpful is Paul Henry, "The 'Adversus Arium' of Marius Victorinus: The First Systematic Exposition of the Trinity," *Journal of Theological Studies* 1 (April 1950): 42–55. Pierre Hadot has added two helpful works, "L'image de la Trinité dans l'âme chez Victorinus et chez saint Augustin," in *Studia Patristica: Papers Presented to the Third International Conference on Patristic Studies Held at Christ Church, Oxford, 1959*, vol. 6, ed. Frank L. Cross (Berlin: Akademie, 1962), and his full length *Marius Victorinus: Recherches sur sa vie et ses oeuvres* (Paris: Études Augustiniennes, 1971).
3. Victorinus does so by using Neoplatonic philosophical categories. See Robert A. Markus, "Marius Victorinus and Augustine," in *The Cambridge History of Later Greek and Early Medieval Philosophy*, ed. A. H. Armstrong (Cambridge: Cambridge University Press, 1970),

His thinking may have also linked Greek and Latin theological formulations.[4]

Victorinus implemented new terminology to express God's various qualities. For example, he denied God's inclusion in one of the four philosophical modalities of being and instead declared God to be above all being.[5] He reasoned that God is not being in that he is the very cause of being. This quality also necessarily elevates God above knowledge and life itself; therefore, God must be that which is not being—in other words, nonbeing. For Victorinus, God existed as what he termed *omnipotent power*, by which he meant that God was above truth, even above all perfections. Thus God, as nonbeing, could be known only through ignorance.[6] At times it seems that Victorinus's conception of God was similar to the "One" of Neoplatonic philosophy.[7]

Trinity. Victorinus's Trinitarian theology has been characterized as "an essay in metaphysics, based on Neo-platonic ontology."[8] Victorinus was able to speak of a Trinity only in that, for him, the Logos was a duality.[9] The unity of the godhead consisted in the *circumincession* ("internal unity") of the persons, a unity that transcends the notion of number.[10] He also made a distinction within the godhead by referring to God as existing *tripliciter* ("threefold"). God's being exists in the process of *status* ("standing" or "being"), *progressio* ("procession" or "going forth"), and *regressio* ("going back" or "returning").[11] In

332; Henry, "Adversus Arium," 45–47. Henry specifically outlines seven Plotinian elements in Victorinus's Trinitarian theology. See also J. N. D. Kelly, *Early Christian Doctrines* (London: Black, 1977), 270.

4. Markus, "Marius Victorinus," 331.

5. Victorinus, *Ad Candidum* 14.1–5 (1027b).

6. Ibid., 14.1–5 (1027b–c). Victorinus refers to this nonbeing as "prebeing."

7. Markus ("Marius Victorinus," 334) says that "the whole ontological scheme falls squarely within its [Neoplatonic thought] tradition of 'negative theology.' The novelty in Victorinus' use of this scheme lies in the way he uses it to establish the consubstantiality of God's Logos with God."

8. J. N. D. Kelly, *Early Christian Doctrines* (London: Black, 1977), 270: "His devotion to Scripture and the Christian revelation obliges him to make drastic modifications of the Neoplatonic scheme." Markus ("Marius Victorinus," 339) says: "Victorinus is prepared to make statements about God which Plotinus could not have countenanced of the One. . . . His theology is scriptural in the second place only."

9. Victorinus, *Adversus Arium* 3.2.12–13 (1099b–d). From the *esse* of the Father comes *vivere* ("to be alive") and *intellegere* ("to know")—a single movement.

10. Ibid., 1.15; 3.1.

11. Ibid., 2.4; 3.4; 4.21. Victorinus, *Hymn* 3.

his attempts to explain the godhead, Victorinus considered the human soul the most helpful analogy for the Trinity.[12]

According to Victorinus, the Father was beyond all knowledge. He was essence, silence, rest, and immobility. Since the Father was beyond knowledge, the Son was responsible to reveal and manifest the Father. Victorinus does admit that the Father has being, or *esse*, and consistently describes it in terms of negative theology. Expressing Victorinus's teaching in terms of Neoplatonic philosophy, this *esse* is the "One."[13]

According to Victorinus, the Son was also referred to as the Logos, that is, the first wisdom. Though distinct from one another, the Logos and the Father are unified. This distinction between Father and Logos, between *esse* and species, is parallel to the distinction between form and substance.[14]

The analogy of the relationship of "potency" to "act" further clarified the relationship between the Father and the Son, that is, the Logos. The relationship between potency and act was consubstantial, which is to say that the Father engendered the act and the act proceeded from potency. Each person was both. Yet the Father was the source of being, and the Son was the activity of being and the source of creation. The Father and the Son are one substance, one consubstantial image of potency in the Father and act in the Son.[15]

From this analysis of the relationship between the Father and the Son, Victorinus developed a theory of the eternal generation of the Son that avoided the charge that such eternal generation necessarily implied change.[16] While eternally generated from the Father, the Son was also

12. Victorinus, *Adversus Arium* 1.32; 1.62. Kelly (*Doctrines*, 271) says: "In it [i.e., the human soul] can be seen the triad *esse*, *vivere* and *intelligere*, determinations or distinctions which are related to each other as the Persons of the Trinity of which it is the image, and which, like Them, are consubstantial."

13. As *esse*, the Father has being. Victorinus, *Adversus Arium* 4.20.

14. Markus, "Marius Victorinus," 334: "In terms of the relation between the Plotinian hypostases, the relation of Father to Son corresponds to the relation of the One to the Intellect. But Victorinus repudiates the tendency implied by the Neoplatonic scheme to subordinate the second to the first hypostasis." See Victorinus, *Adversus Arium* 1.56. The Son, as formed being [on], and the Father, as *esse*, are one substance.

15. At *Adversus Arium* 1.41 and elsewhere, Victorinus makes it clear that this relation of potency to act is equivalent to that of "hidden" and "manifest," which are consubstantial. Since they are consubstantial, Markus ("Marius Victorinus," 336) states that "activity becomes the essential constitutive character of being."

16. Kelly (*Doctrines*, 270) says that for Victorinus *esse* is equivalent to *moveri* ("to move"), and "in relation to the contingent order this movement takes the form of creation, while in

identifiable independently of the Father. The Son was considered life and movement, the manifest form of God as well as the first being.[17]

Victorinus named the third person of the Trinity the Spirit, but the Spirit did not receive as much attention as the Father and the Son. The Spirit was distinguishable from the other two persons in that as the Son revealed the Father, so the Spirit was the voice of the Son.[18] The thinking of Victorinus influenced Augustine's articulation of the Trinity. But a bishop from Milan named Ambrose had an even greater impact on Augustine.

AMBROSE (A.D. 340–397)

Life. Ambrose was the son of a governor of Gaul. When his father died ca. A.D. 354, the remaining family, Ambrose included, moved to Rome. It was there that Ambrose was educated in literature, law, and rhetoric in preparation for following his father into the highest offices of Roman administration. Ambrose soon distinguished himself as an orator and was elected an official of northern Italy.

Despite his popularity as a political figure, Ambrose left government work in A.D. 374 and—to the pleasure of the Cappadocian father Basil the Great—assumed the episcopal chair of what was considered to be the second capital city of Italy, Milan. Prior to his election as bishop, Ambrose was a mere catechumen and had yet to receive baptism.

As bishop of the city, Ambrose sold his personal wealth to care for the poor. Also, he did not seek to win the favor of the imperial government. While serving as bishop, he began to develop a theory of the separation of church and state. He reasoned that the emperor was *in* the church, not *over* the church.

As Theologian. In the midst of episcopal life, Ambrose still found time to write. To Emperor Gratian, who was later murdered by Maximus, he wrote *On the Faith*—a general defense of the divinity of the Son contra current Arian attacks. During this time, around A.D. 381,

---

relation to the Word it is generation."

17. Besides life and movement, he was also "word" and "action." It was when the Son came into relationship with the finite that he made God knowable. See Victorinus, *Adversus Arium* 3.7; 4.20.

18. Ibid., 3.16.

Arianism was still prominent in various regions of the empire. Ambrose also wrote a work titled *On the Holy Spirit*, which depended heavily on the thought of Basil the Great.

Ambrose gave numerous lectures, many of which were transcribed and have been handed down to us today—lectures such as *On the Mysteries* and *On the Sacraments*. These lectures reveal how the sacraments were understood in fourth-century Milan—a time when there was still diversity of thought throughout Christendom regarding the nature of the sacraments.

Ambrose also wrote on Christian ethics in a work titled *On the Duties of Ministers*, apparently modeled after the composition by Cicero with the same name. Though Ambrose was not regarded as a great original theologian, his legacy can be attributed to his work as a bishop and its influence on Augustine.

Many have termed Ambrose's notion of the restoration of man from the state of sin and guilt as *mystical*. He reasoned that the soul is redeemed by an immediate, mystical union with the Redeemer. The most elaborate formulation that Ambrose gave for this relationship is the union of the heavenly Bridegroom with his bride, a figure that Origen had used in a commentary on the Song of Songs.[19]

According to Ambrose, this redemption is initiated by Christ himself. He must seek the soul before the soul can come to him.[20] But this union necessitates the cooperation of the soul. The soul must seek and draw near to Jesus, and for Ambrose this drawing near was done most effectively through ascetic mortification.[21]

It would be a mistake to separate Ambrose's conception of salvation from his views on faith, works, and grace. Of the three concepts, grace played the prominent role for Ambrose. Faith and works depend on

19. Frederick Homes Dudden, *The Life and Times of Saint Ambrose* (Oxford: Clarendon, 1935), 2:625–26.

20. Ambrose says in his *Exposition of the Psalms*: "Come Lord Jesus, seek your servant, seek your weary sheep, seek me, find me, make me, carry me. Come, for you alone can recall the wanderer. Come and seek your sheep, not now through servants and hirelings, but in your own person. Take me in the flesh which in Adam fell. Carry me in the Cross, which brings salvation to those that err, which alone gives rest to the weary, in which alone whosoever dies shall live."

21. Ambrose, *Enarratio Psalm* 36–37: "Let us die with Him, that we may live with Him. Let there be in us, as it were, a daily practice of, and inclination for, dying." Thus the soul may become one with its Redeemer, as Ambrose goes on to say: "made in Him, crucified in Him, buried in Him, buried together with Him, restored to life in Him."

grace. Conversion, reformation, and the daily Christian walk are made possible only through sovereign grace. Even prayer is the operation of grace. The ability to please God is granted by God himself, and the Lord's mercy rescues man from his sin. In short, all goodness in the creature is received from the hand of God, thus leaving no room for man to glory in spiritual or moral achievements.

While emphasizing the role of grace, Ambrose still considered faith and works as necessary for salvation. He regarded faith as intellectual acceptance of revealed truth in addition to direct, personal apprehension of Christ as the Redeemer. This faith flowed forth from the soul as works. This reasoning naturally leads to a tension: the relationship between divine grace and human will. On this relationship, Ambrose's teaching often lacked logic and consistency.

Ambrose also wrote on the church. He reasoned that individual believers are brought into vital union with Christ and receive divine grace through the medium of the church.[22] The church—called the Virgin, Bride of Christ, Second Eve, Mother of All the Living, and City of God—is one, despite its many congregations. Heretics (those defective in faith) and schismatics (those defective in love) are rightly excluded from her.

Ambrose marked the church by certain characteristics.[23] She is *holy*. By this word Ambrose did not mean that the church is reserved for the spiritually perfect, as the Novatianists taught. She is not perfect, but she longs to be. Members of the church are cleansed by baptism, and by grace they exhibit faith, abstain from sin, and walk rightly. The church is apostolic because she preserves the faith and deeds of the apostles. The church is also eternal and transmits the means of eternal life.[24]

AUGUSTINE (A.D. 354–430)[25]

Pre-Conversion. Augustine was born in Thagaste, North Africa, in A.D. 354 to a pagan municipal officer, Patricius, and a devoutly

22. Dudden, *Life and Times*, 636.
23. Ibid., 638.
24. Ibid., 639.
25. See Richard C. Gamble, "Christianity from the Early Fathers to Charlemagne," in *Revolutions in Worldview: Understanding the Flow of Western Thought*, ed. W. Andrew Hof-

Christian mother, Monica. His father would be baptized as a Christian shortly before his death. From his infancy, Augustine was enrolled with the catechumens—those who sought entrance into the church.

At the age of eleven and after years of study at home, Augustine was sent to Madaura, a small city not twenty miles south of Thagaste, for further elementary education. It was in Madaura that Augustine was introduced to Latin literature and engaged in his well-known episode of stealing fruit, which he recounts in *Confessions*. When he was seventeen, Augustine went to Carthage to continue his studies. Almost immediately on his arrival in Carthage, he rebelled against Christianity. He considered Christianity to be the religion of old women. As an exhibit of his masculinity and youthfulness, Augustine took a concubine.

In Carthage, Augustine attended the lectures and meetings of the Manichees and received the education considered necessary for a philosopher. He studied grammar, dialectic, rhetoric, music, geometry, astronomy, and arithmetic. Yet he would attribute the most lasting impression of these years to his reading Cicero's *Hortensius*. Augustine later said that this work had on him the effect of a conversion.[26] In A.D. 375/76, after about four years in Carthage, Augustine left to teach rhetoric at Thagaste.

While in Thagaste, Augustine became greatly influenced by Manichaeism. This religion taught that there were two warring worlds—a good one with a perfect deity, and an evil one with a wicked adversary to the deity. When a person was a Manichaean elect, he thought he belonged to the world of light. But for a while, the Manichaean disciple was trapped in the dark world. Deliverance from this world came only when a man discarded and repudiated his own body as something entirely foreign. Augustine surely saw in these warring worlds a reflection of his own inner struggles, of his deep spiritual longing and entrapment.

But after nine years, Manichaeism left Augustine intellectually dissatisfied, and he began to experience doubts. In search of answers, he sought out their great bishop, Faustus. Augustine left his meeting with Faustus still without the answers he desired, so he began searching

---

fecker (Phillipsburg, NJ: P&R Publishing, 2007), 119–27.
26. Markus, "Marius Victorinus," 342.

for philosophical satisfaction elsewhere. He became a philosophical skeptic,[27] and he would soon become a Neoplatonist.[28]

In A.D. 383 Augustine set sail for Rome. The following year he received an imperial appointment to teach rhetoric in Milan.[29] It was in Milan that Augustine came under the influence of the city's great bishop, Ambrose, and that God drew Augustine to himself.

Christian Biography. Though to this point not drawn to the Christian faith, Augustine found intellectual satisfaction in Christianity when he sat under the teaching of Ambrose. It was Ambrose who taught Augustine an allegorical, or typical, OT exegetical method, which relieved the tensions Augustine had about the OT.

In Milan, Augustine was also introduced to Neoplatonism. This philosophical grid helped him comprehend the relationship between God as spiritual substance and the presence of evil in the world. Evil was understood as a negation. Finally, with an epistemological foundation for his worldview, Augustine made a connection between Plotinus's conception of the *nous*, which was fulfilled in John's notion of the Logos.[30]

Augustine was philosophically and intellectually satisfied by Ambrose's presentation of Christianity. But for Augustine this period was not without its internal struggles, which are recorded in detail in his *Confessions*. God would not let Augustine from his grasp and Ambrose baptized him on Easter in A.D. 387.

Augustine prepared to return to Africa with his mother, who had joined him in Italy. But she died shortly before they sailed for Africa, so in A.D. 388 Augustine returned to Carthage, then traveled to Thagaste. In A.D. 391 he arrived in Hippo, where he established a small monastic community. He also became a presbyter. Four years later, he was consecrated as Valerius's coadjutor bishop and succeeded him soon thereafter.

---

27. Berthold Altaner and Alfred Stuiber, *Patrologie: Leben, Schriften und Lehre der Kirchenväter* (Freiburg: Herder, 1978), 412.

28. Schmidt, *Grundriss*, 112.

29. In *Confessions*, Augustine reflected on his rather quick rise to success as a teacher. His mind experienced tensions between the lure of fame and public reputation and the beginnings he had made in the quest for wisdom.

30. J. G. Davies, *The Early Christian Church: A History of Its First Five Centuries* (Grand Rapids: Baker, 1980), 224.

Meanwhile, at the same time Germanic invasions brought massive changes to the empire. Examining this cultural context is essential to understanding the closing years of Augustine's life.

The Goths invaded the Roman Empire prior to the fifth century. The Germanic tribes admired Roman civilization and sought to assimilate it into their own. In the beginning of the fifth century, Alleric, king of the Visigoths, attacked the weakened empire beginning in the East and conquered Greece as far as Sparta and Constantinople. Alleric began his invasion into Italy, and in A.D. 410 the great city was captured. He pushed his forces south, with his eye on Sicily, but he was stopped only by his own death. Changing direction, his successor led the Goths northward, where they invaded southern Gaul. They settled in southern Gaul by the end of the second decade of the century. But their westward expansion continued into Spain. There were movements of various tribes all the way from England down into Italy, as far west as Spain and as far east as Constantinople. In the year A.D. 455, Rome was again attacked and raided, this time by the Vandals.[31]

Between A.D. 410 and 455, Roman rule had, in many ways, toppled in Britain, France, Spain, and North Africa.[32] Technically, the barbarian kings were servants of the Roman state, as they wished to be affiliated with the great culture and authority of Rome. But it was not the Rome that had been.

In his first ten years in North Africa, Augustine felt the tremors of these shifts in the empire, but he was wholly distracted by theological controversies with the Manichaeans. His next decade was spent in controversy with the Donatists—schismatics who taught that clergy must be perfect to have effective ministry. This controversy was followed by debates surrounding the Pelagian heresy.

The great African thinker died at the age of seventy-six as the Arian Vandals besieged his city. He was spared the knowledge of his home country's devastation and the persecution that came at the hands of the Vandals.[33]

---

31. Jacques Le Goff, *Medieval Civilization 400–1500*, trans. Julia Barrow (Oxford: Blackwell, 1988), 3–36.

32. Ibid., 17.

33. Davies, *Early Christian Church*, 224.

Writings. The corpus of Augustine's literary compositions is vast. Three years before his death, Augustine thought himself to have composed ninety-three literary works and 232 books in addition to his sermons and letters. Most of this massive body of literature has been preserved.

Many consider *On the Trinity* to be Augustine's most significant work. He spent twenty years (A.D. 399–419) composing it. He wrote *On Baptism* (A.D. 400–401) against the Donatists. Against the Pelagians he wrote *On the Spirit and the Letter* (A.D. 412). *On Christian Learning* was an expression of his ideas concerning biblical scholarship.

Augustine's two most popular works are *Confessions* and *City of God*.[34] A literary pioneer, *Confessions* recalls many details from his life; it reveals his sinful youth, conversion to Christianity, and development of thought. *City of God*, published in parts from A.D. 413 to 426, countered the accusation that it was faith in Jesus Christ that brought down the Roman Empire. *City of God* was also the first true theology and philosophy of history aside from the Scriptures.[35] Secular history could never be separated from sacred history in that the true story of the development of humanity was the unfolding of the struggle between faith and unbelief.

Augustine's Theology

Doctrine of the Church. In *City of God*, Augustine outlined the attributes of the church. He argued that there is one holy catholic, apostolic church, and the church's unity is found in the presence of the Holy Spirit. Heretics have no place in the church because, in their unbelief, they deny the unity of the faith. Thus heresy destroys the unity of the church.

For Augustine, the church was also holy. Its holiness was established via union with Christ. The church, however, was without blemish in heaven, not on earth, as not all members of the church were holy. In opposition, the Donatists argued that the church on earth must be absolutely pure. If that were the case, argued Augustine, there would

34. Ibid., 225.
35. James Orr, *The Progress of Dogma* (New York: Armstrong, 1908), 139.

be no church. For Augustine, the church was what he termed a *corpus permixtum*, a "mixed body." Yet the community of believers was also the *communio sanctorum*, the "communion of saints." The true and full number of the elect is the invisible church. There were, in his mind, some Catholics who were *not* elect and some non-Catholics who *were* elect.

Augustine did not, however, have a proper view of baptism. He considered every baptized child a child of God. He proposed that all who were baptized were regenerate, but not all the baptized receive the grace of perseverance—only the justified do.[36] To understand his thought better, we must turn to Augustine's notion of sin and grace.

Sin, Freedom, and Grace: Augustine and Pelagius. To understand Augustine's conception of sin and grace, we begin with Pelagius—an austere British monk and popular teacher in Rome between A.D. 384 and 400.[37] Morality was of primary importance to Pelagius—thus the idea of unconditional free will and corresponding responsibility was the keystone of Pelagius's system of thought.[38]

Pelagius thought that the fall could not produce a bias in man toward evil. He simply denied original sin. He interpreted the phrase "God will have mercy" in Romans 9:15 as, "I will have mercy on him whom I have foreknown will be able to deserve compassion."[39] So there can be no original or hereditary sin, thus leaving human nature unimpaired by the fall.

Pelagius believed that man was not responsible for sin unless that sin was a product of his will. With the elimination of original sin, Pelagianism left humans free to will either that which is good or that which is evil. And with no inherent bias toward evil, humans had the ability to obey God's commandments without committing sin.[40] It was

---

36. Ibid., 144.

37. He was not young at this time and probably died before the year A.D. 420. Some of his works include an exposition of Paul's epistles.

38. Kelly, *Doctrines*, 358. Pelagius himself did not actually try to extricate mankind from the purview of God's sovereignty, even if his followers did.

39. Pelagius, *Commentary on St. Paul's Epistle to the Romans*, as cited by Greg R. Allison, *Historical Theology: An Introduction to Christian Doctrine: A Companion to Wayne Grudem's Systematic Theology* (Grand Rapids: Zondervan, 2011), 456.

40. To be fair, Pelagius did not envision some plateau where the Christian reached the state of perfection here on earth and then sat back; on the contrary, he thought perfection could be maintained only by continuing, strenuous effort.

example alone that was to blame for evil. Children are born as perfect as Adam was before the fall.[41] Adam was naturally mortal, and death was not a result of his sin.[42]

Pelagius held that a command presupposes the power to obey. Since God commands obedience, man must have the ability to obey God's law. Human beings were able, by using reason and free will, to pursue their course and realize their destiny by virtue of their natural powers. The will was a natural human faculty that made choices, maintained itself between good and evil, and was able freely to choose between the two.[43]

Pelagius's followers were responsible for much of the development and dissemination of his doctrine. One of these disciples was Celestius. He emphasized the idea that because Adam was created mortal, he would have died whether or not he had sinned. Another of Pelagius's disciples was Julian of Eclanum, who asserted man's absolute independence from God.

Augustine had developed his thinking on grace and free will prior to Pelagius's criticism. He held that all humankind was affected by Adam's fall into sin.[44] Humanity was organically connected to Adam, and sin flows to all through him. As a result of its Adamic connection, humanity is unable to do that which is spiritually good. That which is spiritually good springs, from God's sight, out of the proper motive of love toward God.[45] There is therefore universal damnation in Adam.

Contra Pelagius, Augustine affirmed biblical election and reprobation. He argued that the reprobate stood condemned both in the guilt of original sin and the guilt of his own sins. In his grace, God chose some and passed over others. Augustine interpreted the statement in 1 Timothy 2:4 that God wants all to be saved to mean that salvation comes exclusively by divine willing. So salvation comes exclusively by unmerited grace. To the contention that this system is unfair, Augustine

---

41. Orr, *Progress*, 156–58.
42. Ibid., 159.
43. Ibid., 155.
44. See Louis Berkhof, *The History of Christian Doctrines* (Carlisle, PA: Banner of Truth, 1969), 133–37; E. H. Klotsche, *The History of Christian Doctrine*, rev. ed. (Grand Rapids: Baker, 1979), 83–96. On grace, see Kelly, *Doctrines*, 352, 357, 365–69 (361–66 for more information on the fall and original sin, and 357–61 for Pelagius).
45. Kelly, *Doctrines*, 361.

appealed to divine mystery and righteousness.[46] The purpose of this salvation is that the chosen will believe and live holy lives.

Augustine also provided distinctions on humanity and sin. He taught that Adam was created without sin and was *posse non peccare*, that is, he had the ability not to sin. But after his original sin, Adam lost that ability. He entered the state of *non posse non peccare*—he was unable not to sin. Given this situation, the will of all humanity needs renewal. For Augustine, humanity's connection to Adam was not federal but realistic. Humanity was germinally present in Adam.[47]

The nature of sin, both original and actual, is voluntary and subtracts from existence. Sin is not the result of sensory experience but of self-love. When the soul loves the self more than it loves God, it falls to the allurement of sin. Concupiscence, the inordinate power of sensuous desire against the soul's law of reason, is a general result of defection from God.[48]

For Augustine, this transforming renewal is produced entirely and solely by God's workings. Sinful humanity stands in need of renewal, which is a work—from beginning to end—of the grace of God. This divine, renewing grace that changes a person is irresistible in that it effectuates its result. Grace does not overpower the will but renews and restores it to freedom. Grace persuades and enables the soul to do what it had been unwilling and powerless to.[49] But irresistible grace does not force the will contrary to its own desires. Grace changes the will so that it yearns for the good.[50] God operates on the will so that, on its own volition, it turns to holiness.

Pelagius held that Augustine's system of thought made men mere puppets of divine grace, and the controversy between his followers and Augustine grew. Initially, Eastern churches were receptive to Pelagius's views. But Augustine sent to Jerome a priest, Crosus, to warn him of

---

46. Allison, *Historical Theolog*, 456–57. For Augustine, election is not limited to those who are in the church and reprobation to those outside the church, for some people who are elect may not be members of the local church; likewise, some may be members who are reprobate. The church helps the elect through the means of grace. See Robert Letham, *Systematic Theology* (Wheaton, IL: Crossway, 2019), 381–82.

47. Orr, *Progress*, 148.

48. Ibid., 147.

49. Ibid., 150.

50. Berkhof, *History of Christian Doctrines*, 135. Roy W. Battenhouse, *A Companion to the Study of St. Augustine* (New York: Oxford University Press, 1955), 216–20.

Pelagius and his views. Although Jerome disagreed with Augustine on a number of theological issues, he agreed with him on the danger of Pelagius. So Jerome wrote against Pelagius; but in A.D. 415 a synod convened in Jerusalem and refused to make a pronouncement against him.[51] Nevertheless, Pelagius's theology, through Celestius, was condemned at the Council of Carthage (A.D. 411–412), in Palestine (A.D. 414–416), in Rome (A.D. 416–418), and at the Council of Ephesus (A.D. 431).

Pelagianism then morphed into semi-Pelagianism, which argued that divine grace and human will are coordinate factors; that predestination is based on foreseen faith and obedience; and that fallen humanity retains enough freedom to cooperate with grace. Semi-Pelagianism, however, was condemned at the Council of Orange in A.D. 530.[52]

While Augustine defended scriptural truth against Pelagian heresy, he still lacked a fully Protestant doctrine of justification because he did not maintain distinctions between justification, regeneration, and sanctification.[53] The doctrine of soteriology had yet to be fully developed.

Trinitarian Theology. For Augustine, the definition of God is connected to the being of God. He is self-existing, which is the very meaning of his name, Yahweh.[54] In *On the Trinity*, Augustine contended that human reason must not be the starting place for understanding the nature of the Trinity, for human reason is defective in at least three ways. First, it operates slowly—so slowly that even a lifetime would not be long enough for a person to reach correct conclusions about God. Second, human reason is darkened by sin and therefore cannot function properly.[55] Third, it is only through contemplation that reason can apprehend the divine, and contemplation requires as a starting point either sensory experience or the intellect. Yet the nature of God is not directly accessible to either sensory experience or the intellect; therefore, Augustine wrote, believers need to turn to revealed truth.

51. Klotsche, *History*, 84.
52. Orr, *Progress*, 161.
53. Ibid., 143.
54. Herman Bavinck, *The Doctrine of God* (Carlisle, PA: Banner of Truth, 1977), 21.
55. Ronald H. Nash, *The Light of the Mind: St Augustine's Theory of Knowledge* (Lexington: The University Press of Kentucky, 1969), 33–37.

If the person who seeks after God chooses to neglect revealed truth, then his or her conceptions of God will be inherently faulty.[56]

In broad strokes, Augustine presented two main themes in *De trinitate*: he first defined the content of the Christian faith, and he then offered analogies to help understand the nature of the Trinity. For Augustine, the content of the Christian faith is founded on the notion of the deity of Christ. Augustine acknowledged that there were difficult passages to understand regarding Christ's deity—for example, passages in which it appears that Jesus does not know the future and in which he seems to reject the notion that he is good. Augustine resolved the tension of these passages by suggesting that the Bible presents Christ not only as the powerful Son of God but also as the humble servant.[57] He proposed that while the Son was sent from the Father, there was no ontological subordination of the Son to the Father.[58] From this foundation, he transitioned to an analysis of the OT theophanies.

Augustine's conception of OT theophanies differed from the views of earlier writers but appropriately underlined his view of Trinitarian equality. He contended that OT theophanies were not exclusively pre-incarnate, earthly appearances of the Son but were also appearances of God the Father.[59] This view led Augustine into addressing the nature of miracles.[60] From there, he defined the notion of "person" and presented arguments for the coequality of the three persons of the Trinity.[61]

Augustine recognized the difficult task of describing God as "person." To do so was to use predication. In the sentence, *The pen is*

---

56. Augustine, *De trinitate* 1.1.2; Rita Beyers et al., eds., *Corpus Christianorum: Series Latina*, 226 vols. (Turnhout, Belgium: Brepols, 1953–) (*CCSL* 50a), 28–29. Scott R. Swain argues that Augustine desired believers to unlearn ordinary human language relative to the Trinity and learn new uses that correspond more properly to biblical discourse. See Scott R. Swain, "Divine Trinity," in *Christian Dogmatics: Reformed Theology for the Church Catholic*, ed. Michael Allen and Scott R. Swain (Grand Rapids: Baker Academic, 2016), 93. See also Battenhouse, *Companion*, 240.

57. Augustine's analysis of the incarnate Son did not permit an actual limitation of Christ's knowledge. For example, he believed that Christ did in fact know the hour of his return to earth in power.

58. All three persons of the Trinity were involved in Christ's sending, including the Holy Spirit's coming as a dove. See Augustine, *De trinitate* 2.5.8–10; *CCSL* 50a, 89–92.

59. Augustine, *De trinitate* 2–3.11. Augustine did not deal with questions such as how the Father, who is "spiritual," took visible form.

60. Ibid., Books 3–4.

61. Ibid., 4.20; *CCSL* 50a, 199–201. See Battenhouse, *Companion*, 243–44.

black, the words *is black* comprise the predicate that describes the pen.[62] Aristotle had already proven ten categories of predication. Augustine deemed adequate only two of those categories—substance and relation—relative to the discussion about God.

To predicate substantially about God goes further than simply asserting the existence of God—it attempts to describe what sort of God exists. Substantial predication speaks of God in the singular; for example, it asserts that God, as God, is great.[63] Relational predication refers to the way in which the three persons of the Trinity are distinguished from one another, or it refers to their relationships to each other.[64] With these means of predication, theologians are able to make distinctions among the three persons of the godhead while still maintaining Trinitarian unity.[65]

It was during a season of tremendous contention in the church—at the hands of Arius and others—that Augustine articulated the coequality of the persons of the Trinity. While he focused on Christ's nature, he did not do so to the neglect of the Holy Spirit.[66] Augustine argued that the Holy Spirit had the same nature as the Father and the Son. The differentiation between the persons was not by degrees of being but in the nature of their causality. He thought of the Father as the "beginning" of the whole divinity and the other two persons in terms of procession and birth. For Augustine, the Holy Spirit became the unifying principle of the godhead, and the Holy Spirit proceeded from both the Father and the Son.[67]

---

62. For more on philosophical predication see Richard C. Gamble, *The Whole Counsel of God*, vol. 2, *The Full Revelation of God* (Phillipsburg, NJ: P&R Publishing, 2018) (WCG2), 992–93.

63. Augustine, *De trinitate* 5.2; CCSL 50a, 208: "Sed aliae quae dicuntur essentiae siue substantiae capiunt accidentias quibus in eis fiat uel magna uel quantacumque mutatio; deo autem aliquid eiusmodi accidere non potest."

64. Ibid., 5.1; CCSL 50a, 206–7.

65. Arianism, said Augustine, was mistaken in part by its inability to distinguish between substantial and relational predication. See Swain, "Divine Trinity," 95–96.

66. Immediately before forwarding his arguments on the equality of the Holy Spirit, Augustine had argued that the Son is an emanation from the omnipotent and was hence himself omnipotent.

67. Augustine, *De trinitate* 4.20.29; CCSL 50a, 199. "Nec possumus dicere quod spiritus sanctus et a filio non procedat; neque enim frustra idem spiritus et patris et filii spiritus dicitur." This double procession—the Holy Spirit proceeds from the Son as well as from the Father, and in Latin *"filioque"*—will be debated later and, sadly, will help cause separation between the Eastern and Western churches. See Battenhouse, *Companion*, 245.

At this point, Augustine's understanding of the nature of the persons of the godhead differed significantly from his Greek-speaking colleagues. He was likely unaware of the complex discussions concerning the nature of *ousia* and *hypostasis*. For him, the distinctions in the godhead were not to be expressed in terms of essence or substance but in terms of relation.

Augustine recognized that his approach to understanding the godhead had inherent problems and limitations. While the Cappadocian presentation had a tendency to lean toward tritheism, Augustine's presentation had the potential of being misunderstood as unitarianism.[68] The term *person* attempts to express the ineffable—to describe God's essence. But God has only one essence—that is, he is God. Thus it could be argued that there is only one person, or one essence, in the Trinity.[69]

Augustine rejected this alternative, but he struggled to express his view in a coherent and readily comprehensible manner. He knew that when a human used the word *person*, it necessitated a relationship to human personality. This relationship led him to his second main theme.

The Bible clearly teaches that humanity was created in the image of God, which, for Augustine, necessarily meant that the three persons of the Trinity are reflected in human nature. But Augustine recognized that every analogy from man to God was a mere reflection and would prove ultimately inadequate. Man would never attain knowledge of God as he truly is. Nevertheless, man was given imperfect and distorted reflections of God—and the first analogy Augustine drew between God and humanity was love. The human mind knows love within itself. So the mind knows God, for God is love.[70] More precisely, the human mind must first know itself to love itself. Thus we see a reflection of the Trinity: the mind itself, the love of it, and the knowledge of it.[71] Augustine saw another Trinitarian analogy in the memory,

68. The Cappadocians used the concept of *ousia* and *hypostasis* as "common" and "particular."

69. Problems with Augustine's teaching on the Trinity will reemerge in the middle and late twentieth century. See the debate about Cornelius Van Til's teaching in a later chapter.

70. Augustine, *De trinitate* 8.10.14; *CCSL* 50a, 290–91.

71. Ibid., 9.4.4; *CCSL* 50a, 297. First, there is equality. The love and the knowledge are equal. Second, there is an identity of essence; the whole mind is involved in knowing and loving itself. Third, they are all in all, being one substance and essence. Fourth, there is an indication of the begetting of the Word and the procession of the Spirit. When true knowledge arises in

understanding, and will. A person has a memory, must understand it, and must will to remember it. The three elements are equal to each other and each one to the whole; otherwise, they could not mutually contain each other.[72] These examples show some of the ways in which Augustine saw humanity as a reflection of the Trinity.

Christ's Generation. Moving from analysis of the persons of the Trinity, Augustine also wrote on Christ's generation, incarnation, and relationship to the Father and Holy Spirit. Augustine asserted that the Son's generation proceeded from the Father, was ineffable, and preserved the power and unity of the Father.[73] There was no priority of the Father in his willing the Son's generation before that generation was accomplished. For Augustine, the Son's begetting from the Father was similar to a fire's begetting its light. As in natural relationships, like begets like. Augustine saw no necessity for inequality between that which was generated and that which generates.

Augustine also asserted that the incarnation was an act of all three persons of the Trinity. At times, he declared specifically that it was the Holy Spirit who was active in the incarnation. Most often, however, he explained that the incarnation was the combined work of the Father and Holy Spirit. In such instances, Augustine's discussion was always within the context of the Son's proceeding from the Father.

Augustine defended unity within the Trinity.[74] The exhibited unity of the Father and the Son was expressed in four basic areas. First, the Trinity was united in substance and will. Augustine found support for this union from Scripture, particularly John 10:30.[75] This verse made clear that even during Jesus's earthly ministry there was perfect oneness within the God-man. The Father and Son's unity of will was

---

a mind, a word or concept is begotten within it—a concept or word that is equal to the mind. See Robert E. Meagher, *An Introduction to Augustine* (New York: New York University Press, 1978), 102–11.

72. Augustine, *De trinitate* 10.11.17–18; *CCSL* 50a, 329–30.

73. The Arian bishop Maximinus countered the doctrine by asserting that the Father, in willing the generation of the Son before the generation itself, is himself prior to the Son. Because the Son is in fact generated, he is necessarily inferior to the Father. The Father is different from the Son because he begets the Son and the Son is begotten by him.

74. In *Contra sermonem Arianorum*, Augustine discussed the unity of knowledge within the Trinity: there was no information that was the exclusive possession of any one person of the Trinity.

75. Augustine exegeted Romans 8:32; Galatians 2:20; John 5:19, 21; and John 17:24.

also essential in Augustine's thought.[76] This unity had its beginning in eternity in that the Son was eternally generated from the Father. Because of the Son's eternal existence, Augustine asserted, the Son had life in himself, as reflected in the testimony of John 5:26.

Second, the persons of the Trinity were also united in eternity, so they exhibit the same power. Their equality in coeternality was expressed in creation and in the sharing of eternal attributes. Augustine resolutely held that the unity of the Father and the Son was manifested in the incarnation—in the very nature of Christ's being born on earth.

Third, there was unity in the incarnation and sending of the Son. The unity of substance that referred back to eternal being and continued in the incarnation extended also in the sending of the Son. Augustine proposed that even though the sending of the Son exhibited a certain prioritization of the Father's will, the Son's obedience did not infer a diversity of nature between the Father and Son.

Finally, the godhead was unified in its works. Augustine asserted that the Son was coeternal and of equal substance with the Father. There was no disagreement between the works of the Father and Son; they were equal. The Father and the Son, as inseparable and equally wise, both choose to make the decisions they make, thus further exemplifying their unity of nature.

In A.D. 325 to 381, the church faced the pivotal question of whether the Son was *homoousios* with the Father. On this point, Augustine was convinced that one had to affirm that Christ's taking the form of a servant was a necessary component for a correct comprehension of the Nicene faith. For Augustine, the term *homoousios* meant quite literally that the Father and the Son are of the same substance. Thus Augustine was determined to demonstrate that God the Father and God the Son are one-and-the-same substance even after the incarnation.

The invasion of North Africa brought Augustine face to face with an Arian bishop named Maximinus. This contact led Augustine to reiterate his earlier works on Christ's unity. His emphasis on the unity of the divinity and humanity of Christ can be seen in his works as early as *Epistle 137*, and in his late work *Contra sermonem Arianorum* he reiterated that Jesus was a unity of human body, soul, and divinity—

76. Manlio Simonetti, "S. Agostino e gli Ariani," *Revue d'Études Augustiniennes et Patristiques* 13 (1967): 66.

a position he substantiated with Scripture.[77] Augustine implemented nearly identical arguments from his earlier work *De trinitate* to defend his conviction.[78]

Doctrine of the Holy Spirit. The early Arians taught that the Holy Spirit was the first work of Christ's creation. In response, Augustine articulated the united Trinity. The doctrine of the divinity of the Holy Spirit developed significantly through Augustine's work.

Augustine defined the Trinitarian unity in a Latin formula similar to one stated in other parts of his writings.[79] These three—the Father, Son, and Holy Spirit—are one God, the Trinity. They are one in that they are united in will, substance, and thought. The unity of the Trinity is seen in the invisibility of the three persons, in that the title *only wise God* may be applied to all three, and in that the Trinity is reflected in the unity of Spirit, water, and blood. The activity of the Trinity is also done in unity. Augustine taught that Jesus Christ and the Holy Spirit work in unity. The Holy Spirit takes part in the activity of the godhead—in the works of creation, the incarnation, and illumination.

The Holy Spirit's involvement in the works of the godhead implies the Spirit's full divinity and therefore his equality with the Father and the Son.[80] Augustine particularly emphasized that there is no inequality between the Son and the Holy Spirit, since the two are united in being and activity. He recognized the differences between the Son and

77. John Thomas Newton ("The Importance of Augustine's Use of the Neoplatonic Doctrine of Hypostatic Union for the Development of Christology," *Augustinian Studies* 2 [1971]: 1–17) was mistaken when he said on page 3 of his article: "This hypostatic union doctrine of the Incarnation becomes a rationale in the thought of Augustine which prevents him from developing any early modified form of the Kenotic theory as that found in Cyril of Alexandria." Already by the time of his *De trinitate*, Augustine had established a kenotic theory—one of the most important points of debate between Augustine and Maximinus. Certainly the hypostatic union did not keep Augustine from developing the kenotic theory.

78. Augustine, *De trinitate* 4.13; *CCSL* 50a, 182: "Quippe dei uerbo ad unitatem commixtus hinc ait [referring to the flesh]: 'Potestatem habeo ponendi animam meam et potestatem habeo iterum sumendi eam. Nemo tollit eam a me, sed ego pono eam a me, et iterum sumo eam.'"

79. Augustine, *Contra Maximinum Arianum* 2.10.2; *Patrologia Latina* 42.759–60: "In Trinitate igitur quae Deus est, et Pater Deus est, et Filius Deus est, et Spiritus sanctus Deus est, et simul hi tres unus Deus: nec hujus Trinitatis tertia pars est unus, nec major pars duo quam unus spiritualis, non corporalis est magnitudo."

80. Maximinus insisted that the Holy Spirit was either subordinate to the Father or to the Son. Augustine would not abide this attack. He utilized various passages from Scripture to support his defense against the argument—passages such as John 16:14; Luke 4:18, 21; and even Matthew 3:16.

175

the Holy Spirit, but he underlined that the differences are not in their respective natures, for in their natures there is equality.

Augustine also defended the fact that the Holy Spirit is equal not only to the Son but also to the Father. This equality is a necessary consequence of the unity of activity and being within the Trinity. In at least one example in Augustine's works, he pronounced that the Holy Spirit is equal to the Father, and he held that nowhere do the Scriptures teach any necessary inferiority in the Holy Spirit's relation to the Father.

Augustine defined the attributes of the Holy Spirit, beginning with his relationship to the other persons of the godhead. According to Augustine, the Holy Spirit proceeds from the Father and is sent from both the Father and the Son. Like the Father and the Son, the Holy Spirit is immutable. He was not created *ex nihilo* or from anything material. From 1 Corinthians 6:19 and 3:16, Augustine argued that the Holy Spirit was fully divine, yet dwells within people. Like the other two persons of the godhead, the Holy Spirit is invisible, even though he has appeared on earth. And perhaps of most importance, the Spirit—in conjunction with the Father—was responsible for the sending of the Son. Augustine associates this sending with Isaiah 48:12–16.

Augustine stressed that the attributes and works of the three persons of the Trinity should not be ascribed exclusively to one of its persons. For example, the Father and the Son send the Holy Spirit, and the Father and the Holy Spirit sent the Son. Yet Augustine credited the Holy Spirit as having several attributes that appear to be particularly his own—the activities of comforting the downcast, intercession, and the proclamation of the gospel.

Augustine's pneumatology can be best understood in conjunction with his Christology.[81] In fact, unless one first understands Augustine's pneumatology, he cannot fully comprehend his Christology. The

---

81. Wilhelm Geerlings, in *Christus Exemplum: Studien zur Christologie und Christusverkundigung Augustins*, Tübinger Theologische Studien Bd. 13 (Mainz: Matthias Grünewald Verlag, 1978), ended part of his investigation of Augustine's teaching with the conclusion that "there is no Augustinian Pneumatology." Such a verdict was premature, although somewhat understandable in that Geerlings emphasized Augustine's Christology in conjunction with his Trinitarian thought. See especially page 74 of Richard C. Gamble, review of *Christus Exemplum: Studien zur Christologie und Christusverkundigung Augustins*, by Wilhelm Geerlings, *Theologische Zeitschrift* 35, no. 6 (Nov/Dez 1979): 374–75.

Holy Spirit filled the Son; the Son and the Holy Spirit have an integral relationship—a unity of being and activity. Especially the mediatorial work of Christ should be considered in conjunction with the activity of the Holy Spirit. In *Tractatus in Johanni Evangelium 74.3*, Augustine states that the grace of the Holy Spirit was necessary for Jesus to perform his activity as mediator. The Holy Spirit was vital in Christ's incarnation, resurrection, and all the intervening activities of Jesus on the earth.[82]

Conclusion. The Princeton theologian Benjamin Breckinridge (known as B. B.) Warfield claimed that Augustine had "not merely created an epoch in the history of the Church, but has determined the course of its history in the West up to the present day."[83] Warfield credited the formulation and articulation of the Trinity entirely to Augustine, with one addition by John Calvin. More recently, Cornelius Van Til said that Augustine possessed a more biblical system of theology than any of his predecessors—even a more biblical view of the Bible itself.[84]

KEY TERMS

circumincession
eternal generation
Donatists
Manichaeans
Pelagians
concupiscence

STUDY QUESTIONS

1. Is the human soul the best analogy for the Trinity?
2. Why does the church need to fight against heretics and schismatics?

82. Geerlings failed to observe this important activity in his extended analysis of the person of Christ.

83. Benjamin B. Warfield, *Calvin and Augustine* (Philadelphia: Presbyterian and Reformed, 1956), 306.

84. Cornelius Van Til, *A Christian Theory of Knowledge* (Nutley, NJ: Presbyterian and Reformed, 1969), 118.

3. Have theologians such as Augustine given too many details about the Trinity?
4. How important is a deep understanding of the Trinity?
5. In what ways do you see Augustine's drawing from the thinking of Victorinus and Ambrose? In what ways can we benefit from their thinking?

RESOURCES FOR FURTHER STUDY

Brown, Peter. *Augustine of Hippo: A Biography*. Rev. ed. Berkeley/Los Angeles: University of California Press, 2000. An excellent biography of Augustine.

Dudden, Frederick Homes. *The Life and Times of Saint Ambrose*. Oxford: Clarendon, 1935. An excellent, full-length biography and theological analysis.

Meagher, Robert E. *An Introduction to Augustine*. New York: New York University Press, 1978. A topical presentation of Augustine's thinking through a selective presentation of primary texts, with elaboration at the end of each chapter.

Van der Meer, Frederic. *Augustine the Bishop: The Life and Work of a Father of the Church*. Translated by B. Battershaw and G. R. Lamb. London: Sheed and Ward, 1978. Takes readers back in time to understand what the city was like, popular piety and how the people worshipped, and how Augustine preached.

6

Early Christian Church Life

IN THE FOURTH CENTURY, the life of the church began to change. This chapter examines the developments in the church with regard to its organization, attitudes, and forms of worship.

CHURCH STRUCTURES[1]

General. After Constantine became emperor of Rome in A.D. 312, a shift occurred in the development of the church.[2] Christianity became the official religion of the Roman Empire. By A.D. 321, churches were legally established, Sunday was honored as a holy day throughout the empire, bishops were permitted to judge in legal matters, and state funds built church buildings. Heretics were now considered civil outlaws.[3] This era of the first "imperial church"—the state church of the Roman Empire—was one of cultural and religious integration.

Synods and Congregations. The legal structure during this time was tied to the church. When issues arose, the emperor called large, empire-wide meetings known as "ecumenical synods." The decisions made at these synods became imperial law. Smaller, provincial synods were supposed to meet twice a year, though they often met less frequently,[4] but their decisions did not carry the weight of law.

---

1. See Richard C. Gamble, "Presbyterianism and the Ancient Church," in *Pressing Toward the Mark: Essays Commemorating Fifty Years of the Orthodox Presbyterian Church*, ed. Charles G. Dennison and Richard C. Gamble (Philadelphia: Committee for the Historian of the Orthodox Presbyterian Church, 1986), 53–62.
2. Karl Heussi, *Kompendium der Kirchengeschichte* (Tübingen: Mohr Siebeck, 1971), 81.
3. Ibid., 81–82.
4. Ibid., 82.

The provinces' capital cities were, most often, the main church centers. In the West, where the church spoke Latin, Rome was the center of power. In the East, power revolved around Alexandria and Antioch. After A.D. 381, the city of Constantinople also rose to prominence.[5]

In the capital city, the chief pastor, referred to as the *metropolitan*, enjoyed privileges over other bishops of smaller churches. Thus bishops became subject to a metropolitan, who often had no connection to their city whatsoever. Bishops were also now employees of the state.[6]

Social Life in the Church through the Fifth Century[7]

Apostolic Age. In the NT, the apostles provided a number of rules for Christian living. They called Christians to abstain from all lusts, renounce idolatry and sin, clothe themselves with righteousness and virtue, and pray. Christians were to subject themselves in a graded series of social relationships: wives to husbands, children to parents, slaves to masters, and all to the civil power. Put simply, the apostles called believers to be holy in every sphere of their religious and common lives.

Based on these apostolic imperatives, a general policy of Christian life developed in the church.[8] The church community was distinct from, and in many ways set against, the pagan community. For example, the Greeks saw work as the activity of servants and slaves. The Romans regarded labors as beneath the dignity of a Roman citizen. But the church gained a new perspective on work. The church saw dignity in even the lowest, most degrading work—that done by slaves. Christians worked hard so as not to be a burden to others. They also sought to obtain the wherewithal to help the needy and to make a good impression on non-Christian workers so as to commend the faith to them.

Within the Christian community, social distinctions were to disintegrate.[9] At this time, the majority of Christians lived as members

5. Ibid., 82–83.

6. Ibid., 83. In A.D. 324, Constantine assumed control of the eastern half of the empire.

7. Philip Schaff, *History of the Christian Church*, 8 vols. (Grand Rapids: Eerdmans, 1979), 3:356.

8. On the Christian's relationship to the state, see Richard C. Gamble, *The Whole Counsel of God*, vol. 2, *The Full Revelation of God* (Phillipsburg, NJ: P&R Publishing, 2018) (WCG2), 514–20. For analysis of the Christian life, see chapters 19–23.

9. Nevertheless, there was no attempt to set aside slavery as a system.

of the lower classes. In the life of the church, however, humble beginnings were no hindrance—some of the pastors of larger churches were former slaves.

The apostolic fathers and the church of the second century also emphasized right conduct. But right conduct was emphasized to such an extent that the Christian life was becoming an observance of a set of rules. We know more about what was forbidden than what was positively suggested for Christians living at this time. Abortion was forbidden. Believers were prohibited from holding certain jobs and professions—as interpreters of omens, enchanters, and astrologers, for example. But no rule prohibited a Christian from being in the armed service.

The church at this time began to emphasize restraint, even from luxurious food and dress. Christians refused to participate in many pagan festivals. They avoided most public shows. Positively, they were encouraged to engage in godly conversation and enjoy nature.

Third Century. As the church grew and developed, so did its rules. Christianity continued to prohibit certain forms of work, and a more complete and comprehensive social transformation became necessary for those who converted to Christianity. The *Apostolic Tradition* taught: "If a man is a pimp, he must desist or be rejected. If a man is a sculptor or painter, he must be charged not to make idols; if he does not desist, he must be rejected. If a man is an actor or pantomimist, he must desist or be rejected. A teacher of young children had best desist."[10] Essentially, every sphere of life was addressed by theologians. Clement of Alexandria and Tertullian even provided complete lists of which foods could be eaten. For example, boiled meat could be eaten, but roasted meat could not be.

Extravagance in clothing was not tolerated. Christian men were not to shave—they were to let their beards grow naturally. Using dice and cards was not permitted; neither was attendance at theaters.[11] Instead, Christians were to lead quiet lives, read Scripture, and speak of godly things.

After Nicaea. Christianity continued to be a religion of the working class, so the church continued to urge hard work and frugality.

---

10. *Apostolic Tradition of Hippolytus*, chapter 16, as cited in J. G. Davies, *The Early Christian Church: A History of Its First Five Centuries* (Grand Rapids: Baker, 1980), 156–57.
   11. Ibid., 158.

The prohibitions against certain occupations continued, with a new addition: moneylending. One of the canons of the Council of Nicaea required any minister who had lent money at interest to be deprived of his office. Many Eastern and Western fathers condemned usury or charging excessive interest.

The church believed food was not to be sumptuous but instead simply a means of nourishing the body. Christians were even encouraged to eat only one meal per day so that only one hour in twenty-four would be spent satisfying the body. In an attempt to sanctify even this one hour, prayers were said before meals. The clothing of a Christian was to be as simple as possible, and no makeup of any kind was to be worn.

For leisure, Christians were to avoid theaters, public sports, and drinking, and they were not so much as to enter a tavern. Instead, they were to rest at home and read the Scriptures. Positively, the Christian home was to be one of hospitality, with time set aside for godly conversation. Christians were encouraged to participate in public good works, such as providing food for the poor and establishing hospitals for the sick.

Union of Church and State. Prior to Constantine, Christianity was an illegal religion, and the church suffered at the hands of the state. Its treatment of the church ranged from severe persecution to mild toleration. So Constantine's integration of the church and the state offered a number of changes for the life of the church.

One positive effect of this integration was that the clergy were now exempt from many public responsibilities. They were under no obligation to serve in the military and were taxed at a much lower rate. Naturally, it was not long before these privileges were abused, thereby resulting in the barring of the wealthy from ministerial service. Another positive effect came in the endowing of church buildings. Believers needed places of worship in which to congregate, and the government provided these buildings. Ministers also received fixed incomes from church and state treasuries and were thus provided with economic stability.

In the pagan world at the time, women were not treated well. But under Constantine, the Bible's teaching on the equality of men and women in the eyes of God bore political fruit, and women were given more equitable rights. In A.D. 321, Constantine granted women the right to control their own property. In A.D. 390, Emperor Theodosius I (A.D. 379–395) gave women rights of guardianship of their children; to this point, such rights had been the sole privilege of men. The rape of widows was now punishable by death, and attempts, though unsuccessful, were made to halt prostitution. Finally, the church also abolished the bloody gladiatorial games.[12]

But this integration of church and state was not without its negative effects. In short, this period of institutional Christianity witnessed the secularization of the church. The church aligned herself with the masses of heathendom, who were now following the so-called *rules* of Christianity without Christian hearts. This secularization took its toll on church leaders. The Christianity of the catacombs and crosses became a Christianity of palaces and prelates.[13] At the time of Bishop Damascus (post A.D. 366), a rich aristocrat in Rome named Iraetextatus claimed that he would gladly become a Christian if he could become the bishop of Rome. The opulence of papal entertainments was more lavish than that even of the emperors.[14]

In many ways, Christianity became acceptable to the masses—and even to the intellectuals. But as Christianity flooded the secular culture, a negative meshing of both cultures occurred. People now wore the same clothes to church as they had worn to the theater. Within the Christian community, morality began to erode. Many bishops began to be concerned more with gaining the favor of the world than pursuing discipline. John Chrysostom, however, was an exception to this trend, and his example of pursuing even the empress with discipline stands in contrast to the laxity that was prevalent in his era.[15] Chrysostom admonished ministers to prevent the unworthy—even the unworthy who had power—from partaking in communion.[16]

---

12. Schaff, *History*, 3:122.

13. Diarmaid MacCulloch, *Christianity: The First Three Thousand Years* (New York: Viking, 2010), 195.

14. Schaff, *History*, 3:127–28; Henry Chadwick, *The Early Church* (Grand Rapids: Eerdmans, 1967), 161.

15. See chapter 4.

16. Chrysostom as cited by Schaff, *History*, 3:358–59: "Though a captain, or a governor, nay, even one adorned with the imperial crown approach the table of the Lord unworthily, prevent him; you have greater authority than he. . . . Beware lest you excite the Lord to wrath, and give a sword instead of food. In addition, if a new Judas should approach the communion,

Ambrose, theologian of Milan, embodied another exception to this general erosion. In ca. A.D. 390, Ambrose refused to allow Emperor Theodosius I to partake in the Lord's Supper, theologically orthodox though Theodosius may have been. Ambrose's reason for the refusal was that following rioting in Thessalonica, Theodosius had seven thousand people executed. Believing his hands to be too stained with blood, Ambrose refused him communion. Eight months after being denied the Lord's Supper, the emperor publicly repented. He announced that from then on, he would wait thirty days before inflicting the death penalty—that life would not be taken in the heat of rage and that, if necessary, the stated penalty could be revoked.[17]

But the Eastern church, in great contrast to its earlier practice of guarding the Lord's Supper, permitted everyone to partake who considered himself worthy. Additionally, in A.D. 390 the Eastern church abandoned its practice of prescribed penance supervised by a deacon or minister.

As this fusion of church and state continued, church discipline began to be enforced by civil penalties. Heresy was considered the worst of crimes against society. And so began an era of the church/state persecution of heretics. The punishments began as relatively mild—banishment and the confiscation of property. But after the rule of Emperor Theodosius I, the death penalty began to be issued. From this moment in history until the eighteenth century, the statewide persecution of heretics was considered a normal legal occurrence.

In his endeavors to spread Arianism throughout the empire, Constantius, Constantine's son, heavily persecuted the orthodox Athanasian party. Emperor Julian the Apostate attempted to restore Rome to its former, pre-Christian virtue and religious practices. He feared that the conflict between the factions of Christianity could result in the dissolution of the empire.

Flavius Theodosius, a man raised in the faith, ruled as emperor of Rome from A.D. 379 to 395. Known as Theodosius the Great, he supported the authority of the Nicene Creed and made pagan idolatry—and all heresy, for that matter—punishable by death. One year into his

---

prevent him. Fear God, not man. If you fear man, he will treat you with scorn; if you fear God, you will appear venerable even to men."

17. Ibid., 3:359.

rule as emperor, Theodosius issued his first edict against heretics. He forbade them from even gathering together. As the years progressed, he would issue no fewer than another fifteen edicts against heretics. He even issued the death penalty for Manichaeans and the Quarto-decimians, who simply held Easter on a different date.

Theodosius was not primarily bent on punishing heretics. His goal was to convert pagans and heretics by terrifying them into submission to the Christian faith. But blood was still shed, the first streams of which flowed in A.D. 385 when followers of a Manichaean sect, known as the Priscillianists, were beheaded.

As foreign and barbaric as this notion of Christian-sanctioned persecution may be to us today, at that time it was advocated almost unanimously by the church. Even Chrysostom, who thought it unwise to execute heretics, supported the banning of pagan assemblies and the confiscation of their property. Jerome, however, advocated the death penalty for heretics; he cited Deuteronomy 13:6–10 in support of his position.[18]

Augustine, a former member of a Manichaean sect, initially opposed the violent persecution of heretics. But his mind soon changed. In his arguments with the Donatists, he soon realized that this group could not be won over with reason. So he began to offer reasons why heretics should, in fact, be physically punished. His primary reason argued that if the state had the responsibility to punish crimes, then it also had the responsibility to punish religious error. He appealed to Galatians 5:19–20 for support by reasoning that both adultery and religious faction stem from the flesh. Shortly after Augustine's change in stance, Pope Leo the Great (A.D. 440–461) also began to advocate the death penalty for heretics.

In early Roman history, emperors acted as priests within the imperial cult. So when the empire put on the garb of Christianity, the emperor assumed a position of authority in the church. This practice began with Constantine, who preached sermons, instituted and deposed bishops, and acted as a patron and the universal temporal bishop of the church. Constantine enjoyed these privileges before he was even baptized![19] His son, Constantius, was called the "bishop of bishops."

18. Ibid., 3:144n2.
19. MacCulloch, *Christianity*, 191.

From this time on, the priesthood and the kingdom became divided. The church controlled doctrinal matters, and the government managed discipline and the rule of the people. But as would be expected, this division was not so simple, and mutual encroachment ensued.

The emperors were actively involved in most church affairs. They participated in disputes, punished heretics, nominated or confirmed influential bishops, and even to a limited extent issued ecclesiastical edicts without calling general councils of the church.[20]

This new state was regarded as a restoration of the theocracy—one birthed in Christian soil. The emperor protected the church, supported her, and had the right to oversee her external affairs. But this oversight went in both directions. As the emperor was understood to be one of the heads of the church, so also the pope and his bishops balanced the emperor and his magistrates. This strong hierarchy within the church kept her from becoming the playground of tyrants.

WORSHIP AND SACRAMENTS THROUGH THE SIXTH CENTURY

Paganization of Worship. Before Nicaea, Christian worship may have seen some influence from the mystery religions, but worship changed after Constantine.[21] With the union of church and state, the church began to introduce glamour and show into Christian worship. In many ways, the church was now in competition with the beauty and elaborate worship of the pagan temple.[22] In addition, pagans entered the church in masses. As a result, worship began to become paganized—the sacraments took on a magical tone, and idols began to be worshiped in iconography.[23]

Formal worship also saw a change in its emphasis. From A.D. 350 to 400, the pinnacle of worship was the sermon. Later, the celebration of the Eucharist, or the Mass, became central to the worship service.[24]

Baptism. Baptism is the sacrament whereby an individual is admitted into the fellowship of the church. There is some discussion among

20. Schaff, *History*, 3:136.
21. Heussi, *Kompendium*, 84–85.
22. Ibid., 85.
23. Ibid., 85–86.
24. Ibid., 86.

NT scholars as to how baptism was administered during the time of the NT.[25] There is no doubt, however, that in the period of the apostolic fathers, baptism was the rite of initiation into the church.

In the second century, baptism was usually preceded by a period of instruction and fasting.[26] Following their time of fasting and being taught, new believers were brought to a place where there was water for baptism. The manner of baptism was not strictly prescribed. The *Didache* says that a believer should be baptized in running water. If it was not available, other water was allowed, with cold water being preferable to warm water. If only a small amount of water was available, then the minister poured water three times on the head. Baptism was to be done in the threefold name of the Father, Son, and Holy Spirit. Often, the new converts being baptized were clothed in white robes.

As time progressed, baptism became, on occasion, more elaborate. In the East, a person being baptized was sometimes dressed in a special robe and crowned with a garland as a symbol of the presence of Christ. But the few records we have of this style of baptism in no way indicate that this practice was normative.

From the third century, we have accounts of baptisms in the writings of Tertullian, Cyprian, and Hippolytus. These three theologians agree that, in baptism, the adult convert was dipped or immersed in water and then gave a confession of his or her faith.

Most often there was a set time in the year for baptisms, namely, around Pentecost or Easter. In preparation for baptism, converts spent a day in prayer and fasting. After immersion, they were anointed with oil and had hands laid on them to receive the Holy Spirit. In Rome, former heathens were given three years of instruction in the Christian faith before they were baptized. Going beyond these basic elements of baptism at the time, some rituals were more elaborate—they involved anointings, exorcisms, and signs of the cross.

---

25. See *WCG* 2:847–54.

26. Davies, *Early Christian Church*, 104: "The second-century fathers believed that baptism was a means of conveying the Holy Spirit, it provided weapons for spiritual combat . . . and was therefore 'spiritual circumcision' in contradiction to the carnal circumcision of the Old Israel; it is a means of rebirth, and was the seal of eternal life. This final term 'seal' was applied frequently to baptism during this period. The word was used of a mark to identify property, like a brand. Since to be initiated is to be stamped with the name of Christ, baptism meant that they had become God's property."

Though infant baptism had not received universal approval, it was in vogue and often occurred within just days of birth, as Cyprian notes. Despite its popularity, Tertullian did not think the baptizing of infants was proper.

After the Council of Nicaea, baptism became quite elaborate. Ceremonies differed based on geographical region, but there were several lines of continuity. The baptized were immersed, often being dipped three times into the water to symbolize Christ's three days in the tomb. The evidence indicates that adult converts were baptized naked, then dressed in white robes after their baptism. A minister anointed the baptized with oil, and they made a confession of faith in Christ and renounced the Devil. Some baptisms involved candles or the exorcism of evil spirits.

In the fifth and sixth centuries, the observance of baptism became more regularized. It included some six constant functions: undressing, anointing with oil, renunciation, blessing of the font, declaration of faith, and putting on of white robes. One of the most interesting elements of early baptism is renunciation. The converts renounced the Devil and all his works. In some churches, converts renounced not only the Devil but also the world and its pleasures.

Lord's Supper.[27] After a convert was baptized, the Lord's Supper was celebrated. Justin Martyr provided a thorough account of how the Lord's Supper was performed in Rome:

> They meet on Sunday because it is the first day in which God, having wrought a change in the darkness and light, made the world and Jesus Christ our Savior on the same day rose from the dead. The service began with readings from the memoirs of the apostles or the writings of the prophets; this was followed by a sermon from the president; then all stood for public prayers. After a kiss of peace, bread and a cup of wine mixed with water were brought to the pastor who offered prayers and thanksgivings to which people responded with the word amen.[28]

The ancient church also celebrated an agape feast, though scholars disagree as to its exact nature. The feast was, at the very least, a

---

27. For NT practice, see WCG 2:854–56.
28. Justin Martyr, *First Apology*, chapter 61, in *Writings of Saint Justin Martyr*, ed. Ludwig Schopp (New York: Christian Heritage Inc., 1948).

quasi-religious gathering. During this feast the church assembled, thanksgiving was given over wine, the bread was blessed and eaten, then the meal was closed with a final thanksgiving.[29]

We have more information about the Lord's Supper in the third century. Worship services began to look more similar to our own: the reading of Scripture, saying of prayers (including those for the emperor), singing of psalms, and sometimes also exchanging the kiss of peace. Then the deacons distributed bread and wine mixed with water.

The simplicity of the Reformation's teaching on the celebration of the Lord's Supper contrasts greatly with its celebration by the ancient church. With the ascension of Constantine, everything changed. The small, persecuted minority that comprised the church became the masses. The celebration of the Lord's Supper changed as well. While the doors had been closed to curious outsiders during the Lord's Supper, now the ceremony was public and formalized. More prayers were said before the Supper, and in the East these prayers became memorized litanies. Often a collection of gifts was taken before the celebration and a psalm sung during the service.

The theology of the Lord's Supper also began to develop. In the West, the notion of transubstantiation was not yet predominant. Augustine made a distinction between the bread and wine's serving as signs and their being taken as real blood and flesh. He believed the elements to be effective symbols that conveyed the invisible grace of God. That grace, however, was not to be identified with Christ's historical body; it was the gift of life.

In the East, however, Chrysostom spoke of "eating" Christ. He also said the wine was identical to the blood that flowed from Christ's side. Chrysostom believed that the nature of the wheat and grapes underwent a sort of change in the celebration of the Lord's Supper. Thus began the doctrine of transubstantiation, which would soon spread to the Western church.

Confession, Prayer, Fasting, and Calendar. Scripture teaches that even though people come to saving faith in Jesus Christ, they are not entirely free from sin. The ancient church wrestled with the possibility of sinless perfection. Some thought that it was possible, while others

---

29. See David P. Moessner, *Lord of the Banquet: The Literary and Theological Significance of the Lukan Travel Narrative* (Minneapolis: Fortress, 1989), 275.

denied that it was. Clement of Alexandria claimed that the goal of Christian maturity was sinlessness. He believed that the mature Christian should no longer face temptations or lusts. The regenerated soul was to mirror God by ruling over its own irrational desires and yearnings for pleasure. But Clement admitted that he knew of no one who had attained perfection while human. On the other hand, Cyprian claimed that perfection was impossible, and he admitted to sinning daily. Pelagius believed that Christians could attain perfection, for if Christ commanded perfection, then it must be possible to achieve.[30] In the *Didache*, Christians are exhorted to confess their sins in the church, particularly before the Lord's Supper. Although we do not have enough information to know exactly what this practice looked like in the early church, we know that the confession of sin was essential to the life of the church.

According to Cyprian, God had ordained means for Christians to walk in maturity—means such as daily Bible reading, prayer, and the singing of psalms and hymns. Of these activities, prayer was the most important, and the early church began to establish set times for prayer, both during the day and at night. Tertullian mentions praying three times a day.[31]

The order of virgins, which developed in this era, constituted another means of measuring Christian maturity. The early church prized celibacy. Athenagoras even said that celibacy brings the believer closer to God. Tertullian recommended celibacy for believers but did not go so far as to reject marriage. Origen agreed—celibacy was simply a better state for the believer to be in. Cyprian contended that celibates had greater rewards waiting for them in heaven. Methodius pointed to the example of Jesus as support for celibacy; he argued that the celibate life was to be preferred for practical reasons. Methodius even equated celibacy with martyrdom. Since Christians were no longer martyred for their faith, celibacy assumed the highest calling of the Christian life. Cyprian claimed that martyrs had a hundredfold reward awaiting them in heaven and virgins a sixtyfold reward.[32]

---

30. Greg R. Allison, *Historical Theology: An Introduction to Christian Doctrine—A Companion to Wayne Grudem's Systematic Theology* (Grand Rapids: Zondervan, 2011), 524–25.

31. Tertullian's three times became expanded in later centuries to seven times, known as the offices of prayer. See ibid., 525–26.

32. Ibid., 527.

Prayer and fasting also marked the life of the early church. The *Didache* exhorts Christians to pray; they were to recite the Lord's Prayer and to pray three times a day. Fasting was a normal practice among the Jews even in Jesus's day, and this practice continued in the life of the early church. The church fasted on Wednesdays and Fridays, in contrast to the Jewish community's fast on Mondays and Thursdays. The goal of fasting was to discipline the body. The money that normally would have been spent on food was used to provide for the poor. Those who fasted did not abstain entirely from food, but they ate only bread and drank only water.

In the early church, most worship occurred in house churches. Sometimes a house was bought communally, and architectural changes were made to facilitate worship. There exists a third-century record of church buildings—and a record of the destruction of church buildings during the Diocletian persecution.

The church began to create uniformity in the practice of penance. It included three elements: confession, penitential exercises, and absolution or reconciliation. For ordinary sins, prayer, almsgiving, and mutual forgiveness were sufficient. Public penance was reserved for graver faults. But many decades passed before a consensus was reached regarding what these "graver faults" were and how the church should respond.

In the last years of the second century, adultery, murder, and idolatry seem to have been treated as irremissible. Callistus of Rome, however, held a more lenient policy toward such sins. Cyprian lamented that by his day morality had so deteriorated that sexual sins and idolatry were regarded as remissible.

The conversion of Constantine changed much in the life of the church. Many at best nominal Christians flooded into the church. The church had to develop new methods of instructing these largely unconverted masses. She sought to present the gospel to these large congregations in creative ways, including through the church calendar. For example, Christmas day was established on December 25 to draw converts away from the pagan solemnities associated with that date. Lent was also added to the calendar, with forty days of nominal fasting, as were Easter, the Feast of the Ascension, and Pentecost.

Monasticism[33]

The monastic movement had its beginnings in Egypt in the fourth century. But it spread rapidly, beginning in the East and moving to the West.[34] Christians began to feel called to a reclusive life withdrawn from the world and its temptations. During the time of state-sanctioned persecution, little within the church drew it toward monasticism. It was relatively easy for the church to stand against the ways of the world under an oppressive system. But when persecution lifted and Christianity became the statewide religion, standing against the world became more complicated. With the rise of Christianity came a concomitant increase in the desire for monastic life.

By the close of the fourth century, there were thousands of monks. What was the draw to this reclusive lifestyle? During its earliest phase of development in the fourth century, the monastic life was considered self-inflicted martyrdom on the part of those who pursued it. The monks engaged in torturous mortification of their natural desires in their seeking the same heavenly glory that the martyrs met through their bloody deaths under persecution.[35] Devout Christians began to use monasticism as a means of living in such a way on the earth, no matter how painful, as to earn the highest heavenly reward. It was a practical way of disengaging from the world and dedicating oneself to holiness and God.[36]

Types. Initially, three types of monastic movements arose. One group engaged in ascetic practices but did not withdraw from social life. Essentially, they were "half monks." Another group withdrew entirely from society and dwelt in caves. They clothed themselves in animal skins and lived on bread and salt. These men were hermits—they lived the monastic life alone, like Saint Antony did. They fled from the world to fight demons in the wilderness. This movement gained

33. See Richard C. Gamble, "Medieval Monasticism," *Tabletalk Magazine*, January 1, 1995, 14–15, 53.

34. Heussi, *Kompendium*, 89–90; MacCulloch, *Christianity*, 203.

35. MacCulloch (*Christianity*, 201) argues that "all Christian monasticism is an implied criticism of the Church's decision to become a large-scale and inclusive organization." He elaborates: "the most 'orthodox' of hermits, simply by his style of life, denied the whole basis on which the Church had come to be organized, the Eucharistic community presided over by the bishop" (ibid., 204).

36. See the previous chapter for information on monasticism.

little traction in the West because of its more extreme climate. The third group lived in cloisters. These men spent their lives in labor and religious devotion. Whatever leftover food was in their monasteries they gave to the poor.[37]

When Augustine returned to North Africa from Italy, he gathered a group who were willing to leave behind their belongings and livelihoods. He then prescribed rules for living, and so were born the Augustinian monks. It is from the Augustinians that Martin Luther would one day come.[38]

From these communities there are shocking tales of self-denial, many of them only stories but ones most likely based in reality. One monk ate only once a week and slept standing up while leaning on his staff. Some never ate bread. Some would deprive themselves of sleep for nights on end. Others would fast for seven days at a time. One monk, named Symeon, spent thirty-six years praying, fasting, and preaching on the top of a thirty-to-forty-foot pillar. He ate once a week. Some monks would spend their entire lives in a cell—they never stepped out of it. They would not cut their hair or trim their beards except at Easter.

Monastic life, however, was not without its spiritual benefits. In one monastery, the monks would rise in the dark of the morning and sing hymns, pray, and read Scripture before heading to work. They paused from work to pray again at 9:00 A.M., noon, and 3:00 P.M. After work, dinner would consist in a simple meal of bread, salt, and occasionally vegetables. They would then sing a hymn of thanksgiving and return to their straw beds for the night.

The climate of the East was more accommodating to the monastic life, but the West also developed a cloister life. The greatest impetus for cloister life in the West came from Benedict.

Benedict of Nursia (A.D. 480–547). At the age of fifteen, Benedict left school to be a monk. As a monk, he experienced a time of temptation to abandon his solitude and be with a woman. Disgusted by his desires, he undressed and rolled naked on thorns and briers until the lustful passions were extinguished. In his life, he established twelve

---

37. Davies, *Early Christian Church*, 184–87.
38. Ibid., 244–45.

cloisters, each with twelve monks and a superior. Tales of his miraculous power abound. Some said he was even able to raise the dead.

In A.D. 529, Benedict wrote the Benedictine rules for these monastic communities.[39] The rules explained how to live a christocentric life and how a monastic community should function—they served as the foundation for monasticism in the Middle Ages. *The Rule of St. Benedict* spoke of the life of a monk as an obedient and humble existence. Monks in these communities were named Black Monks because they wore tunics with black hoods. They fasted two days a week, with "fast" meaning that they ate only one meal that day. The normal meal for a monk was a pound of bread, vegetables, and half a bottle of wine, all consumed in complete silence. Meat was reserved for the sick. A monk had no personal property; even his clothing was owned by the order.[40] In the West the Benedictine monks gave monasticism a permanent form.

KEY TERMS

Benedictine rules
Eucharist
transubstantiation

STUDY QUESTIONS

1. Why could calling large synods be helpful to the church?
2. Was the church more pure before the time of Constantine?
3. Should the church be concerned with how believers eat, dress, and behave?
4. What is the secularization of Christianity?

39. Benedict, prologue to *The Rule of St. Benedict*, as cited by Allison, *Historical Theology*, 528: "If we want to escape the sufferings of hell and reach eternal life, we must hurry to do now what may benefit us for eternity. . . . Never abandoning God's rule, but persevering in his teaching in the monastery until death, we will patiently share in the sufferings of Christ, so that we may deserve to be sharers in his kingdom as well." Evangelism was done by monks such as Saint Patrick in Ireland. Irish monks spread the gospel to others in the British Isles and on to the Continent.

40. Davies, *Early Christian Church*, 244.

5. Should the church and the state be connected in any way?
6. What were the various modes of baptism in the ancient church?
7. How did the ancient church deal with more public sins?
8. Why do you think monasticism developed?
9. What can we learn from the monastic movement?

RESOURCES FOR FURTHER STUDY

This period of church history is very different from our own.

Davies, J. G. *The Early Christian Church: A History of Its First Five Centuries*. Grand Rapids: Baker, 1980. A classic and reliable text.

Allen, George Cantrell. *The Didache: Or, The Teaching of the Twelve Apostles*. London: Astolat Press, 1903.

Benedict. *The Rule of St. Benedict*. Edited and translated by Bruce L. Venarde. Dumbarton Oaks Medieval Library 6. Cambridge: Harvard University Press, 2011.

7

Later Patristic Theology

THIS CHAPTER SUMMARIZES THE development of doctrine during the patristic age—the age of the church fathers. Theologians during this time dove deeply into the doctrine of God—they were particularly concerned to discuss the nature and relationship of the members of the Trinity. This time was one of massive christological debate that began with the Council of Ephesus in A.D. 431 and ended with the Third Council of Constantinople against Monothelitism, which met in the years A.D. 680 to 681. The Council of Chalcedon of A.D. 451 marks the most important point in this tumultuous period.[1]

DOCTRINE OF GOD

Existence and Knowability. The church fathers believed God to be knowable through several mediums. The first was providence. Theophilus and Lactantius argued that the ordered design of the world—season following season and day following night—required a God who ordered such events in his providence.[2]

The church fathers also believed that God was knowable through humanity's self-awareness. Arnobius contended that men—by natural instinct—know that God is the king and ruler of all things. Tertullian believed this innate sense of God to be an even stronger argument than the testimony of creation.[3]

---

1. Aloys Grillmeier, *Christ in Christian Tradition*, vol. 1, *From the Apostolic Age to Chalcedon (451)*, trans. John Bowden (Atlanta: John Knox Press, 1975), 443.
2. Greg R. Allison, *Historical Theology: An Introduction to Christian Doctrine—A Companion to Wayne Grudem's Systematic Theology* (Grand Rapids: Zondervan, 2011), 188–89.
3. Allison, *Historical Theology*, 189.

The third medium through which God could be known, according to the church fathers, was his Word. Tertullian held that Scripture was the best testimony of God's existence, for his Word is clear, full, and commanding.[4]

Augustine used Romans 1:18–23 to argue that all men instinctively know that God exists no matter how much they attempt to suppress that knowledge. He claimed that there is an innate knowledge within men even of God as the Trinity, for humanity reflects the triune nature of God. For example, Augustine saw a reflection of the triune God in the human mind, memory, and understanding.[5]

The later church fathers unanimously affirmed the incomprehensibility of God—that while man can know God, the depths of God can never be exhausted. Aristides referred to the nature of God as *unsearchable*. Lactantius, Cyprian, and Origen taught that the infinite chasm of difference between God and men makes him incomprehensible to humans.[6] Chrysostom claimed that God alone possesses exhaustive knowledge of himself.

Several later patristic authors even held that God was inexpressible, by which they meant that humanity cannot so much as even speak of the divine. Clement of Alexandria taught that human language falls short of describing who and what God is.[7] Arnobius, in agreement, argued that God can only be described by what he is not, the so-called *via negativa* approach.[8] Augustine recognized that human language stammers in its attempts to speak of God in a worthy manner, but even to say that God is inexpressible is still to speak of him![9] Next we will examine the church fathers' understanding of God's attributes.

Character or Attributes. Augustine wrote extensively on the Trinity and doctrine of God. He believed that God's characteristics do not add

4. Tertullian, *Adversus Marcionem* I.xviii, as cited by Douglas F. Kelly, *Systematic Theology*, vol. 1, *The God Who Is the Holy Trinity* (Fearn, Scotland: Mentor, 2008), 16.

5. Allison, *Historical Theology*, 191.

6. Ibid., 189–90.

7. Ibid., 190. See Clement, in A. Cleveland Coxe, ed., *The Ante-Nicene Fathers*, vol. 2, *Fathers of the Second Century: Hermas, Tatian, Athenagoras, Theophilus, and Clement of Alexandria* (Grand Rapids: Eerdmans, 1988), 462–63.

8. Allison, *Historial Theology*, 190; A. Cleveland Coxe, ed., *The Ante-Nicene Fathers*, vol. 6, *Gregory Thaumaturgus, Dionysius the Great, Julius Africanus, Anatolius and Minor Writers, Methodius, Arnobius* (Grand Rapids: Eerdmans, 1988), 421.

9. Allison, *Historial Theology*, 191–92.

to his essence; neither do his attributes, when joined together, compose his essence. Each attribute is true of the totality of his essence and thus cannot be separated from his essence.[10]

Augustine argued that nothing is incomprehensible to the infinite knowledge of God; he compared God's omniscience to mathematical infinity. He also believed God's impassibility to mean that he was beyond human affections and passions.[11] Augustine held that the presence of God is everywhere wholly—not split between Pittsburgh and Philadelphia—meaning that he is omnipresent. While God is omnipotent, reasoned Augustine, there are certain things that he is unable to do: "God is almighty, and yet, though almighty, he cannot die, cannot be deceived, cannot lie. . . . How many things that he cannot do, and yet is almighty! Indeed, for this reason, he is almighty because he cannot do these things."[12]

Trinity.[13] The rise of Arianism generated the need for the Nicene Creed. In its defense, Athanasius spoke of the eternal generation of the Son, which makes it impossible for the Son to be a created being. The Son is equal to the Father in all things yet is distinct from him. "In whatever the Father is, so is the Son, with one exception—the Son is not the Father."[14] The Holy Spirit is not a creature, for he proceeds from the Father and has the same oneness with the Son as the Son does with the Father. The Son and the Spirit are in one another and are never separated; likewise, they are joined with the Father. The Son and Holy Spirit are *homoousios* and consubstantial with the Father. The three are eternal and equal, yet distinct.[15]

The Cappadocian fathers also advanced the discussion of the Trinity. Basil of Caesarea described the relationship between *ousia* and *hypostasis* as the "common" and the "particular." *Ousia* is that which is common to all three persons—for example, their godhead. *Hypostasis*, though, is the special property of each person—for example, fatherhood, sonship, and sanctification. The Cappadocian fathers

10. Ibid., 213.
11. Ibid., 214.
12. Augustine, *On the Creed*, as cited by Allison, *Historical Theology*, 215.
13. For information on the early doctrine of the Trinity, see chapter 3.
14. Allison, *Historical Theology*, 238–39.
15. Joel R. Beeke and Paul M. Smalley, *Reformed Systematic Theology*, vol. 1, *Revelation and God* (Wheaton, IL: Crossway, 2019), 906.

developed the essential notion of mutual indwelling, called *pericho-resis*. This word is used to speak of the union of the three persons in their essence and power, while also allowing for the individuality of each person. The three glorify one another.

Though united, the three persons have unique attributes indicative of their person. Basil thought those attributes to be fatherhood, sonship, and sanctification, while Gregory of Nazianzus considered them to be the Father's unbegottenness, the Son's generation, and the Holy Spirit's procession. Gregory of Nyssa said that the persons of the Trinity are distinguished on the basis of cause and that which is caused. With their careful elaboration of the relationship between *ousia* and *hypostasis*, the three Cappadocians tried to maintain a balanced doctrine.[16]

Augustine made further Trinitarian advances.[17] He laid the groundwork for the double procession of the Holy Spirit. He argued that the Holy Spirit proceeds principally from the Father, but also from the Son. The Holy Spirit is the Spirit of both and, as such, reveals a mutual love with which the Father and Son love each other. The Holy Spirit is the consubstantial love of both the Father and the Son.[18]

Augustine provided a number of analogies for the Trinity. The first analogy he used was he that loves, that which is loved, and love itself. Augustine also used memory, understanding, and will to illustrate the Trinity. Another was mind, knowledge, and love. Yet another was remembering, understanding, and love of God. While Augustine found these analogies to be helpful, he acknowledged that they were only analogies and were thus necessarily insufficient.[19]

The Eastern and Western churches had differences in their theology and theologians. Better than any other Western theologian, Hilary of Poitiers understood the apprehensions that Eastern theologians had

16. Allison, *Historical Theology*, 239–40.

17. The Trinity is "a divine unity of one and the same substance in an indivisible equality; and therefore . . . they are not three Gods, but one God, and yet He who is the Father is not the Son . . . and so He who is the Son is not the Father; and the Holy Spirit is neither the Father nor the Son" (Augustine, *On the Trinity*, as cited by Beeke and Smalley, *Reformed Systematic Theology*, 1:909).

18. Allison, *Historical Theology*, 241–42.

19. Michael Horton (*The Christian Faith: A Systematic Theology for Pilgrims on the Way* [Grand Rapids: Zondervan, 2011], 284) suggests that both Jerome and Augustine failed to understand Cappadocian Trinitarian advances.

with the Western church. He attempted to unite the Eastern church's emphasis on distinct persons within the godhead with the Western church's emphasis on the one essence, or *ousia*, of the godhead.[20] Arianism, adoptionism, and subordinationism all attacked the concept of the Trinity in the Western church. As a result of these attacks, it is no surprise that the Western church emphasized the unity of the divine essence. The Eastern church, however, desired to emphasize the distinctions among the three persons of the Trinity and was concerned that Augustine's analysis marginalized the unique characteristics of each person.[21]

Christology. From the Trinity, we now turn to the doctrine of Christ. Some theologians during this time denied Christ's full humanity. Docetism, which was related to Gnosticism, argued that Jesus only *seemed* to be a man but instead was actually a spirit-type being. Gnosticism taught that the spiritual was good and the fleshly was evil. According to this logic, the Son of God could not take on flesh. Ignatius, on the other hand, claimed that Christ was truly human because he experienced authentic human activities and was physically descended from David.[22] The Gnostics also supported heretical accounts of Christ's life, such as the Gospel of Thomas, Gospel of Judas, and Gospel of Peter.

Arianism posed a great threat to the church during this time. Arius and his followers argued that God is one and could never share his being with another. They believed that God created a son, and through that son he created the world. According to Arianism, that son is exalted and unique because only he was uniquely created. Yet there was a time, before his creation, when the son did not exist. Thus, according to Arius, the son is not eternal or coeternal, and he has a nature and substance that are distinct from the Father's. Arius offered complex biblical support for his teaching.[23]

---

20. Hilary of Poitiers, *De synodis*, as cited by Horton, *Christian Faith*, 287.

21. Horton (*Christian Faith*, 285–86) claims that Augustine's psychological analogies for the Trinity actually lean in a modalistic direction. Horton adds that some contemporary Reformed theologians' seeming failure to comprehend these Eastern vs. Western church distinctions has led to extreme formulations by Cornelius Van Til and John Frame. For more information on contemporary issues, see chapter 26.

22. Allison, *Historical Theology*, 366.

23. Ibid., 368–69. See Robert Letham, *The Holy Trinity: In Scripture, History, Theology, and Worship*, rev. and exp. ed. (Phillipsburg, NJ: P&R Publishing, 2019), 110–17.

Concerned that the empire could rupture over such teachings, Constantine called for a general council—the Council of Nicaea—to decide on these controversies. The council affirmed the deity of Christ and condemned specific Arian beliefs. Though twenty-two bishops came to the council in support of Arius, when the actual statements of Arius were read aloud, they were so shocking that only Arius and two others refused to sign the statement of the general council—the Nicene Creed. As a result, Arius was banished.[24]

Sadly, the victory of this council was short lived. Arianism wavered in the empire but then grew in strength. Attempting to ease religious tensions in the empire, Constantine's posture began to soften toward those the Nicene Creed had exiled. Thus, after modifying his most objectionable statements, Arius was permitted to return from exile.

On his deathbed, Constantine was baptized by an Arian bishop. The "Christian emperor" had gone without being baptized for his entire life. Following his death, an Arian sympathizer, Constantius II, became emperor. Under this new emperor, Arianism flourished. Athanasius continued to oppose Arianism and was banished five times. Despite his ostracism, Athanasius's courage and teaching left a lasting impression in the theological world.[25]

Having determined that the Christ must be fully God and fully man, the church next faced the challenge of articulating the relationship between Christ's divine and human natures. The church was filled with aberrant teachings on the matter. For instance, Apollinarius referred to Christ as "flesh becoming God." In other words, Christ united with a body but not a soul. In place of the soul, Jesus had the divine Word, thus making Jesus no ordinary person.

Gregory of Nazianzus considered this view to be near to Docetism, for if Christ lacked a soul, then he also lacked a mind and will—thus he was not truly human. If Christ was not truly human, then salvation itself was in danger, for the whole of human nature fell and the whole of human nature needed to be redeemed. Apollinarianism was officially condemned at the councils of Constantinople and Chalcedon.[26]

24. Allison, *Historical Theology*, 369–70.
25. Ibid., 371.
26. Ibid., 372–73.

Holy Spirit. This period was also fraught with various errant views of the Holy Spirit. Arius believed the Holy Spirit to be of a different substance from the Father and the Son and thus not divine. His followers viewed the Holy Spirit as a created being. In agreement, Eusebius of Caesarea said that the Holy Spirit is "one of the things which have come into existence through the Son."[27] Dynamic Monarchianism held that the Holy Spirit is a sort of divine influence. Modalistic Monarchianism, on the other hand, claimed that the three persons are one spirit but three different modes of one God. Another group—the Pneumatachians—denied the Holy Spirit's deity but did not consider him a creature.

These views were not left uncontested by the Cappadocian fathers. Basil argued that the Holy Spirit's essence is identical to that of both the Father and Son. Agreeing, Athanasius argued that, in addition to the Son, the Holy Spirit is *homoousios* with the Father; the three persons share one divine essence. Athanasius reasoned that the deity of the Spirit is demonstrated in that believers become partakers of God through his work. Thus in A.D. 362, the Council of Alexandria anathematized those who believed the Holy Spirit to be a creature, one separate from Christ's essence.[28]

But the question was asked: "If the Holy Spirit is consubstantial with the Father as is the Son, then how can the Son and Spirit, who share the same nature, be differentiated?" Gregory of Nyssa emphasized the unity of the divine nature and the diversity of the three persons, thus making evident that they are distinguishable in their personhood but share in essence and glory. Basil insisted on precise language. The Holy Spirit is neither unbegotten nor begotten; rather, the Holy Spirit proceeds from the Father. The Father is unbegotten, the Son is only begotten, and the Holy Spirit proceeds. Neither the Son nor the Spirit is created. Thus the Son and Spirit are distinguished by their mode of origin. Proceeding out of God is not generation but procession "as a breath of his mouth."[29] These notions are a mystery to the human mind.[30]

---

27. Eusebius, *Praeparatio evangelica* 11.20, as cited by Allison, *Historical Theology*, 435.
28. Allison, *Historical Theology*, 435.
29. Basil of Caesarea, *On the Spirit*, as cited by Allison, *Historical Theology*, 436.
30. Gregory of Nazianzus (*Oration* 32.8, as cited by Allison, *Historical Theology*, 436) stated that pursuing these notions makes the inquirer "frenzy-stricken for prying into the mystery

If the Holy Spirit proceeds, then from whom does he proceed? Basil argued that the Holy Spirit is joined to the Father through the Son, and their attributes extend from the Father through the Son to the Holy Spirit. Gregory of Nyssa spoke of the Spirit as proceeding from the Father but receiving from the Son. He differentiated between the Father, who is the cause; the Son, who is directly from the cause; and the Spirit, who is indirectly from the cause. Thus the Holy Spirit proceeds from the Father and receives from the Son.[31]

The creed adopted at Constantinople in A.D. 381 declared that the Holy Spirit is "the Lord and giver of life, who proceeds from the Father; who with the Father and the Son together is worshiped and glorified; who also spoke through the prophets."[32]

Augustine argued that the Holy Spirit is equal in essence and united to the Father and the Son. He held that the Holy Spirit is personally related to, and in communion with, both the Father and the Son. He is not a second Son but proceeds from the Father and the Son; this is the double procession of the Holy Spirit. Augustine explained that the Father and Son are not two separate agents as the source of the Spirit; rather, through one action of the Father and Son, the Spirit proceeds. It was in begetting the Son that the Father made it such that the Holy Spirit would proceed from both. In his work against the Arian bishop Maximinus, Augustine said: "The Father is the author of the Spirit's procession because he begot such a Son, and in begetting him made him also the source from which the Spirit proceeds."[33] Augustine's teaching on the *filioque*, the double procession of the Holy Spirit, was adopted by the Western church at the Third Council of Toledo in A.D. 589.

Creation and Evil. Most of the fathers, though not Augustine, held to a literal, six-day creation. Augustine understood the creation account to be a literary device or pattern.[34] The fathers struggled with the introduction of evil into creation. Arnobius claimed that

---

of God. And who are we to . . . supply an account of the [divine] nature which is so unspeakable and transcending all words?"

31. Allison, *Historical Theology*, 436–37.

32. Ibid., 437.

33. Augustine, *Collatio cum Maximino Arianorum episcopo* 2.14.1, as cited by Allison, *Historical Theology*, 438. For further information on this important text, see Richard C. Gamble, *Augustinus contra Maximinum: An Analysis of Augustine's Anti-Arian Writings* (Ann Arbor, MI: McNaughton and Gunn, 1985).

34. Allison, *Historical Theology*, 254–60.

evil was a mystery. Tertullian held that God created men and women with free will and so could not intervene to stop them from choosing evil. Human freedom was to blame. Origen and Lactantius argued that evil is necessary to produce morally right people and for virtue to advance. Marcion, seeking to resolve the tension of evil and the goodness of God, proposed that there were two gods, one of whom was held responsible for evil. His view was rejected by the church.

Augustine also spoke into the problem of evil. He believed that men possess free will, but he also believed that God knows all that will come to pass. While maintaining the free will of man, Augustine did believe there was an element of compulsion involved, for God's will always comes to pass. He believed that these truths—human free will and divine agency—should be held in tension. Everything that occurs does so according to both divine agency and human willing. Humans who turn from God and abuse their free will do not frustrate the plan of God. Augustine believed, therefore, that God not only foreknew but also decreed the fall of Adam and Eve.

Angels and Demons. Thought regarding angels was diverse. In *Celestial Hierarchy*, Pseudo-Dionysius speculated in detail concerning the heavenly realm out of a belief that the realities of heaven must be reflected here on earth.[35] He thought there to be nine orders of angels, and this structure provided the earthly model for church administration. John Chrysostom believed that angels assist in salvation, serve Christ, and act as examples for Christians. Origen wrote that angels should not be prayed to or for, since angels themselves only want to serve God. But he did encourage believers to pray for angelic protection, for he thought that angels are guardians who lead believers into repentance and assist them in prayer. Origen even thought that at death believers would become like angels.

Later patristic writers attempted to understand the origin of Satan and the fallen angels. Some of the writers attributed the angelic fall to lust for human women. For punishment, these angels were thrust from heaven, cast to earth, and will experience their punishment eternally. The fathers did not believe that Satan was created evil, but he fell and became the head of the fallen angels. He was then instrumental, through

35. Ibid., 307–8.

the form of a serpent, in the fall of man. Evil, then, must have existed in the spiritual or angelic realm before the Adamic fall. Augustine believed that, in number, the angels that fell will be replaced by the redeemed.[36]

Currently, fallen angels, or demons, are preoccupied with working against God. They invent error and false doctrine. They wreak havoc on the earth. They possess unbelievers—not believers—and must be exorcised. Some theologians pursued the monastic life specifically to flee from these demonic and satanic attacks.[37]

One of the most crucial times for the articulation of doctrine was in the twenty-year period between the councils of Ephesus and Chalcedon. We turn to them next.

COUNCILS OF EPHESUS AND CHALCEDON

A century prior to the councils of Ephesus and Chalcedon, the council and creed of Nicaea primarily addressed Christology. In particular, Nicaea hammered out the relationship between the Father and the Son. Contra Arius, the Nicene Creed strongly asserted the consubstantiality of the Father and Son. This claim, while an undeniable victory, required further elaboration. The relationship between Christ's humanity and divinity was still unclear. Thus the church turned her attention to explicating the nature of Christ's incarnation.[38]

Often throughout church history, theological advance occurs as a result of doctrinal disagreement. Articulation on the relationship between Christ's humanity and divinity advanced as a result of a dispute between two theologians: Nestorius, the patriarch of Constantinople, and Cyril of Alexandria.[39]

Nestorius led Constantinople as its patriarch from A.D. 428 to 431. His understanding there to be a distinction between Christ's two natures situated his Christology as Antiochene, meaning that he wanted to press a distinction between Christ's two natures.[40] Nestorius

---

36. Ibid., 306–7.
37. Ibid., 301–5.
38. Grillmeier, *Christ in Christian Tradition*, 1:443.
39. The young Cyril was heavily influenced by Athanasius. See ibid., 1:414–18.
40. See George Leonard Prestige, *Fathers and Heretics* (London: SPCK, 1940), 120–49; Louis Berkhof, *Systematic Theology* (Carlisle, PA: Banner of Truth, 1972), 307. For more on

THE CHURCH DEFINES HERSELF

also disagreed with the common expression *theotokos—mother of God* or *God-bearer*—by arguing that Mary bore a man, the vehicle of divinity, but not God. He refused Mary the long-accepted title *theotokos* because God did not have a mother, was not nurtured in a womb, and could not suffer and die. Instead, he preferred the title *Christotokos—mother of Christ*.

For Nestorius, the incarnation could not involve the impassable Word of God in change or suffering, for both change and suffering would violate the Creator/creature distinction.[41] Nevertheless, Jesus Christ must have real human growth, true temptation, and suffering. Put simply, he must be a real man. Nestorius feared Apollinaris's heretical teaching that the Logos replaced Jesus's human soul—a teaching that was condemned at Constantinople. Teaching that the Word assumed only a body, Apollinaris was condemned on the ground that the Son must have taken on full, unified humanity, including a soul, or there would be no true incarnation. Against Apollinarianism, Nestorius wanted to affirm Christ's integral human nature.[42]

While emphasizing both natures, Nestorius had uncertainties about their union. For him, Christ's divinity and humanity were each their own nature and must somehow exist side by side.[43] The word *nature* was defined as the concrete character of a thing. It was without *prosopon*, "external aspect," and without *hypostasis*, concrete "substance." Thus Nestorius attributed Jesus's human attributes to his human nature and Jesus's divine attributes to his divine nature, but he held that both kinds of attributes may be predicated to the one *prosopon* of the union. His unique solution was that the unity of the two natures was to be found in the common *prosopon*.[44]

Nestorius could subscribe without reservation to Nicene theology. He believed that Jesus was fully divine, had no beginning in time, and as the Son was of the Father's substance. Yet his teaching produced

---

classical Antiochene Christology focusing on Theodore of Mopsuestia, see Grillmeier, *Christ in Christian Tradition*, 1:421–25, 444.

41. Robert Letham, *Union with Christ in Scripture, History, and Theology* (Phillipsburg, NJ: P&R Publishing, 2011), 23.

42. Robert Letham, *Systematic Theology* (Wheaton, IL: Crossway, 2019), 492.

43. The union between the two was not hypostatic but voluntary. *Phusis* is the "humanity of Christ or the divinity conceived of as a concrete assemblage of characteristics or attributes" (J. N. D. Kelly, *Early Christian Doctrines* [London: Black, 1977], 312, 318).

44. Kelly, *Doctrines*, 314–16.

another crisis in the church—one that demanded great deliberation on the part of her theologians. The controversy surrounded the nature of the incarnate Logos. Nestorius could not adhere to a true incarnation, for he put Christ's divinity in a false relationship to his humanity. Thus Christ could not be humanity's redeemer.[45]

Cyril, the patriarch of Alexandria, was a representative of the Alexandrian school, which emphasized the hypostatic union between the divinity and humanity of Christ. He related them to the union between the soul and the body.

Cyril offered the explaination that there were two phases, or stages, of existence in the Logos, namely, preincarnation and postincarnation. Since the incarnate Christ was none other than the eternal Word in a new state, the unity between his two phases of existence was presupposed from the start. There is one nature, the incarnate and divine Word. The union was very real, and the properties participated in each other.[46] Cyril's construction put Christ's unity in first place, but Cyril was still unable to interpret clearly the distinction between Christ's humanity and divinity.[47]

In A.D. 429, the controversy between the Antiochene school, represented by Nestorius, and the Alexandrian school, represented by Cyril, had become so heated that Cyril wrote a letter to monks in Egypt warning them of Nestorius's Christology. A copy of this letter reached Nestorius in Constantinople—and thus began a correspondence of letters between the two men, with the tone of the letters becoming increasingly hostile.

In A.D. 430, Celestine, the bishop of Rome, held a synod in his city. Cyril was asked to carry out the condemnation of Nestorius and sent a provocative letter in his own name as well. In response, Nestorius requested the meeting of a council at Ephesus. But Cyril held a separate gathering, one that anathematized Nestorius, and the document produced at that gathering was accepted by the papal legates.

A summary of this bitter debate reveals that the full deity and humanity of Christ were acknowledged by both sides. The concern was the relationship between the two aspects of his nature. Specifi-

45. Letham, *Systematic Theology*, 493–94.
46. Kelly, *Doctrines*, 319.
47. Grillmeier, *Christ in Christian Tradition*, 1:445; Letham, *Union with Christ*, 24.

cally, theologians questioned the extent of the unity and diversity in the person of Christ regarding his divine and human natures. Cyril and his supporters saw the Antiochene emphasis on Christ's two natures as presenting a danger to the unity of Christ. They therefore created an emphatic unitive Christology and did so by centering it decisively on the Logos. Their opponents saw this emphasis on the unity of Christ's natures as a return to a form of Arianism.

Council of Ephesus (A.D. 431). At the Council of Ephesus in A.D. 431, the fathers created no new formula of belief and did not discuss a concrete statement or creed. But as did the earlier Council of Nicaea, the meeting condemned Nestorius. In particular, it condemned the teaching that Christ was composed of two independent persons who worked together, as was the Nestorian teaching that a true union of Christ's nature does not involve God in change and suffering.[48] The discussion with Nestorius turned on this sentence: "One and the same is the eternal Son of the Father and the Son of the Virgin Mary, born in time after the flesh."[49] The official letter of condemnation read:

> The Holy Synod which, by the grace of God, in conformity with the ordinance of our pious and Christ-loving Kings, is assembled at Ephesus, to Nestorius, the new Judas! Know that because of your godless teachings and disobedience towards the cannons, in accordance with the decree of the statutes of the church on the twenty-second of the current month of June you are condemned by the Holy Synod and dispossessed of any dignity in the church.

Council and Creed of Chalcedon (A.D. 451).[50] The condemnation of Nestorius did not bring an end to the debate. A new theologian entered the dispute—a monk by the name of Eutyches (A.D. 380–456). He held a Christology that was Alexandrian, and an extreme form at that. In one sense, Eutyches was on the complete opposite end of the

---

48. Douglas F. Kelly, *Systematic Theology*, vol. 2, *The Beauty of Christ—A Trinitarian Vision* (Fearn, Scotland: Mentory, 2014), 202.

49. Grillmeier, *Christ in Christian Tradition*, 416. Nicholas R. Needham, in *2,000 Years of Christ's Power*, vol. 1, *The Age of the Early Church Fathers* (London: Grace Publications, 1997), 276–80, traces the historical development of Nestorianism.

50. See R. V. Sellers, *The Council of Chalcedon: A Historical and Doctrinal Survey* (London: SPCK, 1953), 209–26.

spectrum from Nestorius. Nestorius held tightly to the distinct natures of Christ and struggled to piece them together somehow. Eutyches had the opposite problem. He believed that Jesus's human nature existed before the incarnation and thus Christ had two natures prior to the incarnation. But after the incarnation, Jesus possessed only one nature. In this new nature, the divine nature had swallowed up the human one "like a drop of wine in the sea."[51] Thus Eutychus combined Christ's two natures into one nature—a form of *Monophysitism*. At a meeting in Constantinople in A.D. 448, Eutyches had already been deposed as a follower of Valentinus and Apollinarius.

Pope Leo of Rome fervently opposed the teaching of Eutychus. He argued that Eutychus could not deny the distinct natures of Christ, each with their respective properties. Leo also opposed the contention that Jesus had a different human nature. He believed strongly that Christ had to be fully human.[52] In his frustration, Pope Leo sent a letter to Flavian of Constantinople expressing his outrage at the teaching of the single nature of Christ.

As tensions continued to increase regarding the relationship of Christ's human and divine natures, something needed to be done. The emperor stepped in and called the fourth general ecumenical council. Five hundred bishops attended the counsel. Unity was not easily attained in a council of this size, but, despite the challenge of five hundred voices' weighing in, the gathering produced a landmark creed. The council used as sources for the creed Cyril's two letters against Nestorius, Pope Leo's "Tome," the Union Symbol, and Flavian's profession. The creed gave equal recognition to Christ's unity and duality.[53]

Determining the victor in this debate is not as simple as many might assume. Often the Western, Antiochene Christology is seen as triumphant, but that perception is not entirely true. Both views were represented in the creed. From Alexandrian theology, the term *theotokos* was maintained as a designation for Mary. From Antiochene

51. Letham, *Systematic Theology*, 494–95.

52. Daniel J. Treier, "Incarnation," in *Christian Dogmatics: Reformed Theology for the Church Catholic*, ed. Michael Allen and Scott R. Swain (Grand Rapids: Baker Academic, 2016), 226.

53. Kelly, *Doctrines*, 338–43. The Union Symbol was an instrument of agreement that healed the rift between the Antiochenes, who had held to Nestorianism, and Cyril of Alexandria, who was suspected of Apollinarianism. For an English translation of the document, see Kelly, *Doctrines*, 328–29.

thought, the unity of Christ's two, complete natures was upheld. The terms *hupostasis* and *prosopon* were used to express the oneness of person, and *phusis* was used to describe the natures of Christ.[54]

It is beyond the limits of any creed to articulate exhaustively, in formulas of human logic and language, the fullness of the person of Jesus Christ in his *theanthropic* life.[55] The creed's writers knew it was impossible to grasp and explain every nuance of the mystery of the incarnation, so they were content to establish boundaries. In humble recognition that the development of this topic could not be further matured, even through enlightenment from the Lord, the council simply purposed to guard the relationship of Christ's human and divine natures against any conceptions that would truncate or falsely relate them.

The creed articulated and upheld a true incarnation of the second person of the Trinity motivated by the deep love of God. The *telos* ("ultimate aim") of the incarnation was the redemption of the fallen human race and its reconciliation to God. The council did not mix or convert Christ's natures; it did not humanize the divine or deify the human.[56] Excluded was the Nestorian idea of a double nature, one both divine and human. The council was clear: Christ is one divine and human person, with a rational, human soul and an undivided self-consciousness.[57]

The Chalcedonian Creed would proceed to affirm that even after the incarnation and into all eternity, Christ's two natures remain distinct, without confusion or conversion, while also without separation or division. The divine shall remain ever divine, and the human ever human. Yet the two natures continually exist in one common life, and they interpenetrate one another, as do the three persons of the Trinity.

There is only one Christ, one Lord, one Redeemer. There is unity in his distinction, and distinction in his unity. Leo wrote: "The divine and

54. With the death of Celestine in A.D. 432 and the coming of Xystus III, Cyril had submitted his teaching, which had been suspected of Apollinarian leanings by the Antiochenes, and he proved to them that he did not teach change or confusion of the two natures (see Kelly, *Doctrines*, 318). Antiochene language was used in one *prosopon*. With safeguards, *theotokos* was permitted. Nestorius was still condemned probably from the year A.D. 433 (ibid., 341): "One *prosopon* and one hypostasis" comes from Flavian.

55. The term *theanthropic* is a combination of the Greek words, *theos*, "God," and *anthropos*, "man." See Alfred Adam, *Lehrbuch der Dogmengeschichte*, vol. 1, *Die Zeit der alten Kirche* (Gütersloh: Mohn, 1965), 354.

56. Philip Schaff, *History of the Christian Church*, 8 vols. (Grand Rapids: Eerdmans, 1979), 3:750.

57. Schaff, *History*, 3:752–53.

the human are as far from forming a double personality in Christ, as the soul and the body in man, or as the regenerate and the natural life in the believer."[58] The whole work of Christ is to be attributed to his entire person, not exclusively to either his human or his divine nature.

To comprehend how the fathers at Chalcedon distinguished between Christ's nature and person, we remember that Nicaea used the Greek words *hypostasis*, usually translated "person," and *ousia*, "being" or "substance," interchangeably. Eventually they realized that a better expression was one divine *ousia* and three divine *hypostases*. Thus *nature* was distinguished from *person*.

At Chalcedon, the fathers articulated Christ's two natures with four negative expressions: his natures are without confusion, conversion, division, and separation.[59] This fully divine and fully human nature in one person, this *hypostasis*, was termed the *hypostatic union*. As the debates of this time centered on the relationship between the Father and the Son and the natures of the Son, fewer advances were made regarding the doctrine of the Holy Spirit.

In sum, the Chalcedonian Creed embraced "two natures . . . one person," contra Eutychianism. The creed also denied three earlier heresies—Arianism, Apollinarianism, and Nestorianism. Arianism was denied on the ground that Christ is complete in divinity and consubstantial. Apollinarianism was rejected on the ground that Christ is complete in his humanity—he is truly man, with a rational soul and body. And Nestorianism was denounced on the ground that Christ has two natures, without division or separation.[60] The Trinity was understood to be three persons in one divine nature or substance, which they all share in common.

POST-CHALCEDON THEOLOGY

Just as the Council of Nicaea did not end the discussion on the Trinity, so also the Council of Chalcedon did not end the debate on Christology. The Western church embraced Chalcedon and its find-

58. Ibid., 3:754–55.
59. Kelly, *Systematic Theology*, 2:200–204.
60. Allison, *Historical Theology*, 376.

ings. But parts of the Eastern church were still dissatisfied. To them the language of two natures in Christ still reeked of Nestorianism.[61]

Monophysite Controversy.[62] Monophysitism lingered in the Eastern church. Monophysites conceded that after the incarnation, Christ had a composite nature, but they denied that he had two distinct natures. They reasoned that two distinct natures would necessitate a duality of persons.

The Monophysites thought that they were simply following Cyril of Alexandria, who believed that Christ had one nature and one hypostasis. This movement was embraced not only by bishops and theologians but also by the monastic communities of Egypt and Syria. The Monophysite movement was so strong that imperial troops struggled to control a mob in Alexandria that opposed a new patriarch who had signed the Chalcedonian Creed. The rabble eventually lynched the patriarch and installed a Monophysite leader in his place. Syria faced a similar uproar when Monophysites deposed their patriarch and replaced him with one of their own.

To make matters worse, Basiliscus usurped power as emperor (A.D. 475–476) and anathematized Leo's "Tome" and the decisions of Chalcedon. The majority of Eastern bishops endorsed Basiliscus's action, but the patriarch of Constantinople asserted his authority over the claims of Alexandria, Basiliscus yielded, and the rightful emperor was restored.

The restored emperor, Zeno, and the patriarch of Constantinople issued a religious compromise called the Henotikon, which stated that the Nicene Creed, as reiterated at the councils of Constantinople and Ephesus, was a sufficient confession of the faith. The move deprived the Chalcedonian Creed's official status as definitive.

This decision by the Eastern church received a negative reaction from the Western church. Rome's bishop, Felix III, set out to ensure Chalcedonian orthodoxy, and in A.D. 484 he excommunicated the patriarch of Constantinople. The rift grew even deeper between East and West. The Eastern emperor, Anastasius, grew thoroughly convinced of the Monophysite position. As a result, he condemned Chalcedon, deposed

---

61. Williston Walker, Richard A. Norris, David W. Lotz, and Robert T. Handy, *A History of the Christian Church*, 4th ed. (New York: Scribner's Sons, 1985), 173.

62. See Adam, *Lehrbuch*, 354–55.

the pro-Chalcedon patriarch of Antioch, instituted himself as the new patriarch of Antioch, and exiled the patriarch of Constantinople.

In A.D. 519, under a new Eastern emperor, there was an attempt at reconciliation between the Eastern and Western churches. The Eastern church conceded patriarchal status to Rome but still refused Rome's universal authority—the opposing sides were sown together, but with a fragile thread.[63]

The thread was broken under the Eastern emperor Justinian I (A.D. 527–565). He captured Pope Vigilius (A.D. 537–555) and carried him off to Constantinople! Justinian brought about sweeping changes— he outlawed paganism, closed the Platonic Academy in Athens, and attempted to reconcile Monophysite theologians to Chalcedon. In A.D. 533, he published his own official definition of christological faith, which brought a momentary truce to the debating parties.

While the controversy between East and West embraced issues of church power and political control, it was deeply theological at heart—Justinian's truce was more imposed than it was embraced.[64] Monophysite leaders, realizing that they could not survive politically within the empire, began organizing. The Western church condemned Monophysitism at the Second Council of Constantinople, also known as the Fifth Ecumenical Council, in A.D. 553.[65] While legally condemned in the West, there were now independent Monophysite churches in Ethiopia, Syria, Egypt, and Armenia. Furthermore, there were Nestorian churches in Persia.[66]

Monothelite Controversy. The church now faced additional questions regarding the unipersonality of Christ. The relationship between his person and nature remained unresolved. The matter at hand was the will of Christ. Where did it reside? Did Christ have one or two wills? The dilemma can be articulated thus: To say that Christ had but one will seemed to rob him of his human volition, thereby detracting from the integrity of his humanity. But to say that he had two wills appeared to lead down the path of Nestorian error.

63. Walker, *History*, 152–53; Adam, *Lehrbuch*, 363–64.
64. Walker, *History*, 175.
65. Allison, *Historical Theology*, 377. Diarmaid MacCulloch (*Christianity: The First Three Thousand Years* [New York: Viking, 2010], 344–45, 441–42) wrongly treats them as part of the church.
66. Walker, *History*, 178–80.

The Monothelites argued that Christ had one will. They reasoned that because of the unity of Christ's person, there must also be one will within Christ. Their position took two forms: either the human will of Christ merged into the divine, so that the divine will alone acted, or the will of Christ was a fusion of his divine and human wills.[67]

This controversy did not find resolution until the seventh century. At the sixth ecumenical Third Council of Constantinople in A.D. 680 to 681, the doctrine of the two wills was adopted. Those at the council determined that Christ's human will, through its union with the divine will, did not become less human. Instead, his human will was heightened and perfected by its union with the divine will, and the two acted in perfect harmony.[68] In some ways, this union is similar to the will of believers in heaven, whose wills are molded to yearn only for the divine will.

We have reviewed the doctrine of God in the patristic period. We will now investigate the historical development of the other loci of theology during this era.

SCRIPTURE

Canon.[69] Justin Martyr and Polycarp taught that God himself was the ultimate source of the truth of Scripture. Augustine concurred.[70] In opposition to heretics such as Marcion, who rejected the entire OT, Irenaeus and Tertullian underlined the theological unity between the Old and New Testaments. Two marks defined the canon: apostolicity and antiquity.

By this time, apostolic writings abounded.[71] Jerome began his new Latin translation of the Scriptures from the Hebrew OT in A.D. 382.

---

67. Adam, *Lehrbuch*, 366–67.

68. Walker, *History*, 180–82.

69. See Charles E. Hill, "The Truth above All Demonstration," in *The Enduring Authority of the Christian Scriptures*, ed. D. A. Carson (Grand Rapids: Eerdmans, 2016), 61–72.

70. He stated: "For it seems to me that most disastrous consequences must follow upon our believing that anything false is found in the sacred books. . . . For if you once admit into such a high sanctuary of authority one false statement . . . there will not be left a single sentence of those books which . . . may not by the same fatal rule be explained away, as a statement in which, intentionally, and under a sense of duty, the author declared what was not true" (Augustine, *Letter to Jerome* 28.3, as cited by Letham, *Systematic Theology*, 191).

71. For OT canonics, see Richard C. Gamble, *The Whole Counsel of God*, vol. 1, *God's Mighty Acts in the Old Testament* (Phillipsburg, NJ: P&R Publishing, 2009) (*WCG1*), 109–19. For

This translation included the Apocrypha, though he relegated it to secondary status.[72]

Augustine had a broader view of the canon. He believed that not only the Hebrew Scriptures were inspired but also the LXX. His reasoning was that the apostles cited the LXX in Scripture, so it must be inspired. Thus he thought that Jerome should translate from the LXX, not the Hebrew text. As the Vulgate became accepted as Scripture, then the Apocrypha was included.[73]

Inspiration. The patristic writers had developed a full and complete doctrine of inspiration.[74] The fathers all agreed that the Scriptures were given by the Holy Spirit.[75] But they believed that the method of this inspiration was at times quite mechanical. Philo, for example, thought that the OT prophets lost consciousness and wrote in an ecstatic state. Justin Martyr and Athenagoras used the analogy of a musician's playing an instrument to describe the process of inspiration. Irenaus used the word *dictation* to describe the process, and Augustine used the same idea. Hippolytus's view differed from that of the other patristic writers. He held that God prepared the OT prophets for their work.[76]

Authority. Augustine wrote extensively on the authority of Scripture. He understood there to be a distinction between Scripture and nonscriptural works. He believed that even if there were a book relaying the exact truths as those contained in the Bible, that book would not have the same authority. He understood Scripture to have its own particular sacredness and authority.[77]

NT canonics, see Richard C. Gamble, *The Whole Counsel of God*, vol. 2, *The Full Revelation of God* (Phillipsburg, NJ: P&R Publishing, 2018) (*WCG2*), 54–66. The lists included the Muratorian Canon (A.D. 170), Origen's Canon (mid-third century), and Eusebius's canon (early fourth century). Some canonical books were considered to be on the fringe—James, 2 Peter, 2–3 John, Jude, and Hebrews. The first list of NT writings that parallels ours is from Athanasius in A.D. 367. Debate focused on the OT canon. The LXX, begun in the third century B.C., included more books than did the Hebrew Bible. The NT writers knew the LXX and used it in their citations. They did not cite the Apocrypha in the NT, and the Muratorian Canon did not include the OT apocryphal books.

72. Allison, *Historical Theology*, 47–49.

73. Ibid., 49–50.

74. Hill ("Truth above All Demonstration," 78–80) demonstrated how Clement and Pseudo-Justin dealt with nonbiblical "inspired" literature.

75. William Cunningham, *Historical Theology* (Edinburgh: Banner of Truth, 1979), 1:136: "Justin unequivocally professes to hold what we would now call the perfection and sufficiency of the Scriptures as the only rule of faith."

76. Allison, *Historical Theology*, 59–63.

77. Augustine, *Contra Faustum* 11.5, as cited by Hill "Truth above All Demonstration," 84.

Scripture and Tradition. Besides Scripture, the early fathers referred to apostolic tradition, the canon of truth, and church authority. The apostolic tradition was probably an oral source later recorded in Scripture.[78] The canon of truth was a tool used against heresy. Also termed the *rule of faith*, it is a type of creedal statement derived from Scripture. Church authority was also a tool used against heresy. In contrast to heretical novelty, church authority represented a body of sound belief that was not opposed to Scripture and that was a support against heresy.

The concept of authority developed after Irenaeus.[79] The word *tradition* carried with it two concepts. The first was *traditio dei*, or Scripture. This tradition was "vertical." The second was ecclesiastical tradition, which was "horizontal" in nature. From its beginning, the *traditio dei* was the standard for the validity of the ecclesiastical tradition.[80] The patristic writers, however, believed that Scripture and ecclesiastical tradition were from the same source—the Holy Spirit. Thus began to develop the teaching that Scripture and tradition were coextensive in regard to faith and truth.[81] Tertullian, for example, thought that there was a continuous succession of truth leading up to his time. Vincent of Lerin established criteria that would later emerge as the rule of faith—that exegesis and teaching should be assessed and measured against the doctrine that is believed everywhere, always, and by all.[82]

But the rule-of-faith principle soon undermined Scripture's supremacy, especially among the Cappadocians. By the fourth century, Basil the Great admitted that the church was no longer content with recorded

---

78. Allison (*Historical Theology*, 146) incorrectly argues about the time of completion of the canon: "Prior to the completion of the New Testament canon (toward the end of the fourth century)." The canon was complete by A.D. 95 but simply not recognized throughout the whole church.

79. See Heiko Augustinus Oberman, "*Quo Vadis, Petre?* Tradition from Irenaeus to Humani Generis," in *The Dawn of the Reformation: Essays in Late Medieval and Early Reformation Thought*, by Heiko Augustinus Oberman (Edinburgh: T&T Clark, 1986), 259–96.

80. Heiko Augustinus Oberman, *The Harvest of Medieval Theology: Gabriel Biel and Late Medieval Nominalism* (Cambridge: Harvard University Press, 1963), 368.

81. Ibid., 366–67: Oberman was convinced that "Scripture and Tradition are for the early Church in no sense mutually exclusive: Kerygma, Scripture and Tradition coincide entirely. . . . The tradition is not understood as an addition to the Kerygma contained in Scripture but as the handing down of that same Kerygma in living form: in other words everything is to be found in Scripture and at the same time everything is in the living tradition."

82. Letham, *Systematic Theology*, 223.

Scripture but was determined to include practices from unwritten teaching. For example, the church began to pray facing east in anticipation of the resurrection. This practice, and others like it, was based on both written and unwritten precepts handed down from the apostles in mystery. Basil considered it apostolic to adhere to these unwritten traditions. While facing east during prayer may be dismissed as trivial, it offers one example among many of how Basil's instruction relativized Scripture's significance.

As a result of Basil's work, the notion developed that Christians were to be obedient not only to Scripture but also to secret, unwritten ecclesiastical tradition. This idea was promptly integrated into canon law—a century after Basil, Augustine picked up on his remark and mentioned an authoritative, extrascriptural oral tradition.[83]

Gregory of Nyssa damaged the priority of Scripture even further when he claimed that visual revelation should be prioritized over verbal revelation. His reasoning was that greater numbers could understand visually than could understand aurally, and thus God's visible revelation in creation was superior to God's speaking. Gregory's influence resulted in the development of iconography in Greek churches.[84]

Inerrancy. Regarding inerrancy, Augustine understood Scripture to be infallible and argued that it was free from error. For Augustine, finding a mistake in Scripture would have been devastating, for if there were one mistake, then the whole of Scripture could be challenged—and the church would be left with hopelessly subjective judgments. To the patristic writers, inerrancy extended to the entirety of Scripture—the creation account, human origins, and even genealogies. Christians were to believe every word of it.[85]

Clarity or Perspicuity. Augustine acknowledged God's clear revelation while admitting that the Bible also contained ambiguities and obscurities. These obscurities were part of God's plan to help believers in their time of need and to keep them humble. So Augustine developed rules of biblical interpretation. He claimed that if the reader followed these rules, he would grasp the hidden sense without error.

---

83. This passage was handed down into Gratian of Bologna's important *Decretum*. Thus canon law stands on the two pillars of Scripture and tradition (Oberman, *Harvest*, 369–71).

84. Letham, *Systematic Theology*, 224.

85. Ibid., 102–3.

John Chrysostom acknowledged that while there are obscurities, the necessary meanings are plain. He encouraged readers to dig deeply.[86]

Necessity and Sufficiency. The church fathers held that Scripture's sufficiency makes it the standard for Christian belief. True belief must be established by Scripture, and heresy is that which does not conform to Scripture.[87] Since the Scriptures are necessary for the Christian life, the church fathers taught that Christians should read their Bibles each day. Those who thought they did not need to do so because they were not monks were rebuked. The lives of those who neglect the sufficient Word of God are filled with many ills.

Interpretation. The Alexandrian school, begun by Clement of Alexandria, embraced allegory in the interpretation of Scripture.[88] For example, Origen, a member of this school, thought that even though the book of Genesis appeared to be historical narrative, it could not be. The creation account had to be metaphor or figure.[89]

The Alexandrian school taught that there are three levels of meaning found in Scripture. The levels correspond to the human body, soul, and spirit. The first sense, body, is the historical nature of Scripture and edifies simple individuals. The second sense, soul, is an understanding that goes into the soul of Scripture. And the third sense, the most mature, is the spirit, or spiritual law. According to this school of interpretation, not all Scripture may be taken literally. While the three levels all deserve attention, the third sense, which imparts hidden meaning, is the most important. Allegory provided that deeper, and often fanciful, meaning.[90]

The Antiochene school, on the other hand, employed a literal sense of interpretation and was critical of the use of allegory in biblical interpretation. Antiochenes also employed typology in their reading of Scripture because typology did not underappreciate its literal sense. For example, Moses literally gave the Law, but the Law was also a type of

---

86. Allison, *Historical Theology*, 123–25.

87. Ibid., 143–44.

88. Cunningham, *Historical Theology*, 1:147: "It was at Alexandria . . . that the progress of corruption in the interpretation of Scripture, and in the exposition of the scheme of divine truth, was most extensively promoted through the influence of false philosophy."

89. Frances Young (*Biblical Exegesis and the Formation of Christian Culture* [Peabody, MA: Hendrickson Publishers, 2002]) underlines that while there is disagreement between the two schools, nevertheless that disagreement was based upon extensive prior agreement.

90. Allison, *Historical Theology*, 163–65.

Christ. *Theoria*, or the use of insight, aided them in their perception of types. In typology, the Antiochian interpreters held to the literal sense but sought a correspondence between historical fact and spiritual object. The two were to be apprehended together. Their rigid view of understanding typology actually inhibited their perception of legitimate typologies, such the reference to Christ's crucifixion in Isaiah 53:7.[91]

Influenced by Tyconius's *Book of Rules*, Augustine urged interpreters to adhere to the biblical writers' intended meaning.[92] According to Augustine, the Scriptures intend a fourfold meaning: there are eternal truths, facts, future events, and precepts or counsels. The meaning of the literal sense is what the author intended and expressed. The etiological sense is the meaning that explains the reasons for something in the text. The analogical sense is the harmonization of the OT and NT. In his interpretation of the parable of the good Samaritan, Augustine employed allegory. For example, the traveler was Adam, the inn was the church, the oil was the comfort of the Holy Spirit, the innkeeper was Paul, and the Samaritan's return was Christ's resurrection. While this interpretation is allegorical, Augustine also provided guardrails for its use: correspondence to the teaching of the church and the promotion of love for God and others.[93] But Augustine still held to the tradition of adhering to the natural sense of the text. He argued that a person who extracts from Scripture a meaning apart from what the writer intended goes astray.

During Augustine's time, John Cassian (A.D. 365–435) suggested a fourfold exegesis. Cassian posited that there were often three spiritual or figurative senses of Scripture: allegorical, tropological, and analogical. These senses were distinct from the fourth sense—the literal. Jerome emphasized searching for authorial intent in interpretation. He believed that commentators should not impose their own views onto the text but instead should make the biblical author's intention plain and simple.[94] Understanding how patristic theologians understood Scripture, we will now examine how they dealt with the doctrine of humanity.

91. Ibid., 165–66.
92. Tyconius (A.D. 301–400) was a North African Donatist theologian about whom we know little except that he was older than Augustine. His *Book of Rules* gave seven keys for identifying biblical prose and said that knowing these rules would aid the biblical interpreter.
93. Allison, *Historical Theology*, 167–68.
94. Ibid., 168–69.

HUMANITY

Pre-Fall Image of God. Greek philosophy is well known for its dualism, which pitted the bad material, or flesh, against the good immaterial, or soul.[95] In contrast to Greek thinking, Augustine's anthropology became the standard in the early church. Augustine emphasized humanity's goodness in its original creation. Both the body and the soul were servants of God. Augustine believed that the account of Adam's creation has to be accepted by faith.[96]

The origin of the soul had already been debated, and Augustine chose not to take a stand on creationism and traducianism.[97] He believed that neither position was fully revealed in the Scriptures.[98]

Athanasius connected Christ's incarnation with Adam's creation. Adam was created in the image of God—not only by Christ, but also after Christ, the Son of God.[99] He connected the creation of Adam with the atonement of Christ—Christ was made man so that humanity might be made like God.[100]

95. Greek anthropology began in the sixth century B.C. with the Orphic mythology adopted by Plato (427–347 B.C.). Plato held that the soul is divine and the body evil. He believed in successive reincarnations until the soul entered the heavenly realm. "Body" meant shut in prison. The *Epistle to Diognetus* spoke of the soul as imprisoned in the body. Cyprian saw a struggle between them. The body was blamed for troubles and disparaged. Novatian wisely said that it was not the body itself that was evil. See Allison, *Historial Theology*, 326.

96. Augustine, *On the Grace of God and Original Sin*: "For how could I now possibly prove that a man was made of the dust, without any parents, and a wife formed for him out of his own side? And yet faith takes on trust what the eye no longer discovers" (as cited by Letham, *Systematic Theology*, 316).

97. The creationist view was supported by Methodius and Lactantius. This view seemed to help explain the contentious dichotomy between body and soul and argued that since the soul, made in God's image, was joined to a sinful body, a person shares both dignity and depravity. Jerome (*To Pammachius against John of Jerusalem* 22, as cited by Letham, *Systematic Theology*, 344) also argued for creationism, in other words, that God directly creates each individual soul. Tertullian thought that there was a simultaneous transmission of soul and body at generation; this view is called *traducianism*. Gregory of Nyssa was also in favor of traducianism. See Letham, *Systematic Theology*, 345–46.

98. Allison, *Historical Theology*, 327.

99. Athanasius, *On the Incarnation* 3: God "did not barely create men . . . but made them after his own image, giving them a portion even of the power of his own Word; so that having as it were a kind of reflexion of the Word, and being made rational, they might be able to abide even in blessedness" (as cited by Letham, *Systematic Theology*, 334–35).

100. The connection of the first Adam, created in Christ's image, with the second Adam, Christ himself, was an important teaching of the Greek and Syrian fathers. See Letham, *Systematic Theology*, 334–36.

Post-Fall Image of God. There are exegetical tensions regarding the nature of the postlapsarian image of God. Some of the views will be explained below.

Some theologians argued that only believers wholly retain the image of God.[101] Cyprian connected humanity's sin with Adam's. He argued that when an infant is born, he or she has not sinned but has still inherited sin and death from Adam. Gregory of Nazianzus and Gregory of Nyssa, however, denied that infants were born with sin inherited from Adam. Athanasius thought that Adam's sin was that of focusing attention on his body and its desires.

Augustine forged this doctrine in his battle against Pelagius, who focused his attention on the nature of the image of God. For Pelagius, the image of God consists in reason and free will, which are retained by fallen humanity. People themselves have to will something, and they do not need divine grace to accomplish it.[102] Pelagius emphasized that it remains within the ability of man to do good and respond to Christ's call even after the fall because willing and action are exclusively human. People were made by God to be capable of accomplishing his will.[103]

Pelagius had a unique definition of grace. He believed that man has the natural ability to do good, and grace is God's assistance to man in that capacity. He also argued that man has the capacity not to sin. Humanity possesses an absolute free will to choose that which is good or evil. The will can turn to either side, and in his grace God gave man a conscience to help him do good.

For Pelagius, man can choose between right and wrong because he has no internal tendency to sin, no inclination toward evil. Each soul is created uniquely, so the soul has no connection to Adam. Thus babies are not born with a corrupt nature. What may appear to be a sinful nature is simply the fruit of habitual sin. In addition, no one bears the guilt of Adam's sin, for only Adam is responsible for his actions. For Pelagius, Adam was merely a bad example, and his descendants are not obliged to follow him. He even believed that, with grace, people could live sinlessly. He questioned how God could command holiness

---

101. The nineteenth and twentieth centuries produced many challenges to Genesis's account of human creation and the nature of the image. In some ways these challenges are not new.

102. Allison, *Historial Theology*, 345.

103. Letham, *Systematic Theology*, 328–29.

and perfection from his people if they were incapable of being holy and perfect.[104]

As recorded by Augustine, Pelagius's disciple Celestius summarized Pelagian teaching: Adam was created mortal and would have died regardless of whether or not he ate of the fruit. Adam's sin affected no one but himself. There were sinless people who lived in the period of the OT. Infants are in Adam's prelapsarian condition. The whole human race does not die in Adam or rise in Christ.[105] The term *prevenient grace* was introduced in the Pelagian debate.[106]

Augustine opposed Pelagius and his teaching. Augustine was convinced that Adam's sin and its punishment are inherited—that infants have guilty souls, and their sin comes via generation or natural descent, not only by actual imitation.[107] He argued that Adam was born *posse non pecarre*—"able not to sin." But Adam, in his pride, chose to sin. Humanity is now *non posse non pecarre*—"not able not to sin." Augustine taught that unbelievers, using their free will, will always choose evil. From Romans 5:12 he taught that humanity finds itself in the deepest recesses of sin through one man, Adam.[108]

Augustine was convinced, and rightly so, that humanity identifies with Adam and that the whole of human nature was present in Adam. That same human nature was corrupted in Adam. There is now a natural tendency in humankind to turn from God and be drawn to this world—a disobedient lust called *concupiscence*, the inherited corrupt nature that always produces sinful acts when left to free will.[109]

In the end, the church justly condemned Pelagianism. The Council of Carthage in A.D. 418 rejected Pelagius's teaching that death is natural and not divine punishment for sin. The council also rejected his definition of grace, specifically that it is limited to the provision of external help. The Second Council of Orange in A.D. 529 officially condemned Pelagian teachings, specifically that the soul is unaffected by Adam's fall, that grace comes at human request, that for God to

104. Ibid., 346.
105. Ibid., 347.
106. Psalm 59:10 says, "My God will go before me with his mercy." "To go before" in Latin is *preveniere*.
107. Letham, *Systematic Theology*, 381–82.
108. Ibid., 348.
109. Ibid., 348–49.

forgive sins the human will must come first, that a desire to believe is found in human nature not as a result of grace, and that some already have a good will and thus can seek salvation. The council affirmed humanity's total depravity, articulated that humanity cannot believe without the mercy of God, and held that God's grace was necessary to overcome original sin.[110]

After the condemnation of Pelagianism, the church shifted toward what is now termed *semi-Pelagianism* when in A.D. 473 the Synod of Arles condemned the denial of postlapsarian free will and cooperation between divine grace and human free will. Other names associated with semi-Pelagianism include John Cassian, Vincent of Lerins, and Faustus of Rhegium. Semi-Pelagianism taught that Augustine went too far and destroyed any significant free will. Cassian agreed with Augustine that grace needs to assist the will, but he disagreed with Augustine and maintained that the will is free to do or not to do good. There is a harmony between human free will and God's grace, and the human will is always good enough to cooperate with the grace offered. Thus the will still plays a role, though only a minor one, in overcoming sin.

SOTERIOLOGY

Resurrection and Ascension. Docetism challenged the resurrection and ascension of Christ, and the ancient church fought back. Pagans, such as Celsus, thought the idea of the resurrection of Christ was audacious. He questioned why Jesus only *supposedly* appeared to his followers and not to those who opposed him. The Jews put forth the stolen-body theory, which was fought by both Justin Martyr and John Chrysostom. The Nicene Creed asserted the truth of the resurrection and ascension of Christ, and the church determined liturgical remembrances of these events with Easter and ascension sermons.[111]

Justification. At the time of the Reformation, a debate ensued between Protestants and Roman Catholic scholars as to which group was in accord with the ancient church on the doctrine of justification.

110. Ibid., 349–50.
111. Allison, *Historical Theology*, 412–15.

That debate continues to some extent even today. The answer to this question is complicated. Like the loci of theology examined before this one, the church had to work through difficult theological issues.

Augustine developed his mature doctrine of justification in part in reaction to Pelagius. Addressing the will and good works, Augustine did not deny free will. He explained, however, that unbelievers freely exercise only their enslaved will. When justified, the redeemed are then liberated to carry out God's law. The converted, though recognizing their weakness, may satisfy God by faith, as happens with justification. Faith obtains grace, by which the Law is fulfilled. Grace does not make free will void, for grace heals the will. It simply leaves no room for human merit in salvation.

Augustine contributed two important tenets to the church's understanding of justification. First, justification is by grace because of unconditional election. Election is fully sovereign and in no way dependent on anything in man. According to Augustine, the same is true of justification—it is a wholly sovereign work and in no way dependent on man. The unregenerate sinner deserves condemnation and punishment, not grace. Second, justification is a gift, not the result of merit. This gift comes from the working of the Holy Spirit. Augustine entirely opposed grace and merit in his doctrine of justification.[112]

Augustine's teaching here is wholly in line with Protestantism. But his weakness is in part dependent on a mistranslation in Jerome's Vulgate. Where Paul said (in Greek) that believers are *declared* righteous, Jerome translated this verse as they are made righteous. Thus Augustine also viewed justification as making someone righteous.[113]

Clement, Cyprian, Basil, Chrysostom, and Jerome ascribed justification solely to faith in Christ. Christians are saved *sola fide*.[114] The ancient church held that justification is forensic and judicial. Justification also credited Christ's righteousness to the sinner.[115] The fathers properly viewed faith as the sole instrument of justification and justification as divine mercy in contrast to human merit.[116] To argue,

---

112. Horton, *Christian Faith*, 1:86.

113. Ibid., 1:88–91.

114. Ibid., 1:81–82: "The *sola* in *sola fide* therefore had a distinguished pedigree long before Luther."

115. The exception that proves the rule is Clement of Alexandria. See ibid., 1:82–83.

116. Ibid., 1:83–84.

as some Protestants have done, that there is no forensic doctrine of justification in the ancient church is simply mistaken.[117]

Calling. Augustine developed the doctrine of calling. He taught that there was an indiscriminate call to all who heard the gospel. But he also taught that to the elect God makes a second call that unequivocally results in their salvation. God's divine call is effective.[118]

Sanctification. The early church insisted on progress in Christian maturity as a mark of genuine faith. There were high standards for the life of those who received adult baptism. In fact, the fathers described in detail the expected characteristics of a mature believer.

Historians argue that the ancient church tended toward asceticism from biblical grounds. The word *asceticism* means the disdain of anything that is physical and pleasurable. But historians also make clear that the ancient church was influenced by its culture. Platonic philosophy in particular influenced the church toward asceticism, as this philosophy degraded that which was physical and material.[119]

Augustine's view of sanctification was not that the evil body exercised influence on the good soul; rather, he understood the wicked soul to be the root. He knew the erroneous nature of Plato's teaching—he knew that it was not as though the body were evil and the soul or spirit good. Sanctification does not consist in denying the body and focusing on only spiritual matters. Sanctification involves simply living unto God as opposed to living for oneself. This lifestyle requires a lifelong battle, and complete victory over sin will never be won. Augustine spoke of the nature of this battle. After conversion, by God's grace, the human will desires to obey God. God cooperates with the human will that is directed toward God. This relationship is dependent on grace from beginning to end.[120]

117. Alister E. McGrath ("Forerunners of the Reformation? A Critical Examination of the Evidence for Precursors of the Reformation Doctrines of Justification," *Harvard Theological Review* 75, no. 1 [1982]: 219–42) mistakenly asserted: "It is utterly alien to Augustine's thought to speak of a forensic doctrine of justification or of imputed righteousness in the Reformed sense of the term" (see page 220 of his article). Sadly, Allison (*Historical Theology*, 501n17) agrees with McGrath's mistaken notion and quotes him with approval.

118. Allison, *Historical Theology*, 477–80.

119. Allison concluded: "Plato's philosophy exerted a strong impact on the view of sanctification in the early church" (ibid., 524).

120. Augustine, *On Grace and Free Will* 33, in Allison, *Historical Theology*, 529: God "prepares the will, and perfects by his cooperation what he initiates by his operation. . . . In the

For Augustine, the justified person now takes pleasure in righteous deeds and knows that he should perform them. Believers will perform the good. As an outcome of justification, believers have faith working though love. Thus the believer acquires merits through grace. God will reward these merits, and when he does so, "he will crown nothing else than his own gifts."[121]

Perseverance and Assurance. Christians in the ancient church faced many temptations to abandon the church. The first temptation was the horror of martyrdom. But even after those years of martyrdom, the church faced temptations to recede into non-Christian lifestyles. Essentially, two methods were used to encourage the church to continue in the faith, or to persevere. One method used fear as an incentive to continue in Christ, and one underlined the mercy of God.

Many early fathers used fear as a goad. The letter of Barnabas urged believers not to fall asleep in their sins and to be on their guard. Israel was used as an example of failing to walk in God's paths and suffering divine rebuke. Irenaeus warned Christians that the same divine judgment awaited them if they were to turn back to their sinful ways. As Israel had received God's promises and failed, so also might contemporary believers. Irenaeus's presentation of the possibility of the fearful loss of salvation was supposedly a means to counteract pride. Others pointed to what happened to Solomon. He began well but did not end so. Cyprian saw Solomon as a clear warning to believers. And there were also NT arguments that, according to Cyprian, taught the possibility of believers' failing to persevere in Christ.[122]

Augustine articulated the other view with clarity in *On the Gift of Perseverance.* For him, perseverance was a divine gift, one that could be requested in prayer. If given the gift, the believer would continue on to the end, but if the believer lacked the gift, he would not persevere.

---

beginning he works in us that we may have the will, and in perfecting works with us when we have the will. . . . He operates, therefore, apart from us, in order that we may will. But when we will, and so will that we may act, he cooperates with us. We ourselves can, however, do nothing to work good works of godliness apart from God either working that we may will or co-working [with us] when we will."

121. Augustine, *Epistle 194.19,* in Allison, *Historical Theology,* 502n25: "Augustine spoke of eternal life as 'surely the reward of good works.' At the same time, he concluded: 'We are to understand, then, that man's good deserts are themselves the gift of God, so that when these obtain the recompense of eternal life, it is simply grace given for grace.'"

122. Allison, *Historical Theology,* 543–44.

According to Augustine, the gift of perseverance was irrevocable once given, but no believer knew whether or not he truly had it. Augustine reasoned that there are some who obey today but will fall away before the end. This lack of certainty keeps the church humble. Divine predestination constitutes the reason why some persevere and others do not. To the charge of some that such predestination is unfair, Augustine replied that God's judgments are unsearchable. None but God receives credit for his gifts of salvation and perseverance, and none can grasp why God predestines some and not others.[123]

Atonement Theory. Gregory of Nyssa modified Origen's theory and saw Christ's death as an exquisite deception. God tricked Satan, for Satan was ignorant that Christ's deity was enclosed in his flesh. The metaphor Gregory used came from fishing: concealed within the bait is the hook. The ransom destroyed Satan.[124] John of Damascus also used the analogy of the hook, but for him the ransom was paid to God the Father. A trick was still involved, but it was death, not Satan, who was deceived by Christ's deity.

As the decades continued, the substitution theory developed.[125] Augustine presented a full substitution theory. Christ was both the priest who offers the sacrifice and the sacrifice itself. He fulfilled the four aspects of an acceptable sacrifice: to whom it is given, by whom it is offered, what is offered, and for whom it is made. His was a sacrifice for sin that brought redemption to sinners.

Christ's work issued in abundant benefits: believers are delivered from Satan's power, escape from eternal death, and are delivered from God's wrath to reconciliation and friendship with him. Also, since Christ's death was the supreme manifestation of divine love, believers are stimulated to return God's love.[126] Now with an understanding of soteriology, we will move on to the doctrine of the church, called *ecclesiology.*

---

123. Ibid., 547–48.

124. Ibid., 393.

125. Tertullian understood Christ's death as an atonement resulting in freedom from hell and life in heaven. Athanasius also argued that death is the necessary penalty for sinners and that Christ offered his sacrificial blood in place of everyone's. Christ's sacrificial death was a propitiation.

126. Allison, *Historical Theology*, 393–95.

ECCLESIOLOGY

Church Defined. The Nicene Creed used four adjectives to describe the church: unity, holiness, catholicity, and apostolicity. Hippolytus articulated the doctrine of the church's holiness when he protested so-called members of the church who sinned by means of sexual immorality, contraception, and abortion and who had no sense of shame yet still called themselves members of the church. He argued that Jesus's parable of the wheat and tares is a model for understanding the church. There would always be false members within the congregation. Cyprian acknowledged the same parable and model, and he used the reality of tares being among the wheat to encourage members not to become discouraged and withdraw from Christ's assembly but to walk in a more holy fashion.[127]

Clement of Alexandria argued that the notion of the church's universality came from Jesus's parable of the mustard seed. Augustine thought that it came from Christ's words "the whole earth" in Acts 1:8. That the church is catholic or universal means, according to Cyril of Jerusalem, that it extends over all the world, teaches all doctrines, brings the whole of humanity into subjection to Christ, deals with the universal class of sin, and has every kind of spiritual gift.[128] Ignatius said that all true Christians are to belong to this church, and failure to meet with them demonstrates their arrogance and self-condemnation.[129]

Another characteristic of the true church is that she is the mother of believers. Tertullian and Methodius forwarded this teaching, with Methodius citing Revelation 12:1–6 for support. Cyprian was a strong proponent of this teaching and made two classic statements: "He can no longer have God for his Father who has not the church for his mother," and "there is no salvation out[side] of the church."[130] Cyprian's teaching would be important for the church's self-identification.

The church also related to the state. Constantine legalized the church in the fourth century. Now the state gave privileges to the church and influenced her. The church and empire were fairly coter-

---

127. Ibid., 567–68.
128. Cyril of Jerusalem, *Catechetical Lectures* 18.23, in Allison, *Historical Theology*, 568.
129. Allison, *Historical Theology*, 568.
130. Cyprian, *Treatise* 1.6 and *Letter* 72.21, in Allison, *Historical Theology*, 569–70.

minous—those who were members of one were usually members of the other. When the Roman Empire fell one hundred years later, non-Christians blamed its demise on the church.[131]

Augustine offered a comprehensive theology of the church relative to the state. In the light of the Roman Empire's collapse, Augustine presented a massive interpretation of human history that underlined the struggle between the heavenly city, the church, and the earthly city, the people of the Devil. The church was composed not only of people alive in Augustine's day but also the number of all who had been predestined by God since Adam's fall, including the good angels. Those who would be saved would fill up the number of fallen angels. There is a definite, fixed number of the elect—a precise number known only by God.[132]

Augustine acknowledged that the situation in the visible church can appear confusing. There are some in the visible church who may not truly be members, and there are some outside the visible church who will enter. The church is necessary for salvation because she has the sacraments, especially baptism.[133] Christ's church is a fellowship of love. A characteristic of those in Christ's church is the visible demonstration of the love sustained by the Holy Spirit.

The Donatists were heterodox and maintained a different doctrine of the church. They taught that the church had to be truly holy and thus composed only of true believers. Since their church was supposedly holy, it could also solely claim the title *catholic*. Augustine countered that they had separated themselves from the Catholic Church and were thus guilty of schism. A schismatic church is not characterized by love. The Donatists needed to repent and return to the Catholic Church. Augustine's position relative to the Donatists became the church's standard doctrine relative to any schismatic group in the future.[134]

Church Government. To comprehend the later church fathers, we need first to step back and analyze earlier developments. The early church into the third century followed the NT's teaching concerning church office. Christ's church had elders or bishops and deacons. These offices, with equality between the elders and bishops, were articulated

131. Allison, *Historical Theology*, 570.
132. Ibid., 570–71.
133. Ibid., 571–72.
134. Ibid., 572.

by Clement of Rome, the *Didache*, Polycarp, Irenaeus, and Jerome.[135] The bishops were to train others in sound doctrine and to exercise leadership.

But this early position seems to be contradicted by Ignatius of Antioch, who between A.D. 107 and 116 appears to argue for three offices: bishops, presbyters, and deacons. While figures of the Reformation such as John Calvin and nineteenth-century Presbyterian historian William Cunningham dismissed Ignatius's writings as forgeries, there is evidence that they are authentic. Ignatius's writings are difficult to interpret and are not conclusive.[136] Nevertheless, some Protestant historians have argued that Ignatius called for a category of bishop as separate from, and superior to, elder. Grounding the elevation of bishop was a parallel between the authority and relationships of bishop, elders, and deacons with God's relationship to the apostles and deacons. This new system supposedly had the advantage of fostering unity and fighting heresy.[137]

While writers of the later second and mid-third centuries all distinguish between bishops, pastors and deacons, their definitions are inconsistent. As pastors gathered in geographically limited meetings—what one would call a local synod or presbytery today—they appeared to elect a president of the meeting who would be called the bishop. But early theologians do not present bishops as functioning in a higher office than pastors.

Writing in the middle of the third century, Cyprian made a distinction between bishop and presbyter. Yet he was inconsistent; at times he held to the distinction, but in a few places he argued that bishop and presbyter were synonymous.[138] As time progressed, and following cultural examples from the civil sphere, a hierarchical system became standard in the church.[139]

---

135. Clement of Rome's *Epistle to the Corinthians* was written between A.D. 92 and 101, and Polycarp's *Epistle to the Philippians* (ca. A.D. 110) demonstrates two offices: *bishop* and *deacon*. See Richard C. Gamble, "Presbyterianism and the Ancient Church," in *Pressing Toward the Mark: Essays Commemorating Fifty Years of the Orthodox Presbyterian Church*, ed. Charles G. Dennison and Richard C. Gamble (Philadelphia: Committee for the Historian of the Orthodox Presbyterian Church, 1986), 57.

136. See the analysis in Gamble, "Presbyterianism," 57–59.

137. The church needed the bishop's supervision and approval in all situations. See Allison, *Historical Theology*, 590–92.

138. See Cyprian, *Letter* 5.4 and *Letter* 40.1, in Allison, *Historical Theology*, 590.

139. Pseudo-Dionysius also did much to establish the ontological relationships between church offices. He argued that earthly ministry reflected the celestial hierarchy. See Allison,

Issues of church government arose during the strife with Novatian. While he was not theologically heterodox, he separated from the church because, he claimed, it compromised the faith. After times of persecution, Novatian argued that those who lapsed in the face of persecution could never be permitted back into the church fold. Others were milder in response and permitted lapsers to return after they confessed.

Cyprian opposed Novatian and charged him with failing in love. Cyprian used the office of bishop as a marker of theological unity and love. The church is unified, he argued, by one episcopate that is appportioned among all the bishops. The episcopacy was an essential mark of the true church, as supposedly demonstrated by Matthew 16:18–19. Salvation is found only in the church, and Novatian, by separating himself from her, courted disaster.[140]

The *Apostolic Constitutions* of the third through fourth centuries spell out how the church ran and was governed. Under Jesus Christ, the Great High Priest, bishops were put on a par with the OT high priests, presbyters equated with the OT priests, and deacons equated with the Levites. Thus bishops held the responsibility of conducting the church's ministry and were to be obeyed and respected by all the people. Ordination to any church office was placed in the hands of the bishops alone.[141]

At this time, both priests and bishops were chosen with the approval of church members. Both pastors and bishops could baptize. Deacons were not considered part of the priesthood. They carry out what the bishop needed done so that he could concentrate on his own duties. The deacons aided in the distribution of the elements of the Lord's Supper and helped with visitation and the weak. Deaconesses also functioned, following the example of Phoebe, whom Paul mentions in Romans 16:1–2. A deaconess had to be a virgin or the widow of one husband. Deaconnesses accompanied women who talked with male clergy to keep the ministry free from sexual scandal. Also, when a woman was baptized she was received by a deaconess.[142]

Historical Theology, 595.
    140. Ibid., 592–93.
    141. Ibid., 593.
    142. Ibid., 593–95.

The debate between Cyprian of Carthage and Stephen of Rome during the Novatian schism did much to advance Rome's primacy. Cyprian argued that Novatianist sacraments were invalid. Stephen said that even the heretic Novatian's baptism brought grace. A follower of Novatian did not need to be rebaptized to enter the catholic church.

As they argued for their positions, Cyprian said that Christ had given authority to all the apostles as a unity. So the bishops who act in unity share equal authority. Stephen, on the other hand, said that according to Matthew 16:15–19 Jesus gave unique authority to Peter and his successors. Thus the bishop in Rome had priority over all other bishops. Cyprian would not submit to Stephen.

As the church expanded, five important cities assumed authority over their greater geographical areas. The bishops of Alexandria, Antioch, Jerusalem, Rome, and Constantinople became patriarchs. Then a debate erupted as to who had priority among these five. The Council of Constantinople in A.D. 381 said that the bishop of Rome had priority, then the bishop of Constantinople. In A.D. 451 the Council of Chalcedon said that Rome and Constantinople had the same level of authority—a position that Rome rejected.[143]

Rome's primacy was argued by Damasus of Rome (bishop from A.D. 366 to 384), Zosimus, and Leo the Great (bishop from A.D. 440 to 461). Leo says that Peter still ministers through the bishop of Rome. Gregory the Great (bishop from A.D. 590 to 604) used the term *pope* for the bishop of Rome.[144]

Baptism. Moving to the sacraments, baptism was a prerequisite for taking the Lord's Supper. The early church fathers articulated a host of purposes for baptism.[145] They believed that baptism is the instrument of forgiveness for sins[146] and that it delivers one from death.[147] Bap-

143. Ibid., 596–97.
144. Ibid., 597–98.
145. Tertullian, *Against Marcion* 1.28, in Allison, *Historical Theology*, 613.
146. This doctrine was taught by Justin Martyr and Barnabas and codified in the Nicene Creed: "I acknowledge one baptism for the forgiveness of sins."
147. Cyprian said that baptism rescues one from doom and delivers one from hell's judgment. Baptism brings new birth. He said it is the means for the death of the old man and the birth of the new man. John 3:5 was used to demonstrate that baptism was necessary for salvation. Baptism provides the gift of the Holy Spirit. Origen called baptism the "bath of regeneration." Baptism also provides a decisive break from Satan. Unbelievers are in Satan's service and must renounce that service before enlisting with a new master. See Allison, *Historical Theology*, 614–15.

tism is also a symbol of identification with, union with, or imitation of Christ. Basil the Great thought that imitating Christ was essential for an intimate relationship with God. Through baptistm, believers are identified with Christ's resurrection.[148]

By the third and fourth centuries, some additions to these actions included the setting apart of water for baptism; anointing with oil, which Tertullian connected to the OT consecration of priests; and the laying on of hands, which he believed had an OT precedent. Origen and Tertullian said that the water of the sacrament did not provide the Holy Spirit but that it came after baptism via the unction and laying on of hands.[149]

Candidates for baptism, called *catechumens*, had to undergo a period of instruction.[150] By the fourth century, Christianity was legal and many people wanted to join the church. The instruction period kept some of them out. The view began to develop that baptism washed away previous sins but not postbaptismal sins. The renunciation of Satan became more complex, with the person baptized first facing westward and directly denouncing Satan, then turning to the east and professing belief in the Trinity.[151]

Debates concerning infant baptism[152] considered that because of the arduous catechumenical requirements, including fasting, baptism would naturally be available only to adults.[153] A link was seen between baptism and original sin, as well as OT circumcision. Cyprian had equated baptism with circumcision.[154] Augustine used Cyprian's analysis and added that infant baptism was to obliterate original sin in infants. Thus infant baptism became the practice, as codified in the Council of Carthage in A.D. 417.[155]

148. Basil, *On the Spirit* 15.35 and 8.22, in Allison, *Historical Theology*, 615.

149. Allison, *Historical Theology*, 614.

150. Hippolytus said that the instruction normally lasted three years. The students would, among other tasks, memorize the Nicene Creed. See ibid., 616.

151. Ibid., 617–18.

152. Irenaeus's theory of recapitulation may be interpreted to refer to infant baptism. See ibid., 619.

153. Tertullian objected to bringing children for baptism, for they required sponsors to stand in their place. Instead of sponsors' promising on the children's behalf, the point was to delay baptizing children until they became believers. See Tertullian, *On Baptism* 18, in Allison, *Historical Theology*, 618.

154. Cyprian, *Letter* 58.2, 5, in Allison, *Historical Theology*, 619.

155. The Council of Carthage argued against those who said that children do not need baptism because they have not actually sinned. See Allison, *Historical Theology*, 620.

Baptism dealt with both original sin and the actual sins that adults had committed until the time of their baptism. To address the issue of postbaptismal sins, the church began to develop what would become the sacrament of penance, which was especially useful for dealing with the lapsed.

Lord's Supper. The Lord's Supper was observed each week; the elements consisted in bread and in wine mixed with water. This sacrament was available only to baptized believers, who also had to be in good standing with the church.[156]

The precise meaning of the Lord's Supper in the patristic church is difficult to determine. Some early church fathers understood the Lord's Supper to be a sacrifice and connected it to Malachi 1:10–11, contrasting Israel's worthless sacrifices to the true sacrifice among the Gentiles. The nature of that sacrifice is difficult to determine because, on the one hand, Docetism denied the reality of Christ's incarnation. In response, Irenaeus underlined Christ's true incarnation and Christ's being present in the Lord's Supper.[157] Christ's presence was connected to the act of commemoration: the Lord's Supper is a commemoration of Christ's crucifixion and is celebrated in remembrance of his suffering. Christ commanded the Lord's Supper in commemoration of himself.

Augustine wrote extensively about the nature of the sacrament, which applies to both baptism and the Lord's Supper. These sacraments were outward signs of an invisible yet genuine grace.[158] Augustine's understanding of the nature of the sacrament is referred to in Latin as *ex opera operato*—literally, "by the work performed." These words convey the meaning that when a sacrament is performed, it is objectively valid. The sacrament accomplishes its purpose. Thus it is Christ himself who baptizes, and baptism truly forgives sins. Augustine saw baptism as necessary for salvation but held to heretical baptism as legitimate. He believed it was legitimate because of his view of the sacrament's working *ex opera operato*. Baptism accomplishes the forgiveness of sins.[159]

---

156. Ibid., 636–37.

157. Allison wrongly argues that Ignatius held to a one-to-one correspondence between the bread and cup and Christ's body and blood. His citation does not prove that point. See ibid., 638.

158. Ibid., 640.

159. Ibid., 620–21.

Augustine believed that it is Christ himself who serves the Lord's Supper, and he is truly present in it. Holding a realistic view of the Supper, Augustine also held a symbolic view of it, for he denied that the bread and wine offered in the Supper are identical with Christ's historical body and blood.[160] He also taught that the Supper challenged Christians to live in love and unity and as genuine members of Christ's body.

Worship. The church gathered on Sunday. Its earliest worship included readings from the OT and the Gospels along with teaching and admonition, congregational prayer, the Lord's Supper, and financial giving.[161] Eventually, a standardized liturgy was presented in the *Apostolic Constitutions*, which included reading from Scripture, the singing of Psalms, preaching, praying, the holy kiss, and the Lord's Supper.[162]

ESCHATOLOGY

Millennium. By the fifth century, many theologians had become convinced of amillennialism—in other words, that the millennium began with Christ's resurrection and did not have to last for a thousand years on earth. Premillennialism was rejected in part because of its elaborate predictions for the coming of the millennium, especially the Montanists' fanaticism, and also because of the changed relationship to the state, now that Christianity was legal. Another reason for the critique of premillennialism was the theological method coming out of Alexandria, especially from Clement and Origen, who argued against a literal interpretation of the end times. Origen looked for a spiritual meaning, not a literal one.[163]

Augustine was at first attracted to premillennialism but was later scandalized by proponents' descriptions of the millennium. He produced a full amillennialist view of Revelation 20. For Augustine, the one thousand years of the millennium began with Christ's first coming

160. Ibid., 640–41.
161. From Justin Martyr's description in *First Apology* 67, in Allison, *Historical Theology*, 660–61.
162. Ibid., 661–62.
163. Ibid., 687.

and would continue until the end of the world. The first resurrection, mentioned in Revelation 20:5–6, occurs when someone comes to saving faith in Christ. The second resurrection, in verse 5, is the dire fate of unbelievers. Augustine's view reigned in the church for the next thousand years.[164]

Final Judgment and Eternal Punishment. Most early church writers articulated that there would be rewards for the righteous and punishment for the wicked.[165] Origen held a number of unique views on this topic, including the preexistence of souls. Combined with that view, he held that God's punishment for sin was meant to be restorative or rehabilitative, to cleanse evil. Since divine punishment was transformative, he hoped that God's actions would ultimately restore all human and angelic beings. He seems to have held to universal salvation, and his doctrine was condemned in Alexandria in A.D. 400. The Synod of Constantinople condemned his views in A.D. 543 and declared it anathema to think that punishment for the wicked is only temporary.[166]

Augustine's views set the standard for the church for fifteen hundred years. The second death was considered eternal. He described the nightmare of hell: "There, in striking contrast to our present conditions, people will not exist before or after death, but always in death—never living, never dead, but eternally dying. And never can a person be more disastrously in death than when death itself will be deathless."[167] He thought that there would be degrees of happiness among the saved and degrees of misery among the damned.

Augustine dealt with a number of objections to the church's teaching. First, it was argued that endless physical punishment is impossible because the human body cannot take it. Augustine countered that the resurrected body will be miraculously changed and differently constituted. Second, it was argued that it is unjust to be doomed to eternal punishment for sins perpetrated in time. Augustine replied that even in human courts, punishment lasts longer than the time it takes to

---

164. Ibid., 688.

165. Polycarp, Irenaeus, and *The Shepherd of Hermas* held to Christ as the final judge. That judgment would be based on earthly deeds as specifically articulated in the Athanasian Creed. See Allison, *Historical Theology*, 703–4.

166. Ibid., 704–5.

167. Augustine, *The City of God* 13.12.11, in Allison, *Historical Theology*, 706.

perpetrate the crime. He also objected that the question ignores the enormity of Adam's sin—Adam destroyed a good that could have been eternal, thus there must be eternal punishment. Third, some theologians granted that there is divine punishment against the wicked, but they argued that the punishment is meant to be therapeutic and restorative and not eternal. This objection was similar to Origen's thinking. Augustine countered that if divine punishment is purely therapeutic, then even the Devil will be saved. On the other hand, if the Devil will be punished forever, as the Scriptures clearly teach, then so will unbelieving human beings.[168]

THEOLOGICAL METHOD

Stoicism and the Nicene Creed. Douglas F. Kelly argues that the Stoic notion of assent is very close to how many ancient church fathers defined the nature of faith.[169] In fact, Kelly argues that the Nicene Creed, because it begins with "I believe" rather than "I know," indicates that believing, which includes assent, is based on a "Christian adaptation of elements of Stoic epistemology, [which] included both intuitive apprehension of what is there, and also intellectual consent to that supreme Reality that is external to the mind and objectively real."[170] Using these Stoic terms apparently helped fourth-century theologians to communicate biblical realities.

Bridge Builder: Basil the Great. Basil the Great voiced many negative evaluations of Greek thinking yet could be judged a bridge builder. He thought that it was proper to accept useful philosophical notions and to reject the rest of them. While pagan literature must be read selectively, he saw positive value in it.[171]

Philosophical Terms and Theological Method. There is no doubt that the Chalcedonian Creed used the Greek words for *person* and *nature* in a highly technical fashion. The intellectual culture of the

168. Allison, *Historical Theology*, 706–8.
169. Kelly, *Systematic Theology*, 1:45–46. Those church fathers besides Clement include Irenaeus, Hippolytus of Rome, Origen, and particularly Novatian of Rome, who "Christianized certain aspects of Stoic epistemology, ethics and physics."
170. Ibid., 1:46.
171. Ibid., 1:201–2.

time implemented these same words. The methodological question to be asked focuses on whether the theologians of Chalcedon embraced secular philosophical concepts in their implementation of these Greek words.[172] The word *embrace* here would fall into the third level of influence. And the answer to the question is, "No."

Kelly is rightly convinced that when Greek philosophical teaching and categories were brought into Christian theology, the Greek categories and meanings of words were transformed.[173] For example, specific studies on the patristic understanding of divine immutability have demonstrated that there was a marked difference between how impassibility was affirmed in the ancient church and how it was articulated in Greek philosophy.[174] Clearly in the early church, Stoic and other philosophical concepts were used and adapted to fit Christian theology. Christian theologians of the time used the tools available to them. As theology has continued to develop over the next millennium and a half, however, contemporary theologians must be self-conscious and careful if or when they implement pagan thinking into Christian theology.[175]

Conclusion to Part 2. Part 2 began with the new era of early Christianity, when persecution ended and Christianity became the recognized religion of the mighty Roman Empire. We examined how the church and state interacted, as well as the tumultuous development of doctrine. Part 3 will open with the world of medieval Europe.

---

172. Since the early nineteenth century, historians have argued a hellenization thesis that claims the church wrongly embraced Greek thinking.

173. Ibid., 2:205: "I have so far not seen it demonstrated that the quite varied connotations of these words in different strands of Greek thought are ever directly taken over into the official thought of the Church *without a shift in meaning*"; ibid., 2:214: Trinitarian thinking "did not represent the transmutation of Christian doctrine into a Greek mold. Rather, the Church Fathers transformed the Greek terms into instruments that, filled with biblical content, were bearers of [proper] doctrine." Kelly rightly critiques the well-accepted thesis of Harry A. Wolfson, who argued that Philo Judaeus was the main source of patristic thought on the Trinity. See ibid., 2:214–16.

174. Michael Allen, "Divine Attributes," in *Christian Dogmatics. Reformed Theology for the Church Catholic*, ed. Michael Allen and Scott R. Swain (Grand Rapids: Baker Academic, 2016), 72–73.

175. WCG 1:59 describes how the OT itself provides epistemological self-consciousness: "The theologian knows 'facts' about himself and the world around him because God has made him and the world in which he lives. God has also given to him the tools needed to evaluate himself and God's world." WCG 2:955–71 describes how the Bible itself presents realism over against skepticism without needing to rely on Stoic philosophical constructs to build it.

KEY TERMS

Antiochene Christology
Nestorius
Chalcedonian Creed
Eutyches
Monophysites
perichoresis
hypostatic union
prevenient grace
semi-Pelagianism

STUDY QUESTIONS

1. Explain the different ways that God is knowable.
2. What are some of God's attributes?
3. What is the difference between the ontological and the economic Trinity?
4. What were some of the terms used to define the church?
5. Should there be bishops who are of higher authority than pastors?
6. Was there a unified meaning to the Lord's Supper in the ancient church?
7. Would you consider yourself a bridge burner or bridge builder relative to theological method?

RESOURCES FOR FURTHER STUDY

There are some excellent histories of doctrine, but Protestant historical theologians are generally not strong in the field of patristics.

Kelly, J. N. D. *Early Christian Creeds*. London: Longman, 1972. An outstanding scholarly work.

Lampe, G. W. H. "Christian Theology in the Patristic Period." In *A History of Christian Doctrine*, edited by Hubert Cunliffe-Jones, 21–180. 1978. Reprint, New York: T&T Clark, 2006. A very clear and concise resource.

Letham, Robert. *The Holy Trinity: In Scripture, History, Theology, and Worship*. Rev. and exp. ed. Phillipsburg, NJ: P&R Publishing, 2019. On pages 87–250, an outstanding analysis of the development of the doctrine of the Trinity by a British theologian who is a notable exception to general Protestant weakness.

PART 3

The Church and the World

8

New Era with the Decline of Civilization

THIS CHAPTER TRACES THE story of a new era, which dawned following the destruction of Rome and stretched through the fourteenth century. During these centuries, the illiterate invaders of Rome not only learned how to read but also were faced with the saving message of Jesus Christ. These invaders began to build their own kingdoms atop the rubble of Rome. These kingdoms developed into what we now refer to as the feudal system—an economic and political system that characterized this era. Western society also faced a new challenge with the rise of Islam. Christian Europe was attacked from without, thus forcing another defining moment in church history—the Crusades. This chapter will track the interaction between the church and society in this critical era of church history.

INTRODUCTION TO MEDIEVAL HISTORY

Evangelicals often struggle to interpret the Middle Ages. The Reformation, which evangelicals rightly and gladly celebrate, is often viewed as antithetical and as a correction to the medieval system. The question becomes, "Why study the history of a church that was saturated with political and religious corruption?" A simple answer is that the Middle Ages comprise a period of Christ's church, no matter how dark or corrupt they were. God did not abandon his people to stumble about in darkness for six hundred years. The church should not be uncomfortable with or disinterested in the Middle Ages, for the church has much to learn from this era's successes and failures. Studying accomplishments and shortfalls is an essential task of church history. Believers can and should learn from those who have come before us by examining the church throughout all her history. This section will examine the interaction of social and intellectual history and combine that analysis with a conclusion on the historical development of doctrine.

Problem of *Heilsgeschichte* and "Mundane" History. Christians understand human history to be unified and meaningful because God is sovereign over every past, present, and future event. Confident in these presuppositions, the believer does not interpret the events of history as accidental or disconnected, as must the non-Christian. Though believers cannot always trace the hand of God in the exact outworking of his decrees, they can rest in his sovereign reign.

While the church of Christ is not of the world, it remains in the world. The church is rooted in its society and influenced by the changes that take place in the world. As one example of that influence, early in my ministry, church planting and expansion were done without the availability of the internet; it was not yet invented! Now, most visitors find new churches based on internet searches by comparing church against church based on specific and personal criteria.

Culture is a helpful concept to understand as we think about the church in the world. Culture can be defined as that which holds sway and exercises power over people and things. Culture is never static— sometimes a culture changes abruptly, often in the face of catastrophic events. For example, the morning of September 11, 2001, brought unprecedented changes to the American way of life and thought. More recently, a virus has damaged the social and economic landscape in ways no one could have imagined. At other times, decades roll by with more gradual and less noticeable ebbs in the cultural tide. Great changes in culture often present greater opportunities for the preaching of the gospel. Below we will examine some of these cultural shifts in the Middle Ages.

Barbarian Invasion and Conversion (A.D. 430–660).[1] In the year A.D. 430, the great theologian Augustine of Hippo died. By this point

---

1. Jacques Le Goff, *Medieval Civilization 400–1500*, trans. Julia Barrow (Oxford: Blackwell, 1988), 3–36; Nicholas R. Needham, *2,000 Years of Christ's Power*, vol. 1, *The Age of the*

in time, the Roman state had ceased its persecution of the church a century ago. Yet conflicts swept through the church. The negative pressure of doctrinal heresy forced the positive formulation of doctrine and creeds. This two-century era witnessed the growth of magical rites, the occult, and the development of the seven sacraments, which may be best understood as the synthesis of pagan and Christian ideas.

In many ways, Roman political power toppled in Britain, France, Spain, and North Africa when the Visigoths sacked Rome in A.D. 410.[2] The barbarian kings craved the benefits of association with the great Roman culture and thus were technically servants of the Roman state. Nevertheless, what remained was no longer the great Rome of the past. This strange story of Roman decline continued in A.D. 451, when a now-united Roman and German army attacked the barbarian Attila the Hun. Thus, although separation between the Roman and Germanic cultures existed, there was also still an uneasy unity.[3]

In times of war, armies assume prominent roles, and it was the generals who largely controlled the Roman Empire. By the end of the fifth century, the barbarians had conquered Italy, and they continued to dominate the world until the rise of the Emperor Justinian I, who ruled from A.D. 527 to 565.

Justinian I attempted to reconquer the Western empire. He began by seizing North Africa from the Vandals, then reconquered Italy from the Ostrogoths. Theologically, the Vandals and Ostrogoths were Arian, and it was largely through Justinian's victories over them that theological Arianism was extinguished.[4] But after Justinian's death, no one succeeded him in his fight against the Germanic people, and by A.D. 568 the Lombards reinvaded the Italian peninsula.[5]

The conversion of the barbarian Franks, which occurred at this time, can be understood as an epochal event.[6] The Franks, who lived at the end of the century in what is modern France, converted

---

Early Church Fathers (London: Grace Publications, 1997), 287–323. See W. Andrew Hoffecker, ed., *Revolutions in Worldview: Understanding the Flow of Western Thought* (Phillipsburg, NJ: P&R Publishing, 2007), 134–35.

2. Le Goff, *Medieval Civilization*, 17.

3. Ibid., 19.

4. Karl Heussi, *Kompendium der Kirchengeschichte* (Tübingen: Mohr Siebeck, 1971), 116.

5. Justinian I was also against Monophysitism. See Heussi, *Kompendium*, 116; Le Goff, *Medieval Civilization*, 21.

6. Heussi, *Kompendium*, 114–15.

to Orthodox Christianity around Christmas in A.D. 496 under King Chlodovech. Their conversion set the stage for the conversion of the other Germanic tribes.

In the Germanic kingdoms, the king wielded strong influence in the church, and in his person he united the church and the state. There was no official jurisdiction by the pope—the majority of the churches were connected to their national king.[7] By the year A.D. 587, the Visigoths renounced Arianism, so that by ca. A.D. 590 even the Lombards were undergoing conversion. The complete disappearance of Arianism from the West is most often assigned to the year A.D. 660.[8] To understand the period further, we need to examine the growth of papal influence.

Growth of the Papacy (Fourth and Fifth Centuries).[9] Beginning in the fourth century, Bishop Damasus (A.D. 366–384) of Rome began to describe the church there as the *Apostolic See*. He attempted to strengthen the preeminence of the church of Rome among the churches of the West and even extend it over those of the East. As a result, by the end of the fourth century, Rome possessed a preeminent role and authority over the churches of both the Eastern and Western empire.

In a similar manner, Leo I, also known as Leo the Great (A.D. 440–461), insisted on the primacy of Peter among the apostles and that the popes, as Peter's heirs, inherited Peter's role in the church as supreme ruler and teacher. Leo even began to use language such as Peter speaking in and through the pope. The Council of Chalcedon in A.D. 451 maintained that Peter had spoken through the mouth of Pope Leo, thus solidifying the power and authority of the papacy. The issue was settled when the emperor decreed that the pope had supreme power over the provinces of the Western church.

Concomitant with the barbarians' invasion of the Roman Empire was the rise of the power of the bishop of Rome. This power became increasingly solidified as the Roman Empire itself became weaker. There was a seesaw relationship between the power of the pope and

---

7. Ibid., 115.

8. See Williston Walker, *A History of the Christian Church* (New York: Scribner's Sons, 1959), 147; Le Goff, *Medieval Civilization*, 21; Nicholas R. Needham, *2,000 Years of Christ's Power*, vol. 2, *The Middle Ages* (2000; repr., London: Grace Publications, 2004), 16.

9. Walker, *History*, 151.

the power of the Roman Empire: as the power of the empire dwindled, so the power of the papacy, as the visible representation of the power of Rome, increased. The bishop of Rome became the symbol of both apostolic authority and Roman tradition.

This shifting power contributed to a rift between the Eastern and Western church. During the time of Pope Felix III (A.D. 483–492), the church of Rome excommunicated the patriarch of Constantinople. This development was the first recorded schism in the institutional church. It was resolved in A.D. 519 by granting further power to the papacy.

About a century later, Gregory I (A.D. 590–604), also known as Gregory the Great, came to power.[10] By this time the Visigoths and Lombards had abandoned Arianism. Pope Gregory undertook the conversion of the Anglo-Saxons, a task entrusted to a monk named Augustine and his companions.[11] Willibrord and Boniface began the work of the conversion of the land of Frisia, in modern Netherlands, and then Germany during the first half of the eighth century.[12]

Primitive Development. From A.D. 700 to 1050, the papacy was in its primitive stages.[13] In the eighth century, a document named the *Donation of Constantine* was forged and widely used as evidence for papal political authority. This document claimed that in the fourth century, Constantine granted the papacy power over Rome and all the Western empire. The Donation of Constantine began with an account of Constantine's conversion, baptism, and cure from leprosy by the intercession of Pope Silvester. Constantine, in thankfulness, supposedly gave the pope preeminence over the bishops of Antioch, Alexandria, Jerusalem, and Constantinople. He built the Lateran Palace for the pope and gave him the imperial insignia. The insignia was a tangible demonstration that Rome's full imperial power was vested in the pope; he was now ruler of all of Italy and the Western provinces.

---

10. Heussi, *Kompendium*, 119. See Needham, *2,000 Years*, 1:298–304.

11. Pope Gregory I instructed the missionary Augustine "to adapt pagan temples and holidays to Christian purposes." See Douglas F. Kelly, *Systematic Theology*, vol. 1, *The God Who Is the Holy Trinity* (Fearn, Scotland: Mentor, 2008), 207.

12. Le Goff, *Medieval Civilization*, 21; Needham, *2,000 Years*, 2:46–49.

13. R. W. Southern, *Western Society and the Church in the Middle Ages*, The Pelican History of the Church 2 (Middlesex, England: Penguin Books, 1976), 91–100; M. D. Knowles, *Geschichte der Kirche*, Band II, *Früh und Hochmittelalter* (Zürich: Benziger, 1971), 57–68.

To guarantee that this donation would not be violated, the document was placed on Peter's grave.[14]

The Donation of Constantine presents the pope as a universal bishop who acts as teacher, preserver, and godfather of the emperor. It claimed that Peter manifests his power through the papal office, thus making the pope the supreme lord of the West.[15]

Age of Growth. The office of the pope continued to grow from the years 1050 to 1300. One of the highest powers in medieval political life was the ability to give and dispense justice. By this standard, the pope had unrivaled political power, though he lacked the political strength actually to rule the West. In return for loyalty, obedience, and payments, the pope could grant benefits to those whom he chose. Monasteries and religious orders, for example, were given enormous privileges, and popes courted political leaders by allowing the sons of nobility to live as wantonly as they desired.[16]

POLITICAL STRUCTURES IN EUROPE[17]

Frankish Kingdom and Empire (Fifth and Sixth Centuries). From the fall of Rome until Charlemagne, political rule was more localized than it had been during the height of the Roman Empire, when no king had a well-established bureaucracy. The papacy, on the other hand, had skilled administration and exercised great power. Compared with surrounding rulers, the institutional church headquartered in Rome was the strongest reigning organization.

Clovis established the Frankish Kingdom in the fifth century, only for it to be split by later successors.[18] In the early part of the eighth century, one king—Charles Martel—rose to prominence. He was affec-

---

14. R. W. Southern, *The Making of the Middle Ages* (New Haven: Yale University Press, 1992), 93.

15. Southern, *Middle Ages*, 94–95. Saint Peter's tomb was of the highest importance. His bones were very sacred. It was from the tomb that Peter supposedly still performed miracles. While his bones were an active force for union in the West, his persona was entrusted to the pope.

16. Southern, *Western Society*, 121–26.

17. Le Goff, *Medieval Civilization*, 37–55.

18. Stewart C. Easton, *The Western Heritage* (New York: Holt, Reinhart & Winston, 1961), 184–90. For more on Clovis and his Constantine-like conversion, see Needham, *2,000 Years*, 1:290–91.

tionately known as The Hammer. Martel entered an alliance with the Lombards in their effort to fight against the Muslims.

Martel's son was known as Pepin the Short. Despite Pepin's strength, he too had relatively limited authority, even within his own kingdom. The nobles of the Frankish kingdom pushed against any central control asserted over them, so Pepin's power was restricted to royal lands; still, his power was greater than that of any individual lord. Combining this political might with the services of the clergy, he was the strongest among equals. Members of the clergy were especially important to him, for only the clergy possessed even basic literacy skills. Thus they were responsible for writing laws and political recommendations.

To consolidate his power, Pepin the Short requested that the pope crown him king of France. At this time the papacy had its own troubles—the Lombards. The Lombards possessed an effective fighting force and were the ruling faction in Italy. But the pope stood against the Lombards because they occupied large areas of the nation. Seeing the advantages in Pepin's request, the pope commissioned the missionary Boniface to crown Pepin king of the Franks in A.D. 752.[19] With Pepin in power, the pope secured Pepin's support in his fight against the Lombards.

Aware of these plottings, the Lombards moved south toward Rome itself. In A.D. 755 Pepin came to the rescue of Pope Steven II (A.D. 752–757). Pepin and his army crossed the Alps and contained the Lombards, who were fighting under King Aistulf. The two leaders signed a treaty, forcing Aistulf to return occupied land. Pepin and his army then withdrew. But King Aistulf refused to keep his word. So in A.D. 756, Pepin again crossed the Alps and soundly defeated Aistulf, consequently took land from the Lombards, and donated those lands to the pope. This gift became known as the famous *Donation of Pepin*. In fact, a donation of lands won by military conquest was, at the time, considered a legal gift. Thus, thanks to the Donation of Pepin, the papacy legally held vast amounts of land until the nineteenth century.[20] It was likely at this time that Pepin forged the document mentioned earlier—the Donation of Constantine—which gave the

19. Le Goff, *Medieval Civilization*, 21; Needham, *2,000 Years*, 2:46–49.
20. Walker, *History*, 186.

pope direct sovereignty over the western half of the empire.[21] This donation legally lasted as the pope's source of power until the year 1870; it was revived on a much smaller scale in 1929 by the creation of the Vatican City State within the nation of Italy.

With his many victories, Pepin was able to bequeath to his two sons a strong and united kingdom. That kingdom was a recognized ally of the powerful pope—a kingdom that had been blessed by both the church and the nobility.[22]

Holy Roman Empire.[23] King Pepin died in the year A.D. 768. He divided his kingdom between his two sons, Charles, known as Charles the Great, or Charlemagne, and Carloman. Charlemagne led in brilliance during his long reign, which lasted from A.D. 768 to 814. He created legions of loyal nobles and clergy. He reestablished and reigned over a vast empire, with lands greater than those held even by the emperor in Constantinople. He fought the Saxons, defeated the Asiatic tribes, and compelled them both to convert to Christianity. Notably, his only defeat came from the Basques in Spain.[24]

Charlemagne's administrative system was simple. Each free man swore an oath of allegiance to him, and each lord had specific duties to perform for the king. Although Charlemagne was an autocrat, as a ruler he recognized his responsibility to God.[25]

Charlemagne had an interesting relationship with Pope Leo III. The king never considered the pope to be his political superior. At best he viewed the pope as a useful collaborator. Charlemagne granted the pope honor as God's representative and head of the church, but he also felt free to summon synods, declare bishops heretical, and pronounce ecclesiastical sentences out of his own power. In fact, during a time of controversy with Pope Leo III, who was accused of various sins, Charlemagne required the pope to take an oath declaring his innocence. Thus the king sat in judgment over the pope.

---

21. Le Goff, *Medieval Civilization*, 23; Walker (*History*, 186–87) underlined the fact that the document was already known to be false as early as the 1430s.

22. Le Goff, *Medieval Civilization*, 21.

23. Easton, *Western Heritage*, 190–94.

24. See the map from Walker, *History*, 178.

25. Hans von Schubert, *Geschichte der christlichen Kirche im Frühmittelalter* (Tübingen: Mohr Siebeck, 1921), 346.

On Christmas day in A.D. 800, Leo III crowned Charlemagne emperor in Saint Peter's cathedral (later designated a *basilica*) in Rome. Scholars have questioned whether this inauguration was planned by Charlemagne or whether it occurred spontaneously, as the king alleged. Historians have held both positions. Regardless of the initiation of the event, this crowning by the pope established historical precedent. All subsequent emperors felt themselves to be truly crowned only when crowned by the pope himself. It is no surprise, then, that many later popes leveraged this strategic role for personal gain—they often demanded a high price in exchange for a crowning.[26]

Charlemagne held that the church was an essential instrument of government though in every manner subordinate to royal authority. The responsibility of the church was to Christianize the manners and worldview of its Frankish subjects. Education and administration, therefore, were placed in ecclesiastical hands.[27]

Alcuin of York (A.D. 730–804) **and Charlemagne's Court.**[28] Though Charlemagne is well known as a military leader and conqueror, he also reformed both the church and society.[29] He brought to his court many learned men. Perhaps foremost among these men was the English monk and deacon Alcuin, from York.

Alcuin joined Charlemagne's court in A.D. 781. He ran an informal school of the liberal arts in the palace, which Charles frequented. He himself was illiterate and incapable of so much as forming a letter. Alcuin began a process of establishing and expanding monastic schools and libraries throughout the kingdom. His writings provide insight into the nature and curriculum of the famous schools.[30] There were two types of schools: one for boys headed toward ecclesiastical service, and the other for boys aimed at lay leadership.[31] The curriculum included

26. Ibid., 355–57.
27. See Walker, *History*, 189, on the relationship between the church and state; Needham, *2,000 Years*, 2:51–53, 57.
28. Francis Nigel Lee, *A Christian Introduction to the History of Philosophy* (Nutley, NJ: Craig Press, 1969), 127; Needham, *2,000 Years*, 2:54; Le Goff, *Medieval Civilization*, 268: Charlemagne "seems to have tried to unite in his person the double dignity of emperor and priest."
29. Walker, *History*, 188.
30. There were also other schools that flourished during this time, especially the monasteries at Saint Gallen, Corbie, and Fulda.
31. Copleston, *A History of Philosophy*, 2, *Medieval Philosophy* (New York: Continuum, 1950), 1:109.

theology and exegesis, especially for those pupils entering the priesthood. Also included were studies of the *trivium*, grammar, rhetoric and dialectic, the *quadrivium*, arithmetic, geometry, astronomy, and music, thus comprising the seven liberal arts.[32]

Alcuin influenced Charlemagne to think of his realm as the very city of God—something Augustine of Hippo had spoken of four centuries earlier. Alcuin was not a great philosopher or an original thinker, but he was a competent educator.[33]

Not content merely to diffuse education and literacy, Alcuin also collected and copied documents that preserved the heritage of the past. The preservation of large numbers of classical and patristic texts is due to the work of Alcuin and his compatriots.[34] The variety of works held in libraries increased greatly in the ninth century. Their holdings included works pertaining to theology and religion, law and grammar, classical authors, and even logic and dialectic. Alcuin recorded in A.D. 778 that the great library had, in Latin, the logical works of Aristotle, Marius Victorinus, and Boethius.[35]

Alcuin wrote the first medieval treatise on logic, the *Dialectica*. Presumably, he composed this work for use in the *trivium*, which, when he became master of Charlemagne's palace school, Alcuin reestablished as the basis of education. For a season, this work was widely used in teaching, but later it was set aside in favor of newer works.

End of Charlemagne's Era. Charlemagne planned and hoped for peaceful succession, so he divided his empire between his sons. But all his sons died—except for Louis, who was his sole successor. Upon Louis's death in A.D. 840, the empire was divided among his three sons. As a result of these repeated divisions of the empire, it was barely worthy of being referred to as such by the end of the century.[36]

Charlemagne's empire was filled with weaknesses. He did not establish a strong civil service that could rule after him. His officials

---

32. In geometry and astronomy, little work was done in the ninth century, though the *Musica encharidis*, from the last part of the century, advanced the theory of music. See Copleston, *Medieval Philosophy*, 1:109–10.

33. Ibid., 1:108.

34. The Carolingian Miniscule, a beautiful and elegant hand in the field of paleography, was developed at this time.

35. Analysis of Boethius appears in the next chapter.

36. Henry St. Lawrence Beaufort Moss, *The Birth of the Middle Ages: 395–814* (Oxford: Clarendon, 1935), 239–41; von Schubert, *Geschichte*, 361–71.

were not paid for their services but instead were given land as their compensation. So an official could retain the land given to him even when the next emperor sat on the throne. When Charlemagne was no longer in power, the landowners could choose not to serve the current emperor but still retain their land.

After Charlemagne, problems arose from outside the empire as well. The Huns pushed through a corridor of southern Russia and drove the Germanic people to the end of Rome's territory in the West. In addition, the tide of Arabs submerged Syria and Egypt by flowing into North Africa and Spain and settling in the northeast beyond Persia.[37]

Trade and economics were also weakened during this time. By the year A.D. 800, the great Roman road system, which had facilitated economic flourishing, had broken down. Trade did not entirely disappear, for much of the early economic structure in large districts of France and Italy remained. But the economy itself was based on what has been termed a "closed-house economy," in which the needs of life were supplied by the labor of the self-sufficient community and the exchange of goods was subordinate to production. Long-distance trade had almost entirely disappeared, apart from that involving luxury goods—such as spices, jewels, ivory, incense, and works of art—destined for the king's court or the church.

As a result, Britain and northern France—and other more remote regions—existed in a primitive condition of isolated self-sufficiency. Pirates had nearly extinguished all shipping across the Mediterranean Sea. And with the rise of Islam, the Carolingian educational revival faced a bleak future. Education eventually declined to such an extent that many universities and schools disappeared from the landscape.[38]

With the absence of strong central leadership, society developed into strict class rankings—the intermediate ranks essentially vanished, thus creating a chasm between the rich and powerful nobles and the struggling serfs. The collapse of the Roman government in the West brought about a cultural transformation that could be described as a disintegration of the highest layers of civilization. Small fragments of this highest layer remained, but even where they did so, they could in no way be considered a universal pattern.

37. Le Goff, *Medieval Civilization*, 7.
38. Ibid., 128–30.

England to the Norman Conquest. We now move north to Anglo-Saxon England, which mirrored, in many ways, the patterns of change seen in southern Europe. As the seventh century dawned, King Ethelbert of Kent (A.D. 584–616) accepted the Christian faith. Significantly, he also wrote down the kingdom's laws in the common language. In A.D. 627, his successor, King Edwin of Northumbria, also adopted Christianity for the nation.[39] This was the era of the deservedly well-known historian and chronicler Bede, who wrote the *Ecclesiastical History of the English People*.[40] In his philosophy of history, Bede recognized a divine hand that imposed order onto the chaos of history—of both the past and the future.[41]

One consistent trouble for the land came in the form of persistent foreign invasions from the Continent.[42] The sailing Danes, committed pagans, began their raids in A.D. 793.[43] They killed the king of East Anglia and established a subject kingdom in York. By the end of the ninth century, Danish settlers had colonized Yorkshire, Lincoln, Leicester, Derby, Nottingham, Chippenham, and all of east Wessex. The western part of Mercia had an English king who served under Danish authority.[44]

The Danish leader Guthrum accepted baptism and abandoned the attempt to subject English Wessex to his control. He moved to East Anglia, where he established the third Danish colony. He later took control of London.[45]

Things changed when Alfred the Great (A.D. 835–899) took the throne. He compiled the *Anglo-Saxon Chronicle* and built enormous warships, constructed a system of fortress towns, and established permanent garrisons.[46] By the time of his death, he had saved England from Viking paganism and ensured a West-Saxon succession to the throne.[47]

---

39. Helen Cam, *England before Elizabeth* (New York: Harper & Row, 1960), 28; Le Goff, *Medieval Civilization*, 21.

40. Cam, *England*, 29.

41. King Offa is best known for his earthenware dike built at the border with Wales. See Cam, *England*, 30.

42. Ibid., 34–35.

43. Robert Ferguson, *The Vikings: A History* (New York: Viking Penguin, 2009), 31.

44. Cam, *England*, 39–40; Le Goff, *Medieval Civilization*, 43–44.

45. Cam, *England*, 40–41.

46. Ibid., 41.

47. Ferguson, *Vikings*, 136, 201.

Alfred, acknowledging the significant decline in instruction over two generations of Viking invasions, championed advancing education, which he believed should focus on service in public life.[48]

Eventually, Viking linguistic and religious assimilation to English Christianity ensued, with an accompanying reaction against a return to paganism.[49] For instance, heavy penalties were imposed for performing the previously celebrated pagan rituals, such as cremating the dead. Death was also the penalty for forgoing new Christian rites, such as submitting to baptism and abstaining from eating meat during Lent.[50]

As the newly converted Christians inflicted the death penalty on wayward Danish converts, the Danes continued to feel free to kill Christians. Danish raids were unrelenting, and in response, King Ethelred (A.D. 968–1016) treacherously massacred Danish civilians throughout England. His massacre left the kingdom vulnerable from both within and without. Swen Forkbeard, King of Norway and Denmark, took advantage of the weakness by invading England and conquering London. Ethelred fled, thus leaving Swen to become King of England in 1013.[51] England was ruled by Danish kings until 1042.[52]

King Edward the Confessor, Ethelred's youngest son, unified the realm. He administered the nation through nobles called *thegns* and *ealdormen*. As he had no children, King Edward made it clear that he wanted William of Normandy, later known as William the Conqueror, to succeed him. William was related to Edward on his mother's side, but his right to the throne was not undisputed. He landed his forces at Pevensey in 1066; it took five years to subdue the entire nation.[53] The date of William's invasion is still seen as a high-water mark in English history—one as significant to citizens of the United Kingdom as 1776 is to those in the United States.

48. Cam, *England*, 41–44. Ferguson, *Vikings*, 140–42: "Legal parity between the two populations was affirmed, with a fine set at eight half-marks of refined gold for the killing of either a Dane or an Englishman."

49. Ferguson, *Vikings*, 236.

50. Ibid., 51.

51. Cam, *England*, 53; Ferguson, *Vikings*, 276; Le Goff, *Medieval Civilization*, 63.

52. Those Danish rulers include Kings Swein, Cnut, Harold, and Harthacnut. There was a one-month rule by Ethelred's son Edmund Ironside. Some scholars conclude that subjection to Danish rule was not entirely negative. See Cam, *England*, 53–54, 61.

53. Ibid., 55–60, 61.

The Normans were both effective fighters, who brought mounted knights and built fortified castles, and competent administrators.[54] William did not drastically change English laws, for he wanted to be seen as Edward's successor, as ruling in line with Edward's policies. William's noblemen were given lands on the condition that they raise a fixed number of their own fighting men to serve the king each year. They continued to use the serf system to produce wealth.[55] In 1086 William created what would later be called the Domesday Book—a great survey of the land and its owners. Every shire had a royal sheriff and a royal castle. Archbishop Lanfranc worked with William to abolish marriage for members of the clergy, move bishoprics to large cities, and separate lands that observed ecclesiastical laws from those that operated under secular law.

Scotland through the Thirteenth Century. The Scottish kings can be traced back to ca. A.D. 500. Originally from Ireland, they moved into Scotland, where they fought against and assimilated the native Pictish people. In Irish tradition, these kings were not chosen according to the Norman method of primogeniture but instead from the males within four generations of any previous king. From among them, the king was elected by the Scottish earls. The Vikings exercised strong influence in Scotland as well—they conquered and colonized the western isles and parts of northeast mainland Scotland, and they assimilated into their captured territory.[56]

Although during the Middle Ages England and Scotland were legally and politically distinct, the nations were housed on a single island, and tension between the neighbors was inevitable. In 1069 Edgar, rightful successor to the throne of England following the conquest, joined in a rebellion against King William the Conqueror. The rebellion's having failed, Edgar and others fled north to Scotland. But eventually, King Malcolm III of Scotland (1031–1093) and the former King Edgar both made peace with King William.[57] One of the ways that England attempted to usurp Scotland's power consisted

54. Ibid., 68–69.
55. Ibid., 71.
56. Ferguson, *Vikings*, 65, 69, 81.
57. King Malcolm III was followed by William the Lion (1165–1214) and Alexander II (1214–49). See Marion Campbell, *Alexander III: King of Scots* (Isle of Colonsay, Argyll, Scotland: House of Lochar, 1999), 13–14.

in asserting the supremacy of Canterbury as an archbishopric over St Andrews. The pope, however, declared the nation of Scotland to be an independent nation.[58]

King John of England (1166–1216) invaded Scotland in 1216, and King Alexander II of Scotland (1198–1249) captured the English city of Carlisle. But in the midst of this turmoil, in 1221 the King of Scotland married Joanna, eldest daughter of the King of England. Joanna, however, had no children. The King remarried, and his son, Alexander III (1241–1286), assumed the throne in 1249. That Alexander spoke Latin, French, Flemish, and Gaelic points to the diversity of people groups in Britain at this time.[59] In 1251, Alexander married Margaret, daughter of King Henry III of England (1207–1272). Alexander's father-in-law, Henry III of England, attempted to intervene in Scotland by force and intimidation.[60] His attempts were successful. Thus, in fear of an invasion and a Scottish civil war, King Alexander III signed a document submitting to his father-in-law. But because Alexander III was still a minor and no guardians cosigned the document, it was declared to be legally invalid.[61]

In 1256 Gamelin—the bishop of St Andrews—headed to Rome to supress the situation and plead Scotland's cause. Gamelin's efforts were successful, and the pope chastised King Henry and his Scottish allies for what they had done. Eventually he even excommunicated the complicit Scottish counsel.[62] In response, King Henry posted an arrest warrant for Bishop Gamelin to bar him from returning to Scotland.[63]

In 1257, King Alexander III, now sixteen years of age, called for the entire army of Scotland to oppose the English King and his treacherous Scottish allies—an act that restored peace to the region.[64]

58. Campbell, *Alexander*, 25.
59. Ibid., 24–25.
60. Ibid., 68–69.
61. Ibid., 71.
62. Ibid., 83–91, 83: The pope wrote, "We have heard with grief that some of the King of Scotland's so-called counsellors . . . and that Gamelin, Bishop of St Andrews, is spoiled of his goods and driven into exile from his church to the no light injury and contempt of the Holy Name and His apostle. We beseech King Henry to use his influence to right these wrongs."
63. Bishop Gamelin served the king as lord high chancellor until his death in 1271. Fascinating for later Scottish history is that a priest named Alan Wallace, tutor to the Scottish hero William Wallace, served Bishop Gamelin. See ibid., 95–96.
64. Ibid., 97–113.

But in 1272 the English King Henry III died. He was succeeded by his son Edward, who would later be known as the Hammer of the Scots. Alexander III, however, had no sons. Thus his heir was his granddaughter Margaret, Maid of Norway (1283–1290). Her tragic death at sea on a return trip from Scotland would produce a crisis for succession to the Scottish throne.

We have briefly surveyed the early medieval context in Europe and Britain. We will now turn our eyes southward to understand the church's continuing story.

POLITICAL AND THEOLOGICAL STRUCTURES IN THE MIDDLE EAST

Muhammad (d. A.D. 632) **and His Religion.** Muhammad was born in the city of Mecca, on the southwestern coast of central Arabia, in A.D. 571. Already by the time of Muhammad's birth, Mecca was an important religious and trade center.[65] In his early years growing up in this religious hub and working as a merchant, Muhammad encountered Jews, certain types of Christians, and people of eastern religions.[66]

Muhammad's world was one of messianic expectation—the Jews searched for another prophet like Moses, and Christians anticipated Christ's second coming. The Arabs also longed to have their own prophet and authoritative book.[67] When Muhammad claimed to receive personal revelations from God in the cave in which he regularly meditated on Mount Hira, the world was forever changed. His claims to divine revelation began around the year A.D. 610, and two years later he started his preaching ministry. Not everyone received his teaching or prophecy. Some even charged him with demonic possession. Muhammad's harsh condemnations of idolatry threatened the economic power structures of the region that were built on pagan ceremonies and pilgrimages. His teaching engendered such controversy that he fled Mecca in A.D. 622 for Medina.

---

65. Barnaby Rogerson, *The Heirs of Muhammad: Islam's First Century and the Origins of the Sunni-Shia Split* (New York: Overlook Press, 2006), 12.

66. Richard Fletcher, *The Cross and the Crescent: Christianity and Islam from Muhammad to the Reformation* (New York: Penguin Books, 2003), 8–9.

67. Anees Zaka and Diane Coleman, *The Truth about Islam* (Philipsburg, NJ: P&R Publishing, 2004), 32–33.

The city of Medina was an entirely different world from Muhammad's home in Mecca. Muhammad and his preaching met almost unanimous acceptance in Medina, and he slowly began to develop the religion of Islam. He built the first mosque and developed rituals for prayer, burial, daily conduct, marriage, and pilgrimage, all based on the series of visions he received from the angel Gabriel. He also established a yearly cycle of festivals and outlined details of how to rule, how to judge, how to tax and how to govern a state.[68] Men began to swear loyalty to Muhammad—they acknowledged that he was a divine prophet; they agreed to take their disputes to him and defend the community against outside attack.[69] Muhammad's community of followers at Medina grew from eighty impoverished refugees to a movement to be numbered in the tens of thousands.

Before the rise of Islam, Arabia was made up of a patchwork of independent nomadic tribes, with men swearing fealty to their clan leaders. By the time of Muhammad's death in A.D. 632, he had unified the region both politically and spiritually.[70] The Prophet Muhammad began to accomplish what Jesus supposedly had failed to do—establish a kingdom for Allah on earth based on the one true religion.[71] It is interesting that in his lifetime, Muhammad neither performed, nor claimed to perform, any miracles. He never claimed divinity, and he prophesied only of future military campaigns and conquests.[72] But over the years his reputation in that area grew. His followers would later ascribe to him many miracles and even credit him with sinlessness.[73] Let us now examine in some detail Muhammad's teachings.

Book of Islam: the Qur'an.[74] *Islam* means "submission," and at the heart of Muhammad's faith is the idea that men and women must bow to Allah in fear, as slaves bow to their masters. The root of this overpowering necessity of submission is due to Muhammad's understanding of God's supreme oneness. He, in his perfect unity, enjoys the

68. Needham, *2,000 Years*, 2:17–19; Rogerson, *Heirs of Muhammad*, 13–14.

69. Zaka and Coleman, *Truth about Islam*, 39; Fletcher, *Cross and Crescent*, 11; Rogerson, *Heirs of Muhammad*, 11.

70. Rogerson, *Heirs of Muhammad*, 23–24, 27.

71. Zaka and Coleman, *Truth about Islam*, 41; Fletcher, *Cross and Crescent*, 11, 12.

72. Zaka and Coleman, *Truth about Islam*, 43, 51, 85.

73. Ibid., 44–45. Orthodox Islam does not embrace the veneration of Muhammad as a Muslim Christ.

74. Ibid., 20; Needham, *2,000 Years*, 2:20.

elevated status of supreme and only God. He is the omnipotent creator and is separated by an infinite distance from his creation. Thus no relationship exists between a follower of Islam and Allah. God has no desire to make himself known to man or to become man, and he refuses to share his glory with any other being or person. Allah is not seen as a father and thus has no son.[75] He wants nothing and feels nothing. He cannot even be imagined.[76] So he is defined solely by negation.[77]

In the Qur'an, Allah is described as: one, creator, sovereign, merciful, omnipotent, incomparable, omniscient, eternal, invisible, wise, living, loving, avenging, the contriver, the afflicter, the reckoner, the humiliator, the killer at his will, the seizer, the overpowering one.[78]

Muhammad's understanding of God's nature necessitates a complete denial of the Trinity. He held that the idea of the Trinity was no better than an idolatrous pagan notion of many gods.[79] For God to have a son would be unbecoming to God's majesty.[80] Thus, according to the Qur'an, Jesus is not God; neither is he the son of God, nor does he possess divine attributes.[81] The Qur'an also claims that Allah rescued Jesus from the cross, for a prophet (such as Jesus was) would never die such a humble death.[82] Jesus is like Adam.[83] He is also the apostle of Allah to Israel. He is the Messiah. Islam teaches that while his conception was miraculous, still he was a created human being.[84] He was born under a palm tree and spoke as an infant. He was a sign both of mercy and of judgment. He was no more than a servant, but he was a servant raised to honor. Jesus is a word of Allah and a spirit from Allah, and as such, he is to be obeyed. He is a miracle worker by the permission of Allah, who made clay birds fly. He spoke only by Allah's command, was given the gospel, and was a forerunner of

75. Zaka and Coleman, *Truth about Islam*, 60.

76. Ibid., 99.

77. Ibid., 103.

78. Ibid., 100–16, with *Sura* references for each attribute.

79. Fletcher, *Cross and Crescent*, 6: "The austere monotheism of Islam finds the Christian doctrines of Trinity and Incarnation incomprehensible and distasteful."

80. Zaka and Coleman, *Truth about Islam*, 115.

81. *Sura* 5:17; 9:30; 5:116, as cited by Zaka and Coleman, *Truth about Islam*, 59–60.

82. *Sura* 4:157–58, as cited by Zaka and Coleman, *Truth about Islam*, 60.

83. *Sura* 3:59.

84. Zaka and Coleman, *Truth about Islam*, 63–66; *Sura* 19:19. While granting salvation is Allah's prerogative, Ali's commentary grants Jesus that ability.

Muhammad.[85] In Islamic eschatology, Jesus will return—but he will return as a Muslim military figure who will conquer a vast Islamic kingdom.[86]

In Islam there is no necessity for Jesus to function as Redeemer and Savior because the Qur'an does not teach that people have inherently sinful natures. Instead, through careful and obedient participation in the law and obligations of Islam, a person is able to receive the righteousness that qualifies him for the reward of afterlife in paradise. Allah is not, however, obligated to bestow that reward. This reward is a possibility—not a certainty—for the faithful follower. The certainty of reward is only for those who engage in *jihad*, which can be translated "struggle." Muslims understand *jihad* as referring both to the personal struggle for obedience to Allah's will and to the struggle to spread Islam in the world—by preaching, writing, diplomacy, and warfare.[87] The Muslim busies himself with good works—physical acts of worship and public devotion. But in return, Allah does nothing for his followers.[88]

Living as a Muslim. Allah, it is supposed, continually watches over individual Muslim's actions and documents them for the day of judgment. Muslims constantly evoke Allah's name to remind themselves of their obligation to live in total submission to Allah. Their submission is manifested in the five pillars, or duties of Islam: the confession of faith (*shahadah*), prayer five times a day (*salah*), giving to the poor (*zakah*), fasting in the month of Ramadan (*sawm*), and pilgrimage to Mecca at least once (*hajj*).[89] Though Islam is known as a religion of internal peace, it is also a religion of violent *jihad* against outsiders.[90]

Islamic law, known as *shariah*, is believed to be the embodiment of Allah's will. This law is written in the Qur'an and elaborated in the Sunnah and Hadith—both authoritative commentaries. *Shariah* law is considered to be a living body that answers the needs of Islamic

85. Zaka and Coleman, *Truth about Islam*, 62–63.

86. Ibid., 64.

87. Ibid., 107, citing *Sura* 3:146–48, 116; Needham, *2,000 Years*, 2:19.

88. Zaka and Coleman, *Truth about Islam*, 21.

89. Ibid., 120–21; Fletcher, *Cross and Crescent*, 12. For the five pillars of Islam, see Needham, *2,000 Years*, 2:20.

90. Fletcher, *Cross and Crescent*, 13: "a Muslim must practise *jihad*, meaning 'effort' or 'struggle' to convince unbelievers of the way of Islam. Such effort might be peaceful . . . living an exemplary pious life, the undertaking of teaching and preaching; but it might also be coercive and violent, should the unbelievers be stubborn."

society, in both public and private matters. It is the goal of Islam to spread *shariah* law to the whole world, and today Islam has every intention of conquering the West.[91]

The following are examples of *shariah* law from the Qur'an: fornication and adultery require the punishment of one hundred lashes; husbands who fear that their wives are disloyal to them are to admonish them, refuse intimacy, and then beat them; engaging in *jihad* is prescribed and praised; eating pork is prohibited; sons are to inherit twice as much as daughters do; a lewd woman is to be confined to her house until she dies; making pilgrimage to Mecca is a duty; thieves are to have their hands cut off; punishment for those who wage war against Islam is execution, crucifixion, cutting off the hand and foot of opposite sides of the body, or exile.[92] *Shariah* law from the Hadith states that the testimony of a non-Muslim is not valid against a Muslim, Muslims cannot be executed for murdering infidels, and Muslims must kill any Muslim who defects from Islam.[93]

This type of law explains the religiously authorized modern-day death contracts on prominent writers such as Salman Rushdie. The Muslim world awaits the death of Rushdie and others with edicts against them, and it is ready to laud their murderers as champions of Islam. Within Islam, suicide bombers are martyrs who advance the faith by killing infidels. They are honored, and Islamic teaching guarantees them life after death in paradise. The notorious Ayatollah Khomeini said that the purest joy in Islam is to kill and be killed for Allah. What is pejoratively termed "Islamic fanaticism" is in fact nothing but an honest and forthright interpretation of the texts of the Qur'an.[94]

Islamic Conquest of Christian Lands. During Muhammad's lifetime, Christianity had stretched into North Africa and into the East as far as Iraq, which was part of the Persian Empire. Christianity was established as far north and west as remote Ireland and had spread north and east all the way to Russian Georgia.[95]

---

91. Zaka and Coleman, *Truth about Islam*, 127–28, 152–54.
92. Ibid., 129–30; *Sura* 4.11, as cited by Ibn Warraq, *Why I Am Not a Muslim* (Amherst, NY: Prometheus Books, 1994), 297.
93. Zaka and Coleman, *Truth about Islam*, 131.
94. See ibid., 131–32, 140, for the fair conclusion that Islamic law sanctions murderous violence.
95. Fletcher, *Cross and Crescent*, 6–7; Rodney Stark, *God's Battalions: The Case for the Crusades* (San Francisco: HarperOne, 2009), 12.

Motivated by the Qur'an's command to conquer foreign lands, Muslims had conquered the entire Persian Empire and parts of the Roman Empire a mere twenty years after Muhammad's death.[96] By the year A.D. 635, Damascus had been conquered by the Muslims, and the next year Syria and Palestine succumbed. Jerusalem and Caesarea followed in A.D. 638 and Egypt in A.D. 639. Alexandria fell in A.D. 642, and with it came the end of six and a half centuries of Roman rule. Tripoli was under Islamic control the following year, and the last Roman stronghold, Carthage, fell in A.D. 698.[97]

Continuing into the next century, in A.D. 711 the Muslims invaded Spain, which was fully conquered by A.D. 718. In A.D. 721, they crossed the Pyrenees mountains to attack France but were defeated.[98] In their next major attack in A.D. 732, the Muslims conquered lands up to one hundred and fifty miles south of Paris. Under the leadership of King Charles Martel, France's decisive defeat of ten thousand Muslim soldiers was considered critical for the survival of Western civilization. The last Muslim attack on France occurred in A.D. 735.[99] Islamic troops conquered southern Italy and attacked Rome in A.D. 843 and 846. They looted historic and cherished churches and forced the pope to pay a massive tribute.[100] In the eleventh century, Muslims murdered enormous numbers of Jews in Morocco and Grenada, and mass murders of Christian monks and pilgrims were not uncommon.[101] In 1570, tens of thousands of Christian civilians were murdered in Cyprus at the hands of Muslims.[102]

A state conquered by Islam would be declared to be Muslim; however, it often took some two and a half centuries of occupation for even

96. Stark, *God's Battalions*, 12: "I was ordered to fight all men until they say 'There is no god but Allah.'" See Qur'an 9:5: "[S]lay idolaters wherever ye find them, and take them [captive], and besiege them, and prepare for them each ambush."

97. Fletcher, *Cross and Crescent*, 13–15; Stark, *God's Battalions*, 9, 13, 83; Needham, *2,000 Years*, 2:23–24.

98. Fletcher, *Cross and Crescent*, 15; Stark, *God's Battalions*, 12.

99. Stark, *God's Battalions*, 40–42.

100. Southern Italy and Sicily were divided into independent emirates in an occupation that lasted more than two hundred years. See ibid., 23: "Hence the fall of Cyprus (653), Rhodes (672), Sardinia (809), Majorca (818), Crete (824), and Malta (835) were significant losses for the West." See also Le Goff, *Medieval Civilization*, 44.

101. Stark, *God's Battalions*, 29, 84–86, 91.

102. Ibid., 28.

half the Christian or Jewish population actually to convert to Islam.[103] In the earliest phase of Muslim domination, the conquered nations were governed by an elite group of Muslims, while the majority of the population remained Christian.[104] Christians living in a Muslim state ruled by governments appointed by the caliph had to pay an annual poll tax and wear a certain sash to make evident their Christian affiliation. The Muslim rulers allowed for no new churches to be built, and public worship outdoors was forbidden entirely. Christians were denied certain military equipment, and Christian men could have no contact with Muslim women. No one was allowed to disrespect Islam or attempt to convert a Muslim to Christianity.[105]

Critiques of Islam. Islam's history of violence toward other religions began at its very inception with Muhammad, who had approximately seven hundred Jewish men in Medina dig their own graves. He then beheaded them. As early as A.D. 705, the Muslim conquerors of Armenia assembled all the Christian nobles in a church and burned them to death.[106]

But Islam is not repressive only toward those outside the faith—it also seeks to dominate those within. This aspect of Islam can also be traced back to Muhammad. He was both an ambitious and a deliberate man. He desired control and used every means possible to obtain it. He raided caravans, raised a militia, took captives, and ordered public executions. The quiet man who prayed alone in a cave had become a man bent on domination.[107]

This spirit of domination is expressed in Islamic law and the religion's focus on submission. Several consequences flow from the repressive nature of Islam. For one, there can be no Islamic democracy—critical thought, essential to a free society, is unacceptable. Innovation in art and science is discouraged.[108] Women are demeaned: the Qur'an states that the testimony of a woman is of less weight than the testimony of a man.[109] The Qur'an also mandates that women be

---

103. Ibid., 29–32.
104. Needham, *2,000 Years*, 2:26–31; Stark, *God's Battalions*, 27.
105. Fletcher, *Cross and Crescent*, 21.
106. Stark, *God's Battalions*, 29.
107. Zaka and Coleman, *Truth about Islam*, 54–55.
108. Ibid., 151; Warraq, *Not a Muslim*, 294.
109. *Sura* 2.282, as cited by Warraq, *Not a Muslim*, 297.

covered when leaving the house.[110] Muhammad described women in the following manner: "Be friendly to women for womankind was created from a rib, but the bent part of the rib, high up, if you try to straighten it you will break it; if you do nothing, she will continue to be bent."[111]

Interestingly, the Qur'an's account of Joseph and Potiphar's wife is much different from the biblical account. According to the Qur'an, Potiphar did not believe his wife's charge of attempted rape against Joseph. Potiphar then said to his wife: "This is of your women's guile; surely your guile is great." Contemporary Muslim commentators use this story to prove that women are by nature full of guile and deceit. These commentators argue that women are both incapable of and unwilling to change; by nature, they have no choice—at least according to these Muslim commentators.[112] Islam considers women to be inferior to men in every way—a position supported in the Hadiths and perpetuated by Muslim dogma.[113]

The story of Muhammad should sound as a warning. Originally, Muhammad was a quiet pagan in search of the truth. In his quest, he chose to rely on his own understanding rather than the truths of the Christian Scriptures. He knew what the Bible taught concerning God—he knew the debates surrounding the Trinity and the nature of Christ. He spent years dialoguing with Jews and Christians and studying the truths of Scripture. In the end, he allowed his own experience and desires to shape his beliefs about Christ and the Word of God rather than what Scripture actually taught. In doing so, he created one of the most dangerous, vast, complicated, and influential religious sects. Muhammad's religion was an attempt to understand God, yet it violently distorted and rejected the Word of God.

A Response to Islam: The Crusades. Medieval Europe did not stand idle during the militant Islamic expansion. Those who desired to respond to Islam did so in two ways—they fought either with the sword or the pen.[114] While the pope had attempted to begin a crusade

---

110. *Sura* 33.59, as cited by Warraq, *Not a Muslim*, 298.
111. Warraq, *Not a Muslim*, 295.
112. Ibid., 296.
113. Ibid., 293; see the Hadiths, 298–99.
114. Needham, *2,000 Years*, 2:31.

earlier, the first crusade began in 1090 to 1095 and lasted until 1099.[115] Pope Urban II had received a request for help from Emperor Alexios Komnenos (1088–1099).[116] In response, the pope promised that those who died while serving on crusade would be guaranteed entrance into heaven, with no penance to perform after death.[117] As a result of the First Crusade (1096–1099), a Latin kingdom in Jerusalem was established.[118] The pope then called for the Second Crusade (1147–1149). Bernard of Clairvaux helped to rally crusaders through his preaching, but the crusade failed when many died before even reaching Palestine. The Crusaders failed to conquer Damascus in 1148.[119] A fruit of this failure was the ill will that erupted between the Latin-speaking West and the Byzantines. Each side leveled charges against the other.[120]

The Third Crusade lasted from 1189 to 1192. In 1187 the Kurdish leader Saladin—the sultan of Egypt and Syria who had fought against other Muslims—claimed to have received divine revelation instructing him to liberate Jerusalem, which had now been held by the Crusaders for eighty-eight years (1099–1187). Saladin was a great leader and conquered Jerusalem. When the city was under his control, he spared the Christians to demonstrate the moral superiority of the Islamic faith.

In response, in the summer of 1190 King Richard the Lionheart of England set sail to engage in battle in Palestine.[121] Other Crusaders had already begun besieging the nearby city of Acre.[122] In May 1191,

115. Diarmaid MacCulloch, *Christianity: The First Three Thousand Years* (New York: Viking, 2010), 376, 385–86.

116. Needham, *2,000 Years*, 2:185; Walker, *History*, 284–85. MacCulloch (*Christianity*, 383–84) rather provocatively describes Pope Urban's descriptions of atrocities against Christians as "completely imaginary."

117. Walker, *History*, 284; MacCulloch, *Christianity*, 384.

118. Needham, *2,000 Years*, 2:189–92.

119. Walker, *History*, 287; MacCulloch, *Christianity*, 390, 471.

120. Needham, *2,000 Years*, 2:198–99; MacCulloch (*Christianity*, 390, 471) underlined the aggressiveness of Bernard of Clairvaux.

121. King Richard's navy included one hundred and fifty large ships and fifty-three galleys, which arrived in Messina. Three of the large vessels sank and a number of Richard's forces died in a shipwreck off Cyprus in April 1191; those who died included Roger Malus-Catulus, Richard's chaplain, vice-chancellor, and probable leader of the six thousand English-speaking Templar knights. See George Payne R. James, *A History of the Life of Richard Coeur-de-lion, King of England* (London: Bohn, 1854), 71; Hans Eberhard Mayer, "Die Kanzlei Richards I von England auf dem Dritten Kreuzzug," in *Kreuzzüge und lateinischer Osten* 9 (London: Variorum Collected Studies, 1983), 194–95.

122. The crusading armies included Emperor Frederick Barbarosa and King Philip Augustus of France, as well as Richard. See Walker, *History*, 287.

Richard arrived in the Holy Land, where he fell sick with camp fever and nearly died. His great opponent Saladin, as a token of chivalry, sent food to him. Upon recovering, King Richard took the city of Acre and slaughtered all the Muslims.

The Crusaders, deeply steeped in the rituals and rites ingrained in Christianity at the time, took into battle what they believed to be a remnant of Christ's cross. Twenty times they marched into battle with it, and twenty times were victorious. But Saladin lured the Crusaders twenty miles outside Jerusalem to a place called Hattin, where he poisoned the waters, killed thousands of Crusaders, and took the presumed fragment of the cross.

During the Third Crusade, King Richard defeated Saladin at the Battle of Arsuf in Palestine. After taking Acre, the Christians' next goal was securing Jaffa, which would facilitate achieving their ultimate goal—recapturing the city of Jerusalem. At the end of the Third Crusade, in 1192 Richard guaranteed the Christians' rights to the city of Jerusalem.[123]

The Fourth Crusade lasted from 1201 to 1204. The Italian republic of Venice agreed to provide food and transportation for the knights for an entire year.[124] But instead of fighting Muslims, the Crusaders were persuaded to help conquer Constantinople and subdue part of the Eastern church to the Latin West. Thus these Crusaders fought other Christians and were subsequently excommunicated for a time by the pope.[125] The Crusaders' attacks weakened the Eastern Christian Empire and rendered it vulnerable to Islamic attack.[126] In 1209, the pope called for a crusade against the Cathars—a heretical group that had spread through much of Europe and was particularly strong in southern France. This crusade is sometimes referred to as the Albigensian Crusade.[127] The Cathars, whose name comes from the Greek word for "Pure Ones," were dualists.[128] Repeated attempts were made

123. Needham, *2,000 Years*, 2:200.

124. Piers Paul Read, *The Templars* (Cambridge, MA: Da Capo Press, 1999), 186: "The republic would provide a fleet of fifty galleys and transport for 4,500 knights, 9,000 squires and 20,000 foot-soldiers."

125. Needham, *2,000 Years*, 2:201–2; Read, *Templars*, 187, 189: "The restoration of a legitimate ruler was a just cause in the canon of feudal law, and the bishops accompanying the crusade were persuaded to support it."

126. MacCulloch, *Christianity*, 385; Walker, *History*, 288.

127. MacCulloch, *Christianity*, 473–77.

128. Walker, *History*, 300–305; MacCulloch, *Christianity*, 387.

to persuade the Cathars to return to the faith. When these attempts proved fruitless, Pope Innocent called on a French count to expel them by force.[129]

The Fifth Crusade ensued from 1217 to 1221. Its commander was an irresponsible cardinal named Pelagius, whose fight against Egypt ended in failure.[130] The Sixth Crusade (1228–1229) can hardly even be called a crusade. Emperor Frederick II (1212–1250), without bloodshed, negotiated a treaty with the sultan of Egypt for Christian occupation of Jerusalem, Bethlehem, and Nazareth. This peace treaty remained intact until 1244, when these cities were permanently lost to roaming Muslim clans.[131] Acre, the last Christian citadel held in Palestine, was lost in 1291 to the Mamluks. With that loss, the Crusades were over. We can now look back on these efforts and bloodshed as political and military failures.[132] Intimately connected to the Crusades and the Crusaders were the Knights Templar.

Knights Templar. The Knights Templar arose in a time of overall monastic revival. Stephen Harding was an Anglo-Saxon Englishman whose family had been ruined as a result of the Norman Conquest. He traveled to France and eventually became the abbot of Citeaux. The members of the Citeaux monastery were known as Cistercians. The young abbot Bernard arrived at this monastery in 1113.

Under Stephen and Bernard, a renewal of the monastic movement began. The best-known monastery was established by Bernard and twelve others at the valley of Wormwood, which had been known for its robbers. The group changed this name to the "valley of light," or *Clairvaux*. The movement placed a high value on chastity.[133]

Bernard, whose thought will be studied in the next chapter, became an international leader. Hugh, the count of Champagne and later a Templar, endowed the monastery at Clairvaux. Hugh of Payns (1070–1136), founder of the Templars, had written to Bernard from Jerusalem to ask for his help in obtaining papal confirmation and to draw up a so-called "rule of life." Bernard of Clairvaux supported the

129. Read, *Templars*, 189–93.
130. Ibid., 199; Walker, *History*, 289; MacCulloch, *Christianity*, 403.
131. Walker, *History*, 289.
132. Ibid.; Needham, *2,000 Years*, 2:205; Read, *Templars*, 322–23.
133. Read, *Templars*, 96–100.

Templars with his book *De laude novae militae*. The Templars based their thinking on the assumption that the lands of the Middle East had been Christian until they were unjustly seized by the Muslims. The book was filled with descriptions of Christ's life in Palestine.[134] The Templars were supported in England by King Henry I, who at his death established their headquarters in Palestine.[135]

The Knights Templar were connected to the monastic renewal movement of Citeaux.[136] Established as Templars on Christmas day 1119, this small group was also known as "the poor fellow soldiers of Jesus Christ."[137] They were stationed at what they thought was the temple of Solomon.[138] Earlier that year, three hundred unarmed Christian pilgrims to Palestine had been robbed and killed, and another sixty taken as slaves, so one purpose of the Templars was to protect such pilgrims.[139] The knights were fighting for what the church had declared to be a just cause. In 1120 they received an endowment, and eventually their endowments were so widespread that the organization became quite wealthy.[140]

Templar regulations were based on earlier Benedictine and Cistercian orders.[141] Just like monks, the knights ate in silence and fasted on Fridays.[142] While the temple order owned land, no individual could own anything.[143] These noblemen were kept from the noble pursuits of life, such as falconry and hunting. They could not own pointed shoes, shoelaces, gold or silver bridle decorations, or even a food bag constructed of linen or wool. Members had to provide for their own

134. Walker, *History*, 286; Read, *Templars*, 105.

135. Read, *Templars*, 107.

136. There was a rejuvenation because by the end of the century there were twelve hundred monastic communities throughout Europe that were connected to Citeaux. See ibid., 93.

137. Ibid., 91.

138. Ibid., 91–92.

139. Ibid., 92.

140. Ibid., 93, 110,

141. Ibid., 102: "It meant total self-abnegation and, when not engaged in military duties, leading the life of a monk. . . . Married men were allowed to join the Order with permission of their wives, but not to wear the white habit, and widows, though supported by the Order from the benefice brought by their husbands, were, like the knights' other female relatives, to be banned from the Templar houses."

142. Ibid., 103: "Meat was permitted only three times a week: to abstain altogether, as did the Cistercians, would enfeeble them as fighting men."

143. Ibid., 103, 134.

clothing, as well as their own horses, attendants, and equipment. The knights also lived under the absolute power of the grand master.[144]

A Templar had a career similar to that of others in the church; not all the Templars went on crusades.[145] A greater number of the knights were involved in estate management.[146] To become a knight, one had to be the son or descendant of a knight. He also needed to be strong and was expected to be trained before he joined the order.[147]

From the primitive order, which focused on individual salvation, came a shift to a regimental esprit de corps. For example, Rule 340 reads: "Each brother should strive to live honestly and to set a good example to secular people and other [knightly] orders in everything."[148]

A second order was founded as the knights of Saint John, also known as the Hospitaliers.[149] As the crusading orders continued, the Templars and Hospitaliers grew in wealth and soon were among the richest corporate bodies in Europe.[150] They became the bankers of kings, as well as something similar to a protective police force.[151] They offered important civil service.[152]

Such an institution, however, is not without inherent liabilities. Historians have offered various reasons for the Templars' demise:[153] the knights had suffered too many battle losses—they could not hold Jerusalem against the vastly superior Muslim onslaughts;[154] and kings often stole their vast possessions. The Templars had great privileges and enormous wealth—they could build their own churches, keep

144. Ibid., 103, 110–11, 104: "Bernard and the Council fathers seemed more anxious to make monks out of knights than knights out of monks."

145. Ibid., 112.

146. Ibid., 107–8.

147. Ibid., 135.

148. Ibid., 134–35.

149. Ibid., 109–10. The Hospitaliers followed the milder Augustinian rule and built their hospital supposedly at the place where John the Baptist's birth had been announced. While they took care of the sick, they were also a military order.

150. Ibid., 180–81.

151. Ibid., 183–84.

152. Ibid., 184. They obeyed the order's master and had no dynastic ambitions, and some displayed excellent financial acumen. Popes and kings trusted and supported them.

153. MacCulloch, *Christianity*, 387: "Since the eighteenth century, their fate has also been the inspiration for a large amount of deranged conspiracy theory."

154. Disputes between the Templars and Hospitaliers contributed to the fall of Acre. See Read, *Templars*, 248–49.

their own cemeteries, and collect their own tithes.[155] They held more than seven thousand estates in Europe.

The Templars' condemnation by both pope and king did not bring an end to crusading armies. In 1443 Pope Eugenius IV called together an army, which was defeated at the city of Varna. The Hospitaliers lost the Greek island of Rhodes to the Ottoman Turks in 1522 and were given the island of Malta in 1530 by Emperor Charles V. In 1536 they won a battle against the Ottoman ships at the Battle of Lepanto.[156] The Hospitaliers ruled Malta until they were dislodged by Napoleon's army in 1798 and continue to this very day as a legal state and entity subject to the pope.

Interpreting the Crusading Armies. How should believers understand the Crusades? Considering their place in history and especially in today's age, with the continual presence of militant Islam, this question is important.

Harsh criticism of the Crusades began at the time of the Reformation. The first Protestants criticized the Roman Catholic practice of penance and issuing of indulgences. Protestants also properly condemned the Catholic Church for its zeal for earthly wealth and power. The historiographical origins of the idea that the Crusades constituted a religious excuse to seek land and loot likely originated with Lutheran Protestants.[157] Anti-Catholics in France continued to use the Crusades as a means for criticizing the church.[158] And anti-Catholics in England said that the Crusades were a monument to human folly.[159]

Muslim historiography did not portray the Crusades antagonistically until ca. 1900 with European colonialism against the Ottoman Empire. The Ottoman Empire was defeated in World War I, thus losing territory to the United Kingdom and France. The Republic of Turkey was born out of the successful war of independence against

155. Ibid., 185.

156. Ibid., 317–21.

157. Stark, *God's Battalions*, 6–7; Read, *Templars*, 318: "Erasmus . . . condemned the whole concept of crusade, and the Reformation wholly undermined the penitential value of crusading by denying the power of popes to remit penances and forgive sins."

158. Stark, *God's Battalions*, 6.

159. Ibid., 6. David Hume, *The History of England from the Invasion of Julius Caesar to the Revolution in 1688*, Foreword by William B. Todd, 6 vols. (Indianapolis: Liberty Fund, 1983), 1:234, characterized the Crusades as "the most signal and most durable monument to human folly that has yet appeared in any age or nation."

the occupiers. At the end of World War II, when the nation of Israel was carved out of Palestinian lands, anti-Crusader sentiment grew increasingly militant.[160]

Later in the twentieth century, the Crusades have been blamed as the basis for the current Islamic fury and social unrest in the Middle East.[161] They have been represented as a simple case of plunder and colonial expansion that left the supposedly enlightened culture of Islam in ruins.[162] The *New York Times* compared the Crusaders to the holocaust perpetrated by the Nazis as well as to the ethnic cleansing of Kosovo.[163] As President of the United States, Bill Clinton declared that Americans of European descent carry guilt on their shoulders for the Crusades.[164] Others have declared that the Crusades were a natural outflow of Christianity, a violent religion that teaches holy war.[165] The Crusades have been described as a violent deprivation of the lawful Muslim possession of Palestine. Still more have claimed that the Crusades were a European way to demonstrate frustration at the knightly class, or a way to solve a problem connected to that class.[166] Some have also argued that the Crusades were the result of an Arab population explosion.[167]

The opinions expressed above notwithstanding, in thinking through the Crusades, as through all historical events, it is important to remember their social and religious context. From a sociopolitical perspective, understanding that the Crusades were not unprovoked is essential. As noted earlier, Islamic military expansion was endemic throughout Europe and the East.[168] Many Crusaders were motivated to join the war effort to protect their cities and families. At the very least, the Crusades were a concerted political approach to retake lands that had been conquered by Muslims.[169]

160. Stark, *God's Battalions*, 8–9.
161. Ibid., 4.
162. Ibid., 4, 7.
163. Ibid., 5.
164. Ibid., 4–5.
165. Ibid., 6; MacCulloch, *Christianity*, 387.
166. Stark, *God's Battalions*, 6–7. Le Goff (*Medieval Civilization*, 65) says that material causes played an essential role but that special attention should be paid to intellectual and emotional reasons.
167. Stark, *God's Battalions*, 13–14.
168. Ibid., 98: "The sacred sites of Christianity were not secure."
169. Ibid., 8, 32–33; Le Goff, *Medieval Civilization*, 64–70.

Further, it is also important to remember the socioeconomic situation of Europe at this time. Some Crusaders joined the fight in an attempt to earn a better life for themselves and to escape from the poverty and squalor of medieval life, although it is a mistake to believe that the Crusades were undertaken simply to increase the wealth of the Crusaders. The average cost of participating in a crusade was the equivalent of four to five years' annual income.[170] Only 10 to 15 percent of French knights responded to the pope's call to arms. Had there been a real financial incentive, men would have responded in much larger numbers.[171]

Most importantly, the Crusades came at a time when the gospel was not only muted but veritably extinguished in Europe. The church had failed in its mission to proclaim the gospel consistently, faithfully, and accurately. What was proclaimed in place of the true gospel was a ritualistic and paganistic replica of true Christianity. This darkened mirror of Christianity propagated many theological errors—a drive to conquer land in the name of Christ and, in doing so, earn salvation or atone for sin's being some of them. In a sense, like the Muslim expansion into Europe, the Crusades were motivated by religious concerns, but not concerns that were informed by a true understanding of the gospel.

SOCIAL AND ECONOMIC STRUCTURES IN EUROPE

Now with some understanding of the rise of Islam and the Christian response to it, in the final section of this chapter we will round out the social history of the era by turning briefly back in time.

Land and the Crusades: King Otto.[172] Charlemagne inaugurated a second Holy Roman Empire. In A.D. 911, more than a century after Charlemagne's crowning, the title *emperor* was done away with after the death of a king named Ludwig the Child. The Germanic kingdoms

170. Stark, *God's Battalions*, 8, 112.
171. Ibid., 114, 118: "Unlike the Holy Land, Moorish Spain was extremely wealthy, possessed an abundance of fertile lands, and was close at hand. But hardly anyone responded to the pope's summons. Yet only thirty-three years later, tens of thousands of crusaders set out for the dry, impoverished wastes of faraway Palestine. What was different? Spain was not the Holy Land!"
172. Le Goff, *Medieval Civilization*, 56–70.

reverted to electing their own kings. One of those kings, Henry the Fowler, former duke of Saxony, was a successful leader and bequeathed a strong position to his son, Otto I. Otto was chosen as king without opposition.

Otto was the first among Germanic kingly equals, and in his attempt to solidify his power base, he knew that he needed the papacy's help. So he wanted to constitute himself as the protector of the papacy, just as Charlemagne had done previously. His goal was to control even papal appointment.

Otto soon obtained the right to appoint all the higher clergy in his realm, and since they had no regular source of income, the clergy needed the land that Otto alone could give them. We can see plenty of similarities between how Otto and Charlemagne operated. Otto set up a system known as "lay investiture," which was important throughout this period and provokes great discussion within the church as well as in secular history.

In A.D. 951, Otto had an opportunity to march to war in Italy. The Lombards had revived their kingship, and Otto headed south, defeated their king, and married their king's widow. Thus Otto was now also king of the Lombards—a title previously held by Charlemagne. In A.D. 961, Otto fought against the Lombards, although in name he was their king. After defeating them, he forced the pope to crown him emperor. After this time Rome fell silent, as the emperor had established his right to reside over papal elections. He would also refuse papal interference in his choice of German clergy. Hence, Otto I became the lord of both Germany and Italy.

Feudal System.[173] With the disintegration of Charlemagne's empire, power and law grew increasingly localized. Individual landowners began to possess and support their own private armies (what today would be considered private police corps) from their own resources. Territorial law and order were maintained by these private armies. This power, however, was not entirely arbitrary. A network of laws and customs, though not as powerful as sanctions handed down by a monarch, restrained powerful landowners from complete autonomy.

---

173. Easton, *Western Heritage*, 195–204; Le Goff, *Medieval Civilization*, 90–95.

The relationship between the lord and his vassals was the heart of the medieval feudal system.

Feudal law and custom imposed duties on each member of a transaction.[174] There was a moral as well as a material aspect to the sanctions of the feudal system. Vassals' promises were sworn either on the cross or on some holy relics, so that their oaths of loyalty were both sacred and tangible. Breaking either aspect of those oaths incurred punishment.

The feudal system itself was rather ineffective. It suppressed the peasants and lower classes by allowing them few rights, and if a lord did not have a large enough army to enforce his policies and customs, the serfs and lower classes would often rise up against him.

Manorial System.[175] Within the feudal system, the entire class of nobility was ultimately supported by the labor of the peasants. Most feudal lords had given away the largest portions of their land to those under them in exchange for their military service.

Every lord owned an estate, with some estates being larger than others. The lord's serfs cultivated his estate for his personal use. These estates provided the bulk of the lord's income. At times, a feudal lord might own too many smaller estates and himself be unable to control all his lands. In such cases, the lord would appoint supervisors, known as *bailiffs* or *stewards*, who would act as his representatives.

Each estate had a manor house, where the lord and his officials would live. They also had tillable acres, pastures, and forestland. Each manor likely had its own parish church, though the priest—who was appointed by the lord—would live in his own home in town. The peasants lived in small villages, and each village would have a blacksmith, a shoemaker, and other specialized workers.

Not all the tillable land, however, went to the lord. Often only one third, or even as little as one sixth, was given to him. These gleanings were the lord's major source of income. The peasants would work the land for the lord under the supervision of one of their own, whom they chose. The supervisor was given the right to beat peasants who did not work hard enough.

---

174. The Aristotelian view of the universe fit well with both the church and the feudal system. Likewise, the feudal system fit well with the church. See Easton, *Western Heritage*, 219–43.
175. Ibid., 204–9.

The peasants worked the rest of the manorial land for themselves, but whatever they produced from the land was subject to taxation. Each peasant was given a certain number of acres, from six to about thirty. The acres were not self-contained farmland but acre strips of land, some good and some poor. Often each peasant would be given some good and some poor land.

A peasant's small thatched hut in the village would have attached to it a small plot of land, which he could use as he wished. He grew vegetables and kept a few chickens or geese, which provided just enough food to keep him from starving. Peasants consumed a diet of black bread, fresh vegetables if they were able to grow them, porridge, cheese, occasionally meat or fish, and wine.[176]

Status of the Peasant. In theory the peasant was not without rights, but in practice his lord could essentially treat him as he wished. The lord could, if necessary, enforce his own rights in the manorial court, over which he or his steward presided. In the manorial court, serfs could obtain justice against other serfs, and people who lived in the village, known by the old Latin word *villein*, could petition against other villagers. But members of the lower class had no rights against those of a higher class.

While the life of a peasant was difficult, peasants were forbidden to work on Sundays, so each week they always had one day off, in addition to a considerable number of days honoring saints of the church. Such days would feature festivals and dancing in the village, in the street, and in the church or town hall. The lords also entertained their peasantry—especially at harvest time or when the hay was brought in, sometimes after sowing, and usually at Christmas. Usually a festival occurred when the grapes were harvested for making wine. Fairs featuring jugglers and acrobats for entertainment also became common. Despite the difficulties of life in these times, there was psychological security in knowing that each person adhered to the same religion as his neighbors and was in intimate cooperation with them.

176. The staple field crops to which he had access were rye and wheat, planted in the fall, and barley, oats, beans, peas, and sometimes spring rye, planted in the spring and harvested in the fall of the same year. Rye was the cereal used most for the peasants' bread; wheat went to the lords.

Still, lords levied taxes on the peasants—usually a head tax paid annually by all serfs and a direct tax on the property of each peasant. An inheritance tax was also imposed. Furthermore, peasants were required to make many gifts during the various seasons of the year.

Lords also made it illegal for peasants to make their own ovens and build their own mills and winepresses. Thus the serfs were forced to have their flour baked in the lord's oven, their wheat ground at his mill, and their wine made at his winepresses, all, of course, at a charge. Similarly, peasants paid charges for traveling across bridges and tolls for using roads.

One way to escape from this hard life was to stay away from the manor for a year and a day—being gone for that length of time broke the serf's servitude. Staying away for this length of time was especially easy with the growth of towns. Doing so was also possible during the Crusades, when peasants left under the call of arms. Given its oppression, this manorial system was bound to end. The servile status of the peasants and the legal power of the lords disappeared first; and in most Western countries the system did not survive the thirteenth century.

Rise of Towns.[177] During the Early Middle Ages, there was very little industry and trade. By the time of Charlemagne, nearly everything that was produced was from local communities. Goods were purchased by bartering, not with standard coinage.

In the East however, the Byzantine Empire still had industry. One of the only points of contact between the East and West came through the city of Venice. Venice was immune to Muslim attack because it was essentially built on the sea. It traded steadily with Constantinople. It is generally conceded that the ethos of Venice, although geographically located within Italy, was nearer to Byzantine civilization than to that of Western Europe.

The Crusades greatly helped the Italian port cities. At the time of the First Crusade (1095), very few major cities remained in Europe. In the ninth and tenth centuries, the towns had suffered from the Viking invasions, when marauders would ascend from the rivers and attack and destroy cities. With the end of the Viking invasions, the towns could grow again.

177. Le Goff, *Medieval Civilization*, 208–17.

The merchants in the towns became increasingly wealthy through trade, so they found the lords increasingly bothersome. In towns that lacked a strong king, charters were drawn up between towns, and lords established the rights of all parties. It was possible, especially in Italy and Germany, for the towns to have relative political and economic autonomy. This general rule did not hold, for example, in France and England, where there were more strong kings. Only where there was a strong and efficient central government under a king did the towns maintain independence, though of a very limited nature.

These self-governing towns, called *communes*, broke the tradition of the feudal system. Later, these communes would play an important role in the Reformation period. Towns as a whole undertook obligations toward the lord and received privileges in return; this was a distinct break from the feudal system, in which the lord's obligations were always binding on individual persons, not on groups. Towns would now assess taxes, then pay those taxes to the lord. Eventually, the more powerful towns became more like city-states similar to those of the ancient world.

In many towns, the craft guilds became something similar to the municipal government. This development occurred when a charter between a city and a lord was established. The merchant guild, like the later craft guild, was a closed shop. Merchants who did not belong to the guild found themselves excluded from trade within the city. So monopolies held in trade varied from town to town. Price cutting was normally not allowed. The guild had power in that a trader lost his business if he was excluded from the guild. There are records documenting cases of beating those who cut prices.

A young artisan first entered a trade guild by becoming an apprentice to a master upon payment of a fee. Normally the apprenticeship lasted seven years, but sometimes it would last as long as twelve years. In other words, the boy became an indentured servant to the master. It was the task of the master to supervise not only the boy's work but also his morals and behavior. The apprentice would board at the master's home and had to obey him in every matter. When a young man was thoroughly trained in his craft, he became what was called a *journeyman* or *dayworker*, and he was free to leave his master and take work at regular wages wherever he could find it. Alternatively, he could stay on with his master, as was the norm in early times. In certain trades, especially the building trade, it was to the journeyman's advantage to work in foreign cities so that he would improve his knowledge by taking part in building massive churches and public offices.

In the Early Middle Ages, there was plenty of work for the journeyman. So he became a master as soon as he could afford a shop and raw materials and found a wife who could care for his apprentices.

Further Development to A.D. 1500. The years 1000–1300 were ones of economic and social expansion due to a rising population, the availability of metals, such as silver, agricultural production, and a clear definition of powers in the papal office. The concept of the national state began to develop, and education began to advance. The Crusades brought Eastern culture to Europe, thus leading, perhaps, to the Renaissance through the restoration of the Greek classics.

The Middle Ages were also full of conflict, wars, the threat of Islam, and power struggles between kings and popes. For the common person living amid such turmoil, there were uncertainty, fear, plague, and rampant disease. Around 1346, the plague took the lives of twenty-five million people, thus leaving land vacant and the work force ravaged. The church functioned as the place to ameliorate some of life's difficulties, with monks and nuns providing basic healthcare and medicine. But with illiteracy the standard and education practically nonexistent, the common person would not have had knowledge of the gospel—or even a way to gain access to it. Superstition and "Christian" rituals that closely mirrored pagan rites of old arose and gripped the collective mind until the Reformation.[178] From a high point of access, literacy, and education in the Roman Empire, it took Western civilization only a few centuries to fall into dark days.

KEY TERMS

Donation of Constantine
Holy Roman Empire
Muhammad
Crusades

178. Ibid., 35.

feudal system
Islam
Qur'an

STUDY QUESTIONS

1. Can you describe the development of the papacy?
2. Do you think that the Crusades were justified? Why or why not?
3. How did Muhammad's understanding of the nature of God influence the rest of his theology?
4. Do you think that the feudal system was economically and socially just?
5. What were some of the benefits and disadvantages of the apprentice system of labor?

RESOURCES FOR FURTHER STUDY

This chapter focused on medieval economic and social history.

Le Goff, Jacques. *Medieval Civilization 400–1500.* Translated by Julia Barrow. Oxford: Blackwell, 1988. An excellent volume.

Needham, Nicholas R. *2,000 Years of Christ's Power.* Vol. 2, *The Middle Ages.* 2000. Reprint, London: Grace Publications, 2004. An excellent volume among his others, which continue to be some of the most helpful and clear.

Southern, R. W. *Western Society and the Church in the Middle Ages.* The Pelican History of the Church 2. Middlesex, England: Pelican Books, 1976. Although published decades ago, an excellent college-level text on these topics.

9

The Medieval Church to the End of the Thirteenth Century

The Role of the Church in Attaining Salvation

In many ways, the medieval church was a complex system. During the medieval era, it grew to be the most powerful multinational corporation in the world—the church of that era controlled the political, economic, and spiritual climate of much of Europe. But the narrative the church told was relatively simple: there is a God in heaven, a Devil in hell, and an impending judgment of humankind. In many ways, this narrative set the stage for much of the Middle Ages. The whole of medieval human existence was spent toward attaining a favorable judgment on that last day. And the church stepped in to facilitate that aim. The goal of the church was to help humans escape the clutches of hell and enter heaven.

The most pressing question that the church then had to answer was, "How could humans ever receive grace?" The church taught that human beings were saved through grace that was bestowed by God as a heavenly gift, made possible only by Christ's sacrifice. Grace was given to fallen humans only through the medium of the church's sacraments, which they believed to have been founded by Christ himself.

The medieval church, therefore, celebrated seven sacraments—seven channels through which grace dripped into humankind. The first sacrament was baptism, by which a newborn child was supposedly redeemed from original sin. Godparents would accept Christianity on the baby's behalf. The second sacrament was confirmation, which occurred when a child of about the age of twelve accepted the Christian faith personally. The third was partaking of the Eucharist—the most sacred and important of the sacraments, in which bread and wine transformed into the body and blood of Christ through the miracle of transubstantiation. Matrimony—the joining of a man and woman as husband and wife—constituted the fourth sacrament. The fifth was penance, by means of which a sinner would demonstrate his sorrow for confessed sins. The sixth sacrament was extreme unction—an anointing with holy oil that prepared the Christian for death and wiped away any remaining sins. The seventh sacrament, known as *holy orders*, was the ceremony by which laymen were made priests. The laymen were set apart from ordinary men, enabled to celebrate the Eucharist, and granted absolution from sin.

But as this chapter will reveal, the Roman Catholic Church's understanding of grace and salvation created a dilemma for them. Where did people who still had sin in their lives go when they died? To ease this tension, Pope Gregory I (A.D. 540–604) established a new teaching: he said that there was an intermediate place between heaven and earth called *purgatory*. Purgatory was a world in which sins were purged by means of punishment. The duration of this punishment depended on the sinfulness of the person, but the result was a purified soul ready to enter heaven. Thus the medieval church taught that an individual attained salvation through God's grace and the church's sacraments— and, if necessary, purifying punishment in purgatory.

The previous chapter in many ways set the social and economic stage for the theology of this era. This chapter will be largely spent on analyzing a number of medieval theologians and the marks they left on the thinking of the church. But before engaging in an analysis of the individual thinkers, this chapter will seek to understand medieval philosophy and intellectual history.

EARLY MEDIEVAL PHILOSOPHY

Neoplatonism. Neoplatonism was born out of the intellectual struggle of the earlier Greek philosophical schools. Although there were pre-Socratic thinkers, Greek philosophy truly began with Plato. Plato, however, had asked a number of questions that he never answered—questions concerning what he called the *demiurge*, the origin of the world, and space and size as abstract philosophical qualities. Aristotle, his student and successor, followed Plato and presented his own system, much of which was incorporated into the Platonic approach. The Stoics, who also made valuable contributions to the history of philosophy, followed Plato and Aristotle.[1]

But Greek philosophy lacked a systematic completion. It needed to be entirely integrated, and the wisdom that had been accumulated over the eight centuries from the time of Plato needed to be summarized. It could be said that the last of the great Greek pagan philosophers, Plotinus (A.D. 205–270), proved to be that systematician.

Contra Stoic materialism, Plotinus argued for the immortality of the soul. He also stood against some of Aristotle's notions of the soul.[2] In *On the Immortality of the Soul*, Plotinus taught that the soul was entombed in a physical body. Nevertheless, the soul itself experiences suffering, troubles, fears, and desires. The soul has existed from all eternity and descended from heaven to be incarcerated in human bodies. Although it was not good for the soul to have descended from heaven, nevertheless, it has an important lesson to learn while on earth—and to learn it, the soul must encounter evil. By experiencing evil, the soul is able to gain a clearer perception of the good.

In Plotinus's pagan system, salvation comes to the soul as the soul reascends to heaven from the depths to which it fell. The degree of its fall depends on the degree to which the body of the man or woman in which it becomes imprisoned is immersed in sensation. For example, the Epicureans, known as Hedonists, were immersed in sensation and thus fell greatly. The best person, therefore, recognizes his soul's divine nature and works back to a more pure state by leaving the sensory realm and entering the realm of reason and intelligence—via reading historical theology books(!). For example, in physical beauty one can

1. See chapter 1. For more information on the Stoics, see Richard C. Gamble, *The Whole Counsel of God*, vol. 2, *The Full Revelation of God* (Phillipsburg, NJ: P&R Publishing, 2018) (WCG2), 952–54, 975–76.

2. Gordon H. Clark, *Thales to Dewey: A History of Philosophy* (Boston: Houghton Mifflin, 1957), 170–72.

see Beauty itself (Beauty with a capital *B*). Appreciating these forms of that which is eternal, therefore, is positive.

The eternal human soul was produced by what Plotinus referred to as the *divine mind*.[3] This divine mind is the ultimate principle. The mind is the realm of knowledge, and any type of knowledge requires distinctions. This divine mind has duality—a subject and a predicate, required for knowledge. But the mind cannot be the source of true unity. There must be something higher than the mind. Plotinus thought that this higher entity is the One (capital *O*).[4]

The One transcends the world of knowledge, thus making the One strictly unknowable. Statements about something require a subject and predicate, and such statements are inferior to the One. As the philosopher meditates, Plotinus says, salvation is a mystical experience—a trance—and absorption into the One.[5] Neoplatonism, a pagan philosophy, would significantly influence Christian thinking.

Pseudo-Dionysius. The history of medieval philosophy often begins with Pseudo-Dionysius.[6] A Christian convert by the name of Dionysius the Areopagite was in Athens during the time of the apostle Paul's visit to that city (Acts 17:4). During the Middle Ages it was believed that Dionysius wrote a number of works.[7] But the true author of these works is unknown (hence, *Pseudo*-Dionysius). The writings were likely composed near the end of the fifth century.[8] It is not historically possible that they were written by someone who lived in the first century.[9] Patristic and medieval theologians and philosophers, however, did not doubt these works' authenticity, so they were used

3. The soul is an intermediate being between two worlds; it touches the lower world of sense and the higher world, which is next to the world of ideas. This world of ideas and this divine mind are identical. This teaching is slightly different from that of Plato, who saw perhaps some difference between the world of ideas and the divine demiurge. But Plotinus was able to say that his teaching could be squared with Plato's, which is probably the case. See ibid., 172–76.

4. John M. Frame, *A History of Western Philosophy and Theology* (Phillipsburg, NJ: P&R Publishing, 2015) (*HWPT*), 79.

5. Clark, *Thales to Dewey*, 178.

6. Diarmaid MacCulloch, *Christianity: The First Three Thousand Years* (New York: Viking, 2010), 165, 379, 413, 417, 421, 439, 488–89, 561–62.

7. The names of the collected writings were *Divine Names*, *Mystical Theology*, *Celestial Hierarchy*, and *Ecclesiastical Hierarchy*. There are ten letters in the collection as well.

8. Frederick Copleston, *A History of Philosophy*, 2, *Medieval Philosophy* (New York: Continuum, 1950), 1:91–96. Frame (*HWPT*, 125) dates them sometime during the late fifth and early sixth centuries but notes that some date them to 650–725.

9. Copleston, *Medieval Philosophy*, 1:92.

as trusted Christian sources of wisdom. Aquinas cited them some seventeen hundred times![10]

The works of Pseudo-Dionysius were clearly influenced by Neoplatonism and attempted to reconcile Neoplatonist philosophy with the teachings of Christianity. Such attempts at philosophical and theological amalgamation comprise a significant (negative) theme of historical theology.[11] As observed in the first two volumes of *The Whole Counsel of God*, Christianity itself provides answers to the deepest philosophical questions, and theologians should not seek to intertwine the darkness of human wisdom with God's brilliant light.

This pagan philosophical framework affected Pseudo-Dionysius's doctrine of the Trinity. His main aim was finding a "One" principle behind, or higher than, the persons of the godhead. Pseudo-Dionysius said that God in himself is undifferentiated unity.[12] While he did not go so far as to deny the three persons of the Trinity, he emphasized their unity.

Pseudo-Dionysius held to degrees of being; thus God is being in the fullest sense. God has attributes in the most absolute sense, and creation has them in a lesser degree and analogically. Since God is so ontologically distant, Pseudo-Dionysius concludes that God is fundamentally unknown. Man can only speak of him through the *via negativa* ("negative way")—that is, by saying what God is not. Humans cannot conceptualize God, and their only hope of knowing him is through mystical experience—when men abandon words and go beyond even negative concepts.[13] The author also held to a host of mediators between God and humanity, mediators such as cherubs in heaven and bishops and monks on the earth.[14]

Boethius of Rome (A.D. 480–524/25).[15] Boethius, like Pseudo-Dionysius, introduced Greek philosophy, specifically Neoplatonism, into medieval thinking.[16] He was a Christian philosopher born in Rome

10. *HWPT*, 125.

11. See theological analysis in chapters 3 and 7.

12. Copleston, *Medieval Philosophy*, 1:91–96.

13. *HWPT*, 126; Clark, *Thales to Dewey*, 246–47.

14. Francis Nigel Lee, *A Christian Introduction to the History of Philosophy* (Nutley, NJ: Craig Press, 1969), 128.

15. MacCulloch, *Christianity*, 322.

16. Copleston, *Medieval Philosophy*, 1:104. William Edgar and K. Scott Oliphint, *Christian Apologetics Past and Present: A Primary Source Reader* (Wheaton, IL: Crossway, 2009), 1:318:

who had studied at Athens and held a high governmental position under the Ostrogothic king Theodoric. He was later executed for treason.[17]

Boethius translated Aristotle's *Logic*, or *Organon*, from Greek into Latin, as well as Cicero and Porphyry's writings. Boethius's transmission of Aristotle's thought was pivotal for the development of logic in the Middle Ages.[18] There are different types of logic, and a firm grasp of the nature and historical development of logic proves helpful for a better understanding of later theological development.

Aristotle was the developer and systematizer of what is called *classical* or *Aristotelian logic*.[19] Aristotle rejected Plato's world of ideas, and in doing so he needed to find a way to avoid philosophical skepticism. For Aristotle, logic was not a merely formal science of thinking. To make true judgments, there must be some principles on which those judgments depend.[20] A true judgment must have a relationship to reality; thus the laws of thought must also have a relationship to reality.[21]

One of Aristotle's rules of logic is the law of contradiction (also called the "law of noncontradiction").[22] The principle of this law is that the same attribute cannot attach and not attach to the same thing in the same respect. Stated another way, contrary attributes cannot belong to the same subject at the same time. The law of contradiction is not merely a law of thought but primarily a law of being.

From some of Aristotle's works on reasoning, the *Organon* was born. The word *organon* referred to the instrument of science, or the cognitive framework and means through which scientific inquiry is carried out. This process of thought would acquire the more technical term *logic* some years later, by which time it would coincide with our current sense of the word.

From Aristotelian thought developed a tradition that emphasized dialectical or rhetorical argumentation. The searcher for truth moved

---

"Boethius was well aware that, at minimum, to engage the heresies that were making headway in the church, it was useful, if not necessary, to engage them in their own terms."

17. MacCulloch, *Christianity*, 322; Copleston, *Medieval Philosophy*, 1:101. The Ostrogoths were one of the tribes that contributed to the fall of the Roman Empire.

18. He also translated Aristotle's *Categories* and *On Interpretation*.

19. Lee, *Christian Introduction to Philosophy*, 88.

20. See Sir David Ross, *Aristotle* (New York: Routledge, 2004), 33.

21. See chapter 1 on Aristotle.

22. See chapter 1, which defines the law and gives an example.

from a question through a probable argument to a probable conclusion. This type of knowing, and the amount of certainty it engendered, was considered to be the best that could be hoped for in most instances of practical life. Stated differently, there is a certain premise, added to it is a necessary inference, and from those two elements comes certainty.

The field of logic continued to develop after Aristotle's time and in some cases took different directions.[23] One of these different approaches to knowledge was the Stoic, or Ciceronian, approach, which was formulated by Chrysippus (232–206 B.C.). Stoic logic existed separately from Aristotelian logic for a few centuries, but the two types gradually fused in the work of Boethius.[24]

Besides his translations, Boethius also composed an important original work, titled *The Consolations of Philosophy*. His work makes Boethius philosophically significant on a number of fronts.[25] Though he is not often thought of as an independent thinker, he specifically applied philosophical categories to theology; such application became a hallmark of medieval thinking.[26] Boethius's writings contributed to the construction of what would later be termed a "theological science."[27] He also wrote a number of biblical commentaries, and writers began to imitate his literary style.

He also provided some important technical theological terms. The first term concerned God's eternity. He said that God's eternity is "the complete, simultaneous and perfect possession of everlasting life."[28]

23. There was an inherent problem with Aristotle's logic. Clark (*Thales to Dewey*, 162) notes that for Aristotle, "truth is a statement of reality, and reality is all past or present." There is no future reality; therefore, statements like "Caesar will eventually die" are not true. Propositions relative to the future cannot be true.

24. See William Kneale and Mary Kneale, *The Development of Logic* (Oxford: Clarendon, 1962), 177.

25. Copleston, *Medieval Philosophy*, 1:104.

26. Edgar and Oliphint, *Christian Apologetics*, 1:316.

27. Ibid., 1:316: "he sets out to give reason free reign and leaves aside any reference to Christianity. . . . If . . . Boethius did not in fact lose his faith during his imprisonment, it seems clear that his methodology assumes a significant distance, if not an outright separation, between the methodology employed in pure philosophy and that of theology. . . . Boethius offers in the *Consolation* an example of philosophical reasoning that has no foundation in Biblical revelation. . . . Boethius also saw a certain usefulness of philosophy to theology, in that the former is able to help articulate, by way of its terminology and various methodologies, some of the truths of the latter."

28. Boethius, *The Consolation of Philosophy* 5, as cited in *HWPT*, 124; see also Clark, *Thales to Dewey*, 247.

This definition, perhaps dependent on Augustine, is based on the reality that creatures lose part of their lives as they age and as experiences fade into the dark past, but God never loses any part of his life, for he is above time.[29] From these early foundations, medieval thought developed.

MEDIEVAL INTELLECTUAL HISTORY (TENTH THROUGH TWELFTH CENTURIES)

Medieval Universities.[30] Ideas and philosophies were disseminated to future thinkers through universities. People of wealth, however, did not use the university. Family chaplains taught the children of the nobility, and notaries or clerks instructed the children of more ordinary citizens.

Prior to the twelfth century, medieval universities were informally organized. They began with the institution of residential colleges, which were initially intended for poor students. One of the earliest institutions was created in Paris in 1180. The French king recognized the university, and a special law was passed that exempted its members from taxes and gave them special jurisdiction.

Another early university was established by the emperor and confirmed by the papacy in 1158 at Bologne. The papacy regulated all licenses for teaching in the universities and formalized the requirements for the degrees in Bologne, Italy, and Paris in the 1220s. The number of universities continued to expand through the thirteenth century.

In England, Oxford was established in 1214 and Cambridge in the 1230s. Southern France also began a university of medicine at Montpellier in 1220 and of law in the 1230s. In northern France, Orleans became a university and a famous study center for law. In Italy, by 1231 the town of Salerno had established a university along with a school of medicine. Interestingly enough, Germany had no universities at the time; but less formal places of study did exist there—for

---

29. *HWPT*, 124. Frame mentions Boethius's less helpful definition of nature and person, which was intended to aid during his contemporary christological controversies but proved less than helpful in the Trinitarian debate. See ibid., 124–25.

30. John Hine Mundy, *Europe in the High Middle Ages: 1150–1300* (Harlow: Longman, 1973), 464–73; MacCulloch, *Christianity*, 398–403.

example, the Dominican Order, which met in Cologne. In 1253, the northern German town of Lübeck founded a Latin school that would exist for quite some time.

The university curriculum was well established by the mid-thirteenth century. To become a physician, a young medical student would study logic for three years, then devote five years studying Hippocrates, Galen, and practical surgery. Finally, after serving a year-long internship under an experienced physician, he was licensed.

In Paris, studies in theology began with six years in the arts faculty (or division), with the last two years as a bachelor attaining the master's degree. To become a doctor of theology, students spent eight more years in the theology faculty (again, division), with the first four years devoted to biblical exegesis and Peter Lombard's *Sentences* and the next four years serving as a bachelor who taught other students.

Conflicts began to ensue in a fight for control over the universities and schools—did the church have control, or did the city that hosted the university? From as early as 1185 it became common for the church to attempt to monopolize the university's teaching. The church's effort was born out of and continued to reinforce its immature understanding of the need for the university. Sometimes the city councils would actually invade the schools and secularize them.

The master or doctor in the university filled the dual roles of writing the examinations and functioning as the gatekeeper for students being allowed onto the teaching staff. Some of these masters or doctors were highly valued thinkers; others were less so.

In the thirteenth century, ideological battles raged. With the rise of new, entirely trained orders of mendicant (or begging) preachers, the conflict between these preachers and the secular clergy[31] spread into the university. Strongly supported by the popes, members of the mendicant orders forced their way into the faculties of the University of Paris beginning in 1229, when the first Dominican started teaching there.

The Dominican Order, or Order of Preachers, was established in 1217. The Dominicans, who would later become the chief opposition

---

31. The religious clergy were the various orders of monks with different divisions within them, whereas clerics, who were not bound by monastic vows, were called *secular*. For more information, see Mundy, *Europe*, 283–94.

to the Reformation, began with a noble purpose—to preach the gospel to the ends of the earth. They soon became the intellectuals of the Middle Ages, and for their association with the universities and the scholastic method they received vilification in the sixteenth century.[32]

By the 1270s the mendicant orders had split, partly along nationalistic lines. The English teachers of the Franciscan order, for example, attacked Aquinas and asserted that men such as Bonaventura, who was also a Franciscan but was English, were far superior to Aquinas. In the early part of the fourteenth century, Aquinas was canonized on his way toward becoming a saint.

When the power of the academics was high, the professors were not afraid even of the pope himself. As early as the thirteenth century, the power of the university, as the guardian of Christianity itself, was considered to be superior in authority to even the papacy. History, however, demonstrates that the papacy retained its power. In many ways, the universities gave birth to the Conciliar movement, which established church counsels as the highest authority.

Philosophy, Theology, and Learning. During the Middle Ages, philosophers were not particularly interested in studying the natural phenomena of the universe (science) or how things operate (physics). Metaphysics is the study of the reality that lies behind the universe's natural phenomena.

During this time, the intention of the intellectual, especially (but not only) the ordained, was to educate humanity toward Christ. Most thinkers assumed that humanity's reasoning capabilities were able to comprehend some part of the created universe and that, in that comprehension, one viewed the nature of the divine principle itself. So knowledge was almost idolized. This Christian naturalism was suited to an age of intellectual confidence and social growth. Its philosophy was useful to a church that in its leadership of the world was obligated to build rational institutional structures based on natural law and the principles of human behavior. Nevertheless, this philosophical system was not without its problems.[33]

---

32. Jacques Le Goff, *Medieval Civilization 400–1500*, trans. Julia Barrow (Oxford: Basil Blackwell, 1988), 310–11.

33. There was a strong assumption that more wisdom was still to be discovered. This conviction produced a counter belief and the fear of non-Christian learning. For a time, students

This system could not penetrate the various mysteries of nature. It was incapable of determining the origin of the world or the meaning of eternity. It did not help resolve matters of human behavior—such as the foundation of natural determinism and the dilemma of free will and moral responsibility. Here the teaching of the church stepped in to aid philosophy with explanations of the supernatural. The pure naturalism of philosophy and reason and religious supernaturalism, with all its moral imperatives, created something of an intellectual tightrope, though most of this time did not see it as such.

In general, medieval philosophical thought attempted to synthesize a Christian worldview and non-Christian philosophy.[34] The intellectuals of this time were quite successful in this endeavor.[35] But this synthesis of the secular and the sacred did not receive unanimous support. The competing theological or philosophical methodologies of the Middle Ages constituted the first cracks in the chasm that would be evident between the theologies of Protestantism and Catholicism.[36]

Intellectuals sought to understand how God, who was behind all phenomena, related to the structure of human thought. Specifically, they wanted to grasp how various intellectual concepts related to one another.[37] This debate centered on the nature of any concept whatsoever, whether that concept be God or a rock. These concepts were referred to as *universals*.[38]

At first, a fixation on the problem of universals likely seems inconsequential at best and foolish at worst. Moderns shake their heads at the medieval debates over the number of angels that could dance on the head of a pin—as though it were one of the world's pressing

were not allowed to study natural history at Paris because theologians, it was argued, do not need natural science. Thinkers such as Roger Bacon argued that past knowledge was good but far from perfect.

34. Cornelius Van Til, *Who Do You Say That I Am?* (Nutley, NJ: Presbyterian and Reformed, 1975), 62.

35. Colin Brown, *Philosophy & the Christian Faith: A Historical Sketch from the Middle Ages to the Present Day* (Downers Grove, IL: InterVarsity Press, 1968), 20: Greek philosophy left its mark in the form as well as the content of medieval writing. For example, in contrast to Augustine's style, medieval writing was "logical but formal, thorough, but thoroughly dry."

36. Ibid., 12.

37. Ibid., 17–18.

38. See analysis of universals and the one and the many in Richard C. Gamble, *The Whole Counsel of God*, vol. 1, *God's Mighty Acts in the Old Testament* (Phillipsburg, NJ: P&R Publishing, 2009) (*WCG1*), 87–88, and *WCG 2*:1018.

questions! But the problem of universals is not as futile as it may first appear. A universal category, such as genus or species, represents the use of abstraction in human thought. For example, can people talk meaningfully about the likeness of humanity when the topic is abstracted from individual persons? This likeness, considered by the mind, is the idea of species, while considering the likeness of diverse species forms the idea of genus.[39]

These sorts of questions are essential to the philosophical process. The dilemma of how to understand categories dates back to Plato and Aristotle.[40] Porphyry asked whether genera and species, such as man and lion or justice and equality, really existed in nature or whether they were mere speculations.[41] Boethius sought to answer whether abstract categories such as substance, quantity, and relation are actual things or just empty words.

Intelligent conversation and thought cannot help but employ general ideas and words. Permit an example: "The particular object which I see outside is a tree, or more precisely, an oak." Such a judgment affirms that a particular object is of a certain kind, that it belongs to the genus tree and to the species oak. But there may be many other objects, besides the actual one perceived, to which the same terms may be applied. The same ideas may cover many oak trees. Thus objects, like oaks tree, that are outside the speaker's mind are individual, whereas the concepts that classify them are general and universal in character in that they apply indiscrimately to a multitude of individual oak trees.

A further question concerns the relationship between individual objects and the universal concepts that classify them. If the objects are individual and the corresponding concepts general, then universal concepts have no physical foundation in reality—rather, they exist only in the mind. But if the words *tree* and *oak* are mere ideas, then a separation exists between a person's thought and the objects of the thought or the words that express it. Human knowledge, when expressed in universal concepts, is thus of doubtful validity.

39. Copleston, *Medieval Philosophy*, 1:138.
40. Joseph Owens, *The Doctrine of Being in the Aristotelian Metaphysics: A Study in the Background of Medieval Thought* (Toronto: Pontifical Institute of Medieval Studies, 1963), 122–29; and see Herman Bavinck, *Reformed Dogmatics*, ed. John Bolt (Grand Rapids: Baker Academic, 2003) (*RD*), 1:229.
41. This view appeared in a work titled *Introduction to Aristotle's Categories*.

To illustrate the significance of this debate, if a contemporary scientist expresses his knowledge in abstract universal terms—for example, a statement about electrons in general instead of a particular electron—and these terms have no foundation in reality outside the scientist's mind, then science itself is an arbitrary construction that has no relationship to reality. Intellectual skepticism results if someone makes human judgments of a universal character but admits that the foundation of the universal concept exists only in the mind and not in reality.[42]

From the heated debates about concepts and their relationship to objects, there arose two major philosophical factions that would prove significant for theology—realism and nominalism.[43] Those who claimed that the categories or universals were *res* (meaning "thing" or "matter") were called *realists*, a word that bears a different sense than it does in modern English. The realists—Eriugena, Remigius of Auxerre, and William of Champeaux, who all followed Plato—held that the universals, those abstract notions of goodness or beauty or color, were in fact real. They held that what men and women observe and measure on earth are copies of an eternal archetype.[44]

Those who argued that these categories were mere words were called *nominalists*, from the Latin term *nomen* (meaning "name"). The nominalists held that there were no universals, only particulars. The first of these nominalists was a man named Roscellinus (1050–1120). He believed that men were real and could be touched and known, but the category man was a mere notion that had no correspondence in reality.

The nominalists rejected the idea of universals. For them, a true universal is doubtful. There was no universal beauty apart from a beautiful thing. They held that the abstract term *beauty* is merely a manner of speaking.[45] Sadley, Roscellinus applied this debate to the Trinity.

42. See *RD* 1:229.

43. See ibid., 1:223–26, 230; MacCulloch (on Ockham), *Christianity*, 564–65. For late medieval nominalism, see Heiko Augustinus Oberman, *The Harvest of Medieval Theology: Gabriel Biel and Late Medieval Nominalism* (Cambridge: Harvard University Press, 1963).

44. Brown, *Philosophy & Faith*, 18; Edgar and Oliphint, *Christian Apologetics*, 1:339.

45. Brown, *Philosopy & Faith*, 19. Edgar and Oliphint (*Christian Apologetics*, 1:338) state, "nominalism teaches that things sharing the same name are not otherwise related," and (1:339) "Nominalism was no doubt identified first by Plato, who opposed it. He thought that chairs did have something in common, namely, the *form* of 'chairness.'"

He believed that three divine persons cannot be united—thus for him, the Trinity was nothing more than a name. Nominalism developed even further with the thinking of William of Ockham (1287–1347).

Following Augustine, the early scholastic period was dominated by realism. For realists, words designated realities, thus the word *man* refers to an existing object. Men have a common equality, and that common equality is man's essential nature. Concerning God, he was the most universal and the most real.[46] These issues of nominalism and realism are present in much of today's linguistic and analytic philosophies, which are concerned with the precise relationship between language or thought and their corresponding objects.

A group referred to as the *conceptualists*, or at times the *moderate realists*, found a middle course between these competing philosophies. This group included men such as Abelard and Aquinas.[47] They followed Aristotle, who asserted that universals exist in the realm of thought but stand for something in existence to provide unity to the world's diversity. Conceptualism was embraced as an alternative to nominalism and realism.[48] The debate between realism and nominalism extended into the fifteenth century. But nominalism would also appear in another form—empiricism.[49]

These philosophical debates brought about a practical problem—the question of what foundation the thinking person (who was necessarily a member of the church in Europe) should base his thinking on. Was his thinking to be founded on philosophy, theology, or some synthesis of the two? Many argued that natural reason combined with an experience of nature was nearly sufficient to enable man to see God and to understand his world. Thus it was there that the medieval mind could find intellectual certainty.

This information paints the background well for Aquinas's teaching, addressed later in this chapter. There is a natural knowledge with which people are born and then develop. That natural knowledge, however, is different from a further knowledge, which comes by faith. So divine grace perfects natural knowledge. Since God provided both,

46. Clark, *Thales to Dewey*, 87.
47. Edgar and Oliphint, *Christian Apologetics*, 1:339.
48. Brown, *Philosophy & Faith*, 19.
49. RD 1:230–31.

and falsehood cannot come from his hand, then that which comes by faith and that which comes by nature cannot be contrary to one another. In other words, it was believed that theology had its foundation in the light of faith and philosophy in the light of reason. Reason has an ancillary function: describing and defending the faith.[50]

In the thirteenth century, the scholars of the day taught that Plato was mistaken in his belief that the planets were gods and that Aristotle was mistaken in his assertion that the world was eternal. Some had already complained that the professors in Paris cited pagans and less-than-credible philosophers more often than they did biblical and ecclesiastical authority. The complaints, however, came from a small minority. The question of authority and the validity of reason continues to haunt the modern Christian world.

Monasteries and Reform.[51] In the early years of the tenth century, a duke gave a considerable piece of land in Cluny, eastern France (modern day Burgundy), to the abbott of a Benedictine monastery in exchange for prayers to be said for the donor's soul. The land was to be completely free from judicial restrictions and subject to the papacy alone. From this humble inception began the movement of the Cluny monasteries. And as a result, reform swept through the monasteries of all the other orders.

Saint Benedict, the founder of a monastery in Monte Casino, had established a number of rules for monasteries, including the following several examples. He insisted that monks perform manual labor and

50. Aquinas, *Super Boetium de trinitate* 2, 3: "The gifts of grace are added to nature in such a way that they do not do away with it, but rather perfect it. Hence, the light of the faith that is freely infused into us does not destroy the light of natural knowledge implanted in us naturally. For although the natural light of the human mind is insufficient to show us these things made manifest by faith, it is nevertheless impossible that these things which the divine principle gives us by faith are contrary to those implanted in us by nature. Indeed, were that the case, one or the other would have to be false, and, since both are given to us by God, God would have to be the author of untruth, which is impossible . . . . For just as sacred doctrine is founded on the light of the faith, so is philosophy founded on the light of natural reason. Whence it is impossible that those things that are of philosophy can be contrary to those things which are of the faith. This does not mean that in regard to the faith reason or philosophy is considered superior to authority or theology. Rather, reason supports the faith. Its function was ancillary to faith but useful for the work of describing God and defending the faith" (as cited in part by Mundy, *Europe*, 474–75).

51. Le Goff, *Medieval Civilization*, 119–28. Patronage is when a noble can place anyone he wants in a church position because he controls the land around the church building and also pays for the upkeep of the clergy in the church (see MacCulloch, *Christianity*, 363–66.)

sever ties with their past, even with their families. The monks were to be obedient to their abbott and were to worship and pray during set times throughout the day. Under Benedict, monks were not permitted to own personal property. They had to sleep in a dormitory and eat in a common dining room. These rules were enforced in the monastery at Cluny. The first Cluny monastery soon spawned daughter monasteries. The land that was donated to them was free from the normal feudal obligations because it came under church control.

The monastery at Cluny, and its subsequent movement, focused on church reform. Because the monks were considered especially holy, the nobility protected them from violence, thus enabling the monks to preach and increase the scope of their ministries. Not only did the monks nourish the religious life of Europe, but they also trained a number of sincere clergymen to assume high offices in the church. The Clunaic Reform even had hopes of improving the papacy. And it did so to some extent, for Pope Gregory VII (1073–1085) was associated with the Clunaic Reform.

The Gregorian (Clunaic) Reform sought to enforce more strictly two areas of church life. At the time, the secular clergy, priests, and bishops considered celibacy to be almost inhuman—they lived openly with their wives and concubines. The reform movement sought to enforce the church's policy that monks were to be celibate. The movement also sought to restrain the corruption that was rampant in the patronage.[52]

Based on this movement and the number of popes who received training in Cluny monasteries, the pope became the only one who had the right to appoint higher clergy. No more laypersons were to be appointed to church positions. As a result, a quarrel broke out between rulers and the papacy regarding lay investiture.

It must be remembered that at this time the pope himself was subject to emperors. Thus the reformers within the church watched for an opportunity to throw off their bondage to these emperors. This opportunity finally presented itself with the election of the child emperor, Henry IV. In 1059, the papacy announced that henceforth the College of Cardinals would elect the pope. Now only the pope was

52. MacCulloch, *Christianity*, 363–66.

able to appoint the cardinals, and cardinals were appointed for life. This change produced a continuity of policy that could be maintained in the church. The papal appointees of previous popes chose the successor to that office. The emperor had no say in the matter.

Besides the changes in policy on celibacy and simony, a third thrust was integral to the Cluniac Reform—the establishment of a new position: papal legate. The papal legate was a personal representative of the pope and held precedence over all other clergymen in the country. The local clergy and the nobles resented these special ambassadors, but by neglecting or disobeying them they were defying the pope himself. Legates could proclaim announcements from the pope, read papal bulls or decrees, and even excommunicate or enact interdicts on an entire country by the direct authority of the pope. The legates, therefore, could make direct appeals to public opinion and bypass the authority of the local clergy. If the pope had a decree that was likely to be suppressed by local clergy, the papal legate could travel to that region and make the decree known. This type of power in the hands of thoughtful legates made for a very powerful clergy. From the middle of the eleventh century, all the popes were serious reformers.

The young Emperor Henry IV found himself in trouble. His own nobles were constantly rebelling. He struggled to unite Germany and manage his own clergy. To make matters worse, Henry needed money, which for emperors was readily available through simony. Thus Henry pushed aside the movements for reform and sold church offices to pay for his expensive military campaigns. And concerning clerical marriage, he looked the other way. He knew that sooner or later he would have to deal with the pope, but he assumed he could postpone this conflict until he had strengthened many of his weaknesses. But Pope Gregory VII was ready to fight.[53]

Gregory knew of Henry's struggles to manage his own nobles. He also knew that the German clergy, who were not particularly loyal to the pope, would likely not support Henry against the nobles if the pope did support them. So, after laying his groundwork, Gregory excommunicated Henry and deprived him of his kingdom. His papal legates throughout the kingdom announced the emperor's exile. At

---

53. Williston Walker, *A History of the Christian Church* (New York: Scribner's Sons, 1959), 253–56.

the same time, Pope Gregory released all German nobles from their vows of loyalty to the emperor. As a result, one of the nobles took active measures against Emperor Henry. The emperor found himself isolated and deprived of any means for resisting his own nobles. Henry was taken into custody, and the nobles called Gregory to Germany to preside over the election of a new sovereign.

It seemed as though Pope Gregory had succeeded. He was in the process of establishing his right to discipline rulers when Henry escaped and fled to northern Italy. In 1077, Gregory and Henry finally encountered each another, and Henry repented of his sin. This move left Pope Gregory in a difficult situation: as a priest, he had the duty of absolving and forgiving penitent sinners. So Gregory absolved Henry, though it meant the collapse of his policy and the possibility of civil war. After being absolved, Henry returned home, only to consolidate his power, cross the Alps, and drive Pope Gregory into exile. Gregory died in 1085.

Henry V, the next German emperor, continued to have trouble with the pope, whose office persisted in gaining strength. As long as the popes remained reformers, simony and non-celibacy among the clergy were held in check. We need to turn to the great thinkers of the time.

MEDIEVAL THEOLOGIANS

Rhabanus Maurus (A.D. 776–856). Maurus significantly advanced education in Germany. He studied under Alcuin and later taught at Fulda. He become an abbot in A.D. 822. Maurus was then promoted to the position of archbishop of Mainz, where he labored until his death. To help educate priests, he wrote a tripartite *De Institutione Clericorum*, which included an analysis of the seven liberal arts. Most scholars view this period of medieval theological education as relatively unoriginal.[54]

John Scotus Eriugena (A.D. 810–877). In A.D. 810, Eriugena was born in Ireland, which at the time was known as Scotia Major.[55] Around

---

54. Copleston, *Medieval Philosophy*, 1:110–11.
55. Clark, *Thales to Dewey*, 250.

A.D. 845, Charles the Bald, successor to Charlemagne, called Eriugena to replace the famed Alcuin of York at Paris's palace school.[56]

In A.D. 827, a codex of Pseudo-Dionysius had been presented as a gift to the school. This gift prompted the study of Pseudo-Dionysius in the West and facilitated the transplanting of Greek-Christian Platonism into Europe. Eriugena, thoroughly convinced of the value of the work, translated it from Greek.[57] His insights into its meanings were significant.

Eriugena was an influential writer and translator. He made a significant impact on Western mysticism and medieval scholasticism.[58] He helped cast a Neoplatonic and mystical shadow on thought—a shadow that would remain for six centuries.[59] His time spent as a teacher of the church afforded him vast influence on the intellectual community of the empire itself.

Because of his connection with later heretics, Eriugena's writings were condemned in the thirteenth century. His first printed works, which resurfaced in 1681, were listed on the index of forbidden books. In fact, ecclesiastical authorities condemned his *De divisione naturae* (*The Division of Nature*), on at least three occasions. But what made him such a controversial figure?

At the request of the bishop of Reims, Eriugena's first book was written to refute the teaching of predestination as articulated by a priest by the name of Gottschalk. His reply to Gottschalk's teaching was titled *De praedestinatione* (A.D. 851). Those who held a biblical understanding of predestination disagreed strongly with Eriugena's work. This controversy forced the church to return to these philosophical and theological issues. Augustine had written on predestination centuries earlier, but he was just beginning his thoughts on the subject at the end of his life. Even Augustine was not consistent in his stance on the issue. For example, in his later works Augustine wrote that God knew those who would accept Christ and those who would reject

56. Copleston, *Medieval Philosophy*, 1:113.

57. I. P. Sheldon-Williams, "Greek Christian Platonist Tradition," in *The Cambridge History of Later Greek and Early Medieval Philosophy*, ed. A. H. Armstrong (Cambridge: Cambridge University Press, 1970), 519.

58. Ibid., 532–33.

59. Clark, *Thales to Dewey*, 251. Walker (*History*, 192) says that he "developed his own Neo-Platonic philosophy, which his age was too ignorant to judge heretical or orthodox."

him, and God's knowledge of those decrees meant that they would necessarily happen.

Gottschalk was an Augustinian monk. Through his reading of both Paul and Augustine, he developed a clear and consistent doctrine of predestination. He taught that the exact numbers of the saved and the lost were divinely predestined. Gottschalk was repaid for his biblical views with years of torture, imprisonment, and eventually death.[60] Through all his sufferings, he refused to recant. He remained imprisoned for twenty-one years, until his death.[61]

In A.D. 867, Eriugena published the *De divisione naturae*, his greatest work.[62] In it he argued that all nature was divided into four aspects relative to the work of creation. He began with two main groups—the created and the uncreated. In this system, God is in his own category as one who creates and is not created. Eriugena taught that the attributes of God are all superattributes that are not to be confused or thought of as creaturely attributes. God as God is the end of all things. The world is moving toward a consummation, when evil will be judged.[63]

Eriugena next considered those things that are created, then within that category the created things that create and the created things that do not create. Nature that is created but also creates is the form of all things (a thought derived from Plato), which Eriugena equated with the logos. Finally in his system, created nature that does not create is the world in which humanity currently lives.[64]

In *De divisione naturae*, Eriugena taught that students are to begin their investigation with special revelation. They must trust in the revealed word, not in their experiences. But according to Eriugena, the Christian understands the Scriptures through the study of the church fathers, who are essential resources to lean on for comprehending Scripture. Eriugena admitted, however, that the church fathers often

---

60. Clark, *Thales to Dewey*, 251.

61. Sheldon-Williams, "Greek Christian Platonist Tradition," 520. Gottschalk's writings are found in J. P. Migne, *Patrologiae Cursus Completus: Series Latina* (Paris: Garnier Fratres, 1857), 122:439–1022. Eriugena's *The Periphyseon* was written in dialogue form and was intended to investigate Augustine's Neoplatonism and its relationship to Aristotelian logic through Boethius.

62. The work appears in five volumes; see Migne, *Patrologiae Latina*, 122:441–1022. See also Hans von Schubert, *Geschichte der christlichen Kirche im Frühmittelalter* (Tübingen: Mohr Siebeck, 1921), 464.

63. *HWPT*, 127–28.

64. Sheldon-Williams, "Greek Christian Platonist Tradition," 520–23.

disagreed with one another.[65] It is therefore the responsibility of the student to reason between the differing opinions of the church fathers. So reason, he taught, is more foundational than even the authority of the church fathers.[66] In cases of apparent disagreement between revelation and reason, it seems as though Eriugena would have given priority to reason.[67] At the very least, he held reason and the Scriptures to be on the same plane of authority.

In agreement with Augustine, he held to the identity of philosophy and religion, and thus began the philosophical investigation of revealed truth. He taught that even in matters related to God, human experience of God cannot be given preference over the revealed word. He was, therefore, not a self-conscious rationalist.[68]

Eriugena also investigated dialectics. He began with a careful definition: dialectics was the science of disputation, which involved dissecting sentences into genera and species. For him, however, this science gave insight into reality itself.[69] He further held that there was a divine dialectic and that divine activity was the exemplar for human dialectics. By this, Eriugena meant that when scholars divide genera into species, they are not imposing something on nature by their minds. Instead, the human mind is discovering the way the principles of nature are disposed in the divine mind.[70] So when human beings practice dialectics, they are imitating divine activity.[71] In imperfect fashion, human beings think thoughts like God's because humans are made in God's image.[72] This disposition makes both God and the world knowable.

Eriugena's theology proper was a by-product of *The Division of Nature*. Based on his four divisions, God is the uncreated creator. In that aspect, the Father is the first person of the Trinity. As the second division, created creator or the logos, the Son is the second person

---

65. Clark, *Thales to Dewey*, 251.

66. Ibid.

67. Lee, *Christian Introduction to Philosophy*, 129. Eriugena held that God and nature were basically the same. His philosophy had "a thin Christian veneer."

68. Clark, *Thales to Dewey*, 251.

69. Sheldon-Williams, "The Greek Christian Platonist Tradition," 525.

70. Ibid., 526.

71. Ibid., 529.

72. Ibid., 531.

of the Trinity.[73] God also created the earth *ex nihilo* ("out of nothing"); however, the *nihilum* ("nothingness") was his own nature. This *nihilum* is the third division of nature, which is also an aspect of the divine nature. These three aspects are the manifestation of the Trinity in universal nature.[74] Thus Eriugena taught that God and nature are not distinct but one and the same. It would not be a stretch to refer to this view as pantheism.[75]

And yet, as Eriugena contemplated God, he concluded that God is so utterly transcendent that creatures cannot know what he is, nor can they even declare him to be.[76] His doctrine of divine transcendence is so extreme that according to his teaching God is incomprehensible even to himself.[77]

Scholars are divided on how to think about Eriugena's overall philosophical contribution. Several scholars have thought him to be a mere transmitter of Dionysius's thought.[78] Others credit him as having made unique contributions.[79] Based on the historical context in which he found himself, it has been said that he produced a grand system.[80] Some scholars claim that Eriugena has been understudied and merits further investigation.[81]

Eriugena represents a combination of Greek and Latin thought and the prevalent influence of Neoplatonism. He was the first to attempt to merge contemporary thought with past thinking.[82] He also under-

73. Ibid., 527.

74. Ibid., 528; von Schubert, *Geschichte*, 463–65.

75. Von Schubert, *Geschichte*, 463.

76. Herman Bavinck, *The Doctrine of God* (Carlisle, PA: Banner of Truth, 1977), 23: "Affirmative theology is figurative, metaphorical. It is excelled by negative theology. . . . He cannot be reached by human thinking, 'he can be touched but he cannot be grasped by our comprehension.' There is no name which expresses his being. He is incomprehensible and inexpressible."

77. Clark, *Thales to Dewey*, 251–52; Lee, *Christian Introduction to Philosophy*, 129.

78. Clark, *Thales to Dewey*, 251.

79. Sheldon-Williams, "Greek Christian Platonist Tradition," 519: "Eriugena's achievement was remarkable." Copleston, *Medieval Philosophy*, 1:112: "One of the most remarkable phenomena of the ninth century is the philosophical system of John Scotus Eriugena, which stands out like a lofty rock in the midst of a plain."

80. Copleston, *Medieval Philosophy*, 1:112: "But it is all the more remarkable that an isolated case of original speculation on the grand scale should suddenly occur, without warning and indeed without any immediate continuation. If John Scotus had confined himself to speculation on one or two particular points, we might not have been so surprised, but in point of fact he produced a system, the first great system of the M.A."

81. Von Schubert, *Geschichte*, 465.

82. Ibid.

stood true theology and philosophy as one.[83] He was a proponent of Neoplatonism and mysticism, influences that would linger for the next six centuries.[84]

In 1225, Eriugena's *The Division of Nature* was rightly condemned. Eriugena did not understand the biblical doctrine of creation or the Creator-creature distinction. His utterly and radically transcendent view of God led to a *via negativa* theology proper, which is far from biblical.[85]

Anselm of Canterbury (A.D. 1033–1109). Anselm was born in Italy in 1033. At the age of twenty-six he became a monk at Bec, in Normandy, France. His mentor was Abbot Lanfranc, who would later become archbishop of Canterbury (1070–1089). In 1093, Anselm succeeded his mentor to that office.[86]

Anselm favored monastic reform. He stood against a king's ability to appoint bishops for the church. Anselm twice ended up in conflict with kings of England who insisted on their right to appoint bishops. And Anselm, as a result of his position, was twice exiled from England.[87]

Many claim that Anselm was something of an intermediary figure between the theological methods of Augustine and Aquinas. Augustine held that belief preceded understanding (or faith preceded reason); Aquinas sought to reason as far as possible without faith and then add faith to reason. It has been said that Anselm held both positions.

Some have proposed that Anselm's theology was essentially presuppositional.[88] Anselm held that God, as revealed in both creation and Scripture, is the ultimate standard of truth. The statement "I believe that I might understand" makes faith the presupposition of rational

83. Ibid., 467.

84. Clark, *Thales to Dewey*, 250. Von Schubert (*Geschichte*, 463) says that he also translated works by Maximus the Confessor.

85. *HWPT*, 128.

86. Brown, *Philosophy & Faith*, 20–24; H. Liebeschütz, "Western Thought from Boethius to Anselm," in *The Cambridge History of Later Greek and Early Medieval Philosophy*, ed. A. H. Armstrong (Cambridge: Cambridge University Press, 1970), 611–42; MacCulloch, *Christianity*, 416; Douglas F. Kelly, *Systematic Theology*, vol. 1, *The God Who Is the Holy Trinity* (Fearn, Scotland: Mentor, 2008), 65–66. For more information, see Alvin Plantinga, ed., *The Ontological Argument from St. Anselm to Contemporary Philosophers* (Garden City, NY: Anchor Books, 1965).

87. See Walker, *History*, 325–27.

88. For more on the transcendental presuppositional approach, see *WCG* 2:990–1002.

inquiry. Thus faith is the foundation of understanding, not a conclusion from deductions.[89] So when Anselm writes in *Cur Deus Homo* (*Why God Became Man*) that he is leaving Christ out of view, he denies that people can gain faith by reason, even when Anselm offered proofs for his conclusions.[90] In his works, Anselm never leaves the whole of God's revelation out of view, nor does he deny the doctrine of Scripture's self-attestation. Anselm consistently reasoned from a biblical understanding of sin, divine justice, and mercy. His theological method was not always to cite Scripture but to use extrabiblical language to demonstrate the beautiful unfolding of God's plan in the doctrine of the atonement, a rationale that is consistent with Anselm's overall biblical worldview.[91]

Anselm's *Proslogion* presents the ontological argument for God's existence as a prayer: "I am not trying, O Lord, to make my way to your height." This simple prayer reflects Augustinian faith's seeking understanding.[92] Anselm began by defining God via revelation, then built on that which we believe.[93] Anselm's argument, including his response to objections, appears to presuppose Christian truth.[94]

The following is a condensed summary of Anselm's *Proslogion*. The human mind can contemplate God and know that he is (chs. 1–2). The Christian knows that God cannot be thought of as nonexistent, but the fool says that God cannot even be thought of (chs. 3–4). When contemplating God, the believer knows that God is whatever it is better to be than not to be and that this self-existent being has made all other things from nothing (ch. 5). God is sensible even without a body. He is almighty, though there are things that he cannot do. And he is compassionate and impassible (chs. 6–8). God's dealings with the righteous and the wicked are wholly just and merciful (chs. 9–11). God's attributes flow from his life. He alone is uncircumscribed and eternal (chs. 12–13). God is greater than that which can be thought,

---

89. *HWPT*, 129, 130–31.

90. For further analysis, see below.

91. *HWPT*, 132–34.

92. Jasper Hopkins (*A Companion to the Study of St. Anselm* [Minneapolis: University of Minnesota Press, 1972], 18–19) says that the *Proslogion* is dependent upon Augustine.

93. Anselm, *Proslogion* 2: "Therefore, O Lord, who gives understanding to faith, give me, to the extent that you determine helpful, to know that you are as we believe and that you are what we believe. And we believe you to be that which nothing greater can be thought" (my translation; and see Migne, *Patrologiae Latina*, 158:277).

94. *HWPT*, 132.

and he dwells in inaccessible light (chs. 15–16). God possesses all beauty, dwells in the eternity that defines him, and is entirely without parts (chs. 17–19). Thus God is before and beyond all things and is what and who he is (chs. 21–22). God is equally the Father and the Son and the Holy Spirit, and he is the one necessary thing (ch. 23). God, who is the great good, lavishes great good on those who belong to him (ch. 24–25).[95]

Anselm also contributed to the doctrine of the Trinity. In his *De fide trinitatis*, he argues that a person can, at the same time, understand and have faith.[96] In his Trinitarian thinking, Anselm was thoroughly Augustinian. Though Anselm was cognizant of the debates between the Latin West and the Greek East regarding the terms *essentia* ("essence"), *substantia* ("substance"), and *personae* ("persons"), he was personally inconsistent in his use of these terms.

While Augustinian, Anselm nuanced his Trinitarian doctrine. Augustine taught that man was made in the image of God, which includes the soul—comprised of memory, understanding, and will. Anselm wanted to demonstrate that, in contrast, God exists in three persons and one essence. Augustine began with the human mind and moved to the Trinity. Anselm begins with a priori principles, then moves to describe the Trinity as memory, understanding, and love—a variant description that had also been used by Augustine.[97]

Augustine taught that predicates of place and time may be applied to God *per similitudines*, "through likenesses." Anselm agreed. For example, Anselm believed that it was accurate to say that God is sitting above the cherubim. He also agreed with Augustine concerning the procession of the Holy Spirit and intertrinitarian relations. In his definition of intertrinitarian relations, Anselm understood there to be both similarity and distinction between begotten and proceeding.[98] Perhaps the most significant thing he learned from Augustine was the distinction between *dictum secundum substantium* and *dictum secun-*

---

95. But other Reformed scholars have argued that in his *Monologion*, Anselm discusses God's nature without recourse to Scripture's authority. They assert that it is difficult to affirm that he presupposed Christian revelation in his argument. See Edgar and Oliphint, *Christian Apologetics*, 1:366, 368, 373.

96. Aquinas will later disagree and say that a person has either one or the other.

97. Hopkins, *St. Anselm*, 95.

98. Ibid., 98.

dum relatium—that which is said between God's person and relations. This notion dates back at least to Gregory of Nyssa (A.D. 335–394).[99]

Though a contributor to a variety of doctrines, Anselm is best known for his advances on the doctrine of the atonement. His *Cur Deus Homo* speaks as though he does not need information from revelation.[100] This work addresses important questions regarding the atonement—questions such as, "Could God have redeemed humanity in a different way and spared his Son but chose not to?" and "Was God bound by this one method of redemption?"

Book I of *Cur Deus Homo* is comprised of twenty-five chapters. In it, Anselm addresses objections that unbelievers may have to the atonement and seeks to guide them in responding faithfully, while acknowledging that believers' answers will still seem inconclusive and unsatisfying to unbelievers. In chapters 5–7, Anselm explains the nature of redemption and argues that Christ's death demonstrated God's love and delivered humanity from the Devil. Anselm focuses on Christ's voluntary death, his willing obedience, and his satisfaction for sin in chapters 8–11. Next, Anselm addresses the nature of God and whether it would be fitting for him to forgive sins without payment for the debt they have incurred. In chapters 12–14 Anselm concludes that forgiveness without payment is impossible because God is honored in the sinner's punishment. In chapters 15–18 Anselm explores the notion of redeemed humans replacing the number of fallen angels. In the final chapters (19–25), Anselm reaches the center of his argument: humanity is culpable for the fall, and the weight of sin is so great that no man can pay it himself. Man's inability to pay the price for sin, however, does not excuse him, thus creating the necessity for Christ's satisfaction of the debt.

In the first four chapters of Book II, Anselm addresses pre- and postlapsarian humanity. Then in chapter 5 he determines that God must deal with humanity but would not do so under compulsion. In chapters 6–13, Anselm turns to Christology and the nature of the

---

99. He succeeds in going beyond Augustine to face his own problems. See ibid., 120.

100. In the preface he says: "It ends by proving by necessary reasons (Christ being put out of sight, as if nothing had ever been known of him). . . . In the same way, as if nothing were known of Christ, it is shown in the second book, by equally clear reasoning and truth" (Anselm, *Why God Became Man*, Library of Christian Classics 10, ed. and trans. Eugene R. Fairweather [London, SCM Press: 1956], 100).

God-man, who can and does secure salvation. The closing chapters then explain how Christ's sacrificial death truly saves his people, the wonders of the mercy of God, and the validity of the biblical teaching of the atonement.

Augustine proposed the Devil-ransom theory of the atonement.[101] In the Devil-ransom theory, Augustine taught that God was obligated to deal with Satan justly since Satan had claims on humankind. At the beginning of *Cur Deus Homo* Anselm took issue with this theory.[102] The Augustinian theory failed to explain the incarnation in full. Both Augustine and Anselm conceded that God had the ability to save the human race by means other than the incarnation if he willed to do so. Augustine found the incarnation to be fitting since it was more suitable to treat Satan justly. Anselm, however, understood the incarnation as necessary, that is, as freely chosen.[103] Anselm produced what is termed the *satisfaction*, or commercial, theory of the atonement.

For Anselm, sin is withholding from God the honor that is his due. God's honor must be vindicated, either through punishment or satisfaction. If vindication comes through satisfaction, then it must be infinite satisfaction, as can only be given by Christ. Christ perfectly obeyed the law, but his doing so procured no merit because all are to obey. In performing his duty, however, Christ suffered and died, thereby bringing God infinite honor. This work of supererogation brought a reward, and Christ passed this reward on in the form of forgiveness of sins and future blessedness to all who would live according to Christ's commands.[104]

Anselm also advanced the ontological argument for God's existence.[105] He wanted to work out a logical demonstration of God's

101. See chapter 13 of Augustine's *On the Trinity*, 4th ed. (Hyde Park, NY: New City Press, 2002).

102. Hopkins, *St. Anselm*, 27.

103. Ibid., 188–90.

104. The Reformers held to a satisfaction theory, but it differed from Anselm's. The ground for the necessity of the atonement is God's justice not his honor. Christ's death was not merely a tribute to God's honor but endured the penalty of sin. Anselm does not account for Christ's active obedience as a contributing factor—his life had redemptive significance. Neither does Anselm account for how Christ's merit is transferred. It is like a commercial account. There is no accounting for mystical union or for faith. See Louis Berkhof, *The History of Christian Doctrines* (Carlisle, PA: Banner of Truth, 1969), 385–86.

105. Anselm, *Proslogion*, 2–4, in Migne, *Patrologiae Latina*, 158:227–29.

existence deduced from the idea of the most perfect being. That is, God is that than which no greater can be thought, or a being than which nothing greater can be conceived. If this being were simply an idea in the mind, with no corresponding reality, then it would not be the most perfect being, because the being would lack the quality of existence.[106]

Anselm's principle of economy was connected to his ontological argument. This principle taught that whatever is true in the ultimate sense (that is, metaphysically), is necessarily true. Anselm held that the foundation of the universe is economical; there are no unnecessary parts. Think of the difference between an economy car versus a luxury car—the economy car may not have a functioning radio, have roll up windows, and lack air conditioning, but it still has all the essential characteristics of a car.[107]

This ontological argument is, in essence, natural theology—attempting to prove God's existence without an appeal to faith. It is an attempt to find common ground with the unbeliever. The method is to prove something first, in order that the person might believe. Anselm's argument for God's existence adopted a two-step approach: the philosophical foundation for the existence of God was laid, then Christianity was introduced and rested on the strength of the philosophical argument.[108] Anselm, however, stressed the necessity of personal faith in the comprehension of Christian truth. So faith and the use of human reason go together.[109] His approach could be called *revealed theology*.[110]

Abelard (A.D. 1079–1142). Abelard was likely the most well-known intellectual of his time. He was born in northern France and then performed his studies in Paris.

106. Brown, *Philosophy & Faith*, 20.

107. WCG 2:380n246.

108. Brown, *Philosophy & Faith*, 33. Frame rightly disagrees with this analysis in a number of his writings.

109. Ibid.

110. There are continuing debates concerning this argument. Historically, the ontological argument was restated and adapted by Descartes and Leibniz and was refuted by Aquinas and Kant. For more information, see ibid., 21; Kelly, *Systematic Theology*, 1:66–76; Peter A. Lillback, "Calvin's Development of the Doctrine of Forensic Justification," in *Justified in Christ: God's Plan for Us in Justification*, ed. K. Scott Oliphint (Fearn, Scotland: Mentor, 2007), 53. Edgar and Oliphint (*Christian Apologetics*, 1:369) conclude: "It is not overstating the matter to say that Anselm's ontological argument . . . remains central to any philosophical theology and apologetic that seeks to do justice to the truth of Christianity and the question of God's existence."

Abelard had two major teachers. The first was Roscellinus or Roscelin of Tours (1050–1120). Even though nominalism as a movement truly began with William of Ockham (1285–1349), Abelard was a nominalist who opposed both Eriugena and Anselm. Abelard was also a student of William of Champeaux (1070–1121). William was an extreme realist. Abelard rejected William's teaching and modified Roscellinus's.[111] As mentioned earlier, Roscellinus believed men to be real, but he believed the category of humanity was contrived. He believed it impossible for three persons to be united; hence he thought that there were three gods. Roscellinus was essentially a tritheist.[112] To him, the Trinity was nothing more than a name; that is, a universal is a mere word.[113]

Abelard struggled with the question of universals. He disagreed with the nominalists, who believed that a universal is a mere word. Instead, Abelard believed universal is a term that could be predicated of things. Humans understand a universal when their minds sift through evidence derived from the senses and find shared traits of individual things. The universal denotes something real, even if it lacks separate essence. The universal denotes a condition or a state that a number of individuals have in common.[114]

Abelard submitted the Christian faith to reason and unified theology and philosophy. He did not think that believers could fully comprehend God's truth, but they could understand it consonant with faith. For him, Christian belief was an estimate, not a mere opinion—a mental approximation of the truth that will be revealed in full at the last day.[115]

During his years as a teacher, Abelard was convicted of having had an affair with one of his students, a girl named Heloise. When she became pregnant, Abelard was beaten and castrated by her uncle and guardian.[116] When their son was born, they named him Astrolabe. It

111. Clark, *Thales to Dewey*, 261.
112. Lee, *Christian Introduction to Philosophy*, 129.
113. Abelard also got into a scuffle with Bernard of Clairvaux. Bernard secured Abelard's second condemnation at a council in 1141. See Walker, *History*, 329.
114. Ibid., 328.
115. Ibid., 329.
116. Nicholas R. Needham, *2,000 Years of Christ's Power*, vol. 2, *The Middle Ages* (2000; repr., London: Grace Publications, 2004), 254–55; for Abelard's "History of My Calamities," see 284–85; for Abelard's preface to *Sic et Non*, see 286–87.

was after Abelard's physical humiliation in 1122 that he composed *Sic et non* (in English, *Yes and No*). In it, Abelard addresses more than one hundred and fifty theological questions. He set apparently contradictory statements from the Bible or from the church fathers alongside one another and reconciled the contradictions using reason.[117] Abelard's logical finesse was put on display in this work and others like it.[118]

Abelard also studied ethics. By this time, sin had already been defined as transgressing God's law, either in ignorance or with intent. In contrast to this classic definition, Abelard argued that guilt can only be imputed when there is full knowledge of and intention to transgress the law of God.[119] His reasoning came from Christ's very words on the cross, "Forgive them, for they do not know what they do" (Luke 23:34). Abelard's ethics were thus based on the notion of human free will.[120] He held that it is human beings' intentions, rather than their actual acts, that determine whether their actions are good or evil.[121] This teaching shows the nature of nominalist ethics. Since there are no universals, the terms *good* and *bad* are deprived of any meaning whatsoever. They are signs that denote God's commands. Abelard's faulty definition of sin led to subjectivity and moral relativism.

Abelard also spent time studying the atonement. In agreement with Anselm, he rejected the notion that in the atonement, God was paying a just ransom to Satan. But he also rejected Anselm's theory of the atonement. Abelard held that Christ's incarnation and death on the cross were the highest expression of God's love toward underserving sinners. He believed that these loving actions were intended to awaken

117. Some of his other works include *Introductio ad theologiam* and his ethical treatise *Scito te ipsum*, or *Know Yourself*. See James Ramsay McCallum, *Abelard's Christian Theology* (New York: Richwood Publishing, 1976); John Marenbon, *The Philosophy of Peter Abelard* (Cambridge: Cambridge University Press, 1997). MacCulloch (*Christianity*, 398) notes: "the word [theology] was first given currency in the 1120s by the Paris theologian Peter Abelard when he used it as title of a controversial discussion of Christian thought, his *Theologia Christiana*."

118. Edgar and Oliphint, *Christian Apologetics*, 1:339: "Abelard is arguably the greatest logician since antiquity."

119. Abelard, *Ethics*, Book I: "if someone forces someone in religious orders, bound by chains, to lie among women, and he is led into pleasure—but not into consent—by the bed's softness and the touch of the women around him, who can venture to call this pleasure nature has made necessary a 'sin'? . . . Nothing taints the soul but what belongs to it, namely the consent that we've said is alone the sin, not the will preceding it or the subsequent doing of the deed" (as cited by Edgar and Oliphint, *Christian Apologetics*, 1:349–50).

120. Ibid., 1:341.

121. Walker, *History*, 330; Edgar and Oliphint, *Christian Apologetics*, 1:339.

human love for God in return. This theory is called *exemplarism* or the "moral influence theory" of the atonement.[122] This theory would reemerge in the nineteenth century.

Despite his other erroneous beliefs, he was ultimately condemned for his teaching on the Trinity. He was accused of being nearly Sabellian. Abelard called the Father Goodness, the Son God's Ideas, and the Holy Spirit the World Soul.[123]

During his lifetime Abelard had few followers, likely because he was condemned twice. But his dialectical method and attempts to contain vast amounts of teaching into a systematic theology formed a bridge between earlier scholasticism's preoccupations with individual questions and the great comprehensive surveys that were to follow in the next century.[124]

Bernard of Clairvaux (A.D. 1091–1153).[125] Bernard of Clairvaux was born into a noble family near Dijon, France, in 1091. Around 1112–1113, Bernard entered the Cisterian monastery. In 1115, he established a monastic house in Clairvaux in which he served as abbot. He drew up the rules for the Knights Templar in 1128. At the pope's request, he preached from 1146 to 1147 in support of the Second Crusade. While he strongly opposed Islam, Bernard believed that heretics and Jews should be persuaded, not coerced, into accepting the Christian faith.[126] Bernard was a powerful figure in his own time; some thought of him as the uncrowned emperor of Europe. He was even considered to be a miracle worker. Bernard was made a saint in 1174 and a doctor of the church in 1830.

Perhaps the most widely known of his writings are his *Sermones in Cantica Canticorum* (eighty-six sermons on the Song of Songs). He interpreted the book as an allegory of spiritual love between Christ as the bridegroom and the soul united to Christ as his bride.[127] Some of his other works include *De diligendo Deo;*[128] *Steps of Humility*

122. Walker, *History*, 330; *HWPT*, 143.

123. Walker, *History*, 329; Lee, *Christian Introduction to Philosophy*, 130; Clark, *Thales to Dewey*, 264. Frame (*HWPT*, 143) mentions that *Introductio* was condemned in 1140 "mainly because of its speculative discussion of the doctrine of the Trinity."

124. Walker, *History*, 330.

125. See Lee, *Christian Introduction to Philosophy*, 139; Walker, *History*, 294.

126. Needham, *2,000 Years*, 2:198–99.

127. Ibid., 2:195.

128. See excerpt in ibid., 2:213–14.

and Pride; *On Grace and Free Will*;[129] sermons on Titus;[130] and *De consideratione*, a treatise that critiqued the papacy's mixing of earthly activities with its proper divine tasks.[131] His poetic work survives in some of his hymns.[132]

Bernard is remembered as a mystic. Medieval mysticism has roots that can be traced back at least as far as the earliest days of Christianity, if not even further to pre-Christian, Greek and Hebrew thought.[133] Most fundamentally, mysticism offers an alternative to scholasticism. Bernard opposed the scholastic approach of Abelard's *Sic et Non*.[134] Some of his frustration may have stemmed from a perceived over-intellectualization of theology.[135] As opposed to this intellectual approach, mysticism expresses the heart's longing for an encounter with God.[136] The goal of mysticism is the vision of God. Stated another way, mysticism expresses a desire for intimate communion with God. The means to this intimate communion is often through self-renunciation, illumination, then finally union with or vision of God.[137] Bernard's mysticism did not follow Pseudo-Dionysius's desire for the mind to contemplate

129. See excerpt in ibid., 2:212–13.

130. See excerpt in ibid., 2:211–12.

131. Walker, *History*, 295. Needham (*2,000 Years*, 2:197) quotes Calvin's *Institutes*, 4.2.11, concerning this treatise: "Bernard speaks as though the very truth itself were speaking."

132. Some hymns perhaps from his pen include: "Jesus the Very Thought of Thee," "O Sacred Head Now Wounded," and "Jesus, Thou Joy of Loving Hearts."

133. There is abundant literature on the history of mysticism. See Margaret Smith, *Introduction to the History of Mysticism* (London: SPCK, 1930). It is argued by some that non-Christian Greek thinkers influenced certain church fathers. Particularly important was Neoplatonism. For more information on the importance of Neoplatonism and Pseudo-Dionysius to the development of mysticism, see William Ralph Inge, *Christian Mysticism: Considered in Eight Lectures Delivered before the University of Oxford* (London: Methuen, 1899), 9–11. See also his *Mysticism in Religion* (Chicago: University of Chicago Press, 1948).

134. "Peter Abelard is a persecutor of the Catholic faith and an enemy of the cross of Christ. Outwardly he is a monk but inwardly he is a heretic. . . . With Arius [he] distinguishes grades and steps in the Trinity; with Pelagius he prefers free will to grace; with Nestorius he divides Christ. . . . Thus traversing almost all sacred subjects he boldly attacks them from end to end and disposes of each in a damnable manner" (Bernard of Clairvaux, *Letter 331*, as cited by Arthur Cushman McGiffert, *A History of Christian Thought* [New York: Scribner's Sons, 1953], 2:224).

135. Ray C. Petry, ed., *Late Medieval Mysticism* (London: SCM Press, 1957), 47: "For all of these, love's possession, or the experience of divine companionship, rather than the mind's comprehension of God, is paramount. . . . Furthermore, *scientia* . . . must give way to *sapientia*."

136. A similar expression was found in the rise of classic liberalism in the nineteenth century. Cold scholasticism had taken over the German universities, and there was a heartfelt need for communion with God. Liberalism, however, was not anchored in the Christ of Scripture.

137. Ibid., 19. For more information on the triple way, see Evelyn Underhill, *Mysticism: A Study in the Nature and Development of Man's Spiritual Consciousness* (Cleveland: Meridien

God but was more practical in nature—Bernard longed for the soul to experience divine love.[138] Mystical union was like a marriage between the human soul and the Word of God.[139] Some claim that Bernard shifted the emphasis in Latin piety from the exalted Christ to the human, suffering Christ.[140]

During Bernard's lifetime, sixty-eight new Cistercian monasteries were established.[141] Luther and Calvin would be greatly influenced by Bernard's work.[142]

Peter Lombard (A.D. 1096–1160). Peter Lombard was born in Lombardy, northern Italy, and studied in Bologna, Reims, and Paris. He was likely a student of both Hugh of Saint Victor and Abelard and a friend of Bernard.[143] In 1140 he became a teacher in Paris. Then in 1159, he began as a bishop of Paris.[144]

His important work *Four Books of Sentences* (1150–1152) trained theologians for theological discussion. Lombard organized the book according to topics, then under each topic came an assortment of the opinions, or sentences, of a variety of theologians on that specific matter. The topics ranged from the doctrine of God to created beings, or God's works, to salvation and the incarnation to the sacraments and last things.[145]

Books, 1955), 298–443. Petry (*Medieval Mysticism*, 22–45) traces the historical development of late medieval mysticism.

138. Walker, *History*, 294–95.

139. This theology is seen through his sermons on the *Canticles*, as well as in *The Grades of Humility*. Petry, *Medieval Mysticism*, 51–53: in the mystical union is "the destruction of man's *proprium*, the obliteration of his private singularity or individual possessiveness, and his metamorphosis into unity of spirit with God"; the soul is first drawn by God and in response "the soul seeks out the Word in order to accept the corrections that he will mete out to her."

140. Needham, *2,000 Years*, 2:195.

141. He popularized adoration of the Virgin Mary even though he opposed the notion of the immaculate conception (ibid., 2:195–96).

142. Needham (ibid., 2:194) quotes Luther's statement, "In his sermons Bernard is superior to all the teachers, even to Augustine himself, because he preaches Christ so excellently," and (ibid., 2:199) cites Luther's *Commentary on Galatians*: "Bernard [is] a man so godly, so holy, so pure, that we should commend and prefer him before all the theologians of the church."

143. Hugh of Saint Victor (1090–1141) was an important author and theologian who guided students in their reading and study for the Parisian school in *Didascalicon de studio legendi*; wrote on the sacraments in *De sacramentis Christianae fidei* and on Noah's ark; and composed a commentary on Pseudo-Dionysius.

144. Walker, *History*, 331.

145. The tables of contents of these massive volumes are available online at Franciscan archive.org. Full Latin texts are also available online. For the most recent English translation, see Peter Lombard, *The Sentences, Books 1–4*, trans. Giulio Silano, 4 vols. (Toronto: Pontifical

He taught that metaphysics should be proven from the Scripture and defended by Christian reason. But Lombard held that true knowledge was higher than faith.[146] He learned his dialectical method from Abelard's *Sic et Non*, and from Hugh of Saint Victor he learned reverence for church tradition and authority.[147] He was the first Catholic theologian to articulate the seven sacraments—baptism, communion, confirmation, penance, marriage, ordination, and extreme unction. This list of sacraments was accepted by the Roman Catholic Church in 1439 at the Council of Florence.

Lombard's view of penance differed from that of contemporary Catholic teaching. He did not understand penance to be the priestly cleansing of sin by absolution; rather, penance was the priest's declaration of what was brought about by the Holy Spirit. Lombard taught that the sacraments were not mere signs but in fact causes of grace in the lives of believers. His position on the nature of the sacraments would be developed into the thirteenth-century notion of *ex opera operato*—that a sacrament is effective by virtue of the offering of it.[148]

Richard of Saint Victor (A.D. 1110–1173). Richard of Saint Victor wrote *On the Trinity*. Building on the work of Boethius, he stressed the individual distinctions within the Trinity. He explained that the Father gives without receiving; the Son both gives and receives; and the Holy Spirit receives love.[149] He taught that the three persons are truly distinct in their personal properties, yet those properties are incommunicable—in other words, each person is identical with the self-existent being of the one true God.[150]

Alexander of Hales (A.D. 1180–1245). Sometime between 1220 and 1225, the Franciscan theologian Alexander of Hales composed the four-volume *Glossa super Sententias* on Lombard's *Sentences*. He also

---

Institute of Mediaeval Studies, 2007–2010). See Walker, *History*, 331; K. Scott Oliphint, *Thomas Aquinas* (Phillipsburg, NJ: P&R Publishing, 2017), 4.

146. Lee, *Christian Introduction to Philosophy*, 130.

147. Walker, *History*, 331.

148. Needham, *2,000 Years*, 2:256–58.

149. Richard said that the divine person is "something that exists through itself alone, singularly, according to a rational mode of existence" (as cited by Michael Horton, *The Christian Faith: A Systematic Theology for Pilgrims on the Way* [Grand Rapids: Zondervan, 2011], 284n35).

150. Scott R. Swain, "Divine Trinity," in *Christian Dogmatics: Reformed Theology for the Church Catholic*, ed. Michael Allen and Scott R. Swain (Grand Rapids: Baker Academic, 2016), 99n81.

began writing a book titled *The Summa of Universal Theology*, which was not completed until after his death. In this work Alexander implicitly and explicitly quotes Augustine more than six thousand times.[151] Alexander's work reflects the developments made by Lombard. In his contributions to the fields of ethics and philosophical thought, Alexander went beyond the dialectical method and semantics. His thought was informed by Aristotle's metaphysics in new and innovative ways.[152]

Francis of Assisi (A.D. 1181/82–1226). Born Giovanni Bernardone, Francis of Assisi was a lighthearted and joyful child raised in a wealthy household. But in 1202 Giovanni was captured as a prisoner of a war; as such, he suffered tremendously. After his mistreatment during the war, he fell ill. These years of hardship furrowed his disposition. Around the year 1206, Giovanni committed his life to seeking for God. After having sold all his possessions, he was convinced of two things: he was called to preach about the kingdom of God and repentance, and he was to live in abject poverty. He longed to imitate Christ—in his poverty, in his love, and in his humble deference to the religious authorities placed over him. In 1209 he wrote a rule for monastic life, and in 1210 he submitted an application to the papacy to establish an organized order. This new order of humbler brothers was founded around a simple goal: to deny the world and follow Christ. The Order of Lesser Brothers received papal approval.

Francis longed to see Muslims convert to Christ and so sent missionaries to the Muslim world. He even went to the court of the Egyptian sultan to plead that he convert to Christianity.

While his *fratres minors* ("friars minor") organized, Francis withdrew further and further from the world. Supposedly, he received marks on his hands, feet, and side—the stigmata—that imitated Christ's wounds. Several years after receiving them, he died in a small hut outside Assisi.[153]

Peter of Spain (A.D. 1210/20–1277). Standard historiography of the past has argued that this Peter of Spain is Petrus Juliani, one-time

151. Jacques-Guy Bougerol, "The Church Fathers and *Auctoritates* in Scholastic Theology to Bonaventure," in *The Reception of the Church Fathers in the West: From the Carolingians to the Maurists*, ed. Irena Dorota Backus (Leiden: Brill, 1997), 1:301.

152. Marcia L. Colish, *Studies in Scholasticism* (Aldershot, England: Ashgate, 2006), 5, 106.

153. Walker, *History*, 313–16.

dean of the cathedral chapter at Lisbon who studied under Albert the Great. Peter worked his way into elite ecclesiastical circles as the physician to Pope Gregory X and in 1276 became that pope's successor. He took the name Pope John XXI. One year later, the roof of his study collapsed on him and he died from the injuries that he suffered. But contemporary scholarship is quite uncertain as to whether Peter of Spain is Pope John XXI.

Consensus has grown regarding the import of Peter of Spain's *Summulae logicales* (*Summaries of Logic*; ca. 1246) to the development of scholasticism. This work has been the subject of much scholarship because of the backlash it received during the Renaissance and Reformation. Northern European humanists condemned scholastics and scholasticism, and the name they associated most readily with scholasticism was Peter of Spain.

Historical theologians correctly identify scholasticism with figures such as Thomas Aquinas and Bonaventura. But during this period, foundational to all higher study was the course in the liberal arts. It was in this curriculum that Peter of Spain's *Summulae logicales* played a prominent role. This text was read by thousands of students, and presses printed edition after edition of it in Paris. It would not be an overstatement to say that this work was foundational to all philosophical study.

Peter wrote the definition of scholastic philosophy that is repeated more often than any other definition: "Dialectic is the art of arts and the science of sciences, possessing the way to the principles of all curriculum subjects."[154] The locus is foundational to the scholastic method; and according to Peter, who perhaps was influenced here by Cicero, a locus is the seat of an argument or that from which a convenient argument is drawn toward the question proposed. An argument is a means for implying a conclusion so as to create conviction regarding a doubtful matter. Peter's thought on this matter would later be followed by the writer and theologian Peter Ramus.[155]

---

154. Beginning of *Summulae logicales*.

155. Ramus constantly denounced Peter of Spain; nevertheless, Ramus's understanding that dialectic is the center and core of philosophy recapitulated Peter's opening words in the *Summulae*. There are now two English translations available: Francis P. Dinneen, *Language in Dispute: An English Translation of Peter of Spain's Tractatus* (Amsterdam/Philadelphia: Benjamin's Publishing, 1990), and Brian P. Copenhaver, Calvin G. Normore, and Terence Parsons,

THOMAS AQUINAS (A.D. 1224/25–1274)[156]

Biography. Somewhere near the end of 1224 or the very beginning of 1225, Thomas, son of the count of Aquino, was born in the family's castle near Naples, Italy. At age five he was sent to the Benedictine abbey of Monte Cassino for his studies. He remained there until in 1239 Emperor Frederick II expelled all the monks, thus forcing Thomas to leave as well. He then studied for a time in Naples.[157] In 1243, Aquinas joined the Dominican order.

Under Dominican guidance, he studied under Albertus Magnus of Bavaria (1193–1280) at the University of Paris (1245–1248).[158] He then traveled to the German city of Cologne, where he remained until 1252.[159]

After his time in Cologne, Aquinas returned to Paris to continue his studies. From 1252 to 1254, he studied as a lecturer on Scripture, or *baccalaureus biblicus*. Then from 1254 to 1256 he studied the *Sentences* of Peter Lombard as *baccalaureus sententiarius*. At the end of this time, Aquinas received his license to teach as a member of the theology faculty.[160] In the same year, he was granted his magister (master's degree) and lectured as a professor of the Dominican Order. He likely earned his doctorate in 1257. In 1259, Aquinas left Paris to lecture with the *studium curiae* attached to the papal court in Rome until 1268. This position afforded him the opportunity to travel.[161] Next he taught for a time again in Paris, then in Naples in 1272. In 1274, he died en route to the Council of Lyons.[162]

---

eds., *Peter of Spain Summaries of Logic: Text, Translation, Introduction, and Notes* (New York, Oxford University Press, 2014).

156. Lee, *Christian Introduction to Philosophy*, 132.

157. K. Scott Oliphint, *Thomas Aquinas* (Phillipsburg, NJ: P&R Publishing, 2017), 3. He had already studied the church fathers, and while at Naples he was introduced to Greek and Arabic philosophy.

158. Lee, *Christian Introduction to Philosophy*, 131; see Clark, *Thales to Dewey*, 268.

159. Lee, *Christian Introduction to Philosophy*, 131; Clark, *Thales to Dewey*, 268–69; Walker, *History*, 244; Brown, *Philosophy & Faith*, 24. Oliphint (*Aquinas*, 4) says that in Paris he began the study of Pseudo-Dionysius.

160. This degree is still given in modern Switzerland, and it is the degree that certifies a student as a pastor. Today, a person cannot lecture on the theology faculty with only this lesser degree.

161. Copleston, *Medieval Philosophy*, 1:302–3.

162. Walker, *History*, 245.

Aquinas was apparently a simple, religious man. He was canonized in 1323 and made a doctor of the church in 1567. In 1879 Pope Leo XIII decreed Aquinas's thought the official philosophy of the Roman Catholic Church,[163] which considers his great abilities to have been supernatural gifts.[164]

Writings and Contributions. Aquinas wrote more than sixty works, some of which were multivolume sets.[165] He wrote commentaries on Isaiah, Jeremiah, Lamentations, Job, the Psalms, Matthew, and John.[166] He also wrote commentaries on Boethius's short treatise on the Trinity and his longer *De hebdomadibus*.

The *Summa contra Gentiles* was written between 1259 and 1264 in the context of Dominican missionaries' preaching against Muslims, Jews, and heretical Christians in Spain.[167] In the first three sections, Aquinas explores what human beings can understand about God apart from special revelation. He determines that without special revelation, humans can grasp God's existence and perfections, that God is the Creator, and that there is a providential ordering of creatures toward their end, which is God. In the final section, Aquinas explains that only revelation provides information on the Trinity, the incarnation, redemption, the sacraments, and eschatology.[168]

In ca. 1265, Aquinas began writing *Summa theologiae* as an introduction to theology in an attempt to supplant Lombard's great four-volume work.[169] But Aquinas never completed the work because of a supposed mystical experience in 1273.

In his contributions, Aquinas sought to offer knowledge of God, human origins, and destiny. Though he taught that this knowledge was found in reason, he held that reason was inadequate without supplementary revelation. Aquinas also taught that the Scriptures are the final authority, but they must be interpreted in the light of the writings of the church fathers, the decrees of the councils, and papal definitions.[170]

---

163. Ibid., 340.
164. Oliphint, *Aquinas*, 10.
165. Ibid., 1.
166. Ibid., 5: "His understanding of Scripture was, in significant ways, overshadowed by his speculative thinking."
167. Walker, *History*, 341.
168. Needham, *2,000 Years*, 2:265. Oliphint, *Aquinas*, 6.
169. Needham, *2,000 Years*, 2:265.
170. Walker, *History*, 341.

Aquinas possessed a unique ability to synthesize previous thinking. He also held that there was no contradiction between philosophy and theology, for both came from the hand of God, and truth is one. In fact, he produced a synthesis of faith and reason that affords Aristotelian philosophy its own authority and integrity.[171] Two of Aquinas's more significant contributions consisted in his argument for God's existence and his doctrine of analogy relative to the doctrine of God.

Anthropology and Soteriology. Earlier Platonic-Augustinian notions of the soul argued that it was superior to the body. The soul was considered to be categorically other and to possess a unique status and nearness to God. In contrast, Augustine held that the soul was not independent of the body, regardless of its immaterial nature. He taught that each soul is formed by God and united to a body as one substance—a psychosomatic unity.[172]

Aquinas believed that before the fall, Adam possessed *donum superadditum*, a special "superadded gift." This gift was personal knowledge of God, eternal life, and spiritual joy. This gift also enabled Adam to seek the highest good. Humanity, with the *donum superadditum*, is in the likeness of God.

To Aquinas, prelapsarian Adam was not as perfect as later Protestants would hold. Aquinas taught that even in the garden, Adam was unable to remain good without divine aid. When Adam sinned, he forfeited the *donum superadditum*, and the result was that he, and his posterity along with him, turned toward lower, more base aims. This inherent, vile corruption poisoned the ability of Adam's descendants to please God. Aquinas believed, however, that original sin is not personal guilt but sin by analogy. Thus unbaptized infants who die are not cast into eternal punishment or welcomed into heaven—they are sent to limbo.

Augustine separated human beings into two categories—those under sin and those under grace; but he maintained three categories for humanity—fallen man as sinner, redeemed and spiritually endowed man under grace, and man as pure nature. The third category refers to people whose minds are no different from the mind of pre-fall Adam.

---

171. Ibid., 341–42; Brown, *Philosophy & Faith*, 25. MacCulloch (*Christianity*, 412) says: "the work of Aquinas had the eventual effect of ending the official Church's fears about the challenge which Aristotle's thought appeared to present to Christian faith."

172. Walker, *History*, 343.

Aquinas believed that even after the fall, Adam and his posterity retained the ability to attain natural virtues, such as prudence, courage, self-control, and justice.[173] Man was still crafted in the image of God. This view of man helped Aquinas explain how Aristotle created his great system of ethics without special revelation. Even without grace, humanity, as image bearers of God, can formulate helpful systems of ethics.

Aquinas held that when a fallen person's sins are forgiven through free and unmerited grace, the *donum superadditum* is also restored, and the power to practice Christian virtue is divinely infused. This infused grace is love, placed in the soul by participating in the sacraments, and the human disposition or *habitus* of love, where the sinner is made acceptable to God and can live in obedience.[174]

Humanity can now merit, by free obedience, greater grace. Aquinas also taught that man could resist divine grace. So a person accepts grace through a combination of free will and grace. Aquinas also believed that God wills all to be saved and that Christ died for all without exception. So then, why are not all saved? Because man, in his free will, can reject extended grace. Thus only that grace that is not pushed away is effective.

The redeemed sinner can perform works that are God-pleasing and fully meritorious, works called *merita de condigno*. These actions merit the reward of eternal life. Such works are only possible by the prevenient and cooperating grace of God. Thus grace and merit work in conjunction. The faith that justifies is faith that is formed by works of love. If those works are missing, then the person does not possess justifying faith.[175]

Arguments for God's Existence.[176] Aquinas was convinced that God's existence is not inherently evident to human beings; it requires proof.[177] Aquinas's position is contradicted by Paul's statement in Romans 1:17–20.

---

173. Ibid.

174. Walker (ibid., 343–44) underlined that here Aquinas disagreed with Lombard, who argued that instead of infused grace the Holy Spirit indwelt the redeemed soul.

175. Ibid., 344.

176. Robert L. Reymond, *A New Systematic Theology of the Christian Faith* (Nashville: Thomas Nelson, 1998), 135: "By it [the arguments] he attempted to demonstrate from sense data alone without any *a priori* equipment the existence of God."

177. Brown, *Philosophy & Faith*, 26; Aquinas, *Summa theologiae* I Q. 2 Art. 1. For the underlying procedure used in the fivefold proofs, see Kelly, *Systematic Theology*, 1:80–81.

Aquinas presented his arguments for the existence of God in the *Summa theologiae* and *Summa contra Gentiles*.[178] In *Summa theologiae*, his first argument is sometimes referred to as the "argument from motion." It is self-evident that an object moves from actuality, through motion, to potentiality. For example, a baseball that is sitting on a bench is not fulfilling its potentiality, but it achieves its full potentiality when it is thrown. No potentiality can become actuality without something that or someone who moves it. Aquinas reasoned that since there is change in the world—that is, since the world has moved from stillness to motion—God is the first mover.[179] Stated another way, rest is the normal state, so every event or motion must have a cause. Nothing causes, moves, or designs itself. Thus God is the first cause, or Aristotle's unmoved mover.[180]

Aquinas's second argument was the way of efficient causality.[181] The being of something is caused by that which has being itself. In other words, there must be a first efficient cause of all, and that first cause is God.[182]

His third argument is from necessary and possible existence, or different modes of existence. At some future time, every living thing may not be. The cause of the first living thing must have being of itself; necessary existence must be the same as being. In other words, since there is temporal existence, there must be eternal existence.[183] Necessary existence must necessarily exist, while contingent existence may, or may not, exist. Something exists whose existence is necessary; thus God necessarily exists.[184] God is that which is eternally existent.

The fourth argument flows from degrees of being, known as the "argument from gradation." There are some things that are better, or nobler, than others. For example, a rock is less noble than a lion. There must be something more noble than the lion, something from which the lion receives its nobility. That which is the cause of all

178. Oliphint, *Aquinas*, 56–57.

179. Greg R. Allison, *Historical Theology: An Introduction to Christian Doctrine—A Companion to Wayne Grudem's Systematic Theology* (Grand Rapids: Zondervan, 2011), 193–94.

180. Oliphint, *Aquinas*, 58–60; *HWPT*, 147; Kelly, *Systematic Theology*, 1:81–84.

181. *HWPT*, 147n47.

182. Oliphint, *Aquinas*, 61–62; Kelly, *Systematic Theology*, 1:84–85; Allison, *Historical Theology*, 194.

183. Oliphint, *Aquinas*, 64; *HWPT*, 148; Kelly, *Systematic Theology*, 1:85–90.

184. Allison, *Historical Theology*, 195–96.

being, goodness, and nobility is called *God*.[185] Stated differently, by a hierarchy of being, there must be a best or perfect being, and that being is God.[186]

The fifth proof is not an a posteriori cosmological argument but a teleological argument. It is called the "argument from providence" and is a slight variation of the second proof. It follows this line of thinking: This world is moving toward a meaningful end by a great intelligence; God, who is the one moving the world, is the ultimate efficient cause.[187] In other words, since all things are directed toward their end, God is the being who directs them toward that end.[188]

It would be impossible to calculate the number of books that have been written toward analyzing and critiquing Aquinas's proofs.[189] The first of Aquinas's arguments is cosmological—it reasons from the natural world to God.[190] Aquinas followed Aristotle by beginning with the senses. But when Aristotle reasoned for a prime mover, Aquinas found a personal God. Aquinas's first argument—for an unmoved mover—depends on an antedated Aristotelian worldview.[191] Additionally, in his proofs Aquinas used the word God in an ambiguous fashion. While a Christian acknowledges that God created the heavens and the earth and is creation's efficient cause, to use the word God in the place of Aristotle's unmoved mover is to import senses into the term God that may not be at all identical.[192]

It has been debated whether Aquinas's first argument is purely philosophical. Some have argued for its philosophical nature, while others see

185. Oliphint, *Aquinas*, 64–65; *HWPT*, 148; Kelly, *Systematic Theology*, 1:90–92.

186. Allison, *Historical Theology*, 195–96.

187. Oliphint, *Aquinas*, 65–66; Kelly, *Systematic Theology*, 1:92–95.

188. Allison, *Historical Theology*, 197.

189. Frame (*HWPT*, 149) says that there are three ways to know God's nature: by causality, by eminence, and by negation. Arguments 1–3 and 5 were by causality and 4 by eminence, thus ascribing to God the maximum perfection.

190. Ibid.; Oliphint, *Aquinas*, 81.

191. Brown, *Philosophy & Faith*, 27. David Hume, in *Enquiry Concerning Human Understanding* (1777), was critical of Aquinas. He asked whether Aquinas's first cause was the same as a prime mover, or as a great designer, or as the Christian God? Logically, a cause of something cannot have attributes that are beyond what we see in its effects. The maker of something—for example, the carpenter of a house—and the designer—the house's architect—are not necessarily identical.

192. Brown, *Philosophy & Faith*, 29. For an extensive critique of the five ways, see Oliphint, *Aquinas*, 78–89.

it as an argument among Christians.[193] Initially, it seems likely that his first argument is made among Christians, but that assertion contains both a cloaked agenda and an incorrect presupposition. The latter assumes that Aristotle was correct concerning causality and a first mover and invokes that insight to demonstrate God's existence as known to reason. The ground for this assertion is that rational and revealed truths cannot disagree—an assertion that is simply incorrect.[194] In sum, Aquinas's proofs are neither convincing nor demonstrable of the God of Scripture.

Knowledge of God. For Augustine, human understanding of God presupposes embracing the truths of Christianity (that is, faith). Augustine left no room for autonomous philosophy or the unaided use of human intellect. Anselm, in agreement with Augustine, emphasized that commitment to and faith in God are prerequisites to understanding the central truths of Christianity. Faith and reason go hand in hand for apprehending religious truth.[195] This approach has been called "revealed theology."

Aquinas took the opposite position. For him, faith in God needed to be founded on the independent results of human reasoning. Aquinas's approach presupposed that fallen humanity is able to reason properly and to interpret human experience apart from God's revelation.[196]

Aquinas believed that God's existence can be proved by the person who is willing to understand the facts and draw correct conclusions. Some have described Aquinas's method as a two-story approach. In it, the bottom or first floor is human beings' ability to reason, not divine revelation. If humans would just use their reason to observe the world around them, then they would conclude that a god exists. Then the second floor, from divine revelation, would teach them who God is. This approach is referred to as *natural theology*.[197] Thus natural

---

193. Oliphint says that it is purely philosophical. Richard Muller, however, counters that Aquinas's first argument is made on the basis of reason but has a theological and biblical backdrop and is an argument among Christians. See Oliphint, *Aquinas*, 61–62, and Richard A. Muller review "Aquinas Reconsidered," *Reformation21* (February 19, 2018).

194. See Richard A. Muller, "Aquinas Reconsidered (Part 3)," in *Reformation21* (March 5, 2018).

195. Brown, *Philosophy & Faith*, 33.

196. Greg L. Bahnsen, *Van Til's Apologetic: Readings & Analysis* (Phillipsburg, NJ: P&R Publishing, 1998), 47; see also 193n75 and, on the mind of man as potentially participating in the mind of God, 333.

197. Brown, *Philosophy & Faith*, 35–36.

theology, based on human cogitation or philosophy, is the intellectual superstructure.[198] But whether theologians use Augustine's or Aquinas's approach, there are still problems to be solved. One such problem is the use of language. Besides arguments for God's existence, the doctrine of analogical language is significant.

Since the time of Aquinas, theologians have admitted that when humans use language about God, they speak in a special fashion. Valid statements about God are not univocal, or identical in meaning.[199] But such statements are also not equivocal, or absolutely diverse—rather, they are what is generally termed *analogical*.[200]

Theologians have offered complex and nuanced definitions of what it means to say that language about God is analogical.[201] The term *analogical* is most often used to mean an agreement, correspondence, resemblance, or similarity between two things.[202] So in language, *analogical* means a general correspondence or resemblance between the language that is used concerning the subject and its object, which in this case is God.[203] Thus humans can speak meaningfully about God even if their language is only analogical, or poetic.[204]

An analysis of Aquinas forces the question of whether human knowledge is analogical to God's knowledge.[205] In other words, is

198. Ibid., 34: "From Aquinas onwards it became accepted in large sections of the church that natural theology with its secular philosophical arguments provided the intellectual basis of Christian faith."

199. Reymond (*New Systematic Theology*, 96) says that Aquinas was certain that "nothing can be predicated of God and man in the univocal sense. Rather, only analogical predication is properly possible when speaking of the relationship between them." See Aquinas, *Summa theologiae* 1.13.10 R obj. 3, as cited in *HWPT*, 153.

200. We do not use univocal language for God. God is our Father but certainly not in the same sense as is our biological father. Equivocal language would become meaningless. For the exegetical foundation of this position see *WCG* 1:95–96, and for further elaboration see *WCG* 2:26–27.

201. For example, some say that there is proper proportionality in saying that God's wisdom is related to his nature as human wisdom is related to his nature. There is attribution in that God's wisdom is like ours because God is the cause. There is resemblance in that divine wisdom is like human wisdom in some ways. See *HWPT*, 153.

202. Reymond (*New Systematic Theology*, 97) argues that the use of the word *analogy* requires that "in some sense a univocal feature exists between them. . . . For all their differences, they have something in common. . . . The success of any analogy turns on the strength of the univocal element in it." I agree.

203. Brown, *Philosophy & Faith*, 30–32.

204. On language about God as poetic, see *WCG* 2:344–47.

205. This is the issue of the Clark–Van Til debate. For more information, see Fred H. Klooster, *The Incomprehensibility of God in the Orthodox Presbyterian Conflict* (Franeker,

there an exact correspondence between God's knowledge of things and man's knowledge of those same things?

First, it must be noted that the concept of knowing has multiple applications. Knowing may refer to what is known, the method or criteria of knowing, or the act of knowing.

When it comes to the what of knowledge, there is an identity of thought between God and man. It can legitimately be said that what a man knows, God knows, despite the fact that God and man are metaphysically different.[206] A man can know actual truth, not an analogy of truth. The truth that a man knows is also known by God. A man knows something to be true by the same standard that God knows it to be true—the standard's being the very mind of God.[207]

But discontinuity enters in regard to the method or criteria of knowing, as well as in the acts of knowing.[208] Specifically, God's knowledge is prior to and necessary for man's knowledge. Humanity's knowledge is secondary and derivative. God's knowledge is self-validating. Man's knowledge is dependent on God's prerequisite, self-validating knowledge.[209] Most importantly, however, God can be known by man.[210] The relationship can be described as *analogical* if by that term one means that man knows both truthfully and reliably.[211]

According to Aquinas, human beings can know God in three ways. Humans can have an immediate vision of God, which only occurs by supernatural grace. Immediate visions of God occur very rarely on earth, and even those who receive visions of God remain incapable of comprehending God. The second method by which humans can know God is faith. This knowledge is derived from special revelation. But even knowledge based on special revelation provides no knowledge of God's essence. On earth, human knowledge of God is mediated. People cannot know God as he is in himself, but they can know him only as

---

Netherlands: Wever, 1951).

206. Bahnsen, *Van Til's Apologetic*, 228.

207. Ibid., 228–29: "By the same standard or 'point of reference' for both man and God (namely, God's own mind)."

208. Ibid., 226.

209. Reymond, *Systematic Theology*, 98.

210. Bahnsen, *Van Til's Apologetic*, 225.

211. Some argue that Van Til denied that man qualitatively knows something as God knows it. There is a qualitative distinction between the content of human knowledge and God's knowledge. See Reymond, *Systematic Theology*, 98, citing the complaint against Clark.

the first and most eminent cause of all things. There is no knowledge of God's being as such, nor is there a name that adequately expresses his being. Positive names for God indicate God's being, but God is knowable only through his representations in his creatures.[212] Third, humans can know God by means of natural reason.[213] Aquinas argued that philosophers have discerned truths about God. The apostle Paul even says that unbelievers know truths about God (see, for example, Romans 1:19–20). But the truths about God that the philosophers have discerned are only partial. The full truths about God are that he exists and that he is the judge. The philosophers have yet to discern these truths.[214]

In general, scholasticism held that God was unknowable. After the Reformation, the Roman Catholic Church adopted Aquinas's doctrine of God's unknowability. The teaching was officially adopted by the Lateran Council, convened by Pope Innocent III.[215]

Herman Bavinck believes that the doctrine of God's incomprehensibility, so far as it was developed at this time, was true. He lamented, however, that this truth was ignored by later scholastics, who left no room for God's incomprehensibility. They made it a divine attribute like all the others.[216] But besides this difficult and advanced teaching on God's nature, Aquinas also taught on the sacraments.

Sacraments. Following Aristotle, Aquinas determined that each of the seven sacraments has both matter and form. The matter may be bread, wine, or water, and the form is comprised by the words of institution. When the priest intends to offer the sacrament and an adult intends to receive its grace, then the sacrament *ex opera operato* ("from the work performed"), by means of the work, conveys that

212. Bavinck (*Doctrine of God*, 24) says, against Aquinas, "Duns Scotus affirmed that there was indeed a quidditative, albeit imperfect, knowledge of God" and Aquinas was certain that "nothing can be predicated of God and man in the univocal sense. Rather, only analogical predication is properly possible when speaking of the relationship between them."

213. Aquinas, *Summa theologiae* I q.12 13, as cited by Bavinck, *Doctrine of God*, 23, and *RD* 2:39. There are truths about God "which the natural reason is . . . able to reach . . . In fact, such truths about God have been proved demonstrably by the philosophers, guided by the light of the natural reason" (Aquinas, *Summa contra Gentiles* 1.3.2, as cited by Bahnsen, *Van Til's Apologetic*, 184n58).

214. Kelly, *Systematic Theology*, 1:163–67.

215. Bavinck, *Doctrine of God*, 24–25.

216. Ibid., 24.

grace.[217] Three sacraments leave a mark on the believer's soul: baptism, confirmation, and holy orders.

Since the Fourth Lateran Council in 1215, transubstantiation has been the dogmatic teaching of the Roman Catholic Church. Peter Lombard used the word *conversion* to describe the change in the elements. Aquinas clarified, however, that when a duly ordained priest uses the proper words, the accidents (characteristics perceived by the senses) of the matter—the bread, and the wine—remain unchanged, but the substance is transformed into the very body and blood of Christ. Further, the doctrine of concomitance established that Christ is fully present in each one of the elements, so the use of only bread was sufficient to convey grace.[218]

The Eucharist became the most cherished sacrament because of the teaching not only that it conveys grace but also that Christ himself is present in the bread. The church, therefore, deemed it proper to adore the consecrated bread during the procession on the Feast of Corpus Christi, and Aquinas wrote a liturgy to that effect. It was believed that the Mass continued the incarnation and represented Christ's passion without the shedding of actual blood.

The sacrament of penance involves confession, contrition, earnest resolve to amend, satisfaction, prayer, and alms. According to church law, penance required confession to a priest at least once a year. When the sinner evidenced contrition, confession, and a willingness to offer satisfaction, then the priest, speaking as Christ's representative, pronounced absolution. Without such pardon, those who committed deadly sins were denied the assurance of salvation. After absolution, the priest would impose works of satisfaction.[219]

In addition to penance, by the time of Aquinas the Roman church had a century-old system of indulgences. This system had started during the First Crusade. The church taught that an indulgence would remit part or all of a sinner's temporal penalty, including purgatory. Aquinas taught that Christ's superabundant merits, in addition to the

217. Walker, *History*, 345.

218. The doctrine of concomitance, from the Latin "to accompany," is that both the bread and the wine convey both Christ's body and blood and that the body is not only in the bread and blood only in the wine. See ibid., 345.

219. Ibid., 346.

merits of the saints, comprise a treasury of good works from which a portion may be transferred to the sinner by the church's authority in the person of the pope or his bishop.[220]

Other Theologians

Bonaventure (A.D. 1221–1274). Bonaventure was born in Italy in 1221. He would go on to hold the Franciscan chair in Paris beginning in 1254, the position of minister general of the Franciscans in 1257, and the position of cardinal bishop in 1273.[221] He was canonized in 1482 and made a doctor of the church in 1587.

Bonaventure's works include his well-known *Commentary on the Sentences* (1250), the official biography of Francis of Assisi, and an expanded, authoritative commentary on the Franciscan rule. His brief *Journey of the Mind to God* became a classic of Franciscan spirituality.[222] Philosophically, this work is Augustinian rather than Aristotelian, meaning that he did not need a philosophical system to undergird his theology. Again like Augustine, he held that intellectual and moral certainty require divine illumination of the mind and conscience.[223] This book was also a mystical work in that it focused on the two important components of mysticism: God as the supreme reality, and the soul's progress toward union with God. The mind, through meditation and prayer, with divine grace, begins by gazing on the traces of God in the world, only to catch sight of him within itself. Then the mind finally rises above itself to the Trinity. In the final state, intellectualism ceases and the soul unites with God in the ecstasy of love.[224]

Bonaventure was a contemporary of Aquinas.[225] The latter taught that the existence of God could be demonstrated using arguments from

---

220. Ibid., 347.

221. Ibid., 338.

222. At one time it was believed that he also wrote *Meditations on the Life of Christ*, which was in fact written later by another Franciscan—John de Caulibus. See MacCulloch, *Christianity*, 417.

223. Walker, *History*, 338.

224. Ibid., 339; Needham, *2,000 Years*, 2:261.

225. David Knowles, "The Middle Ages 604–1350," in Hubert Cunliffe-Jones, *A History of Christian Doctrine* (1978; repr., New York: T&T Clark, 2006), 270: "Bonaventure was the first to present a comprehensive scheme of Christian doctrine resting upon an explicitly formu-

creation. The Trinity, however, could be known only through faith and thus required special revelation to grasp. But Bonaventure had a different approach. He distrusted Aristotle's metaphysical philosophy.[226] If God is known only as first cause or prime mover, Bonaventure argued, then God is not known at all. God is not the prime mover but a Trinity. Bonaventure believed that arguments that conclude with an abstract god are false. Thus he still integrated philosophy and theology, but he did so by positing Christ as the medium not only of theology but also of philosophy.[227]

John Duns Scotus (A.D. 1266–1308).[228] John Duns Scotus was born in the small town of Duns in Roxburghshire, Scotland. The pejorative *dunce* was birthed during the later rise of Renaissance humanism when Scotists argued against humanists who were deemed incapable of scholarship.[229] Duns Scotus joined the Franciscans in 1281 and ten years later became a priest. He studied at Oxford and Paris, where he would also lecture on the *Sentences* between 1300 and 1303. He taught in Paris as a master of theology in 1305 and two years later moved to Cologne, Germany.[230]

For Aquinas, the intellect was the supreme part of the human being. But for Duns Scotus, the will was supreme. Dun Scotus's teaching concerning the human will extended to his analysis of God. He argued that God's will is not constrained by his intellect. God is omnipotent and can freely will anything that is not contrary to his nature. So when God wills something, that something is good simply because God wills it. This teaching stood in opposition to Aquinas, who taught that God wills something because that thing is good; in other words, first God intellectually determines something to be good, then wills it.[231]

Likewise, Aquinas's notion that the sacraments must intrinsically contain and convey grace also limits God's will. Slightly, but importantly different in Duns Scotus's thinking, the proper performance of

lated outlook on the universe, on the metaphysical constitution of beings, and the process of cognition in the senses, mind and soul."

226. Copleston, *Medieval Philosophy*, 1:242.

227. Ibid., 1:258.

228. Lee, *Christian Introduction to Philosophy*, 138; Clark, *Thales to Dewey*, 284–94.

229. For more information on humanism, see Part 4.

230. Walker, *History*, 349.

231. Ibid., 350–51. For a deep analysis of Scotus's view of God's being, as well as his proofs for God's existence, see Kelly, *Systematic Theology*, 1:100–18.

the sacrament is the condition, when fulfilled, that God will bestow grace. Duns Scotus said that the sacraments were not instrumental causes of grace, but in the divine covenant God promises to be present when the sacraments are duly performed.[232]

Duns Scotus's Augustinianism comes to the fore in his argument that salvation is not based on the quality of someone's soul but on God's free acceptance of him. God has chosen in eternity who will be saved and who will not be saved.[233]

John M. Frame is critical of Duns Scotus, and rightly so. For Duns Scotus, God's will is superior to his intellect. Given that superiority, Duns Scotus argued, God, of his own supreme free will, could have given human beings a different set of ten commandments than the ones he issued. Frame notes that such a view violates Scripture. God's moral law reflects his very being—the moral law is given in order that human behavior can reflect God. He argues that Duns Scotus's voluntarism—giving preeminence to the will—does not flow from the conviction of divine sovereignty but from a faulty view of human freedom.[234]

Scholars mark Duns Scotus's era as the beginning of late scholasticism and the introduction of the debate between the *via antiqua* ("old way") and *via moderna* ("modern way").[235] This debate will be best understood when seen in the context of a significant thinker, William of Ockham.

William of Ockham (A.D. 1285–1349).[236] William of Ockham was born near London in 1285. He joined the Franciscans while he was still young and earned his master of theology degree at Oxford.

232. Walker, *History*, 351.
233. Ibid., 352.
234. *HWPT*, 156. With Frame, I hold that neither the will nor the intellect is supreme. The whole person wills and thinks.
235. Another Franciscan at this time was Nicholas of Lyra (1270–1349), who was the head of the order in France and wrote a commentary on the entire Bible. He argued that there was a double-literal sense to the OT. The text has a literal sense, which in turn signifies Christ. He complained that the literal sense has been practically obliterated because of the method of exegesis commonly passed on by others. See Allison, *Historical Theology*, 169–72.
236. Bavinck (*Doctrine of God*, 24) quotes William of Ockham: "Neither divine essence nor divine quiddity, nor anything that pertains to the very nature of God, nor anything that is in reality God, can here be known by us in such a manner that nothing else than God presents itself to the reason." Ockham stressed the independence of personality. See Van Til, *Who?*, 65; Lee, *Christian Introduction to Philosophy*, 138; Clark, *Thales to Dewey*, 284–85.

The chancellor, however, brought theological charges against him, and Ockham had to defend himself at Avignon. While in Avignon, he became embroiled in the issue of Franciscan poverty and was excommunicated.[237]

Two aspects of Ockham's thought would sink roots into the church's thinking for the next several centuries: his view of salvation, and the nature of how one knows. Naturally, his view of salvation was dependent on his doctrine of God. Ockham embraced Duns Scotus's distinction between God's absolute power and his ordained power. God, by his absolute power, could have made salvation dependent on hatred of him rather than love of him. God was bound to nothing but himself. Flowing from Francis's notion of the great mercy of God toward his people came Ockham's belief that God, in his plan of salvation, willed that he would save men and women who do their very best in their state of nature, thus acquiring semi-merit, or merit *de congruo*. After those who do their best move on to a state of grace, they can acquire full merit, or merit *de condigno*. In this final state they would earn salvation. Ockham reasoned that God does not deny grace to those who act according to that which is in them. Thus Ockham did not embrace Duns Scotus's or Augustine's notion of eternal predestination. For Ockham, election is dependent on God's ordained will, but that willing is also conditioned on God's foreknowledge of a person's good acts. For Ockham, eternal predestination is divine foreknowledge of human behavior. Such a doctrine, he thought, preserved human freedom and dignity.[238]

As a Franciscan, Ockham rejected the Dominican adaptation of Greek philosophy to Christianity seen in the works of Aquinas. In essence, he rejected earlier Greek notions of the foundations for epistemology. Greek and Christian thinking before him understood knowledge as being mediated through universals. Humans know a particular through a universal. While there was discussion and divergence on how humans come to know a universal, Greek and Christian thinkers before Ockham agreed that these universals have some type

---

237. The Franciscans held to the doctrine of absolute poverty—that Christ and his apostles had no personal or shared property. Pope John XXII declared this doctrine heretical and excommunicated the general of the order, as well as Ockham.

238. Walker, *History*, 353–54; MacCulloch, *Christianity*, 564–65.

of extramental reality.[239] In contrast, Ockham proposed a principle of economy now referred to as *Ockham's razor.*[240]

Ockham believed that only individual things that exist are actually real—there is no need to postulate universals. Ockham called knowledge of individual things "intuitive cognition." Knowledge of the individual thing comes first in both thought and reality. Ockham believed that, at best, universals exist as a content of the mind. Since in Ockham's system universals by nature are mental and linguistic, he and his successors were called *nominalists.*[241] Ockham's beliefs challenged the traditional manners of thinking—that God's existence could be proven by natural reason.[242] Instead, he believed that any knowledge of Christian doctrine came through faith and Scripture alone.

Thomas à Kempis (A.D. 1380–1471). Born in the Rhineland of western Germany, Thomas à Kempis was sent to school in the Netherlands by his father, who was a blacksmith. The eastern Netherlands saw the birth of a religious movement known as the Modern Devotion. This movement began with Gerard Groote (1340–1384), a highly educated Carthusian who was critical of clerical immorality. Within his own home, he formed a group of women who worked to provide for themselves and lived in service to God and society. Their goal was to live in religious community, while not separating themselves from society. Florentius Radewijns, a parish priest, further organized the movement into the Sisters and Brothers of the Common Life. The movement spread through the Netherlands and into Germany. The Brothers specialized in educating young men and would go on to influence Luther and Erasmus.[243]

Thomas à Kempis's book *The Imitation of Christ* is the prime example of the thinking of this movement. The work consists of four parts, three of which deal with the inner life and one of which deals with the Eucharist. À Kempis admonished his readers to live simply,

---

239. *HWPT,* 156–57. The medieval debate included extreme realism—the universal is a reality found in all particulars of its class; extreme nominalism—universals are not real things but only names; and conceptualism—universals are mental concepts symbolized by words.

240. Walker, *History,* 355: "Plurality is not to be postulated without necessity," or "Whatever can be done with fewer assumptions is done in vain with more."

241. Ibid., 356; *HWPT,* 158.

242. *HWPT,* 159.

243. Walker, *History,* 363–64.

deny themselves, and obey humbly those in authority over them.[244] As now we turn from this brief survey of several medieval theologians, we will focus on the Late Medieval Period.

LATE MEDIEVAL PERIOD: SOCIAL, ECONOMIC, AND POLITICAL ISSUES

Economic Changes. Industrial developments and global events occasioned the broadening of economic possibilities. Trading corporations—such as the Hanseatic League and the English Merchants of the Staples—began to develop. Banks grew as coins began to be used more commonly. The bubonic plague—the so-called Black Death of this era—sparked an interest in automation because of the enormous depletion of the labor force. In addition, the discovery of America opened up a new part of the world for trade and industry.

Improvement in the weather, which had been miserable for the first half of the fourteenth century, also had its effect on the economy. Gradually, industry began moving out of the city to escape guild regulations, which slowed production. New achievements in navigation equipment, such as the compass and quadrant, spurred expeditions, such as the rounding of the Cape of Good Hope. The financing industry saw innovations, such as the practice of discounting and the use of credit and bills of exchange, known as "promissory notes." At this time, the Netherlands constituted the hub of industry and economic life.

The greatest multinational corporation at the time—the medieval church—controlled the economic climate of this period. Lands were held as papal states, and once bishoprics and monasteries were established, they could not escape papal control. One-third of England's land belonged to the church, as did half of Scotland. By decree, the English king Henry VIII abolished the church's ownership of this land; the Scots received it back by paying for it through taxes.

During the church's so-called Babylonian Captivity (1309–1377), Pope John XXII began collecting taxes from the church, while annates, amounting to the first year's worth of a bishop's income, were also

244. Steven Ozment, *The Age of Reform, 1250–1550* (New Haven: Yale University Press, 1980), 97.

collected. The church also generated income through legal appeals and the sale of indulgences.

By the year 1500, the economy was rife with problems. Specifically, uncontrolled spending combined with declining revenue. Local church revenue suffered as a result of decreased farm production on the monastic lands and higher taxes on wool. Bishops had to pay for dowries for their illegitimate children, and the papacy borrowed money at lending rates of up to 30 percent despite the church's admission that the practice of usury was wrong.

Social Changes. The fourteenth century witnessed a shift in the balance of power within social structures. The nobility found themselves in a difficult financial situation—their income from tenants was fixed, prices and wages were up, and laborers were scarce in the wake of the plague. As a result, the nobility had an abundance of land, little cash, and few workers. So nobles began to work in the court or the church, both of which institutions offered a steady income. Serfs could now flee to the city for freedom. Some serfs became swept up in utopian ideas of prosperity, and at times their zeal manifested in revolts. The lower nobles could and did become mercenaries. Interestingly, the men in this class could also marry daughters of successful merchants; the marriages resulted in a close connection between the lower nobility and the rising middle class.

To protect itself, the middle class developed monopolies, chiefly by means of small charter trading companies. As demand for their products increased, the middle class strengthened. Members of the middle class tended to join with the gentry who had land, which helped both the lower nobles and the middle class ascend the social scale. Unrest among the middle class would provide fertile ground for the Reformation.

The discovery of America—the New World—had economic, social, and particularly religious ramifications. As new cultures were encountered, new ideas and superstitions began to develop. The plague that swept through Europe only furthered these superstitions. And the church's doctrine of transubstantiation and its sale of indulgences added to the already brimming climate of superstition.

Social unrest increased as the commoners became involved with astrology, alchemy, necromancy, charms and curses, witchcraft, and satanism. Fear and uncertainty were prevalent at every level of society. This atmosphere of fear also tilled the ground for the Reformation, which would settle the fears that the Roman Catholic Church had failed to address.

The Thomistic view of society (recalling the thinking of Thomas Aquinas), which held that social hierarchy was divinely established and should thus be maintained, also played a role in the social change of the period. But the middle class longed to advance and was thus antagonistic to the church's status-quo approach.

Political Change: Feudalism. In the medieval feudal system, the king owned all the land, so he had the right to divide the land and grant it to whomever he wished. Often a king would reward his best soldiers with a gift of land to guarantee their loyalty to him. The land that was granted for service to the king was a called a *fief*.

A number of advances contributed to the decline of the local kings and the feudal fief system. It could be argued that the growth of a monetary system, as opposed to a barter system of trade, choked out feudalism. In addition, advances in archery and machines of war, such as canons, rendered traditional armies obsolete.

A king now had the ability to receive money instead of military support from his nobles, and he could use that money to hire mercenary soldiers. To save on costs and to increase their effectiveness against new forms of weaponry, militaries began using infantry more than armor and cavalry. With the increase in the usage of coins, the king also taxed the middle class on their wealth. This improvement centralized the political structure, thus resulting in the rise of a stronger yet more limited number of monarchies.

The nobility experienced high rates of death from engaging in wars, so the middle class became increasingly important to the monarchy, both for its money and its administrative assistance. The lack of political competitors vying for the nobles created an environment favorable to absolutism, a system of government the church championed.

The church supported this system for a number of reasons. In general, the church wanted the political rule of the people to mirror and reinforce the ecclesiastical absolutism of the papacy. Absolutism comported well with the feudal way of life, which the church sought to maintain. Absolutism maintained order and tended to secure privi-

335

leges for the church. For instance, when a bishopric went vacant, the church would approve a candidate, who would then be appointed by the king. This tight relationship between the church and the state ensured that the wealthy new bishop would pay both the king and the pope.[245] The church viewed the state as an arm of the church; the state was the moon and the church was the sun. The church believed itself to have been entrusted with both the spiritual and the civil sword, and absolutism tended to facilitate this view.

With the rise of centralized monarchies came the national state. Centralized wars, wars between kings, and an increasing unity of language among the peoples also contributed to the rise of national states. And with the rise of national states came city-states as well. City-states developed in Switzerland and in imperial cities of the Holy Roman Empire. These cities were in constant political turmoil. The unrest would allow the Reformation to flourish in those lands, for no organized civil power could spend the time to extinguish it.

CHURCH AND POPULAR CULTURE

For three to four hundred years prior to the Protestant Reformation, efforts were made to reform the church. Peter Waldo, along with the Waldensiens of France and Italy, and John Wycliffe of England, along with his Lollards, provided impetus for the burgeoning movement of theological reform that was spreading throughout Europe. These groups began to cooperate and feed off each other. Jerome of Prague took Wycliffe's ideas to Bohemia, where they were then taken up by John Hus.

A desire for moral reform within the church occasioned the rise of new expressions of monasticism. Some of the significant leaders and orders within monasticism were Savonarola of Florence; the Brethren of the Common Life in the Netherlands; the Fraticelli or Little Brothers—a fringe group that sought to carry on the tradition of Francis of Assisi; the Carthusians; the Third Order or Order of the Penitents; the Ora-

---

245. In this political mix, legislative bodies lost their power and influence, since the king had the right of patronage. Kings changed rapidly due to the short life expectancy which characterized that time.

tory of Divine Love; and the Oratory's subsidiary group focusing on the reform of the secular clergy, the Theatines.[246]

These groups were limited in what they could accomplish in their own day, in part because some of these groups wanted nothing more than to return to medieval piety. But that desire was not the only thing preventing deeper reform. It was also hampered by the lack of a middle class and by church-instigated governmental persecution, which drove these movements underground or defeated them altogether. The social climate of the time was simply not right for true reform in the church.

Worldly Elements in the Church. The prevalent attitude toward the church at this time was captured in a simple phrase: "the nearer to Rome, the farther from grace." The church had, in many ways, become nothing more than a well-oiled, mechanical ceremony. And a lucrative ceremony at that. The sale of indulgences and the practice of patronage catered to the corruption of church leaders. Many sought church office because it offered a lucrative career. But pull back the curtains of this ceremony and one sees rampant immorality. It was typical for a church leader to have a concubine, and sexual licentiousness was boldly embraced by church officials. So it should come as no surprise to learn that the church placed little emphasis on teaching. Though friars taught occasionally, bishops filled a pulpit only four times each year. The rate of illiteracy among the priests was disturbing, especially to the literate middle class. Many members of the clergy used pilgrimages as religious excuses to escape from wives and children.[247] For an institution that had the express purpose of extending grace to humanity, the church was rotting from the inside out. Things had to change.

Humanism and Literature. The times witnessed a rise of individualism, or the cult of the *virtuoso*, grounded in the notion that reason itself could make man *quasi divino*—"seemingly divine." But this emphasis on the individual undermined the corporate nature of the church.

As a consequence of the Crusades, a number of classical writings were discovered during this time. Scholars began to study Roman classical writings and patristic works, and the study of these ancient

---

246. For a detailed account of these orders, see Kenneth Scott Latourette, *A History of Christianity*, 2 vols. (Peabody, MA: Prince, 2005).

247. Read, for example, Geoffrey Chaucer's *The Canterbury Tales*, rev. ed. (New York: Penguin Classics, 2003).

manuscripts resulted in the development of the historical-grammatical method of exegesis. This method stood in contrast to the fourfold exegetical method (allegorical, moral, spiritual, and literal) of the Middle Ages. Northern humanists began to study Scripture in its original languages due to the unavailability of other classical texts. Printing also underwent great advances during this time.

Much of the popular literature of the Middle Ages consisted of morality and miracle plays. But the fifteenth and sixteenth centuries saw the development of romance, pastoral poetry with the theme of a return to nature, the novella, satire, humor, and irony. This literary development was due to the introduction of paper in 1300 and moveable type in 1450 by Johannes Gutenberg.

This time was also one of progress and advance. Music developed both technically and popularly. Thanks to the influences of Aristotle and Pythagoras, and to nominalism's emphasis on individual phenomena, science lurched forward. Advances in anatomy were made by Copernicus and Vasallieu and in chemistry by Parcelcius.

As culture and technology began to ripen, the church—by now a Goliath of an economic and political machine—was rotting spiritually. The first winds of reform were blowing against the church, but true reform had not yet come. It was on the way. Before we examine its development, in the next chapter we will explore more of the theology of this time.

KEY TERMS

metaphysics
negative theology
universals
sacrament
ransom to Satan

STUDY QUESTIONS

1. How do you evaluate the rise of monasteries? In what ways were they helpful in their own time period?

2. Do you have a favorite medieval theologian?
3. What were some of the weaknesses of medieval thinking?
4. How do you evaluate Aquinas's five arguments for God's existence?
5. How many senses of Scripture are there?

RESOURCES FOR FURTHER STUDY

In general, Protestants are not fond of this period in the church's history. It is an era of decline, but it is still the narrative of Christ's church.

Abelard, Peter. *Ethical Writings*. Translated by Paul Vincent Spade. Indianapolis: Hacket, 1995. Especially his "Ethics" or "Know Yourself" and his "Dialogue between a Philosopher, a Jew, and a Christian," which wrestles with ethics and the nature of ultimate good and evil.

Anselm. *Proslogion*. In *Christian Apologetics Past and Present: A Primary Source Reader*, by William Edgar and K. Scott Oliphint, 365–83. Wheaton, IL: Crossway, 2009. Includes a very helpful introduction to *Proslogion*.

Boethius. "A Treatise against Eutyches and Nestorius." In *The Theological Tractates*, edited by G. P. Goold and translated by H. F. Stewart, E. K. Rand, and S. J. Tester, 72–129. Cambridge: Harvard University Press, 1973. A primary source with helpful introductions.

Petry, Ray C., ed. *Late Medieval Mysticism*. London: SCM Press, 1957. For mature Christians, it contains enjoyable readings from Bernard of Clairvaux's writings, such as "On the Love of God" and "Of the Three Ways in Which We Love God," on pages 47–74.

10

Medieval Theology

THIS FINAL CHAPTER OF Part 3 will compile medieval reflections on the various doctrines of systematic theology. Like the preceding patristic era and the eras still to come, the Medieval Period both advanced theologically and began to slip down theological slopes that made evident the deep need for a reformation.

DOCTRINE OF GOD

Existence. Medieval theologians offered various arguments for God's existence. In the *Proslogion*, Anselm argued that God is the being "than which nothing greater can be conceived." This is a classic a priori argument—that is, an argument that is prior to or which makes no appeals to human experience. It is also an ontological argument.[1]

Aquinas's arguments, on the other hand, are a posteriori, which is to say that they are based on human experience. A posteriori arguments assert general principles based on the observation of particular instances. As such an argument, Aquinas's reasoning moves from observations of the world to assertions of God. These arguments were presented in chapter 9.

Knowability. Medieval theologians were captivated by how and in what ways God can be known. Pseudo-Dionysius developed a new approach to thinking about God, the *via negativa*, or the "negative way." He argued that God, because he is the cause of all things,

---

1. Greg R. Allison, *Historical Theology: An Introduction to Christian Doctrine—A Companion to Wayne Grudem's Systematic Theology* (Grand Rapids: Zondervan, 2011), 192–93.

is beyond definition, even beyond denial. Thus Pseudo-Dionysius believed that theologians must reject positive assertions about God. Though Pseudo-Dionysius used the *via negativa*, his ultimate aim was to become speechless and unknowing because, he believed, even the language of Scripture that defined or described God was bound by limitation.[2]

In *Journey of the Mind to God*, Bonaventure outlined that he was convinced, and rightly so, that reflection on the world gives the person doing the reflecting a deeper knowledge of God. He believed that contemplation of the image of God in humanity was an avenue to knowledge of God. But for Bonaventure, the best way to know God—a way even better than through cognitive knowledge—was through a mystical experience.[3]

Duns Scotus made a distinction between theology that humans can know—theology *ad nostra*—and theology *in se*—theology as God has in himself. In this distinction, Duns Scotus emphasized that only God has a mind proportionate to knowing God.[4]

Aquinas spoke of the beatific vision. By this expression he meant that it is possible, by grace alone, to have a vision of God through which the intellect can understand God's essence by God's uniting himself to it. Aquinas preferred this method of understanding God.[5]

Written anonymously in the latter half of the fourteenth century, *The Cloud of Unknowing* argued that God's reality was hidden from human feeling and knowledge. The author argued that an understanding of God comes only through love, not through knowledge. This argument exemplifies *apophatic* theology.[6]

Trinity. Medieval theologians also developed the doctrine of the Trinity. The Latin term *filioque*, which means "and the Son," was introduced in A.D. 589 at the Third Council of Toledo. *Filioque*, which articulated that the Spirit proceeds from the Father and the Son together, concerned the mode by which the Holy Spirit related to

2. Ibid., 190–91.
3. Ibid., 198.
4. Michael Allen, "Knowledge of God," in *Christian Dogmatics: Reformed Theology for the Church Catholic*, ed. Michael Allen and Scott R. Swain (Grand Rapids: Baker Academic, 2016), 10.
5. Allison, *Historical Theology*, 197–98.
6. Ibid., 198.

the other two persons of the godhead.[7] It was this teaching, at least in part, that would spark the East–West schism of 1054.[8]

In *On the Trinity*, Boethius (A.D. 480–524) explained that because God is not separate in substance, there is only one God. In this work, Boethius defined the divine person as "an individual substance of a rational nature."[9] Plurality in God is a predicate to relation. The Trinity's relationships bring number to the Trinity, but the Trinitarian relationship is of individuals. Thus Boethius held to unity and diversity as well as equality and distinction within the godhead, as Anselm would later do.[10] Eastern theologians criticized this Western definition of person because it emphasized the three persons' autonomy rather than their love and community.

Building on Augustine's Trinitarian formulations, Peter Lombard seemed to regard the divine persons as triple repetitions of the same substance. He thus insufficiently regarded their personal attributes. He argued that not only God the Son but also God the Father or God the Holy Spirit could have been made man—and could still be made man.[11] Lombard's argument ignored the biblical teaching that only the Son is the proper subject of the incarnation.

Aquinas argued that while God's existence could be known by natural reason, the Trinity could not be so known. Aquinas, who leaned on the thinking of Boethius, said that the word *person* signifies a relation as subsisting. If applied to humans, this definition might lend itself to tritheistic conceptions, but Aquinas rejected such a notion. The term *person* is useful both to convey the sense of Scripture and to refute heretics. *Person* also speaks truthfully about God's being because God is the most perfect being, and the use of *person* cannot be limited to creaturely notions. Furthermore, when applied to God, the word *person* refers to a particular individual, in other words,

7. The phrase was condemned by Patriarch Photius I of Constantinople in A.D. 864. Thomas Aquinas held a strict doctrine of *filioque*. It became official doctrine in the West at the Second Council of Lyons in 1274. See Michael Horton, *The Christian Faith: A Systematic Theology for Pilgrims on the Way* (Grand Rapids: Zondervan, 2011), 304.

8. There was a serious attempt to reunite the East and West at the Council of Florence in 1439 when a joint statement on the *filioque* was approved, but there were other reasons that kept the two parts of the church from reuniting. See Allison, *Historical Theology*, 243–45.

9. Boethius, *On the Trinity*, as cited by Horton, *Christian Faith*, 283.

10. Allison, *Historical Theology*, 244.

11. Lombard, *Sentences* 3.1.3, as cited by Horton, *Christian Faith*, 286.

that which distinguishes this one from that one. The word connects to God's relations, particularly to relations of origin that distinguish the three persons.[12]

Four relations apply to the godhead: paternity, filiation, spiration, and procession. By an act of the divine intellect, there is paternity and filiation. By an act of the divine will, the Holy Spirit spirates from the Father and the Son and proceeds from the Father and the Son. Generation and spiration are distinct relationships. While there is complete equality among the three persons, the Father is the principal member of the Trinity.[13]

Convened in 1215, the Fourth Lateran Council established the Athanasian Creed. This council also embraced the part of Cappadocian theology that defined God as one in essence and three in person.[14]

Christology. While significant advances had been made in the ancient church at the Councils of Nicaea, Constantinople (the first through the third), Ephesus, and Chalcedon, medieval theologians continued to focus their writings on the second person of the Trinity. From a soteriological perspective, Anselm's *Cur Deus Homo* defended the classical notion of Christ as fully God and fully man.[15]

Aquinas held to the traditional belief of Christ's two natures.[16] He focused on the *communicatio idiomatum* ("communication of the properties"). He argued that it was proper to speak of Christ's human experience when referring to him as God and of his divine experience when referring to him as man. The divine nature did not become human, nor did the human nature become divine. The two natures maintained their respective properties. Yet that which is said of either nature may also be said of the one person, Jesus Christ.[17]

Holy Spirit. In *On the Procession of the Holy Spirit*, Anselm argued that the Holy Spirit is the Spirit of God. God is Father, Son, and Holy Spirit; thus the Holy Spirit must be from all three persons. But the

12. Scott R. Swain, "Divine Trinity," in *Christian Dogmatics: Reformed Theology for the Church Catholic*, ed. Michael Allen and Scott R. Swain (Grand Rapids: Baker Academic, 2016), 97–98.

13. Allison, *Historical Theology*, 245.

14. Horton, *Christian Faith*, 287: "The Father is one (*alius*), the Son another (*alius*), and the Holy Spirit another (*alius*), yet there is not another thing (*aliud*)."

15. Allison, *Historical Theology*, 377–78.

16. He argued against Eutychianism and Nestorianism.

17. Ibid., 377–79.

Holy Spirit cannot be from himself. Thus Anselm reasoned that the Holy Spirit is from the Father and the Son. Yet neither can the Holy Spirit be from the Father through the Son. There is but one divine nature; thus the Holy Spirit cannot be from one divine nature and through another. John writes that the Father would send the Spirit in his name and that Jesus would send the Spirit from the Father. Thus, Anselm concluded, Jesus's sending and the Father's sending were one.[18]

The *filioque* was reiterated in 1215 at the Fourth Lateran Council—but theologians from the East disagreed with the term. The disagreement sparked a controversy that resulted in Photius of Constantinople's excommunicating Pope Nicholas I because Photius was convinced that neither the Scriptures nor the church fathers supported the notion. In his mind, the term *filioque* made the Son a second source, or principle, of the Holy Spirit. The West, however, denied this charge. Aquinas countered that "the Father and the Son are one principle of the Holy Spirit."[19]

Attributes. Anselm affirmed God's impassibility and simplicity and the divine inability to change. His theology of the atonement was grounded in divine impassibility. While he affirmed divine foreknowledge, he believed that this foreknowledge did not necessitate human sin. If foreknowledge did necessitate sin, Anselm thought, human freedom and responsibility would be compromised. But he was convinced that God's foreknowledge was compatible with human freedom.[20] Concerning divine omnipotence, Anselm taught that God's inability to sin did not decrease his power, for the so-called "power to sin" is actually impotence, not power.

Aquinas also affirmed God's simplicity.[21] How theologians interpret divine simplicity significantly influences their theology of God. Humans cannot conceive God's properties in a univocal, or "same," way. Nor

---

18. Ibid., 439–40.

19. Aquinas, *Summa theologiae*, I. 36. IV, as cited by Allison, *Historical Theology*, 440.

20. He argued: "So it is necessary that it shall happen freely and there is no conflict whatsoever between a foreknowledge which entails a necessary occurrence of a free exercise of an uncoerced will. For it is both necessary that God foreknows what shall come to be and that God foreknows that something shall freely come to be" (Anselm, *On the Compatibility of the Foreknowledge, Predestination, and Grace of God with Human Freedom*, as cited by Allison, *Historical Theology*, 215).

21. He said that God's "nature does not differ from his attributes, nor [does] his essence differ from his existence. There is no composition of genus and species in him, nor one of subject

do they understand God's properties in equivocal or absolutely different ways. Instead, all such language about God is analogical—that is, a word taken in one sense is put in the definition of the same word taken in other senses.[22] While God is simple, Aquinas said, God is perfectly good, omnipresent, omniscient, merciful, omnipotent, and perfectly blessed. And some divine attributes are mirrored, albeit imperfectly, in human beings. For example, God is truthful, and humans can be truthful, but their truthfulness is analogous, not univocal.[23]

Creation. In the *Monologion*, Anselm attempted to prove from reason that creation was *ex nihilo* ("out of nothing"). Aquinas taught that the godhead created, but the three persons had distinct roles in creation. He also wrestled with whether creation was accomplished in one day, following Augustine, or in seven days. As might be anticipated, all the medieval theologians believed in an earth that was between four thousand and fifty-five hundred years old.[24]

Providence and Evil. Anselm wrestled with the dilemma of God as the potential author of evil and the unjust punishment of evil. He resolved this tension by claiming that evil was nonexistent. He held that "good" human actions are the result of the goodness of God, while "bad" human actions are the result of man's own fallen intentions. Thus there is compatibility between human free choice and the grace of God. If a person does good, then God is to be praised for his goodness and man is to be praised for his cooperation with divine grace. He argued that evil deeds can be attributed solely to human beings' wicked choices.[25]

Aquinas taught that God's providence is directed to accomplish his design. God preserves all that exists, and he is the first, or causal, agent. God uses secondary means to control the universe. Thus human choices are within his providential plan.

God does not will evil to be done, but God wills to permit evil. While God is not the cause of evil, he did create a world in which

---

and accident. Therefore, it is clear that God is in no way composite, but is altogether simple" (Aquinas, *Summa theologiae*, I. q.3. a.7., as cited by Allison, *Historical Theology*, 216).

22. Aquinas, *Summa theologiae*, I. q. 13. a. 10, as cited by Allison, *Historical Theology*, 216–17.

23. Allison, *Historical Theology*, 217–18.

24. Ibid., 260–62.

25. Ibid., 284–85.

the good could fall. He did not cause the fall of Adam and Eve; they were responsible for their disobedience and were thus rightly judged.[26]

Angels and Demons. The spiritual or angelic sphere was a special focus of study during this time, thanks to the detailed work of men like Aquinas and Lombard. Medieval theologians believed there to be a hierarchy among the angels—John of Damascus and Pseudo-Dionysius elaborated this hierarchy.[27]

In *On the Devil's Fall*, Anselm argued that the Devil longed for more than he received and thus led a host of angels out of heaven with him. Anselm reasoned that these fallen angels must be replaced with an equal number of the redeemed. Christ's strong work was needed to restore this celestial harmony.[28]

Aquinas taught that God created by means of his intellect and will. He thought that angels were created by God's intellect—therefore they are purely intellectual and without physical nature. These angels, immense in number, are more like God than men. Aquinas taught that angels could move instantly from place to place. And while they possess free will, they are not lured by temptations, because it takes physical bodies to be so influenced. While on earth, guardian angels protect people from demons. And upon death, humans hope to be taken up into the order of the angels.

DOCTRINE OF SCRIPTURE

Canon. During the medieval era, the Latin Vulgate was the accepted biblical text. But because the Catholic Church had supposedly determined the bounds of the canon, the church's authority was considered equal to the canon's. The apocryphal literature was also included as part of the canon even though this literature could not be found in the Hebrew Bible. Jerome had explained that the Apocrypha should not be used to establish doctrine; nevertheless, the doctrines of purgatory and prayers for the dead were established by the apocryphal writing of 2 Maccabees. In addition, the Vulgate's translation of the

26. Ibid., 283–84.
27. Ibid., 309–12.
28. Ibid., 308–9.

NT was poor. Based on the Vulgate's mistranslation of Matthew 4:17, the sacrament of penance found its way into the life of the church.[29]

Inspiration and Authority. The medieval church held to the doctrine of divine inspiration. Photius of Constantinople, John Scotus Eriugena, Peter Abelard, Gabriel Biel, and John Wycliffe were all convinced that God spoke in Scripture.[30]

The early medieval church adhered to the supremacy of Scripture over the teaching of the church fathers.[31] Aquinas taught that the Christian faith was founded on infallible truth and that the Scriptures are incontrovertible truth. He held that writings of earlier theologians were useful but should not be approached with the same level of trust and dependence. The Scriptures are free from error, while other writings must be approached with a critical eye.[32] As the Middle Ages continued, the church began to drift from these convictions regarding the authority of Scripture and the fallibility of man.

Some looked to the papal interpretation of the Scriptures as their highest authority. Others departed from the authority of Scripture in search of an oral tradition they believed to have been passed down from the apostles. The bishops also began to be considered sources of authoritative doctrine. Even more, general church councils were thought to be authoritative.[33]

The crisis of biblical authority reached a high point with the Waldensians. Peter Waldo (1140–1205), a merchant, was the ostensible founder of a unique group of medieval Christians. His followers, known as the Waldensians, were a barefoot, or at best sandaled, group who fasted three times a week, took no oaths, prohibited the shedding of blood, and prayed only the Lord's Prayer. They abandoned observation of the Mass, prayer for the dead, and any belief in a purgatory. They taught that if the priest who was administering the sacrament was unworthy, then he offered an invalid sacrament. The Waldensians held the Bible as the only law for life.[34]

---

29. Ibid., 50–51.
30. Ibid., 63–64.
31. Demonstrated in the writings of Aquinas, Eriugena, and Gerson (ibid., 82–83).
32. Robert Letham, *Systematic Theology* (Wheaton, IL: Crossway, 2019), 191.
33. Allison, *Historical Theology*, 86–87.
34. Williston Walker, and Richard A. Norris, David W. Lotz, and Robert T. Handy, *A History of the Christian Church*, 4th ed. (New York: Scribner's Sons, 1985), 230.

In response to the Waldensians, the Council of Toulouse was called in 1229. The ruling of this synod forced the Waldensians out of the church and excommunicated them for preaching without licenses. Since this movement was born from laymen's simply reading the Bible, the church forbade the laity even to possess the Scriptures, except for the Psalter.[35] To keep people from error—or, negatively expressed, to keep power—the church also forbade vernacular translations of Scripture.[36]

Inerrancy and Clarity. While Anselm and Aquinas both taught that the Scriptures were wholly true, Peter Abelard had a more complex view of Scripture.[37] His *Sic et Non* established contrary sources of authority.[38] Medieval theologians held that, in general, the Scriptures were obscure. The medieval church taught that while some portions of Scripture were clear and accessible, much of Scripture was veiled, some of it even impenetrable. Each portion of Scripture had a different value. In an age of prevalent illiteracy, the responsibility rested with priests to interpret the Bible for the laymen. Not only was its interpretation the responsibility of the priests, but also the privilege of even reading Scripture was granted to the priests alone.

Despite the church's ruling on translation, John Wycliffe (1330–1394) translated the Bible from the Vulgate into English.[39] At least one hundred and fifty of his manuscripts remain today.[40] Wycliffe's English translation of the Bible received criticism because Wycliffe was a layman, not a priest. The church's argument, already in place for a century now, was that the priests alone could guard against heretical teaching.[41]

In his great work *De veritate sacrae scripturae*, John Wycliffe developed the doctrine of inerrancy. He argued that the Scriptures were dictated by God and that each part of Scripture, not simply the heart of the message, was breathed out by divine authority. Each sentence,

---

35. Allison, *Historical Theology*, 125–28. See Henri de Lubac, *Medieval Exegesis: The Four Senses of Scripture* (Grand Rapids: Eerdmans, 1998).

36. It was at this time that the church also started an inquisition. See Walker, *History*, 231.

37. Ibid., 103.

38. Allison, *Historical Theology*, 104.

39. Heiko Augustinus Oberman, *The Harvest of Medieval Theology: Gabriel Biel and Late Medieval Nominalism* (Cambridge: Harvard University Press, 1963), 372–73.

40. See Walker, *History*, 268.

41. Allison, *Historical Theology*, 125–28.

even each word of the Scripture, is of the highest authority.[42] Wycliffe proposed a mechanical theory of inspiration—that the prophets and authors spoke the words of God. He contrasted that high view of Scripture with the much lower view of the authority of human laws given by the church. The contributions of Wycliffe were significant for Martin Luther's later development.[43]

Wycliffe was by no means an innovator of these rich doctrines, for a high view of Scripture—even a mechanical view—had already been established in the patristic period. Wycliffe did, however, teach that a text's meaning often dwelt beneath the literal meaning of the text.[44]

Necessity and Sufficiency. In the Early Medieval Period, an understanding of the sufficiency and necessity of Scripture was tied to the assumption that the Bible should be read and interpreted alongside the church's tradition. They wrongly argued that God first inspired the Scriptures, then inspired the church to interpret the Scriptures correctly. Scripture's necessity and sufficiency were soon eclipsed by Christ's supposed "unwritten teaching."

Aquinas believed in the necessity of theological science based on divine revelation. Both Duns Scotus and Gabriel Biel affirmed Scripture's necessity and sufficiency. Gerald of Bologna (d. 1317), a Thomist, and Thomas Netter Waldensis (d. 1413), a Carmelite, both believed that divine revelation could be given outside Scripture. This view overthrew Scripture's sufficiency and necessity. Bologna and Waldensis thought that Scripture was necessary only for the well-being of the church, not for its very existence.[45]

Interpretation. A tradition held by theologians such as Rabanus Maurus, Hugh of Saint Victor, Aquinas, Nicholas of Lyra, and John

42. See John D. Woodbridge, *Biblical Authority: A Critique of the Rogers/McKim Proposal* (Grand Rapids: Zondervan, 1982), 47.

43. Alexander Ganoczy and Stefan Scheld, *Die Hermeneutik Calvins: Geistesgeschichtliche Voraussetzungen und Grundzüge* (Wiesbaden: Steiner, 1983), 13. There is still debate concerning the meaning of Wycliffe's view of Scripture. It has been called *fundamentalistic* by some, and others find that word grossly anachronistic. I agree. See E. Gordon Rupp, "Christian Doctrine from 1350 to the Eve of the Reformation," in *A History of Christian Doctrine*, ed. Hubert Cunliffe-Jones (1978; repr., New York: T&T Clark, 2006), 291.

44. A high view of Scripture does not always keep theologians from bad hermeneutics. Wycliffe did not have bad hermeneutics, but Origen did—and Origen held to what could be called *inerrancy*.

45. Allison, *Historical Theology*, 147–51.

Wycliffe insisted that the spiritual sense of the text is based on and presupposes its literal sense. Nevertheless, most medieval interpreters followed in the footsteps of Origen and Augustine by adhering to the multiple-sense approach of interpretation.[46]

While Gregory the Great promoted a threefold approach to interpretation, John Cassian and the Venerable Bede argued for a fourfold approach. The four senses were: (1) the letter or history; (2) the allegory, where true faith is hidden; (3) tropology, or the moral meaning; and (4) the anagogy, which leads readers to heavenly matters.

Aquinas created a variation of this fourfold approach.[47] Foundational to it was the notion that there were two basic levels of meaning: the literal and the spiritual. He then divided the spiritual sense into three categories of meaning: (1) the allegorical; (2) the tropological, or moral; and (3) the anagogical, from the Greek *anagōgē*.[48] Aquinas insisted that the spiritual sense was based on and presupposes the literal sense.

In the twelfth century, a competing school arose at the Abbey of Saint Victor, which was known as the Victorines. At this school, Hugh of Saint Victor (1090–1141) criticized those who sought the hidden meaning of the biblical text. He emphasized its literal sense. He had two prominent followers, Richard and Andrew. Influenced by the Jewish school of Rashi (1040–1105), these men were the first to stand against a purely allegorical interpretation of OT passages. They still argued, however, that the best interpretation was the one that remained within church tradition.

For example, on the literal or historical level, the word *hand* was understood simply to be a member of the body, but it was also understood metaphorically to refer to the right hand of God—a reference to the power of God. In the Middle Ages, both interpretations for the word *hand* were considered as conveying the literal meaning of the biblical text. The metaphors did not diminish the truth of the text but supposedly elevated the reader for contemplating truth.

46. Of course, the Christian Platonists of Alexandria loved to use allegory, as well as the cabalistic interpretation of the Bible, which was later welcomed by Pico Della Merindola.

47. See Gerald Bray, *Biblical Interpretation: Past and Present* (Downers Grove, IL: InterVarsity Press, 1996), 129–57. Philip Edgcumbe Hughes, *Lefèvre: Pioneer of Ecclesiastical Renewal in France* (Grand Rapids: Eerdmans, 1985).

48. Allison, *Historical Theology*, 169–70.

The spiritual sense was then built atop the literal meaning. As mentioned previously, the spiritual sense had three further divisions. The allegorical meaning most often related the OT to the NT. For example, Abraham's offering of Isaac as a sacrifice pictured the Father's sacrifice of Christ. The moral sense provided instruction for life in the church. The anagogical sense literally meant "a climb" or "ascent upward." So the anagogical sense took statements of Scripture and tied them to eternal glory. For example, according to an anagogical interpretation, the physical city of Jerusalem is, in fact, the heavenly Jerusalem. The anagogical sense could be understood to constitute something of an eschatological meaning. For example, Hugh of Saint Victor said that the length of Noah's ark, three hundred cubits, was a sign of the cross, since that number is represented in Greek by the letter *T*, which is shaped like a cross. Guibert of Nogent (d. 1124) taught that the darkness on the face of the deep in Genesis is a "sign of the darkness of sin and worldliness which clouds men's minds, and in the ground which sprouts from the earth, a sign of the fruitfulness of the Word of God when worldly cares have been cast away."[49]

Scripture and Tradition. A distinction was made between Scripture and tradition as early as Irenaeus, as discussed previously in chapter 7. The patristic church asserted that both Scripture and tradition come from the Holy Spirit and thus failed to recognize the unique nature of the Scriptures.

In the early fourteenth century, the church began to address the precise relationship between the authority of Scripture and the church. There were two competing theories that, for lack of better terms, have been labeled Tradition I and Tradition II. Tradition I was the combination of Scripture and its historical interpretation—a view evident already in the patristic church. All theologians until the beginning of the fourteenth century held to Tradition I.[50]

Originating with Basil, Tradition II allowed for authoritative, extra-biblical, oral tradition.[51] Tradition II considered Scripture, ecclesiastical tradition, and church or canon law as equal in authority. Medieval

---

49. Hugh of Saint Victor, *Selected Spiritual Writings*, ed. Aelred Squire (New York: Harper & Row, 1962), 67.
50. Tradition I is not the Protestant notion of *sola scriptura*. See Oberman, *Harvest*, 376–77.
51. Ibid., 371–73. Asserting the existence of this tradition gave prominence to the bishops.

scholars debated whether this clarification of terms constituted a theological disintegration.[52] Despite arguments made in favor of Tradition II, from a Protestant perspective this expansion of authority marked a disintegration.

The debate over Scripture and authority was intimately intertwined with theological and political issues. Theologically, the discussion of authority centered on one fundamental sentence by Augustine: "I would not believe the gospel unless the authority of the Catholic Church moved me to that belief." This statement could be, and has been, interpreted as asserting church authority over the authority of Scripture. Politically, there was a struggle for power between Pope John XXII and the Holy Roman Emperor. The pope excommunicated the emperor and demanded that he relinquish his crown.

Marsilius of Padua (ca. 1275–1342) wrote a work titled *Defensor pacis*, in which he demonstrated the empire's independence from papal authority. *Defensor pacis* also established principles for determining the relationship between Scripture and the church.[53] Marsilius acknowledged the existence of divine and human law. He defined divine laws as those that bind the church, such as a statement from the NT. Human or church laws, on the other hand, were those given by the pope, cardinals, priests, or the church at large.

Marsilius decided that church or human laws must be seen in connection with the gospel and the persuasion of the Holy Spirit. Authority for human laws, like the authority that comes from human preaching, comes from Christ and the Holy Spirit. In a sense, the Holy Spirit gives the authority to the preaching, and that preaching then becomes part of the church.

Marsilius held that the NT was the final authority in the church and that the bishops held no higher power. He believed that Peter was not ranked above the other apostles and likely never even visited Rome. Marsilius thought the NT made room for clergy to own their own estates, and he was convinced that the pope held no bind-

---

52. Ibid., 374: "Yet it was certainly not a sign of late medieval disintegration that more and more doctors realized that they had to come to terms with a dual concept of tradition." See Heiko Augustinus Oberman, "*Quo Vadis, Petre?* Tradition from Irenaeus to Humani Generis," in *The Dawn of the Reformation: Essays in Late Medieval and Early Reformation Thought*, by Heiko Augustinus Oberman (Edinburgh: T&T Clark, 1986), 282.

53. Ganoczy and Scheld, *Hermeneutik Calvins*, 12.

ing authority or truth. He argued that instead the supreme authority was a church council.[54] Marsilius's work is studied to this day as an important treatise on political theory.

William of Ockham, who had been excommunicated by Pope John XXII, realized that both Traditions I and II were present in the church, and he clarified the discussion. Battle lines were drawn as to who had the highest authority to define extrascriptural tradition.[55]

Ockham was clear that there were certain criteria that had to be met for the general binding of church teaching. The criteria were: (1) that such teaching be given by revelation of God found in Scripture; (2) that the teaching has been assumed by the universal church; and (3) that, in combination with the first two general principles, it generally diminish the authority of the pope. Ockham held that the pope did not possess more authority than the gospel.[56] Depending on their confessional position, historians either hail or condemn Ockham's views.[57] Ockham's respect for the authority of Scripture has led some to identify his teaching with the *sola scriptura* stance of the Reformation, but doing so is reading something back into Ockham's teaching that simply was not there.[58]

In *De sensu litteralae sacrae scripturae*, Jean Gerson (1363–1429) maintained that the Scriptures ought to be the domain of the clergy.[59] He emphasized contemplation, moral renewal, and the practice of piety as a way of life.[60]

54. Walker, *History*, 264.

55. One could hold to Tradition II and be a curialist (the pope) or conciliarist (a council). See Oberman, *Harvest*, 376.

56. Others see Ockham as bowing to the authority of the church in his *Dialogus inter magistrum et discipulum*; see ibid., 366: "Holy Scripture contains all the truths of faith; a complementary unwritten tradition is transmitted through the apostles and their successors. . . .There is good reason to believe that Occam himself favored the second position [Tradition II]."

57. Ibid., 362–63.

58. Ibid., 361, 364. Wycliffe held to a theology of merit. See Heiko Augustinus Oberman, *The Dawn of the Reformation: Essays in Late Medieval and Early Reformation Thought* (Edinburgh: T&T Clark, 1986), 213.

59. Fritz Hahn, "Zur hermeneutik Gersons," *Zeitschrift für Theologie und Kirche* 51 (1954): 34–50.

60. Interestingly, it has been asserted but not substantiated by E. Gordon Rupp that "there are interesting resemblances between his preaching and that of the next great French preacher, John Calvin" (Rupp, "Christian Doctrine," 296). Important also is Gabriel Biel (1420–1495), who is known as the last of the great scholastics.

DOCTRINE OF HUMANITY

Pre-Fall Image of God. The doctrine of humanity suffered during this time because of the influence of a dualism between flesh and spirit introduced by Platonic philosophy. Historically, the church has wondered about the origin of the soul. Aquinas was a proponent of the idea that God creates each soul directly. He also argued that there was a difference between what he termed the *sensitive soul*, produced by the body, and an *intellectual soul*. According to Aquinas, God created the intellectual soul.[61] Aquinas also understood there to be a distinction in humanity between the image of God and the likeness of God. The image of God is found in the spirit, mind, or intellect; the likeness of God is found in the soul, emotions, and body. The image of God comprises reason, free will, moral agency, and civic virtues.[62]

Following Aristotle, Aquinas believed that the soul was the focus of the body—that is, the intellectual principle in a person, or soul, is the person's proper form. As a higher faculty, the soul should exercise natural control over the body.

In his prelapsarian state, Adam's reason was subject to God, his emotions were subject to reason, and his body was subject to his soul. But according to Aquinas, this original state was one of grace. Medieval theologians held that Adam was not created with freedom in righteousness, but Adam, as well as all creation, needed a supernatural gift, a *donum superadditum*, to continue in Edenic paradise.[63] God gave this gift, which was nothing short of likeness with God.

Post-Fall Image of God. Medieval theologians wrestled with the meaning of "original sin." A common understanding at the time was that original sin inherits the corruption of Adam's nature, not the actual sin of Adam. Original sin was construed as a habit by means of which people's lower nature dominates their reason. The central idea of original sin was not the corruption of human nature but the loss of the *donum superadditum*.[64]

---

61. Dependent on Aristotle, Aquinas said that the soul must not be nonsubsistent, for otherwise the soul would perish with the body. See Letham, *Systematic Theology*, 344.

62. Aquinas, *Summa theologiae* 1a.93–94, as cited by Letham, *Systematic Theology*, 329–30.

63. Horton, *Christian Faith*, 421–22.

64. Herman Bavinck, *Reformed Dogmatics*, ed. John Bolt (Grand Rapids: Baker Academic, 2003) (*RD*), 3:95–96.

In *Cur Deus Homo* Anselm used an analogy from feudalism to define the nature of sin: sin is a debt owed to God. To satisfy a wronged feudal lord, a thief must repay to the lord more than what he stole from him. Men and women owe God righteousness, or uprightness of the will.[65]

Aquinas defined a sinful act as a voluntary choice that violates reason or moral law. A sin departs from the proper end or goal, which is God. Viewing sin as a voluntary act, Aquinas rejected a genetic view of inheriting Adamic sin: humans are responsible for their own sins. He believed that, at birth, people inherit their human nature from their first parents—that all humans are born of Adam and "are as so many members of one body."[66]

Aquinas also developed the distinction between mortal and venial sin. The distinction went as follows: If ultimately the sin turns the sinner from the greatest goal—God—then it is a mortal sin and deserves eternal punishment; if, however, the sinner sins without turning away from God, then the sin is a venial sin and does not merit eternal punishment.[67]

ATONEMENT

Resurrection and Ascension. Aquinas argued that Christ's ascension affected believers' salvation in two ways: on the believers' part, and on Christ's part. For believers, the ascension secured faith, hope, love, and a deeper reverence for Christ, because in his ascension believers see Christ not as a man but as the God of heaven. For Christ, the ascension prepared for believers' ascension, initiated his intercession for believers, and paved the way for endowing spiritual gifts.[68]

Atonement Theory. The ancient church generally held to the ransom theory of the atonement. This theory asserts that Satan "owns" sinners and Christ must buy them back through his death on the cross.

Anselm recognized problems with this view but also held that God cannot simply forgive sin out of his mercy without reference to his

---

65. Allison, *Historical Theology*, 350–51.
66. Aquinas, *Summa theologiae* 1a2ae.81.1, as cited by Letham, *Systematic Theology*, 382–83.
67. Allison, *Historical Theology*, 351–52.
68. Aquinas, *Summa theologiae*, as cited by Allison, *Historical Theology*, 415–16.

honor. God had every right to damn all humanity and thereby satisfy his justice.

Anselm argued that man cannot pay the debt of sin. Even if he fasted and prayed, he would only give God his due. In addition, no sinner can make another sinner righteous. So humankind is helpless and needs a true God and man. Jesus Christ—the God-man—is the only one capable of offering satisfaction. His death was a sufficient and necessary satisfaction willingly offered to God. Christ thus obtained a reward, which he does not need. For believers to embrace Christ grants them satisfaction and redemption.[69]

Anselm's satisfaction theory made improvements over the prevalent ransom theology, but it was still defective. He argued incorrectly that the motivation for Christ's sacrificial work was to restore the number of lost angels to heaven—God needed to replace the fallen angels to restore original creation.

Abelard rejected both the ransom and satisfaction theories. He proposed instead the moral-influence theory, which argued that sinners must have their love for God stimulated—Christ's incarnation and death on the cross was love's crowning act and provided the instigation for sinners' love for God. For Abelard, there was no necessary connection between Christ's death and the forgiveness of sins; Christ's death was simply an extreme act of love that was designed to stimulate a response of love. Bernard of Clairvaux opposed Abelard and his moral-influence theory. As a result, the moral-influence theory was condemned in 1140 at the Council of Seno even before Abelard's death.

Aquinas developed Anselm's notion that Christ's work of infinite satisfaction could be applied to an infinite penalty. He called Christ's work a *supererogation*. But he mistakenly held that for the application of Christ's work, sinners must cooperate with that work. Believers' faith and love, combined with their faithful participation in the sacraments, unite them to Christ's atonement.[70]

Election and Reprobation. In *The Compatibility of God's Foreknowledge, Predestination, & Grace with Human Freedom*, Anselm

69. Allison, *Historical Theology*, 395–97.
70. Aquinas, *Summa theologiae* III.48.ii, as cited by Allison, *Historical Theology*, 398: "Christ's suffering works its effect in them to whom it is applied through faith, love, and the sacraments of faith."

demonstrated the compatibility of predestination and human freedom. Predestination occurs by necessity and includes the predestining of both good and evil. Anselm held that God predestines evil acts in the sense that he does not forcefully deliver people from temptation.

Anselm made a distinction between God's causing a thing by constraint or force and his causing a thing as a consequence of something else. God does not by force or constraint damn reprobates against their will. Instead, he damns reprobates as a consequence of their freely and willfully performed evil deeds. In the same way, the elect are not saved through force or against their will but as a consequence of their willful faith in Christ. Thus Anselm reasoned that predestination does not inhibit free choice.

Aquinas understood divine providence as leading people to two ends. Humanity, given its own nature, cannot be saved by that nature; it must be directed to salvation by another nature. Divine direction toward eternal life is referred to as *predestination*. Humanity can, however, sin and die according to its own nature, and God's permitting some to walk unhindered down this path is referred to as *reprobation*. Both decrees—predestination and reprobation—include divine willing.

Aquinas denied that God predestines people based on their divinely foreseen good works. To say that the basis of predestination is foreseen good works would be to confuse effect and cause: believers' good works are not the cause of their having been predested but an effect of it. God predestines in his mercy and reprobates in his justice.[71] Aquinas also distinguished between the decree of predestination and the actualization of the decree. The decree cannot be furthered by prayer, but prayer can assist in the actualization of the decree.[72]

Justification. Aquinas's doctrine of justification departed substantially from Augustinian theology, which underlined grace received by faith alone, with resulting good works.[73] Aquinas defined justification as a movement from the state of unrighteousness to the state of righteousness. Relying on Aristotle, Aquinas explained that every movement requires a mover. In the case of justification, the end goal—eternal

71. Allison, *Historical Theology*, 460.
72. Ibid., 460–61.
73. Ibid., 504–5.

life—is impossible for a sinful human nature to attain. Thus God's grace is the "mover" required to achieve the end goal.

While Aquinas emphasized the necessity of God's grace, he also called for human cooperation in salvation. God initiates the movement, or process, by infusing a sinner with grace, the sinner responds by moving toward God and away from sin, and then the sinner receives forgiveness. Aquinas taught that the infusion of grace makes the human nature righteous in a way that transcends forensic imputation, which is a mere declaration. God's love is so great that it produces an effect. There is a synergism between grace and human action. A justified person is not simply declared righteous in justification but is actually made righteous.[74]

Aquinas also believed that people can perform deeds that deserve merit. He developed the distinction between *condign* merits—true, worthy merits performed through grace—and *congruent* merits—human works merely reckoned as merits. He held that condign merit results in eternal life.[75]

Aquinas also developed the notion of purgatory. Purgatory was a place of temporal punishment for souls that needed cleansing from venial, forgivable sins. The living could help the dead trapped in purgatory through prayer, masses, and almsgiving. In addition, indulgences could be purchased to remit this temporal suffering. By the time of the Reformation, teaching on purgatory was standard in the Catholic Church.[76] Ultimately, the idea of purgatory derived from paganism.[77] While defenders of the notion of purgatory may provide various arguments in favor of the doctrine, it is nowhere recorded in Scripture.[78] Nevertheless, the Second Council of Lyon (1274) and the Council of Florence (1438) made the doctrine of purgatory part of the official teaching of the church.

Perseverance. Augustine taught that God grants to the saved perseverance in the faith. Aquinas, however, stressed habitual grace in addition to God's continuing grace. Habitual grace is infused through the

74. Ibid., 507: "Thus, justification was not confined to this life but could be completed after death."

75. Ibid., 505–6.

76. *RD* 4:609.

77. Ibid., 4:632.

78. Ibid., 4:633.

sacraments and nurtures the soul to will that which is good. Habitual grace, though, is unable to reform the will sufficiently to persevere. Aquinas believed that free will made perseverance a possibility but by no means a certainty. A freely willing person could, for example, give in to passions and choose that which is not right. Thus, according to Aquinas, free will renders perseverance possible, but not certain, for saved yet sinful humans.[79]

THE CHURCH

East–West Split. The split between the two worlds of Christendom hinged on the matter of church authority. The East refused to submit to the pope and disagreed with the Roman Catholic Church's push to amend the original Nicene Creed to reflect language of submission to the pope.

Furthermore, the Latin church claimed that the Holy Spirit worked in its midst and that it was the sole source of salvation. Pope Eugene IV (1383–1447) argued that the sacrament of confession must be engaged by a bishop, who, supposedly following Acts 8:14–18, gave the Holy Spirit by the laying on of hands. The Holy Spirit was linked to the Catholic Church's sacraments; thus, under the guidance of the pope, the church could not err in doctrine, and the Roman Catholic Church must be the sole standard of doctrine and practice.[80]

Church Government. Pope Innocent III (1198–1211) claimed superiority over the emperor. Medieval kings, however, did not affirm papal superiority. For example, King Edward I of England and King Philip IV of France opposed Pope Boniface VIII (1294–1303). In fact, Philip IV captured the pope and attempted to force his resignation. With urging from Philip IV, Pope Clement V moved the papal court to Avignon, France, where it remained for nearly seventy years. This time was one of papal decadence. In 1378 the church returned to Rome, only to split and see a contingent return to Avignon. As a result of the division, the church now had two seated popes. In 1409, the Council of Pisa deposed both the pope in Rome and the one in Avignon and elected

79. Allison, *Historical Theology*, 548–49.
80. Ibid., 440–41.

a third pope, thus giving the church three popes reigning simultaneously, with the third one located in Pisa. But the Council of Constance deposed all the papal claimants and elected a new pope in 1417, thus reuniting the papacy. This so-called Great Schism or Great Western Schism lasted from 1378 to 1417. This season of schism elevated the authority of councils, hence the term "conciliar movement" was applied to the period. But Pope Pius II ended the reform movement by delegitimating all appeals to councils.[81]

Ecclesiology Proper.[82] Aquinas defined the church as a "congregation of the faithful." The church has four attributes, or marks, and three divisions. The divisions are: on earth, the militant church; in heaven, the triumphant church; and in purgatory, the expectant church.[83] Aquinas opposed the church's increasing involvement in secular matters.

New ecclesiologies began to develop as a result of the church's increasing spiritual bankruptcy. For example, in his commentary on the Song of Songs, Bernard of Clairvaux argued that the book was an allegory of the church. Joachim of Fiore (1135–1202) developed an ecclesiology that was based on history. He divided history into three ages, each with forty-two generations. The first historical age was the time of the OT, which he considered the time of God the Father. The second age, that of the NT and the Son of God, was drawing to a close. He believed that the Antichrist was coming to unleash tribulation, and in preparation for that event God would raise up new preachers and hermit monks. Joachim believed the third historical age began in the sixth century with Saint Benedict. He understood the Franciscan and Dominican orders as corresponding to the two witnesses of Revelation 11:3–12 and taught that the third age would come to its consummation in 1260 with the return of Christ. The new church would heal the East–West split and supposedly usher in the conversion of the Jews.[84]

Three new ecclesiologies were ruled heretical. The first group comprised the Cathari, or Albigenses. Both a crusade and an inquisition were waged against them. They believed in two gods—a good god and

---

81. Ibid., 598–601.
82. There were also three new monastic orders: the Carmelites, Cluniacs, and Cistercians. The Carmelites, named after Mount Carmel in Israel, were mendicants.
83. *RD* 4:621.
84. Allison, *Historical Theology*, 572–75, 689–90.

an evil one. They denied Christ's humanity and bodily resurrection, and they advocated the exclusive use of the NT. The second unacceptable understanding of ecclesiology, from the perspective of the Roman Catholic Church, was that of the Waldensians. They refused to submit to bishops or acknowledge the pope as the head of the church, denied Mass for the dead and purgatory, and established their own competing hierarchy and ministry. The third "heretical" ecclesiology was that of the dissenters John Wycliffe and John Hus. Wycliffe still held to the ancient Augustinian understanding of the threefold church, comprised of those in heaven, on earth, and in purgatory. Nevertheless, he taught that membership in the visible Catholic Church in no way guaranteed salvation or true church membership. In fact, Wycliffe was convinced that the pope was the Antichrist. Wycliffe wrote on the necessity of pastors' holiness. He believed that pastors should live frugally and be dependent on the giving of the church. The main task of the pastor, according to Wycliffe, was to preach the gospel, which he considered more important than even prayer and the sacraments.[85] Building on Wycliffe's views, John Hus argued that the elect were still the elect, no matter what the Roman Catholic Church might say about them.[86] The church did not lie dormant in the midst of this opposition—she defended herself and claimed infallibility and indefectibility, even in the case of heretical popes.[87]

Baptism.[88] According to the Constitution of Padua in 1339, baptism could be celebrated at any time of the year, and parents were to present their children for baptism within eight days of birth. Hugh of Amiens challenged the legitimacy of infant baptism, but the church was not deterred. Anselm also supported infant baptism.

Aquinas taught that baptism could be by immersion, sprinkling, or pouring. He believed that the person's attitude toward the sacrament was more significant than its method. Aquinas connected baptism to

---

85. Ibid., 601.

86. Ibid.

87. Ibid., 576–77.

88. Charles Hodge, *Systematic Theology*, 3 vols. (London: Clarke, 1960), 3:498–508, 546–57; Edmund P. Clowney *The Church* (Leicester: InterVarsity Press, 1995), 287–89; Robert Lewis Dabney, *Systematic Theology* (Edinburgh: Banner of Truth, 1985), 726–817; John Bannerman, *The Church of Christ*, 2 vols. (Carlisle, PA: Banner of Truth, 2015), 1:232–33.

the remission of original sin. For him, the ceremony of adult baptism included reciting a catechism.[89]

Lord's Supper. In A.D. 831, Paschasius Radbertus wrote *On the Body and Blood of the Lord*, in which he argued that the bread, after proper consecration by the priest, was the body of Christ—it was born of Mary, crucified on the cross, and raised from the tomb. He believed the same was true of the wine—it became Christ's very blood. His argument was that Christ did not say that the bread and wine were mere figures of his body, so the assumption must be that they were truly the flesh and blood of Christ. The elements' reality is flesh and blood, and their figure is bread and wine.

Radbertus's view did not go unopposed. Writing a book with the same title, *On the Body and Blood of the Lord*, the Benedictine monk Ratramnus argued that Christ's body sits at the right hand of the Father and thus cannot not be present on the altar. Ratramnus did hold, however, that the faithful still receive Christ's body and blood mysteriously.[90] The church adopted Radbertus's view. In the eleventh century, that view was again opposed, this time by Berengar of Tours. In 1059 Berengar was defeated, forced to retract his teaching, and made to take an oath that the body and blood of Christ are "in truth" made present in the bread and wine of the Lord's Supper.[91] With the last opposition denounced, the Roman Catholic Church now elevated the Lord's Supper above the other sacraments out of the belief that Christ's actual body and blood are constituent parts of the sacrament.[92]

The church then began to wrestle with how this miracle of the Lord's Supper occurs practically. One view, referred to as *impanation*, argued that the substance remains the same and that the body and blood are truly there but hidden. The church rejected this notion.

The Catholic Church taught that the nature and substance of the elements are transformed in the celebration of the Lord's Supper—the bread and wine cease to exist as such. The understanding was that the word *substance*, following Aristotle, refers to the essence or defining nature of a thing. The word *accident* is the characteristic of something as

---

89. Allison, *Historical Theology*, 621–23.
90. Ibid., 641.
91. Clowney, *Church*, 287.
92. Allison, *Historical Theology*, 642.

it is perceived by the senses—its appearance, smell, and texture. Hence in the Lord's Supper, the accidents remain the same, but the substance is transformed into Christ's body and blood. In 1140, this substantial change was called *transubstantiation* and, in 1215 at the Fourth Lateran Council, was accepted as the official teaching of the Roman Catholic Church.[93] Aquinas was the prominent proponent of transubstantiation.[94]

The council also decreed that, once each year, people should first confess their sins and then partake of the Eucharist. In the thirteenth century, people were given only the bread during the Lord's Supper. The cup was withheld to avoid spilling the wine and thus desecrating the blood of Christ. The church justified its withholding of the cup via the doctrine of concomitance, which stated that the full presence of Christ was fully in each element. Bonaventure argued that since Christ cannot be divided, the whole Christ is indivisibly present in each element. Hence the church's argument was that by not offering the cup, the church was not withholding the full presence of Christ.

Wycliffe strongly opposed the doctrine of transubstantiation and, in particular, the idolatry it bred: priests claimed to possess the power to transform bread into the body of Christ, and people worshipped the consecrated bread.[95] Sadly, even as theological advances were made in the Middle Ages, the doctrine of the sacraments declined.[96]

ESCHATOLOGY

Individual. The Roman Catholic Church teaches that heaven is for those who are perfectly pure. The imperfectly pure, or those with

93. Clowney, *Church*, 288: "Thomas Aquinas drew his solution from his understanding of Aristotle, and the distinction between substance and accident. Cows may come in different colors, sizes and shapes, but the differing outward aspects are accidental. They may change radically, yet the animal still remains substantially a cow. Using that distinction, Thomas could maintain that the Eucharist was really and substantially the body of Christ, even though the accidental appearances remained those of bread and wine."

94. Aquinas, *Summa theologiae*, III.75.iv., as cited by Allison, *Historical Theology*, 644–45: "For the whole substance of the bread is changed into the whole substance of Christ's body, and the whole substance of the wine into the whole substance of Christ's blood. Thus, this is not a formal, but a substantial conversion; nor is it a kind of natural movement."

95. Allison, *Historical Theology*, 641–46.

96. Herman Bavinck, *Gereformeerde Dogmatiek* IV (Kampen: Kok, 1911), 510, 524: "The development of the doctrine of the sacraments indicates that the further in time they went the further from the Scriptures they went" (my translation).

venial sins, must undergo cleansing. That cleansing would last as long as the purification required.

The intermediate state developed into the notion of gradual purification, which developed into the notion of purgatory. The concept of purgatory continued into the Middle Ages with the pope's being given jurisdiction over it.[97] The *limbus patrum*, "fringe of the fathers," was where the OT saints waited for Christ, thus supposedly explaining his descent to hell.[98] The church also taught that on the outskirts of hell existed a place called the *limbus infantum*, where all unbaptized babies live—even babies of non-Christian parents. The Catholic Church has still not defined the *limbus infantum* with precision.[99]

The concept of purgatory is a natural outflow of the Roman Catholic doctrine of justification. According to the Catholic Church, justification is the infusion of supernatural grace that enables the Christian to do good works and earn eternal life.[100] The idea of purgatory arose from the church's need to answer the question of the destination of deceased believers whose lives have not yet been purified.

The Roman Catholic Church maintains different categories for veneration of a being or person. God is adored (*latria*), Mary deserves *hyperdulia*, or extra veneration, the saints are venerated, or offered *dulia*, and the relics of the saints deserve religious devotion. The cult of the martyrs began as a practical celebration of the communion of saints.[101] The invocation of saints began as requests for their assistance but soon developed into veneration of them.[102] The veneration of the saints included prayer, fasting, vigils, feasts, gifts, pilgrimage, and procession. The purpose of venerating the saints consists in obtaining favor and benefit from God.[103]

General. The ancient and medieval church generally held to amillennialism. The church also believed in a coming, renewed universe. Aquinas defended the notion of the renewal of man and his environ-

---

97. Louis Berkhof, *Systematic Theology* (Carlisle, PA: Banner of Truth, 1972), 680–86.
98. Ibid., 681.
99. Ibid., 687.
100. *RD* 4:634.
101. Ibid., 4:621.
102. Ibid., 4:627: "The saints are objects of religious veneration (*cultus religiosus*), even if it is not called worship (*latria*) but veneration (*dulia*)."
103. Ibid., 4:622.

ment from Scripture, reason, and correspondence. In this renewed world the sun and moon will no longer move, but they will be brighter. Further, the church taught that on the new earth there will be no more animals or plants.[104]

Final Judgment. In the Middle Ages, the view of eternal punishment held that it is excruciating; it involves the pain of the loss of the beatific vision and the constant pain of the senses. And fear of eternal punishment motivates people to stop sinning, serves God's justice, and stimulates gratitude.[105] The fear and terror of eternal punishment were manifested in the art and literature of the time—in Michelangelo's fresco *The Last Judgment*, Dante Alighieri's narrative poem *The Divine Comedy*, and John Milton's great and classic book *Paradise Lost*.[106]

Aquinas responded to a number of objections regarding eternal judgment—objections such as since sin is temporal, so also should punishment be temporal, and since the sin of wicked people is so great, they should simply be annihilated. Aquinas modified and used Aristotle's argument that punishment relates to the dignity of the one offended: since God's majesty is infinite, punishment must be infinite in duration, for it cannot be infinite in intensity.

THEOLOGICAL METHOD

Bridge Builders and Burners. In the patristic period, some sought to build bridges between Christianity and pagan philosophy, and some opposed any such synthesis. This healthy opposition to synthesis was devastatingly absent during medieval times. As a whole, thinkers during the Middle Ages moved to unite a Christian view of the world and life with unbelieving thought.

Pseudo-Dionysius sought to reconcile Neoplatonism and the teachings of Christianity. As a result of his dependence on Neoplatonism, Pseudo-Dionysius had a weak doctrine of the Trinity. While he never denied the existence of three persons in the Trinity, he emphasized their unity in seeking to find the "One" behind the Trinity. This emphasis was similar to the teaching of Plotinus but found little support in Scripture.

104. Allison, *Historical Theology*, 726–27.
105. Ibid., 708–9.
106. Ibid., 709–11.

Pseudo-Dionysius, following Neoplatonism further, considered God to be so transcendent that he was ultimately unknowable—believers, by means of the *via negativa*, were reduced to knowing what God is not. So the solution to how to know God was not through God's self-revelation in Scripture and in the person of Jesus Christ but through mystical contemplation.

Boethius also introduced Greek philosophy, specifically Neoplatonism, into his thinking. In particular, he applied philosophical categories to theology, and these philosophical categories became a hallmark of medieval theology. His writings contributed to the construction of what would later be termed "theological science."

Early medieval learning pushed theologians to consider new methods of organization, which resulted in scholasticism. Scholasticism is not a theology but a methodology. Medieval theology developed alongside the rise of scholasticism. Abelard's dialectical theological method, as well as his attempts to synthesize vast amounts of teaching into a systematic theology, bridged the gap between early scholasticism's preoccupation with individual questions and the great comprehensive surveys that were to come in the next century. The massive works of Aquinas and Lombard are monuments of vast theological learning.

In addition to the quest for theological structure that occurred during this time, there were also explorations of differing methodological approaches. Relative to theological method, Anselm acted as an intermediate figure between Augustine, who argued for faith first and then reason, and Aquinas, who advocated for reason apart from faith for as long as possible, then finally the supplementation of reason with faith.

Christian scholarship in the university became heavily influenced by naturalism, which fit well with the era of intellectual confidence and social growth. In many ways, naturalism was useful to the church in its attempts to build institutional structures based on natural law. Nevertheless, naturalism had problems of its own. It had no ability to penetrate the mysteries of nature, determine the origin of the world or the meaning of eternity, or even solve questions concerning human behavior.

In conclusion, the medieval theological method was brilliant and vast. But this method was built on a synthesis of biblical thought and philosophical notions. Only time would tell the damage this unsteady foundation would cause.

Conclusion to Part 3. This third part, called *The Church and the World*, described a new era, which followed the toppling of the peace of Rome. In God's providence, the illiterate invaders of Rome learned not only letters but also the saving message of Jesus Christ. The victors attempted to build new empires atop the ashes of Rome. These new kingdoms would develop into the feudal system—an economic and political system that would continue throughout this entire era. Western society faced the rise of Islam as Europe faced Muslim invaders. This struggle resulted in yet another defining moment—the Crusades.

This section also tracked the development of the medieval church until the end of the thirteenth century by exploring early medieval philosophy, the centrality of the university and monastery, the role of Scripture in the life of the church, and many of the prominent theologians and thinkers who left their mark on church history. The final chapter traced medieval reflections across the doctrines of systematic theology. While theological advances were being made, the foundation of the church was beginning to rot from philosophical paganism. The need for a reformation was becoming increasingly apparent.

KEY TERMS

> a priori argument
> a posteriori argument
> *via negativa*
> beatific vision
> *filioque*
> mechanical theory of inspiration
> satisfaction theory of the atonement
> purgatory

STUDY QUESTIONS

1. What are the arguments for the *via negativa*?
2. Can you give biblical arguments for the *filioque* clause? Should the Western and Eastern church have split over this word?
3. Should church tradition play any role at all in scriptural interpretation?

4. Are there multiple senses to Scripture? What do you think of the fourfold sense?
5. Would Adam necessarily have fallen into sin?
6. How do you evaluate Aquinas's doctrine of justification?
7. Can you explain how Christ is truly present in the sacraments?

RESOURCES FOR FURTHER STUDY

The Medieval Period produced two massive systematic theologies and a number of treatises on specialized topics. Aquinas's *Summa theologiae* is huge in extent! Peter Lombard's *The Sentences* is also gigantic. Both authors have much to offer for the mature theologian.

Aquinas, Thomas. *Summa Theologiae: A Concise Translation*. Edited by Timothy McDermott. Notre Dame: Christian Classics, 1989.

Lombard, Peter. *The Sentences, Books 1–4*. Translated by Giulio Silano. 4 vols. Toronto: Pontifical Institute of Mediaeval Studies, 2007–2010.

PART 4

Post Tenebras Lux

11

Crisis among God's People

POLITICS IN GENERAL

Pre-Reformation. The Hundred Years' War between France and England ended in 1453. Before that time, political society in Europe existed in the form of a feudal monarchy. In feudal society, the king's vassals owned important public powers as their legal right—a right that was usually inherited. This division of power constituted a central characteristic of feudal society. In this system, the king did not hold the type of absolute power as, for instance, the emperor of Rome had held earlier; rather, the king was the chief lord among a number of lords.

The situation changed in 1453. There was a rapid building of the state, and by the end of the Habsburg–Valois Wars with the Peace of Cateau-Cambrésis in 1559, the political society of Europe consisted of sovereign states.[1] These Renaissance-era kings of France, Spain, and England were referred to as "new monarchs" who ruled over new monarchies. What makes their rule new and different from that of previous regimes is a matter of academic debate. The following characteristics constitute the generally accepted understanding of the new monarchies.

The first characteristic is that internal diversities were eliminated so that the lesser nobles were now very much subjected to the sovereign.[2] Second, law emanated from the sovereign. Two Latin statements

1. Steven Ozment, *The Age of Reform, 1250–1550* (New Haven: Yale University Press, 1980), 248–58.
2. Geoffrey R. Elton, *Reformation Europe: 1517–1559* (New York: Harper & Row, 1963), 297.

describe the political situation as it applied to law: *Princeps legibus solutus est* (meaning that the prince is not bound by the law), and *Quicquid principi placuit legis habet vigorem* (meaning that the will of the prince has the force of law).[3]

Another characteristic of the new monarchies was their keeping of a permanent mercenary army. In the feudal system, the lesser lords had the legal right to command their own armies and wage war; now in the new monarchies, that right was partially or primarily lost. This loss of military strength greatly weakened the influence of the lesser lords.

A final defining aspect of the new monarchies was the development of various financial institutions.[4] Since warfare was expensive and nearly constant, princes and nobles had to raise vast sums of money continuously. Their approach to fundraising was threefold: they drew rent money from the royal domain; levied taxes directly—the most important means; and borrowed from newly developing financial institutions. Because of declining value from rental income, the role of rent money became less important than was direct taxation. Direct taxation came from customs duties and sales taxes that were placed on a multitude of commodities.

The custom of royal borrowing was slightly different from modern definitions of borrowing. Quite often borrowing consisted of the king's asking for a gift of a certain amount from wealthier citizens of the larger cities.[5] For example, when King Henry VIII of England went to war with France in the early 1520s, he asked for gifts from the clergy, and the most prominent and very wealthy Cardinal Wolsey "donated" a huge amount of money for the cause.[6] When a prince or church noble gave such a gift, he did so at his own behest, however personally reluctant he may feel.

Taxation. The practice of taxation during this time also deserves special attention. Establishing taxation by the king without the consent

---

3. The political theorist Jean Bodin (1530–1596), while living in the Reformation era, still defined sovereignty as "the power to make law." Only natural law and divine law bound a sovereign prince. See Eugene F. Rice, *The Foundations of Early Modern Europe 1460–1559* (New York: Norton, 1970), 93.

4. Ozment, *Age of Reform*, 182–90.

5. Rice, *Foundations*, 100–102.

6. Jasper Ridley, *Statesman and Saint: Cardinal Wolsey, Sir Thomas More and the Politics of Henry VIII* (New York: Viking Press, 1983), 116–17.

of the nobles has been considered by some to be the defining factor in the transition from feudal monarchy to modern monarchy. One of the best examples of that transition occurred in France during the reign of King Charles VII, who ruled from 1422 to 1461.

The Estates General, which was similar to the English Parliament, was established in France as a representative assembly that gave consent for taxation. Because of his added power and the nation's financial emergency, King Charles wrung out of them recognition that the crown needed a constant income. The immediate circumstance from which this concession was born was the termination of the Hundred Years' War. Funds were desperately needed to pay for expensive artillery and to compensate the soldiers who had fought. But once the principle that the king could constantly seek funds became established, that privilege continued to be invoked long after the immediate crisis of war was over. Of course, the change did not come overnight. In theory, the Estates General still had to give consent for taxation, but in practice there arose an expectation and demand from the king for a certain amount of money each year.

Basic economics tells us that there are two traditional forms of taxation. The first is a standard percentage for all people no matter their income—for example, a state sales tax. The other is a progressive tax—for example, a federal income tax. With progressive taxation, as an individual's income rises, the proportion of his taxes supposedly rises.[7]

A third form of taxation at this time was an inverse progressive tax. That is, the person who was least able to pay taxes paid proportionately the most tax. In an aristocratic state, the few have the majority of power, and the wealthiest aristocrats or nobles had the most power. They were therefore able to manipulate the government to their greatest financial advantage by avoiding heavy taxation themselves and placing the burden on the masses.[8] In France this tax was collected primarily from the provincial estates that were geographically farthest from the crown and had proportionally less power. With the increasing strength

7. For example, those with an annual income of more than one million dollars (seminary professors and the like) pay a much higher percentage of income tax than do common workers.

8. Rice, *Foundations*, 102–4. In France this tax, called the *taille*, became further established during the reigns of Kings Francis I (1494–1547) and Henry II (1519–1559).

of the king and his army, and with the decreasing military power of the provincial nobles, there was little the provincial governors could do to protect their income. Now that we have a picture of the general political and economic structure in Europe as a whole, we need to examine some specific countries.

England. There are a few peculiarities about England's politics that make its history different from the history of some of the other European countries. One fact that contributed to England's political solidarity is that the younger sons of English nobility did not inherit the privileges and estates of their fathers; rather, these younger sons become commoners. This situation created a constantly growing middle class, some of the members of which were well educated. Suddenly, with the descent of the nobles' sons to the middle class and the rise of some of the serfs to the middle class, a tremendous consolidation of class and power occurred within the country.

A critical development in English history prior to King Henry VIII's reign was an uprising in 1497 because of high taxes. This uprising was quelled, and as a result of the successful subjugation of the taxed classes, "England entered the sixteenth century as a compact nation."[9]

Spain. Although Spain was relatively immune from and resistant to Reformation thought, its history will shed light on the cultural setting of the time. Spain had for centuries been under Muslim domination. In the beginning of the tenth century very few of Spain's states were under Christian rule. But from then until the dawn of the Reformation, slowly the Christians began recovering their land. At the time of the Reformation there were within Spain five main states: Castile, Aragon, Portugal, Navarre, and Granada. Granada, which comprised only about 2 percent of the country's geographical area, was at that time the sole Muslim state.

There were exceedingly great periods of warfare in Spain, and attendant with that warfare came personal violence and lawlessness. Lands were wrested from the Muslims via two methods: (1) direct involvement by the crown—when lands were won, they reverted directly to the sovereign; and (2) the winning of the land by individual nobles. These private nobles made warfare their life's work and became known

9. Thomas M. Lindsay, *History of the Reformation*, 2 vols. (Edinburgh: T&T Clark, 1963), 1:20–22.

as the Grand Masters. At times their power may have overshadowed that of the sovereign.

To ensure law and order in the realm, solidify her own holdings, and protect the people, Queen Isabella (1451–1504) instituted a group called the Holy Brotherhood. This group was made up of commoners and was similar to a mounted police; they were a cavalry force consisting of one horseman for each one hundred houses. This brotherhood had their own judges, and these police themselves performed the sentences imposed on criminals. The legal power of the brotherhood actually exceeded that of the nobility; when the brotherhood made a decision, the nobles were not legally able to overrule it. The queen's idea was brilliant not only because it solidified her holdings and power but also because the brotherhood enjoyed tremendous popular support—it effectively secured the towns from crime. With the level of popular support so high, the nobles' power was gradually whittled down.

Furthermore, Queen Isabella also unilaterally began to strip the wealthy Spanish church of many of its riches. In combination with her marriage with Ferdinand of Aragon, nearly all of Spain was united under their rule, with the brotherhood's continuing as an institution and serving as Spain's standing army.[10]

Within Spain, there was an increasing desire for national unity and for religion to be used as the means to that unity. But the presence there of competing religions worked against that ideal. Jews, Christians, and a sizable group of Muslims all lived in Spain. So in 1478 Pope Sixtus IV sponsored the establishment of an inquisition in that land.[11] The Jews were compelled to become Christians, and within about twenty-five years virtually all the Muslims in Spain had become nominal Christians, though it would take another century for the presence of Islam to be eradicated.

After Isabella's death in 1504 there was a period of anarchy, which was not suppressed until the reign of Holy Roman Emperor Charles V. Fortunately, Charles V's troubles in Spain will aid the Reformation in Germany.

Italy. Although Italy and Germany were vastly different in some respects, they shared a common lack of political unification. Many of

10. Ozment, *Age of Reform*, 184.
11. Lindsay, *Reformation*, 1:598–600.

their politicians thought there were to be two supreme authorities in the world: the pope as the ultimate spiritual authority, and the emperor as the ultimate political authority. Though the emperor was at least in principle the head of the state in Germany, this type of thinking kept both Germany and Italy from having one single ruler over the nation. In Italy, the presence of the pope in Rome, with his claims of political sovereignty, made the emergence of one supreme political ruler all the more difficult.

Italy was divided into five states. In the north were Venice, Milan, and Florence. In the center was the pope's sovereign territory as its own political entity. No king or noble had any power there. In the south was Naples. While it may appear strange to us today, the papal state in that time was viewed by the rest of the world as merely one temporal power among other temporal Italian powers.[12]

PROSPECTS FOR CHRISTIANITY IN A.D. 1500

Crisis. In 1500, Christian missions in the Far East were collapsing. Islamic power was growing. The Turks were constantly hammering at the gates of Vienna on the east of the empire. Skepticism and unbelief were rampant. In general, the earlier pillars of religion and political power were crumbling. Political turmoil continued in Europe, which experienced a tremendous rise in nationalism. The Holy Roman Empire was becoming less powerful, and the individual nations, with the exception of Germany and France, were becoming more powerful. Individual powerful cities were also becoming increasingly important in the overall economic scheme. Many cities boasted great productivity among their handworkers and artisans. The merchants in northern Italy and northern Germany became powerful groups.

Economic and social changes abounded. The social classes began to experience shifts in identity and constituency. The power of the nobility had greatly declined, and discontent reigned among the lower nobility and peasantry. The church was not helpful in allaying this discontent.

---

12. See Rice, *Foundations*, 114–16. That the papal states were viewed simply as sovereign territories proved significant for Italy's political history. It reflected the treatment of those papal states by other Italian powers, especially during the reigns of Alexander VI (1492–1503), Julius II (1503–13), and Leo X (1513–21).

One of the most significant developments in human history was the invention of printing, which occurred in the West around 1450. Printing spread rapidly and broadly and revolutionized the known world. One of the most famous products of the innovation appeared in 1456, with the printing of Gutenberg's famous Latin text of the Bible.[13] The leap forward in technology that accompanied the printing press is comparable to the digital revolution in recent decades—for example, I composed my doctoral dissertation on an electric typewriter, and now we transmit texts on the internet and download them directly to our smartphones.

Portions of the Bible began to appear in vernacular translations. Contrary to popular belief today, Martin Luther was not the first person to give Germany a Bible in the vernacular—a complete but inferior edition appeared before he began his great work. Other, better translations were available to people in the Netherlands. Circulation of vernacular Bibles was not wide, owing partly to the church's opposition to such translations. For example, there was opposition in England to Wycliffe's translation, as well as to his teaching in general. Nevertheless, the invention of printing formed a strong pillar for the later foundation of the Reformation.

Forerunners of the Reformation. Certain men of the age are classified as forerunners of the Reformation.[14] These men were, in general, located in northwest Germany and the Rhine Valley. While there are a number of noteworthy examples of such forerunners, we will limit our focus to four of them.

13. Nicholas R. Needham, *2,000 Years of Christ's Power*, vol. 3, *Renaissance and Reformation* (London: Grace Publications, 2005), 25.

14. Heiko Augustinus Oberman, *Forerunners of the Reformation* (Philadelphia: Fortress, 1981), 1–20. Academic discussion of the notion of forerunners of the Reformation requires historiographical nuancing. A forerunner, in contrast to a humanist, advances Protestant teaching. Judging continuity or discontinuity from the Middle Ages to the Reformation depends on the definition of the term *forerunner*. Karl Ullmann's nineteenth-century, two-volume work argued that medieval Christianity became a false religion of law, and Luther's reformation was one of the grace of Christ with no connection to the religion of medieval times. Ullmann was critiqued in his own century, and the critique continued into the twentieth. Three German scholars dominated early twentieth-century historiography: Adolf von Harnack, Friedrich Loofs, and Reinhold Seeburg. Heiko Oberman stood alone at the end of the twentieth century in late medieval and Reformation historiography. He wanted to avoid two extremes: confessional blinders and an unreasonable predilection for discontinuity. Oberman served for a number of years on the governing board of the Meeter Center for Calvin Studies in Grand Rapids, Michigan.

John Pupper of Goch (1400–1475) was trained by the Brethren of the Common Life, founded by the Dutch deacon Gerard Groote (1340–1384), and functioned as a sort of prior in an Augustinian nunnery. He held to the supreme authority of the Bible and maintained that the church had introduced artificial distinctions among classes of people in order to further itself. Pupper sought to eliminate any double standard of morality between the clergy and laity.[15]

John Ruchrath of Wesel (d. 1479) was a preacher at the great cathedrals of Mainz and Worms and was later a professor at the fairly new University of Basel. Ruchrath and Pupper were similar in their views, though Ruchrath was the more popular of the two. He taught that salvation was by grace; God predestined those who would be saved; and even excommunication by the church could not thwart God's will. His teaching would be classified as *antisacerdotal* in that he rejected indulgences and the so-called "treasury of merit." He held to the authority of Scripture over human opinion.[16] Ruchrath was tried for heresy and condemned; he then recanted publicly and was sentenced to prison, where he died.

Wessel Gansfort (1420–1489) was associated with the devotional movement of Thomas à Kempis.[17] Gansfort was an excellent and driven student who studied Greek and Hebrew on his own initiative. He studied in Cologne, Louvain, and then Paris, where he also instructed.

Luther later published Gansfort's writings and spoke very highly of them. Gansfort's work showed that he held to justification by faith alone; predestination of individual believers; the priesthood of all believers; the infallibility and supreme authority of the Bible; the existence of the invisible church; and the fact that the Holy Spirit, not the

---

15. Luther published fragments of the works of Pupper of Goch; see Oberman, *Forerunners*, 18. See also Heiko Augustinus Oberman, *The Dawn of the Reformation: Essays in Late Medieval and Early Reformation Thought* (Edinburgh: T&T Clark, 1986), 139.

16. His position was complicated. On the one hand, he said: "As long as it seems to me that the pope or theologians or any school asserts a position contradicting the truth of Scripture, my concern for scriptural truth obliges me to give it first place. . . . But in every case I owe more respect to canonical Scripture than to human assertions, regardless of who holds them." Yet he also said: "I know very well that Scripture alone is not a sufficient rule of faith. I know that some things which were not written were handed down by the Apostles and that all these teachings ought to be received into the rule of faith just like Scripture. These two things, together with what can logically be deduced from them, constitute the only rule of faith" (Oberman, *Forerunners*, 99–100, 105).

17. See the analysis of à Kempis in the previous chapter.

church, bestows salvation. Gansfort rejected the Catholic doctrine of the keys to the kingdom and its penitential system for the absolving of sins. He also showed the errors in the Vulgate to the residents of a nunnery! Gansfort taught on the theological faculty at Heidelberg until his views got him into trouble, whereupon he left.

The fourth important forerunner of the Reformation was Rudolph Agricola (1444–1485). His best-known work is the *De dialectica inventione libri tres*.[18] In general terms, one of the objects of his writing was to turn aside older methods of teaching and produce something that would be more meaningful for contemporary university students.[19] The means of making that change was Agricola's development of the *topoi*, or "commonplaces." This change moved away from Aristotelian classification, which depended on categories or predicaments. These *topoi* or loci were the key notions of any given subject.[20] Although perhaps not Agricola's intent, the result of his work was a gradual methodological change in university instruction. The topics now absorbed the other logical disciplines and were able to embrace the entire intellectual process. Studying the topics became the most important way of studying a matter.[21]

Humanism, Renaissance, and Humanist Reformers. Italy was the scene for the rebirth of European culture and society.[22] The Italian Renaissance had repercussions in Germany primarily through a migration of teachers. The Renaissance as a comprehensive development was not an elevation of autonomic man against God, nor was it in general an anti-Christian movement.[23] The Renaissance in its simplest expression was a current to recapture the sources of Western civilization. The presence of paganism was observable in Italy, but there were also some Christian elements spurring the developments of the day.[24]

18. He also wrote the *De formando studio*.

19. A practical consideration of this new approach was also that it was easily printed by the new printers.

20. Walter J. Ong, *Ramus, Method, and the Decay of Dialogue: From the Art of Discourse to the Art of Reason* (Cambridge: Harvard University Press, 1958), 104. Agricola was not the first one to move away from the categories. Boethius's *Commentaries* and *On Topical Differences* had earlier modified the Aristotelian system.

21. Ong, *Decay of Dialogue*, 106.

22. Needham, *2,000 Years*, 3:20–21.

23. Ozment, *Age of Reform*, 17.

24. Ibid., 305–7.

Though linked to the changes in Italy, the German Renaissance was different in kind. The reason for the difference was rather basic: if the cry of the Renaissance was *ad fontes*, "to the sources," where would a German turn? The Germans had no written language during the heyday of the classics and therefore had no original sources from that period—so they turned to the Bible. The German Renaissance was, according to most, more biblical than classical in its emphasis, and it also tended to be more scholarly than was the Renaissance in other countries.[25] This latter trend was demonstrated in the tremendous increase of German universities established at the time. There was also concern in Germany and northern Europe for moral improvement combined with a yearning to get behind the problems of medieval theology. This goal set up inherent tensions, which resulted in fights between university faculties.

Humanist studies played a crucial role in the Reformation.[26] One class of humanist can be termed the "humanist reformer." As a group, these scholars advocated a reform of both life and morality, but not of doctrine.[27]

One of the first humanist reformers was the German-born Johann Reuchlin (1455–1522). A child prodigy, he wrote a Latin lexicon at the age of twenty. Also skilled in the biblical languages, he wrote both a Greek and the first printed Hebrew grammar.[28] Reuchlin became a lawyer and a diplomat rather than a theologian and at the time of his death was a university professor.

As a Hebrew scholar, Reuchlin attempted to stem the rife anti-Semitism of his day. As a result, he fell into controversy with Johannes Pfefferkorn, a converted Jew. Pfefferkorn was on a mission to suppress Judaism and sought to destroy all copies of the Talmud. He persuaded Emperor Maximilian I to decree that all Jews had to submit their books to government authorities.[29] The complexities of the situation resulted in a prolonged battle of pamphlets between Pfefferkorn and Reuchlin.

25. Elton, *Reformation Europe*, 283–84.
26. Ozment, *Age of Reform*, 290–317.
27. See Oberman, *Dawn*, 1–38.
28. His *Rudiments of Hebrew* was published in 1506.
29. Ozment, *Age of Reform*, 303; Needham, *2,000 Years*, 3:29.

Reuchlin's views were not well received by some of the authorities of the day. The conservative faculty of Cologne accused him of heresy. In 1520, Pope Leo X condemned one of his statements as heretical. Reuchlin also found himself at odds with some of the more prominent reformers. Though Melanchthon was his student, Reuchlin opposed both Melanchthon and Luther.

In tracing the progression of humanist reform to England, one discovers several reformers who were influential in the humanist revolution. John Colet (ca. 1467–1519) studied from 1493 to 1496 under the leaders of the movement in Italy. In England, he lectured at Oxford on the Greek texts of the Pauline epistles. He was then in 1504 dean of Saint Paul's in London, where he founded the famous Cathedral School. From his pulpit, he denounced corruption in the church. Because his attacks were both well founded and accurate, he was cited for a heresy trial—but the church's citation was overruled by King Henry VIII.[30]

Sir Thomas More (1478–1535) was a devout layman and a famous humanist.[31] More was trained in law at Oxford. He was an enthusiast for the Greek language and in particular for Paul's epistles. Ironically, however, his writings are not known for emphasizing Scripture. Further, More opposed the Reformation. Eventually, he became chancellor of the British realm during the reign of King Henry VIII. In the controversy between Henry and the pope regarding Henry's desire to divorce his wife, More sided with the pope; consequently, he lost his life under Henry's sentence of death.

More is most famous for his great literary production *Utopia*, dating to 1516. Purported to be a place discovered by a Portuguese explorer, Utopia was a land where everyone was treated alike; all property was held in common; the work day consisted of six hours; there was perfect family discipline; and all religions that maintained belief in providence, virtue, and immortality were tolerated. In Utopia priests were allowed to marry, and all images of God were prohibited.

The humanist movement also flourished in France—but there it looked different due to the country's academic centralization. Except

30. Needham, *2,000 Years*, 3:32.
31. See Richard C. Gamble, review of *Statesman and Saint: Cardinal Wolsey, Sir Thomas More and the Politics of Henry VIII*, by Jasper Ridley, *WTJ* 45, no. 2 (Fall 1983): 455–56.

for the University of Paris, there were no academic institutions capable of lending sufficient intellectual impetus to the movement of French humanism. For example, while the study of Hebrew and Greek had been introduced there, the strongly intellectual school was still under the domination of Rome and thus highly controlled.

John Major (1469–1550) was a Scottish theologian who taught in Paris. It is possible that Major taught John Calvin when Calvin was there. Major did teach Erasmus, and certainly Major's thought was available to Calvin while Calvin was in that great city of learning. Some argue that Major pushed for a movement back toward the authority of the church.[32] He responded negatively to Luther's judgment concerning the weightiness of Scripture in comparison to church tradition.

Despite the lack of push for reform from the universities, there were individual teachers of Greek who forwarded the French Renaissance movement.[33] One of these teachers was Faber Stapulensis, also known as Jacques Lefèvre d'Étaples (1455/60–1536), a widely educated scholar and a contemporary of Reuchlin. Lefèvre was greatly interested in the Greek NT and theology in general. He desired to maintain the absolute supremacy and authority of Scripture and so attempted the formulation of a theology based directly on the Bible. In his writings, Lefèvre advocated what would become the Reformation doctrine of justification by faith, though he retained a belief in purgatory. In 1509 he published a Psalter and in 1512 a reform-leaning exegesis of the Pauline epistles. He also translated the Bible into French.[34]

Lefèvre was a rather timid man; nonetheless, he criticized as abusive the Catholic teaching on fasting, celibacy, and merit from good works as a means of attaining salvation. He even took his stand against the sacrificial conception of the Mass. His theology proved him to be too anti-Catholic for Paris, and in 1525 he was forced to flee to Strasbourg.

---

32. The argument is made by Alexander Ganoczy and Stefan Scheld in *Die Hermeneutik Calvins: Geistesgeschichtliche Voraussetzungen und Grundzüge* (Wiesbaden: Steiner, 1983). Thomas F. Torrance, in *The Hermeneutics of John Calvin*, ed. A. I. C. Heron and Iain R. Torrance (Edinburgh: Scottish Academic Press, 1988), 36, argues for John Major's influence on Calvin.

33. Needham, *2,000 Years*, 3:31.

34. Philip Edgcumbe Hughes, *Lefèvre: Pioneer of Ecclesiastical Renewal in France* (Grand Rapids: Eerdmans, 1985); Needham, *2,000 Years*, 3:30.

Lefèvre's bifold Psalter was an important advance in biblical studies; it also made some contributions to hermeneutics. Lefèvre postulated
a twofold literal sense of the biblical text, termed its *duplex sensus
literalis*.[35] He argued that the literal and spiritual senses coincide so that
the true sense of the Psalms is not allegorical or tropological; rather,
it is the sense that the Holy Spirit, speaking through the prophet,
intends. The interpreter's task is to elucidate this sense as far as God's
Spirit enables.[36]

In his commentary on the Psalms, Lefèvre defended himself against
the charge of wasting his time because of the availability of the famous
patristic commentaries on the same book. He noted that his writing
was quite different from theirs. Specifically, while they were diffuse,
he tried to be succinct; while they propounded multiple senses, he
sought to find the single sense the Holy Spirit intended to convey to the
prophet's mind. He also argued that the church fathers had a paucity
of texts, while he had many, thus making it easier for him to recover
the single, original sense.[37] Lefèvre was convinced that the biblical text
should be handled with sober respect because it is the Word of God.
It should not be interpreted with the fourfold sense propounded by
the ancient church. He insisted on the close bond between words and
their meanings.[38]

Luther's writings give abundant evidence of Lefèvre's influence
on Luther's method of scriptural interpretation.[39] "In all essential
respects," says Hughes, "Luther's hermeneutical theory coincides with
that of Lefèvre."[40] Hughes also sees Lefèvre as contributing to Calvin's
exegetical theory when he (Hughes) maintains that the emphasis on
the primacy of the literal or natural sense of the biblical text was a
distinguishing trait of Reformed exegesis. But Hughes was unable
to provide the same type of support for Lefèvre's direct influence on
Calvin as he was for Lefèvre's direct influence on Luther.

35. Hughes, *Lefèvre*, 55.
36. Ibid., 56.
37. Ibid.
38. Ibid., 59: Lefèvre "affirmed the fundamental importance of the literal or natural sense
of Scripture."
39. Ibid., 60: "For Luther, as for Lefèvre, Christ is the key to the Psalter and to the Scriptures in their entirety."
40. Ibid., 61. Hughes's conclusion is an important, and proper, contrast to that of Gerhard
Ebeling.

All these foregoing humanists were pioneers of the Reformation. They were afraid, however, to rebel against the church though they objected to its abuses. There is yet another humanist reformer who stands head and shoulders above the rest.

Desiderius Erasmus of Rotterdam (A.D. 1466–1536) was the most important humanist of the Germanic territories.[41] His writings were wildly popular, and examining his life and significance shows the theological trends of his time.[42] Erasmus was probably born at Gouda, near Rotterdam, around 1466 and died in 1536. His father was most likely a priest who lived with his mother for some time but whose marriage to her was prevented by the church. At an early age, Erasmus went to a school run by the Brethren of the Common Life. He greatly disliked monastic education, which environment would later prove to be his lot. The Bishop of Cambrai was interested in the young student and took him to Paris's Collège de Montaigu as his private secretary.[43]

Later, Erasmus entered the University of Paris. From there he went to Cologne, where he became the tutor to English students. A turning point came in 1499, when he traveled to England and met the humanists Sir Thomas More and John Colet. After returning to the Continent, he began his critical writings on the church and culture.

After five years, Erasmus returned to England and was appointed guardian of the royal physician's sons. In this capacity, he accompanied them on a tour of Italy and tutored them as they traveled. In 1503 Erasmus wrote one of his first books, *The Handbook of the Christian Soldier*. After the Italian tour, he was appointed Lady Margaret's Professor of Divinity at the University of Cambridge—a faculty chair that still exists. By this time, Erasmus's reputation as a witty and popular

---

41. For more information, see Roland Bainton, *Erasmus of Christendom* (Peabody, MA: Hendrickson Publishers, 2016); H. Hillerbrand, ed., *Erasmus and His Age: Selected Letters* (New York: Harper & Row, 1970); George Faludy, *Erasmus of Rotterdam* (New York: Stein and Day, 1970); Johan Huizinga, *Erasmus and the Age of the Reformation* (New York: Harper & Row, 1957); Ernst W. Kohls, *Die Theologie des Erasmus*, 2 vols. (Basel: Reinhardt, 1966); Albert Rabil, *Erasmus and the New Testament: The Mind of a Christian Humanist* (San Antonio, TX: Trinity University Press, 1972); J. D. Tracy, *Erasmus: The Growth of a Mind* (Geneva: Droz, 1972); and Manfred Hoffmann, *Rhetoric and Theology: the Hermeneutic of Erasmus* (Toronto: University of Toronto Press, 1993).

42. Needham (*2,000 Years*, 3:33) says that 2.5 million copies of his 226 works circulated.

43. Ibid., 3:36.

lecturer was well established. Despite his personal charisma, he never became a close friend of anyone. By the time Erasmus returned to the Continent in 1515, he was an established, famous scholar whose literary work was supported by various patrons. He is well known for his brilliant satires on affairs in the church, most famously expressed in his 1509 bombastic work, *In Praise of Folly*, which deals with the sloth and corruption of the monasteries and the dire threats by the popes.[44] Also noteworthy, and indicative of his great skill, is his *Adages*, a multivolume collection of Latin proverbs.

What we would consider to be his chief work, however, along with his criticism of the Catholic system, came to fruition in 1516 with the first published Greek NT. So it would come out before another text that had been scheduled for publication, Erasmus's manuscript of the Greek NT was published quickly rather than edited carefully.[45] In producing his edition, Erasmus used three twelfth-century NT manuscripts that were not particularly accurate. Luther used the second edition of Erasmus's NT for his German translation. The Textus Receptus is based on the fifth and sixth editions of the same.[46] From Basel, where Erasmus had worked on his Greek NT and texts of the early fathers, he moved north to Freiburg im Breisgau when the city became Protestant. He returned to Basel in May 1535 and died there in 1536.

Erasmus's theology was not thoroughly Augustinian. He believed that mankind possessed freedom of the will and that this freedom was the ability to turn either to or from salvation. Erasmus said that he was not a Pelagian—he only wanted a tiny bit of salvation to be not purely by grace. He believed that the beginning and end of salvation were entirely by grace but that the middle consisted of a mix of grace and human cooperation.[47] Perhaps in tandem with his belief that humanity works to some extent for salvation, Erasmus's writings do not contain the doctrine of justification by faith.

---

44. He also produced, in 1517, a hilarious work called *Julius Excluded*, in which Pope Julius is excluded from heaven.

45. Cardinal Ximines had completed his edition of the NT but had waited for the completion of the OT in Greek before publishing his work. So Erasmus was the first person to publish a Greek NT. For Erasmus's works, see Carter Lindberg, *The European Reformations*, 2nd ed. (Malden, MA: Wiley-Blackwell, 2010), 52.

46. Needham, *2,000 Years*, 3:134–35.

47. This view destroys the believer's assurance of salvation; if salvation in any way depends on the believer's own ability to maintain it, then that salvation is capable of being forfeited.

Erasmus's religion amounted to a simple proclamation of the teachings of the Sermon on the Mount. The goal of Erasmus's *philosophia Christi* was more than pious moralism. His hope was holiness in Christ, without which all are outside the pale.[48] Sadly, Erasmus proved to be a religious opportunist who remained in the Catholic Church until the bitter end. His position is best expressed in his own words: "When the popes and emperors decree what is right, I obey, which is the course of true piety; but when they command what is wrong, I submit, and that is the safe course."[49] While Erasmus's theology was not admired by the Reformers, his exegetical works and method were studied in detail.

Erasmus as Exegete. Erasmus played an important role as an exegete. According to him, certain tools were necessary for proper interpretation and biblical exegesis: a pious mind; a knowledge of Latin, Greek, and Hebrew; acquaintance with ancient wisdom, which included rhetoric, dialectic, music, arithmetic, and nature; and finally, listening to the ancient Christian fathers.[50]

Erasmus argued in his *Ratio* that the patristic commentators were superior to the scholastic and more recent commentators.[51] Origen and Jerome were his two favorites.[52] Jerome was the first of the fathers edited by Erasmus, and this edited work came out at the same time as Erasmus's Greek NT. The edition included a biography of Jerome that presented a strong justification of Jerome's synthesis of classical and Christian learning.[53] We know that Erasmus never loved Augustine

48. It has been well argued that Erasmus was very important in Zwingli's earliest hopes for reform and that it is from Erasmus's foundation that the Swiss Brethren grew and developed. See Kenneth R. Davis, "Erasmus as Progenitor of Anabaptist Theology and Piety," *Mennonite Quarterly* 47 (1973), 164: "This same 'design' . . . appears also to have been part of the goal of the early Zwinglian . . . reform movement," and "the realization of this design becomes the very essence of the reform drive of the Swiss Brethren, the Anabaptists."

49. Erasmus, "Letter to Richard Pace (July 5, 1521)," in *Voices of the Reformation: Contemporary Accounts of Daily Life*, ed. John A. Wagner (Santa Barbara, CA: Greenwood Press, 2015), 30.

50. Rabil, *Erasmus*, 109.

51. "The ancients, on the basis of the solid foundation of Scripture, raise a strong edifice into heaven: the moderns by the foolish arguments of men or even by flatteries not less foolish than monstrous, are raised to infinity by a superstructure" (H. Holborne, *Erasmus' Collected Works*, 189–90, as cited by Rabil, *Erasmus*, 102).

52. Rabil, *Erasmus*, 103.

53. Ibid., 105; see Lindberg, *European Reformations*, 162.

with the same depth that he loved Origen and Jerome. Nevertheless, he still learned from Augustine's exegetical methods.[54]

There were, for Erasmus, many senses of Scripture. He held this view as early as 1499.[55] For him, even the old fourfold distinctions of Scripture were not adequate to express all the nuances in Scripture.[56] Erasmus's earliest works—*De cotemptu mundi* (1488), various letters written from Paris between 1495 and 1499, and *Enchiridion militis Christiani*, or *Handbook of a Christian Knight* (1503)—demonstrate that he held to a basic dichotomy between the flesh and the spirit.[57] While this dichotomy became a hallmark of Erasmus's life, a relative change in emphasis occurred as he matured.[58]

In the *Enchiridion* Erasmus emphasized allegory almost exclusively. The allegorical method provided a way to use the classics.[59] After writing the *Enchiridion*, Erasmus began to see the importance of grammar in biblical interpretation, and grammatical interpretation became more important to him. This difference was most dramatically displayed in his introduction to the NT, where it seems that the spiritual and literal interpretations stand in tension with each other.[60]

Erasmus's method of allegorical interpretation was relatively new. At this point Erasmus was dependent on Augustine's *On Christian Doctrine*.[61] He believed that there were three, perhaps four, allegorical

54. Rabil, *Erasmus*, 107.

55. See P. S. Allen, H. M. Allen, and H. W. Garrod, eds., *Erasmi Epistolae*, 12 vols. (Oxford: Oxford University Press, 1906–1958), 1:255ll15–17. In a letter to the Englishman John Colet, Erasmus said: "The holy books are so rich that various meanings can be elicited from them and none of these should be rejected if only it is probable and not contrary to piety" (as cited by Rabil, *Erasmus*, 109).

56. Erasmus commented in the *Ratio seu compendium verae theologiae* (1518): "It is not enough to examine how eternal truth (on which men are divided) shines variously in different ways: according to the historical sense, which is simple, the tropological, which pertains to habits of common life, the allegorical, which discusses secret things about the mystic head and body, the anagogical, which touches upon the celestial hierarchy. But we must also consider in the case of each of them, the steps, the differences, and the method of discussion (as cited by Rabil, *Erasmus*, 101n3).

57. Ibid., 19–20.

58. Ibid., 57.

59. Ibid., 101.

60. Erasmus urged interpreters to follow the example of Origen, who did not hesitate to "correct" historical "errors" in the text. But in a passage added in 1523 Erasmus says that readers should imitate Origen or Ambrose except in that their method was "excessive and frequently more injurious to the historical sense than is right" (ibid., 102n3).

61. Charles Bene, *Erasme et Saint Augustin* (Geneva: Droz, 1969), 435–36.

functions. He saw Scripture as difficult and hidden but believed that with great effort the pious mind could understand it.[62] For allegory moves beyond the grammatical and historical interpretation to apply everything to Christ, and it presupposes a pious mind as a condition for penetrating the mysteries.

Erasmus was convinced that there are passages of Scripture that must be taken allegorically. He cited one such example as John 2:19, where Christ says that in three days he will raise a temple. The disciples knew that this statement was not meant literally. Also, Erasmus maintained that Paul understood circumcision allegorically when he (Paul) maintained that one who is truly circumcised is one who was free from desires and passions.[63]

Erasmus believed that allegory can help interpret those Scriptures that, if taken literally, would in his opinion be absurd. It cannot be literally true, for example, that God created light on the first day but the sun and moon only much later. Despite these positive benefits, thought Erasmus, allegory should not be forced on a passage.[64]

Another tenet in Erasmus's interpretation was the primacy of Scripture's moral meaning. Erasmus focused attention on redirecting the believer's life through action rather than through knowledge. Even if not every passage has an allegorical meaning, he said, every passage does have a moral meaning. In fact, he upheld the value of the allegorical meaning of a passage precisely for the building up of moral life. The moral interpretation was not as limited as the literal and allegorical methods were.

62. Erasmus said in the *Ratio*, 259–60: "Now by means of tropes and allegories and similes and parables, Scripture is hidden or indirect, sometimes to the point of obscurity of a mystery, whether this is aimed at Christ, whom Scripture announces through the word of the prophets . . . or whether he wished to exercise our laziness for results acquired by great effort; or whether by this plan, he wished that his mysteries and secrets be hidden from the profane and impious and in such a way that in the meantime hope of understanding might not be blocked for pious searchers; or whether this kind of speech was especially pleasing because, while it is especially efficacious for persuading, it is equally revealed to the learned and the unlearned."

63. Rabil, *Erasmus*, 111.

64. E. Gordon Rupp, *Luther and Erasmus*, Library of Christian Classics (Philadelphia: Westminster John Knox Press, 1969), 38: "Erasmus went so far in his treatise against Luther as to declare that 'there are some secret places in the Holy Scripture into which God has not wished us to penetrate more deeply and if we try to do so, then the deeper we go, the darker and darker it becomes, by which means we are led to acknowledge the unsearchable majesty of the divine wisdom, and the weakness of the human mind.'"

In the final analysis, for Erasmus the Scriptures were divine and not human. He thought human methodology could help people understand the Scriptures, but the reader's having knowledge does not mean that the reader is wise.[65]

In conclusion, Erasmus always bowed to the church's judgment. He washed his hands of Luther when the latter became embroiled in controversy, and he even went so far as to state that he would agree with the church if it taught Arianism. Here was a gifted man but one who was grievously weak in his convictions. Tragically, there is no indication whatsoever that this profound scholar, who labored extensively in the Scriptures, ever understood the gospel. Erasmus wrote in 1523: "It does not make sense to incur death for the paradoxes of the Lutherans and of Luther." He further stated: "If I were a judge I would not dare to condemn a man to death for taking a stand on any of these issues; nor would I be willing to suffer death for them myself."[66]

KEY TERMS

new monarchy
forerunners of the Reformation
Renaissance

STUDY QUESTIONS

1. What were some of the reasons why Europe was ripe for reformation at the opening of the sixteenth century?
2. Are you surprised that there were forerunners to the Reformation? Why are they important?
3. What were some of the ways that humanism and the Renaissance contributed to the Reformation?

65. Rabil, *Erasmus*, 113.
66. Oberman, *Forerunners*, 37–38.

RESOURCES FOR FURTHER STUDY

There are two excellent biographical works from this era in addition to primary source material.

Ridley, Jasper. *Statesman and Saint: Cardinal Wolsey, Sir Thomas More and the Politics of Henry VIII*. New York: Viking Press, 1983. An eminently readable, scholarly account of Sir Thomas More and Cardinal Wolsey.

Hughes, Philip Edgcumbe. *Lefèvre: Pioneer of Ecclesiastical Renewal in France*. Grand Rapids: Eerdmans, 1985. Written by a believing scholar who presents Lefèvre's life and thought in context.

Erasmus. *The Adages of Erasmus*. Compiled by William Barker. Toronto: University of Toronto Press, 2001. Full of fascinating information, as with Erasmus's many other entertaining and edifying works.

12

The German Reformation

MARTIN LUTHER (A.D. 1483–1546)

Luther's Life. Luther, of middle-class German parentage, was not necessarily destined to ecclesiastical life. He was studying at the University of Erfurt on the way to becoming a lawyer—a career choice that could produce considerable wealth and prestige. It was a good move for a young man from the middle class. During a terrifying thunderstorm, during which lightning struck the ground near to Martin, he promised the local patron saint that he would become a monk if he were saved. He stuck to his promise and entered the Augustinian monastery. The Augustinians were an observant order, which means that they took serving as monks seriously. Luther was not only a monk but was also ordained as a priest in 1507.

Because he had already begun studying at Erfurt's university, it was decided in 1508 that he would continue his education in theology.[1] The Renaissance had produced a flowering of newly established universities, particularly in Germany. Luther went to the one at Wittenberg, which had just been founded in 1502. Later, in 1510–11, the Augustinians sent Luther to Rome. While there is academic debate as to whether the trip to Rome affected Luther, it is clear that he was perceptive and knew that there were problems in the capital of Christendom.[2]

Luther, although not a brilliant scholar, completed all the education necessary to receive the doctor's degree in 1512 and immediately began work as a professor of theology. It is precisely at this point that

---

1. Carl R. Trueman, *Luther on the Christian Life* (Wheaton, IL: Crossway, 2015), 31–33.
2. Ibid., 34.

knowledge of Luther's biography is important for understanding his later ministry as a reformer as well as his doctrine of the church. The medieval educational system was vastly different from our own. There was only one kind of doctor in those days—the doctor of theology. Theology was the queen of the sciences, and theology was controlled by the church. With the receipt of the doctor's degree came an oath of loyalty to the university (still a practice in the old European universities), as well as an oath of loyalty to the church, particularly to the pope.[3] But Wittenberg's new university, although having papal approval to grant degrees, did not require an oath of loyalty to the pope. Luther's doctoral degree was actually a doctor of biblical studies, and just like any other doctor he had to swear an oath of loyalty—but his oath was to the Scriptures. Years later, when he faced enormous pressure to repudiate his findings, he was able rightly to retort: "All I did was what you told me to do." As he swore an oath to enter the monastery, in similar fashion he swore an oath of loyalty to the Word of God. In his own mind, he was never a rebel.

As professor of theology, Luther began to study Greek and Hebrew. He memorized vast sections of the Scripture. In later life he felt that he had the whole NT and much of the OT committed to memory. From 1513 to 1515 he taught on the Psalms. He went on to teach Romans and Galatians from 1515 to 1516. A popular preacher, he was made the vicar over eleven monasteries and also served as the people's priest in Wittenberg.

Luther's deep involvement in pastoral work was the catalyst for one of his most famous theological controversies. The controversy involved selling indulgences. Luther's parishioners bought them even though selling them was prohibited in the immediate area. Luther rightly believed that the theology behind indulgences cheapened God's grace, and he wrote his *Ninety-five Theses* condemning the practice. Many Protestants commemorate October 31, 1517, when Luther nailed the document to the church door in Wittenberg, as the beginning of the Protestant Reformation. The theses themselves were not particularly revolutionary—Luther argued that his view against indulgences actually accorded with the pope's. The theses also addressed other issues,

3. Carter Lindberg, *The European Reformations*, 2nd ed. (Malden, MA: Wiley-Blackwell, 2010), 54–60.

such as Luther's rejection of scholasticism and the use of Aristotle in theology.[4] Still, the *Ninety-five Theses* ignited a pamphlet war with Johann Tetzel, the indulgence hawker.

In the spring of 1518, Luther attended the general meeting of the Augustinian chapter in Heidelberg. There he was able to communicate his theology in greater detail and influenced future reformer Martin Bucer. In the fall of that year, Luther met with one of the most brilliant lights of the Roman Catholic Church, Cardinal Cajetan, at the Imperial Diet that met at Augsburg. By this time it was clear to the authorities that Luther was not to be won back to the Roman fold. The plan was to have him arrested and taken to Rome, but because Luther's prince would not turn him over, he escaped.[5]

In January 1519, the death of Emperor Maximilian focused attention away from theology and toward politics. The Leipzig Debate followed in July. The debate was called by Andreas Carlstadt, dean of the theology faculty at Wittenberg, who sought to defend Luther's *Ninety-five Theses* from their cricitism by professor Johannes Eck. The Wittenbergers arrived at the debate with armed students. In his debate with Eck, Luther admitted that the papacy and councils could err. He now realized that his sole authority was Scripture and that he was aligned with the condemned Czech reformer Jan Hus. As a result of the debate, Luther was condemned with a papal bull in July, 1520. Citing Psalm 74:22, the bull opened with the call for the Lord to rise up; it condemned forty-one of Luther's errors from his *Ninety-five Theses* and other writings.[6]

Meanwhile, Luther composed three substantial pieces that outlined his own theological position and in December publicly burned the papal bull along with the books of canon law. The war was about to begin.[7] In 1521, a meeting of the Imperial Diet that included the young new emperor, Charles V, was assembled at Worms. There Luther

4. They were written in Latin and were not posted to arouse the public. They were translated and then published in German without his permission. See ibid., 61–72, and Owen Chadwick, *The Reformation* (New York: Penguin Books, 1990), 43–47. For the contents of the *Ninety-five Theses*, see Denis R. Janz, ed., *A Reformation Reader* (Minneapolis: Fortress, 2008), 88–93.

5. Trueman, *Luther*, 39–40.

6. Ibid., 41–42.

7. Those writings include: *The Babylonian Captivity of the Church; An Appeal to the German Nobility;* and *The Freedom of the Christian.* For the last text, see Janz, *Reformation Reader*, 105–13. See also Chadwick, *Reformation*, 52–55; Trueman, *Luther*, 42–44.

received his final condemnation.[8] He was able to escape from the city with armed men who protected him. Condemned by the church and state, Luther was now viewed as an outlaw, his meagre goods were confiscated, and his life was forfeit. The elector Frederick left before Luther was finally condemned so that he could claim ignorance of the proceedings.[9]

Now in hiding, Luther worked on his German translation of the NT. But the movement for reform needed his leadership, and he returned to Wittenberg in 1522. There he labored as a pastor and teacher without much incident until 1525. In that year he faced three major issues: conflict with Erasmus, which culminated in Luther's magisterial *Bondage of the Will*; being forced to take a position on the Peasants' War; and, on a positive note, his marriage to the former nun Katharina von Bora, who had fled from a monastery.[10] The printed NT saw the light of day in September 1527, and the initial three thousand copies sold immediately. The second edition came out in December.[11]

In 1530, Emperor Charles V asked the Lutheran princes to provide a confession of faith. Luther's colleague Philip Melanchthon wrote the Augsburg Confession that was presented to Charles at the Diet, but he rejected it, even though it was adopted by the Lutheran leaders. The Reformational union was called the Schmalkaldic League, and it protected Luther and his people until Luther's death in 1546.[12]

Luther's Reformation in Germany. With the monumental break from Rome, Luther had to face the question of how to rearrange church order. In 1523 he published the *Little Baptism Book* and *Concerning the Order for Public Worship*. Preaching formed the central part of the worship service. He wrote German hymns and put Psalms to music. In 1525, with another minister he issued the first Protestant catechism. All this material became standardized in what was called the Deutsche Messe, or German Mass.[13]

---

8. Lindberg, *European Reformations*, 75–83.

9. Chadwick, *Reformation*, 55–56; Lindberg, *European Reformations*, 83–85.

10. Lindberg, *European Reformations*, 96. For two recent biographies of Katharina's fascinating life and her influence on Luther, see Ruth A. Tucker, *Katie Luther: First Lady of the Reformation* (Grand Rapids: Zondervan, 2017), and Michelle DeRusha, *Katharina & Martin Luther: The Radical Marriage of a Runaway Nun and a Renegade Monk* (Grand Rapids: Baker, 2017).

11. Lindberg, *European Reformations*, 87.

12. Trueman, *Luther*, 51.

13. Chadwick, *Reformation*, 72–73; Trueman, *Luther*, 102–4.

The changes were not relegated to the church alone. The church and the state were intimately interrelated. Beginning in 1527 official commissions of theologians and statesmen inaugurated what is called "civil visitation." Saxony and Thuringia were the Reformation centers in North Germany, while the Rhineland and Baden were the prime centers in the south. Through the visitations, Luther learned of the people's great theological ignorance.

In 1528 Melanchthon, with Luther's input, issued new instruction maintaining that the final decision in ecclesiastical matters rested with the state. In those states that had Protestant princes, Catholic worship was not to be tolerated publicly, though a man could maintain his private beliefs. There was to be no anti-Trinitarianism. There was to be freedom of conscience. Belief in the Trinity gave full citizenship rights, so Catholics retained civil rights.

In 1529 Luther put together some charts and tables for children's instruction based on the Ten Commandments and the Lord's Prayer. This work became his *Shorter Catechism*. He also composed a *Larger Catechism*. Practical material, such as Bibles, catechisms, songs, and orders of worship, had been hitherto nonexistent for the youngest members of the church.[14]

The German Reformation was not without its impact on education. There was a reversal of the humanist tendency of digging into the classics. Because of the so-called "simple gospel" that was being so widely preached, anti-intellectualism spread through the land. Illustrating the change is the fact that in the year 1520 there were 529 students at Wittenberg's university, but five years later enrollment had dropped to 171. This reduction may be due in part to the lack of certain ecclesiastical employment for Protestant students. Also, some who thought of going into the church were now free to go into business or commerce. Luther disliked the educational trend. He underlined the need for an educated clergy. He appealed to the German municipalities to maintain strong schools.[15]

This time was also one of distressing social problems. Peasant discontent was growing, as was unrest among the lower nobility. There

---

14. Trueman, *Luther*, 109–13.

15. Luther even translated Aesop's *Fables* (his translation being published after his death) to aid children's education.

was a new economic atmosphere abroad. The peasants, who had few economic and civic rights, began to think that their liberties in Christ should entail freedom from much of the bondage under which they suffered. The peasant organization, named after the humble sandal they wore—the *Bundschuh*—was suppressed. In the summer of 1524, isolated peasant bands rose in revolt.[16] By the spring of 1525, conditions were extremely bad. The peasants published a declaration of their rights called the Twelve Articles.[17] Based on Erasmus's teaching, the Twelve Articles maintained that the peasants were purchased by Christ and were therefore not to be treated as pieces of property; that they should be granted more hunting, fishing, and firewood rights; that the inheritance tax and its incumbent great services to the nobility should be abolished; that the common land must be returned to common use; that the community should have the right to choose its own priest; and that only the title "great" was to be retained by the nobility, with all the others abolished. The signers said they would withdraw any article that was shown to be contrary to the Bible. There was no response from the authorities. Open warfare erupted in 1525 between the peasants and the great landowners, with the peasants encouraged by Thomas Müntzer.[18] He called on them to slaughter the nobles, whom he called the Canaanites—the people the ancient Israelites had been charged to slaughter when they entered the Promised Land.

Luther needed to take a position in the midst of this crisis. He urged a peace based on the Twelve Articles. He admitted that the lords were guilty of suppressing the principles embodied in the articles but meanwhile urged both parties to nonviolence.

Nevertheless, civil war broke out. Luther's former colleague at Wittenberg, Carlstadt, was banished from Saxony, and Carlstadt allied himself with Müntzer in south Germany.[19] Although Luther was himself from peasant stock, he lived with the anti-peasant party. Angry at their bloodletting, he wrote a strong paper against the robbing, murderous bands of peasants. They had killed a noble in the

16. Chadwick, *Reformation*, 59–62; Trueman, *Luther*, 49.
17. See Lindberg, *European Reformations*, 108, 151, 156.
18. For more information on Müntzer, see below.
19. On Carlstadt and Müntzer, see Lindberg, *European Reformations*, 130–52; Trueman, *Luther*, 46–49, 101, 151–52.

sight of his own family, and he was against peasants who functioned as both judge and executioner. The peasants thought they had been betrayed by their leader and thus lost sympathy for both Luther and the Reformation. After a period of extreme violence on the part of the nobles, Luther tried for a course of moderation, but it was too late. Tens of thousands of peasants were killed, and in a pitched battle at Frankenhausen, Müntzer was captured and then executed.[20]

Luther faced continued theological and political opposition. In November 1522 the Imperial Diet that met at Nuremburg was unable to force the Protestant electors to turn Luther over for judgment even though he had been condemned by the earlier Edict of Worms. They did call for a general council of the church. The January 1524 Diet at Nuremburg tried again to enforce the edict of Worms against Luther but failed.[21]

In the spring of 1524, Luther wrote to Erasmus both commending and admonishing him. Later in September Erasmus published his work on free will, in which he stated that the ethical ends of religion were most certain and that although the will is the slave of sin, it is still free to some extent. Luther replied in December 1525 with *De servo arbitrio*, in which he stoutly maintained that the will of man is so bound by sin that it is not free to do right even though his own position on the bondage of the will is offensive to natural reason.

The next phase in Luther's life, from June 1526 to March 1529, is bracketed by the first and second meetings of the Diet of Spires. On the one hand, the First Diet of Spires was a positive move for the Protestants, who urged the repeal of the Edict of Worms. The Diet agreed that reform was urgently necessary; private masses were to be abolished, clergy should be free to marry, and communion for the people should be celebrated in both kinds (the bread and the wine).[22]

Emperor Charles V, who was strongly behind enforcing the Edict of Worms, did not attend the Diet because he had been at war against King Francis I of France. The victorious emperor was signing a treaty

---

20. Nicholas R. Needham, *2,000 Years of Christ's Power*, vol. 3, *Renaissance and Reformation* (London: Grace Publications, 2005), 129; Lindberg (*European Reformations*, 157) puts the number at one hundred thousand.

21. Needham, *2,000 Years*, 3:134.

22. Lewis W. Spitz, *The Renaissance and Reformation Movements* (St. Louis: Concordia, 1971), 53.

with France while the Diet met. The treaty was a strongly anti-Lutheran compact with very hard terms for the French. But almost immediately after signing the peace agreement, King Francis I visited the pope in Rome and was absolved from responsibility to abide by the treaty's terms. So the following spring, in 1527, Charles V's mercenary army of twenty thousand men invaded Rome and imprisoned the pope until he agreed to call for a general council of the church.[23]

Two years later, in March 1529, the Second Diet of Spires met and voted to continue the Edict of Worms.[24] This was a grave setback for those who supported change, and the Lutheran commissioners were not willing to accept these terms. They handed in a document, or *protestation*, in which they demanded that the terms of the First Diet of Spires be upheld. It is due to this protestation that the Lutherans became known as Protestants.[25]

An Imperial Diet was called to meet in the important city of Augsburg in the spring of 1530. The emperor, who had been preoccupied with the Turkish threat to Vienna, arrived in June. Luther, who was still banned from the empire, could not attend the Diet. Melanchthon was the spokesman for the German Protestants. He said that the main differences between the Protestants and the Catholics were just in form. Melanchthon desired that members of the clergy be allowed to marry, the laity be allowed to receive the communion cup, and the right to private interpretation of Scripture be granted.

The emperor ordered the Protestants to present a confession of their faith within four days.[26] Anticipating that demand, the Lutherans had reworked an earlier document, called the Marburg Articles or Articles of Schwabach, and provided the first evangelical confession to appear during the Reformation. That important document, called the Augsburg Confession, is the historic Lutheran creed to this day.[27]

The confession had a conciliatory attitude toward the doctrines of Rome. Luther called it a soft-stepper because of its irenicism. None

---

23. Lindberg, *European Reformations*, 219–20.

24. Ibid., 220–21.

25. Philip Schaff, *History of the Christian Church*, 8 vols. (Grand Rapids: Eerdmans, 1979), 7:691; Thomas M. Lindsay, *History of the Reformation*, 2 vols. (Edinburgh: T&T Clark, 1963), 1:371; Needham, *2,000 Years*, 3:137.

26. Chadwick, *Reformation*, 65.

27. Lindberg, *European Reformations*, 222–25.

of the articles was particularly concerned with setting forth Scripture as the sole authority and supreme rule of faith and practice. The confession emphasized the Catholic doctrine of the Trinity and Christology. It condemned the Anabaptists, who believed in extrabiblical revelation, and those who taught that children could be saved without baptism. It held, in continuity with Catholic teaching, that baptism was indispensable for salvation. Part II rejected the sacrificial Mass, clerical celibacy, monastic vows, and the secular power of the bishop if it interfered with his spiritual power. Article IV, on justification, however, stated clearly that "men are freely justified for Christ's sake through faith."[28] The original text has been lost and was apparently even more pro-Catholic than the text we have today.[29] Some claim that in that orginal version Melanchthon's view of transubstantiation was almost the same as the Catholic view.

The emperor thought that the confession was far too strong, and he reached no agreement with the Protestants. The Diet recessed from September until April 15, 1531, to give the Protestants time for further consideration. If they would not change, they were to be devastated by fire and sword. The emperor published an edict that enforced the old Edict of Worms by condemning Lutheran teachings as heretical. To make the situation even more complicated, a number of cities, including Strasbourg, disagreed with the Augusburg Confession regarding the Eucharist and refused to sign it.

Enough tension had been building for the Roman Catholic hierarchy to attempt to force a general council of the church.[30] A council was called to meet in 1535, but the Protestants would not participate.[31] In 1537 Pope Paul II (1534–1549) called a general council of the church to settle differences. Luther had the courage to say that he would attend, but the council was postponed indefinitely. In the absence of a council, Luther was asked to write theological articles as a basis for dealing with the emperor, for the emperor was seeking Protestant military support against France. In the end, a council did not meet until 1545.

28. Lindsay, *Reformation*, 1:366–68.
29. The present text of the confession was first published in 1531 and is known as the *Augustana Invariata*. A revision, known as the *Augustana Variata*, was published in 1540.
30. Up to the time of the Council of Trent in 1545, the Catholic Church had not made a definitive statement on the nature of justification.
31. Spitz, *Renaissance*, 483–91.

Lutheran Progress and Regress. The Protestants of Europe were not totally unified on matters of doctrine. A Swiss movement, contemporary with the one in Germany, had developed but with different nuances, particularly on the Lord's Supper.[32] Melanchthon, as leader of the Lutherans, and Martin Bucer of Strasbourg, as leader of the Swiss, held a series of conferences. Their positive discussions were given final documentary form as the Wittenberg Concord in May of 1536. The Wittenberg Concord was satisfactory to the Lutheran leaders and agreed that the Lord's Supper was a sacramental union in which the body of Christ was truly present and offered. It also maintained that the unworthy received the body and blood of Christ in the sacrament. This concord was the basis of union between Strasbourg and southern Germany and the northern German movement—it placed Strasbourg more in the Lutheran camp than the Zwinglian or Swiss camp.

The Reformation movement was progressing and gaining approval until a major setback occurred: the famous Protestant noble, Philip of Hesse, committed adultery with a number of women. After 1525, Philip stopped taking the Lord's Supper because of his sin. In 1539 he decided to marry a seventeen-year-old woman named Margarita von Zelle. But Margarita's mother refused to approve the marriage unless Philip received formal relinquishment of his present marriage. Philip consulted with Martin Bucer, who at first opposed the marriage but then said that there were OT examples of polygamy and that he was uncertain of the NT's teaching on the matter. Pope Clement VII recommended marriage in such cases. Philip of Hesse then consulted with Luther but did not present all the facts. Luther thought that Margarita might simply be a concubine seeking legalization and, while he thought the marriage was a bad idea, recommended that a secret marriage was better than none if Hesse could not remain free from sin.[33]

The disastrous wedding was arranged. Several nobles were invited to visit Philip and were surprised to find that, in fact, they had been invited to a wedding. The wedding was supposedly a secret, but such a secret could never be kept. Once word was out, a conference was called. Luther argued that a good, strong lie was necessary to hide his approval of the marriage. He held that his advice was similar to that

---

32. Luther had already met with the Swiss in 1529. See chapter 13.
33. Chadwick, *Reformation*, 71–72.

of a secret confessional, so it was better for him to lie than to divulge that he had approved. But Philip was very much opposed to lying. At this point, the emperor became involved and offered a quid-pro-quo solution: for a pardon, Philip was to promise that there would be no alliance of the Schmalkaldic League with England or France. Word spread of Philip's agreement with the emperor, and it destroyed public confidence in the Reformation movement.[34]

The Colloquy of Regensburg was a meeting that held out hope of bringing the Lutheran and Catholic churches together. Emperor Charles V called for the conference in the spring of 1541. Melanchthon and Bucer represented the Protestants, and there was good progress until they came to the doctrines of transubstantiation and the spiritual priesthood of believers. Even the conciliatory Melanchthon was strong on these points, and there was no partial agreement or toleration that was acceptable to either Luther or the Catholics. Charles V now knew that the Lutherans could never be brought back to the medieval church.

By 1544, Luther was more than sixty years old, and political and theological turmoil continued to boil around him. At the Diet of Spires in that year, the emperor gained the promise of Protestant military assistance against the Turks and the French by permitting the secularization of all church properties in the realm. In September, he made peace with the French in a treaty that contained a secret clause: the French were never to lend military aid to the German Protestants. One year later, he made peace with the Turks.[35] This development helped bring about the Schmalkaldic War when in 1546 the emperor launched an attack on Saxony and Hesse. The Protestants rallied as one, but they lacked skilled military direction. By being slow to react, they lost their best chance of victory, for they allowed Charles V to use troops from both Italy and Holland.

Having scattered the Protestants, the emperor intended to subdue both the pope and the Protestant (Schmalkaldic) League with a general council called to begin in 1545. The pope rebelled at this attempt, and in response he formed an alliance with France. While this move left Emperor Charles V furious, he could do nothing about the council.

34. Lindsay, *Reformation*, 1:381.
35. The year 1545 is also notable for the great council of the Roman church, the Council of Trent. This conclave was soon highly unsatisfactory to the Protestants.

He did, however, gather an army about him and march to the Italian border. Trent, the city where the Catholic theologians met, was fearful.

In the midst of these political and military troubles, Luther was called to mediate a dispute between two counts who were quarreling over an inheritance. After traveling in the bitter cold to Eisleben to adjudicate their conflict, Luther died at the age of sixty-three.[36]

Even after Luther's death, political turmoil continued. At home, Duke Maurice of Ducal Saxony was attacking John of Saxony. In the spring of 1547, John's forces were surprised and routed, and he was taken prisoner. He gave over his territories to Maurice and was himself sentenced to death. Philip of Hesse was also captured and sent with John to Holland. Thus the Schmalkaldic War brought to utter defeat the Protestant (Schmalkaldic) League.

Hoping to end all religious conflict, Charles V opened the Imperial Diet in 1547. It adopted a law called the Augsburg Interim, which would supposedly meet Protestant needs even though it had been produced by Catholic authors. In substance it taught the absolute supremacy of the pope, the doctrine of transubstantiation, that there were seven sacraments, and the adoration of the Virgin Mary as well as saints. There were a few Protestant concessions—communion could be celebrated in both kinds, clergy could marry, and indulgences and purgatory were not mentioned. It also contained a statement of justification by faith. These concessions comprised at best a meager compromise that was carried through by the exclusive political might of the emperor. In southern Germany the city of Constance was forced to become Catholic, and Martin Bucer had to flee Strasbourg for England.[37] Committed Lutherans fled or went into hiding. Many gathered at the city of Magdeburg in northern Germany, where the emperor's power was weak, and from that city published a flood of Protestant literature.

After a few years of regrouping, in 1552 the Protestants gathered arms and pushed against the emperor. They liberated Philip of Hesse and nearly captured the emperor.[38] The situation caused political chaos, and it began to appear that the only hope for peace was for the two religions to tolerate each other.

36. Ibid., 1:384–85.
37. Ibid., 390.
38. Ibid., 393.

Emperor Charles was worn out from the strife and by the Diet of Augsburg in 1555 turned religious matters over to his successor, Ferdinand. The Protestant princes demanded a religious settlement and achieved what is termed the Peace of Augsburg. This accord lasted for six decades. The peace provided recognition of the evangelical position as summarized by the Augsburg Confession, Protestant territory conquered by the Catholics was returned, and importantly, the nobility were given the right to determine the religion of their territory. This rule is summarized by the Latin phrase *cuius regio, eius religio*, "whose is the rulership, his is the religion." If a person did not agree with his noble, he was free to move away. At this juncture the emperor retired to a Catholic monastery, and the empire was divorced from Spain and the Netherlands.

Interpretations of Luther. Luther strove for self-understanding as he vacillated between self-confidence and self-accusation. He had a sensitive nature yet also an iron will. The two often seemed to be in conflict, but this tension was necessary for him to see himself both as a reformer and as a Christian. Luther was plagued by the question as to why he was right and so many others were wrong.[39] He had confidence in his calling yet was also cognizant that he was following the biblical message. He wrestled with the same tensions in his intellectual life. He was aware of his position as a doctor of the church yet at times seemed intellectually unable to grasp nuances of the scriptural text. This inability was especially seen in the strife over the Lord's Supper. He was driven to get to the bottom of the biblical text, yet often he knew he was incapable of doing so.

During Luther's era there was a complex view of anthropology. The common understanding of the Late Middle Ages was that there were two types of clerics or educated people. On the one hand there was the monk—supposedly, one who entirely rejected himself for the sake of the kingdom of God. On the other hand there was the radical opposite: the Renaissance strong man full of self-affirmation. There was no way in the Late Middle Ages or Renaissance period to bridge the separation between the two ideologies of personhood. But in many ways Luther bridged that gap through his faith in God. From his

---

39. This self-questioning was seen at the Diet of Worms when Luther, thinking in Latin, asked himself, *non sum solum sapis?*—"Am I alone wise?"

certainty of forgiveness came self-confidence of the highest sort. Yet he knew that all he had comprised was only a gift—a gift he was not worthy to receive. Thus we see Luther creating a new self-perception or even a new anthropology: men and women can now be confident because they are God's instruments, and that confidence is no longer limited to the religious monk or well-educated Renaissance man but is freely offered to all God's children.

Luther as Exegete.[40] All Protestants held to the view that the church was founded on the teachings of the prophets and apostles and the authority for church teaching must come from the Bible. But what did the slogan *sola scriptura* really mean? Luther's exegetical methodology was complex. As a doctor of theology he was aware of the medieval tradition of the fourfold sense of Scripture. Formally rejecting the fourfold sense, Luther said that the Scriptures must have one literal sense.[41]

During Luther's time, there were two traditions concerning the nature of the literal sense. The tradition that followed Faber Stapulensis (d. 1536) and the ancient church maintained the *sensus literalis propheticus*, that is, the prophets of the OT as they spoke were always referring to the coming Christ. We sometimes call this sense the *typological* sense.[42] The other camp followed Nicholas of Lyra (d. 1349) and maintained that the literal sense should follow a historical-factual approach.[43]

Luther followed the school of Stapulensis—and for a very simple reason: Luther had one exegetical goal in all his works, namely, to make Christ present to the reader as the one who justifies and is the

---

40. Gerald Bray, *Biblical Interpretation: Past and Present* (Downers Grove, IL: InterVarsity Press, 1996), 197–200.

41. Luther stated: "[The Holy Spirit's] words cannot have more than one, and that the very simplest sense, which we call the literal, ordinary, natural sense. We are not to say that the Scriptures or the Word of God have more than one meaning. We are not to introduce any metaphorical, figurative sayings into any text of Scripture, unless the particulars of the words compel us to do so. For if anyone at all were to have power to depart from the pure, simple words and to make inferences and figures of speech wherever he wished [then] no one could reach any certain conclusions about any article of faith" (as cited by Daniel Fuller, "Biblical Theology and the Analogy of Faith," in *Unity and Diversity in New Testament Theology: Essays in Honor of George E. Ladd*, ed. R. A. Guelich [Grand Rapids: Eerdmans, 1978], 195–213).

42. Heinrich Bornkamm, *Luther und das Alte Testament* (Tübingen: Mohr Siebeck, 1948), 74–75.

43. See Fritz Hahn, "Faber Stapulensis und Luther," *Zeitschrift für Kirchengeschichte* 57 (1938): 356–432.

single subject of the Bible's content. Knowing Luther's goal helps one understand his deep struggle concerning including the book of James in his NT canon. Since James spoke of a justification that, at first glance, appears to include works in addition to the pure grace of Christ, or at least does not make the doctrine clear, Luther thought the book must be rejected—for certainly Luther's hermeneutic could not be altered!

Luther condemned the use of allegory in interpretation and specifically rejected Origen's and Jerome's exegesis. But even though in theory Luther rejected allegory, he implemented it frequently and used it until his last lecture. Allegory may be used, according to Luther, after the analogy of faith is applied and when the goal is to clarify other passages that are unclear. The following examples illustrate Luther's use of allegory: In Deuteronomy 1, Luther used certain etymological derivations of various names and places to mean at one time the Law and the gospel, and at another place the old and new man. In Deuteronomy 3, when the Bible says that Moses will not go over the Jordan, it means that the Law does not go into the kingdom of God. The golden calf at Deuteronomy 9:16, for Luther, is the teaching of righteousness by works. The OT principle of an eye for an eye actually means that God will heartily punish heresy. That someone who is recently engaged should not go to war means that new converts should not be made preachers of the Word. That someone should not plow with a donkey and an ox tied together, as recorded in Deuteronomy 22:10, means that one should not teach, at the same time, faith plus works. There are other examples from his works until 1545.

For Luther, allegory was permissible if it helped find Christ in every passage of Scripture. Fortunately, his use of allegory reduced as he matured. Luther's rule for implementing allegorical exegesis was that allegory is permitted, or even commanded, when the text makes no other useful sense. He supported this implementation of allegory because he was convinced that Paul used this method—as, for example, in 2 Corinthians 3:13, where Paul discusses the veil of Moses. Luther also cited Paul's reference to Sarah and Hagar in Galatians 4:22–24. Of course this justification for allegory's use was the same argument used by Justin Martyr in the earliest period of church history.[44]

44. Bornkamm, *Luther*, 81. For more on Luther's exegesis, see Richard C. Gamble, "The Sources of Calvin's Genesis Commentary: A Preliminary Report," *Archiv für Reformationsge-*

Concerning his biblical text, we know that Luther had in his possession one of the Froben Bibles of Basel. Johannes Froben was a humanist publisher of that great city, and in 1498 and 1509 he put out two German editions of the Bible. The Bible that Luther used is not quite what we would imagine today. The text was the Vulgate, and on top of that text was Anselm's interlinear gloss.[45] The *Glossa Ordinaria*, which was first written by Walafrid Strabo (d. A.D. 849), is a collection of sentences and extracts of various church fathers explaining the Scriptures sentence by sentence and was placed on the left-hand margin of the page.[46] The *Postil*, a commentary written by Nicholas of Lyra, was to be used as a supplement to the *Glossa Ordinaria*. The *Postil* stressed the importance of the literal or historical interpretation of the text. Lyra was a converted Jew, could read Hebrew, and used Jewish commentaries to help him interpret the text. The *Postil* was placed on the right-hand margin.[47]

Luther's Theology. Luther's theological method may be summarized by his symbol, which was a rose. His theological system was not systematic but concentric. The system, like a rose, had a center with surrounding pieces. While Luther praised Melanchthon, the two men did not approach theology from the same perspective. Luther said that theology was a paradoxical discipline. Theology was always pastoral and spoke to the people's needs. This approach was perhaps a reaction against scholasticism.

Luther thought that humanity can, through nature, know certain things about God, especially his power and justice. Thus he did not deny the existence of natural theology. But he held that God's provision for human need depended on supernatural revelation. For Luther God was, to some extent, still hidden from humanity—because special revelation is an accommodation. God does not fully reveal himself as he is in himself. For example, Moses was only able to see God's back. God is to be known only in Jesus. Christ is the ultimate revelation of

---

schichte 84 (1993): 206–21.

45. Wilhelm Pauck, ed., *Luther: Lectures on Romans* (Philadelphia: Westminster John Knox Press, 1961), xxx: "The interlinear gloss was a paraphrase of the text stressing the specific meaning of the different words, the logical connection between them, and the interrelation of the several parts of sentence."

46. Ibid., xxv.

47. Ibid., xxixn17.

the masked God, but Christ is not exhaustively revealed in Scripture. Even the Holy Spirit also ministers to believers through masks.

The paradoxical nature of theology is that the law of God is salutary to life yet also actually a hindrance. This paradox makes the law/gospel distinction very important. God's law convicts believers of sin—the main function of that law. While God's law is beneficial, its effect will never be life. It condemns men and women before God.

There is discussion among scholars as to whether Luther teaches the third use of law, namely, how it functions as direction for believers in their effort to live a holy life. This emphasis is primarily a Reformed one, though Luther does hold to something close to the third use of law because he was strongly against antinomianism. The third use of law cannot invalidate the second use, Luther insisted. He and Reformed theologians at least agreed that God's law was foundational for civil righteousness and the condemnation of sin.

Luther's anthropology begins with the distinction between the inner and the outer person. The inner person is as he stands before God, or *coram Deo*. The outer person is man as he stands before others, or *coram hominibus*. The inner person is completely free, for the relationship between God and the inner man is one of pure grace and mercy.[48] For Luther, believers know that they have a secure relationship with God. The outer person is the servant of all, with his orientation being toward his neighbor. For medieval man to have a vocation or calling meant to become a priest or a monk; in contrast, Luther saw every honorable job as a calling, just as is the job of a priest. For Luther, no job held greater spiritual value than another job.

Also important for Luther was distinction between the Word and the Spirit. Christ can only be found in the written Word of God—nowhere else. In other words, for Luther there could be no Pentecostalism, no way of experiencing the Spirit apart from the Word. Luther was strong in his condemnation of Thomas Müntzer, who, he claimed, swallowed the Holy Spirit feathers and all.[49]

48. According to medieval theology, humans are pilgrims on the way to judgment. They could not know what the verdict was going to be in the final judgment; they could hope and work but could not know. There was no solid assurance. Assured righteousness from the sacraments could perhaps meet the standards of God's judgment.
49. Lindberg, *European Reformations*, 141–42.

ANABAPTISTS

Thomas Müntzer (A.D. 1489–1525). After World War II, and particularly during the 1960s and 1970s, historical and theological research on the life and writings of Thomas Müntzer reached a pinnacle in Germany. Interest in him came especially from the former East Germany, where Müntzer was viewed as an early Marxist revolutionary. It was said that every school child in East Germany knew the name of Müntzer—there are monuments to him, and the city where he ministered was changed to bear his name.

Despite all this attention, Müntzer studies have only relatively recently come into full bloom.[50] There is now a critical edition of his collected writings, the first volume of which was published in 1968; it presented not only his main writings and letters but also some material that had not been published previously. Better editions of some of these collected writings were also published in the 1970s. Further critical work on Müntzer's letters and other writings was finally completed only a few years ago.[51] A one-volume collection of Müntzer's works in English, with introductions and notes, was compiled and edited by Matheson.[52] This work is most helpful, since Müntzer's German is difficult for even contemporary German scholars to read.

Many are able to associate Thomas Müntzer's name with radical Anabaptism. But beyond that association, knowledge of him is limited, so a brief biographical introduction is in order. Probably born in 1489, Müntzer most likely received his bachelor and master of arts degrees, as well as his bachelor of theology degree. He was ordained to the priesthood and traveled in what was the western border of East Germany. He obtained further theological training in Wittenberg, probably from late 1517 through 1518, where he met and studied with Luther and Melanchthon. In 1519, Luther wrote a letter of support for Müntzer while the latter was pastoring in a small town. Further

---

50. Peter Matheson, *The Collected Works of Thomas Müntzer* (Edinburgh: T&T Clark, 1988). Matheson asserts that "the world of Müntzer studies is in ferment" (xii).

51. Wieland Held and Siegfried Hoyer, eds., *Quellen zu Thomas Müntzer* (Leipzig: Evangelischen Verlagsanstalt, 2004); Siegfried Brauer and Manfred Kobuch, eds., *Thomas Müntzer Briefwechsel* (Leipzig: Evangelischen Verlagsanstalt, 2010); Armin Kohnle and Elke Wolgast, eds., *Schriften, Manuskripte und Notizen* (Leipzig: Evangelischen Verlagsanstalt, 2017).

52. Matheson's *Collected Works* comprises the first full English translation.

travels and ministry followed, but Müntzer's arrival in the city of Zwickau is important for recreating his biography.

Zwickau was a very important city. Müntzer pushed the Reformation there and had to flee in 1521. Eventually, he made it to the great city of Prague, where the citizens were supposed to be more receptive to this new gospel. There Müntzer had time to develop his thought more fully. Already he was emphasizing different theological points from those of Luther.[53]

After being chased out of different cities for his views, Müntzer finally landed in Allstedt. In 1523, he was working out the implications of his belief in the priesthood of all believers. One result of his understanding of the doctrine was the translation of all worship services into the German language so that no one was passive during worship. Also in 1523 he got married. In the spring of 1524, citizens started to burn church icons; as usual, the city authorities were against this act. Called before the Duke Johann in July, Müntzer preached to him in the hope of a positive judgment for reformation. It did not ensue, and Müntzer had to leave Allstedt. He went from there to the imperial city of Muhlhausen.

In Muhlhausen, Müntzer continued the same program for reform. As opposition grew stronger, he became convinced that it was time to fight back. He enlisted the support of the people and started to engage in armed combat. Müntzer himself became fiercely opposed to the higher classes, probably because of their opposition to reform. He was convinced that he carried the sword of Gideon against the nobility. Müntzer raised a peasant army of thousands and led them against Frankenhausen. He preached to his men that they were not fighting for themselves but for God. Six thousand of Müntzer's men were killed, and only six soldiers of the opposition died. On May 27, 1525, Müntzer was beheaded in front of the door of the city of Muhlhausen.

Two characteristics undergird Müntzer's theology: mysticism and apocalypticism. Much of sixteenth-century theology was apocalyptic, meaning that Christ's return was imminent. Even Luther interpreted some parts of the Bible apocalyptically. For example, in his commen-

53. Abraham Friesen, *Thomas Müntzer: A Destroyer of the Godless* (Berkeley: University of California Press, 1990), 94.

tary on Genesis Luther attributed all the diseases that had come to Germany as a sign of the near return of Christ. In the second half of the sixteenth century, however, apocalypticism in general had died down.

There were points of agreement and dependence between Luther and Müntzer. Luther provided Müntzer with some ideas, but scholars agree that Luther did not provide the larger context of his thought.[54] On the various issues related to works righteousness, they agreed; but they held different understandings of the importance of the imitation of Christ. According to Müntzer, Luther was an accommodator with worldly authority and had his eyes set on the things of the earth, not of God. In the end, Luther openly opposed Müntzer. Luther wrote a pamphlet against Müntzer and his work in Allstedt, and, of course, Müntzer returned the action in kind.

Müntzer's first major writing was *The Prague Manifesto*, written in November 1521.[55] There are four extant editions of this work: two in German (one long and one short), one in Latin, and one incomplete Czech text. The *Manifesto* is an unusual piece. Written in the style of a prophet, it stated that unless Müntzer's readers listen to him, the Turks will overtake them within a year. With all the social and religious change occurring in the world, Müntzer truly believed that the end of the world was coming. In the *Manifesto* he argued that there was a distinction between the written Word of God and other types of revelation that come from the Holy Spirit. He did not think that God's speaking should be confined to the text of Scripture.[56] The work was also Protestant in that Müntzer argued for the priesthood of all believers. He insisisted that this priesthood should be characterized by deep piety—there had to be a clear difference between the way Christians lived in contrast to non-Christians.

Another important work by Müntzer was titled the *Sendbrief an die Bruder zu Stolberg* (*Letter to the Stolberg Brothers*). This sermon

54. Ibid., 1–8.

55. Matheson's *Collected Works* is well done. He gives the German in footnotes when translations are difficult and provides other good information.

56. Matheson, *Collected Works*, 34: "Müntzer demands not a dumb God, which is all that the dead letter of Scripture can offer, but a God whose work is eternal and alive, who speaks directly to man. This notion derives ultimately from Meister Eckhart and Dominican mysticism, though Müntzer probably received it from the Book of Spiritual Poverty wrongly attributed to Tauler."

presented to the nobility outlined much of his theological and political thought. Using Romans 13 for his text, he was convinced, unlike Luther, that there should not be a great divide between civil government and the church. Luther was always against opposing an unjust or unchristian government. Not so Müntzer.[57] If the government did not protect the true believers and punish the wicked, then it ceased to be government. At this important point he and Luther held opposite exegetical interpretations of the passage.[58]

Earlier critical scholarship presented two pictures of Müntzer. On the one side was Müntzer the revolutionary, who wanted to establish a better society for the poor. The other portrait was Müntzer the theologian, who was consumed by apocalyptic piety. Some scholarship wants to build a bridge between these disparate pictures, since both identities were necessary for Müntzer's drive to construct a new primitive Christian community of believers.[59]

Schleitheim Confession and German Anabaptist Developments. The Schleitheim Confession was written in 1527 by Michael Sattler (1490–1527), a former Benedictine monk. Its seven points comprised the most representative summary of Anabaptist belief. The first point was that baptism was for believers only. Infant baptism was the highest and chief abomination of the pope and was a more grave error than mistakes in the doctrine of justification or the Eucharist. The second point emphasized the importance of the ban, or excommunication. Third, the confession outlined the breaking of bread, or the Lord's Supper, which was simply a memorial meal. The fourth was a requirement for separation from the evil world—the good cannot mix with the bad. The fifth point concerned pastors, who were shepherds elected by the community. Sixth came the refusal to bear the sword, which automatically meant that a Christian could not serve in civil office. The final point was against taking oaths.[60] In the confession,

57. Hans-Jürgen Goertz, *Thomas Müntzer: Apocalyptic, Mystic and Revolutionary* (Edinburgh: T&T Clark, 1993), 128.

58. Lindberg (*European Reformations*, 141) argues that humanist rhetoric provided the structure of Müntzer's theology. The concept of *ordo rerum*, which underlined the proper relationship between beginning and end, was a fundamental hermeneutical category. While Luther was also influenced by humanist rhetoric, for him it was simply a tool for biblical exegesis.

59. Goertz, *Müntzer*, 161.

60. Lindberg, *European Reformations*, 192–93, 204–5.

behavioral matters were considered more important than doctrinal ones. Soteriology, the Trinity, and even Christology were not clearly articulated.

There were other German Anabaptist developments. Melchior Hoffman (1495–1543), a native of Swabia in southern Germany, became a Lutheran preacher in Livonia (Latvia) in 1523. He was preaching in Kiel in 1527 when Carlstadt met him. In 1530 he was rebaptized and maintained the Anabaptist position regarding this matter. Around 1533 he began to preach in the Netherlands and declared that the New Jerusalem was soon to come to Strasbourg. Elijah would also return, and the Lord would come soon afterward. Hoffman therefore went to Strasbourg—either to welcome Elijah or become Elijah. There he was imprisoned and, ten years later, died.[61]

The excitement he had created spread through the lower Rhine Valley so that the Duchy of Jülich-Cleves banished all Anabaptists. But the chief preacher of Münster in Westphalia was won over, and the city became a haven or refuge for Anabaptists, led by Jan Matthys, a baker from Haarlem. Matthys said the kingdom was to be set up immediately and sent out preachers to proclaim its advent. He called himself Enoch, the second of Melchior Hoffman's two witnesses. The city council lost control of the situation to the Anabaptists in February 1534. The bishop of Münster was driven out but gathered troops and surrounded the city. A long siege began.

Due to the military emergency, Matthys assumed greater control of the city. Community of goods was established. One day he had a vision in which he was commanded to preach the gospel and attack the bishop's army. The next day he did so with only twenty men. Finis!

Jan of Leiden then took command of the situation. With much pomp he divided the city into twelve tribes, over each of which was a judge who held the power of life and death. In July he ordained that widows might be united to married men to increase the population for war. The women were to choose their own husbands. Before long, Jan himself had fifteen wives.

Soon Jan of Leiden considered himself the Messiah. He sent apostles into the surrounding country; they were summarily executed. By this

---

61. Ibid., 190, 207–8, 286.

time, a grave food shortage threatened the city. Rats were being eaten. After more than a year of siege, the city fell in June 1535. Hand-to-hand fighting featured in the last stand, during which a large portion of the population was massacred. Jan was captured and caged by the victorious bishop. He was then sent on an exhibition tour, after eight months of which he was tortured to death. The cage holding his body was hoisted to the top of the steeple of the Lambertikirche in Münster—and was still there at the beginning of World War II.

Unfortunately, people thought that all Anabaptists were like these radicals. This supposition was not true; nonetheless, the movement suffered a serious setback. These events broadened the differences between the Lutherans and Anabaptists. They were finally forced into compulsory subscription to the Augsburg Confession.

Menno Simons (A.D. 1496–1561). Menno was born in what is known today as the province of Friesland in the Netherlands. We do not know much about his background except that his family was in comfortable enough circumstances to send him to school to train for the priesthood.

In 1524, when he was twenty-eight years old, Menno was ordained as a priest and installed in a church. He was at that time fully committed to the Roman Catholic Church and had apparently never read the Bible. At that time, the Bible was considered dangerous. His conversion, similar to Zwingli's before him, was a gradual affair. Like any intellectual of the period, he certainly entertained questions concerning the Roman church, and one focus of his questioning involved the nature of the Lord's Supper. After two years in ministry, he acquired and read a book by Luther. At this time, he also began to read the NT.

In 1531, when Menno was thirty-five, the first Anabaptist was martyred. This particular Anabaptist had come from Germany. His martyrdom made a great impression on Menno, since prior to this time he had not heard of a second baptism. Menno's biographers maintain that he had yet to question basic Roman teaching on this point. Menno began to study the NT in earnest and to ask a number of questions of other priests. He also began to read the writings of the church fathers and saw that their post-Constantinian teaching that infant baptism was important in washing away original sin was not to be found in the Bible.

413

In 1533 the radical sect of the Münsterites erupted. Their teaching spread north to Holland as well, and some of them took over a small convent in the Netherlands by force of the sword. They were routed by the authorities, and many of them were killed. That Menno's brother was killed with them made a great impression on Menno.[62] After further study he resolved to withdraw from the Catholic Church on Sunday January 30, 1536. Concerning his decision, he commented:

> The gracious Lord granted me His Fatherly Spirit, aid, power and help, that I voluntarily forsook my good name, honor and reputation which I had among men, and renounced all the abominations of Anti-Christ, Mass, infant baptism, and my unprofitable life, and willingly submitted to homelessness and poverty under the cross of my Lord Jesus Christ—Behold, my reader, thus the God of mercy, through His abounding grace which He bestowed upon me, a miserable sinner, has first touched my heart, given me a new mind, humbled me in His fear, taught me in part to know myself, turned me from the way of death and graciously called me into the narrow path of life, into the communion of his saints. To him be praise forever more.[63]

One of Menno's most important writings was a small book titled *Foundation of Christian Doctrine*.[64] It was first written in 1539–1540 in Dutch and revised in 1558. It appeared at the same time as the publication of Calvin's second edition of *Institutes*. Menno's purpose was much the same as Calvin's—he hoped the book would end the persecution of the brethren. *Foundation of Christian Doctrine* was printed in German in the eighteenth century and appeared in at least three English translations before 1871. The book is divided into three parts: the first is a call to biblical faith, the second a refutation of Catholicism, and the third and final an appeal for toleration.

Menno's teaching on infant baptism was clear. He was convinced that only those who could fully understand the gospel, those who turned from darkness to light, those with a living and active faith,

---

62. Ibid., 210.
63. John Horsch, *Mennonites in Europe* (Scottdale, PA: Mennonite Publishing House, 1950), 185–92.
64. Lindberg, *European Reformations*, 286.

were to be given this sign.[65] This teaching necessarily excluded infant children—baptism was a symbol of death to sin and new life in Christ, and infants could not bear this mark.[66] Furthermore, there was no biblical warrant to perform such an act on children.[67] Menno felt forced to reject infant baptism and to condemn those who practiced it. According to him, infant baptism perverted God's ordinance, did violence to the Word of God, and misused his name.[68] His rejection of the doctrine and his opinion of those who still clung to such supposedly false teaching were strong and specific.[69]

This brief description does not fully summarize Menno's extensive teaching on the nature and function of baptism. But in most sixteenth-century polemics—and this one is no exception—the debaters were reacting against their own religious background. To understand Menno, we need to understand his context in the Roman Catholic Church.

It was erroneously taught in the Catholic Church that baptism was for the remission of original sin, a teaching that all Protestants rejected. Menno's cry was for all Protestants to listen more carefully to the Bible's teaching. In addition, perhaps because of Luther's and Erasmus's influence, for Menno the Bible was the NT but not necessarily the OT. Thus theological continuity between the OT and the NT was not searched for or greatly appreciated. For these theological points, Menno and his followers were willing to die—and they did.

Menno's views on baptism came from a peculiar theological method, which he described. Having first heard of believer's baptism

65. Menno Simons, *The Complete Writings of Menno Simons*, ed. J. C. Wenger, trans. Leonard Verduin (Scottdale, PA: Herald Press, 1984), 123: "For where there is not faith through love working obedience (again we speak of those who have come to years of understanding) there is no promise."

66. Ibid., 123–24: "Therefore beware, for the symbolism of baptism is to bury sin, and to rise with Christ in a new life, things which can by no means be said of infants. . . . As Paul says, in Christ Jesus neither circumcision availeth anything, nor uncircumcision, but a new creature."

67. Ibid., 123: "For we are no more commanded to baptize infants than Israel was to circumcise female children."

68. Ibid., 120: "Young children are without understanding and unteachable; therefore, baptism cannot be administered to them without perverting the ordinance of the Lord, misusing His exalted name, and doing violence to His holy Word. In the New Testament, no ceremonies for infants are enjoined, for it treats in both doctrine and sacraments with those who have ears to hear and hearts to understand . . . faith does not follow from baptism, but baptism follows from faith."

69. Ibid., 123–24: "For those who maintain that the baptism of irrational children is a washing of regeneration do violence to the Word of God, resist the Holy Ghost, make Christ a liar and His holy apostles false witnesses. . . ."

after receiving his theological education, he attempted to determine whether there was what he considered a NT foundation for the practice. He searched the church fathers and then went to Luther, who "taught me that children were to be baptized on account of their own faith." Then he went to Bucer, who taught something like a dedication doctrine—in other words, that children were set apart—and finally to Heinrich Bullinger, who "pointed to the covenant and to circumcision."[70] In each case Menno noted a particular theological method: "When I noticed from all these that writers varied so greatly among themselves, each following his own wisdom, then I realized that we were deceived in regard to infant baptism."[71] Notice his phrase: "each following his own wisdom."[72] In short, Menno wanted to avoid taking a theological position based on anything but his own conception of the teaching of Scripture. That desire is perhaps the reason why he later got into controversy concerning the doctrine of Christ.

In his *Reply to Micron*, Menno summarized his conclusion in thirty-one points. His method was consistent: his teaching was always "according to the Scriptures."[73] Micron, according to Menno, was not following Scripture; rather, "he [Micron] uses philosophy and not the Scriptures as was the case in the first matter."[74] Likewise, Menno's problem with infant baptism was that he did not see a clear NT warrant for the doctrine.[75]

Definition and Classification. Having had a brief glimpse of a few Anabaptist leaders, we would do well to categorize the broader movement. The term *Anabaptist* was meant as a pejorative title. No Anabaptist thought of himself as a "rebaptizer." He thought there might have been a christening or some other papal rite that was given to babies. In the Justinian code, it was a capital offense to rebaptize.

---

70. Simons, "Reply to Gellius Faber," in *Complete Writings*, 669.

71. Ibid., 696: "Behold, thus are the advocates of infant baptism divided among themselves." For more on baptism, see chapter 15, Reformation Theology.

72. Ibid., 695: "ordinance to suit their own taste."

73. Simons, "Reply to Micron," in *Complete Writings*, 865–67. Martin de Cleyne, or Martin Micron, was a Zwinglian who held two debates with Menno and published an account. This work appeared in 1556. See ibid., 835–36.

74. Simons, "Reply to Faber," in *Complete Writings*, 694: "for all they philosophize and propose about it is mere deceit."

75. Ibid.: We need "a commanding word, by which all things are to be judged that are to please the Lord."

If we do not want to use the word *Anabaptist* to describe this movement, what should we call it? The "left wing of the Reformation" is too political a term. George H. Williams chose a good categorization with the title of his book, *The Radical Reformation*. Williams also used a helpful principle to characterize the movement, namely, the different Anabaptist movements' attitude toward authority.

Anabaptists proper were those who looked to the Bible as their authority. Within that category there were three subgroups. The first group was termed *evangelical* and included the leaders Hubmaier, Simons, and Grebel. The second group was classified as *revolutionary*, which embraced Hoffman. The third group was called *contemplative*, which included Hans Denck.

A second category of Anabaptists looked to the Holy Spirit as their primary authority and were termed *spiritualists*. In that category there were also three subgroups: the *revolutionary* included Carlstadt and Müntzer; the *evangelical* embraced Swenkfield; the *rational* included Franck and Paracelsus.

The final category of Anabaptists were the *evangelical rationalists*, who turned to reason as their authority. This group included Servetus, Ostellio, and Soccinius. All in this group tended toward anti-Trinitarian thinking.

The Roman Catholic historian Joseph Lortz said that Protestantism is the triumph of subjectivism, and Anabaptism is only an extension of that principle. His analysis is incorrect, but it is true that in many Anabaptist circles the doctrine of forensic justification was not emphasized. All Anabaptists rejected the Catholic tradition of church and wanted to go "back to the Bible." Sixteenth-century people saw Anabaptists as anarchist and chaotic. Besides the Lutheran reformation in Germany and the Anabaptist movement throughout Europe was a Swiss movement, which will be analyzed in the following chapter. The Lutheran and Swiss movements intersected in the city of Marburg, Germany.

EUCHARISTIC CONTROVERSY: MARBURG (A.D. 1529)

Circumstances and Need. The Reformation in German-speaking Switzerland developed and solidified slowly, while in the north, Luther's work was effective in Germany. In the light of these developments, the idea of a union between the forces of Luther and those of the Swiss reformer Ulrich Zwingli had been considered for some time. Zwingli sought out such a union, and in 1529 the German Prince Philip of Hesse, who himself would later cause many problems because of his adultery, thought it wise to try to consolidate the Swiss and German Protestants for defensive purposes. September 1529 was set as the date for a German–Swiss conference at Philip's Marburg fortress.

Agenda Debate and Theological Unity. Stenographers were present for all sessions and provided three volumes of transcripts. This conference was not public, though others took part. Zwingli thought they ought first to consider the question of the Eucharist. Luther thought it more to the point to discuss the whole Reformation movement.

Luther drew up a formula of concord to be signed by those in attendance. All those present subscribed to a statement of the great points of doctrine on which they were agreed, but the problem of the Eucharist proved to be the point on which the conference broke down. There were fifteen topics, and fourteen were agreed on. It is often said that the difference at Marburg was on one half of a point.

Breakdown on the Eucharist. All present at the colloquy had rejected the Catholic notion of transubstantiation, which holds that the bread and wine actually become the body and blood of Christ through a miracle that takes place in the celebration of the Lord's Supper. In that teaching, then, Christ is subsequently sacrificed on the altar. But rejecting this doctrine is easier than creating a new one! How were Christians of the sixteenth century to understand Christ's own words, "This is my body?"

Zwingli and Luther could not agree on the interpretation of Christ's words. Luther's position was that the bread and wine were the body and blood of Christ through consubstantiation as opposed to transubstantiation. Understanding the *communicatio idiomatum*, or "communion of properties," is important for grasping Luther's interpretation. Luther argued that Christ's glorified human nature received from his divinity the property of omnipresence. Part of the glorification of Christ's resurrection was the gift of physical omnipresence. In other words, the physical resurrected body of Christ is everywhere and can therefore be in the bread. Just as divinity can be everywhere through omnipresence, so also can Christ's body be everywhere. *Consubstantiation* was the view that the body and blood of Christ were in, with, and under the bread and wine. The infrequently used but related English word *ubiquity* comes from the Latin word *ubique*, which means "everywhere."

Zwingli asserted that the body and blood of Christ are neither locally included in the elements nor sensibly present in them; rather, they are symbols through which believers have communion in Christ's body and blood. The bread and wine are not naturally united with the physical body and blood of Christ. Zwingli held that Christ's body was resurrected and is physically present at the right hand of God the Father—and thus could not be present in the elements.[76]

Zwingli thought that Luther's notion destroyed the real nature of a body. The definition of a body is necessarily limited by space and time. Luther thought that he was true to the words of Jesus' statement, "This is my body," but Zwingli countered that Luther was unfaithful to the Scripture since Jesus is seated at the right hand of God in heaven. Three days were spent discussing the sacrament without any agreement. Zwingli and the Basel reformer Oecolampadius pointed out that Christ did not mean to say that the bread was actually his body.

Conference Conclusion. Zwingli, with tears in his eyes, extended the hand of fraternal fellowship to Luther, who refused the offer. Luther felt he could not join in Christian fellowship with anyone who denied what was, to him, a fundamental article of the Christian faith.[77] While sometimes it is thought that Luther's famous statement "You have a different Spirit" was addressed to Zwingli, it was actually addressed to Bucer. Luther meant that he had the Holy Spirit, and Bucer had the spirit of the Evil One.

MARBURG A.D. 1529: ZWINGLI AND LUTHER

Hunched over his desk the student gazed up on the lofty castle.
Upon that mount great theologians discuss important issues.
The drop of cool wine seemed to calm him from the hassle.

76. See Richard C. Gamble, "Switzerland: Triumph and Decline," in *John Calvin: His Influence in the Western World*, ed. W. Stanford Reid (Grand Rapids: Zondervan, 1981), 55–74.
77. Luther's failure to embrace Zwingli despite their theological differences may also be related to Luther's falling out with Carlstadt. Carlstadt was considered by Luther to be an

While all appeared tranquil to the student down below,
Inside the stoney walls a battle raged—over truth—
With consequences well beyond grandchildren to bestow.

The student sliced his cheese and bowed his head,
And wondered to himself if they could make a difference.
He doubted, but it would be better with some more bread.

Such verbal violence for stones too heavy a load,
Soon to incarnate and engulf all the German lands
Like white hot lava from the mountain top it flowed.

The student never felt the heat.

A dozen generations have flown and the lava is cool.
A few know what happened there;
But no one seems to teach it now in school.

The discerning understand what the old events mean.
The lofty debates surely made a mark.
To the four corners of the earth the divergences are seen.

Now tranquil stand the silent rocks up there.
But strife o'er "truth" is not abating,
For that which is for one with others he cannot share.

On elbows propped his eyes gaze on Marburg's stone.
Theologians no longer lead these lands,
Yet heart is stirred again to engage before a call from home.

The student saw the light.[78]

---

instrument of the Devil. Carlstadt went to Zurich and was received by Zwingli. Zwingli must
therefore also be an instrument of the Devil.

78. Poem ©2000 Richard C. Gamble.

GERMAN DEVELOPMENTS AFTER LUTHER'S DEATH

Theological reformation brings with it theological controversies. The antinomians maintained that after salvation God's law was no longer operative for believers. Luther may have given some ground for this view in his early writings. His companion, Agricola, defended the view in its extreme form, namely, that there was no validity to the OT and that its law was not necessary because of overpowering grace. The common call of his group was, "To the gallows with Moses." Fortunately for Agricola, he gave up his view in 1541. The church would stuggle with antinomianism for a long time after Agricola.

Next was the synergistic controversy started by the position Melanchthon took in his monumental *Loci communes*. There he said that there was in man a "faculty . . . of applying himself toward grace."[79] Pfeffinger of Leipzig (1555) followed this lead and said that man to a certain extent cooperates with God in his conversion. This view was condemned in 1559 under Flaccius's leadership. The Formula of Concord (1577) at Article II decided against synergism.

Yet another conflict was the controversy over the Eucharist, a controversy also starting with Melanchthon. Luther held that Christ's body was present in the Lord's Supper but also that his body was everywhere present in a spiritual sense and not only in heaven at God's right hand. Apparently, the 1530 Augsburg Confession maintained consubstantiation—but the original text is lost. In 1540, Melanchthon issued a new text of the Augsburg Confession in which he had made some changes. The text is called Melanchthon's *Variata* (meaning "altered"). This version was more Reformed and spoke of the "body and blood of Christ being truly exhibited" in the sacrament. This view became known as *crypto-Calvinism* by many and was attacked by the Lutherans in the 1550s. Melanchthon's view was held at Wittenberg for a long time, but the view gradually lost ground.

A final controversy concerned theologian Georg Mayor or Major, who declared in 1552 that good works are necessary for salvation, since it is clear that no one is saved by bad works and that no one is

---

79. There he supposedly said that humanity could apply himself toward grace. For more information, see William G. T. Shedd, *A History of Christian Doctrine*, 2 vols. (Minneapolis: Klock & Klock, 1978), 2:40.

saved without good works. This controversy was largely over words. Opponents said that good works are harmful in reference to salvation. In 1562, Mayor admitted that he had made unwise statements.[80]

Key Terms

Peasants' War
Council of Trent
Schleitheim Confession
Augsburg Confession

Study Questions

1. How many senses do the Scriptures have?
2. How do you define the literal sense of Scripture?
3. How diverse was the Anabaptist movement? What are some of the categories that can define it?
4. Is Martin Luther's view of the Lord's Supper the only legitimate one? Should churches split over their views of the Lord's Supper?
5. The Lutherans, Reformers, and Anabaptists wrote confessions and catechisms. Are they important today?

Resources for Further Study

Martin Luther's writings are vast! His commentary on Genesis covers seven volumes. Suggested shorter readings include the two listed below.

Augsburg Confession. In *The Book of Concord: The Confessions of the Evangelical Lutheran Church*, edited by Robert Kolb and Timothy Wengert, 28–103. Minneapolis: Fortress, 2000. Includes an introduction by the editors and translations of the Latin and German texts.

80. See E. H. Klotsche, *The History of Christian Doctrine*, rev. ed. (Grand Rapids: Baker, 1979), 207.

Luther, Martin. *The Freedom of the Christian* and *Small Catechism*. In *A Reformation Reader*, edited by Denis R. Janz, 105–13, 118–29. Minneapolis: Fortress, 2008.

Schleitheim Confession. In *A Reformation Reader*, edited by Denis R. Janz, 208–11. Minneapolis: Fortress, 2008. A confession of the Swiss Anabaptists.

13

Post Tenebras Lux

THE SWISS REFORMATION

Sixteenth-century urban life was, in comparison with life in the West today, a time of great physical stress. Calvin listed the many afflictions of his own day: "A thousand maladies there are that beat incessantly upon us, one after another. Now the plague tortures us, now war, now ice or hail strikes down our crops and threatens us with poverty; now through death we lose wives, children, other relatives; sometimes our houses are set afire."[1]

Ulrich Zwingli (A.D. 1484–1531).[2] The Reformation in German-speaking Switzerland had its beginnings in the city of Zurich under the leadership of the great reformer Ulrich Zwingli. Zwingli's death preceded even the first edition of Calvin's *Institutes*.[3] To understand the Swiss Reformation, we must also remember that the German-speaking capital city, Bern, was more powerful than were both Zurich and Geneva.

1. Ford Lewis Battles, *The Piety of Calvin* (Phillipsburg, NJ: P&R Publishing, 2018), 63.

2. For some primary sources in English, see Ulrich Zwingli, *Commentary on True and False Religion* (1929; repr., London: Labyrinth Press, 1981), preface, introduction, and reply to Emser; *On Providence and Other Essays* (1922; repr., London: Labyrinth Press, 1983)—six documents; and *Ulrich Zwingli: Early Writings*, ed. Samuel Macauley Jackson (1912; repr., London: Labyrinth Press, 1987), preface and life of Zwingli—fourteen documents. Secondary sources include: W. P. Stephens, *The Theology of Huldrych Zwingli* (Oxford: Clarendon, 1986), and Ulrich Gäbler, *Huldrych Zwingli: His Life and Work* (Philadelphia: Fortress, 1986).

3. See G. R. Potter, *Zwingli* (Cambridge: Cambridge University Press, 1976); G. W. Locher, *Die Zwinglishche Reformation im Rahmen der europäischen Kirchengeschichte* (Göttingen: Vandenhoeck & Ruprecht, 1979); Stephens, *Theology of Zwingli*; Gäbler, *Life and Work*.

Zwingli was born at Wildhaus, a subcanton of Taggenburg. His father was an alderman-farmer and his uncle the village priest and Ulrich's first tutor. Zwingli's educational preparation for the priesthood was not exceptional. At the age of ten he left home for school in Basel and later went to a school in Bern. He received his university education at the city of Vienna. In 1504, young Zwingli received his bachelor of arts degree and in 1506 his master of arts. It was only then, at the age of twenty-two, that he was permitted to begin theological studies. This training enabled Zwingli to read the Mass in Latin and to repeat the creeds as well as to hear confessions. He was offered a position as priest at the relatively small town of Glarus, where he labored for ten years (1506–16).[4]

Glarus was a small town in an important nation. Switzerland had developed into one of the great powers of Europe. Its army was reputed to be nearly invincible. The Swiss Confederation had become the virtual ruler of the Milanese territories, and importantly for the movement of Reformation, Zwingli had acted as a chaplain to one of their campaigns in Italy during June 1513 and perhaps later in 1515.

For that decade in Glarus, Zwingli performed the normal duties of his office, including daily Mass, hearing parishioners' confessions, performing marriages, and burying the dead. This period of pastoral responsibility at Glarus was very fruitful for his learning. He had time to study both Greek and Hebrew, in addition to meditating on the Bible and reading the works of the church fathers. In 1513, at age twenty-nine, he began to study Greek so that he might read the NT in its original language. He was interested in the notion of the Italian humanist Picco that Jesus's statement "This is my body" is not a literal expression but might be a figurative one. At this time, Zwingli also read some of Erasmus's writings. His sermons at Glarus became increasingly political and anti-mercenary. He criticized the alliance his nation had made with France and the whole idea of Swiss mercenaries' being sought by various countries.

In 1515 Zwingli met Erasmus at Basel. At this time Zwingli was already somewhat doubtful as to whether the Roman Catholic Church

---

4. A priest had to be at least twenty-three years of age, and one became a priest by the confirmation of the bishop. Zwingli apparently received this confirmation in September 1506, but he was some four months short of the required age. See Potter, *Zwingli*, 23n1.

was sound and faithful. In the following year he moved to Einsiedeln, approximately fifteen miles to the west and the seat of a great monastery, and he left a substitute in his place at Glarus. Here, too, was a shrine to the Virgin Mary and the site of many pilgrimages. Zwingli deepened his study of the Greek NT, read the church fathers, and realized that there was great need for reform in the church.

By 1518 Erasmus had finished his Greek NT, which would soon become important not only for Zwingli but also for the entire Christian world.[5] Zwingli's attitude toward this new book, the Greek NT, was one of great excitement.

At this time he was entering the heights of his intellectual prowess. He had now mastered the Greek language. It has been speculated that no one north of the Alps knew Greek better than Zwingli—not even the famous Erasmus.[6] Zwingli also began to read the Greek church fathers, particularly Origen, Cyril of Alexandria, and John Chrysostom. Later, Chrysostom would come to be important also for Calvin's development in the area of scriptural exegesis.[7] As Zwingli continued to grow in knowledge, his dissatisfaction with the Roman Catholic Church mounted increasingly. In addition to his deepening personal knowledge, his intellectual contacts were becoming more numerous as well.[8]

In December 1518 Zwingli was elected to fill the position of "people's priest" in Zurich.[9] Thus he moved from his relatively unimportant country church in Einsiedeln to the great cathedral of Zurich. In the discussions surrounding Zwingli's appointment, the unhappy fact of

5. "It was this New Testament, added to [the] study of Saint Augustine's treatise on the Fourth Gospel," notes Potter (*Zwingli*, 40), "that opened his eyes and impelled him to fill his sermons with the new-found glad tidings." Potter (ibid.,) goes on to state: "The Vulgate he knew already and extremely well, but here was the real thing, the divine word exactly as the Holy Spirit had guided the pens of the evangelists."

6. Ibid., 42–43.

7. See John R. Walchenbach, "John Calvin as Biblical Commentator" (PhD diss., University of Pittsburgh, 1974).

8. The well-known printers Froben and Amerbach of Basel and the great scholar Beatus Rhenanus of Strasbourg were in communication with him. While he continued to study the Hebrew language, he also exchanged his ideas with the Hebraists Wolfgang Capito and Conrad Pellican.

9. The election date was December 11; he was elected by seventeen out of twenty-four votes. Philip Schaff (*History of the Christian Church*, 8 vols. [Grand Rapids: Eerdmans, 1979], 8:38) incorrectly gives the date as December 10. Thomas M. Lindsay (*History of the Reformation*, 2 vols. [1963; repr., Edinburgh: T&T Clark, 1964], 2:29) mistakenly says that the year was 1519.

his unchastity came to light. It is relatively certain that Zwingli committed a sexual sin, but some historians of the nineteenth century painted a picture of Zwingli as having frequent lapses in that regard. Their general portrait of his moral life was rather unfavorable. Those historians, however, committed the all-too-frequent blunder of reading history from the presuppositions of their own cultural milieu. The morality of the priesthood altogether throughout the fifteenth and early part of the sixteenth century was simply atrocious. Zwingli did sin, to which he confessed, from which he repented, and, as far as we know, the likes of which he never committed again. His confession, repentance, and continuing chastity stand in contrast to his competition for the position of people's priest in Zurich, namely, a man purported to be the father of eight children! Compared to his contemporaries, Zwingli was not a particularly immoral man; rather, he lived the life of the sinful common person of that era.

The city of Zurich had a population of about six thousand—not small for that time.[10] Zurich was a strong and somewhat prosperous city that minted its own coins, which were of a consistent quality.[11] Zurich, since medieval times, still relied heavily on its strong walled fortifications for protection. Zurich was also, as far as Late Middle Ages cities went, a rather unique town in its relationship to the papacy. This trade and manufacturing city had somehow managed to subordinate the ecclesiastical authorities to the rulers of the city, a situation unheard of at the time. As difficult as it may be to believe, church properties were taxed.[12] The city could even inspect convents if it so desired. Whereas the pope would never permit these peculiarities in other European cities, it was probably his desire to keep the flow of Swiss soldiers coming to the aid of the church that forced the ecclesiastical authorities to tolerate these abnormalities.

Zurich had already joined the Swiss Confederation back in 1315 and was, as much as was possible in the 1500s, democratically run.[13]

---

10. Potter (*Zwingli*, 53) estimates that the city proper had slightly fewer than six thousand inhabitants and that there were approximately sixty thousand people living in the countryside surrounding Zurich.

11. Manufacturing coins was a symbol of power. For example, the city of Basel, not too far away, had its coins minted by its bishop.

12. Lindsay, *Reformation*, 2:29.

13. Schaff, *History*, 8:39.

A senate, or council, composed of the masters of the thirteen trade guilds ruled the town. There were twelve trade guilds in Zurich and one guild that represented the patriciate. These guilds still exist in Switzerland, but their functions today are limited to purely social and cultural events. The Burgermeister, or mayor, also had great powers in Zwingli's time, and a council of 212 members convened for special occasions or in times of crisis.[14] Yet in spite of its well-developed governmental structure, Zurich remained a rather rude and licentious city.[15]

Having arrived in Zurich in December, Zwingli officially began his work on January 1, 1519,[16] his thirty-fifth birthday.[17] His ministry there began with a direct break from the medieval tradition of preaching from prescribed pericopes or preestablished biblical texts.[18] Furthermore, he noted that he would not follow the scholastic interpretation of passages in the Gospels but would instead endeavor to make Scripture its own interpreter.[19]

Although safe and secure from outside invasion, the city of Zurich underwent a surprise attack from the inside. The bombardment came from the pulpit of the great cathedral and the mouth of Zwingli. Zwingli's earlier reading of the Greek NT had begun to take its toll as he continued to question his church's teachings. Although it is difficult to find a tower experience in Zwingli's life similar to what happened to Luther, it is clear that Zwingli was an evangelical when he arrived in Zurich.[20] Zwingli himself testified that he had begun preaching evangelical doctrine before he arrived in the city and, in fact, before he had heard of Luther.[21]

14. Lindsay, *Reformation*, 2:29.

15. Schaff, *History*, 8:40n1.

16. Ibid., 8:40, calls it his thirth-sixth birthday. See Potter, *Zwingli*, 60.

17. Schaff, *History*, 8:40.

18. That Saturday he preached a sermon on Christ's genealogy and announced that he would then begin (the following day) to preach a series of sermons from the Gospel of Matthew. See Potter, *Zwingli*, 60.

19. Lindsay, *Reformation*, 2:30.

20. Zwingli's "conversion" was perhaps more gradual and certainly more connected to Renaissance humanism. Stephens (*Theology of Zwingli*, 21) says: "There is no agreement about when or how Zwingli became a reformer. Some place the date as early as 1515 or 1516, others as late as 1521 or 1522. Some see the decisive influence in Erasmus, others in Luther or Augustine." See Wilhelm H. Neuser, *Die reformatorische Wende bei Zwingli* (Neukirchen-Vluyn: Neukirchener Verlag, 1984), 77–84.

21. Stephens, *Theology of Zwingli*, 22: "Zwingli seems to have read Luther hastily, to have looked to him for the confirmation of his own views, and to have admired him primarily

Another decisive turning point, both in Zwingli's own life and for the city, was the outbreak of the plague in August 1519. One quarter of the city's population was doomed to a hideous death. Zwingli was infected with the dreaded disease in September, as was his brother Andrew, who subsequently died. God brought Ulrich Zwingli to death's door, perhaps to give him the vision that he needed to help guide thousands in Switzerland from death unto life. Zwingli beautifully described his experience in what is called his *Pestlied*, or *Song of the Plague*.[22]

Zwingli's reforming preaching was beginning to take effect, as evidenced by the complaints that were immediately raised against him. But Zwingli convincingly argued to government officials that he was not inventing new doctrine.[23] In 1520, it was determined that the priests of Zurich should preach the Gospels and Epistles without human explanations, which probably meant that they were to avoid using the scholastic theologians as resources. Zwingli was appreciated enough to be elected to the canonry as an official cleric of the cathedral, thus giving him the right of citizenship. At the same time in Germany, the condemned Luther was kidnapped from the city of Worms and spirited away to the Wartburg Castle. Luther was condemned, but Zwingli continued to operate from within the hierarchy of the Roman Catholic Church.[24]

The next significant event for the Reformation in Zurich is almost humorous. The "great theological question" concerned eating sausage! How much trouble can one sausage get you into, anyway? Well, if Luther had the troublemaker Tetzel, Zwingli had his sausages.[25]

---

for the boldness of his stand against the pope."

22. There was a break from his traditional Catholic background in the *Pestlied*. There is no calling on the Virgin Mary or reliance on the Roman church. There is a trust in God and Zwingli's utter giving of his life to him. An English translation appears in Potter, *Zwingli*, 70. German and English texts appear in Schaff, *History*, 8:44–46. The German text is found in Ulrich Zwingli, *Huldreich Zwinglis Sämtliche Werke*, hg. Emil Egli und Georg Finsler, *Corpus Reformatorum* 88–89 (Berlin/Leipzig/Zurich: M. Heinsius Nachfolger, 1904), 1:67–69.

23. In many ways, also, he had not left all things Roman Catholic. For example, he did not preach against the theory that was behind selling indulgences—a point to which Luther had arrived two years earlier. At this point, Zwingli was not a thoroughgoing Reformer; he still associated with the bishop's advisor Farer (Fabri). See Potter, *Zwingli*, 66–67.

24. Ibid., 73.

25. It is true that the sausages of southern Germany and northern Switzerland are the epitome of comestible delight, but if in early 1522 Zwingli's friends would have known the trouble those sausages could get them into, perhaps they would have restrained themselves.

The story follows these lines. During the 1522 Lenten season of fasting, some sausage was eaten during an evening meal at the printer Froschauer's house in clear violation of church law. The authorities legally determined this act to be a violation of law, and the offenders were to be punished.

Punishment could have easily been avoided provided that confession, repentance, and perhaps even a little money would have been offered. But this repentance did not happen. In fact Zwingli, who had been present at the meal but did not partake of it, condoned the printer's actions and made a public issue of the matter. He let loose with a pamphlet on the Christian's freedom in the matter of food and declared that the gospel of Christ had overthrown the demands of Roman church law.

If sausages can get a sixteenth-century priest into trouble, imagine what a woman could do! Zwingli had decided that what he rightly called *innovations* in the church, such as fasts, should not be arbitrarily or forcibly imposed on people. Doing so was *ultra vires* (beyond the church's legal power), or inhuman.[26] He was also convinced that celibacy should not capriciously be required of men and women. Because of this view, in 1522 he secretly married a woman named Anna Reinhart (b. 1484), widow of Hans Meyer von Knonau. On July 2 of that year, Zwingli, along with ten other priests, petitioned the bishop, as well as the Swiss Diet, or federal government, not only for the preaching of the gospel freely but also for the allowance of marriage for members of the clergy.[27] The great humanist Erasmus supported this protest.

As expected, however, the petition was not granted. Open rebellion against authority followed, with two priests getting married in 1523.[28] Zwingli's "secret" marriage was made public in 1524.[29]

Meanwhile, Zwingli's fame as a preacher and writer grew and grew. His deep study of the Greek NT text proved fruitful. The sermon he preached in September 1522 titled "Of the Clarity and Certainty of the

26. Ibid., 77.
27. Schaff, *History*, 8:48; Lindsay, *Reformation*, 2:33.
28. Schaff, *History*, 8:48. A priest named Reubli of Wyticon was wed on April 28, 1523, and Leo Jud was married in September of the same year.
29. Ibid., 8:48–49.

Word of God" demonstrated Zwingli's attitude toward Scripture. For Zwingli, as with Luther and later Calvin, the Bible was the infallible Word of truth and without error in all its parts. At the disputation of Zurich in 1523, Zwingli announced that he had with him the infallible and impartial judge, Holy Writ, in Hebrew, Greek, and Latin. Some scholars have lamely attempted to deny that Zwingli and the other reformers had such a high view of Scripture.[30]

He wrote the *Apologeticus archeteles*, or *The Beginning and the End*, which, among other things, supported the *sola scriptura* principle.[31] The importance of this booklet lies in its strong statements on the authority of Scripture.[32] Here Zwingli asserted scriptural authority as plainly as Luther had ever done.[33] In this work Zwingli made a defense for the gospel based on the harmony and order found in Zurich.[34]

His work titled *The Clarity and Certainty of the Bible* also appeared. Consequently, opposition to his, and to others', evangelical preaching grew. In fact, in the year that Zwingli was married, a Protestant minister outside Zurich's territory was imprisoned and tortured for seven months for his supposedly heretical preaching. In spite of this opposition, Zwingli and his ideas continued to advance.

Zurich Reformation (A.D. 1523–1528): **Theological Issues.** In January 1523, a well-organized debate that scholars call the first public disputation occurred between Zwingli and those who wished to support the church of Rome.[35] Attending the disputation were more than six hundred people, amounting to over 10 percent of the city's entire population.

30. The crucial topic of debate concerns the relationship between the objective Word of God, or written Scripture, and the subjective activity of the Holy Spirit in convincing the sinner that Scripture actually is the "Word of God." Geoffrey Bromiley is mistaken in his introduction to Zwingli's sermon in *Zwingli and Bullinger*, ed. G. W. Bromiley (Philadelphia: Westminster Press, 1953), 57. There Bromiley says, "And that means in the last resort the Word is present in fullness only where it is the living and miraculous utterance of God himself." This interpretation of Zwingli, while interesting, obviously reflects the influence of the Swiss theologian Karl Barth on Bromiley and is not in accordance with Zwingli's own doctrine of the Word of God.

31. This work is most likely dated to August 1522 (see Lindsay, *Reformation*, 2:33); Locher (*Zwinglishche Reformation*, 691) puts the date at August 23. For the text, see *Corpus Reformatorum: Zwingli*, 1:249–384.

32. Schaff, *History*, 8:48.

33. Potter, *Zwingli*, 86.

34. Ibid., 85–86; see also Locher, *Zwinglishche Reformation*, 108–10.

35. Schaff, *History*, 8:53; Lindsay, *Reformation*, 2:34; Potter, *Zwingli*, 100.

For this debate, Zwingli prepared what may be considered the first public statement of the Reformed faith. The text is called the Sixty-seven Articles or Conclusions (*Schlussreden*).[36] These articles insisted that the Word of God was the only rule of faith and that only Christ is the Savior. Additionally, the articles directed an attack on the papacy, the Mass, fasts, purgatory, and other abuses.

On the side of the Reformation, Zwingli and three others were present.[37] On the Catholic side, the bishop of Constance sent theologian Dr. Johann Faber along with three counselors.[38] The debate's outcome was that the city fathers declared Zwingli's teaching theologically sound, and he was encouraged to continue in the same manner of preaching. Likewise, other preachers in the city were urged to sermonize only that which could be proven from the Scriptures.[39]

Afterward, Zwingli prepared a defense of his articles in response to theological charges brought against them by the Catholic Dr. Faber.[40] Thus 1523 could be seen as the year in which the Swiss Reformation began, and Zwingli may unhesitatingly be classified as a reformer.[41]

After the first disputation, Zwingli, in true Swiss fashion, carefully attempted to educate the people of Zurich through both spoken and printed sermons. He preached strongly against the worship of images, for example, but did not want action to precede education. He felt that as the people and magistrates were informed, so also the magistrates would legislate against various abuses.[42] As is often the case with religious fervor, however, some Zurichers defied the law in their zeal to destroy images and actually defaced and destroyed what was considered church property.[43] The Roman mass was also generally neglected throughout the city.[44]

---

36. Given January, 29, 1523. The text is in *Corpus Reformatorum: Zwingli*, 1:458–65. See Schaff (*History*, 8:52–54), who gives a short list of the most important articles, translated in Arthur C. Cochrane, *Reformed Confessions of the 16th Century* (Philadelphia: Westminster Press, 1966), 36–44. See also C. S. Meyer, *Luther's and Zwingli's Propositions for Debate* (Leiden: Brill, 1963).

37. Schaff, *History*, 8:53.

38. Ibid.; Lindsay, *Reformation*, 2:34; see Potter, *Zwingli*, esp. 102–3.

39. Schaff, *History*, 8:54; Lindsay, *Reformation*, 2:34.

40. See Schaff, *History*, 8:54n3.

41. Potter, *Zwingli*, 125.

42. Lindsay, *Reformation*, 2:34.

43. Ibid.; Schaff, *History*, 8:54n4.

44. Schaff, *History*, 8:54.

Perhaps because of this disruption, a second disputation was scheduled for October 26, 1523.[45] This disputation drew an even larger crowd than the first, with between eight hundred and nine hundred men taking part, including at least three hundred and fifty clergy and ten doctors of theology.[46] The disputation lasted until October 28. On the first day of debate, Zwingli attacked the use of images in the churches. The second day of disputation centered on the Roman mass, and Zwingli argued that it was not a sacrifice but instead a memorial of the Lord's death.[47] As a result of the disputation, the Mass was not immediately abolished, but idols were to be carefully removed from the churches in an orderly manner. In addition, a commission was established to study the matter of the Mass and worship and thereafter to write a paper on the commission's findings for the government. The writing committee included Zwingli, supplemented by two other ministers.

The paper that resulted from this committee's assignment was Zwingli's *Brief Christian Introduction*.[48] This paper deals mainly with the nature of salvation and the error of having images in worship. Because images had led to the sin of idolatry in the church, their destruction was a necessity. Because of the need to change the Mass, Zwingli also commented on what would later become an important element in his later theology. The Lord's Supper was presented not as a repetition of Christ's sacrifice but rather as a faithful remembrance of Christ's acts.[49] The *Introduction* was sent to all the ministers of the Swiss cantons (the Swiss word for *provinces* or *states*), to the bishops of the local areas, and also to the faculty of the University of Basel, the only Swiss university established at the time.[50]

A third public disputation arose in January 1524. The attendance at this disputation was much smaller than those at the previous two disputations. Those who still advocated the Mass were informed that

45. Lindsay, *Reformation*, 2:35; Schaff, *History*, 8:54.
46. Potter, *Zwingli*, 131.
47. Lindsay, *Reformation*, 2:35. The Mass was ably defended by Martin Steinli of Schaffhausen, with Konrad Schmid's offering an eloquent defense of a more moderate position. See Schaff, *History*, 8:55.
48. *Corpus Reformatorum: Zwingli*, 1:541–65.
49. Lindsay, *Reformation*, 2:35–36.
50. Schaff, *History*, 8:56.

they could no longer object to the will of the magistrates, who had now legislated against it; though the advocates were not commanded to give up their old beliefs, their actions could be legislated.

A unique feature of the three Zurich disputations was that they were conducted in the Swiss German dialect, whereas Latin was the means of communication at the German disputations. Also, laypeople were invited to the Swiss debates. As a result, in Switzerland the laypeople, that is, the magistrates and the educated—not only the clergy and princes—were in many ways the catalysts for reformation. Yet in both Germany and Switzerland the magistrates and the people desired reformation.

It was after the third disputation that the structures of the old Catholic worship were dismantled. By June of 1524 the process was fairly complete; it included the removal of the church organs and the termination of the choir's singing in Latin. Furthermore, the buildings were stripped of icons and left whitewashed for pure worship by the saints.[51]

Zurich Reformation: Social and Political Issues. Like a great locomotive that gradually gains momentum, the movement toward reform in Zurich was now moving powerfully. There was a general cry from the clergy to have all the images removed from the churches. Again Zwingli was victorious, and even though the second disputation did not provide a real exchange of arguments between the Catholics and Zwingli, he wrote the *Brief Christian Introduction*, which outlined salvation by faith and the respective duties of ministers and governments.[52] His introductory sermon to the second disputation, titled "The Shepherd," was also published at this time. By June 1524, under Zwingli's recommendation, the city council ordered the removal of all images from the churches. Later in the year, monks and friars were permitted to relieve themselves of their monastic vows. Most of them did, so the state laid charge against the monastic houses. In January 1525, Zwingli's supporters finally gained a majority in the city council.

If 1523 did not evidence strong enough movement toward reform, then certainly the year 1525 could mark the beginning of the Swiss Reformation. That was the year of the first evangelical Lord's Supper

51. See Potter, *Zwingli*, 140.
52. This work came out in November 1523.

celebrated in Zurich. It was also a year of continued literary activity for Zwingli. Against a group called the Anabaptists, he wrote *On Baptism, On Rebaptism and Infant Baptism, Answer to Hubmaiers Booklet on Baptism*, and two other small works on baptism. Perhaps the most important of these writings was his anti-Catholic *Commentary on True and False Religion*, which saw the light of day in March of the same year.

Zwingli had an active preaching ministry. He began preaching on Matthew and probably used John Chrysostom's famous *Homilies on Matthew* as his source.[53] By this time Zwingli's Greek was quite good, and he began studying Reuchlin's *Rudimenta Hebraica*.[54] During the week he preached on the Psalms, and on Fridays he preached in the marketplace so that the villagers could hear him.[55] After Matthew, he proceeded to the book of Acts and then advanced to the Pauline epistles. Within four years he preached through the entire NT with the exception of the Book of Revelation. His preaching was a welcome innovation that made him very popular with the people.

Zwingli's evangelical preaching can be classified as a positive move toward reformation. There was also what we could call a negative move away from the power and authority of the church in Rome. Yet tracing the lines and movements of reform is sometimes complex. In Germany, for example, Tetzel's sales of indulgences may rightly be described as the immediate catalyst for the Reformation there. The same, though, cannot be said for Switzerland. Even at this time, Zwingli did not disagree in principle with selling indulgences. He did not get into trouble with the Catholic authorities on indulgences and for his actions had even received the approval of Dr. Johann Faber, the general vicar of Constance.[56] Later, however, he did have the Catholic indulgence peddler Samson expelled.

His first real attack against the existing Roman system came against the paying of tithes. Zwingli declared tithes to be merely voluntary offerings.[57] Thereafter followed addressing the issue of eating the for-

---

53. Schaff, *History*, 8:40.
54. Ibid.
55. Lindsay, *Reformation*, 2:30.
56. Schaff, *History*, 8:43.
57. Zwingli had been reading Hus's *On the Church*. See Lindsay, *Reformation*, 2:31.

bidden sausage at the printer's house during Lent in 1522.[58] Zwingli supported his friends by publishing the *Selection or Liberty concerning Foods; an offence and scandal; whether there is any Authority for forbidding Meat at certain times* (*Von Erkiesen und Fryheit der Spysen*).[59] This was Zwingli's first printed book, in which he asserted that in matters of indifference Christians have the right to abstain from certain activities. In this little work he appeals to abundant scriptural texts for doctrinal support.[60]

The bishop of Constance was very unhappy with the way the Council of Zurich handled this crisis. He felt that they compromised the church in their recognition that fasting was not imposed in the NT even though the practice had the weight of tradition behind it. The bishop protested to the small council (or senate, composed of the leaders of the guilds) by asserting that the church had authority to rule in such matters and that therefore the church should be obeyed. Zwingli appeared before the special council of 212 members and continued to argue for liberty of conscience.

At this point in time, the council resolved to abide by its compromise. It also requested that the bishop hold a meeting with his clergy so that a resolution might be obtained. This event was very important in the Swiss Reformation. "This resolution of the Council," argues Lindsay, "really set aside the Episcopal authority and was a revolt against the Roman Church."[61] Zwingli now found himself in a very difficult and dangerous situation. He had obviously caused trouble between the Roman church and the city, and his having done so did not help his popularity. The pope could have both condemned the city and pronounced all loyal Catholics apostate. This move, called "the ban," was an effective means of papal control.

Meanwhile, an important, nontheological, economic issue was festering under the surface of religious strife. Zwingli had participated in a military campaign as a chaplain and after that experience was convinced that the mercenary system itself was an evil for his country.

---

58. Potter, *Zwingli*, 75.

59. Lindsay (*Reformation*, 2:31) gives the date of the publication as April 16, 1522.

60. Some of those scriptural passages were 1 Corinthians 8:8; 10:25; Colossians 2:16; 1 Timothy 4:1; and Romans 14:1–3; 15:1–2. See Schaff, *History*, 8:47.

61. Lindsay, *Reformation*, 2:32.

He took his protest to the civic authorities against such service. When Zurich's officials inclined to his position, they realized that a decision against mercenary service would now alienate them from the rest of the Swiss Confederation.

In God's good providence, however, events moved to aid Zwingli's striving against the mercenary system. In 1521, the French king was permitted to recruit sixteen thousand mercenary soldiers from all over Switzerland despite official protests from the city of Zurich. Although the allowance was sanctioned by the Swiss Confederation, Zurich prohibited recruiting men in their area. Many Zurichers were unhappy at both their loss of money and their separation from the other cantons. During this time, Zwingli's life was frequently threatened.[62]

The pope, who was not only a spiritual leader but the prince of wealthy estates as well, had also pleaded with Zurich for a body of soldiers to help defend his territory in Italy. The city's government refused the pope's plea just as it had that of France. This time Zurich's judicious decision saved the day.

The decision was wise because the thousands of Swiss mercenaries hired by France were employed to go into Italy and fight against the pope's hired men! Thus the pope's Swiss mercenaries were set to fight against the Swiss mercenaries hired by the French! Had Zurich acquiesced to either the pope or the French king, it would have been Swiss battling to the death against Swiss! To consolidate anti-mercenary feeling, those men from Zurich who performed mercenary service on either side—which service was officially forbidden—returned home with neither monetary reward nor honors from France or Rome! These misadventures turned the city against all foreign mercenary service, and the council forbade all such future service permanently.[63]

Zurich's permanent prohibition of mercenary activity in January 1522 may appear at first glance to be a purely political/social decision; but that was not the case. The ruling was also of great religious significance. For it was at this point that Zurich made a decided break with the papacy. Since the Middle Ages, Switzerland had provided the pope with a personal body of guards, which is still the case today. Given the fact that through history the pope was not a purely religious leader

62. Ibid.; see also Locher, *Zwinglishche Reformation*, 93.
63. Lindsay, *Reformation*, 2:32.

but actually a political figure—in fact, a violent political figure—the importance of a group of trusted personal guards for him is self-evident. Zurich had always provided the pope with half the number of these bodyguards. Because Zurich now forbade all foreign military service, this half of the pope's guard was perhaps withdrawn. "When the long connection between Zurich and the papacy is considered, this decree was virtually a breach between the city and the Pope. It made the path of the Reformation much easier," argues Lindsay, "and Zwingli's open break with the papacy was only a matter of time."[64]

Reformation in Bern. Bern is the Swiss capital, and the 1528 disputation there was decisive for the overall success of the Swiss Reformation.[65] In the light of Bern's great political power, Zurich's reformation was more secure as a result of its acceptance in Bern. But the disputation was also helpful for Zurich because there Zwingli had an opportunity to present his own views on the nature of the church.

Zwingli's position, that each local church was within a confessing community of churches, was met with favor in Bern. The local church thus became relatively independent in its own affairs. This shift was indeed a radical move from the episcopal system—and with Christian history of a thousand years! Even with granting local autonomy, thought Zwingli, because the church commonly confessed Christ, church unity throughout the Swiss Confederation could be maintained.

Also noteworthy were the different ideas on the church held on the one hand by Zwingli and on the other hand by the Basel reformer Johannes Oecolampadius (1482–1531). Oecolampadius wanted more independence of the church from the city magistrates regarding church discipline. This issue would become increasingly important in the years to come.

The Bern disputation also sheds light on Zwingli's views of the Swiss group called the Anabaptists. "Concerning the Baptists who left us," Zwingli said, "the point is that they are not of us and are not a church but rather a mutilated, withdrawn pack" (my translation).[66] The

---

64. Ibid., 2:32–33.
65. Bruce Gordon, *Clerical Discipline and the Rural Reformation: The Synod in Zurich, 1532–1580* (Bern: Lang, 1992), 40c.
66. "Desshalb ouch der Touffer kilch und sunderung, die von uns ussgangen sind, drumb, das sy nit von uns sind (1 John 2:19), nit ein kilch sind, sunder ein zerschnittne, abgetrettne, rott" (*Huldreich Zwinglis sämtliche Werke*, vol. 6, as cited by Gordon, *Clerical Discipline*, 40).

previous chapter outlined the development of Anabaptism in Germany and the Netherlands. In December 1524, a number of radicals were calling themselves by the simple title *brethren* or *Christian*. One of their leaders, Felix Mantz, wrote his *Petition of Protest and Defense* to the Council of Zurich that same month. In January, Zwingli and Bullinger debated Mantz and three other leaders in what has become known as the First Baptismal Disputation. There was no hope that Zwingli or the magistrates could be won to their opinion.

Neither was there any hope that the Swiss Anabaptists would be deterred; nevertheless, in January 1525 they started the action by celebrating the Lord's Supper and rebaptism. Their baptism was a simple pouring of water on the head combined with the Lord's Supper, with common bread and wine. All was to be performed in the simplest fashion possible in imitation of the NT accounts. In contrast, the Mass was still read in Latin in the parishes of Zurich, since the time was before Zwingli's celebration of a Reformed Lord's Supper.

These Anabaptist leaders were effective. Records demonstrate that from 1525 their hearers had a deep conviction of sin and a longing for forgiveness. On January 30, Mantz and another leader were arrested. There was apparently another disputation, at which Zwingli argued that there was no second baptism. The Anabaptist leaders countered by saying that second baptism is what is recorded in Acts 19:3–5. Mantz remained unconvinced by Zwingli's arguments. While Mantz was in prison, at least forty more adults had been rebaptized. He was released but again imprisoned in March, and what is called the Second Baptismal Disputation occurred. Mantz somehow escaped from the authorities, but the Anabaptist leadership was banished from the area. They traveled east to what is called the Grisons. Mantz was arrested there and was imprisoned until October 1526.

Although the Anabaptists had been scattered, a form and direction of the movement was now taking shape. The Swiss Anabaptists were convicted that all who had experienced divine forgiveness were, in obedience to the Great Commission, to proclaim repentance and true believer's baptism among all people no matter what limitations were imposed by the Magisterial Reformers.[67]

67. George Hunston Williams, *The Radical Reformation* (Philadelphia: Westminster Press, 1962), 137–55.

Fundamental to Zwingli's rejection of the Anabaptists was his definition of the church. Zwingli believed that the church is truly a mixture of those set apart as Christ's but that among this group there are also the impious. It is in fact a mixed group.[68] This view did not conform to the Anabaptist notion of the church as those, and those alone, who are saved.

Civil War and Zwingli's Death. Unlike pluralistic modern nations, no state in the sixteenth century thought that there could be more than one religion within its realm. Religion was too important to the fabric of society. We can easily ask whether our present pluralistic experience is a true advance. However that question is answered, the answer in Zwingli's day was clear. Switzerland was to have one religion and one alone. The clouds of civil war were about to belch forth their thunder.

Civil war erupted, and in 1531 the Zurichers lost to the Catholic cantons. Zwingli was captured, cut into four pieces as a traitor to the nation, and then burned as a heretic. There was a concomitant negative reaction against the city by Zurich's rural inhabitants. They believed that it was the city's war, not theirs, for which they must now offer help, pay, and suffer the consequences of defeat. Anti-clericalism, which had been rampant in the early part of the sixteenth century (as well observed in the peasant uprisings of the 1520s), was now directed against Zurich's Protestant clergy.

Reformations in Saint Gallen and Basel. The earliest reformer of the town of Saint Gallen was Joachim von Watt (1484–1551). Like Zwingli, he was sent to Vienna for university when he was seventeen years old. There identifying himself as a humanist, he changed his name to Vadianus. He had a successful literary career before he decided to study medicine. In 1517, at the age of thirty-three, he graduated as a medical doctor from a program that was a more theoretical and less practical course of study than medicine is today.[69]

Vadian left the academic world of Vienna in 1518 and came home to be the town physician. Saint Gallen had fewer than five thousand inhabitants, but as Vadian was away on his honeymoon the plague swept through the city and killed seventeen hundred of its inhabitants.[70]

68. Gordon, *Clerical Discipline*, 53.
69. E. Gordon Rupp, *Patterns of Reformation* (London: Epworth, 1969), 359–60.
70. Ibid., 364.

As a humanist, Vadian became Erasmian and read Luther. He was in contact with Zwingli in 1511, and by 1523 they were corresponding regularly. He was president of the second Zurich disputation in October 1523, where he made the closing speech.[71] He was a member of the city council in 1521 and mayor in 1525. Reforming edicts came from his direction in 1526. At a debate in Bern in 1528 he was again president.[72]

Vadian had heard of Calvin as early as 1536 and thought it important for Calvin to be united with the Zurich theologians on the nature of the Lord's Supper. Calvin, on his part, found Vadian to possess keen judgment in desiring that union. Calvin had high regard for him—and dedicated the work *De scandalis* to Vadian. While not a particularly good theologian, Vadian published some theological works. He was a very good local historian and a scholar to the very end.[73]

The Basel Reformation was led by the great scholar and reformer Johannes Oecolampadius (1482–1531). Born in Germany as Johannes Heussgen, he, like Vadian, changed his name. To identify himself as a humanist, Heussgen took the name Oecolampadius. He studied theology at Heidelberg and began work as a preacher in 1510. He left this post for further studies at Tübingen in 1513.[74]

In the summer of 1515 Oecolampadius went to the city of Basel. His task was to help launch Erasmus's Greek NT, and he provided a great number of the textual annotations.[75] Oecolampadius was not as famous as Erasmus, but they worked together as scholars. Oecolampadius indexed Erasmus's nine-volume edition of Jerome's works.[76] While in Basel he studied at the university and eventually obtained his doctor's degree.[77] He publicly supported Luther in 1519 and published a Greek grammar in 1520. Oecolampadius was a well-

---

71. Ibid., 367.

72. Ibid., 372.

73. Ibid., 375–77. He published a large history of the famous abbey in Saint Gallen in 1529 and a work on the Lord's Supper in 1535.

74. Diane Poythress, *Reformer of Basel: The Life, Thought, and Influence of Johannes Oecolampadius* (Grand Rapids: Reformation Heritage Books, 2011), 1–5.

75. Rupp, *Patterns*, 9: "A large number of the Hebrew *adnotations* came from Oecolampadius, perhaps over 100, a high proportion in the gospel according to St. Matthew."

76. Ibid., 10: he "had been a scholar of Reuchlin and a colleague of Erasmus, and thus in personal contact with the two finest luminaries of the new learning."

77. Poythress, *Reformer of Basel*, 5–6.

established scholar who had fully mastered both the Hebrew and Greek languages.[78]

After completing his work with Erasmus in Basel, Oecolampadius spent some time as a cathedral preacher in Augsburg, as an Augustinian monk, and in hiding in a castle in Germany, but he returned to Basel in 1522 and joined the theological faculty the following year.[79] His public lectures on Isaiah were very popular and drew literally hundreds of listeners. The city was moving toward reformation.

Owing to Oecolampadius's leadership and publications, by 1525 the city was ready for reformation.[80] Three years later, with Zwingli, Oecolampadius attended the Bern disputation of 1528, and the following year the Mass was abolished throughout the whole city of Basel. In that same year Oecolampadius also became the main cathedral preacher and attended the Marburg Colloquy with the other Swiss delegates.[81]

Oecolampadius revolutionized liturgy and discipline.[82] He almost succeeded in establishing a system of church discipline that depended on church authority. A twelve-member consistory was set up to administer discipline and consisted of an equal number of ministers, magistrates, and representatives of church laymen.[83] Sadly, Oecolampadius died in November 1531.

Early Reformation in French-Speaking Switzerland. Oftentimes God uses extraordinary people to do extraordinary service in his kingdom. Guillaume [William] Farel (1484–1565) was just such a person. There is a statue of him in front of the main church in the city of Neuchâtel, where Farel lived for most of his life. The statue really

78. Rupp, *Patterns*, 8. Poythress (*Reformer of Basel*, 5) says that at this time he spoke German, Greek, Latin, Aramaic, some Swiss German, Italian, French, and Hebrew. This accomplishment would rival any contemporary humanist.

79. Poythress (*Reformer of Basel*, 8–9) recounts that Eck wrote to Rome to say that Oecolampadius was more dangerous than Luther. She also correctly suggests that Oecolampadius had instituted liturgical reforms at his church in Basel, thus creating the earliest Protestant liturgy (ibid., 13).

80. He published a commentary on Isaiah, broke with Erasmus over Luther, did not object to a priest's being married in the city, held a Protestant service each Sunday, and wrote a work on the Lord's Supper (see ibid., 14–19).

81. Ibid., 14–29.

82. He was instrumental in establishing the singing of the Psalms in Basel and Strasbourg, and he established ecclesiastical ordinances. See ibid., 20–21, 26–27, 29–30.

83. T. H. L. Parker, *John Calvin: A Biography* (Philadelphia: Westminster Press, 1975), 62.

captures the man's spirit as it depicts him standing erect, with his arms raised high above his head and his hands holding a huge Bible. It is as though he is about to catapult the Bible into orbit or else crash it down on the city.

Farel's statue, however, reminds us of what the Scriptures say about another, even greater man of God—Moses. After Moses received the Ten Commandments, the people of Israel sinned terribly. Moses threw down the tablets in anger, and God's judgment fell upon the people. The impression one gets from the statue is that Farel, like Moses, is about to bring down God's wrath on the people of Neuchâtel. But instead of the Ten Commandments alone, Farel has the whole Bible!

Actually, the parallel between Moses and Farel is not reflected exclusively in the statue but is in many ways seen in their ministries. Both at the time of the Hebrews' exodus from slavery in Egypt and during the Protestant Reformation, God dealt with his people in rather unique ways. In both cases, by a mighty hand and an outstretched arm God removed his people from bondage and delivered them to a new land. This type of language describes what happened at the exodus but can in truth be applied to the Reformation as well. Through the preaching of the Word of God, men and women came in great numbers to know Jesus Christ and his work—the true exodus that was reflected so many years earlier in the exodus from Egypt.

Continuing the parallel between Moses and Farel, both leaders were concerned about their successors. Moses needed Aaron. Farel had Calvin. This observation does not mean that Calvin was the theological successor of Farel, as though Farel were the tutor and Calvin the student. Farel realized that even though he was older than Calvin, it was Calvin who had the superior intellectual gifts. But Farel was first on the scene at Geneva, and it was Farel who twisted Calvin's arm into staying.

Farel began the Reformation in Geneva. He had first visited the city in 1532, and by sixteenth-century standards it was fairly large. With about ten thousand inhabitants, it was as large as Basel or Zurich.[84] It was on Good Friday in the year 1533 that Farel held the first Protestant service in Geneva—in a garden.

84. Ibid., 54; see also William Monter, *Calvin's Geneva* (New York: Wiley & Sons, 1967).

The spread of the gospel in Geneva bore some violent fruit. In May a riot broke out in which a Roman Catholic churchman, called a *canon*, was killed. The Roman bishop of Geneva had the ringleaders arrested, but the city magistrates argued that in the case of murder the episcopal court had no jurisdiction. Seeing that he would not be able to try the murderers, the bishop left Geneva and never returned. In fact later, the city had the culprits executed.[85]

Geneva had been in alliance with the cities of Fribourg and the Swiss capital of Bern.[86] Fribourg, a strongly Catholic city, had protested Farel's presence in Geneva, but his actions there were approved by the city of Bern. After various disputations and riots, it was discovered that an episcopal notary had documents signed by the bishop—documents that authorized the appointment of a military governor from Fribourg over the city. Infuriated, Geneva refused to continue its alliance with Fribourg, thereby leaving Bern the sole protector of the city.

The bishop of Geneva, however, would not give up his power in the city without a fight. He aligned himself with Savoy, gathered troops, and attacked the city. This attack failed. A number of other attacks were also attempted, but all without success.

The magistrates wrote to Rome, protested the actions of their bishop, reported his absence, and declared the office of bishop vacant. But Rome chose to ignore the letter. The magistrates established their own mint in 1535, thus proclaiming their independence from the Roman hierarchy.

Charles of Savoy was not ready to lose Geneva; he mustered a troop of five hundred mercenaries and besieged the city in late 1535. Geneva appealed to Bern for help but received none. They then turned to King Francis I of France. A small cavalry force was sent, but after its attempt to cross the Alps during the winter, and after being attacked by Savoyard troops, only seven men and the commander succeeded in reaching Geneva. Their "generous" offer of protection under French rule was voted on and subsequently turned down by the city.

This futile attempt by France aroused Bern to action. Assembling a force of six thousand soldiers, she liberated Geneva from the Savoy

---

85. Alexandre Ganoczy, *The Young Calvin*, trans. David Foxgrover and Wade Provo (Philadelphia: Westminster Press, 1987), 106–7.

86. Parker, *John Calvin*, 56.

troops in February 1536. As a result of Farel's preaching and disputations, the citizens of the newly liberated city voted in May of that year to live according to the gospel.[87]

Although Geneva was now legally a Protestant town, it was such in name only. As Calvin was saying farewell to the Company of Pastors, he testified many years later: "When I first came to this church there was almost nothing. They were preaching and that is all. They were good at seeking out idols and burning them, yet there was no other Reformation. Everything was in an uproar."[88]

Certainly, the Geneva at the time of Calvin's death could not be described in the same terms that Calvin used to describe the city on his arrival. Ford Lewis Battles stated the situation very clearly:

> Not a few supporters of the old faith remained; others merely wanted to be free of all restraints to live the kind of lives they pleased. There were Anabaptists who clamored to be heard and more sophisticated thinkers who wished to give up Trinitarianism. There was great reluctance even among some of the political leaders to translate Farel's and Calvin's blueprint for the city into reality. And great pressures, political and religious, were being brought from the outside to bear on newly-reformed Geneva.[89]

What were some of the effects of Calvin's sojourn in this Protestant city? How did he come to stay there in the first place? Answers to those questions are in the following chapter.

Other Swiss Reformers. Martin Bucer (1491–1551) was born into a relatively poor family in 1491. While in his late teens, he determined to become a Dominican monk. But in 1520 Bucer left the monastery, and two years later, in 1522, he married. In 1523 he was excommunicated from the Roman church and went to Strasbourg.

The Reformation had already begun in that city through the preaching of Matthaeus Zell. In Strasbourg, this preaching was very important for the Reformation. In either 1524 or 1525, the Mass was abolished in the parish churches, though it was still permitted in the monastic churches.

---

87. Ford Lewis Battles, "Introduction to the *Confession of Faith of 1538*" (n.p., 1972), ii.
88. Ganoczy, *Young Calvin* (cited with different translation), 108.
89. Battles, "Introduction," ii.

Bucer developed a thoroughly Protestant service. He created an evangelical form of confirmation based on proper instruction and confession, which lead to confirmation. Church government progressed through the use of elders. Finally, by 1529 the Mass was suspended altogether in the city. In 1548, because of the Schmalkaldic War, Bucer had to flee to England. While there, he wrote the important political work on Christ's reign, *De regno Christi*, in 1550. He died in 1551.[90]

Wolfgang Musculus (1497–1563) had studied in the Benedictine monastery. After reading Luther he left the monastery in 1518. From 1529 to 1531 he studied at Strasbourg and served as a preacher in Augsburg from 1531 to 1548. Having to leave Germany because of the Augsburg Interim in 1548, he went to Switzerland and was appointed professor of theology at Bern in 1549. There he labored for the rest of his life. Musculus's major theological work was his *Loci communes sacrae theologiae*, which came out one year after Calvin's final edition of the *Institutes*.[91]

Peter Martyr Vermigli (1500–1562) studied at the great centers of Padua and Bologna.[92] He lived in Italy for forty-three years. Fully trusted by the Roman authorities, he probably functioned as consultant to the *Consilium* of 1537, and he was later appointed to the first delegation that represented the Catholic side at the Colloquy of Worms in 1540.

Everything changed in the year 1542, when a papal bull came out against his successful reforms in the city of Lucca. That reforming work was so powerful that it may have directly contributed to the resurgence

90. Hastings Eells, *Martin Bucer* (New York: Russell and Russell, 1971); D. F. Wright, ed., *Martin Bucer: Reforming Church and Community* (Cambridge: Cambridge University Press, 1994).

91. Richard A. Muller, *Post-Reformation Reformed Dogmatics*, vol. 1, *Prolegomena to Theology* (Grand Rapids: Baker, 1987), 41.

92. John C. McLelland and G. E. Duffield, eds., *The Life, Early Letters and Eucharistic Writings of Peter Martyr* (Oxford: Sutton Courtenay Press, 1989); Marvin Anderson, *Peter Martyr: A Reformer in Exile (1542–1562)* (Leiden: Brill, 1975); John C. McLelland, *The Visible Words of God: An Exposition of the Sacramental Theology of Peter Martyr Vermigli* (Grand Rapids: Eerdmans, 1957); John C. McLelland, ed., *Peter Martyr Vermigli and Italian Reform* (Waterloo, ON: Wilfrid Laurier University Press, 1980); Donald Nugent, *Ecumenism in the Age of the Reformation* (Cambridge: Harvard University Press, 1974); Robert Kingdon, *The Political Thought of Peter Martyr Vermigli* (Paris: Droz, 1980); and J. P. Donnelly, *Calvinism and Scholasticism in Vermigli's Doctrine of Man and Grace* (Leiden: Brill, 1976). While he was a prior near Naples, he encountered Juan de Valdes's new ideas.

of the Roman Inquisition.[93] Vermigli was summoned to appear, and fled north, first to the city of Basel and then to Strasbourg. By the end of the year he succeeded Wolfgang Capito as professor of theology at the university there.

Five years later, Thomas Cranmer invited Vermigli to England. He taught for six years at the University of Oxford as a Regius Professor of Divinity until 1553. While there, he upheld Protestant teaching on the Lord's Supper (1549), helped work through the vestment controversy (1550), helped revise the prayer book (1552), and then aided in the formulation of the Forty-two Articles (1553).[94]

With the rise of Queen Mary, Vermigli was forced to leave England and return to Strasbourg for the next three years (1553–1556). Vermigli's good friend Martin Bucer, leader in Strasbourg, had already died in 1551. After Bucer's death, one contemporary said, "The two most excellent theologians of our times are John Calvin and Peter Martyr."[95] But since Vermigli could not sign the Wittenberg Concord, he also had to leave that city, and he ended his career in Zurich, where he labored from 1556 to 1562. After his death, a dogmatic treatment titled the *Loci communes* was gathered out of his writings and published in 1576.[96]

Vermigli was an able churchman. He prepared a statement on Christ's presence in the Lord's Supper for his Huguenot supporters at the Colloquy of Poissy in the fall of 1561. Catherine de' Medici called the meeting to resolve the simmering conflict between Catholics and Protestants over the advance of Protestant doctrine in France. Beza and Vermigli led the Reformed delegation, but sadly the meeting ended in a stalemate and served as a prelude to the civil war that would soon break out.[97] Vermigli's views, which, based on constitutional principles, upheld the magistrates' right to resist tyranny, were widely distributed.[98]

---

93. Frank A. James III, *Peter Martyr Vermigli and Predestination* (Oxford: Clarendon, 1988), 3.

94. Ibid., 4.

95. Ibid., 5. See Richard C. Gamble, "Sacramental Continuity among Reformed Refugees: Peter Martyr Vermigli and John Calvin," in *Peter Martyr Vermigli and the European Reformations: Semper Reformanda*, ed. Frank A. James III, 97–114 (Leiden: Brill, 2004).

96. Muller, *Post-Reformation*, 41.

97. William Johnson and John H. Leith, eds., *Reformed Reader: A Sourcebook in Christian Theology* (Philadelphia: Westminster John Knox Press, 1993), 320.

98. Ibid., 351: "Kingdon offers the judgment that Vermigli mediated between Lutheran and Reformed theorists, and he notes that Vermigli's stance is less radical than many of the later

Key Terms

public disputation
indulgence
mercenary service

Study Questions

1. What role did public disputations play in the Swiss Reformation?
2. Zwingli was killed in a civil war. Do you think that the issues were important enough that blood should have been shed over them?
3. The Swiss Reformation occurred a long time ago at a faraway place. Could such reformation come to your city?

Resources for Further Study

Poythress, Diane. *Reformer of Basel: The Life, Thought, and Influence of Johannes Oecolampadius.* Grand Rapids: Reformation Heritage Books, 2011. An excellent work in which Dr. Poythress introduces this very important Basel reformer to the English-speaking world.

Bucer, Martin. *De regno Christi.* In *Melanchton and Bucer,* edited by Wilhelm Pauck, 174–394. Philadelphia: Westminster John Knox Press, 1969. A wonderful, and in many ways timeless, treatise on the implications of Christ's mediatorial kingship over all areas of life written to help the English Reformation.

Reformed. Part of the reason for Vermigli's less radical position, as Kingdon implies, may be that he wrote prior to the St. Bartholomew's day massacre of 1572."

14

Reformations in Geneva, the UK, and the Netherlands

JOHN CALVIN (A.D. 1509–1564) AND THE REFORMATION IN GENEVA

Calvin's Life to A.D. 1536.[1] Born in 1509, John Calvin was an exceptionally bright young student. He obtained funding to study Latin in Paris and then attended the Collège de la Marche of the University of Paris. His father moved him from Paris to study law first at Orléans and then in Bourges. He completed his legal education in 1532.

The great humanist Erasmus wrote a commentary on the stoic philosopher Seneca's work *De Clementia*, and in Erasmus's concluding paragraph he invited others who might be able to add to what Erasmus had written also to write a commentary.[2] Calvin took up the challenge, and before the publication of his 1536 *Institutes of the Christian Religion* he produced a full-length commentary on *De Clementia* (1532).[3] The number of copies printed was small and partially subsidized by Calvin.

1. See Richard C. Gamble, *Articles on Calvin and Calvinism*, vol. 1, *The Biography of Calvin* (New York/London: Garland, 1992).
2. W. De Greef, *The Writings of John Calvin*, trans. Lyle D. Bierma (Grand Rapids: Baker, 1993), 85: "Perhaps what drew Calvin to Seneca was the Christian humanists' sensitivity to Stoic ideas. Calvin himself never offered an explanation.... Above all Calvin hoped through this commentary to establish his reputation as a humanist scholar."
3. John Calvin, *Commentary on Seneca's De Clementia*, trans. and ed. Ford Lewis Battles and André Hugo (Leiden: Brill, 1969). See Francois Wendel, "Le Commentaire sur le De Clementia de Seneque," in *Calvin et l'humanisme* (Paris: Presses Universitaires de France, 1976), 37–62.

What role does this earlier publication play toward understanding the writer and man Calvin, as well as the later composition of the *Institutes*? The question is complicated. It was part and parcel of sixteenth-century literary genre for humanists to address kings and emperors. Seneca's text was a perfect one for Calvin, the trained lawyer, to try his hand at writing to the king of France. The Roman emperor Nero had the philosopher Seneca as his helper. Perhaps Seneca could help again, this time in the garb of sixteenth-century France. It is true that writing a scholarly commentary on an ancient text takes a classic sixteenth-century humanist approach; and one scholar sees Calvin's commentary as the product of just that approach, not as the writing of a Reformer, while arguing that the commentary is nothing but a humanist study of an ancient text.[4]

But against the conclusion that this text is only a humanist one, it is highly probable that this was Calvin's first Christian apology, written to the King Francis I.[5] In the commentary, Calvin compared and contrasted Stoic and Christian concepts of providence and reflected on the human conscience's having a natural law.[6]

There are a number of literary similarities between Calvin's earlier *De Clementia* commentary and the first edition of the *Institutes*. One important Protestant theme, developed earlier by Ulrich Zwingli in his *Commentary on True and False Religion*, was the relationship between true and false religion. In his commentary on Seneca, Calvin cited various philosophical authorities on the meaning of those two contrasting terms.[7]

4. Alexandre Ganoczy, *The Young Calvin*, trans. David Foxgrover and Wade Provo (Philadelphia: Westminster Press, 1987), 179: "His commentary on the *De Clementia* is the epitome of a humanist study of an ancient document." Like Erasmus, "Calvin knows how to dwell in the serene heights of the scholar; he does not like 'the profane crowd,' and he does not descend into the arena of the burning issues of the day."

5. Ford Lewis Battles, "Introduction" to *Institutes of the Christian Religion, 1536 Edition*, by John Calvin, trans. and annot. Ford Lewis Battles (Grand Rapids: Meeter Center/Eerdmans, 1986), xxii. Acknowledging that Josef Bohatec had stated the thesis earlier, Battles (ibid.) concludes: "Let us for the moment suppose that the Seneca Commentary was Calvin's first apology to Francis I."

6. De Greef, *John Calvin*, 85.

7. Battles, "Introduction," xxiii: "But when we look at the clear Christian use to which this material is later put in the *Institutes* (1.12.1) we must admit that the fundamental issue of true versus false religion was already on Calvin's mind in early 1532."

There are two other important matters in this work. One is the nature of the human soul, and the other is the relationship between divine governance and human rule of this world.[8]

Calvin's comments and analysis in this commentary were similar to the last chapter of the 1536 *Institutes*, the chapter on governance. From his work on Seneca, Calvin was familiar with the classical form of the monarchy. If the 1536 *Institutes* is, at least in part, a political apology for the French evangelicals, then this background analysis of government was very important.[9]

Another early work, called the *Psychopannychia*, on the topic of soul sleep, was published in 1542 and 1545, although it had been composed earlier.[10] Neither the 1534 nor the 1535 edition is extant.[11] The doctrine of soul sleep, held by a number of French evangelicals, was that when the body dies, the soul also dies or goes to sleep. Calvin wrote to defend the soul's immortality and assert the continuing life of the soul independently of the body after death. For Calvin, the soul was preeminently identified with the image of God. That identification solidified the soul's immortality.[12] Calvin sent a number of drafts of the work to different reformers, including Wolfgang Capito of Strasbourg, for advice concerning publication of the manuscript. Capito, in a letter to Calvin dated 1534, dissuaded him from publishing it and sent him back to the drawing board. Calvin continued to revise the manuscript during his Basel sojourn in 1535. In the preface to his commentary on the Psalms, Calvin gave his readers an account of the work's literary history.

During his early travels Calvin had returned to Paris, probably in September 1533.[13] In those days there was heated strife between the

8. Ibid., xxi–xxiv.

9. Ibid., lviii: "Unquestionably Calvin is here reworking from this new evangelical Christian vantage point the whole classical teaching on the monarch." See his chart of classical sources used by Calvin in Ford Lewis Battles, "The Sources," in *Interpreting John Calvin*, ed. Robert Benedetto (Grand Rapids: Baker, 1996), 86–88.

10. De Greef, *John Calvin*, 166; Battles, "Introduction," xl.

11. Ganoczy, *Young Calvin*, 179: "Thus we may affirm that with this study Calvin presents himself for the first time as a true 'biblical' humanist, from this time on engaged in contemporary controversies."

12. Battles, "Introduction," xlii: "As God never dies, never sleeps, so the image of him in man must be ever watchful until the blessed reunion of soul with body at the general resurrection."

13. Ganoczy, *Young Calvin*, 77–78. A letter written by Calvin to Mr. Daniel of Orléans gives us quite a bit of detail on this time in Paris.

traditional Sorbonne theologians and other theologians who could be called Reformists.[14] Nicolas Cop, the rector, or president, of the University of Paris was supposed to deliver an address on All Saints' Day, November 1, and he did so. The president was Calvin's longtime friend. His address was basically a sermon expounding the lectionary's gospel reading of the day—Matthew 5:1–12. Cop's discourse began in most beautiful words: "Something great, something far excelling expression or even comprehension by mind or thought is the Christian Philosophy, a philosophy divinely given by Christ to a man, to show forth the true and surest felicity."[15] Although the speech was delivered by Cop, we know from the manuscript that it was actually written by Calvin.[16] Within forty-eight hours of the address, a heresy complaint was leveled against Cop to the Paris Parliament due to the sermon's Reformed tone. A price was set on Cop's head, and both Calvin and Cop had to flee the city.[17] Word of the scandalous message had reached King Francis I. The king was clear concerning his desires, and he specifically mentioned Cop's address: "Its further spread [Lutheran heresy] we wish with our might and power to prevent. And to that end we wish and understand that such grievous punishment should be meted out that it would be a correction to the accursed heretics and an example to all others."[18]

Another early writing was Calvin's Latin preface to Pierre Robert Olivetan's French Bible.[19] This preface was printed in June 1535 and appeared only in that edition. In it, Calvin stated that the Bible should be in the common tongue, which was contra contemporary Roman

14. Ibid., 76. Some of the "traditionalists" were even banned from Paris. The main Reformist preacher at that time and place was Gerard Roussel. Roussel had finished a series of sermons in the spring of 1533 at the king's palace, and they were an enormous success.

15. John Calvin, *Institutes of the Christian Religion, 1536 Edition*, trans. and annot. Ford Lewis Battles (Grand Rapids: H. H. Meeter Center/Eerdmans, 1986), 364. It has been suggested that this introduction is similar to Erasmus's foreword to the third edition of his Greek NT. There are also possible connections to a sermon by Luther delivered on the same day in 1522, to Melanchthon's *Loci communes*, as well as to Bucer's *Commentary on the Gospels*. See De Greef, *John Calvin*, 86.

16. Some scholars incorrectly argue that at this point in his life Calvin was still not a radical Reformer. The thesis is defeated by that fact that the young Frenchman had to flee the capital. If he were still a Catholic, at least as King Francis I understood that word, then he and Cop could have stayed. In 1534, Calvin gave up his benefice with the Roman church. But even this decisive act is not yet strong enough for some interpreters. See Ganoczy, *Young Calvin*, 77–78, 85.

17. De Greef, *John Calvin*, 86–87.

18. Battles, "Introduction," xviii.

19. Ibid., appendix IV, 373–77.

Catholic teaching.[20] It was wrong, in Calvin's opinion, to deprive the people of the light and comfort of the Word of God.[21]

As we have examined some of Calvin's earlier writings, we must acknowledge that there is debate as to whether Calvin was converted at the time he wrote his commentary on Seneca. Much of the scholarly debate revolves around the meaning of the word *conversion*. T. H. L. Parker placed Calvin's conversion in late 1529 or early 1530. Saxer placed it in 1532, with the time of the publication of *De Clementia*. Scholl and Ganoczy see his conversion with the first edition of the *Institutes*.[22]

Calvin's association with Cop in late 1533, however, ensures this as the latest date possible for his conversion. No one would have risked his life for the sake of humanism. It is even clear that Calvin was already converted when he wrote the early *Psychopannichia*, and certainly no unconverted Roman Catholic would have said that the bishop of Rome was guilty of sin by hiding the Scriptures from the people, as Calvin did in his Latin preface to Olivetan's French Bible.[23]

Calvin's best-known literary work is the *Institutes of the Christian Religion*. It was probably composed late in 1534 or early 1535 and was published in Latin in 1536.[24] Some argue that the *Institutes* was

20. There was a French edict against "the Lutherans" in 1535. See William S. Barker, "The Historical Context of the *Institutes* as a Work in Theology," *A Theological Guide to Calvin's Institutes*, ed. David W. Hall and Peter A. Lillback (Phillipsburg NJ: P&R Publishing, 2008), 1–15.

21. De Greef, *John Calvin*, 91: "He declares the bishop of Rome and his priests to be guilty because they have hidden the light under a bushel."

22. Ganoczy, *Young Calvin*, 8–9.

23. For more information, see Richard C. Gamble, *Articles on Calvin and Calvinism*, vol. 2, *Calvin's Early Writings and Ministry* (New York/London: Garland, 1992).

24. Two evangelical works were published in French before the *Institutes*: Farel's *Sommaire* in 1525, and a work by Francis Lambert in 1529. There was probably not an earlier French edition before the Latin text appeared. Battles ("Introduction," xxxviii) notes: "A lively debate among scholars of a generation ago discussed whether in fact such a French work was ever published. The first extant French edition of the *Institutes* is dated 1541, a translation of the second Latin edition of 1539. However, Calvin adapted from the 1536 Latin the Geneva *Catechism* of 1537. Obviously, he found the 1536 *Institutes* too long and complicated for a mere catechism; in fact, even the 1537 Catechism proved too learned for this popular use and was replaced, as Calvin gained pastoral experience at Geneva and Strasbourg, by the familiar Genevan question-and-answer type of catechism." Concerning the relationship of Farel to Calvin, Battles noted no dependence. Again, Battles (ibid., xxxviii) says: "While there may be some echoes of Farel's tone and general position, Calvin's work seems to owe nothing to it in style, structure or even content, although two such works, covering as they do the same field from the same general theological vantage point, would necessarily overlap."

first written either as a catechism or an apology—or as a combination of the two.

Those who argue that it was primarily a catechism cite that it was probably written before there were any French martyrs, thus there was no need at that time for an apologetic work.[25] There can be little doubt that Calvin intended the first edition to be a catechism. The *Institutes* identified the faith of French Protestants.[26] Calvin rejected the institutional Roman church and at the same time rejected its opposite extreme, the disruptive spiritualism of what he called the *catabaptists*.[27]

On the other hand, King Francis I saw the French evangelicals simply as Anabaptist rebels, not like the organized German Protestants.[28] King Francis's persecution began in early 1535. Thus the political situation surrounding the years 1535 to 1536 required a defense of the French evangelicals. The Swiss Anabaptists were already known, as were the terrible events of the kingdom of Münster, which fell in June 1535. There was therefore a need to plead the Protestant case before the king to stop the persecution. Thus the purpose of the first *Institutes* was both catechetical as well as apologetic.[29]

Calvin in Geneva: A.D. 1536–1538. On Good Friday of 1533, William Farel held the first Protestant service in Geneva.[30] By 1536, Geneva was legally a Protestant town—but in name only.[31] The story of Calvin's coming to Geneva is truly remarkable. Calvin was traveling to another place when he had to make a detour through the city on the lake. He had no prior intention of visiting Geneva at all.

When William Farel heard that Calvin was in town, he went to visit him at the local hotel. There Farel took matters into his own hands.

---

25. Benjamin B. Warfield, *Calvin and Calvinism* (New York: Oxford University Press, 1931), 380–82.

26. E. David Willis, "The Social Context of the 1536 Edition of Calvin's *Institutes*," in *In Honor of John Calvin, 1509–64, Papers from the 1986 International Calvin Symposium, McGill University*, ed. E. J. Furcha (Montreal: McGill University Press, 1987), 134.

27. Battles, "Introduction," xlv.

28. De Greef, *John Calvin*, 196.

29. Battles, "Introduction," xl: "Calvin's response to this question: How can the true evangelicals be proved of a different stamp from their more radical brethren? took two forms. He first set out to deal with what he considered the most damning theological aspect of the question in his *Psychopannychia* written in 1534–35 and published finally in 1542. He then mounted a more comprehensive literary campaign in the 1536 *Institutes*."

30. See chapter 12.

31. Ganoczy, *Young Calvin* (cited with different translation), 108.

Calvin was not an exceptionally bold fellow but had obvious talents for writing. He felt called to be a scholar. But Farel had other ideas for him. Farel knew that he could not handle all the work of reforming Geneva by himself. He desperately needed some help. Calvin was perfect for the job—except that Calvin did not think so! Farel used the most persuasive words that he could find to convince Calvin to stay and help in the work of reformation, but it was all to no avail. Farel then did the only thing left for him to do: he told Calvin that if he did not stay in Geneva and help with the reforming work, God would curse Calvin's studies.

This declaration was the ultimate admonition. Calvin truly believed that God had spoken to him through Farel. It was clear to Calvin that God wanted the young author of the *Institutes* in Geneva.[32] Calvin, eventually installed as a pastor, found great delight in his full-time church responsibilities.[33]

Calvin went to work immediately. He began his lectures on Scripture at Saint Pierre Cathedral in September 1536. He and Farel then composed a confession of faith, which was accepted by the city in November 1536.[34] Following the production of that document, the two ministers presented "Articles concerning the organization of the Church and of Worship at Geneva proposed by ministers at the Council, January, 1537." These articles proposed a catechism.

So some of the fruits of Calvin's first sojourn in Geneva were that the city had adopted a solid Protestant confession of faith, excommunication was established, and the Psalms were sung in public worship. Since many in the city were illiterate and could not read music,

32. T. H. L. Parker, *John Calvin: A Biography* (Philadelphia: Westminster Press, 1975), 57. See Williston Walker, *John Calvin: The Organizer of Reformed Protestantism* (New York: Putnam, 1906), 158.

33. See Parker, *John Calvin*, 58: "his pastoral ministry was for the glory of God and the upbuilding of the Church." Parker reminded his readers that "Too often Calvin is represented as a remote planner organizing the Church life of the city according to a rigid ecclesiastical polity, with Geneva as an area designated for Reformed experiment. Such a doctrinaire figure Calvin was not"; and Ganoczy, *Young Calvin*, 111: "At the end of 1536, Calvin was called to be an ordinary preacher, a pastor of the church of Geneva. This time he accepted without hesitation. His promotion was in all probability an act of the council, and it was not accompanied with any ceremony of ordination with the laying on of hands or any other liturgical rite."

34. For more information, see Walker, *John Calvin*, 184–92; François Wendel, *Calvin: The Origins and Development of His Religious Thought* (London: Collins, 1974), 52; F. Bruce Gordon, *Calvin* (New Haven: Yale University Press, 2009), 71.

a children's choir was established to help teach the adults how to sing by ear.[35] During the time of public worship, all the shops and stores were to remain closed.[36]

The first Genevan catechism, from 1537, addressed thirty-five topics. Calvin included Bible references. During his ministry at this time, he suffered a great loss when his brother Charles died on October 1, 1537.[37] In 1542 there came a second Genevan catechism, which followed a question-and-answer format. That catechism also included sample prayers.[38]

The Reformation brought about structural changes to the church; they included instituting church offices, the Company of Pastors, and discipline. Calvin established four church offices to reform the Genevan church: pastor, teacher or doctor, elder, and deacon. The pastor was to preach the Word of God, admonish and exhort, and administer the sacraments. The teacher was to instruct the faithful in sound doctrine and prepare students for ministry and civil government. The duties of the elders were "to keep watch over every man's life, to admonish those whom they see leading a disorderly life, and where necessary, to report to the assembly which will be deputized to make fraternal correction." The deacon was charged with caring for the poor and sick and with putting an end to begging.

The church of Geneva included what was termed the Venerable Company of Pastors and the Consistory. The Company of Pastors had strictly ecclesiastical functions. Primarily, the members worked in education and the examination of candidates for ordination. The *Consistory*, a term still used in Continental Reformed churches, or the *Session*, used by Presbyterians, was not confined to pastors but had lay

---

35. Parker, *John Calvin*, 63.

36. Ibid., 64.

37. Walker, *John Calvin*, 57. Because Charles refused Catholic last rites, he was buried with the criminals. See Ganoczy, *Young Calvin*, 118.

38. John H. Leith, foreword to *John Calvin: Instruction in Faith (1537)*, trans. and ed. Paul T. Fuhrmann (Louisville: John Knox Press, 1992), 9–13. The catechism was translated from Latin into English by Elijah Waterman and published in Hartford, Connecticut, by Sheldon & Goodwin, 1815. To his translation Waterman attached an appendix arguing that the "Catechism commonly called Dr. Alexander Nowell's which was sanctioned in the Convocation of Bishops and Clergy in 1562, and published in 1570, as a standing summary of the doctrines of the English Church is in substance the Catechism of Calvin enlarged." Thanks to the Huntington Library of Pasadena, California, for providing access to the Waterman translation.

members as well; in fact, elders comprised a majority in the Consistory. The Consistory's duty was to maintain ecclesiastical discipline; its court was the controlling power in the church. The Consistory court, however, did not have the right to pronounce civil punishment.

By reforming the church in these specific ways, Calvin was moving to reform Genevan society as well.[39] His reforming method utilized ecclesiastical discipline. The objective of Calvin's church discipline was to protect the church as a body of believers, to protect the individual Christian within the church, and to bring offenders to repentance.

The manner of discipline was first through private admonition of the offender, then through admonition before witnesses, and finally, when admonition failed, through excommunication. The grave sentence of excommunication was implemented for only the most serious crimes. Since one of the objects of discipline was to bring the offender to repentance, care had to be taken in the community's response to those punished.[40]

The people of the church were further protected in that the pastors were not exempt from discipline. This innovation was important and welcomed over the Catholic system. Calvin wanted the clergy to be liable to civil jurisdiction, for he believed they should provide the very best of examples to the people.

Calvin made it clear that his objective for church discipline was that those who lived shameful lives should not be numbered as Christians, since living a shameful life dishonors God. Second, evil people corrupt the good. Third, the dishonor of separation from the church may spark repentance.[41] The goal of discipline was to return the sinner to the fellowship of the church. Calvin insisted that physical force may not be used to compel conversion. A middle ground was sought for church discipline: "neither laxly nor rigorously, but rather in a pastoral spirit."[42] But this first stage of reform ended abruptly when Calvin and Farel were expelled from Geneva.

---

39. Parker, *John Calvin*, 62: "Discipline, then, was essential to the life of the Church. Where there was no discipline there could continue no Church."

40. See Richard C. Gamble, "Switzerland: Triumph and Decline," in *John Calvin: His Influence in the Western World*, ed. W. Stanford Reid (Grand Rapids: Zondervan, 1981), 55–63.

41. Willem Balke, *Calvin and the Anabaptist Radicals* (Grand Rapids: Eerdmans, 1981), 51.

42. Ibid., 52.

Expulsion and Strasbourg: A.D. 1538–1541. In 1538, Calvin and Farel were ousted from Geneva. Their expulsion came as a result of two actions. First, there was a change of leadership in the church of the Swiss capital city, Bern. In Bern, there were some unique parts of worship. Baptism was administered at the font, unleavened bread was used in the Lord's Supper, and four church festivals from Rome were still celebrated: Christmas, Easter, Ascension, and Whitsun. Bern, the powerful capital of Switzerland, wanted the church at Geneva to conform to its style.

Second, there was an election in February 1538, and four new Genevan syndics took their seats. The newly elected syndics were pro-Bern.[43] Without the ministers' counsel, and against their advice when informed, the city adopted the Bernese rituals.

Calvin and Farel would not agree to the Bernese innovations. They were asked to use unleavened bread at the Easter communion, but they refused to do so. They were ordered to use it or, if they failed to comply, were forbidden to preach. They refused to use it and still preached, but they did not celebrate the Lord's Supper on Easter. The next day, Monday, they were to be expelled—after replacements could be found. On Tuesday, the city decided not to wait for replacements, and the ministers were to depart within three days.[44] After making a trip to Bern, Farel headed to Neuchâtel, where he would minister for the rest of his life. Calvin had hoped to reside in the fair city of Basel but left for Strasbourg.[45]

Looking back historically, Calvin's first sojourn at Geneva had simply been a disaster. As the year 1537 began, Farel presented the Genevan magistrates with a reform program. First, the citizens had to assent to the new confession of faith, and a program of religious education was instituted. But already by early 1538 the magistrates had turned against the ministers—a betrayal that was very difficult for Calvin psychologically.

---

43. Wendel, *Calvin*, 55.

44. Parker, *John Calvin*, 66; Ganoczy, *Young Calvin*, 120–22; Wendel, *Calvin*, 56.

45. In the French-speaking cantons, Farel, who agreed with Calvin, was not successful in getting the new ideas introduced into the government of the city of Neuchâtel. For more on Farel, see David W. Hall, *Calvin in the Public Square: Liberal Democracies, Rights, and Civil Liberties* (Phillipsburg, NJ: P&R Publishing, 2009), 38–44.

Calvin found refuge as a French speaker within the German-speaking city of Strasbourg. Calvin and the Strasbourg reformer Martin Bucer (1491–1551) were very good friends. Bucer was the older brother, and Calvin was very much indebted to him. Regarding Bucer, Calvin said in a letter to Heinrich Bullinger of Zurich

> I will not proclaim at this moment the rare and manifold virtues which this man possesses. Let me just say that I would do a great deal of injustice to the church of God if I were to hate or despise him. I will remain silent as to how he made himself serviceable to me personally."[46]

Both men were theologians of the church. They agreed on many issues, including the nature of the Lord's Supper. Bucer cosigned Calvin's *Confessio fidei de eucharistia.*

Because he was older, a question has perplexed scholars: did Martin Bucer influence Calvin, or did Calvin influence Bucer? The answer to the question is that Bucer was clearly the early leader, particularly while Calvin was at Strasbourg, but in time there was no longer a mentor-subordinate relationship.[47]

Life in Strasbourg was, for Calvin, full of pastoring, writing, and preaching. He was pastor to the four hundred or so French refugees in the city, and he spent quite a bit of time in caring for their souls. Each day he lectured or preached, and he prepared for preaching twice on Sunday.[48] This hardly seems like a relaxing time in modern terms, but it was a breath of fresh air for the weary Calvin. Calvin enjoyed the city of Strasbourg and applied for citizenship. The honor was granted, and Calvin anticipated staying at this city on the Rhine for the rest of his life. It was while he was in Strasbourg that his commentary on Romans appeared, and, more importantly, it was in Strasbourg where he met the wonderful Idelette de Burre, who would become his wife.

---

46. Willem van't Spijker, "Bucer's Influence on Calvin: Church and Community," in *Martin Bucer: Reforming Church and Community*, ed. David F. Wright (Cambridge: Cambridge University Press, 1994), 32: "The '*communio*' that existed between Bucer and Calvin was based on their shared '*communio cum Christo*.'"

47. Van't Spijker, "Bucer's Influence," 33: "Calvin realized Bucer's ideals when the latter was hindered from doing so in Strasbourg."

48. Parker, *John Calvin*, 68.

In Strasbourg, Calvin was able to institute many reforms in worship and life so that the refugees under his care could come before God in a manner that Calvin was convinced was more biblical and honoring to God. There was a monthly communion service, and the people learned how to sing the Psalms to God's glory, as Calvin worked on the 1539 Psalm book for singing the Psalms.[49] Worship was joyous and well ordered.[50]

Calvin also completed a new edition of the *Institutes*. The first edition, which contained only six chapters, had sold out within the first year. The second edition was finished by the end of July 1539 and grew to seventeen chapters.[51]

In 1539 came an edict aimed at purging the French kingdom against the "diabolical" errors of the Lutherans. A year later, in 1540, came the Edict of Fontainebleau, which began the repression of heresy by the French Parliament. Happily, Calvin married Idelette the following year.[52] She was a widow whose loving husband had died of the plague in 1540.

Meanwhile, back in Geneva, affairs were not flowing smoothly for the city. Its leadership had ousted Calvin and Farel and replaced them with ministers who were controllable and incompetent. Political affairs proceeded smoothly for a while, but the deterioration of church life began almost immediately. Also, in God's providence, two of Calvin's main opponents met humiliating deaths after his departure. The city's spiritual life began to deteriorate more and more. Finally, even those who had opposed Calvin and Farel realized the city's dire need of leaders of their caliber.

Recall to Geneva: A.D. 1541–1554.[53] The city was divided into three districts, with one church for each section. Geneva was served by five ministers and three assistants. Calvin was the chief minister at the

49. Walker, *John Calvin*, 225–26.
50. Ganoczy, *Young Calvin*, 126–27; Parker, *John Calvin*, 68–69. A metrical Psalter was published in Strasbourg in 1539.
51. Parker, *John Calvin*, 72–73.
52. Bernard Cottret, *Calvin: A Biography* (Grand Rapids: Eerdmans, 2000), 140.
53. Bruce Gordon, *Clerical Discipline and the Rural Reformation: The Synod in Zurich, 1532–1580* (Bern: Lang, 1992); William Monter, *Calvin's Geneva* (New York: Wiley & Sons, 1967); Ronald S. Wallace, *Calvin, Geneva & the Reformation: A Study of Calvin as Social Reformer, Churchman, Pastor and Theologian* (Grand Rapids: Baker, 1988); Harro Höpfl, *The Christian Polity of John Calvin* (New York: Cambridge University Press, 1982), 90–102.

Cathedral of Saint Peter. On Sundays, sermons were preached first at daybreak, then at 9:00 A.M., and finally 3:00 P.M. at both Saint Peter and Saint Gervais cathedrals. The third church, La Madeleine, did not include the daybreak sermon. At noon, between public worship services, the children were catechized. Thus each Sunday at Saint Peter and Saint Gervais there were three services, with only two sermons. The newly converted Genevans requested more sermons, so in 1542 Calvin tried to preach two different sermons on Sunday mornings. That heroic effort lasted for only two months. It appears that thereafter he preached the same sermon twice on Sunday mornings.

Sermons were also preached on Mondays, Wednesdays, and Fridays. There was a weekly required Bible study for the ministers of the city as well as the countryside, and every three months there was a time of mutual examination of each other's lives.

We do not know much about Calvin's life from this early time. In 1546, Calvin preached through the book of Isaiah passage by passage, and probably from 1546 to 1548 he preached through the Psalms that had recently been put into meter. We believe that during this period Calvin preached without a manuscript or even notes, probably directly from the Greek or Hebrew text.

Ecclesiastical ordinances were published to be a set of guidelines for discipline among the ministers. For example, a section of one of these sets reads:

> In order to obviate all scandals of conduct it will be needful to have a form of discipline for ministers, as set out below, to which all are to submit themselves. This will help to ensure that the minister is treated with respect and the Word of God is not brought into dishonor and scorn by the evil fame of ministers. Moreover, as discipline will be imposed on him who merits it, so also there will be need to suppress slanders and false reports that may unjustly be uttered against those who are innocent. But first of all it must be noted that there are crimes which are altogether intolerable in a minister and faults may be endured provided that a fraternal admonition is offered.[54]

54. Philip Edgcumbe Hughes, *The Register of the Company of Pastors of Geneva in the Time of Calvin* (Grand Rapids: Eerdmans, 1966), 38.

The new Protestant ministers were different from the Catholic priests. In the old system, priests were not under civil jurisdiction—basically, the civil and spiritual worlds could ignore each other. Not so in the new Genevan regime. The magistrates worried that the ministers in Calvin's Geneva would become new popes. Power is never given—it is always earned or taken. Would Calvin take power, earn power, or, like he did a few years earlier, lose power and again be expelled? This issue was not resolved in Geneva until the very end of Calvin's life.

A new French king named Henry II was crowned in 1547, and his ascension initially brought further repression on the Protestants. The Edict of Châteaubriant, passed under this king, severely strengthened persecution of Protestants, whom Henry regarded as dangerous heretics. The edict commanded the confiscation of property of those who fled to Geneva to escape persecution in France and forbade those left behind to contact them. Henry imposed heavy censorship of the press and even forbade the discussion of religious topics over meals at home.

The Genevan Consistory met each week. The issues with which the consistory dealt were usually domestic.[55] Some specific issues included different aspects of marital strife and breaking the sanctity of the home. An ancillary problem consisted in church disruptions, such as murmuring against the sermon.[56] Also connected were problems with gambling and usury.[57] Under the category of marital strife, some of the issues addressed concerned engagements, such as whether proper or legal engagements had been made. Sub issues included whether the father had paid the bride's dowry in full. One issue dealt with a unique instance of a wife's attempted suicide.[58]

Dealing with premarital sex took the greatest portion of the consistory's time. When there was no pregnancy, were the charges of sin leveled against a young man true? When the liaison produced a child,

---

55. One exception related to family matters when a wife insisted that since the church was the body of Christ, she should belong, for carnal enjoyment, to all the men of the church. See Robert M. Kingdon, ed., *Registers of the Consistory of Geneva in the Time of Calvin, Volume 1, 1542–1544* (Grand Rapids: Eerdmans, 2000), 309, 312–13.

56. See Kingdon, *Registers*, 312–13 (for speaking against ministers), 60, 72–74, 75, 245 (for muttering at the sermon).

57. Pierre Truffet agreed that he needed to have fun.

58. Ibid., 280–81.

were adequate financial provisions made for the mother and her baby? Should marriage between the couple occur?[59]

The era was a time of great violence. The consistory's records read like stories out of any contemporary soap opera—in one account, a husband threatened to pull his wife's nose off. There are further examples of domestic strife, including wife beating, which, sadly, was generally tolerated.[60] There was at least one case of husband beating.[61] Reconciliation always required the shaking of hands or giving of hugs.[62]

Many of the issues were resolved via the "punishment" of attending sermons.[63] Preaching was available four days per week. Piety was checked by means of church attendance, naming who had preached and on what text he had preached, and the ability to recite the Lord's Prayer in the common language (French, of the Genevan dialect). These measures were followed by one's knowing the confession of faith in French. Almost none of those brought before the consistory were able to satisfy the ministers at the initial meeting with them. They were then given from one week to three months to improve. Consistorial punishment included being forbidden to take the Lord's Supper.

This time was also one for polemics. In 1544, either Balthasar Hubmaier's booklet *Concerning the Christian Baptism of Believers* or the 1529 Schleitheim Confession was published in French and circulated in the area.[64] That winter, Farel had asked Calvin to write against the Anabaptists. Anabaptists had made some inroads near Neuchâtel, where Farel was ministering.

The story goes something like this: The area around Neuchâtel had become Protestant in 1536, but the pastor there was incompetent and actually turned some people away—not only from Catholicism but also from Christianity itself! Sometime during that period, Anabaptist

59. Ibid., 29, 33, 37, 40–42, 47, 54, 57, 233, 260, 286, 326.
60. Ibid., 34, 40, 242, 253, 256, 269, 297, 304, 318, 319–22, 366, 394–95—although wife beating was forbidden (see 336).
61. Ibid., 242, 260.
62. Ibid., 46, 50, 53, 75, 78–80, 240, 291.
63. Ibid., 19, 26 (prayer and attendance).
64. Aimé Louis Herminjard (*Correspondance des Réformateurs dans les Pays de Langue Française* [Nieuwkoop: De Graaf, 1965]) says that it is Hubmaier, while Balke (*Calvin and Anabaptists*) says that it is the Seven Articles. Based on correspondence between Farel and Calvin, Farley agrees with Balke. See John Calvin, *Treatises against the Anabaptists and against the Libertines*, ed. and trans. Benjamin Wirt Farley (Grand Rapids: Baker, 1982).

thought began to spread, and the pastor was not able to present any counterevidence to their charges. In an exchange of pulpits with a pastor from a nearby town—a pastor who was scheduled to baptize an infant—that pastor was confronted by shouts from the congregation as to where there was NT evidence for baptizing infants. A debate occurred in the spring between Farel and the Anabaptists. Calvin's *Against the Anabaptists* was a reality by June 1.

Of course, Calvin knew about the Anabaptists before this time.[65] He had already made references to them in the 1536 *Institutes*.[66] While in Strasbourg Calvin publicly debated Anabaptists, and as a result some people had their children baptized.

In 1545 some of Calvin's friends started to write down his sermons, and his first printed sermons stem from that time. The reason for their publication was Calvin's concern for the church in France. He had already translated the *Institutes* into French in 1541 and wanted his French sermons printed and distributed there. Also, between December 1546 and February 1547, the Company of Pastors developed regulations that were intended to supplement the Ecclesiastical Ordinances of 1541. These new regulations were adopted by the city council in May.[67] But a personal shadow fell over the Calvin home as Idelette departed from her earthly struggles in 1549.

This period was also one of intense theological debate. There were theoretical theological struggles with Pierre Caroli.[68] During this period of ministry Calvin endured the Bolsec controversy (1551), and the following year heresy charges were brought against the *Institutes*. Amazingly, at the trial the city council was undecided and procrasti-

---

65. Walker, *John Calvin*, 201–2. They had already disrupted his ministry in Geneva. See Wendel, *Calvin*, 53.

66. Calvin, *Treatises*, 21. Balke summarizes areas in which Calvin knew that he was different from the Anabaptists. Those areas include: the nature of the church, the role of discipline, infant versus believer's baptism, the rightful place of the oath, civil authority, taxes, laws, the problem of pacifism, and opposition to tyranny.

67. Hughes, *Register*, 53. December through February 1547: they "were intended to complete the Ecclesiastical Ordinances of 1541 by adding certain rules appropriate to the life of the country churches. The application of the general ordinances of 1541 in a setting very different as regards customs and mental outlook from that of the urban population had raised numerous difficulties. . . . They were not formally adopted by the Council of Two Hundred until 17 May."

68. Walker, *John Calvin*, 183–215; Richard C. Gamble, "Calvin's Controversies," in *Cambridge Companion to John Calvin*, ed. Donald K. McKim (Cambridge: Cambridge University Press, 2004), 188–206.

nated in making a judgment. The pressure mounted to the point that Calvin threatened to resign, but finally in November the magistrates said that the *Institutes* were "good and holy."

Then Calvin endured the Servetus affair and in 1553 got into serious trouble when he refused to give communion to a prominent Genevan named Berthelier. In 1554 life in Geneva got better for Calvin when after a minor riot Calvin's opponents fled the city and were condemned by the magistrates. Even Calvin the preacher got into trouble. He was rebuked for his sermons.

Final Ministry. Churches began to be organized in France in 1555, and by early 1559 scholars estimate that there were at least seventy-two organized congregations. That year saw the first general synod of France, and Geneva was asked to send nineteen ministers to that nation. In the following year, they requested another dozen. By the next year, 1561, there were requests for ninety ministers! A national French church was created in the midst of a very hostile state. The first massacre of Protestants came in 1562. By 1566, scholars document that at least one hundred and twenty ministers were serving there.

Calvin's final years in Geneva comprised a time of great strengthening of the church in the city as well as a period of internal and external political opposition.[69] Beza said that Calvin preached 286 sermons and delivered 186 lectures on theology per year. If we round down the number of sermons, we can calculate that 250 sermons equals five sermons per week for fifty weeks per year. If an academic year consisted of 49 weeks, then Calvin lectured on the Scriptures three or four hours per week. Truly this life was one of service to the bride of Christ!

Calvin also wrote commentaries on most of the NT and much of the OT. He had developed a distinctive hermeneutic that can be summarized as *brevitas et facilitas.*[70] Expositions of Scripture were to be accommodated to the ability of the recipients. They were to be clear and easily understood. These are some of the reasons why Calvin's commentaries are still read by many with great benefit.

---

69. For more information, see Richard C. Gamble, *Articles on Calvin and Calvinism*, vol. 3, *Calvin's Work in Geneva* (New York/London: Garland, 1992).

70. See Richard C. Gamble, *"Brevitas et Facilitas*: Toward an Understanding of Calvin's Hermeneutic," *WTJ* 47, no. 1 (Spring 1985): 1–17, and "Exposition and Method in Calvin," *WTJ* 49, no. 1 (Spring 1987): 153–65. Both articles also appear in Richard C. Gamble, *Articles on Calvin and Calvinism*, vol. 6, *Calvin and Hermeneutics* (New York/London: Garland, 1992).

During his busy life of pastoring, teaching, and preaching, Calvin continued to revise his *Institutes*. The *Institutes* first appeared in 1536 with six chapters; subsequent editions grew to twenty-one chapters. The final edition featured a new arrangement—the massive tome was put into four books: *The Knowledge of God the Creator, The Knowledge of God the Redeemer in Christ, The Way in Which We Receive the Grace of Christ*, and *The External Means or Aids by which God Invites us into the Society of Christ and Holds us Therein*, each one with separate chapter divisions and sectional subdivisions.[71] From the first edition to the last, the *Institutes* quintupled in size and its arrangement changed, yet the book remained the same at its heart by reflecting Calvin's desire that it train men and women to know God and love him more deeply and thus come truly to know who they are as God's creation.

REFORMATION IN ENGLAND[72]

Merchants began to bring Lutheran information into England as early as the 1520s.[73] Henry Tudor attempted to establish stability in his realm. Because many nobles had died in the previous wars, he added to the nobility and worked for economic recovery. England had still claimed much of France, and Henry VII realized that taking over France required a strong England. He was succeeded by his son, Henry VIII.

King Henry VIII (A.D. 1509–1547). Henry had not been trained to be king. His older brother Arthur was meant to rule and had received great preparation to do so. Arthur was married to Catherine of Aragon, the daughter of the king and queen of Spain. When Arthur died, it

---

71. "The order was suggested by the consecution of topics in the Apostles' Creed and follows what is called the Trinitarian method of arrangement, or the order of God's revelation as Father, Son and Holy Ghost. The discovery of this simple principle of arrangement gave the final touch to the *Institutes* as a work of art and permitted it to make its due impression upon the mind of the reader" (Benjamin B. Warfield, "The Literary History of Calvin's Institutes," *The Presbyterian and Reformed Review* 10 [April 1899]: 205).

72. See Richard C. Gamble, review of Statesman and *Saint: Cardinal Wolsey, Sir Thomas More and the Politics of Henry VIII*, by Jasper Ridley, *WTJ* 45, no. 2 (Fall 1983): 455–56.

73. Carter Lindberg, *The European Reformations*, 2nd ed. (Malden, MA: Wiley-Blackwell, 2010), 294.

was arranged for Henry VIII to marry her.[74] So in 1509 the talented, charming, and cruel Henry married Catherine, his brother's widow. Catherine was seven years older than he was. They had a son in 1511, but the boy died after seven weeks. Further sons also died. A son was needed for a peaceful succession, and since Queen Catherine was about forty years old, Henry knew a divorce was needed. He was convinced that God had cursed the marriage because, in canon law, one was not supposed to marry a person who was already or had been related by marriage. He petitioned the pope for a divorce.

In 1527, the Emperor Charles V captured Rome and Pope Clement VII. Catherine was Charles's aunt, and therefore Charles pressured the pope not to grant the divorce. The emperor's pressure worked, and by 1529 the divorce was simply not forthcoming. Politically, this refusal caused Henry to move closer to severing relations with Rome: Henry claimed that the papacy had usurped power and questioned whether it was right for law, even canon law, to be adjudicated outside the realm.

In 1532, Thomas Cranmer was appointed archbishop of Canterbury. Cranmer was a Protestant and had been increasingly identifying himself with the teachings of the Continental Reformation—but in England church affairs were still under the crown. In the same year came the Restraint of Appeals, which meant that a petitioner could not appeal outside the realm, specifically, not to Rome. Cranmer's appointment had been helped by the Boleyn family, whose daughter Anne the king had been courting. In May 1533, Cranmer declared Henry and Catherine's marriage to be against the law of God, and Henry was subsequently free to remarry. He married the then-pregnant Anne Boleyn, and Cranmer crowned her queen in June 1533. Her yet-unborn child would be the future Queen Elizabeth.[75] Later, Henry and Catherine's annulment would cause strife—their child, the future Queen Mary Tudor, was now illegitimate. But if the marriage had not been annulled, then the future Queen Elizabeth would be illegitimate. Further, the pope and Charles V were infuriated by Henry's actions— the pope excommunicated Henry, who would now need to establish his own church. The seeds of unrest were planted.

---

74. J. J. Scarisbrick, *Henry VIII* (Berkeley: University of California Press, 1968), 4–7.
75. Lindberg, *European Reformations*, 304–5. Some say that Anne held an evangelical faith—her chaplains were Protestant.

In 1536, the Ten Articles were established to govern the church. In key areas the articles sound Protestant: they affirmed justification by faith alone; they argued that the sources of authority were the Bible, the ecumenical creeds, and the four great ecumenical councils; and transubstantiation was not mentioned in the discussion of the Lord's Supper. In the following year, *The Bishops' Book*, which was to guide theology, denied purgatory. Here was the high-water mark of King Henry's move in theology.[76]

Meanwhile, Anne was not able to produce a viable heir—her son was stillborn, and she was executed for adultery in May 1536. Eleven days later, Henry married Jane Seymour. Jane produced the future King Edward VI. Now with a son to take the throne, Henry reverted and became more sympathetic to Catholicism. The Six Articles, which reaffirmed Catholic teaching on the Lord's Supper and the necessity of vows of chastity for priests, were made law in June 1539. Anyone who denied transubstantiation was to be punished by death, and married priests were given one month to "put away" their wives.

Thomas Cromwell arranged for Henry to marry Anne of Cleves, who was in Germany. The courtship was conducted by long distance. Henry had her portrait, but apparently the portrait was not quite accurate. When the forty-nine-year-old Henry saw her face in person, he was somewhat distressed and called her his "Flemish mare." The marriage was annulled in July 1540. This disastrous marriage precipitated Cromwell's beheading.

Only eighteen days after the annulment of his marriage with Anne of Cleves, Henry married seventeen-year-old Catherine Howard, who was Anne Boleyn's first cousin and lady-in-waiting. The Howard family was intensely Catholic. In 1542, Catherine was beheaded for adultery. In 1543, Henry married his last wife, Catherine Parr. She was apparently a fine and devout Protestant, but Henry was committed to his Protestant-and-Catholic mixed religion—in the same year a new *King's Book* was issued; it was thoroughly Catholic. Transubstantiation was never permitted to be attacked. Ultimately, though Henry had

---

76. Neelak Tjernagel, *Henry VIII and the Lutherans* (St. Louis: Concordia, 1965), 163–67. During King Edward VI's reign a new confession of forty-two articles was composed that was strongly Calvinistic. These articles were put aside under Mary I's reign. Finally, the Church of England adopted Thirty-Nine Articles of Religion in 1571.

no fundamental problems with the papacy, his main concern was not theology; rather, it was with securing his dynasty, and he was willing to reject the papacy to do so. Henry VIII became increasingly unwell due to his obesity, boils, and gout, and he died in 1547 at the age of fifty-five.[77]

King Edward VI (A.D. 1547–1553). Edward took the throne in 1547 at the age of nine, and a council of regents was established. The duke of Somerset and brother of Jane Seymour, Edward Seymour, became prominent. He made himself lord protector of the realm. Somerset had Reformed leanings, and knowledge of the Bible spread under his leadership. He established a commission to discuss liturgical reform. In that same year, Calvin's friend and fellow reformer Peter Martyr Vermigli was invited to become a professor at Oxford University, where he brought a decidely Protestant and Reformed biblical teaching.

In September 1548, the bishops approved a new prayer book. In 1549 it was approved for the whole of England. Innovatively, it suggested that all worship was to be performed in English. The theology of the prayer book is described as "studied ambiguity," as vestments were maintained. But Protestants, encouraged by the reformers John à Lasco, John Knox, and Martin Bucer, Regius Professor of Divinity at Cambridge, soon felt that the prayer book was inadequate.[78]

Theological polarization in England was rising. Nationalistic Englishmen wanted to follow distinctive English slowness and ambiguity. On the other hand, internationals wanted England to follow the Continental Reformation more closely. The movement toward more reform was aided in 1550 when the duke of Northumberland ousted Somerset. Northumberland was more radical, and in 1552 the church issued a second prayer book. Its theological principle was that everything without scriptural principles should be omitted. This book is the foundation for the modern prayer book.[79]

Queen Mary (A.D. 1553–1558). After the death of Edward, Mary followed as queen from 1553 to 1558. Mary sought to restore Catholicism and viewed the pope as the head of Christianity. She is known as Bloody Mary due to the roughly two hundred martyrs killed dur-

77. Ibid., 242–44.
78. Lindberg, *European Reformations*, 306–7.
79. Ibid., 307–8.

ing her reign. Under Mary, Nicholas Ridley and Hugh Latimer were martyred in Oxford. Thomas Cranmer recanted his Protestantism; in the end, though, he renounced his recantation and was condemned to be burned at the stake. He plunged his right hand, with which he had signed his recantation, first into the flames as a sign of his anguish over renouncing Protestantism. Many Protestants were exiled, and many fled to the Continent and to Scotland. In 1554, Queen Mary married king Philip of Spain but in 1558 died without an heir.

Queen Elizabeth (A.D. 1558–1603). Mary's half sister, Elizabeth I, reigned from 1558 to 1603.[80] Under her reign, Protestantism in England was assured, and there was general joy and relief among Protestants.[81] All public worship was to be according to the *Book of Common Prayer* of 1559.[82] More radical Protestants thought her reforms were merely a good beginning to the work that needed to be accomplished, but Elizabeth thought the Reformation was completed. Tension grew between theologians in the English church who desired further reformation, and Elizabeth's push for stability and compromise would grow throughout her reign and lay the groundwork for religious civil war in the next century.

REFORMATION IN SCOTLAND

To the north, England's cousin was allied with France, England's enemy. Politically, the Scottish nobles held great power—more so than the English. The Scottish monarch was not much more powerful than were the most powerful lords of the land. When the monarch was a minor, the government was often in the hands of regents. The real governing was done by a powerful noble who ruled in the monarch's name.

This was the case with Mary, Queen of Scots. Her father was King James V, who was the son of King James IV and Margaret Tudor, King Henry VIII's sister. James V became king at only one and a half

---

80. She spoke French, Latin, and Italian. See ibid., 311.

81. Roland Bainton (*Women in the Reformation* [Minneapolis: Fortress, 1971]) gives evidence of her piety.

82. Lindberg, *European Reformations*, 313.

years of age when his father was killed at Flodden Field. His mother and her second husband served as regents. James V married Mary of Lorraine, or Guise, in 1538 and reigned until he died at the age of thirty in 1542. Thus in that year their daughter, Mary, became queen when she was only six days old and was under her mother's regency until 1561.[83]

Henry VIII had always had his eye on obtaining Scotland.[84] To secure Scotland from English aggression, it was agreed that Mary should be sent to France to wed the future French king.[85] There she was sent in 1548; she married King Francis II in 1558 when she was sixteen and he was fourteen. Francis died in 1559, and at his death Mary became queen of France. She returned to Scotland in 1561.

Precursors to the Scottish Reformation. Patrick Hamilton (1504–1528), one of the most famous Scottish reformers, studied in Paris and Marburg and was a relative of the Stuarts with a distant claim to the throne. He returned to Scotland and began to preach his new understanding of the doctrine of grace; his preaching caught the attention of church authorities. He was called before a church council and charged with holding to Luther and Melanchthon's views. Hamilton maintained their truth and was subsequently condemned as a heretic. The views for which he was condemned were that: man has no free will; there is no purgatory; the pope has no power to loose or bind souls; the pope is the Antichrist; every priest has the pope's power; the pope's laws have no strength; Christians are in a state of grace; penance is devilish; auricular confession is not necessary for salvation; there is no salvation by works; and Christians can be assured of salvation. Hamilton was burned at the stake in St Andrews in 1528—on the same day that he was convicted by the council.

Born around the same time as Hamilton, John Knox was ordained to the priesthood in 1530.[86] He was educated at Glasgow University, where he studied under John Major.[87] Perhaps he was ordained as a knight of Saint John, for he carried a two-handed sword as George

83. Antonia Fraser, *Mary Queen of Scots* (New York: Greenwich House, 1969), 3.
84. The Scots had been defeated by the English at Flodden a generation earlier, then at Solway Moss in 1542, then at Pinkie Cleugh in 1547.
85. Fraser, *Mary*, 30.
86. Donald Macmillan, *John Knox: A Biography* (London: Andrew Melrose, 1905), 13–14.
87. Ibid., 15–16.

Wishart's protector.[88] Knox labored as a tutor and became a Protestant in about the year 1543, when reading Scripture in the vernacular was allowed. He witnessed the martyrdom of George Wishart in March 1545. For Knox, the Roman church was the great Antichrist.[89]

With Queen Mary still a child, Scotland was ruled by a Protestant regent, the earl of Arran. But the true power lay with the Catholic Cardinal Beaton and the queen dowager, Mary of Lorraine.[90] In 1546, some radical Protestants murdered Cardinal Beaton, chancellor of the realm, and took his castle at St Andrews. This move was both religious sacrilege and political treason. The bishop's castle at St Andrews was held for a year by resisters. In April 1547, Knox joined them as the minister of the one hundred and fifty defenders of the castle. In July 1547 the castle fell, and Knox was condemned to be a French galley slave.[91] There were three hundred slaves, who were housed in a ship that was one hundred and fifty feet long and fifty feet wide. The Roman Catholic crew of the ship carried a picture of the Virgin Mary and made the Protestants kiss the image. Someone threw it into the sea—presumably Knox, who yelled, "let our Lady now save herself; let her learn to swim." In March 1549, after nineteen months of slavery, Knox was released.[92]

Knox became a minister in the Church of England and served as the royal chaplain of England's King Edward VI (1547–1553) from 1551 until Edward's death. Knox was one of six chaplains to the king. He gave three to four hour-long sermons at court and was offered the bishopric of Rochester, which he refused.[93] After King Edward VI died,

88. Ibid., 17: he "acted first as a notary . . . but in later years his Catholic adversaries railed at him as one of the 'Pope's Knights,' and as having received Orders by which he 'were umquhile called Sir John." 26. Jasper Ridley, *John Knox* (Oxford: Clarendon, 1968), 44: "to stay with Wishart and defend him to the end with a two-handed sword. . . . Wishart, Ormiston, and Calder were imprisoned in Edinburgh Castle. Calder gained his freedom by making over his man-rents to Beaton. Ormiston escaped over the Castle wall in broad daylight. Wishart was taken to St Andrews, condemned as a heretic, and strangled and burnt."
89. Macmillan, *John Knox*, 18: "Theology became the absorbing interest, to the exclusion of Arts and Letters"; ibid., 19: "Their minds were both Hebraistic and Hellenistic; while the Scottish mind was Hebraistic only."
90. Ibid., 20.
91. Ibid., 30.
92. Ibid., 35–36, 40: "Terms were arranged between the two Governments, and some time in the month of February 1549 Knox gained his freedom, and in 1550 all his fellow-prisoners were allowed to leave France."
93. Ibid., 53–59.

at the ascension of Mary Tudor, Knox went into exile and began to develop the notion that armed rebellion might be necessary against a wicked ruler.[94]

While in exile, Knox pastored English exiles in Frankfurt, Germany. In worship, Knox desired to follow the simple Swiss tradition, which appealed to the more Puritan-leaning members of the congregation. But other members of the congregation desired to follow the English *Book of Common Prayer*.[95] One prominent member stated that the church "would do as they had done in England, and their church should have an English face."[96] Tensions erupted in congregational unrest, and Knox was eventually voted out of the church by those who wanted to follow the English church closely.[97]

From 1555 to 1559, Knox served in Geneva as a minister of the Church of England. He held that there was no more Christian community than that of Geneva. As Knox viewed the world from Geneva, he saw Catholics as triumphing and idolatry as increasing. From his perspective, he saw that these horrible things were caused by evil women, that is, Catherine de Medici, Bloody Mary of England, and Mary, Queen of Scots. In response, in 1558 he prepared *The First Blast of the Trumpet against the Monstrous Regiment of Women*, which was followed by a second "blast." Knox's theory on the evils of women in political leadership may be the most radical theory of revolution in sixteenth-century Reformation thought. The timing of these works was less than ideal. Mary of England died, and Elizabeth came to the throne. She never forgave Knox for his condemnation of female rulers.

In 1559 Knox returned to Scotland. There, Queen Regent Mary of Guise was doing all she could to suppress Protestantism and promote Catholicism.[98] The Protestant response was a call to arms.[99]

In 1560 Mary of Guise died, thus leaving Scotland without a ruler, since her daughter had become queen of France.[100] The Scottish

94. Ibid., 72. See also, Richard C. Gamble, "The Christian and the Tyrant: Beza and Knox on Political Resistance Theory," *WTJ* 46, no. 1 (Spring 1984): 125–29.

95. Ibid., 77.

96. Richard Cox, as cited by Macmillan, *John Knox*, 81.

97. Macmillan, *John Knox*, 80–81.

98. Ibid., 137–41, 150.

99. Ibid., 138.

100. Ibid., 178–79.

Parliament, left to act on its own, enacted Protestant laws: it ratified a Presbyterian confession of faith, abolished papal power and the Mass, and established a Presbyterian church. Protestantism represented a minority, but it had won over some powerful lords. The acts of this parliament were not strictly legal, for the crown had to accept the actions—and the new Queen Mary was unwilling to do so.

Mary after the Reformation. Mary returned to Scotland in August 1561. She had been refused safe conduct by the English Queen Elizabeth, who felt threatened by Mary's remote claim to the English throne.

Once back in her native land, Mary sought to restore Catholicism, and she celebrated the Mass in her palace. Not surprisingly, there was tension between Knox and the queen. Apparently, she had danced at the news that some Protestants had been massacred by her uncle while they were worshipping. Knox renounced this action from the pulpit, and she called him to appear before her. Because she wanted to be privately admonished, he replied that he had been called to public ministry, not to wait on princes and whisper in their ears.[101] Some who had attended Mass were arrested, and Knox was summoned again.

Queen Mary married Henry Stuart, Lord Darnley—great grandson of King Henry VII—in 1565. Their son James was born in 1566 and would become James VI of Scotland. Lord Darnley died in a strange accident. The home in which he slept had a basement filled with gunpowder, which mysteriously exploded and destroyed the whole house. The impact of the explosion on Darnley was that, having escaped the house with his life, someone strangled him to death outside in the garden!

Due to the strange circumstances surrounding Darnley's death, Mary was suspected of murder and adultery, and she had to abdicate the throne in favor of her one-year-old son. She managed to escape to England in 1568. Queen Elizabeth provided housing for her, but the two women never met.

Elizabeth was motivated to keep Mary off the Scottish throne. If Catholicism were to prevail in England or Scotland, then Elizabeth's

---

101. J. H. S. Burleigh, *A Church History of Scotland* (Edinburgh: Hope Trust, 1988), 184: "Mary had strong views as to the obedience due from subjects to their princes, and Knox's views were equally strong on the duty of a preacher to declare the truth of God's Word and to rebuke sinners. . . . Four times he was summoned to the royal presence on account of such utterances and in the Fourth Book of his History he has set down what took place."

throne would be in jeopardy, since according to the Catholic Church she was an illegitimate child; as such, she could not reign. Elizabeth had been excommunicated, and the pope called on the devout to overthrow her.[102] England, therefore, supported the Reformation in Scotland as well as in England.

Reformation Parliament. In 1560 the Scots Confession of Faith was approved.[103] It was written by five men, but primarily by John Knox.[104] This confession has the notion of *semper reformanda*, in other words, that the church should be always reforming. Scripture was "the mouth of God," so the confession acknowledged that doctrine and practice should change if shown from Scripture that it was wrong. The first General Assembly was also held in 1560, with only six ministers and thirty-six elders present.

DUTCH REFORMATION[105]

Charles V (A.D. 1500–1558). The Netherlands, at this period of history, consisted of both Dutch- and French-speaking populations that were divided into seventeen states, known as *provinces*. The Emperor, Charles V, was the sovereign over the Netherlands. Specifically, he was the individual sovereign over each of the seventeen Dutch provinces. Charles was popular in the Netherlands. He had been raised there and understood their customs.

Philip II (A.D. 1527–1598). There was a dramatic change when Philip II succeeded Charles V. Philip II was raised in Spain and spoke only Spanish. He introduced reforms in the church, including the

---

102. Burleigh, *History of Scotland*, 181.

103. For the text of the confession, see Arthur C. Cochrane, *Reformed Confessions of the 16th Century* (Philadelphia: Westminster Press, 1966), 166–68. See also Burleigh, *History of Scotland*, 155: "The Scots Confession contains twenty-five articles of which twelve treat of what may be called the basic doctrines of the Catholic faith: God and the Trinity (one Substance in three Persons); the Creation and Fall of man and the prophetic promises of redemption; the Incarnation (two Natures in one Person); the Passion, Resurrection, and Ascension of Christ, and His return to judge the earth; Atonement through the death of Christ and Sanctification through the Holy Ghost. All this, though there are traces in it of distinctively Calvinist emphases, is entirely orthodox and in accord with the Catholic creeds."

104. Burleigh, *History of Scotland*, 154.

105. For more information, see Richard C. Gamble, *Articles on Calvin and Calvinism*, vol. 14, *Calvinism in France, Netherlands, Scotland, and England* (New York/London: Garland, 1992).

addition of more bishops. This was a sound plan; however, the Dutch bishops had more than exclusively church power. They were wealthy, and in the nobility's mind the office of *bishop* was a good place to install their sons. The nobility did not like threats to what they considered their historical pregogative. Philip also raised taxes.

So within about a year of Philip's ascension as emperor in 1566, mobs broke into the churches. They too were against the increased taxes. But there was little personal violence here, in contrast to what happened in France. To remedy the situation, a duke of Alva, known as the Iron Duke, was sent to the Netherlands in 1567 to keep order. He arrived with a large, well-trained Spanish army. Dutch opposition against Philip II and the duke of Alva focused on William of Orange.

William of Orange (A.D. 1650–1702). William's father was a German count of Nassau. Orange is located in the southern part of France. William belonged to a prestigious Dutch family—he was a *Stadtholder*, which was like being an English viceroy. In the monarch's absence, William functioned in the monarch's name. Thus William was not just a nobleman—constitutionally, he was second in power to the king.

The Revolt and Alignments. The revolt against Emperor Philip II began in earnest in the year 1572, somewhat against William's will. The situation had been complicated by radicals forced out of England called the Sea Beggars, who were encouraged to grab Dutch ports. With the Dutch tinderbox smoking, William looked around for allies in his forthcoming struggles.

William would have needed to sign the Augsburg Confession to receive German support, which would have alienated the Calvinists. He knew that much of his support was found in the Calvinists—so he turned to France and Admiral Gaspard de Coligny.

The French rose to support William, but they were all wiped out in the Saint Bartholomew's Day massacre of 1572. William then turned his attention to England. England was willing to give him moral support in his struggle against Emperor Philip but no money. England's move indicates that the British considered the Spanish too powerful to be conquered. Also, the more Spain fought with Holland, the more secure England was against Spain.

Goals. William's goals and method were very clear. His ultimate goal was not to overturn Philip II's reign but to force him to recognize traditional Dutch rights. The Dutch revolt, therefore, was not the same as the French revolt.

A new element in William's approach was a desire to have religious toleration extended throughout the seventeen provinces. Specifically, William allowed Roman Catholic, Reformed, and even Anabaptist groups some political toleration. The duke of Alva's response was much more typical of the day—he said that he would rather see the Netherlands destroyed than have it be a servant of the Devil.

William's method was to unite all the Dutch nobles against Philip II. William needed to underscore the political nature of their revolt. He knew that the southern provinces were vulnerable to Spanish attack. Yet the Calvinists wanted to see the conflict as a holy crusade. William knew, however, that such an attitude would alienate the rest of the nobility. The best tactic, he thought, was to paint Emperor Philip as a Spanish oppressor on Dutch soil. At first his strategy appeared to work.

Warfare. In 1574, however, the Spanish forces pushed to split Holland in two. That the city of Leiden held out kept the Spanish from instant victory. But the people of Leiden soon began to starve. In desperation, they broke the retaining dykes. This daring action was a remarkable military move. The Dutch navy fought against the Spanish army! William said that he would honor Leiden and founded their fine university in 1575.

Key Terms

Thirty-Nine Articles
Presbyterianism
episcopacy

Study Questions

1. Is the essence of Christianity individual salvation, or should the church be concerned about social issues?
2. What should be the relationship between the church and the state?
3. What were Henry VIII's motivations for breaking with the Roman church?

Resources for Further Study

Calvin, John. *Institutes of the Christian Religion*. Edited by John T. McNeill. Translated by Ford Lewis Battles. Philadelphia: Westminster Press, 1960. Should be read by all seminarians.

————. *The Golden Booklet of the Christian Life*. Published and distributed for many years as an anonymous text of Christian piety, though not many people knew that it is simply a part of the *Institutes*.

15

Reformation Theology

DOCTRINE OF GOD

Existence and Knowability. Luther said that people can know God by observing creation and his sustaining creation. But he believed that knowledge of God from creation results in false worship. People can at best know that God exists; they have general knowledge, but true and particular knowledge of Christ comes through Scripture.

Scripture reveals a portion of God that is hidden and revealed. God in his own nature and majesty is hidden; he does not want to reveal that nature, and that nature is of no concern for creation. True knowledge of God is found in Christ.[1]

Creation. Martin Luther rejected Augustine's account of creation. He held to a young earth and creation *ex nihilo*.[2]

Calvin argued for creation *ex nihilo* based on what Moses said in the Hebrew text. The verb that he used was not *to form* but *to create*. He also held to a young earth and to six days of creation, and he was against instantaneous creation. He developed a theology of creation that advocated appreciation of creation and a moderate use of creation's gifts. In Calvin's day, there were believers who were overly restrictive about using the world's goods, and Calvin feared that this perspective unjustly bound conscience. There are colors and smells that simply delight—they go beyond necessary use. On the other hand, there was not to be limitless freedom.[3]

---

1. Greg R. Allison, *Historical Theology: An Introduction to Christian Doctrine—A Companion to Wayne Grudem's Systematic Theology* (Grand Rapids: Zondervan, 2011), 198–99.
2. Ibid., 262–63.
3. Ibid., 263–65.

Providence and Evil. Luther's view of providence was not at odds with the church's view, but his view of the will was very different from that of Erasmus. Erasmus had argued that the will is sufficiently free to cooperate with God's grace. In *The Bondage of the Will*, Luther argued that at its best, the human will is corrupt. While the will can move toward a relative good like civil law, it can never move toward God in a way that God respects. Erasmus's view cheapens grace.[4]

Calvin saw God as ordaining all events by his providence and viewed providence as compatible with human responsibility. Calvin acknowledged the interpretive problems presented by biblical statements which indicate that God repents. Those statements seem to teach that God's plan does not stand firm. Calvin concluded that God never repents, that such language is anthropomorphic, and that there are biblical examples that demonstrate God's plan when he repents—such as sparing the Ninevites and Hezekiah. In those two examples God wants them to repent before they perish.[5]

Christology. The Lutherans and Reformers disagreed on the communication of properties. Luther taught that Christ's human body obtained omnipresence in union with his divine nature. Calvin and the Reformers rejected that communication.[6]

Attributes. There was no fundamental disagreement with the medieval church on God's attributes. Calvin did not want theologians to try to limit God by their own imaginations. Sinful and finite human beings are deeply inclined to remake God in their own image. The Bible teaches that God is unchangeable, yet he repents. At such times, God accommodates himself to human capacity. Scripture uses anthropomorphisms.[7]

Theologians make distinctions in God's way of knowing, between God's necessary and free knowledge. God's natural/necessary knowledge includes several types of truth. It includes all actual things in the past, present, and future, as well as all possible things that could be. This type of truth includes that a circle cannot be a square, as well as knowledge of all possible future contingent choices and events that involve an act of human willing.

4. Ibid., 286.
5. Ibid., 288–89.
6. Ibid., 379–80.
7. Ibid., 218–19.

God's free knowledge is that which he has decreed will necessarily take place. It is knowledge of what will be. This knowledge is a subset of all possibilities known to him. It includes all actual future, contingent choices and events that involve an act of human will.

Holy Spirit. Catholics and Protestants agreed on the Trinity and specifically on the personhood and deity of the Holy Spirit and his procession from the Father and the Son. Their contention was the relationship between the Word of God and the Holy Spirit. Luther presented the outward and inward work of the Holy Spirit. The outward work is through preaching, and the inward work is by faith. The Holy Spirit was necessary for salvation. Also, the Holy Spirit works sanctification in believers, in other words, the application of the benefits of Christ's work.[8]

Benjamin B. (B. B.) Warfield characterized Calvin as the theologian of the Holy Spirit. Calvin criticized the Catholic Church for its preference of the Spirit of God over the Word of God. He made a number of contributions to the doctrine. The internal witness of the Spirit for the Word of God transcends arguments for the certainty of Scripture. This witness goes beyond human ability, it seals true certainty on the heart. There were also fanatics who went too far by separating the Spirit from the Word, and Calvin refuted them.[9]

Trinity. Calvin was heavily involved in Trinitarian debate with Michael Servetus, as well as with Socinianism.[10] He carefully studied patristic theology—that of both Eastern and Western theologians—and he was able critically to examine earlier Western thinking. Brilliantly, he was able to combine God's essential unity, a Western emphasis, with the distinct reality and mutuality of the persons, an Eastern emphasis. He described the way in which the Father, Son, and Holy Spirit are God by using the Greek term *autotheos*, or "self-God," woodenly expressed. Each divine essence is self-existent. Thus for Calvin there is a shared divine essence, while each person has unique, distinguishing

8. Ibid., 441–42.
9. Ibid., 442–44.
10. For information on Calvin and Servetus, see Richard C. Gamble, "Calvin's Controversies," in *The Cambridge Companion to John Calvin*, ed. Donald K. McKim (Cambridge: Cambridge University Press, 2004), 196–98.

attributes. The three share the same essence, while the Father is the source of the persons of the Son and Spirit.[11]

DOCTRINE OF SCRIPTURE

Canon. The Reformers held to the authority of the Hebrew text of the OT scriptures over the Septuagint and rejected the Apocrypha. The Greek text of the NT was authoritative. The Council of Trent anathematized all who did not hold the Apocrypha as authoritative.[12] The church did not have authority over Scripture. The church did not establish the canon of Scripture.

Inspiration and Authority. Inspiration was not a point of debate between Protestants and Catholics. Later authors wrote of God as the principal or efficient cause and humans as the instrumental cause of Scripture. In this complementary work came the verbal plenary inspiration of the Scriptures. Inerrancy also flowed out of this doctrine. Both Luther and Calvin maintained that the Scriptures held supreme authority.[13] Practice and doctrine were to be found in Scripture alone. Thus they rejected the notion of purgatory and praying for the dead. They held that the truth and authority of the Bible comes from the Bible itself and the internal testimony of the Holy Spirit.

But Müntzer disagreed with the Magisterial Reformers on Scripture's inspiration and authority. From humanist rhetoric, he developed a complex notion of the proper order of things relative to revelation. He held that knowledge of God is not teachable and that believers must hear God's word not from a book but from God's own mouth. A mystical, inner-oriented hearing is primary and necessary. God's communication is not limited to the age of inscripturization but continues into the present. Thus he believed that Scripture is only a part of the whole of God's continuing revelation.[14]

11. Michael Horton, *The Christian Faith: A Systematic Theology for Pilgrims on the Way* (Grand Rapids, Zondervan, 2011), 288–90.

12. Allison, *Historical Theology*, 51–54.

13. For Luther, see Robert Kolb, "The Bible in the Reformation and Protestant Orthodoxy," in *The Enduring Authority of the Christian Scriptures*, ed. D. A. Carson (Grand Rapids: Eerdmans, 2016), 90–98.

14. Carter Lindberg, *The European Reformations*, 2nd ed. (Malden, MA: Wiley-Blackwell, 2010), 141.

The Catholic Church moved away from its earlier position and saw the church as a superior authority to Scripture. Catholic polemicist Johannes Eck said, "Scripture is not authentic without the authority of the Church, since canonical writers are her members." The church "provides the whole meaning and the authority of Sacred Scripture."[15] This position was engraved by the Council of Trent, which held to two sources of authority or two authoritative divine revelations: the Scriptures and unwritten tradition, and the church's own interpretation of Scripture as the only authoritative interpretation.[16]

Inerrancy and Clarity. Neither Luther nor Calvin would countenance any errors in Scripture. They interacted against the Socinians, who allowed for error in portions of Scripture—parables, historical events, morals, and descriptions of scientific matters.

In *The Bondage of the Will*, Luther asserted a twofold clarity to Scripture. There is an external clarity, which means that nothing written in Scripture is obscure or ambiguous. The internal clarity comes to those who possess the Holy Spirit. Scripture's clarity is presupposed, for Christ does not want his word to be obscure to his people.

But asserting Scripture's clarity did not mean that the reader can comprehend God in all his being or that the meaning of every text is obvious. Scripture's clarity does not imply that all mysteries are resolved. Erasmus wrongly believed that the passages that describe God's incomprehensibility meant that the Scriptures were obscure. Positively, the Reformers knew that clearer passages enlighten more obscure passages.[17]

Zwingli's printed sermon *Of the Clarity and Certainty of the Word of God* (1522) underlined the effect of reading Scripture. Scripture is clear and enlightens the reader and assures the reader that what he reads is true and worthy of trust because it comes from God. Thus there is an external Word that is read and preached. Not all believe this Word. The internal word is believed in the heart and illuminates. The clarity of Scripture is a function of the internal word.[18]

---

15. Johannes Eck, *Enchiridion locorum communium 1525*, as cited by Allison, *Historical Theology*, 91.

16. Allison, *Historical Theology*, 92–93.

17. Ibid., 128–30.

18. Ibid., 131–32.

Calvin did not pen a work on the clarity of Scripture but took the biblical teaching for granted. He strongly opposed the Catholic position that the Bible is incomprehensible to the laity. He appealed to divine accommodation as support for Scripture's clarity. Scripture is clear because to know God there is a need for special revelation of him that goes beyond general revelation. Also, Scripture is clear because its style is simple or humble. Thus the untrained can understand it.

But OT revelation was more obscure than NT revelation. All Scripture is obscure for those without the Holy Spirit. In asserting clarity or perspicuity, Calvin did not claim that it was easy to interpret Scripture. God accommodated himself to believers, and there is in the Bible a bare and open divine revelation, with nothing obscure, thus giving God's people certainty.[19] The Protestant view meant that the Bible needed to be translated into the common language, accompanied by the encouragement of laypeople to read, hear, and understand God's Word.

The Catholic Church opposed all this teaching. It prohibited translations in the Netherlands (1526), England (1530), France (1548), and Spain (1551). In 1546, the Council of Trent made the Vulgate the official Bible and declared that only the church had the right to interpret it.[20]

Necessity and Sufficiency. Luther stood against Catholic teaching and underlined the sufficiency of Scripture. He held that the Bible is different from all other alleged sources of revelation or instruction. It is superior to the church. The Augsburg Confession maintains Scripture's sufficiency for the remission of sins. The Formula of Concord taught the supreme authority of Scripture. Yet it also affirmed the Apostles', Nicene, and Athanasian creeds. Luther also stood against the fanatics who thought that the Spirit of God spoke directly to believers apart from the Word.[21]

Calvin agreed with Luther and thought the Scriptures were sufficient and necessary. He opposed the notion that church councils could not err. He too opposed fanatics and argued that the Word and the Spirit are joined. He said that Scripture alone is the source and standard for the Christian faith; this assertion is called the "formal

19. Ibid., 132–34.
20. Ibid., 134–35.
21. Ibid., 151–53.

principle of Protestantism." He argued that special revelation gave a clearer picture of God than does general revelation. He also urged parishioners to listen and submit to divinely appointed preachers.[22]

Interpretation. Luther was trained in the medieval, fourfold approach to Scripture and used allegory. As he matured as a Reformer, he developed theologically and rejected allegory.[23] He developed a literal or grammatical-historical meaning. "We should strive, so far as it is possible," Luther said, "to get one, simple, true, and grammatical meaning from the words of the text."[24]

In addition, he thought that Romans communicated the purest gospel; that knowing the topics and worldview of the NT was important to exegesis; that interpreters should implement a christological interpretation for all the Scriptures; that one should carefully consider the context of the passage being interpreted; and that it is important to distinguish law from gospel. Law is that which expresses divine demands while emphasizing human inability. Gospel is that which expresses God's promises by underscoring that Jesus Christ has met all God's demands.

Luther disagreed with the Catholic position that scriptural interpretation belongs to the pope and that theology should be done with regard to Scripture, church tradition, and the ancient church fathers' exegesis. Instead, thought Luther, there is a need for the right kind of person—one who has godliness.[25]

In the Reformed tradition, Zwingli spoke of God's Word as having a true and natural sense. He also spoke of the significance of the biblical context.[26]

Calvin rejected allegory and pressed for the biblical authors' intent. He wanted to open the minds of the biblical authors. His principles included a proper theological framework, or theological structure,

---

22. Ibid., 153–55.

23. Ibid., 174, cites Luther's words in the Genesis commentary but fails to see how Luther still used allegory. For better analysis, see Richard C. Gamble, "The Sources of Calvin's Genesis Commentary: A Preliminary Report," *Archiv für Reformationsgeschichte* 84 (1993): 206–21.

24. Luther, *Lectures on Genesis: Chapters 45–50*, as cited by Allison, *Historical Theology*, 173. Luther's hermeneutic influenced his insistence on a literal interpretation of the words of the Lord's Supper.

25. Allison, *Historical Theology*, 174.

26. Ulrich Zwingli, "Of the Clarity and Certainty of the Word of God," in *Zwingli and Bullinger*, trans. G. W. Bromiley (Philadelphia: Westminster Press, 1953), 87.

provided by the *Institutes*.[27] The notions of brevity and clarity, that biblical interpreters were to imitate God's own method of speaking, were important to Calvin.[28]

The internal testimony of the Holy Spirit makes certain to the reader or hearer God's special revelation in the Scriptures. The Holy Spirit confirms the Word to us. The Spirit and the Word belong inseparably together.[29]

The Heidelberg Catechism built on Calvin's thinking and defined the nature of faith as sure knowledge and firm confidence worked through the Holy Spirit by hearing the gospel.[30] For Calvin and the authors of the Heidelberg Catechism, the written Word of God touches the ears, but through the work of the Holy Spirit it touches the heart as well. There is in Calvin and the Heidelberg Catechism the view that this internal testimony of the Spirit does not prevail over the outward written Word of God. For this internal testimony serves not as a further source of revelation but rather as a certifier or confirmer of the words of the human witnesses who wrote the Scriptures.

A not well-known but important creedal document accepted by all the Reformed churches is the Second Helvetic Confession, first written by Heinrich Bullinger in 1562 and revised in 1564. This confession was the first to put forward formal principles for interpreting Scripture.[31] The confession taught the classic doctrine that Scripture

27. John Calvin to the Reader, *Institutes*, 1:4. See Thomas F. Torrance, *The Hermeneutics of John Calvin*, ed. A. I. C. Heron and Iain R. Torrance (Edinburgh: Scottish Academic Press, 1988), cited by Allison, *Historical Theology*, 175.

28. For more information, see Richard C. Gamble, "*Brevitas et Facilitas*: Toward an Understanding of Calvin's Hermeneutic," *WTJ* 47, no. 1 (Spring 1985): 1–17; "Calvin as Theologian and Exegete: Is There Anything New?," *Calvin Theological Journal* 23, no. 2 (1988): 178–94; "Exposition and Method in Calvin," *WTJ* 49, no. 1 (Spring 1987): 153–65; "The Sources of Calvin's Genesis Commentary: A Preliminary Report," *Archiv für Reformationsgeschichte* 84 (1993): 206–21. See also Richard C. Gamble, *Articles on Calvin and Calvinism*, vol. 6, *Calvin and Hermeneutics* (New York/London: Garland, 1992).

29. John Calvin, *Institutes of the Christian Religion*, ed. John T. McNeill, trans. Ford Lewis Battles (Philadelphia: Westminster Press, 1960) (*Institutes*), 1.7.4, 1.9.2, 1.9.3.

30. Heidelberg Catechism question and answer 21.

31. Second Helvetic Confession, chapter 2: "The apostle Peter has said that the Holy Scriptures are not of private interpretation (2 Peter 1:20), and thus we do not allow all possible interpretations. . . . But we hold that interpretation of scripture to be orthodox and genuine which is gleaned from the scriptures themselves (from the nature of the language in which they were written . . . the circumstances in which they were set down, and expounded in the light of like and unlike passages and of many and clearer passages) and which agree with the rule of faith and love, and contributes much to the glory of God and man's salvation." For more

is its own interpreter, a doctrine that underlined the distinctive and unique authority of Scripture.[32]

DOCTRINE OF HUMANITY

Pre-Fall Image of God. Luther moved away from the medieval tradition of viewing human beings as rational animals while holding to reason as that which distinguishes us from beasts. A better approach is theological, rather than philosophical—a theological approach that views humanity as made in the image of God. Such an approach gives humanity its highest dignity.[33]

Human nature is composed of body, soul, and spirit. The human spirit is the highest and noblest part, from where faith and the ability to comprehend eternal things comes. The soul is where reason dwells, and the body is tasked to carry out what the soul knows and the spirit believes. Humanity is a holistic dualism between the body and the soul, which is of a different substance from the body but which loves the body. Luther held the traducianist position that the soul is generated at conception. At the fall, the image of God was so deeply corrupted that it was almost completely obliterated. Through the gospel people can be remade in the divine image.[34]

The *duplex cognitio dei*, or "twofold knowledge of God" and man, was important for Calvin. Adam knew himself as he comprehended himself as God's creature. His self-identity was bound up in his relationship to God.[35]

Post-Fall Image of God. Martin Luther rejected the semi-Pelagian notion of free will. *The Bondage of the Will* embraced Augustinianism and argued that the will is enslaved to sin and cannot on its own reverse that thinking and turn to God. He thought that the will was

---

background information on this creed, see Philip Schaff, *The Creeds of Christendom* (Grand Rapids: Baker, 1984), 3:396–420.

32. See G. C. Berkouwer, *Holy Scripture*, ed. and trans. Jack B. Rogers (Grand Rapids: Eerdmans, 1975), 165.

33. Allison, *Historical Theology*, 330–31.

34. Ibid., 331.

35. Allison (ibid., 332–33) argues that by examining what is restored we understand more of the image. In regeneration the image is restored, but full restoration awaits heaven. Because we are created in the divine image, we can love as the Bible teaches us to love.

like a horse that can have only one rider, God or Satan. If Satan is riding, then there is no hope for such a perverse will.

Luther's notion of original sin was that the human nature is pervasively corrupted. Even though it appears to be unfair, human beings are condemned for Adam's sin.[36] Even the regenerated remain thoroughly sinful. His Latin phrase designating the regenerated was *simul iustus et peccator*.[37]

Calvin continued in the Augustinian tradition. Apparently, he thought that Adam's sin was pride. It was also unfaithfulness to God's Word. Original sin is transmitted not from parent to children but because of federal headship in Adam.[38] Thus all humans are justly condemned in Adam, which is not to say that they are liable for another's sin. Even newborn babies are under condemnation. Also, actual sins flow from this original sin.

Calvin affirms that sin affects the whole of human nature, including the will and reason. His view is known as *total depravity*. He also held to total inability. Humans sin necessarily but not under compulsion. Humans want to sin. Adam did not fall by necessity. It is not God's fault that Adam fell but Adam's fault.[39]

The Council of Trent held to many Protestant teachings but disagreed concerning the role of the will in salvation. The council denied total depravity and total inability. They thought that the will could cooperate with God's grace in salvation.[40]

Faustus Socinus (1539–1604) and the Socinians had a Pelagian view of sin. Original sin should be rejected because it contradicts human reason. Adam's sin was his alone, and it did not affect anyone else.[41]

---

36. "Original sin is nothing but the utter maliciousness and the inclination to evil that all human beings feel in themselves" (Martin Luther, *What Luther Says*, ed. Ewald M. Plass [St. Louis: Concordia, 1959], 3:1297, as cited by Allison, *Historical Theology*, 353–54).

37. See A. Chacko George, "Martin Luther's Doctrine of Sanctification with Special Reference to the Formula 'Sinul iustus et peccator': A Study in Luther's Lectures on Romans and Galatians" (ThD diss., Westminster Theological Seminary, 1982).

38. *Institutes*, 2.1.8, Library of Christian Classics (LCC) 1:215: "a hereditary depravity and corruption of our nature, diffused into all parts of the soul, which first makes us liable to God's wrath, then also brings forth in us those works which Scripture calls 'works of the flesh'" (as cited by Allison, *Historical Theology*, 355).

39. Allison, *Historical Theology*, 354–56.

40. Ibid., 356.

41. Ibid., 357.

ATONEMENT

Atonement Theory. The Reformation is well known for the "penal substitutionary theory" of the atonement. This view, developed by Luther, is similar to Anselm's satisfaction theory, but instead of grounding the atonement in God's honor Luther grounded it in God's justice. Our holy God hates sin and always acts against it. There is an eternal penalty to pay for sin.

Humanity is cursed for sin and cannot pay this penalty on its own. Christ, however, can and did pay the penalty. He substituted for humanity, paid the penalty, and suffered divine wrath against sin. Christ's sacrifice was a propitiation.[42]

Calvin, too, held to the penal substitutionary theory. He located Christ's saving work in his larger work of the threefold offices of prophet, priest, and king. It was as priest that Christ reconciled sinners to a righteous God through his sacrificial death. Calvin defined Christ's work as substitution, cleansing, expiation and propitiation. Christ's work included his life of obedience, although that life was not the key element of his atoning work. Christ's death in place of sinful humanity was voluntary. "The guilt that held us liable for punishment has been transferred to the head of the Son of God."[43] Also, Christ's crucifixion was meaningful because it was a cursed way to die. He became subject to the curse and thus removed God's wrath against believers. "We have in his death the complete fulfillment of salvation, for through it we are reconciled to God, his righteous judgment is satisfied, the curse is removed, and the penalty paid in full."[44]

The Socinians developed a heretical atonement theory called "the example theory." Socinus's problem with the Reformers related to the doctrine of God. According to the Socinians, if God's justice is satisfied, then there is no need for mercy in the atonement. We know that God is merciful; therefore, Christ did not need to suffer punishment to satisfy divine justice. God can and does forgive sin without demanding that justice be satisfied. Divine justice and mercy are issues of the divine will, and God can simply choose not to exercise his justice. Socinus

---

42. Ibid., 398–99.
43. *Institutes*, 2.16.5, LCC 1:509–10, as cited by Allison, *Historical Theology*, 400.
44. *Institutes*, 2.16.13, LCC 1:520, as cited by Allison, *Historical Theology*, 401.

said that the Reformers had the wrong view of justice. It is wrong to say that justice is an infinite divine attribute. God chose to exercise his mercy instead of his justice. Christ's death was cruel when there was no need of satisfaction. Such a God is base and sordid.

Socinus's view also included a false image of Jesus, who was simply a very holy man equipped with divine power but was not God himself. This man was a powerful example of virtue and integrity and is thus a model or example that moves us to break with sin and lead a holy life. Thus the cross is not about a substitutionary death by God's Son but an example that is intended to lead others to embrace forgiveness. The atonement was not objective reality but a subjective influence moving us to receive divine forgiveness.[45]

Election and Reprobation. Luther supported unconditional election. He wanted people to view election as a comfort. They were to pay careful attention to trusting in Christ for their salvation.[46] Unconditional election is contrasted to conditional election, which asserts that God knows who will have faith and then elects them on that basis.

John Calvin is well known for his doctrine of election, but interpreters today correctly say that election is not Calvin's main doctrine. Calvin taught that predestination is a biblical teaching, that it is part of God's eternal and unchangeable decree, that it is unconditional, that it is individual, and that the Bible teaches both election and reprobation.[47] God does not simply foreknow the future but actually ordains events. The reprobate are such because of God's will as well as the reprobate's own evil. Calvin's view of predestination magnifies God's grace, inclines believers toward humility, and gives confident hope.[48]

The Council of Trent opposed predestination. They thought it rash presumption for anyone to believe for certain that he or she is predestined. That knowledge is only obtained by special revelation.

45. Allison, *Historical Theology*, 402–3.

46. Martin Luther, *The Bondage of the Will*, trans. James I. Packer and O. R. Johnston (Old Tappan, NJ: Revel, 1957), 317, as cited by Allison, *Historical Theology*, 461. Luther opposed Erasmus's view of limited human freedom.

47. Allison, *Historical Theology*, 463.

48. Ibid., 464–65. See Joel R. Beeke, *Debated Issues in Sovereign Predestination: Early Lutheran Predestination, Calvinian Reprobation and Variations in Geneva Lapsarianism* (Göttingen: Vandenhoek & Ruprecht, 2017), 83–164.

Anyone who thought otherwise was declared anathema.[49] Anabaptists also opposed election in the Waterland Confession, a 1577 Dutch Mennonite document that denounced unconditional election and reprobation.[50]

Theodore Beza (1519–1605) developed the "supralapsarian theory" of election.[51] Supralapsarianism says that the divine decrees of election and reprobation precede the divine decree to create humanity and permit humanity's fall. His view was attacked because it posited an absolute decree dependent only on God's will. The decree of election and reprobation were before the decrees of creation and permission of the fall. Opponents argued that supralapsarianism made God the author of sin, and God's authoring sin would be unjust and unloving of God.[52]

Jacobus Arminius (1560–1609) affirmed conditional election and opposed supralapsarianism as well as infralapsarianism because he thought the whole notion should be rejected. Infralapsarianism argues that the divine decree of election and reprobation succeeds the divine decree to create humanity and permit humanity's fall. Rejecting classic Calvinism, he made his own formulations.[53]

Regeneration, Conversion, and Calling. Luther struggled with Romans 1:17 on the righteousness or justice of God. He had a tor-

49. Canons and Decrees of the Council of Trent, sixth session, in Schaff, *Creeds*, 2:103, as cited by Allison, *Historical Theology*, 466.

50. Allison, *Historical Theology*, 466.

51. For a classic study of the issues, see Walter Kickel, *Vernunft und Offenbarung bei Theodor Beza: Zum Problem der Verhältnisses von Theologie, Philosophie und Staat* (Neukirchen-Vluyn: Neukirchener Verlag, 1967), 9, 10: "The ground for such a development to orthodoxy must be searched for in the influence of a rationalistic humanism, or more precisely, a Melanchthonian Aristotelinism." See also Heinrich Heppe, *Reformed Dogmatics* (Eugene, OR: Wipf & Stock, 1977), xxx: "H. Meylan says in his book about Claude Aubery that Beza did not use Aristotelian philosophy principally but condemned its misuse. E. Bizer says that Beza inserted Aristotelian philosophy in his theology."

52. Allison, *Historical Theology*, 466–67.

53. The Five Articles of the Remonstrants, followers of Arminius, came out in 1610. The Synod of Dordt was the Calvinist reply. It affirmed total depravity, unconditional election, limited atonement, irresistible grace, and perseverance of the saints. See Peter Y. De Jong, *Crisis in the Reformed Churches: Essays in Commemoration of the Synod of Dort (1618–1619)* (Grand Rapids: Reformed Fellowship, 1968); W. Robert Godfrey, *John Calvin: His Influence in the Western World* (Grand Rapids: Zondervan, 1982), 95–122. Also, Baptists affirmed "a fully Calvinist theology of predestination" in the First London Confession and the Second London Confession. The General Baptists had an anti-Calvinist theology of predestination (Allison, *Historical Theology*, 469). Some in the Baptist tradition affirm election but either ignore or disagree with reprobation.

mented conscience. He linked regeneration with saving faith: apart from faith there is no regeneration. Conversion requires awareness of sin before God does his work. Luther distinguished between an inward and an outward call. Sin binds our wills, and no one can embrace the gospel. God himself must intervene and draw sinners to himself.[54]

Calvin held to repentance as following faith and as born of faith. He held to a general call and an effective call. The effective, or particular, call is for the elect.[55]

Justification.[56] Luther distinguished two kinds of righteousness: *alien* and *actual. The Freedom of a Christian* demonstrated the paradoxical relationship between alien and actual righteousness. The believer is subject to none, on the one hand, and is servant of all, on the other hand. Luther's opponents accused him of denying the importance of good works. His *Treatise on Good Works* addressed the question and said that good works were found in common activities, such as eating and drinking. His view of justification broke with the Roman Catholic notion of merits and called for a new church.[57]

Calvin joined Luther's condemnation of the Catholic notion that justification comes from faith joined with good works. The Catholics confused justification and sanctification and taught an infused righteousness rather than imputed righteousness. This position viewed justification as a reward that could be merited. Calvin's affirmation that good works follow from justification helped to blunt Catholic criticism. Calvin held that there is an inseparable connection between justification and sanctification.[58]

There are some structural differences between Reformed and confessional Lutheranism on the importance of the doctrine of justification. Both camps hold justification by faith as an essential doctrine, but Lutherans view justification as the fulcrum for their theological

54. Allison, *Historical Theology*, 483–85.

55. See Richard C. Gamble, "Calvin on Irresistible Grace," *Reformed Theological Journal* 25 (2009): 14–21.

56. See Richard C. Gamble, "The Very Gate of Paradise to Me: The Development of Protestantism's Teaching on Justification by Faith," *RPTJ* 4, no. 1 (Fall 2017): 8–42, on justification in Luther and Calvin.

57. Allison, *Historical Theology*, 509–12.

58. Heinrich Bullinger's *The Grace of God that Justifies Us for the Sake of Christ through Faith Alone, without Good Works, while Faith Meanwhile Abounds in Good Works* appeared in 1554 (see ibid., 512–13).

system. While justification is not a central dogma in the simplistic sense of an axiom from which all other doctrines can be deduced, still, in the Lutheran Book of Concord, justification provides the glue that holds the system together.[59]

The Council of Trent denounced the Protestant doctrine. It held that baptism was necessary for justification, as was prevenient grace, which prepared for justification. Justification could then increase daily or through unfaithfulness become lost.[60] All Protestants were condemned to hell.[61]

Sanctification. Calvin's view of "initial salvation" (regeneration and adoption) combined with sanctification, which flows from and confirms salvation. Regeneration's object is to demonstrate agreement between God's righteousness and our obedience, which confirms our adoption as sons. We have been adopted to live a life of imitation of Christ, which includes inward conformity to him.[62] Practically, Calvin advised daily advance in sanctification. Even slight progress is still progress. Progress was achieved by self-denial, on the one side, and devotion to God, on the other side. Believers need to bear the cross. But this attitude is not a Stoic one.[63]

The Council of Trent had a different theology. For Catholics, sanctification was progress in obtaining greater degrees of justification. A Catholic mysticism developed as taught by Ignatius of Loyola, Teresa of Avila, and John of the Cross.[64]

Perseverance. Luther correctly said that the Catholic Church taught that no one could be certain about his or her salvation until the final

59. Carl R. Trueman, "A Tract for the Times: James Buchanan's *The Doctrine of Justification in Historical and Theological Context*," in *The Faith Once Delivered*, ed. Anthony Selvaggio (Phillipsburg, NJ: P&R Publishing, 2007), 42–43.

60. From Canons and Decrees of the Council of Trent, sixth session, the decree on justification reads: "Justification itself . . . is not remission of sins merely, but also the sanctification and renewal of the inward man, through the voluntary reception of the grace, and of the gifts, by which an unjust man becomes just . . . Of this justification, the . . . instrumental cause is the sacrament of baptism, which is the sacrament of faith, without which [faith] no man was ever justified" (as cited by Allison, *Historical Theology*, 487–88).

61. Allison, *Historical Theology*, 514.

62. See Richard C. Gamble, "Calvin and Sixteenth-Century Spirituality: Comparison with the Anabaptists," *Calvin Theological Journal* 31, no. 2 (1996): 335–58, and "Calvin's Spirituality," *Reformed Theological Journal* 25 (2009): 5–13.

63. Allison, *Historical Theology*, 532–34.

64. Examples include Ignatius, *Spiritual Exercises*; Teresa of Ávila, *The Way of Perfection* and *Interior Castle*; and Saint John, *Dark Night of the Soul*. See ibid., 535.

judgment. He denounced this "monster of uncertainty" and argued that if a person's sins were laid on Christ's back, then they cannot be on ours as well. The Catholic Church thought his position was presumptuous and evil.[65]

Calvin taught that perseverance was not given as a reward for faithfulness or helped by human willingness but was entirely a divine gift. He said that the Catholic Church was wrong for teaching that God works in the believer's life as long as he cooperates with divine grace. There is no cooperation between God and the believer in perseverance. Perseverance is grounded in election, a truth that gives great assurance. There are people who have professed to be believers who have fallen away. But they were never true believers.[66]

The Council of Trent denied that people could know the decree of election in this lifetime and that there is human cooperation in salvation. It charactized assurance as heresy and said that making such a claim condemned one to hell. Fear and uncertainty keeps people from pride. Also, mortal sin causes the person to lose his or her justifying grace.[67]

Arminius did not teach that a true believer could completely lose his salvation but thought that there were passages in Scripture that leaned in that direction.[68] The fifth article of the Articles of the Remonstrants said that whether believers can return to the present evil world, lose a good conscience, and be devoid of grace "must be more particularly determined out of the Holy Scripture, before we ourselves can teach it with the full persuasion of our minds."[69]

DOCTRINE OF THE CHURCH

Marks. Luther had established seven marks for a true church: the church possesses the Word of God, baptism, the Lord's Supper, the

65. Ibid., 549–50.
66. Ibid., 550–52.
67. Ibid., 553.
68. Arminius, *The Writings of James Arminius*, 1:254, as cited by Allison, *Historical Theology*, 555.
69. *Five Arminian Articles*, article 5, in Schaff, *Creeds*, 3:548; see Allison, *Historical Theology*, 555.

public exercise of the keys—specifically discipline, the church calls ministers, prayer, public praise and thanksgiving, and possession of the cross—and the church endures misfortune and persecution so that it may be more like Christ. Eventually, the first three marks were judged to be essential for a true church, and the two elements of proper preaching and sacraments constitute the church.[70]

Calvin, following Augustine, distinguished between the visible and the invisible church. The church was to be charitable with her members and not engage in a witch hunt to expel inauthentic members.[71] Martin Bucer added church discipline as a mark. The Belgic and Scottish confessions include, besides true preaching and proper sacraments, the third mark of discipline.

Calvin wrote about the marks of the true church. This Christian community is physical by necessity. God speaks to his people through physical ministers.[72] The church is like a mother who feeds and nourishes believers.[73] Yet his conception is more complicated by the presence of the invisible church within the physical, visible church.[74]

Believers must have a firm conviction that through God's work they have received forgiveness of sins and have therefore been engrafted into the body of the church.[75] Within the church there is forgiveness of sins.[76] The church has three supporting structures—she is founded

70. The Augsburg Confession reads: "The church is the congregation of the saints in which the gospel is rightly taught and the sacraments rightly administered. And unto the true unity of the church, it is sufficient to agree concerning the doctrine of the gospel and the administration of the sacraments" (Martin Luther, *On the Councils of the Church*, as cited by Allison, *Historical Theology*, 578–79).

71. *Institutes*, 4.1.8, as cited by Allison, *Historical Theology*, 579.

72. *Institutes*, 4.1.4, 1017: "As he did not entrust the ancient folk to angels but raised up teachers from the earth thus to perform the angelic office, so also today it is his will to teach us through human means."

73. Ibid., 1016.

74. Ibid., 1013–15.

75. Ibid., 1035: "Consequently, we must firmly believe that by God's generosity, mediated by Christ's merit, through the sanctification of the Spirit, sins have been and are daily pardoned to us who have been received and engrafted into the body of the church."

76. Ibid. "Forgiveness of sins, then, is for us the first entry into the church and Kingdom of God. Without it, there is for us no covenant or bond with God. For thus he speaks through the prophet . . . (Hos. 2:18–19, cf. Vg). . . . Thus in the Creed forgiveness of sins appropriately follows mention of the church. For as one reads in the prophet, only the citizenry and household of the church obtains this (Isa. 33:14–24). . . . Now I say that it ought first to be built up, not that there can be any church without forgiveness of sins, but because the Lord has promised his mercy solely in the communion of saints."

on God's election, connected to Christ's steadfastness, and, finally, based on the firm foundation of God's promises.[77]

Calvin was convinced that after the believer's initial union with Christ, the believer needed help—so that his faith might increase and he might move on toward the goals of the Christian life. To all those ends, God gave the church.

Christ's church is necessary to the Christian life. As with a mother, it is through the church that we have come to life.[78] Also as a mother does for her children, the church preserves and protects believers.[79] In continuity with parenting imagery, Calvin also used the image of father and applied it to pastors. Specifically, the pastor is like a father who cuts his children's meat at a meal.[80]

The true church is built up by the preaching of God's Word within the context of God's prescribed order.[81] In the church's public worship, God's people are brought up to God's presence.[82] The benefits that obtain to God's people through preaching and the sacraments come through ministers.[83]

Born to life in the church, nurtured and nourished in the church, parented in the church, Christians must therefore give back to the church that which is her due. Since God is the common Father of believers and Christ is the head over all the members of the church, all members should treat each other with love as brothers.[84] Those

77. Ibid., 4.1.3, 1015.

78. Ibid., 4.1.4, 1016: "For there is no other way to enter into life unless this mother conceive us in her womb, give us birth, nourish us at her breast, and lastly, unless she keep us under her care and guidance."

79. Ibid.: "Not only does the Lord through forgiveness of sins receive and adopt us one for all into the church, but through the same means he preserves and protects us there."

80. Ronald S. Wallace, *Calvin's Doctrine of the Word and Sacrament* (Eugene, OR: Wipf & Stock, 1997), 115–17.

81. *Institutes*, 1019: "We must hold to what we have quoted from Paul—that the church is built up solely by outward preaching, and that the saints are held together by one bond only: that with common accord, through learning and advancement, they keep the church order established by God (cf. Eph. 4:12)."

82. Ibid.: "Nevertheless, he laments that he burns, is tormented and well-nigh consumed, with this single trouble, vexation, and sorrow. Surely, this is because believers have no greater help than public worship, for by it God raises his own folk upward step by step. . . . This benefit so belongs to the church that we cannot enjoy it unless we abide in communion with the church."

83. Ibid., 1036. "Thirdly, it is dispensed to us through the ministers and pastors of the church, either by the preaching of the gospel or by the administration of the sacraments."

84. Ibid., 4.1.3, 1014f.

united to Christ must be loyal to the visible church and with each other.[85]

Calvin connected sound preaching in the church to Christ's kingship. The symbol of a potentate's power was then, and still is today, his scepter. The Scriptures are that "scepter" of Jesus Christ.[86] The Protestant pastor, as the one who keeps Christ's scepter, should be treated with honor because of the task.[87] Yet his honor is derived from God; it is not original to the man himself.[88] Any place where the Word of God is not respected could never be called a church of Jesus Christ.[89]

God's Word has to be heard by the congregation. By the notion of hearing the Word, Calvin meant taking sound waves into the ears, then moving to actions that are done with the heart and hands. If the Word of God is not heard, then that assembly where it is spoken is in fact no longer a church.[90] Calvin also believed that preaching the Word would produce love within the church.[91]

There is a true hearing of preaching. From the congregation's perspective, preaching includes difficult parts. Sometimes a sermon is difficult to hear because the words cut to followers' hearts. Nevertheless, the people must not rebel.[92] While a preacher may be called

85. Ronald S. Wallace, *Calvin's Doctrine of the Christian Life* (Edinburgh: Oliver & Boyd, 1959), 245ff.

86. *Institutes*, 4.2.4, 1046: "Since the church is Christ's Kingdom, and he reigns by his Word alone, will it not be clear to any man that those are lying words (cf. Jer. 7:4) by which the Kingdom of Christ is imagined to exist apart from his scepter (that is, his most holy Word)?"

87. John Calvin, *Necessity of Reform*, in *Selected Works of John Calvin: Tracts and Letters*, vol. 1, *Tracts*, ed. and trans. Henry Beveridge (Grand Rapids: Baker, 1983), 216: "Let pastors, then, have their due honor—an honor, however, not derogatory in any degree to the supreme authority of Christ, to whom it behooves them and every man to be subject. For God declares, by Malachi, that the government of the Israelitish Church was committed to the priests, under the condition that they should faithfully fulfill the covenant made with them, viz., that their 'lips should keep knowledge,' and expound the law to the people (Mal. 2:7)."

88. Ibid.: "Pastors are mistaken if they imagine that they are invested with the government of the church on any other terms than that of being ministers and witnesses of the truth of God."

89. *Institutes*, 4.2.7, 1048: "Who has without exception dared to call that assembly 'church' where the Lord's Word is openly and with impunity trodden under foot?"

90. Ibid., 4.2.3, 1044: "For the Lord nowhere recognizes any temple as his save where his Word is heard and scrupulously observed."

91. Ibid., 4.2.5, 1047: "Now this communion is held together by two bonds, agreement in sound doctrine and brotherly love."

92. Calvin, *Sermon on 2 Timothy 3:16*: The people "must not say, 'Ho! That is too hard to be borne. You ought not to go on like that,'" said Calvin; rather, "those who cannot bear to be reproved had better look for another school-master than God." While pleasant

by God and preach only the Word, nevertheless that preaching may bear little fruit in the congregation's life. The right attitude on the congregation's part is imperative. The congregation must be willing to obey God—with no reserve.[93] The congregation is not a passive audience during preaching.[94]

Calvin rightly believed that there is power in the Word that is independent of the recipient.[95] There can be a satanic hardening of the heart against the Word.[96] The Word of God as preached must be obeyed. To hear and not obey is like being a warrior who owns fine armor but hangs up the armor and leaves it to rust.[97]

In his historical context, Calvin and his pastoral colleagues were faced with a severe problem. Present-day pastors face it as well. Calvin was convinced that the church of Christ has the right to demand certain things of her members—because the church speaks with authority. Her commands are to be obeyed by God's people.[98] Calvin, and all believers, had to submit to the voice of God in the church.

The Roman church made such obedience impossible. That church insisted that its laws should be obeyed—even if they were unjust and injurious. The Roman church contended that those ecclesiastical laws may not be rejected. The Genevan ministers had to resolve the dilemma. It was resolved in affirming that the true church was wor-

---

preaching is desired, that may not be God's way for the people. "There are many who will not stand it." Calvin went on, "'What! Is this the way to teach? Ho! We want to be won by sweetness.' You do? Then go and teach God his lessons! These are our sensitive folk who cannot bear a single reproof to be offered to them. And why? 'Ho! We want to be taught in another style.' Well then, go to the devil's school! He will flatter you enough—and destroy you" (translated by T. H. L. Parker, *The Oracles of God: An Introduction to the Preaching of John Calvin* [London: Lutterworth, 1947], 61–62; see this resource for more information on proper hearing).

93. LeRoy Nixon, *John Calvin: Expository Preacher* (Grand Rapids: Eerdmans, 1950), 65: "Yet the preaching might have little or no effect, if the attitude of the congregation were not all that it should be. The congregation makes or breaks the effect of a sermon, according to whether or not they come in the right attitude. The only proper attitude for hearing a sermon is the attitude of willingness to obey God completely and with no reserve."

94. T. H. L. Parker, *John Calvin: A Biography* (Philadelphia: Westminster Press, 1975), 95.

95. Wallace, *Word and Sacrament*, 92.

96. Ibid., 93.

97. Wallace, *Christian Life*, 219.

98. *Institutes*, 4.2.10, 1050: "For if we think of the church in this way—that we should reverence its judgment, defer to its authority, obey its warning, be moved by its chastisements, and keep its communion scrupulously in all respects—then we cannot admit that they have a church without the necessity of subjection and obedience to it awaiting us."

thy of believers' submission to its authority, but the Roman church was not.[99]

Where true and effective ministry is found, it will bring good fruit in the lives of the congregation's members. Calvin specified that type of fruit. Men who had previously lived notorious lives had been changed. Even those who had been good and respectable had also seen improvements. Third, men and women who had lacked clear consciences could now enter God's presence with joy in their hearts.[100]

Church Government. The first issue of church government is the church's relationship to the state. The Lutheran and Reformed churches are sometimes called "magisterial churches" because of their view of the union of church and state. The Roman Catholic Church united church and state as well but held that both church and state were to be united under one head, the pope.[101]

The Anabaptists had a different view—one that separated the church and the state. They argued that because the state is inherently wicked, Christians cannot become involved in civil government.[102]

99. Ibid., 4.10.23, 1201: "But here also the Lord best confronts them with the truth of his word, and delivers us out of such bondage into the freedom that he has purchased for us by his sacred blood, the benefit of which he has more than once sealed by his Word."

100. Calvin, *Necessity of Reform*, 200–201: "But is there no fruit in this, that many who are truly pious feel their obligation to us, in that they have at length learned to worship God with a pure heart, and to invoke him with a calm conscience, have been freed from perpetual torments, and have been furnished with true delight in Christ, so as to be able to confide in him? But if we are asked for proofs which every eye can see, it has not fared so unhappily with us that we cannot point to numerous sources of rejoicing. How many who formerly led a vicious course of life have been so reformed as to seem converted into new men? How many whose past lives had been free from censure, nay, who were held in the highest estimation, have, instead of retrograding, been able to testify by their conduct that our ministry has proved neither barren nor unfruitful?"

101. The Catechism of the Council of Trent 1566 says: "[Christ] placed over his church, which he governs by his invisible Spirit, a man to be his vicar, and the minister of his power: a visible church requires a visible head, and, therefore, the Savior appointed Peter head and pastor of all the faithful . . . desiring that he, who was to succeed him [Peter] should be invested with the very same power of ruling and governing the entire church" (as cited by Allison, *Historical Theology*, 581).

102. The 1529 Schleitheim Confession reads: "The government magistracy is according to the flesh, but the Christians' is according to the Spirit. Their houses and dwelling remain in this world, but the Christians' are in heaven. Their citizenship is in this world, but the Christians' citizenship is in heaven. The weapons of the conflict and war are carnal and against the flesh only, but the Christians' weapons are spiritual, against the fortification of the devil" (Allison, *Historical Theology*, 580).

They cannot swear allegiance to the state. They would not become involved with the state churches—either Catholic or Protestant.[103]

As to church government, Luther did not change the method of church government under the Catholic system; he established bishops in his churches, but they were not to be concerned with matters of civil government. There was to be no mixing of church power and the power of the sword.[104]

Calvin said that God could have chosen to rule over the church directly but chose instead to rule through ministers. Calvin used Paul's list of five offices, from apostles to teachers, but held that only the last two are ordinary offices of the church. The offices of apostle, prophet, and evangelist were for the beginning of his kingdom. Calvin differentiated between pastors and teachers, or doctors: teachers are not involved in discipline and administration of the sacraments but only in scriptural interpretation to keep doctrine pure. Pastors performed all those functions.[105] A gospel call included the ministers declaring a person fit to receive such a call and receiving one from the people. Such a person could be called either a *bishop*, *presbyter*, *pastor*, or *minister*, since those words are interchangeable. This was the first break with episcopal government. Calvin added two other offices, *elder* and *deacon*. The deacons took care of the poor. The city and church of Geneva established a hospital and cared for thousands of refugees.[106]

The situation in England was more complex.[107] By 1534 England had officially broken with the pope, and in the Supremacy Act Parliament acknowledged that the king was and ought to be the supreme head of the Church of England.[108] The situation was again complicated

103. The Anabaptists also had their own view of the pastor's role in the church. Pastors are "to read, admonish and teach, warn, discipline, excommunicate from the church, lead in prayer for the advancement of all the brothers and sisters, serve communion, and in all things see to the care of the body of Christ, in order that it may be built up and developed, thereby silencing its detractors" (from the Schleitheim Confession, as cited by Allison, *Historical Theology*, 604).

104. Allison, *Historical Theology*, 602.

105. See Richard C. Gamble, *Articles on Calvin and Calvinism*, vol. 10, *Calvin's Ecclesiology; Sacraments and Deacons* (New York/London: Garland, 1992).

106. Allison, *Historical Theology*, 602–3.

107. King Henry VIII was angry that the pope refused to grant him an annulment to his marriage with Catherine of Aragon. In 1531 Parliament had recognized Henry as the "Supreme Head of the Church of England as far as the law of Christ allows."

108. The Supremacy Act removed the earlier phrase, "as far as the law of Christ allows" (Allison, *Historical Theology*, 604–5).

when a queen took power and Queen Elizabeth had the archbishop of Canterbury designated the highest church official, with the regent's being the supreme governor. This was a specifically Protestant episcopal form of government. But the English Puritans were dissatisfied with the situation. They desired to purify the church and rid it of what they considered Catholicism. The Puritans were divided into groups—the Separatists said church and state should be separate. A group known as the Independents wanted to stay in the Anglican church but reform it along Presbyterian or Congregationalist lines. The Congregationalists argued that individual congregations were the highest source of authority.[109]

English Baptists came out of the Separatists group. John Smyth and Thomas Helwys had, in 1607, fled to Holland, where they had practiced infant baptism but changed to believer's baptism. In 1611 Helwys founded the first Baptist church in London. It was Arminian in theology, thus a General Baptist church. There were particular Baptist churches that were Calvinist.[110]

Baptism. Luther supported infant baptism and argued that while there is not a positive biblical command for the sacrament, it must be practiced for two reasons. First, it was wrong to say that the church had been mistaken for a thousand years—and Christ would not allow that to happen. Doing so would be to say that there was no true baptism and thus no true church. Second, while there was insufficient scriptural support to begin the practice had it not already been instituted, still, Scripture had enough to say about it so as to preclude discontinuing the practice. Christ told his diciples to let the children come to him; he said that all nations are to be baptized; and the NT gives examples of household baptisms. Thus Luther's understanding of the nature of baptism is difficult to comprehend.[111]

109. Robert Browne fled persecution and took his congregation to Holland in 1580. He articulated congregationalism. John Robinson of Scrooby, England, also fled to Holland, but part of the group set sail on the Mayflower in 1620 and settled in Plymouth Colony as Congregationalists.

110. Ibid., 605–6.

111. Luther's *Small Catechism* (1529) reads: "It works forgiveness of sins, delivers from death and the devil, and gives eternal salvation to all who believe, as the Word and promise of God declare. . . . It is not water . . . that does it, but the Word of God which is with and in the water, and faith, which trusts in the Word of God in the water. For without the Word of God

501

Relative to faith and baptism, Luther presented a number of answers concerning infants' having faith.[112] One was the faith of the children's sponsors, their parents or others. The sponsors believe in the place of the infants. This faith is vicarious. But this view was deemphasized toward the view that the infant children actually believe. His argument was that since the sacrament was valid, the infants must have faith. Their faith is Christ's gift to them. That infants can have this faith is apparently proven by John the Baptist in his mother's womb.[113]

But Luther eventually denied the importance of faith for the validity of the sacrament.[114] He disagreed with the Catholic insistence that baptism was absolutely necessary for salvation, but he argued for its necessity against those who would dispense with it as something only external and not necessary.[115]

There was a lot of interaction between the Swiss Anabaptists and the early leaders of the Swiss Reformation. In Switzerland, the first believer's baptism was in 1521.[116] Believer's baptism was outlawed in Zurich in 1525 and pronounced punishable by death. In that same year, Oecolampadius of Basel did not think that Scripture compelled infant baptism or believer's baptism, so both should be allowed.[117] The Schleitheim Confession of 1527 argued that baptism was for believers only and that infant baptism was an abomination. Menno Simons's *Foundation of Christian Doctrine* taught that baptism was

---

and water is nothing but water, and no baptism: but with the Word of God it is a baptism." The same teaching appears in Luther's *Large Catechism* (1529). See ibid., 623–24.

112. Luther, "Of Infant Baptism," says in his *Large Catechism*: "Faith clings to the water, and believes that it is baptism, in which there is pure salvation and life: not [salvation] through the water . . . but through the fact that it is embodied in the Word and institution of God, and the name of God inheres in it" (see ibid., 624).

113. Timothy George, *Theology of the Reformers* (Nashville: Broadman, 1988); Allison, *Historical Theology*, 624.

114. In his *Large Catechism* Luther says: "For not on that account [i.e., the lack of faith] does baptism become invalid; but everything depends upon the Word and command of God. Baptism is nothing else than water and the Word of God in and with each other; that is, when the Word is added to the water, baptism is valid, even though faith be lacking. For my faith does not make baptism, but receives it." We take the infant to baptism with hope: "We bring the child to be baptized with the conviction and the hope that he will believe, and we pray that God will give him faith. But we do not baptize on the strength of this belief, but only on the fact that God has commanded it" (as cited by Allison, *Historical Theology*, 624–25).

115. Ibid., 625.

116. George, *Reformers*, 624.

117. Diane Poythress, *Reformer of Basel: The Life, Thought and Influence of Johannes Oecolampadius* (Grand Rapids: Reformation Heritage Books, 2011), 18–19.

only for those with a living faith and was a symbol of dying to sin and living to Christ, which infants could not exercise. Infant baptism did violence to God's Word. Menno was convinced that both Lutheran and Reformed defenses of the practice were unacceptable.

Given the complexity of Luther's view and earlier discussions in Switzerland, Calvin gave a lot of thought to the nature of baptism. He saw baptism as a sign of initiation into the church.[118] Baptism functions as token and proof of cleansing from sin, mortification, and testimony. Baptism is a sign of salvation, remission, and cleansing of sins. Baptism is also a promise of salvation[119] and a proof and sign of the believer's cleansing.[120] Christ's great purity destroys the believer's filth.[121]

There is a relationship between baptism and repentance. Contemporary Roman Catholic theology taught that regeneration consisted of a combination of baptism paired with human repentance and the power of the keys. In contrast, Calvin emphasized the primary importance of baptism. The Catholic theological mistake birthed the fake sacrament of penance.[122]

There was also a connection in Calvin's mind between the cleansing via baptism and the mortification of a believer's flesh.[123] The cleansing is an offering of mercy from God but not a license to sin.[124] Those

118. Calvin gives a clear and precise definition of baptism in the *Institutes*, 1303: "Baptism is the sign of the initiation by which we are received into the society of the church, in order that, engrafted in Christ, we may be reckoned among God's children."

119. "Calvin, *Institutes*, 1304: "It is to receive baptism with this promise: 'He who believes and is baptized will be saved' (Mark 16:16) . . . And by Peter: 'Baptism . . . saves us' (1 Peter 3:21)."

120. *Institutes*, 1304: "Baptism brings three things to our faith which we must deal with individually. The first thing that the Lord sets out for us is that baptism should be a token and proof of our cleansing; or (the better to explain what I mean) it is like a sealed document to confirm to us that all our sins are so abolished, remitted, and effaced that they can never come to his sight, be recalled, or charged against us. For he wills that all who believe be baptized for the remission of sins (Matt. 28:19, Acts 2:38)."

121. Ibid., 4.15.3, 1305–6: "For Christ's purity has been offered us in it; his purity ever flourishes; it is defiled by no spots, but buries and cleanses away all our defilement."

122. Ibid., 1306: "We have been cleansed of our sins by Christ's blood. Yet what is the sign and testimony of that washing but baptism? . . . which in our first regeneration was given us through baptism alone . . . as if baptism itself were not the sacrament of penance!"

123. Ibid., 1325: "Scripture declares that baptism first points to the cleansing of our sins, which we obtain from Christ's blood; then to the mortification of our flesh, which rests upon participation in his death and through which believers are reborn into newness of life and into the fellowship of Christ. All that is taught in the Scriptures concerning baptism can be referred to this summary except that baptism is also a symbol for bearing witness to our religion before men."

124. Ibid., 1306: "By this Paul does not deny that we obtain in Christ continual and unceasing forgiveness of sins even unto death; but he indicates that he was given by the Father

who are baptized, therefore, are not free to live lives of sin.[125] Also, baptism is a public profession of one's faith.[126]

For Calvin, baptism held the benefits of adoption and also nourished the believer's hope in God. Baptism was also a pledge and earnest. Finally, baptism united one to Christ.[127] The mark and pledge of baptism is universal in its being a sign of adoption.[128] Calvin emphasized baptism as a pledge of being joined to Christ and clothed with Christ.[129] Adoption teaches believers to rely and lean on Christ.[130] Calvin was convinced that this knowledge should make God's people treasure their adoption over everything else in the world.

Calvin promoted the very helpful notion of individual believers calling their baptism to mind in that such memories fortify believers in their divine forgiveness.[131] This great assurance is of practical aid when believers have guilty consciences.[132]

---

only to poor sinners who, wounded by the branding of conscience, sigh for the physician. To them the mercy of God is offered. Those who, counting on impunity, chase after the occasion and license to sin, provoke nothing but God's wrath and judgment."

125. Calvin, *John Calvin's Sermons on Ephesians*, trans. Arthur Golding (Edinburgh: Banner of Truth Trust, 1973), 2:13–15, 194–95: "And therefore all they that name themselves as belonging to the church, and yet nevertheless are disorderly and dissolute persons shall one day feel what a sacrilege it is to have so profaned their baptism, which God had ordained for their salvation."

126. *Institutes*, 1325: "All that is taught in the Scriptures concerning baptism can be referred to this summary except that baptism is also a symbol for bearing witness to our religion before men."

127. Ibid., 3.25.1, 987: "Christ, the Sun of Righteousness, shining through the gospel and having overcome death, has, as Paul testifies, brought us the light of life. Hence we likewise by believing 'pass out of death into life,' being 'no more strangers and sojourners, but fellow citizens of the saints and of the household of God' who 'made us sit' with his only begotten Son 'in heavenly places,' that we may lack nothing for full happiness."

128. Calvin, *Sermons on Ephesians*, 2:13–15, 194–95: "Although baptism does not serve for any one people, city, or country in particular, yet we are marked out by God when he gives us the use of his sacraments to assure us of his adoption, and to nourish the hope he has given us by his gospel."

129. Ibid.: "It is true that they who retreat from our Lord Jesus Christ in a way make their baptism vain, but that will cost them very dearly, because the pledge and earnest that God gives us to show we are joined to our Lord Jesus Christ and are clothed with him (as it is said in the twelfth chapter of the first Letter to the Corinthians) is too precious a thing to be so misused."

130. Ibid., 214–15. "God tells us and assures us that he has adopted us in order that we should lean wholly upon him." Yet that connection is made in the context of "pure worship."

131. Ibid., 1305: "We ought to recall the memory of our baptism and fortify our mind with it, that we may always be sure and confident of the forgiveness of sins."

132. Ibid., 1306: "Therefore, there is no doubt that all pious folk throughout life, whenever they are troubled by a consciousness of their faults, may venture to remind themselves of their

More specifically, in baptism God's people "put on Christ." First, it is a token of renewal and mortification when believers groan under the branding of conscience.[133] The notion of "putting on Christ" means that believers share or participate in Christ's death and burial.[134] But this putting on of Christ does not mean only sharing in his death. It also means that believers share or participate in Christ's life and blessings.[135]

Baptism is a token of the believer's union with Christ. Knowing that believers share in Christ's life and death—and thus in all his blessings—is an advantage to the believer's faith.[136] But to be so united to Christ requires knowledge that salvation is truly a Trinitarian work.[137]

Regarding baptism's efficacy, Calvin had to deal with many problems that developed during the days of medieval theology. Beginning in the ancient church, it had been taught that baptism was a cleansing for all past sins. Because of that erroneous view, baptism was often held off till the end of life. Calvin reminded his readers that baptism's efficacy did not reach back only into the past.[138]

---

baptism, that from it they may be confirmed in assurance of that sole and perpetual cleansing which we have in Christ's blood."

133. Ibid., 1307: "Hence, Paul proves that we are children of God from the fact that we put on Christ in baptism (Gal. 3:26–27)."

134. Ibid.: "Baptism also brings another benefit, for it shows us our mortification in Christ, and new life in him. . . . Through baptism Christ makes us sharers in his death, that we may be engrafted in it (Rom. 6:5, cf. Vg.). . . . He uses this same argument in another place: we were circumcised and put off the old man after we were buried in Christ through baptism (Col. 2:11–12)."

135. Ibid.: "By these words he not only exhorts us to follow Christ as if he had said that we are admonished through baptism to die to our desire by an example of Christ's death, and to be aroused to righteousness by the example of his resurrection. . . . So those who receive baptism with right faith truly feel the effective working of Christ's death in the mortification of their flesh, together with the working of his resurrection in the vivification of the Spirit (Rom. 6:8). . . . Thus the free pardon of sins and the imputation of righteousness are first promised us, and then the grace of the Holy Spirit to reform us to newness of life."

136. Ibid.: "Our faith receives from baptism the advantage of its sure testimony to us that we are not only engrafted into the death and life of Christ, but so united to Christ himself that we become sharers in all his blessings."

137. Ibid., 1308: "But we obtain regeneration by Christ's death and resurrection only if we are sanctified by the Spirit and imbued with a new and spiritual nature. For this reason we obtain and, so to speak, clearly discern in the Father the cause, in the Son the matter, and in the Spirit the effect, of our purgation and our regeneration."

138. Ibid., 1305: "But we are not to think that baptism was conferred upon us only for past time, so that for newly committed sins into which we fall after baptism we must seek new remedies of expiation in some other sacraments, as if the force of the former one were spent.

So ends a brief examination of Calvin's view of baptism in general. But Calvin also wrote about the nature and purpose of infant baptism. He acknowledged God's fatherly care toward our children even after our death; he said, therefore, that believers should be grateful to God and instruct their children in the ways of piety.[139] Promises were connected to infant baptism. And God has promised to adopt our infants as his own.[140]

Calvin wrote at a time when segments of the church taught that baptism was necessary for salvation—and Calvin stood against that teaching. It was the divine promise that was important to salvation, not the sign of that promise.[141] Calvin viewed infant children of church members as belonging to Christ's church even if they died in infancy without the benefit of having been baptized. The ground for that membership is the divine promise.[142] He was convinced that children, even of only one believing parent, are considered by God to be holy.[143]

Calvin made a connection between baptism and circumcision. He explained the difference between the manner in which Abraham received circumcision following his profession of faith and Isaac's receiving circumcision as a hereditary right because of the form of

---

. . . But we must realize that at whatever time we are baptized, we are once for all washed and purged for our whole life."

139. Ibid., 1359: "From this would grow up not only an impious ungratefulness toward God's mercy but a certain negligence about instructing our children in piety. For when we consider that immediately from birth God takes and acknowledges them as his children, we feel a strong stimulus to instruct them in an earnest fear of God and observance of the law."

140. Ibid., 1321: "God declares that he adopts our babies as his own before they are born, when he promises that he will be our God and the God of our descendants after us (Gen. 17:7). Their salvation is embraced in this word. No one will dare be so insolent toward God as to deny that his promise of itself suffices for its effect"; and 1359: "Accordingly, unless we wish spitefully to obscure God's goodness, let us offer our infants to him, for he gives them a place among those of his family and household, that is, the members of the church."

141. Ibid., 1321: "For men will think that Christ has come not to fulfill the promises but to abolish them (cf. Matt. 5:17), seeing that the promise which was then effective enough of itself to confer salvation before the eighth day (Gen 17:7; cf. v. 12) now would not be valid without the aid of a sign."

142. Ibid., 1323: "From this it follows that the children of believers are baptized not in order that they who were previously strangers to the church may then for the first time become children of God, but rather that, because by the blessing of the promise they already belonged to the body of Christ, they are received into the church with this solemn sign."

143. Ibid., 1329: "For this same reason, the children of Christians are considered holy; and even though born with only one believing parent, by the apostle's testimony they differ from the unclean seed of idolaters."

the divine promise.[144] As God continued to develop the theology of circumcision, he revealed that circumcision was also a sign to cut the foreskin of the heart in demonstration that Israel was God's chosen people.[145] Circumcision of the heart—not done by human effort—demonstrated circumcision's true meaning. Thus the nature of the promises of circumcision, including forgiveness of sins and suppression of the flesh, has the same nature as the promies of baptism. Both circumcision and baptism are seals of divine promise and grace.[146]

Both circumcision and baptism are literal signs, and neither is more spiritual than the other. The two sacraments signify the same truth and fulfillment.[147] Baptism fulfills the same office.[148] Baptism and circumcision have the same inner mystery, promises, use, and efficacy.[149] Baptism, like circumcision, is appointed for infants.[150] Both sacraments

144. Ibid., 1347: "The latter by hereditary right, according to the form of the promise, is already included within the covenant from his mother's womb"; and 1326: "When the Lord commands Abraham to observe circumcision, he previously states that he will be God to him and his descendants, adding that he possesses the abundance and sufficiency of all things."

145. Ibid., 1326: "That circumcision is the sign of mortification."

146. Ibid.: "We have, therefore, a spiritual promise given to the patriarchs in circumcision such as is given us in baptism, since it represented for them forgiveness of sins and mortification of flesh. Moreover, as we have taught that Christ is the foundation of baptism, in whom both of these reside, so it is also evident that he is the foundation of circumcision. For he is promised to Abraham and in him the blessing of all nations (Gen. 12:2–3). To seal this grace, the sign of circumcision is added. . . . We therefore conclude that, apart from the difference in the visible ceremony, whatever belongs to circumcision pertains likewise to baptism."

147. Ibid., 1333: "Clearly, if circumcision was a literal sign, we must estimate baptism to be the same. For the apostle, in the second chapter of Colossians, makes neither more spiritual than the other. For he says that we were circumcised in Christ not by a circumcision made with hands, when we laid aside the body of sin which dwells in our flesh. This he calls the 'circumcision of Christ.' . . . What do these words mean, except that the fulfillment and truth of baptism are also the truth and fulfillment of circumcision, since they signify one and the same thing?"

148. Ibid., 1327: "For circumcision was for the Jews their first entry into the church, because it was a token to them by which they were assured of adoption as the people and household of God, and they in turn professed to enlist in God's service. In like manner, we also are consecrated to God through baptism, to be reckoned as his people, and in turn we swear fealty to him. By this it appears incontrovertible that baptism has taken the place of circumcision to fulfill the same office among us"; and 1333: "They pretend that circumcision was a figure of mortification, not of baptism. . . . From this we gather that baptism is put in place of circumcision in order to represent to us what circumcision signified to the Jews of old. In asserting a difference between the covenants, with what barbarous boldness do they dissipate and corrupt the Scripture!"

149. Ibid., 1339: "Therefore, setting aside these absurdities of theirs, let us cling to the resemblance between baptism and circumcision, which we see most completely in accord with respect to the inner mystery, the promises, the use, and the efficacy."

150. Ibid., 1353: "Circumcision, which is known to correspond to our baptism, had been appointed for infants (Gen. 17:12)."

are founded on Christ, the head.[151] Both sacraments have meaning in the promise of the covenant. As there were promises to the children of old, so the covenantal promises apply to Christian children.[152]

A controversial topic was how the sign of baptism could be given to children who could neither understand nor swear to the obligations of the covenant. Calvin argued that believers' children were able to be partakers in the covenant.[153] His argument was that there is a group of people who are heirs of the kingdom of heaven and possess a token of adoption. As Christ embraced the children, so he signified their common possession along with adults.[154] Infant children of believers are not barred from Christ's kingdom simply because they have not received the waters of baptism. The ground for salvation is not baptism but the covenant.[155] It is a blessing to children to be baptized because it can strengthen them and give them greater zeal for the kingdom.[156]

Lord's Supper. Luther's 1520 *Babylonian Captivity of the Church* opposed three teachings of the Catholic Mass. The first was that the

151. Ibid., 1334: "In this way we ought to understand all the earthly promises . . . as the head to which they refer, should always hold the first place."

152. Ibid., 1332: "For he expressly declares that the circumcision of a tiny infant will be in lieu of a seal to certify the promise of the covenant. But if the covenant still remains firm and steadfast, it applies no less today to the children of Christians than under the Old Testament it pertained to the infants of the Jews. . . . It is most evident that the covenant which the Lord once made with Abraham (cf. Gen. 17:14) is no less in force today for Christians than it was of old for the Jewish people, and that this word relates no less to Christians than it related to the Jews. . . . For God's sign, communicated to a child as by an impressed seal, confirms the promise given to the pious parent, and declares it to be ratified that the Lord will be God not only to him but to his seed; and that he wills to manifest his goodness and grace not only to him but to his descendants even to the thousandth generation."

153. Ibid., 1347: "Or (to put the matter more clearly and briefly), if the children of believers are partakers in the covenant without the help of understanding, there is no reason why they should be barred from the sign merely because they cannot swear to the provisions of the covenant."

154. Ibid., 1356: "But I return to that principle that only those who are members of Christ are heirs of the Kingdom of Heaven; then Christ's embrace (Matt. 19:13–15; Mark 10:13–16; Luke 18:15–17) was the true token of adoption, by which infants are joined in common with adults."

155. Ibid., 1323, "Infants are not barred from the kingdom of Heaven just because they happen to depart the present life before they have been immersed in water. Yet we have already seen that serious injustice is done to God's covenant if we do not assent to it, as if it were weak of itself, since its effect depends neither upon baptism nor upon any additions."

156. Ibid., 1344: "If they happen to grow to an age at which they can be taught the truth of baptism, they shall be fired with greater zeal for renewal, from learning that they were given the token of it in their first infancy in order that they might meditate upon it throughout life."

church withheld the cup from the laity. The Catholic Church defended its view from Aquinas's notion of concomitance, according to which the bread alone contained all that was necessary for the taking of communion.[157] The second problem was with transubstantiation. The Catholic Church held that transubstantiation was the only legitimate view. Luther strongly disagreed.[158] The third problem was that it was wrong to view the sacrament as a good work and sacrifice.[159]

Luther retained the word *Mass* for the supper and still held that Christ was truly and completely present in the supper.[160] His view is called *consubstantiation* and maintains that the body and blood of Christ are in, with, and through the elements but are not substantially changed. Luther's views were not accepted by all Protestants, as we learned from the Marburg Colloquy in the previous chapter.

The *Consensus Tigurinus*, or Swiss Agreement, was born out of theological adversity. In a sense, the unhappy ending of the Marburg Colloquy was still to be resolved. Luther and Zwingli had agreed in 1529 on almost every point of theology except the Lord's Supper. All was quiet on that front until 1544 to 1545, when Luther attacked Zwingli's notion of the Lord's Supper with his *Kurzes Bekenntnis vom Abendmahl* ("Short Confession on the Lord's Supper").

Zwingli had already been dead for more than a decade when Luther's work appeared, so it was fairly difficult for him to defend himself! Bullinger, his successor and son-in-law, closely followed Zwingli's views. Bullinger responded to Luther with his *Wahrhaftes Bekenntnis der Diener der Kirche zu Zürich . . . insbesondere über das Nachtmahl* ("The True Confession of the Pastors of Zurich . . . Concerning the Lord's Supper"). Bullinger rejected the Lutheran view

157. William of Champeaux in the twelfth century taught concomitance. It was the general practice in the thirteenth century also and was supported by Aquinas.

158. Martin Luther, *Luther's Works*, ed. Jaroslav Pelikan and Helmut T. Lehmann, 56 vols. (St. Louis: Concordia, 1968), 36:29: "What is asserted without the Scriptures or proven revelation may be held as an opinion but need not be believed"; and 36:31: "It is an absurd and unheard of juggling with words to understand bread to mean the form or accidents of bread. . . . [It is not] right to enfeeble the words of God in this way, and by depriving them of their meaning to cause so much harm" (as cited by Allison, *Historical Theology*, 647–48).

159. Luther, *Luther's Works*, 36:38: "What we call the mass is a promise of the forgiveness of sins made to us by God and such a promise as has been confirmed by the death of the Son of God" (as cited by Allison, *Historical Theology*, 648).

160. Allison, *Historical Theology*, 649.

of consubstantiation. He also probably rejected the idea that the sacrament can be a direct means of grace. The fundamental principle of the Lord's Supper, for Bullinger, was as a religious illustration and a stimulant to faith; the entire content of the sacrament consisted in the remembrance of Christ. For the believer, the real presence of Christ was in the Lord's Supper, but the unbeliever received only bread and wine. It was through the work of the Holy Spirit that it was possible for believers to be partakers of Christ.

Fighting between the German Lutherans and the Swiss was not healthy from any perspective, except perhaps from Luther's. Calvin, perceptive of the danger, began to explore the possibility of an accord with the Lutherans or at least Swiss unity on the Lord's Supper. But Calvin's thoughts on the supper agreed neither with Luther's nor with Bullinger's. The prospect of agreement with the Zurich reformers was therefore not very great.

There were deep theological issues that had to be worked through. It is clear that Calvin and Bullinger rejected the Lutheran notion of consubstantiation. While repudiating that idea, Calvin nevertheless affirmed with the Lutherans that the flesh of Christ was given in the Lord's Supper. Christ was indeed truly present in the sacrament.

The issue yet to be resolved with the Lutherans was whether Christ's resurrected body was in heaven or on the earth. Calvin affirmed that the body of Christ remained solely in heaven and retained its human properties while there. Could there be an alternative to the either/or issue? Can the believer truly partake of Christ if Christ is in heaven and not on the earth?

Thankfully, Calvin saw an answer to this question. According to Calvin, it was found in the Holy Spirit's action in regard to the Lord's Supper. Christ did not come down to the church from heaven but, instead, by the power of the Holy Spirit lifted the church to himself in heaven. In the Lord's Supper the church partakes of Christ in a spiritual, heavenly manner. There is a real presence of Christ in the Lord's Supper, but it is a heavenly mode of presence. Believers feed on Christ in the heavenlies.

Calvin was quick to point out that an unbeliever did not receive this presence of Christ. It was not that the unbeliever was not offered the body and blood of Christ, however, for both the evil and the good are offered them. True reception of Christ's body and blood comes by faith alone, with the receiver himself being the obstacle that keeps him from enjoying the gift. Partaking by the unbeliever, however, does not mean that he receives it to his own detriment, as some Lutherans maintained.

Calvin began discussions with Bullinger in Zurich in early 1547. Bullinger gave Calvin a copy of his *De sacramentis*.[161] Calvin, not able to agree with Bullinger's conception, submitted a draft of his own position in twenty-four propositions.[162] Bullinger made annotations to Calvin's text and sent it back. Calvin revised the text again in January 1549. Calvin thought that the project was important enough to travel again to Zurich, with Farel, in May. Agreement between Calvin and Bullinger was confirmed within a few hours. This understanding between them on the Lord's Supper is summarized in the *Consensus Tigurinus* and united Switzerland with respect to the doctrine of the Lord's Supper.

What can be concluded from an analysis of the contents of the *Consensus Tigurinus*? Did Calvin's understanding of the sacrament of the Lord's Supper become normative throughout Switzerland, or did Bullinger's? Two differing conclusions have been drawn concerning the *Consensus*: either it was a complete triumph for Calvin's doctrine, or there was honest give-and-take between Bullinger and Calvin in their agreement. To say that there is no Bullingerian influence in the *Consensus* would not be accurate, though it is also clear that Calvin's understanding of the Lord's Supper is presented in the document. The *Consensus* asserts that in the sacrament there is a real union of life with Christ and that the signs are not empty; they are means of grace and convey the benefits of redemption.[163]

Calvin had much to say about the Lord's Supper. With Luther, he knew that Roman transubstantiation must be rejected. We cannot chew

161. This work was written in 1546.

162. It was sent to Zurich in June 1548. There are a number of similarities to Calvin's teaching. On the marks of the church; the church triumphant and militant. Calvin was hopeful that an agreement could be reached among the Protestants, at least among the Protestants of Switzerland.

163. For more information on polemics regarding the Lord's Supper, see Gamble, "Controversies," 193–96, and Richard C. Gamble, "Sacramental Continuity among Reformed Refugees: Peter Martyr Vermigli and John Calvin," in *Peter Martyr Vermigli and the European Reformations: Semper Reformanda*, ed. Frank A. James III (Leiden: Brill, 2004), 97–114.

Christ's body with our teeth.[164] He was convinced that God adopts believers into his own household in baptism, and as a good householder God also sustains and preserves believers with the food of life.[165]

The visible elements make the believer's secret union with Christ more certain, and these elements feed their souls.[166] As the bread and wine nourish bodies, so also does Jesus Christ offered in the Lord's Supper give true food for the soul.[167]

Worship. Luther's German Mass normally included singing a hymn or psalm; singing the *Kyrie eleison* ("Lord, have mercy"); readings from the Bible; singing another hymn; a reading from one of the Gospels; singing the Apostles' Creed; a sermon; reciting the Lord's Prayer; an admonition about the Lord's Supper; partaking of the supper with the singing of the *Sanctus* ("Holy"); a final hymn or the *Agnus Dei* ("Lamb of God"); and a benediction.

Calvin.[168] Protestants are well known for the Reformation's principles of *sola scriptura* ("Scripture alone") and *sola gratia* ("grace alone"). There is another important Reformation principle as well: *soli Deo gloria* ("glory to God alone"). This last phrase refers to the believer's Christian walk here on earth. For if there is any good in us, if we perform any deeds that would be considered pleasing in God's sight, then we acknowledge that he is the one working in us and performing these works. Thus to God alone will be the glory.

164. *Institutes*, 1372: "The Fourth Lateran Council (1215), . . . affirmed transubstantiation (canon 1)"; and 1405: "And first we must not dream of such a presence of Christ in the Sacrament as the craftsmen of the Roman court have fashioned—as if the body of Christ, by a local presence, were put there to be touched by the hands, to be chewed by the teeth, and to be swallowed by the mouth."

165. Ibid., 1360: "For as in baptism, God, regenerating us, engrafts us into the society of his church and makes us his own by adoption, so we have said, that he discharges the function of a provident householder in continually supplying to us the food to sustain and preserve us in that life into which he has begotten us by his Word."

166. Ibid., 1361: "Since, however, this mystery of Christ's secret union with the devout is by nature incomprehensible, he shows its figure and image in visible signs best adapted to our small capacity. Indeed, by giving guarantees and tokens he makes it as certain for us as if we had seen it with our own eyes. For this very familiar comparison penetrates into even the dullest minds: just as bread and wine sustain physical life, so are souls fed by Christ."

167. Calvin, *Sermons on Ephesians*, 175: "Jesus Christ is the true food of our souls; that just as our bodies are sustained and nourished with the bread and wine, so we have our spiritual life of the very substance of God's Son."

168. Ibid., 668. See Hughes Oliphint Old, *The Patristic Roots of Reformed Worship New American Edition* (Black Mountain, NC: Worship Press, 2004).

Soli Deo gloria also refers to how God's people are to worship. As we worship him, we see the need to give him all the glory and not to worship man and human institutions. This phrase must be understood with the backdrop of the Roman Catholic Church of the sixteenth century.

For Calvin, God's activity in dealing with humanity in history—namely, God's entering into a relationship through the covenant—is significant. God entered into a relationship with Abraham and his descendants not because there was something inherently better about Abraham but because God, in his mercy, desires to perform this gracious act. God entered a covenantal relationship with Abraham, and the conditions of that covenant are binding on Abraham. He must continue in a certain way of life if he is to remain in the covenant with God.

Connected with God's entering into covenant with man and telling him that he must live in a certain manner is God's giving the law to man. God gave to Abraham and his descendants a law by which all the affairs of life could be directed. This law of life is inherently connected to the covenantal relationship in which Abraham found himself. The law is not to be understood exclusively as a collection of commands about how to live but is included in the covenant of grace itself.

Calvin understood the law as covenantal law.[169] For him, Moses was the promoter of the promises given to Abraham and a type of renewer of the covenant.[170] According to Calvin, all worship is connected with the law, and the law is connected to the covenant. Thus for Calvin, there is no boasting in obedience to the law. It is God who makes a person righteous, it is God who works in one's heart, and it is God who teaches us how to be righteous.

---

169. *Institutes*, 2.7.1–5. W. Niesel, *The Theology of Calvin*, trans. H. Knight (Grand Rapids: Baker, 1980), 93: "The law of God is embedded in disgrace and loyalty which he shows toward his people, the church; God in guiding entering into a covenant with his people makes an absolute claim upon them. This divine demand is the meaning of the law." *Institutes*, 2.7.1: "By the term law, I understand not only the Ten Commandments, which prescribed how one should live in piety and justice, but the whole cultus of religion which God communicated through Moses."

170. *Institutes*, 2.7.1. Niesel (*Theology of Calvin*, 93–94) says that Moses's role is actually sealing the covenant between God and his people and, as a prophet of God's covenant, demonstrating the mercy of God to the people.

Thus covenant and worship are united.[171] According to Heinrich Bullinger (1504–1575), a Reformer in the city of Zurich after the death of Zwingli and important to the English church, the covenant is a two-sided contractual relationship. In other words, there is reciprocity in the contractual relationship, as, for example, in God's covenant with Abraham in Genesis 22.[172]

Calvin defines the nature of true worship in this way: "The worship of God is said to consist in the spirit, because it is nothing else than that inward faith of the heart which produces prayer, and next, purity of conscience and self-denial, that we may be dedicated to obedience to God as holy sacrifices."[173]

There is to be no self-invented worship. Calvin's thesis is summarized in one sentence: "From this we gather that a part of the reverence that is paid to him consists simply in worshiping him as he commands, mingling no inventions of our own."[174]

Calvin was certainly not the first person to argue against self-invented worship.[175] Earlier, Zwingli had articulated the same principle, and Bucer in Strasbourg was crystal clear in his views against human ceremonies.[176] Oposition to self-invented worship was also shared by the Anabaptists of this time.[177]

---

171. J. Wayne Baker, *Heinrich Bullinger and the Covenant: The Reformed Tradition* (Athens, OH: Ohio University Press, 1980); Heinhold Fast, *Heinrich Bullinger und die Täufer: Ein Beitrag zur Historiographie und Theologie im 16. Jahrhundert* (Weierhof: Mennonitischer Geschichtsverein, 1959); Gottfried Locher, *Die Theologie Huldrych Zwinglis* (Zurich: Zwingli-Verlag, 1952); John Murray, *The Covenant of Grace: A Biblico-Theological Study* (London: Tyndale Press, 1954); Hans Heinrich Wolfe, *Die Einheit des Bundes: Das Verhältnis von Alten und Neuen Testament bei Calvin* (Neukirchen-Vluyn: Neukirchener Verlag, 1958); Tjarko Stadtland, *Rechtfertigung und Heiligung bei Calvin* (Neukirchen-Vluyn: Neukirchener Verlag, 1972).

172. Ernst Koch, *Die Theologie der Confessio Helvetica Posterior*, Beiträge zur Geschichte und Lehre der Reformierten Kirche (Neukirchen-Vluyn: Neukirchener Verlag, 1968), 388–40.

173. Calvin, *Commentary on the Gospel According to John*, vol. 1, trans. William Pringle (Edinburgh: Calvin Translation Society, 1847), reprinted in *Calvin's Commentaries* vol. 17 (Grand Rapids: Baker, 2003), 161.

174. Calvin, *Institutes,* 1202.

175. See Old, *Patristic Roots*, 24: "The most important criticism which the Strasbourg Reformers had of the old forms of worship was that they were of "merely human origin. . . . The Reformers wanted to worship according to the commandments of God."

176. Zwingli, *Apologia* (CR LXXXIX), and Bucer, *Grund und Ursach*, as cited by Old, *Patristic Roots*, 25.

177. For example, see Hans Denck, "Divine Order," in *Early Anabaptist Spirituality: Selected Writings*, ed. Daniel Liechty (New York: Paulist Press, 1994), 133–34.

For Calvin, self-invented worship included human traditions as well as what he called "false humility."[178] As Calvin freely articulated his position against self-invented worship, he was also quick to observe that human nature screams against God's prohibition of that very thing. He stated plainly, "We have a propensity to such worship."[179] Such a propensity, such a desire and pulling, thought Calvin, was like the church's being drawn toward the abyss. His fear of this human desire was based on his conviction that the kingdom of God "is taken away whenever He is worshiped by laws of human devising, inasmuch as He wills to be accounted the sole lawgiver of His own worship."[180]

ESCHATOLOGY

Individual. The Reformers rejected the notions of purgatory, an intermediate state or place people go after dying. Instead, the Reformers taught that deceased believers go to heaven and the unregenerate to hell. There could be a difference of degree of blessedness and curse before the final judgment.[181] But since the notion of purgatory is wrong, the connected notions of offerings and prayers for the dead are also wrong. Such prayers and veneration are pagan in origin.[182] Calvin also rejected the notion of soul sleep.[183] Soul sleep argues that the soul

178. Calvin, *Commentary on the Epistles of Paul the Apostle to the Philippians, Colossians and Thessalonians,* ed. and trans. John Pringle (Edinburgh: Calvin Translation Society, 1849), reprinted in *Calvin's Commentaries* vol. 21 (Grand Rapids: Baker, 2003), 201–2: "Self-invented worship, humility and neglect of the body . . . human traditions . . . are agreeable to us on this account, that they are in accordance with our understanding, for anyone will find in his own brain the first outlines of them. This is the first Pretext. . . . The second is humility, inasmuch as obedience both to God and men is pretended, so that men do not refuse even unreasonable burdens. . . . Traditions appear to be admirable exercises of humility. . . . For it should be a settled point among all the pious, that the worship of God ought not to be measured according to our views; and that, consequently, any kind of service is not lawful, simply on the ground that it is agreeable to us."

179. Calvin, *Commentary on Colossians,* 2:23, 203ff.: "It is of importance to consider here, how prone, nay, how forward the mind of man is to artificial modes of worship. The zeal of men, therefore, for superstition is surpassingly mad, which could not be restrained by so plain a declaration of God from breaking forth, as historical records testify."

180. *Institutes,* 1201.

181. Louis Berkhof, *Systematic Theology* (Carlisle, PA: Banner of Truth, 1972), 681.

182. Later, it became a Jewish practice. It is still held by the Greeks, the Lutherans, and many Anglicans. Tertullian had already rejected intercession for the dead. *RD* 4:638–39.

183. *RD* 4:611. See previous chapter.

is in a state of unconscious repose at death instead of its remaining rationally and religiously active.[184]

General. During the Reformation, some, called *chiliasts*, limited Christ's reign to one thousand years.[185] Both Luther and Calvin were amillennialists and denounced premillennialism. The chiliast position held that there would be a limitation to the wicked's punishment and to the elect's blessedness.[186] Calvin thought that such a position casts reproach on Christ.[187]

There will be inequality of reward for the faithful in heaven.[188] There is a specific relationship between a believer's actions on the earth and his or her heavenly reward.[189] These doctrines call for sobriety of analysis and battle against laziness.[190]

On the other hand, both Luther and Calvin held to judgment and punishment of the reprobate. Luther rightly emphasized God's graciousness even in judgment. In his commentary on the Gospels, Calvin did not think that the eternal fire for the reprobate was literal. The issue involves a deep sense of God's fury coming down against the wicked. Both Luther and Calvin held that there would be a renewing of the heavens and the earth. Calvin, as expected, rebuked excessive speculation on the nature and extent of that renewal.[191] The final section of this chapter focuses on how theology should be structured.

---

184. Berkhof, *Systematic Theology*, 688–90.

185. *Institutes*, 2:995.

186. Ibid.: "Now their fiction is too childish either to need or to be worth a refutation. And the Apocalypse, from which they undoubtedly drew a pretext for their error, does not support them. For the number 'one thousand' [Rev. 20:4] does not apply to the eternal blessedness of the church but only to the various disturbances that awaited the church, while still toiling on earth. On the contrary, all Scripture proclaims that there will be no end to the blessedness of the elect or the punishment of the wicked [Matt. 25:41, 46]."

187. Ibid.: "Those who assign the children of God a thousand years in which to enjoy the inheritance of the life to come do not realize how much reproach they are casting upon Christ and his Kingdom"; and see ibid., 995n9 for Heinrich Quistorp, *Calvin's Doctrine of the Last Things* (Louisville: John Knox Press, 1955), 158–62.

188. *Institutes*, 2:1005.

189. Ibid., 2:1006.

190. Ibid.: "As far as I am concerned, I not only refrain personally from superfluous investigation of useless matters, but I also think that I ought to guard against contributing to the levity of others by answering them."

191. Allison, *Historical Theology*, 727–28.

THEOLOGICAL METHOD

Issues with *Sola Scriptura*. The Christian faith has always needed a solid grounding. The question at the time of the Reformation was whether Scripture alone was adequate for that task or whether it needed either tradition and/or human reason as well. Since Protestants assumed that the Bible was comprehensible to the common man, the Bible had to be taught in a way that would expound the true meaning of the text. Also, theological principles had to be defended through the Scriptures.[192]

Both Protestants and Catholics agreed that the Bible was interpreted from within a theological context. The question was whether the context was discovered from within the biblical text or was imposed on it from without.[193] *Sola scriptura*, Scripture as the only rule for faith, was articulated before the reformation by John Wycliffe.[194] But Protestants interpreted the rule in two ways.[195]

The classic Lutheran and high church Anglican view was that if a church practice was not forbidden and could be justified by tradition or reason, then it was permitted. In contrast, the Reformed tradition argued that only what is allowed in Scripture is permitted in church practice. Some scholars term the Reformed tradition an "unrealistic attitude."[196]

Some also wrongly argue that the Magisterial Reformers were unclear in their definition of divine inspiration.[197] As well, they supposedly accorded to tradition the same authority as the biblical text.[198]

---

192. Gerald Bray, *Biblical Interpretation: Past and Present* (Downers Grove, IL: InverVarsity Press, 1996), 189–90: "the principle of Scripture alone meant that the Bible contained its own theological system, which ought to be developed independently."

193. Ibid., 191.

194. Ibid..

195. Bray argued that high church Anglicans believed it possible, or even necessary, "to allow practices which were not expressly forbidden by Scripture and which could be justified on the basis of tradition or reason. For them, Scripture was an ultimate court of appeal against abuse rather than a handbook outlining daily life and practice." Cranmer held what he termed the "moderate view"—observable in the Forty-two Articles 1553 and the Thirty-Nine Articles of 1571. See ibid., 192.

196. Ibid..

197. Bray argued that the patristic fathers were unclear and that lack of clarity continued. Ibid., 195: "but little attempt had been made to clarify what this meant."

198. Bray (ibid., 196) argues that Luther and Calvin held that the biblical books were written by the men to whom they were attributed, which was "a clear case of tradition being accorded the authority of the text itself." But Bray's statement is clearly contradicted by Calvin's discussions of the authorship of the books of Hebrews and Revelation, the very examples that Bray cites!

The argument then follows that the Reformers' simple view of biblical infallibility developed in the following century into total inerrancy.[199] Yet a careful examination of Calvin's exegetical methods and hermeneutic clearly demonstrates that he held to a complex and nuanced view of biblical inerrancy.[200]

Full System of Theology. Some mistakenly argue that the Reformers did not supply a fully developed theological system.[201] It can readily be granted that Luther, brilliant theologian that he was, did not produce anything like a classic systematic theology.

Nevertheless, contemporaries such as Oecolampadius and Erasmus were already wrestling with how best to craft theological works. They were both repulsed by late scholasticism and were interested in finding a new way.[202] Oecolampadius found many similarities between the theologies of the Cappadocian fathers and his own theology. Fascinatingly, he almost went to Luther's university at Wittenberg as professor of Hebrew. Perhaps the German Reformation would have had a different flavor had he gone there.[203]

Melanchthon's *Loci communes* certainly qualifies as a systematic theology, but it does not compare with the breadth or depth of an Aquinas or a Lombard. Neither the 1520s nor the 1530s were yet a time for massive Protestant systematic theologies. It was difficult for

199. The ancient doctrine of "verbal inspiration" (from which the healthy church had apparently recovered), like some type of internal parasite, "reappeared with a vengeance" in the early seventeenth century" (ibid., 197).

200. Ibid., 196: "There are no errors or discrepancies of any kind, on any matter whatsoever, in the biblical text." Calvin and Reformed theology after him recognized hosts of problems and apparent discrepancies, but Calvin's view of revelation prohibited any errors. Such a view of inerrancy is not a development of later, cold, Reformed scholasticism but must be seen in the sixteenth century. It was combined with a philosophical presupposition, namely, that "religious truth could not be divorced from secular truth." Thus biblical truth had to be "scientifically" exact: numbers had to be exact, not approximations. Ibid., 197: "As a result of this approach, statements of Scripture could be taken out of their context and used to elaborate theories on matters far removed from the original intention of the writers." Bray's caricature sounds more like Origen's allegory, not inerrancy! He will then wrongly argue that the Swiss Consensus Formula (1675) took things too far and that the document produced a counter reaction.

201. Richard A. Muller (*Post-Reformation Reformed Dogmatics*, vol. 1, *Prolegomena to Theology* [Grand Rapids: Baker, 1987], 17) argues that the Reformers "did not provide [those generations] with a fully developed theological system."

202. E. Gordon Rupp, *Patterns of Reformation* (London: Epworth, 1969), 11: "and [it] was in part the attempt of the new learning to find a dogmatic norm in the period before the infiltration of philosophy, and especially of Aristotle, into theology."

203. Ibid., 13.

the early Reformers to find the peace and quiet necessary to think long and hard on difficult and complex theological issues. As the decades rolled on, Calvin found the time to expand his *Institutes*. But those mistaken authors assert that even Calvin's *Institutes* was "not a full system of theology."[204] This argument simply cannot be sustained. Calvin's *Institutes* is different from earlier medieval writings and later works of Reformed orthodoxy. Yet it is methodologically consistent and comprehensive in its theological sweep. It develops all the loci of systematic theology and rightly should be judged as a full system of theology.[205] Moving ahead in time, we shall now turn to Calvin's successor.

Theodore Beza (A.D. 1519–1605) **and Peter Ramus** (A.D. 1515–1572). Peter Ramus was a controversial professor in Paris. His teaching was debated, and eventually the French king interdicted his lectures in 1544. The decree against Ramus was canceled in 1547 by the next king, who appointed him as *regius* professor; as such, he lectured to large crowds. He was converted to Protestantism in ca. 1561, taught at Heidelberg in 1570, and was then killed in the Saint Bartholomew's Day massacre in 1572. Ramus can be considered a transitional figure who tried to reform logic and move from the medieval adoption of Aristotle.[206] By the first quarter of the seventeenth century, logic was divided among the Aristotelians, the Ramists, and the semi-Ramists.[207]

204. Muller, *Post-Reformation*, 13.

205. See Richard C. Gamble, "Calvin's Theological Method: The Case of Caroli," in *Calvin Erbe und Auftrag: Festschrift für Wilhelm Neuser*, ed. Willem Van't Spijker (Leuven: Peeters, 1991), 130–38; "Calvin's Theological Method: Word and Spirit: A Case Study," in *Calviniana: Ideas and Influences of Jean Calvin*, ed. Robert Schnucker, Sixteenth Century Essays and Studies 10 (Kirksville, MO: Sixteenth Century, 1988), 63–75; and "Calvin as Theologian and Exegete," 178–94.

206. Paul Oskar Kristeller, *The Classics and Renaissance Thought* (Cambridge: Harvard University Press, 1955), 17: "The attempts at a reform of logic, due to Valla, Agricola, Ramus and Nizolius . . . were in part guided by rhetorical considerations, but represent an episode of great historical significance"; ibid., 43 note: "There was a persistent tendency . . . culminated in Ramus and Nizolius to reform Aristotelian logic with the help of rhetoric, and during the latter part of the sixteenth century as well as much of the seventeenth, Ramism was a serious rival of Aristotelian logic in the schools of Germany, Great Britain and America"; and ibid., 63: "Ramus used at least the name of Plato in his bold attempt to replace the traditional Aristotelian logic of the schools."

207. Charles B. Schmitt, *Aristotle and the Renaissance* (Cambridge: Harvard University Press, 1983), 2: "Lorenza Valla, Luther, Corpernicus, Ramus, and Bruno were among the notable critics, but it was only in the seventeenth century that Bacon, Galilei, and Descartes succeeded in mounting an attack which was to prove fatal to the Arisotelian system, though not equally

Current opinion concerning the relationship between Theodore Beza and Ramus follows this line of thought: that Beza, who drank deeply from the fount of Aristotle, necessarily rejected Ramus because of Ramus's intension to reject Aristotle's method.[208] But the question needs to be asked whether this view is in fact a proper interpretation of Beza's thinking. In the light of the study of Calvin's hermeneutical positions and the solidifying Reformed hermeneutic, it is at least possible to argue that Beza rejected Ramus's new logic not because Beza's theology was wedded to the rigors of Aristotelian thinking, but because his hermeneutical method itself prohibited him from adopting Ramus's system.[209]

There was a tremendous change in the way that education was done at the time of the Reformers, and Ramism was part of an overall pedagogical system that Beza, as rector of the Genevan Academy, wished to reject from the system at Geneva. As Calvin and later Beza rejected the loci method of Scriptural exegesis, that rejection was, in fact, rejecting Ramism as well.

Conclusion to Part 4. Part 4 consisted of five chapters on the Reformation. We can see that God in his providence prepared the Western world for the coming Reformation with political developments, economic developments, and social/intellectual developments—besides the work of the theological forerunners of the Reformation. The German and Swiss reformations had similarities and differences due in part to the personalities of the leaders and the different nations to which they belonged. The same can be said for the Reformation in other lands. We noted that the Protestant reformations also included the

---

so to all of the individual parts"; and 90: "Academic skepticism revived by Ramus and his circle among others"; see also Muller, *Post-Reformation*, 44.

208. For example, Walter J. Ong, *Ramus, Method and the Decay of Dialogue: From the Art of Discourse to the Art of Reason* (Cambridge: Harvard University Press, 1958), 28: "However, it was Ramus' fierce anti-Aristotelian record, rather than this mild theology, which led Beza to warn him away from Geneva for a time." It has been argued that Ramus wanted to be simple and applicable. Joel R. Beeke and Randall J. Pederson, *Meet the Puritans* (Grand Rapids: Reformation Heritage Books, 2006), 43: "Ramism sought to correct the artificial sophistry of the Aristotelianism of the day, characterized by a breach between life and thought, between knowing and doing, and, in the case of the religious life, between theology and ethics."

209. For Calvin's hermeneutic, see chapter 14. There is a reason why Lutherans more readily adopted Ramus's method but not that of the Calvinists. The Lutherans and Reformed had different exegetical methods. The situation was more complicated in the Netherlands. William Ames adopted Ramism, but it declined after his death.

non-magisterial Anabaptist tradition. Finally, we saw a basic unity among the Protestants as they stood against a resurgent Roman Catholic Church and that they were willing to pay for their newly found freedom in Christ with their own blood. Next, Part 5 explores the theologically exciting time of post-Reformation theology.

KEY TERMS

consubstantiation
Heidelberg Catechism

STUDY QUESTIONS

1. Do you think that the Reformers were correct in putting so much emphasis on Scripture over any type of tradition?
2. What did the Council of Trent teach about election and reprobation?
3. What did Arminius teach about election and reprobation?
4. Lutherans and Anglicans kept bishops in their church organizations. How do you evaluate their decision?

RESOURCES FOR FURTHER STUDY

Bierma, Lyle D. *An Introduction to the Heidelberg Catechism*. Grand Rapids: Baker, 2005. An excellent introduction and commentary on the Heidelberg Catechism.

Hughes, Philip Edgcumbe. *Theology of the English Reformers*. Grand Rapids: Eerdmans, 1966. An accurate presentation of the fathers of the English church written by a Bible-believing member of that church.

Williams, George Hunston. *The Radical Reformation*. Philadelphia: Westminster Press, 1962. The classic work that accurately describes in detail the thinking of the Anabaptists.

Since the 1970s, a group of scholars has met every four years to discuss and debate Calvin's theology. The papers presented at those meetings are published by various editors and represent the finest scholarship possible. Some of the more recent titles are:

Huijgen, Arnold, and Karin Maag. *Calvinus frater in Domino*. Göttingen: Vandenhoeck & Ruprecht, 2020.

Selderhuis, Herman J. *Calvinus Pastor Ecclesiae*. Göttingen: Vandenhoeck & Ruprecht, 2016.

PART 5

The Church after the Reformation

16

Seventeenth-Century Cultural and Philosophical Backgrounds

ENLIGHTENMENT

The era from the Reformation to the Enlightenment experienced remarkable changes. There was a rise in secularism, worldliness, and the implementation of natural philosophy.[1] In general, religious and church life began to become less important to people. The Enlightenment offered them a new worldview—a worldview of humankind's autonomy.[2] This transformed worldview embraced science and rejected religion.[3] The changes that took root at the time of the Enlightenment have flowered into the problems that plague contemporary society.[4] Some have interpreted the Enlightenment as a largely positive intellec-

1. Karl Heussi, *Kompendium der Kirchengeschichte* (Tübingen: Mohr Siebeck, 1971), 325.
2. John M. Frame, *A History of Western Philosophy and Theology* (Phillipsburg, NJ: P&R Publishing, 2015) (*HWPT*), 214: "God revealed in Scripture not only a way of salvation, but a worldview capable of philosophical articulation. The way of salvation presupposes the worldview. . . . This metaphysic dictates an epistemology and ethic in which divine revelation is the supreme authority, and the worst error is the denial of revelation, that is, the claim of human autonomy. But in the fall human beings embraced intellectual autonomy, so that in their thought and practice they lived by their own wisdom rather than God's. To atone for that sin, God sent his Son, Jesus Christ, who died to suffer the penalty we deserved and to regenerate the hearts and minds of his elect people. Those who believed renounced their claim to autonomy and sought, however inconsistently, to live and think as followers of Jesus."
3. Heussi, *Kompendium*, 322.
4. Douglas F. Kelly, *Systematic Theology*, vol. 1, *The God Who Is the Holy Trinity* (Fearn, Scotland: Mentor, 2008), 223.

tual movement.[5] But regardless of one's interpretation, the Enlightenment was a major force that is still manifesting its fruit today.[6]

All across Europe, nations were undergoing profound shifts in cultural, religious, and philosophical thought. At the end of the eighteenth century, the French Revolution came partially as a result of the radical discontinuity between the piety of the Reformation and the carnality of the Enlightenment.

What began with the disintegration of the inner life of the institution of the Roman Catholic Church turned into a full-fledged counter-reformation, which helped pave the way for the Enlightenment.[7] The Enlightenment in France had a distinctly anti-religious and anti-church accent—in fact, the revolution in France was brimming with hatred toward the church and the Christian faith. One of the reasons for this antagonism toward Roman Catholicism was the intimate connection between the church, the deprived socio-economic status of the people, and the corrupt political regimes.[8] It was difficult for the intellectual elites of that time to overthrow the baggage of their inherited cultural Christianity. Unfortunately, it seems that the Protestant theological leaders of the time did not recognize this cultural shift. Theology in general was less unified, and it lost relevance to many.[9]

Generally speaking, the development of German idealism, the rise of positivism in England, and the thought-world of Rousseau in France stand as the middle expression of the development of the Enlightenment. As is apparent from this disparate list, the middle workings of enlightenment were by no means unified. The Enlightenment was,

5. E. D. Hirsch (*Validity in Interpretation* [New Haven: Yale University Press, 1967]) saw the Enlightenment as a constructive and positive movement to be continued into the present.

6. The Enlightenment's influence on Kant was very strong (see Kurt D. Schmidt, *Grundriss der Kirchengeschichte* [Göttingen: Vandenhoek & Ruprecht, 1963], 433). Douglas Kelly evaluates it negatively—see Kelly, *Systematic Theology*, 1:224: "The Renaissance, which came into its own only in the Enlightenment, worked a far deeper split within Western Christendom than did the sixteenth-century Protestant Reformation. . . . Both Protestant and Catholic populations were inundated by this new form of pagan secularism, and their most basic beliefs and practices came under heavy attack from this new religion which said it was not a religion. . . . So far as I know, no alternative religion ever had such success in debilitating Christianity and in replacing it"; and ibid., 1:225: "Leading Renaissance Humanists started a trend that the later Enlightenment would follow: use the classical past to criticize the more recent (Christian, medieval past), so as to weaken the thousand-year-old Catholic synthesis."

7. Schmidt, *Grundriss*, 392.

8. Heussi, *Kompendium*, 331.

9. Ibid., 323.

however, an international movement, unified or not. With the increased accessibility of books and the advance and circulation of newspapers, enlightenment rippled across Europe.[10]

The Enlightenment was not without its reactionary movements. Pietism, for example, should be considered, at least in part, a reaction against the Enlightenment.[11] Even the generally positive movement of Pietism unwittingly contributed to the increase in secularism. As the Pietists fought to keep God close on a devotional level, they permitted a separation from him in the scientific sphere.[12] Pietism took many forms—organized Methodism in England was Pietism at its high point.[13]

RATIONALISM

In General. The great nations of France, Holland, and England all rose in economic and political power during this time. The Enlightenment was in full bloom in England by the end of the seventeenth century, though it took on a different flavor from the movement that was evolving on the Continent, particularly in France. The Enlightenment in England was in many ways a counter reaction to what is termed *rationalism.*

Rationalism holds that reason is the ultimate authority for truth and falsehood, for right and wrong. Knowledge for rationalists is a priori, that is, it comes from innate principles known previously. Rationalists build their scientific systems on reasoning and self-evident truths. They believe that the mind has innate principles that affect this classification process. Founded on the earlier mathematical ideals of Galileo, rationalism views knowledge as based on logic alone.

René Descartes (A.D. 1596–1650). The French-born René Descartes, with his famous *cogito ergo sum*, "I think therefore I am," would become known as the "father of rationalism." Descartes was the son of a councilor in the parliament of Bretagne. He was a devout Catholic and spent most of his intellectual life in the Netherlands. His

10. Ibid., 324.
11. *HWPT*, 176.
12. Schmidt, *Grundriss*, 431.
13. Heussi, *Kompendium*, 323.

writings include the *Discourse on Method* (1637); *First Philosophy* and *Meditations* (1641); and *Principia* (1644).[14] He is credited with inventing coordinate geometry.[15]

Descartes had two main goals. First, he wanted to advance the science of mechanics by generalizing the mathematical method. Second, based on the advances in the science of mechanics, he wanted to create a greater understanding of the overall operations of nature. Descartes had read Francis Bacon's works on scientific method. He thought that Bacon's error was to begin with the empirical facts of the natural world. Descartes believed that he should have begun with general principles that provide the foundation for analysis.

One of the major philosophical questions asked throughout the ages has been, "What does the human being really know?" Descartes had his own answer to this question.[16] He believed that it was possible that an evil genius could convince people that they were awake when they were asleep. But Descartes reasoned that even if he were the victim of an evil genius, still he could not doubt that he was doubting. Doubt is a thought process, thus doubting proves the very existence of thought. So Descartes concluded that doubting proves the existence of a thinking subject.[17]

Descartes's answer to the question, "What does the human being really know?" was that the person can only know that which he fully understands.[18] The human mind is presented with many interrelated objects of ideas. The objects of ideas must therefore be separated and analyzed individually to be truly understood. He understood questioning or doubt as the beginning of knowledge; from there, a solid epistemological foundation could be built.[19]

14. He is labeled a rationalist philosopher by Colin Brown, *Philosophy & the Christian Faith: A Historical Sketch from the Middle Ages to the Present Day* (Downers Grove, IL: Inter-Varsity Press, 1968), 49; also by Francis Nigel Lee, *A Christian Introduction to the History of Philosophy* (Nutley, NJ: Craig Press, 1969), 148.

15. Brown, *Philosophy & Faith*, 50.

16. Schmidt, *Grundriss*, 438. He was probably reacting against Montaigne's newly introduced skepticism.

17. *HWPT*, 179.

18. René Descartes, *Discourse on Method*, part ii, trans. Laurence J. Lafleur (Indianapolis/New York: Bobbs-Merrill, 1960), 3–60.

19. Ibid., part iv. See Williston Walker, *A History of the Christian Church* (New York: Scribner's Sons, 1959), 427; Brown, *Philosophy & Faith*, 50.

That foundation was that he thinks, and because he thinks, he therefore exists. This line of logic is known by the Latin phrase Descartes used to sum it up: *cogito ergo sum*. This was the one certain principle that Descartes held. In a sense, the phrase means that reason is the basis for all knowledge, and whether something is reasonable becomes the critical measure for everything.[20] From his so-called "epistemological certainty" of undoubted principles, Descartes was convinced that he could deduce all knowledge. There would be disagreements between scholars in details, and it was at this point where experimentation could be helpful. Descartes argued that after a conception was doubted, it could be approved. An adequate proof must have the certainty of mathematical demonstration.[21]

Descartes, as a faithful Catholic, expanded his supposedly undoubted principle.[22] His arguments for God's existence are found in the *Discourse on Method* and *Meditations*. With modifications from the causal and ontological arguments, he argued that since he, as a finite being, existed, then an infinite being was implied.[23] Furthermore, since God is a perfect being, he would not deceive us.[24]

Descartes's system was not without deficiencies. One of his weaknesses was that he did not sufficiently appreciate experimentation. His notion of overall mechanics involved too much speculation. Second, Descartes also had difficulty understanding the relationship between the human body and human ideas.[25] For example, in regard to his statement *cogito ergo sum*, there is no reason to conclude *ergo sum* (therefore I exist) on the basis of *cogito* (I know, or doubt). It may be true that it appears to me right now that I am reading a book and do not feel particularly hot or cold. Nevertheless, from these sensations, why must I necessarily exist? Third, Descartes needed God for epistemological certainty. This weakness is perhaps his most important one. While it is true that all thinkers lean on God for certainty,

20. Schmidt, *Grundriss*, 438.

21. Walker, *History*, 428.

22. Frame (*HWPT*, 180) claims that Descartes had hoped that the Roman Catholic Church would adopt his philosophy in place of that of Aquinas.

23. René Descartes, *Meditations*, part iii, trans. Laurence J. Lafleur (Indianapolis/New York: Bobbs-Merrill, 1960), 61–143; Brown, *Philosophy & Faith*, 51.

24. Descartes, Discourse, part iv; Brown, *Philosophy & Faith*, 51.

25. Walker, *History*, 427; *HWPT*, 182.

what Descartes did with this truth was wrong. Descartes separated knowledge of God from God's self-revelation in Scripture. Rather than using supratemporal revelation, the foundation for epistemological certainty became immanent reasoning.[26] Descartes's ideas were absorbed and developed by someone quite different from a French Catholic.

(Baruch) Benedictus (de) Spinoza (A.D. 1632/34–1677). Holland was known for its tolerance of ideas.[27] Baruch Spinoza was a Dutch Jewish philosopher, and because Holland offered Jews freedom, he lived in the enlightened city of Amsterdam. But his free thought resulted in his expulsion from the synagogue. In 1663, Spinoza published his famous book *Principles of Philosophy*. This work was followed in 1670 by the *Tractatus theologico-politicos*. His most important writing was published in 1677 after his death, his *Ethics* (*Ethica, ordine geometrico demonstrate*).[28]

Spinoza began his work in a fashion similar to that of Descartes, as they were both rationalists.[29] He wanted to begin with what he called clear and distinct ideas. There were certain notions that Spinoza, like Descartes, thought to be self-evidently true.[30] Spinoza's self-evident truth was that there is substance, and this substance can be called either *God* or *nature*. Spinoza said, "For, whatever is, is in God, and without God nothing can be, or be conceived."[31] During his lifetime, Spinoza was attacked as an atheist—a charge that he denied.

As God was a logical implication for Descartes, Spinoza intended to start with God, and he used an ontological argument similar to that of Descartes.[32] This God or *substance* that Spinoza said existed was not the Christian or Hebrew God. For Spinoza, God was not

26. Schmidt, *Grundriss*, 438; *HWPT*, 180: "In all this argumentation, Descartes ultimately appeals to his own subjective consciousness as the ultimate criterion of truth. Here there is no role for Scripture."

27. For background information, see Dan Levin, *Spinoza: The Young Thinker Who Destroyed the Past* (New York: Weybright and Talley, 1970), 1–99.

28. Brown, *Philosophy & Faith*, 53; *HWPT*, 183.

29. Gordon H. Clark, *Religion, Reason and Revelation* (Jefferson, MD: Trinity Foundation, 1986), 52.

30. Brown, *Philosophy & Faith*, 54.

31. Spinoza, *Ethics*, Part I, proposition viii, note 2, as cited by Brown, *Philosophy & Faith*, 55.

32. *HWPT*, 183.

the cause of all things; rather, God was what Spinoza would call "an indwelling of all things."

For Spinoza, god as substance was self-existent and self-authenticating. This substance also determined right and wrong. Spinoza's god connected metaphysics and epistemology, for Spinoza united god's self-existence with self-authentication. Fascinatingly, while Spinoza's understanding of God was misguided and unhelpful, he came close to the biblical presentation of God as self-attesting.[33]

Philosophers call Spinoza's position *pantheism*. Spinoza argued that God cannot be personal—in direct contradiction of Scripture. Furthermore, Spinoza encouraged critical Bible study and denied individual immortality.[34] He gladly used the scalpel of historical criticism on Scripture.[35] He desired to distinguish scientific thought from the dogmas of religion; thus he reduced religion to the role of love and pious sensitivity.[36]

Gottfried Wilhelm Leibniz (A.D. 1646–1716). Leibniz can fittingly be classified as a universal genius. He was both a diplomat and a philosopher and had vast correspondence with the finest minds of Europe.[37] He hoped for the reunion of Catholicism and Protestantism.[38] He should be credited, likely alongside Newton, with the honor of discovering infinitesimal calculus, and he did excellent work on symbolic logic, though his manuscript on the subject was lost for a long time. He is also credited with creating the Prussian Academy in Berlin.

Even though Leibniz did not develop a comprehensive philosophical system, he wrote a significant amount. His best philosophical work was a brief *Essais de Théodicée*, also known as his *Monadology*. It was written in Amsterdam in 1710 and was first published in 1714, then again in 1720.[39] As a rationalist, Leibniz wanted to find the one most fundamental component or substance of the world.[40] Leibniz saw

---

33. Ibid.
34. Brown, *Philosophy & Faith*, 58; Heussi, *Kompendium*, 328.
35. Levin, *Spinoza*, 185.
36. His thinking would influence Kant; see Heussi, *Kompendium*, 328. Unfortunately, in the second half of the eighteenth century Spinoza's critical thinking exercised an important role in German spiritual life.
37. *HWPT*, 185.
38. Walker, *History*, 428.
39. Heussi, *Kompendium*, 333.
40. *HWPT*, 185.

the world as composed of an infinite number of invisible substances, similar to what we call *atoms*, which he termed *monads*.[41] Unlike the contemporary notion of atoms, Leibniz argued that monads had various levels of consciousness.[42] In the monad scale of being, the highest was god, which he viewed as the original, simple substance that produced all monads.

Leibniz's religion was connected to his method. Though Leibniz stood against Pietism, he nevertheless defended some traditional notions of biblical revelation. He supported the doctrine of Christ's incarnation and the theology of the sacraments. He was, however, critical of miracles. Leibniz's theological method separated what he termed "revealed theology" from natural theology. This separation, which was important for deism, helped Leibniz see Jesus Christ not as the incarnate God but rather as the most important teacher of religion. Thus his theology was similar to that of John Locke—a combination of deism and fragments of orthodox Christianity.[43]

EMPIRICISM

In General. Thinkers at this time observed what seemed to them to be large gaps between some of the minute conclusions of the scientists and the broad axioms that were presented by the rationalist philosophers. For these thinkers, there appeared to be common prerequisites to scientific study that were matters of human experience, not of mathematics or some type of innate knowledge.[44] Empiricism arose as a movement set in contrast to rationalism. Knowledge for empiricists was mainly a posteriori, that is, information gained by means of a sort of empirical inquiry. The need to comprehend the visible was

41. This view was unlike that of Spinoza, who saw one substance.

42. Walker, *History*, 428. Frame (*HWPT*, 186) argues that the monads are actually minds, thus making Leibniz an atomistic idealist.

43. Heussi, *Kompendium*, 334. *HWPT*, 188: "Similarly, everything that every monad thinks or does is part of its nature. . . . A monad will not act in response to another monad, but only according to its own nature. . . . For God makes each monad to reflect the entire universe from its own perspective"; and ibid., 189: "This is Leibniz's solution to the problem of evil: evil is logically necessary to the achievement of a good world."

44. Gordon H. Clark, *Thales to Dewey: A History of Philosophy* (Boston: Houghton Mifflin, 1957), 357.

foundational to the rise of empiricism. In general, empiricists deny innate knowledge and understand the mind to be an empty file that must be filled by sensory experience.[45] Empiricists underline experience in all human knowledge by positing that all knowledge is based on experience alone.[46] They are convinced that humans obtain all their knowledge through the senses. People can only know, excepting the use of pure logic, whether something is true or false based on testing the idea in experience.[47] Empiricists are skeptical of innate knowledge and see the mind as a blank to be written on by sensory experience.[48] Summarizing their differences, rationalists begin with metaphysical axioms and from them deduce what can be known (epistemology) and what should be done (ethics). Empiricists begin with what can be known, then move to metaphysics and ethics.[49]

Thomas Hobbes of Malmesbury (A.D. 1588–1679). The English philosopher Thomas Hobbes should not be understood as a pure empiricist—though he was inclined toward scientific studies and showed traces of empiricism in his thought.[50] He was, in fact, drawn to mathematics and Continental rationalism.

His father, also named Thomas Hobbes, was a somewhat disreputable clergyman. The elder Hobbes fell into conflict with another pastor, fled his church, and left his wife and three children in the care of his wealthy, unmarried brother. By this point, however, young Hobbes had already left home to study at Oxford. He graduated in 1608. Upon graduation, Hobbes began work as a tutor and in that capacity had the opportunity to tour the Continent in 1610. On this trip, he was exposed to scientific and critical studies, which stood in contrast to his Oxford scholasticism.

He began philosophical work in 1629, and by 1637 he was an independent scholar.[51] He published his groundbreaking *Leviathan* in 1651. The *Leviathan* asserted many principles of the now well-known

---

45. *HWPT*, 177–78.
46. Brown, *Philosophy & Faith*, 60; Clark, *Thales to Dewey*, 360.
47. Brown, *Philosophy & Faith*, 60–62; and see Schmidt, *Grundriss*, 437.
48. *HWPT*, 177–78.
49. Ibid., 191.
50. Ibid., 189.
51. Heussi, *Kompendium*, 329.

social contract theory.[52] While holding to the sovereign right of kings, Hobbes argued for natural equality among men, and he asserted that political power should be representative and founded on consent.[53]

Blaise Pascal (A.D. 1623–1662). Pascal was a theologian, philosopher, and scientist.[54] As a theologian, like Descartes, Pascal was Roman Catholic. But his approach to religion was very different from that of Descartes.[55] Pascal was exposed to Jansenism—a movement that renewed interest in Augustine in Catholic France.[56] In 1653, the pope condemned Jansenist teaching. In 1654, what we might refer to as Pascal's definitive conversion took place. He discovered what he called the God of Abraham, Isaac, and Jacob and not that of the philosophers and men of science.[57]

Between the years 1656 and 1657, Pascal published his *Provincial Letters*, in which he defended Jansenism against its opponents. His *Provincial Letters* were then placed on the Roman Catholic index of forbidden books. His chief work, called *Pensées sur la religion*, was collected by editors and published in 1669 after Pascal's death.[58]

Pascal developed what is now his famous wager: risk your life on the possibility that Christianity might be true. We can neither see God nor prove the truth of the gospel to exclude every doubt. We can only

52. *HWPT*, 191n49: "The idea of a social contract can be found among Greek philosophers (Epicurus), and later in Hugo Grotius (1625), John Locke (1689), and Jean-Jacques Rousseau (1752). But these could not agree with one another or with Hobbes about the character of the state of nature, the nature of human rights (either within or beyond the state of nature), or the elements of the social contract."

53. Ibid., 192: "He puts epistemology before metaphysics." Frame then comments on his own philosophy: "The biblical philosophy that I advocate in this book would take a third option: neither metaphysics nor epistemology is prior to the other. . . . Both these disciplines have legitimate implications for each other. The biblical epistemology presupposes the biblical metaphysics, and vice versa. But their unity is evident only through divine revelation, which stands above human life and presents a complete worldview."

54. Ibid., 223: "In 1647, Descartes visited the family when Pascal, then twenty-four, was ill. They disagreed on philosophical and scientific matters, but the next day Descartes returned and ministered to Pascal as a physician"; and 224: "A principle called Pascal's Law states, 'When there is an increase in pressure at any point in a confined fluid, there is an equal increase at every other point in the container.'"

55. Brown, *Philosophy & Faith*, 56.

56. Pascal's sister joined the Jansenist convent at Port Royal in 1651 (see *HWPT*, 225; Schmidt, *Grundriss*, 391). That Jansenism was destroyed by the intrigues of the Jesuits was a victory for the Roman church. Yet that victory carried with it some sad fruit. It probably helped to set up the French Revolution.

57. Brown, *Philosophy & Faith*, 58.

58. Ibid.; Heussi, *Kompendium*, 310; *HWPT*, 225.

find out Christianity's truth by staking our lives on it.[59] According to Pascal, though Christianity cannot be demonstrated, the evidence makes its truth exceedingly probable.[60]

In direct opposition to the rationalists, Pascal did not support metaphysical proofs for God's existence.[61] He judged such proofs to be overly complex, with little, if any, evident impact. Even if they did influence a soul, an hour later that same person would be afraid that he had made a mistake. Pascal held that knowledge of God reached without Jesus Christ has little or no value. Those who know God through a mediator are aware of their wretchedness.[62] Pascal argued that there is a vast difference between knowing God and loving him.[63] The truth of Christianity is deeper and richer than mere argumentation. Some Christian philosophers assert that Pascal was attempting to recall his era to biblical religion. Pascal seems to echo the cry of the Reformers just a century earlier.

As a philosopher, Pascal in his epistemology transcended both rationalism and empiricism in that he saw knowledge as gained not simply from axioms (rationalism) or from introspection into ideas (empiricism). Human knowledge comes from the body, the mind, and what he termed the *heart*, or love. For Pascal, true knowledge included commitments of the heart.[64]

Unfortunately, Pascal's voice was not heard by his generation. Even today Pascal is treated strangely; he is considered something of an intellectual oddity and is thought of as outside the mainstream of European intellectual development. Nevertheless, he is also credited with being one of the most profound thinkers of his time.[65] Pascal's epistemology—his recognition that knowledge is not mere deduction

59. Brown, *Philosophy & Faith*, 58.

60. *HWPT*, 226–29. The wager goes beyond intellectual assent to heart commitment. Concerning Christianity as "probable," a partial truth, Frame argues that partial truths are both legitimate and unavoidable in the apologetic enterprise, contra Cornelius Van Til, who objected to arguments for Christianity based on probability. Throughout *Christian Theistic Evidences*, Van Til stands against Bishop Butler's supposedly neutral notion of probability. Butler's point was that Christianity is probably true—which is all that reasonable people should require.

61. Ibid., 226.

62. Pascal, Pensées, 212, as cited by Brown, *Philosophy & Faith*, 59.

63. Ibid., 60.

64. *HWPT*, 230.

65. Brown, *Philosophy & Faith*, 60. Schmidt (*Grundriss*, 392) has a different opinion.

from axioms or introspection into ideas but includes the heart—was beyond his time.[66]

John Locke (A.D. 1632–1704) was the son of a small country landowner and lawyer. Locke studied at the University of Oxford during a time when Puritanism was a strong influence. In fact, the great John Owen was the vice chancellor of Oxford when Locke was a student. Locke's formal study was in the field of medicine; his theological writings demonstrated that he was a man of Christian faith.[67] He was eventually awarded a doctoral degree.[68]

During England's time of political upheaval, Locke chose to reside for a time in Holland. While there, he had time to write his philosophical works. His most famous writing is titled *An Essay Concerning Human Understanding*, published in 1690. He wrote many other treatises as well.[69]

Locke was the pioneer of the empiricist approach to knowledge. At Oxford, he had been impressed by the work of the rationalist René Descartes. But his own approach was a rejection of Decartes's rationalism.

66. *HWPT*, 231: "In these remarkable *Pensées*, Pascal introduces themes that are new to the history of philosophy and will be taken up by others: (1) He is one of the first Christian thinkers to take seriously the implications of modern science. (2) He is one of the first philosophers to take into account sophisticated concepts of mathematical probability. (3) He is one of the first thinkers to take seriously the subjective or existential dimension of knowledge, not as a barrier to understanding, but as a necessary basis for it."

67. John Locke, *A Commonplace-Book to the Holy Bible on the Scripture's Sufficiency Practically Demonstrated*, 5th ed. (New York: American Tract Society, 1858). See *HWPT*, 191–96, and 218: "Locke believed that God is able to reveal himself in word as well as in the world, and that God's verbal revelation is fully authoritative." On that same page, however, Frame notes that Locke is also called the father of deism: "But he also said that human reason is the test that enables us to judge among purported revelations. When we apply that test, we discover that Christ's teachings are essentially the fulfillment of the moral law of nature, discovered by reason. Anyone should be considered a Christian, then, who believes in God and in Jesus as Messiah. The essence of Christianity, therefore, is *reasonable*, that is, simple and accessible to everyone."

68. Brown, *Philosophy & Faith*, 61.

69. Those works include the *Letter on Toleration* (1689), *The Reasonableness of Christianity* (1695), *Paraphrases and Notes on the Epistles of St. Paul* (1705–7), and *A Discourse on Miracles* (1706). See *HWPT*, 218: "In his *De Veritate* (1624), he proposes to discuss 'Truth, as Distinguished from Revelation.' In *De Religionis Gentilum* (1645), he lists five principles by which we can recognize truth in the religions of the world: (1) God exists. (2) We are obligated to worship him. (3) The essence of worship is practical morality. (4) When we sin, we should repent of it and abandon it. (5) God will reward and/or punish our misdeeds in this world and/or the next. . . . In 1695, he published anonymously a book called *The Reasonableness of Christianity*. This book actually defends the notion of special revelation, which Cherbury and others rejected."

The main issue for Locke was to determine whether there were primary or self-evident truths to man. He rejected the notion of innate ideas.[70]

Locke's view of the human mind was that it was not filled with preconceived notions but was, instead, a blank slate.[71] This blank slate received impressions from outside it.[72] He denied innate ideas, such as God's existence, the concepts of number, morality, and logical contradiction. He conceded that the ideas may be universal, but that possible characteristic did not mean that they were necessarily innate.[73]

While empiricism holds that all knowledge is based on experience alone, it does recognize different types of experience. For example, there is sensation and the mind. There were thus two loci, or focal points, of knowledge—ideas (ideas of sensation), and the mind's reflection on those ideas (ideas of reflection). Locke argued that all ideas come from the mind's reflection on them.[74]

The human mind has no other immediate object than its own ideas. For example, sound is a physical sensation and exists only in a perceiving ear.[75] The human mind takes simple ideas and acts on them by either compounding them, abstracting them, or relating them. Thus, expressed as simply as possible, "knowledge is the perception of the agreement or the disagreement of two ideas."[76] In other words, white is not black.[77] This epistemological theory is sometimes termed the "representative theory of knowledge."[78]

70. Clark, *Thales to Dewey*, 358–59.

71. *HWPT*, 193.

72. John Locke, *An Essay Concerning Human Understanding* I, i–iv: "Let us suppose the mind to be white paper, void of all characters, without any *ideas*. How comes it to be furnished? Whence comes it by that vast store which the busy and boundless fancy of man has painted on it, with an almost endless variety? To this I answer in one word, from *experience*; in that all our knowledge is founded, and from that it ultimately derives itself. Our observation employed either about *external sensible objects*, or about the internal operations of our minds, perceived and reflected on by ourselves, is that which supplies our understanding with materials of thinking. These two are the fountains of knowledge, from whence all the *ideas* we have, or can naturally have, do spring" (as cited by Brown, *Philosophy & Faith*, 61).

73. Clark, *Thales to Dewey*, 359–60. Clark said that Leibniz read this work and responded against it in his *New Essays on the Human Understanding*.

74. Ibid., 361: "Empiricism proceeds on the assumption that experience, in particular sensation, puts the mind in contact with reality."

75. Ibid., 363.

76. Locke, *Essay* IV. I.2, as cited by Brown, *Philosophy & Faith*, 62.

77. Clark, *Thales to Dewey*, 367.

78. Brown, *Philosophy & Faith*, 62: "The mind itself has no direct knowledge of the outside world, for it is never able to bypass the senses and stand outside them. What the mind perceives

But knowledge is not this simple. For example, knowledge of a book is a compound idea of brown, of leather, and of a certain shape. To make this knowledge more complex, students have experienced hundreds of books in a library, ascertained their common qualities, discarded their individual peculiarities, and then formulated the abstract notion of book.[79] In the case of a book, how does the color brown come together with the shape rectangle? The answer to the question is in the notion of substance. Locke said that substance serves the important function of uniting qualities so that a thing can be said to exist. The notion of substance also helped Locke explain individuation—that one book is different from another.[80]

In addition to the mind and its ideas, Locke reflected on a number of religious topics. He drew a distinction between faith and reason. Reason was ascertaining the certainty of propositions via deduction from ideas obtained by either sensation or reflection.[81] Faith included assent to propositions. But the ground for the assent relative to matters of faith was the credibility of the proposition's proposer, who is God, who speaks those propositions through divine revelation.[82]

Locke also had a well-developed theory of the relationship between reason and revelation. For him, reason is a natural revelation in which God communicates truth that can be grasped by the natural faculties. On the other hand, revelation is an enlarged natural reason providing a new set of discoveries communicated immediately by God—discoveries that reason vouches the truth of by the testimony and proofs it gives that the discoveries come from God.[83]

---

is the data conveyed to it by the senses, upon which it then gets to work and interprets."

79. Clark, *Thales to Dewey*, 364.

80. Locke, *Essay* II, xxiii, 1; Clark, *Thales to Dewey*, 365.

81. Locke, *Essay* IV.18.2, as cited by Brown, *Philosophy & Faith*, 63: Reason is "the discovery of the certainty or probability of such propositions or truths, which the mind arrives at by deduction made from such ideas, which it has got by the use of its natural faculties, viz. by sensation or reflection."

82. Ibid.: "Faith is the assent to any proposition not thus made out by the deductions of reason, but upon the credit of the proposer, as coming from God, in some extraordinary way of communication. This way of discovering truths to man, we call Revelation."

83. Ibid., IV. Xix.4, as cited by Brown, *Philosophy & Faith*, 63–64. Specialists debate Locke's relationship to scholasticism. Sell says that Locke was not a scholastic. For a scholastic "revelation supplements the discoveries of natural reason; . . . Rather, he was like those (Reformed) who held that natural theology is not the rational foundation of system but 'because its truths belong to the higher truth'" (Alan P. F. Sell, *John Locke and the Eighteenth-century Divines* [Cardiff: University of Wales Press, 1997], 74, 303). According to Sell, Locke did not

Locke's system is, however, subject to criticism. Did Locke really know himself or anyone else? It appears that he is, at least in part, dependent on a modified rationalist notion of *cogito* for self-consciousness.[84] Also, is it possible that our ideas are bare visions of things that have no corresponding reality? Does even one idea that I have in my mind exactly conform to a real external object? Locke would say that for mathematics, which gives real knowledge, such correspondence is not necessary. There are truths relative to a triangle, for example, whether such a triangle actually exists in reality. But Locke also asserted that only when people's ideas of things conform to real things do people have real knowledge of them. Thus, while there is knowledge, there is not much of it.[85]

George Berkeley (A.D. 1685–1753). Berkeley was born in Ireland, and at the age of twenty-two he started teaching at Trinity College, Dublin. He finished his philosophical works by the time he was twenty-eight years old. Later in his life, in 1728, he attempted to establish a missionary college in Bermuda. He eventually became a bishop of the Church of England.[86]

Berkeley rejected abstract ideas, such as Plato's forms. For him, there was no man in general, but only individual men.[87] His view of reality was that human beings did not actually perceive objects but instead have internal sensations of those objects. There was, in his opinion, no matter. From those internal sensations, people have convinced themselves that things do, in fact, exist outside themselves. Berkeley's teaching is termed *idealism*, i.e., the world is nothing but mind.[88]

---

make reason the arbiter of revelation. Sell's view stands in contrast to Nicholas Wolterstorff's interpretation of Locke in Nicholas Wolterstorff, *Reason within the Bounds of Religion* (Grand Rapids: Eerdmans, 1976), 24–29.

84. Clark, *Thales to Dewey*, 368.

85. Ibid., 368–69.

86. George Berkeley's chief philosophical works include: *An Essay towards a New Theory of Vision, A Treatise Concerning the Principles of Human Knowledge,* and *Three Dialogues between Hylas and Philonous* (see Brown, *Philosophy & Faith*, 64). Berkeley accepted much of Locke's teachings. Yet he perceived that there were problems inherent in Locke's thinking, and he both criticized and modified those theories. He was critical of Locke's theory of abstract ideas and particularly critical of "abstracting" (see Clark, *Thales to Dewey*, 369).

87. *HWPT*, 196–97.

88. Ibid., 197–98.

Things exist as far as they are perceived by someone.[89] When unseen by human eyes, an object is always observed by the all-seeing God.[90] Thus for Berkeley, existence required being perceived or perceiving.

Some philosophers would say that with this one stroke Berkeley had, on the one hand, denied the existence of matter and, on the other hand, proved God's existence.[91] His thesis was certainly novel and, to most, brilliant. Nevertheless, his thinking is not without its difficulties.

First, Berkeley could not answer the question as to whether the objects that people perceive with their minds are in fact the same as those that are perceived by the Infinite Mind. If there was not an exact correspondence between the two, then it made the human objects of perception hollow. Second, Berkeley's theory violated common assumptions concerning both human behavior and objects. For example, the farmer knows that objects exist in reality, and he knows that reality is not immaterial. Third, the only possible conclusion to Berkeley's system is that all anyone could know is himself and his own perceptions. No one can stand outside himself. Ultimately, a person cannot even know whether anyone else exists.[92] While Berkeley had interesting theories, it seems wiser to include objects in our worldview. In fact, there is an intelligible reality outside ourselves.

British Deism. The word *deism* must be carefully defined.[93] Overall, the earliest deism can be favorably compared to Thomas Aquinas's

---

89. Brown, *Philosophy & Faith*, 66; *HWPT*, 197.

90. In *Principles of Human Knowledge* I., iii, Berkeley says: "the table I write on, I say, exists, that is, I see and feel it; and if I were out of my study I should say it existed, meaning thereby that if I was in my study I might perceive it, or that some other spirit actually does perceive it" (as cited by Brown, *Philosophy & Faith*, 65).

91. *HWPT*, 198: "What he does is to prove God's existence by cosmological arguments with idealist modifications. Our sense experience, he says, is orderly, regular, and predictable. We cannot explain this in terms of abstract substances and forces. So what might account for it? The only thing we know that has the power to order reality is mind. So the First Cause must be, like us, a mind. . . . So God keeps all the being of ideal reality in place. . . . In this way, Berkeley offers his idealistic philosophy as a Christian apologetic. . . . Berkeley recognizes that the functioning of the world requires not only a First Cause (Locke), a guarantor of truth (Descartes), an impersonal world system (Spinoza), or a 'cosmic accountant' (Leibniz), but a *person* who communicates with us mind-to-mind. . . . But Berkeley's philosophy does not *begin* with God. . . . But there is no place for an authoritative word from God in Berkeley's theory of knowledge."

92. Brown, *Philosophy & Faith*, 65–66; *HWPT*, 195.

93. Schmidt, *Grundriss*, 442–43.

natural theology. Deism was established and built on reason, and from that foundation various phases and developments were added.[94]

Lord Herbert of Cherbury (1583–1648) is considered to be the first deist. In his *On Truth*, he held that God's hand imprinted certain notions on all human minds. Those common notions have been imprinted independently of God's special revelation in the Bible. It is those notions that form the foundation for all true religion. Included in Cherbury's common notions is the belief that God exists, that it is our duty to worship him, that sin is evil, that there is a need for repentance and for expiation, and that there will be eternal rewards and punishments. Lord Herbert also considered it a common notion that the practices of virtue and piety were essential parts of religion.[95]

There is probably a similarity of thought between Lord Herbert's ideas and those of Spinoza and Descartes. Unlike Descartes and Spinoza, however, Lord Herbert attempted to relate his common notions specifically to classical Christianity.[96]

In England, early deism had many advocates. To describe themselves, the British deists used the phrase *free thinkers* instead of *deists*. According to these free thinkers, their movement attempted to understand religion more complexly than had been done before. In parallel

---

94. *HWPT*, 217: "This word [deism] refers to the view that God created the world and established in that world a system of natural laws (causal and ethical), but does not thereafter enter into nature or history"; ibid., 219: "These deist authors flatly rejected the claim of the Scriptures to be the infallible written Word of God. For them, God's revelation is located in the natural world, not in a book. It is general revelation, not special revelation. Thus, all revelation is accessible to reason alone. . . . But among the deists, not only is it permissible to claim rational autonomy, but autonomous reason is sufficient as an authority for theology, just as for the rationalist and empiricist philosophers autonomous reason is sufficient for our understanding of the world. For the deists, Scripture has no divine authority at all. . . . To the deists, then, Christianity is a 'republication of the religion of nature.' . . . God exists, says Cherbury, and he will reward our goodness and punish our wickedness. But what of forgiveness? No news of divine forgiveness can be discovered through a rational analysis of nature. Nor evidence of miracle, nor prophecy. . . . It is hard to imagine a more drastic alteration of the Christian system of belief. . . . There is no gospel here, and no grace. . . . There can be no personal relationship with such a God. The deist God, indeed, has very few personal characteristics. . . . This *heresy* is certainly more serious than any heresy of the past. For deism does not merely question individual doctrines. It repudiates Christ himself and denies that there is any gospel of salvation. . . . But in the academic-intellectual establishments, deism became a popular, even flourishing position."
95. C. Gregg Singer, *A Theological Interpretation of American History* (Phillipsburg, NJ: Presbyterian and Reformed, 1981), 25.
96. Brown, *Philosophy & Faith*, 74.

to Kant's later notion of enlightenment, the movement thought that it was naive to adopt the previous generation's religious beliefs.[97]

The foundation of the deist system was natural religion. In that natural religion, the thinker would only take into his or her system that which was deemed reasonable. Some wanted to create a religion that did not rely on or use any special revelation. Perhaps because of this desire, the Bible came under attack by many of the early deists.[98] The criteria for a reasonable, natural religion were established on the principles of God, while holding to the notions of eternity and a principled system of ethics.

In parallel thinking, if someone invites you to dinner and serves roast beef, potatoes, a salad, and vegetables, it would be most rude to ask, "Where is the apple pie?" Such an addition to the meal would be pleasant, but unnecessary. For the deists, the Trinity and the incarnation were peculiar church dogmas that were unnecessary—they were the apple pie of this reasonable religion. But these doctrines could not be part of this reasonable religion on another basis: they were judged to be unreasonable. So for most deists, the Lord Jesus became the beautiful, yet purely human, prophet of this reasonable, natural religion.[99]

This chapter has traced seventeenth-century intellectual history, particularly that which stands in contrast to the contemporary development of Reformed theology. An analysis of rationalism and empiricism appears in chapter 19.

---

97. Heussi, *Kompendium*, 329.

98. That does not mean, however, that their attacks went unpunished. For example, in 1729 one author was sentenced to a year in jail for blasphemy. Unable to pay off his debts, he spent the rest of his life in prison. Some of the earliest biblical criticism is found in Anthony Collins's writings (*The Scheme of Literal Prophecy Considered* [1726]; *Discourse of the Grounds and Reasons of the Christian Religion* [1724]; and six discourses on the "miracles of our saviour"). These works attacked the existence of hell by saying the word indicates states of mind, not places. It is at this point that even the resurrection of Jesus Christ is attacked. Thomas Sherlock wrote *Trial of the Witnesses of the Resurrection of Jesus*. Sherlock's conclusion is one that we use today. He was able to demonstrate that the actions of the disciples represent a clear and sincere testimony to their experience. See Brown, *Philosophy & Faith*, 77–78.

99. Heussi, *Kompendium*, 330.

KEY TERMS

Enlightenment
empiricism
deism
rationalism
monad

STUDY QUESTIONS

1. Can you make an argument that empiricism is a better philosophy than is rationalism? Can you make an argument that rationalism is better than empiricism?
2. What was Descartes's place of epistemological certainty?
3. Have you ever met a deist? Does deism still exist today?

RESOURCES FOR FURTHER STUDY

Clark, Gordon H. *Thales to Dewey: A History of Philosophy*. Boston: Houghton Mifflin, 1957. A book that in some ways is hard to beat when it comes to a college-level presentation and that includes a classic explanation of rationalism and empiricism (pages 301–94).

Frame, John. *A History of Western Philosophy and Theology*. Phillipsburg, NJ: P&R Publishing, 2015. A much more expansive analysis of "Theology in the Enlightenment" (on pages 214–50) than is reviewed in our short chapter above.

Hoffecker, W. Andrew, ed. *Revolutions in Worldview: Understanding the Flow of Western Thought*. Phillipsburg, NJ: P&R Publishing, 2007. Contains an excellent contribution titled "Enlightenments and Awakenings: The Beginning of Modern Culture Wars" (pages 240–80).

17

Seventeenth-Century Reformed
Theology and Controversies

THE SEVENTEENTH CENTURY SAW a flowering of Reformed theology, as theologians reflected on the development of doctrine post-Reformation. Men such as John Owen and Francis Turretin made great strides in this area. They offered a careful and refined definition of even the most basic concept of *theology*. The century also was a time of refining, sometimes by fire, of theological ideas. By the start of the eighteenth century, multiple church councils had met, confessions were penned, and heresies were uncovered and confuted—the basic form and structure of what it meant to be non-Catholic, whether Reformed, Lutheran, Baptist, Presbyterian, or Independent, was established.

JACOB ARMINIUS (A.D. 1560–1609) AND THE REMONSTRANTS

Context and Life. When Jacob Arminius was fifteen years old, his family was killed by Spanish troops. His friends saw to his training at the University of Marburg and the University of Leiden. After this basic education, he was sent to Geneva, where he studied under Theodore Beza. He also studied for a year at the University of Basel under Grynaeus. He ended up spending about four years in Switzerland and achieved outstanding academic credentials. He then spent fifteen years in pastoral ministry in the Netherlands.

In 1603, Arminius was called to succeed Junius as professor of theology at the prominent University of Leiden.[1] He was rigorously

1. Williston Walker, Richard A. Norris, David W. Lotz, and Robert T. Handy, *A History of the Christian Church*, 4th ed. (New York: Scribner's Sons, 1985), 539–40.

examined by the strict Calvinist Franciscus Gomarus before his installation.[2] Not long afterward, however, his teaching came under scrutiny. His view of election, while not precisely Pelagian, differed noticeably from mainstream Calvinism. Although national synods were called to investigate his teaching, none was able to convene. Arminius died before the controversy could be adjudicated.

Theology. During Arminius's lifetime, most of his work remained unpublished. Arminius held that original sin infected all people—he saw a relationship between Adam and his posterity. But original sin did not, in reality, condemn anyone, because God ushered all humanity into a state of possible reconciliation through the covenant of grace he made with Adam and his posterity. God promises forgiveness of sins to all who remain in the covenant. Since infants have not broken this covenant, they are not liable to condemnation. Arminius held that God's prevenient grace eliminated original sin and total depravity for all until they reach the "age of accountability."[3]

For Arminius, predestination is grounded in God's foreknowledge. God determined to save those whom he foresaw would believe and persevere—predestination was conditioned on a person's acceptance or rejection of Christ, not a divine decree. Grace enabled human cooperation, but the cooperation was a result of renewal by the Holy Spirit.[4]

Remonstrants. After Arminius's death, forty-three of his followers met in 1610 to pen a remonstrance to the states of Holland requesting protection for their views.[5] The remonstrance contained five points affirming that: (1) God elected a group of those who would believe and obey, not individual people; (2) Christ died for each person; (3) faith is a divine gift; but (4) the gift of faith is resistible; and finally (5), there

2. Robert Godfrey, "Calvin and Calvinism in the Netherlands," in *John Calvin: His Influence in the Western World*, ed. W. Stanford Reid (Grand Rapids: Zondervan, 1982), 104. See Carl Bangs, *Arminius: A Study in the Dutch Reformation* (Nashville: Abingdon Press, 1971); Richard A. Muller, *God, Creation, and Providence in the Thought of Jacob Arminius* (Grand Rapids: Baker, 1991).

3. Greg R. Allison, *Historical Theology: An Introduction to Christian Doctrine—A Companion to Wayne Grudem's Systematic Theology* (Grand Rapids: Zondervan, 2011), 357.

4. See Arminius's "An Examination of the Treatise of William Perkins Concerning the Order and Mode of Predestination" (1602), as cited by Godfrey, "Calvin and Calvinism," 105.

5. By the end of the sixteenth century, Roman Catholicism was made illegal throughout the Netherlands, but the Reformed faith still represented a minority. Its adherents did not reach the 50 percent mark until about 1650. See ibid., 103.

is uncertainty whether all believers will persevere in their faith.[6] In response to these five points, those who opposed Arminius's teaching crafted the seven-point Counter-Remonstrance. The Netherlands found itself deeply embroiled in controversy. The majority of ministers held to the Counter-Remonstrance, but the Remonstrant minority was protected by the government. Their erroneous teaching led to the need for a unified Reformed response. This response came in the 1618–19 Synod of Dordrecht.

Theological Background of the Synod of Dordt. Before moving to an analysis of that synod, we must first examine the development of some of the relevant doctrines. In a previous chapter we discussed how Pelagius was an austere British monk and a popular teacher while in Rome.[7] Morality was for him of the highest importance, and he judged that Augustine's system made men mere puppets who are wholly dependent on the movements of divine grace. The keystone of Pelagius's system, therefore, was the idea of unconditional free will and corresponding responsibility.[8]

In Pelagius's system, the fall created no human bias toward evil. He simply denied original sin and interpreted the phrase "God will have mercy" in Romans 9:15 as "I will have mercy on him whom I have foreknown will be able to deserve compassion."[9] By eliminating original sin, Pelagius supposed that there was free will to do either that which is good or that which is evil. Likewise, with no bias toward evil, it would then be possible for a human being to obey God's commandments without committing sin.[10]

Augustine, in contrast to Pelagius, held to biblical election and reprobation. The reprobate were condemned because of the guilt of

6. Ibid., 105; Walker, *History*, 541.

7. He was in Rome from A.D. 384 to 409, was not young at this time, and probably died before the year A.D. 420. Some of his works include an exposition of Paul's epistles and other letters.

8. J. N. D. Kelly, *Early Christian Doctrines* (London: Black, 1977), 358. Pelagius himself did not actually try to extricate mankind from the purview of God's sovereignty even if his followers did.

9. Pelagius, *Commentary on St. Paul's Epistle to the Romans*, as cited by Allison, *Historical Theology*, 456.

10. Pelagius did not envision some plateau where the Christian reached the state of perfection here on earth and then sat back; on the contrary, the state of perfection can only be maintained by continuing, strenuous, effort.

original sin, in addition to their own sins. Salvation was exclusively by unmerited grace. God chooses some and passes over others. Salvation has a purpose—that those chosen will believe and live holy lives.[11] Grounded in these beliefs, the ancient church condemned Pelagianism.[12]

Nevertheless, there was diversity of opinion on the nature of divine election. In the fifth century, a position termed "semi-Pelagianism" arose.[13] Proponents of semi-Pelagianism rejected Pelagianism but found fault with Augustine's theology because God wills that all men be saved, not just some. They reasoned that since God wills all to be saved, those who do perish are damned against his divine will. Thus they argued that divine predestination must be ordained in the light of the human behavior that God foresees.[14] These views were the roots of Arminius's thinking.

While the Second Synod of Orange in A.D. 529 condemned semi-Pelagianism, the synod fell short of advancing full Augustinianism. The synod was reluctant to support double predestination and specifically anathematized the notion that some are foreordained to evil by divine power, or reprobation.[15]

In the medieval church, Anselm of Canterbury defined sin as a debt owed to God. He conceived God as something of a feudal lord.

---

11. Augustine interpreted 1 Timothy 2:4, that God wants all to be saved, that salvation comes exclusively by God's will. To answer objections that such a situation is unfair, Augustine appealed to divine mystery and that God is wholly righteous (see Allison, *Historial Theology*, 456–57). As to who belong to the elect and who to the reprobate, the answer was not exclusively those who are in the church and those who are outside the church, because some may be elect and not be members of the local church, while some may be members who are reprobate. The church helps the elect through the means of grace.

12. Pelagiasm particularly as articulated by Pelagius's disciples Celestius and Julian of Eclanum. Celestius was condemned at Carthage in A.D. 412, Pelagianism was condemned in A.D. 418, and the teaching was anathematized at the Council of Ephesus in 431. See Kelly, *Doctrines*, 361, 69; Cornelis Venema, *Chosen in Christ: Revisiting the Contours of Predestination* (Fearn, Scotland: Christian Focus, 2019), 171.

13. Kelly, *Doctrines*, 370.

14. Ibid., 371. The position was begun by John Cassian (A.D. 360–435). Spearheaded by Faustus of Rhegium (d. A.D. 495), this group agreed with Augustine on the fall, original sin, and salvation by grace. But Faustus considered Augustinianism fatalistic. In the Augustinian system, he argued, God was to blame for human evil and was accountable for our misery. As a counter to Augustine, he proposed distinguishing between predestination, foreknowledge, and permission. God has foreknowledge of events and human decisions, but that foreknowledge is not the same as predestining those events and decisions. God only wills the good—he does not will evil events and wicked decisions but merely permits those evils. When men and women do evil, they are the ones who are responsible for their actions and thus bring condemnation on themselves.

15. See earlier analysis in chapter 7.

To satisfy such a lord, the thief must pay him back more than he has stolen. God cannot simply forgive sin out of his mercy without reference to his honor. Anselm argued that God could damn everyone—doing so would satisfy his justice. He believed that satisfaction for sin was necessary; this theory is generally termed the "satisfaction theory."[16]

But humanity cannot pay the debt of sin. Even if someone fasted and prayed, he or she would give to God only his due. And no sinner can make another sinner righteous. Mankind is helpless and needs a true God and man to accomplish this work. Jesus Christ—the God-man—is the only one capable of offering satisfaction. His death was a sufficient and necessary satisfaction willingly offered to God. Christ thus obtained a reward, which he himself did not need. Embracing Christ grants satisfaction and redemption. While Anselm was the first one to work out a complete theory of atonement, his thinking still had flaws, which were to be later improved upon.[17]

It was the great medieval theologian Peter Lombard who used the phrase, "Christ's atonement was sufficient for all, but efficient only for the elect."[18] This expression concerning the nature of Christ's work became the theological standard.

The established Catholic position at the time of the Reformation was that Christ died for all, but not everyone received the benefit of his death.[19] While standing against Roman theology, Calvin did not study the design of the atonement but taught that redemption was subordinate to the eternal decree of election.[20] Calvin did not see a problem with the notion that Christ's death was sufficient for all but only efficient for the elect. This statement, and its theological structures, would come to the fore half a century after Calvin's death.

Calvin and his successors had to address Socinianism's errant teaching on the atonement. The Socinians argued that salvation came by

16. See earlier analysis in chapter 7. But God needs to replace the fallen angels; his doing so restores original creation.

17. Allison, *Historical Theology*, 395–97. Louis Berkhof, *Systematic Theology* (Carlisle, PA: Banner of Truth, 1972), 385.

18. Venema, *Chosen in Christ*, 246n64. See Richard A. Muller, *Calvin and the Reformed Tradition* (Grand Rapids: Baker, 2012), 70–106.

19. J. Van Genderen and W. H. Velema, *Concise Reformed Dogmatics*, trans. Gerrit Bilkes and Ed M. van der Maas (Phillipsburg, NJ: P&R Publishing, 2008), 526.

20. Archibald Alexander Hodge, *The Atonement* (Philadelphia: Presbyterian Board of Education, 1867), 374.

Christ's revelation of the way of faith and obedience. Christ was to inspire his disciples to a similar life. This thinking, called the "example theory," rejected the notion of retributive justice in God and posited instead that God could simply pardon whom he willed without requiring satisfaction for sin.[21] The Socinians opposed the doctrine that Christ made satisfaction for sin.[22]

Synod of Dordt (A.D. 1618–1619). These theological issues all came to a head at the Synod of Dordt.[23] The synod has been called "the most important development in the post-Reformation period of Reformed orthodoxy."[24] To ensure that the Remonstrants had a fair trial, the Dutch invited an international delegation to investigate the matter, and their meeting in Dordt was the only truly ecumenical synod of the Reformed church. Theologians came from England, German-speaking Switzerland, Geneva, and Germany.[25] They not only answered the five points of the Remonstrants but also addressed other crucial church issues.[26] The synod's decision against Arminianism was unanimous.[27] Its deliberations are summarized under five headings: *total depravity, unconditional election, limited atonement, irresistible grace,* and *perseverance of the saints.*[28] The canons, or heads of doctrine of the synod,

21. Berkhof, *Systematic Theology*, 387; *RD* 3:347.

22. *RD* 3:348–49. The Socinians first argued that the doctrine was against Scripture. Second, they argued that satisfaction was not necessary. Third, they thought that satisfaction was also impossible. Fourth, it was a harmful doctrine because it supposedly elevated a merciful Christ over a demanding God.

23. Two recent helpful analyses on the synod and its work are: Peter Sammons, *Reprobation: from Augustine to the Synod of Dort—The Historical Development of the Reformed Doctrine of Reprobation* (Göttingen: Vandenhoeck & Ruprecht, 2020), and Joel R. Beeke, *Debated Issues in Sovereign Predestination: Early Lutheran Predestination, Calvinian Reprobation and Variations in Geneva Lapsarianism* (Göttingen: Vandenhoeck & Ruprecht, 2017).

24. Venema, *Chosen in Christ*, 213.

25. For an excellent analysis of the work of the British delegation to the synod, see Anthony Milton, *The British Delegation and the Synod of Dort (1618–1619)*, Church of England Record Society 13 (Suffolk: Boydell Press, 2005).

26. The *Pro-Acta*, decisions made before Arminius's followers arrived, addressed a standardized Dutch Bible translation, the need for catechetical instruction, baptizing pagan children, preparation for ministry, and what to do with "dangerous" books. The *Post-Acta*, decisions made after they arrived, established a text for the Belgic Confession, addressed questions of Sabbath observance, and adopted a new church order that incorporated the church's right to discipline herself. See Godfrey, "Calvin and Calvinism," 107–9.

27. Ibid., 109.

28. John V. Fesko, "The Ground of Religion: Justification according to the Reformed Tradition," in *The Doctrine on which the Church Stands or Falls: Justification in Biblical, Theological, Historical, and Pastoral Perspective*, ed. Matthew Barrett (Wheaton, IL: Crossway,

serve, along with the Heidelberg Catechism and Belgic Confession, as the confessional foundation for all the Continental Reformed churches.

Regarding the atonement and predestination specifically, the Remonstrants' view began with faulty exegesis of Romans 9—they argued that divine election is based on an act of faith in response to a gospel call and that Jacob and Esau were types illustrating this case.[29] Theologians call this view "conditional predestination." From this defective exegesis, the Remonstrants argued for a flawed view of God's will and decree in holding that God, by an antecedent will, willed all humanity to be saved, but by a consequent will, with the knowledge of who would repent and believe, God elected some. As they would express it, Christ died for all men, for God wills the salvation of all men.

But a biblical conception of limited atonement focuses on the Bible's teaching concerning those for whom Christ died. The real issue is the work of Christ as sacrifice—for whom did Jesus Christ offer himself as a sacrifice? The question can be more precisely asked, "Did Christ come to make the salvation of all men possible, to remove the obstacles which stood in salvation's way, merely to make provision for salvation?" The biblical answer to the question is that Christ's sacrifice was effective for those for whom it was offered. Proper exegesis and theology demonstrate that the Bible uses words that are universal in form but that cannot be interpreted as meaning "all men" distributively and inclusively.[30]

In fact, every theological system, in some way, actually limits the atonement. For example, if the atonement was intended to save all men and women but did not do so, then its power is limited. If the atonement was intended to save only the elect, then its design is limited. God, in the perfect council of himself, intended the atonement to be limited.

After this cursory discussion of limited atonement, it must be admitted that even within the Reformed faith there are differences in interpretation and various nuances regarding the scope of the atonement. For

2019), 716. Arminius had a faulty doctrine of faith. Fesko questioned: "In technical terms, is faith the very thing that God receives as righteousness, or is faith a metonym for Christ and his righteousness?" In the section on rejection of error 4 in head 2, the synod rejected those who denied that we are justified before God and saved through faith, insofar as faith accepts Christ's merit. They rejected Arminius's notion of faith.

29. Venema, *Chosen in Christ*, 232.

30. See Richard C. Gamble, *The Whole Counsel of God*, vol. 2, *The Full Revelation of God* (Phillipsburg, NJ: P&R Publishing, 2018) (WCG2), 572–73.

example, not long ago a prominent Reformed scholar said that Canon #2, on Christ's death, "has often been characterized as teaching a limited atonement. The canons were not primarily on the limited nature of Christ's death but on the effectiveness of it."[31] While it is true that this canon underlines the effectiveness of Christ's work, proper interpretation of this canon does not fall into a dichotomy of either limited atonement or effective application; rather, a theologically responsible balance will argue that it holds to both limited atonement and effective application.

More problematic is a statement made by a Reformed theologian who argued: "I prefer not to use the term limited atonement because it is misleading. I rather speak of *definite redemption or definite atonement*."[32] Undoubtedly, Christ's work of redemption is applied to a definite number of people. But the theologians at Dordrecht correctly recognized—and we must hold to—the certainty that the atonement is, in fact, limited. It is limited either in its extent or in its power. Though the phrase *limited atonement* demands careful explanation, it is not inherently ambiguous. To say that the title is misleading blunts the advantage of the precision of the original canon as well as the excellent expansion in the later Westminster Confession of Faith.[33] In conclusion, limited atonement is a pillar of biblical teaching that was worthy of spirited defense against the Remonstrants in the early seventeenth century. It remains worthy of vigorous defense today.

Arminius's theology sprouted and matured in an era of great theologians and great theological writing. The rest of this chapter will examine some of the many voices contributing to the theological choir during this time.

WILLIAM AMES (A.D. 1576–1633)

Life and Writings. From 1594 to 1598, William Ames was trained at Christ's College at the University of Cambridge. He received his master's degree in 1601 under William Perkins and was invited to be

---

31. W. Robert Godfrey, "The Synod of Dordt," *Tabletalk Magazine* 42, no. 6 (June 2018): 72–75.

32. R. C. Sproul, "TULIP and Reformed Theology: Limited Atonement," *Tabletalk Magazine*, April 8, 2017.

33. See chapter 18 for the work of the Westminster Assembly.

a fellow of the college in 1607.[34] Ames was already a nonconformist opposed to various high-church practices of the Church of England, such as the required wearing of vestments. Because of his Puritan views and his Latin translation of *English Puritanism*, Ames was taken into custody and suspended. In 1610, he immigrated to Leiden in Holland and remained there until his death.[35] Ames worked as chaplain to the British community at The Hague, but in 1618 he was dismissed through English political pressure. English authorities continued to block him until 1622, when he was inaugurated at the new Friesland University of Franeker.[36] In 1626 he was made rector of the university. At Franeker, he did not get along with his colleague Maccovius—either theologically or in lifestyle.[37] Ames felt the need to leave his academic post and went to Rotterdam in 1632 to assume the role of pastor of an independent congregation.[38] But in 1633 he caught a fever when his house was flooded, and he died. His widow sailed in 1637 for Salem in the Massachusetts Bay Colony in America and was granted forty acres of land.[39]

Ames was a productive writer. His works included a long polemical book against Catholics, *Bellarmine Disarmed*, and *Conscience, with the Power and Cases Thereof*. His final works were *Lectures on the Psalms of David* and *A Fresh Suit against Human Ceremonies in God's Worship*.[40]

Theological Controversies. Ames serves as a model for classic English Puritan teaching. He provided theological leadership on at least three fronts: (1) the nature of liturgical worship, (2) theological arguments against Rome, and (3) the nature of theology.[41]

---

34. Joel R. Beeke and Randall J. Pederson, *Meet the Puritans* (Grand Rapids: Reformation Heritage Books, 2006), 39.

35. William Ames, *The Marrow of Theology*, trans. John Dykstra Eusden (Durham, NC: Labyrinth, 1983), 4; Beeke and Pederson, *Puritans*, 40.

36. John Dykstra Eusden, foreword, preface, and introduction to *The Marrow of Theology*, by William Ames, trans. John Dykstra Eusden (Durham, NC: Labyrinth, 1983), 6.

37. Ibid., 8. For example, Ames opposed Maccovius's heavy use of alcohol.

38. Ibid., 9; Beeke and Pederson, *Puritans*, 43.

39. Eusden, introduction, 10. Ames's wife took his library to the new world, and it provided part of the nucleus for the new Harvard College's library. See Beeke and Pederson, *Puritans*, 44.

40. *De conscientia et eius jure vel casibus: libri quinque* (1630); ET, *Conscience with the Power and Cases Thereof: Divided into Five Books* (London, 1643). See a good summary in Beeke and Pederson, *Puritans*, 46. His final work sums up issues between the Puritans and Richard Hooker.

41. See Keith L. Springer, *The Learned Dr. William Ames* (Urbana, IL: University of Illinois, 1972); Kelly M. Kapic and Randall C. Gleason, *The Devoted Life: An Invitation to the Puritan*

In ecclesiology, Ames met John Robinson (1576–1625), pastor of the English Separatist congregation at Leiden, who was known as a Brownist. Following the teaching of Robert Brown, Robinson thought it necessary to separate from the Church of England due to its corruption. It was no longer possible or helpful to work for reformation from within the church. Robinson believed that participation in other churches' sacraments was wrong because their sacraments were invalid.[42] Ames was a non-separatist—he believed that congregations must be purified but still remain within the established church. He was zealous for church reform and simplicity in worship, stood opposed to ecclesiastical hierarchy, favored a degree of independency, and was a Sabbatarian.[43]

Ames was also involved in the Arminian controversy. He defined Arminianism as a dangerous error tending toward heresy, but he did not go so far as to label it heresy unless it lapsed into Pelagianism.[44] He thought that the Dutch Remonstrants failed to give God's power its rightful, primary place. He thought that there was spiritual preparation necessary if grace was to be experienced—contra his colleagues Gomarus and Johannes Maccovius.[45]

Concerning the nature of the knowledge of God, Ames believed it permissible to use philosophical terms to explicate God's nature. God's essential attributes are *subsistentia* ("reality" or "source of subsisting") and *efficientia* ("efficient power"). God's essence and subsistence are linked and comprise God's sufficiency or divine completeness. Ames strove to analyze God's working power.[46] For example, he noted that God does not do certain things even when he has the power to do them—an observation that differentiates between the divine *potentia absoluta* ("absolute power") and *ordinate* ("ordained power").[47]

Classics (Downers Grove, IL: InterVarsity Press, 2004); Eusden, foreword, vii.

42. Eusden, introduction, 5.

43. Ibid., 19.

44. Ibid., 8.

45. Ibid., 6–7.

46. Ibid., 22. Ames will also use a description of the Trinity from Calvin's *Institutes*.

47. Ibid., 23. See Richard C. Gamble, *The Whole Counsel of God*, vol. 1, *God's Mighty Acts in the Old Testament* (Phillipsburg, NJ: P&R Publishing, 2009), 513, 663; WCG 2:370–71: God's absolute power is his "ability to perform whatever is in harmony with himself. A second way in which theologians describe God's power is by use of the term actual or ordinate power. That power means that he is able to do what he decrees. The Bible is full of examples of God exercising this type of actual power."

Ames argued in favor of Ramian logic in contrast to Aristotelian logic. For Ames, understanding the component parts in dialectics leads to right thinking, and understanding the parts of theology leads to a better Christian life. Dialectical thinking helps people better understand their spiritual condition.[48]

Marrow of Theology. In 1623, Ames's *Medulla Theologica* (*Marrow of Theology*) appeared in Latin. This text made vast strides in defining doctrines and became the standard theological textbook for New England Puritans for more than a century.[49] Ames's theology had its roots in Augustinian thought, specifically his just war theory. His work also demonstrates a partial dependence on late medieval theology, including the theology of Thomas Aquinas.[50]

After a brief foreward, in which Ames describes his purpose in writing as to instruct and stir conviction, he defined *theology*.[51] For Ames, theology is not speculative but practical. Theology is the art of living: "every art has its rules to which the work of the person practicing it corresponds. Since living is the noblest work of all," he thought, "there cannot be any more proper study than the art of living." A person's highest life is lived to God, thus the nature of theological life is living to God.[52] The human will is the subject of theology and the final end of theology refers directly to the practice of Christianity.[53]

Ames then discussed the nature of faith. He determined that faith is resting—it is a choice that involves the whole person. It is not confined to the intellect.[54] Faith as belief is through the Holy Spirit's persuasion.[55] God's authority is the proper and immediate ground of all truth that is to be believed.

Against the Remonstrants, Ames taught that predestination does not presuppose its end but causes it. It is a decree of God concerning humankind's eternal condition, a decree that manifests his special

48. Ibid., 18, 38, 42.
49. Ibid., 1; Beeke and Pederson, *Puritans*, 47.
50. Eusden, introduction, 15–17; see Beeke and Pederson, *Puritans*, 49.
51. Ames, *Marrow*, 69.
52. Ibid., 77: "Since the highest kind of life for a human being is that which approaches most closely the living and life-giving God, the nature of theological life is living to God."
53. Ibid., 78: "The first and proper subject of theology is the will."
54. Ibid., 80.
55. Ibid., 81: "The final dependence of faith, as it designates the act of believing, is on the operation and inner persuasion by the Holy Spirit." See Beeke and Pederson, *Puritans*, 49.

glory.[56] Election is the predestination of certain people so that God's glorious grace may be shown in them. Calling is the gathering of men together in Christ so that they may be united with him. Calling is both internal and external and is at times termed *conversion*. Calling is received as both passive and active—it is passive in regeneration, is active in faith, and results in repentance.[57]

For Ames, justification is God's gracious judgment by which he absolves the believer from sin and death and reckons him righteous and worthy of life for Christ's sake. Christ's righteousness is imputed to the justified and apprehended by faith.[58] Justification begins in God's mind, is then pronounced in Christ's resurrection, and is actualized when faith is born and the Holy Spirit witnesses to one's spirit. The nature of justifying faith is not simply assent or trust but reliance on Christ. Justification does not erase the blame or the effects of sin, but it removes the obligation to undergo eternal death.

Ames claims that adoption is God's gracious judgment by which he gives the faithful the dignity of sonship because of Christ's work. He then argues that sanctification is a real change in man from the sordidness of sin to the purity of God's image. The nature of sanctification is that it pertains to the whole man, first to the soul, then to the body. The Holy Spirit is the principle efficient cause, and faith is the serving cause of mortification and vivification.

Glorification is the real change in man from misery to eternal happiness. Glorification has its starting point in redemption, begins in the present life, and is completed in the next life.[59] Redemption is real deliverance, and in glorification "the life that results from the pronouncement and award is given to us: we have it in actual possession."[60] In summary, Ames's *Marrow* provided a robust and faithful exposition of theology. There is little wonder why this excellent book was so foundational to theology in America.

56. Ames, *Marrow of Theology*, 152.
57. Ibid., 158–59. Because of this receiving, calling is termed *conversion*. See the discussion in *WCG* 2:648.
58. Ibid., 160.
59. Ibid., 171.
60. Ibid., 172. Another important theologian who comes after Ames is the Swiss theologian Johannes Wollebius (1586–1629), whose clear and concise *Compendium theologiae Christianae* was used extensively. See Richard C. Gamble, "Switzerland: Triumph and Decline," in *John Calvin: His Influence in the Western World*, ed. W. Stanford Reid (Grand Rapids: Zondervan, 1981), 69.

GISBERTUS VOETIUS (A.D. 1589–1676)[61]

Biography and Works. Gisbertus Voetius attended the University of Leiden, where he studied under the Calvinist Francis Gomarus (1563–1641) and Jacob Arminius (1560–1609). In 1611 he began his pastorate at Vlijmen, and as the youngest delegate to the Synod of Dordt in 1618–19, he sided with Gomarus.[62] He was a faithful pastor who preached as many as eight times per week.

Voetius's first book was published in 1634 and titled *Proof of the Power of Godliness*.[63] He then moved to Utrect, where he carried a part-time preaching schedule.[64] He became a professor of theology and Oriental science in Utrect in 1636; his inaugural lecture was titled "On Piety Joined with Science." He spent his first years as a professor in theological combat, particularly against Arminians and Catholics. In the next decade, he critically addressed the new philosophical method of René Descartes. Voetius also opposed Cocceius's method.[65] Voetuis was orthodox, scholastic, and pietistic.[66] His theological method demonstrates the complexity of the time. He leaned toward Aristotelianism rather than the logic of Ramus.[67] He is also credited with developing the first comprehensive mission theology.[68] He stood against Erastian-

61. For further information on Voetius, see Joel R. Beeke, "Toward a Reformed Marriage of Knowledge and Piety: The Contribution of Gisbertus Voetius," *Reformation and Revival* 10, no. 1 (Winter 2001): 125–42; Beeke and Pederson (*Puritans*, 45) comment that Voetius "was profoundly influenced by Ames's ideas."

62. Beeke and Pederson, *Puritans*, 802: Voetius defended Maccovius, "whose supralapsarian conception of predestination was of a more logically rigid nature than that of most other delegates."

63. Godfrey, "Calvin and Calvinism," 111–12.

64. Beeke and Pederson, *Puritans*, 803.

65. Ibid., 804–5; and see below.

66. While a Pietist, he still opposed De Labadie. See Godfrey, "Calvin and Calvinism," 113; William Johnson and John H. Leith, eds., *Reformed Reader: A Sourcebook in Christian Theology* (Philadelphia: Westminster John Knox Press, 1993), 13n8: "Voetius did, however, repudiate Labadie's separatism, thus reflecting another Reformed dispute in this period: that between Presbyterians and Independents"; and Beeke, "Reformed Marriage," 133.

67. Beeke and Pederson, *Puritans*, 800: "He leaned on the humanistic Aristotelianism of Leiden rather than on Ramism, which insisted on the purely instrumental and non-autonomous role of philosophy. Voetius did not accept the conviction of other Calvinists, such as William Ames, who felt that Peter Ramus was a safer guide than Aristotle for methodology in doing theology. . . . And [he] consequently regarded the Ramist controversy as superfluous. . . . He offered intellectual scholasticism combined with piety like devotion moderna."

68. J. A. B. Jongeneel, "The Missiology of Gisbertus Voetius: The First Comprehensive Protestant Theology of Missions," *Calvin Theological Journal* 26, no. 1 (1991): 47–79.

ism and for the separation of the church and the state, and his final years saw the publication of his three-volume *Politica Ecclesiastica* (1663–1676).[69]

Controversy with Descartes. The issue between Descartes and Voetius was whether human cogitation is the foundation for reason or Scripture.[70] In 1642, Voetius persuaded the academic senate to condemn the Descartes system of philosophy because it opposed scholastic and Aristotelian philosophy, and further, its implications were dangerous for theology. Descartes wrote a long letter to Voetius in response and personally attacked Voetius in the second edition of his *Meditations*. The strife between the two was theological. Following Augustine and Anselm, Voetius's method was faith seeking understanding, not striving for Aristotelianism. In contrast, for Descartes, faith could not be fully grasped by reason. Reason must not be bound or hindered by faith. For Descartes, faith was to be autonomous. As noted in a previous chapter, Descartes argued that his method would provide epistemological certainty. In opposition to that view, Voetius argued that human reason is clouded by both sin and error; therefore, humans cannot attain perfect knowledge. Instead, it is in the Scriptures that truth is found.

Reformed scholars hold differing opinions on Voetius. Robert Godfrey said that "he failed to help the church develop tools for effectively understanding and coping with modern systems of thought." Further, Godfrey claimed that "Voetius's dedication to Aristotle in both philosophy and science today seems simply reactionary and obscurantist."[71] Joel Beeke, however, has said that Voetius is as essential to Dutch Reformed theology as Owen is to English theology.[72]

Voetius was controversial in his own life as well. In addition to his battling Descartes, there were fifty years of controversy in Holland between the Voetians and the followers of Johannes Cocceius.[73]

69. Godfrey, "Calvin and Calvinism," 113.

70. B. Hoon Woo, "The Understanding of Gisbertus Voetius and René Descartes on the Relationship of Faith and Reason, and Theology and Philosophy," *WTJ* 75, no. 1 (Spring 2013): 45–63.

71. Godfrey, "Calvin and Calvinism," 112.

72. Beeke and Pederson, *Puritans*, 799.

73. Rowland S. Ward, *God and Adam: Reformed Theology and the Creation Covenant* (Melbourne: New Melbourne Press, 2003), 77. Van Genderen and Velema (*Dogmatics*, 542) observe: "Cocceius made a significant attempt to break with the scholastic way of thinking

JOHANNES COCCEIUS (A.D. 1603–1669)

Biography and Works. Johannes Koch, or Cocceius, was born in Bremen in northern Germany. He specialized in Biblical Hebrew and served as professor of biblical philology at Bremen from 1630 to 1636, then as professor of Hebrew at Franeker,[74] where he was taught by William Ames. He also taught at the University of Leiden.[75]

In 1648 he wrote *The Doctrine of the Covenant and Testament of God* (*Summa doctrinae de foedere et testamento Dei*) at Leiden. He presented what would today be called a "biblical theology."[76] His theological method has had lasting influence.[77] Significantly, Cocceius developed covenantal theology. He followed an exegetical method based on the theme of covenant and developed it into a theological paradigm.[78] He also pressed the distinction between the Law and the gospel, which resulted in his more liberal view of the Sabbath.[79]

Covenant of Works. Cocceius viewed the covenant of works with Adam as one-sided, or monopleuric. What he termed the "law of nature" required human obedience. It was a universal covenant. God was in no way obligated to reward Adam, but a reward could well

---

and present a biblical theology. To him, the covenant and testament of God were the most important theological subject matter. In covenantal theology, of which Cocceius was the most prominent representative, the covenant (*pactum*) between the Father and the Son was firmly ensconced."

74. Johnson and Leith, *Reformed Reader*, 9–10.

75. Ward, *God and Adam*, 77.

76. J. I. Packer, "Introduction: On Covenant Theology," in *The Economy of the Covenants*, by Hermann Witsius (Escondido, CA: The Den Dulk Christian Foundation, 1990), v: He worked out "in detail what we would call a biblical-theological, redemptive-historical perspective for presenting covenant theology . . . but muddied his exegesis by allegorical fancies and marginalized himself by needless attacks on the analytical doctrine-by-doctrine approach to theological exposition that was practised by his leading contemporaries in Holland"; Ward, *God and Adam*, 77: "Over against the tendency to use systematic theology as an interpretative grid, Cocceius aimed to draw his theology from careful contextual exposition of Scripture in the light of the unfolding purpose of God in Christ. He was thus in many ways the founder of Biblical theology."

77. Heiner Faulenbach, *Weg und Ziel der Erkenntnis Christi: Eine Untersuchung zur Theologie des Johannes Coccejus*, Beiträge zur Geschichte und Lehre der reformierten Kirche 26 (Neukirchen-Vluyn: Neukirchener Verlag, 1973); Charles McCoy, "Johannes Cocceius: Federal Theologian," *Scottish Journal of Theology* 16, no. 4 (1963): 352–70; Gottlob Schrenk, *Gottesreich und Bund im altern Protestantismus vornehmlich bei Johannes Cocccejus* (1923; repr., Giessen: Brunnen, 1985).

78. Johnson and Leith, *Reformed Reader*, 9–10.

79. Ward, *God and Adam*, 77.

be expected. There were two sacraments in the covenant of works: (1) paradise as a pledge of the heavenly city, and (2) the tree of life as a pledge of eternal life.[80]

He argued in his system that as a result of human sin, the covenant of works was undone. Because of the eternal intertrinitarian pact between the Father and the Son, a new covenant—one of grace—was instituted. Because of Christ's surety, this covenant was unbreakable. The first economy of the covenant of grace, through circumcision and the Passover, prefigured salvation through Christ. Cocceius's covenantal theology emphasized the need for human obedience and deemphasized the pretemporal decrees.[81] As Cocceius was a proponent of biblical theology, he opposed the more systematic theological methods of Voetius and others.

Church life was tumultuous on the Continent, and Cocceius and Voetius were in the very eye of the hurricane. Across the pond in the United Kingdom, religious debate erupted into full-fledged civil war. A key figure in the debates and controversies was Samuel Rutherford.

SAMUEL RUTHERFORD (A.D. 1600–1661)[82]

Samuel Rutherford's life is a mirror of all the tumultous events that swept through Scotland in the middle of the seventeenth century. Rutherford was born at Nisbet in Roxburghshire and was educated at the University of Edinburgh from 1617 to 1621. He obtained the master's degree in four years.[83] Two years after graduation, Rutherford

---

80. Ibid., 115.

81. Johnson and Leith, *Reformed Reader*, 126. Apparently, Cocceius had a view that has been termed "continual creation"; see ibid., 174: "Similarly, Jonathan Edwards defends 'continual creation.' . . . Some Reformed theologians have criticized Edwards' position for its failure to distinguish God's creating from God's upholding of the world." For a critique of Edwards, see Hodge, *Systematic Theology*, 1:577–81.

82. For information on Rutherford, see: O. K. Webb, "The Political Thought of Samuel Rutherford" (PhD diss., Duke University, 1964); D. Strickland, "Union with Christ in the Theology of Samuel Rutherford: An Examination of His Doctrine of the Holy Spirit" (PhD diss., University of Edinburgh, 1972); J. M. Ross, "Samuel Rutherford," *The Month* 236 (July 1975): 207–11; Kingsley G. Rendell, *Samuel Rutherford: The Man and His Ministry* (Fearn, Scotland: Christian Focus, 2003); C. E. Rae, "The Political Thought of Samuel Rutherford" (MA thesis, University of Guelph, 1991); John Coffey, *Politics, Religion and the British Revolutions: The Mind of Samuel Rutherford* (Cambridge: Cambridge University Press, 1997).

83. Thomas Murray, *The Life of Samuel Rutherford* (Edinburgh: Oliphant, 1828), 13.

became professor of humanity at his alma mater, a university that was then only forty years old.[84] In 1625 he began to study theology, and within two years he was pastoring in the rural town of Anwoth, Kirkcudbrightshire, where he ministered for a decade.[85] He was married in 1626, but his wife died in 1630.[86]

During this time there was tension between those who desired to reform the Scottish church and the followers of King Charles I, who desired to bring the Scottish church more in line with the English church. After a visit to Scotland in 1633, the king concluded that the Scottish style of worship was too bare and austere. So he proposed revisions, which were approved by the archbishop of Canterbury, William Laud. Their proposal was at first opposed by the older bishops. In 1634, Rutherford and a colleague were threatened to be forced to appear before the local Court of High Commission. To avoid the threat, Rutherford simply had to renounce Presbyterianism. He refused.[87] As time advanced, bishops opposing the king lost their influence, and the king mandated a new book of canons. New canons and a promised liturgy, submitted by Laud, were approved by the king in 1635 and were to be strictly observed in Scotland.[88]

In 1636 Rutherford was called before the court a second time, and this time he was deprived of his office. This sentence was not deemed sufficiently severe, so he was called to appear in Edinburgh, where that decision was confirmed. The charges against him, presented by

84. Ibid., 16.

85. Ibid., 18–23. It is not certain whether he was ordained by bishops or by an independent presbytery. J. D. Douglas (*Light in the North* [Grand Rapids: Eerdmans, 1964], 49) says "without giving any engagement to the Bishop." Murray (*Life*, 36–37) says he did not submit to bishops. He was always ready to confess faults and never made such a confession. The bishop was induced by Lord Kenmure and Lord Kirkcudbright. Bishops were given seats in Parliament. Ministers were made privy counsellors, lords of session, and judges in courts of exchequer. Bishops determined pastors' stipends. It is probable that through Kenmure he was admitted without acknowledging bishops.

86. Murray, *Life*, 49; Beeke and Pederson, *Puritans*, 722–23.

87. Murray, *Life*, 84–85. As he faced ejection, he wrote: "It hath pleased the Lord to let me see, by all appearance, my labour in God's house here at an end; and I must now learn to suffer, in the which I am a dull scholar. . . . I seek no other thing, but that my Lord may be honoured by me, in giving a testimony. I am willing to do him more service; but seeing he will have no more of my labours, and this land will thrust me out, I pray for grace to be acquaint with misery, if I may give so rough a name to such a mark of those who shall be crowned with Christ."

88. Ibid., 113–14.

the bishop of Galloway, were: nonconformity, preaching against the Articles of Perth, treason, and authoring the *Exercitationes apologeticae pro divina gratia* (Amsterdam, 1636), which criticized Arminianism and vexed the Church of England's clergy.[89]

During the three-day trial, Rutherford appeared before the court but declined their jurisdiction and refused to give the bishops their titles. In July 1636, he was deprived of office, expelled from gospel ministry, forbidden to preach in Scotland under pain of punishment for rebellion, and confined to Aberdeen.[90] Immediately after the trial he wrote: "With submission to my Lord's will, my kind Lord hath now bestowed upon me, even to suffer for my royal and princely King, Jesus."[91] Rutherford's opposition was not political, for he freely obeyed the king. Instead, his opposition was religious, as Rutherford was convinced that the theology of the bishops, as well as of the hierarchy itself, was contrary to the Word of God.

While confined in Aberdeen, Rutherford ministered in private homes and engaged in public debates. He wrote letters to friends.[92] His successes while in Aberdeen drew further ire, and it was determined that he should be banned even farther north or expelled from the country. These plans, however, were not implemeneted.[93] The bishop tried to impose an Arminian-leaning minister on the congregation at Anwoth. Claiming that Rutherford was still their legal pastor, the congregation opposed this imposition.[94]

The king, meanwhile, attempted to impose on Scotland the new liturgy promised in the canons, and he began in the city of Edinburgh. The people rejected the new liturgy. The rejection was so widespread that the Presbyterians were emboldened to do away with the Articles

89. The *Exercitationes* was apparently printed in a second edition that same year in Franeker. Another edition appeared later in 1651. Ibid., 73, 88–89.

90. Murray, *Life*, 87; James Reid, *Memoirs of the Lives and Writings of Those Eminent Divines Who Convened in the Famous Assembly at Westminster in the Seventeenth Century* (Paisley, Scotland: Young, 1815), 2:346–49; J. D. Douglas, *Light in the North* (Grand Rapids: Eerdmans, 1964), 49: "the town consists either of Papists or of men of Gallio's naughty faith"; Beeke and Pederson, *Puritans*, 724.

91. Murray, *Life*, 91.

92. Now famous, the letters were not published during Rutherford's lifetime. See Samuel Rutherford, *The Letters of Samuel Rutherford* (Banner of Truth, 1984).

93. He commented on his captivity: "I know, and am persuaded, it is for God's truth, and the honour of my king and royal prince Jesus, I now suffer" (Murray, *Life*, 102).

94. Ibid., 111–12.

of Perth and the canons. When petitions to the king were ignored, the Scots organized tables of commissioners from the various estates. The tables then renewed the covenant of 1580. Beginning at Greyfriars in Edinburgh, this new covenant spread throughout Scotland in a matter of days.[95] Unable to sway his subjects, who were on the brink of civil rebellion, the king withdrew his canons, his liturgy, and his court of high commission. He even summoned a general assembly to meet at Glasgow in November 1638, with a parliamentary meeting promised for the following spring. In the midst of this turmoil, Rutherford slipped out of Aberdeen in 1638.[96]

In that same year, the General Assembly, which determined that it could meet without the king's permission, overturned the earlier laws moving Scotland toward episcopacy; deposed, suspended, or excommunicated the country's fourteen bishops; and determined that ministers could no longer serve in a civil appointment or office. They also elected Rutherford as professor of divinity at St Andrews.[97] He initially declined the position out of his desire to stay in his pastorate at Anwoth. The following year, however, the assembly confirmed his appointment.[98] He accepted the position on the condition that he be allowed to preach once a week. He said that he could not be hindered from preaching, so he was permitted both tasks.[99]

Meanwhile, hostilities broke out between English and Scottish forces. The Scots were led under the banner, *For Christ's Crown and Covenant*. After a skirmish near Berwick, the Scots were victorious, and peace was reached in June of 1639.[100]

In 1640 a charge was made against the Scottish society meetings, and Rutherford defended those private meetings in a treatise.[101] This controversy formed the background for his work titled *A Peaceable and Temperate Plea for Paul's Presbytery in Scotland*, published in 1642.[102]

---

95. Ibid., 120–26.
96. Ibid., 133.
97. For details on the assembly, see ibid., 133–46.
98. Ibid., 158–59.
99. Reid, *Memoirs*, 2:345–51; Beeke and Pederson, *Puritans*, 725. Rutherford's *Disputatio de divina providentia* is from his lectures during this time. See Murray, *Life*, 169.
100. Murray, *Life*, 175.
101. Reid, *Memoirs*, 2:351; Murray, *Life*, 178–80.
102. Murray, *Life*, 186–87.

He was also remarried that year to Jean M'Math Montgomery—"a woman of great worth and piety."[103]

The promised Scottish Parliament was not called by King Charles, so the decisions of the General Assembly were not confirmed. But the Scottish Parliament still met, even without permission. In fact, King Charles was preparing for war, which broke out in August 1640, with further military victories gained by the Scots. During the peace negotiations held in London, many Londoners heard Scottish preaching and were swayed to the Presbyterian system.[104]

Cognizant that further civil war was about to erupt within his kingdom, King Charles traveled to Scotland and promised to agree to all the Scottish legal changes, thus earning for him goodwill in the northern part of his kingdom.[105] He also promised to sign the *Solemn League and Covenant*, a technical document agreeing to bring England into conformity with the theology and practice of the Scottish church.[106]

As civil war errupted in England, the Westminster Assembly began in July 1643.[107] Rutherford's wife was with him in London for the assembly, and two of their children died during their time in London.[108] Rutherford attended the assembly until October 1647—longer than any other Scot. He remained in London the entire time.[109]

Rutherford was quite productive during the time of the assembly, when he wrote *Lex Rex* and other books.[110] In 1644, *Lex Rex* was published as a reply to Bishop John Maxwell. Maxwell argued that the royal prerogative is derived from God alone and demands total

103. She was the widow of Sir Hugh Montgomery, first Viscount Montgomery (Murray, *Life*, 191–92). None of their six children survived their father, nor did the daughter from the first marriage (Beeke and Pederson, *Puritans*, 721–25).

104. Murray, *Life*, 195–200.

105. Ibid., 200.

106. Ibid., 200–206.

107. Such an assembly had been hoped for in 1642, but the king would not sanction it. Thus they went ahead the following year (ibid., 207). On the documents and polity, see ibid., 210–12.

108. Ibid., 234; Beeke and Pederson, *Puritans*, 725.

109. Murray, *Life*, 216.

110. Beeke and Pederson, *Puritans*, 726; Murray, *Life*, 228–33. These books included *The Due Right of Presbyteries* (a defense of Presbyterianism against independency); *The Divine Right of Church Government and Excommunication*; *Survey of the Spiritual Antichrist* (a defense against antinomianism and various sects); and *The Trial and Triumph of Faith* ("a book of sermons on Christ's saving work in the Cananite woman"). He also probably composed his *Rutherford's Catechism* (Edinburgh: Blue Banner, 1998) during this time.

obedience. Rutherford's reply caused massive tumult.[111] A new form of statist absolutism had arisen in England beginning with Henry VIII; it reached fruition with King Charles I, who held to a monarch's absolute rights beyond any restraints.[112] Rutherford had the audacity to argue for limitations on the divine right of kings. Since the people consent to a king's crown, the people may also resist a tyrant.[113]

In 1644 Rutherford wrote *The Due Right of Presbyteries, a Peacable Plan for Scotland*.[114] In this work he argued that the civil magistrate has spiritual and supernatural ends. He modified his position in *Divine Right of Church Government* (1646) after attending the Westminster Assembly.[115]

Upon his return to St Andrews, Rutherford succeeded Robert Howie as principal of New College.[116] A year after his return, he wrote a work against antinomianism titled *A Survey of the Spirituall Antichrist*. Prefixed to this work was a lengthy apologetic for his position in earlier publications against so-called "freedom of conscience."[117]

111. Douglas, *North*, 50: "What he did in effect was to call Scotland to a Holy War which would rescue England from the tyranny of Episcopacy, and bring her to the true religion. . . . *Lex Rex* is the plea of the Covenanters for the majesty of the people; for the truth that the law, and no autocrat on the throne, is king; for the creed that limitless sovereignty is the property of God alone." It was reissued with different titles in 1648 and in 1657.

112. Monarchs with the same notions include Philip II of Spain, Francis I of France, and Emperor Charles V. The notion reached a high point with King James VI of Scotland/I of England. See Douglas F. Kelly, *Systematic Theology*, vol. 1, *The God Who Is the Holy Trinity* (Fearn, Scotland: Mentor, 2008), 227.

113. Beeke and Pederson, *Puritans*, 726; and see 730 for the summary.

114. Murray, *Life*, 109, 218.

115. Douglas, *North*, 56; see Coffey, *Politics, Religion, and British Revolutions*. Some of his other writings include *The Trial and Triumph of Faith* (1645), on Matthew 15. *The Divine Right of Church Government and Excommunication* (1646) was against Erastianism and argued that church discipline should lie with ministers, not the civil magistrate. *Christ's Dying and Drawing Sinners to Himself* appeared in 1647.

116. Robert Howie was the principal author of the 1616 Scottish Confession of Faith drawn up by the General Assembly of Aberdeen. See John Macleod, *Scottish Theology* (Edinburgh: Banner of Truth, 2015), 59; Ian Hazlett, "A New Version of the Scots Confession, 1560," *Theology in Scotland* 17, no. 2 (2010): 35. Howie retired from active teaching in 1641 but kept his salary and title until his death around 1647 (Murray, *Life*, 244–45). For more on Howie, see Mark W. Elliott, "Spiritual Theology in Bruce, Howie, Johnston, Boyd, and Leighton," in *The History of Scottish Theology*, vol. 1, *Celtic Origins to Reformed Orthodoxy*, ed. David Fergusson and Mark W. Elliott, 210–24 (Oxford: Oxford University Press, 2019).

117. Published in 1648. Murray, *Life*, 252: "He continued to plead the divine right of presbytery, and to urge the opinion, that all contrary sects were heretical, and ought not to be tolerated."

In 1649 Rutherford wrote a book against religious freedom titled *A Free Disputation against Pretended Liberty of Conscience*. It was also against all forms of church polity except Presbyterianism.[118] He was convinced that there was no place for religious minorities. He differed from Richard Hooker, who had already recognized some liberty for dissent fifty years earlier.

One week before King Charles I was executed in 1649, Scotland passed the Act of Classes, which excluded non-covenanters—those who would not sign the *Solemn League and Covenant*—from both civil and military office.[119] Five days after Charles I was executed, the Scottish Parliament hailed Charles II as king.

In June 1650, Charles II arrived in Scotland and, prior to his coronation, signed the *Solemn League and Covenant*. In response to this move, in September 1650 Oliver Cromwell invaded Scotland and defeated the Scots at Dunbar. In the light of this armed attack from England, and in fear of ongoing conflict, King Charles II encouraged his followers to repeal the Act of Classes. Meanwhile, in October a group of ministers protested that the soon-to-be crowned king had accepted terms too hastily and needed to prove that he had changed his non-covenantal principles.

In December, the church's General Assembly removed the Act of Classes by passing a public resolution. Those who allowed supporters of King Charles I to return to public office in Scotland and supported the Scottish coronation of King Charles II were termed Resolutioners. Many of the Resolutioners were convinced that Presbyterianism could only be advanced by the king, since Cromwell supported an independent form of church government. Charles II was crowned on January 1, 1651, at Scone.[120]

Rutherford opposed these actions. Those who joined in opposition, coming mostly from the southwest of Scotland, became known as the Protesters. Strife between the two groups reached a crisis in 1651, when

118. Ibid., 253.

119. For more information, see Richard C. Gamble, "The Clash of King and Kirk," in *The Practical Calvinist: An Introduction to the Presbyterian and Reformed Heritage*, ed. Peter A. Lillback (Fearn, Scotland: Mentor, 2002), 217.

120. Immediately before the coronation, the king visited St Andrews, and Rutherford gave him an address in Latin on the duty of kings (Murray, *Life*, 270–71).

four Protester ministers were deposed or suspended.[121] Rutherford and the Protesters were barred from attending the General Assembly of 1651—then claimed that the assembly was invalid.

Independency gained power in England, and in 1652 Cromwell expelled the Presbyterians from the House of Commons.[122] The breach was not yet healed at the General Assembly meeting of 1653, which was the last to occur until the Restoration, by order of Cromwell.[123] Rutherford, who was in a great minority, wrote against the Resolutioners.[124] Through all this tumult, Rutherford's pen never slowed. In 1655, his *The Covenant of Life Opened* was released. The year 1658 saw his *A Survey of that Survey of the Summe of Church Discipline of Mr. Thomas Hooker*.[125] His last work appeared the following year— *Influences of the Life of Grace*.[126]

Oliver Cromwell died in 1658, and his son Richard succeeded him for a year. But there was a swift move to reestablish the monarchy and return to the religious practices of the days prior to the civil war. Rutherford's violent opposition to the Resolutioners resulted in trouble for him when the monarchy was restored in 1660. A group of twelve Protesters gathered at Edinburgh and were arrested. They were eventually released.[127] The Scottish Parliament met on January 1, 1661, and recalled the "Solemen League and Covenant" and abolished Presbyterianism. By the Act Rescissory, they determined that all acts of Parliament since 1638 promoting Presbyterianism and the *Solemn League and Covenant* were annulled and illegal.[128]

With these significant changes, Rutherford's end was in sight. He was charged with treason; he was deprived of his church, faculty position, and stipend; his *Lex Rex* was ordered to be burned; his

121. Bailey wrote a 1657 tract about it titled "A True Representation of the Rise, Progress, and State of the Present Divisions of the Church of Scotland" (ibid., 277).

122. Ibid., 241.

123. Ibid., 282. There is a 1656 letter from Rutherford to a minister in London describing the events from Rutherford's perspective (ibid., 288). Cromwell never took sides in the debate. He did deprive excommunication of civil penalty (ibid., 291).

124. This work, titled *Testimony of the Ministers of Perth and Sterling*, bore seventeen signatures. Rutherford stated on his deathbed that he felt very alone in the conflict. No one at the college or in the presbytery agreed with him (ibid., 296–300).

125. Ibid., 301.

126. Ibid., 302.

127. Ibid., 263, 310–11.

128. For more information, see Gamble, *Practical Calvinist*, 218.

presbytery was overthrown; and he was confined to house arrest. Rutherford was not alone. A number of prominent ministers were hanged. Rutherford was charged to appear for judgment, but he was already on his deathbed.[129] A few weeks before his death, he wrote *A Testimony Left by Mr. Samuel Rutherford*.[130]

If Rutherford is one of the most famous Scottish theologians of the seventeenth century, John Owen is one of the most famous English theologians of the time. He may be one of the most famous English Reformed theologians ever.

JOHN OWEN (A.D. 1616–1683)

Biography. John Owen was born the son of an Anglican minister at Stradhampton, Oxfordshire. He studied at Oxford, where in 1632 he earned the bachelor of arts and in 1635 the master of arts. In 1637 Owen left Oxford as a result of his refusal to submit to Archbishop William Laud's high-church discipline.[131]

In March 1642, Owen began his career as an author with the publication of *A Display of Arminianism*. Shortly thereafter, he married his first wife. The couple would eventually have eleven children, but only one of their children survived into adulthood. Owen served as a minister in Fordham, Essex, in 1643, as well as at Coggeshall, Essex. After preaching before Parliament, Owen was appointed dean of Christ Church, University of Oxford, by the House of Commons in 1651. He became vice-chancellor of the university in 1652 and received the doctor of divinity the following year. With the restoration of the monarchy in 1660, Owen spent the remaining years of his life in relative obscurity and, as some have argued, in a sad experience of defeat for having seen much of his life's work reversed.[132] In 1820

129. Murray, *Life*, 313, 323; Beeke and Pederson, *Puritans*, 727–28. Douglas, *North*, 58: "In 1661 the Restoration Government called in all copies of *Lex Rex* as a work poisonous and treasonable; its author had six months earlier been cited to answer the charge of treason, and only fast-failing health prevented his ultimate encounter with the royal hangman."

130. Murray, *Life*, 316.

131. Peter Toon, *God's Statesman: The Life and Work of John Owen—Pastor, Educator, Theologian* (Exeter: Paternoster, 1971).

132. Andrew Thomson, *John Owen: Prince of Puritans* (repr., Fearn, Scotland: Christian Focus, 2004); Crawford Gribben, *John Owen and English Puritanism: Experiences of Defeat*

his complete works were published in twenty-three volumes, and a twenty-four-volume set appeared in 1850.[133]

Atonement. Owen made significant contributions to the doctrines of justification and sanctification. To combat the view of conditional, or hypothetical, universalism as advocated by John Cameron and Moises Amyraout, in 1647 Owen wrote his treatise *The Death of Death in the Death of Christ*.[134] Owen's response to the heterodox teaching was strong and clear: salvation comes only by divine agency; God is both merciful and just and does not offer salvation to all; hence, Owen reasoned, any suggestion of a universal atonement is a contradiction.[135]

In 1649, the Puritan Richard Baxter had attempted to resolve some of the problems connected with soteriological antinomianism in Britain when he published *Aphorisms on Justification*. Baxter's work was meant to oppose the antinomians yet also to accommodate parts of their teaching in places where Baxter deemed possible. But accommodation is only possible when the two theological principles are not entirely antagonistic. Several scholars have argued that Baxter's attempt to accommodate antinomian teaching wrongly moved the ground of justification. Baxter's work was then defended by others, thus fanning the flames of debate.[136]

In 1652, Owen also wrote *A Dissertation on Divine Justice*. This treatise marked a shift from his earlier position found in *The Death of Death*.[137] The theological issue at hand was whether Christ's death was because of God's will or because of his vindicatory justice. The WCF did not explicitly speak to this debate.[138] Historically, Calvin had grounded the necessity of Christ's death not on God's vindicatory justice but on an act of God's will. Many seventeenth-century British theologians adopted Calvin's position—theologians including Ruther-

---

(Oxford: Oxford University Press, 2017).

133. Edward Hindson, ed., *Introduction to Puritan Theology* (Grand Rapids: Baker, 1976), 141–43.

134. John Owen, *The Works of John Owen*, ed. William H. Goold, 16 vols. (Edinburgh: Banner of Truth, 1965), vol. 10.

135. Johnson and Leith, *Reformed Reader*, 224.

136. Owen, *Works*, 5:3.

137. See Carl Trueman, "John Owen's Dissertation on Divine Justice: An Exercise in Christocentric Scholasticism," *Calvin Theological Journal* 33, no. 1 (1998), 89.

138. Ibid., 91.

ford and Twisse. But Owen became convinced that this position was fundamentally incorrect and thus wrote his *Dissertation*.

Justification. Published in 1677, Owen's *The Doctrine of Justification by Faith through the Imputation of the Righteousness of Christ: Explained, Confirmed, and Vindicated* was the fruit of three decades of his lecturing, preaching, and publishing.[139] He began this work by explaining that he was not attempting to interact with anyone in particular. Instead, his stated aim was simply to open the Scriptures.[140] Owen emphasized the significance of this doctrinal debate.[141] To him the issue was whether salvation is related to anything that sinners do or is found solely and exclusively in Christ. The proper conclusion, according to Owen, is that salvation must be found solely in Christ.

But the doctrine of justification by faith in Christ is also the fundamental principle of the Christian's daily walk.[142] In that light, believers must be convinced that they are walking correctly so that they may maintain clear consciences.[143] The path to correct teaching, according to Owen, is the study of Scripture and the reflection on our experience of biblical truths.[144]

The first step to a proper understanding of justification is for believers to remember that they are to appear before God Almighty as judge. Understanding God as judge, with all his greatness, power, majesty, righteousness, and holiness, will drive the lost sinner to inquire what the Scriptures promise to them as their relief and refuge.[145] Believers must understand that they are devoid of any righteousness in themselves.[146] Righteousness, so as to enable one to appear before God, must be of divine type and origin.[147] Owen reasoned that a proper view of God and man will safeguard men from a number of errors, including Pelagianism and Socinianism.[148]

---

139. See Whitney G. Gamble, "John Owen on Justification by Faith," in *Handbook of John Owen*, ed. John Tweeddale and Crawford Gribben (Edinburgh: T&T Clark, forthcoming).
140. Owen, *Works*, 5:4.
141. Ibid., 5:5.
142. Ibid., 5:10.
143. Ibid.
144. Ibid., 5:11.
145. Ibid., 5:13, 19.
146. Ibid., 5:26.
147. Ibid., 5:27.
148. Ibid., 5:20–23.

Owen began with the original covenant in the garden of Eden to explain that the way of renewed fellowship between a sinless God and sinful humanity may be beyond reason, but it is still comprehensible.[149] In fact, Owen argued that unless the history of redemption is understood and believed, it is not possible to have a proper view of justification.[150] Thus Owen taught that such knowledge is not reserved for theologians and academics but is also meant by God for common believers.[151]

Specifically, Owen taught that in union with Christ, the redeemed sinner's iniquity is imputed to Christ, and Christ's righteousness is imputed to the sinner.[152] The union of Christ and the sinner is so intimate that believers should, and must, see themselves as truly righteous in God's eyes. Owen commented:

> Being ingrafted unto Christ, fastened, united unto him, he makes his things ours, communicates his riches unto us, interposeth his righteousness between the judgment of God and our unrighteousness: and under that, as a under a shield and buckler, he hides us from that divine wrath which we have deserved, he defends and protects us therewith; yea, he communicates it unto us and makes it ours.[153]

This union is a sweet protection by which believers are hidden "under the precious purity of the First-born, our eldest brother, . . . fragrant with his sweet savor, and have our sin buried and covered with his perfections, that we may present ourselves before our most holy Father, to obtain from him the blessing of righteousness."[154]

While this union with Christ, in which sin is given to Christ and his righteousness is given to believers, is an entirely divine act, still, by faith believers are meant to perform what is required of them.[155] The free, unmerited justification through and in Christ is not inconsistent with the demand for personal holiness and obedience, exercised

149. Ibid., 5:44–47.
150. Ibid., 5:47–48.
151. Ibid., 5:49.
152. Ibid., 5:35.
153. Ibid., 5:39.
154. Ibid., 5:39.
155. Ibid., 5:40.

through faith, in the life of the believer.[156] Grace is the motivation for this life of obedience.[157]

One of the main questions of Owen's time was the ground of justification—whether it is founded on Christ's active obedience, his fulfillment of God's law in its entirety, or on his passive obedience, his suffering and death.[158] Theologians agreed that the believer's sin is given to Christ, but there were some who argued that the Gospels are silent concerning Christ's righteousness imputed to believers.[159] Within the Reformed community, some argued that only Christ's suffering and death, his passive obedience, is imputed to sinners.[160] Johannes Piscator (1546–1625), a German Reformed professor at Herborn, and the Scotsman Robert Rollock (1555–1599) both argued that remission of sins is found only in Christ's passive obedience.[161] For them, Christ's righteousness is not imputed to the believer.[162] Owen, however, recognized that the only true ground for eternal life is perfect obedience to the Law. God requires this righteousness for one's appearing before him. If Christ's active obedience is not imputed, then a human-merit system can be introduced.[163]

Owen moved to the causes and objects of justifying faith. He understood true faith, as presented in Scripture, to be twofold. The first type of faith is simple believing. This faith does not purify the heart or work in love and is thus ultimately inadequate. This type of faith is sometimes referred to as "historical faith" because it is similar to the faith that someone has regarding historical information.[164] "Justifying faith" is entirely different.[165]

Owen set up his definition of justifying faith in opposition to the Catholic view, which understood faith simply as an assent to divine

156. Ibid., 5:53.
157. Ibid., 5:54.
158. See chapter 18 for an account of the debate on this issue at the Westminster Assembly.
159. Ibid., 5:58–60. This was Socinus's objection.
160. Ibid., 5:63.
161. Buchanan, *The Doctrine of Justification: An Outline of Its History in the Church and of Its Exposition from Scripture* (1984; repr., Edinburgh: Banner of Truth, 1991), 174; Robert Letham, *The Westminster Assembly: Reading Its Theology in Historical Context* (Phillipsburg, NJ: P&R Publishing, 2009), 39, 217.
162. This position also seems to be Gataker's (see Letham, *Westminster Assembly*, 91).
163. Buchanan, *Justification*, 175.
164. Owen, *Works*, 5:71–72.
165. Ibid., 5:73–74.

revelation.[166] Justifying faith includes assent, but it is also much more.[167] True faith requires that the justified sinner understand that there is not simply forgiveness in general but forgiveness specifically for him.[168] Justifying faith comes only after conviction of sin.[169] To have justifying faith, one must first hear the Law's rigorous demands.[170] Through the Law the eyes of sinners are opened to the stench of their sin; however, the sinner's subsequent repentance is neither preparation for nor a condition of the believer's justification.[171]

The proper object of faith is Christ and his work.[172] Faith is an act of the soul in which people who are convicted of their sins look to Christ for propitiation for those sins.[173] Justifying faith is exercised in the prayer that sinners offer when they request that Christ's benefits of mediation be applied to them.[174] Faith is the instrumental cause of justification, and the cause of faith is God's grace. The object of our faith is given to us by God, but the use of it is our own.[175] We are justified by the imputation of Christ's righteousness, which is apprehended by faith. Faith is not the condition of the imputation, nor is it a disposition for its introduction. In other words, faith is not a congruous merit.[176]

The effect of faith is pardon for sin, and the means of communicating Christ and his benefits are the promises of the gospel.[177] Owen concluded that believers come to God the Father in Christ's name so that they may be "made partakers of what he hath designed and promised to communicate unto poor sinners by him. And this represents the complete object of our faith."[178]

Sanctification. Owen's teaching on justification is clear and helpful, but he is perhaps most famous for his work on sanctification. Specifically, his treatises that deal with two aspects of sanctification,

166. Ibid., 5:80.
167. Ibid., 5:81.
168. Ibid., 5:84.
169. Ibid., 5:74.
170. Ibid., 5:75.
171. Ibid., 5:79, 82.
172. Ibid., 5:85, 89.
173. Ibid., 5:91.
174. Ibid., 5:92.
175. Letham, *Westminster Assembly*, 110–11.
176. Ibid., 112.
177. Owen, *Works*, 5:87.
178. Ibid., 5:92.

perseverance and mortification of sin, are examples of stellar theological thinking. In response to John Goodwin's 1642 work on justification, *Imputatio fidei*, in 1654 Owen wrote *The Doctrine of the Saints' Perseverance Explained and Confirmed*. Goodwin, not to be confused with the Westminster divine Thomas Goodwin, wrongly maintained that God did not impute Christ's righteousness to believers but, instead, imputed believers' faith for their righteousness.[179]

Owen began his long work by defining *perseverance*.[180] For saints, perseverance to the end is a result of God's unchangeable decree, which is rooted in God's unchangeable character.[181] Perseverance is bestowed on believers by grace. This grace comes to the believer because he has a principle of new life and the habit of faith.[182]

In believers' salvation, Christ gives the Holy Spirit and all that accompanies salvation, takes their sin upon himself, and actively imputes his righteousness to them. He takes them into an everlasting covenant, with innumerable promises that he will be their God and he will preserve them to be his people.[183] Each day he increases faith, love, and holiness within them, strengthens them, and cares for them in their backsliding with the healing balms of the gospel. In the light of those promises and covenant, God will keep in gospel obedience those who are his own.[184]

Owen demonstrated from patristic sources that this teaching has been the position of the church throughout her history.[185] Ambrose, for example, saw perseverance seated in predestination, Christ's complete redemption, and his continual intercession.[186] Medieval teaching did not break from this pattern.[187]

The doctrine of perseverance seals God's mercy and grace to believers in the new covenant, based on God's unchangeableness and faithfulness. Believers must know this doctrine, for it affects their practical walk with God. It causes them to realize that they have been built

179. Ibid., 11:2
180. Ibid., 11:21.
181. Ibid., 11:22–28.
182. Ibid., 11:20–21.
183. Ibid., 11:22.
184. Ibid., 11:23.
185. Ibid., 11:58.
186. Ibid., 11:59.
187. Ibid., 11:70.

on a rock.[188] God supplies his children with what they need for this walk, but they, knowing their frailty, must be humble.[189] While there are some who fall away and others who are crippled with doubt, we can do all things through him who strengthens us. Believers can have a measure of assurance through their own conscience concerning their walk with God.[190] Those in Christ can have confidence that while Adam was in a covenant of works, believers in Christ are in the permanent covenant of grace.[191]

God has given believers faith that as Christ was raised, so also will they be raised to new life, as well as faith that God has already made them entirely new creatures. Believers are indwelt by the same Spirit who dwells in Christ—Christ as the head and believers as members of the body. By that indwelling of the Spirit, believers know that God will always be faithful to supply his children with what they need.[192]

Owen then began defining *indwelling sin.* Indwelling sin is deep within believers and, sadly by nature, is a familiar friend.[193] It touches and meddles with every inch of believers' lives.[194] It draws them into war and makes their flesh its captive. Believers have no natural power to incline their hearts to Christ, to do any spiritual good.[195] But despite indwelling sin, saints presently enjoy spiritual glory from two vantage points. Extrinsic to believers is God's favor and free acceptance in Christ. Within believers is sanctification, the fruit of love, faith, and obedience to him.[196] The believer can rest in knowing that these benefits cannot be broken or withdrawn. And as though that were not enough, believers also have the mercy of the covenant of grace. Thus, while believers can entangle themselves with shameful and sinister sins, they can never fall from the state of regeneration. They cannot move from being a child of God to a child of the Devil. This permanent state is one of the defining characteristics of the covenant of grace.[197]

188. Ibid., 11:78–80.
189. Ibid., 11:81.
190. Ibid., 11:84–86.
191. Ibid., 11:88–89.
192. Ibid., 11:98–99.
193. Ibid., 11:105.
194. Ibid., 11:106.
195. Ibid., 11:107–12.
196. Ibid., 11:117–18.
197. Ibid., 11:118–19.

Owen made four arguments as to why believers persevere. First, they persevere as an outflow of the immutability of the divine nature. God's nature does not change. He cannot and will not change his love toward those whom he has graciously accepted.[198] Believers have been utterly transformed in their regeneration. Believers were dead in their sins, but they are now alive in Christ. A saint's continuation depends on God's irrevocable grace, not on that believer's efforts.[199] The grace shown toward believers is based on God's character—his power and immutability.[200] Second, perseverance is based on the immutability of God's purposes. Those who are effectually called are necessarily saved. The opposite is also true: those who remain in wickedness were never called.[201] Third, perseverance is a result of the covenant of grace. God promises to be his people's God forever.[202] All the conditions of the covenant are met by God, not by men.[203] Fourth, perseverance is rooted in God's promises. God's gospel promises are demonstrations of God's love for sinners through Christ in a covenant of grace, in which he promises to be their God.[204] Christ atones for believers, and then the Holy Spirit abides in them and pours out on them all the things necessary for bringing them to enjoy him.[205] The promises of perseverance are of two kinds: God's continuing favor toward us—justification— and the believer's continuing obedience to God—sanctification. These promises are wholly dependent on God, not the believer.[206]

The focus of perseverance is on Christ's work.[207] Christ has paid the debt of sin in full, thus there is no condemnation. God's vindicatory justice has no charge against Christ's people. Christ's work cannot be separated from his procuring the Holy Spirit for his people. And the Spirit unchains believers from the power of sin so that it may no longer reign over them.[208] Believers must, then, learn to view them-

198. Ibid., 11:120–23.
199. Ibid., 11:124–25.
200. Ibid., 11:126–27.
201. Ibid., 11:174.
202. Ibid., 11:207.
203. Ibid., 11:210–17.
204. Ibid., 11:232.
205. Ibid., 11:227.
206. Ibid., 11:235–38.
207. Ibid., 11:290–96.
208. Ibid., 11:297.

selves as having died in Christ, been raised with him, and entered his holy place.[209] This explanation summarizes the believer's union with Christ.[210] In that union, the ruling of original sin, or the old man, is crucified and destroyed. Sin no longer has dominion.[211]

In the final and most significant section of his analysis, Owen stated that believers' mystical union with Christ is the Holy Spirit's personally dwelling within them—the anticipated promise of the covenant of grace.[212] Owen outlined how the Spirit guides and directs believers in the manner of their walk. Externally and morally, the Word of God establishes the way for life. Internally and efficiently, the Holy Spirit directs, leads, and carries believers along this path.[213] The Spirit leads believers to understand and embrace biblical truth, which then supports and strengthens them.[214]

Significantly, the Holy Spirit also restrains believers. There are times when believers fail in their duties; they are inclined toward evil and turn from the Spirit's guidance. Living within believers is an innate wildness that provokes them to run from God. But then something, or someone, stops their running and they cannot keep going. This saving restraint is from the indwelling Holy Spirit, who daily renews God's people in sanctifying grace.[215]

In addition to the saints' perseverance, Owen wrote famously on a topic that became the title of another book, *The Mortification of Sin*, published in 1656, two years after *Perseverance*. During this time, Owen was the dean of Christ Church and vice-chancellor of Oxford University, and he led regular lecture series for his young students on this topic. In this work, Owen has a wonderful expression: "Be killing sin or it will be killing you."[216] Even though believers have died and are alive in Christ, there can be no repose from the work of fighting sin. The effort cannot be half-hearted or simply done when it is

209. Ibid., 11:299.
210. Ibid., 11:336–41.
211. Ibid., 11:307.
212. Mystical indwelling is different from his essential filling of all things and his energetical operation of all things (ibid., 11:330). Also, the Spirit's power is stronger in some than in others and at times gives more strength or less to the same person (ibid., 11:336).
213. Ibid., 11:342.
214. Ibid., 11:344–48.
215. Ibid., 11:348–50.
216. Ibid., 6:50.

convenient; rather, it must be the constant endeavor of the believer.[217] Sin always strives for the utmost—and those who let their guard slip will be conquered. There is a contest for believers' lives and souls.[218]

Owen gave a sharp warning: when mortification proceeds from self-strength with a goal of self-righteousness, it is the epitome of false religion.[219] He then transitioned to the topic of indwelling sin. Believers have indwelling sin, which must be put to death. To put indwelling sin to death means that its power and strength must be choked and killed by the Holy Spirit. Christ's cross, by both merit and example, kills indwelling sin, but this work is carried out by degrees through all our days.[220]

Mortification is a constant duty even for the most sanctified of believers. The struggle is to keep indwelling sin from having life and power to produce works of the flesh.[221] Mortification is the weakening of habitual sins so they no longer flare up.[222] To accomplish this mortification, believers must recognize that sin is a dreadful enemy and must be destroyed. Believers must pay attention to sin even in the moments when sin is not seducing them—they must study sin's subtleties, strengths, opportunities, reasonings, strategies, and excuses. Mortification is always standing at the ready to fight sin by apprehending the sin, leading it to God's law and Christ's love, condemning it, and then putting it to death.[223] Believers can also ask God for the spiritual gifts that counter and offset sins. For example, they might plead for heavenly mindedness in their struggle with the love of this world.[224] There are two keys to true spiritual mortification of sin. The first is to hate sin simply because it is sin. The second is to love Christ in the cross.[225]

217. Ibid., 6:51.
218. Ibid., 6:54–55: "Let not man think he makes any progress in holiness who walk not over the bellies of his lusts."
219. Ibid., 6:47, 58: "Such outside endeavors, such bodily exercises, such self-performances, such merely legal duties, without the least mention of Christ or his Spirit, are varnished over with swelling words of vanity for the only means and expedients for the mortification of sin, as discover a deep-rooted unacquaintedness with the power of God and mystery of the gospel. The consideration hereof was one motive to the publishing of this plain discourse."
220. Ibid., 6:48.
221. Ibid., 6:49–50.
222. Ibid., 6:73–74.
223. Ibid., 6:77.
224. Ibid., 6:83. Of course, mortification can only be accomplished by a believer.
225. Ibid., 6:86–88.

As believers mortify the flesh, there is an increase in the power and comfort of their spiritual life. Mortification is a gift of Christ and the work of the Holy Spirit. The Holy Spirit causes believers' hearts to yearn for the fruit that is contrary to the flesh. The Spirit is a fire who ignites the roots of our deep-seated lust. He gives believers communion with Christ in his death and fellowship with him in his sufferings. Mortification is his work, yet it involves the believer's obedience.[226]

As a careful doctor of souls, Owen concluded that there are two basic problems in the Christian life. On the one hand, believers lack the power to walk obediently with God, and on the other hand, they lack peace and comfort in the Christian life. One reason for the problems is that sin weakens and darkens the soul and hinders believers' duty.[227] In contrast, mortification prunes via divine grace and makes room for the tender branches to grow.

Owen vividly described some dangerous marks of indwelling sin. Sometimes believers' own hearts plead with them to countenance their sin. God might rebuke the believer for a particular sin; then, instead of running to Christ's blood for pardon, the believer finds another way to throw off and escape God's yoke. A believer who frequently falls into sin's seduction exhibits a dangerous symptom of calloused, habitual, and deeply rooted sin. Finally, when within a believer there remains a lust that the believer knows God has dealt with in the past, the continued presence of that lust is a very dangerous symptom of indwelling sin.[228] When believers have a deep-seated, particular lust, it is commonly because they are generally negligent regarding all their sins.

Owen offered numerous antidotes to rotten patterns of sin. Mortification will not occur without both sincerity and diligence. If believers are negligent in the areas where they are not presently struggling, then there will be no relief in the current area where they are battling. Believers must have a clear and abiding sense in their minds and consciousness of the guilt, danger, and evil of sin. When neither sermon nor sickness makes believers' hearts tender, there is a very real danger that they are hardened by sin's deceitfulness. An

226. Ibid., 6:61–62.
227. Ibid., 6:64.
228. Ibid., 6:90–95.

unmortified lust harms the believer's soul. Believers grieve God when they harbor his enemies in their hearts, when Jesus's love for believers is foiled, and when his adversary is gratified. Believers then become of less value to Christ in the church and kingdom.

Owen wanted believers to load their consciences with the guilt of sin. To do this, he said they must meditate on God's holy law.[229] They must think on their sin, then think of God's law and its purity and ask our gracious God that they might be changed. They must drag their lusts to the gospel—not for relief, but for further conviction. Consider Christ on the cross, then weep.[230] Owen further advised believers to meditate on truths that serve to fill them with self-abasement and thoughts of their own vileness. This is where the use of a later theological term—the *Creator/creature distinction*—is helpful. God is infinitely high and holy, and his creation is infinitely distant from him. Owen rightly says that believers cannot bear the brilliant rays of God's glorious being. Believers must remain in awe of his majesty. No matter how advanced believers are in piety, they know little of him and have almost no familiar communion with him.[231] As humans, we have trouble with the weak rays of the sun—how much more the glistening beams of God's infinite brightness!

Even though God has revealed himself to us and has given us ways to speak about him, we do not know him as he is. How can we comprehend even that which he has revealed? Take the Trinity, for example—the subsistence of distinct persons in the same individual essence, which is altogether mysterious. We only know him by what he has done, not for who he is. We know him by the good that he has done for us rather than by his essential goodness. What we know of him, we know by faith.[232]

Positively, Owen urges believers to reflect on God's continual patience toward them throughout their life. Believers have sinned and sinned and sinned, yet God's forgiveness is continually lavished on them. Given God's deep mercy, Owen urged believers not to be

229. While Owen does not mention doing so, a great practice is regularly to read through the WLC on the Ten Commandments.
230. Ibid., 6:103–4.
231. Ibid., 6:110–11.
232. Ibid., 6:112–15.

content with their present spiritual condition. There is no place in the believer's life for anything but humility.[233]

God gives good gifts to his children, and believers are his children. When we as believers are wounded by our sin, when we are ashamed for the things that we have done that alienate us from him, then we look to him and his covenantal promises and our hearts are gently quieted. Considering those promises is the salve that cures our wounds from sin.[234] While some unbelievers may have greater theological knowledge than some believers, unbelievers do not know as they ought to know; they have no true communion with God. True believers know God in their hearts as a father in an intimate covenantal relationship, as a father who rewards his children.

It is Christ who, by faith, will kill our sin. "His blood is the great sovereign remedy for sin-sick souls. Live in this," Owen pleaded, "and you will die a conqueror; yea, you will, through the good providence of God, live to see your lust dead at your feet."[235] With the eyes of faith, we contemplate what Christ has done to mortify our lusts. By faith, we expect relief from Christ. We ourselves cannot mortify our sin because it comes by his grace. And he is ever tender, kind, and merciful.[236] He has promised us relief, he died to destroy the Devil's work, and he always fulfills his word. The means of that promised relief lies in Christ's ordinances of prayer, worship, and sacraments.[237]

One of the keys to mortification is to understand what the NT means when it says that believers are crucified with Christ. Through Christ's crucifixion and subsequent resurrection, he procured the Holy Spirit for believers to mortify sin. In his own suffering and crucifixion, Christ embodied the perfect example of a mortified life.[238] "Look on him under the weight of our sins, praying, bleeding, dying," Owen pleaded; "bring him in that condition into your heart by faith; apply his blood so shed to your corruptions. Do this daily."[239]

233. Ibid., 6:105–6.
234. Ibid., 6:119–22.
235. Ibid., 6:131.
236. Ibid., 6:133–34.
237. Ibid., 6:135–36.
238. Ibid., 6:137: Christ did so "efficiently, in that from his death virtue comes forth for our crucifying; in the way of a representation and exemplar we shall assuredly be crucified unto sin, as he was for our sin."
239. Ibid., 6:138.

As Owen drew his great work to a conclusion, he reminded his readers that mortification is exclusively the work of the Holy Spirit. Only the Spirit convinces believers' hearts of the evils of sin and lust. Believers cannot mortify sin through rational considerations. While Owen did not use the following example, note that any one of us may go on a diet or resolve to exercise more, but we cannot convince ourselves of the deep evils of our sin. It is the Spirit who convinces the soul of the evil of lust and "cuts off all its pleas, discovers all its deceits, stops all its evasions, answers its pretenses, makes the soul own its abominations and lie down under the sense of it."[240] It is the Spirit alone who brings Christ's cross into our hearts with its sin-killing power, and it is the precious Holy Spirit who is the great author and finisher of our sanctification.[241] Owen's work is a great aid to the Christian walk.

Biblical Theology. Reformation exegesis, as done by Calvin and Bullinger, was biblical-theological.[242] Owen followed this Reformed tradition with what he considered to be his greatest and most enduring contribution to Reformed theology, *Theologoumena pantodapa*, published in 1661.[243] In the nineteenth century, J. P. Gabler coined the technical term *biblical theology* to distinguish it from *dogmatic theology*, and that is the English name given to Owen's work, originally published in Latin.[244] Owen's method of "doing" theology as outlined in his *Biblical Theology* is extremely insightful and helped provide a model for the three-volume *Whole Counsel of God*.[245]

Owen's title page was meant to be descriptive of the work. He endeavored to set out theology's true nature, as well as a God-honoring method to create it.[246] A proper method was necessary to avoid frustration.[247] Owen also noted that since the ancient church, there had been competition between Plato's method and Christ's. To twist the gospel

240. Ibid.
241. Ibid., 6:139.
242. J. I. Packer, foreword to *Biblical Theology*, by John Owen (Morgan, PA: Soli Deo Gloria, 1996), xii.
243. Ibid., xviii.
244. Ibid., xi.
245. See the analysis in Richard C. Gamble, *The Whole Counsel of God*, vol. 2, *The Full Revelation of God* (Phillipsburg, NJ: P&R Publishing, 2018) (WCG2), 7–8, 29.
246. J. I. Packer, foreword to *Biblical Theology*, xxiii.
247. Ibid., xxvi.

to conform to Plato is to harm the church.[248] In coming to Christ, there must be a change in the way one thinks.[249] Proper theological method must implant in the brain and heart a yearning to live for God. Even pagan philosophers argued that method and life cannot be separated.[250]

Owen's formal definition of theology is: "The doctrine of God with regard to himself, his works, his will, his worship, as well as our required obedience, our future rewards and punishments, all as revealed by God himself to the glory of His name."[251] True theology is simply the pure teaching of God's Word, apprehended with believers' rational faculties as God has illuminated them.[252] Because true theology is, by definition, heavenly, then there can be no humanity added in—all theology revolves around God.[253] One cannot understand theology unless it is revealed to him or her by divine grace and design. All theology flows from the fact that God wishes himself to be known, and he has given Scripture to his people in order to accomplish that purpose. Thus, the believer's thoughts and theology must conform to Scripture as the revelation of the divine mind.[254] Theology is a spiritual science that makes the practitioner proficient in the gospel's mysteries and produces holy wisdom.[255] Theology must be performed by someone deeply in love with Christ.[256] That person then molds his thinking and life to Christ's pattern.[257]

Due to the heavenly nature of theology, Owen thought that it was far removed from the method of the technical sciences.[258] Theology does not consist in formalized propositions constructed as theses,

248. Ibid., xxxviii: "Already in the ancient church it was the complaint of many that Christians tried to put on Christ in such a way as not to put off Plato. Nor can it be denied that no one has ever twisted the gospel into conformity with pagan philosophy without great loss of truth and harm to the Church."

249. Ibid., xl: "With the world, indwelling sin, and early education all arguing the same way, it requires the power of the gospel of grace to change a man's thinking."

250. Ibid., xliii.

251. Ibid., 16–17.

252. Ibid., 17.

253. Ibid., 16.

254. Ibid., 15.

255. Ibid., xliv.

256. Ibid., xlvi: "Let us proclaim it boldly—the man who is not inflamed with divine love is an outsider to all theology."

257. Ibid., xlvi–xlvii: "Who will make this his decision, to make God's truth loveliest, fairest, his most-beloved, to know her well and mold himself in her pattern."

258. Ibid., 8–9.

proofs, and distinctions.[259] The theology of Christianity is simple—it ridicules subtle Aristotelian philosophy. Theology goes beyond what the natural man knows.[260] The student of theology must be instructed by the Holy Spirit. And one who is instructed by the Holy Spirit and made familiar with things that are outside the normal person's comprehension, that person is a theologian.[261] God's mysteries are divine truth and need not, and should not, be forced into either scientific or philosophical molds.[262] Owen was cognizant that his method and understanding of theology could be controversial—in his day, such startlingly simple reliance on Scripture as the basis for all theology was not commonplace.[263]

Communion with God. Owen wrote many treatises and books—space does not permit an analysis of them all! But one more work by Owen must be mentioned. Owen's *Communion with God* is a beautiful treatment of the triune God's communion with his people. Owen began by stating that the three persons of the godhead are the object of faith, but he emphasized that God the Father is the cause of and special object of faith. The Father's love flows from his character. First, God loves his own.[264] Second, this fatherly love is the fountain of all other graces.[265] His love is consistent with his character—it is constant, kind, and gentle.[266]

To have communion with God, the believer must receive the Father's love by faith and express gratitude for it. One of the ways that Owen speaks of receiving the Father's love is through the word *rest*. The believer rests in the full assurance of God's love. Even in the midst of adversity, he can rest and not grumble, for he can still delight in God.[267] Owen

259. Ibid., xlv.
260. Ibid., 7.
261. Ibid., 11.
262. Ibid., 12: "As long as scholars are willing to carve out the mysteries of divine truth as revealed from the mind of God and force them into the straitjackets of man-made and man-pleasing rules of science, or else to shackle them to I know not what philosophies (with which by nature it can have nothing in common), they will achieve nothing but to make a subject which should be most clear and certain to a rational mind, and render it most muddy, cloudy, ambiguous, labyrinthine, and obscure."
263. Ibid., xlviii.
264. Owen, *Works*, 2:6, 15–16, 21.
265. Ibid., 2:14.
266. Ibid., 2:23–25, 27–28.
267. Ibid., 2:17–18.

noted that the Father's love cannot be diminished, but it is changeable in its communication to his people. God still loves the believer when the believer sins, but God does not love that person's sin.[268] In response to this lavish, fatherly love, the believer is obligated to love God in return.[269]

While packed with theological insight, Owen's text is also eminently practical. He argued that many believers are ignorant of the mercies that are theirs in God the Father. Some can view the Father's love only as purchased through Christ's blood. But it is the Father's love that is the source of divine yearning to have communion with his people. Thus, while still holding to the Father's majesty and greatness, believers should not be ignorant of this fatherly compassion and love. The Trinity is self-sufficient, but still, the Father yearns for communion with his people and desires their happiness.[270] Knowing this truth produces change in the believer. When the believer's heart knows that God the Father's chief property toward him is love, then, "it cannot help but choose to be overpowered, conquered and embraced by him."[271] For Owen, to think often and much on the Father's love is a powerful motive to the end of the believer's holiness.[272]

FRANCIS TURRETIN (A.D. 1623–1687)[273]

Biography. Francis Turretin had the privilege of studying at the world's finest universities: Geneva, Leiden, Utrecht, Paris, Samur, Mon-

268. Ibid., 2:23–24.

269. Ibid., 2:20–23.

270. Ibid., 2:27–28, 32: "Assure yourself, then, that there is nothing more acceptable to the Father than for us to keep our hearts filled with him as the eternal source of all that rich grace which flows out to sinners in the blood of Jesus."

271. Ibid., 2:32–33: "So do this: set your thoughts on the eternal love of the Father and see if your heart is not aroused to delight in him. Sit down for a while at this delightful spring of living water and you will soon find its streams sweet and delightful."

272. Ibid., 2:37.

273. For further bibliography, see Samuel Alexander, "Turretin," *The Biblical Repertory and Princeton Review* 20 (1848): 452–63; John W. Beardslee, "Theological Development at Geneva under Francis and Jean-Alphonse Turretin (1648–1737)" (PhD diss., Yale University, 1956); Charles Eugene Edwards, "Turretin's Theology," *Princeton Theological Review* 26 (1928): 142–49; John Oliver Nelson, "The Rise of the Princeton Theology: A Genetic Study of American Presbyterianism until 1830" (PhD diss., Yale University, 1935); Martin I. Klauber, "Francis Turretin on Biblical Accommodation: Loyal Calvinist or Reformed Scholastic?," *WTJ* 55, no. 1 (Spring 1993): 73–86.

tauban, and Nimes.[274] In 1648 he was called to be a pastor of the Italian congregation in Geneva, and in 1653 he was appointed professor of theology at the university in Geneva.[275] His major theological work is the *Institutio theologiae elencticae* (1679–1685). His four-volume *Opera* in 1702 also contains a disputation, *De sacra scripturae authoritate*, which is a clear and compelling account of the verbal plenary inspiration of Scripture.[276] In this work, Turretin argued that the process of copying was protected by God. Divine preservation, however, was distinct from divine inspiration.[277] In 1675, Turretin worked with J. H. Heidegger to write the Helvetic Consensus Formula.[278]

As Theodore Beza was accused of beginning Reformed scholasticism, so Francis Turretin's theology has been wrongly judged by some to be a departure from John Calvin's theology. Some have incorrectly asserted that Calvin and Turretin held antithetical views on the doctrine of Scripture, but there is work to be done in analyzing the theological continuity between Calvin and Turretin.[279]

Analysis of the *Institutio*. In his excellent work on theology, Turretin defined theology as "a system or body of doctrine concerning God and divine things revealed by him for his own glory and the salvation of man."[280] He acknowledged a universal desire to know God. He believed that creatures were designed to worship him, thus necessitating theology. Furthermore, Turretin distinguished between the knowing subject—humans who can know—and the most knowable object—God.[281]

True theology is divided into two categories: *archetypal* and *ectypal*. Archetypal theology is God's essential knowledge of himself and that which he has decreed to reveal about himself. Ectypal knowledge is an image of the archetypal. It is the finite and created ideas of creatures

274. His father Benedict (1588–1631) was the Genevan delegate to the Synod of Dordt. While at Geneva he studied with John Diodotie and Frederick Spanheim.

275. He replaced Trochin.

276. Richard Muller, *Post-Reformation Reformed Dogmatics*, vol. 1, *Prolegomena to Theology* (Grand Rapids: Baker, 1987), 49; Johnson and Leith, *Reformed Reader*, 31.

277. Allison, *Historical Theology*, 64–69.

278. For more information on the document, see Gamble, "Switzerland," 70.

279. Ibid., 70–71.

280. Francis Turretin, *Institutes of Elenctic Theology*, ed. James T. Dennison, trans. George M. Giger (Phillipsburg, NJ: P&R Publishing, 1997), 1:2.

281. Ibid., 1:3–4.

concerning the Creator. Furthermore, true theology is divided into (1) natural, innate, and acquired knowledge of God, and (2) supernatural knowledge of God found in Scripture that transcends human reason.[282]

Focusing on natural theology, Turretin argued that men and women are born without innate knowledge; they are born with blank slates. He concluded that humans develop theology through interaction with the world. Such knowledge is sufficient for people to know that God exists and that he deserves to be worshipped. But this knowledge cannot save. In fact, the natural person stifles this knowledge deep within so that sin may be given more free reign.[283]

God and divine things comprise the object of theology. That object may be considered materially, when God is the primary object considered, or formally, when Scripture is the mode used to consider. This fact makes theology a distinct science, superior to all other sciences.[284] But theology is not something known, as in Aristotle's five intellectual habits; rather, it is something believed, as it is based on revelation, not human reason.[285] Furthermore, theology is both theoretical and practical. God is to be both known and worshipped.[286]

Middle Knowledge. Turretin participated in a debate on middle knowledge relative to the doctrine of God. The Catholic theologian Luis de Molina (1535–1600) had developed the notion of God's middle knowledge, which supposedly eased the apparent contradiction between human free will and predestination. There are, according to Molina, three ways in which God knows.

God's natural knowledge is that knowledge he possesses of all actual things—past, present, and future—but all possible things as well. God's free knowledge is his knowledge of the things that he has decreed will necessarily take place; it is his knowledge of what certainly will be. God's middle knowledge is his knowledge of all things that can take place involving an act of the human will. God knows these options before he freely chooses to decree something about them. God's middle

282. Ibid., 1:4–5.
283. Ibid., 1:6–9.
284. Ibid., 1:16–18.
285. Ibid., 1:18–20.
286. Ibid., 1:20–23.

knowledge includes what would be if circumstances were not what they are. Middle knowledge includes all conditional future choices and events—choices and events that involve some act of human will.[287]

Lutheran theologians sided with Molina regarding middle knowledge, but Turretin and Reformed theologians rejected it. Middle knowledge was rightly rejected because, while it grants that God knows what free agents will do, that knowledge is without a special decree that precedes it. God has predestined choices and events according to his good pleasure, not because he has foreknown that free agents would believe or obey. Middle knowledge comes not from God, but from the willing itself.[288]

With middle knowledge, human choice does not necessarily originate in divine foreknowledge or predestination, though it coheres with both; rather, choices stem from the created being freely willing to do an action. God foreknew that choice, because the being's freely chooses to do that thing in the circumstance in which he finds himself.[289]

Turretin and Reformed theologians, against Lutheran theologians, rejected middle knowledge because it asserts that both humans and angels make choices apart from a special decree that precedes them. Middle knowledge practically eliminates God's sovereignty because choice is prior to decree and springs from the will itself.[290]

Turretin also faced a number of opponents relative to the doctrine of God. The Socinians argued about God's knowledge of future contingent things that depend on human choices. The Socinians said that God cannot have this type of knowledge. They wanted to preserve the human will from any causal conditions that might incline the will to one direction. Thus God's decree cannot thwart human decisions. Turretin argued that God has infallible knowledge of the future.[291]

Turretin also addressed an eschatological issue that was dividing Protestants. The issue regarded the state of the earth at the end of time. The Lutheran position was that it would be destroyed. The other position, and the one that Turretin supported, was that the earth would be

287. Allison, *Historical Theology*, 221.
288. Ibid., 222.
289. Ibid., 221–22.
290. Ibid., 222.
291. Ibid., 220.

significantly transformed. He concluded also that speculation should be limited in such matters.[292]

PETRUS VAN MASTRICHT (A.D. 1630–1706)

Biography. The Schoning family was from the city of Mastricht but was forced to flee in 1579 when Spanish troops overthrew the city. Upon settling in Cologne, the family adopted the family name *van Mastricht*. The young Petrus attended the University of Utrecht and studied under Gisbertus Voetius. Upon completion of his studies, Petrus accepted a call to be an assistant pastor in Xanten in 1653. After nearly a decade there, he moved to Glückstadt in Schleswig-Holstein, where he pastored from 1662 to 1667.

He then received an invitation to Brandenburg to become a professor of Hebrew and practical theology at the University of Frankfurt (Oder), where he taught for three years. He left there to teach a number of subjects as a member of both the theology and philosophy faculty at the fifteen-year-old University of Duisburg. He remained in Duisburg from 1670 to 1677. After a decade of university instruction, Petrus was then called by the University of Utrecht, where he stayed for the rest of his life.[293]

Writings. His first theological publication, from 1666 and abbreviated the *Prodromus*, or *Forerunner*, is a shorter work on human creation, humility before God, and walking with God; it was written using a similar method as his later work.[294] In 1669, he wrote his second volume on preaching, *Methodus concionandi*, while teaching at Frankfurt (Oder). A third work, on the nature of saving faith, appeared in 1671. His philosophical writing against Descartes, aptly named *The Gangrene of the Cartesian Novelties*, appeared in 1677 and was later reprinted. His most significant work, *Theoretical-Practical Theology*, is now appearing for the first time in English.[295]

292. Ibid., 729.
293. Adriaan Neele, "Life and Work," in *Theoretical-Practical Theology*, vol. 1, *Prolegomena*, by Petrus van Mastricht, ed. Joel R. Beeke, trans. Todd M. Rester (Grand Rapids: Reformation Heritage Books, 2018), xxvi–xxxvii.
294. Ibid., xxix.
295. Petrus van Mastricht, *Theoretical-Practical Theology*, trans. Todd M. Rester, ed. Joel R. Beeke (Grand Rapids: Reformation Heritage Books, 2018).

HERMANN WITSIUS (A.D. 1636–1708)

Biography. Hermann Witsius was born in 1636 in West Friesland.[296] His studies began under his uncle; then, at the age of fifteen, he went to the University of Utrecht at the time when Voetius was a professor there and studied Syriac and Arabic. He wrote an oration in the Hebrew language at the age of eighteen. In 1654, he then studied at Groningen under Samuel Maresius.

Witsius was ordained in 1657 at the age of twenty-one. He began his ministry at Westwoud and was married in 1660. In 1661 he moved to the large congregation at Wormeren, where he offered public lectures that were published. Two of these works were *The Practice of Christianity* and *On the Regenerate and Unregenerate*. In 1666 Witsius moved to Goes, Zeeland, and two years later to Leeuwarden, the capital of West Friesland.

In 1675 Witsius was appointed a pastor and professor of theology at Franeker. His inaugural address, "On the Character of a True Theologian," was published by the Free Church of Scotland in 1856 and given, free of charge, to divinity students.[297] He was then called from 1680 to 1698 to a professorship at Utrecht, where his wife died in 1684. He had two sons, who died young, as well as three daughters.[298] After Utrecht, he taught as a professor of theology at Leiden from 1698 to 1707. He performed no pulpit work there—he was a sickly man and suffered a stroke six years before his death. His health declined to the extent that he had to retire in 1707; he died one year later.[299]

His major dogmatic works were *De oeconomia foederum Dei cum hominibus libri quattuor* (first edition, 1677; second edition, 1685; third edition, 1694); the two-volume *Exercitationes sacrae in*

---

296. "Memoir of Witsius," in *Sacred Dissertations on the Apostles' Creed*, trans. Donald Fraser (Edinburgh: A. Fullarton & Co, 1823), xi–xxix; reprinted Escondido, CA: Den Dulk Foundation, 1993), 1:xi: "Before he was 15 he could not only speak and write the Latin language correctly, but was minutely acquainted with Greek and Hebrew."

297. Beeke and Pederson, *Puritans*, 811, 823.

298. Witsius, "Memoir of Witsius," 1:xi–xiv. Witsius could also preach in French.

299. Ibid., 1:xi: "He spent many nights totally without sleep, and spared no effort to advance literature and piety. His great labors and frequent watchings, ill suited to a feeble constitution, were probably carried to an injudicious excess."

symbolum, quod apostolorum dicitur (1681); and another work on the Lord's Prayer (1689).[300]

Theological World. Witsius's theology follows the Dutch theologian Cocceius's in many ways. As mentioned earlier, there was great controversy between Cocceius and Voetius. But Witsius saw value in both their approaches. Like Cocceius, Witsius used the covenant as his organizing fulcrum.[301] He agreed with Cocceius on the nature of the eternal covenant, which was centered on the agreement between the Father and the Son.[302] Christ took the obligations of the covenant of works as surety for the elect. To fulfill those responsibilities, he had to become man and place himself under the Law. A multilateral covenant of redemption was foundational for the unilateral covenant of grace. The covenant of grace is between the triune God and the elect.[303] Thus one can conclude that Witsius, in balanced form, represented Cocceius's covenantal thought.[304]

Economy of Covenants. In Witsuis's work *Economy of the Covenants*, he defined a covenant as a mutual agreement between parties with respect to a matter. Specifically, a covenant is an agreement between God and man to obtain ultimate blessedness, with threats against anyone who despises that blessedness.[305] Divine-human covenants are monopleuric in initiation, while dipleuric in administration.[306] The covenant of works had essential aspects: God and man were the parties, the condition of the covenant was perfect obedience, the promise of the covenant was eternal life, and death was the penal sanction.

300. Muller, *Post-Reformation*, 49. His work on the Lord's Prayer was first published in English in 1736. See Ward, *God and Adam*, 142. He taught that the covenant of works was abiding. See Hermann Witsius, *The Economy of the Covenants*, 2 vols. (Escondido, CA: The den Dulk Christian Foundation, 1990), l.ix.151.

301. J. I. Packer, "Introduction: On Covenant Theology," in *The Economy of the Covenants*, by Hermann Witsius, 2 vols. (Escondido, CA: The den Dulk Christian Foundation, 1990), 1:v: "Witsius concedes to the Cocceans who had insisted 'that the only way to organize theology and set out Christian truths was in terms of the historical unfolding of God's covenant dealings.'" Beeke and Pederson, *Puritans*, 812: "In governing his concept of systematic theology by the concept of covenant, Witsius uses Coccean methods while maintaining essentially Voetian theology."

302. Ward, *God and Adam*, 115–16. Following Cocceius, he also rejected Twisse's idea that God's freedom was so great that he could have forgiven sin without satisfaction. He agreed with Cocceius that the Sabbath was a third sacrament given as a pledge of blessed rest with God.

303. Johnson and Leith, *Reformed Reader*, 228.

304. Ward, *God and Adam*, 77.

305. Witsius, *Economy*, 1.1.5–5, 9.

306. Ibid., 1.1.15.

The covenant also included as sacraments of paradise the tree of life, the tree of the knowledge of good and evil, and the Sabbath.[307] The *pactum salutis* (the covenant of salvation), enacted between God the Father and God the Son in eternity, was foundational.[308]

Regarding human salvation, Witsius discussed union with Christ and election.[309] He stated that election is in Christ, and Christ is the elect of God. The names of the elect are written in what he calls the "book of life of the Lamb." He uses *book of life* as a technical term "because the Lamb takes up the first page of that book, is the head of the rest of the elect."[310]

WILHELMUS À BRAKEL (A.D. 1635–1711)

Theological Understandings. The next great theologian to contribute to the story is Wilhelmus à Brakel, a deeply pious man for whom the name of Jesus was sweeter than honey.[311] À Brakel saw the time from Adam to Christ as an age of promise in which Christ's nature, as well as his suffering and death, were presented to God's people so that they could become familiar with him and believe in him.[312] À Brakel understood the OT era as having begun at the first promise in Paradise, not at Mount Horeb.[313] He argued that the time before Mount Horeb should not be called the time of promise, nor should there be a difference in meaning between the words *covenant* and *testament*.[314]

The OT church (OT Israel, or "the church under age," as understood in the Reformed tradition) can be separated into different epochs. Adam was in a covenant of works. A new covenant was announced in

---

307. Ibid., 1.6.
308. Ibid.
309. "Witsius offers an exposition of faith completely orthodox in content but woven in the rich language of piety that characterized the late seventeenth century Dutch Reformed" (Johnson and Leith, *Reformed Reader*, 242; Witsius, *Economy*, 3.4.7).
310. Witsius, *Economy*, 3.4.2; 1:325; and see 1:342–43.
311. Wilhelmus à Brakel, *The Christian's Reasonable Service*, trans. Bartel Elshout, 4 vols. (Grand Rapids: Reformation Heritage Books, 1995), 1:xxi: "For à Brakel the name of Jesus is sweeter than honey; you can almost sense the inner stirrings of His soul when he exalts Jesus as the Father's unspeakable gift to fallen sons and daughters of Adam."
312. Ibid., 4:373.
313. Ibid., 4:385; and see 4:387.
314. Ibid., 4:385.

Genesis 3:15. In that new covenant a promise was made to the woman (Eve). There was to be a seed of the woman who would crush the head of the serpent (Satan). That promised seed is Christ.

There is also a distinction between the church before and after Abraham. Before Abraham, the church was comprised of different nationalities, much as in the NT church. À Brakel understood there to be six transformations after the time of Abraham.[315] This was a time of national covenant when "the covenant of grace [was] established with that particular nation."[316]

Types and Shadows. À Brakel guided his readers in thinking through the nature of OT types and shadows. Christ was not defined by the types—it was the types that were defined according to Christ. The pious Israelite saw the image of Christ in the type. À Brakel used an analogy of a man by a fence who can see the shadow of a person. From the shadow, the person can determine whether the shadow is male or female and whether the person is standing or sitting. In the same way, the OT sacrifices were shadows of Christ.[317] For determining types, à Brakel utilized hermeneutical rules, which were as follows: students of the Bible are to think soberly and not allegorize; even the word *type* does not always mean that the referent is a type; in the NT, there are allusions that are not necessarily types; there is allegory in the Bible; allegories are not types.[318] A type has to be carefully defined. It is "something ordained of God prior to the coming of Christ, to typify the Savior who was to come." To be a type, it had to be appointed by God as such.

À Brakel argued that there are some biblical characters who should not be considered types. For example, Adam, Abel, Enoch, and Noah are not types of Christ. In addition, Adam and Eve's garments were not types of Christ's righteousness. The ark is not a type of Christ, and neither is Hagar. Also, the flood was not a sacrament of the covenant of grace, nor was it a type of baptism.[319]

À Brakel also noted that there were OT shadows. The nature of these shadows was not punitive nor burdensome but one of divine

315. Ibid., 4:395.
316. Ibid., 4:375.
317. Ibid., 4:374.
318. Ibid., 4:377–81.
319. Ibid., 4:382.

blessing. These shadows were instructions about Christ—instructions depicting Christ and leading the faithful to him.[320] Since in the OT sins were atoned for by Christ prior to his incarnation, "the sacrifices and typical ministry of . . . [them] had to cease and be annulled by virtue of their fulfillment through Christ."[321] À Brakel understood there to be an essential continuity between the Mosaic covenant and previous postlapsarian covenants. In other words, the OT did not begin at Sinai.[322] He denied that the Ten Commandments constituted a covenant of works.[323]

The OT sacrificial system pointed to Christ. When someone offered a sacrifice, he was to remember his sins and be humbled. Those offering knew that their sacrifices could not remove sin, but the shadows of the sacrifices whispered of their substance in Christ. In this fashion, all OT sacrifices were of an identical nature. "Religion prior to and after Moses does not differ as to nature and sort—nor is there a difference between the state of the church prior to and after Moses."[324]

In the midst of these theologians' lives, ministry, and theological writings, there were some further doctrinal controversies that played out. These controversies established what would, and what would not, be Reformed Orthodoxy.

THEOLOGICAL DEBATES: ANTINOMIANISM

Antinomianism goes back to the garden of Eden; it began with Adam, who defied God's law. In the sixteenth and seventeenth centuries, antinomianism was a complex and dangerous reality.[325] Antinomianism denies "in some way the ongoing relevance of some part or even the whole of the moral law."[326]

---

320. Ibid., 4:393.

321. Ibid., 4:388–89.

322. Ibid., 4:389–92: "The essence of this covenant was no different from the covenant God made with Abraham, Isaac, and Jacob, and with Israel at Horeb." He also addressed many objections to his position.

323. Ward, *God and Adam*, 133; see also à Brakel, *Reasonable Service*, 3:44.

324. À Brakel, *Reasonable Service*, 4:394.

325. Mark Jones, *Antinomianism: Reformed Theology's Unwelcome Guest?* (Phillipsburg, NJ: P&R Publishing, 2013), 1.

326. Whitney G. Gamble, *Christ and the Law: Antinomianism at the Westminster Assembly* (Grand Rapids: Reformation Heritage Books, 2018), 1.

In Germany. Debate erupted in the sixteenth century between the team of Luther and Melanchthon against their former colleague Johann Agricola (1494–1566). Agricola had been with Luther when he posted his ninety-five theses; he studied under Luther at Wittenberg and functioned as Luther's private secretary. Agricola had been given essential work to advance the German Reformation in the 1520s. He was nominated to the significant post of professor of theology at Wittenburg in 1526 but lost the post to Melanchthon.[327]

The theological questions centered on whether preaching the Law was required for repentance and salvation and whether the moral law was still binding on Christians.[328] Luther and Melanchthon rightly taught that the Law must be preached with the gospel. A true theologian and preacher could not preach one without the other. Melanchthon's view—that preaching the Law produces repentance—was falsely characterized as Roman Catholic.[329] Agricola disagreed with his colleagues and argued that preaching the gospel, not the Law, produces repentance. Agricola also held that good works are not necessary for the Christian.[330] In response to Agricola's claims, in 1539 Luther wrote a public letter titled *Against the Antinomians.*[331] This controversy lingered for a number of decades in Germany.

In England. In the seventeenth century many English theologians wrote against antinomianism. The antinomian movement underlined Christ's completed work of redemption to the point that there was little room for God's law to function as the guide for life and conduct.[332] The situation was exacerbated when press censorship was lifted in 1642, antinomian publications subsequently flooded London, and

327. Herman Hanko, "Johann Agricola and Antinomianism (1)," *The Standardbearer* 78, no. 16 (May 15, 2002): 373–75.

328. Jones, *Antinomianism*, 32: "Divines such as Girolamo Zanchi (1516–1590) and André Rivet (1572–1651) did not hold that the moral law as given by Moses was binding on Christians."

329. Ibid., 6.

330. Herman Hanko, "Johann Agricola and Antinomianism (2)," *The Standardbearer* 78, no. 18 (July 1, 2002): 472–76.

331. There had been an earlier public disputation on antinomianism at Wittenberg. See Luther's "First Disputation Against the Antinomians," December 18, 1537. http://www.lutheran press.com/docs/SDEA-prev-Ch1.pdf.

332. Whitney G. Gamble, "The Theology of the Westminster Confession of Faith in its Context," in *The History of Scottish Theology*, vol. 1., ed. David Fergusson and Mark W. Elliott (Oxford: Oxford University Press, 2019), 267.

hundreds went to hear antinomian preachers.[333] The English debate became theologically complicated and has been variously interpreted.[334]

One of the first issues was whether justified sinners could be chastised by God for their sin. Antinomians denied that they could be, while the Reformed gave a positive answer.[335] Another antinomian position was that God cannot "see" the believer's sin, thus he cannot become angry with that believer. Yet another question was the role of faith. The Antinomians did not view faith as the lone instrument of justification;[336] rather, they asserted that justification is found in the eternal divine decree, and the believer needs simply to remember that decree.[337]

The Westminster Assembly spent many hours debating this theology.[338] In the first few weeks they wrestled with what to do with the antinomian preachers—and especially with the issue of whether they were heretics.[339] They debated issues relative to the imputation of Christ's active and passive obedience.[340] They also had to untangle confusion concerning the relationship between the OT and the NT and the relationship between good works, the Law, and justification.[341]

In the English context a new term—*neonomian*—was coined to refer to a further twist in debate.[342] Neonomians spoke of the duties of the gospel.[343] The neonomians taught that Christ's atoning death

333. Whitney G. Gamble, "The Significance of English Antinomianism for Anna Trapnel," *Reformation & Renaissance Review* 17, no. 2 (2015): 155–66.

334. Jones, *Antinomianism*, 25–26, 36, 125–27. For a critical review of his work, see Whitney G. Gamble, "Missing the Point?," review of *Antinomianism: Reformed Theology's Unwelcome Guest?* by M. Jones, *European Journal of Theology* 21, no. 2 (2014): 192–93.

335. W. Gamble, *Christ and Law*, 3–4; and 4: "Antinomianism contorted the biblical presentation of redemption. It bifurcated the Old and New Testaments, conflated justification and sanctification, confused the nature of justifying faith, and denied punishment for sin."

336. See ibid., 109–31.

337. W. Gamble, "Westminster Confession," 268.

338. For the earliest antinomian formulations by John Eaton, see W. Gamble, *Christ and Law*, 14–20; for debates in the 1630s, see ibid., 31–37; for a deep and detailed analysis of the theological issues facing the assembly, see ibid., 39–64.

339. Ibid., 65–84, 84: "The spectre of antinomianism created in the divines an urgency to explain clearly and carefully the doctrine of justification, the place of faith and works in salvation, the nature of the relationship between the Old and New Testaments, and the role of Christ's work in redemption."

340. Ibid., 87–108.

341. Ibid., 133–54.

342. Buchanan, *Justification*, 176: "It has often been said that the publication of Dr. Crisp's writings gave rise to the Neonomian Controversy." The term was first used by Isaac Chauncy (1632–1712) to describe Richard Baxter.

343. Jones, *Antinomianism*, 11–12.

was sufficient to bring all men and women to salvation. Christ procured a new law—the law of grace, which was different from the law of works. In this new law, the terms of salvation are easier. God no longer requires perfect obedience from sinners—instead, he requires sincere, even imperfect, obedience. Christ is still the believer's legal righteousness; it is the sinner's plea against the old law's demand. But "the immediate ground of our justification is, not the imputed righteousness of Christ, but the inherent, personal righteousness of the believer himself, which begins with faith, grows with sanctification, and is completed and made sure only by final perseverance."[344] John Owen was opposed to antinomianism, but neither was he a neonomian.[345] Similarly to Owen, William Ames argued for the necessity of good works simply because they were commanded.[346] The wretched heresy of antinomianism was a significant movement across Europe.[347]

Theological Debates: Pietism

In General. Pietism was the reigning theological school in Germany from 1692 to 1730. Some of Pietism's roots can be located in Roman Catholic mysticism, a sub-category of the movement called Jansenism, and in English Puritanism and Quakerism. In general, Pietism broke away from scholasticism, emphasized the emotional aspects of humanity and Christianity, and had a negative view of the Christian's relationship to the world. Pietism was also a countermovement to seventeenth-century German Lutheranism.[348]

344. Buchanan, *Justification*, 177–78.

345. Jones, *Antinomianism*, 12n29. On Owen's opposition to antinomianism and his scholastic distinctions used in the debate, see Gert van den Brink, "Impetration and Application in John Owen's Theology," in *The Ashgate Research Companion to John Owen's Theology*, ed. Kelly M. Kapic and Mark Jones (Farnham, England: Ashgate, 2012); ibid., 12: "Thus, the antinomian debates in the latter part of the seventeenth century revealed that just as there is a spectrum of antinomian theology (Saltmarsh vs. Crisp), so also is there a spectrum of neonomian theology (Baxter vs. Williams), as well as slight disagreement among orthodox theologians in expressing certain points of Reformed theology (Goodwin vs. Owen)."

346. Jones, *Antinomianism*, 69.

347. The NT's use of the indicative and imperative addresses many of the issues; see *WCG* 2:645–75, 738, 799; and the whole of chapter 22, 2:862–908; see also *WCG* 2:572.

348. D. Martyn Lloyd-Jones, "Ecclesiola in Ecclesia," in *Puritan Papers*, ed. J. I. Packer, 5 vols. (Phillipsburg, NJ: P&R Publishing, 2004), 4:85.

There are at least four characteristics to seventeenth- and eighteenth-century Pietism. Pietism first emphasized lively internal religion, which meant religion of heart-piety, self-introspection, and private devotions. The second main characteristic of Pietism was the significance of personal works of piety. Third, there was a revulsion against the world and its pleasures, which could be classified as the delights of cultivated society. Specifically, Pietism looked down on going to the theater and playing cards. The final characteristic was a distinct relationship to the state church. Pietists usually remained within the established or state churches, developed a church within the church (or *ecclesiola in ecclesia*), and practiced a limited form of Separatism.[349]

German Pietism: Philipp Jakob Spener (A.D. 1635–1705). Spener is the person most closely associated with the German movement. He was a Lutheran marked by the thought and piety of northern Germany but was originally from Alsace, in the south. He was educated in Strasbourg, Basel, and Geneva. He was influenced in part by asceticism and Calvinism, but English Puritanism influenced him the most significantly.[350] He began to attempt to exercise church reform in the city of Frankfurt but was frustrated in his attempts by the city's government.[351] While working within the restrictions placed on him, he focused his attention on increased catechetical instruction. In 1670, in an effort to deepen individuals' spiritual life, he gathered a group of people for Bible reading, prayer, and discussion of the Sunday sermons. These circles met in homes and were called the *collegia pietatis*, from which we derive the term *pietism*.[352] In spite of Spener's opposition, some of his disciples withdrew from the established church's worship and sacraments. The tension escalated to such a level that some of his meetings faced police opposition. In 1686, he was glad to accept a call away from Frankfurt to the city of Dresden.[353]

---

349. Walker, *History*, 445. This relationship to the state church is complicated. Martin Bucer also developed the notion of a church within the church, but he is not usually classified as a Pietist.

350. Such influence came particularly through the German translation of Lewis Bayly's widely read *The Practice of Piety* and also probably through some of the translated works of Richard Baxter. See Lloyd Jones, "Ecclesiola in Ecclesia," 4:83.

351. Walker, *History*, 445.

352. Ibid., 446.

353. Ibid., 447.

For a while, Dresden offered Spener a quieter, less confrontational life. But soon he was opposed by the two Saxon universities at Leipzig and Wittenberg. When in 1691 he was invited to Berlin by Elector Frederick III, later King Frederick I of Prussia, Spener was once again eager to leave.

With his final transition to the city of Berlin, Spener entered a vigorous literary battle with his opponents, who were now termed the *orthodoxists*.[354] Though Spener was a true Lutheran, his opponents did not see him as such, and they accused him of heresy. He focused on Scripture, not the Lutheran creeds. The heart was what was important to Spener; he considered intellectual differences to be relatively insignificant. His minimization of intellectual differences stood against a cultural movement that held that sound teaching carried the greatest significance.[355] Nevertheless, Spener was instrumental in establishing a university in Halle that began in 1691 and formally opened in 1694.

There was also the perception that Protestant scholasticism addressed the head and forsook the heart. This perception gave rise to Lutheran and Reformed Pietism, associated with Spener's work *Pia desideria*, which he wrote in 1675.[356] Leveling sharp criticisms at the state of the Lutheran church in Germany, Spener suggested in this work a number of reforms.[357] The pious had to combat the evils of governmental interference, as well as the poor example of the unworthy lives of some of the clergy. He argued that theology itself was the seedbed for controversy and was thus unhelpful.[358] Genuine Christianity was best seen in the believer's life. There had to be evidence of a person's regeneration. Like the English Puritans, Spener called church members to be moderate in their food, drink, and dress and to reject dancing

354. That title had also been used in the ancient church.

355. Ibid., 446; Lloyd-Jones, "Ecclesiola in Ecclesia," 84.

356. Allison, *Historical Theology*, 537.

357. Karl Heussi, *Kompendium der Kirchengeschichte* (Tübingen: Mohr Siebeck, 1971), 336: "He wanted intensive Bible reading, remembering that Christianity does not lie in our knowledge but in what we do; there was also to be more love in religious disagreements. Spener urged a change in theological study with greater emphasis on practical living and on a life that is closely connected to God's love. There must be reform in preaching with less emphasis on rhetoric so that it is more comprehensible to the laity" (my translation). Walker (*History*, 447) uses the phrase *ecclesioloe in ecclesia*.

358. Walker, *History*, 446.

and playing cards, all of which were considered *adiaphora* (or "things indifferent") at that time by the Lutheran church.

The German Pietist movement continued and flourished under a younger leader—August Hermann Francke (1663–1727). After having visited Spener in Dresden, Francke began a group at the University of Leipzig called the *collegium philobiblicum* ("gathering of Bible lovers"). By 1689, Francke lectured regularly to the students and townspeople and thus gained a following in the surrounding area. As a result of the beginnings of turmoil, the city released an edict forbidding the meeting of these groups, called *conventicles*. Francke was also strongly opposed by the theology faculty and in 1690 left Leipzig for Erfurt.

In Erfurt, Francke faced further opposition to the extent that in 1691 he faced expulsion. Through the influence of Spener, Francke joined the new university at Halle and pastored in the neighboring village. Until his death, Francke kept Halle a center of Pietism.[359] In 1695 he began the first of his schools for children living in poverty. His schools, all of which were run in the spirit of Pietism, would go on to become well known. At the time of his death in 1727, there were 2,200 children in these schools. Franke also established an orphan house that could house up to 134 orphans. These schools are in operation to this day.[360]

Halle University was founded on zeal for missions. The first Protestant missionaries to India originated in this movement in 1705. During the eighteenth century, more than sixty-four foreign missionaries were sent out from Halle University.[361] Overall, the German Pietist movement touched the German Reformed churches in the southwest and Scandinavian lands. But with Francke's death, the movement began to decline. No one stepped into the place of Spener or Francke as leader of the movement.[362]

---

359. Ibid., 448.
360. Lloyd-Jones, "Ecclesiola in Ecclesia," 84. The orphanage idea was imitated in other lands.
361. Walker, *History*, 448.
362. Ibid., 449.

Theological Debates: Imputation of Adam's Sin

Following the death of John Calvin, one area of dispute within the Reformed community concerned the nature of the transmission of Adam's sin to his posterity.

Original Sin. The debate first centered on Joshua Placaeus (1596–1658), a professor at the theological academy in Saumur, France. His definition of original sin was that it "consisted simply in the depravity derived from Adam and did not include the imputation of the guilt of Adam's first sin."[363] Based on this definition, original sin would be limited to the human propensity to sin and would not include the reality that humanity received legal culpability for our father Adam's sin.

Placaeus argued that inheriting culpability for Adam's sin, known as *immediate imputation*, was not the classic position of the Reformed creeds. He argued that this teaching of immediate imputation was not found in the Gallic, Belgic, Scottish, or Helvetic confessions.[364] With a learned and respected professor's opposing the traditional Reformed stance, the Reformed community was forced to pause and assess who had made a false step—Placaeus or his opponents. Placaeus argued that he had not denied the imputation of Adam's first sin and was not out of accord with the Synod of Dordt. To understand the controversy better, the terms of the debate should be carefully defined.

Mediate versus Immediate Imputation. Placaeus's position was that Adam's first sin was mediated to his posterity through the inheritance of a corrupt nature, which means that the imputation of Adam's sin is the effect of the hereditary corruption.[365] This position is referred to as *mediate imputation.*

On the other hand, immediate imputation claims that Adam's first sin was transmitted to his children immediately, that is, without the mediation of hereditary corruption. The imputation of Adam's first sin is the cause of the corruption.[366] With the terms defined, we can

---

363. John Murray, *The Imputation of Adam's Sin* (1959; repr., Nutley, NJ: Presbyterian and Reformed, 1977), 42. For more information, see Robert L. Reymond, *A New Systematic Theology of the Christian Faith* (Nashville: Thomas Nelson, 1998), 436–37.

364. Murray, *Imputation*, 46.

365. Ibid., 43.

366. Ibid.; Turretin, *Elenctic Theology*, 1:614–16; and see the *Formula Consensus Helvetica*, 1675, Canones X, XI, XII, in James T. Dennison Jr., comp. "The Formula Consensus Hel-

see that the issues involved have consequences for the nature of God, sin, and salvation.

Imputation of Guilt and Justice in Punishment. As is often the case in complex theological arguments, there are a number of technical terms that must be understood in order for one to comprehend the debate. The Latin word *reatus* refers to the legal blame or penalty for certain actions. The *reatus* is the obligation to receive a penalty. The word *poenae* refers to the justice involved in the condemnation, and the more familiar word *culpa* is the genuine guilt or condemnation that comes to the perpetrator of wicked actions. From the technical terms, the historical unfolding also helps one to comprehend the crisis.

Beginning with the Reformation, Calvin's teaching on imputation was clear and concise. Unless someone is worthy of blame, unless there is some connection between the person and the act or sin that is blameworthy, there is, or should be, no liability to the person for the sin's penalty.[367] Calvin's position was followed by others.[368]

The English theologian John Owen nuanced this basic teaching. He held that the guilt imputed to Adam's posterity was specifically found in the obligation to satisfy divine justice. Owen refused to distinguish between *reatus culpae*, receiving blame or penalty for committing the act, and *reatus poenae*, receiving blame for the sake of divine justice.[369] The differences between the two ideas are not immediately evident. The distinction hinges on the biblical, albeit abstract, notion of God's infinite justice.

The act of sin is an affront to divine honor. As such, it is only just for God to condemn sin. In agreement with Owen, the Dutch theologian Petrus van Mastricht held that blame was simply the medium or pathway between the concepts of guilt for the act or

---

vetica (1675)," in *Reformed Confessions of the 16th and 17th Centuries in English Translation,* 4:516–30 (Grand Rapids: Reformation Heritage Books, 2014).

367. *Institutes,* 2.1.8, as cited by Murray, *Imputation,* 81: "Whence it follows," he said, "that it is properly accounted sin in the sight of God because there is no *reatus* [blame] without *culpa* [actual guilt]."

368. Murray, *Imputation,* 81. Calvin's position was followed by Jerome Zanchius, the Leiden Synopsis, and W. Amesius.

369. Owen, *Works,* 5, as cited by Murray, *Imputation,* 74. Owen's rejection was apparently a response to the abuse of the distinction by the Roman Catholics—to support their notion of purgatory. For more information, see Murray, *Imputation,* 79.

sin, on the one hand, and the just condemnation flowing from the guilty act, on the other hand.[370] Van Mastricht carried great influence in Holland.[371]

From a human perspective, it seems evident that if there is an obligation for someone to receive punishment, then there must be some type of involvement in the actual committing of the crime or sin.[372] In reference to Adam's sin and posterity, the two are related beyond a mere satisfaction of God's justice, or *reatus poenae*, "but must also include, as the antecedent and ground of that *reatus*," Professor Murray said, "involvement in the *culpa* of Adam's transgression."[373] Thus it does not appear that Owen was correct. As can be imagined, debate surrounding the atonement continued on. This theological thread was revisited in the nineteenth century.[374] Theologians not only wrestled with human guilt and its application for man but also debated the very nature of God's being.

THEOLOGICAL DEBATES: GOD'S BEING

Seventeenth-century theologians knew that they had to articulate the relationships between God's attributes as well as comprehend his providence. In the past, theologians often demonstrated a preference for one of God's attributes over another. Such imbalance was always

370. Van Mastricht said: "*Reatus* is therefore the *medium quid* between *culpa* and *poena*, for it arises from *culpa* and leads to *poena*, so that it is at the same time the *reatus* of *culpa* and of *poena* and, as a medium, intervenes between these two termini and takes its name from both equally. . . . *Reatus* is therefore the liability in punishment arising from the *culpa* which sin entails. . . . In reality, the *reatus culpae* is simply the *reatus poenae*. . . . We should expect from this definition of the relations of *culpa*, *reatus*, and *poena* that *reatus poenae* could not be conceived of apart from *culpa*" (as cited by Murray, *Imputation*, 80).

371. Ibid. The same definition is found in the Liden Synopsis.

372. Ibid., 83: "*Reatus* and *poena* and, if we will, *reatus poenae*, always presuppose *culpa* and that, therefore, our involvement in the *reatus*, the obligation to penalty, of Adam's sin means that we were also involved in the *culpa* of his sin. . . . If we have the *reatus* in common with Adam we must likewise have his *culpa*." Lutheran theologians took the same position.

373. Ibid., 84.

374. More information is found in chapter 20 on nineteenth-century theology. Murray points out that the Hodges disagree with the seventeenth-century formulations. See Murray, *Imputation*, 83n134: "This lengthy monograph is devoted to a large extent to criticism of Dr. Hodge's position"; 84: Hodge is divergent "from the older Reformed theologians"; 85: Hodge's position "appears to the present writer illegitimate."

to the detriment of the church.[375] Some theologians—such as Origen, Augustine, and Roman Catholic theologians—understood God to be absolute essence.[376] Others emphasized the significance of God's will. These theologians were the Socinians, the Remonstrants, and the rationalists. Still other theologians, such as Erasmus, held to God as absolute reason or absolutely moral.

In contrast, the task of the biblically faithful theologian is to "proceed from the principle of the harmony of all God's attributes, and consistently to adhere to this principle despite all the problems."[377] When that pathway is followed, theology maintains a biblical balance.

God's providence was studied under three subjects in the post-Reformation period. *Preservation* is God's providence that sustains all creation. *Concurrence* is how God works with his creation in terms of primary and secondary causes. Secondary causes do not act independently of God, but concurrence is when God acts together with that which he created in a way that is consistent with the nature of each thing.[378] *Government* is God's providential ruling in each creature's life for his glory and for the elect person's salvation.

The idea of providence triggered some theological discussions. Reformed and Lutheran theologians held opposite positions regarding the relationship between divine foreknowledge and the divine decrees. The Lutherans claimed that divine foreknowledge is not dependent on the divine decree, while the Reformed held tightly together providence and the decree.[379] A second area was providence and the presence of evil. Three methods were adopted to address this issue: the first method was to distinguish between an action, the effects of the action, and the nature of the action; the second was to distinguish between proximate (or near) and remote (or distant) causes; a third was to distinguish between divine permission and divine action. This third method does

---

375. For more information on God's attributes, see Richard C. Gamble, *The Whole Counsel of God*, vol. 1, *God's Mighty Acts in the Old Testament* (Phillipsburg, NJ: P&R Publishing, 2009) (*WCG1*), 653; WCG 2:343–51.

376. See Charles Hodge, *Systematic Theology*, 3 vols. (London: Clarke, 1960), 1:373.

377. RD 2:182.

378. Allison, *Historical Theology*, 290.

379. Ibid.: "Specifically, they made a distinction between the providence of God and his divine foreknowledge while acknowledging that God both possesses exhaustive foreknowledge and sovereignly determines all that happens."

not mean that God permits evil but, rather, that he does not restrain the bad actions from occurring.[380]

Immutability. This era also wrestled with the nature of God's immutability—and specifically whether God changes his mind. Going back to the ancient church, the semi-Pelagians argued that God was changeable in his will, not his being. For the semi-Pelagians, God's will was, or at least could be, dependent on the will of man. Following the Reformation and the rise of the theology of Jacobus Arminius, this controversy poured back into the church.

As we consider the thoughts of God, the fact that he does not change—namely, that he is immutable—does not in any way insinuate a lack of activity or immobility in God. While God remains unchangeable, this truth in no way means that he does not care about his people on earth. He is not ignorant of the changes on the earth and in the lives of those who dwell on it.

Yet the Bible teaches that God, as the Creator of the world, exists beyond time, which began at creation. He exists beyond space, which likewise had a chronological beginning. His being, therefore, is beyond any type of temporal becoming. In his very being, God is different from creation. Certainly he can, and does, reach down to us, but he is not like us. As a practical example, consider that because he is beyond space, time, and change, he can hear at the same time prayers offered in Korean in Korea and in English in America.[381]

Infra- and Supralapsarianism. Some theologians at the time of the Reformation wondered about the relationship between Christ as himself elect and Christ as the Mediator of the elect. The question was whether or not Christ was foreordained to be the Mediator in order to bring about the salvation of his people. Was the election of believers then logically prior to the foreordination of Christ as the Mediator?[382]

---

380. Ibid., 290–91.

381. Herman Bavinck, *The Doctrine of God* (Carlisle, PA: Banner of Truth, 1977), 149; Hodge, *Systematic Theology*, 1:391: "Though unchangeable in himself, God lives the life of his creatures, and is not indifferent to their changing activities." Sadly, going beyond the notion of God's simply changing his will, there have been more recent denials that assert the changeability of God's being. It is argued that God changes in his being through creation, incarnation, and redemption. For those theologians, God stands "in reciprocal relationship" to man; is dependent on the universe for his knowledge of reality; for him there is a past, a present, and a future; like any man, he becomes angry; and, in general, his disposition answers to that of man.

382. Bavinck, *The Doctrine of God*, 406.

Alternatively, perhaps Christ was also an object of election, whereas he was foreordained to be not only the Mediator but also the head of the church. If so, did Christ's election logically precede the election of the church?[383] Logically in God's mind, which came first—Christ's election as the Mediator, or the election of believers?

Some may consider this discussion to be bankrupt of importance. But the Princeton theologian Charles Hodge would disagree with an impetuous dismissal. If we do not understand God's plan for creation and providence, or if we do not understand his plan of salvation from beginning to end, then it is difficult for us to understand our own salvation and even more difficult to share it with others. "It [understanding this plan] must determine our theology," argued Hodge, "and our theology determines our religion."[384] How theologians answer these questions places them on a continuum between the views of infralapsarianism and supralapsarianism.

Infralapsarians assert that God, to demonstrate his glory, determined to create the heavens and the earth and men and women. Then, still prior to creation, God decreed to permit the fall of Adam and his posterity, after which he decreed to predestine some. The decree of predestination comes after the decree to permit the fall. Thus the order of decrees in the mind of God is as follows: decree to create man, decree for man to fall, then decree to predestine.[385] The theologians at Dordt sided with infralapsarianism.[386]

Supralapsarians assert that God, in a demonstration of his grace and justice, includes the decree to create and to permit the fall in the

383. Ibid.

384. Hodge, *Systematic Theology*, 2:314–15: If "we are ignorant of the great end aimed at in the scheme of redemption, or of the relation of the several parts of that scheme; or if we misconceive that end and that relation, all our views must be confused or erroneous. . . . If the end of redemption as well as of creation and of providence, is the production of the greatest amount of happiness, then Christianity is one thing; if the end be the glory of God, then Christianity is another thing. The whole character of our theology and religion depends on the answer to that question."

385. Ibid., 2:316–20. Infralapsarians do not include in the decree of predestination the decree to permit the fall. Theologians who are usually considered infralapsarian include van Mastricht and Turretin. See Robert Lewis Dabney, *Discussions of Robert Lewis Dabney* (Edinburgh: Banner of Truth, 1991), 1:296–97.

386. Hodge, *Systematic Theology*, 2:317. See WCF chapters 3, 6, 7; WSC Q. 19, 20, which is clearly infralapsarian; Berkhof, *Systematic Theology*, 123, 130. Debates on infra- and supralapsarianism will continue in the nineteenth century.

decree of predestination.[387] Their order is as follows: God decreed to elect some, to create them as well as the reprobate, and then to permit the elect to fall.

There are problems with both infra- and supralapsarianism.[388] At times I long simply to dismiss the debate, but then I remember Hodge's words. There is, however, an alternative to choosing one position or the other. The questions being asked by the theologians are themselves methodologically flawed.

Since the Scriptures clearly teach the Creator/creature distinction, how beneficial is it for the creature to attempt to determine the pattern of thought in the mind of the Creator—a pattern that is "thought" before there was any creation? In reality, this debate is excessively speculative. In this matter, Reformed theologians were as guilty as their medieval counterparts who debated the number of angels that could dance on the head of a pin! Bavinck rightly said that both groups are mistaken.[389] Both positions look to a certain group of biblical texts for support while demeaning, or dismissing entirely, an entirely different set of texts.[390]

The Problem of Evil and the Order of God's Decree. A connected issue is the relationship between evil and the order of God's decree. The question involved here is whether or not God authors sin. If God's providence cannot be limited to bare permission, then some think that he must be the author of the crimes and sins that instruments of iniquity perform.[391] In the *Institutes*, Calvin struggled with this age-old question.[392] While Calvin refused to limit God's providence to bare permis-

---

387. Berkhof, *Systematic Theology*, 118. Theologians connected with supralapsarianism are Beza, Martyr, Voetius, Witsius, and Comrie.

388. Ibid., 125: "God's electing love is sovereign; it consists in the sovereign counsel of his own will and is not determined by any foresight on his part of autonomous activity or absence of activity on the part of men. The process of salvation moves from electing grace as fountain, to its goal in the praise of the glory of God's grace in the glorification of those who are the objects of electing love and the participants of redeeming grace." See Bavinck, *Doctrine of God*, 359.

389. Bavinck, *Doctrine of God*, 383: "Both supra and infra err when they regard the various elements of God's counsel as subordinately related to each other. Both are one-sided: supra emphasizing God's sovereignty; infra, God's righteousness, holiness and mercy."

390. Ibid., 386. The supralapsarians presented their view because they considered it to come closer to the teaching of Scripture, and Calvin especially came to his views, which were not fully developed supralapsarian, by his deep reflection on human sin.

391. See ibid., 235, 389; and John Murray, *Calvin on Scripture and Divine Sovereignty* (Grand Rapids: Baker, 1960), 66.

392. *Institutes*, 1.18.3: "And I have already sufficiently shown that God is called the author of all these things which these censors wish to happen merely by his idle permission" (as cited

sion, he also rejected the notion that God was the author of sin. Calvin held that God ordained Adam's fall: "I so assert it as by no means to concede that God was the author."[393] Calvin further confessed that no human mind is able to answer adequately this troubling question.[394]

All Protestants reject certain ideas regarding the relationship between God and sin. They reject the notion that God is the author of sin; that man was created unto damnation; and that the decree of reprobation was the cause of sin, thus making sin the efficient cause of reprobation. To be consistent, the supralapsarian should place the decree of reprobation in its entirety before the decree to permit sin. Calvin thought that reprobation rested on sin. Sin is the proximate cause of damnation, thus Calvin should not be considered a supralapsarian.[395]

Supralapsarian and infralapsarian theologians both distinguish between condemnation and reprobation. Condemnation is the execution, in time, of the decree of reprobation. But supralapsarians will further divide the one decree of reprobation into various parts: a preceding purpose and a subsequent purpose.

THEOLOGICAL METHOD

The seventeenth century was full of deep theological insight. It would be appropriate to conclude this chapter with a brief analysis of the nature of theological method during the era.

Earlier Scholarship. By the 1960s, Protestant scholasticism was ridiculed by those who were influenced by neoorthodoxy, such as the followers of Karl Barth.[396] They viewed the theology of the era as a betrayal of the Reformation in the name of Aristotle. At the risk of

---

by Murray, *Calvin on Scripture*, 67).

393. Murray, *Calvin on Scripture*, 67; see *Institutes*, 1.18.3.

394. Calvin, *De aeterna Dei praedestinatione*, col. 316: "But how it was that God, by his foreknowledge and decree, ordained what should take place respecting man, and yet so ordained it without his being himself in the least a participator of the fault, or being at all the author or the approver of the transgression; how this was, I repeat, is a secret manifestly far too deep to be penetrated by the human mind, nor am I ashamed to confess our ignorance. And far be it from any of the faithful to be ashamed to confess his ignorance of that which the Lord envelops in the blaze of his own inaccessible light" (as cited by Murray, *Calvin on Scripture*, 67).

395. Murray, *Calvin on Scripture*, 62.

396. See chapter 22 for an analysis.

oversimplification, they argue that the Reformers Calvin and Luther set aside Aristotle, but many seventeenth-century theologians—the scholastics—welcomed him back.[397]

This situation introduces a difficult question for evangelical theologians. When asked whether the period of Protestant scholasticism was one of the preservation of Reformational thought, many are afraid to recognize discontinuity between the Reformation and scholasticism, for when they do, they then supposedly side with neoorthodoxy.

It is true that in the seventeenth century Calvin's influence had greatly diminished.[398] There was also a change in the genre of theology. Theology had become less rhetorical and pastoral and more logical, technical, and dialectical. The theologians of the age were not ignorant of these changes. They felt that theology was a science unto itself, with a right to its own distinctive theological vocabulary, even if they did not go so far as to think that preaching should become as technical.

There are two competing views concerning the origins of seventeenth-century orthodoxy. The first view is that it arose from the political and theological needs of Protestants, particularly against Rome and other Protestants. In warfare, combatants use, and rightfully so, whatever weapons are within arms' reach. In this case, Aristotle was within reach.[399] A larger group of scholars claim that scholasticism developed from principles inherent within Protestantism itself. Those principles concerned the importance of a highly educated clergy.[400]

In the 1980s, scholars thought that they did not have a good definition of *scholasticism*. At that time, scholasticism was identified with

397. Karl Barth said that his followers have thrown Aristotle out and repurified theology once again. For an analysis of Barth's thinking contrasted to Richard Muller's analysis, see Kelly, *Systematic Theology*, 1:159–60.

398. Ferguson commented on Calvin's method in contrast to the scholastic method: "But one cannot help feeling that there was a loss of the genius of Calvin's life project of producing commentaries on the text of scripture and developing and perfecting the *Institutes* as a companion to scripture. His deeply expository approach to theology had led him to write a *summa pietatis* as distinct from a *summa theologiae*" (Sinclair B. Ferguson, *The Whole Christ: Legalism, Antinomianism, and Gospel Assurance—Why the Marrow Controversy Still Matters* [Wheaton, IL: Crossway, 2016], 54).

399. This position is the one held by John W. Beardslee, *Reformed Dogmatics: J. Wollebius, G. Voetius, and R. Turretin* (New York: Oxford University Press, 1965), in this country and by Hans Emil Weber, *Reformation, Orthoxdoxie und Rationalismus*, 2 vols. (Leipzig: Gutersloh, 1937–1951), in Germany.

400. Representing this position are Ernst Troeltsch, P. Althous, and Ernst Beizer.

having six tendencies: it was a priori—scholasticism was the search for basic principles; it had a strong dependence on Aristotle; it was a stress on logic that threatened, or seemed to threaten, *sola scriptura*; it had an increasing speculative fascination with attempting to ascertain God's will; it treated Scripture historically, that is, as a body of propositions from which a philosophy may be built; finally, it represented a shift from the centrality of faith to an assent to truth.[401]

Later Scholarship. Beginning in 1987, Richard Muller, then of Fuller Theological Seminary, argued that Protestantism after 1565 needed to grow to survive. Its foundation was confessional, but it needed to create a complete systematic theology that was lacking in the Reformers.[402] Muller divided Reformed scholasticism into two historic periods, early (1565–1630/40) and high (to the end of the seventeenth century). These periods are both, in some ways, like and unlike the theology of the Reformation.

These periods are unlike the Reformation because, while Protestant, they also draw on the theological constructs of the Medieval Period—for example, on the doctrine of the Trinity. They are also more fulsome in that they cover all doctrines of systematic theology, not simply those contested with the Catholics.[403] The term *scholastic* was used by these Protestant writers to describe their own system, which was detailed and distinct from other theological systems, such as biblical/exegetical theology or catechetical theology.

The term *scholastic* was not meant to draw philosophy into dialogue with theology, as was the case in the thirteenth century—it is not medieval scholastic but Protestant scholastic; it therefore does not propose one key doctrine to unlock the nature of theology, nor is it attached to one particular philosophical system.[404] Muller concluded that a change in form and method does not necessarily mean a change

---

401. Brian Armstrong, *Calvin and the Amyraut Heresy: Protestant Scholasticism and Humanism in France* (Madison: University of Wisconsin Press, 1969).

402. Muller, *Post-Reformation*, 13. Muller's second volume in this series came out in 1993.

403. Ibid., 14–17.

404. Ibid., 18. Influence also came from Peter Ramus (1515–1572). Ibid., 1:30: "Ramism is characteristic of the striving of early orthodoxy toward a careful and viable enunciation of theological method." Beeke and Pederson (*Puritans*, 469) comment: "Ramism had won the support of the Puritans, due to its practicality. Ramus . . . had reformed the arts curriculum by applying it to daily life. He proposed a method to simplify all academic subjects, offering a single logic for both dialectic and rhetoric to make them understandable and memorable."

in substance;[405] rather, there is doctrinal continuity and methodological discontinuity. Yet he admits that methodological change also brings about doctrinal change.[406]

Muller's analysis of the Reformers concludes that their "system as such was not fully developed nor had theology yet received a full Protestant treatment as an academic discipline."[407] Reformational theology had strong homiletical and catechetical motives. Calvin's *Institutes* and Bullinger's *Compendium* were intended to be instruction in the "basic teachings of Scripture," "preparations for biblical study," and "forms of catechetical instruction." They are both written in a discursive style, not in a sophisticated dialectical model.[408]

In Reformed orthodoxy, "these characteristics are no longer as obvious in the system. . . . Preaching and teaching of piety have been separated from instruction in doctrine by the increasing need to deal with the language of technical school-theology."[409]

Most scholars have sided with Muller. Even John Frame, who is no friend of scholasticism, says that while there was a different feel to post-Reformation literature, there is nevertheless not a great chasm between them.[410] It was a drive toward academic respectability, which is not wrong in itself. But the quest for academic respect has, at times, led to compromise with non-Christian thought.

KEY TERMS

Arminianism
antinomianism
Pietism
imputation

405. Muller, *Post-Reformation*, 20.
406. Ibid., 23.
407. Ibid., 28.
408. Ibid., 29. See Muller's criticism of Calvin's strained discursive style by the final edition of the *Institutes*.
409. Later writers, such as Zanchi and Walaeus, produced both introductory doctrinal instruction and systems of theology. See Muller, *Post-Reformation*, 29.
410. John M. Frame, *A History of Western Philosophy and Theology* (Phillipsburg, NJ: P&R Publishing, 2015) (*HWPT*), 175.

STUDY QUESTIONS

1. Was the Synod of Dordt correct to condemn Arminian theology? Why or why not?
2. Was Voetius correct to oppose Descartes and his thinking? What are the dangers to Descartes's philosophy?
3. In the seventeenth century, there was no separation of church and state. How should contemporary Christians think about the relationship between the church and the state?
4. Voetius and Cocceius and their followers debated theological method. Why is theological method important?

RESOURCES FOR FURTHER STUDY

This chapter is unbelievably rich in primary theological texts. There are a number of great multivolume theological systems that can be studied with much profit.

Ames, William. *The Marrow of Theology*. Translated by John Dykstra Eusden. Durham, NC: Labyrinth, 1983. A single-volume theological classic.

Hodge, Charles. *Systematic Theology*. 3 vols. London: Clarke, 1960. Replaced Turretin's *Institutio* at Princeton.

Owen, John. *Biblical Theology*. Morgan, PA: Soli Deo Gloria, 1996. Another single-volume theological classic.

Rutherford, Samuel. *Loveliness of Christ*. Edinburgh: Banner of Truth, 2007. Although his theological works are heavy, I strongly recommend reading this small portion of his letters. Rutherford's depth of piety and heart for ministry are unparalled.

Turretin, Francis. *Institutes of Elenctic Theology*. Edited by James T. Dennison. Translated by George M. Giger. 3 vols. Phillipsburg, NJ: P&R Publishing, 1992–1997. Formerly the standard theological textbook at Princeton.

Van Mastricht, Petrus. *Theoretical-Practical Theology*. Translated by Todd M. Rester. Edited by Joel R. Beeke. Grand Rapids: Reformation Heritage Books, 2018. In Jonathan Edwards's view, even better than Turretin.

Witsius, Hermann. *The Economy of the Covenants*. 2 vols. Escondido, CA: The den Dulk Christian Foundation, 1990. A much smaller theological system that does not intend to cover all the loci of systematic theology but gives an eye-opening analysis of the importance of the covenant.

18

Westminster Confession of Faith

RATIONALE FOR STUDYING THE WESTMINSTER CONFESSION OF FAITH

Relevance and Adequacy. Many theologians and congregations question whether any confession is fit to meet the needs of the contemporary church. In particular, many have wondered whether something as old as the Westminster Confession of Faith (WCF) is suited for the modern church. It is true that the WCF was written in a particular historical situation and context. As seen in the previous chapter, it was a theologically rich era. For more than three hundred years, Presbyterians have asserted that the WCF is a theological high-water mark that has yet to be transcended.

Nevertheless, we must grant that all human writings, no matter how thorough, are fallible and that the Holy Spirit has continued to work in the church to enlighten her. Murray's answer to the question was that "creedal confession must keep pace with the challenge of heresy."[1]

Conflicting Views of the Role of the Confession. Paul Woolley, the first church historian at Westminster Theological Seminary, had a rather low view of the WCF. He agreed that confessions are helpful for stating truth that is useful for living—their primary purpose is educational and evangelistic.[2] But to force a person to adopt a confession is, in Woolley's words, "utterly perverse."[3] Woolley believed

1. John Murray, "The Theology of the Westminster Confession," in *Scripture and Confession*, ed. John Skilton (Nutley, NJ: Presbyterian and Reformed, 1973), 126.
2. Paul Woolley, "What Is a Creed For? Some Answers from History," in *Scripture and Confession*, ed. John Skilton (Nutley, NJ: Presbyterian and Reformed, 1973), 96–97: "A creed is often said to be a standard."
3. Ibid., 97: "But as soon as something becomes necessary as a means to a desirable end it begins to take on an aspect of coercion. . . . Instead of a joyous affirmation we have a manda-

612

that "[confessions] are harmful when they are perverted to prevent freedom of study, as is still sometimes done today."[4]

On the other hand, Robert Godfrey, another prominent historian, understands the usefulness of confessions differently: "For some who belong to the Westminster school of theology," he states, "there is a weakness in understanding both the role and the content of the confessions in the life of the Reformed churches."[5] This weakness in understanding is summarized by the expression *sympathetic-critical*, was held by the twentieth-century Dutch theologian Klaas Schilder, and was picked up by others.[6] Godfrey held that theologians should have a sympathetic-critical relationship to the Reformed tradition but not to the catechism.[7] There ought to be a distinction between a theologian's tradition and confession—the systematic theologian's relationship to the confession ought to be neither critical nor sympathetic-critical. Godfrey believed that instead systematic theologians should be confident of their confession because they have subscribed to it as their confession. He argued that it was wrong to view a denomination's confession as a brief systematic theology that was liable to updates at any given time.[8] He also believed that it was wrong to permit exceptions to the confession's teaching, for that practice "weakens the proper function of the confession as a clear testimony to what the church believes. It also tends to relativize and undermine the authority of the confession in the life of the church."[9]

HISTORICAL CONTEXT OF THE ASSEMBLY

Sixteenth- and Seventeenth-Century England.[10] In the 1534 Act of Supremacy, King Henry VIII had himself recognized as the supreme

---

tory deprivation of freedom."

4. Ibid., 122.

5. W. Robert Godfrey, "Westminster, Justification, and the Reformed Confessions," in *The Pattern of Sound Doctrine*, ed. David VanDrunen (Phillipsburg, NJ: P&R Publishing, 2004), 140.

6. Godfrey cites Richard Gaffin, John Frame, and Tim Trumper.

7. Godfrey, "Reformed Confessions," 141.

8. Out of fairness, Godfrey belongs to the Dutch Reformed tradition and is not Presbyterian. In that tradition, not only the office-bearers but also all members of the congregation subscribe to the confession, and office-bearers are not permitted exceptions to the confession.

9. Godfrey, "Reformed Confessions," 142–43.

10. For background information, see chapter 14.

head of the Church of England. As a result of this document, the king, or his designated subordinate, had the right to investigate, correct, and discipline the clergy. To that end, in 1549 King EdwardVI held a general commission. For the next twenty years, their work was mostly visitation, but eventually it became a permanent commission called the Court of High Commission. The court grew in number and power and consisted mostly of bishops and canon lawyers. A summons to appear before the court included the obligation to answer all questions posed, even if doing so meant committing perjury. The penalties imposed were most often fines or imprisonment, as the court was not permitted to torture or inflict death.

English delegates attended the Synod of Dordt in 1618–19. Arminianism had been disrupting England, but in 1622 King James I directed that no one was to preach on issues relating to predestination.[11] In 1625, his son Charles I (1600–1649) became king. Charles's wife, Henrietta Maria, was a Catholic. He appointed William Laud as archbishop of Canterbury. Together they pushed the English church toward high-church ritualism and, theologically, toward Arminianism. Laud's moves were unpopular with many theologians, who consistently petitioned Parliament to do something to address the need for religious reform. In 1641 Parliament passed the Triennial Act, which dissolved the despised Court of High Commission, impeached Archbishop Laud, and demanded that the king summon Parliament every three years. What followed was the English Civil War, one of the last great wars of religion.

Scottish Background. While Scotland was far behind England economically, its schools and universities were not greatly inferior.[12] The University of St Andrews had been established in 1414, followed by Glasgow in 1451 and Aberdeen in 1495.

Educational changes occurred as a result of the Reformation. In 1560, the University of Edinburgh was established and in 1583 was

---

11. Whitney G. Gamble, "The Theology of the Westminster Confession of Faith in Its Context," in *The History of Scottish Theology*, vol. 1., ed. David Fergusson and Mark W. Elliott (Oxford: Oxford University Press, 2019), 265.

12. While schools existed in the major towns by the time of the Reformation, it was 1616 before the Privy Council of Scotland mandated schools for every parish, and seventeen years later that act was confirmed by Parliament. See Thomas Murray, *The Life of Rutherford* (Edinburgh: Oliphant, 1828), 4.

served by the celebrated Robert Rollock (1555–1599) as principal. In 1593, Marischal College, now part of the University of Aberdeen, was established as an imitation of Protestant arts colleges of the Continent. The express purpose of Marischal College was to train ministers for the church. The college was led by the very able Robert Howie (1565–1647). In 1607, Howie moved from Aberdeen to take the principalship of St Andrews following Andrew Melville, who was at this point locked in the Tower of London.[13] In 1639, Samuel Rutherford joined the St Andrews faculty. By the 1640s, the University of Edinburgh had six professors—a principal representing divinity, four regents in philosophy, and one regent in the humanities.[14] This educational milieu serves as the backdrop for the era's political situation.

In 1603, King James VI of Scotland/I of England united the two crowns. He claimed absolute power over the church, drew ministers into Parliament, and gave the ministers in attendance bishoprics, thus bringing episcopacy into Scotland.[15] In 1603, James VI took leave of his Scottish kingdom with the promise to return. But he returned only once—in 1617 to impose English-style worship.

In 1618, a plan—called the Five Articles of Perth—was formed to conform Scottish worship to the English pattern. Innovations included

13. Howie authored many works, including *Problema de eorum qui fide iustificati sunt, sanctificatione: una cum collatione sanctificationis et respiratione* (Basel, 1588); *De iustificatione hominis coram Deo* (Basel, 1590); *De reconciliatione hominis cum Deo* (Basel, 1591); and *De aeterna Dei praedestinatione aphorismi theologici* (Basel, 1591). See J. K. Cameron, ed., *Letters of John Johnston and Robert Howie* (Edinburgh: Oliver & Boyd, 1963).

14. Entrance required knowledge of Latin. All texts were in Latin, and lectures were delivered in Latin. In November, the young men gathered in the common hall, a topic was given in Scots, and they had to translate it into Latin. They translated for three hours in the morning. In the afternoon they read their essays out loud. Ramean philosophy was predominant. The academic year lasted from October until August, and eight to ten hours per day were required in the classroom, listening to prelections, or holding disputations. Disputation was of the highest importance. Proceeding to the next year required an entrance examination. The professor of humanities taught Latin, Roman literature, and Greek. He probably taught the first two years for a few hours each day. They had to know Greek by the end of the first year and for entering the second year were examined by translating from Greek into Latin. The day before graduation was spent in examination on all subjects. On the night before graduation they would sign the Confession and hear about how they did in the daytime exams. Upon their being sustained, their names were enrolled. Then they would hear the topic of disputation for graduation day. Graduation morning was spent in disputation either attacking or defending the thesis. In the afternoon they took the opposite position (Murray, *Life of Rutherford*, 5–14).

15. James Reid, *Memoirs of the Lives and Writings of Those Eminent Divines Who Convened in the Famous Assembly at Westminster in the Seventeenth Century* (Paisley, Scotland: Young, 1815), 2:286.

kneeling at the Lord's Supper, celebrating five holy days, private baptism, private Lord's Supper, and episcopal confirmation.[16] The people responded with violent religious protests that would mar Scotland for generations to come. King James died in March 1625.

Religious unrest ushered in a movement that culminated in the National Covenant, which was signed in Edinburgh in February 1638.[17] That same year, Alexander Henderson preached in St Andrews that the Scots can only do what is warranted by God: "Try [test] anything that the magistrates impose upon you, before you obey it, if it is warranted by God or not; because God is the only superior over you."[18] The scene was set for civil war and significant religious shift. The English Parliament called for a meeting of ministers at Westminster Abbey in London, now known as the Westminster Assembly, to revise the Thirty-Nine Articles, which were the foundation for English worship and polity.[19] The Scots participated and as well sent an army to help the parliamentary forces based on England's signing the Solemn League and Covenant of 1643.

Westminster Assembly Members

Many of the invited delegates chose not to participate, for the king had forbidden this assembly.[20] Still, there were more than one hundred English divines and half a dozen Scottish commissioners.

English Members. Thomas Gataker (1574–1654) was born in London; he was the son of an Oxford-trained pastor who was well

16. Reid, *Memoirs*, 2:290–91.

17. The National Covenant was a protest against attempted changes by the King and Laud to force the Presbyterian Church of Scotland to the liturgical and episcopal forms of England, specifically bishops, the *Book of Common Prayer*, and the book of canons. While it opposed the changes, it affirmed continuing loyalty to the king. That November, after thirty-six years, the Scottish church held its first free General Assembly.

18. J. D. Douglas, *Light in the North* (Grand Rapids: Eerdmans, 1964), 40–41.

19. For more in-depth information concerning the Westminster Assembly, see Richard C. Gamble, "The Second Use of the Law in Scottish Context," *RPTJ* 1, no. 1 (Fall 2014), 18–27, and Richard C. Gamble, "He Is Not Lord over Evil Is He?," *RPTJ* 3, no. 1 (Fall 2016), 27–38.

20. Reid, *Memoirs*, 1:47: "Many of the most learned Episcopal divines were nominated, along with the Presbyterians and Independents; and Archbishop Usher, Bishops Westford, Prideaux, and Brownrigg, Doctors Holdsworth, Hammond, Sanderson, and others; but they refused, because the king had declared against it."

known for self-denial and being willing to forsake everything to follow Christ. Thomas was bright and finished school at the age of sixteen. In 1590 he was sent to Saint John's College, Cambridge. There he was trained in Greek and Hebrew. His father died while Thomas was in college, thus leaving him with insufficient funds to continue his education. Others however, seeing the promise of this young scholar, contributed to his education.[21]

In 1596, Sidney College was established at Cambridge. Before it was even erected, Thomas was selected as a fellow. While the college was being built, he served as a private tutor and was advised to seek ordination. Feeling unfit for the high office, he at first declined but then submitted. The college was finished in 1599, and he began his work as tutor. He also began to preach in the towns near Cambridge. He eventually left the college to become a private chaplain in London. From 1601 to 1611, he preached to the lawyers of Lincoln's Inn. He was particularly keen to help Sabbath observance. In 1603, he took a bachelor of divinity degree at Cambridge but declined to pursue the doctor of divinity for economic reasons. His salary with Lincoln's Inn was not high.[22] In 1611, Gataker was married and took the rectory of Rotherhithe in Surrey, near London Bridge. During this time, he was afflicted with an almost perpetual headache. From his preaching at Lincoln's Inn, he developed a discourse titled *Of the Nature and Use of Lots* (1619). His work was attacked by John Balmford, and in 1623 a reply was published. In 1624, he published *A Discussion of the Popish Doctrine of Transubstantiation* as well as *A Short Catechism.*[23] He nearly died of colic in 1642 but was well enough to attend the Westminster Assembly in 1643. He was offered the mastership of Trinity College, Cambridge, the highest post attainable at the college, yet declined to take it. Humbly, neither would he permit a portrait of himself to be painted. Over the course of his long life, he authored more than forty works.[24]

---

21. Ibid., 1:284–86.

22. Ibid., 1:286–90.

23. Ibid., 1:291–99. He began an elaboration of Romans 3:28 in 1640 but was reluctant to publish it. It was published after his death by his son. He also produced *An Antidote against Error Concerning Justification* (London, 1670).

24. Ibid., 1:309–15. In 1698 Herman Witsius collected Gataker's works into one volume, titled *Opera critica.* It is true that Gataker had a distinctive view on the remission of sins as

William Gouge (1575–1653) was another prominent Westminster Assembly member. In 1595 he went to King's College, Cambridge. While a student, he read five chapters of Scripture in the morning, five after dinner, and another five before he went to bed. He became a fellow after three years. Having studied Hebrew with a rabbi at the college, he then taught Hebrew. During the first year of his fellowship, he began a commonplace book for divinity that summarized each chapter of Scripture. He remained at Cambridge for nine years.[25]

Gouge was married and led his family twice daily in worship. Ordained in 1607, he began ministry at Blackfriars in London, where he stayed until his death. He preached twice on Sundays and held a weekly public lecture for thirty-five years. He yearned for all his sons to enter the ministry, which he considered to be the highest calling. Gouge held strongly to the Sabbath.[26] To allow his servants to prepare for the Sabbath and retire early, he did not ask them to cook a hot meal on Saturday evening.[27]

Elected to the Westminster Assembly in 1643, Gouge would sometimes moderate when the prolocutor was absent. When the assembly voted against episcopacy, the bishops refused to ordain anyone who would not support the crown. A committee was established in 1644 to ordain, with Gouge as a member. He published Finch's book, The Calling of the Jews, and was cast into prison for nine weeks by Bishop Neile.[28] Gourge was the author of at least sixteen publications, mostly sermons, along with a substantial commentary on Hebrews and two catechisms.[29]

Charles Herle (1598–1659) was educated at Exeter College, Oxford, from 1612 to 1618.[30] As a minister in Devonshire, he suffered

---

subsequent to justification and was opposed to the active obedience of Christ's being imputed to the believer in justification. But he chose to remain silent about his opinon. See Robert Letham, *The Westminster Assembly: Reading Its Theology in Historical Context* (Phillipsburg, NJ: P&R Publishing, 2009), 91–92; Reid, *Memoirs*, 1:299.

25. Reid, *Memoirs*, 1:343–48. He received the bachelor of divinity in 1611 and the doctor of divinity in 1628.

26. Ibid., 1:344–45.

27. Ibid., 1:351.

28. Ibid., 1:363.

29. Titles included *The Whole Armour of God*, a treatise on Ephesians 6:10–20 (1616); and *Eight Treatises on Domestic Duties* (1622). See Joel R. Beeke and Randall J. Pederson, *Meet the Puritans* (Grand Rapids: Reformation Heritage Books, 2006), 288.

30. Reid, *Memoirs*, 2:24–30.

as a Puritan nonconformist. He then pastored in Winwick, Lancashire, at a church with a very wealthy living. He was elected to the assembly, and when Dr. Twisse died in 1646, Herle was elevated to the role of prolocutor. After the assembly, he resumed his pastorate in Winwick.

In 1651 the earl of Derby, Herle's patron, raised an army for King Charles II. He sent a lieutenant with forty horses to Winwick, but they did not plunder his home. When the earl's forces were defeated, the same lieutenant was wounded and was treated by Herle's family at Winwick.

Herle was a moderate Presbyterian who believed that Jesus Christ himself, as king and head of the church, had appointed a church government that was distinct from the civil magistrate. He authored four small books and several published sermons.

William Twisse (1578–1646) was educated at Oxford, and after acting as chaplain to King James I's daughter Elizabeth of Bohemia, he began to pastor in England. As the civil war began, he was forced to give up his manse to soldiers; he died impoverished, for all that he had and owned was plundered by the king's soldiers.[31]

Theologically, Twisse was supralapsarian.[32] Some of his writings include *Vindiciae gratiae, potestatis, ac providentiae Dei* (Amsterdam, 1632) and *An Examination of Mr. Cotton's Treatise Concerning Predestination* (London, 1646). When King Charles II was restored to power, he had Twisse's and others' bones dug up from the collegiate church of Saint Peter and tossed into a hole.[33]

Richard Vines (1600–1655) was trained at Cambridge's Magdalen College. He taught as a schoolmaster at Hinckley in Leicestershire, then served as a minister in Weddington, in Warwickshire. As the civil war broke out in 1642, he was driven from his house and forced to take shelter in Coventry, about ninety miles northwest of London.[34] In 1644 he became master of Pembroke Hall, Cambridge, but was

---

31. Ibid., 1:37–55.

32. Ibid., 1:54: "And yet he says, 'That he reckons that controversy, relative to the order of God's decrees, to be merely *apex logicus*—a logical nicety,' as he calls it"; and 1:55: "Dr. Owen opposes Dr. Twisse, concerning this point, in his Dissertation on Divine Justice; where he speaks very honourably and respectfully of him as his most learned antagonist."

33. Ibid., 1:57–58. At his death his children were to be given one thousand British pounds from Parliament's public funds, but they never received it.

34. Ibid., 2:192.

turned out in 1649 for refusing The Engagement.[35] Vines argued for the divine right of presbytery.[36] He was averse to printing anything of his own, yet he authored twelve printed sermons, a collection of twenty sermons on the Lord's Supper, and a number of smaller pieces.

Scottish Commissioners. By their own decision, the Scots refrained from becoming members of the assembly.[37] Alexander Henderson (1583–1646) was trained at St Andrews University, and in 1611 he was a professor of philosophy and rhetoric.[38] In fact, Henderson entered the ministry while he was still unconverted. He was inclined to episcopacy and was a parson at Leuchars by the patronage of Archbishop Gladstanes. The people rebelled against his installation to such an extent that they bolted the doors. Undeterred, Henderson came in through the window. While pastoring, Henderson secretly went to hear a Presbyterian preach, and the word cut like a sword into his heart.[39] There was an immediate change in his ministry, and he became a convinced Presbyterian.

Henderson was called before the Court of High Commission in St Andrews in 1619 for coauthoring the *Perth Assembly*, a booklet against the court. The authors defended themselves well and left without a charge against them.[40] Nearly twenty years later, in 1637 Henderson

35. Johannes G. Vos, *The Scottish Covenanters* (Pittsburgh: Crown & Covenant, 1995), 61–63. The Engagement of 1648 was when Scottish nobles visited the king at the Isle of Wight and made a secret treaty to raise a Scottish army to help the king regain his throne in England. Those who participated in the plan were called Engagers. The Scottish Parliament passed an act requiring everyone to support The Engagement, but the General Assembly actually said that The Engagement was sinful and condemned it.

36. Reid, *Memoirs*, 2:194.

37. The ruling elders included John Campbell (1598–1662), first earl of Loudoun and chancellor of Scotland; Archibald Johnston/Lord Warriston (bap. 1611; d. 1663)—for more information, see David G. Whitla, *Archibald Johnston of Warriston, the National Covenant, and the Formation of British Puritanism (1611–38)*, St Andrews Studies in Reformation History (Leiden: Brill Academic, forthcoming); John Maitland/Viscount Maitland/Earl Lauderdale (1616–1682); and George Winram of Liberton/Lord Liberton (d. 1650). See Robert S. Paul, *The Assembly of the Lord: Politics and Religion in the Westminster Assembly and the 'Grand Debate'* (Edinburgh: T&T Clark, 1985), 441.

38. Robert Low Orr, *Alexander Henderson: Churchman and Statesman* (London: Hodder & Stoughton, 1919); Anonymous, *Lives of Alexander Henderson and James Guthrie: With Specimens of their Writings* (Edinburgh: John Greig, 1846).

39. Reid, *Memoirs*, 2:284–88. Bruce was excluded from ministry in Edinburgh (when the king was there). In 1605 he was ordered to Inverness for four years. Andrew Melville and John Davidson were imprisoned.

40. Ibid., 2:291.

was told to inaugurate new liturgical changes in worship within two weeks or be charged with rebellion. He presented a petition to the privy council objecting to the liturgical changes. The privy council eventually agreed with Henderson. The group became known as the Petitioners.[41]

On March 1, 1638, at Greyfriars Church in Edinburgh, many signed the *National Covenant*, written by Henderson and Archibald Johnston, a lawyer.[42] The *Covenant* was a solemn agreement rejecting the attempt by Charles I and Laud to force English church practice and liturgy on the Scottish church. The marquis of Hamilton was the king's high commissioner to suppress those signers, known as Covenanters. He met with Henderson to dissuade him but was unsuccessful. In fact, the king's attempted suppression excited the Covenanters all the more. The city council of Edinburgh decided to have Henderson join with Andrew Ramsay as pastor in Edinburgh without the advice or consent of the bishops.[43] In July of that year, Henderson was sent to Aberdeen, a city that did not receive the *National Covenant*, where he debated with the doctors. After the debate, one hundred people signed the *Covenant*.

In November, the Petitioners called a general assembly and Scottish Parliament in Glasgow. The bishops issued a declinature against the legality of the assembly, which the marquis of Hamilton insisted be read as the first order of business. After much commotion, the declinature was not yet read, and Henderson was elected moderator of the assembly. The king's commissioner entered a protest. When it was read, the assembly had a reply ready. The question was posed, "whether this assembly found themselves the judges of the Bishops, notwithstanding their declinature." They abolished episcopacy with a great speech by Henderson.[44]

The royal commissioner dissolved the meeting in the name of the king and forbade further meetings. The Petitioners did not obey, and the bishops excommunicated all of them.[45] Undaunted, not only did

41. Ibid., 2:293.
42. Edwin Nisbet Moore, *Our Covenanter Heritage* (Fearn, Scotland: Christian Focus, 2000), 37: "Henderson drafted *The Solemn League and Covenant*, which the Scottish church, Westminster Assembly, and the civil governments in England and Scotland promptly adopted."
43. Reid, *Memoirs*, 2:295.
44. Ibid., 2:300–301.
45. Ibid., 2:298, 303, 305: "A proclamation was issued against the Assembly, and published with great solemnity . . . in Glasgow."

the Petitioners abolish episcopacy, but they also denounced the Court of High Commission, renounced the Articles of Perth, and declared the canons and the liturgy unlawful. The royal superstructure, built by Kings James and Charles, was dismantled to its very foundation.[46] Henderson was called, in the king's name, "the prime and most rigid Covenanter in the kingdom." Archbishop Laud said that Henderson "hath shewn himself a most violent and passionate man, and a Moderator without moderation."[47]

The king immediately planned a counter move and began to raise an army against the Covenanters. The Scots prepared in the winter of 1639, and Henderson wrote a number of tracts defending their actions.[48] Before war erupted, King Charles offered peace, and in June 1639 Henderson served as a commissioner from the Scottish army to present a treaty. The treaty was signed, and the Scottish army disbanded. Henderson, along with thirteen others, was called by order of the king to meet with him. It was a trap, and the people stopped them by taking their horses.[49] In August, another general assembly was called to meet in Edinburgh. This assembly condemned episcopacy as unlawful and contrary to the Word of God and provided yet another defense to the royal commissioner.[50]

In 1640, Henderson was made rector of the University of Edinburgh as war against the king was renewed. A treaty was offered to the king, and Henderson was again one of the commissioners.[51] Negotiations for the treaty were held in London. During that time, a paper drawn up by Henderson was delivered to the English leaders—a paper explaining what had happened in Scotland and outlining plans for carrying out the same in England. One of the stipulations of the treaty with the king was a plan for greater religious uniformity.[52] Negotiations took more than nine months, and a spiritual revival broke out while the Scots were still in London.[53] Henderson negotiated with the king

46. Ibid., 2:314.
47. Ibid., 2:314–15.
48. Ibid., 2:315. Henderson's tracts included "Instructions for defensive arms."
49. Ibid., 2:316.
50. Ibid., 2:320.
51. Ibid., 2:323.
52. Ibid., 2:324.
53. Ibid., 2:325.

to have income from the bishops diverted to the Scottish universities. Henderson returned to Edinburgh in July 1641.[54]

The General Assembly met the following month. Henderson read a letter from London ministers that expressed hope that Scottish-style discipline could be established in England.[55] Thus Henderson proposed a new confession, catechism, and directory for worship. The king left England to cultivate his crown in Scotland and was present for the meeting of the Scottish Parliament. He attended Presbyterian public worship and appointed Henderson as his personal chaplain. Each morning and evening, Henderson led the king and his family in worship.[56] The king gave the bishops' money to the universities and slightly elevated some of the nobles.

In 1642 the English Parliament agreed to abolish episcopacy and requested that Scottish ministers help in the soon-to-be-called Westminster Assembly. Henderson met with the king and the other Scottish commissioners at Oxford.

In January of the following year, Henderson gave the king a humble petition from the Scottish General Assembly, and the king replied unfavorably. Their ill-treatment convinced the commissioners that the royal party was dangerous, so they entered an alliance with the English Parliament. In August, commissioners came from the English Parliament to the Scottish General Assembly; Henderson again moderated the assembly. They carried a declaration of both English houses of Parliament showing a desire for the reformation of religion and invited Scottish ministers to join with their divines.[57] Henderson presented a draft of the covenant, and it was eventually adopted.[58] He assisted commissioners of the two houses of Parliament with a treaty with the king at Uxbridge. The king was unwilling to abolish episcopacy even

54. Ibid., 2:326.
55. Ibid., 2:327.
56. Ibid., 2:330.
57. Ibid., 2:333.
58. Ibid., 2:334: "The English at first were for a civil league, and the Scots for a religious Covenant. This at length obtained the assent of the three Committees, of the English Parliament, of the Convention of Estates, and of the General Assembly. Being adopted by them, it was immediately transmitted to the General Assembly and Convention. And being introduced into the Assembly by a very grave and appropriate speech from the Moderator, it was received with the highest applause, and adopted with tears of much joy."

though he had agreed to it in Scotland. Thus the treaty was suspended, the king returned to London, and civil war ensued.[59]

In the spring of 1646, the king lost the war and left for Newcastle. He called on Henderson, as his chaplain, to come to him. The king and Henderson wrote papers to each other that debated episcopacy, but the king refused to denounce it. In July, Henderson stopped negotiating with the king and left for Scotland. He died in Scotland eight days later. In 1662, the king's commissioner had Henderson's tombstone defaced.[60]

Robert Baillie of Lamington (1599–1662) was the great-great-grandson of King James II. His own great-granddaughter would later marry Bonnie Prince Charlie.[61] Robert was from a family of lesser nobility. He completed his university studies and received church orders from Archbishop Laud in 1622, and he was made a regent of philosophy at Glasgow. In 1637 he was invited to preach to the General Assembly in Glasgow in favor of the *Book of Common Prayer*, but he refused and was considered anti-episcopal.[62]

In 1639 and 1640 he was a chaplain to the Covenanters. During this time, he carried a sword and Dutch pistols in his saddle. He was present for the negotiations with the king. In 1640 he was sent to accuse Archbishop Laud for attempting intrusions in Scotland. He attended the Westminster Assembly from 1643 to 1646.[63] Baillie played a peculiar role during the assembly. Ardently desiring covenanted uniformity, he was the iron fist for Presbyterianism.[64] Baillie held private talks with Thomas Goodwin, but "for that toleration they aime at we cannot consent."[65] He became a Resolutioner and in 1661 was appointed principal of Glasgow.[66]

---

59. Ibid., 2:336–37.

60. Ibid., 2:338–41. Paul, *Assembly*, 440: "One may agree that Alexander Henderson was the wisest and perhaps most moderate of the Scottish Commissioners, but we should recognize that in putting forward their modest claim to toleration, the writers of *An Apologeticall Narration* were presenting a new and still very unpopular idea."

61. See F. N. McCoy, *Robert Baillie and the Second Scots Reformation* (Los Angeles, CA: University of California Press, 1974).

62. Reid, *Memoirs*, 2:271.

63. Ibid., 2:274. He apparently spoke to the assembly only once. See W. Gamble, "Theology of the Westminster Confession," 269.

64. Paul, *Assembly*, 441, and 444: "To him the Scottish cause and the Presbyterian cause were one."

65. Ibid., 445.

66. Reid, *Memoirs*, 2:275.

George Gillespie's (1613–1648) father was a thundering preacher.[67] Gillespie was educated for the ministry at St Andrews and initially served as a chaplain to nobles. Then in 1638, he was ordained by a presbytery in open defiance of the archbishop of St Andrews. At the age of twenty-four, Gillespie wrote the anonymous *A Dispute against the English Popish Ceremonies Obtruded upon the Church of Scotland* (1637). It destroyed the opposing arguments and was received without so much as a response. Immediately, the book was condemned to be burned because it stirred the hearts and affections of the subjects from their due obedience and allegiance.

In 1644, Gillespie published *One Hundred and Eleven Propositions Concerning the Ministry and Government of the Church*. Then his *Aaron's Rod Blossoming*—a three-hundred-page, careful argument against the Erastian position—was published in 1646. Again, the book silenced all his opponents.[68] Gillespie's power was not limited to his pen; he was also a skilled debater on the floor of the assembly.[69] In 1648 he was elected moderator of the Scottish General Assembly. His widow was to receive one thousand British pounds from the English Parliament at his death, but she never received the promised amount.[70]

CONTROVERSY AT THE ASSEMBLY

Preaching and the Ministry. The Westminster divines addressed many controversies during their years of service in London. During this time of British history, the church and the state were connected

---

67. W. D. J. McKay, *An Ecclesiastical Republic: Church Government in the Writings of George Gillespie* (Edinburgh: Rutherford House, 1997); W. D. J. McKay, "George Gillespie and the Westminster Assembly: The Defence of Presbyterianism," *Scottish Bulletin of Evangelical Theology* 13, no. 1 (1995): 51–71.

68. Douglas, *North*, 46–47.

69. In a debate at the assembly on church discipline, Selden had wrongly argued that Matthew 18 "contained no warrant for ecclesiastical jurisdiction, but concerned the ordinary practice of the Jews in their common civil courts." Gillespie summarized Selden's arguments, "then steadily, point by point, he completely refuted it, proving that the passage in question could not be interpreted or explained away to mean a mere reference to a civil court, and that the Jews both possessed and exercised the right of spiritual censures." Selden said in reply, "that young man, by this single speech, has swept away the learning and the labour of ten years of my life" (Douglas, *North*, 41).

70. Reid, *Memoirs*, 2:278–83; Douglas, *North*, 38.

closely. In England's case, however, the state was preeminent. But there was immense opportunity for ecclesiastical reform, as Parliament was interested in making changes. A parliamentary committee began removing scandalous clergy from their congregations. Ministers were expelled for moral failure, ineptitude, divisions, and pope-like behavior. In addition, any lay preachers were removed from their congregations. Those who were removed from their pulpits were replaced by trained men who were not satisfied to administer the sacraments without a sermon. These new ministers were willing to preach sermons, not simply read the preaching of another man. In fact, the chief task of the minister was to preach. Their ministry of the Word and prayer was intended to give hope to the spiritually impoverished.[71]

The Westminster divines had distinct ideas on preachers and the nature of preaching. For them, the preached word was the word of God. It was a demonstration of the Spirit and of power. They were convinced that preaching is the most effective regular means of grace.[72] History is filled with precedent for preaching reform. For example, John Calvin saw the preacher as relaying the message of God. Even though the message is relayed through a man, it carries divine authority.[73]

Calvin's views had received varied responses. King Edward VI embraced his views, Queen Mary strongly rejected them, and Queen Elizabeth was coldly indifferent to his view of preaching.[74] Calvin's views were picked up in William Perkins's book *The Art of Prophesying*.[75]

Church office in England was different from that in much of the rest of the Continent. England maintained a system of church patronage and benefices, or livings. Some occupants were rectors and others vicars.[76] Those rectors or vicars who were appointed by patrons did not

71. Chad Van Dixhoorn, *God's Ambassadors: The Westminster Assembly and the Reformation of the English Pulpit, 1643–53* (Grand Rapids: Reformation Heritage Books, 2017), 1–8.

72. Ibid., 9. He has a section defining *puritanism* and how that term relates to the members of the assembly (ibid., 10–16).

73. Ibid., 17–21.

74. When Archbishop Grindal attempted to introduce Zurich-inspired "prophesying" to improve preaching, Elizabeth insisted that these plans cease because England needed at best only a handful of preachers (ibid., 22).

75. Ibid., 27–28.

76. A vicar received part of the income from a benefice, while a rector received, by right, all the income. Ordination was performed by the bishop with an archdeacon, deans, and two prebendaries. After the laying on of hands, the patron would pronounce the prelate's name for

necessarily need to be clergy. This system encouraged pluralism, whereby ministers would attend to more than one parish at a time. Rectors who were inducted into livings had financial burdens.[77] And induction into a living did not involve a license to preach.[78] But under King James VI/I, who appreciated preaching, there were improvements for the church.[79]

Archbishop William Laud believed that the sacraments were more important than preaching, so serious reformers contended for structural change within the church. Put simply, preaching needed to improve.

When the assembly was summoned on July 1, 1643, England was in economic and political trouble. As a result of the war that began in 1642, England was experiencing various kinds of suffering. The war also opened doors for social and religious radicalism.[80]

Under Charles I, the English church spiraled toward Arminianism and Roman Catholicism. There was now an opportunity within the church for deep and structural reform. The problem was that London was being overrun by radicalism.

The necessary reforms included the reorganization of discipline that would be pastoral and remedial in addition to a process to approve prospective ministers. The majority of divines saw the need to restructure the entire episcopal system—a structural change that would have been impossible under the previous monarchs.[81]

The majority at the assembly wanted to dislodge bishops as supposed overseers of preachers who did not themselves regularly preach. Now preachers, in conjunction with overseers, called *ruling elders*, would lead in all phases of church government and pastoral practice.[82]

---

appointment. Induction followed when the priest's hands were placed by the archdeacon on the church door (ibid., 24, 46).

77. Rectors had to pay their patrons legal costs for a deed of presentation, then a fee of institution to the bishop, a fee of induction to the archdeacon, and finally a fee of the first year's income to the crown. The bishop would "visit" each parish at least once in three years. On his first visit to the new rector, the bishop would receive a modest fee. Each subsequent visit yielded one half the amount of the first fee (ibid., 46–47).

78. The license to preach came from the archbishop or one of the two universities. Most ministers were not permitted to preach (ibid., 48).

79. Ibid., 24–26.

80. Ibid., 28–33. Of course King Charles had managed to rule without Parliament from 1629 to 1640. See ibid., 36.

81. Ibid., 33–36.

82. While there was a desire to dismantle episcopacy, there was still diversity of opinion on what type of Presbyterianism should be established. For more information see Chad Van Dixhoorn, "Presbyterian Ecclesiologies at the Westminster Assembly," in *Church Polity and*

The preaching of the Word was an integral part of the Westminster Assembly. Each day from 6:00 to 8:00 A.M., there was preaching and prayer. Probationary sermons were given between 8:00 and 9:00 A.M. before the start of plenary sessions.

As pastors were plundered and displaced by royalist troops, the assembly would examine those pastors and certify them competent to inherit the parishes of those who had been ejected. As time progressed, a system was established. First the assembly would certify the preacher, then the congregation would approve the appointment, and finally Parliament would approve the placement.[83] Even after presbyteries were established, Parliament insisted on the assembly's certification so that they could, in some measure, maintain control over the ministry of the church. Thus candidates for ministry had to sustain two sets of ordination exams.[84]

By the fall of 1643, a committee submitted twenty-one procedural rules for examining ministerial candidates. One of the rules was worded in such a way as intentionally to exclude Congregationalists.[85] Eventually, some candidates could be given probationary approval for a period of six to twelve months. But there were at times tensions with Parliament when a politically well-connected candidate was rejected by the assembly while receiving the support of a parliamentary house.[86]

There were essential characteristics for ordination. A man called to ministry was called to pulpit ministry. Such a man needed to be godly and Christlike in character. Congregations needed to have confidence that the sermons they heard from these men were the very words of God. All of this work applied to English pastors and congregations, not to those in Scotland.[87]

Independency versus Presbyterianism.[88] There was a group who could be called *divine right* (or *jus divinum*) Presbyterians, who believed that the

---

Politics in the British Atlantic World, 1635–66, ed. H. Powell and E. Vernon (Manchester: University of Manchester Press, 2020), 104–29.

83. Van Dixhoorn, *God's Ambassadors*, 41–43.

84. Ibid., 49–50.

85. The eighth question asked whether the church and ministry of England were true. Such an affirmation of a visible church as a regional collection of congregations was not possible for Congregationalists. For an analysis of all twenty-one questions, see ibid., 53–56.

86. Ibid., 59–61.

87. Ibid., 173–75.

88. For more information, see Robert S. Paul, *The Assembly of the Lord: Politics and Religion in the Westminster Assembly and the 'Grand Debate'* (Edinburgh: T&T Clark, 1985), appendix V, 565.

basic structure, even many of the details of church governance, had been prescribed by Christ in the NT. Thus it was the obligation of the church to follow the pattern established by Christ. Another sizeable group in the assembly comprised what could be termed "pragmatic Presbyterians." These men were opposed to episcopacy in its present English form but hesitant to assert scriptural authority for Presbyterian distinctives.

The Independents were another small, yet influential group; they opposed any form of church authority beyond local eldership. They were, however, willing to engage in more regional consultative connections. Finally, there was another group called the Erastians, who argued that the civil magistrate had the God-given right to determine the form and functions of church government.[89] With each group still in its infancy, confusion ensued when some of the Independents defined *presbytery* as the elders of a local congregation.[90]

The first point to remember when analyzing the deep confusion and unharmonious voices of assembly members relative to church government is that the Scottish commissioners were not greeted by convinced Presbyterians at the time of the Westminster Assembly. Many of the English members still had a deep and abiding sympathy for episcopacy. Commenting on their position, Robert Baillie said, "the greatest and most countenanced part were much Episcopall."[91] Nevertheless, episcopacy would not be tolerated. The struggle would be between the Independents and Presbyterians.

Both groups were in favor of having presbyteries and synods and recognized that these assemblies were to be, in some sense, higher or superior ones. But the issue was the nature of the local congregation's subordination to the higher court and the reaches of the coercive or juridical powers of the higher assemblies.[92] The differences were summarized in a letter by Robert Baillie: "The Independents have entered

89. For a very helpful introduction and the text of the *Directory for Church Government*, see Wayne R. Spear, "The Westminster Assembly's Directory for Church Government," in *Pressing Toward the Mark: Essays Commemorating Fifty Years of the Orthodox Presbyterian Church*, ed. Charles G. Dennison and Richard C. Gamble (Philadelphia: Committee for the Historian of the Orthodox Presbyterian Church, 1986), 83–93.

90. Paul, *Assembly*, 301n137, and 339: "Burroughs apparently argued for a covenanted church under its own 'presbytery' and was not in favor of having elders ruling who were not in immediate pastoral relationship with the particular congregations."

91. Ibid., 439.

92. Ibid., 434–35, and 448: "The Independents had gone a long way, although they may not have conceded absolutely the juridical power of presbytery over congregations."

their dissent only to three propositions: 'That in Ephesus was a classical Presbytrie; That there is a subordination of Assemblies; That a single congregation has not all and sole power of ordination.'"[93]

A main point of debate was excommunication. The Presbyterians argued that someone who has been excommunicated should have the right of appeal. The Independents believed that church discipline had to be confined to where the person lived and worshipped. The individual believer is not a member of any higher fellowship. Excommunication must come only from a particular congregation. Independents were opposed to excommunication as a right of superior assemblies.[94]

Both groups claimed *jus divinum*.[95] The political issue was that the Independents did not want to accept the Presbyterian form of government, as practiced in Scotland, because they rightly feared that their position would not be secure within the new religious establishment.[96]

In April of 1644, the Independents and Presbyterians held private meetings.[97] As the problem grew worse, a committee of accommodation was established. But the Scottish commissioners were determined that any agreement would be predicated on the acceptance of Scottish Presbyterianism.[98]

To understand this debate, which may seem opaque to contemporary readers, we must first realize that, at this time, religious intolerance was assumed. It was inconceivable to the seventeenth-century English or Scottish mind that multiple religions could be practiced within the same nation.[99] Both Independents and Presbyterians were convinced that intolerance was a virtue, not a vice, and neither party hesitated to utilize force to assert its position.[100] These sinful men who gathered

93. Robert Baillie, December 26, 1644, as cited by ibid., 437.
94. Ibid., 435n229.
95. Ibid., 449. Nye made a speech in which he said that Presbyterianism could not fit with a civil state. He asserted that to draw a kingdom under one national assembly was pernicious (see Paul, *Assembly*, 446, citing a letter by Baillie).
96. Ibid., 436.
97. There were three Independents: Goodwin, Burroughs, and Bridge, and the Scottish Commissioners, together with assembly members from Parliament, Lord Wharton, Sir Henry Vane, and Oliver St. John.
98. Ibid., 445–46, 447.
99. Ibid., 440n13: "Religious intolerance was not regarded as evil but as commitment, and intolerance was therefore endemic to seventeenth-century religion."
100. Ibid., 440: "Baillie was entirely justified in pointing to the intolerance of the New England Congregationalists. . . . Once we recognize that intolerance was regarded as a virtue

to enlist God-honoring changes, often through contentious debate, did not labor in vain.

FRUIT OF THEIR LABORS: CONFESSION, CATECHISMS, DIRECTORY OF CHURCH GOVERNMENT

Confession of Faith. The Westminster Confession of Faith (WCF) was sent in 1647 to the English Parliament and the General Assembly of the Church of Scotland. It was adopted without amendment by the Scottish church. The English Parliament required a list of proof texts, and after it received them, the Confession was adopted, with some omissions, in 1648. The Scottish Parliament also ratified the Confession without amendment. The WCF—a compilation of thirty-three chapters that address every essential point of doctrine—is the apex of theological summaries.[101] It is the most faithful secondary summary of the teaching found in God's Word, and it is a document of great value to study, no matter a person's denominational affiliation.[102]

Catechisms. The Larger Catechism (WLC), written in a question-and-answer format, was to be more exact and comprehensive than the shorter version. The Shorter Catechism (WSC), based on the WLC but written for children, was also written in a question-and-answer format. It contained 107 questions and their answers. The WSC was sent to Parliament just over a month after the WLC was sent; it was

rather than a vice, and that liberty of conscience was understood as an excuse for license. . . . [we see that] Baillie had no compunction about using force . . . any more than Cromwell had any compunction."

101. For more information, see Archibald Alexander Hodge, *The Confession of Faith* (Edinburgh: Banner of Truth, 1978); Benjamin B. Warfield, *The Westminster Assembly and Its Work* (New York: Oxford University Press, 1931); John Murray, "The Theology of the Westminster Confession," *Scripture and Confession*, ed. John Skilton (Nutley, NJ: Presbyterian and Reformed, 1973), 125–48; Robert Letham, *The Westminster Assembly: Reading Its Theology in Historical Context* (Phillipsburg, NJ: P&R Publishing, 2009); Wayne R. Spear, *Faith of Our Fathers: A Commentary on the Westminster Confession of Faith* (Pittsburgh: Crown & Covenant, 2013); Chad Van Dixhoorn, *The Minutes and Papers of the Westminster Assembly, 1643–53* (Oxford: Oxford University Press, 2012); Chad Van Dixhoorn, *Confessing the Faith: A Reader's Guide to the Westminster Confession of Faith* (Edinburgh: Banner of Truth, 2014); John R. Bower, *The Confession of Faith: A Critical Text and Introduction* (Grand Rapids: Reformation Heritage Books, 2020).

102. The best short summary of its contents is found in W. Gamble, "Theology of the Westminster Confession," 270–75.

approved by the Church of Scotland in July 1648 and the Scottish Parliament early the following year.[103]

Directory. *The Directory for the Public Worship of God* and *The Form of Presbyterial Church Government* were both completed in December 1644. In 1645, the *Directory* was approved and established by Parliament and the Scottish General Assembly, and the *Form* was approved by the General Assembly. *A Directory for Church-Government, Church-Censures, and Ordination of Ministers* was completed in July 1645 and adopted by the General Assembly of Scotland in 1647. Fascinatingly, it has not been printed in Scotland for more than two hundred years, and it has never been printed in America. It contains some overlap with the *Form of Church Government.*[104] *The Directory for Family Worship* was not approved by the Westminster Assembly but was added by the Church of Scotland, which deemed it necessary.

PRESBYTERIAN HISTORY AFTER THE WESTMINSTER CONFESSION OF FAITH

King Charles I escaped from prison and provoked the Second English Civil War (1648–1649). He was defeated yet again, then executed. The monarchy was abolished, and the Commonwealth was ushered in.

Commonwealth. While fighting continued in Scotland and Ireland, sometimes referred to as the Third English Civil War, the Commonwealth lasted from 1649 to 1660. In 1653, Oliver Cromwell (1599–1658) dissolved the Rump Parliament and was declared to be the lord protector. This time in British history is referred to as the Protectorate. The Protectorate Parliament was dissolved in 1659.

Restoration. After the death of Oliver Cromwell, his son became the second lord protector. But he was unable to retain power and resigned after nine months. In 1660 General George Monk, who had

---

103. Douglas F. Kelly, "The Westminster Shorter Catechism," in *To Glorify and Enjoy God: A Commemoration of the 350th Anniversary of the Westminster Assembly,* ed. John L. Carlson and David W. Hall (Edinburgh: Banner of Truth, 1994), 101–26; John H. Leith, *Assembly at Westminster: Reformed Theology in the Making* (Richmond, VA: John Knox Press, 1973).

104. See J. R. DeWitt, *Jus Divinum: The Westminster Assembly and the Divine Right of Church Government* (Kampen: Kok, 1969).

governed Scotland under Cromwell, marched his soldiers south and organized the Convention Parliament. This parliament declared that Charles II was now king since his father had been executed.

Thus the monarchy was restored to King Charles I's son Charles II (1630–1685). He was crowned in 1661. Many who had signed the previous king's death warrant were hanged, drawn, and quartered. Cromwell's corpse was hung in chains.

The Church of England was restored as the national church in England, backed by the Clarendon Code and the Act of Uniformity in 1662. Many in England were glad to be done with the Presbyterians and the Independents. Episcopacy was reinstated in Scotland as well. When King Charles II died, he was succeeded by his younger brother, King James VII/II (1633–1701). In 1668 he secretly converted to Catholicism and attended Anglican services until 1676. He worked for liberty for Roman Catholics and nonconformists, while he brutally persecuted the Presbyterian Covenanters. He had a Roman Catholic son who was prepared to succeed him.

Glorious Revolution. In 1688, the union of English Parliamentarians and William III of Orange-Nassau deposed King James II. They placed on the throne the Protestant Mary II Stuart (1662–1694), the daughter of James II. Her husband, William (1650–1702), invaded with a Dutch fleet and took the throne with his wife; they became King William and Queen Mary.[105] Their enthronement led to the Revolution Settlement, thus creating an Anglican Church of England and a Presbyterian Church of Scotland.[106]

Marrow Controversy. Turning from political turmoil and shifts in power, it will be helpful briefly to address a controversy that surrounded a book published in ca. 1647. With the approbation of many, an Independent named Edward Fisher published *The Marrow of Mod-*

---

105. In 1690, James II made one attempt to recover his throne at the battle of the Boyne in Ireland. After that defeat he lived in France. These changes resulted in the English bill of rights and the Hanoverian succession. Sophia of Hanover was a granddaughter of James VI/I. William and Mary and Mary's sister Anne had no children, and the house of Stuart was Catholic. Sophia's son became King George I. The Scottish Parliament did not want to abandon the house of Stuart, and the parliaments united in 1707. No Catholic monarchs are allowed.

106. Not all Scots would enter this newly formed Church of Scotland, which failed to address very important legal and theological issues. For more information, see Richard C. Gamble, "The Clash of King and Kirk," in *The Practical Calvinist: An Introduction to the Presbyterian and Reformed Heritage*, ed. Peter A. Lillback (Fearn, Scotland: Mentor, 2002), 215–32.

ern Divinity. This book was an attempt to strike a balance between the errors of antinomianism and real neonomianism, or legalism.[107] The book was republished in the eighteenth century and provided the impetus for focused debates on various views already held in the church.[108]

The General Assembly of the Church of Scotland was deeply opposed to this work—so much so that, in 1720, they prohibited anyone from speaking positively of the work.[109] This prohibition brought about a counterreaction by approximately a dozen supporters, who are now known as the Marrow Men.

The most important spokesman of the group was Thomas Boston (1676–1732). Sinclair Ferguson says that there were two main issues to the debate. First, for all who come to Christ there is fullness of grace; and second, there is not only fullness, but also freedom.[110]

The debate encompassed at least two significant theological issues. First, one cannot speak lightly of the law of God as being abrogated (the antinomian position), for the Law is an expression of God's very will and nature as the just governor of all.[111] Second, the debate also contained a number of issues related to Christ's work and the believer's forensic justification.[112]

God's plan in justification was to overrule the fall, for his own glory, with a manifestation of all his moral perfections.[113] There is a twofold revelation in justification. First, God perfectly manifests his moral attributes in total harmony. This manifestation transcends simply dispensing life to the righteous and punishment for the wicked. Second, God reveals his essential Trinitarian nature and manifests distinct operations of each of the three persons in the work of justification.[114]

---

107. James Buchanan, *The Doctrine of Justification: An Outline of Its History in the Church and of Its Exposition from Scripture* (1984; repr., Edinburgh: Banner of Truth, 1991), 182; Mark Jones, *Antinomianism: Reformed Theology's Unwelcome Guest?* (Phillipsburg, NJ: P&R Publishing, 2013), 13. Sinclair B. Ferguson (*The Whole Christ: Legalism, Antinomianism, and Gospel Assurance: Why the Marrow Controversy Still Matters* [Wheaton, IL: Crossway, 2016], 33) says that part one came out in 1645 and part two in 1648.

108. Buchanan, *Justification*, 183.

109. Ferguson, *Whole Christ*, 32.

110. Ibid., 42.

111. Buchanan, *Justification*, 288.

112. Ibid., 292.

113. Ibid., 293.

114. Ibid., 293–94.

This eternal covenant determined the plan and regulated the provisions of the elect's salvation.[115]

Believers must remember that this covenant, wrought for their salvation, was the manifestation of his lovingkindness and tender mercy. Our salvation is a free movement of mercy in the mind of God. God's love ordained the end, and his omniscient wisdom provided the means for the accomplishment of salvation. It was not that the covenant of salvation was the cause of his love. Stated another way, it is not that Christ's great work of redemption prompted the Father's love.[116] The Marrow Controversy split the church in Scotland and sparked significant soteriological advances.

Conclusion to Part 5. After the Reformation, the church lived in a vibrant time politically, socially, and intellectually. It was an era of great scientific and philosophical advance. Philosophers grappled with how best to comprehend the world, whether through empiricism or rationalism.

The church's theologians had the time and opportunity to reflect on the great issues of the faith. Unlike in the earlier period of the Reformation, when the Reformers had to fight for their very existence, most theologians in this time enjoyed state-sponsored salaries. This era also saw the convening of grand theological conferences, such as the Synod of Dordt and the Westminster Assembly. In these conferences, state churches solidified a full-orbed reformation of religious life.

Yet behind the progress of this rich season, storm clouds were forming in the heavens. The raindrops of the Enlightenment would soon give way to the rolling thunder of deeply developed rationalism and empiricism and the lightning bolt of Immanuel Kant's answer to the philosophical and theological dilemma.

KEY TERMS

jus divinum
Solemn League and Covenant

115. Ibid., 294.
116. Ibid., 295–96.

STUDY QUESTIONS

1. What were the political circumstances that forced the English Parliament to seek Scotland's aid?
2. What do you think of the Westminster Larger Catechism's analysis of the Ten Commandments?

RESOURCES FOR FURTHER STUDY

The Westminster Confession of Faith is available through many online resources. Students of the confession should realize that most American denominations have modified the original confession and for historical accuracy should investigate what the divines actually wrote. Also, most American Presbyterian denominations have modified the original directory for worship, and students may want to read the divines' own directory to compare.

Heppe, Heinrich. *Reformed Dogmatics*. Eugene, OR: Wipf & Stock, 1977. The best means for grasping the theology of WCG3 Part 5. This classic text has been in English translation for fifty years and is the gold standard for an overall grasp of the theology of the seventeenth century. Heppe choose twenty-eight loci of theology moving from natural and revealed theology to glorification. In each section he has arranged snippets of primary text that elucidate the thinking of all the theologians mentioned through each part plus many others.

Moore, Edwin Nisbet. *Our Covenanter Heritage*. Fearn, Scotland: Christian Focus, 2000. An insightful examination of the historical circumstances and thinking of the Presbyterians.

Muller, Richard A. *Post-Reformation Reformed Dogmatics*. Vol. 1, *Prolegomena to Theology*. Grand Rapids: Baker, 1987. Another great resource.

Vos, Johannes G. *The Westminster Larger Catechism*. Phillipsburg, NJ: P&R Publishing, 2002. A very helpful study of the Westminster Larger Catechism.

PART 6

The Church in the Modern Western World

19

Eighteenth Century

As WE LEAVE THE beauty of the Reformed theology of the seventeenth century, we now turn our attention to movements that were held at bay for a time before unleashing their furor against God and his Word.

RATIONALISM IN FRANCE

Voltaire (A.D. 1694–1778). A key figure for the French Enlightenment was Francois-Marie Arouet, known by his nom de plume, Voltaire. Voltaire lived a quite colorful life. At the age of twenty-one, he found himself imprisoned for having insulted the king. He was then exiled for three years (1726–1729). For Voltaire, this time in exile was philosophically determinative, for it was in this time that he encountered English deism. He eventually returned to Paris but was forced to leave again. He then spent a significant part of his life in the region of Lorraine. After these humiliations, Voltaire returned to Parisian power, was named the historiographer of France, and was elected to the French Academy. In 1750, he moved to Germany and spent two years as the philosopher-poet for Frederick the Great of Prussia. A little later, he moved to Calvin's Geneva, and from the year 1759 until his death he lived just across the French border. For half a century, Voltaire was a dominant force as a playwright for the French stage. He wrote poetry, edited a large philosophical dictionary, and played an important role in the compilation of the thirty-five-volume *Encyclopedia* by Diderot.[1]

---

1. Gordon H. Clark, *Religion, Reason and Revelation* (Jefferson, MD: Trinity Foundation, 1986), 47. Voltaire is the author of *The Bible Finally Explained* and *God and Man*.

Theologically, Voltaire was passionately anti-Catholic—he saw only corruption and deceit in the Catholic Church. He did not, however, abandon God altogether. Voltaire said that he would always be convinced that a watch proves a watchmaker and the universe proves the existence of a God. Thus Voltaire believed that God was necessary for the foundation of human thought and must be believed in. He held to a natural theology.[2]

Jean-Jacques Rousseau (A.D. 1712–1778). Rousseau was also a fascinating character with a colorful personal life. Born in Geneva, he was for a time a member of the Roman Catholic Church, but then he became Protestant, only to transition later to becoming a deist. Refusing to care or take responsibility for all five of his illegitimate children, he entrusted them to orphanages. He was a musician, a political theorist, and, generally, a man of letters.[3] Rousseau was forced to leave France because both of his works, *Emile* and *The Social Contract*, were condemned.

In 1750, Rousseau wrote *Discourse on the Arts and Sciences*. This work answered the question posed by the Academy of Dijon as to whether scientific and liberal-arts studies have positive or negative moral effects on a student.[4] He began with an acknowledgment that there had recently been great progress in these fields.[5] Nevertheless, he argued that cultural progress corrupts human morals.[6]

A dozen years later, his treatise *Emile* appeared. In this work, Rousseau outlined a pattern of education that was based on *natural instincts*, by which expression he meant removing the child from the corrupting influences of society. In this philosophical novel, the young student Emile had yet to encounter everyday aspects of European life, such as church bells or military toys, for Rousseau held that both items

2. Colin Brown, *Philosophy & the Christian Faith: A Historical Sketch from the Middle Ages to the Present Day* (Downers Grove, IL: InterVarsity Press, 1968), 86; Karl Heussi, *Kompendium der Kirchengeschichte* (Tübingen: Mohr Siebeck, 1971), 332.

3. Brown, *Philosophy & Faith*, 81.

4. Five years later, in 1755, he wrote *Discourse on Inequality*. A work titled *Political Economy* appeared in 1758.

5. Jean-Jacques Rousseau, *A Discourse on the Moral Effects of the Arts and Sciences* (London: Dent, 1961), 120: "It is a noble and beautiful spectacle to see man raising himself, so to speak, from nothing by his own exertions; like the sun, encompassing with giant strides the vast extent of the universe. All these miracles we have seen renewed within the last few generations."

6. Ibid., 123: "Our minds have been corrupted in proportion as the arts and sciences have improved."

were symbols of a corrupt society. Armed with a tutor and living in the country allowed Emile's natural instincts to be channeled in what Rousseau thought was the right direction.[7]

The Social Contract was also published in 1762. The reverberating effects of this book would be difficult to overstate. The notion of the social contract has led to the destruction of some of the finest aspects of Western civilization.[8] Earlier debates concerning the need for divine authority for law were set aside. He argued that laws should no longer be rooted in divine law but instead in the will of the people.[9] Such a theory may sound at first appealing, as this rationale is foundational for law even within the United States. He argued that the social contract was the underpinning of any good society and culture, for the social contract would integrate a just government with sufficient freedom for the majority. This thinking laid the foundation for the horrors of the French Revolution.[10]

In conclusion, even long after his death Rousseau exercised great influence in European politics and literature because of his attractive and persuasive writing style. He was also influential in the area of religion. His natural religion placed man on center stage. From the intellectual leaders of France, we move across the channel to England.

EMPIRICISM IN BRITAIN

Bishop Joseph Butler (A.D. 1692–1752). While his name may not be familiar, Joseph Butler was the most influential Christian apologist of his day. Since his day, his method of evidences has controlled the discipline of apologetics.[11] His *Analogy of Religion, Natural and*

7. Brown, *Philosophy & Faith*, 82.

8. It wrongly places political authority on the backs of a feckless majority instead of on natural law—or even better, on God's Word. Since Rousseau despised God and his Word, he had to find some other place to establish right and wrong.

9. Jean-Jacques Rousseau, *The Social Contract*, trans. G. D. H. Cole (London: Dent, 1961), 7: "Since no man has a natural authority over his fellow, and force creates no right, we must conclude that conventions form the basis of all legitimate authority among men." 15: "whoever refuses to obey the general will shall be compelled to do so by the whole body."

10. Brown, *Philosophy & Faith*, 83.

11. Cornelius Van Til, *Christian Theistic Evidences* (Phillipsburg, NJ: Presbyterian and Reformed, 1978), 5.

Revealed, to the Constitution and Course of Nature (1736) defended Christianity against contemporary deism. In this book, Butler creates an analogy between Scripture's teaching and the deist's notion of natural revelation.[12] He argues that there are features of this life that resemble features of the afterlife. As an example, since early life on the earth is a training ground for later life, we can safely infer that this life is a training ground for the next life.[13]

The *Analogy* began with the concept of *probability*. The apologetic claim for Christianity is the modest one that there is at least a chance of its being true, a practical presumption in its favor. And in everyday life, intelligent people most often act on things that are only considered probably true. Christianity is on a par with those probable facts of everyday life.[14] Butler refers to the facts of everyday life as the constitution and course of nature. For Butler, it is the foundation for understanding facts. He was also an empiricist.[15] Empiricism does not deny reason but is convinced that knowledge is founded on experience rather than on rational principles.[16] Butler's arguments for Christianity, however, are based on facts.[17] But reason also plays an essential role—it judges the meaning, morality, and evidence of revelation.[18]

Concerning the soul's immortality, Butler reasoned that because in life we have undergone many changes yet continue to live, it is prob-

12. John M. Frame, *A History of Western Philosophy and Theology* (Phillipsburg, NJ: P&R Publishing, 2015) (*HWPT*), 233.
13. K. Scott Oliphint, foreword to *Christian Theistic Evidences*, by Cornelius Van Til, edited by K. Scott Oliphint (Phillipsburg, NJ: P&R Publishing, 2016), xxxiii.
14. Van Til, *Evidences*, 7.
15. Butler had read Samuel Clarke's book, which tried to prove God's existence by way of Cartesian a priori reasoning. Even after corresponding with him, Butler found those arguments unconvincing (ibid., 9–10).
16. Ibid., 31: "At an earlier point he absolutely rejected the validity of *a priori* reasoning."
17. Ibid., 31–32: "After it has been shown that miracle and fulfilled prophecy are facts, that is, that such things as have been recorded have actually taken place, these facts must be shown to be in analogy with the facts as we observe them in the 'constitution and course of nature.' The tool with which we do the work of comparing one 'fact' with another 'fact' of a different nature is the 'faculty of reason, which is the candle of the Lord within us.'"
18. Butler, *Analogy*, 240, as cited by Van Til, *Evidences*, 12–13: "Reason can, and it ought to judge, not only of the meaning, but also of the morality and the evidence, of revelation. First, it is the province of reason to judge of the morality of the scripture; i.e., not whether it contains things different from what we should have expected from a wise, just and good Being; for objections from hence have been now obviated; but whether it contains things plainly contradictory to wisdom, justice, or goodness; to what the light of nature teaches us of God."

able that we shall also survive death. This argument is from likeness, or continuity—which is an argument from the known to the unknown based on a principle of continuity.[19]

As Butler considered Adam and creation, he presupposed what he referred to as an "Author of nature," for he was a Christian writing against deists who also believed in a god.[20] Moving to man's original state, Butler believed that Adam had a propensity toward that which was not virtuous.[21] For Butler, this natural propensity toward certain objects was likely the explanation for Adam's original sin—essentially, an Arminian stance toward the fall.[22] One fact of experience, according to Butler, is the power of contrary choice, or the so-called "freedom of the will."[23] Butler did not acknowledge any corruption of human nature after the fall. He believed that human reason is in the same condition as it was in creation, and the human will, while admittedly weakened by habitual sin, is as inclined toward the good as it was at creation.[24] Butler did not even mention the need for regeneration.

When his opponent was wholly ignorant of the Christian faith, Butler's apologetic approach was to demonstrate the corroboration of natural religion by Scripture. If it can be demonstrated to the opponent that natural religion and Scripture cooperate, then the opponent would no longer perceive a conflict between reason and revelation.[25] For Butler, Christianity's practice is reasonable.[26]

Butler's methodology seems commendable, for it appears to give the Christian apologist and unbelievers the common ground of fact as a starting point. Butler believed that believers and unbelievers can

19. But Van Til argues that it is not legitimate for an empiricist to assume a general continuity in the course of nature (Van Til, *Evidences*, 13–15).

20. Ibid., 17.

21. Butler, *Analogy*, 120, as cited by Van Til, *Evidences*, 21: "Mankind, and perhaps all finite creatures, from the very constitution of their nature, before habits of virtue, are deficient, and in danger of deviating from what is right: and therefore stand in need of virtuous habits, for a security against this danger."

22. Van Til, *Evidences*, 22.

23. Ibid., 11.

24. Ibid., 25.

25. Ibid., 29.

26. Ibid., 30: Butler has shown, "that there is more than a presumption. He has shown that there is a great positive probability for the truth of Christianity. And that is all that reasonable men should require. If they require more they forget that satisfaction 'in this sense, does not belong to such a creature as man.'"

settle differences over simple appeals to facts. In addition, we can use the same method of procedure to analyze those facts.[27]

The foundational defect of Butler's methodology is that "it begins by assuming that the enemies of the gospel of Christ are right in holding that man is, or may be, self-explanatory, and that the facts of his environment are, or may be, purely chance-produced and directed."[28] It is the Arminian, not the Reformed, who would want to use Butler's method. The Arminian believes in a more finite God, not a sovereign or absolute God. Arminians believe sinners capable of discerning between good and evil apart from regeneration. Butler's method is similar to that of Aquinas.[29]

David Hume (A.D. 1711–1776). Hume was born in Edinburgh, Scotland, and began university there at the age of twelve. He graduated three years later. His professional career was rather peculiar. He served as a secretary to a general, as a librarian in Edinburgh, and even worked for the British Embassy in Paris. He was a friend of the prominent thinker Jean-Jacques Rousseau, and at one time he brought the French philosopher to London.[30] Unfortunately for Hume, Rousseau falsely accused him of attempted murder.

During his lifetime, Hume was better known as a historian than as a philosopher.[31] He was disappointed with the reception of his philosophical work, written when he was from twenty-one to twenty-five years of age and titled *Treatise of Human Nature* (3 vols., 1739–40). Hume also wrote the more famous, and from his own statements, more mature, *An Enquiry Concerning Human Understanding*, as well as *An Enquiry Concerning the Principles of Morals* (1751), *Dialogues Concerning Natural Religion*, and finally *The Natural History of Religion* (1757).

In one sentence, we may describe David Hume as both an empiricist and a skeptic.[32] He argued that there were no abstract ideas. A

27. Ibid., 62.
28. Oliphint, foreword, xxxiii.
29. Van Til, *Evidences*, 62–63.
30. See chapter 19.
31. Bertrand Russell, *A History of Western Philosophy* (New York: Simon & Schuster, 1945), 686.
32. Gordon H. Clark, *Thales to Dewey: A History of Philosophy* (Boston: Houghton Mifflin, 1957), 382; Charles W. Eliot, *English Philosophers*, Harvard Classics 37 (New York: Collier, 1910). See David Hume, *Enquiry Concerning Human Understanding*, Section II, "Of the origin of ideas" (Chicago: Encyclopedia Britannica, 1955), 316–20.

person, a self, can know only from experience; therefore, there can be no unknown physical substance and unknown spiritual substance.

Earlier, Berkeley had said that the existence of the self is self-evident. But Hume argued that there is no reason, from human experience alone or from pure empiricism, to assert the self-evident nature of the existence of the human self.[33] From human experience alone, for example, no one can determine the existence of a human spirit. Not only can people not know the self, but it is furthermore mistaken to say that the self is in some sense eternal. There is, in experience, no ground for asserting the eternality of the human soul.[34]

Hume's denial of the existence of a spiritual substance means that God's existence must also be denied. The British philosophers Locke and Berkeley had thought that because beauty, order, and wisdom exist in the universe, God's existence must also be possible. Against their thought, Hume argued that the ontological argument for God's existence is not convincing. He recognized that a believer could reason against his argument by suggesting that the presence of a half-finished house demonstrates the existence of an architect and builder. Hume replied, however, that in the case of a house, this assertion is true because many people have experiences of half-finished houses; but when it comes the universe, can someone say that there is necessarily an architect and builder? He argued that the answer is no, because no one has seen an unfinished universe.[35]

There are fatal flaws in Hume's thinking, and his philosophical foundation severely limits knowledge. Hume's philosophy does not allow for the possibility of knowing other persons. For example, no one else can know my toothache. Neither can I understand someone else's experience, for example, of the color red.[36] I am not confident that Hume even knew himself.[37] Hume was not at all certain that humans

---

33. Clark, *Thales to Dewey*, 382–85.
34. Ibid., 386.
35. Ibid., 389–90.
36. Ibid., 384.
37. "When I enter most intimately into what I call myself, they always stumble on some particular perception or other. I never can catch myself at any time without a perception, and never can observe anything but the perception" (Hume, *Treatise* I, i, as cited by Brown, *Philosophy & Faith*, 68). His idea of substance was also peculiar: "Substance is nothing but a collection of simple ideas, that are united by the imagination, and have a particular name designed to them,

possess a soul.[38] He denied that anyone could believe in miracles.[39] Hume truly had a great philosophical mind, but during his lifetime he was neither popular nor famous.[40] One of his more popular competitors was the movement we refer to as *deism*.

Hume's Reply to Butler. Hume held Butler in high regard. They shared a common opposition to a priori reasoning. Nevertheless, Hume rejected Butler's arguments for Christianity presented in the *Analogy*.[41]

Butler believed that the course of nature would remain the same into the future. Hume, however, argued that such a presumption was founded on custom, at best, and that there is no logical relationship between the past and the future.[42] Hume's point was simply that no one can know how future events will occur. Expecting future events to follow the pattern of history is reasoning founded on nonrational grounds.[43]

If Hume's thesis is correct, then it is quite destructive to Butler's argument. Could Butler have countered Hume? The simple answer is no, because Butler's argument is inconsistent in itself. Only if the God of the Bible is in control can someone assume that the future will follow established patterns. Butler was unable to make that assumption at the start of his argument.[44]

---

by this we are able to recall, either to ourselves or others, that collection" (Hume, *Treatise* I, i, 6, as cited by Brown, *Philosophy & Faith*, 68).

38. *HWPT*, 201: "Hume replaces metaphysics with psychology. . . . He was not only skeptical about necessary connection, but also skeptical about the existence of the *mind* or *soul* in the traditional metaphysical sense. . . . So he defined *soul* minimally, to agree with his experience, as a *bundle* of perceptions. . . . Though accused of atheism during his life, he often took pains to express his theology in . . . traditional terms."

39. Ibid., 202: "Hume argues that there can never be sufficient evidence to affirm that a miracle has taken place. . . . He says that no miracle has had witnesses of sufficient character, education, and intelligence to warrant our belief."

40. Ibid., 204: "I think his best contribution to philosophy is his refutation of the *is-ought* fallacy. . . . But in the end I must concur with Hume's own judgment that his work is nothing more than an expression of his own subjective feeling"; and 204n80: "I argue that moral obligation can come only from the biblical God, the personal absolute . . . and that therefore all attempts to derive morality from other sources commit the *is-ought* fallacy."

41. Van Til, *Evidences*, 34–35: "Hume was not willing to accept any positive construction of knowledge even to the extent of reasonable probablility."

42. Ibid., 38. Oliphint, in Van Til, *Evidences*, 38n15: "sensation cannot establish the cause-and-effect relationship."

43. "Our reasoning is based upon past experience. Past experience is nothing but an accumulation of brute facts which have been observed as happening in a certain order. Why should not the events of the future be entirely different in nature from the events of the past?" (as cited by Van Til, *Evidences*, 40).

44. Ibid.: "His main assumption, that the constitution and course of nature may be expected to remain in the future what it has been in the past, rests upon an uncritical remnant of apriorism."

Butler assumed there to be an "Author of nature." This assumption was legitimate when speaking to deists but not comprehensible by a full empiricist.[45] Hume was also critical of Butler's notion of a future life, as pure empiricism requires absolute neutrality concerning the future. Hume's pure empiricism even destroyed certainty with regard to laws, for experience cannot produce a law. A pure empiricist such as Hume would admit that there is some sort of regularity of events, but nothing such as a law could be guaranteed.[46] The empiricist is forced to be indifferent to the future.

Hume also objected to miracles, for it is God who produces miracles, and God cannot be proven to exist.[47] Even if all the Bible's miracles were proven to have occurred, an empiricist such as Hume would reply that even natural events have a strangeness inherent to them. An empiricist would argue that we simply need to be more open to the possibilities of chance.

Hume did believe, however, that using an a posteriori method could perhaps prove the existence of a finite god. According to Hume, this god is like us and is therefore subject to limitations. Such a god could resemble both our evil and our good. Using an argument from the analogy that god is like us cannot actually carry thinking into the unknown. A necessarily existent god would have to rely on information that is unknown to us. The god of a posteriori reasoning must be penetrable by man's mind.[48] We have briefly encountered both rationalism and empiricism; now let us move forward to an analysis of both.

ANALYSIS OF RATIONALISM AND EMPIRICISM

Response to Skepticism. Many responsible philosophers posit that philosophy's task is to combat a relentless human drive toward skepticism.[49] During the seventeenth and eighteenth centuries, it was believed that only two philosophical options were strong enough to

45. Ibid., 41.
46. Ibid., 47n27. Oliphint's comment.
47. Ibid., 49.
48. Ibid., 52–59.
49. For example, see Avrum Stroll, *Epistemology: New Essays in the Theory of Knowledge* (San Francisco: Harper & Row, 1967), 2–3.

restrain the tide of skepticism. Epistemological certainty, as an answer to the skeptic, could be built on either law—inexorable, unyielding law—or on fact. Law, on the one hand, universally resists the human will toward skepticism. And fact, on the other hand, is an individual resistant that is repeated in innumerable variations.

Descartes believed it was necessary to drive out skepticism, and as a rationalist he wanted to avoid recourse to sensory experience. His *cogito* was supposedly the antidote to despair; it was a solid, epistemological foundation. Descartes went the way of using law. Law is related to mathematics, and Descartes believed that mathematics would provide the vehicle for truth. Spinoza and Leibniz followed Descartes. They applied mathematical and logical criteria to every aspect of life. They searched for necessary truth.[50] Leibniz formulated the rationalist principle with his proposition called an *identity*, which today we refer to as a *definition*. An example of an identity is that all right angles are equal; this proposition is also known as a *tautology*.

An identity is different in kind and character from the facts of observation. Observed facts, and the empirical rules generalized from them, can be logically denied without contradiction. But a necessary truth, like an identity, is established by the principles of logic and is thus undeniable. Reason, therefore, seems to be firmly established.

If someone proves God's existence based on apriorism, then everything else that exists is necessarily proven.[51] If God's existence is sufficient reason for creation to exist, then God must entail creation. But that which is necessary cannot entail that which is contingent.[52]

In contrast, for certainty the empiricist turned not to law but to fact.[53] Locke, Berkeley, and Hume all insisted on the primacy and sufficiency of sensation for genuine knowledge. They understood the process of knowledge to be as follows: sensation comes to the mind,

50. Lev Shestov, *Athens and Jerusalem* (New York: Simon & Shuster, 1966), 51.

51. Oliphint, in Van Til, *Evidences*, 47n28: "That is, if one seeks to conclude that the existence of God is necessary, based on the contingent existence of man, that necessity is dependent on the contingent in order for it to be defined as necessary. The two poles, therefore, of necessity and contingency mutually entail each other."

52. Van Til, *Evidences*, 48: "A priori reasoning on non-Christian assumptions, no less than a posteriori reasoning upon non-Christian assumptions, leads to the apotheosis of chance and thus to the destruction of predication."

53. See E. A. Singer Jr., *Experience and Reflection* (Philadelphia: University of Pennsylvania Press, 1959), 3–10.

then the senses furnish the mind with simple ideas concerning those sensible qualities. Locke believed that the mind compares the simple ideas received from sensory experience, and from those simple ideas the mind makes more complex knowledge.

Only Apparent Answers. Rationalism's attempt to avoid skepticism—by using a mathematical definition, for example, of a triangle or square—in no way guaranteed the existence of an object. The rationalist needed to find at least one object or fact that exists only and exclusively by its definition. If such an object or fact existed by definition, then rationalism would be the most true way of conceiving reality. Thus the rationalists turned to the classic ontological argument for God's existence as that one existent entity that exists simply by definition and supposedly validates rationalist philosophy.[54]

Empiricism cannot answer the question of how the blank mind, or tablet, performs as it is intended to do. According to empiricists, the blank mind does not have anything within it in which to place the data of raw sensory experience. There is no inherent mental grid to organize information—no receptacle in what is, by definition, a blank mind.

A very simple way of demonstrating this problem is to hold a rose. When holding the rose, the hand feels slight pressure on the fingers' nerve endings from the weight of the rose. The holder, however, does not know how the feeling in the finger is actually related to the rose. The eye sees the rose's red color but cannot know for certain that it is not the color green. The nostrils detect a delightful flowery perfume but cannot know that this smell is not actually that of dung.[55]

Empiricism, therefore, has unjustifiably assumed there to be some type of law-like characteristic that distinguishes between something and nothing. Empiricism can correctly be judged to be "an outworn and outmoded superstition."[56]

Similarity and Failure. While the methodologies utilized by proponents of rationalism and empiricism are quite different, they are not without their similarities. Rationalism argues that knowledge is derived

54. Clark, *Thales to Dewey*, 325: "Only in the definition of God can we conceive of the coincidence of an existent with its essence, which can give the hope of passing from definition to a real existing world."

55. Upon hearing this example, a student of mine said that his dog and I may have different judgments about smell!

56. E. D. Harris, *Nature, Mind and Modern Science* (London: Allen and Unwin, 1954), 452.

from self-evident principles, and empiricism claims that knowledge is a product inductively constructed from sensory data. They both seek epistemological certainty, as well as universal application. Both methods ground their epistemological certainty in humanity.

The two are also seemingly interdependent. Rationalism needs empiricism—the rationalist's bare logic in no way guarantees the existence of an object—and empiricism's definition of fact depends on the rationalistic view of law. The two are seemingly pairs of contradictory hypotheses that are mutually dependent on each other for validity. Nevertheless, the reality is that neither rationalism nor empiricism was able to defeat skepticism. In the coming pages, we will observe Immanuel Kant's stepping into the midst of this debate and simply dismissing both Continental and British rationalism. But first we will return to the walls of the church—not everyone in the world was wrestling with these philosophical debates.

COUNT ZINZENDORF (A.D. 1700–1760) AND THE MORAVIANS

Count Nicholas Ludwig von Zinzendorf had an estate and permitted German-speaking Moravians to build a village on his land, a village that they named Herrnhut. By 1727 the Moravians had grown to a sizable number, and Zinzendorf began to assume leadership of this growing community. The year 1727 is also the year given for the birth of the Moravian church.

Herrnhut. The Herrnhut society considered itself to be something of a united body of Christian soldiers. They wanted to be a community that was separated from the world but also one that was always ready to send its soldiers into the world for Christ's kingdom. In some ways, the community was similar to a Protestant monasticism, although members were bound under no vows. The members held daily prayer and worship. The children of the community were separated from their parents and raised like children in an orphanage were raised.

There was tension in this new community concerning the formal structure of their church. Zinzendorf was influenced by German Pietism and thus wanted to create the church within the formal structure of the Saxon, or state, Lutheran Church. But opposition against this society arose from both the state Lutheran Church and from some in the community, and there was pressure from within Herrnhut to separate from the state church.[57]

The willingness to go anywhere as a Christian soldier produced a tremendous mission movement. This community sent missionaries to the West Indies, Greenland, and Georgia in the United States.[58]

Zinzendorf Banished. The tensions between Zinzendorf and the state church were too high, and in 1736 Zinzendorf was banished from Saxony.[59] He traveled to western Germany and, the following year, was ordained as a bishop in Berlin. Then he traveled to West India and London. By December 1741, Zinzendorf had crossed the Atlantic headed to New York, then went to a new mission in Pennsylvania named Bethlehem—the American headquarters of the movement. After establishing seven or eight congregations and planting schools, Zinzendorf left America in January 1743.[60]

In 1747, Zinzendorf was recalled from banishment when the Moravian body accepted the Lutheran Augsburg Confession. The Moravians became part of the state church, while having their own services. Zinzendorf died in Herrnhut in 1760.[61] While not all will agree with how the German count organized and structured his community, the Moravians, without question, advanced the gospel around the world. Staying within Germany, we will now look at a rather different movement.

GOTTHOLD EPHRAIM LESSING (A.D. 1729–1781)[62]

Lessing is well known as an essential figure in the development of German drama and theater—he liberated them from their simple

57. Williston Walker, *A History of the Christian Church* (New York: Scribner's Sons, 1959), 450–51.

58. The mission to Georgia was led by August Gottlieb Spangenberg (1704–1792).

59. D. Martyn Lloyd-Jones, "Ecclesiola in Ecclesia," in *Puritan Papers*, ed. J. I. Packer, 5 vols. (Phillipsburg, NJ: P&R Publishing, 2004), 85. Zinzendorf did not develop a church within the church but eventually broke from it and joined with the United Brethren or Moravian Brethren.

60. Walker, *History*, 452.

61. Ibid., 453.

62. Heussi, *Kompendium*, 346; see also Kurt D. Schmidt, *Grundriss der Kirchengeschichte* (Göttingen: Vandenhoek & Ruprecht, 1963), 450–52.

imitation of French works.[63] But for our purposes, we will examine how Lessing unwittingly changed the face of NT studies.

The *Fragments*. Lessing worked as the librarian at the great Herzog August Biblothek in Wolfenbüttel, one of the world's great libraries.[64] There he came upon the *Fragments* of H. S. Reimarus (1694–1768) and had them published. Reimarus painted a shocking picture of Jesus Christ. He argued that Jesus was a psychologically unbalanced enthusiast who was killed at the hands of the ruling Roman and Jewish authorities. Further, his disciples, who were knaves, recognized the financial and political power that was available to them, and they pretended that Jesus was raised from the dead and ascended into heaven. Thus Christianity is not based on fact at all but instead on a massive fraud. In the light of the fact that the entire religion is a fraud, he contended that it is healthy for society to expose the charade.[65]

Reimarus's work was foundational for subsequent German NT studies. He focused on what he considered to be the kernel of the biblical message, namely, the eschatological message bound up in Jesus's proclamation of the nearness of the kingdom of God. Reimarus dismissed as later embellisment all that went beyond this fundamental eschatological message.

Reimarus included in those supposed later additions miracles as well as testimony to Christ's divinity. Thus the true historical Jesus was merely a good man who possessed an enthusiasm for life and provided wonderful teachings that should be studied and preserved.[66] Jesus's message was distorted by his overzealous followers.

Reimarus's teaching should be soundly rejected. If someone's philosophical and theological presuppositions prohibit the possibility of the miraculous, then those presuppositions prohibit the possibility of Christianity itself. In the cases of Reimarus and his later disciple Albert Schweitzer, their presuppositions concerning the miraculous

---

63. Brown, *Philosophy & Faith*, 86.
64. I had the great privilege of being a fellow of the library in 1993.
65. Ibid.
66. Reimarus's teachings were in many ways seen in parts of British deism. The scholar J. S. Semlar answered the challenging research concerning Jesus and his followers. The true issues involved here concern whether or not miracles can occur—miracles such as a virgin birth, a resurrection from the dead, or the turning of water into wine.

have so influenced their research as to vacate their work of almost all value.[67]

Other Writings. In 1780 Lessing wrote *Die Erziehung des Menschengeschlects* (*The Education of the Human Race*). Those who followed the Enlightenment believed Lessing to be one of their own. But Lessing considered the theology of the Enlightenment to be unwarranted in its conclusions and muddled in its thinking.[68]

His most important play was *Nathan the Wise.* The play presents a Muslim, a Jew, and a Christian. The wise Jew, Nathan, supposedly proves the point that no one knows which of the three religions truly possesses God's truth. Nathan reasons, therefore, that the only way to determine the validity of each religion is through the actions of the believers of the religion.[69] Such relativism presented in a popular format was detrimental to Christianity.

Lessing's most important pamphlet was "On the Proof of the Spirit and Power." In it, he separated truths revealed in history from truths manifest from reason. For example, one can believe that Jesus performed miracles—and even that he was resurrected from the dead. But believing those particular historical facts does not require that same person to believe in Jesus's deity or in the Trinity. Lessing has the epistemological objection that miracles, or any historical event for that matter, cannot be used as the springboard for leaping to even larger theological truths.

This pamphlet worked in conjunction with the play *Nathan the Wise.* Lessing ackowledged that religions may make historical claims, but he was convinced that those claims, made in the religions' scriptures, were not epistemologically strong enough to elicit faith, which requires veracity at all times and places. Thus there is always a separation between the facts or truths of history and the nature of faith.[70] This separation is known as *Lessing's ditch.* Faith, for Lessing, cannot be established based on mere historical events. He believed there is

67. Brown, *Philosophy & Faith*, 87.

68. His relatively famous phrase was "Flickwerk von Stuempern und Halbphilosophen," as cited by Leonhard P. Wessel, *G. E. Lessing's Theology: A Reinterpretation* (The Hague: Mouton, 1977), 155. Heussi, *Kompendium*, 346: "Dem Christentum war er persönlich immer ferner gerückt" ("He was always turned further and further away from Christianity").

69. *HWPT*, 220–21.

70. Ibid., 221–22.

a ditch that lies between history and faith—historical claims cannot verify any religion.

In response, believers know that Christ is truly revealed in the Scriptures, which are self-authenticating. We know by faith that the historical events are true. Though Lessing opposed the Christian faith, a contemporary German thinker named Immanuel Kant proved to cause even more damage to the Christian faith.

IMMANUEL KANT (A.D. 1724–1804)[71]

Many eighteenth-century thinkers were deists, who denied the Trinity and adhered to a strict natural law. Some of those thinkers later became simple atheists. It was here that Immanuel Kant was influential.

Biography and Writings. Kant was born and died in Königsberg, which was at the time located in East Prussia. He was the son of a saddler of Scottish ancestry and had something of a pietistic upbringing. Kant served as an instructor from 1755 to 1770. He was then made a professor of logic and metaphysics. He continued as a professor until shortly before his death. Kant was a sociable man, but he never married. He followed a strict pattern of life.

Kant was educated in the rationalist tradition,[72] but he fell under the influence of the thinking of Hume, whose writings caused him supposedly to awaken from his slumbers.[73] He understood there to be a line of demarcation between mathematics and metaphysics. Kant became convinced that all speculation about the great metaphysical themes of *God*, *freedom*, and *immortality* was nothing but a waste of

71. Francis Schaeffer, *How Should We Then Live?* (Westchester, IL: Crossway, 1983), 160; William Dennison, "Reason, History, and Revelation: Biblical Theology and the Enlightenment," *Kerux: The Journal of Northwest Theological Seminary* 18, no. 1 (May 2003): 3–25.

72. His first philosophical period supported the teaching of Leibniz and Wolff. Philosophical primacy was given to mathematical truth. Mathematical truth was the origin of the world, and there was little place for considering individual humans. See Herman Dooyeweerd, *A New Critique of Theoretical Thought*, vol. 1, *The Necessary Presuppositions of Philosophy*, trans. David Freeman and William Young (Philadelphia: Presbyterian and Reformed, 1953), 335, 360.

73. *HWPT*, 252–53: "Kant's early work reflected these rationalist emphases, which he later described as *dogmatic* speculation. At some point, however, Kant read David Hume, who, he said, roused him from his dogmatic slumbers. Hume's skepticism was a frontal challenge to Continental rationalism. No longer could philosophers simply assume that logical deduction from carefully chosen axioms would lead them to certainty about the structure of the world."

time. Kant agreed with the empiricists in holding that all knowledge begins with experience. Nevertheless, he did differ from the empiricists. He held that while the raw material of knowledge comes from outside of us, the mind is involved in processing that material by means of its own concepts, not concepts taken from sensory experience.[74]

Kant's writings are vast. His monumental *Critique of Pure Reason* was written in 1781 to set out an enlightened approach to human knowledge. He seemed to have one foot in the old world of rationalism and empiricism and the other foot in the modern world.[75] A few years after 1781, he addressed another significant philosophical question: "What is the Enlightenment?" His answer was: "The Enlightenment is man's leaving his own culpable immaturity."[76]

Kant then turned his attention to the field of ethics. His first book on the topic was *Fundamental Principles of a Metaphysic of Morals*, which was published in 1785. In 1790 he published *The Critique of Judgment*, which dealt with questions regarding aesthetics and purpose in the universe. But it was a work he published three years later that got him into trouble: *Religion within the Limits of Reason Alone*.[77] This book was intended to be the third of four steps in shifting the way humans think. The first book was intended to change metaphysics, and the second, ethics.[78] In this work on religion, Kant claimed to respect Christianity, but he sought to wed it to the control of reason.[79] The King of Prussia censured the work and forced Kant to claim that his purpose was to commend Christianity. Nevertheless, Christianity

74. Brown, *Philosophy & Faith*, 93.

75. The second, revised edition of Kant's *Kritik der Reinen Vernunft* (ed. Erich Adickes [Berlin: Reimer, 1889]) appeared in 1787. For an English translation, see Immanuel Kant, *Critique of Pure Reason*, trans. Paul Guyer and Allen W. Wood (Cambridge: Cambridge University Press, 1998).

76. Immanuel Kant, "Beantwortung der Frage: Was ist Aufklärung?" *Berlinische Monatsschrift* 2 (1784): 481–94. The citation is from Immanuel Kant, *Gesammelte Schriften*, Bd. VIII (Berlin: Reimer, 1900), 35: "Aufklärung ist der Ausgang des Menschen aus seiner selbstverschuldeten Unmündigkeit. Unmündigkeit ist das unvermögen, sich seines Verstandes ohne Leitung eines andern zu bedienen."

77. *Die Religion innerhalb der Grenzen der blossen Vernunft.*

78. He wrote of his plan to C. F. Stäudlin, theology professor at Göttingen: "My long-standing plan for the reappraisal, incumbent upon the field of pure philosophy centered upon dealing with three tasks. What can I know? (Metaphysics) What should I do? (Ethics) And What may I hope? (Religion)," with the fourth field being anthropology (as cited by Brown, *Philosophy & Faith*, 92).

79. Kant, *Gesammelte Schriften*, XI: 429, no. 574.

was commended only in that the Bible was deemed the best vehicle for public instruction in morality.[80]

Kant also lectured for twenty years on anthropology. Based on these lectures, in 1798 he published a work titled *Anthropology*, which was the fourth and final plank of a massive, structural change in Western thinking.

Kant was one of the greatest thinkers of all time and perhaps the most important thinker of the modern era. His thinking has influenced every area of Western intellectual heritage—in particular, the organization of Christian thought. Moving from Kant's biographical background, we will examine four themes of his teaching: the significance of the Enlightenment, the two worlds, his consequent analysis of knowledge and judgment, and his analysis of God's existence.

Enlightenment. Many of the significant movements of history bear mottos that encapsulate the movement in several words. The motto of the Renaissance was *ad fontes* "back to the sources," and the Reformation was marked by the five *solas*. The Enlightenment's motto could be called "dare to use your own understanding."

Kant argued that this important and developed Enlightenment mode of thought applied to religion in general and Christianity in particular.[81] Any new generation of thinkers should not be bound by the previous generation's creeds. To be bound by previous dogmas offended human nature. Human nature and thought should be stretching toward the future, not shackled to a dead past. An enlightened generation longs to be liberated from the bondage of the past and marches boldly into the future. But according to Kant, his own generation was not very enlightened, and it could only become so when it rejected external authorities and judged everything according to individuals' own understandings.[82]

Two Worlds. Kant presented his notion of the *primacy of practical reason*, based on his earlier *Critique of Pure Reason*, which was in many ways dependent on earlier Greek philosophy.[83] Kant determined

---

80. Brown, *Philosophy & Faith*, 92.

81. *HWPT*, 251: "The dominance of Christian thought . . . came to an end in the early seventeenth century, with a convulsion initiating 'modern' philosophy and the period of its initial dominance, otherwise known as the *Enlightenment*."

82. Brown, *Philosophy & Faith*, 91.

83. Cornelius Van Til, *The Great Debate Today* (Nutley, NJ: Presbyterian and Reformed, 1971), 21: "In Greek thought, it is man that makes himself the final reference point in predication.

that scientific knowledge existed within the realm of phenomena. This phenomenal world was subordinated to the realm of the spirit, which he termed the *noumenal* realm. The noumenal realm was that of free personality, in contrast to the phenomenal realm of impersonal law.

Kant, however, believed that it is impossible to have knowledge of any world beyond that of space and time, or the phenomenal. This world beyond cannot be grasped by any of our concepts, or even by any one person. All that we can know is that the noumenal exists. By its very definition, that world is beyond our experience. Kant said that the mind errs whenever it attempts to make a judgment about the noumenal world, about matters that are beyond experience.

Kant created a distinction between things as they are in themselves and things as they appear to us. Things as they are in themselves belong to the noumenal world—a reality that exists apart from anyone's experience of it. The world that we experience is the phenomenal world. It is all things as they appear to us; it is the real world. Thus Kant held the opposite position that Plato held. Plato had argued that the real world is the one that is in heaven—he referred to it as *the world of forms* or *ideas*—and the world as we experience it in space and time is merely a shadow of that true world.

Kant believed that thinkers can obtain intellectual certainty only in the phenomenal world. Men and women can use their reasoning here with confidence. Specifically, the phenomenal world is always apprehended by and with the mind. The mind exercises certain functions—called the *transcendental categories*—that are necessary for understanding the phenomenal world. The transcendental aesthetic is the notion of space and time in which raw sensory data are placed. It can be thought of as the bed or home in which sensory data rest. The transcendental analytic categories are those of *unity*, *causality*, and *possibility*. The mind uses these categories rationally to analyze the new sensory data. In other words, the mind prescribes these categories, which are also termed *laws of nature*. Putting together the transcendental aesthetic (or new data) and analytic (or categories) is the transcendental unity of *apperception*. It is the category of unity of

---

... The Aristotelian notion of the analogy of Being assumes that God and man are participants in one Being that in depth of metaphysical conception precedes them both. It is the same abstract principle of continuity that is still employed by Kant."

experience, or the single synthesis in the mind of the multiplicities of raw sensory data. These transcendental categories supposedly resolve the philosophical problem of the one and the many.

But what does all this mean practically? For Kant, notions such as *plurality* and *cause-and-effect* do not originate in the world of sensory experience but in the mind itself. Specifically, causes and their effects occur not because of some force that moves events and objects within the world—they occur merely because the mind arranges experience in a certain order. All knowledge's structure is contributed from the mind.[84]

Kant's thinking was without a doubt both creative and brilliant. But it is not immune to critique. Kant's belief in two worlds—one knowable, called the *phenomenal*, and one unknowable, called the *noumenal*—forced him to become both a skeptic and an irrationalist. He was a skeptic in that he said there was a world that existed that was beyond our ability to know. He was irrational in that he spoke of the unspeakable and discussed the unknowable. Kant also had no ability to explain how the noumenal and phenomenal worlds interact. Using other philosophical terms, Kant could not combine form and matter.

Kant's distinction between the scientific world (the phenomenal) and the world of freedom, religion, and God (the noumenal) produced an antagonism between the two that was detrimental to Christianity.[85] Since the two worlds were so opposed, Christianity could supposedly be detached from any type of historical or scientific accuracy. Christianity did not need to be accurate; it could function well if, for example, it simply promoted human freedom and morality. Also, Kant's two worlds supposedly gave later theologians a way to speak biblically within a framework that was far from biblical. *Revelation* could become some type of nonpropositional influence that originated in the noumenal realm. *Grace* could be a mystical experience from an unknown noumenal sphere. Finally, *faith* could be the realization that the ultimate cannot be found in the world of sensation, the phenomenal world.[86]

84. There are actually twelve categories by which the mind understands experience and shapes the data (see *HWPT*, 258).

85. Dooyeweerd, *New Critique*, 1:378.

86. Kant's analysis has a wide impact. *HWPT*, 252: "His distinction between *phenomena* and *noumena* . . . reappears in Schopenhauer's distinction between *idea* and *will*, Wittgenstein's distinction between *fact* and *the Mystical*, Heidegger's distinction between *technology* and *poetry*,

Analysis of Knowledge. Kant's aim in *The Critique of Pure Reason* was to examine human processing of sensory experience, or what we call *knowledge*.[87] To summarize, knowledge's raw material consists in the outside world, that is, that which is perceived by the senses. He referred to this raw material as the *synthetic element*. The mind then employs various forms or categories to process this raw material, or synthetic element. These forms that the mind implements are pure concepts of the understanding. Some of those categories include the intuition of time and space, or quantity and quality.[88] An example (not used by Kant) would be catching a ball: one must use space or distance to connect the proximity of the thrower and analyze the speed and weight of the ball over time to be able to catch the ball.

When the human mind uses these mental forms to process the synthetic element or new sensory data, then the mind knows the synthetic element. But as the mind knows the data, the mind does not actually perceive those objects from sensory data as they are in themselves.[89] Those things or objects from sensory data are perceived through the grid of the mental forms. It is as though people look at every object through rose-tinted glasses. People see the world through the coloration of their mental forms.[90] There is no *thing in itself*.

Kant further separated human knowledge into two types. There was what he termed *a priori* (that is, innate) knowledge and *a posteriori* knowledge (from sensory experience).[91] A priori knowledge supposedly comes before, or without, any prior sensory experience. Mathematical

---

Gadamer's between *techne* and *phronesis*, Barth's between *Historie* and *Geschichte*, the distinction Buber and Brunner made between the *I-it* and the *I-thou*, and in the various neo-Gnostic and neopagan distinctions between *the many* and *the one*."

87. Immanuel Kant, *Kritik der reinen Vernunft*, 480: "Und so enthält das Wirkliche nichts mehr, als das bloss Mögliche. . . . Denn sonst würde nicht eben dasselbe, sondern mehr existiern, als ich im Begriffe gedacht hatte, und ich könne nicht sagen, dass gerade der Gegenstand meines Begriffs existire"; and 481: "aber für Objekte des reinen Denkens ist ganz und gar kein Mittel, ihr Dasein zu erkennen, weil es gänzlich *a priori* erkannt weden müsste, unser Bewusstsein aller Existenz aber, gehöret ganz und gar zur Einheit der Erfahrung, und eine Existenz ausser diesem Felde kann zwar nicht schlechterdings für unmöglich erklärt werden, sie ist aber keine Voraussetzung, die wir durch nichts rechtfertigen können."

88. Dooyweerd, *New Critique*, 343.

89. Kant, *Critique*, in Theodore Meyer Greene, *Kant Selections* (New York: Scribner's Sons, 1929), 55: For "while much can be said *a priori* as regards the form of appearances, nothing whatsoever can be asserted of the thing in itself, which may underlie these appearances."

90. Brown, *Philosophy & Faith*, 95.

91. Kant is building on medieval foundations. See chapter 9.

proofs are good examples of a priori knowledge, for they are known without direct experience.[92] A posteriori knowledge is knowledge that comes by sensory experience. The expression *a posteriori* itself derives from *posterior*, meaning "after." Tasting food and seeing color are examples of a posteriori knowledge. When we bite into an apple, we make a judgment about its sweetness, and when we look at the apple, we judge whether it is colored red or green. According to Kant, these two types of knowledge are quite different from each other. A priori knowledge is entirely independent of experience. If there is a priori knowledge that has no admixture of knowledge by experience, then it is pure knowledge.[93] Thus pure knowledge is only a priori.

Kant's advances in epistemology—of how people know—had enormous consequences. They formed something of a bulwark against Hume's skepticism. Yet Kant's system failed. It can be said that Kant gave a more sophisticated representative theory of knowledge than did Locke, but Kant is just as liable to the criticisms that are leveled against that theory.[94] For Kant and his followers, there is no knowledge of anything that goes beyond immediate experience, and even within that very limited sphere, there is still no knowledge of the thing itself.[95] To better understand Kant's epistemology, we need also to see the nature of judgment.

Analysis of Judgment. Kant believed that there were two types of judgments. The word *judgment* is a predication or assertion about a subject or knowledge claim. A thinker can make either an *analytic* or a *synthetic* judgment.[96]

In an analytic judgment, the predicate is logically and necessarily present in the subject. The simplest analytic judgments are definitions. For example, Hoosiers are Indianans. The predicate *Indianans* is logically contained in the subject *Hoosier*. Another example is that

---

92. Greene, *Selections*, xxxiv. The rationalists had insisted that true philosophical knowledge has to be necessary and universal and cannot come by mere empirical generalizations from sensory experience.

93. Kant, *Critique*, in Greene, *Selections*, 27: a priori knowledge is "independent of all experience, and not of this or that experience only. Opposed to this is empirical knowledge, or such as is possible *a posteriori* only, that is, by experience. Knowledge *a priori*, if mixed up with nothing empirical is called pure."

94. Brown, *Philosophy & Faith*, 96.

95. Ibid., 97.

96. Dooyweerd, *New Critique*, 340.

roses are flowers. The predicate *flower* is logically contained in the subject *rose*.

A synthetic judgment is a statement in which the predicate is not present in the subject. For example, some Hoosiers are fat. The predicate *fat* is not contained in the definition of *Hoosier*. This judgment is synthetic because not all Hoosiers are fat. Or consider another example: some roses are red. The word *red* is not contained in the definition of *rose*. Not all roses are red.

This information is admittedly complicated, but there is a purpose in understanding it: Christians need to be prepared to defend the faith against unbelievers who will likely wield Kantian philosophy (or some form of it) against us. This section is intended to help or at least introduce Christians to Kant's system of thought, since he is one of the foremost thinkers of the Enlightenment.

God's Existence. Kant believed that there are basically only three proofs for God's existence and that all three of the proofs are inadequate. The *ontological argument* is that the definition of a necessary being implies that the necessary being exists. This argument was articulated in the Middle Ages and was held by Descartes, but it was disassembled by Kant. Kant demonstrated that the ontological argument only proves God's existence if one assumes it from the beginning. He argued that God may exist, but this existence cannot be known a priori;[97] rather, Kant believed, one must learn of God's existence from outside the human mind, that is, by external sensation or the synthetic element.

While Kant was wrong, in that God has made man in his image and his existence is known to all men, there is something to be said for his attack against the ontological argument. I can believe that I have a million dollars in my bank account, but my belief does not mean that I actually have the million dollars. The fact that I can conceive something does not mean that thing exists.[98]

Kant formulated the *cosmological argument* for the existence of God as follows: if anything exists, an absolutely necessary being must also exist. Now I, at least, exist; therefore, an absolutely necessary

---

97. Kant disagreed with Anselm who argued that the ontological argument demonstrated knowledge of God without experience.
98. Brown, *Philosophy & Faith*, 98.

being must exist. Kant thought that the argument was plausible but problematic. Specifically, this argument makes use of the earlier, deficient ontological argument when it attempts to leap from the notion or concept of a *necessary being* to an actually *existent necessary being*.[99] Furthermore, it is not possible to conceive what such a being is like. There are natural forces that produce effects yet remain a mystery.

The *teleological argument*, however, commanded Kant's respect. For him it breathed purpose and meaning into life and scientific investigation. The visible creation manifests signs of order and purpose. The nature of those observable purposes are such that they cannot not have been self-devised. They point beyond themselves to an intelligent, free being. But Kant concluded that this argument was only a disguised ontological proof, thus natural theology's attempts to prove God's existence are null and void. Nevertheless, while Kant held that God cannot be proved, he also conceded that God cannot be disproved.[100]

Kant wondered whether God could be known apart from sensory experience. In itself, this question would have been too simple.[101] So Kant divided the question. He questioned whether existence is logically an attribute of the subject, God. Kant's answer was no. His reasoning was that some subjects could be only mental states, without a corresponding reality outside the mind. We can think of examples of things that exist in our minds that do not have corresponding realities outside our minds.[102] Kant concluded, therefore, that God's existence cannot be known apart from experience. He said that existence cannot be an attribute of any subject.

Kant said that God may exist, but that knowledge cannot be on an a priori analytic basis. Instead, one must learn of God's existence from outside the human mind. That knowledge supposedly comes only through sensory experience.[103] Kant applied his thoughts about God in

---

99. *HWPT*, 262.

100. Brown, *Philosophy & Faith*, 99.

101. His actual formal question was, "Is the existence of God an analytic a priori?"

102. For example, J. R. R. Tolkien's world in his *Lord of the Rings* trilogy first existed in the author's mind, then in the minds of those who read his books, and then in the minds of those who saw his movies. While the world may seem very real to the watcher in a movie theatre, it, of course, does not exist in reality.

103. I disagree with Kant. The earlier philosophers were correct when they asserted that knowledge of God's existence is innate. Yet knowledge of God also includes sensory experience. The two should not be separated.

the opening words of *Religion within the Limits of Reason Alone*.[104] He was convinced that if modern man was really to live as though he had come of age, then he must throw away all external and pseudo authorities. He must heed what his own reason tells him is right. He no longer needs God to advise him or offer incentives. Kant, however, lived in a Germany with a state-supported church. All German citizens were to be either members of this church or at the very least not antagonistic to it. So Kant still made room for God.

And Kant found other reasons to believe in God. For Kant, God's existence was not found through sensory experience but instead through humanity's general sense of the *moral imperative*. An imperative is a command; stated more precisely, it is an objective moral principle formulated in the form of a command. Kant distinguished between a *hypothetical* and a *categorical* imperative. For example, a hypothetical imperative is when a student tells a professor that he wants to make a grade of *A* in his class. Then the professor looks the student in the eye, points his finger, and commands in a loud voice, "Study hard!" This command is relative in that it is not binding on all people. This imperative relates to the particular student who wants to make a good grade.

A categorical imperative is a rational principle that is valid for all people under all circumstances. It is not a matter of acting according to your conscience but of rigidly adhering to a rational principle.[105]

For Kant, God was thus useful for a unified notion of how to behave in the world.[106] Kant believed that there was nothing wrong with presupposing certain things that belong to the noumenal world, about which we have no certainty, and yet are helpful for making moral decisions. We can still aim at, or something may point to, the idea of an absolute being. Responsible people act as though God exists. Kant believed that we ought to act as though such a being will reward us, even though he admitted that we cannot know anything about such

104. Kant said that "So far as morality is based upon the conception of man as a free agent who, just because he is free, binds himself through his reason to unconditioned laws, it stands in need neither of the idea of another Being over him, for him to apprehend his duty, nor of an incentive other than the law itself, for him to do his duty" (as cited by Brown, *Philosophy & Faith*, 100).

105. The categorical imperative has for Kant the same status that the clear and distinct ideas had for Descartes and the rationalists. Kant accepted it as self-evidently true. It is self-evident that if everyone were to pursue self-seeking and suicide, then life would be impossible.

106. *HWPT*, 263.

a being.[107] But Kant did not want God to exist in every part of life. We should not act as though God can give an authoritative divine revelation.[108]

Regarding Kant's categorical imperative, the question needs to be answered as to why anyone should obey it. Kant seems to be advocating that people adhere to categorical imperatives because they create a more pleasant existence for everyone. But if that were the case, then the categorical imperative would be nothing but a modified hypothetical imperative. Thus the categorical imperative could be simply an expression of what the speaker happens to think is desirable.[109]

Kant argued that people should obey the categorical imperative for its own sake. But can we not ask whether it is enough simply to ask what we should do? What authority stands over and above me and demands that I should behave in some particular way? The question of *oughtness* addresses the transcendent. It is not, as Kant told his readers, an autonomous principle of the will but something that comes to man from outside himself.[110]

Jesus taught, in continuity with the OT, that the first great commandment is to love God. The second is to love the neighbor as the self. The human individual has an internal awareness of the necessity to love both God and neighbor. Sadly, this internally known necessity is not always, or even sometimes, acted on. So Kant is in one sense correct in his assertion. People inherently know that they should behave in a certain fashion.

So how does Kant think that he knows what he calls the *categorical imperative*? According to his own teaching, he knows it not based on external, authoritative revelation or even results from Paul's teaching. He knows it, he argues, because of his own construction of religion or Christianity. Sadly, this construction is far from the actual Christian faith.

---

107. Van Til, *Great Debate*, 3–5, 9. The idea of a *first cause*, the idea of an *absolute being*, or the idea of a *final purpose* for the universe are *limiting concepts*.

108. There is a fascinating cultural context to Kant's philosophy. The German people have been known for their sense of duty. Since many other cultures do not have this same sense, where then is their sense of God?

109. This question connects to postmodernism's notion of laws as the construct of the majority's desires.

110. Brown, *Philosophy & Faith*, 101.

At the end of the summary on rationalism and empiricism, I mentioned that Kant stepped into the middle of a watershed epistemological debate. Kant was not able to bridge the divide. Our discussion now crosses the Atlantic Ocean and settles in early America.

JONATHAN EDWARDS (A.D. 1703–1758)[111]

Biography. Jonathan Edwards was born into a family deeply rooted in New England.[112] At the age of six he began the study of Latin, and by thirteen he knew Greek and Hebrew. A month before his thirteenth birthday, young Edwards began as a student at Yale University.[113] After graduation, in the year 1722, he started preaching in New York, and two years later he became a tutor at Yale.[114] In 1727 the young scholar married Sarah Pierrepont.[115] About twenty years later, in 1746, Presbyterians founded the College of New Jersey, and in 1757 Edwards became president of the college that would soon be known as Princeton University.[116]

Jonathan Edwards habitually spent more than twelve hours a day in some form of study. His usual method of study was to formulate and arrange his thoughts on a given problem by writing.[117] While Edwards's literary output was vast, in this chapter we will focus on one book that has profound significance for any study of the doctrine of human nature.

Freedom of the Will.[118] Early Arminians taught that God grants faith to those he has foreknown will exercise it, and Christ's work of

111. See Harold Simonson, *Jonathan Edwards, Theologian of the Heart* (Grand Rapids: Eerdmans, 1974); George M. Marsden, *Jonathan Edwards* (New Haven: Yale University Press, 2003).

112. Edwards's great-grandfather had already lived in New England. Timothy, Jonathan's father, had graduated from Harvard College and was a pastor. See Iain H. Murray, *Jonathan Edwards: A New Biography* (Edinburgh: Banner of Truth, 1987), 4–7.

113. Initially, Harvard was the training place of American pastors.

114. Ibid., 41.

115. Ibid., 91.

116. Ibid., 284.

117. Paul Ramsey, introduction to *Freedom of the Will*, by Jonathan Edwards, ed. Paul Ramsey (New Haven: Yale University Press, 1957), 7.

118. I had the privilege of taking a seminar on this book in seminary under Dr. John Gerstner. Edwards's anthropology was determinative for my presentation of human actions and choices

salvation made it possible for everyone to be saved. Arminians did believe that grace is necessary for salvation, but they held that man can resist this extended grace. Grace is also necessary to continue in Christ, but people can also resist this grace. Perseverance, therefore, is conditional. Conditionality is the distinguishing mark of Arminianism.

In 1752 to 1753, Edwards wrote *Freedom of the Will* against such beliefs.[119] Two pillars are foundational to this work: proofs from Scripture and proofs from reason. Edwards set before his readers the following either/or situation: either God is shut out of this world, or absolute human free will is shut out. Either human will is king, or God's providence is king.

Edwards defined the word *freedom* relative to the will very carefully. For him, freedom meant the ability to do that which we will, to move our will according to our pleasure. Edwards firmly held that humans had such freedom. Free will is that act of volition wherein the person is "free from hindrance or impediment in the way of doing, or conducting in any respect, as he wills."[120] In other words, Edwards believed that people are free to do what they will but not to do what they do not will.

The issue of a prior cause does not come into play with his definition of freedom. Freedom is simply limited to choosing according to a person's pleasure, not determining the roots or foundation of that pleasure.

Edwards also believed that the determination of the will by the agent is consistent with morality and that morality, in fact, requires this determination. Relative to making moral choices, Edwards also spoke about the freedom of indifference. There are choices that people make that are not worthy of praise or blame, such as choosing the color of a shirt in the morning.

Relative to cause in making choices, Edwards was rightly convinced that a person always chooses his or her perceived highest good. No event can occur without a cause, and Edwards held that one's perceived highest good is the cause or motive for choice. Willing is a

---

after the fall in Richard C. Gamble, *The Whole Counsel of God*, vol. 1, *God's Mighty Acts in the Old Testament* (Phillipsburg, NJ: P&R Publishing, 2009) (*WCG1*), 220–28.

119. Edwards, *Freedom of the Will*, 9–10.

120. Ibid., 163.

bit different. The willing is not determined by the greatest apparent good. Determination relative to the will is the connection between an internal act of choosing and the subsequent external action. The will is determined by the strongest motive present to the mind.[121]

To summarize the meaning of moral responsibility relative to action in Edwards's thinking, when a person makes a fully conscious moral choice, he or she totally identifies with that choice. The choice is not based simply on what he or she wants but on who he or she is as a person.[122] Thus, when it comes to exercising faith in Jesus Christ, an unregenerate sinner cannot choose Christ. He or she hates him and does not find bending the knee to him to be her highest good. It is only after the Holy Spirit does the work of regeneration in that person that his or her will is transformed so that he or she views Christ as the pearl of great price and his or her will freely chooses Christ. Edwards's views against Arminianism were opposed by two of his contemporaries.

THE WESLEYS AND THE DEVELOPMENT OF METHODISM

At the end of chapter 17 we examined German Pietism. At roughly the same time, England experienced a similar expression of Pietism. Different religious societies began to form in England, and by the year 1700 it was estimated that there were one hundred piety societies meeting in the city of London alone.[123] The societies met as a way for people to practice and express their piety in the face of a corrupt state church. In 1702, Samuel Wesley formed a society. The clergy did not look favorably on the societies, and by 1710 their numbers began to decline.

Life before Field Preaching. John Wesley (1703–1791) was the older brother of Charles Wesley (1707–1788). John, a fellow of Lincoln Col-

---

121. Ibid., 148.

122. Ibid., 428: "not so properly because they are from us, as because we are in them, i.e., our wills are in them; not so much because they are from some property of ours, as because they are our properties."

123. Justo L. Gonzalez, *A History of Christian Thought* (Nashville: Abingdon Press, 1975), 3:280: First established in 1678, "The purpose of these societies was not to take the place of the church, but rather to supplement the worship of the church with the devotion, study, and experience of smaller groups."

lege, Oxford, was ordained as an Anglican priest in 1728.[124] Charles, while at Oxford, had formed a club that began as a study group but soon became increasingly organized. The student members visited prisoners and fasted. In early 1735, George Whitefield (1714–1770) joined the club.[125]

In 1735, the Wesley brothers sailed as missionaries to Georgia, one of the American colonies. While on board, they encountered the Moravians. During a terrible storm at sea, the Wesley brothers noticed the Moravians' calm.[126] The Wesleys' own religious state was unsettled by the encounter. In 1738, both John and Charles were converted. The Wesleys were greatly influenced by Luther's commentary on Romans, which determined the Wesleys' estimate of the normal way to enter the Christian life.[127]

John then sailed to Germany to meet with the Moravians. He met Count Zinzendorf and spent enough time to make judgments about the Moravians; in the end, he determined that he could not become a Moravian.[128] He never intended to set up societies, pejoratively called Methodist societies, in opposition to or in competition with the Church of England. He still agreed theologically with the Anglican Thirty-Nine Articles and the liturgy and piety of the *Book of Common Prayer*.[129]

Field Preaching and Theology. The Wesleys' friend George Whitefield had started field preaching, and he invited the brothers to join him in Bristol. There John Wesley found his calling, which continued to the end of his ministry. His preaching produced dramatic results. He was fearless in the face of opposition.[130]

Yet he was wrestling with whether predestination is absolute or conditional. Wesley also struggled with whether man can resist the grace of God and with the matter of the perseverance of the saints. He did not appreciate the theology of the Synod of Dordt. Wesley

---

124. Walker, *History*, 454–56; Schmidt, *Grundriss*, 524–26.

125. Walker, *History*, 457; Gonzalez, *Christian Thought*, 3:287; V. H. H. Green, *John Wesley* (London: Thomas Nelson, 1970), 9–37.

126. Green, *Wesley*, 38–44.

127. Walker, *History*, 458–59.

128. Ibid., 459: "Wesley was too active in religious attitude, too little mystical, too outreaching to men in their wider needs." See Gonzalez, *Christian Thought*, 3:281.

129. Gonzalez, *Christian Thought*, 3:283.

130. Green, *Wesley*, 67–91; Walker, *History*, 459.

concluded that predestination is always conditional and depends on the individual's beliefs. Wesley could not accept unconditional predestination because of the implications it has for unconditional reprobation. He believed that a man's resistance to grace is the cause of his unbelief, not God's reprobation.[131]

If Wesley were to assert that man made the first movement of faith, he would be a Pelagian. At its best, Pelagianism makes God's grace unnecessary, and at its worst it makes grace the result of human merit. This was rank heresy, and Wesley had received enough training to know it. So he rejected this view. Arminianism, condemned by the Synod of Dordt and the opponent of Jonathan Edwards, was Wesley's solution. The answer for the Wesleys was the notion of universal, prevenient grace, a grace that is given to all humans. Because all men have this grace, all are capable, through the working of that grace, to move to the further grace of belief. That belief then leads to justifying faith, then eventually to the assurance of salvation.[132] The Wesleyan movement spread throughout Great Britain and made its way to America. Let us now conclude this chapter with an analysis of early American thinking on some important issues.

EIGHTEENTH-CENTURY AMERICA

Law, Liberty of Conscience, and Religion in Early America. New England was charged with tension over religious liberty. For example, in 1636 Roger Williams, who opposed enforced religious conformity, was ejected from Massachusetts.[133] He went to England to obtain a charter for the state of Rhode Island. Thirty years after his ejection from Massachusetts, Rhode Island's charter guaranteed full religious liberty.[134] Yale College, mentioned earlier in connection with Edwards, had been established by Puritan Congregationalists when Harvard was no longer theologically conservative.[135]

131. Gonzalez, *Christian Thought*, 3:284.
132. Ibid., 3:285.
133. Edwin S. Gaustad, *Faith of Our Fathers: Religion and the New Nation* (San Francisco: Harper & Row, 1987), 23.
134. Ibid., 24.
135. Ibid., 19.

In New York in particular, the Dutch maintained control for the first forty years. Then in 1664, the English assumed power. But even after 1664, the Dutch Reformed churches were still powerful, and they deemed the Quakers to be as much a political and social threat as they were a theological one.[136] The powerful politician William Penn saved the Quakers.[137] In 1682, the charter of the Commonwealth of Pennsylvania granted the liberty of conscience and the liberty not to worship, but it did not grant the liberty to labor on Sunday.[138] It could be said that Pennsylvania emphasized liberty of conscience for the society, while Rhode Island upheld individual liberty.[139] The population of Maryland had originally been largely Roman Catholic, but by the mid-eighteenth century, Anglican churches outnumbered Catholic churches by three to one.[140]

The southern states housed mostly Presbyterians. The Presbyterians, unlike the New England Congregationalists, were less favorable to liberty of conscience in religious matters. At least until the American Revolution, Presbyterians considered the American colonies still obliged to uphold the Westminster Confession of Faith, which was decidedly against tolerating Roman Catholics. But the WCF was not in favor of ecclesiastical independence either. While the new nation was struggling to determine issues relative to the church and the state, it appears that God himself was also doing a mighty work in the land.

Great Awakening. The Great Awakening of the 1740s was a movement considered by many to be the beginning of the modern American evangelical movement.[141] While praised by many, this movement was not a full expression of the whole counsel of God.[142] Jonathan Edwards was a great theologian of the movement, but he had no comparable political/social leader. The reason for this lack was because the movement never aspired to establish a Christian view of society. These colonists were reluctant to become involved in political and social issues.[143]

---

136. Ibid., 17, 25.
137. Ibid., 26.
138. Ibid., 27.
139. Ibid., 28.
140. Ibid., 16.
141. The Great Awakening actually curtailed the movement for religious liberty (ibid., 31).
142. Richard L. Ganz and William J. Edgar, *Sold Out* (Ottawa: Onward Press, 1990), 91.
143. Ibid., 92.

There were at least three reasons for their reluctance. First, they concluded that formal externals, such as worship, education, and government, are essentially insignificant. One only has to look to these people's past to get an idea of how they might have reached such a conclusion. They believed that attention to such external details had enslaved them in their prior unbelief.[144] The second reason for their reluctance was that they identified Christ's reign exclusively with the church and understood the Devil to be in control of all else.[145] The third reason consisted in the movement's failure to combat entrenched Enlightenment thinking—the Enlightenment blamed the church for political problems.[146]

These reasons help explain why some decades later, by the time of the American Revolution, evangelicals were quite willing not to be involved in public affairs. There was a desire to separate the church from the state. They longed for Roger Williams's *wall of separation.* They wanted the truth of the church to be on one side of the wall and the autonomous society to be on the other.[147]

American Culture: Thomas Jefferson (A.D. 1743–1826). As we investigate eighteenth-century American culture, we find a truth that is constant in every century: culture gets shaped by relatively few elites.[148] There is a lot of mythology surrounding the life of Thomas Jefferson, America's third president. He was born into a wealthy family and was college educated. When he was fourteen years old, his father died, thus leaving him twenty-seven hundred acres in Virginia and a number of bondservants.[149] His financial inheritance came to him from three prior generations of slaveholders.[150]

Jefferson was a man of great wealth. During most of his adult life, he owned approximately ten thousand acres and from one slave to

144. Ibid.
145. Ibid., 93.
146. Ibid.
147. Ibid., 93–94.
148. There are a number of important and omitted national religious and political leaders, including John Adams (see David M. McCullough, *John Adams* [New York: Simon & Schuster, 2001]) and George Washington (see Peter A. Lillback, *George Washington's Sacred Fire* [King of Prussia, PA: Providence Forum Press, 2006]).
149. Marvin Olasky, *The American Leadership Tradition* (Wheaton, IL: Crossway, 1999), 29.
150. Richard Hofstadter, *The American Political Tradition* (New York: Vintage, 1957), 18.

two hundred slaves.[151] This wealth provided him the leisure to write. One of the major questions about Jefferson concerns his position on slavery. Some scholars have adamantly maintained that he was in favor of abolishing it as an institution, and there is some justification to that claim. He did write up a draft of a law gradually to emancipate the slaves, but that law was never even introduced into the legislature for discussion.

Jefferson was a talented and complex man. He was both a thinker and a practical man. He was an outspoken proponent of mass education. Although he wanted general education, he wanted America to remain largely a rural country. He thought that Americans should leave the manufacturing to Europe. He saw merchants, land speculators, and even the working class as corrupt. He did not like cities but instead had a love for the land. He believed that farmers were the only honest and dependable people. Jefferson, thus, thought that if a society separated human nature from what he would consider its proper or natural environment—a thought that echoes Rousseau's *Emile* in terms of the cultivation of the soil and the ownership of real property—then that society would experience troubles. Democracy, like society in general, should not be separated from the farm and the soil.

The rise of modern industrial capitalism did to Europe and the United States exactly what Jefferson had feared it would do. Industrial capitalism began to push society further and further away from the actual cultivation of the land.[152] Jefferson was convinced that a life lived away from the farm and the soil had an artificial basis. So it is no surprise that Jefferson had an agricultural, agrarian vision for society. One of the inherent problems with Jefferson's view of democracy was that it lacked a sturdy economic foundation. While his dreams for society might be considered quaint, his thoughts on religion were nothing short of wicked.

Jefferson's faith did not inhibit his keeping slaves or carrying out an adulterous lifestyle.[153] Jefferson also took issue with organized religion—as often happens with human beings, his worldview stemmed from his experience. Jefferson had an unpleasant relationship with

151. Olasky, *Leadership Tradition*, 25.
152. Hofstadter, *Political Tradition*, 18.
153. Olasky outlines two different adulteries (see Olasky, *Leadership Tradition*, 25–27).

an Anglican clergyman, and it resulted in his overall distaste for the Anglican church.[154] He also had strong feelings against Presbyterians.[155] He was a deist, and it has been correctly claimed that deism was foundational for the American Revolution as well as for the rise of American democracy itself.[156]

Jefferson longed for the United States to purify itself of its past and to become Unitarian.[157] As president, he disagreed with his predecessors Washington and Adams regarding government-sponsored religious services. In a letter dated January 1, 1802, and likely without knowing it, he nodded his agreement with Roger Williams. He wrote that since religion "is a matter which lies solely between man and his God," the legislature should build "a wall of separation between Church and State."[158] As Peter Lillback has demonstrated, this phrase has caused trouble in America for more than two hundred years.[159]

The eighteenth century, like every century that has preceded it, was full of turmoil and changes. The power of ungodly thinking seemed to gain a stronger headwind even in the midst of apparent ecclesiastical progress. These changes laid the foundation for an even more tumultuous nineteenth century.

KEY TERMS

noumenal realm
phenomenal realm

154. Ibid., 31, 36.
155. "The Presbyterian clergy are loudest, the most intolerant of all sects, the most tyrannical and ambitious; ready at the word of the lawgiver, if such a word could be now obtained, to put the torch to the pile, and to rekindle in this virgin hemisphere, the flames in which their oracle Calvin consumed the poor Servetus"(*Jefferson's Extracts*, 393 to William Short, April 13, 1820, as cited by Gaustad, *Faith*, 48, 177).
156. C. Gregg Singer, *A Theological Interpretation of American History* (Phillipsburg, NJ: Presbyterian and Reformed, 1981), 24.
157. Olasky, *Leadership Tradition*, 43. Jefferson argued "that Americans had within their grasp the opportunity for a purification of Christianity as significant as that achieved more than two centuries earlier by Luther and others" (Gaustad, *Faith*, 8).
158. Gaustad, *Faith*, 46: "Jefferson first employed the metaphor, then endeavored for the rest of his life to give that metaphor as much brick and mortar as he possibly could." Olasky, *Leadership Tradition*, 24.
159. Peter A. Lillback, *Wall of Misconception* (King of Prussia, PA: Providence Forum Press, 2007).

analytic judgment

synthetic judgment

STUDY QUESTIONS

1. If you had to choose between rationalism and empiricism, which one would you choose?
2. How do you evaluate the Christians of Herrnhut?
3. What is *Lessing's ditch*? Does his thought make sense to you?
4. How do you evaluate Kant's philosophical thinking?
5. Is divine revelation possible in Kant's philosophical world?
6. Do the Wesleys have a proper view of grace, the human will, and salvation?
7. Do you think that America was founded on Christian principles?

RESOURCES FOR FURTHER STUDY

This chapter had to analyze much non-Christian thinking to set the background for the development of theology. A high point of the chapter was the life and writings of Jonathan Edwards. Yale University Press has been producing excellent texts of his writings, which now fill more than twenty-six volumes.

Edwards, Jonathan. *Freedom of the Will*. Edited by Paul Ramsey. New Haven: Yale University Press, 1957. Briefly analyzed in this chapter.

———. *The Works of Jonathan Edwards*. Vol. 22, *Sermons and Discourses, 1739–42*. Edited by Harry S. Stout and Nathan O. Hatch. New Haven: Yale University Press, 2003. Sermons always worth reading.

Lillback, Peter A. *George Washington's Sacred Fire*. King of Prussia, PA: Providence Forum Press, 2006. Gives historical, biographical, and theological analysis of the first president.

20

Nineteenth Century

Nineteenth-Century European Thought

Nineteenth-century European thought was profound and complex. Secular thought advanced more and more, but in small pockets the church was able to stand against this powerful, intellectual movement of unbelief.

Romanticism and Schelling.[1] When considering worldviews and cultural movements, the word *romanticism* does not signify two lovers' speaking and behaving in an intimate and lovely fashion. Instead, romantic thinkers posit that the point of contact with reality is not with or through the intellect but through intuition, or perhaps mystical intuition. To romantics, therefore, God, or reality, is not equated with the intellect or understanding but with feeling.[2]

At the age of eighteen, Friedrich Wilhelm Joseph von Schelling (1775–1854) wrote his dissertation at Tübingen on the fall of Adam. While there, he shared a room with Georg Hegel, and the two became friends. A few years later, Schelling wrote *On the Possibility of an Absolute Form of Philosophy* and *Of the I as the Principle of Philosophy*.[3] As the nineteenth century began, he published *Ideas for a Philosophy of Nature*.[4] He also published his *Lectures on the Method*

---

1. See Francis Schaeffer, *How Should We Then Live?* (Westchester, IL: Crossway, 1983), 162.

2. That philosophy helps us understand why Schleiermacher will later give up *religion* for *religious experience*. Gordon H. Clark, *Thales to Dewey* (Boston: Houghton Mifflin, 1957), 443–44, 470.

3. The German titles of these works are *Über die Möglichkeit einer Form der Philosophie überhaupt* and *Vom ich als Prinzip der Philosophie*.

4. Friedrich Wilhelm Joseph von Schelling, *Lectures on the Method of Academic Studies*, trans. E. E. Harris and P. Heath (Cambridge: Cambridge University Press, 1988).

of Academic Studies. His works were later compiled by his sons into fourteen volumes.[5]

Schelling was a romanticist and deist who developed something called *identity philosophy*. According to this philosophy, absolute reason is the principle that holds together the real and the ideal, the object and subject, the natural and the spiritual. This absolute reason unites all contradictions and is referred to as *God*. The incarnation of the Son of God and the Trinity simply made no sense to Schelling. To him, the incarnation and the Trinity were abstract speculations that somehow became necessary truths.[6] Schelling's philosophy stood contra German classicism, which was itself a reaction against the Enlightenment and came from the roots of Greek thought, with an added Christian coloring. It promoted a humanistic ideal, which was reached not through religious or moral ways but instead through aesthetic development.[7] Schelling's philosophy also stood against the thinking of his friend Hegel.

Georg Wilhelm Friedrich Hegel (A.D. 1770–1831).[8] Beginning in 1818, Hegel was a professor of philosophy at the University of Berlin. By this point he had already written *The Phenomenology of the Spirit* (1807). Hegel helped restore the Enlightenment.[9]

Hegel was opposed to the romantic movement. The romantics believed that there was a system of thought with no inherent contradictions and where everything fit together nicely.[10] In contrast, Hegel constructed a tremendous philosophical system. He understood philosophy and religion to have the same object. To Hegel, the main difference between the two was that religion worked from the less important or lower form of *Vorstellung*—which is usually not trans-

---

5. Richard Falckenberg, *Geschichte der neueren philosophie von Nikolaus von Kues bis zur Gegenwart* (Leipzig: Veit, 1927), 361–66.

6. Karl Heussi, *Kompendium der Kirchengeschichte* (Tübingen: Mohr Siebeck, 1971), 350.

7. The famous literary figure Johann Wolfgang von Goethe (1749–1832) belonged to this group, as did the philosopher Johann Gottlieb Fichte (1762–1814). Fichte thought that God was not the substantial ground for the world but was a mere moral guide. Fichte's position brought accusations of atheism, and he moved closer to Spinoza's philosophy, where God was seen as *absolute being* (see ibid., 348–50).

8. See Karl Loewith, *From Hegel to Nietzsche: The Revolution in Nineteenth-Century Thought* (London: Constable, 1965); Warren C. Young, *A Christian Approach to Philosophy* (Grand Rapids: Baker, 1969), 193.

9. Heussi, *Kompendium*, 350; Clark, *Thales to Dewey*, 440.

10. Clark, *Thales to Dewey*, 444.

lated into English but means *preliminary presentation*—and philosophy used a higher form, the *Idea*.[11] The broad panorama of human history, according to Hegel, was not a mixture of isolated and unrelated pieces. He believed history instead to be a unity—prior events are embraced and then modified by later events. He applied this understanding to the history of philosophy, he believed that Plato and Augustine, and Descartes and Kant did not stand in actual philosophical contradiction to one another; rather, their philosophies were aspects, phases, or moments of a much larger organic unity. For Hegel, truth, like the flow of history, was not static; it was always moving and developing. While true contradictions were possible, they were not contradictions in the normal sense of the word. Hegel believed that one part of the contradiction folded in on or developed out of another part, because propositions cannot be true in isolation from each other. Hegel believed that propositions must be ordered or structured in some type of systematic form.

The dialectical method originated in kernel form in Kant, was used by Fichte, and was then perfected by Hegel.[12] The thesis begins with a sentence or a point. When the thesis is analyzed, however, one finds in it an antithesis. To find a resolution of the tension, one must look for a higher meaning, which is located in the synthesis of the statements. The synthesis then becomes the new thesis, and the process begins again.[13]

Hegel did believe that there could be a time when one finds a synthesis that does not have an antithesis. At this point, one has reached the end of the method.[14] In Hegel's system, each thought closes out its counter-thought. But this first thought is in some form of relationship to its counter-thought. If the first thought is not in a relationship to the counter-thought, then the first thought makes no sense. An example of this method comes from nature: the bud is not a flower, but the bud is in the flower.[15]

---

11. Malcolm Clark, *Logic and System: A Study of the Transition from Vorstellung to Thought in the Philosophy of Hegel* (The Hague: Martinus Nijhoff, 1971), 27–35.

12. Clark, *Thales to Dewey*, 440.

13. John M. Frame, *A History of Western Philosophy and Theology* (Phillipsburg, NJ: P&R Publishing, 2015) (*HWPT*), 272.

14. Clark, *Thales to Dewey*, 441.

15. Ibid., 442–43.

Humanity, in Hegel's terms, is self-alienated spirit. Hegel believed that man is truly God but is alienated from himself because he does not realize this truth. As history reveals itself, man becomes less alienated to himself because the self becomes God.[16] Hegel followed Kant's anthropology in some senses and viewed humanity's self-realization as a God-like being as a major philosophical theme. His system identifies the self with God—God is within humanity, yet, coterminously, humanity is a slave to self.

While Kant saw conflict within humanity, what he saw was an inner conflict. Hegel, on the other hand, saw conflict in humanity as the subject, with an alien world as the object. Kant was concerned for the individual struggle for absolute self, while Hegel's philosophy of history involved the whole of humanity.

Objects play an important role because man finds himself at enmity with objects. Objects are thought to be extensions of man himself, and they are striving against man as man realizes his positional relationship in regard to the world and to the objects. Humankind ascertains this problem and realizes that he is in essence the whole of nature and the universal spirit, which is itself God or the absolute spirit.

Humanity is not simply God-like, as Kant thought; for Hegel, humanity is God itself. As humanity strives to become God, humanity strives for true self-identity. Hegel concluded that Jesus was the only historical man to realize his true divinity and that this divinity was within all humankind.[17]

Hegel's system understood world history to be the striving of humanity to become fully God. He held that one is not fully God until one realizes that he is God. The historical process of God's self-realization is a process of knowing. Hegel interpreted the progress of human self-knowledge as God's passage to self-knowledge. Instead of seeing a divided self, as Kant taught, Hegel saw a self-alienated spirit. The divine creativity, which belongs to spirit, serves its self-centered need to become conscious of itself. Spirit as conscious subject, humanity, confronts spirit as external object, world. This subject-object relationship is one of the self-alienation of spirit.

16. Robert C. Tucker, *Philosophy & Myth in Karl Marx* (Cambridge: Cambridge University Press, 1961), 31.
17. Ibid., 41.

Hegel's solution to the problem was through an act of knowing. In that act, he claimed, there is a change from subject-object to subject-subject. Human freedom is to recognize that the object is in fact a second self. Philosophy has as its goal knowing no presence other than the self. This ultimate freedom excluded the possibility that more than one being could become fully free. As humanity moves Godward, spirit assumes all the worldly objects and transcends them in acts of knowing. The self then comes to know itself as absolute being in the history of the world, and God becomes fully God.[18]

An important component of Hegel's thinking is sometimes referred to as the *dialectic of aggrandizement.* Man's reaching for God, or attaining what would be his true self, is indeed dialectical. Hegel believed this contradiction to be the moving force on the earth. The dialectic of aggrandizement is dealing with the elevation of man or his self-realization, in opposition to self-alienation, and the dialectic that is in that process. Man knows who he is in relationship to God, yet there is contradiction in actual life experience. Man knows that, in effect, the self is God, but the self is not consciously aware of that fact in life and is thus alienated from his real self. This, in essence, is true dialectic.[19]

Many Protestant theologians of this time wanted to align themselves with Hegel's philosophy. After his death, a new movement came about with a group known as young, or post, Hegelians.[20]

Post-Hegelians. Hegel is significant if for no other reason than that he is the catalyst for much of the philosophy that followed him. The first group, in general, responded positively to him. In the latter half of the twentieth century, though, there was a reactionary movement against Hegel.[21]

As a pessimist, Arthur Schopenhauer (1788–1860) taught that this world was the worst of all possible worlds—he does not fit well as a post-Hegelian. Schopenhauer was a romantic and regarded the intellect as superficial. He tried to find refuge in some deeper form of life. For him, the deeper form, or major aspect, of humanity was the human will, which was neither rational nor moral. Schopenhauer

18. Ibid., 45.
19. Ibid., 73–85.
20. Heussi, *Kompendium*, 368.
21. Clark, *Thales to Dewey*, 471.

believed nature to be blind and purposeless and science to be superficial. For him, human life had no goal—his philosophical legacy was a strong irrationalism.[22]

Ludwig Feuerbach (1804–1872) held a number of beliefs that were anti-Hegelian. For example, Feuerbach believed that man has real being as man; man is not God. And when man realizes that he is not God, he is freed from self-division. It is the projecting of the self as absolute that produces alienation. As to the relationship between God and humanity, Feuerbach took Hegel's thought and stood it on its head.[23] Feuerbach argued that man was not elevating himself to the position of God, rather, God was revealing himself in man. As man realizes his divinity, God is realizing himself. Feuerbach said that the only truth in Hegel is found when there is an exchange of terms, or when God and man are interchanged.

In his two works, *The Essence of Christianity* (1841) and *The Essence of Religion* (1851), Feuerbach criticized contemporary theologians he claimed were merely doing anthropology. In other words, their God was simply a projection of themselves.[24]

Feuerbach taught that man is alienated from God because there is no real separation between the two, but man feels alienated because religion causes him to believe as much.[25] God is man in the state of self-alienation, the revealed man, and the idealized image of positive attributes of the species. God is the ideal of what men should be. He is man in communion with man.

Feuerbach eventually accepted a purely physiological explanation for human thought. He was a nominalist; thus to him, universals were nothing but names. He believed real existence not to be found in abstract self-consciousness but in sensation alone. Since there are true men who never philosophize and philosophers who stop philosophizing, he concluded that human nature is primarily emotional, not intellectual.

22. Ibid., 470–71; Heussi, *Kompendium*, 369; Gordon H. Clark, *Religion, Reason and Revelation* (Jefferson, MD: Trinity Foundation, 1986), 181.
23. Tucker, *Karl Marx*, 92.
24. Cornelius Van Til, *Christianity and Barthianism* (Philadelphia: Presbyterian and Reformed, 1962), 4–5. Barth said that Feuerbach did not understand the significance of death or of evil (Karl Barth, *Die Theologie und die Kirche* [Munich: Kaiser, 1928], 237).
25. Tucker, *Karl Marx*, 93.

True reality is that man is limited and temporal. Humanity suffers, senses, and inevitably dies. The body has already unconsciously determined even what appears to be conscious choosing. Feuerbach believed that "Der mensch ist was er isst," or "Man is what he eats." He also had a different goal for history than did Hegel. For Hegel, the goal of history was the self-realization of God in man. For Feuerbach, it was the self-realization of man as man.[26]

David Friedrich Strauss (1808–1874) was the first radical who wrote predominantly religious material—his aim was to destroy Christianity.[27] In 1846, his *Leben Jesu, kritisch bearbeitet* (1835–1836) was published in three volumes in English.[28] While Strauss admitted that there is truth in Christianity, as there is truth in other religions, he concluded that, in effect, the supposed historical facts of Christianity are mere myth.[29] While Strauss denied the Christian faith for himself, he granted that there is a role for religion to play in society. He considered religion to be a feeling of dependence in a naturalistic universe.[30] These lesser-known, anti-Christian thinkers will be eclipsed by the next massive force in nineteenth century thought: Karl Marx.

Karl Marx (A.D. 1818–1883) was born in the Rhineland of Jewish parents who later converted to Lutheranism. He studied law at the University of Bonn but then traveled to Berlin to read philosophy and history. He eventually received a doctorate at the University of Jena for a dissertation on the ancient Greek philosophers.

Although Hegel had died five years before Marx arrived in Berlin, Marx would later write that Hegel's intellectual legacy still weighed heavily among students and scholars. Young Marx associated with a group of Hegelians who referred to themselves as *free spirits*. Several times Marx turned to the work of journalism, but his journalistic efforts often resulted in failure. What made Hegelianism irresistible to

---

26. Ibid., 51.

27. Barth wrote on Strauss in Karl Barth, *Protestant Thought* (New York: Harper, 1959), 356; Clark, *Thales to Dewey*, 472.

28. Colin Brown, *Philosophy & the Christian Faith: A Historical Sketch from the Middle Ages to the Present Day* (Downers Grove, IL: InterVarsity Press, 1968), 152. For more on Strauss, see Richard C. Gamble, *The Whole Counsel of God*, vol. 2, *The Full Revelation of God* (Phillipsburg, NJ: P&R Publishing, 2018) (WCG2), 118, 414.

29. Clark, *Thales to Dewey*, 473.

30. Ibid.

Marx was the notion of the deity of humanity. Marx was captivated by the thought of man beyond limits.

In 1848 Marx was arrested, tried for sedition, and acquitted—still, he was expelled from Germany. He spent the rest of his life in comparative poverty in London, where he frequented the British Museum to gather material for his great analysis of capitalism—*Das Kapital* (1867).[31]

Although intellectually indebted to Hegel, Marx rejected Hegel's notion that all reality is a product of the absolute spirit. Instead, Marx followed Feuerbach in understanding materialism to be the basic principle of reality. Marx made a radical step for his time: he made no attempt to find a place in his thought for religion in general or Christianity in particular. Instead, he denounced religion as an enemy.[32]

But Marx did tolerate religion as long as it was understood to be the handiwork of man. He saw religion as an extension of human self-consciousness or self-awareness. This felt need for extension had its roots deep in human society. Humans live in a world of man, of the state, and of society in general. It is this human society, or state, that produces religion. Marx saw religion as being particularly helpful as an expression of suffering, a protest against oppression, and the cry of the human soul against a soulless existence. But Marx believed that Judaism is an inferior extension of Christianity. He believed that Christians are so blinded by their religion that they are unable to see their true relationship to God—Christians, in their own blindness, have set up for themselves a dreadful god of money and greed. Thus Marx thought of religion as a dreaded opium of the people. He thought that when men and women were truly happy, their religion would disappear.

Marx believed that money is both the supreme being of the world and the cause for man's economic woes, along with private property. He thought that property ownership did nothing but cause strife in society.[33] Though a proponent of communism, Marx did not advocate a raw communism, which would entail even women's being seen as communal property.

---

31. Marx had met Friedrich Engels (1829–1895) soon after arriving in London, and together they wrote an enormous number of pamphlets and polemical works. Engels owned a prosperous textile factory and was thus able to support Marx (see Brown, *Philosophy & Faith*, 135).

32. Ibid.

33. Marx saw this result especially in France but also in England.

Marx argued that the state is an extension of the people, not people an extension of the state. This seed of an idea would grow into the cry that there had to be a complete revolution in order to have a proper state.[34] Marx called for a revolution at the hands of the proletariat—the propertyless working class of society.

The term *alienated labor* referred to the workforce that was estranged because their wages were dealt from the hands of greedy capitalists. Marx provided an excellent example of such. He said that a working man needs to labor only half a day to produce the requirement of his wage. But because he works an extra and unnecessary half day, his labor contributes negatively toward himself and positively toward the capitalist.[35]

Following seeds sown by Marx, Friedrich Engels and Vladimir Lenin would develop the doctrine of dialectical materialism. Based in what he considered to be Hegelian thought, Marx was convinced that reality is never static but always moving, most often upward. So society is always evolving, sometimes in sudden leaps and lurches.[36] For example, society had transitioned—had progressed, according to Marx—from the feudal system to capitalism, and from capitalism to socialism, and then finally from socialism to communism. The change was dependent on class struggle. Marx, an impoverished German transplant living in nineteenth-century England, brought about global change in the economic, political, and ecclesiastical spheres.

Friedrich Nietzsche (A.D. 1844–1900) studied theology as a Roman Catholic at the University of Bonn. But during Easter communion in 1865, Nietzsche refused to participate. Following that turning point, Nietzsche abandoned religion and began to study language.

Nietzsche had syphilis and by the age of thirty was already a partial invalid. His health required him to remain in bed for thirty-six hours every two to three weeks. Life was by no means easy for him. Because of his ill health, after nine years of teaching Nietzsche resigned from his professorate at the University of Basel and lived off a small pension.[37] He spent the summers in the Swiss Engadine mountains.

---

34. Tucker, *Karl Marx*, 104, 192.
35. Ibid., 18–19.
36. This process is demonstrated in Hegel's *Logic* (see Brown, *Philosophy & Faith*, 135).
37. Ibid., 138; *HWPT*, 329.

Nietzsche loved Richard Wagner's music because it took away his pain, even if only for a moment. At an opening of Wagner's new music, however, Nietzsche fell suddenly ill. The powerful music was apparently no longer enough to keep the pain at bay. Thus Nietzsche turned against Wagner. As a result, he discovered what he termed *life anew* and a new philosophy, called "the will to power."

In 1882, Nietzsche met the twenty-one-year-old Lou Almay Salamay. He considered her his protégée. With a psychologist friend, the three of them took a vacation in Italy. On the trip, Nietzsche proposed marriage to Lou, but she turned down his offer and claimed to have no desire at all to marry. It was not long, however, before Lou left Nietzsche for his psychologist friend. This rejection wore on Nietzsche psychologically.

In 1888, Nietzsche left the mountains and traveled to Italy, where he started a new system of values, a new morality. The project was called "the transvaluation of all values." He expanded his idea of the will to power by noting that power itself is good and weakness is bad. He thought of Christianity as the religion of pity. He opposed pity because pity is only felt when people are deprived of strength.

He then wrote *The Antichrist* and *The Twilight of Idols*. He believed it to be his task to describe morality to a society that existed without divine sanctions. But the task was impossible for him. His great mind led him to a cul-de-sac. Eventually declared to be clinically insane, by 1889 his letters betray his own madness. He envisioned himself to be a god combatting suffering on behalf of mankind. He believed every man ought to be a god unto himself. The human condition lies somewhere between man's being an animal and being what he deemed the *Übermensch*—which might be translated something like "superman."

Nietzsche was moved to an asylum, then to his mother's home. For eleven years, he lived in a vegetative state with his sister Elizabeth. In 1900 Nietzsche died of a stroke. Elizabeth then reedited his literary works and published a collection of them called the *Will to Power*.[38]

Nietzsche's notion of the will to power is not infrequently seen in today's world. He began with philosophical skepticism. He was

---

38. His sister, a strong German nationalist and anti-Semite, had written a two-volume biography about her brother before he died. The titles of some of his works include *Human, All Too Human: A Book for Free Spirits*. A second part, *Assorted Opinions and Maxims*, was

not convinced that language, or even logic, granted access to the true nature of things. In agreement with Kant, he held that there was no knowledge of the thing in itself, but he went beyond Kant and denied the existence of any universal categories within experience. Thus the whole process of knowing is simply an invention of the will.[39]

For Nietzsche, facts did not exist—only interpretations. As a result, the categories of *true* and *false* are inapplicable. The fruit of Nietzsche's philosophy was a loosening of moral and intellectual certainty. People were no longer sure of good and evil, or of right and wrong. Nietzsche believed that we are not determined by outside forces. This conclusion means that traditional philosophy, as well as religion, disappear. For him, God is dead, and God's funeral means the absolute freedom of man. He viewed traditional Christianity as a barrier to exercising our will to power. In his *Thus Spoke Zarathustra*, he proposed the ideal of self-overcoming. He believed that humanity could transcend itself. The will to power was to obtain this self-knowledge, or self-mastery. Let us now return across the ocean to the United States.

NINETEENTH-CENTURY AMERICAN THOUGHT

This section will outline the intellectual world of nineteenth-century America through the lens of two intellectual leaders in the fields of law and education.

Oliver Wendell Holmes (A.D. 1841–1935) came from an outstanding family. His father, Dr. Oliver Wendell Holmes Sr., published hundreds of poems, wrote three novels, and was dean of the Harvard Medical School. Dr. Holmes had a strong distaste for Calvinism, which had been the religion of his father. As dean, he admitted Blacks to the medical school but dismissed them after being pressured to do so.[40]

---

published in 1879, and a third part, *The Wanderer and His Shadow*, followed in 1880. *The Joyful Wisdom* was published in 1882; *Beyond Good and Evil* saw the light of day in 1886; *The Twilight of the Idols* followed in 1888; *Towards a Genealogy of Morals* came in 1887; *Ecce Homo* in 1888; and *The Antichrist: Attempt at a Critique of Christianity* in 1895.

39. HWPT, 330.

40. Louis Menand, *The Metaphysical Club: A Story of Ideas in America* (New York: Farrar Straus Giroux, 2001), 7–10.

The early life of his son was cultivated and homogenous. The young Holmes was the consummate product of the pre–Civil War idealistic world. But that world bled to death on the field of battle. He returned from the war as a changed man to a changed America. "He told me," Einstein reported, "that after the Civil War the world never seemed quite right again."[41] Holmes personally faced the specter of death on more than one occasion during the Civil War, when he was shot in the chest, the neck, and the foot. Within the envelope of those nearly fatal experiences, he discovered that he had no need of religion.

He rejected the intellectual life of prewar Boston and became convinced that disinterested inquiry provided answers.[42] His principle legal work was *The Common Law*, which was published in 1881.[43] Holmes was praised by John Dewey as one of the "greatest American philosophers."[44] His influence, however, in no way supported the church. Holmes was convinced that the NT had failed society, that the obligation to duty has nothing to do with God and his law, and that nobility of character is the doing of one's duty without thought toward an end or reward. Uncertainty became his certainty. At the end of life, he thought that the performance of his duty was all that he could ask for. Proper belief, he thought, could change, because the best beliefs are adaptable to circumstances.[45]

John Dewey (A.D. 1859–1952) was another prominent American at this time. He was born in Vermont and graduated in 1879 from that state's university in a class of eighteen, which included both his brother and cousin. He attended graduate school at Johns Hopkins University in Baltimore. From there he went to teach at the University of Michigan at Ann Arbor, then at the University of Chicago. While teaching in Chicago, he opened the University Elementary School, which was immensely successful.[46] Dewey eventually ended up at Columbia University in New York.[47]

41. Ibid., 69.
42. Ibid., 59.
43. Ibid., 64.
44. Ibid., 437.
45. Ibid., 23–27, 37–38, 54, 64.
46. Ibid., 320: "By 1902, there were 140 students, 23 teachers, and ten graduate students working as assistants; it had become an international sensation; and it was known as the Dewey School."
47. Ibid., 235–38, 304.

Dewey found himself at home in modernity. As both a philosopher and an educator, he longed to provide a method for dealing with humanity's problems.[48] His most wide-ranging philosophical book was *Experience and Nature*, published in 1925, when he was sixty-six years old. He retired from Columbia in 1930.

If Dewey is known for anything, it is as an educator. Most people would know his name through the Dewey Decimal System of classification in libraries. But he was much more than an educator. His thinking had a deep and epistemologically developed foundation. Dewey had established the elementary school in Chicago to test a theory regarding the unity of knowledge. He was convinced that each academic subject is an aspect of a greater whole of knowledge.[49] For his predecessors, however, the unity of knowledge was tethered to a divine will or some sort of absolute. Dewey rejected this earlier theory. His conception of the unity of knowledge was that knowing is tied to doing.

He was convinced that knowledge is a by-product of activity. It is not disembodied information, because then it is cut off from the activity in which it has its meaning. Dewey was convinced that separating knowing from doing is both socially pernicious and philosophically erroneous.[50] He desired goal-directed activity. For example, the academic subject of chemistry should be connected to the activity of cooking. There is a symbiotic relationship between learning and doing. His bestselling book, *The School and Society* (1899), has never been out of print to this day![51] We have briefly examined nineteenth-century German thinking and American pragmatism. Let us now turn to see how theology developed both on the Continent and in America.

Nineteenth-Century German Theology[52]

Some evangelical scholars have argued that the barren state of nineteenth-century German theology was nothing more than the con-

48. Ibid., 237.
49. See Clark, *Thales to Dewey*, 517–23.
50. Menand, *Metaphysical Club*, 322.
51. Ibid., 328.
52. See Richard L. Schoenwald, *Nineteenth-Century Thought: The Discovery of Change* (Englewood Cliffs, NJ: Prentice Hall, 1965).

tinuation of the sterile state of eighteenth-century theology and philosophy.[53] Nineteenth-century German scholars worked diligently in the field of biblical criticism. For them, history, whether biblical or secular, was a story of events that could be meaningfully interpreted so as to enrich the present through critical and imaginative reconstruction.[54] Only a handful of believing scholars figure in this period. This section will focus its attention on the development of liberalism.[55]

Friedrich Daniel Ernst Schleiermacher (A.D. 1768–1834).[56] Friedrich Schleiermacher was the grandson of a minister and son of a Reformed army chaplain who had been originally trained by the Moravians. Schleiermacher began to be influenced by Enlightenment thinking when he started his studies at the University of Halle.

He blossomed in the social and cultural life of the great capital city of Berlin.[57] His *Addresses on Religion to Its Cultured Despisers* (1799) was written to his friends, those so-called "cultured despisers of religion."[58] In this work, Schleiermacher critiqued the worldview of his colleagues in Berlin and presented an apology for his life. He argued that a life that was not affected by personal religion was impoverished and artificially sterile. The book was a success.[59] After producing this work, he was asked to help translate Plato's dialogues from Greek. His time in Berlin came to an unhappy end when he fell in love with a pastor's wife, who refused to divorce her husband to be with him. He then fled the city and accepted a pastoral position that gave him more time to write.[60]

---

53. Edward J. Young, *An Introduction to the Old Testament* (Grand Rapids: Eerdmans, 1964), 21.

54. Richard R. Niebuhr, "Friedrich Schleiermacher," in *A Handbook of Christian Theologians*, ed. Martin E. Marty and Dean G. Peerman (Nashville: Abingdon Press, 1985), 17.

55. One was C. F. Keil, who wrote with high regard for the Bible's integrity and trustworthiness.

56. See Friedrich Schleiermacher, *The Christian Faith*, ed. H. R. Mackintosh and J. S. Stewart, 2 vols. (New York: Harper, 1963). See also Richard R. Niebuhr, *Schleiermacher on Christ and Religion* (New York: Scribner's Sons, 1964), and Karl Barth, *The Theology of Schleiermacher* (Grand Rapids: Eerdmans, 1982).

57. Niebuhr, "Friedrich Schleiermacher," 19; Williston Walker, *A History of the Christian Church* (New York: Scribner's Sons, 1959), 487. He arrived in 1796.

58. *HWPT*, 294. Frame rightly remarked that he was so intent to find common ground that he compromised biblical teaching. God's existence and personal immortality were for him not essential.

59. Niebuhr, "Friedrich Schleiermacher," 19. He published *The Soliloquies* in 1800.

60. Ibid., 20.

In 1804, Schleiermacher was appointed to the University of Halle, where he taught until 1807. There he began the *Brief Outline of the Study of Theology* and also published a small booklet titled *Christmas Eve*. In the latter work, he struggled with the historicity of Jesus.[61]

He returned to Berlin as pastor of Trinity Church and in 1810 was appointed as a professor of theology at the new University of Berlin, where he joined his colleague Friedrich Hegel in the philosophy department.[62] He remained at the University of Berlin until his death.

In 1817, the Lutheran and Reformed churches of Prussia were united.[63] Schleiermacher was hopeful that Protestant theology could develop as a result of this union. After the merge, his *The Christian Faith according to the Principles of the Evangelical Church* was published in two parts (1821, 1822; revised in 1830).[64]

Schleiermacher proposed a new type of religious understanding.[65] He overturned two traditional opinions concerning the nature of religion itself and Christianity in particular.[66] The first view he overturned was what might be termed *classic religion*. This view held that religion, whether Judaism, Christianity, or Islam, is based on an assent to authoritative truths in combination with living a life of obedience to God's will. The other view of religion that Schleiermacher overturned, generally known as *rationalist Christianity*, was an acceptance of natural theology and living a universal morality based on reason. Both classic and rationalist Christianity held to belief in eternal life and longed for eternal felicity.[67] Schleiermacher challenged both views because of his very different view of God.

Schleiermacher's position developed as he examined the world around him. He observed antithesis: he saw both that which is changing

---

61. Ibid., 20–21.
62. Ibid., 23.
63. *HWPT*, 294.
64. Niebuhr, "Friedrich Schleiermacher," 23.
65. Ibid., 18.
66. Walker, *History*, 629–31.
67. Because he was convinced that the Reformation failed to apply its insights to the doctrine of the Trinity, Schleiermacher called for renewed reflection on that doctrine. His project was to subject older articulations of that doctrine to "a new formulation of the concept of God more generally" (Friedrich Schleiermacher, *The Christian Faith* [Edinburgh: T&T Clark, 1989], 749, as cited by Scott R. Swain, "Divine Trinity," in *Christian Dogmatics: Reformed Theology for the Church Catholic*, ed. Michael Allen and Scott R. Swain [Grand Rapids: Baker Academic, 2016], 79).

and that which is permanent. From these antitheses, Schleiermacher saw on one side the absolute and eternal, which is called *God*, without whom all life and thought would be chaos. On the other side he saw the world, without which all would be empty. For Schleiermacher, God was immanent in the world.[68]

Connecting theology with anthropology, Schleiermacher thought that the human—in contrast to the great absolute—feels small, finite, and limited. The human feels dependent, and it is this dependence that is the basis for religion. Religion is primal experience—it is a feeling of absolute dependence.

Schleiermacher held that religion belongs to the realm of feeling and emotion.[69] Religion is neither a body of doctrines, either revealed from God or somehow rationally certified, nor an ethical system. He did grant, however, that behavior and belief are derived from religion. A new task came with this new definition: religion's goal was now to bridge the finite with the universal. And the task of Christian doctrine was to interpret these fundamental religious experiences intellectually.

Christian faith was no longer to be established in Scripture; the Christian Scriptures themselves came out of that particular religion and are an expression of that religious feeling. In Christianity, this sense of dependence was defined in terms of faith in Christ as Savior.

Since all religions express this feeling, however, the differences between religions are only in degree of adequacy for meeting this human need. Schleiermacher believed that Christianity is the highest of all religions and best expresses the feeling of absolute dependence; therefore, the word *God* is the verbal signifier for this feeling of dependence. *God* is that on which humans are or feel dependent.[70] He held that God is not knowable through reason, or through the study of the objects of truth, but through feeling, called *Gefühl*. Put simply, religion is a person's inborn sense of that which is true and eternal, which

---

68. Walker, *History*, 630: "The Absolute is throughout all. God is therefore immanent in His world." But Frame says that Schleiermacher's God is utterly transcendent.

69. Cornelius Van Til, *The Great Debate Today* (Nutley, NJ: Presbyterian and Reformed, 1971), 60: "The dogmatic principle of Schleiermacher's Christian Faith is human experience rather than the revelation of Christ through Scripture."

70. Niebuhr, "Friedrich Schleiermacher," 19. *HWPT*, 294: This *Gefühl* can mean *feeling* or *religious consciousness*—"He understands it to be a sense of the unity (ultimately God) that underlies all the diversities of experience."

finds its source in something more profound than mere metaphysical philosophy and officially sanctioned theological systems.[71]

The first view of religion that Schleiermacher rejected was that the Scriptures are authoritative. Schleiermacher held that Scripture *became* authoritative based on faith. Faith is the foundation for Scripture, not the other way around. The NT simply records the original feelings that Jesus's disciples had about him. By faith, someone can read those words from the Bible and receive inward illumination, but the words themselves are not objectively God's word. There is no propositional revelation. Thus theology's content comes from the believer's religious feeling.[72]

Schleiermacher's theological method was circumscribed by a philosophical grid based on his work in Plato combined with the systems of Kant and Hegel.[73] Kant was rightly concerned, thought Schleiermacher, to rescue religion from the burning critique of science. Kant demonstrated that religion is distinctive, a different sphere of life from either science or even from ethics. Schleiermacher tried to take all the Christian doctrines and insert them into Kant's scheme. For Schleiermacher, religion was very narrowly circumscribed, thus keeping it separate from the other disciplines. Religion had its own sphere and was thus insulated from the others.[74]

Moving to his doctrine of Christ, Schleiermacher's theology did not have a foundation in natural theology with a second story of faith, as did Aquinas's theology. Schleiermacher's theology was not static but was constructed on the notion of Christ as the saving act for all men. Christ is the one who bridges the finite with the universal.[75] Yet Schleiermacher's Christ did not need a resurrection.[76] For Schleiermacher, to be truly Protestant was also to be truly christological. To be Protestant was to put Christ first, to put man's relationship to Christ above everything else. Christ must be the believer's great prophet, priest, and king.

---

71. Niebuhr, "Friedrich Schleiermacher," 17–18.

72. *HWPT*, 295–97.

73. Niebuhr, "Friedrich Schleiermacher," 20.

74. But Schleiermacher did not get any further than Kant did because this religion was still simply a projection of the autonomous man. Man is still the final judge in this religion.

75. Walker, *History*, 631.

76. Van Til, *Great Debate*, 61.

Regarding salvation, Schleiermacher's view of immortality was also different from classic Christianity's. Immortality for him was simply a quality of life and not necessarily connected to duration of time. Sin was sensuous consciousness, the opposite of absolute dependence. It was part of human nature.[77] He did not believe that salvation came through historical events, such as the incarnation, crucifixion, and resurrection.[78] He held that people are not saved by something external to them but by an enhancement of religious feeling, something within. What Jesus does in salvation is to show believers that we are like him and can become more like him. Christ is no different from who we are.[79] Through conversion, the believer lives a new life of fellowship in Christ. His sins are forgiven, and he lives as a child of God. It is in Christ that he is justified and sanctified.[80] For Schleiermacher, Christianity is the theology in which Christ and faith in Christ are central—on Christ hinges the interpretation of human life.[81] In conclusion, Schleiermacher made God continuous with or immanent in the world. His thinking is what is termed *classic theological liberalism.*

Problem of the *Historical Jesus*. The previous chapter presented Lessing's publication of H. S. Reimarus's manuscript.[82] According to Reimarus, Jesus was nothing more than a political pretender to the title Messiah, connected to the zealots.[83] Reimarus's research was groundbreaking in its impact—it has influenced NT studies even to today.

Ferdinand Christian Baur (1792–1860), professor at the University of Tübingen, was another pioneer in this subject. For him, the fourth gospel was the most important document that demonstrated Jesus's life.[84] In fact, the fourth gospel became the benchmark by which the Synoptics were judged.[85] Baur developed the notion that John's gospel

---

77. *HWPT*, 297–98.

78. Ibid., 299

79. Ibid., 298.

80. Van Til, *Great Debate*, 58–59, citing the *Christian Faith* (1928).

81. Van Til, *Great Debate*, 61.

82. Robert B. Strimple, *The Modern Search for the Real Jesus: An Introductory Survey of the Historical Roots of Gospel Criticism* (Phillipsburg, NJ: P&R Publishing, 1995), 20–22.

83. Jörg Frey, *Die Johanneische Eschatologie I*, Wissenschaftliche Untersuchungen zum Neuen Testament 96 (Tübingen: Mohr Siebeck, 1997), 1:29.

84. Strimple, *Modern Search*, 38–40. *HWPT*, 301n21, argues that "Baur developed a Hegelian triad in which Peter was the thesis, Paul the antithesis, and Luke the synthesis."

85. Frey, *Eschatologie*, 1:34. Frey argues that Baur was in some sense dependent on Luther here. Of high importance were the miracles and the eschatological concepts that fit in well

could not have been written by an eyewitness.[86] Thus, in Tübingen, the picture of Jesus was the spiritual one of John.[87] Specifically, dependent on Hegel, Baur understood the different Johanine sayings to be the dialectical unfolding of John's controlling *logos* idea.[88] At the time, Baur's interpretation of John found little following in Tübingen.[89]

David Friedrich Strauss (A.D. 1808–1874) was Baur's student even before Strauss attended the University of Tübingen.[90] Under Baur, Strauss acquired an appreciation for the ancient classics and for the field of textual criticism. In 1825 he began his studies at the University of Tübingen, where he read and revered the works of Schleiermacher and Hegel. After graduating, Strauss accepted a professorship and taught Latin, Hebrew, and history. But only one year later, in 1831, Strauss left this position for the opportunity to do further study under Schleiermacher and Hegel in Berlin. Almost immediately upon Strauss's arrival in Berlin, Hegel died.

In 1829, Strauss continued the discussion that had begun with Reimarus.[91] Strauss, largely dependent on the thinking of Hegel, reasoned that the contents of philosophy and religion were the same—while one expressed itself in the form of concepts (*Vorstellung*), the other expressed itself in expressions (*Begriffe*). While Strauss did not establish a new dialectic, he nevertheless held to a dualistic relationship between *Vorstellung* and *Begriff*. Employing source-critical judgments of the Synoptic Gospels, Strauss began to paint a radical portrait of Jesus.[92]

Germanic, liberal Christianity was plunging headlong into theological and text-critical darkness. And they did so with a deaf ear turned to those who cried out in warning. One of these voices of warning came from the northern realms of Denmark.

---

with German idealism. The best expression from John was God's relationship to the world and humanity. As John 17:2 says, the communication of eternal life is in the message of human knowledge of God. John's eschatological theology was thought to unite the disconsonant notions of adoption with opposition to God as well as the present and the future. And at 1:37 Frey notes that the movement to see John's theology as the hermeneutical criterion for interpreting Jesus's words in the synoptics stood against Ritschl's judgment.

86. See *WCG* 2:315.
87. Frey, *Eschatologie*, 1:37.
88. Ibid., 1:35.
89. Ibid., 1:36.
90. Strimple, *Modern Search*, 27–29.
91. Frey, *Eschatologie*, 1:30.
92. Ibid., 1:31.

Søren Kierkegaard (A.D. 1813–1855).[93] Søren Kierkegaard's father was a wealthy businessman in Copenhagen. Immediately following the death of his wife, he married his servant. Four months after his marriage to his servant, she gave birth to a son, whom they named Søren. This moral scandal stained the reputation of the Kierkegaard home. Søren was a weak child growing up and is remembered to have walked with a limp.[94]

Though Kierkegaard is regarded for his work as a philosopher, his training was as a theologian. Thus some of his works were written with a distinctly theological tone. In his book *Fear and Trembling*, Kierkegaard focused his attention on Abraham's sacrifice of Isaac. Kierkegaard wrestled with the tension between God's command to murder and his promise of offspring through Isaac, Abraham's only son by Sarah. From this tension, Kierkegaard wrote the well-known phrase, "the teleological suspension of the ethical." By this expression he meant that Abraham was willing to suspend the ethical—to do that which he knew was unethical, namely, to murder his son—because he trusted the righteous *telos* of God. He also wrote *Either/Or*, *The Stages of Life*, *Repetition*, and *The Philosophical Fragments*, which prepared the way for his *Concluding Unscientific Postscript*.

Kierkegaard was convinced that true NT Christianity was essentially unknown among the Danes, and he wanted them to know what it meant to be an authentic Christian.[95] He was particularly interested in what authentic Christianity was within a so-called "Christian society"—that is, within European Christendom.[96] Kierkegaard found a

93. See Walter Lowrie, *Søren Kierkegaard*, 2 vols. (New York: Harper, 1962); Walker, *History*, 649.

94. Martin J. Heinecken, "Søren Kierkegaard," in *A Handbook of Christian Theologians*, ed. Martin E. Marty and Dean G. Peerman (Nashville: Abingdon Press, 1985), 125–26.

95. Ibid., 127; see also Richard Lints, "The Age of Intellectual Iconoclasm: The Nineteenth-Century Revolt against Theism," in *Revolutions in Worldview: Understanding the Flow of Western Thought*, ed. W. Andrew Hoffecker (Phillipsburg, NJ: P&R Publishing, 2007), 310–11. *HWPT*, 314: "True beliefs were the sum total of religion . . . the spiritual corruption of the church weakened the church's witness to the sanctity of the individual . . . the paradox of the eternal entering time"; and 315: "People had heard true doctrine all their lives, but they weren't taught to choose the good. . . . So Kierkegaard's question of how one can become a Christian in Christendom is the question of how one's will can be changed."

96. *HWPT*, 317–18: "Religion B is what Kierkegaard considers to be true religion, *transcendent* religion, governed by faith alone. It comes from God himself—his paradoxical act of bridging the 'infinite qualitative difference between time and eternity.'"

model to that end in the ancient Greek philosopher Socrates. Socrates posed so many questions that he forced people to think. Thus the title of *Either/Or* was written against Hegel's notion of a historical/philosophical synthesis.[97] Kierkegaard wanted to question that synthesis.

While Schleiermacher was, in a general sense, more theologically formative, Kierkegaard, who remained within post-Kantian theology, could be considered the father of dialectical theology.[98] In the nineteenth century, Kierkegaard presented a new sort of Christ. His Christ sums up all human interpretation.[99]

Kierkegaard taught that the Christian faith is absolute paradox, or contradiction.[100] By this description he meant that while God does not have internal or external contradictions, humans do. For example, the paradox of the incarnation is inexplicable for man.[101] Similarly, humans must be transformed in order to grasp that Jesus died in the stead of humans.[102] As VanTil wrote, "That which seems to be impossible logically and that which seems to be meaningless factually become, when taken together, the source of all meaningful predication."[103]

Kierkegaard taught that there is an absolute qualitative difference between God and humanity.[104] There is no simple continuity between the two, and thus there is divine elusiveness.[105] Despite this difference,

97. On Kierkegaard's *Either/Or*, see *A Kierkegaard Anthology*, ed. Robert Bretall (New York: Random House, 1946), 21: "Starting from a principle is affirmed by people of experience to be a very reasonable procedure; I am willing to humor them, and so begin with the principle that all men are bores. Surely no one will prove himself so great a bore as to contradict me in this. This principle possesses the quality of being in the highest degree repellent, an essential requirement in the case of negative principles, which are in the last analysis the principles of all motion."

98. Van Til, *Great Debate*, 108–9. Van Til (ibid., 103) also credited him as a founder of later twentieth-century existentialism: "Modern existential philosophy follows Kierkegaard in setting the idea of Existence over against that of Essence."

99. *HWPT*, 313: "Kierkegaard's thought is very different from anything that has come before. . . . It is easier to identify what Kierkegaard is not than what he is."

100. Søren Kierkegaard, *Papers and Journals: A Selection* (New York: Penguin Books, 1996), 14: "The idea of philosophy is mediation—Christianity's is the paradox."

101. Heinecken, "Kierkegaard," 137; see also Van Til, *Great Debate*, 109–10.

102. Heinecken, "Kierkegaard," 138.

103. Van Til, *Great Debate*, 110.

104. Heinecken, "Kiergegaard," 138–39. *HWPT*, 318: "He cannot be reached through science or philosophy, but can be grasped only in passionate inwardness"; and 318n59: "God, therefore, understands the paradoxes of time and eternity, but they are beyond the power of *human* reason to understand."

105. Søren Kierkegaard, *Concluding Unscientific Postscript* (Princeton: Princeton University Press, 1992), 224: "God has absolutely nothing obvious about Him, that God is so far from

Kierkegaard believed that there remains a place of meeting for God and man: they meet in an ethical relationship. The question is whether or not man obeys God.[106]

Kierkegaard opposed Descartes's notion that humanity is primarily a thinking thing. Kierkegaard understood humans to have an active will as those who make choices. If humans were only thinking beings, then humans would be devoid of relationships, and relationships—particularly those in Christ—are the essence of what makes a person human. Kierkegaard held that there could be no isolated, cognitive subject that is out of relationship with the world.[107] In reaction against the prevailing idea that if one was born a European, he was a Christian, Kierkegaard taught that each person must enter the kingdom of God alone. Humans die alone, and they come to faith alone.[108]

Kierkegaard also held that reality cannot be grasped by reason, for reality is mere chance, and chance cannot be systematized into logic. Human existence is made up of free decisions, and genuine choice is between two true alternatives. Such decisions are not determined by rational thought.[109] Kierkegaard believed that reality must be grasped individually. Personal decisions are needed.[110]

Kierkegaard's view of humanity encompassed three stages: the *aesthetic*, the *ethical*, and the *religious*. Each stage had its own presupposed concepts of rationality. A person could move from one stage to the next via a leap. In the first stage, human beings live a sensuous life. As they move to the ethical stage, life becomes governed by society's rules—humans live a moral life, one in which they are willing to sacrifice their personal interests for a higher cause. The life of Socrates is an excellent example of this ethical stage of human existence. In the final stage, the person lives in an intimate relationship with God; this final stage requires a leap of faith.[111]

---

being obvious, that He is invisible." His invisibility is related to His omnipresence. "God's visibility would annul his omnipresence."

106. Van Til, *Great Debate*, 107.

107. Ibid., 102–3.

108. Heinecken, "Kierkegaard," 140.

109. *HWPT*, 314–315: "Rational analysis is capable of describing choice, but I think Kierkegaard is right in saying that rational analysis does not determine choice."

110. Clark, *Thales to Dewey*, 486.

111. *HWPT*, 315–17. Don Juan from Mozart's *Don Giovanni* exemplifies aesthetic.

Truth was subjective for Kierkegaard. While some interpreters have argued that Kierkegaard did not deny truth's existence independently of the knower, he seems to think of truth as having two different meanings, or senses. First, there is *subjective* truth, which is a quality of the knower rather than of the object.[112] Subjective truth is believed with passion—so much so that it determines the very lifestyle of the one who holds it. Second, there are *facts of history*, which exist independently of a person's knowledge. For example, God exists regardless of whether anyone believes in him. Kierkegaard did not identify truth with historical objectivity.[113] He denied even the existence of historical objectivity; for him, history could only offer probability. And for this reason, Kierkegaard had problems with objective revelation.[114]

The meaning of what he calls the *Christ event* is not to be identified with any other ordinary historical event.[115] For Kierkegaard, the wonder of the Christ event is that eternal truth enters into relationship with individuals. Individuals enter into this relationship by believing that which is beyond understanding, and thereby they are transformed. Further, this transformation means living a life of fellowship with Christ. And in this life, sin is no longer reduced to guilt but is a breaking of fellowship with the one who transformed the person.[116]

Kierkegaard's doctrine of revelation is related to his doctrine of God and truth. Since in Kierkegaard's thinking God is qualitatively different from and beyond humanity, God does not reveal himself directly and provide instruction. In fact, Kierkegaard believed that it is not Christianity but paganism which taught that God is directly related to man.[117]

112. *HWPT*, 319.

113. Kierkegaard, *Postscript*, 208–9: "It is subjectivity that Christianity is concerned with, and it is only in subjectivity that its truth exists, if it exists at all; objectively, Christianity has absolutely no existence. . . . Christianity teaches that the way is to become subjective, i.e., to become a subject in truth. Lest this should seem a mere dispute about words, let me say that Christianity wishes to intensify passion to its highest pitch; but passion is subjectivity, and does not exist objectively."

114. *HWPT*, 318n60: "He denies the historicity of the story of the fall in Genesis 3."

115. Van Til, *Great Debate*, 103, 112. Note that it is the meaning which is being talked about. Perhaps Kierkegaard affirmed that Jesus came in ordinary history; but it transcends ordinary history when it becomes meaningful for the individual.

116. *HWPT*, 318.

117. Kierkegaard, *Postscript*, 224: "All paganism consists in this, that God is related to man directly, as the extraordinary is to the astonished observer."

Kierkegaard believed that God could not reveal himself to man through the simple medium of historical fact and human knowledge,[118] for God is not discovered in propositional truth. Divine revelation was more than mere propositions or facts for Kierkegaard.[119] Instead, when God reveals himself, humans either respond in great offense or submit and place all their faith in him. For Kierkegaard, revelation is discerned in what he called *inwardness*—an inwardness that involves transformation.[120]

Kierkegaard emphasized that faith could not be founded on doctrine. If it were, he reasoned, then faith would be a purely intellectual exercise. Instead, the object of faith is an existing person, and the answer of faith is not the validity of a set of doctrines. The answer of faith is whether or not Christ existed.[121] Since faith is beyond understanding—for who could understand the incarnation?—then faith is always uncertain. The answer of faith must be addressed with passion, for it is the nature of a relationship. Kierkegaard believed that one must give up everything to follow God.[122]

Given his views of God, humanity, truth, and reality, it is no surprise that Kierkegaard opposed Hegel's philosophy.[123] Kierkegaard articulated several reasons for his opposition. First, he regarded Hegel's thought as a speculative philosophy, abstracted from everyday life.[124] He inverted the Hegelian dialectic in all his pseudonymous

118. Van Til, *Great Debate*, 104, 106.

119. Some say that he was not against objective revelation (see Heinecken, "Kierkegaard," 140).

120. Kierkegaard, *Postscript*, 224: "But the spiritual relationship to God in the truth, i.e., [is] in inwardness"; *HWPT*, 315.

121. Kierkegaard, *Postscript*, 230: "The object of faith is not a doctrine, for then the relationship would be intellectual, and it would be of importance not to botch it, but to realize the maximum intellectual relationship. The object of faith is not a teacher with a doctrine; for when a teacher has a doctrine, the doctrine is *eo ipso* more important than the teacher, [N.B.: here is the problem] and the relationship is again intellectual, and it again becomes important not to botch it. The object of faith is the reality of the teacher, that the teacher really exists. The answer of faith is therefore unconditionally yes or no. For the answer of faith is not concerned as to whether a doctrine is true or not . . . it is the answer to a question concerning a fact."

122. *HWPT*, 317.

123. Ibid., 314: "Hegel thought (or so Kierkegaard understood him) that to choose is to take the next step in the rational dialectic, from thesis to antithesis to synthesis. . . . But for Kierkegaard, this picture destroys the essence of choice."

124. Kierkegaard argued against speculative philosophy, which would defend itself by saying that there is no paradox when a matter is viewed eternally. In response, Kierkegaard (in *Postscript*, 222) said, "I admit that I am not in a position to determine whether the speculative

writings. Second, Hegel's teaching reconciled the church with the state—a reconciliation that produced mediocre citizen-Christians.[125] Hegel was a socialist, and his thinking disregarded the individual.[126] Third, Kierkegaard disagreed with Hegel's notion that the incarnation could fit into a rationally comprehensible system. Kierkegaard believed that human reason could not determine what is possible and impossible.[127]

The final section of analysis concerns Kierkegaard's apologetic. He is an example of a classic fideist. He believed that Christianity could not be rationally defended and considered any defense of the faith to be a shameful and insidious betrayal. Christianity had to be proclaimed only. Nor did he permit a natural theology.[128]

There has been some discussion among interpreters as to whether or not Kierkegaard was an irrationalist.[129] It seems that this debate is a minor one in the light of Kierkegaard's destructive notions of God, truth, humanity, salvation, and the authority of Scripture.[130]

Albrecht Ritschl (A.D. 1822–1889).[131] It has been said that Albrecht Ritschl was the most prominent theologian of the last quarter of the

---

philosopher is right, for I am only a poor existing human being, not competent to contemplate the eternal either eternally or divinely or theocentrically, but compelled to content myself with existing." Speculative philosophy failed "to take time to grasp what it means to be so critically situated in existence as the existing individual."

125. Clark, *Thales to Dewey*, 387.

126. *HWPT*, 313.

127. Van Til, *Great Debate*, 102. Heinecken ("Kierkegaard," 127) rightly said: "If the Hegelian interpretation of Christianity were true, then all anyone had to do to become a Christian would be to think straight."

128. Heinecken, "Kierkegaard," 142–43. Van Til, *Great Debate*, 112–13: "We now no longer start with natural theology and try to discover whether God exists. We now no longer walk backward down the ages to look for the historical Jesus."

129. Since he was against Hegelian philosophy, some evangelical thinkers, such as Gordon Clark, consider him to be an irrationalist. Frame argues that Kierkegard is not an irrationalist; see *HWPT*, 319: "Note that he does speak twice of the God of Christianity as the 'true' God and the traditional Christian view of God as a 'true conception.' So he is not indifferent about truth in the normal sense, Aristotelian truth in contrast with falsity." See also Heinecken, "Kierkegaard," 141: "This is Kierkegaard's so-called irrationalism—that reason is not the final arbiter, but existence itself in all its arbitrariness. God himself is love and not reason. The Logos that became flesh is not the world reason but the creative Word that brings into being that which it speaks."

130. Clark (*Thales to Dewey*, 488) rightly says that his view "results in the destruction of Christianity's objective historicity."

131. See Hugh Ross Mackintosh, *Types of Modern Theology: Schleiermacher to Barth* (London: Nisbet, 1956).

nineteenth century.[132] He was the son of a Lutheran preacher and bishop. Young Ritschl studied at the universities of Bonn, Halle, and Heidelberg. But his education at these universities left him dissatisfied.

Ritschl stumbled upon Hegelianism at the University of Tübingen under the brilliant professor Ferdinand Christian Baur (1792–1860). Baur understood Hegel's notion of *thesis, antithesis,* and *synthesis* to be a fundamental theme throughout all history—biblical history included. This view was used to understand the NT better. For example, the thinking of the original apostles who held to messianic Judaism was the thesis. The views of Paul were the antithesis to the original apostles' thinking. And the synthesis of the two can be seen in the ancient church, which merged the competing views. Baur's Hegelian presupposition concerning the flow of history resulted in a redating of the books of the NT.[133]

Though Ritschl began in NT studies, he gradually moved into systematic theology. In 1864 he left the University of Bonn to teach at Göttingen, where he remained for twenty-five years. Ritschl's magnum opus was *The Christian Doctrine of Justification and Reconciliation,* which was published in three volumes from 1870 to 1874. This work was so significant, and so controversial, that it engendered both a school and a counter school.[134] Ritschl founded what is now referred to as *the old liberalism,* or *old modernism.* He influenced a number of well-known disciples, including Wilhelm Herrmann and Adolf von Harnack, discussed below.

Ritschl's first book was in the field of NT studies, and in agreement with Baur he argued for Lukan priority among the Gospels. But several years later he changed his mind and proposed Mark as the earliest gospel.[135] This change was prompted by his rejection of Baur's interpretation of the development of early doctrine's being the synthesis of the Petrine thesis and Pauline antithesis.[136] He then proceeded to study Christ and his work. Ritschl sought to discover the historical

---

132. A. Durwood Foster, "Albrecht Ritschl," in *A Handbook of Christian Theologians,* ed. Martin E. Marty and Dean G. Peerman (Nashville: Abingdon Press, 1985), 49.

133. Walker, *History,* 489.

134. Ritschl also produced a three-volume history of Pietism.

135. For more information on Ritschl, see Horton Harris, *The Tübingen School* (Oxford: Clarendon, 1975), 101–12.

136. Walker, *History,* 493.

Jesus.[137] He believed Jesus to have been primarily a religious teacher who spoke on brotherhood and ethics.[138] To Ritschl, Jesus was fully human, even the ideal man. For him, as for the other Tübingen professors, the Bible was a merely human book.

With regard to salvation, Ritschl taught that a person examines Jesus's life, then makes a value judgment about him. He held that Jesus's deity is an ethical value judgment, and his righteousness is a human righteousness. Humans share in Jesus's divine nature when they enact Jesus's works. In redemption, God acts to restore the broken familial relationship between God as father and humanity as brother. Ritschl believed in a purely human Jesus—thus he preached a works-based salvation.[139]

Ritschl believed that Christians are answering the wrong question when they define Christ as preexistent, or as having two natures, or as being a member of the Trinity—they are answering a question that the early church, or for that matter the NT writers, never asked. He believed that these questions can only be answered by metaphysical speculation. The proper attitude toward Christ, he thought, is to recognize him as he is: a revelation of the nature of God, or in other words, a pattern of love.

In sum, Ritschl sought to meld two aspects of Christianity that are often difficult to bring together. On the one hand, he was an intellectual who was well respected by scholars for his search for the historical Jesus using the most scientific historical scholarship. On the other hand, he apparently was a pious man with a strong relationship with Christ. He is reported to have lived and taught a synthesis between vibrant Christian faith and new knowledge.[140]

Ritschl agreed with Schleiermacher that religious consciousness is the foundation of religious convictions, yet he followed Kant more closely than he followed Schleiermacher. Ritschl disagreed with the notion that the individual moral consciousness is normative; instead for him, it is the Christian community—the church—that is normative, not the individual. In other words, Ritschl had more of a social

137. Ritschl dismisses biblical teaching about Jesus's virgin birth and two natures as simple impositions of Greek philosophical thinking. See *HWPT*, 301.

138. Strimple, *Modern Search*, 50–51.

139. *HWPT*, 301–2.

140. Walker, *History*, 637.

and ethical focus than did Schleiermacher. This different focus caused Ritschl to reject as valueless what he considered to be speculative philosophical theology. He apparently believed that philosophy could offer a first cause, but a first-cause god is far from a loving Father. He rejected metaphysics as an aid to Christian truth.[141]

Prominent Ritschlians. Johann Georg Wilhelm Herrmann (1846–1922) was professor of theology at the University of Marburg.[142] In 1895 his most famous writing, *The Communion of the Christian with God*, was translated into English.[143] Many of his articles were collected into a volume that was published in 1966.[144] Herrmann, while also influenced by Kantian thought, developed Ritschl's thinking in the most meaningful and unique way. To him, religion was an individual, inner experience of the overpowering work of Christ. He believed that theology's task is to put words to that experience.[145]

A fascinating insight about Herrmann comes from an unexpected source—the biography of Westminster Theological Seminary's founder J. Gresham Machen, who studied under Herrmann in Marburg. "It is hardly an overstatement," wrote Ned Stonehouse about Machen, "to say that Wilhelm Herrmann was responsible for one of the most overwhelming intellectual and religious experiences of [Machen's] life." Liberalism, as presented by Herrmann at Marburg, became attractive and heart-gripping because of Herrmann's overpowering, fervent religious spirit.[146] Machen, trained at Princeton Theological Seminary and

---

141. Ibid., 638.

142. Ibid.

143. The German title is *Der Verkehr des Christen mit Gott*. The fourth edition came out in 1903. *Christlich-Protestantische Dogmatik* appeared in 1906 and was revised in 1919.

144. Wilhelm Herrmann, *Schriften zur Grundlegung der Theologie*, Teil I (Munich: Kaiser, 1966).

145. Heussi, *Kompendium*, 409.

146. N. B. Stonehouse, *J. Gresham Machen: A Biographical Memoir* (Grand Rapids: Eerdmans, 1954), 105; see 106–8 for his quoting letters from Machen, including the following: "Such an overpowering personality I think I almost never before encountered—overpowering in the sincerity of religious devotion. Herrmann may be illogical and one-sided, but I tell you he is alive. I am now engaged in the perusal of Herrmann's book, *Der Verkehr*. . . . I can't criticize him, as my chief feeling with reference to him is already one of the deepest reverence. Herrmann refuses to allow the student to look at religion from a distance as a thing to be studied merely. He speaks right to the heart; and I have been thrown all into confusion by what he says—so much deeper is his devotion to Christ than anything I have known in myself during the past few years. But certain I am that he has found Christ; and I believe that he can show how others may find Him—though, perhaps afterwards, in details, he may not be a safe guide." Later, Machen said,

scheduled to return to teach there, was overwhelmed by this learned professor who had a deep fervor and moral earnestness.[147] Meeting Herrmann caused Machen to become skeptical about the possibility of entering ordained ministry—Herrmann was a liberal theologian, yet he held such an apparent and deep piety.[148] This contradiction threw Machen into an intellectual crisis. Herrmann was likely in his mind years later when Machen distinguished between liberalism and Christianity.[149]

Adolf von Harnack (1851–1930), a professor in Berlin, has been called "the prince of church historians."[150] His multivolume *History of Dogma* is considered a magisterial work, and his *What Is Christianity?* is a classic example of advanced liberal theology.[151] Von Harnack's shorter booklet, *Thoughts on the Present Position of Protestantism*, opens up the Ritschlian school. Like Kierkegaard, von Harnack believed that the state church in Germany was in trouble—that is, was threatened by the spirit of Catholicism. Specifically, Roman clericalism, ritualism, "the alluring union of exalted piety and solemn secularity, and the substitution for religion of obedience" were enticing his Protestant church.[152]

He argued that these Catholic temptations were foreign to the original principles of Protestantism.[153] Old Protestantism would never have turned away from the truth; it was built on confessions that were drawn from Scripture. The old Protestants longed for the Bible to be understood and available to all. The original Protestant church was defined by the doctrine that von Harnack termed *Theologia Sacra*.[154] The old Protestants wanted the church to have intellectual understanding, assent, and complete trust in the teachings of

---

"In my opinion, *Der Verkehr* is one of the greatest religious books I ever read. . . . He has gotten hold of something that has been sadly neglected in the church and in the orthodox theology."

147. Ibid., 108.

148. Ibid., 105.

149. Ibid.

150. See Wilhelm Pauck, "Adolf von Harnack," in *A Handbook of Christian Theologians*, ed. Martin E. Marty and Dean G. Peerman (Nashville: Abingdon Press, 1985), 86–111.

151. *History of Dogma*, in seven volumes, appeared in English from 1894 to 1899. *What Is Christianity?* appeared in 1901.

152. Adolf von Harnack, *Thoughts on the Present Position of Protestantism*, trans. Thomas Bailey Saunders (London: Black, 1899), 32–46.

153. Ibid., 8–9.

154. Ibid., 20. *Theologia Sacra* had a sacred text (the Bible) which required a sanctified intelligence to comprehend it. Yet there was already some tension concerning the sanctified intelligence because to some extent the natural intelligence could rightly grasp the Scriptures.

Scripture.[155] But *Theologia Sacra* had died, and in its place was a lesser theology. Von Harnack, as a trained historian, traced the roots of this demise. He argued that inherent in the work of theology, discernable already in the writings of the church father Origen, was a necessary secular element wrapped up in all human investigation. This element was the supposedly required science—or organizing principle—of biblical and theological interpretation.[156]

Von Harnack argued that immediately after the Reformation, the Anabaptists, who perceived the methodological difference, tried to divide *Theologia Sacra* into two parts. The first part was what the Anabaptists termed *spiritual intuition*, or the *inner light*, and the second was *natural knowledge*. Though von Harnack supported this division, it was condemned by magisterial Protestantism.[157]

Protestantism continued to move away from *Theologia Sacra* because it sought to create an impartial record of the facts. This goal resulted from the historical sense, which was connected to the scientific perception of facts. Thus Protestantism held that no creed was to be foundational to an exposition of the Scriptures, for such a creed would only adulterate the purity of the text. The only methods or tools that should be allowed in interpretation, therefore, were philological and historical. According to von Harnack, this move indicated an alteration of the meaning of *knowledge* itself.[158]

Thus the departure from *Theologia Sacra* was due both to the shift of science (or historical sense) and the development of the church itself. There was a growing distaste for and depreciation of theology within the church. Theology, therefore, began to be pushed into the background and viewed as barren and unproductive. Sadly, for many in the church theology simply did not matter.[159] And what filled the void that theology left?

Positively, the church replaced theology positively with philanthropy, and negatively, with nondogmatic Christianity. The church claimed that theology smothered the vivid realization of the forces

155. Ibid., 18–20.
156. Ibid., 21.
157. Ibid., 22.
158. Ibid., 23–25.
159. Ibid., 26–27.

of religion. Von Harnack thought this movement against theology was necessary. While never mentioning names, von Harnack leaned on the thinking of Schleiermacher and Kierkegaard and claimed that this movement was necessary because of the one-sidedness of the old Protestantism, "which sought to make religion depend exclusively on doctrine."[160] In other words, religion had become exclusively cold and intellectual. And theology was to blame.[161]

According to von Harnack, Ritschl helped to restore what he considered to be a proper Protestantism by strengthening both doctrine and religious feeling, which should never have been segregated.[162] But Ritschl was an exception, and von Harnack despaired that Ritschl's thinking was no longer prevalent.[163]

Ernst Peter Wilhelm Troeltsch (A.D. 1865–1923) **and the *History of Religions* School.** The *history of religions* school directly opposed Ritschlian theology. The school sought to understand Christianity as simply one more iteration of an ancient Near Eastern religion. Its proponents included Hermann Gunkel in OT, Wilhelm Bousset in NT, and Ernst Troeltsch and Johannes Weiss. Of these men, Troeltsch was the theologian. He was a professor in Bonn from 1892 to 1894, then went to Heidelberg, and finally, in 1915, accepted a call to the University at Berlin. His *Glaubenslehre* was the primary theological document of the history of religions school.[164]

Troeltsch was a follower of Kantian thought. Like Kierkegaard, he argued for a dualism of faith and knowing, but he did so because he valued the history of religions, not in opposition to metaphysics. Troeltsch understood Christianity to be one religion among many; he held that God's revelation was not found exclusively in Judaeo-Christianity but could be found in the religious life of other peoples and traditions. He believed that Christianity did not have any absolute, transhistorical authority. Troeltsch understood theology to be neither philosophical nor scientific.[165]

160. Ibid., 28.
161. Ibid., 47–51.
162. Ibid., 56.
163. Ibid., 29–31.
164. This work was first published in Munich in 1925 and was reprinted more than five decades later; see Ernst Troeltsch, *Glaubenslehre* (Aalen: Scientia Verlag, 1981).
165. Jacob Klapwijk, Einleitung zu *Glaubenslehre*, von Ernst Troeltsch (Aalen: Scientia Verlag, 1981), ix.

Johannes Weiss (A.D. 1863–1914). Weiss a professor at Marburg, was convinced that the oldest Christology was adoptionistic.[166] In other words, he believed that the oldest NT teaching concerning Jesus of Nazareth was that he was a mere man, albeit a very special man. But through his resurrection, Jesus was elevated to the position of Messiah. Thus Jesus became the *adopted* Messiah. Weiss emphasized the notion of adoption because it stood in contrast to natural sonship, which comes at the time of birth. His point was that Jesus was not born the Messiah—or even born the Son of God. Instead, at a moment in history, through an act of God's will, Jesus *became* the Messiah. Weiss argued that this way was how the early church thought of Jesus, and he pointed to passages such as Acts 2:22 for support.[167]

To Weiss, the loftiest NT expression of Jesus was that he was God's organ, a concept that can be seen throughout the Gospels.[168] But Jesus was also given the titles *prophet, second Moses,* and *servant of God.*[169] Weiss believed that Jesus, as the Son of Man, was in a unique relationship to the Father. In that relationship, Jesus possessed a revelation that was the call of Jubilee.[170] Because of his unique relationship to the Father, Jesus had the ability to reveal this knowledge of the Father to others. But Weiss was clear in his belief that while Jesus was on earth, he was no Messiah-king—either for Israel or the world. His exaltation would only come after his death.[171]

Weiss traced his thinking back to Psalm 2:7.[172] In the OT, the king of Israel was a son of God. In Psalm 2, this son is adopted when he is crowned. Thus, argued Weiss, when Jesus was elevated to God's right

---

166. J. Weiß, *Das Urchristentum* (Göttingen: Vandenhoeck & Ruprecht, 1917), in which see the chapters "Die Lehre von der Auferstehung am dritten Tage," 60, and "Die Lehre vom Tode des Messias," 75.

167. Ibid., 86.

168. Ibid.

169. Ibid.: "The highest that can be said about Jesus is that he expelled the demons in the power of the Spirit, that he was a prophet who was powerful in word and deed, and that through him God called his people home."

170. Ibid., 87: "Jesus is designated as 'unique among the sons of men' and as 'the Son' of the 'Father'. He and the Father had a unique relationship of intimate knowledge."

171. Ibid., 88: "[While on earth] "he was not yet the Messiah-King either of Israel or of the world. Jesus was a man elect of God who manifested the highest power and revelation who would, after his death, be elevated to the position of Son of God and be designated the messianic King."

172. Ibid., 85: "This earlier teaching [of Psalm 2] is made clear at Acts 2:36 when Jesus is elevated to the position of Messiah. This is the earliest Christology that we have."

hand, he was also then elevated to the position of Son of God. He pointed to Acts 13:33 for further confirmation of this belief: "This he has fulfilled to us their children by raising Jesus, as also it is written in the second Psalm, 'You are my Son, today I have begotten you.'"[173]

But Weiss believed this earliest view had been changed, even in the writings of Paul. In Romans 1:3–4, Weiss saw Paul as attempting to hold in tension two views: that Jesus was the Son of God from the beginning (Paul's view), and that in the resurrection Jesus became the Son of God.[174]

Weiss also used Acts 10:38 to show that Jesus's crowning came after his death, though his anointing and designation as future king occurred as early as his baptism in the Jordan.[175] But Weiss saw Saul and David as earlier types of this coming king. As such, Saul and David were first anointed as kings by prophets long before they actually were made kings. Weiss saw the same pattern in the anointing of Jesus. Jesus's kingship was tucked away, revealed to only a few.[176] While nineteenth-century German theology experienced a massive move away from biblically faithful theology, the Netherlands saw the opposite with a flowering of mature and careful biblical teaching.

NINETEENTH-CENTURY DUTCH THEOLOGY

Abraham Kuyper (A.D. 1837–1920).[177] In 1837, Abraham Kuyper was born into the home of a pastor in the Netherlands. At the age of eighteen, he began his studies at the University of Leiden in theology and literature.[178] Whatever faith Kuyper had coming into the university quickly came under attack—not in a blatant, hostile way, but subtly

173. Ibid., 86.
174. Ibid.
175. Ibid., 88.
176. Ibid.
177. See W. Robert Godfrey, "Calvin and Calvinism in the Netherlands," in *John Calvin: His Influence in the Western World*, ed. W. Stanford Reid (Grand Rapids: Zondervan, 1982); Catherine M. E. Kuyper, "Abraham Kuyper: His Early Life and Conversion," *International Reformed Bulletin* 5 (April, 1960): 19–25; L. Praamsma, *Let Christ Be King: Reflections on the Life and Times of Abraham Kuyper* (Thorold, ON: Paideia Press, 1985); R. E. L. Rodgers, *The Incarnation of the Antithesis: An Introduction to the Educational Thought and Practice of Abraham Kuyper* (Edinburgh: Pentland Press, 1992).
178. Frank Vandenberg, *Abraham Kuyper* (Grand Rapids: Eerdmans, 1960), 14.

and slowly. Modernism, a highly rational theological liberalism, began to pull at Kuyper intellectually. Its effect was so subtle and persistent that, upon his graduation, Kuyper would be deemed a liberal by any evangelical standard. This newfound liberalism for Kuyper was only reenforced when he entered the seminary. The seminary of the University of Leiden stood against the old orthodoxy that had for so long been a hallmark of the Netherlands. Many of the faculty at the seminary went so far as to deny the historicity of the bodily resurrection of Jesus.

After seminary, Kuyper went on to do doctoral work.[179] During his doctoral studies, one of his professors asked him to write what turned out to be a prizewinning essay on the nature of the church in the writings of John à Lasco, a Polish Reformer. When Kuyper began work on this project, he soon found that there were no complete texts of à Lasco's works in any of the great libraries of Europe. Through personal connections, however, Kuyper was able to acquire a collection of à Lasco's works. And he poured himself—both heart and mind—into writing this essay. He researched to the point of exhaustion. When he finished the piece, he nearly collapsed. He required six weeks of complete rest and several months off work to recover fully. His pursuit of this project gives readers a small window into the personality and drive of the young Kuyper.

Kuyper earned his doctorate at the age of twenty-five. He was then called to a small country church at Beesd. But his theological leanings had not swung back; theologically, he was still a liberal. He did not view Christ in the way that Scripture presents him; Kuyper believed Jesus was a good example who died for what he believed in.[180] But in this small country church were many strong believers who were not impressed with this young man's doctorate or his facility in the Dutch language. One of his parishioners, the daughter of a miller, was so unsettled by Kuyper's theology that she refused even so much as to speak to him. But the others in the congregation shepherded this member of the congregation and reminded her that their pastor, too, had an immortal soul and needed to be cared for. That reminder was all the encouragement she needed. When Kuyper came to visit the

179. Ibid., 22–30.
180. Ibid., 31.

miller's daughter and her family, she boldly witnessed to him of the assurance and deep love of God in Christ Jesus.[181]

Though her testimony was nothing new to Kuyper intellectually, assurance and peace were foreign to him experientially. The testimony of this woman, and of others in the congregation like her, unsettled him. Over time, the minister became the one ministered to. Kuyper began to listen to his congregation, and his heart burned within him. Sometime in the early years of his ministry, after learning to listen to the humble yet earnest believers of his church, Kuyper fell before the throne of grace and begged for mercy for Christ's sake. He was converted to Christ.

After his conversion, Kuyper immersed himself in the theology of John Calvin and in the preaching of the Word of God. He had finally found peace. But his conversion made him aware of the needs of his own denomination, the state church, that had begun to rot with liberalism. He sought to pastor his own flock and to labor toward the reformation of the larger church.

The four years he spent in this small church afforded him the time to write and help republish à Lasco's corpus of works. Kuyper was becoming well known as a gracious pastor, a powerful preacher, and a careful scholar. As his reputation spread, he was soon called to a much larger church in Utrecht.

Kuyper pastored in Utrecht until 1870. During his three years there, he preached, cared for the souls of his congregation, and taught catechism classes for the children. But during this time he also began several new endeavors that would shape the rest of his life.[182] He began to do editorial work for a weekly magazine that addressed religious and political affairs. He also joined a Christian political party. The matter that pulled Kuyper into politics regarded schooling.

Kuyper was convinced that Christian children should have the right to attend Christian schools. He disliked the humanistic educational philosophy of the public schools. He believed that the best way to teach children about the earth and the stars and the mountains and the sea was by teaching them about the Creator and Sustainer of all

181. Ibid., 33.
182. For a summary of Kuyper's writings during this period, see James Bratt, ed., *Abraham Kuyper* (Grand Rapids: Eerdmans, 1998), 19–124.

good and perfect things—something that, he was convinced, could only be done in a Christian school. This conviction required political involvement.[183]

After three years in Utrecht, Kuyper was again called to a larger church, this time in Amsterdam. This transition asked more of him and gave him a much larger congregation to minister to. He gladly accepted the call. While there, conflict broke out between liberal and conservative churches in Amsterdam. Right in the middle of this conflict was Kuyper. He offered brilliant defenses of historic biblical and Reformed Christianity. He also became increasingly involved in his editorial and political work.[184] It was in Amsterdam that Kuyper's life took a turn. He was a talented speaker and debater, concerned for the rights of the Christians in Dutch society, and well known through his pastoral and editorial work. It is in Amsterdam that his political career developed.

In 1874, Kuyper was elected to the Dutch Parliament. And so at the age of thirty-six, Abraham Kuyper took his required oaths of office.[185] What led Kuyper into politics? He was an ordained minister with an ever-growing ministry. To accept a seat in Parliament meant that he would be forced to walk away from the pastorate. Were earthly concerns pulling him from the pulpit?

Kuyper longed to see a reformation in the church and to see justice done in Holland in Christ's name. He was not concerned for justice merely for the sake of justice, and he was under no illusion that the church would establish a political kingdom on the earth. He simply felt compelled by the Word of God to step into this office that had been offered to him. The party he represented was a small minority, so ambitions of great victories were likely not on his mind. But his party stood for Jesus Christ and a justice and righteousness based on the Word of God.[186]

Although Dutch law forced Kuyper to forfeit his ministerial credentials, his labors in the church did not cease. He now served as a

---

183. Vandenberg, *Kuyper*, 47–49.
184. Ibid., 50–61.
185. Ibid., 62–70.
186. His party was called the Anti-Revolution party, in contrast to the cry of the French Revolution: "No God, no Master."

ruling elder in the church, and that role gave him the right to vote in both the local and larger governing bodies of the church. His fight for the church's conservative cause had not ended. He also continued to edit the weekly newspaper. In sum, after being elected to the Dutch Parliament, much of Kuyper's ministry remained the same.

Kuyper continued to promote Christian education throughout his governmental career. He joined with the Catholics in this fight, and together they took power away from the liberal theologians. Kuyper was in agreement with the Catholics on education—specifically, in their fight for state subsidies for parochial schools.

All these years later, Kuyper had still not learned moderation in his work. He entered all his tasks with zeal and energy. But as a freshman in the political world, and with the hopes of believers resting on him to enact change, Kuyper once again worked himself to exhaustion. He was a full-time politician, a full-time editor, and almost a full-time laborer in the church.

Further, his governmental actions were not received well by many. The press referred to him as a "white-washed tomb"; he was accused of trying both to establish a republic and to overthrow the Dutch monarchy. Some thought he was attempting to become the next Cromwell. The pressures were simply too much for Kuyper too bear.[187] He broke down physically. He sold his home in Amsterdam, and his doctor advised him to leave Amsterdam for a vacation. He was gone for fifteen months, most of which time he spent in Switzerland. He referred to this period as his year in exile.[188]

This season was beneficial for Kuyper. It does not seem to have resulted from a spiritual breakdown; instead, he simply needed to learn that there were physical limits to what he was capable of accomplishing. Upon returning to Amsterdam, Kuyper resigned from Parliament. Sadly, there was little that he could accomplish in politics at this time because of the current political climate, and Kuyper knew it. So he began his work once again as an editor. There would be no more breakdowns in his future.

At this point in Kuyper's life, education remained one of his chief concerns. Kuyper wanted to see the development of Christian grade

187. Vandenberg, *Kuyper*, 71–79.
188. Ibid., 80.

schools. But while in Switzerland he began to dream even further; he wanted to see a Christian university established. In his time, a university included graduate schools of medicine, law, and theology. And universities in Holland required extensive credentials—beyond those that even modern colleges in America require.[189] To establish a Christian university in Holland was Kuyper's new vision.

Within three years of his return from Switzerland, the Free University of Amsterdam was established. The word *free* did not mean that the school charged no tuition but that it was free of both state and church control. This university was established on the Bible as expressed in the Calvinistic confessions of Holland. The professors were not only to be Christians, but also they were required to know how to teach their subjects from a holistically Christian perspective.

The school began humbly and small, as would be expected. But it quickly began to grow. Kuyper was the first rector, and the position rotated each year to a different member of the faculty. Many have said that this university was the greatest contribution of Kuyper's life. The believers in Holland knew that the educated would always control government, science, religion, and the arts. They looked at the godless, humanistic educational system and knew that unless there were Christian alternatives to education, the nation would rot spiritually.[190] Thus the establishment of Free University in 1880 marked a milestone in the history of Holland.

In 1886, Kuyper was instrumental in a movement called the Doleantie. The people were in *doleantie*, from the Latin word meaning "to feel sorrow"—they were in mourning because of the theological liberalism of their parent denomination. In 1892, a denomination formed out of the Doleantie movement—a denomination called the Reformed Churches of the Netherlands, with approximately one hundred thousand members.[191] From 1893 to 1894, Kuyper published his monumental, three-volume *Encyclopedia of Sacred Theology*. He

---

189. In modern times in America, some men have held similar visions—for example, those who founded and established Oral Roberts University, Liberty Baptist University, and The Master's University and Seminary.

190. Vandenberg, *Kuyper*, 91–103. American evangelicals know the truth of Kuyper's thoughts as they view the impact that godless humanism has had in American higher education.

191. Ibid., 115–44; see Bratt, *Kuyper*, 11; James Edward McGoldrick, *God's Renaissance Man: The Life and Work of Abraham Kuyper* (Auburn, MA: Evangelical Press, 2000), 87–97.

continued to lecture in theology, seek reform for the church, and fight for Christians' civil standing. The political world had shifted. Now the overriding concern in politics was the issue of suffrage.[192]

In the late 1880s and 1890s, questions as to who had the right to vote—or *suffrage*—were dominating Holland.[193] Kuyper advocated for more citizens to be granted that significant right.[194] He wanted to push suffrage forward so that the head of every household had the right to vote, thus granting the vote to thousands who currently did not have it. Even this effort was perceived as extreme liberalism. But he considered the issue to be so important that he decided to run for a seat in the second house of Parliament in 1894, and he was elected.

In the 1890s, Kuyper traveled to the United States to lecture at Princeton and other schools. It was also during this decade that Kuyper lost his dear wife at the age of fifty-eight. In a letter to a friend, Kuyper confided that since his wife's death, the poetry had gone out of his life.[195] In 1901, Protestants held the largest number of seats in Parliament in Holland, so the queen asked Kuyper to be prime minister. Thus a new day dawned in Dutch history and in the life of Kuyper as well.[196]

During his time as prime minister, Kuyper served his country faithfully through a rather difficult season. Mass strikes paralyzed the nation, and the queen nearly died. Kuyper had to deal with activities connected to the Boer War in South Africa. But he used this position to help Christian schools survive in the Dutch community.

After a brief four-year period, the liberals regained power, and Kuyper was forced to step down as prime minister at the age of sixty-eight. It would have been a fitting time to retire. But not for Kuyper. Upon leaving his position in the government, he finally had the freedom to achieve one of his life's goals—travel the Holy Land. He wrote a two-volume description of the land while traveling around the Mediterranean for nearly a year. This work is still valuable to historians today.

192. Vandenberg, *Kuyper*, 157–69.

193. Women did not get the right to vote in the United States until the early part of the twentieth century.

194. In Holland, women did not have a chance to vote, but neither did all men. A voter had to meet certain qualifications of age, education, and economic position.

195. Ibid., 205.

196. For a brief presentation of Kuyper's political thinking, see Bratt, *Kuyper*, 205–362. Kuyper's political speeches were collected in four volumes.

He also continued to write for his newspaper, though he had stepped down as editor when he was elected prime minister. This release from politics also gave him the time to write many other theological books and pamphlets that are still treasured by many.

It was not very long before Kuyper found his way back into governmental office, and he held a number of different posts after serving as prime minister. In all this time, Kuyper remained faithful to his convictions and to the Word of God. As the second decade of the twentieth century began, Kuyper's strength declined. But even then he continued his ministry until his death in 1920. He would never retire. So it was with many lasting memorials that the Lord called his servant Abraham Kuyper home to him.[197]

Herman Bavinck (A.D. 1854–1921).[198] Herman Bavinck was born into a minister's family and to a father who had left the state church in 1834. The Bavinck family was influenced by what is referred to as the Second Reformation, or Reformed Pietism. Bavinck studied at Kampen briefly, and at the age of twenty he attended the University of Leiden, where he completed his doctoral work in 1880. Bavinck wrote his dissertation on Zwingli's ethics. The time at the liberal university in Leiden apparently cost him spiritually as he was confronted with robust systems of thought contrary to his upbringing.[199] After one year in a pastorate in Friesland, at the age of twenty-eight he was elected to teach at the seminary at Kampen in 1882. He became a minister of the *Gereformeerde Kerken* when that denomination was established in 1892.[200]

---

197. Some of his writings include the already mentioned *Encyclopedia of Sacred Theology*; *Lectures on Calvinism*, also known as the Stone Lectures; *The Holy Spirit*; *Commentary on the Heidelberg Catechism* (4 vols); and *Book of Revelation* (4 vols). From 1872 he was editor-in-chief of *De Standaard*. He also edited *De Heraut*—a weekly Christian paper. He kept that editorial work for fifty years. His weekly mediations for *De Heraut* were collected into a book titled *To Be Near unto God*, published in English by Presbyterian and Reformed in 1979.

198. See R. H. Bremmer, *Herman Bavinck als Dogmaticus* (Kampen: Kok, 1961); H. E. B. Dosker, "Herman Bavinck," *Princeton Theological Review* 20 (1922): 448–64. There are some excellent biographies as well: V. Hepp, *Dr. Herman Bavinck* (Amsterdam: W. Ten Have, 1921); Ron Gleason, *Herman Bavinck: Pastor, Churchman, Statesman, Theologian* (Phillipsburg, NJ: P&R Publishing, 2010); and James Eglinton, *Bavinck: A Critical Biography* (Grand Rapids: Baker Academic, 2020).

199. John Bolt (editor for Herman Bavinck), *The Last Things: Hope for This World and the Next* (Grand Rapids: Baker, 1996), 10.

200. John Bolt, *Bavinck on the Christian Life* (Wheaton, IL: Crossway, 2015), 21–38.

Before 1892, Bavinck traveled to Berlin with Geerhardus Vos, of Princeton Theological Seminary, to hear lectures by Julius Kaften, Eduard Zeller, and Friedrich Paulsen. In 1892 he came to North America and was visited by Vos and his daughter.[201] Bavinck remained at the seminary in Kampen until going to the Free University of Amsterdam in 1902 to replace Abraham Kuyper, who had just been elected prime minister. His monumental *Reformed Dogmatics* was first published from 1895 to 1899. The second edition was released between the years 1906 and 1911. In 1904, at the age of fifty, Bavinck wanted to focus on more practical theology and thus produced *Principles of Psychology*.

In 1908, Bavinck traveled to Princeton to deliver the famous Stone Lectures. These lectures were published as *Philosophy of Revelation*.[202] He also wrote *Christianity, War, and the League of Nations*; *Victory of the Soul*; *Following of Christ*; and *Modern Life*. He was a member of the Royal Academy of Sciences (1906), was knighted by the queen, and became a member of the upper chamber of the Dutch government (1911), the equivalent of the United States Senate. Bavinck taught until his death in 1921.[203] His last words were reportedly: "My dogmatics avails me nothing, nor my knowledge, but I have my faith, and in this I have all."[204]

NINETEENTH-CENTURY THEOLOGY AT OLD PRINCETON SEMINARY

There are similarities and differences between the theology of Abraham Kuyper and Herman Bavinck, of old Amsterdam, and the theologians of old Princeton.[205] The adjective *old* is applied to both Amsterdam and Princeton because neither the current Free Univer-

---

201. Bolt, *Last Things*, 23–24.
202. Herman Bavinck, *The Philosophy of Revelation* (Grand Rapids, Eerdmans, 1953). He also wrote *Modernisme en Orthodoxie*, as well as *Our Reasonable Faith*, a one-volume summary of his dogmatics, which appeared in English in 1956. His *The Certainty of Faith* was published in English in 1980.
203. Johan D. Tangelder, "Dr. Herman Bavinck 1854–1921: Theologian of the Word," *Christian Renewal* (January 29, 2001): 14–15.
204. Dosker, "Herman Bavinck," 459.
205. See Richard B. Gaffin, "Old Amsterdam and Inerrancy?," *WTJ* 45, no. 2 (Fall 1983): 219–72.

sity of Amsterdam nor the current Princeton Theological Seminary embraced the theology of their past. Old Princeton understood the facts of history, the arguments of reason, and even objective science all as validation of the truthfulness of Scripture. The Dutch, however, did not agree with this approach.[206] They held to an antithesis between believing and unbelieving thought.

Princeton Seminary was established with very specific educational goals.[207] From the original "Plan of the Seminary," approved in 1811, their goals were twofold: to promote piety and to promote literature.[208] Seventy years later, Princeton had the largest student population of all the Presbyterian seminaries.[209] By the time of Princeton's centennial in 1912, the school had enrolled upwards of one thousand more students than any other seminary in the United States.[210] The Princeton ideal was to be where piety was joined with solid learning.[211] Old-Princeton theology has been summarized as: "devotion to the Bible,

206. Mark A. Noll, *The Princeton Theology, 1812–1921: Scripture, Science, and Theological Method from Archibald Alexander to Benjamin Breckinridge Warfield* (Grand Rapids: Baker, 1983), 41: "Warfield held that history, reason, and objective science could demonstrate the validity of Scripture as divine revelation. Individuals convinced by such demonstration could then rely on Scripture to construct theology. Kuyper and Bavinck, to the contrary, placed very little store by Warfield's kind of evidentialist apologetics."

207. David B. Calhoun, *Princeton Seminary*, 2 vols. (Edinburgh: Banner of Truth, 1994), 1:84: "In addition to much analytical study of the English Bible, students took courses in Hebrew and Greek, Biblical criticism (including both textual criticism and interpretation), and Bible history (described as 'Sacred Chronology,' 'Sacred Geography,' 'Jewish Antiquities,' and 'Oriental Customs')"; and 1:85: "Second-year students continued to study the original languages of Scripture and added systematic (didactic) theology and biblical and church history. The third-year curriculum included systematic (didactic and polemic) theology, church history, church government, pastoral care, and homiletics."

208. As cited by Noll, *Princeton Theology*, from "Plan of the theological seminary," 56: "It is to afford more advantages than have hitherto been usually possessed by the ministers of religion in our country, [the normal method of ministerial preparation prior to seminaries was through pastoral tutors] to cultivate both piety and literature in their preparatory course; piety, by placing it in circumstances favorable to its growth, and by cherishing and regulating its ardor; literature, by affording favorable opportunities for its attainment, and by making its possession indispensable."

209. David B. Calhoun, *Princeton Seminary*, 2 vols. (Edinburgh: Banner of Truth, 1996), 2:67: "In 1880 Union NY had 144 students, Western had 136, Andover 126, and Princeton had 172—the same as it had been 20 years earlier."

210. Mark Noll, "The Spirit of Old Princeton and the Spirit of the OPC," in *Pressing Toward the Mark: Essays Commemorating Fifty Years of the Orthodox Presbyterian Church*, ed. Charles G. Dennison and Richard C. Gamble (Philadelphia: Committee for the Historian of the Orthodox Presbyterian Church, 1986), 237.

211. Calhoun, *Princeton Seminary*, 2:405.

concern for religious experience, sensitivity to the American experience, full employment of the Presbyterian confessions, seventeenth-century Reformed systematicians, and the Scottish philosophy of Common Sense."[212]

Archibald Alexander (A.D. 1772–1851).[213] Archibald Alexander was the first professor at Princeton. Though he had memorized the Westminster Shorter Catechism (WSC) as a boy, he considered his childhood to be one of spiritual ignorance. In the Virginia Presbyterian community in which he grew up, for example, there was not to be so much as a discussion of a conversion experience.[214] Things changed when he turned seventeen. He left home and served as a tutor to a wealthy Baptist family, and he began to attend their church. Alexander first heard about new birth in a conversation with a minister of this Baptist church. When he returned home to Virginia, he discovered that a spiritual revival had swept through the valley he grew up in. And he determined to engage in prayer until he, too, could experience salvation. Alexander did undergo a spiritual change, and he felt a call on his life for pastoral ministry. He served as a pastor in Philadelphia from 1807 to 1812. His goal as a pastor was to inform the understanding as well as impress the heart.[215] In worship, he believed that people's emotions could not be smothered if true piety existed there.[216]

In 1812, Alexander began his time at Princeton with just three students, and for his thirty-nine years as a professor, he remained intrigued with religious experience.[217] In his first year at Princeton, Alexander taught every subject, but Samuel Miller arrived to his aid the following year. The text that Princeton used for systematic theology

212. Noll, *Princeton Theology*, 13; see also David F. Wells, ed., *The Princeton Theology* (Grand Rapids, Baker, 1989), 13–35.

213. J. W. Alexander, *The Life of Archibald Alexander* (New York: Scribner's Sons, 1854); Charles Hodge, "Memoir of Archibald Alexander," *Biblical Repertory and Princeton Review* 27 (January 1855): 133–59; Lefferts A. Loetscher, *Facing the Enlightenment and Pietism: Archibald Alexander and the Founding of Princeton Theological Seminary* (Westport, CT: Greenwood, 1983).

214. W. Andrew Hoffecker, *Piety and the Princeton Theologians* (Phillipsburg, NJ: Presbyterian and Reformed, 1981), 2: "He was reared among Presbyterians who looked disparagingly upon conversion experiences."

215. Ibid., 11.

216. Ibid., 13.

217. Ibid., 1. "None of the other Princetonians showed a greater preoccupation with the subject of religious experience than Archibald Alexander."

was Francis Turretin's multivolume theology in Latin.[218] He also taught apologetics, which he considered preliminary to theology.[219] His work in apologetics was published in 1825: *A Brief Outline of the Evidences of the Christian Religion*. While being the systematician, he spent one evening each week listening to and critiquing student sermons.[220]

During his years as a professor, Alexander maintained an exemplary personal devotional life. He began his time with a daily reading from Scripture, from other literature, and with prayer. Then he read the Bible in Greek and in Hebrew. He then chanted the Psalms in Hebrew from a Bible given to him by Charles Hodge. He would also regularly seclude himself for a day of prayer and fasting.[221]

In his inaugural address for the seminary, Alexander focused on John 5:39, where Jesus commanded his followers to search the Scriptures. He pointed out that the command is indefinite—thus all people are to search the Scriptures. But he said that some are bound more strongly to this duty, particularly ministers and teachers. Alexander directed his inaugural address to those who were bound to an even greater degree to this passage.

The task he set before himself in this address was monumental—his purpose was to prove that the Scriptures contain the truths of God and to ascertain the nature and extent of those truths.[222] He also addressed those who invalidated the Scriptures as the only rule of faith and practice; this group included Roman Catholics, rationalists, and those who thought that they were capable of being divinely inspired.[223] He explained how the Scriptures could be exegeted so that the reader can ascertain their full and true meaning, a task now known as *hermeneutics*.[224]

218. While Alexander considered Turretin's work ponderous, scholastic, and in a dead language, working through the text made students strong and logical divines (Calhoun, *Princeton Seminary*, 1:91).

219. His textbooks were Samuel Clarke, William Paley, and Joseph Butler's *Analogy* (ibid., 1:88–89).

220. Ibid., 1:96.

221. Hoffecker, *Piety and Princeton*, 7.

222. Noll, *Princeton Theology*, 74–75.

223. Ibid., 79–80.

224. Ibid., 81–83: Having looked briefly at the history of Reformed exegesis, Alexander concluded that "good sense and the analogy of faith are the guides which we should follow in interpreting the Bible." He included, of course, acquisition of the biblical languages and historical helps.

Alexander outlined the character and abilities necessary for the teacher of God's Word. First, he must be a man of learning—with a knowledge of Latin and the ability to engage in literary conversation.[225] He must also be illuminated and assisted by the Holy Spirit. Alexander held the strong conviction that students of theology must hold their studies of God's Word close in hand with their pious devotion to the Word. The theological student must possess sincere and ardent piety.[226] He must truly pray without ceasing and search for knowledge to strengthen the church, not to puff himself up.[227]

Alexander thought and wrote much about the nature of religious knowledge. He was rightly convinced that there are two kinds of religious knowledge: (1) knowledge of the truth that is revealed in Scripture, and (2) the impression that such truth makes on the mind, that is, when the mind rightly apprehends that truth.[228]

Alexander believed that there must be a balance between the head and the heart. For Alexander, objective truth, or scriptural teachings comprehended with the mind, and subjective truth, or the emotional integration of that teaching into the believer's life, go together like a hand in a glove.[229] In other words, Alexander understood there to be a complementary relationship between doctrine and life experience. He believed that doctrine manifests itself in experience, and the two types of knowledge check and balance each other. Christian experience could mislead, but not when the head guides the heart with sound doctrine, or especially what Alexander called "fundamental doctrines."[230] But he also held that doctrine without piety is vacuous.[231] This balance of

225. Ibid., 84. Noll mentions that Samuel Miller had the same opinion of clerical status.

226. Ibid., 85: "The conclusion from these premises is that the student of sacred literature should be possessed of sincere and ardent piety."

227. "There is no person who needs more to be in the constant exercise of prayer than the Theological student; not only at stated periods, but continually in the midst of his studies, his heart should be raised to heaven for help and direction. A defect here, it is to be feared, is one principal reason why so much time and labor are often employed in theological studies with so little profit to the church. That knowledge which puffeth up is acquired; but charity, which edifieth, is neglected" (as cited by Noll, *Princeton Theology*, from the "Inaugural Address," 85).

228. Hoffecker, *Piety and Princeton*, 23–24.

229. Ibid., 19.

230. Ibid., 33: "Two characteristics distinguish fundamental doctrines: 1. That the denial of them destroys the system. 2. That the knowledge of them is essential to piety."

231. Ibid., 14–15: "The lack of acts of devotion and piety has both religious and ethical overtones which are closely interwoven. Speculative faith effects no moral transformation and produces no religious acts of humility, praise, and love."

piety and knowledge can be traced back through the Reformed tradition to John Calvin.[232]

Alexander seems to have followed a *via media* ("middle way") approach to the mind and heart. He did not speak much about his religious feelings. Nevertheless, he sought to forge a strong tie between religious truth and religious experience.[233] In other words, he believed there was a middle way between rigid speculation and undiscerning enthusiasm.[234]

Alexander condemned the theologically orthodox Presbyterians who remained deficient in experience. The Christian faith is a dead faith if it is speculation alone, deprived of all experiential knowledge. "Religious knowledge is only truly 'religious' and 'knowledge' in the fullest sense, when the feelings and the affections are excited. Only then do discernible acts of devotion and piety result."[235] Alexander left an indelible mark on Princetonian piety, and his vision was not lost with his successors.[236] Princeton sought to produce graduates who were both eminently logical and men of pious affections and tender feelings.[237]

Samuel Miller (A.D. 1769–1851). Samuel Miller was an active churchman before he arrived at the new Princeton Seminary. A graduate of the University of Pennsylvania and ordained in 1793, he began his pastoral work in New York. In 1806 he was elected moderator of the General Assembly. Then in 1813, he was elected professor of ecclesiastical history and church government at Princeton, where he served faithfully for thirty-five years. For a number of years, he worked to amend the *Form of Government* with two other ministers before

232. Ibid., 33: "In this description, Alexander succinctly captures the essence of the Princeton theology and the Princeton Piety. In juxtaposing doctrine and piety in this way, Alexander continues the Reformed tradition extending back to John Calvin himself."

233. Ibid., 25–26: "This correspondence between the truth and experience received strong emphasis in Alexander's writings and is central to the via media that he attempted to forge."

234. Ibid., 29: "Alexander's two-front attack in the area of religious experience established a pattern that was to be the permanent Princeton model for any discussion of religious experience. His purpose was to forge a via media between a cold speculation and a burning enthusiasm."

235. Ibid., 14.

236. Ibid., 8: "These sources reveal a continuing personal concern for the experiential element in religion from his own conversion experience to the general practice of piety. . . . One is struck by the . . . references to feelings and emotions in Alexander's account"; and 9: "This principle that experience was to be based on an intellectual apprehension of the objective truths of Christianity was to become a sine qua non in the Princeton piety."

237. J. W. Alexander, *Thoughts on Preaching* (repr., Edinburgh: Banner of Truth, 1988), 42.

the revisions were accepted by the assembly in 1821. In 1832, Miller published a book on the office of ruling elder.[238] He also published *The Utility and Importance of Creeds and Confessions: Addressed Particularly to Candidates for the Ministry* in 1839.[239]

Charles Hodge (A.D. 1797–1878). Charles Hodge was the greatest Princeton professor.[240] His religious experience began early.[241] As a boy, Charles faithfully attended church. He memorized the catechism and was examined in it by his pastor, the famous Dr. Ashbell Green. As a teenager, his widowed mother sent him to Princeton to continue his education. During his time there, Hodge proved himself to be an exceptionally diligent student. In 1821, at the age of twenty-four, he felt the call to ministry placed on him. He was then ordained and began teaching at Princeton.[242] In 1822, Hodge was inaugurated as professor of Oriental and biblical literature. This new chair required him to teach OT Hebrew language and literature, in addition to Greek language and NT literature. He also lectured on Romans, Corinthians, and hermeneutics. In his inaugural address, Hodge stated that his aim was to illustrate the importance of piety in the interpretation of Scripture.[243] He stated that piety was the fruit of an inward operation of the Holy Spirit and manifested itself in humility and candor.

After teaching for four years, Hodge was convinced that he needed further study. So in 1826 he placed his wife and two children in the care of his brother and mother in Philadelphia, and he sailed to Europe for two years of further study.[244]

---

238. Samuel Miller, *An Essay on the Warrant, Nature and Duties of the Office of the Ruling Elder in the Presbyterian Church* (Jackson, MS: Presbyterian Heritage Publications, 1987).

239. Kevin Reed, "Biographical Sketch of Samuel Miller," in *Holding Fast the Faithful Word: Sermons and Addresses by Samuel Miller*, ed. Kevin Reed (Grand Rapids: Reformation Heritage Books, 2018), ix–xxxii.

240. See W. Andrew Hoffecker, *Charles Hodge: The Pride of Princeton* (Phillipsburg, NJ: P&R Publishing, 2011).

241. Archibald Alexander Hodge, *The Life of Charles Hodge* (New York: Scribner's Sons, 1880), 94: As "far back as I can remember, I had the habit of thanking God for everything I received, and asking him for everything I wanted. I prayed walking along the streets, in school and out of school, whether playing or studying. I did not do this in obedience to any prescribed rule. It seemed natural." He remembered uttering profanity only once, when he was thirteen or fourteen years old.

242. Calhoun, *Princeton Seminary*, 1:109–11.

243. Hodge, *Life of Charles Hodge*, 94: "It is the object of this discourse to illustrate the importance of Piety in the Interpretation of Scripture."

244. See ibid., 103–201; Calhoun, *Princeton Seminary*, 1:117.

Commenting on his graduate studies in Germany during those years, Hodge said: "It is this vital connection between piety and truth that is the great and solemn lesson taught by the past and present state of the German churches."[245] Like Alexander before him, Hodge was convinced of the need for an intimate connection between piety and doctrine, particularly as a result of his time in Germany.[246] Hodge warned his students against sin, but he also warned against the temptation to take religious truth and analyze it metaphysically. To do so would harden a student's heart.[247] In 1834 Hodge was awarded the doctor of divinity degree and from 1834 to 1838 was aided in Hebrew by Joseph Addison (J. A.) Alexander, Archibald Alexander's son. In 1838, J. A. Alexander was installed as professor of Oriental languages and literature, and in 1840 Hodge assumed the chair of exegetical and didactic theology.

Hodge and his wife had eight children. Archibald Alexander (A. A.) Hodge, Charles's oldest son, was ordained to the ministry and in 1847 became a missionary to India. While Archibald was in India, in December of 1849 Charles's wife died. Following Archibald Alexander's death in 1851, Hodge acquired the chair of polemic theology as well.[248] The years of 1848 to 1855 were not as productive for Hodge. He sought recreation in reading novels, playing backgammon, and, in the summertime, croquet on the lawn.[249]

In 1835 Hodge published the first edition of his *Commentary on Romans*. In 1836 an abridged edition was published, and in 1841 the

---

245. Noll, *Princeton Theology*, 108–10.

246. Ibid., "Lecture to theological Students," 111: "The correspondence between opinion and character is strikingly observable in the various religious parties in that section of the church. . . . Wherever you find vital piety, that is, penitence, and devotional spirit, there you find, the doctrines of the fall, of depravity, of regeneration, of atonement, and the Deity of Jesus Christ. I never saw nor heard of a single individual who exhibited a spirit of piety who rejected any one of these doctrines. There are many who have great reverence for Jesus Christ and regard for the scriptures, but having no experience of the power of the gospel, they have no clear view nor firm conviction of its doctrine; they are vacillating on the borders of two classes of opinion, exactly as they are in feeling."

247. Ibid., 112: "Holiness is essential to correct knowledge of divine things, and the great security from error. . . . Again, beware of any course of life or study which has a tendency to harden your hearts and deaden the delicate sensibility of the soul to moral truth and beauty. There are two ways in which this may be done, a course of sin, and indulgence in metaphysical speculations on divine things. . . . Thus also religious truth, viewed in the general, produces devotion; metaphysically analyzed it destroys it."

248. Hodge, *Life of Hodge*, 92–95, 204–5, 238, 321.

249. Ibid., 377.

work was translated into French.[250] In 1839 to 1840, Hodge published *Constitutional History of the Presbyterian Church*. By 1840 he had published thirty-six articles in the *Repertory*. In 1841, *The Way of Life* was published. His other biblical commentaries followed, including commentaries on Ephesians (1856), 1 Corinthians (1857), and 2 Corinthians (1859).[251]

Archibald Alexander Hodge speculated that his father had begun to project writing a systematic theology by the year 1864, when he was already sixty-seven years old. The writing itself likely began in 1867, and the first volume was sent to the publisher in December 1870. Charles was then seventy-three years old. The manuscript of the last volume was completed in October of 1872. Charles Hodge held that the systematician had to be first and foremost a biblical exegete.[252]

As an intellectual and spiritual leader in the Presbyterian church, Hodge was not exempt from playing a significant role in ecclesiastical controversy. The Old School–New School Controversy began in 1835. The New School supported revivalism and a modified Calvinism that was more open to revivalism. The Old School, led by Hodge and the men of Princeton, was not supportive of revivalism. There had been a plan of union that included synods controlled by New School theologians, but the General Assembly of 1837 refused to recognize these new synods. The new synods then exited the meeting and held their own general assembly. The dispute flowed into the court system, and in 1839 Pennsylvania's supreme court determined that the Old School assembly was the true representative of the Presbyterian church.[253]

Some other controversies that he faced involved the constitutionality of church boards and the nature of eldership, during which he debated with the learned Old School Southern theologians James Henley Thornwell and Robert Jefferson Breckinridge.[254] There was also debate as to

250. In 1864 a revised second edition appeared.

251. Ibid., 400.

252. Ibid., 323. Hodge made "acquisitions in the original languages of Scripture and in the science and practice of biblical exegesis, which are professedly the basis of systematic theology, and yet are the qualifications in which the vast majority of speculative theologians have been more or less deficient."

253. Calhoun, *Princeton Seminary*, 1:213–55.

254. Breckinridge argued for what is termed a *two-office* view of the eldership: there is one order of elder with diversity of office. Hodge countered that Breckinridge's view was not supported either in the Bible or in the church's constitution and that here are three distinct

whether Catholic baptism should be accepted. Hodge argued that it should be.[255] He disputed with Charles Finney concerning the liberty of the human will and with Horace Bushnell and Edwards A. Park concerning total depravity and the nature of religious truth.[256] Also, from 1836 to 1849, Hodge wrote three articles addressing the grave theological/political issue of slavery, and later he wrote an article on the topic for the General Assembly of 1864. His consistent position was that the Bible opposed both pro-slavery arguments and the abolitionists. He thought the abolitionists were wrong to say that slaveholding is a sin, because the Bible regulates slavery according to biblical requirements.[257] A continuing controversy revolved around the nature of subscription to the Westminster Confession of Faith.[258] Toward the end of his public ministry, in 1874 Hodge wrote a pamphlet against the scientist Charles Darwin, whose theory of evolution Hodge deemed atheistic.[259]

James Waddel (J. W.) Alexander (A.D. 1804–1859). Waddel was a professor at Princeton and the greatest Princeton preacher. He was the oldest son of Archibald Alexander and spent much of his life focusing on the intimate relationship between preaching and piety. He taught that eloquence in the pulpit required earnestness.[260] He wrote, "No man can be a great preacher without great feeling,"[261] and he understood there to be a difficult balance between systematic theology and practical application in preaching.[262]

offices. See Hodge, *Life of Hodge*, 401–4; Calhoun, *Princeton Seminary*, 1:299–301, 383–84. Calhoun mentions that when the northern and southern churches split, the north followed the three-office view and the south the two-office view.

255. Calhoun, *Princeton Seminary*, 1:303–4.
256. Ibid., 1:305–7, 313–14, 315–16.
257. Ibid., 1:326–27. Calhoun concludes: "The Princetonians were, as they often claimed, 'friends of the slaves,' but they failed to align themselves clearly and positively with the oppressed in the face of real injustice and tyranny."
258. Hodge, *Life of Hodge*, 406–8.
259. Ibid., 576; Calhoun, *Princeton Seminary*, 2:15–20. *What Is Darwinism?* appeared in 1874.
260. Alexander, *Thoughts on Preaching*, 6: "The great reason why we have so little good preaching is that we have so little piety. To be eloquent one must be in earnest. . . . We have loud and vehement, we have smooth and graceful, we have splendid and elaborate preaching, but very little that is earnest."
261. Ibid., 20.
262. Ibid., 186: "Books on systematic theology give the classified results of biblical investigation. To the production of these systems, either in the head, in the sermons, or in the printed book, all exegetical research is subsidiary. Fondness for [systematics] will be very much in proportion to the strength, clearness, and harmonious action of the intellect. No man can

In his preface to the wonderful book *Thoughts on Family Worship*, Alexander commented, "In a period when the world is every day making new inroads on the church, it has especially invaded the household." He taught that family worship is part of the covenant and appears in the remotest corners of gospel history. As examples, he pointed to family worship in the lives of Noah, Isaac, Abraham, and Job. He also saw the practice throughout the book of Deuteronomy, particularly in chapter 6, as well as in the sacrament of the Passover.[263] The same theology of family worship is taught in the NT and was continued by the fathers of the ancient church.

Alexander also taught that the Reformers highly valued family devotion.[264] Above other European countries, Scotland truly treasured family worship, as seen in its 1647 *Directory for Family Worship*.[265] The elements of family worship consisted of prayer, then the reading of the Scriptures with a plain catechizing, which could also include admonition and rebuke.

As early as 1596, records demonstrate that when elders visited homes, they would ask whether the families had family worship. Alexander, too, was a strong proponent of catechism within the home.[266] He held that when family worship is disregarded, worldliness fills the void;[267] that family worship helps correct and supplement the absence of individual reflection on God in the home;[268] and that it also benefits the piety of the person who leads the family in these devotional activities.[269]

---

be said to know anything truly, which he does not know systematically. Every sermon is, so far as it goes, a body of divinity. . . . Systematics will teach a man to think, and strengthen him to preach. When studies are miscellaneous and desultory, there is the more reason for [systematics], in order to give unity to the varied acquisitions."

263. J. W. Alexander, *Thoughts on Family Worship* (Grand Rapids: Reformation Heritage Books, 1998), 13.

264. Ibid., 21.

265. Ibid., 22. The *Westminster Confession of Faith* (Atlanta: Committee for Christian Education and Publications, Presbyterian Church in America, 1986) (*WCF*), chapter 26, paragraph six, states: "God is to be worshiped everywhere, in spirit and in truth: as in private families daily, and in secret each one by himself."

266. Alexander, *Family Worship*, 24.

267. Ibid., 28.

268. Ibid., 32: "Summon a family to the worship of God, at stated hours, and you summon each one to seriousness of reflection, of which he might have been wholly robbed, by the hurry of the day's business."

269. Ibid., 34: "No one need wonder, then, that we place a family-prayer among the most important means of reviving and maintaining the piety of him who conducts it."

Another reason Alexander used in support of family worship was that a parent's prayers could awaken the piety of a child.[270] His reasoning continued: "unspeakable good would ensue, if every father could feel himself to be the earthly, but divinely-appointed, head-spring of religious influence to his household," and when he does, the father "has assumed his rightful place as an instructor, a guide and an exemplar in devotion."[271] This teaching applies to families without children as well. He continues, "better a roofless than a prayerless house: better beg one's bread, with prayer, than deny God by a neglect of this chief means of domestic prosperity."[272] Alexander observed that this family worship also influences the intellectual abilities of the family. He recalls a day when uneducated weavers and dyers—factory workers—argued over minute divisions of theology.[273]

Archibald Alexander (A. A.) Hodge (A.D. 1823–1886). After graduation from the College of New Jersey and Princeton Seminary, Hodge sailed to India as a missionary, but he returned in 1850 after only three years.[274] He then served in various churches from 1851 to 1864.

His *Outlines of Theology* are sermons that he preached on Sunday evenings.[275] He was rightly convinced that theology could be preached, and this volume demonstrated that reality. Hodge's theological principles were as follows: the Scriptures are the standard for all religious knowledge; Christ's person and work are the center of theology; salvation is by free grace; and theological knowledge has a practical end—to advance personal holiness, more effective service, and God's greater glory.[276]

In 1864, Hodge was called as professor of systematic theology to Western Theological Seminary in Pittsburgh, where he served for thirteen years.[277] In 1867 he wrote *The Atonement*.[278] In 1869 he wrote

---

270. Ibid., 36: "When yet a child, no one means of grace, public or private, so awakened my attention, as when the children were prayed for day by day."

271. Ibid., 47.

272. Ibid., 57.

273. Ibid., 92.

274. Calhoun, *Princeton Seminary*, 1:268, 279.

275. Ibid., 2:52, 75.

276. Archibald Alexander Hodge, *Outline of Theology* (repr., Edinburgh: Banner of Truth, 1991), 16.

277. Calhoun, *Princeton Seminary*, 2:51–52. Chapter 23 contains analysis of his inaugural address.

278. For more information on his view of the atonement in its historical context, see Richard C. Gamble, "The Doctrine of the Atonement from the Westminster Assembly to the

A Commentary on the Confession of Faith, an invaluable resource on the WCF that is still used today.[279]

Hodge arrived at Princeton in November 1877.[280] In 1881 he coauthored an article with B. B. Warfield on the nature and character of inerrancy to counteract the teaching of Charles Augustus Briggs. Hodge believed that it was proper to distinguish between the origin of Scripture, which included historical circumstances and the interaction of divine and human factors, and inspiration itself. Inspiration was the superintendence of God over the various authors' writings. God especially formed each writer to communicate his particular part of Scripture. Each author was precisely prepared by the Holy Spirit. The authors were active in their thinking and writing, thus producing a Bible that is "an errorless record of the matters he designed them to communicate, and hence constituting the entire volume in all its parts the word of God to us."[281]

KEY TERMS

romanticism
dialectical method
will to power
religious feeling

STUDY QUESTIONS

1. What do you think of Marx's view of humanity?
2. What do you think about John Dewey's epistemology or how students should learn?
3. Why do you think that Schleiermacher wanted to overturn older ways of viewing Christianity?

Twentieth Century," in *The Faith Once Delivered*, ed. Anthony T. Selvaggio (Phillipsburg, NJ: P&R Publishing, 2007), 254–56.

279. Calhoun, *Princeton Seminary*, 2:52, 75, 101.

280. His inaugural address there was titled "Dogmatic Christianity, the Essential Ground of Practical Christianity" (see ibid., 2:49).

281. Inspiration was also "the constant attribute of all the thoughts and statements of Scripture," and "accounts for nothing whatever but the absolute infallibility of the record . . . in the original autograph" (*Presbyterian Review* 2 [April 1881], as cited by Robert Letham, *Systematic Theology* [Wheaton, IL: Crossway, 2019], 211).

4. Is Kierkegaard correct that truth is subjective?
5. Would you side with Hodge and the three-office view of eldership or with Thornwell and the two-office view?

RESOURCES FOR FURTHER STUDY

Nineteenth-century Dutch and Princetonian theology is a delightful place in which to spend hours reading and meditating.

Alexander, J. W. *Thoughts on Preaching*. Reprint, Edinburgh: Banner of Truth, 1988. Formative to sound preaching for generations.

Bavinck, Herman. *Reformed Dogmatics*. Edited by John Bolt. Grand Rapids: Baker Academic, 2003. The gold standard for the Reformed tradition.

Eglinton, James. *Bavinck: A Critical Biography*. Grand Rapids: Baker Academic, 2020. A welcome addition from a fine scholar and powerful communicator.

Hodge, Archibald Alexander. *A Commentary on the Westminster Confession of Faith*. Carlisle, PA: Banner of Truth, 1958. A one-volume work helpful to anyone in the Presbyterian or Reformed traditions.

Hodge, Charles. *Systematic Theology*. 3 vols. London: Clarke, 1960. Historically, considered so powerful and foundational that only recently have conservative Presbyterians ventured to write their own systematic theologies.

Kuyper, Abraham. *Common Grace: God's Gifts for a Fallen World*. Edited by N. D. Kloosterman. Bellingham, WA: Lexham Press, 2015.

———. *Pro Rege: Living under Christ the King*. Edited by John H. Kok. Bellingham, WA: Lexham Press, 2016. Demonstrates Kuyper's reputation for his views on Christ's mediatorial kingship.

———. *Heidelberg Catechism. E Voto Dordraceno: Toelichting op den Heidelbergschen Catechismus*. 4 vols. Amsterdam: J. A. Wormser, 1892–95. A multivolume commentary helpful to anyone in the Presbyterian or Reformed traditions.

21

Early Twentieth Century

MANY HAVE SOUGHT TO understand the theological transition between the nineteenth and twentieth centuries. Some have drawn together two main strands of thought from this period: historical criticism and the search for a valid religious experience. But this transition can be more fittingly described in three dominant categories: confessional believers, represented here by the old-Princeton theologians; the so-called "mediating theologians"; and the unbelieving existential rationalists.[1] The confessional believers represented traditional evangelicals. The rationalists were more destructive to the Christian faith—they denied much of the veracity of the Bible. And the mediating school was birthed in the writings of the nineteenth-century theologian Friedrich Schleiermacher.[2] This mediating school would one day be known as *classic liberalism*.

This was a unique season for the world. Following World War I, wealth was concentrated in the United States, and labor was plentiful. This cultural milieu set the stage for the theology that would develop in the coming years.

---

1. No model is perfect. The issues are made more complex with influences of Pietism and theologians such as Ernst Wilhelm Hengstenberg (1802–1869), in Germany, who was a confessional orthodox.

2. That group would include the German-speaking theologians Neander, Tholuck, and Dorner (Williston Walker, Richard A. Norris, David W. Lotz, and Robert T. Handy, *A History of the Christian Church*, 4th ed. [New York: Scribner's Sons, 1985], 491).

EARLY TWENTIETH CENTURY: ECONOMIC, SOCIAL, AND INTELLECTUAL BACKGROUNDS

Victorian England. Victorian England acted as a sort of model for most of the United States. So to understand the social backdrop of the United States and other European countries, it is necessary to pause and understand several aspects of British culture and customs.

Victorian England was a civil and humane society.[3] Queen Victoria believed it to be her duty to guide her nation in the way of virtue.[4] At this time, England was divided in a class-based system, even among the lowest of classes. But Victorian culture honored the dutiful task of working and providing for a family.[5] Victorian English culture held that all work was sacred, even in the most menial of professions.[6] This value-rich ideology ran throughout the classes.

Victorian society focused on both the self and the family. While self-interest was permitted, self-discipline, control, and respect were revered. The family was cherished during this time—so much so that cherishing family became almost a civic religion.[7] The extent of civil liberties was largely dependent on people's control of their appetites. The less internal control there was, the more need there was for external control.

These Victorian values had social consequences. Until 1829, London had no police force, but by 1856 police forces existed throughout the country. Between 1857 and 1901, indictable offenses in England declined by nearly 50 percent. Even though the population of England increased from nineteen million to thirty-three million, the number of crimes dropped significantly.[8] The rate of illegitimacy decreased from 7 percent to 4 percent. As the family was esteemed so highly, most homes now had two parents present. This brought a stability to the home, even among the lower classes.[9]

3. Gertrude Himmelfarb, *The De-Moralization of Society: From Victorian Virtues to Modern Values* (New York: Knopf, 1995), 18.
4. Ibid., 27–28.
5. Ibid., 31–32.
6. Ibid., 30, 35, 38.
7. Ibid., 51, 53–57.
8. Ibid., 39.
9. Ibid., 41–42.

This age of virtue, however, was not the fruit of evangelical piety.[10] Instead, formal religion had been eclipsed by the general advance of public morality.[11] These reforms were largely the fruit of a secular religion that believed that progress in science would promote the welfare of society. Watching from Europe, Nietzsche predicted that this Victorian society would soon swerve into disarray.[12] Sadly, the outbreak of World War I changed Europe and America.

World War I. In the summer of 1914, France mobilized nearly three million reserve soldiers into battle. With these three million soldiers went many of France's technicians and managers, and so went the French economy. By the end of August 1914, half of France's factories closed. Germany had conscripted 5.25 million men into service, thus bankrupting the German economy. Russia found itself in the same situation, with grain production in 1915 at less than two-thirds of what it had been in 1914.[13] Despite its minor role, the United States mobilized more than four million men and spent a total of $33 billion on the so-called Great War—double what the federal government had spent during its first one hundred years of existence.[14]

By the end of the war in 1919, eight hundred thousand German civilians deteriorated at the hand of disease and malnutrition. The war had claimed ten to thirteen million lives and wounded nearly twenty million more. The emotional consequences of this global devastation could not be mended with a treaty or transition.

In this great world war, governments learned new methods of manipulation, with one of them being the dissemination of propaganda. To some extent, every government wielded this manipulative

10. Ibid., 6, 9–10, 12–13.

11. Ibid., 26–27: "George Eliot uttered the classic statement of this secular ethic when she said that God was 'inconceivable,' immortality 'unbelievable,' but duty nonetheless 'peremptory and absolute.'"

12. Ibid., 188: "Nietzsche looked down on those 'English flatheads,' those 'little moralistic females à la Eliot,' who thought it possible to have a morality without religion. 'They get rid of the Christian God and now believe all the more firmly that they must cling to Christian morality'; they become 'moral fanatics' to compensate for their religious emancipation. For the moment 'morality is not yet the problem.' But it would become a problem once they discovered that without Christianity there is no morality. 'When one gives up the Christian faith, one pulls the right to Christian morality out from under one's feet.'"

13. John A. Garrity, ed., *Columbia History of the World* (New York: Harper & Row, 1988), 469.

14. Ibid., 469.

tool. Governments learned that if they held the strings of the media, they could manipulate their citizens into believing whatever the government wanted them to believe.[15]

For example, in April 1918 the London *Times* reported that German citizens were boiling down bodies of dead allied soldiers for their fat. British citizens at large fell for this false narrative. Similar propaganda would contribute to the start of World War II just twenty years later.[16] The massive social and economic changes during this time also generated new ways of thinking.

Idealist Philosophy. Scholars struggle to date the beginnings of idealism as a philosophical movement. Some trace its roots all the way back to ancient Greece, while most now consider idealism to have arisen after the debates of rationalism and empiricism, often starting with Kant.

In general, idealists argue that each and every fact stands in relation to other facts. When isolated, a fact is meaningless—entirely unintelligible.[17] In essence, idealism is a counter-philosophy to empiricism. Even Plato struggled with this philosophical problem. Initially, Plato argued that the ideal world is the world that is fully known. It is known without reference to the sensory world. This form world is real, despite its separation from material objects. On the far side of the spectrum, Plato thought that there is another world of pure nonbeing and ignorance and that the sensory world is between these two. But Plato would later deny the independence of the ideal world. He understood that the two worlds were unintelligible apart from one another. Just as the notion of a husband is only intelligible in the light of a wife, so were the ideal world and the world of nonbeing dependent on each other.[18] Yet Plato could not find a rational connection between the two worlds.

Idealism began to develop after the rise of rationalism and empiricism. Idealists were convinced that Kant had made advances over earlier philosophy as he stood against both rationalists and empiri-

---

15. Ibid., 473.
16. Ibid.
17. Cornelius Van Til, *Christian Theistic Evidences*, ed. K. Scott Oliphint (Phillipsburg, NJ: Presbyterian & Reformed, 2016), 67–70.
18. Ibid., 74.

cists. But Kant also proposed that there are two worlds: the noumenal and phenomenal. Kant, like Plato, was unable to draw a connection between these vastly different worlds. Idealists searched out methods of connecting Plato's and Kant's two worlds. Hegel believed that he found the connection that others were unable to find—he found it in the supplement of an absolute mind.[19]

Hegel believed that the absolute mind was real and engaged in the process of self-development. For Hegel, the real is both rational and the culmination of the dialectical process of consciousness. Thus he believed that the real is the rational and the rational is the real.[20]

In addition, Hegel believed that the ideas of *pure being* and *nonbeing* are both empty and interchangeable. He taught that when these notions are brought together, however, they gain meaning. The principle of dialectic brings the two into contact. When they are no longer isolated but are combined through interpenetration or dialectic, being and nonbeing, identity and diversity, and pure affirmation and pure negation have a life and meaning to them. Being and nonbeing experience a common reality and meaning in *becoming*. In this way, Hegel merged rationalism and empiricism, or fact and principle. His a priori was held not independently of facts but with the assistance of facts. The diversity of the factual provided meaning to the rational.[21]

Hegel's absolute idealism was attacked by Kierkegaard and generated further intellectual developments. F. H. Bradley (1846–1924) and Bernard Bosanquet (1848–1923) both expanded idealist thinking in their monumental works on logic. They argued that thinkers need a comprehensive a priori for any knowledge. Beginning with simple counting, they argued that numbers are not meaningful without a finite goal. Counting has to occur within a numerical system as a whole.[22] The philosophy of idealism would maintain its dominance for some time.

19. Ibid., 72–73.
20. Ibid., 72n33.
21. Ibid., 75n40; 76n43: "The Absolute idealists, in seeking to solve the impasse between the *a priori*, or unifying principle, so prevalent in rationalism, and the *a posteriori*, or principle of diversity, so present in empiricism, argued that any fact, or any number of facts, is what it is by virtue of its relation to the whole."
22. Ibid., 76: "If we are to add information to our store of knowledge, we need the system of knowledge in order to relate a new fact to the system of facts already known."

But idealism was attacked by a movement called *analytic philosophy*, which was also significant for twentieth-century British and American thinking.[23] Thus the theologians who follow here were living in economically, socially, and intellectually tumultuous times.

Early Twentieth Century: Old Princeton Seminary

Introduction: The Rise of American Fundamentalism and Modernism. At the end of the nineteenth century and the beginning of the twentieth, a movement called *fundamentalism* arose in the United States. It was a reactionary movement against mainline churches and denominations that had rejected a number of basic Christian teachings. Many of these mainline denominations questioned, and often dismissed, the virgin birth, authority of the Scriptures, veracity of miracle accounts, and bodily resurrection of Jesus Christ. Those who still believed in these basic scriptural teachings were derogatively labeled *fundamentalists*, a name that came from a series of pamphlets written by more than sixty authors, published between 1910 and 1915, and titled *The Fundamentals*.[24] The articles, largely written by non-Presbyterian authors, were written on biblical doctrines such as Christ's deity, sin and salvation, biblical inspiration, creation and evolution, and evangelism and missions.[25] While the old-Princeton authors, studied below, supported the fundamentalist movement, they did not consider themselves to be fundamentalists but simply those who upheld Scripture and the Westminster Confession of Faith.[26] The great Princeton theologian J. Gresham Machen was one of the first to

23. Names associated with analytic philosophy are G. E. Moore (1873–1958), who wrote *Principia Ethica* in 1903, as well as Bertrand Russell (1872–1970) and Ludwig Wittgenstein. Wittgenstein is analyzed in chapter 22.

24. On fundamentalism, see A. James Reichley, *Religion in American Public Life* (Washington, DC: Brookings Institute, 1985). See also George M. Marsden, *Fundamentalism and American Culture: The Shaping of Twentieth-Century Evangelicalism, 1870–1925* (New York: Oxford University Press, 1980).

25. See Peter A. Lillback, "J. Gresham Machen, Fundamentalism, and Westminster Seminary," in *Christianity and Liberalism*, by J. Gresham Machen, legacy edition (Philadelphia: Westminster Seminary Press, 2019), 191–93.

26. Marsden (*Fundamentalism*, 138) underlined how Machen was accepted in fundamentalist circles as he was offered the presidency of Bryan University in Tennessee and was discussed as a possible president of Moody Bible Institute.

be categorized as a fundamentalist.[27] It seems that Machen was the only twentieth-century Reformed theologian to permit himself to be so categorized.

A movement from within the Presbyterian church arose against the five fundamentals set forth in 1910 by the General Assembly. A committee of Presbyterian ministers composed the Auburn Affirmation of 1924, which was signed by 1,274 ministers. Proponents of the Auburn Affirmation argued that these five fundamentals were not the only valid theories—other theories also merited confidence and fellowship in the church. The signers of the Auburn Affirmation advocated for an expanded understanding of what the fundamentals of Christianity are. As Machen, who violently opposed the Auburn Affirmation would soon make clear in *Christianity and Liberalism*, the issue was not simply of one possible theory of truth versus another. The signers of the Auburn Affirmation, by rejecting the five fundamentals, were rejecting Christianity in favor of liberalism.[28]

Also involved in this debate was a complex group that could be labeled the Social Gospelers. Walter Rauschenbusch, a professor at the Baptist Rochester Seminary, summarized well the teaching of the Social Gospel in his two books, *Christianity and the Social Crisis* (1907) and *A Theology for the Social Gospel* (1917). Rauschenbusch was more conservative than many of the movement's critics gave him credit for being. The Social Gospel movement was primarily concerned with working toward the kingdom of God,[29] a kingdom embodied by the realm of love and the commonwealth of labor.[30] That kingdom needed to socialize people properly because the then-current social structure helped perpetuate sinful situations. Rauschenbusch, likely influenced by John Dewey, stressed that the validity of Christian theology is judged by what Social Gospel theologians do.[31]

27. C. Allyn Russell, *Voices of Fundamentalism: Seven Biographical Studies* (Philadelphia: Westminster Press, 1976), 147.

28. For the persuasive argument that the two movements represent two distinct sets of hermeneutical presuppositions, see Vern S. Poythress, "Christianity and Liberalism and Hermeneutical Presuppositions," in *Christianity and Liberalism*, by J. Gresham Machen, legacy edition (Philadelphia: Westminster Seminary Press, 2019), 263–65.

29. Walter Rauschenbusch, *Christianity and the Social Crisis in the 21st Century*, ed. Paul Rauschenbush (New York: HarperOne, 2007), 54–55.

30. Reichley, *Religion in American Public Life*, 208.

31. Marsden, *Fundamentalism*, 92.

Benjamin B. Warfield (A.D. 1851–1921).[32] Benjamin B. (B. B.) Warfield was born in Lexington, Kentucky, into a pious family. The children in his family were expected to memorize the Westminster Shorter Catechism (WSC) by the age of six, then learn the scriptural proofs, and then move on to the Westminster Larger Catechism (WLC). Warfield studied science at Princeton. It was not until he continued his studies in Germany that he decided to pursue ministry. He graduated from Princeton Seminary in 1876, married, and then did graduate work in Leipzig. He accepted his first teaching post at Western Seminary in Pittsburgh, where he remained for nine years. He then served as professor of didactic and polemic theology at Princeton for another thirty-three years.[33] Throughout his career, he held the Westminster Standards in the highest regard.[34]

Warfield was a prolific writer, but he is best known for his work on the doctrine of inspiration.[35] Much of his work on inspiration was the result of a controversy Warfield had with the teachings of Charles A. Briggs (1841–1913). Briggs had studied under higher critics in Germany and was intent to expose Presbyterian churches to its teachings. In debates with the Princeton theologians, Briggs accused them of distorting the teachings of the WCF. He held that their views of inspiration and authority were rooted in Reformed scholastic theology, not the standards.[36] In this debate, Warfield explained earlier views of

32. See Fred Zaspel, *The Theology of B. B. Warfield: A Systematic Summary* (Wheaton, IL: Crossway, 2010); Kim Riddlebarger, *The Lion of Princeton: B. B. Warfield as Apologist and Theologian* (Bellingham, WA: Lexham Press, 2015).

33. See David B. Calhoun, *Princeton Seminary*, 2 vols. (Edinburgh: Banner of Truth, 1996), 2:113–24; John M. Frame, *A History of Western Philosophy and Theology* (Phillipsburg, NJ: P&R Publishing, 2015) (*HWPT*), 242, 404.

34. See Benjamin B. Warfield, *The Westminster Assembly and Its Work* (New York: Oxford University Press, 1931); Arthur W. Kuschke, introduction to *Selected Shorter Writings of Benjamin B. Warfield*, 2 vols., ed. John Meeter (Nutley, NJ: Presbyterian and Reformed, 1979), 1:xiii–xv.

35. His selected writings published by Oxford include *Revelation and Inspiration*, which contains articles on the idea of revelation as well as exegetical articles on the biblical notion of inspiration; *Biblical Doctrines*, with articles on the Trinity, predestination, faith, and the person of Christ; and *Christology and Criticism*, which opens historico-critical studies of Christ's person and work. Warfield was a brilliant historical theologian as well. See his *Studies in Tertullian and Augustine* and *Calvin and Calvinism*. The Oxford collection is ten volumes in total. For more information on Warfield's view of the atonement in its historical context, see Richard C. Gamble, "The Doctrine of the Atonement from the Westminster Assembly to the Twentieth Century," in *The Faith Once Delivered*, ed. Anthony T. Selvaggio (Phillipsburg, NJ: P&R Publishing, 2007), 256–58.

36. Jack B. Rogers and Donald K. McKim, *The Authority and Interpretation of the Bible* (San Francisco: Harper & Row, 1979), 353.

inspiration and inerrancy. Although Briggs was suspended from the ministry, he had set the stage for doubting the authority and inspiration of the Bible. The rise of higher criticism and the developments of evolution posed a formidable threat to fundamental biblical doctrines, and Warfield stepped in to defend the faith and a high view of Scripture.[37]

William B. Greene (A.D. 1854–1928). William Greene was from New England and trained at Princeton College and Seminary. He was ordained in Boston and ministered there from 1880 to 1883. He then pastored Tenth Presbyterian Church in Philadelphia until 1892. Greene served Princeton Seminary as Stuart Professor of the Relations of Philosophy and Science to the Christian Religion from 1892 until his death in 1928. While he did not write many books, he reviewed hundreds of them in *The Princeton Theological Review* and wrote dozens of articles and pamphlets.[38]

In 1903, old Princeton's Presbyterian church made revisions to the WCF.[39] Their revisions added weight to a movement for a reunification of the Cumberland Presbyterian Church and the Presbyterian Church in the United States. Warfield had written against the union by arguing that Cumberland Presbyterian Church's confession was undeniably Arminian. Some argued that doctrine was of no assistance to the Christian life. In 1905, Greene responded to this belief with a fascinating address on the relationship between doctrine and the Christian life. He argued that each doctrine has a practical application and that doctrine is foundational to piety.[40]

As the professor of apologetics and ethics, Greene acted as the faculty's voice and conscience on social issues. He insisted that the church's primary task is not fundamentally or chiefly social but the preaching of the gospel of individual salvation. He did believe, however, that the church could not remain indifferent to the struggles and questions of

37. For excellent analysis, see Jeffrey A. Stivason, *From Inscrutability to Concursus: Benjamin B. Warfield's Theological Construction of Revelation's Mode from 1880 to 1915* (Phillipsburg, NJ: P&R Publishing, 2017).

38. Calhoun, *Princeton Seminary*, 2:214.

39. Those revisions included new chapters titled "Of the Holy Spirit"; "Of the Love of God, and Missions"; and "Declaratory Statement." The statement softened the confession's strong position on election. There were also deletions about refusing a lawful oath and about the pope's being the Antichrist.

40. Calhoun, *Princeton Seminary*, 2:250–51.

society. Greene thought that faithful preaching must not shy away from the texts in which God has made a pronouncement on social reform, and it must elaborate social principles from scriptural texts in which social reform is not explicitly mentioned.[41]

In 1893, Greene presented an inaugural address that revealed his views on apologetics. Greene believed that the foundation of apologetics is man's rational faculty, which has self-evident and universal application to all human beings.[42] He held that reason is an even stronger evidence for the Christian faith than an external authority. But he admitted that reason, if left to itself, can lead humans no further than their consciousness of guilt.[43] Greene presupposed that there must be a rational basis for the acceptance of divine revelation.

While Greene embraced the principles and theology of the Reformation, his apologetic approach did not match this theology. He did not fully realize the effects of the fall on human thinking and reasoning, and he assumed that common-sense beliefs were valid.[44]

Geerhardus Vos (A.D. 1862–1949).[45] Jan Vos, the father of Geerhardus, was from the Dutch-German Reformed tradition and was trained at the seminary of the secession church in Kampen.[46] In 1881, Geerhardus graduated from the gymnasium in Amsterdam and then immigrated with his family to the United States. As a young boy, he was influenced by poets; he would write poetry for the rest of his life in both Dutch and English.[47] Vos attended seminary in Grand Rapids, Michigan, for two years before transferring to Princeton Seminary, where he completed the master of divinity program in two years. The capstone of his seminary education was a book written for the Hebrew prize and titled *The Mosaic Origin of the Pentateuchal Codes*. He

---

41. Ibid., 2:260–64.

42. K. Scott Oliphint, foreword to *Christian Theistic Evidences*, by Cornelius Van Til (Phillipsburg, NJ: P&R Publishing, 2016), xv.

43. Calhoun, *Princeton Seminary*, 2:134–35.

44. Oliphint, foreword, xvi.

45. See Danny E. Olinger, *Geerhardus Vos: Reformed Biblical Theologian, Confessional Presbyterian* (Philadelphia: Reformed Forum 2018).

46. James T. Dennison Jr., *The Letters of Geerhardus Vos* (Phillipsburg, NJ: P&R Publishing, 2005), 13.

47. Vos wrote a number of volumes of poetry in Dutch and English. See George Harinck, "The Poetry of Theologian Geerhardus Vos," in *Dutch-American Arts and Letters in Historical Perspective*, ed. Robert P. Swierenga, Jacob E. Nyenhuis, and Nella Kennedy (Holland, MI: Van Raalte Press, 2008), 69–80.

returned to Europe, and after studying for a year in Berlin he obtained a doctorate in Semitics from the University of Strasbourg.

In 1888, Vos was appointed professor of didactic and exegetical theology at Calvin Theological Seminary in Grand Rapids. There he taught for nearly twenty-five hours per week in the areas of philosophy, dogmatics, systematics, and non-Christian religions. He taught his seminary courses in Dutch, and on the weekends he preached in English.[48]

In the fall of 1893, at the age of thirty-one Vos began teaching at Princeton Seminary. During his time as a professor at Princeton, he never preached outside the seminary's chapel. Vos's life was in fairly constant flux, and he was never well known.[49] While his writings were not vast compared to some of his Princeton colleagues, each of his volumes had a deep profundity to it.[50]

In many ways, this three-volume *The Whole Counsel of God* series has been modeled after Vos's vision set forth in his *Biblical Theology*. Vos argued that the best way to understand God's self-revelation is in the manner by which God has unfolded it—historically.[51]

As is always the case for professors, Vos encountered theological controversies, first from within his own denomination—the Presbyterian Church (USA). In 1923 he protested his presbytery's nomination of his colleague Charles Eerdman as moderator of the General Assembly. Also, Vos likely agreed with B. B. Warfield that J. Ross Stevenson was not a fitting choice for the presidency of Princeton Seminary.[52] His heart

48. Calhoun, *Princeton Seminary*, 2:139. Vos's five-volume *Reformed Dogmatics* (ed. and trans. Richard B. Gaffin [Bellingham, WA: Lexham Press, 2012–2016]) is an English translation of his mimeographed Calvin Seminary lectures.

49. Dennison, *Letters of Vos*, 13, 28, 52.

50. Some of his writings include *The Teaching of Jesus Concerning the Kingdom of God and the Church* (New York: American Tract Society, 1903); his sermons, titled *Grace and Glory*, rev. ed. (Edinburgh: Banner of Truth, 2020), first published in 1922; *The Self Disclosure of Jesus* (New York: George H. Doran, 1926); *Pauline Eschatology* (Princeton: Princeton University Press, 1930); and *Biblical Theology*, 3rd ed. (Edinburgh: Banner of Truth, 2014), first printed in 1934 and again in 1948. The theme of *Biblical Theology* was already articulated in his inaugural lecture, "The Idea of Biblical Theology as a Science and as a Theological Discipline," at Princeton in 1894. For more information on Vos's view of the atonement in its historical context, see Gamble, "Doctrine of the Atonement," 258–60.

51. There are more than two hundred and fifty references to Vos in *WCG2*. On his philosophy of redemptive history, see Richard C. Gamble, *The Whole Counsel of God*, vol. 2, *The Full Revelation of God* (Phillipsburg, NJ: P&R Publishing, 2018), 62–65.

52. Dennison, *Letters of Vos*, 20n27; and 35 for more information on Warfield and Stevenson.

broke as he watched the Princeton he loved rot internally. He considered futile any attempt at reforming the Presbyterian Church (USA).[53]

J. Gresham Machen (A.D. 1881–1937).[54] John Gresham Machen was born in Baltimore to a wealthy and prominent family. He was educated in classics at Johns Hopkins University. In 1902 he began seminary at Princeton, and after graduating he studied further at the University of Marburg in Germany. Machen served as the professor of NT at Princeton Seminary between 1906 and 1929. He had been deeply influenced by his studies under Wilhelm Herrmann in Germany, and because of the doubts that boiled up from those studies, he postponed his ordination until 1914.

Machen wrote *The Origin of Paul's Religion* (1921), a brilliant critique of the liberal notion that Pauline thought is based on Greek philosophy and opposed to the teaching of Jesus. His *New Testament Greek for Beginners* (1923) was used by seminaries for decades and is still in use today by some schools. *Christianity and Liberalism* (1923) was a true theological blockbuster. For Machen, liberalism was not simply a variant form of Christianity, like the Baptist and Presbyterian traditions, for example; to Machen, liberalism was an affront to Christianity. It preached another gospel and another Christ.[55] Machen believed that Christianity is a rational religion, not one based on feeling.[56] In 1932, he published an article titled "The Importance of Christian Scholarship." In this work, he argued that humble, excellent Christian scholarship is essential for evangelism because the facts of the gospel are foundational to the Christian faith, not a religious

---

53. Ibid., 35–36.
54. See Ned B. Stonehouse, *J. Gresham Machen: A Biographical Memoir* (Grand Rapids: Eerdmans, 1954); Paul Woolley, *The Significance of J. Gresham Machen Today* (Nutley, NJ: Presbyterian and Reformed, 1977); D. G. Hart, *Defending the Faith: J. Gresham Machen and the Crisis of Conservative Protestantism in Modern America* (Phillipsburg, NJ: P&R Publishing, 2003); and D. G. Hart, ed., *J. Gresham Machen: Selected Shorter Writings* (Phillipsburg, NJ: P&R Publishing, 2004).
55. J. Gresham Machen, *Christianity and Liberalism* (New York: Macmillan, 1923), 81: "Jesus was not for Paul merely an example for faith; He was primarily the object of faith. The religion of Paul did not consist in having faith in God like the faith which Jesus had in God; it consisted rather in having faith *in Jesus*. . . . The plain fact is that imitation of Jesus, important though it was for Paul, was swallowed up by something far more important still. Not the example of Jesus, but the redeeming work of Jesus, was the primary thing for Paul."
56. K. Scott Oliphint, "Machen and Philosophy," in *Christianity and Liberalism*, by J. Gresham Machen, legacy edition (Philadelphia: Westminster Seminary Press, 2019), 205.

experience. Further, good scholarship is also essential to apologetics and to the establishment and growth of a healthy church. And the preaching of such a church should concentrate on a transcendent God, human misery and guilt, and the mystery of salvation in Christ.[57]

Machen lived in a time of great controversy. In a struggle for denominational control, the modernists insisted on reorganizing the Princeton board of directors and added two signers of the Auburn Affirmation. This move was more than Machen could stand, and in protest he founded Westminster Theological Seminary in 1929. Not long thereafter, because of unfaithfulness in his denomination's foreign mission board, he founded the Independent Board for Presbyterian Foreign Missions. The leadership of his denomination had had enough of Machen's protest; they turned on him and ejected him from fellowship. Thus, in 1936, Machen founded the Orthodox Presbyterian Church. Not long afterward, he died of pneumonia at only fifty-five years of age.

At the beginning of the twentieth century, American evangelical Protestantism wore a different face than it did for many decades afterward. In many ways, the religious culture of America at this time was far different from what it is in the twenty-first century. Furthermore, there were significant differences in the religious climate of the American north and south. This reality was reflected in a northern and southern Presbyterian church, as well as in northern and southern branches of many evangelical denominations.[58]

Machen was not only an excellent churchman and NT scholar, but he was also vitally concerned with the social issues of his day. He was a foundational figure in twentieth-century Protestantism, particularly within the Presbyterian church. His writings on social issues began in 1918. Machen is also helpful when viewed as a north/south figure. Most of his working life was spent in New Jersey, but he was born south of the Mason-Dixon line and can very much be identified with southern concerns as well.[59] We will briefly examine a number of his positions articulated in writing between 1918 and 1933.

---

57. See Sandy Finlayson, "Machen and Scholarship," in *Christianity and Liberalism*, by J. Gresham Machen, legacy edition (Philadelphia: Westminster Seminary Press, 2019), 221–24.

58. *HWPT*, 292–93.

59. For example, in a letter to G. H. Hospers, Machen stated that the southern states in the Civil War were "acting in the plainest possible exercise of constitutional rights, and that the

In 1918, at thirty-seven years of age, Machen wrote a letter to congressman John R. Ramsen—a letter that was recorded in the congressional minutes. He wrote to the congressman concerning the Susan B. Anthony amendment addressing women's suffrage. Machen still struggled with whether or not it was proper for women to receive the right to vote—certainly, the social climate a century ago was vastly different from today! But that issue was not Machen's reason for writing his letter. He was concerned with the process of how constitutional changes were made. He was convinced that the question of suffrage ought to be granted to states. And he was confident that the men of New Jersey were against it; after all, they had voted against it in 1915. Machen was convinced that a national referendum would defeat the issue.[60]

The importance of this letter is Machen's basic principle behind the letter, not his view on women's suffrage. This letter makes evident Machen's desire for the protection of individual liberty. This liberty can be protected by states' rights and by referendum, both of which Machen advocated. He was decidedly against the notion of a minority ruling over a majority. This simple conviction would reverberate throughout his writings.

In 1924, Machen dealt with a number of social issues, including child labor and social progress. He held that there were other evils that had been only temporarily arrested. One such example was the (misnamed) child-labor amendment. This amendment was "designed to give Congress power to limit, regulate, and prohibit the labor of persons under 18 years of age."[61] Machen was convinced that this amendment constituted the government's attempt to usurp family rights, and he held that this type of legislation should be made only by the states. Some of his other attempts at reform included the repeal

---

real revolution was entered into by those who endeavored to prevent such plainly guaranteed rights" (as cited by Russell, *Voices of Fundamentalism*, 147).

60. Congressional record, as cited by Russell, *Voices of Fundamentalism*, 147. Machen closed the letter with these words: "In short, the present amendment represents an attempt to avoid a popular [male] vote (which could be overwhelmingly negative) on an exceedingly momentous question. The suffrage leaders are absolutely unscrupulous in their choice of means. All fairness, all true democracy, all united effort in the present war are abandoned ruthlessly in the interest of an ill-timed and unintelligent feminism. Do such leaders really represent the women of this country? For my part I do not believe it for a moment" (ibid.).

61. Ibid., 148.

of New York's Lusk laws, which placed private teachers under state supervision and control; the invalidation of the Nebraska language law, which made it a crime to study any language besides English before the eighth grade, even in private schools; and the prevention of the establishment of a federal department of education.

Machen outlined the issues of fundamentalism and social progress in an excellent article titled "Does Fundamentalism Obstruct Social Progress?" from 1924. The theological and social situation of this era was colored by events of the preceding century. The question Machen addressed in the article is understandable in the light of his context. Many considered fundamentalism, which stood against the Social Gospel movement, to be against social progress. Machen was called on to defend fundamentalism relative to social issues. But was Machen even a fundamentalist? He began the article by declaring himself to be a fundamentalist, yet only within certain parameters. He wrote that a fundamentalist was not necessarily a premillennialist but instead was one who "definitely and polemically maintained a belief in supernatural Christianity as over against the Modernism of the present day."[62]

In this article, Machen attacked the Social Gospel without so much as naming it. He understood that many consider historic Christianity to be inimical to social progress. Many had established a sort of dichotomy: the older evangelism sought to win individuals, while the newer (and supposedly better) evangelism endeavored to bring down the kingdom of God on the earth through the improvement of physical conditions and the reparation of broken relations.[63] Machen was convinced that this is a false dichotomy. He wrote that Christianity is "social as well as individual. . . . When a man is rescued inwardly from the world, he is not, according to Christian teaching, allowed to escape from the world into a place of mystic contemplation, but is sent forth again into the world to battle for the right."[64] He ensured that his readers understood that Christianity always insists on the individual soul's rights.

62. J. Gresham Machen and Charles P. Fagnani, "*Does Fundamentalism Obstruct Social Progress?*" *The Survey Graphic* 5 (July 1924): 391.
63. Ibid., 392.
64. Ibid.

Machen concluded the article by responding to the contention that fundamentalism, or as he called it, "historic Christianity," is doctrinal rather than practical. Machen thought that even this objection betrayed narrow-mindedness. The church, Machen argued, was not caught in a dichotomy between analyzing the basis of its faith and relieving people's physical distresses; rather, "as a matter of fact she ought to do both. Neglect of either one will certainly bring disaster." He later said that "if the intellectual defense of our faith causes us to neglect our duty to the poor, we have made ourselves guilty of a great sin." Machen longed for a revival of religion akin to the Reformation, and when it comes, he said, "it will destroy no fine or unselfish or noble thing; it will hasten and not hinder the relief of the physical distresses of men and the improvement of conditions in this world."[65] In this same article, however, Machen emphasized that no matter the practical problems, no matter how pressing the economic need, mindfulness of the soul was of the utmost importance.

Two years later, in 1926, Machen appeared in Washington before a congressional committee to speak against a federal department of education.[66] Although he perceived the monopolistic control of education by the state to be the worst infringement, he was also opposed to a permanent military draft. Machen held this view not because of pacificist convictions but because he believed that the draft was an invasion of personal liberty.[67]

Prohibition was another pressing issue of the day. The Prohibition movement, which began when fourteen states prohibited the consumption of alcohol prior to the Civil War, reached its high-water mark in 1919 when the Eighteenth Amendment to the United States Constitution was ratified. The amendment prohibited the manufacture, sale, or transportation of intoxicating liquors.[68] On this issue, American evangelicals (in general) spoke with one voice. Evangelicals were generally silent on many other topics, but on prohibition, men even such as Dwight L. Moody, who was a strong contender for the separation of church and politics, pressed for the prohibition drive.

65. Ibid.
66. Russell, *Voices of Fundamentalism*, 148.
67. Ibid., 149.
68. Reichley, *Religion in American Public Life*, 217.

Most would expect Machen, a fundamentalist, to have joined the march for prohibition and speak out on the evils of alcohol consumption. But Machen did neither one. In 1926, his Presbytery of New Brunswick entertained a resolution to endorse the prohibition amendment. Machen voted against endorsing it. His negative vote was received with criticism, which prompted his writing a response. This response gives insight into his position on the relationship between the church and social issues. Machen wrote that his negative vote was not meant to express an opinion on prohibition itself but, rather, was intended to express that the church should not, in its corporate capacity, as distinguished from the activities of its individual members, be on record with regard to political questions of this nature. The church should not step foot into the political field.[69]

Machen believed that individual Christians could, and sometimes should, endorse legislation, as exemplified by Machen on the matter of suffrage. But he advocated that a distinction be made between acting as citizens in the public arena and the actions of the corporate ecclesiastical body. Machen's position on church involvement in the political field would help determine Presbyterian social policy following his death. Many held to a broad understanding of the limits of the political field, thus limiting the jurisdiction of the church's activity to the bounds of the individual soul.

In the following decade, Machen believed that the foremost social problem was an encroaching denial of individual liberties. In 1933 he made his major address on the church and social issues. He presented a paper titled "The Responsibility of the Church in Our New Age" to the American Academy of Political and Social Science. The paper sought to explain the nature of the church and the new age. With regard to the church, Machen believed that some old things were worth retaining—for example, he held that Homer and the Amiens Cathedral are superior to contemporary art nouveau. In the political

---

69. Machen said: "The Church, I hold, ought to refrain from entering, in its corporate capacity, into the political field." For support, he cited chapter 31, Article 4, of the WCF. It reads as follows: "Synods and councils are to handle or conclude nothing, but that which is ecclesiastical; and are not to intermeddle with civil affairs which concern the commonwealth, unless by way of humble petition in cases extraordinary; or by way of advice for satisfaction of conscience, if they be thereunto required by the civil magistrate" (see *Westminster Confession of Faith* [Atlanta: Committee for Christian Education and Publications, Presbyterian Church in America, 1986]).

and social sciences, Machen believed that civil and religious liberty should be maintained.[70]

Then also in 1933, Machen defined the church.[71] For him, the church was radically doctrinal, intolerant, and ethical.[72] Machen found it easiest to define the church with negatives—by what she is not. The church was neither a society of general welfare nor to be engaged in political activities.[73] Furthermore, the church was not to offer any official pronouncements on the political or social questions of the day, and the church should not be expected to cooperate with the state in any matter involving force. Thus, when the church becomes a mechanism for political measure, "the Church is turning aside from its proper mission, which is to bring to bear upon human hearts the solemn and imperious, yet also sweet and gracious, appeal of the gospel of Christ."[74] Yet the church was also to be radically ethical and to express that quality in love. "It will offer men simple benefits," said Machen, "it will never pass coldly by on the other side when a man is in bodily need. But it will never be content to satisfy men's bodily needs."

In sum, Machen was a pioneer of many sorts and a man of extraordinary talent. He was a careful and insightful scholar, the founder of Westminster Theological Seminary, and the founder of a new denomination that preserved conservative Presbyterian theology. He was also a man who was vitally concerned about the social issues of his day. He held that political activity in social issues was to be carried out by individual Christians, not by the church at large.

EVANGELICAL AND REFORMED THEOLOGY

Modern Evangelical Theology. The roots of American evangelical theology can be traced to a number of places: in eighteenth-century

70. J. Gresham Machen, "Essentials for Prosperity," *The Annals of the American Academy of Political and Social Science* 165 (January, 1933): 2: "To those lovers of civil and religious liberty, I confess that I belong," said Machen, "in fact, civil and religious liberty seems to me to be more valuable than any other earthly thing—than any other thing short of that truer profounder liberty which only God can give."
71. Calhoun, *Princeton Seminary*, 2:221–35.
72. Machen, "Essentials for Prosperity," 6.
73. Ibid., 7.
74. Ibid., 9. See his "Essentials for Prosperity," 2ff. Later he asserted nine.

England, concomitant with the rise of the Wesleyan movement;[75] in the Pietist movement in eighteenth-century Germany; and, more recently, in nineteenth-century thought.[76] In the 1920s, nearly all the members of the Association of Theological Schools (ATS), the main accrediting body for seminaries in the United States and Canada, were connected either with university graduate schools or were large, mainline, financially endowed seminaries. After World War II, the first American evangelical seminary was accredited: Fuller Theological Seminary in California.[77] Thus it could be argued that modern evangelical theology as an institutionalized movement is a post–World War II phenomenon.

Evangelical theology in early twentieth-century America was marked by certain characteristics. One of those characteristics was that evangelical theology transcended denominational boundaries. In the United States, evangelicals were found throughout an array of mainline denominations, including the United Methodist Church, the United Presbyterian Church, the Evangelical Lutheran Church, and the Southern Baptist Church. Yet there were opponents to both fundamentalism and evangelicalism in each one of these denominations. At times, evangelical theology was tied more closely to transdenominational or parachurch institutions than to ecclesiastical bodies.[78]

Within modern evangelicalism, evangelical theology is still widely held in Baptist churches, in earlier Methodist churches (though sadly not in the contemporary United Methodist Church), and within the Wesleyan tradition. Most fundamentalists hold to a premillennial view of the end times. In the Presbyterian world, fundamentalism more

75. On the Wesleyan movement, see T. A. Langford, *Practical Divinity: Theology in the Wesleyan Tradition* (Nashville: Abingdon Press, 1984).

76. On Pietism, see F. E. Stoeffler, *The Rise of Evangelical Pietism* (Leiden: Brill, 1965), and also his *German Pietism during the Eighteenth Century* (Leiden: Brill, 1973).

77. It is interesting that there are more students enrolled in evangelical seminaries than there are in the mainline seminaries. But the mainline seminaries twenty years ago had seven times more endowment funds than did evangelical seminaries (as reported by Dr. Dan Aleshire, former executive director of the Association for Theological Schools, in a lecture presented in Orlando, Florida, in August 2001). On the influence of Fuller Seminary, see Iain H. Murray, *Evangelicalism Divided: A Record of Crucial Change in the Years 1952–2000* (Edinburgh: Banner of Truth, 2000), 24–26.

78. Two examples are the institutions of Fuller Theological Seminary in California and Dallas Theological Seminary in Texas. Other examples of strongholds of evangelical theology are the parachurch institutions of InterVarsity Christian Fellowship, Campus Crusade for Christ, The Navigators, and the widespread publication *Christianity Today*.

closely aligns itself to the new-school branches in contrast to what is termed *old-school* Presbyterianism.[79]

Reformed Theology. In general, the term *Reformed theology* is much easier to define than is *evangelical theology*. Reformed theology has its roots in the Reformation of the sixteenth century and stands atop the shoulders of men like John Calvin and John Knox.

In the United States, Reformed theology is most often associated with particular denominations, which include the large and smaller Presbyterian churches as well as the large and smaller Continental Reformed denominations—such as the Christian Reformed, Reformed Church of America, and other smaller groups.

Though there are many denominations that have adopted the title *Reformed*, it goes without saying that not all theology that claims to be Reformed is actually so. The old-Princeton theologian B. B. Warfield defined Reformed theology simply as "biblical Christianity come into its own."[80] Yet even this definition is not received without contention. Reformed theology is generally represented by those individuals and denominations that hold to the classic Reformed and Presbyterian confessions—namely, the Westminster Confession of Faith, the Belgic Confession, the Heidelberg Catechism, and the Canons of Dordt, in conjunction with the more modern notion of biblical inerrancy.

The Relationship between Reformed and Evangelical Theology. Reformed and evangelical theology have much in common. The Reformed confessions uphold and cherish all the major theological marks of evangelicalism. The two also stand in agreement that a profession of faith in Jesus Christ should bear impact on a person's life. Both movements also value individual and corporate piety and the separation of church and state.[81] But Reformed and evangelical theology are not without their differences.

---

79. Murray, *Evangelicalism Divided*, 1–24.

80. One of Warfield's best definitions of the Reformed faith is found in Benjamin B. Warfield, "A Brief and Non-Technical Statement of the Reformed Faith," in *Selected Shorter Writings of Benjamin B. Warfield*, ed. John E. Meeter, 2 vols. (Phillipsburg, NJ: P&R Publishing, 1970), 1:407–10.

81. Evangelical theology is a bastion of church/state separation. Machen's support for a strong separation of the church and the state has been earlier noted. Granted, the British and Continental Reformed tradition is historically less strong on the issue of church/state separation. In fact, the WCF as originally written was against it.

The Reformed confessions are neither fundamentalist nor evangelical in nature, for Reformed confessions articulate a particular relationship between theology and life. Also, Reformed theology does not have a limited notion of piety; instead, it believes that piety should pervade the individual life. In contrast to classic Anabaptist theology, Reformed theology teaches that Jesus Christ, in his mediatorial kingship, has dominion in every sphere of life, including the political, cultural, and educational.[82] Both Continental Reformed thought and British Presbyterianism are firmly united on the mediatorial kingship of Christ.[83]

While there is much that weds Reformed and evangelical thought, their disagreements have at times fostered antagonism and fear. Many evangelicals and fundamentalists feared the work of liberal theologian Walter Rauschenbuch in his *A Theology for the Social Gospel* (1917), for to them his truncated theology of the Social Gospel sounded far too similar to Reformed theology.[84] Evangelicals and the Reformed also viewed prohibition differently. Evangelical theology was unified in its stance against alcohol, but within the Continental Reformed community and other Presbyterian groups, alcohol was simply a part of life.[85]

The Reformed community also had its fears of evangelicalism, particularly in relation to the individual and society and the role of

82. The 1529 Schleitheim Confession of the Anabaptists and Mennonites asserted that civil government is outside the perfection of Christ and that Christians were not to participate in civil government. As observed in the previous chapter, Abraham Kuyper is an example of opposition to this position with his proper cry for the crown rights of King Jesus.

83. American Presbyterianism, even in the smaller conservative denominations, has not always kept in line with this classic Presbyterian teaching.

84. On the Social Gospel movement, see the classic work of William Temple, *Christianity and Social Order* (New York: Hammondsworth, 1942). For evangelical comment on the movement, see David F. Wright, ed., *Essays in Evangelical Social Ethics* (Exeter: Paternoster, 1979).

85. The issue of prohibition produced tremendous stress within the Presbyterian church in the 1930s. At the third and fourth general assemblies of the Orthodox Presbyterian Church (OPC), there were overtures from seven presbyteries urging the church as an institution to take a stand for total abstinence by all her ministers and elders. The OPC's fourth General Assembly approved a motion to take no action at that time. The issue did not surface in that particular denomination for another five years. The OPC General Assembly eventually elected a committee to study the "relationship of the OPC to society in general and to other ecclesiastical bodies in particular, with a view to bringing to the next assembly recommendations suggesting ways and means whereby the message and methods of our church may be better implemented to meet the needs of this generation and the OPC may have an increasing array of influence and make a greater impact on life today." After much effort and many meetings, the committee produced a majority report and a minority report and concluded that the committee should not be continued. There was no official answer to the broader or narrower questions of alcohol consumption.

doctrine in the church and life. Machen openly labeled himself a fundamentalist. And recognizing the evangelical fear of the Social Gospel, Machen opposed it. Yet Machen held that while Christianity does seek after the individual soul, it is in no way inimical to social progress.[86] He believed that the choice between the individual soul and the progress of society was a false dichotomy; for him, Christianity was both individual and social.[87] The deep issue for Machen was to affirm that Christianity was doctrinal rather than practical, that is, there is no dichotomy between the basis of faith or doctrine and relieving physical distress. On these topics, tensions continue between these two groups even today.

SOCIALISM, EXISTENTIALISM, AND THE BREAKDOWN OF ABSOLUTES

This final section analyzes the early twentieth century and examines American and European thinkers who stood against Christ and his gospel. Every one of these thinkers arrived at different answers to life's pressing questions, but every one of their answers led only to despair and hopelessness.

W. E. B. Du Bois (A.D. 1868–1963). At the age of sixteen, W. E. B. Du Bois was the valedictorian of his high school in Massachusetts. He went on to attend Fisk College, from where he graduated at twenty years of age. Two years later, in 1890, he received his second bachelor's degree from Harvard, where he also earned a master's degree the following year. He then received a scholarship from President Rutherford B. Hayes to study at the prestigious University of Berlin, where he spent two years. In Berlin, he studied with the most prominent social scientists of his day. In 1895, at the age of twenty-seven, he returned to the United States to finish his doctorate at Harvard. He was the first African American to receive the doctorate from Harvard.

After completing his education, Du Bois taught at Wilberforce College in Ohio for two years, then received a special fellowship from the University of Pennsylvania to research African Americans living

---

86. Machen, "Does Fundamentalism Obstruct," 392.
87. Ibid.

in Philadelphia. In 1899 his research culminated in his book *The Philadelphia Negro*. In 1897, he transitioned to a position at Atlanta University, now Clark Atlanta University, where he built a sociology department. He created a full-scale exhibit of African American achievements for the 1900 Paris World's Fair, a project funded in part by the United States government.

In 1910, Du Bois was appointed director of publications and research for the NAACP and edited *The Crisis Magazine* for twenty-five years. Following World War I, he attended the Paris Peace Conference as a representative of the NAACP. He also held the first Pan-African meeting at the Paris Conference. He was intrigued by the successes of the 1917 Russian Revolution, and in 1927 he visited Russia. By 1930 Du Bois had grown dissatisfied with the NAACP movement and resigned in 1934. He then taught at Atlanta University until he was forced to retire in 1944 at the age of seventy-six.

As would be expected from his ties to Russia and communism, Du Bois was formally investigated by the Federal Bureau of Investigation (FBI) in 1942. The Department of Justice harassed him and pressured him to register as a foreign agent. He refused to do so. In 1945, he was elected as international president at the fifth Pan-African Congress. He visited communist China in 1953 and returned with nothing but favorable things to say about Joseph Stalin—Du Bois claimed that few men of the twentieth century even approached Stalin's stature. At age eighty-two, he ran for the United States Senate in New York on the American Labor Party ticket, and in 1958, at ninety, he helped establish a left-wing political coalition in New York. In 1959 he received the Lenin Peace Prize, and he joined the Communist Party USA in 1961.

In 1963 Du Bois left the United States and became a citizen of Ghana and an official member of the Communist Party in Ghana. The night before Martin Luther King's "I Have a Dream" speech, Du Bois died. He was honored in 1992 by a postage stamp bearing his image, and in 1994 the library of the University of Massachusetts Amherst was named in his honor.[88]

88. Robert Gooding-Williams, "W. E. B. Du Bois," in *The Stanford Encyclopedia of Philosophy*, ed. Edward N. Zalta, Spring 2020, https://plato.stanford.edu/archives/spr2020/entries /dubois/. Access date April 12, 2020.

Du Bois authored twenty-two books, five of which were novels, and established or edited four journals. In 1903 he authored *The Souls of Black Folk*; and in 1935 he wrote a Marxist interpretation of the post–CivilWar era in the South titled *Black Reconstruction* (1935), which examined in a positive light the work of African Americans during that period. In 1940, Du Bois wrote his autobiography, titled *Dusk of Dawn*, which explored his notions of the African and African-American quest for freedom.

Du Bois felt like a stranger to American life.[89] His goal was to transform White America's perception of and attitude toward Black Americans.[90] Thus, in vivid and powerful descriptions, Du Bois wrote of the desperate condition of the African American. His writing spoke into African Americans' questions and hurts. The following is a brief examination of his economic, political, sociological, educational, and religious views.

Du Bois was primarily concerned with the (unequal) distribution of the world's goods. He looked out on a world with a chasm between the very rich and the very poor, and he blamed private ownership for the disparity.[91] He believed that, inherently, private ownership made the rich richer and the poor very much more so.[92] Hence he advocated communist ownership of goods to ensure that the greatest number of people could benefit.[93] He was convinced that deep down, the civilized world knew that there ought to be public ownership of capital.[94] His plan for the transition to public ownership began with the public utilities and certain monopolies; then eventually, enacting the plan would culminate in the public ownership of land.[95]

---

89. W. E. B. Du Bois, *Dark Water: Voices from within the Veil* (Mineola, NY: Dover Publications, 1999), v.

90. Ibid., vi.

91. Ibid., 57.

92. Ibid.: "Today, therefore, we are challenging this ownership; we are demanding general consent as to what materials shall be privately owned and as to how materials shall be used."

93. Ibid., 56: "Our great ethical question today is, therefore, how may we justly distribute the world's goods to satisfy the necessary wants of the mass of men"; and 58: "What I had to show was that no real reorganization of industry could be permanently made with the majority of mankind left out. These disinherited darker peoples must either share in the future industrial democracy or take over the world."

94. Ibid., 86.

95. Ibid., 91–92: The communist movement should be from carefully crafted transitions to "the use of taxation to limit inheritance and to take the unearned increment for public use

He also called for African Americans to escape the perils inherent to servile work.[96] He considered their work to be, in essence, serfdom.[97] Though Du Bois himself was not a Christian, he used religious rhetoric to convince African Americans of the injustice of their working conditions.[98] In his day, Black men were paid 25 to 75 percent less than White men for the same work. This wage discrepancy broke down the family unit. The system had made it economically impossible for the man to be the sole provider for his household. The pushes and pulls of the culture forced African-American families to take on a different dynamic from that of White families. In African-American homes, the mother and father, by necessity, functioned differently in their roles.

Du Bois also had strong views on political theory. He taught that democracy's responsibility was to bring justice to all human beings within a nation and that democracy could not bar a class of people from justice simply because they were judged, incorrectly, to be inferior.[99] He was convinced that to argue that African Americans were unfit to vote merely because they were poorly educated was a defective argument.[100] He taught, instead, that democracy was founded on the worth, not the intelligence, of individual citizens, and these citizens have the right and the ability to judge the merits of their leaders' actions.[101] Du Bois saw the struggle of a majority-rule democracy to be to address minority

---

beginning (but not ending) with a 'single tax' on monopolized land values; the training of the public in business technique by co-operation in buying and selling, and in industrial technique by the shop committee and manufacturing guild."

96. Ibid., 64. Du Bois somehow instinctively hated servile work. He was convinced that it was because he was raised in New England rather than in the Carolinas that he was able to escape its taint; and 69: "Here the absurdity ends. Here all honest minds turn and ask: Is menial service permanent or necessary?"

97. Ibid., 66: "In 1880, 30 percent were servants and 65 percent were serfs. The percentage of servants then rose slightly and fell again to 21 percent who were in service in 1910 and, doubtless, much less than 20 percent today. This is the measure of our rise, but the Negro will not approach freedom until this hateful badge of slavery and medievalism has been reduced to less than 10 percent."

98. Ibid.: "The paths of salvation for the emancipated host of black folk lay no longer through the kitchen door with its wide hall and pillared veranda and flowered yard beyond."

99. Ibid., 82, 84.

100. Ibid., 81: "We say easily, for instance, 'The ignorant ought not to vote.' We would say, 'No civilized state should have citizens too ignorant to participate in government,' and this statement is but a step to the fact: that no state is civilized which has citizens too ignorant to help rule it. Or, in other words, education is not a prerequisite to political control—political control is the cause of popular education."

101. Ibid., 83.

positions, for a democracy reflects and represents all those whom it governs, not just the majority.[102] He thought that a mature democracy would learn to heed the concerns and cares of its minorities.[103] The theoretical foundation for laws, he said, has no reference to any type of divine authority but simply to brute fact, to science, and to human wants.[104] While there may be certain natural laws, most laws are simply the fruit of self-interest established to serve the powerful.[105]

In regard to sociology, Du Bois considered the African American's economic and sociological disadvantages to be nearly insurmountable.[106] He was convinced that a woman's right to vote was not a privilege but a necessity. He had heard the arguments against women's right to vote, and he was shocked that even some women could agree with those arguments,[107] which he dismissed as pure, blinding ignorance. Du Bois was not ignorant of the cost, however, that would be involved in gaining the right for women to vote.[108]

In 1918, African-American women faced insult and abuse. Du Bois considered it to be unforgivable (both on earth and in heaven) to deny African-American women the simple courtesy offered to White women. He believed that only prostitutes faced treatment similar to that of African-American women![109] As a result of mistreatment, one in seven Black women was separated from her husband as compared to one in ten White women.[110] The broken homes of the African-American community resulted in childless wives and husbandless mothers. Du Bois longed for the home that had free, married women with children.[111]

102. Ibid., 87.
103. Ibid., 88.
104. Ibid., 90. Du Bois asked what a democracy was to do when there was a fully functional democracy where all groups could vote. "In matters of Truth and Faith and Beauty, the Ancient Law was inexcusably strait and modern law unforgivably stupid. . . . This does not say that everything here is governed by incontrovertible 'natural' law which needs no human decision as to raw materials, machinery, prices, wages, news-dissemination, education of children, etc."
105. Ibid., 91. Few know who makes the powerful inner rules. Some hold these rules to be "natural . . . a part of our inescapable physical environment. Some of them doubtless are; but most of them are just as clearly the dictates of self-interest laid down by the powerful private persons who today control industry."
106. Ibid., 105.
107. Ibid., 84.
108. Ibid., 85.
109. Ibid., 100.
110. Ibid., 104–5.
111. Ibid., 107.

He believed that a woman's freedom to work, and to be paid reasonably for her work, was worth a high price.[112]

Du Bois also believed that the educational system had failed. He believed that system had begun working simply to reinforce the status quo rather than to develop the mind fully and robustly.[113] In addition, the rotting of the educational system was also a result of the South's determination to promulgate the ignorance of African Americans.[114] As long as African-American children were kept from school, there could be no advance.[115] He called for a complete change of thought regarding education. No longer should humans merely exist for work, rather, work should be a tool used to promote human flourishing and democracy.[116]

Regarding Christianity and faith, Du Bois looked on White Christianity as an utter failure.[117] After all, the Southern Presbyterian church witnessed the tragedy of slavery and stood by.[118] In his eyes Christianity had failed, and Du Bois proposed a new faith—one of humanity that would transcend all forms of prejudice based on color.[119] Since no one knows whether there is a resurrection, he asserted, continuing life should be seen in the training of the next generation.[120] Du Bois believed that if Christianity were to continue within the Black community, it would need to be distinct from all White expressions of faith.

112. Ibid.

113. He was writing before/during the time of John Dewey. Ibid., 121: "We say, morally, that high character is conformity to present public opinion; we say industrially that the present order is best and that children must be trained to perpetuate it." Du Bois argues that, in contrast, "the object of education is manhood and womanhood, clear reason, individual talent and genius and the spirit of service and sacrifice."

114. Ibid., 122.

115. Ibid., 124.

116. Ibid., 123.

117. Ibid., 20–21, 36: "Missionaries and commerce have left some good with all their evil. In black Africa today there are more than a thousand government schools and more than thirty thousand mission schools, with a more or less regular attendance of three-quarters of a million school children"; and 40: "The real effort to modernize Africa should be through schools not churches."

118. Ibid., 99: "The Presbyterian synod of Kentucky said to the churches under its care in 1835: 'Brothers and sisters, parents and children, husbands and wives, are torn asunder and permitted to see each other no more. These acts are daily occurring in the midst of us. The shrieks and agony often witnessed on such occasions proclaim, with a trumpet tongue, the iniquity of our system. There is not a neighborhood where these heartrending scenes are not displayed. There is not a village or road that does not behold the sad procession of manacled outcasts whose mournful countenances tell that they are exiled by force from all that their hearts hold dear."

119. Ibid., 40.

120. Ibid., 114.

In sum, Du Bois was a brilliant spokesman who fought against injustice and cast light on the blind spots of Christianity. He was correct in his assessment that Southern Presbyterianism and Southern Baptists were wrong to watch racial atrocities unfold before their eyes; nevertheless, Christianity itself cannot be discounted because Christians throughout history have failed to live in accordance with biblical values. But for answers, Du Bois did not seek to call for biblical reform; instead, he looked to Marxism and communism. This chapter now turns to another movement that sought to address more of humanity's questions.

Historical Background and General Description of Existentialism. The roots of twentieth-century existentialism are often traced back to the nineteenth-century Danish thinker Søren Kierkegaard (examined in the previous chapter).[121] The writings of Feodor Dostoyevsky (1821–1881) also contributed to the beginnings of the existentialist movement. In Germany, Nietzsche's preoccupation with the dilemma of human existence also pushed the existentialist movement into motion. Nietzsche's answer to the dilemma of existence was his declaration that God is dead.[122]

The roots of existentialism may go even deeper than any of these individuals' thinking—they may go to a sense of dissatisfaction with rationalistic humanism. The world no longer seemed to make sense. The individual found himself in a hostile world in which he was fighting for survival (and losing). The atrocities of World War I—with its bloody trenches and choking mustard gas—destroyed any lingering sense of romance that war carried with it and only contributed to the sense of disorientation.

Thus existentialism began in Germany in the wake of World War I. Its most popular exponents, however, were French thinkers following the second world war.[123] Existentialism is as much a tendency or

121. See Francis A. Schaeffer, *How Should We Then Live?* (Westchester, IL: Crossway, 1983), 163.

122. Colin Brown, *Philosophy & the Christian Faith: A Historical Sketch from the Middle Ages to the Present Day* (Downers Grove, IL: InterVarsity, 1968), 183.

123. Walter Kaufmann, ed., *Existentialism from Dostoevsky to Sartre* (Cleveland: Meridian, 1956); E. L. Alan, *Existentialism from Within* (London: Routledge/Kegan Paul, 1953). Frederick C. Copleston, *Contemporary Philosophy: Studies of Logical Positivism and Existentialism* (London: Burns & Oats, 1963), 127.

an attitude as it is an organized philosophical movement.[124] There is tremendous diversity among those who refer to themselves as *existentialists*. They range from self-proclaiming atheists to Christians, from those who refer to existentialism as a philosophical system to those who do not. An existentialist seeks to practice philosophy no longer as a detached spectator but as an actor in the middle of a drama. Many of the French existentialists protested against any and all systems of external authority.[125]

In sum, existentialism protested against modern society. It decried organized industry and political bureaucracies for hindering individual expression. It pushed back against modern society for pressing the individual into conformity. But as to a response, existentialists were not united, though many would lean into the philosophy of Karl Marx.

Martin Heidegger (A.D. 1889–1976).[126] Heidegger was a powerful and novel thinker, a brilliant philosopher, and a committed Nazi. He changed the way that many understood philosophy. But not all were favorable to Heidegger—there are more critical commentaries written of him than of anyone apart from Aristotle.

In 1909, Heidegger enrolled at the University of Freiburg in Breisgow as a student of Catholic theology. He then changed his course of study to mathematics, then again to philosophy. The main professor of philosophy at the University of Freiburg was Edmund Husserl, who had begun the philosophical movement of *phenomenology*. Husserl greatly assisted Heidegger's philosophical career.

Then World War I erupted. Heidegger began the war as the postal censor in Freiburg. He was then moved nearer to the front to be a meteorologist. His job was to determine wind direction to assist in the use of poison gases.

After the war, Heidegger married and moved to Marburg, where he assumed the position of associate professor of philosophy. But he had little taste for city life and would often retreat to a small hut in the Black Forest. This retreat became his spiritual refuge, his place of solitude. He began to see himself as a son of the Black Forest—he wore peasant clothing and chopped his own wood.

---

124. Brown, *Philosophy & Faith*, 181.
125. Ibid., 183.
126. Schaeffer, *How Should We Then Live?*, 168.

In 1928, after the retirement of Husserl, Heidegger filled the philosophy chair in Freiberg.[127] While in that city, Heidegger had an affair with a brilliant, Jewish student named Hannah Arendt. She would play a key role later in his life. Heidegger assumed the role of rector in April 1933, just several months after Hitler became chancellor of Germany. Heidegger's predecessor as rector had resigned in protest to Nazi actions.[128] But Heidegger was a committed Nazi.[129] In a disproportionate estimate of his own abilities, he believed that he could guide and control Hitler. He believed that if a government had the right philosopher as its guide, then the state would be successful; this belief revealed his deeply classical Greek thought. He was quickly disillusioned, however, and in the next year he stepped down as rector.

By 1944, Hitler's days were numbered. Freiberg was bombed and the university abandoned. Heidegger returned to the city, and reality along with it, and appeared before a de-Nazification committee. For months he faced investigations and interviews. The pressure was simply too much; Heidegger broke down in nervousness and attempted suicide. He was banned from teaching for five years. These days were the darkest ones of his life.

When the war had finally ended, French philosopher Jean-Paul Sarte (see below) cited Heidegger as being philosophically helpful. This support returned credibility to Heidegger and his thinking. He resumed teaching, and he began to gain respect internationally. After Heidegger apologized to Hannah Arendt for his actions, she, who was now living and writing in New York, helped to promote his work in the United States.

In the 1920s Heidegger left the Catholic Church and his teacher Husserl along with it. Over the course of his career Heidegger wrote a number of significant works, the most prominent of which was *Sein*

127. Husserl was Jewish. Heidegger differentiated individual Jews from Jewish culture. He was against the Jewification of German culture. Husserl, as a Jew, was banned from entering Freiburg buildings—and Heidegger did not stop the practice. Heidegger called for a notion of community—so did the Nazis. Individual authenticity moved to the *Volk*, or the *people*.

128. Thirteen professors had been forbidden the vote for the office of rector simply because they were Jewish.

129. The reason given for his allegiance to the Nazis is that Hitler, and the party, viewed themselves as rural, too, and claimed to offer a rural type of life.

und Zeit, or *Being and Time* (1927).[130] It was a masterpiece in philosophical writing, and a well-timed masterpiece at that. The world felt lost in the rubble of World War I. The philosophy of phenomenology had been abandoned, and *Being and Time* spoke into the disillusionment of the late 1920s. In this work he asked one question: What is meant by the verb *to be*? Had familiarity cloaked the mystery of this verb? His aim in this book was to interpret both time and being—and the book made Heidegger's name what it is today. All the intellectuals read this work and interacted with it. It generated excitement all over the world.[131]

Heidegger understood humanity to be caught up into a larger process. Human beings, as they exist in society, are both free and enslaved. Heidegger longed for humans to recognize their freedom and to realize their destiny in the light of their impending death.

Kant had earlier argued that space and time are of equal importance, and Heidegger disagreed. He believed that space is insignificant. Instead, he understood time and existence to be connected. Humans' being is in the process of becoming. He did not believe in a fixed human essence and saw Aristotle's *rational animal* as an abstraction.

Humans participate in practical actions and tasks. They really live in those things—they look forward to those events and tasks.[132] Heidegger argued that rural people in particular have a grasp of themselves and the world. Nevertheless, they are a minority. He believed that those who live in the city lose their sense of individuality. They are pressed into conformity and crushed by anxiety and inauthenticity. He warned his readers that they might lose themselves. In the 1920s, this book was breathtaking and prophetic.

Heidegger has been criticized by both friend and foe for perceived failures in his *Being and Time*. First, his technical terminology has proven to be a stumbling block to readers. Second, and more funda-

---

130. *HWPT*, 348: "To [Heidegger], the deepest question is: 'Why is there something rather than nothing?' . . . *Human being* he called *Dasein* ('being there')."

131. Martin Heidegger, *Vom Wesen Des Grundes. The Essence of Reasons: A Bilingual Edition, Incorporating the German Text*, trans. Terence Malick (Evanston, IL: Northwestern University Press, 1969).

132. *HWPT*, 348n44: "Heidegger, like the pragmatists, thinks that to know a thing is initially to know its use in my life."

mentally, many have critiqued his philosophical methodology. Every good philosopher's method is related to his goal. In *Being and Time*, Heidegger's goal was to elucidate the very nature of human being, and specifically to do that in a "concrete manner."[133] His goal was based on a threefold assumption: that man as being is responsible for his being, is thoroughly temporal in his being, and is able to leap from time to being itself.[134]

Heidegger's method is most often labeled as *phenomenological*. He attempts to elicit man's temporal being from universal structures of experience, which he asserts are the temporal horizon of human awareness. The thinker is somehow able to venture beyond temporal awareness to a deeper underlying structure. Unfortunately, Heidegger's disciples remain unaware of how they are to step into this deeper underlying structure.

While students have wrestled with Heidegger's suggestions, they conclude that the enterprise of *Being and Time* is unfinished.[135] Nevertheless, since this book was one of Heidegger's early writings, many of his followers hoped that he would provide answers to the how? question in his later works.

Just two years after *Being and Time* was published, Heidegger wrote *Vom Wesen des Grundes* (*The Essence of Reasons*). In this work he analyzed whether there is purpose in being. Heidegger did not believe that there is true human purpose in what has been called (after Kant) the "phenomenal realm of space and time." Instead, based on the thinking of the poets, he believed that humans can enter a realm of transcendence that is above the phenomenal world. The thinking person can look forward or upward to an absolute purpose.

In many ways, Heidegger's *Introduction to Metaphysics* (1953) dealt with the same issues as *Being and Time*.[136] In this work Heidegger critiqued Western philosophy's attempt to arrive at being by analyzing and transcending the opposites of being: becoming and appearance. Instead, Heidegger proposed a path similar to that of early Greek

133. Martin Heidegger, *Being and Time* (New York: Harper & Row, 1962), 1.

134. John M. Anderson, introduction to *Discourse on Thinking* (New York: Harper & Row, 1966), 16.

135. Ibid., 17.

136. Martin Heidegger, *Introduction to Metaphysics* (New Haven: Yale University Press, 1959).

philosophy: the thinker should simply intuit being. Yet again, his followers were unable to find this (supposedly) intuitive path.[137]

After these two failures, Heidegger shifted from his initial position. He redefined, in a major change, the defining character of human
being.[138] He believed there was a need to search for what he termed
a *new ground of meaning*.[139] Heidegger's search for a new ground
of meaning culminated in one of his later writings, *Discourse on
Thinking*.[140]

In *Discourse on Thinking*, Heidegger proposed that humanity's
nature is to be found in relationship to something else, something
beyond. He believed that inherent to human nature is a yearning
for transcendence that could be a transcendence to being. In other
words, he thought that to understand humanity, humans must transcend humanity.[141]

Heidegger's philosophical insight merits recognition. After many
years of search and struggle, and devouring the history of Western
philosophy along the way, Heidegger finally reached a foundational
philosophical truth. Both individually and collectively, human self-
awareness is incomplete when the locus of identity is strictly temporal
and inter/intrahuman. As Augustine rightly observed, the human heart
is restless until it finds its rest in God.

In 1976, Heidegger died. Many have struggled to think well about
his life, about this former Nazi who wrote insightful books. It should be
remembered that interesting books are written by not only good men.
Jean-Paul Sartre was another thinker who was on the quest for being.

Jean-Paul Sartre (A.D. 1905–1980).[142] Jean-Paul Sartre was born in
the early twentieth century in Paris. He studied psychology, history of
philosophy, logic, philosophy, ethics and sociology, and physics at the
École Normale Supérieure in Paris. Beginning in 1931, Sartre taught
at a number of French schools. But with the start of World War II he

---

137. Anderson, introduction, 19.
138. Heidegger confessed this as "forsaking an earlier position" in Martin Heidegger,
Unterwegs zur Sprache (Stuttgart: Pfullingen, 1959), 98–100.
139. Anderson, introduction, 20.
140. *Discourse on Thinking* was first published as *Gelassenheit* in 1959 (ET, New York:
Harper & Row, 1966).
141. Anderson, introduction, 22–23.
142. Schaeffer, *How Should We Then Live?*, 167.

was drafted into the French army. In 1940 he was captured by German troops. He was a prisoner of war for nine months, during which time he read Heidegger's *Being and Time*. Because of problems with his eyes, however, he was released from the German prison; upon his release, he returned to Paris to continue teaching.

Sartre's main philosophical work is *Being and Nothingness: An Essay on Phenomenological Ontology* (1943). In that work he covers the nature of being, nothingness, humanity, truth, and absolutes.

Sartre understood *being* to be full, opaque, and free from distinction—something without qualification or limitation.[143] Only being can come from being.[144] And by *nothingness*, Sartre meant *nonbeing*, or *negation*. Nothingness is real, or a component of the real. Humans are always present before the specter of nothingness. More specifically, sheer nothingness is not.[145] Thus the very origin of nothingness is a paradox, for the introduction of nothing requires a being, as nothingness cannot come from being. And Sartre taught that the being that introduced nothingness is human reality, or human consciousness.[146] Nothingness is connected to ignorance, or a lack of knowledge, which is a kind of nonbeing. This concept of *nothingness* helped formulate Sartre's definition of humanity.

Humanity is defined in terms of freedom, said Sarte. True humanity is freedom.[147] The human being is, and can be, detached from the world.[148] Humans can negate the world, and by doing so they attain freedom. When a person thinks about humanity, he or she knows that existence precedes essence. Man first exists, then he defines himself. There is no human nature as it is itself, "since there is no god to conceive it."[149] Humans are always free to choose a new essence, to decide what they will be.[150]

Since what Sartre calls nothingness—that is, making distinctions—comes into the world by humanity, humanity cannot be being. Man

---

143. Jean-Paul Sartre, *Being and Nothingness* (Secaucus, NJ: Citadel, 1977), 74.
144. Ibid., 23.
145. Ibid., 22.
146. Ibid., 24.
147. Ibid., 440.
148. Ibid., 24.
149. Jean-Paul Sartre, *Existentialism Is a Humanism* (New Haven: Yale University Press, 2007), 22. On the previous page, Sartre had made clear that he represents atheistic existentialism.
150. Sartre, *Being and Nothingness*, 510.

is thus . . . nothing. Man is what he wills himself to be. Each person's essence, however, is in the past.[151] Man defines himself in his present choices. Thus nonbeing is entwined in being.[152]

Regarding truth, Sartre understood truth to be a type of nonbeing. He reasoned that because truth concerns being, and something that is about being cannot be being itself, truth must be nothing. Because truth makes distinctions—for example, a table is not a grapefruit—truth cannot be in being.

Sartre had a problem dealing with absolutes. He insisted that the starting point of existentialism is found in the saying of the Russian Dostoyevsky, "If God did not exist, everything would be permitted."[153] Sartre was convinced that the true atheist must also disregard Christian morality.[154] He believed that all humans must individually establish their own value systems. He also taught that authentic humans must make real choices, for even avoiding a choice is in itself making a choice. Every choice that a human makes transforms him into the person he is becoming. Thus Sartre held that humans are the product of what they do, think, and choose.[155]

Sartre believed that humans make choices against the backdrop of lingering death from a sense of deep anxiety. Choices are made as part of humans' lonely existence. For Sartre, death marks everything and, in the end, demonstrates the unintelligibility of reality; death is the foundation of the absurd.[156] As a consistent atheist, Sartre demonstrates the agony or even horror of life without Christ.[157] Here, unbelieving thought has continued its deep downward spiral toward the abyss.

151. *HWPT*, 352: "We cannot live in the present without remembering the past; but the past *is not*. Nor can we live without anticipating the future; but the future, also, *is not*. . . . Sartre argues that existentialism is the best defender of responsibility."

152. Sartre, *Being and Nothingness*, 21.

153. Sartre, *Existentialism*, 28–29.

154. He was highly critical of earlier French atheists who still wanted some type of a priori law. They thought morality was needed. Sartre (*Existentialism*, 29) asserted: "If however, God does not exist, we will encounter no values or orders that can legitimize our conduct."

155. Sartre, *Being and Nothingness*, 510.

156. Sartre, *Existentialism*, 74–75; 78: "Since God does not exist and we all must die, everything is permissible."

157. *HWPT*, 357: "Existentialism, springing out of Kierkegaard and Nietzsche by way of Husserl, begins with the conviction that human consciousness, particularly the experience of choice, gives the philosopher access to levels of understanding unavailable to previous thinkers."

KEY TERMS

idealist philosophy
fundamentalism
Auburn Affirmation
Social Gospel
communism
existentialism

STUDY QUESTIONS

1. What were some of the economic, social, and intellectual problems that faced the West in the first decades of the twentieth century?
2. Are the five fundamentals sufficient to describe Christianity at the beginning of the twentieth century? Are they sufficient today?
3. Should Machen have founded an independent board for foreign missions, a new seminary, and a new denomination?
4. What do you think of Du Bois's analysis of problems in African-American society and his answers to those problems?
5. Existentialism as a philosophy is not as popular as it was in the middle of the twentieth century. Are there any parts of existentialism that you find attractive?

RESOURCES FOR FURTHER STUDY

Each one of Geerhardus Vos's works is nothing short of a treasure.

Vos, Geerhardus. *Grace and Glory*. Rev. ed. Edinburgh: Banner of Truth, 2020. Vos's sermons—a spiritual feast for all Christians.
———. *Pauline Eschatology*. Princeton: Princeton University Press, 1930. Should be read by every seminary student.

22

Middle Twentieth-Century Theology

APPROXIMATELY HALF THE THEOLOGIANS addressed in this chapter were born in the nineteenth century, with a few of the later ones living into the twenty-first century. The late 1960s will be used as a cutoff date of sorts for the scope of this chapter. The theologians addressed here come from European, British, and American backgrounds. Represented are theologians from within and outside the conservative Presbyterian tradition.[1]

RUDOLF BULTMANN (A.D. 1884–1976)[2]

Biography and Writings. Rudolf Bultmann studied at the universities of Marburg, Tübingen, and Berlin. He began teaching in 1912, and

1. Given the richness of philosophical and theological reflection during this era, and in the light of this chapter's length, a number of worthy theologians have not been presented, including Dietrich Bonhoeffer.
2. Some primary sources by Bultmann include: *Faith and Understanding*, trans. L. P. Smith (New York: Harper & Row, 1969); *Commentary on John* (Philadelphia: Westminster John Knox Press, 1971); *The History of the Synoptic Tradition*, trans. John Marsh (New York: Harper & Row, 1963); *Jesus Christ and Mythology* (New York: Scribner's Sons, 1958); *History and Eschatology: The Presence of Eternity* (New York: Harper & Row, 1957); *The Theology of the New Testament*, trans. K. Grobel, 2 vols. (New York: Scribner's Sons, 1951, 1955); *Theologie des Neuen Testaments*, 5 Aufl. (Tübingen: Mohr Siebeck, 1965); *Essays, Philosophical and Theological* (New York/London: Macmillan/SCM Press, 1955); *Existence and Faith* (London: Fontana, 1964); *Faith and Understanding: Collected Essays*, trans. L. P. Smith, Library of Philosophy and Theology (New York/London: Harper & Row/SCM Press, 1969); *Jesus and the Word* (New York: Scribner's Sons, 1934); *Primitive Christology in Its Contemporary Setting* (Minneapolis: Augsburg Fortress, 1975); *The Johannine Epistles: A Commentary* (Minneapolis:

in 1921 he returned to Marburg as professor of New Testament. He taught at Marburg until his retirement in 1951. Following his retirement, Bultmann lectured at Yale in 1951, then at Edinburgh in 1955.[3]

One of his earliest books was titled *Geschichte der Synoptischen Tradition*, published at Göttingen in 1921. Bultmann worked in form criticism, which had been advocated earlier by Johannes Weiss. Bultmann concluded that all the Gospels, including Mark, were theological, not historical, documents.[4]

Twenty years later, in *Das Evangelium des Johannes*, Bultmann argued that gnostic influences had entered into the thought world of the fourth gospel. In this gospel, any notion of history was sacrificed to theology.[5] Bultmann determined that modern readers can know almost nothing concerning the life and personality of Jesus. He added, "and it is even denied that he ever claimed to be the Messiah."[6]

Bultmann denied the direct revelational significance of any of the so-called *facts* in the NT. He conceded that the information of the NT could, nevertheless, bear meaning for a reader, but that meaning would need to be related only to the existential meaning.[7] For Bultmann, the notion of faith was not dependent on historical reality.[8]

Bultmann was concerned to hold in balance his skeptical attitude toward the factual or historical content of the gospel narratives while yet maintaining his belief in the overall message of the NT. He was convinced that the present form of the NT was repulsive to contemporary readers. To get any of them to listen to the Christian message,

---

Augsburg Fortress, 1973); *Second Letter to the Corinthians* (Minneapolis: Augsburg Fortress, 1985); *What Is Theology? Fortress Texts in Modern Theology* (Minneapolis: Augsburg Fortress, 1997); *New Testament and Mythology and Other Basic Writings*, ed. Schubert M. Ogden (Minneapolis: Augsburg Fortress, 1984); and Rudolf Bultmann and Karl Kundsin, *Form Criticism: Two Essays on New Testament Research*, trans. Frederick C. Grant (New York: Harper & Row, 1962). See also John Macquarrie, *The Scope of Demythologizing: Bultmann and His Critics* (New York: Harper & Row, 1961); Stanley N. Gundry and Alan F. Johnson, eds., *Tensions in Contemporary Theology* (Chicago: Moody, 1976); Robert Reymond, *Introductory Studies in Contemporary Theology* (Philadelphia: Presbyterian and Reformed, 1968).

3. John Macquarrie, "Rudolf Bultmann," in *A Handbook of Christian Theologians*, ed. Martin E. Marty and Dean G. Peerman (Nashville: Abingdon Press, 1985), 445.

4. Macquarrie, "Rudolf Bultmann," 445.

5. Bultmann was convinced that John's teaching was primarily eschatological. Scholars continue to debate Bultmann's finding, as exhibited by the works of Jörg Frey.

6. Bultmann, *Jesus and the Word*, 8, as cited by Macquarrie, "Rudolf Bultmann," 446.

7. Macquarrie, "Rudolf Bultmann," 446.

8. Ibid.

therefore, that message would have to be presented to them in a new and different form.

Myth and Existential Interpretation. Bultmann believed that the real history of Jesus had been transformed into a myth. The actual facts concerning the historical Jesus had been changed into a story of a divine, preexistent being who became incarnate, atoned for human sin, rose from the dead, then ascended into heaven. This same one would return from heaven, judge the earth, and inaugurate a new age. Bultmann argued that this view of a person could not be held in modern thinking—it must be relegated to the undifferentiated thinking of a prescientific age.[9] This theological situation, of course, presents a dilemma. If Christianity belongs to a so-called "prescientific age," and contemporary Christians no longer live in that age, then the connection between the two worlds—between Christians and the Christian faith—appears to have been severed. The options are that Christians must either abandon Christianity or transform it. Bultmann did not want to reject Christianity. He was convinced that there is still truth to be found in the text of the Bible, no matter how deeply that truth is hidden. There is an essential message in the Bible—a message that can be separated from its historical accidents and mythical exaggerations. For Bultmann, the task of pulling back the mythical tapestry was not an attempt to discover some sort of historical substratum. According to him, the entire message is a myth, and thus the Christian task is to liberate Christianity from the myth—in other words, to *demythologize* the Christian faith.[10]

Myth is related to an existential interpretation. Bultmann believed the biblical creation account to be a myth. But by *myth*, he did not mean that it is merely an interesting, fabricated account of creation. He believed myths should be interpreted as expressions of our creaturely dependence. For Bultmann, the resurrection is a myth, and the discovery of an empty tomb is mere legend.[11] These myths comprise a primitive way to express an aspect of humanity's self-awareness.[12]

9. Ibid., 447.
10. Ibid., 448.
11. Rudolf Bultmann, *Kerygma and Myth* (New York: Harper, 1961), 7: "What primitive mythology is, that a divine being should become incarnate and atone for the sins of men through his own blood!"
12. Macquarrie, "Rudolf Bultmann," 453.

Bultmann desired to translate the Bible from mythical language into understandable words. He defined *demythologizing* as a method of interpretation and exegesis.[13] The NT text must be made meaningful for human existence. To reach his goal, Bultmann was indebted to the Marburg philosopher Martin Heidegger.[14] Heidegger helped Bultmann formulate a proper analysis of human existence by using what is now called an "existential interpretation."[15] With it, Bultmann supposedly did much to make the NT meaningful to the contemporary reader. Nevertheless, he failed to provide sufficient answers to the fundamental hermeneutical question: he was unable to resolve the problem of the historical Jesus.[16] Part of the hermeneutical problem lies in the issue of the nature of history itself. Bultmann saw a need to change the concept of *history*.

Eschatology. Bultmann's method of demythologizing might be applied to broader concepts. Following the work of Johannes Weiss and Albert Schweitzer, Bultmann regarded eschatological myth as both fundamental and pervasive in the NT.[17] Jewish apocalyptic literature provided the foundation for understanding the world as a great cosmic drama. Shortly, supernatural intervention will bring the present age to an end. There will be a final judgment, and men will be assigned to destinies of either bliss or torment. The first disciples' expectation of an imminent end proved to be wrong, and to modern thinkers the whole belief reeks of absurd superstition. As Bultmann said, "History did not come to an end, and, as every schoolboy knows, it will continue to run its course."[18] Bultmann viewed NT mythology as something remote and unintelligible to minds that are accustomed to post-mythical thinking.

How did Bultmann handle the problem of the eschatological myth? When Bultmann analyzed the Gospel of John, which he thought to have been written at the end of the first century, he noticed that the

13. Rudolf Bultmann, *Jesus Christ and Mythology* (New York: Scribner's Sons, 1958), 45. See also Rudolf Bultmann, "The Problem of Hermeneutics," in *Essays, Philosophical and Theological*, by Rudolf Bultmann (New York: MacMillan, 1955), 234–61.

14. For more on Heidegger, see chapter 21.

15. Macquarrie, "Rudolf Bultmann," 448–50.

16. Cornelius Van Til, *The New Hermeneutic* (Nutley, NJ: Presbyterian and Reformed, 1974), 1–2.

17. Macquarrie, "Rudolf Bultmann," 451.

18. Bultmann, *Kerygma and Myth*, 5, as cited by Macquarrie, "Rudolf Bultmann," 452.

eschatological anticipation of Christ's immediate return had begun to fade. The hope that was present in the earlier gospel accounts was more crude than the eschatology found in John. Thus the author of the fourth gospel began to think of the purely future eschatology as entering into the here and now of Christian experience. This different eschatological outlook in the Gospel of John provided the basis for Bultmann's claim that his hermeneutic of demythologizing was present even in the Scriptures themselves.[19]

Christology. Bultmann did assert that Christ is God. But that assertion was not a metaphysical pronouncement relative to the second person of the Trinity; rather, to assert that Christ is God is, he said, a declaration of one's attitude toward the Christ—a value judgment made by someone who experiences atonement. Thus Christology should be interpreted existentially and subsequent to soteriology. God addresses believers through the dead and risen Christ. God still speaks through the NT's mythological formulations. This kerygmatic word from God supposedly presses each hearer to make a radical decision.[20]

Bultmann's thinking became the norm for NT research through much of the twentieth century. His disciples filled the chairs of seminaries and universities across the Western world. His unbiblical scholarship and analysis remained unquestioned, apart from a few rather lonely and muffled voices. Living and writing at about the same time was the Swiss theologian Karl Barth.

KARL BARTH (A.D. 1886–1968)[21]

Many consider Karl Barth to be the most important theologian of the mid-twentieth century—or even that entire century.[22] No one

19. Macquarrie, "Rudolf Bultmann," 453.
20. Ibid., 455.
21. See Georges Casalis, *Portrait of Karl Barth* (New York: Doubleday, 1963); Wilhelm Pauck, "A Brief Criticism of Barth's Dogmatics," in *From Luther to Tillich: The Reformers and Their Heirs* (New York: Harper & Row, 1984), 146–51. See Alexander T. McKelway, "Magister Dialecticae et Optimarium Partium (Recollections of Karl Barth as Teacher)," *Union Seminary Quarterly Review* 28, no. 1 (Fall 1972): 93–98; John C. Bennett, "A Non-Barthian's Gratitude to Karl Barth," *Union Seminary Quarterly Review* 28, no. 1 (Fall 1972): 99–108.
22. Daniel Jenkins, "Karl Barth," in *A Handbook of Christian Theologians*, ed. Martin E. Marty and Dean G. Peerman (Nashville: Abingdon Press, 1985), 396.

else in the twentieth century could claim to have even neared his theological attainments. He began a new era in the history of theology.[23] Barth aggressively reinterpreted both classical theology and classical ecclesiology. He did not back down from attacking his opponents, yet he is also considered to have been an ecumenical theologian.[24]

Life and Writings. In 1891, Barth's father was appointed professor of NT in Bern, so Karl attended university there. He would also attend Berlin, Tübingen, and Marburg. He studied alongside Herrmann and Weiss and with the philosophers Cohen and Natorp. He then entered a rural Swiss pastorate, where he served from 1911 to 1921.

Barth's first major publication, his commentary on Romans, appeared in August 1918 and ignited a blaze in Europe. Shortly thereafter, he began his teaching career in Germany. His *Christian Dogmatic* first appeared in 1927. *Die Theologie und die Kirche* quickly followed in 1928, and some would suggest that this work is one of the best introductions to his thought.[25] Also in 1928 Barth wrote a short explanation of the book of Philippians.[26] As the Nazi regime ascended to power, Barth was dismissed from the University of Bonn. He moved back to the Swiss city of Basel, where he taught from 1935 until his retirement in 1962.[27]

Barth wrote a history of modern thought in addition to his enormous multivolume *Church Dogmatics*. The *Dogmatics* is considered to be particularly significant for a number of reasons. One reason is its length, which also may be its weakness, as many find its fourteen volumes to be somewhat intimidating. Second, Barth sought to demonstrate God's sovereignty and initiative in revelation. Barth is considered a scholar who would always return to the text of Scripture.

---

23. John M. Frame, *A History of Western Philosophy and Theology* (Phillipsburg, NJ: P&R Publishing, 2015) (*HWPT*), 363: "The new movement went by various names. Barth called it *crisis theology* and *theology of the word*. Ibid., 364: "Whatever we may call it (it is now commonly called *Barthianism*), it was easily distinguishable from what had gone before. When Barth published his *The Epistle to the Romans* in 1919, Karl Adam, the Roman Catholic scholar, later remarked that it 'fell like a bombshell in the playground of the theologians.' It began a new era in the history of theology."

24. *HWPT*, 402–5; Jenkins, "Karl Barth," 406.

25. A. D. R. Polman, *Barth*, An International Library of Philosophy and Theology (Philadelphia: Presbyterian and Reformed, 1960), 9.

26. *Erklärung des Philipperbriefes* (ET, Atlanta: John Knox Press, 1962).

27. Jenkins, "Karl Barth," 396.

Yet he does not return to Scripture as evangelicals might do, for he denies its inerrancy.[28]

Presentation of Evangelical Theology. A helpful introduction to Barth's theology is his mature work on evangelical theology. Barth's method was first to define theology and then transition to evangelical theology. He taught that theology was a science that, like other sciences, seeks to apprehend a specific object and its environment in the manner directed by the phenomenon itself. More specifically, theology is a science that seeks to apprehend and speak of God, but there are many conceptions about God, and thus many theologies.[29]

In some ways, Barth believed that each thinking person is a theologian. Theology is who or what receives a person's highest loyalty, but it is also related to more philosophical worldviews. Even the denial of God's existence by philosophers "would in practice merely consist in transferring an identical dignity and function to another object."[30]

Barth preferred to call his theology *evangelical* theology. True evangelical theology came to final expression in the NT, though it was informed by the OT, and evangelical theology was rediscovered at the time of the Reformation.[31] The term *evangelical*, especially relative to theology, is a broad category. Barth said that some Protestant theology should not be labeled as evangelical, and some Catholic theology should be so labeled. Characteristic of evangelical theology is the scientific study of God—a scientific study that acknowledges God, who reveals himself to readers in the gospel and who communicates and acts in the midst of them.[32] Since there are many theologies, there are two proofs that are useful for testing which competing theology is the best one.

The best theology would be the most powerful one, but if it were to proclaim itself the only one, then it would certainly not be the one

---

28. Ibid., 401: "He is certainly not a fundamentalist. He insists that it is essential that the Bible should be open to critical examination from all sides."

29. Karl Barth, *Evangelical Theology: An Introduction* (New York: Holt, Rinehart and Winston, 1963), 3.

30. Ibid.: "There is no man who does not have his own god or gods as the object of his highest desire and trust, or as the basis of his deepest loyalty and commitment. . . . There is no philosophy that is not to some extent also theology."

31. Ibid., 5.

32. Ibid., 6: "Who himself speaks to men and acts among and upon them. Wherever he becomes the object of human science, both its source and its norm, there is *evangelical* theology."

true theology.[33] Concerning the second proof, evangelical theology cannot claim complete authority, for God himself is the only complete authority. Evangelical theology is modest because its subject, God, determines it to be so. Barth reasoned using negatives. Theology is not sovereign over God. God prohibits theology "from boasting that each one is the most correct or even the only correct theology." Also, evangelical theology is not a philosophy of religion.[34]

Evangelical theology has three subordinate presuppositions. The first is that human life is in the midst of what he termed an *insoluble dialectic*. This dialectical tension is the importance of human existence for theology. Second, evangelical theology requires faith in the God who authenticates himself. Third, theology uses reason, which makes theology possible. Barth also refers this third presupposition to humanity's spiritual capacity.[35]

Barth warned, however, that these three themes cannot become dominant. Evangelical theology cannot relate God to man. Instead, its task is to relate man to God. If theology were to relate God to man, it would surrender itself to a new Babylonian captivity.[36] Theology must recognize the mystery of the freedom of its object, who is God.[37] It is God who determines the nature of theology. Barth taught that God made himself known in the history of his deeds, which prove his existence and essence. Thus God is not a thing or an idea or even a sum of truths.[38] Theology will also not describe the divine procession in temporal isolation; rather, theology will be dynamic, and never static. God has done things in the past and will continue to do things in the future. Yet there is unity in the past and future because there is unity in God.[39]

33. Ibid., 4–5. Already in Barth there is some hesitation to make an absolute claim.
34. Ibid., 7.
35. Ibid., 7–8. His first reason sounds like Søren Kierkegaard's thinking. The dialectical tension that is the importance of human existence for theology gave rise to his series by the name *Theologische Existenz Heute*.
36. Ibid., 8.
37. Ibid., 9.
38. Ibid.: "God can be called the truth only when "truth" is understood in the sense of the Greek word *aletheia*. God's being, or truth, is the event of his self-disclosure, his radiance as the Lord of all lords, the hallowing of his name, the coming of his kingdom, the fulfillment of his will in all his work. The sum of the truths about God is to be found in a sequence of events."
39. Ibid., 10: "Theology must describe the dynamic interrelationships which make this procession comparable to a bird in flight, in contrast to a caged bird. . . . The God of the Gospel

According to Barth, God is neither self-sufficient nor self-contained. While he has no equal, he is also not wholly other, for he is a God who demonstrates mercy and is for humanity. He confronts man as a divinity with humanity. God is as lowly as he is exalted. He is friendly toward humanity.[40] "Evangelical theology is concerned with Immanuel, God with us! Having this God for its object, it can be nothing else but the most thankful and happy science!"[41]

Thus God is the object and starting point for evangelical theology. Theology is a language bound to God, who both makes possible and determines theology. The Word is the first determination of the place of theology. While theology is a human response to God, it is the Word of God which is heard and to which the believer responds.[42] Theology is a human reproduction, analogy, or reflection of the Word of God.[43]

Notion of the *Word of God*. Barth's theology of the Word of God is different from that of most Christians.[44] For most Christians, the Word of God is first the Bible. Second, believers would likely think of Christ himself as the incarnate Word of God. Barth, however, refers to the Bible as the witness of the Word, which is not the same as God's Word itself. For Barth, it is this Word of God, not the Bible, that regulates his theology.[45] But if the Word of God is not the Bible, then what is it? Barth said that it is the word that God has spoken, speaks, and will speak. It is also the work of God upon men. It is a simple, single, unambiguous, word. "In this Word, God's work itself becomes speech."[46]

Barth believed that the biblical writers of both the Old and New Testaments were elected and set apart by God to speak of what they had seen and heard.[47] Evangelical theology's concrete concern is the

---

rejects any connection with a theology that has become paralyzed and static."

40. Ibid., 11.
41. Ibid., 12.
42. Ibid., 16.
43. Ibid., 17.
44. See Polman, *Barth*, 16–30.
45. Barth, *Evangelical Theology*, 18.
46. Ibid., 19. In other words, the event becomes God's Word.
47. Barth's emphasis is that the biblical writers recorded what God had done, "not confirmations of their own religious, moral, or political preferences, or their optimistic or pessimistic views, opinions, and postulates!" (ibid., 27). This statement demonstrates how his theology was against the notions of liberal biblical criticism, especially the history of religions.

"Logos of God in their witness."[48] Thus for Barth, theology has no direct information about the Logos; it has only indirect information. The biblical writers could only echo the acts of God.[49] What the OT writers wrote, and what was eventually accepted as canonical, is an authentic testimony to the Word of God.[50]

Barth and Schleiermacher. Barth knew Schleiermacher's theology well.[51] While Schleiermacher focused on God's immanence, that is, God in humanity's experience, Barth focused on God's transcendence. Barth contended that Schleiermacher began from the wrong epistemological certainty of self-consciousness and then asked about knowing God.[52] Schleiermacher's old-liberalism theology was anthropocentric, not properly christocentric.[53] Old liberalism optimistically praised men and believed that they only needed proper teaching.

Critical Analysis. In contrast to the old theology, Barth initially seemed intent to return to Scripture. But he did not start with Christ as found in Scripture.[54] Barth said that God "calls into existence and action his holy and faithful human partner. In the midst of his people he lets one become man."[55] This statement is a denial of Christ's eternal preexistence and seems to whisper of the ancient heresy of adoptionism. Furthermore, Barth was a christological modalist; he said, "With him he expresses the same solidarity that a father has with his son; he affirms that he, God, is identical with this man."[56]

Barth also had a poor view of the Trinity. Calvin had advanced Trinitarian thinking to embrace strengths from both Eastern and

48. Ibid., 26.

49. Ibid., 27.

50. Ibid., 28. What Barth means can be seen in the following hypothetical example: I am in a car accident outside a seminary building. From inside the building, a seminarian hears the screech of the brakes and the crash and rushes out. He sees the event and then writes a narrative of it. In a similar fashion, the biblical writers have echoed acts and events. The contemporary Bible reader does not have the event itself.

51. Barth lectured on Schleiermacher at the University of Göttingen in 1923/1924. Those lectures were published in English as *The Theology of Schleiermacher* (Grand Rapids: Eerdmans, 1982).

52. *Die Christliche Dogmatik im Entwurf*, vol. 1 (Munich, 1927) as cited by Cornelius Van Til, *Christianity and Barthianism* (Philadelphia: Presbyterian and Reformed, 1962), 2.

53. Van Til, *Christianity and Barthianism*, 3.

54. Ibid., 9.

55. Barth, *Evangelical Theology*, 21.

56. Ibid., 22.

Western theology.[57] Because of his view of Scripture, which emphasizes God's absolute subjectivity in self-revelation, Barth's theology deprecates a biblical notion of the plurality of divine persons. While not an outright modalist, Barth still collapses the persons into the divine essence.[58]

In sum, Christ desires for his church to have a true word from God, which has been given to her in the pages of Scripture. But Barth grants to the church only a testimony to such a word. And even this testimony Barth corrodes, for he argues that the testimony of the biblical authors differs widely from one author to the next.[59] For Barth, the Bible is filled with human thought and speech that is oriented toward the Word of God but is not the actual Word of God.[60] For Barth, the Bible is a polyphonic testimony to the Word of God.[61]

But there is no epistemological certainty in this view—a problem that even Barth may have recognized. He admitted that the central affirmations of Scripture are not self-evident. Instead, theologians have to search for the truth of the Word found in the Bible. To aid in this search, Barth suggested that readers of Scripture use their "conjectural imagination."[62]

Frame rightly categorizes Barth as a theologian who used conservative terminology to promote his nonconservative theology.[63] Barth claimed that his theology was based on Scripture, not feeling or philosophy.[64] But regardless of how conservative and familiar his vocabulary may seem, the substance of his theology is no different from modernism.[65]

57. See chapters 14 and 15 on Calvin and the Trinity.

58. Jürgen Moltmann charges Barth with being too influenced by Augustinian Trinitarian thought and a notion of person obtained via idealism. See Michael Horton, *The Christian Faith: A Systematic Theology for Pilgrims on the Way* (Grand Rapids: Zondervan, 2011), 295.

59. Barth, *Evangelical Theology*, 30.

60. Ibid., 31.

61. Ibid., 33.

62. Ibid., 35.

63. *HWPT*, 364: "This is a prime example of . . . *conservative drift*, the tendency of liberal thinkers to advance their cause through the use of conservative terminology."

64. Ibid., 365.

65. Ibid., 365–66: "Cornelius Van Til's *The New Modernism* argues by its very title that the theology of Barth is no different from Ritschlianism, except in vocabulary"; and 365n9: "Modernism hears man answer without anyone having called him. It hears him talk to himself." Karl Barth, *Church Dogmatics*, vol. 1, *The Doctrine of the Word of God* (New York: Scribner's Sons, 1956), 1.1, 68.

PAUL TILLICH (A.D. 1886–1965)[66]

Life and Writings. Scholars have claimed that Paul Tillich is fundamental to contemporary theology.[67] He served as a professor of philosophy and theology at Berlin, Marburg, Dresden, and Frankfurt. Then in 1933, he traveled to America at the age of forty-seven as a refugee from Hitler's Germany. After mastering the English language, he taught at Union Seminary, Harvard, and finally Chicago. His mature thought is presented in his three-volume *Systematic Theology* (1951–1963).[68]

Method. Like Bultmann, Tillich was convinced that he had to communicate effectively to the current generation. He rejected Barth's thinking along with any notion of literalistic supernaturalism. He perceived a need for a new theological structure. That new structure would synthesize human wisdom and experience with biblical religion. Some have called his method *correlation*. He would incorporate a dialectical approach and assert that Christian symbols somehow provide the answers to contemporary problems.[69] In summary, Tillich was convinced that Christianity speaks into every contemporary philosophical issue. Christianity answers human struggles with reason, questions of ontology, personal identity, and even the concept of *history*.[70]

OSCAR CULLMANN (A.D. 1902–1999)

Life and Background.[71] Oscar Cullmann was born into a Lutheran home in Strasbourg. He studied in his native city and in 1924 graduated

---

66. Some of his writings include: *Biblical Religion and the Search for Ultimate Reality* (Chicago: University of Chicago Press, 1955); *A Complete History of Christian Thought* (New York: Harper & Row, 1968); *The Courage to Be* (New Haven: Yale University Press, 1952); *The Eternal Now* (New York: Scribner's Sons, 1963); *Morality and Beyond* (New York: Harper & Row, 1963); *The Religious Situation*, trans. H. Richard Niebuhr (New York: H. Holt and Co., 1932).

67. Vernon C. Grounds, "Pacesetters for the Radical Theologians of the Sixties and Seventies," in *Tensions in Contemporary Theology*, 2nd ed., ed. Stanley N. Gundry and Alan F. Johnson (Grand Rapids: Baker 1986), 82.

68. Williston Walker, Richard A. Norris, David W. Lotz, and Robert T. Handy, *A History of the Christian Church*, 4th ed. (New York: Scribner's Sons, 1985), 545.

69. Grounds, "Radical Theologians," 83–85.

70. Ibid., 85.

71. Professor Cullmann had recently retired from the faculty when I began my studies in Basel. He helped me in my studies and kindly read my dissertation. After my graduation, we corresponded for nearly twenty years. Because of that relationship this section is longer than

from its university. His first article was published in 1925 on *Formge-schichte*.[72] He may have already thought that the NT should not be thought of in terms of the dominant, early twentieth-century philosophy.

Cullmann then went to Paris to teach Greek and to study at the Sorbonne. In 1926 he was appointed director of the Thomasstift. In 1930 he finished his doctoral dissertation, *Le problème littéraire et historique du Roman pseudo-Clémentin*.[73] Immediately, Cullmann became professor of NT at Strasbourg. In 1938, he became professor of NT and ancient church history at the University of Basel.

Beginning in 1949, Cullmann also became the full-time professor of the history of early Christianity at the École des Hautes Études in Paris.[74] In 1953, he was given the same chair at the Sorbonne. He also frequently lectured at the Waldensian seminary in Rome.[75] He lectured in French at Paris, in German at Basel, and in Italian at Rome. He also lectured in masterful English in the United States in 1954, 1959, and 1964. Two *Festschriften* were published in his honor.[76] Before 1955, Cullmann was given honorary doctorates by both Edinburgh and Manchester. In March 23, 1959, *Time Magazine* published an article on him. A follow-up article was published just one week later, again in *Time Magazine*.[77] Cullmann was made commander of the French Legion of Honor in the 1970s and a member of the Institute of France. In 1993, he was the first Protestant to receive the Prix International Paul VI from the Paul VI Institute.[78]

Time and History. Cullmann wrote four articles that presented the basic principles of *Heilsgeschichte*, or *salvation history*. These articles

---

some of the others. For more information, see Theodore Martin Dorman, *The Hermeneutics of Oscar Cullmann* (San Francisco: Mellen, 1991); and Matthieu Arnold, *Oscar Cullmann: Un docteur de l'Eglise* (Lyon: Olivétan éditiones, 2019). For a deeper analysis of Cullmann's *State in the New Testament*, see Richard C. Gamble, *The Whole Counsel of God*, vol. 2, *The Full Revelation of God* (Phillipsburg, NJ: P&R Publishing, 2018) (WCG2), 520, 779–86.

72. Oscar Cullmann, "Formation de la Tradition Evangelique," *Revue d'histoire et de Philosophie Religieuses* 5 (1925): 564–79.

73. The work was published in Paris by Librarie Félix Alcan in 1930.

74. In 1950 he was professor of NT in the Faculté Libre de Théologie Protestant.

75. S. C. Guthrie Jr., "Oscar Cullmann," in *A Handbook of Christian Theologians*, ed. Martin E. Marty and Dean G. Peerman (Nashville: Abingdon Press, 1985), 338.

76. These celebratory volumes are *Neotestamentica et Patristica*, ed. W. C. Van Unnik (Leiden: Brill, 1962); and *Oikonomia: Heilsgeschichte als Thema der Theologie*, ed. Felix Christ (Hamburg: Reich, 1967).

77. These articles appeared in the magazine's religion section; the first article was titled "Christian Solidarity" and the second, "New Sayings of Jesus."

78. He also appears in the *Petit Larousse* dictionary.

were the initial thoughts of his first book.[79] That book, *Christus und die Zeit*, appeared in 1945 and was translated five years later as *Christ and Time*.[80] In that work, Cullmann presented what he considered to be the biblical notion of time and history, in contrast to the Greek notion. By examining words such as *day, hour, season, time, age, now*, and *today*, Cullman discovered what he considered to be the biblical concept of *history*. History began with creation, then moved through a succession of redemptively decisive events, called *kairoi*, and is to conclude with the eventual consummation of all things.[81] Thus there was a threefold linear concept of *time* in Judaism: creation, *kairoi*, and consummation. Then a major change occurred in Christianity: within that threefold notion of time, Christ became time's midpoint. The biblical timeline has three sections: the period stretching endlessly or eternally backward from creation, the limited time between creation and the end of the world, and the period stretching endlessly forward from that end. According to Cullman, history is central to the biblical concept of *salvation*. There is a succession of individual saving events that is the pattern of *Heilsgeschichte*.

The Greek philosophical meaning of *time* was quite different from the biblical concept.[82] The Greek view of time was circular.[83] Time was a constant repetition of events that occurred without direction or goal. In addition, time and salvation were related in Greek thought. In the Greek mind, salvation came by escaping from the prison of time. Redemption, conceived as divine actions within human time, was impossible.[84]

Contra much contemporary scholarship, Cullmann argued that neither the apostle John nor the book of Hebrews incorporated a Greek conception of time.[85] Cullmann understood the biblical and

79. *Königsherrschaft Christi und Kirche im Neuen Testament* (Zollikon/ Zürich: Evangelische Verlag, 1941); "Eschatologie und Mission im Neuen Testament," *Evangelisches Missionszeitung* 85 (July 1941): 98–108; "Die Hoffnung der Kirche auf die Wiederkunft Christi," *Verhandlüngen des Schweizerichen Reformierten Pfarrvereins*, 83 (1942): 26–50; *Les premieres confessions de foi chrétiennes* (Paris: Presses Universitaires de France, 1943), 18–73.

80. Oscar Cullmann's, *Christus und die Zeit* (Zurich: Evangelischer Verlag, 1945) became *Christ and Time*, trans. Floyd Filson (Philadelphia: Westminster Press, 1950).

81. Cullmann, *Christ and Time*, 39.

82. Ibid., 49–50.

83. Ibid., 51.

84. Ibid., 52.

85. But Gnosticism attacked the biblical notion of time, and Gnosticism was fought against especially by Irenaeus. Ibid., 55: "The first apostasy from the Primitive Christian understanding

the Greek conceptions of time to be antithetical.[86] The two competing concepts could not be reconciled.[87] This biblical notion of time was lost from the early church writer Irenaeus until the federal theology of Johannis Cocceius.

The difference between the Jewish and the Christian concepts of time lies in the placement of this midpoint. For the Jews, the midpoint lies in the future with the anticipated Messiah, and then comes the end of history. But for the church, Jesus Christ is the midpoint, and there is no chronological end of history.[88] To illustrate the concept, Cullmann used D-Day as an analogy. In World War II, one decisive battle was fought that would determine the outcome of the entire war. After that battle, fighting may have lingered, but all sides knew the ceasefire would inevitably come.[89] In Christ's death and resurrection, history has such a beginning of the end. All subsequent events in history are eschatological. This state of affairs is what is termed the "already-but-not-yet."

In contrast to Barth, Cullmann rejected the conceptual distinction between *time* and *eternity*. Barth stressed the temporal quality of eternity; he said that eternity was unending duration.[90] For Cullmann, eternity was not qualitatively different from time.[91] When it is, the Platonic conception of timeless eternity is wrongly introduced.[92] In summary, with less speculation than either Bultmann or Barth, and rejecting their philosophical categories, Cullmann wanted to discover the nature of biblical redemptive history. To do that, the Christ-event has to be the temporal midpoint of the historical process.[93]

History and Prophecy. Having briefly examined mid-twentieth century struggles and the supposed solutions of Bultmann and Barth, Cullmann offered refreshing answers to many of their theological

---

of time is not found in Hebrews nor in John. . . . These writings are not controlled by a Hellenistic slant. The first apostasy comes rather in Gnosticism."

86. Ibid., 56: "Whoever takes his start from Greek thought must put aside the entire revelatory and redemptive history."

87. Ibid., 58: "There can be no real reconciliation when the fundamental positions are so radically different."

88. Ibid., 59, 81–82 (see the chart on 82); and 101: "In Judaism, this solidarity is not anchored in a time line whose mid-point is a historical fact."

89. Ibid., 84.

90. Ibid., 62–63.

91. Ibid., 63.

92. Ibid.

93. Ibid., 12–18.

questions. While Cullmann adopted current literary conventions and distinguished between history, saga, and myth, he made it clear "that between these various items Primitive Christianity makes no distinction. In this respect it considers Adam to be upon the same plane as is Jesus of Nazareth."[94] Given those realities, Bultmann argued that the story needed to be changed. Not so with Cullmann.[95] He argued that Christians have to deal with this reality, as it is essential to the concept of *salvation*.[96]

Cullmann said that there is a way to deal with the fact that scholars today distinguish between history and myth, while the primitive church did not. The answer lies in what Cullmann termed *prophecy*. Again, the word *prophecy* has special meaning for primitive Christianity. Cullmann distinguished between two types of prophecy: (1) that which was primal and eschatological, especially the creation narrative and John's revelation; and (2) revealed prophecy concerning history, which fell in the middle between the bookends of primal and eschatological prophecy.

In this middle section, the facts are open to historical testing. But the main assertion of the OT, namely, that Israel was chosen by God, cannot be tested by historians. Similarly, the reality that Jesus is the Son of God also remains "concealed from the historian as such."[97] In other words, the middle section is historical, but it is history that has been interpreted theologically, or history seen through the eyes of faith.[98] "Taken as one whole, they yield the picture of Jesus the Son of God."[99] But Cullmann was not satisfied with simply interpreting the middle, prophetic-history part—he also analyzed primal prophecy from this perspective.

94. Ibid., 94: "The historical sense is completely lacking in the authors of the Primitive Christian writings, and hence for them a distinction between history and myth is *a priori* remote."

95. Ibid., 95. Bultmann handled it incorrectly. Adam becomes "the ever valid psychological fact of human sin." His method strips those histories "of their character as redemptive *history*. . . . In the NT point of view is not the essential thing in the figure of Adam the fact that a second Adam comes *after* him?" He sees the redemptive history "to be as much a dispensable framework as is the outmoded world view of the Bible" and tries to find an essential kernel.

96. Ibid.: "The placing of history and myth together upon one common line of development in time belongs to the essential core of the Primitive Christian conception of salvation."

97. Ibid., 96–99.

98. Ibid., 98: "Without the presupposition of a revelation such a presentation of history is meaningless, and the interpretation which it gives of the history, that is, the thing that is the essential in it and that influences the entire presentation, can only be believed."

99. Ibid., 99.

He found that the creation account can no longer be viewed simply or merely as a primitive myth. "It is concentrated in a historical act."[100] It is brought together at Colossians 1:17–19. Thus creation plays a role between the time after the resurrection and the future return of Christ. This situation is what Paul specifically addressed in Romans 8. Paul understood there to be a relationship between the Holy Spirit and creation. Creation shares in the waiting liberation of Christ's return. It too is groaning, participating in the already-but-not-yet.[101] The same connection to history can be found in the book of Revelation. While the book was written in a nonhistorical framework, it contains clear historical references—such as, for example, references to the Roman Empire. Unlike so many of his colleagues, Cullmann concluded that, like the creation, "this eschatological drama is to be thought of as a development in time."[102]

Baptism. Three years after *Christ and Time*, Cullmann's work on baptism appeared. Within two years it was translated into English.[103] The purpose of the research was to defend pedobaptism against Karl Barth's *Die kirchliche Lehre von der Taufe.*

Cullmann argued that baptism did not originate with Jesus, but it had a distinctively Christian meaning attributed to it—it is essential to remember that Christian baptism is only possible after the resurrection. John the Baptist's baptism was anticipatory, because he was baptizing prior to the resurrection. The cross is the occasion of Jesus's general baptism: "Jesus' solidarity with His whole people is demonstrated in this baptism through death and resurrection."[104] Cullmann thought that Christ's baptism in some sense affects all people; but application to the individual is still necessary.

Since faith follows baptism, Cullman argued that the baptism of infants is justified. Individual baptism is necessary to show participation in the body of Christ. In Colossians 2:11–12, Paul makes clear

100. Ibid., 102.

101. Ibid., 102–3.

102. Ibid., 105. Cullmann rejected, for example, E. Lohmeyer's 1926 commentary on Revelation which chose to see this drama exclusively as mythology.

103. Oscar Cullmann, *Die Tauflehre des Neuen Testaments—Erwachsenen und Kindertaufe* (Zurich: Zwingli-Verlag, 1948); and *Baptism in the New Testament*, Studies in Biblical Theology 1 (Naperville, IL: Allenson, 1950). The text of *Baptism in the New Testament* is now available on the internet at biblicalstudiesorguk.blogspot.

104. Cullmann, *Tauflehre*, 19–20.

that baptism is the fulfillment of and replacement for the OT rite of circumcision. After Pentecost, baptism expressed acceptance into the covenant people (circumcision) and the cleansing of sin (proselyte baptism). Both infant and adult baptism have equal biblical attestation, but "the baptism of adults, whose parents at their birth were already believing Christians, is not demonstrable."[105]

Christology of the New Testament. Cullman's next major work was *The Christology of the New Testament*.[106] In this book, Cullmann established that the pressing question for the NT writers was, "Who is Christ?" The question in the minds of the writers of the NT regarded what Christ does, not his nature. The NT reflects the self-estimate of Christ and the estimate of him in and by the primitive Christian community. This reflection is not metaphysical but kerygmatic and confessional. The Christology of the NT is functional; it deals with historical events.[107]

The NT documents are both confessional and historical. Christ was not fit into any conceptual scheme; rather, all concepts were readjusted to him. And when readers recognize the radical newness of NT theology, they can see the NT's difference from either timeless mythology or nonhistorical kerygma.

Contra Bultmann, the Gospels actually reveal Jesus's mind. Jesus knew that he had to carry out God's plan of salvation. His disciples did not understand his real identity. During Jesus's life, it was finally not so much the past or future events of redemptive history as it was the present on which the thinking of the church concentrated—the time between the comings. So profound was the cultic experience of the present Lord that it was from this center that the whole line of redemptive history was given its christological interpretation.[108]

For Cullmann, there was a line of NT christological development. It began with Jesus's messianic self-consciousness (in contrast to the view of Schweitzer and others) and his disciples' early premonitions during his earthly ministry. It moved to the disciples' Easter experi-

105. Cullmann, *Baptism*, 70.
106. The German text appeared in 1956. The English translation was published in Philadelphia by Westminster Press in 1959.
107. Guthrie, "Oscar Cullmann," 345.
108. Ibid., 347.

ence—the believing community's experience of the Lord in worship—to a deep theological reflection, particularly in John and Hebrews, on the connection between Christ and all *Heilsgeschichte*.[109] *Heilsgeschichte* exposes the development of NT Christology and the deficiency of the older approach of imposing a dogmatic scheme on NT data.

Salvation in History.[110] The purpose of this work was to present a viable alternative to Bultmann's existentialism and to make a contribution to dialogue with Roman Catholic scholars. In the prolegomena, Cullmann addressed how the NT writers treated the OT. On one side, Gnosticism dealt with both the OT and NT as documents in which could be found truths in mythological dress. In contrast, the NT writers dealt with the OT through the lens of their belief in Jesus Christ and a *Heilsgeschichte* or a *Christusgeschichte*. Neither was there any union with Greek–Oriental syncretism.[111]

Cullmann was convinced that the contemporary church could learn from how the early church dealt with Marcion. While that past culture was different from his own, nevertheless, the message of Christ was "a scandal for philosophical thinking then, just as it is today."[112] In fact, in many ways the entire history of Christianity could be interpreted through the lens of the scandal of *Heilsgeschichte*.[113] Cullmann traced the development of the contemporary debate on eschatology. Focusing on the nature of the kingdom of God, Cullmann believed a number of options were available. The first option was Schweitzer's position. Schweitzer understood Jesus's eschatology as futuristic, a view characterized as *consequent eschatology*.[114] Schweitzer had a number of disciples.[115] But he and they failed to recognize the historical centrality

---

109. Ibid., 348.

110. See Edward W. H. Vick, review of *Salvation in History*, by Oscar Cullmann, *Theologische Zeitschrift* 1 (1966): 75–78.

111. Oscar Cullmann, *Heil als Geschichte*, 2. durchgesehene Aufl. (Tübingen: J. C. B. Mohr, 1967), 6–7.

112. Ibid., 9.

113. Ibid., 10. Cullmann actually named those theologians who so ordered their interpretation of theology in this fashion: from Irenaeus through Augustine, the Protestants Coccejus, Bengel, and others.

114. Ibid., 14–15.

115. Ibid., 19. One of his followers was M. Werner, who traced the Schweitzer position through church history in *Die Entstehung des christlichen Dogmas* (Bern/Leipzig: Haupt, 1941; 2. Aufl., 1953).

of Christ. Neither did the school grasp the *already* of the kingdom; rather, it waited in anticipation for the *not yet.*

Charles H. (C. H.) Dodd resolved the dialectic of the kingdom in the other direction, sometimes referred to as *realized eschatology,* though Dodd preferred the term *inaugurated eschatology.* According to this view, there is no future consummation. For Dodd, some of the NT writings—Paul, Hebrews, and 1 Peter, to name several—were closer to Jesus's realized eschatology than were others.[116] Even more than Dodd, however, Bultmann saw a radical division within the NT books.[117] This division produced the principle of dividing the various NT writings.[118] Bultmann held to a present and coming tension, but it was not historically bound—it was an existential tension of deciding now either for or against the kingdom.[119] The final option, which Cullmann held, understood the kingdom of God to be both present and future for the NT writers.[120]

The second section of Cullmann's work is the history of the notion of *Heilsgeschichte.* The fundamental data is the event, then follows the prophetic/apostolic interpretation of the event. These events link up in a series that shows constants and contingents. Continuity in *Heilsgeschichte* is not simply linear—it allows for both revisions and expansions.[121]

The third part demonstrates the very nerve center of the present work—the tension between the *already* and the *not yet,* which is central to the entire NT.[122] There is a relationship between the Old and New Testaments, between Jesus and the later NT writings. Cullmann used the relationship between *event* and *interpretation* as a key principle

---

116. Cullmann, *Heil als Geschichte*, 16: "In this way Dodd attempted to bring Platonism and eschatology into harmony."

117. Ibid., 18. See Bultmann's *History and Eschatology*, as cited by Cullmann, *Heil als Geschichte*, 27.

118. Ibid., 29.

119. Ibid., 27. Bultmann wrote against Cullmann in "Heilsgeschichte und Geschichte. Über O. Cullmanns *Christus und die Zeit*," *Theologische Literaturzeitung* 73 (1948): 659–66; *HWPT,* 405: "The Heilsgeschichte of Vos and Cullmann occurred in space and time; the *Geschichte* of Barth and Bultmann enters space and time only in a word of proclamation, a word that becomes true for the church only 'from time to time.'"

120. Cullmann (*Heil als Geschichte*, 19) adds W. G. Kummel to this list, *Die Eschatologie der Evangelien* (Leipzig: J. C. Hinrichs Verlag, 1936).

121. Oscar Cullmann, *Salvation in History* (New York: Harper & Row, 1967), 66–116.

122. Ibid., 175.

to offer a schematic description of how *Heilsgeschichte* had already developed in the OT.

The principle examines an event, of which a prophet must be an eyewitness. There is the revelation of a divine plan in and with this event, and a connection of this event with earlier revelation given to other prophets. This principle of interpretation was then applied to the NT. Jesus reinterpreted OT *Heilsgeschichte* in the light of his understanding of himself. The early church reinterprets the *Heilsgeschichte* of Jesus in the light of his resurrection, then subsequently in the light of its later experience.

Cullmann's fourth section is an examination of the NT evidence. It is a section overrun with controversy with the Bultmannian school. Cullmann saw that school as a mere reinterpretation of Schweitzer's futuristic eschatology. He asserted instead that Jesus's preaching contains present and future elements, both of which imply *Heilsgeschichte*. Contra Bultmann, Cullmann did not consider the Pauline and Johannine writings to stand at odds with the Lucan and other NT writings. Jesus teaches that the kingdom has come in his person, yet the kingdom is still not yet because Jesus expects an end to come. Cullmann rightly concluded that Schweitzer, Bultmann, Dodd, and other scholars had allowed philosophy to influence their understanding of the NT.[123] As a Lutheran scholar who watched the world endure two world wars, Cullmann next wrote a smaller book on the church's relationship to the state.

Church and State. Cullmann took a particular interest in the church and state.[124] He believed that the church can be best understood within its historical nexus—between the resurrection and return of Christ. The church exists in this in-between in eschatological tension, caught between the already fulfilled and the not yet consummated.[125] The Holy Spirit, the celebration of the Lord's Supper, and even the preaching of the Word are all evidences of this tension that the church exists within. Preaching is both the proclamation of the good news that Christ is

---

123. Cullmann, *Heil als Geschichte*, 22–24.

124. Oscar Cullmann, *The State in the New Testament* (London: SCM Press, 1957); and "The Kingship of Christ and the Church in the New Testament," in *The Early Church*, ed. A. J. B. Higgins, 105–40 (London: SCM Press, 1956).

125. Guthrie, "Oscar Cullmann," 348–49.

victorious and a somber warning of his final coming. Thus the church has a part in the divine redemptive activity in history. While the church may often appear insignificant and ineffective, she is the center of God's activity in the world.[126] Christ reigns not only over the church "but also . . . over the world of political powers—and at a deeper level over the invisible demonic 'powers' which the NT sees as standing behind the state."[127] Hence the state must stay within its defined limits.[128] In the final work we will analyze in this chapter, Cullmann focused his attention on the authorship of the Gospel of John.

The Johannine Circle. According to Cullmann, the gospel criticism of his day had shattered the notion of the literary unity of the Gospel of John.[129] Redaction criticism concluded that the fourth gospel was a composition of various edited versions, which resulted in stylistic peculiarities, misplaced verses and chapters, and differing theological concepts. Generally speaking, there are three ways to explain this curious state of affairs: (1) there were multiple redactions,[130] (2) there were several conflicting sources,[131] and (3) the original order can be restored by rearranging verses and chapters.[132] Cullmann, however, offered his own resolution. He was convinced that the author was a man of strong personality who utilized either common oral or written

---

126. Ibid., 349.

127. Ibid., 350.

128. Ibid., 351. For an analysis of Cullmann's view of the state, see *WCG* 2:516–20.

129. Cullmann had already retired from full-time teaching by the time of this publication and had already written many articles on John's gospel. Oscar Cullmann, *The Johannine Circle*, trans. John Bowden (Philadelphia: Westminster Press, 1975), x: "the earliest Christianity is rooted in a marginal form of Palestinian Judaism, and it has guided all my work on the milieu and the spiritual home of the Gospel of John in a particular direction. . . . At that time . . . we did not know more or less heterodox Judaism as well as we do now, after more recent discoveries of manuscripts. . . . We cannot follow the Tübingen school in dividing earliest Christianity into Palestinian Jewish Christianity and Hellenistic Gentile Christianity"; and contra a gnostic origin, x: "it cannot be related to earlier works by other scholars on gnostic influences on Judaism."

130. Cullmann (*Johannine Circle*, 2, 5) suggests that the last verses of chapter 21 indicate a "circle" of disciples who published the gospel.

131. The sources include the Synoptics plus special Johannine sources or traditions. See ibid., 5–7, 8: "If I am right in supposing that at least the content of the farewell discourses (chs. 14–17) comes from him—of being inspired by the 'spirit of truth' to reveal the deeper meaning and significance of these facts, so that he can deal with the speeches of Jesus in a sovereign manner . . . even if the author has made use of written or oral traditions, he has adapted them entirely to his purpose and given them his own distinctive stamp."

132. Ibid., 8: "On the one hand what we may regard as a logical order may not necessarily correspond to the thought and practice of the author."

traditions, as well as special traditions that might include personal reminiscences. This author was responsible for the main lines of the text in its present state. Cullmann supposed that after the author's death, a redactor or redactors completed the work by adding chapter 21.[133] Cullmann argued that the Gospel of John should be understood as an account of the life of Jesus.[134]

Cullmann was convinced that John's purpose was different from that of the Synoptics because John had a particular theological purpose. Cullmann emphasized that the Paraclete inspired John to write. John's goal was to strengthen the faith of the church.[135] John was convinced that, under the power of the Holy Spirit, he could develop the words of Jesus beyond what Jesus actually spoke.[136] This left Cullmann with an even more difficult question—was John's gospel historically accurate?[137]

Cullmann considered it significant that John claimed to present facts in his gospel, not allegory. John viewed the events he narrated as following a foreordained divine timetable.[138] He was certain of the veracity of his own account.[139] Regardless of the fact that John claimed

133. Relative to the work of a redactor, Cullmann (ibid., 10) underlined that if a view attributed to a later redactor "did not seem to him to be *irreconcilable* with other statements in the original gospel, is it really so much more difficult in some cases to suppose that the author of the original Gospel might have made this combination *himself?*"

134. Ibid., 11: "The conception of this account is his work."

135. Cullmann disagreed with Käsemann, who supposed that the author was engaged in a polemic against the mainstream church and asserted that John as an individual author had the conscious aim to speak of the incarnate Christ and his exalted presence in the church (ibid., 15, 17).

136. Ibid., 18: "On the ground of this conviction that he is being guided by the Paraclete in this remembrance, the evangelist can allow himself to develop the discourses beyond what the incarnate Jesus said. Without indicating any transition, he can suddenly introduce his own words (e.g., in 3.13, in the conversation with Nicodemus, where Jesus as incarnate speaks of the one who has ascended into heaven). The risen Christ speaks *through* the evangelist. Through him the Christ continues the teaching which he gave during his incarnation."

137. Ibid., 20: "We have defined the purpose of the evangelist as being both to give an account of the words and deeds of Jesus and to demonstrate their significance for the church."

138. Ibid., 21: "In this case *history*, *facts*, are the *object* of theological consideration. . . . During this brief period of activity every moment is of supreme significance for the salvation of the world"; and 22: "The same may be said of the geographical area of Jesus' activity, of his going to and fro between Judaea and Galilee, and perhaps also of 4.4, where the author says that Jesus *had to* go through Samaria. He had to meet the woman of Samaria there at Jacob's well, whereas the Jews were accustomed to make detour so as not to have to go through Samaria, which was excommunicated by the Jews. He had to meet the woman in order to prepare the ground for the future mission in Samaria."

139. Ibid., 22: "The evangelist is evidently convinced that he is reporting facts because he is relying on traditions or reminiscences which appear to him to be certain."

to have recorded history, scholars have doubted his claim. Their doubts are often a result of the fact that the author uses history to serve theological purposes. Cullmann reminded his readers that while earlier twentieth-century scholarship downplayed the fourth gospel's historical reliability, several more recent authors had affirmed its reliability. Cullmann then argued for the historical reliability of the Gospel of John[140] and even criticized those who denied its historical veracity.[141]

Cullmann proposed that to understand the text, its literary characteristics must first be understood. Focusing on twentieth-century authors, he presented a number of theories regarding the language of the Gospel of John.[142] He denied that the gospel was a translation from Aramaic or that it was based on Hebrew poetry.[143] He reasoned that the best explanation for the gospel's literary character, as distinct even from that of the Synoptics, is its theological aim within its literary milieu.[144]

Regarding its literary milieu, earlier scholarship had suggested that John's gospel was either Hellenistic or Judaistic. Scholarship then thought it to be either Palestinian or Hellenistic Judaism. More recent

140. Ibid., 24: "In connection with the Johannine *discourses* of Jesus, which are so different from the synoptic preaching of the kingdom of God, I have already remarked that the evangelist feels justified in acting in a sovereign manner and himself speaking in the name of Jesus without indicating the transition. . . . Nevertheless, in certain cases we must ask whether it is not possible to imagine a more intimate teaching given by Jesus to the Twelve, apart from the preaching to be found in the synoptics, which had a different character."

141. Ibid., 25: "But it is equally perverse to deny any historical value at all to the Gospel of John because of the theological perspectives in which events are shown."

142. Ibid., 26: "Bultmann assumes that both the *semeia* source and the passion narrative were written in a Greek heavily permeated by Semitisms, whereas the original language of the revelation discourses was Aramaic. . . . Up to the first decades of the twentieth century, modern critical works exclusively assigned the Fourth Gospel to the Hellenistic sphere"; and 27: "On reading the Gospels one gains the impression that the language is generally Semitic, although on closer inspection some similarities with Hebrew can also be found in Koine Greek and in the Septuagint: the rare appearance of subordinate clauses, the placing of the verb before the subject . . . the repetition of the personal pronoun, and so on."

143. Ibid., 28: "Several scholars have used the rules of Hebrew poetry to define the rhythm, the alternation of strophes and the parallelism of Johannine style more closely. . . . [It] has attempted to describe the forms of Johannine poetry. . . . These proposals for reconstructing Johannine rhythm and the Johannine strophes do, however, seem to me to be burdened with too many subjective and hypothetical elements."

144. Ibid., 29: "The theological perspective also explains the Johannine manner of narrating events, which is very different from that of the synoptic gospels. . . . Language, style and literary characteristics may thus be explained primarily in terms of the theological aim of the evangelist, though they are also shaped by the conceptions of the Johannine circle which are determined by the particular milieu in which he is rooted."

scholarship is less certain that the question must have an either/or answer, for Palestinian Judaism is not as homogeneous as had previously been thought. Current scholarship demonstrates that the author of the fourth gospel was familiar with many OT themes, knew Jerusalem and Jewish worship and customs, and had contact with what some call *sectarian Judaism*, as seen in the Qumran community.[145] The author also seems to have been connected to John the Baptist and his disciples. This connection seems to have been so close that Cullmann speculates that John likely belonged to the Baptist's disciples.[146]

Cullmann rejected the idea of a gnostic background for John's theology. Such scholars argue that John was influenced by a Mandaean redeemer myth.[147] While John's gospel is directed toward a gnostic world of thought, it is far different from Gnosticism itself.[148]

Cullmann next examines John's theology within the early Christian community. The Tübingen school incorrectly placed the historical analysis of early Christianity within a Hegelian philosophical structure. While the Tübingen school's influence has waned, remnants of its ascendancy remain. The historical complexity of the situation cannot mean, for example, that in Palestine there was a monolithic Gentile Christianity set over against a homogeneous Jewish Christianity. Cullmann deems it unlikely that the first Christians were entirely from *official Judaism*; rather, John's gospel indicates that his thinking originated in a group of people who were from nonconformist Judaism and who, after coming to faith in Christ, remained distinct from their fellow believers who came out of official Judaism. In Acts 6, these two groups were identified as the Hellenists and Hebraists, and thus these two groups have been together from the very inception of the church.

145. Ibid., 32: "But the references to Old Testament themes are much more numerous, especially those related to the book of Exodus. . . . References are rightly made by scholars to the wisdom literature"; and 33, relative to Qumran: "Various fundamental conceptions have been compared, particularly 'dualism' and the idea of the 'spirit.'"

146. Ibid., 37: "This [Samaritan] religion is in some respects especially close both to the Gospel of John and to heterodox Judaism."

147. Ibid., 35: "Bultmann, in particular, attaches great significance to the influence of the Mandaean redeemer myth on Johannine theology. . . . At any rate, the 'redeemer myth' is not to be assigned the dominant role in the explanation of Johannine christology accorded to it by Rudolf Bultmann and his pupils, simply because of the use of kindred concepts in the Gospel of John."

148. Ibid., 39: "The Gospel of John is not simply a product of gnostic syncretism." Cullmann also contradicted Käsemann's notion that John is a gnostic gospel (see ibid., 58, 61).

John's gospel should be identified with those Hellenists of Jerusalem.[149] In fact, Cullmann connected the message of the martyr Stephen (Acts 7) with the theology of John and his circle.[150] He also connected the Hellenists' mission to the Samaritans with Johannine theology.[151]

There is much here that is useful to the evangelical who is involved in discussions with ministers who are in mainline denominations or with those who were trained in the higher critical traditions. While Cullmann does not think that the author of the fourth gospel was John the son of Zebedee, one of the twelve disciples, his analysis of authorship as someone who holds to the tenets of higher criticism gives the evangelical valuable information and perspective.[152]

In his consideration of authorship, Cullmann examined the internal and external evidence as well as the historical and theological content of John's gospel.[153] He wrongly concluded that the author could not be one of the twelve disciples. Nevertheless, Cullmann was convinced that the author had to be considered a disciple even if he was not one of the inner twelve.[154] Through his research, Cullmann, like so many evangelicals, concluded that the author was John the Beloved Disciple (who was not the John who was one of the Twelve).[155] He was convinced that the author was an anonymous John who represented another theological tradition not contained in the Synoptics.[156] As Peter was an eyewitness, a leader of the Twelve, and the main spokesman in the Synoptics, so also John was an eyewitness, a former disciple of John the Baptist, and the leader of those first Christians who originated

149. Ibid., 39–42; and 43: their threefold similarities were "1. In theological conceptions. 2. In an interest in the mission to Samaria. 3. In the common roots of Stephen's speech and the Gospel of John in heterodox Judaism, above all in Samaritan theology."

150. For Cullmann's analysis of Stephen's speech, where he finds similarities in theology of place and Christology, see ibid., 43–46, 52.

151. Cullmann also views the success of Philip's mission work with the Samaritans as connected to Johannine theology (see ibid., 46–49).

152. For more extensive interaction with Cullmann's theory as well as Ridderbos, see WCG 2:282–90.

153. Cullmann, *Johannine Circle*, 63–70.

154. Some have thought of Lazarus or John Mark as the Beloved Disciple, for example.

155. He rejected the notion that information about the Beloved Disciple was a later insertion and that the Beloved Disciple was some type of symbolic, ideal figure (contra Bultmann and a host of others; see ibid., 72–76).

156. Unlike the false gospels that tried to attach themselves to a well-known disciple, the Gospel of John had an *anonymous* author, which was for Cullmann a convincing demonstration that the author was a historical figure (see ibid., 77, 80).

from another Jewish tradition with closer ties to Samaria. In contrast to most, if not all, of his fellow critical authors, Cullmann demonstrated that the Gospel of John could very well have been written by an eyewitness. Cullmann pushed against the notion of most, if not all, liberal commentators that the author was not an eyewitness and was, at best, a distant source for the gospel.[157] As Cullmann concluded his work, he demonstrated rather convincingly that the Gospel of John is a historically trustworthy source of information on the life of Jesus.[158]

Theological Method and Interpretation. At this point, it should be rather apparent that the theological method of Oscar Cullmann is dissimilar to the method of Rudolf Bultmann. Cullmann does not want modern interpreters to judge the NT writings by our own philosophical or theological ideas. Bultmann argued that the message of the NT is not believable to the modern mind, while Cullmann argued that students should not be primarily concerned with the believability of what they read. Even if the text sounds strange or contradictory to the modern interpreter, the message of the text must be understood. This stance placed Cullmann in opposition to the trends of nineteenth- and early twentieth-century exegesis, and to the Bultmann school in particular.[159] In fact, many of Bultmann's followers were antagonistic toward Cullmann.

Evangelicals ought to consider the life and works of Cullmann and appreciate his bold opposition to liberal scholarship. He accused earlier scholars of finding in the NT only their own presuppositions.[160] His method was not to distinguish between that which is historically genuine and that which is false, that which is essential and that which is nonessential, or a primitive shell and an eternal truth.[161] Nevertheless, evangelicals must still be cautious. Cullmann was also a form critic. Despite all that evangelicals may be able to agree with him on, he did not believe the text of the NT to be the inerrant Word of God.[162]

---

157. Ibid., 76–85.

158. Ibid., 86–94.

159. Guthrie, "Oscar Cullmann," 339.

160. Ibid.: "They stripped off as disposable 'form' whatever did not agree with, and discovered as 'kernel' whatever did agree with, their own ideas about which of the events and words of the New Testament were scientifically and historically demonstrable, rationally and morally acceptable. As a result, the 'historical Jesus' they were so concerned to discover turned out to be only a reflection of nineteenth-century idealism."

161. Ibid.

162. Ibid., 340.

PROCESS PHILOSOPHY AND THEOLOGY

Process philosophy began in England and spread to the United States. It was born in nineteenth-century liberalism and philosophy. Process theologians often use biblical language to advocate certain ethical themes and manipulate biblical concepts in order to squeeze them into their philosophical systems.[163] Process theologians have been especially critical of classical theism in arguing that classical theism cannot resolve the dilemma of how God is both compassionate and passionless. Anselm resolved this dilemma by explaining that God is compassionate in terms of human experience but not compassionate in terms of his being. Aquinas's solution was that God loves without passion. Process theologians argue that in classical theism God only appears to be compassionate. Systematic theology's task is to answer such probing questions. Turning to process theology for answers is a dead end.

Alfred North (A. N.) Whitehead (A.D. 1861–1947). Whitehead was the prominent figure of the process philosophy movement.[164] Born in Britain, Whitehead was a mathematician, logician, and philosopher best known for his work in mathematical logic and the philosophy of science. In 1885, Whitehead began teaching at Trinity College, Cambridge, where he would spend the next twenty-five years. During this time, he worked primarily on mathematics and logic.[165] In 1890, Bertrand Russell arrived at Cambridge and the two men began to collaborate. They authored the three-volume *Principia Mathematica* (1910, 1912, 1913) and made contributions to twentieth-century logic and metaphysics.[166]

163. *HWPT*, 445: "Process theology is riddled with naturalistic fallacies, because it is unclear on the source (or reality) of ethical *norms*"; and 445–46: "The ethics of process theology is a form of utilitarianism, an approach to ethics often criticized for its lack of straightforward ethical norms."

164. Others were Gottlob Frege and Bertrand Russell. Charles Hartshorne finished doctoral studies in 1925 and heard Whitehead's lectures after his doctoral studies.

165. Whitehead's 1898 *A Treatise on Universal Algebra* (Cambridge: Cambridge University Press, 1898) had resulted in his election to the Royal Society.

166. "One of the great scientific documents of the twentieth century," Linsky, Bernard and Andrew David Irvine, "*Principia Mathematica*," in *The Stanford Encyclopedia of Philosophy* (Winter 2020 Edition), ed. Edward N. Zalta, https://plato.stanford.edu/archives/win2020/entries/principia-mathematica/, accessed March 12, 2020.

In 1910, Whitehead transitioned to the University of London. During his time in London, he focused primarily on the philosophy of science and education. Then, from 1924 to 1937, he taught at Harvard. There he worked on general philosophical issues, including his comprehensive metaphysical system, which he referred to as *process philosophy*.[167]

In *Principia Mathematica*, Whitehead demonstrated that he was a philosophical atomist who determined the smallest constituent of reality and, from that point, attempted to build reality as a whole. For him, the smallest component of reality consisted in atomic processes, from which individual facts and things were abstractions.[168] Thus he believed that facts and concepts should not be sharply divided. Everything in the world flows together, and objects of experience are deeply connected to other things in the environment. The world is made up of processes.

Actual occasions or entities are the final, real things which make up this world.[169] They are occurrences within time and space that enter into relationships with one another. Actual occurrences are in process, are changing, and everything actual is in a similar state of flux. Thus nothing is already in being, for no actual occasion is independent of a cycle of change.[170] Everything is in a process of becoming. Actual entities or occasions are in the process of becoming, since they are in interaction with other entities. They consist in a unification of past entities into a single experience.[171] Knowledge of such occasions and entities is what Whitehead termed a *prehension*. While actual entities

167. Some of his better known writings were: *The Concept of Nature* (Cambridge: Cambridge University Press, 1920); *The Principle of Relativity with Applications to Physical Science* (Cambridge: Cambridge University Press, 1922); *Science and the Modern World*, rev. ed. (Cambridge: Cambridge University Press, 1932); *Religion in the Making* (New York: Macmillan, 1926); *Symbolism, Its Meaning and Effect* (New York: Macmillan, 1927); *The Aims of Education and Other Essays* (New York: Macmillan, 1929); *The Function of Reason* (Princeton: Princeton University Press, 1929); *Process and Reality: An Essay in Cosmology* (New York: Macmillan, 1929); *Adventures of Ideas* (New York: New American, 1933); *Nature and Life* (Chicago: University of Chicago Press, 1934); *Modes of Thought* (New York: Macmillan, 1938); *Essays in Science and Philosophy* (New York: Philosophical Library, 1947).

168. *HWPT*, 439–40.

169. Whitehead, *Process and Reality*, 28, as cited in *HWPT*, 440.

170. There are no Aristotelian substances.

171. *HWPT*, 441: "This is a process of *becoming* in which the occasion perishes before it reaches a state of *being*. Then the occasion that perished is replaced by others that continue the universal process."

perish, nevertheless they are still available for others to prehend, thus giving a type of objective immortality to actual entities.[172]

Whitehead held that besides actual occasions and entities, there are two other modes of being—eternal objects and God. It is in the eternal objects (similar to Plato's forms) that process philosophers find some type of permanence. Yet these eternal objects are not substances but potentials or possibilities.[173] Eventually, process philosophy made its way into theology.

God in Process Thought. Whitehead needed a god to account for how the possibilities or eternal objects became available to actual entities. His god has a primordial and consequent nature. Its primordial nature pertains to qualities that transcend any particular world, qualities that are related to and likely dependent on the eternal objects. Its consequent nature is physical, as it carries out the eternal ideals in a particular world. While this god is a necessary being, nevertheless, it is dependent on this world for its concrete nature.[174] The god of process thinking is certainly not the God of the Bible.[175] Some process theologians attempt to leave hints of continuity with traditional theism by speaking of themselves as *neoclassical theists*. They use the word *pantheism* to describe their view of the relation of God and the world, a view that is foreign to the classical or older notion of *God*.[176]

LUDWIG WITTGENSTEIN (A.D. 1889–1951)[177]

Biography. Ludwig Wittgenstein was the youngest of eight children, the son of the wealthy Karl Wittgenstein. He was born in Vienna, where

172. Ibid., 442: "So Whitehead is a *panpsychist*, like Berkeley and Leibniz; he believes that mind, or something significantly analogous to mind, exists in all reality."

173. This view excludes the person as a true individual. *HWPT*, 443: "Personal human existence is a 'serially ordered society' of occasions of experience."

174. Ibid., 443–44.

175. A classic presentation of process theology is given by John B. Cobb Jr. and David Ray Griffin, *Process Theology: An Introductory Exposition* (Philadelphia: Westminster Press, 1976). *HWPT*, 445n116: "There is no such thing as creation out of nothing in process theology. . . . God and the world have both existed eternally, for they are correlative. So when process thinkers talk about God's *creative activity*, their concept is closer to the traditional concept of providence. God's *creativity* is like that of a human artist, who makes beautiful things out of various existing materials, as in Plato's *Timaeus*."

176. *HWPT*, 444–45.

177. See *WCG* 2:97–98.

he was then homeschooled until he was fourteen. He was sent to Linz to finish high school, then attended the Technische Hochschule in Berlin until 1908. After his time in Berlin, Wittgenstein traveled to Manchester, England, where he studied from 1908 to 1911.[178] Beginning in 1912 he studied at Trinity College, Cambridge, for a year and a half.[179] It was then that World War I broke the headlines, so he left Cambridge to serve in the Austrian army. He also spent some time in Norway.

After the war he worked as a schoolteacher, then worked full time for two years building a mansion for his sister. In 1929 he returned to Cambridge, where he remained as a fellow of Trinity College until 1936. He spent another year in Norway, then returned to Cambridge to succeed G. E. Moor. He remained in that position at Cambridge from 1939 to 1947. Wittgenstein possessed an unusual and forceful personality. He was relationally complex—he avoided making acquaintances but also needed friendships.[180] He had an earnest drive to create.[181] Many contemporaries have considered him to be something of an enigma.[182] In 1949, Wittgenstein was diagnosed with cancer. After his diagnosis he traveled to Ireland, where he died in seclusion in 1951.

Writings. Some of Wittgenstein's early influences were Plato, Schopenhauer, Spinoza, and Tolstoy.[183] He had become a Schopenhauerian epistemological idealist but then changed to Frege's conceptual realism.[184] His earliest published work—the *Tractatus Logico-Philosophicus*—was finished by the end of World War I and published several years later. An English translation of this work was made in 1922. The *Tractatus* consisted of several theses, such as:[185] "The world

178. Georg Henrik von Wright, *Ludwig Wittgenstein: A Memoir, with a Biographical Sketch* (Oxford: Oxford University Press, 1962), 5–6.

179. *HWPT*, 468: "Wittgenstein left Cambridge to fight for Austria in World War I, but he carried with him through the war a set of papers on which he wrote the only book published during his lifetime, the *Tractatus Logico-Philosophicus*, a book that comes to 111 pages in the Internet edition, including introductions, but not indices."

180. Von Wright, *Ludwig Wittgenstein*, 18: "I believe that most of those who loved him and had his friendship also feared him."

181. Ibid., 20.

182. Ibid., 22.

183. Ibid., 21.

184. The move was from holding that what a person knows about an object exists only in that person's mind to the teaching that universals (concepts) have real and independent existence.

185. *HWPT*, 469: "The *Tractatus* attempts to establish rigorous limits to meaningful language. . . . A meaningful proposition is either an *elementary proposition* or one that can be reduced to one. . . . Elementary propositions are statements of what Russell called *atomic*

is all that is the case"; "What is the case—a fact—is the existence of a state of affairs"; "A logical picture of facts is a thought"; "A thought is a proposition with a sense"; "A proposition is a truth-function of elementary propositions"; and "What we cannot speak about we must pass over in silence."[186] The work centered on two philosophical issues: the first was the theory of truth-function, and the second was language as a picture of reality.[187]

Wittgenstein published two small works more than a decade later—the *Blue and Brown Books*, representing his Cambridge lectures delivered between 1933 and 1935 and published in two volumes. After his death, a number of notebooks were published, some antedating the *Tractatus*. Wittgenstein's thought is divided into his earlier and later periods. Some scholars have claimed that the later Wittgenstein has no philosophical ancestors.[188]

MICHAEL POLANYI (A.D. 1891–1976)[189]

Biography. The best way to begin to comprehend Michael Polanyi is to think of him as a scientist who grew dissatisfied with how philoso-

---

facts. . . . This is merely to restate Hume's argument that you cannot derive *ought* from *is*—you cannot derive ethical obligations from statements of facts"; further, 471: "Wittgenstein admits that what he has tried to do violates his own criteria for meaningful language"; and 472: "On that criterion, the *Tractatus* had solved all philosophical problems. The rationalism of this claim correlates with the irrationalist claim that answers to foundational questions are mystical."

186. Ludwig Wittgenstein, *Tractatus Logico-Philosophicus* (New York: Harcourt, Brace & Company, 1922), 31, 171, 189.

187. *HWPT*, 470: "Statements of this sort fall into a category that Wittgenstein called *the Mystical.* . . . The Mystical of Wittgenstein is similar to the noumenal world of Kant. . . . But they have done us the favor of showing us that God and revelation make no sense at all in a philosophical scheme presupposing human autonomy. . . . Wittgenstein recognizes that his own book falls prey to the same criticisms he has made of ethical, metaphysical, and religious language. . . . The *Tractatus* aims to show the relation between language and the world. But as we have seen, *world* has a problematic status in this book. . . . So Wittgenstein's special language, his perfect language, not only excludes ethical, religious, and metaphysical language, but also excludes attempts to show the relation between language and reality. Yet that exclusion applies to the *Tractatus* itself. . . . In Wittgenstein's view the perfect language can only state facts. It cannot refer to relations between language and fact, even though those relations are indeed facts of a higher order. . . . But the *Tractatus* is precisely an attempt to state in language the relationships between language and fact."

188. Von Wright, *Ludwig Wittgenstein*, 15.

189. For further analysis of Polanyi, with a particular focus on theological issues, see Richard C. Gamble, "Critical Realism and the New Perspective," *RPTJ* 1, no. 2 (Spring 2015): 4–12.

phers explained his own field of endeavor. From this dissatisfaction, Polanyi developed an entire epistemological system.[190] But he was not a normal scientist—or even a normal philosopher, for that matter.

Polanyi was born into a Jewish home in Hungary in the final years of the nineteenth century. He was trained as a physician in Budapest, and he served as such in World War I. In 1920 he began research in Germany. Three years later, he was elected to the Kaiser Wilhelm Institute for Physical Chemistry. After a decade, Polanyi began to see firsthand the problems connected with National Socialism. So in 1933 he moved to England.[191] One of his brothers immigrated to Brazil, another to Italy, and the third to the United States. His older sister was a specialist in the field of rural sociology. While Michael was in England, in 1944 he was made a fellow of the Royal Society. He also taught as a professor of physical chemistry and social studies at the University of Manchester.[192]

During this time, the way in which science was comprehended is generally termed *positivism*. Polanyi, however, felt that positivism tended too greatly toward reductionism. The notion that all ideas derive from a single homogeneous type did not resonate with the way in which

190. Jerry H. Gill, *The Tacit Mode: Michael Polanyi's Postmodern Philosophy* (New York: State University of New York Press, 1999), 53: "The whole of Polanyi's work is to be understood as an attempt to counteract this one-sided emphasis on objectivity in modern epistemological thought by establishing the personal dimension of cognitive activity"; Marjorie Greene, introduction to *Knowing and Being*, by Michael Polyani (Chicago: University of Chicago Press, 1969), xiii: "It was, indeed, the problem of the organization of science which moved Polanyi, in the first instance, to embark on philosophical reflection"; Eugene Webb, *Philosophers of Consciousness* (Seattle: University of Washington Press, 1988), 30–31: "His own career was that of a scientist who eventually turned to reflection on the cognitive process he had experienced in the practice of science. . . . From his own description of it, it seems that Polanyi's interest in philosophical reflection on science and cognition in general developed in large part out of his dissatisfaction with the currently prevalent account, which was that of positivism."

191. The details of Polanyi's early years are not clear (at least to me). Drusilla Scott, (*Everyman Revived* [Grand Rapids: Eerdmans, 1985], 2) says that he was raised in Hungary and entered the University of Budapest in 1909. Webb (*Philosophers*, 26–27), however, hints that Polanyi's father had already emigrated to Switzerland after the 1848 revolt, studied engineering there, then married a Russian countess, who had also fled to Switzerland (because she tried to blow up the Tsar!). The question seems to be, Was Polanyi born of a dispossessed Jewish family that had emigrated from Hungary and then raised in Switzerland? As to his formal education, Scott has his training entirely in Hungary, with a move to Germany in 1920. Concerning the move to England, Polanyi must have had tremendous linguistic abilities to continue a career in yet another language (his third) at age forty-one.

192. Webb, *Philosophers*, 26–31.

he thought or did science. In addition, positivism did not seem strong enough to bear the burden of a comprehensive philosophical system.[193]

Polanyi's first major publication appeared in 1946 under the title *Science, Faith, and Society*.[194] The University of Manchester wisely changed his duties after its appearance so that he no longer had to teach.[195] This change allowed him time to work on the Gifford Lectures for 1951 to 1952; they later became the book *Personal Knowledge*.[196] In large part, this volume was a reaction to Albert Einstein's theory. Polanyi was convinced that Einstein's work, moving from absolute time and space to relativity, illustrated well the way scientific knowing takes place but also undermined the philosophical rule of positivism.[197]

Polanyi understood that science was performed in this way: the scientist begins with a question that searches for a rational order, then the scientist moves to a solution to the question. Polanyi recognized that in working as a scientist, there were times when he knew more than he could fully explain. Such knowledge, labeled *tacit* knowledge, could not be accounted for by philosophers. Polanyi's thinking continued to develop, and at the end of the 1950s he produced *The Study of Man*, which investigated what he termed *focal* and *subsidiary awareness*.[198]

By the middle of the twentieth century, Polanyi had a well-developed epistemology and philosophy of science. He stood against eminent contemporaries such as Karl Popper. But Polanyi's critiques touched every major philosophical figure; for example, he opposed Descartes's system of doubting and even the thinking of Kant.[199]

193. Ibid., 32.

194. Michael Polanyi, *Science, Faith, and Society* (1945; repr., Chicago/London: University of Chicago Press, 1964).

195. Scott, *Everyman Revived*, 3.

196. Michael Polanyi, *Personal Knowledge: Towards a Post-Critical Philosophy* (1958; repr., Chicago: University of Chicago Press, 1962). There is, of course, much more in this trend-setting study.

197. Already in 1912, Einstein had responded very positively to the paper by the twenty-one-year-old Polanyi on the third law of thermodynamics. Correspondence between the men continued. See Scott, *Everyman Revived*, 2.

198. Michael Polanyi, *The Study of Man* (Chicago/London: University of Chicago Press, 1959). Some of his other major works include *The Logic of Liberty* (London: Routledge/Kegan Paul, 1951); *Knowing and Being*, ed. Marjorie Greene (London: Routledge/Kegan Paul, 1961); and *The Tacit Dimension* (Chicago/London: University of Chicago Press, 1966).

199. Webb, *Philosophers*, 32–39.

Researchers describe Polanyi's philosophy as a commentary on the fact of human consciousness.[200] During his own time, he was critiqued by analytic philosophers and by those who doubted whether tacit knowledge is really knowledge at all.[201] It is fascinating that the Polanyi name continues to have an impact in the West. In 1986, ten years after Polanyi's death, his son won the Nobel Prize for Chemistry.[202]

Science's Reign. In 1959, Polanyi equated the impact that Christianity had on the world in the first three centuries A.D. to the influence that science has exercised on the West in the last three centuries. Sadly, he was likely correct. In his analysis, science is now the supreme intellectual authority.[203] According to Polanyi, science's pathway to this pinnacle is easily traceable. Science began with rebellion against authority. After a successful rebellion, it led reforms that aided every aspect of human culture. Science's reform movement was based on the presupposition of empirical induction, with the goal of developing a mechanistic theory of the universe. Yet Polanyi thought that this movement of liberation had now turned pathological.[204] Given that science could be salutary for a time, he was convinced that eventually people would realize that science's principles were, in his words, nonsensical and absurd, and manifestly so.[205] One reason for his displeasure with scientific rationalism was that its adherents had to profess that everything can, and must, be explained by physics and chemistry.

But physics and chemistry cannot account for human consciousness, not to mention for morality and human responsibility. Instead of admitting scientific rationalism's inherent limitations, many scientists have simply denied the existence of human consciousness. For they know that acknowledging the human conscious would endanger their field, so they deny consciousness and coterminously embrace scientific

200. Such a dismissal does not take Polanyi's own assertions seriously. He claimed to present to the world "a new theory of knowledge," ("Faith and Reason," *The Journal of Religion* 41, no. 4 [1961]: 241), a claim based on what seems to me to be a mountain of evidence that had begun in 1946.

201. Webb, *Philosophers*, 40–52.

202. Ibid., 26–31.

203. Michael Polanyi, "The Two Cultures (1959)," reprinted in *Knowing and Being*, 40–48. He made his point clearly: "'It is contrary to religion!'—the objection ruled supreme in the seventeenth century. 'It is unscientific!' is its equivalent in the twentieth."

204. Polanyi, *Knowing and Being*, 41.

205. Ibid., 41–42. His critique was blunt: "Eventually the truth-bearing power of its absurd ideals was bound to be spent and its stark absurdity to assert itself."

bigotry.[206] While Polanyi ridiculed such shortsightedness, his critical knife would cut even more deeply into the fabric of the scientific world. He argued that disregarding truth in favor of scientific ideals has led to modern nihilism. And Polanyi laid these charges at nihilism's feet: an unnatural division of the human masses, the severing of families, and ruined friendships as no conflict has done before. Furthermore, while such personal destruction is quantifiable, Polanyi feared an even greater future terror: the decimation of entire cities and civilizations through atomic weapons. This possibility loomed on the horizon because there was no longer sufficient common philosophical ground between the nations bearing the heavy burden of their own atomic weapons.[207]

Polanyi did not, however, leave his reader without hope. There was still the possibility that science could repent and recognize that claiming a criterion of objectivity in fact forced denying reality to any moral claims. Polanyi could see change as a possibility only by one path: the way of revising the worthless claims of science.[208]

Critique of Pure Kant. Deeply embedded within Kant's *Critique of Pure Reason* lies the seed of its own destruction. The seed is the agency of personal decision used when someone classifies a particular incident under a general concept. According to Polanyi, Kant referred to this agency twice—first when it was cited as that which constitutes our so-called *mother-wit*, and again when Kant asserted that it was a skill so deeply hidden within the human soul that he termed this agency *nature's trick*.[209] Polanyi could not comprehend how Kant could simply admit the existence of this powerful mental agency—one that was exempt from analysis or reason. He was also perplexed as to how generations of Kant scholars left unchallenged this submission of reason to some unaccountable decision-making.[210]

---

206. Ibid., 42.

207. For more on Polanyi's development of this idea, see his "Beyond Nihilism (1960)," in *Knowing and Being*, 3–23.

208. Polanyi, *Knowing and Being*, 46. Polanyi, however, did not seem to hold out much actual hope for revision. His footnotes contained the narrative of an encounter that he had at the meeting of the American Association of the Advancement of Science (in 1956). His challenges proved ineffective. If the master himself was incapable of convincing scientists to change, who could hope for lesser lights to be successful?

209. Immanuel Kant, *Critique of Pure Reason*, A.133 and A.141, as cited by Polanyi, *Knowing and Being*, 105.

210. In fact, the situation was not too perplexing for Polanyi. He attributed the Kantian silence to their instinctive preference "to let such sleeping monsters lie, for fear that, once

Thus Polanyi assumed the responsibility to explain this agency of unformalizable mental skills.[211] His approach was multifaceted. First he attacked the notion of strict scientific objectivity by critiquing the classical theory of mechanics—the mathematical formulae by which the planet's motions are governed. Mechanics recognizes that observation and theoretical predictions will have deviations. So the question the scientist must face is whether the deviation is random or indicative of certain trends. It is the process of determining the nature of the deviation where Polanyi admits that strict statistical analysis can determine regularity and randomness while he also argues that the application of those mathematical rules cannot be prescribed by strict rules.[212] Furthermore, the notion of randomness itself means randomness in relationship to potential order. That potential order, Polanyi asserts, is also an informal act of personal interpretation.[213]

His second prong of analysis revolved around human recognition of significant shapes. After discussing camouflage, background figures, Rubin's face/vase, and horizon and rest, Polanyi made a direct connection to Kant's *inscrutable power*.[214] The connection came via Ames's figures of a man and boy in a room where the boy looks taller than the man. The key to understanding the illusion lies in the clues and assumptions that observers make when they view the object. There are no exact rules for the use of the clues.[215] Specialists, however, have noted some general principles relative to the interaction between background and figure; these principles are summarized in the notion that humans have a tendency to overlook things that are unprecedented.[216]

---

awakened, they might destroy their fundamental conception of knowledge" (Polanyi, *Knowing and Being*, 106).

211. At a later place, he defined Kant's unaccounted-for agency this way: "The mother-wit to which Kant surrenders the application of rules to experience and of that inscrutable power hidden in the bosom of Nature, by which he accounts for our capacity to form and apply universal conceptions—th[is is] tacit power" (ibid., 112).

212. After a pattern has been chosen (for example, direction or periodicity), the scientist's computations will yield a numerical value for the probability of the pattern. But there are no *rules* to determine the pattern! See ibid., 107–8.

213. Ibid., 109.

214. Ibid., 110–11.

215. Ibid., 112.

216. Ibid., 113. Polanyi states the principle precisely: "Whenever we are focusing our attention on a particular object, we are relying for doing so on our awareness of many things to which we are not attending directly at the moment, but which are yet functioning as compelling clues for the way the object of our attention will appear to our senses."

Polanyi was able to present many scientific examples of this tendency emphasizing the important function of peripheral impression used as clues. He described this art as that which helps humans, relative to perception, make sense of the world.[217] Of significance to Polanyi was the fact that the main clues are inside the body and cannot be experienced in themselves.[218] It was from this wealth of analysis that Polanyi turned on Kant and doubted that Kant was correct in his despair relative to elucidating this agency. While much can be known about it, very little can be articulated with exactitude. Polanyi concluded his analysis by tying the opening rifle shot aimed at Kant to a frontal blast focused on scientific work in general, and epistemology in particular.[219] According to his penetrating analysis, what is needed is nothing less than a set of new definitions of the nature of experience and eternal reality.[220]

Polanyi and Austin. As a philosopher of language, John Langshaw Austin (1911–1960) developed much of the current *speech-act theory*. He was educated at Balliol College, Oxford, and became White's Professor of Moral Philosophy at his alma mater after World War II. With Wittgenstein, Austin advocated an examination of the way people use words to understand a given word's meaning.

Austin's philosophical interests were different from those of Polanyi, and thus it is not easy to make connections for comparison. Nevertheless, Ian Ramsey did just that in a chapter titled "Polanyi and J. L. Austin."[221] He found the following similarities: a shared critical attitude toward scientific detachment; a shared notion that knowledge is descriptive information regarding supposedly objective facts; and a

217. Ibid., 114–15.
218. Ibid., 115.
219. Ibid., 118: "It is customary today to represent the process of scientific inquiry as the setting up of a hypothesis followed by its subsequent testing. I cannot accept these terms"; and 119: "My own answer to this paradox is to restate an ancient metaphysical conception in new terms."
220. Ibid., 120. *HWPT*, 482: "Polanyi . . . rejected the positivist notion of objective scientific knowledge, arguing that personal commitments are necessary to scientific discovery. . . . So scientific knowledge presupposes personal knowledge."
221. See Ian Ramsey, "Polanyi and J. L. Austin," in *Intellect and Hope: Essays in the Thought of Michael Polanyi*, ed. A. Langford and W. Poteat (Durham: Duke University Press, 1968). Ramsey summarized the difference: "Austin was the more analytical and critical, more professional linguistic philosopher than the synthetic, constructive scientist with a background in social studies" (ibid., 170).

shared recognition that some assertions have a self-involving character. In sum, they were both repulsed by an oversimplified empiricism and its ontology.[222] Specifically, Polanyi argued that when a psychiatrist recognized a disease—say, for example, an epileptic seizure—there were no precise, specifiable criteria for such recognition. The psychiatrist needed something more, and that more was understanding.[223]

Understanding came when the psychiatrist comprehended all the observed particulars, in other words, when he came to an awareness of the entity as a whole. This type of understanding, according to Polanyi, is specifically excluded by positivistic epistemology because that system refuses "to acknowledge the existence of comprehensive entities as distinct from their particulars."[224] Yet for Polanyi, this complex was the central act of knowing.

Ramsey chose a similar situation from Austin's writings. As Polanyi had a psychiatrist identifying an epileptic seizure, Austin had a goldfinch flying onto a branch. Different answers may be offered to answer the question of how a person knows that the bird is a goldfinch. A proper answer had to steer between too definite an answer—because it has a red head, which reason would be stereotyped empiricism—and lean toward one that simply "recognized" that the bird was a goldfinch "from its red head."[225] The two answers, according to Austin, differ materially because the words *like, from,* or *by* possess an essential "vagueness."[226] The issue for Austin is recognition, not proof by descriptive assertion.[227]

In this way, Ramsey was able to identify the similarity between Austin's *recognition* of the goldfinch and Polanyi's psychiatric *comprehension* of the epilepsy. Both would concur that the details were only part of the story and would disagree with a simplistic positivism that made the particulars out to be the whole story.[228] Ramsey gleaned a second example from Polanyi's article "The Creative Imagination"

222. Ibid.

223. Ibid., 171–72.

224. Polanyi, "Faith and Reason," 240, as cited by Ramsey, "Polanyi and Austin," 172.

225. Ramsey, "Polanyi and Austin," 173–74.

226. J. L. Austin, *Philosophical Papers* (Oxford: Oxford University Press, 1961), 53, as cited by Ramsey, "Polanyi and Austin," 174.

227. It seems that for Austin, to *recognize* is not necessarily the same as to *know.*

228. Ramsey, "Polanyi and Austin," 175.

(1966), in which Polanyi focused on ordinary perception. Ramsey saw that focal attention, or comprehension or tacit awareness, is "clearly a kinsman of Austin's 'recognition' which goes beyond the features which may be separately described."[229]

A second major place of agreement between the two thinkers is found in the notion of self-involvement. There was a connection between Polanyi's notion of personal knowledge and Austin on convictional language. They both recognized "the ultimacy for epistemology of the personal act of affirmation, of the speech act."[230]

Ramsey's intention was not simply to compare these two leading philosophers. Instead, his aim was to underline their weaknesses—weaknesses that would supposedly be strengthened by adopting Ramsey's own notion of *disclosure*.[231] Specifically, adopting Ramsey's notion of disclosure gives to Austin "reference" and offers to Polanyi "more than a 'psychological point.'"[232] Further, Polanyi's concept of *tacit knowledge* and the knowledge of particulars would be able to be better related through the avenue of disclosure.[233] Yet Ramsey's own suggestions are no stronger than those of Polanyi.

In conclusion, this brief philosophical analysis of such diverse areas as process philosophy, Ludwig Wittgenstein, Michael Polanyi, and J. L. Austin demonstrates that after two and a half millennia of exploring, scientists and philosophers are still desperately searching for epistemological certainty. They have yet to find a rock on which to stand. Understanding the historical contours of this search is beneficial for believers as they approach unbelievers with the gospel of Christ. The next section will examine the life and thinking of a theologian who spent his life helping others to see that Christ alone is the place of security.

229. Ibid., 176–77.
230. Ibid., 193. See earlier remarks also at 183, 190.
231. Ibid., 170: "My own concept of disclosure can be used to interpret the insights of both Austin and Polanyi in a way that avoids the crude metaphysics which Austin rejected, while clarifying and developing Polanyi's discussion at certain crucial points"; and 177: "It is at this point that I believe that the accounts of both Polanyi and Austin are inadequate, and where I am bold enough to suggest that by an appeal to the concept of disclosure . . . both will discover a supplement which each needs." For more on Ramsey's argument for "disclosure" as a move beyond either one, see also 171, 175.
232. Ibid., 179.
233. Ibid., 183.

CORNELIUS VAN TIL (A.D. 1895–1987)

John Frame, a student of Cornelius Van Til, said of him, "Van Til is perhaps the most important Christian thinker since Calvin."[234] Van Til helped press the worldview of Scripture into every corner of thought and practice. His life and works merit attention, appreciation, and absorption.

Biography. Cornelius Van Til was born in Grootegast, Netherlands, as the sixth son of a dairy farmer. When Cornelius was just ten years old, his family immigrated to the United States and began farming in Indiana. He was the first of his family to pursue higher education. He attended Calvin College in Grand Rapids, Michigan, and Princeton Theological Seminary. He earned his bachelor of theology degree in 1924 and his master of theology in 1925.[235] Coterminously, he attended Princeton University and obtained his master of arts in 1924 and his doctorate in philosophy in 1927.

While a student at Princeton, Van Til wrote a paper on covenant theology and human freedom that laid the foundation for some of his later work.[236] While studying at Princeton, he began to develop a Reformed epistemology that was based on Bavinck's previous, groundbreaking work. He argued that humans in different biblical states or categories—such as pre-fall Adam, the unregenerate, and the regenerate—think in distinct manners. In addition to articulating the antithesis between believing and unbelieving thought, Van Til's thesis addressed the Trinity, the organic connection between creation and covenant,

---

234. John M. Frame, *Cornelius Van Til: An Analysis of His Thought* (Phillipsburg, NJ: P&R Publishing, 1995) (*CVT*), 44, 46, 47: "I would not advance this parallel between Van Til and Kant if Van Til's thought were on a level of sophistication far below that of the German philosopher. . . . Students of philosophy who give Van Til's work a careful examination will find the sheer intellectual quality, subtlety, and penetration of his work not one bit inferior. Indeed, Van Til's intellectual caliber reinforces the comparison . . . thus laying a necessary foundation that ought to be the basis for all subsequent Christian reflection."

235. He wrote his master's thesis under the systematic theologian C. W. Hodge, successor to B. B. Warfield and grandson of Charles Hodge. John R. Muether, *Cornelius Van Til: Reformed Apologist and Churchman* (Phillipsburg, NJ: P&R Publishing, 2008), 52: His doctorate was awarded "after he defended his dissertation on 'God and the Absolute.'"

236. Ibid., 54: "He located the 'philosophical basis for covenant theology' in a 'transcendental realism' that avoided the pitfalls of both pragmatism and idealism"; and 55, concerning biblical epistemology: "Autonomy and creatureliness are incompatible, no matter how intoxicated modern thinking is with the former."

and the proper use of reason. In his thesis, Van Til also appropriated and rejected aspects of the works of both Warfield and Kuyper .[237] By the time he finished his Princeton University dissertation, Van Til was already aware of problems in the old-Princeton apologetic approach and was on his way to address those weaknesses.[238]

Upon graduating, Van Til accepted a pastorate at a church in Michigan. As a pastor in the Dutch tradition, Van Til conducted a ministry that combined preaching, house visitation, and catechetical instruction.[239] After only one year as pastor of this congregation, Princeton called Van Til to return to teach apologetics. Had Machen remained the chair of apologetics at Princeton, Van Til would likely never have served there. But he did return, and succeeding W. B. Greene he sought to change the direction of Princeton's apologetic methodology.[240] In the midst of the controversy engulfing the direction and character of that great seminary, Van Til sided with Machen.[241] After just one year, Princeton offered Van Til a full-time teaching position, which he declined in order to return to his church in Michigan.[242] He claimed that the purpose of all his advanced study was simply to help him more faithfully minister the Word of God.[243] But Van Til knew that he was needed back east. He promised Machen to help at the

237. Ibid., 55, 56: "Aquinas led to Bishop Butler's analogy, which begot Charles Hodge, who produced Buswell and Clark"; and 80: "Van Til's article, 'Nature and Scripture,' outlines and defends a distinctively Reformed approach to natural revelation based on the first chapter of the Westminster Confession of Faith."

238. K. Scott Oliphint, "The Consistency of Van Til's Methodology," *WTJ* 52, no. 1 (Spring 1990), 27–49, and his "Cornelius Van Til and the Reformation of Christian Apologetics," in *Revelation and Reason*, ed. K. Scott Oliphint and Lane G. Tipton (Phillipsburg, NJ: P&R Publishing, 2007), 280.

239. Muether, *Van Til*, 58.

240. Ibid., 59.

241. See chapter 21 on Machen. Muether (*Van Til*, 62) cited a letter to Machen from Ned B. Stonehouse, who said: "and no doubt will be asked to fill any vacancy which may occur in the department of philosophy of the college or the department of theology or apologetics in the seminary . . . and should leave after a short period of time from two to ten years of service." Muether (ibid., 63) also cited Van Til's reflection on teaching with Machen: "But we could not help but imbibe something of his spirit of unreserved devotion to the one goal of lifting up the banner of Christ on top of the highest mountain."

242. Muether, *Van Til*, 60. *CVT*, 22, 23: "Van Til was enormously reluctant to leave Spring Lake, but after much correspondence and personal visits by Allis, Stonehouse, and Machen himself, Van Til, several days before the opening exercises, accepted the offer."

243. Cornelius Van Til, "My Credo," in *Jerusalem and Athens: Critical Discussions on the Theology and Apologetics of Cornelius Van Til*, ed. E. R. Geehan (Nutley, NJ: P&R Publishing, 1971), 8, as cited by Muether, *Van Til*, 58–59.

new Westminster Theological Seminary for one year, while his church eagerly awaited his return.[244]

Naturally there was antagonism between the new Westminster and the old Princeton.[245] Some have thought that Machen was against Van Til's new apologetic method.[246] But Machen appears to have supported Van Til's new direction.[247] Van Til's apologetic method and his position at Westminster Seminary were secure.[248] Immediately before the establishment of the Orthodox Presbyterian Church (OPC) in 1936, there was trouble at Westminster Seminary. Machen's strong ecclesiastical position—in opposition to his denomination's direction,

244. Muether (*Van Til*, 67) cited the Christian Reformed magazine *The Banner*, which commented: "We are not unwilling to sacrifice our very best men if thereby we can help to make Westminster a stronghold of Calvinism in a country where positively Calvinistic schools are so rare."

245. Ibid., 73: "Van Til's lengthy review he countered, was a perversion of his position and a dishonoring of the Princeton tradition"; further, 73–74: "Van Til's unworthy motives, Mackenzie went on to charge, displayed less zeal for the Reformed faith than antagonism to his former employer. As the Auburn Affirmation continued to 'haunt' Van Til 'like a nightmare,' Mackenzie said, Van Til created a new heretic 'unknown to the Westminster divines'; Mackenzie termed it a 'modern Princetonianist'"; and 74: "Charles Bouma, editor of the *Calvin Forum*, . . . pronounced Princeton's Barthian phase as 'on the wane.'"

246. Ibid., 68: "Allan MacRae . . . maintained that Machen privately told him in 'the strongest language' that he 'stood with Warfield and against Van Til.' . . . Had Machen devoted the time to studying the matter, he would certainly have asked Van Til to leave. . . . If, as Machen contended, indifferentism to doctrine made no heroes of the faith, Van Til went a step further in arguing that indifference to apologetic method made ineffective defenders of the faith. . . . Van Til suffered Arminian apologetics no more gladly than Machen welcomed evangelical moderates. Reformed theology could do better than that."

247. Ibid., 70: "Going even further, Machen hoped to submit to Van Til's instruction. 'I wish I could take your courses in Evidences. I need it, and I am sure it is greatly to the benefit of the Seminary that you are offering it.'"

248. Ibid., 72: "Together, [Van Til and Murray] expressed common indebtedness to the biblical theological approach of Geerhardus Vos, and each oriented his own approach to systematic theology around the history of redemption"; further, 129: "Taking his cue from Vos, Van Til argued that there was no human knowledge that was not revelational"; 131: "Eschatological life, Vos had taught Van Til, is more than merely another stage in the culmination of the benefits of redemption; it is life of a different order. . . . The creation-fall-redemption paradigm of neo-Calvinism could not fully account for the qualitative difference of the resurrected life, life in the consummate state"; 130: "It may not be too great a stretch to imagine, therefore, that Vos provided Van Til with the tools to comprehend not only redemptive history but also the story of Western philosophy. In neither soteriology nor epistemology is neutrality possible"; and finally, 72: "Murray embraced Van Til's understanding of analogical knowledge and his notion of the interrelation of general and special revelation. Murray affirmed the self-attestation of Scripture and even articulated a form of circular reasoning in his article in *The Infallible Word* (1946) in what John Frame described as 'the most explicitly Van Tillian passage in Murray's writings.'"

which moved toward a split in the mother church—caused the resignation of nearly half the members of the seminary's board.[249]

Van Til had been teaching at Princeton and Westminster for nearly ten years when Machen had his troubles with the Presbyterian Church (USA) and left the liberal-leaning denomination to start the OPC. Unhappy with his own denomination—the Christian Reformed Church—Van Til joined Machen in the young OPC and never left.[250] Machen, however, lived only a short time after the establishment of the OPC, and with his death there was a vacuum of power in both the church and seminary. At the age of forty-one, Van Til was now the senior faculty member at Westminster. The church was also experiencing both internal and external troubles. Externally, the church was beginning to face the increasingly influential educational philosophy of John Dewey. Van Til was convinced that Dewey and evolution were destructive to Christian education.[251] And within the church, there was strife with some members who held to premillennial dispensationalism.[252] The OT scholar Allan MacRae, for example, contended with Van Til's amillennialism.[253] In addition, Wheaton College president J. Oliver Buswell and others began to question the direction of apologetics at Westminster and, to make matters worse, even wrongly claimed that Van Til was rejecting the theology of Hodge.[254] The new denomination and seminary, just ten years old at this time, began to be questioned.[255] In the midst of this strife, Van Til began to grow concerned that the OPC was becoming less Reformed.[256] In 1944, the Synod of the Christian Reformed Church invited Van Til a way out of the controversies by replacing Louis Berkhof as professor of Systematic Theology at Calvin Theological Seminary.[257] Van Til declined this

249. Ibid., 75.

250. Ibid., 77–78.

251. Ibid., 81. For information on Dewey, see chapter 20.

252. The controversy became public when O. T. Allis published an article against dispensationalism in January 1935 (ibid., 82).

253. Ibid., 87.

254. Buswell misunderstood Van Til; Buswell claimed that Van Til excluded the underlying assumptions of Hodge and others and so asked whether he also excluded Machen's analysis (ibid., 85–86).

255. Ibid., 96.

256. Ibid., 117.

257. Ibid., 98; and 99: "Murray was bold enough to advise that Van Til not abandon his calling in apologetics because he was simply not qualified to specialize in systematic theology."

appealing offer and remained at Westminster, where he would teach for another thirty-five years. One enduring fruit of those thirty-five years was Van Til's groundbreaking apologetic method.

Apologetic Method. Van Til defined apologetics as "the vindication of Christian theism against any form of non-theistic and non-Christian thought."[258] Part of Van Til's vision was to establish the Reformed faith as a self-sustaining system.[259] He believed that a Protestant theology required a Protestant apologetic. Van Til described his own system as follows:

> Throughout my aim has been to show that it is the historic Reformed Faith alone that can in any adequate way present the claims of Christ to men for their salvation. The Reformed Faith alone does anything like full justice to the cultural and missionary mandates of Christ. The Reformed Faith alone has anything like an adequately stated view of God, of man, and of Christ as the mediator between God and man. It is because the Reformed Faith alone has an essentially sound, because biblical, theology, that it alone has anything like a sound, that is biblical, method of challenging the world of unbelief to repentance and faith.[260]

John Frame reacted to the teaching of Van Til by saying: "I was amazed to find that the same Bible that presents the message of salvation also presents a distinctive philosophy, including metaphysics, epistemology, and ethics, one which alone makes sense of human life."[261] According to Frame, Van Til's apologetic made four advances: in (1) the metaphysics of knowledge,[262] (2) the ethics of knowledge,[263] (3) the argument for Christianity,[264] and (4) his critique of unbelief.[265]

258. Cornelius Van Til, *Christian Theistic Evidences* (Phillipsburg, NJ: P&R Publishing, 1978), 1.

259. Cornelius Van Til, *The Defense of the Faith* (Philadelphia: Presbyterian and Reformed, 1955), 84: "What point of contact is there in the mind and heart of the unbeliever to which the believer may appeal when he presents to him the Christian view of life?"

260. Cornelius Van Til, *Toward a Reformed Apologetics* (Philadelphia: privately printed, 1972), 3, as cited by Muether, *Van Til*, 211.

261. *CVT*, 15.

262. Ibid., 53: "In my opinion, his account of the metaphysics of knowledge merits superlative commendation."

263. Ibid.

264. Ibid.

265. Ibid., 51.

Van Til rejected the old-Princeton apologetic.[266] Some have claimed that Van Til did not create a new Reformed apologetic but simply adapted Bavinck's robust system found in his four-volume *Reformed Dogmatics*, which was not at the time available in English.[267] Others believe that he brought about a Copernican revolution in apologetic methodology.[268] Van Til rejected the old-Princeton apologetic as expressed in the methodology of Bishop Butler.[269] Butler believed that there was a high probability that Christianity was true,[270] but he held that even if there was only a slight chance that the claims of Christianity were true, then well-reasoning people should act on its precepts.

As an empiricist, Butler understood knowledge to be founded on experience.[271] Butler wrote:

> Reason can, and it ought to judge, not only of the meaning, but also of the morality and the evidence, of revelation. First, it is the province of reason to judge of the morality of the scripture; i.e., not whether it contains things different from what we should have expected from a wise, just, and good Being . . . but whether it contains things plainly contradictory to wisdom, justice, or goodness; to what the light of nature teaches us of God.[272]

For Butler, facts do not testify to the existence of God. Facts are simply fact that awaits interpretation.[273]

---

266. Comparing old Princeton and old Amsterdam on the use of reason, Van Til said: "In short, because I hold to the appeal to reason as autonomous to be both illegitimate and destructive from the point of view of [the] Reformed faith that I am bound to reject [Valentine] Hepp's position [old Amsterdam] as well as that of old-Princeton apologetics. But happily I can do so in view of the theology that I learned from old Princeton and Amsterdam" (Muether, *Van Til*, 162–63).

267. Muether, *Van Til*, 115–16.

268. Oliphint, "Reformation of Christian Apologetics," 280: "Any historical survey of Christian apologetics would show that, since Aquinas, the church has done little to develop the discipline of apologetics until Van Til. . . . Van Til's influence will be seen by future generations as a 'Copernican revolution,' in apologetics."

269. For more on Bishop Butler, see chapter 19.

270. Van Til, *Evidences*, 7.

271. Ibid., 31. Butler rejected a priori reasoning. Butler's appeal is to fact. Miracle and fulfilled prophecy are facts.

272. Butler, *Analogy*, 238–39, as cited by Van Til, *Evidences*, 12.

273. Van Til, *Evidences*, 16. Oliphint, "Reformation of Christian Apologetics," 59n57: "A brute fact is a mute fact. That is, it is a fact that does not 'say' anything; it has no meaning, unless and until a person gives meaning to it. . . . For Van Til, there are no brute facts because

Van Til was convinced that Butler's own faith was suspect. Butler held a deficient view of humanity's original state, an essentially Arminian soteriology, and the belief that human reason (post-fall) was in basically the same condition as it was pre-fall.[274] Butler also taught that human will is inclined toward good.[275] He argued that if someone foreign to Christian beliefs were presented with evidence from natural religion, as corroborated by Scripture, that person would find no conflict between reason and revelation. In sum, Butler believed that Christian practice is reasonable and that Christianity's truthfulness is highly probable.[276]

Hume's skepticism, however, undermined both empiricism and Butler's apologetic method. Hume had a high regard for Butler. The two shared an opposition to a priori reasoning, as they both believed that all knowledge comes from sensation.[277] Hume and Butler also believed that each sensation has no systematic relation to other sensations, and likewise each particular idea recalls other particular ideas to create general ideas. This theory eliminated the possibility of cause-and-effect. Each sensation must be discreet.[278] The theory also meant that there is no logical relation between the past and the future. While Butler believed that nature could be expected to remain the same in the future, Hume countered that such an expectation was merely custom.[279] Hume held that the human expectation that tomorrow will be like today is nonrational.[280]

---

every fact is a created fact. As created, every fact carries with it God's own interpretation. God speaks the facts into existence, and he speaks through that which he has created"; and 77n49: "It is the case . . . that brute facts are meaningless, nonsense, and of no value, in that their meaning, sense, and value must be found in the 'system' in which they exist. . . . The only real way to make sense of facts is to understand them in terms of the Christian system of thought."

274. Van Til, *Evidences*, 21–22.

275. Ibid., 25: "There is no mention of the need of regeneration anywhere in Butler's *Analogy*."

276. Ibid., 30–31.

277. Ibid., 33–35. Oliphint, "Reformation of Christian Apologetics," 35n8: "What made Hume more radical in his empiricism is that he argued that knowledge of facts could have only an empirical foundation; nothing else could be added to, or synthesized with, our sense experience in order for us to claim to know."

278. Van Til, *Evidences*, 36–37. Oliphint, "Reformation of Christian Apologetics," 38n15: "We do not have cause and effect because there is no necessity in the second ball moving. For various reasons, it might have remained where it was. Thus sensation cannot establish the cause-and-effect relationship."

279. Van Til, *Evidences*, 38.

280. Ibid., 40.

Van Til found two dominant inconsistencies in Butler's arguments. First, Van Til explained that Butler's notion that the course of nature will remain constant in the future rests on an unwarranted presupposition, or, stated differently, on an uncritical remnant of apriorism.[281] Second, Butler held to an author of nature—another unwarranted presupposition.[282] One might argue that, based on humanity's contingent existence, God's existence is necessary—that is, the necessary is dependent on the contingent in order for it to be defined as necessary. If that were the case, then necessity and contingency would mutually entail each other, which by definition is impossible.[283] "Thus," Van Til wrote, "we are back at chance as the most fundamental concept in philosophy. A priori reasoning on non-Christian assumptions, leads to the apotheosis of chance and thus to the destruction of predication."[284]

Hume was critical of using miracles as a proof for Christianity. He reasoned that even if all the biblical miracles actually occurred, their validity would merely demonstrate the strange nature of natural events, not the truthfulness of the Christian faith.[285] Hume also denied the argument from design as a proof for the existence of God. An a posteriori method will never prove an absolute deity. It can, at best, prove a finite god who is subject to limitations. Based on experience, there is no way to bridge the chasm from the finite to the infinite.[286]

Van Til believed that Butler's methodology was tied to an Arminian understanding of God and that such a methodology would only flourish when and where Arminianism flourished.[287] But Butler's methodology was appealing in that it appeared to provide common ground with unbelievers on the issue of fact. In other words, the believer and the unbeliever could appeal to facts to settle their dif-

281. If someone were to try to defend Butler and concede that he was an inconsistent empiricist, Van Til had an answer at hand. Can we grant an apriorism to escape Hume's skepticism? Ibid.: "The 'reasonable use of reason' . . . was entirely uncritical"; further, 44: "A pure empiricism can give no presumption for anything to happen in the future. A pure empiricism would require us to be entirely neutral as to the future"; and 48: "On an empirical basis there can be no positive presumption that the future will be like the past and the unknown like the known."
282. Ibid., 41.
283. Ibid., 47n28.
284. Ibid., 48.
285. Ibid., 49.
286. Ibid., 52–53.
287. Ibid., 61.

ferences.[288] Yet, as will be seen shortly, Van Til rejected even the existence of brute facts.

Van Til rejected the old-Princeton apologetic based on his theological notion of God's aseity. He was convinced that divine aseity is a key to proper theology and apologetics. God is the fullness of being; he is self-contained. And for Van Til, this aseity included his Trinitarian being.[289] As self-contained, God spoke this world into existence from nothing, providentially controls creation, and procured redemption for the elect through Christ.[290] Divine aseity distinguishes the biblical worldview from its alternatives. Since apologetics seeks to prove God's existence, God must be presented as he is: *a se*. Such a God, and only such a God, provides a Bible that is self-authenticating.[291] Van Til was convinced, and rightly so, that Scripture's testimony about itself should be accepted based on its own authority.[292] The God of the Bible is in no way dependent on the world—a view that contrasts with both polytheistic and monistic worldviews.

Divine aseity bears with it epistemological implications. God knows himself and the world by knowing himself. He knows that which is possible by knowing his own power; he knows that which is actual by knowing his own eternal plan; and he perfectly knows the temporal accomplishment of his plan. He does not need creation even for his knowledge of creation. But humans, as his creation, need to know the Creator to know themselves or anything else. In Romans, Paul makes clear that all people know God, and they do to some extent. Yet to understand God exhaustively lies beyond the bounds of human ability. He is utterly incomprehensible.[293]

Divine aseity also has implications for methodology in apologetics. Because of the doctrine of aseity, apologists can presuppose God's

288. Ibid., 62. See K. Scott Oliphint, *Covenantal Apologetics: Principles and Practice in Defense of Our Faith* (Wheaton, IL: Crossway, 2013), 110–13, 117–22.

289. It also includes God as personal. Frame says that Van Til correlates *personal* with *self-contained*. John Frame, "Divine Aseity and Apologetics," in *Revelation and Reason: New Essays in Reformed Apologetics*, ed. K. Scott Oliphint and Lane G. Tipton (Phillipsburg, NJ: P&R Publishing, 2007), 120n21, 121: "So the phrase 'self-contained ontological Trinity,' summarizes the content that the apologist is called to defend."

290. Ibid., 115–19.

291. Ibid., 123.

292. Ibid., 124: "God's word is self-attesting because it is self-contained."

293. Ibid., 122. For further information on God's incomprehensibility see *CVT*, 97–113.

revelation in Scripture, not shy away from any biblical distinctives in their apologetic, and demonstrate that compromising these doctrines leads to incoherence in all terrains of knowledge.[294] Many have pointed out the circularity in reasoning of accepting the Bible's testimony about God. Van Til, however, maintained that in basic principles all systems are circular, and that unless the biblical worldview is presupposed, human thinking deteriorates into incoherence.[295] But he also granted that there are good, rational reasons to believe the message of Scripture, and he allowed for supplemental evidences and rational arguments in apologetics.

Divine aseity exposes the poverty of non-Christian thought. The issue is the self-contained ontological Trinity. Many unbelievers have felt the need for something *a se* that is not God. Such a pseudo-god could be the universe, something within the universe, or something supposedly external to the universe. These human idols, however, cannot philosophically produce that which is necessary. Any principle from within the world cannot account for the world itself.[296]

In sum, a range of philosophical theories attempt to explain how people come to know. But knowledge comes from both sensory experience and categories of thought that are in no way derived from sensory experience.[297] These epistemological categories relate to presuppositions, which fit well into a proper apologetic presentation.[298] Van Til's apologetic is simply reasoning based on Scriptural presuppositions.[299] The first presupposition that Van Til proposes is that the Bible is the foundation for truth.[300] Thus, God exists. The Bible immediately

---

294. Frame, "Divine Aseity," 119.

295. Ibid., 124.

296. Ibid., 128–29.

297. *CVT*, 132–33, 135.

298. Ibid., 134: "Clearly, then, any twentieth-century apologist worth his salt would have to deal in a serious way with the concept of presupposition, distinguishing it from other aspects of human knowledge, and distinguishing his own view from the many other possibilities available"; and 135: "Therefore, if presuppositionalism denotes apriorism, Van Til is not a presuppositionalist."

299. Muether, *Van Til*, 181: "His reasoning by presupposition was a radical challenge to the foundationalism of mid-century evangelical thought that was generally following in the train of Enlightenment rationality." *CVT*, 116, 136; and 133: "It was in the idealist literature that *presupposition* became a common philosophical term."

300. Van Til taught that humanity has an incorrect view of itself. The Scriptures are needed for a correct view. The Scriptures alone can show humanity what it needs in terms of making sense of human experience. Van Til, *Defense of the Faith*, 85–86; and 88, quoting John Murray,

speaks of the existence of God as a given. And God reveals himself authoritatively in his Word. So all human meaning and intelligibility are due to him.[301] Granted, thinking begins with consciousness in a temporal sense. But consciousness cannot be correctly interpreted apart from God, and consciousness does not need to provide normative standards.[302]

Van Til also analyzed the ethics of epistemology. He held that knowledge has an ethical aspect. Humans have knowledge of God, which is most often good, but even such knowledge can be ethically depraved.[303] Van Til held that there are two types of people: the sheep and the goats—believers and unbelievers. These two types of people have two different ways of knowing. The unregenerate have a corrupt heart; the things that they do, think, and know are not for the glory of God. To do actions well, they must be done to and for God's glory. Thus the Devil may speak truth, but because of the wickedness of his heart, he falsifies even the truth that he does speak.[304] Van Til believed that human depravity is an ethical, not a metaphysical, issue. He held that the fall did not leave an inch of the human person unscathed.[305]

Evidences. The apologetics curriculum at old Princeton consisted of two courses: evidences, and apologetics proper. As Van Til developed the second course at Westminster, he informed Machen that he would organize the course differently from the course he took as

---

"The Inspiration of the Scripture," *WTJ* 2, no. 2 (May 1940): 90. "It would appear, therefore, that the truer, more effective and, on all accounts, more secure defense of Christianity and exposition of its essential content is not to take our starting point from those terms that will express the essential creedal confession of some of its most widely known historical deformations but rather from those terms that most fully express and give character to that redemptive religion which Christianity is. In other words, Christianity cannot receive proper understanding or its exposition proper orientation unless it is viewed as that which issues from, and is consummated in the accomplishment of, the covenant council and purpose of Father, Son and Holy Spirit." See also *CVT*, 135.

301. *CVT*, 128; and 129: "Thus Van Til unleashes the great vision of Kuyper, to bring all areas of human life under the sway of Christ."

302. Ibid., 139.

303. Ibid., 202: "Yet what is meant by knowing God in Scripture is *knowing and loving* God: this is *true* knowledge of God: the other is *false*."

304. Ibid., 203: "Knowledge itself must be sought with the proper goal, standard, and motive if it is to be true in the fullest sense."

305. Ibid., 204.

a student.[306] In the past in this course, evidences were based on the notion that some issues—such as the ability of human reason rightly to judge evidence and to reason from causality to the external world and then to God—are built merely on common sense.[307] The great Princeton theologian Charles Hodge claimed that these truths of common sense are given in the constitution of human nature; they are universal and unalterable and thus provide a sufficient foundation to defend Christianity.[308]

But this philosophical foundation, referred to as *Scottish common-sense realism*, faced challenges in the nineteenth century and still does today. One such challenge is evolutionary thinking. Darwinism attempted to poke holes in a sense of certainty that a sovereign God controls creation. Darwinism claimed that there might be an intelligent designer, but there also might not be. Later evolutionary thinking went so far as to deny the so-called *universal* or *common-sense* notion of an intelligent designer. Old Princeton believed that the existence of an intelligent designer was common sense, but evolutionists simply disagreed and stated the contrary. Philosophically, common-sense realism is incapable of settling a dispute about common sense.

Van Til was convinced that because of the depth of human sinfulness, those who examine the evidence for Christianity in a reasonable manner are not certain to conclude that the Christian faith is in fact true. This notion contradicted the old-Princeton approach.[309] In his introduction to *Evidences*, Van Til addressed the issue head-on. He taught that despite mountains of philosophical teaching, there are not several possible universals that could give facts their meaning, but only one: the triune God of Scripture. He referred to facts apart from God

---

306. Van Til, *Evidences*, 1: Christian theistic evidences is "the defense of Christian theism against any attack that may be made upon it by 'science.'"; and 3: "When we speak of evidences as the vindication or defense of Christian theism against science we take the word science in its current meaning."

307. Concerning Van Til's work on Christian evidences, K. Scott Oliphint (in foreword to *Christian Theistic Evidences*, by Cornelius Van Til [Phillipsburg, NJ: P&R Publishing, 2016], xviii) says: "No one else, at the time of the writing of Van Til's syllabus on evidences, had dealt such a deathblow to these notions [the neutrality of reason]. . . . But even Bavinck had elements of a neutral notion of the real within his theology." Scottish common-sense realism began with the philosopher Thomas Reid (1710–1796).

308. Ibid., xviii–xx.

309. Ibid., xxi.

as *brute facts*. He defined brute facts as facts without interpretation and relation to anything else and thus impossible and unknowable.[310] Since according to Van Til there are no brute facts, he reasoned that proper scientific methodology is available only on Christian presuppositions. Christianity does not contend with science on the facts themselves but on the principles that control science, or what is termed the "philosophy of science."[311]

This conclusion naturally leads to the issue of the apologetic starting point. Unbelievers do not understand the depth of their sin. In their minds, they have merely fallen from original righteousness. Further, unbelievers do not have a proper view of the surrounding world, for general revelation gives neither a full nor a true account of God, nor does it give a full or true account of humans and their world.[312]

Van Til was convinced that it is not appropriate to begin apologetics with a common ground of knowledge, as Catholic apologists sought to do.[313] He held that Protestant theologians such as Karl Barth and Gordon Clark also began in incorrect places.[314] Evangelicals of his own day were not much better. They held that, to some extent, human self-consciousness, as well as objects in the world, are intelligible without a consciousness of God. They believed that with a reasonable use of reason, one can properly understand creation—and when one applies his reasoning abilities to the facts of Scripture, "there is every likelihood that he will become a Christian."[315] But Van Til lamented that dry bones cannot revive themselves—the unregenerate mind cannot find its way to God by reason.[316]

Common Grace and the Antithesis. Abraham Kuyper was well known for his pioneering work on common grace. Even Kuyper, how-

310. Van Til, *Evidences*, 1–2.
311. Ibid., 4: "Our contention will be that a true scientific procedure is impossible unless we hold to the presupposition of the triune God of Scripture."
312. Van Til, *Defense of the Faith*, 89; and 90: There is thus "a fundamental difference of opinion between Romanism and Calvin on the origin and nature of the 'disturbance' in human nature."
313. Ibid., 93–94.
314. Van Til considered Clark a rationalist and Barth an irrationalist and that both shared a defective starting point in a false doctrine of creation (Muether, *Van Til*, 127).
315. Van Til, *Defense of the Faith*, 96.
316. Ibid., 97, quotes B. B. Warfield's powerful words on the dry bones in his chapter on "Christian Supernaturalism" in *Studies in Theology* (New York: Oxford University Press, 1932), 25–48.

ever, was inconsistent in his analysis by allowing for at least relative agreement between believers and unbelievers in certain fields of study.[317] For example, Kuyper spoke of the neutrality of weighing and measuring, but Van Til countered that even purely scientific activities such as weighing and measuring cannot escape the impact of the fall.[318] Van Til sought to reexamine common grace and establish it on the firmer foundation of Christ and his work, combined with the biblical notion of antithesis.[319] But Van Til abstained from Kuyper's and his followers' critique of human culture.[320] Van Til was strong on the antithesis.[321] The question of the antithesis addresses how the fall affects human thought—an issue of the ethics of knowledge. Correctly, he believed that the ultimate criterion of truth is God's revelation. Unbelievers, however, reject this standard and adopt their own authority as the ultimate criterion.[322]

Nevertheless, some scholars are critical of Van Til's handling of the antithesis.[323] While Van Til embraced common grace, sometimes he was so strong in his approach that it came across as though he thought unbelievers knew absolutely nothing.[324] Though even Van Til may at times have struggled with consistency in his analysis, he was correct that Christians should analyze unbelieving thought from a principial or systemic position. The matter is not whether an unbeliever can weigh an object as correctly as a believer can, for there cannot be degrees of correctness when the issue is principial.[325] Thus a believer can agree with certain ideas from unbelievers—for they do not speak all propositions falsely—while simultaneously rejecting their basic or core system of thought.[326]

Clark Controversy. Beginning in 1944, Van Til and others stood against the Christian philosopher and theologian Gordon Clark (1902–

---

317. He also rejected Kuyper's notion that "the New Jerusalem of the consummated state would receive into the heavenly kingdom even some works of reprobate culture through God's work of common grace" (see Muether, *Van Til*, 155).

318. *CVT*, 195.

319. Muether, *Van Til*, 153.

320. Ibid., 154.

321. *CVT*, 42, 44.

322. Ibid., 187–89, 197.

323. Ibid., 187, 199, 201, 212, 215, 222: "On this point, Hepp is right and Van Til wrong."

324. Ibid., 189, 196, 198.

325. Ibid., 208, 210.

326. Ibid., 209–11.

1985).[327] Van Til accused Clark of grounding his thinking on Greek philosophy.[328] Clark also seemed to hold an aberrant position on the nature of faith, for he was satisfied to define faith as mere assent to Christian doctrine.[329] The controversy also involved issues relative to a qualitative difference between God's knowledge and human knowledge.[330] In reply, Clark argued that in Van Til's system of thought, humans have a mere analogy of God's knowledge, not a one-to-one correspondence. And a mere analogy of God's knowledge can only result in unmitigated skepticism.[331]

In 1957, Clark reopened the debate with Van Til. He accused Van Til of being influenced by Barthianism and claimed it was Barth's influence that caused Van Til to teach that unbelievers could not know the truth. Clark argued that there must be an identical point of coincidence between human and divine knowledge.[332]

This debate significantly affected Presbyterianism and has naturally attracted the analysis of a number of Reformed scholars.[333] Some of them, such as Robert Reymond, appear to have misunderstood some of the nuance of this debate.[334] Others critically assert that Frame's analysis of the controversy did not reckon with the broader ecclesiastical debate in the OPC.[335] In many ways, the actual debate concerned the nature and emphasis of this budding denomination largely in reference to whether the OPC would be Reformed (and agree with Van Til) or veer toward evangelicalism.[336]

327. Muether, *Van Til*, 102.
328. *CVT*, 46–47, 134.
329. Muether, *Van Til*, 102.
330. Ibid., 103.
331. Ibid., 104–5.
332. Muether, *Van Til*, 109. See Gordon H. Clark, "The Bible as Truth," *Bibliotheca Sacra* 114, no. 454 (April 1957): 163
333. See the pro–Van Til analysis by his nephew and my former colleague Fred H. Klooster, *The Incomprehensibility of God in the Orthodox Presbyterian Conflict* (Franeker, Netherlands: Wever, 1951).
334. Reymond incorrectly understood Van Til's notion of analogy and concluded with Clark that Van Til's position would lead to skepticism. See Robert L. Reymond, *The Justification of Knowledge: An Introductory Study in Christian Apologetic Methodology* (Nutley, NJ: Presbyterian and Reformed, 1976), and the analysis in Muether, *Van Til*, 110.
335. Muether, *Van Til*, 106. *CVT*, 102: "It should be noted, however, that the General Assembly did not revoke Clark's ordination or declare his view to be out of accord with the Westminster Standards."
336. Muether, *Van Til*, 107–8.

Barthianism.[337] In addition to the works he had already written against the thinking of Karl Barth, in the mid 1940s Van Til published a full-length book, *The New Modernism*, addressing Barthian theology.[338] In it, Van Til expressed his concern that evangelicals were adopting portions of Barthian theology without realizing that each of these parts related to a larger whole.[339] Van Til knew Barth's works to be replete with superficial similarities to orthodox Presbyterianism, and they made Barth's errors even more subtle and dangerous. But Barth's doctrine of Scripture differed greatly from that of evangelicalism.[340] Barth was also committed to Kantian philosophy, which undercut his entire theological agenda.[341]

The controversy reached its peak in 1962, when Barth lectured at Princeton Seminary and Van Til released his *Christianity and Barthianism*. Despite Van Til's writings, Barth's theological system was largely accepted by both the religious left and right. Barth himself said that Van Til did not understand him and that he could not understand Van Til.[342] Further discussion of Van Til's doctrine of God will come in chapter 29.

JOHN MURRAY (A.D. 1898–1975)

Biography. Even in the late twentieth century it would have been unnecessary to introduce the theologian John Murray to evangelicals. Yet the march of time has continued, and it is likely that contemporary readers know little about John Murray, the Scotsman who spent his life teaching systematic theology at Westminster Theological Seminary.

Born in the Highlands at the end of the nineteenth century, Murray was raised in a family deeply committed to the Presbyterian church. In 1880, John's father, Alexander, became an elder at age twenty-seven in the Free Church of Scotland. Alexander Murray served for fifteen

---

337. See earlier analysis of Barth in this chapter.
338. Barth had written against the Kuyperians, who, claimed Barth, had misunderstood the relationship between reason and revelation—and Van Til wrote against Barth in 1937 by accusing the dialectical theology of Barth and Brunner of having conquered old Princeton (ibid., 143–45).
339. Ibid., 120–22, 188.
340. Ibid., 123.
341. Ibid., 129.
342. Ibid., 190–91.

years as a ruling elder in the Free church. But along with his minister and forty to fifty others, he joined the Free Presbyterian Church and started a new congregation. When there was no teaching elder available to preach, Alexander would exhort from the Word. Alexander's son John was born three years after Alexander joined the Free Presbyterian Church. Of the seven children before him, John was one of the few raised to speak the English language instead of Gaelic.[343]

John was not born into a wealthy home. Like most in the region, the family's standard meal was potatoes and herring. Despite this relative lack of wealth, in 1910 God provided for young John to attend Dornoch Academy. He would leave on his bicycle on Monday morning, travel the fourteen miles to school, and stay there through Friday evening.

When World War I exploded on the Continent, John embraced his national duty; he followed the example of his older brothers and enlisted. He was sent across the ocean to fight in France before the end of the year. These days were difficult for John Murray. He recounted falling asleep while leaning against a tree and still wearing his pack. But he was rewarded for his efforts with promotion to lance corporal. He was listed as missing in action in July 1918, while the last large-scale German offensive began. He was blinded in one eye by shrapnel and was honorably discharged on December 10, 1918.

The veteran entered the University of Glasgow in the autumn of 1919 and completed the normal four years of university work in three. During his time at Glasgow, Murray became a communicant member of the Free Presbyterian Church of Scotland. He preached for the first time in 1922 and in the following year became a candidate for gospel ministry. At the time, the Free Presbyterian Church had no denominationally sponsored theological seminary. Thus, in the autumn of 1923, John and five others went to study with a theological tutor by the name of Reverend Wick. Then, in May of 1924, the Synod of the Free Presbyterian Church voted to send John to study at Princeton Theological Seminary in the United States.

Murray trained at Princeton for three years and obtained both the bachelor of theology and master of theology degrees in 1927. His

343. John Murray, *Collected Writings of John Murray*, ed. Iain Murray, 4 vols. (Edinburgh: Banner of Truth, 1976–1982), vol. 3.

three years at Princeton were years of theological tumult in America's Presbyterian church. The notorious Auburn Affirmation was produced in 1924. In 1926, J. Gresham Machen was elected by the faculty to the chair of apologetics, but the General Assembly declined to confirm his appointment. The faculty of Princeton Seminary also censured their president, J. Ross Stevenson, for his part in the General Assembly's action against Machen. But in the midst of the debate, Murray's years at Princeton were a time of tremendous opportunity. During this time, the Princeton faculty consisted of C. W. Hodge (Charles Hodge's grandson and B. B. Warfield's assistant for twenty years) in systematic theology; Gerhardus Vos as the chair in biblical theology; O. T. Allis and Robert Dick Wilson in Old Testament; and W. P. Armstrong and J. Gresham Machen in New Testament.[344]

During summer breaks, Murray ministered to North American Scottish immigrant congregations. His desire was to enter pastoral ministry, though in God's providence he never did. Two matters kept Murray in the academic world. The first was his academic giftedness. Princeton Seminary had awarded him the Gelston-Winthrop Fellowship for post-graduate study, and he used the funds to study at the University of Edinburgh. Following Murray's year in Scotland, C. W. Hodge called him back to Princeton to serve as his assistant in theology. Thus, during the 1929 to 1930 academic year, Murray began his teaching career in systematic theology at Princeton Seminary.

The second matter that kept Murray from the pastorate was his inability to be ordained back in Scotland. The Free Presbyterian Church found him to be theologically unacceptable for his supposedly lax views on the Sabbath.[345] So with the doors closed at home and an invitation to join the new Westminster Theological Seminary, Murray remained in the United States. At Machen's death in 1936, in many ways leadership of the conservative Presbyterian church in America's north, at least in the area of systematic theology, fell on the strong shoulders of John Murray. He continued his teaching career at Westminster Seminary

344. Ibid., 3:19–27.

345. The issue was whether it was acceptable to use public transportation to attend worship. Given the North American context, Murray said that it should be allowed, although he himself would not use it. The Synod of the Free Presbyterian Church disagreed and gave Murray until October 1930 to change his views. He did not (ibid., 3:33–36).

until his retirement in 1966. He married in that same year and took his bride with him to Scotland, where he died in May 1975.

Writings. Two figures played prominent roles in Murray's development. One was the systematician B. B. Warfield, and the other was his teacher Gerhardus Vos.[346] Iain Murray wrote shortly after John Murray's death, "All that John Murray wrote was intended to promote the obedience of faith."[347] To that end, Murray wrote widely on theological and practical topics.[348] Special recognition should be given to his unparalleled work titled *Redemption Accomplished and Applied.*[349] After his death, The Banner of Truth Trust gave to the church a magnificent tribute in the form of a four-volume set of the *Collected Writings of John Murray.*[350] Most recently, Westminster Seminary has transcribed fifteen audio recordings from Murray's preaching and produced them under the title, *O Death, Where Is Thy Sting?*[351]

Machen and Murray on Social Issues. It is interesting to compare the differing thoughts of J. Gresham Machen and John Murray on social issues. Born into a less-than-wealthy family in the Scottish

346. Murray had missed by only two and a half years the chance to study with this towering figure. Murray's high regard for Warfield was clear. See Murray's review of Warfield's *The Person and Work of Christ* in *Collected Writings*, 3:358–59: "In the case of so versatile a theologian as Warfield, it is rather difficult to select one particular locus in theology and say that his greatest contribution lay in that particular field. But there is much to be said in favor of the judgment that Dr. Warfield's devotion and scholarship as a theologian reached their zenith in the exposition and defense of the Biblical doctrine of inspiration." In the reviewed work there are also three sermons, and Murray's comments reveal his esteem: "Dr. Warfield's sermons reveal something in his character which might easily escape those who are acquainted only with his specifically theological output. It is his devotional fervor." His sermons "evince an exceptional combination of exegetical insight, expository skill, fervent piety and practical application."

347. Murray, *Collected Writings*, 1:xiv.

348. Some of Murray's books include *Christian Baptism, The Covenant of Grace, Divorce, Principles of Conduct, The Imputation of Adam's Sin, Calvin on Scripture and Divine Sovereignty*, and his monumental two-volume commentary on Romans.

349. For expanded information on his view of the atonement, also comparing this work with his later research in the *Collected Writings*, see Richard C. Gamble, "The Doctrine of the Atonement from the Westminster Assembly to the Twentieth Century," in *The Faith Once Delivered*, ed. Anthony T. Selvaggio (Phillipsburg, NJ: P&R Publishing, 2007), 261–73.

350. Volume 1, *The Claims of Truth*, includes chapters on Scripture, Christ, Westminster Seminary, the gospel, Christian life, the moral law, church, and contemporary issues. Volume 2, *Select Lectures in Systematic Theology*, has chapters on humanity, common grace, redemption, and the church. Volume 3 contains a charming life of Murray, as well as select sermons and reviews. The final volume, *Studies in Theology and Reviews*, contains sixteen assorted studies in theology and Murray's reviews from 1954 to 1967.

351. This title was published in Philadelphia by Westminster Seminary Press in 2017. I cannot overstate how indebted I am to his writings.

Highlands, Murray came from a cultural-economic class that differed from Machen's. But Murray attended the same seminary as Machen and also pursued graduate studies outside the United States, just as Machen had done. He was even Machen's colleague at Westminster Seminary for more than half a decade.

Murray and Machen interpreted differently the same passage of the Westminster Confession of Faith relative to the church and political activity. Understanding their differences will shed light on the development of twentieth-century Presbyterian social action.

In an article on the relationship between the church and the state, Murray held to the separation of church and state functionally.[352] But he also stated that, "while this diversity of function and of sphere must be recognized, guarded, and maintained, the larger unity within which this diversity exists must not be overlooked."[353] He was convinced that both the church and the state must promote the interests of God's kingdom. While no one would disagree with this goal in principle, the question regards the implementation of such principles.

Murray was convinced that when laws that transgress God's law are made and the God-given rights of citizens are not protected, the institution of the church must oppose those laws. The church must condemn the state's action or inaction, confront the civil magistrate on the given issue, and then promote correctives.

Murray held that in the case of political corruption, the church does not have the option to stand aside. For political corruption is public sin, and the church neglects its vocation if it does not denounce the corruption as such. Murray held that the church must be involved in the political sphere, and to say that it should not be concerned "is only [a] misconception of what is involved in the proclamation of the whole counsel of God."[354]

Murray understood that his position appeared to be inconsistent with the Westminster Standards at chapter 31, section 4—precisely

352. John Murray, "The Relation of Church and State," *Collected Writings of John Murray*, ed. Iain Murray, 4 vols. (Edinburgh: Banner of Truth, 1982), 1:254, 255: "Each must maintain and assert its autonomy in reference to the other and preserve its freedom from intrusion on the part of the other." He specifically says, "To put the matter bluntly, the church is not to engage in *politics*."

353. Ibid., 1:254.

354. Ibid., 1:255.

where his former colleague Machen had earlier cited them.[355] Murray confessed that his opinion may have surpassed the function originally envisioned by the framers of the confession. But he did not think that his position was inconsistent with the standards and, for that matter, did not see any reason for his position to be abandoned. Murray's defense of his position was bifold. First, the church felt that in the confession it was appropriate to define the role of the magistrate and to articulate the extent of the magistrate's abilities. Thus, throughout history, churches that have held to the Westminster Standards have thought it proper to resist the state when it has tried to infringe on the rights of the church.

His second and weightier argument was that it is a function of the church to declare the whole counsel of God in political matters —as already recognized by the Westminster divines. The divines had neither wanted nor intended the church to determine civil affairs, but they did hold that the church could speak to civil affairs by the use of the pulpit and the press.[356] The church could declare the religious and moral implications of political measures. But the WCF also stated that the church could directly appeal to the civil magistrate in specific governmental activities—an action that goes beyond the simple function of the proclamation of the whole counsel of God.

Thus, though Murray did not address the issue of prohibition, it is apparent that he would have disagreed with Machen on the principle of a presbytery's right to endorse a specific piece of governmental legislation. It is quite probable that he would have voted with Machen against the resolution supporting prohibition, but on different grounds.

Like Machen, John Murray was a man concerned for the society around him. Yet their differing opinions are noticeable on the matter of church/state relations. Within conservative Presbyterianism in America's north, there was strong historical precedent in the twentieth century to support what could be called a *church-as-activist* view (the view maintained by Murray), which holds that it is of fundamental importance for the church, as the church, to address social ills. On the other hand, Machen was a proponent of the view that active individual

355. See the analysis of Machen in chapter 21.
356. There are two means of declaring the Word of God, "namely the pulpit and the press" (ibid., 1:257).

Christians, in contrast to the corporate church body, should become involved in such matters.

These issues are still relevant to theological discussion today. The Presbyterian church is still largely divided on the matter and still generally follows the positions established by Murray and Machen. In the fall of 1988, for example, more than fifty years after Machen's death, a presbytery of the OPC determined that

> support of abortion, homosexual rights, the Equal Rights Amendment, and the National Education Association is clearly contrary to Scripture, and that all persons who support those positions stand in opposition to the Lord God and His declared revelation in the Bible, and that those persons in the eldership of the church (represented by this presbytery) who identify with that political party and its candidates who now support those positions be reminded of the seriousness of their being publicly identified with those positions, of the grievousness of this public support and of how this support seriously mitigates against our stand for the Lord Jesus Christ.[357]

It would certainly be interesting to hear what Machen would think about an OPC presbytery's making such a political pronouncement!

But both Machen and Murray agreed that action taken in the field of public justice and civic righteousness in the name of Christ is an important aspect of the Christian life. Machen certainly modeled that concern in a consistent manner, as seen by his political actions as an individual, as did Murray. This chapter next transitions to a figure in the conservative Presbyterian church whose fame surpassed even that of Van Til and Murray.

FRANCIS SCHAEFFER (A.D. 1912–1984)

Biography. Francis Schaeffer was born in January 1912 in Philadelphia. At the age of about eighteen, he became a Christian through simply reading his Bible. In 1935 he graduated from Hampden-Sydney College, in Virginia, and was married. He then studied for two years

357. Minutes as cited in *Journey Magazine*, March/April, 1989, 4.

under Machen, Van Til, and Murray at Westminster Seminary. In 1937, however, he left Westminster and headed to Faith Theological Seminary, newly founded in Wilmington, Delaware, from where he graduated in 1938.

Schaeffer was ordained in the Bible Presbyterian Church. He then served as a pastor in Grove City, Pennsylvania, until moving in 1941 to Chester, Pennsylvania. In 1943 he moved to St. Louis, Missouri, and then the family moved again in 1948 to become missionaries in Switzerland. In 1954 Schaeffer received a doctor of divinity degree from Highland College, in Long Beach, California. In 1955 he founded the famous L'Abri Fellowship in the Swiss Alps. He received an honorary doctor of letters degree from Gordon College, Wenham, Massachusetts, in 1971. And in 1977 Schaeffer led a speaking tour across the United States on his important film and book, *How Should We Then Live?*[358]

Writings. Schaeffer's first major book, *The God Who Is There* (1968), critiques contemporary culture. In this book he explains how mid-to-late twentieth-century thought has replaced reason with so-called "modern mysticisms." Schaeffer presents Christianity as an avenue for a meaningful and authentic life in the midst of this mysticism. His other works include *Escape from Reason* (1968), a more in-depth historical analysis of the crisis of thought in his day, beginning with Aquinas's dualism; *Death in the City* (1969), a biblical exposition foundational for cultural critique; *The Church at the End of the 20th Century* (1970); *True Spirituality* (1971); and *He Is There and He Is Not Silent* (1972). Then in the 1980s he wrote *A Christian Manifesto* and his last book, *The Great Evangelical Disaster* (1984).

Development of Modern Science. *The Church at the End of the 20th Century* was one of Schaeffer's most significant books. He began this work with a discussion of the development of modern science, then told of its demise. He argued that modern science arose out of a Christian mentality. Galileo, for example, observed the richness and beauty of the universe and felt compelled to worship the beauty of the Creator. The result of this type of worldview, relative to science, was certainty of the uniformity of natural causes.[359] There were two more

---

358. Lane T. Dennis, *Letters of Francis A. Schaeffer* (Westchester, IL: Crossway, 1987), 25–28.
359. Francis A. Schaeffer, *The Church at the End of the 20th Century* (Downers Grove, IL: InterVarsity Press, 1970), 9; and specifically, 13: "Man on the basis of reason could understand

results from this Christian mentality: that nature was important, and that there was a distinction between nature as object and the human self as observer. Schaeffer believed that this foundation provided an objective basis for knowledge.[360]

But the first modern mathematician, Leonardo da Vinci, began a countermovement. Da Vinci sought an infinite reference point in rationalism or humanism and believed that he had found it in mathematics.[361] Schaeffer argued, however, that such a search is futile, for man can never begin with a particular and then derive a universal no matter whether the topic is metaphysics or morals.[362] Others in the countermovement pushed toward a closed and determined creation. Rousseau viewed the world as a merely autonomous machine. The Marquis de Sade held to a specifically chemical determinism. So since everything is determined, he reasoned, then whatever is, is right. With such a philosophy, "you cannot say that anything is right or wrong. Morality is dead. Man is dead."[363] Nietzsche, influenced by this philosophy, agreed and wrote words that still reverberate today: "God is dead." Schaeffer countered that the results of such a philosophy only drive a person mad. If God is in fact dead, then man is left with no answers.[364]

According to Schaeffer, the end of science came when, to the notion of the uniformity of natural causes, the phrase *in a closed system* was added. As science morphed into psychology and the social sciences, man found himself in the machine of the universe. In this closed machine, there was no longer room for beauty, love, or even for God himself.[365]

Schaeffer addressed humanity's end: as a machine in a machine world. On the one hand is the universe, which is a closed machine. It is determined. On the other hand is humanity's longing for autonomous freedom. He attributes the beginning of this longing to Kant

---

the universe because a God of reason had created it." By this statement Schaeffer meant that the system is open with a personal God; it is not a closed system (see ibid., 14).

360. Ibid., 10. Bacon believed that man was fallen but was still wonderful.

361. Ibid., 11. Rationalism is "that man begins from himself and tries to build all the answers on this base, receiving nothing from any other source and specifically refusing any revelation from God."

362. Ibid.

363. Ibid., 14.

364. Ibid., 15. Michel Foucault is similar; he says that the only freedom is in insanity.

365. Ibid., 13.

and sees its development in the mid-twentieth century with the start of the student freedom movement of the 1960s. Schaeffer predicted that this yearning for autonomous freedom would lead only to selfish and ugly behavior.[366] Thus the lines of struggle were clear: an autonomous machine and its determinism on the one side, and the human desire for autonomous freedom on the other.[367]

But such a presupposition concerning the world did not explain either the universe or humanity.[368] Yet this presupposition concerning the world and humanity is foundational to the French existentialist's struggle.[369] The struggle is also demonstrated in the chaotic universe portrayed in mid- and late-twentieth century art. But in reality, the world is likely not so chaotic.[370] Similarly, mid- to late-twentieth century philosophy portrayed humanity as a machine that is determined either chemically, socially, or psychologically. Because this philosophy suppresses human aspirations, it produces within the human heart a terrible, cosmic, final alienation.[371] It was no wonder, according to Schaeffer, that college students revolted for being treated as mere machines.[372] If there is no personal creator, then humanity is left with "the impersonal plus time plus chance."[373]

This particular view of the world had never appeared in the history of thought, according to Schaeffer. It is a new way of looking at knowledge. Earlier philosophers had searched for a unified-field concept,

366. Rousseau wrote about raising children—and put his own in an institution. The French painter Gauguin did the same as Rousseau. He went to Tahiti and left his family hungry in Paris. He had an illegitimate son in Tahiti. The son would later sign his paintings "Gauguin." See Gaugan's painting *What? Whence? Whither?* in Boston's Museum of Fine Arts (ibid., 12). For information on the high Renaissance and the problem of nature and grace, see Francis A. Schaeffer, *Escape from Reason* (Chicago: InterVarsity Press, 1968).

367. Schaeffer, *Church at the End*, 12.

368. Schaeffer's phrase is the "mannishness of man." He explains it as human "aspirations." He wants to be more than a cog in a wheel: "He wants a relationship to society or the university other than that of a small machine being manipulated by a big machine" (see ibid., 16).

369. Ibid., 13. For example, Sartre poses the basic philosophical question as to why there is something rather than nothing (nonbeing).

370. Ibid., 14.

371. Ibid., 16. The alienation has been expressed by Alberto Giacometti and Charlie Chaplin. Mortimer Adler, in *The Difference of Man and the Difference It Makes* (New York: World Publishing, 1971), said that if we cannot find something different about man, something that makes him more than a machine, then we will treat him as a machine.

372. These presuppositions can be challenged, but Christian presuppositions are presented as unthinkable (Schaeffer, *Church at the End*, 14).

373. Ibid., 15, 18.

that is, a concept that would incorporate the entirety of the world and knowledge. Philosophers now, however, accept a dichotomy and begin with a divided universe—they have largely given up hope of finding a unified field of knowledge.[374] Neither is there any optimism from that particular philosophical vantage point. When unbelievers begin with reason and rationality, they are certain to arrive at pessimism.[375] They are convinced that there is nothing in reason or rationality that would lead to optimism. If unbelieving humans want optimism, they must proceed from a different angle. To reach beauty or even God, which is pure optimism, unbelievers become convinced that humans must begin in the realm of nonreason.

Believers also respond to this world in mysticism, which, according to Schaeffer, is a leap into the nonrational. As modern thinkers long for some ground for optimism and disregard optimism and faith as having any connection to reason, they feel the need to leap to the nonrational—to leap "upstairs."[376] "He feels forced to make the leap against his reason."[377]

Mystics are those who feel the need to leap into the nonrational, which is different from classical Christian mysticism. The movement began with Rousseau and Kant, but it matured in Kierkegaard and his followers.[378] It began with the philosophers but eventually was picked up by the artists, particularly the postimpressionists. In music, this movement can be seen in Debussy; in literature it is evident in the work of T. S. Eliot; and it pervades film.[379] The work of Aldous Huxley and the rise of psychedelic drug use were not escapes but the

374. Ibid., 17.

375. By the word *rationalism*, Schaeffer (ibid., 18) means "that man should understand the world by starting totally from himself. . . . Beginning with rationalism, rationally you come only to pessimism. Man equals the machine. Man is dead."

376. In *The God Who Is There*, "upstairs" means that which "deals with significance or meaning, but is not open to contact with verification by the world of facts or reason" (Schaeffer, *Church at the End*, 18).

377. Ibid. Because he holds to a closed system (impersonal plus time and chance), he feels "really damned, caught in his own kind of hell," and leaps upstairs.

378. Ibid., 17.

379. The fruit of generational alienation, says Schaeffer, can be observed in the music of John Cage, the liberalism of Malcolm Muggeridge, the works of French author Albert Camus, and movies such as Antonioni's *Blow-up!* The good films "are the awful ones, because they teach that there is no truth, no meaning, no absolutes, that it is not only that we have not found truth and meaning but that they do not exist" (ibid., 18, 22–25).

manifestations of human longing for even a small taste of optimism.[380] This movement even spilled over into theology, particularly in the work of Karl Barth. He taught that faith is a leap into an upper-story building. In a strange sense, this type of theology and psychedelic drugs were offering a similar experience—an upper-story leap: "both are trips, separated from all reason."[381]

In the 1960s there was evident tension between the twenty-somethings and the older generation. Schaeffer notes that the older generation behaved as though the old Christian world remained, even though it lay in rubble.[382] This generation operated on the memory of what used to have been, though, interestingly enough, it did not truly hold to traditional Christian beliefs or ethics. The younger generation regarded this older generation as plastic and contrived, for they advocated a worldview without even believing in it. They were the silent majority, "but they are weak as water."[383]

More than fifty years ago, Schaeffer observed that Western culture was moving toward a complete loss of freedom.[384] What he referred to as "the new left" had developed out of the hippie and free-speech movements.[385] He believed that whether it was the new left or the right-wing elite who assumed control, the end would be the same.[386] The danger for evangelicalism was to drift into the establishment elites.[387]

Schaeffer believed that these cultural trends called for a Christian revolution. For the revolution to be successful, Christians had to recognize that there was a difference between cobelligerents—those fighting for a similar cause—and true allies. Thus Protestants and

380. Ibid., 20. Huxley wrote *The Humanist Frame*. For Huxley, taking drugs was what Schaeffer would call an "upper-story leap."

381. Ibid., 21: "They are left upstairs with only connotation words and no content. For them any concept of a personal God is dead, and any content about God is dead. They are cut off from any categories of absolute right and wrong and thus they are left with totally situational ethics." Evangelicals face temptations this way.

382. Ibid., 23. The old Christian world was one in which Puritan writer Samuel Rutherford's *Lex Rex* could be looked on to build a solid Christian political theory, for example. Rutherford held that God's Word could guide human thought in all areas of life. A similar worldview was articulated by the Dutch theologian Abraham Kuyper. Sadly, already by the 1960s all non-Christians and many professing Christians had abandoned such solidly biblical thinking.

383. Ibid., 20.

384. There will be a need for philosopher kings, such as John Kenneth Galbraith (ibid., 30).

385. Ibid., 32.

386. Ibid., 33–34.

387. Ibid., 35.

Catholics could function as cobelligerents in the fight against abortion, even if they were not true allies. He also believed in the importance of the Kuyperian antithesis between the way of life of a committed Christian against paganism, as well as the need for a true Christian community, and the significance of taking truth seriously.[388] A poor revolution would occur if believers neglected any of these things.[389] He believed that when the church began to take the creeds seriously, it would begin to have a distinctly Christian view of both God and humanity.[390] Schaeffer also thought that the church was busy discussing matters that were already twenty to thirty years in the past and needed to begin to engage with the current discussion.[391]

Finally, Schaeffer introduced what he termed the "line of despair," dated from 1890 to 1935. Before this time, in both the United States and Europe, people believed in absolutes. Yet the landscape and thinking had changed, and the church was caught unprepared. One of the reasons the church was not prepared was because of the failure of classical apologetics.[392] The line of despair began with philosophy and ends with theology, beginning in Europe and spreading to the United States.[393]

EVANGELICAL AND REFORMED THEOLOGY

The previous chapter introduced some of the similarities between fundamentalism, evangelicalism, and Reformed theology. As time passed, some of these similarities and differences became more pronounced. The last chapter ended with tensions between the groups, and the next section resumes the conversation.

Reformed Fear: Segregation. In 1959, C. Herbert Oliver, a Black minister in the Presbyterian church, wrote a book on race relations

---

388. Ibid., 36–39.

389. Ibid., 40–41.

390. Ibid., 45–50. Also, a vibrant church cares for other people, ibid., 85–87.

391. Ibid., 81.

392. Francis A. Schaeffer, *The God Who Is There* (Downers Grove, IL: InterVarsity Press, 1968), 18: "The philosophers came to the realization that they could not find this unified rationalist circle, and so, departing from the classical method of antithesis, they shifted the concept of truth and modern man was born"; and 20: "What Hegel taught arrived at just the right moment of history for his thinking to have its maximum effect."

393. Ibid., 13–16.

that opposed segregation. The book was titled *No Flesh Shall Glory*. In it he wrote:

> As segregation is basically inhuman and unnatural, a thoroughgoing system of absolute segregation throws all morality and decency to the wind in its dealing with the segregated group. It is hard to understand how a conscience even remotely influenced by Christian teachings can do this. The segregationist who wishes to improve the intelligence and educational standards of a segregated group is also faced with a painful dilemma, for education and segregation cannot be blended: they are mutually exclusive. Where enlightenment thrives, segregation cannot stand. Where segregation is most complete, intellectual growth is most effectively crushed.[394]

Since much of American evangelicalism centered in the South, many perceived segregation as a particular problem within evangelicalism.[395]

Unity: Abortion. Prior to the infamous Roe vs. Wade decision of the United States Supreme Court in 1973, perceptive leaders of conservative Presbyterianism knew that abortion was a critical social issue that needed to be addressed.[396] Congregations were encouraged to educate themselves on the issues and take appropriate action.[397] Little

394. C. Herbert Oliver, *No Flesh Shall Glory* (Philadelphia: Presbyterian and Reformed, 1959), 62. In 1966, the Reformed Presbyterian Church, Evangelical Synod, produced a general assembly report strongly condemning segregation.

395. Segregationism was not only an evangelical problem, however. Note the views of B. B. Warfield, as a southern Presbyterian, against integration at Princeton Seminary.

396. For example, in 1968 a committee was established in the OPC to investigate the issue and develop a position paper. That paper took a strong stand against abortion even before it became legally possible to obtain one. The opening paragraph of the report is truly prophetic; it says, "If abortion is murder, even in some cases, then the current pace of abortion liberalization could lead to a slaughter of defenseless human beings worse than the atrocities of Hitler, Stalin or Herod the Great." A minority report requested that the church follow the same pattern that it did in the 1930s regarding alcohol. The minority report also asked whether it is right for the church to encourage enforcement of religious principles by state legislation and called that avenue a very dangerous course. See *Minutes of the Thirty-fifth General Assembly, May 14–17, 1968* (Philadelphia: The Orthodox Presbyterian Church, 1968).

397. After presenting a lengthy theological analysis of pertinent scriptural passages, the committee of the OPC recommended three actions. They proposed that their general assembly adopt a resolution against abortion and that further study of the matter should be carried out by congregations, sessions, and presbyteries so that "questions may be better instructed concerning the scriptural principles involved, and so that they might be motivated to take appropriate action relative to pending civil legislation or other pertinent situations in their communities" (ibid.).

more than a year later, the Supreme Court ruled in favor of abortion throughout the United States, and for the last fifty years the country has stood by as millions of babies have been lawfully slaughtered.

With one voice, American evangelicals decried the court's decision. Yet within the conservative Presbyterian church, there was debate on whether or not it was the place of the institutional church, as a church, to make pronouncements on social issues.[398]

In conclusion, American Reformed theology must continually address pressing questions. After Machen's death, conservative American Presbyterianism debated the matter of whether or not to require church members to abstain from drinking alcohol. Some were in favor of such a requirement, while others resolved not to enforce what they perceived to be a nonbiblical requirement on church members. Even though sobriety was praised, drunkenness condemned, and many ministers and elders chose to abstain from drinking alcohol, the church refused to enforce such abstinence.

It is apparent that the main division between evangelical and Reformed thought concerns the relationship between the individual Christian and society. But tensions do not end here. There are tensions and differences not only between evangelical and Reformed traditions but also within each movement. Maintaining unity in the believing community is an uphill battle, but one worth fighting!

REVIVAL AND DESTRUCTION

The thesis of the following section is that without a revival of Reformed theology, evangelical theology will self-destruct. Initially, it may seem both arrogant and premature to predict the demise of American evangelical theology. But the intention of this section is to demonstrate that this thesis is neither rash nor without reason. To

---

398. The OPC had a minority report to the abortion report. "It therefore appears to the author of this minority report that the church is on the verge of doing what it refused to do in 1937, on the verge of adding additional sense to the scriptural catalog." The minority report stated later, "the report accompanies this by an encouragement to the enforcement of religious principles by state legislation. Setting the fate of the church upon this path may perhaps be expected of people who have not known what it is to live under a denial of religious freedom but it is a very dangerous course nevertheless, and the study of history provides plenty of supporting evidence" (ibid.).

accomplish this goal, it will be necessary to ask some challenging questions of evangelical theology.

The Future of Evangelicalism. There were some rather disturbing trends in American evangelical theology at the end of the twentieth century. No evangelical would knowingly abandon the Scriptures. But in practice, many evangelicals have abandoned the Bible's teaching because they no longer find it adequate to meet the challenges of life. For example, many so-called *evangelicals* have abandoned Scripture in the practice of Christian counseling and nurture. "They do not think the Bible is sufficient for achieving Christian growth," said the Presbyterian leader James M. Boice (1938–2000), "so they turn to secular therapy groups."[399] Evangelicals also often practically abandon the Scriptures in worship. Boice again writes, "So many pastors tone down the hard edges of biblical truth in order to attract greater numbers to their services. They major in entertainment."[400]

Many American evangelicals have also conformed to what could be referred to as "the pattern of this age."[401] In Romans 12:2 Paul wrote, "Do not conform any longer to the pattern of this world." In this passage, it is possible that Paul could have been referring to personal ethical issues; today, such issues might include the use of tobacco or the consumption of alcohol. Paul is not merely advocating personal piety, however, but a complete reformation of the mind.[402]

399. James Montgomery Boice, *Whatever Happened to the Gospel of Grace?* (Wheaton, IL: Crossway, 2001), 24. More could be said concerning the crisis in the area of Christian counseling. The issue is best noted in some of the debates between the approach of nouthetic counseling and other evangelical approaches that incorrectly consider a biblical approach too simplistic.

400. Ibid., 25; and 29–30, where he later asserts: "Evangelicals used to be defined by their theology. . . . Today they search for ministers with entertainment and management skills. They flock to dynamic pulpit personalities rather than to those who exhibit godly character." It appears to me that the issue of worship is one of the most divisive in American evangelicalism today.

401. Ibid., 28; and 36, where later he elaborates by saying that evangelicals have deserted the Reformation gospel because of their "obsession with the culture, a consumer mentality, and a recasting of the gospel in worldly terms to appeal to unbelievers—the chief problem is that we have forgotten God and are not really living for his glory."

402. Iain H. Murray, *Evangelicalism Divided: A Record of Crucial Change in the Years 1952–2000* (Edinburgh: Banner of Truth, 2000), 255. Boice (*Gospel of Grace*, 42) makes a similar assertion. George Marsden (*Evangelicalism and Modern America* [Grand Rapids: Eerdmans, 1984], 45), pronounces a bitter critique when he says that it seemed in the 1970s "as if the evangelicals were as busy following the course of the liberals as offering an alternative to it" (as cited by Murray, *Evangelicalism Divided*, 251).

Secularism. One example of this evangelical conformity is secularism. Secularism has influenced American evangelical theology to the extent that it dictates how evangelicals construct their churches, arrange those churches' interior designs, and even write and deliver sermons.[403] In addition, many evangelicals have been conformed to materialism. In American evangelicalism, pastors of large churches are often highly paid and relatively powerful. While a pastor should be well cared for, many pastors of the larger churches in a presbytery earn up to three times the income of the presbytery's average pastor.[404]

Another example of evangelical conformity is the rise of the need for academic respectability. Certainly a rise of academic abilities in evangelicalism is not a negative trend. But what cost will American evangelicals pay to obtain such academic respectability? The cost of academic respectability is often the abandonment of a high view of Scripture. Young scholars are often pressed to abandon the doctrine of inerrancy in their pursuit of higher academic degrees.[405]

Many prominent professing evangelicals now argue against the verbal inspiration of Scripture. In his *Scandal of the Evangelical Mind*, well-known professor and former OPC elder Mark Noll argued that the old-Princetonian preoccupation with biblical inerrancy was misguided and should be replaced with "what is essential to Christianity, [which is] a profound trust in the Bible as pointing us to the savior."[406] Karl Barth would not have disagreed with this statement.

The British evangelical scholar Alistair McGrath holds a similar view. McGrath wrote of Charles Hodge, "Hodge's analysis of the authority of Scripture is ultimately grounded in an acknowledged and implicit theory of the nature of language, derived from reflecting the enlightenment agenda."[407] Well-known theologian David Wells laments,

---

403. Boice, *Gospel of Grace*, 55; Murray, *Evangelicalism Divided*, 255.

404. Most American evangelical churches have a membership of fewer than two hundred persons.

405. Murray, *Evangelicalism Divided*, 174, 187. See Carl R. Trueman, "The Impending Evangelical Crisis," *Evangelicals Now* (February 1998): https://www.e-n.org.uk/1998/02/features /the-impending-evangelical-crisis/. Accessed December 19, 2019.

406. Mark Noll, *The Scandal of the Evangelical Mind* (Grand Rapids: Eerdmans, 2008), 491, as cited by Murray, *Evangelicalism Divided*, 195.

407. Murray, *Evangelicalism Divided*, 196–97.

The stream of historic orthodoxy that once watered the evangelical soul is now damned by a worldliness that many failed to recognize as worldliness because of the cultural innocence with which it presents itself. . . . It may be that Christian Faith, which has made many easy alliances with modern culture in the past few decades, is also living in a fool's paradise, comforting itself about all the things God is doing . . . while it is losing its character, if not its soul.[408]

Critical Thinking. Sadly, it seems that many American evangelicals have lost the ability or will to look at the world in a thoughtful manner. While this assertion is strong, if modern evangelicals were compared to evangelicals of the nineteenth century, the deterioration of thoughtfulness would be evident, and shockingly so. The nineteenth-century American public could form opinions on complex issues such as slavery and the limits of the federal government because they had been trained to read the printed page.[409] Increasing mindlessness is not the problem of evangelicals only but also of America at large. But since evangelicals exist within American society, they suffer at the hand of this malady. They have not escaped from their own culture's problem.[410] Boice again writes, "Sadly, the dominance of television in our culture has had its impact on the churches and on preaching, where the services are now increasingly designed to be entertaining and the preachers are told to win people by helping them to have a good time."[411]

In the Southern Presbyterian Church in 1923, more than fourteen thousand young people could recite the Westminster Shorter Catechism from memory. Now, as Iain Murray says, "a biblical illiteracy prevails even among those who come as students to seminaries."[412]

Pragmatism. Much of American evangelicalism has also adopted pragmatism. The practice of calling people forward at evangelistic

---

408. David F. Wells, *No Place for Truth* (Grand Rapids: Eerdmans 1993), 11, 68; Murray, *Evangelicalism Divided*, 256.
409. Boice, *Gospel of Grace*, 54.
410. Neil Postman, *Amusing Ourselves to Death: Public Discourse in the Age of Show Business* (New York: Penguin, 1986). Says Boice, "The chief cause of our mindlessness is television. . . . In other words, television is not only mindless: it is teaching us to be mindless too" (*Gospel of Grace*, 51, 54). See also Boice's *Mind Renewal in a Mindless Age: Preparing to Think and Act Biblically* (Grand Rapids: Baker, 1993).
411. Boice, *Gospel of Grace*, 59.
412. Murray, *Evangelicalism Divided*, 209.

crusades is inherently the fruit of American pragmatism.[413] Boice laments that "church growth theorists hold seminars in which preachers are taught to think of the masses as their market and the gospel as something that needs to be attractively packaged to sell."[414] American evangelicals were eager to cultivate associations with people who were considered to be famous, whose names would catch the public's eye. Murray writes in regard to the ministry of Billy Graham (1918–2018), "Friendship was sought with all whose high profile could reflect with advantage on the message he preached."[415] This seeking after the famous and well-known has proven to be disastrous.[416] In addition, American evangelicals grew pragmatic in their decisions to work alongside liberals, Roman Catholics, and Jews in ministry.[417]

Evangelicals have also adopted new forms of old errors. For example, in the eighteenth century, an erring theologian taught that all who believe that Jesus died for sins as testified by the apostles are justified, regardless of the effect such a belief has on their lives. Zane C. Hodges (1932–2008) taught this same theological error at Dallas Theological Seminary, no matter the opposition he received from other evangelicals.[418] Hodges and others at Dallas Seminary opposed any demand for repentance and faithfulness because, they argued, such demands would add works to faith.[419] No Protestant, evangelical or Reformed, wants to connect works to faith salvifically. Yet every evangelical should understand that the nature of faith demands repentance from sin and

---

413. Ibid., 51–54. Murray cites Billy Graham's public relations director: "In our crusades and work we need every instrument of modern mass communications. We've got the greatest product in the world to sell—salvation for men's souls through Christ. Why shouldn't we sell it as effectively as we promote a bar of soap?" (ibid., 54).

414. Boice, *Gospel of Grace*, 57.

415. Murray, *Evangelicalism Divided*, 59.

416. Judgments by Billy Graham have unfortunately proven to be sadly mistaken. For example, consider what he said concerning a meeting with former president Bill Clinton: "It was a time of warm fellowship with the man who has not always won the approval of his fellow Christians but who has seen his heart and desire to serve God and do his will" (ibid., 63).

417. Ibid., 76.

418. Boice, *Gospel of Grace*, 142. Zane C. Hodges wrote *The Gospel Under Siege: Faith and Works in Tension* (Dallas: Redención Viva, 1992); *Dead Faith: What Is It?* (Dallas: Redención Viva, 1987); and *Absolutely Free!* (Grand Rapids: Zondervan, 1989). John MacArthur has rightly opposed Hodges in his book called *The Gospel According to Jesus* (Grand Rapids: Zondervan 1994).

419. Boice, *Gospel of Grace*, 142–44. This position is also related to the erroneous teaching concerning the "carnal Christian."

a new desire to walk with Christ. The evangelical church needs to remember that wrong belief is just as dangerous as unbelief.[420]

A Return to Rome? American evangelicals have even come alongside the Roman Catholic Church. In March 1994, a twenty-five page document titled *Evangelicals and Catholics Together: The Christian Mission in the Third Millennium* (or *ECT*) was published.[421] Twenty-five evangelical and Catholic leaders endorsed the document, including J. I. Packer. In addition, *Christianity Today* supported *ECT*. But California pastor and teacher John F. MacArthur immediately rejected it. He wrote a book against *ECT* titled *Reckless Faith*. "There was now," judges Iain Murray, "a fundamental difference among evangelicals."[422]

Conclusion. Without a revival of Reformed theology, American evangelical theology will destroy itself; or perhaps it has already done so. It is not my intention to provide the answers needed for the continuation of American evangelical theology. But all proper theology must give God ultimate glory. As long as American evangelical theology cannot give proper glory to God, it will be doomed to failure. Many American evangelicals do give God glory, only then to mix in human ability. The result is that the glory loses its brilliant luster. Until evangelicals join their voices with Reformed theology and proclaim *soli Deo gloria*, perhaps evangelicalism's demise should go unlamented.[423]

While there are apparent theological differences between Reformed and evangelical thought, it is time for the two groups to cooperate more extensively. Consider, briefly, the account of Abram and Lot in Genesis 13. Abram and Lot settled with their flocks and men between Bethel and Ai. But though the two men had a good relationship, their vast herds resulted in limited pastureland, which only created strife among their hired men (v. 7). The quarreling resulted in their need to separate—a painful experience for Abram.[424]

At the time, Abram and Lot were a microcosm of the church, for they were the people of God on the earth. So God's people today should heed the lessons of this narrative. Though Abram and Lot

---

420. Murray, *Evangelicalism Divided*, 259.
421. Billy Graham preceded *ECT* in finding common ground with Roman Catholics. See Mark Noll, "The Innocence of Billy Graham," *First Things* 79 (January 1998): 37.
422. Murray, *Evangelicalism Divided*, 224.
423. Boice, *Gospel of Grace*, 167.
424. See *WCG*, 1:319–20.

were personally at peace, their men quarreled. Notice a seemingly disconnected piece of information that the narrator provides in verse 7: "there was strife between the herdsmen of Abram's livestock and the herdsmen of Lot's livestock. At that time the Canaanites and the Perizzites were dwelling in the land." This phrase has nothing to do with the livestock or the conflict. But the narrator is teaching the reader something. Abram and Lot were in enemy territory. And as their enemies—the Canaanites and Perizzites—were on all sides of them, the laborers fought against each other.

In the same way, the church is surrounded by the enemy, and he is dangerous. Peter writes: "Your adversary the devil prowls around like a roaring lion, seeking someone to devour" (1 Peter 5:8). Yet one of the dominant themes of the NT is unity within the church because this area is where the church struggles most. The church far too often quarrels with one another in the land of the enemy. In Christ, the church must relate to each other as adopted family members. Unlike the separation that occurred between Abram and Lot, Reformed and evangelical Christianity must unite and work toward the common ends of strengthening the church and advancing God's kingdom. For outside true evangelicalism and Reformed theology is a destructive movement that plagued the Evangelical Theological Society in North America twenty years ago. The following pages will address some of the theologians who were part of this movement.

JOHN MACQUARRIE (A.D. 1919–2007) AND JOHN HICK (A.D. 1922–2012)

John Macquarrie: Biography and Writings. John Macquarrie was born in Scotland and studied philosophy and theology at the University of Glasgow. He began his doctoral program in theology at the University of Glasgow after serving in World War II. In the early 1960s he taught at Union Seminary in New York, and in 1970 he became Lady Margaret's Professor of Divinity at Oxford, where he remained until his retirement in 1986.

He was a prolific author. In 1955 he wrote *An Existentialist Theology: A Comparison of Heidegger and Bultmann* (London: SCM

Press). In the 1960s and 1970s, he wrote further on existentialism, the language of theology, ethics, and theology proper. Of his writings, his most important was *Principles of Christian Theology*.

John Hick: Biography and Writings. Born in England, John Hick was trained in philosophy at the University of Edinburgh, then completed his studies in 1950 at Oxford. He served as Danforth Professor of the Philosophy of Religion at Claremont Graduate University, in California, and as H. G. Wood Professor of Theology at the University of Birmingham. He also taught at Cornell University, Princeton Theological Seminary, and Cambridge University.

Hick wrote a number of books. In the 1950s and 1960s, he wrote on the topics of God's existence, the nature of faith and knowledge, and the problem of evil. In the 1970s he turned his attention to the philosophy of religion, eternal life, and Christology. In the following two decades, he worked on interpreting religions.

Macquarrie on the Doctrine of God. John Macquarrie's *Principles of Christian Theology* intends to present an entire system of thought; the following analysis will focus only on his doctrine of God.[425] He believed that God's nature could best be known through an understanding of the word *being*. God's name as revealed in Exodus 3:14 should be comprehended as an ongoing process of being in both time and history that is neither a fixed nor stationary condition.[426] Macquarrie argued that people come to know being as it is declared and manifested through the symbols of revelation.[427] Variation in being's self-disclosure results in a variation of symbols.[428]

Macquarrie taught that people are first confronted with being when they realize the nothingness of both themselves and this world and then being overwhelms them in revelation. Though humans have not seen nor noticed it, being has been there. Being itself is distinct from

425. After an introduction, the first part of his work is philosophical theology that addresses the tasks of philosophical theology, the nature of human existence, the nature of revelation, being and God, the language of theology, and religion and religions. The second part is symbolic theology that includes its tasks, the Triune God, creation, God, the world and evil, the person and work of Christ, the Holy Spirit and salvation, and the last things. The third part is applied theology.

426. John Macquarrie, *Principles of Christian Theology* (New York: Scribner's Sons, 1966), 180.

427. Ibid., 149.

428. Ibid.

any particular being—that is, a person—and cannot be conceptualized. Being is known as presence and manifestation.[429] This being includes becoming, has taken time into itself, and expands and realizes itself in history.[430]

Traditionally, God was viewed anthropomorphically, as someone much like ourselves, and locatable at some certain spatial place, for example, the sky. Traditional theism toned down the anthropomorphic elements, and God became a metaphysical person without a body who dwelt beyond the world, yet intervenes in the concerns of the world. God was still thought of as a being.[431] But science has destroyed this conception of God by claiming that the world is self-regulating and does not require such an entity. Still, Macquarrie observed that such a being would not be ultimate because men could still inquire about his being.

God should not be conceived of as a being, no matter how exalted or high, but as Being, which is more ultimate than any particular being. Being is not a property, therefore it must be thought of as incomparable. Being is transcendent, which is mysterious in that it is above all categories, yet it is not an incomprehensible blank. Being is the prior condition to all beings, which makes it more "beingful" than anything that simply is (i.e., a being).

Macquarrie maintains that while Being is transcendent it must also be immanent. It must be immanent because Being gives itself with and through particular beings. Without the beings in and through which it appears and in which it is present, it would be impossible to distinguish Being from nothing.

God is not simply being but may be comprehended as holy Being. This holy Being is not a particular being, that is, person, thing, or a property of beings, but a prior condition to any particular being, and it is thus transcendent. God is described as holy Being when he confers being and goes out from himself as primordial Being into creation;[432] therefore, God, as holy Being, must of necessity be both transcendent and immanent.[433]

429. Ibid., 78.
430. Ibid., 191.
431. Ibid., 106.
432. Ibid., 235.
433. Ibid., 130.

Holiness has relation to the traditional divine attributes. The adjective *holy* points to the mystery of God plus humans' response to that mystery when it confronts them. Human response to this mystery has two aspects. First, humans experience the holy as it demands of them, overpowers them, and judges them; second, humans experience God's holiness in that it empowers them. The first response is humans' experience of divine wrath, which exhibits God's righteousness and justice. The second response is God's grace toward men, which exhibits his love and mercy. All these attributes are rooted in Macquarrie's notion of God's *letting be*.

With his philosophical notions, Macquarrie is forced to redefine traditional categories of God. For example, God's omnipotence means that he "is the source and also the horizon of all possibilities, and only those as excluded that are inconsistent with the structure and dynamics of God himself."[434] He defines God's omniscience as that God, as Being, transcends and occupies every perspective at once. By omnipresence, Macquarrie means that God is not restricted to the empirical world or factual situations as is man. God's immutability must be comprehended in relationship to his dynamism. While immutable, God cannot be static or monolithic.[435]

Macquarrie defines God's immensity as humans' inability to measure him, and his infinity points to the contrast between beings and Being that "lets be." Macquarrie does not want his readers to understand God's eternality to mean his timelessness. Instead, he wants them to think of his eternality as a mere comparison between being and Being.[436] God may also be seen as containing time. For the beginning of creation is not a past time, but Being. At all times, he is that which

---

434. Ibid., 189.

435. He suggests that a better and more biblical term than *immutable* or *consistent* would be *faithful*. Faithful is (ibid., 190): "God's unchangingness through change, so to speak." He says that God does not undergo fundamental changes, yet faithfulness must be understood in terms of a history of action. Macquarrie's language is confusing—he seems to be saying that God changes but does not make a fundamental change but changes faithfully. He does not provide a consistent definition of the nature of fundamental change but gives as an example a God of wrath becoming a God of grace. Macquarrie does not even discuss holy Being in terms of being primarily wrath-full or grace-full but in the terms that define God as Being. Being is not defined as wrath or even special grace. It appears that to reinforce his own conception of immutability, Macquarrie implements classical metaphysical terminology that he does not embrace as proper for God.

436. Ibid., 188.

"lets be."[437] For Macquarrie, God is dynamic and enters into a world of beings. God's eternality, termed *letting be*, moves from primordial Being to expressive Being to bring men and women to Being.[438] God's essence is to "let be." People call him God and "recognize him as holy Being, calling forth our worship, because he pours out Being."[439] God is holy, righteous, and merciful in his acts of providence. Divine providence asserts that there is a God who is ordering history. And as humans live in accordance with God's directing of events, his providence is grace to them; but as humans push against God's working in history, his providence is judgment against them.

Another approach to the analysis of Being is what being is not. First, Being is not a particular being. Second, Being is disclosed in existing, and existing is not beholding, considering, or seeing, for being concerns involvement and participation. In addition, Being is not a property of being, such as *hardness*, or a class, such as *humankind*. Finally, the word *being* is not synonymous with God, for God is not a neutral designation as Macquarrie maintains that being is.[440]

In terms of God's mystery, Macquarrie believed that God in his Being is incomparable and suprarational in his transcendence but is also immanent. He said that "the discussion of the attributes in relation to the mystery of God points us to the paradoxical, or dialectical character that belongs to every adjective applied to the incomparable, which nonetheless draws near in revelation and presence."[441]

Macquarrie also spoke of God in Trinitarian terms. Being is dynamic, stable, and formulated in terms of primordial Being, understood as the Father in the Trinity; expressive Being, who is Jesus Christ; and unitive Being, who is the Holy Spirit. God is not a being but transcendent and immanent Being. The Trinitarian formula came into existence to express the belief of the Christian community that God, who created all things, became incarnate in the man Jesus Christ and

437. Ibid., 199–200.
438. See ibid., 103, for his trying to explain eternality by the characteristic of being as the prior condition of any beings. This characteristic he calls *letting be*, which is something that is "positive and active, as enabling to be, empowering to be, or bringing into being."
439. Ibid., 183.
440. Ibid., 98–102, 105, 170.
441. Ibid., 187.

that God still dwelt with the community and guided it;[442] therefore, the doctrine of the Holy Trinity was created to elucidate a picture of God. But it must be judged only in terms of what it affirms, because it points to something beyond what it specifically expresses. In addition, it must also be judged in relation to the errors that it excludes.[443]

Macquarrie claimed that the early doctrine of the Holy Trinity expressed the unity of God as one substance or essence. All three persons of the Trinity are fully God, and none is subordinate to the others. He argued that the Father, Son, and Holy Spirit must be understood in terms of Being, not in terms of three beings.[444] But there is an inherent problem in understanding the terminology of the early conceptions for the Trinity. Those formulations use the term *persons* to portray the diversity of the Trinity. Since the word *person* does not mean the same today as it did then, Macquarrie provides alternatives—words such as *movement* and *mode*.

He termed God the Father *primordial Being*. Primordial Being refers to the concept of *letting be*: "The Father as primordial Being is the depth of the mystery of God."[445] Macquarrie claimed that God the Father, the primordial Being, is revealed in and through the other persons of the Trinity. He referred to the second person of the Trinity, the Son, as expressive Being. He said, "The energy of primordial Being is poured out through expressive Being and gives rise to the world of particular beings, having an intelligible structure and disposed in space and time."[446]

The second person of the Trinity may also be understood as the Logos or Word, which gains expression through the beings and is also generated by the Father, which separates the Logos from the beings. The hidden primordial Being flows out through the being of Jesus Christ, and his being is connected or caught up into Being itself.[447] There has never been a time when the Logos was not the Son or was not united with the Father as primordial Being. Expressive Being took part in the creation and the reconciliation, or new creation. Also, while

442. Ibid., 175.
443. Ibid., 176.
444. Ibid.
445. Ibid., 182.
446. Ibid.
447. Ibid., 183.

expressive Being has always been active, at a given time approximately two thousand years ago there was a new and decisive revelation of that activity in the person of Jesus of Nazareth.[448] This event was the climax of God's reconciling work and provides the revelation on which the Christian community of faith determines its way of understanding holy Being.[449]

Macquarrie taught that Jesus of Nazareth was the symbol of Being. He understood Christ to be the revelation, or symbol, of God. The event of Jesus Christ is the highest point of God's providential activity—the very focal point of the disclosure of the mystery of Being.[450] The Gospels provide information concerning this Jesus of Nazareth, and theology depends on the identity of this Jesus. If no importance were attached to the historical life or existence of Jesus of Nazareth, then he was nothing but another mythical redeemer—some type of Mithras or Osius. The Gospels claim that Jesus taught men to live with supreme self-giving love, and he exemplified this lifestyle in his very existence.[451]

There were a number of critical moments of revelation in the life of Jesus. First came the nativity, or the virgin birth, which pointed to Christ's origin in God. Second came the baptism, which initiated Christ's vocation. Third came the temptation, which affirmed Jesus's humanity. Fourth came the transfiguration, when the divinity and humanity of Christ—the very Being—drew near to the disciples.[452] But it is in the passion where the connection between Christ's person and work becomes evident, where the historical dimension of Christology is manifested, as well as an affirmation of Christ's humanity and the revelation of the human Jesus, who is also the Jesus of Christian faith.[453]

448. Ibid., 178.

449. Throughout *Principles of Christian Theology*, Macquarrie refers to God as *he* yet gives no indication as to why God should be a *he* instead of a *she* or an *it*. Classical theology always refers to God as *he*, but if God is holy Being, how does Being become male?

450. Ibid., 249.

451. Ibid., 352–53; it was in him that there occurred reconciliation—the crucial event in the relationship between God and creatures.

452. Ibid., 257–64.

453. Ibid., 265. There are two prominent motifs in the passion. The first is Christ's obedience as he agonizes over his Father's (primordial Being's) will. Yet Christ is perfectly obedient to the Father's will, even to the agony of the cross. The second motif in the passion is Christ's absolute self-giving. His obedience to submit to the cross is also the highest expression of giving himself to others (ibid., 280–82).

This Christ can be further understood through his titles. As Macquarrie understands it, the resurrection and the ascension are moments, with the resurrection pointing to life being attained through death and with the ascension portraying the man Jesus as the transparent revealer of God.[454] The faith community gave five titles to Jesus of Nazareth. The first one was Messiah, which involves an understanding of the human Jesus as fulfilling the OT conception of a ruler who would restore the prosperity of the nation. Macquarrie viewed the title Son of Man as apocalyptic and as encouraging a supernatural understanding of Jesus as a heavenly being.[455] Son of God is possibly of Hellenistic origin indicating some sort of God-man.[456] The titles Lord and Word have the greatest universality because they have both Greek and Jewish connotations. Lord means God in the OT and is used for a particular cultic deity in the Greek religion. Through the Word, God acted for and communicated himself to the Hebrews, and this title represents the governing principle of the world for the Greeks.[457]

Concerning the third person of the Trinity, Macquarrie taught that if the Son is generated by the Father, then the Holy Spirit is said to proceed from the Father and the Son.[458] *Procession* was used as a generic term, with *spiration* as the specific procession of the Holy Spirit from the Father. He terms the third person of the Trinity *unitive Being*—for the function of the Spirit is to maintain the unity of Being with the beings. This unity is a unity of freedom—a unity comprehending a diversity of free, responsible beings. The Spirit promotes a higher level of unity between Being and the beings, for it proceeds from primordial Being and from expressive Being, as the agent of bringing into being every particular being and leads the beings into a higher or richer unity with Being.[459]

The Father, or primordial Being, and the Son, or expressive Being, were both active in creation. The Holy Spirit, unitive Being, also par-

454. Ibid., 265–67.
455. Macquarrie should add that the title Son of Man was the mode in which Jesus addressed himself, not necessarily a title given to him in the last verse of the first chapter of John's gospel.
456. Ibid., 268–69.
457. Ibid., 269.
458. Ibid., 179.
459. Ibid., 204.

ticipated in creation, for the Spirit's activity is mentioned as "moving over the waters" (Macquarrie's words). The Spirit, as unitive Being, lifts the whole creation toward God, thus bringing the beings into unity with Being. The highest point of the unity built by the Holy Spirit is the free, conscious communion of existent beings with Being, a communion termed, in effect, the "adoption as sons." Yet the Spirit works in all levels of creation; that work may be understood as a striving in creaturely beings below conscious thought.[460] Macquarrie taught that in relation to people's lives, the Spirit is God at his closest to humans. Through the Spirit, humans can hear the voice of Being from beyond themselves. The Spirit communicates the being of Christ as the focus of holy Being; it arouses the realization of being's kinship with Being. The next section will focus on the arguments that Macquarrie and Hick offer for God's existence.

Arguments for God's Existence. John Hick rehearsed various arguments for belief in the existence of God. He began with Anselm's ontological argument, which he affirmed.[461] By definition, it is true that the most perfect being that there is exists. Yet it needs to be proved that this perfect being is God. There is therefore a distinction between something that exists in the mind only, and something that exists in reality. The most perfect conceivable being must exist both in reality and in the mind.[462]

The second form of the argument adds God's necessary existence. The concept of God's *necessary existence* is defined in terms of his aseity. Hick maintains that aseity is derived from "the Latin *a se esse*, 'being from oneself.'"[463] First, the concept of *aseity* understands God as dependent on nothing other than himself for existence. Nothing created him, and nothing can destroy him; God is and is all-conditioning. In other words, God determines all states and circumstances of all

---

460. Ibid., 295.

461. It runs in this manner. God is a being than which nothing greater can be conceived. Anselm had two important points: the word *greater* does not mean spatially larger, and there is a difference between the idea of the "most perfect being" and the idea of the "most perfect conceivable being." John H. Hick, *The Philosophy of Religion* (Englewood Cliffs, NJ: Prentice Hall, 1970), 16.

462. Ibid., 16–17.

463. Ibid., 7. But Hick's Latin translation is not quite correct, for "being from oneself" is translated *a se entis*; *a se esse* would mean "to be from oneself." Nevertheless, there are two important elements in the concept of *aseity* or "self-existence."

things. Second, God is eternal, which means that he has no beginning or end and that he is outside time.[464]

The second argument for the existence of God is Thomas Aquinas's first-cause argument. Aquinas attempted to prove that given the general structure of the world, it is logically necessary that there must be a god. In this argument, Aquinas argued that everything that happens has a cause, and every cause has a cause, and so on, either going on for infinity or until arriving at a first cause. Since there cannot be an infinite regress of causes, there must be a first cause, which is God.

Contemporary followers of Aquinas have modified his first-cause argument. The endless series of causes is seen as being in need of a reality that is self-explanatory. They have redefined the endless series not as necessarily being a regress of events in time but as an eternally inconclusive regress of explanations. According to the later Thomists, if there is no self-explanatory reality, then the universe itself is unintelligible.

Aquinas's third proof consisted in the cosmological argument. In it he maintained that each item of the world could or could not have existed in the same or different form—that is, everything in the world is contingent. Since all things are contingent, because each item did not exist in some time period, there must have been a time when nothing existed. If that conclusion is true, then since presently there are things in existence, there must be something that is noncontingent, and that something is God.

Hick then moved to the teleological argument, or the argument from design. This argument appeared as early as Plato and is still in use today. Hick used William Paley's version of the argument, employing the analogy of the watch. The analogy goes as follows. There are no natural reasons why a watch would be lying in a deserted place; therefore, humans must assume that an intelligent mind made the watch. Hick, in his understanding of Paley, gives certain qualifying statements. He qualifies that for humans to assume an intelligent maker of a watch, they need not have seen a watch, nor does the watch need to work correctly, nor do even all the parts of the watch need to be discovered. A designed watch, no matter how foreign or well-functioning, betrays

464. Ibid., 7–8.

the work of a creative hand. Since the world is as complex as a watch, then there must be a watchmaker, who is God. A broader variation of the argument had been presented by F. R. Tennant and Richard Swinburne. In the light of moral, aesthetic, religious, biological, and cognitive experience, it is most probable that there is a god. Theism alone accounts for man's moral and religious experience and the material universe; therefore, theism is the most likely worldview.[465]

Another argument used to prove God's existence is the moral argument. There are two basic forms of this argument, but the argument as a whole maintains that because of man's sense of obligation to his fellow men, there must be a god as the ground of this obligation. The first form of the argument begins with either objective moral values or the fact of human conscience and proceeds to a God who is a transcendent ground of value or the voice of conscience. The second form of the argument claims that if humans recognize a sovereign claim of moral values on their lives, then from such a presupposition God's existence may be postulated.[466]

In contrast, there are arguments presented against God's existence. There are two influential interpretations of religious experience viewed as such. The first is the sociological theory of religion, with Émil Durkheim (1858–1917) as the principle proponent. This theory argues that society fabricates gods that are imaginary for the purpose of controlling individuals. He claims that society, not God, transcends the individual's personal life and gives the individual a moral imperative. Thus society has been symbolized as God.[467] The second counter was offered by Sigmund Freud (1856–1939), who saw religion as a mental defense against nature. He explained that if the forces of nature, such as death, could be transformed into beings of sorts, then humans could deal with them and not be paralyzed by them. Freud argued that the Judeo-Christian religion projected the personality of the father on the universe—so that adults can now deal with the universe in the same way that a child deals with his father. He proposed that if humans

---

465. Ibid., 26–27.

466. Ibid., 28. There are also special public events, such as miracles and visions, which are thought of as proofs for God. These proofs, however, cannot be valid for those who have not experienced such an event (ibid., 37).

467. Ibid., 30–32.

could understand religion as such, then they could confront the world as it truly is, without the need for a god or gods.[468]

With the advances in the scientific realm, science and religion have often given conflicting testimonies of reality. Scientifically based findings have directly contradicted nonscientific assertions found in the Bible. Either the Bible is not divinely inspired, or scientific testimony is incorrect. Since science is not necessarily incorrect, then Christian faith may be regarded as a relatively harmless psychological phantasy. Nature may be studied without reference to God, and science can reject the notion of a god.[469]

John Macquarrie taught that there are two main types of arguments for the existence of God. There are the a priori theories, such as Anselm's, that are based on pure reason alone and on the concepts that belong to it apart from any experience of the world, and there are a posteriori theories, such as those of Saint Thomas, in which reason constructs its theories on the basis of physical experience.

Macquarrie believed that it was beneficial to examine the proofs in the entire context of the given theologian's thought. For example, Aquinas may have been attempting to correlate theology and philosophy, not necessarily attempting to provide a cogent demonstration of God's existence. In other words, he may have been attempting to show the compatibility of faith and reason.

Macquarrie's summary of the arguments for God's existence is that the a posteriori arguments offered by Aquinas, which begin with the world and seek to argue to God, have been developed into a cosmological argument, which proceeds from the limited status of things in the world to an unlimited God, and a teleological argument, which asserts that the world's order needs a creative intelligence. Macquarrie prefers those arguments to Anselm's because they begin with empirical evidence rather than abstract ideas.[470]

Karl Barth understood Anselm's ontological argument as intended for Christians, not necessarily to persuade unbelievers to accept Christianity. Also, Barth held strong opinions concerning the notion of arguments for God's existence. He believed that apologetics, in terms

468. Ibid., 33–34.
469. Ibid., 37–38.
470. Macquarrie, *Principles*, 41.

of arguments such as Anselm's, should be used only within the church against heresy. Barth taught that when interacting with unbelievers, Christians should begin with the Scriptures and Christ, nothing more, for he believed that attempting to find a common ground of argumentation with those outside the church distorts the gospel.[471]

Emil Brunner disagreed with Barth. Brunner taught that believers should look for a point of connection with unbelievers so that the gospel might be received. These points of contact might be the various ways that God is working in the world or in his providence, in history or general revelation, or even in evolutionary theory.[472]

On Religious Language.[473] Hick and Macquarrie believed that there are two fundamental problems inherent to religious language. The first problem is the unique sense that descriptive terms pose when applied to God. The second is the basic function of religious language. The statement "Henry is the king of England" could be verified as to its truth or falsity by asking an Englishman. But the words "God is king" cannot be so verified. Apparently, the word *king* is used differently to describe God, or such statements make no sense at all.[474]

Aquinas maintained that there is a difference in a word when applied to God and when applied to a created being. The term *univocal* describes the use of words with identical meaning, while *equivocal* describes the comparison of words used with entirely different meanings. Apparently, neither one of these terms is satisfactory to describe the meaning of descriptive terminology applied to man and God.[475]

The best word for this relationship is *analogical*, which means that there is some quality that corresponds to both levels of existence. For example, a person might be described as loving, or such a person might do or say certain things that could be described as loving. At the same time, God is also described as loving. The term *loving* is used in an analogical sense here, for certainly God does not do all the things that humans do when humans are considered loving, nor do humans love with the perfect, immense love with which God loves. According

471. Ibid., 281.
472. Ibid., 259.
473. For an introduction to the problem of religious language, see *WCG* 2:343–49.
474. Hick, *Philosophy of Religion*, 12.
475. Ibid., 8.

852

to Hick, analogical language does not contribute anything but limited statements about God.[476]

Paul Tillich believed that religious language is symbolic, and he held that there are two different types of symbolic language: symbols and signs. Both types point to something beyond themselves, but a symbol participates in that to which it points, while a sign does not. For a symbol, Hick provided the example of a nation's flag, which is enveloped in the might of that country. And for a sign, he gave the example of a red light, which indicates an external connection—namely, where to stop.[477]

Symbols have a complex meaning. They participate in or are enveloped by that to which they point, but they are also only useful for a specific period of time. At some point in history, symbols cease to exist. Symbols are like art, which communicates a level of reality that is opened only via this means of communication but also expands a love and understanding of art.[478]

Hick argued that religious language can be only symbolic, with one exception—for if humans speak of anything that is of ultimate concern (part of Tillich's definition of religion), then they can only point toward it, while still being ultimately connected to it.[479] Tillich's thought on religious language has two divisions. There is a negative aspect, which warns against anthropomorphism. This aspect explains that humans may never adequately apply literal language to God because humans are finite, and God negates part of humans' definition or meaning in that he is infinite.[480] Positively, God has metaphysical and moral attributes, and according to the theory of incarnation, humans can look to Christ for God's moral attributes. As Christ is good, so humanity can observe how God is good. As Christ spoke in parables, so humans may think of God in parables.[481]

Macquarrie himself developed a threefold analysis of religious language. First, when a person makes a locution, he is expressing

476. Ibid., 84.
477. Ibid., 85–88.
478. Ibid., 71–72.
479. Ibid., 72. The one exception—the only literal thing we can say about religious experience, or God—is that we may say that God is *Being-itself*, according to Hick's understanding of Tillich. Yet Hick does not explain specifically what Tillich meant by Being-itself.
480. Ibid., 73.
481. Ibid., 74–75.

something that would have otherwise not been known to anyone except the individual who is speaking. That individual may speak in an impersonal way, like a scientist or mathematician, that does not convey psychological information but instead merely expresses what is empirically verifiable. Or an individual may express in his locution his personality, feelings, and emotions.[482]

Theological language fits within the second category because it expresses total existence. Total existence is the whole range of man's mode of being in the world. Macquarrie refused to concede, however, that religious statements express only emotion, for religious statements also express the insights the individual has concerning the structure of reality. If the individual were not to discern what his language was communicating or attempting to communicate, then his language would be, in effect, illegitimate. Macquarrie asked the question, "If there is something legitimately to be communicated by religious language, what is it?"

His answer was that theological language refers to Being.[483] Being is expressed in religious language in reference to individuals expressing that Being. Being, or assertions about Being, are not assertions of empirical fact, but by stretching ordinary (i.e., scientific) uses, language develops and becomes capable of sophisticated expression.[484]

Religious language, therefore, is somewhat different from either normal or scientific language.[485] Theological language communicates the comprehension of Being that has been appropriated by the individual in the attitude of faith. Believers must be cautious to relate theological language to the frame of reference of the nonreligious, not just to those who share in a community of faith. For Hick, religious language is also difficult to describe, but its significance lies in the impact that it makes on human experience.[486]

482. Macquarrie, *Principles*, 114.
483. Ibid., 115.
484. Ibid., 116.
485. Ibid., 117: Macquarrie justifies this assertion by maintaining that "in our doctrine that Being is present and manifest in the beings, and . . . indeed it is only in and through beings (including our own being) that we can have any understanding of Being. The presence and manifestation of Being in beings, or alternatively expressed, the participation of beings in Being, justifies the logic of a language of Being."
486. It is impossible to verify an encounter with God, for we can never measure unlimited love or any other of God's attributes. But as Christians our belief concerning God's nature is

SCHUBERT M. OGDEN (A.D. 1928–2019)

Life. Schubert M. Ogden was born in Ohio and educated at Ohio Wesleyan University. He studied theology under Charles Hartshorne (1897–2000) at the divinity school of the University of Chicago. Hartshorne's work was significant in the development of process philosophy and theology.[487] Ogden was also influenced by Bultmann both as a student and a friend. Ogden taught for several years at Chicago's divinity school, but he spent most of his extensive career at the Perkins School of Theology at Southern Methodist University.

Writings. Beginning with the publication of his dissertation on Bultmann in 1961, Ogden researched the doctrine of God in the 1960s, the theology of liberation in the 1970s, Christology in the 1980s, and theological methodology in the 1990s.[488] Ogden was intent to answer

---

based on God's self-revelation to us through Jesus Christ. We may indirectly verify the authority of Christ in an experience of the reign of Christ in the kingdom of God the Father. If that kingdom becomes a matter of fact, then it will not be susceptible to logical proof, and here is possibly the evidence needed to exclude rational doubt. In conclusion, Hick maintains that the locution "God exists" must be seen in the light of what he calls "making a difference." Only as we determine the difference that God's existence makes in human experience can we bring this question into proper focus (Hick, *Philosophy of Religion*, 103–5).

487. Ogden and Hartshorne held a colloquium and then wrote a book, *Theology in Crisis: A Colloquium on the Credibility of God* (New Concord, OH: Muskingum College, 1967). In that volume, Hartshorne said that human life itself may be seen as a sample of reality. He maintained that human life is the only part of nature that we know by being it—we know human life from within as well as from without. Also, in constructing a model of reality we are to read human consciousness, thought, and feelings into it. Likewise, when we attempt to conceive God, we are trying to understand a reality that is vastly different, both quantitatively and qualitatively, from ourselves. Third, human life is social, as exemplified by language itself, and also by one's relationship to one's own body. Also, Hartshorne understood that any earthly society needs rulers—otherwise there is chaos. So God is a cosmic ruler who rules the universe, and in this theory God's love is manifest in that he is involved in social relations—he rules by his goodness and his love. Yet God is so far only seen as a big brother; therefore, God must also be viewed as being superior in principle. Superior in principle means that God is exalted in principle above all other individuals. Of course, this exaltation does not rule out God's increasing in value himself, for Hartshorne believes that whatever value anyone actually has, God will actually have. He also maintains that God can and does change. If one admits that God can change, thus denying the idea that God is perfect, then God can acquire value from the world. Hartshorne also asserted that all facts about God are contingent facts—for they are true, but they could have been false. It is true that Washington crossed the Delaware River, but conceivably he could not have done. So is our understanding of the facts about God. See Ogden, *Theology in Crisis*, 20–26.

488. See Mark Taylor, "The Boundless Love of God and the Bounds of Critical Reflection: Schubert Ogden's Contribution to a Theology of Liberation," *Journal of the American Academy of Religion* 57, no. 1 (Spring 1989): 103–47; Franklin Gamwell, "On the Theology of Schubert M. Ogden," *Religious Studies Review* 23, no. 4 (October 1997): 333.

two questions: whether or not contemporary Christian witness is consistent with the earliest apostolic witness, and whether contemporary Christian witness is credible.

Ogden wrote on the nature and attributes of God. He defined God's nature by two essential characteristics. First, God is related to humans' lives in the world, and because of that relationship humans' own selves and actions make a difference as to God's actual being; and second, God's relatedness to humans' lives is in itself related to nothing, and because of that unrelatedness, neither humans' selves nor humans' actions make a difference as to God's existence.[489]

Ogden believed that God is best understood as being strictly analogous to the human self. God is related to the universe of other beings as the human self is related to the body. In previous classical metaphysics, God was understood as the timeless absolute. But Ogden contended that God is the living dynamic God of Holy Scripture, not a timeless absolute; for the distinctions of past, present, and future may properly be applied to God, whose being is the eminent instance of historical being.[490] In the light of the modern doctrine of God and the analogy of being, God must be viewed as radically different from past metaphysical conceptions.

Classical metaphysics denied that God could in any sense be understood to be temporal and relative, which denial, according to Ogden, starkly contradicted Scripture's representation of God as the eminent Self or Thou. Ogden understood God as both absolute and relative, which he held to be complementary, not contradictory, characteristics. God's absoluteness is understood by Ogden to be the abstract structure or identifying principle of his lofty unabsoluteness, or eminent relativity. This understanding of God demonstrates how the Thou—with the greatest conceivable degree of genuine relatedness to others, namely, relatedness to all others—is for that very reason the most truly absolute Thou that any mind can conceive.[491]

The testimony of Scripture represents God as the necessarily existent. God's reality is spoken of in terms of myth that contains both concrete

---

489. Schubert M. Ogden, *The Reality of God and Other Essays* (New York: Harper & Row, 1966), 180.
490. Ibid.
491. Ibid., 144.

and imaginative terms, representing him as a supreme person who freely creates the world and redeems it. God is seen as the ultimate end and source of whatever is or could ever be. God is universally immanent as sovereign Creator and Redeemer of all things.[492] God is necessary, and without the affirmation of his reality, the witness of Scripture would not be the same, for in Scripture, God is understood to be the ultimate source and end of all that either is or could ever be. This theory is contrasted with the classical theistic view of God as being nothing but necessary and not having real internal relations with contingent beings. Ogden believed that Scripture could be appropriately interpreted only if God's nature is understood as having a contingent as well as a necessary aspect.

Concluding his remarks on God's nature, Ogden wanted his readers to understand that God exists both necessarily and contingently—by reason of his internal relations to wholly necessary creatures. God's existence is not dependent on anything; the only thing that is contingent is what God is. By this assertion Ogden meant the actual state of the infinite number of states possible for God, which is contingent on his own decisions and on the free decisions of the creatures who comprise his world.

Ogden sought to understand the reality of God so that the conception may respect all that is legitimate in modern secularity while also respecting the distinctive claims of the Christian faith. His method for doing so was to claim that God is understood as the perfect instance of creative becoming. Instead of God's being merely the barren Absolute, which is related to nothing, Ogden claimed that by definition God is related to everything in a similar fashion as to how humans relate to their bodies. In addition, he believed that God is not utterly unchangeable but should be understood to be continually in the process of self-creation by uniting all past actuality with the abundance of future actuality.[493]

Since God is a living and growing God, it is also implied that God is eminent or perfect reality. If God is the eminently temporal and changing One, where time and change have no end, then he is also eternal and unchangeable.[494] God's only environment is wholly internal, which means that he can never be localized in any particular space

492. Ibid., 122.
493. Ibid., 59.
494. Ibid.

and time but instead is omnipresent; therefore, God is not only the eminently relative One but there is also a sense, according to Ogden, in which he is absolute.[495]

Finally, God may be seen as eternal, impassive, immaterial, and immutable, or what is termed the *metaphysical Absolute*. Ogden's term, in opposition to the classical definition, conceives God as the supremely relative Self or Thou, which includes the Absolute as the visionary or abstract principle of his own concrete identity.[496]

KEY TERMS

amillennialism
myth
existential interpretation
Heilsgeschichte
brute fact
line of despair

STUDY QUESTIONS

1. How do you view Bultmann's view of Christ and Scripture?
2. What is the *Word of God* for Barth?
3. What do you think of Cullmann's notion of *already-but-not-yet*?
4. What is wrong with process theology?
5. What are the strengths of the old-Princeton apologetic and Van Til's apologetic method?
6. Do you think that Machen or Murray has the stronger position on social issues?

RESOURCES FOR FURTHER STUDY

Cullmann, Oscar. *The State in the New Testament*. London: SCM Press, 1957. A shorter work that is of value even though Cullmann was not an evangelical.

495. Ibid.
496. Ibid., 61.

Van Til, Cornelius. *Christian Theistic Evidences*, ed. K. Scott Oliphint, 2nd ed. (Phillipsburg, NJ: P&R Publishing, 2016); *The Defense of the Faith*, ed. K. Scott Oliphint, 4th ed. (Phillipsburg, NJ: P&R Publishing, 2008); *Christian Apologetics*, ed. William Edgar, 2nd ed. (Phillipsburg, NJ: P&R Publishing, 2003). Edited works that are much more accessible and easier to read than Van Til's original writings.

Murray, John. Pure gold—all his writings.

23

Modern Theology

THIS CHAPTER SUMMARIZES THEOLOGICAL development beginning in the eighteenth century and continuing to the end of the twentieth century. This era in the church will see a number of faithful theologians who demonstrate and uphold the beauty and richness of God's Word for the life of the church. But during this time, a number of thinkers will attempt to mar the clarity and authority of Scripture by seeking to esteem human reason and put subjectivity in its place. Believing in the inspired Word of God became a badge of shame and antiquated thought, but there would continue to be men who "considered the reproach of Christ greater wealth than the treasures of Egypt" (Heb. 11:26).

DOCTRINE OF GOD

Character or Attributes. Schleiermacher's belief that God is a feeling of dependence on the absolute began a novel view of God's attributes—namely, that the attributes of God are only how feelings relate to him.[1] Concomitant with these changes, some modern theologians wrongly created an ontological hierarchy of God's attributes.[2] Specifically, they

---

1. Friedrich Schleiermacher, *The Christian Faith* (Edinburgh: 1928), 196: "All attributes which we ascribe to God are to be taken as denoting not something special in God, but only something special in the manner in which the feeling of absolute dependence is to be related to him" (as cited by Greg Allison, *Historical Theology: An Introduction to Christian Doctrine—A Companion to Wayne Grudem's Systematic Theology* (Grand Rapids: Zondervan, 2011), 223.

2. God's being and his attributes are identical. Richard C. Gamble, *The Whole Counsel of God*, vol. 2, *The Full Revelation of God* (Phillipsburg, NJ: P&R Publishing, 2018) (WCG2), 384: "They are not, and cannot be, in some type of an 'economic' or functional relationship,

argued that love is ontologically higher than his other attributes. So love became the supreme attribute. And within this schema it began to be argued that God essentially could not even express wrath—so God's wrath cannot even be real. While these theologians did not entirely dismiss God's justice, they significantly relaxed it. And they believed that the love of God is more important than his holiness, righteousness, and wrath.

Albert Knudson (1873–1953) was a Methodist theologian connected with Boston University and what is termed the "school of Boston personalism." Knudson formulated a unique conception of the relationship between God's love and justice in his *The Doctrine of God*.[3] He considered it pharisaical to believe that God, in his righteousness, would dispense rewards and punishments to humans according to what they deserved. Instead, Knudson believed that Jesus disregarded distributive justice, for (again, according to Knudson) forgiving love cannot be bound by retribution; rather, love transcends the law and graciously bestows favors despite demerits, and God's love overcomes his holiness, righteousness, and wrath.[4]

Hans Küng (1928–2021), a Swiss Roman Catholic theologian, also prioritized God's love over his righteousness and holiness. In *On Being a Christian*, he explained Christ's death on the cross not as a sacrifice but as the deepest expression of love.[5]

Process philosophy emphasized the significance of becoming—a process—over being or stability. Alfred North (A. N.) Whitehead, the founder of process philosophy, believed that God has a primordial and consequent will. Charles Hartshorne (1897–2000), who studied at Harvard under Whitehead, took process philosophy and developed it into process theology.[6] Process theology then continued to develop with men like Macquarrie, Hick, and Ogden. Karl Barth, however,

---

because the two are identical with each other." To insert either functional or being hierarchies produces massive difficulties. Albrecht Ritschl wrongly said that God's love was ontologically higher than his other attributes.

3. Albert C. Knudson, *The Doctrine of God* (New York: Abingdon Press, 1930).

4. Allison, *Historical Theology*, 223–24.

5. Hans Küng, *On Being a Christian*, trans. Edward Quinn (Garden City, NY: Doubleday, 1976), 435: "A love, that is, which cannot be defined abstractly but only with reference to this Jesus" (as cited by Allison, *Historical Theology*, 224).

6. Allison, *Historical Theology*, 226.

stood against process theology because it made God contingent to the created order.[7]

More recently, *open theism* has been held by evangelicals such as Clark Pinnock and John Sanders. Sanders's view, called *presentism*, posits that God has omniscience but not exhaustive foreknowledge.[8] Since future human actions are not yet real, there is nothing yet to be known. So these theologians redefine divine omnipotence as God's knowing all that he can know.[9] This view denies God's exhaustive foreknowledge and leaves the future open to possibility; thus it should be rejected, as was done by John Frame in *No Other God: A Response to Open Theism* (Phillipsburg, NJ: P&R Publishing, 2001).

Christology. This era witnessed a number of aberrant christological views. In the nineteenth century, the Lutheran theologian Gottfried Thomasius (1802–1875) developed what is called *kenotic Christology*. In this view, he argued that the Son of God could not have maintained his full divinity in the incarnation. Thomasius taught that in the incarnation Jesus divested himself of relative divine attributes, such as omnipotence, omniscience, and omnipresence, while maintaining his immanent divine attributes—those that characterize God in himself—such as his absolute power, holiness, and love.[10]

Johannes Weiss argued that the early church understood the preresurrection and preexaltation Jesus as a mere man. They often refer to Acts 2:22 for support. But Weiss taught that the early church's understanding of the nature of Christ changed even as early as the thinking of Paul, as seen in Romans 1:3–4.

Along with his reinterpretation of religion as a whole, Schleiermacher thought that Christology also needed to be reformulated. Thus he redefined Christ's sinlessness as a gradual but complete submission of his self-consciousness to his God-consciousness. He made Christ out to be like all men but distinguished only by "the constant potency of his God-consciousness, which was a veritable existence of God in him."[11]

---

7. Ibid., 227.

8. John Sanders, *The God Who Risks: A Theology of Providence* (Downers Grove, IL: InterVarsity Press, 1998).

9. Allison, *Historical Theology*, 229.

10. Ibid., 381–82.

11. Friedrich Schleiermacher, *The Christian Faith*, ed. H. R. Mackintosh and J. S. Stewart (Edinburgh: T&T Clark, 1928), 385, as cited by Allison, *Historical Theology*, 382.

In the so-called "quest for the historical Jesus," H. S. Reimarus attempted to separate the real Jesus of Nazareth from the disciples' dreams and writings of him.[12] Martin Kähler (1835–1912) distinguished the historical Jesus from the Christ of Scripture and claimed that there were no sources available that would provide reliable and authentic insight into the actual life of Jesus of Nazareth.[13] Albert Schweitzer (1875–1965) taught that Jesus attempted a violent inauguration of the kingdom of God. Schweitzer claimed that Jesus sought to bring all history to a close, but he failed.[14]

Rudolf Bultmann advanced the dichotomy between the historical Jesus and the kerygmatic Christ of faith. Bultmann taught that the historical Jesus was not as significant to the church as the preached Christ. But he believed that the preached Christ was fragmentary and legendary. Thus the mythological elements of the preached Christ had to be removed via demythologizing.[15] Though Bultmann may have asserted that Christ is God, to him the assertion was not a metaphysical pronouncement relative to the second person of the Trinity but a declaration of a person's attitude toward the Christ.

Creation. It was during this time that the onslaught against a young earth, six-day creation began. In 1813, Georges Cuvier in *Theory of the Earth* proposed what is referred to as *catastrophism*, or that a relatively large number of floods occurred. His view gained wide support—so much so that it was the standard view of geologists by the 1820s. In *Principles of Geology* (1830–1833), Charles Lyell proposed an opposite view, called *uniformitarianism*, that proposed that geology should not be invoked to account for any catastrophes, not even the Noahic flood.

Some Christians responded with novel interpretations of long-held biblical proof texts. Thomas Chalmers proposed the *gap theory*, which argued that there were vast geological ages before Genesis 1:3 and a recreation of the geological ruins in six literal days. George Stanley

12. Reimarus was published in 1778 by Lessing in *Wolfenbüttel Fragments* (see Allison, *Historical Theology*, 383).

13. Martin Kähler, *The So-Called Historical Jesus and the Historic, Biblical Christ,* trans. Carl Braatan (Philadelphia: Fortress, 1964), in Allison, *Historical Theology*, 383.

14. Albert Schweitzer, *The Quest of the Historical Jesus: A Critical Study of Its Progress from Reimarus to Wrede,* trans. W. Montgomery (London: Black, 1910), in Allison, *Historical Theology*, 383.

15. Allison, *Historical Theology*, 383–84.

proposed that the days of Genesis 1 were representative of vast geological ages. This view became known as the *day-age theory*. John Fleming proposed the *tranquil-flood theory*. In this theory, Fleming argued that while the flood in Genesis was worldwide, it was peaceful and had no enduring geological effects. In his new *local-flood theory*, John Pye Smith proposed that the flood was a catastrophic event that was geographically localized to the Mesopotamian Valley.[16] Then in 1859, Charles Darwin released *On the Origin of Species*. In this revolutionary work, he argued that all life evolved according to natural selection as random mutations produced changes without purpose or design over a long period of time. This worldview stood in direct contradiction to biblical claims.[17]

Some believers thought that they could keep science and faith distinct in their thinking, thus enabling them to hold both evolution and the Bible to be true. But within fifteen years of Darwin's *On the Origin of Species*, Charles Hodge released a book written in response to Darwin. Hodge denounced atheistic Darwinian evolution. Though Darwin and his immediate followers may not have been self-proclaimed atheists, his theory excludes all design from nature and is thus atheistic.[18]

William G. T. Shedd sought to harmonize the biblical narrative of creation and current science. He understood Genesis 1:1 to be creation *ex nihilo* and believed that then, in Genesis 1:2, began the original composition of the physical universe. Shedd did not believe that the six days of creation were literal days but rather were lengthy periods of time. Thus he held to an old earth. But he still rejected naturalistic evolutionary theory. He made a distinction between how the inorganic world developed and that of biological life. Biological life developed with divine creative acts.[19]

Later, Benjamin B. (B. B.) Warfield also sought to harmonize the Bible and evolutionary theory. For he believed that if it were truly science, then it must harmonize with Scripture. Thus he thought that believers could hold to a nuanced view of evolution. Warfield justified his approach by saying that evolution held simply that all humans have

16. Ibid., 267–68.
17. Ibid., 269.
18. Ibid.; Charles Hodge, *What Is Darwinism?* (NY: Scribner, Armstrong, and Co., 1874).
19. Allison, *Historical Theology*, 269–70.

a common ancestor. Believers could nuance this approach by requiring God's constant oversight in the process, along with his occasional supernatural interference in the making of something new. Warfield thought it possible that Adam could have developed from hominids, but Adam was distinguished by being given a human soul.[20] Warfield merely hoped that scientists would begin to acknowledge the existence of mystery and recognize the need for some higher power. Thus Warfield believed in an old earth and rejected the notion that the genealogies of Scripture were intended to determine the age of the earth.[21]

Today, there is a range of interpretive approaches to the creation account in Genesis. Herman Ridderbos and Meredith Kline advanced the *framework hypothesis*, which contends that the week of creation is an anthropomorphic, artistic arrangement that was never intended to be understood as a literal week.[22] Charles Hodge, James Orr, Augustus Hopkins (A. H.) Strong, and Davis Young (son of Edward Joseph [E. J.] Young) advocated a *day-age theory* in which a day could be understood to be a much longer period of time. This thesis is predicated on the assumption of an old earth. Some of their arguments are as follows. They claim that the Hebrew word for *day* can, and often does, denote an extensive period of time. They also argue that the first three days cannot be seen as ordinary days, as the events said to occur on each day are hard to imagine as having been accomplished within a twenty-four-hour period. They also think that the seventh day of God's rest was thousands of years long.

Belief in a young earth and literal six-day creation, however, has not been entirely abandoned. Many believers still hold that the earth is but several thousand years old. In addition, there is a strengthening intelligent-design movement.[23] But properly exegeting creation accounts is difficult, and many in the evangelical church are still wrestling with the issues.[24]

20. An elder in the OPC adopted a similar view that was rejected as heterodox in the early 1990s. More information on that controversy can be found at the OPC web site.

21. Ibid., 270–71.

22. Ibid., 272.

23. Ibid., 272–76.

24. For more information on the narrative of creation, see Richard C. Gamble, *The Whole Counsel of God*, vol. 1, *God's Mighty Acts in the Old Testament* (Phillipsburg, NJ: P&R Publishing, 2009) (*WCG1*), 147–57.

SCRIPTURE

Canon. In the 1770s, Johann Salomo Semler introduced a division between the Bible and the Word of God in his *Treatise on the Free Investigation of the Canon*. Historical criticism cast suspicion on the OT canon. Hugo Grotius doubted that Solomon wrote Ecclesiastes. Spinoza denied Mosaic authorship of the Pentateuch. Johann Gottfried Eichhorn (1752–1827) viewed OT canonization as an entirely human process.[25] Schleiermacher devalued the OT to such an extent that he denied its inspiration. He believed that the OT infected Christianity with legalism.

Reimarus's life of Jesus was nothing short of wicked—but was sadly still foundational for German-language NT studies. Reimarus proposed that the kernel of the biblical message is the eschatological portions of Scripture. Anything that goes beyond this eschatological kernel is a later embellishment. But B. B. Warfield was a champion of biblical inspiration. He introduced a complicating factor into the nature of apostolicity. He proposed that it is not the writings themselves that make them apostolic but the determination by the apostles that they are canon. In other words, the issue was not apostolic authorship but imposition by the apostles as law. Herman Ridderbos said that Christ delegated authority to his apostles as authorized bearers of divine revelation. The canon is not a product of the church, but the church is a product of the canon.[26]

Brevard Childs, though not an evangelical, had great influence on evangelicals. He disapproved of the historical-critical approach for the following reasons. First, this approach concentrated on the history of Hebrew literature rather than on the canonical text itself. Second, it failed to see the role of the canon in Israel's life. Third, the historical-canonical approach disregarded religious factors that influenced the shaping of the OT canon. The canon formed Israel's identity, and the religious community shaped the literature. The same critique applies to the NT canon. His method, called a "canonical approach," focuses on the final canonical form of the Bible as received by the church.[27]

---

25. Allison, *Historical Theology*, 54–55.

26. Herman N. Ridderbos, *The Authority of the New Testament Scriptures* (Grand Rapids: Baker, 1963); Allison, *Historical Theology*, 56.

27. Brevard S. Childs, *Introduction to the Old Testament as Scripture* (Philadelphia: Fortress, 1979); also *The New Testament as Canon: An Introduction* (Valley Forge, PA: Trinity

Inspiration. Classic biblical teaching was disregarded out of antisu-pernatural presuppositions. Miracle accounts began to be deprecated because they were beyond human reason. With biblical criticism's assumption that the Scriptures were not inspired, focus began to shift to the Bible's human authorship. Scholars at this time seemed to have only two options: the first was to believe in a type of mechanical inspiration and be humiliated by all the historical-critical scholarship that continued to uncover errors in Scripture, and the second was to reject inspiration and gain academic respect.

Schleiermacher's reformulation of the doctrine of Scripture strongly opposed classic historic teaching. His reformulation rejected that the Holy Spirit inspired the OT law or history, held that only portions of the prophets were inspired, and taught that genuine faith could only be founded on an experience of Jesus, not Scripture.

Theologians began to follow Schleiermacher in pulling Scripture out from its foundational place for the Christian faith and thus felt the freedom to begin to question even its most basic truth claims. This move sparked a new type of teaching. Scholars began no longer to view the Bible as inspired or infallible but as the historic manifesta-tion of God in Christ. But in an attempt not to sever all ties with the historic Christian faith, a general, undefined sense of inspiration was maintained. But inspiration began to be treated as similar to human inspiration, like a person's being inspired to write a poem or song. As some poets are better than others (though all may be, in one sense, considered to be inspired), so scholars believed that there are differing degrees of biblical inspiration. Some portions of Scripture are more inspired than others. But with this more broad and fuzzy use of inspi-ration, the concept of *absolute infallibility* was discarded. Scholars were convinced that Scripture is filled with human imperfections.[28]

In the nineteenth and early twentieth centuries, James Bannerman and B. B. Warfield battled this modern concept of *inspiration*. They sought to retether the doctrine of Scripture to the historic Christian faith. They argued that inspiration gives Scripture a supernatural char-acter, thus making it both a divine and human book. All Scripture is

Press International, 1994), cited by Allison, *Historical Theology*, 56–57. For more on Childs's method, see WCG 1:129–30.

28. Allison, *Historical Theology*, 69–72.

867

God-breathed, and the biblical authors were taken up and carried along by the Holy Spirit in their writing. They held that the Bible was not 50 percent divine and 50 percent human. There was a confluence of the two.[29]

In the twentieth century, Karl Barth articulated a unique theology of Scripture. Protestants have always believed that the Word of God is first the Bible, and Christ is the incarnate Word of God. But Barth claimed that the Bible is a witness to revelation and became the Word of God. He believed that the Bible is human words and human speech. He did not think that there is any direct identity between the human words of Scripture and the actual words of God.[30] He referred to the Bible as the "witness of the Word," which is not the same as its being the Word of God itself. And Barth held that theology is regulated by this word—the very Word of God—not the Bible, which he believed is just the witness to the word. Barth taught that God alone could reveal himself to people, though his revelation was not immediate or through any other medium. So though he believed that the Bible is not an instrument of direct impartation, he still considered it to be a genuine witness. To him, though the Bible is errant, God used it despite its limitations. The Bible contains human thought and speech oriented toward the Word of God for Barth—not the actual word of God. Such a view of the Bible is nothing short of disastrous—it offers no epistemological certainty.

In the late 1970s, Jack Rogers and Donald McKim argued that inerrancy was a relatively late historical teaching that began with Turretin and then developed at Princeton.[31] Rogers and McKim were adamant that inspiration was not the teaching of the church. John Woodbridge wrote of Rogers and McKim that "those authors had blatantly misrepresented the major figures of the church and the affirmation of the inspiration and inerrancy of Scripture."[32]

Authority. In the nineteenth and twentieth centuries, the Roman Catholic Church sided against the Protestant notion of biblical author-

29. Ibid., 75–76.
30. Emil Brunner also opposed the orthodox doctrine of verbal inspiration.
31. Jack B. Rogers and Donald K. McKim, *The Authority and Interpretation of the Bible* (San Francisco: Harper & Row, 1979).
32. John D. Woodbridge, *Biblical Authority: A Critique of the Rogers/McKim Proposal* (Grand Rapids: Zondervan, 1982), 27–28.

ity. In the place of the authority of Scripture, Vatican Council I pronounced papal infallibility. In addition, the Catholic Church taught that tradition bears the weight of divine authority.[33]

The traditional Protestant position is that Scripture leads to salvation. Schleiermacher, however, reversed this order and argued that faith preceded biblical authority. With this reordering, he elevated experience above objective divine revelation. Hence Schleiermacher led the way for subjective experience to be considered authoritative. As was their norm, old Princeton opposed any diminution of biblical authority.[34]

In the twentieth century, the Swiss theologian Emil Brunner (1889–1966) declared that the day when theological controversies were settled with the words "It is written" was no more. He replaced the authority of Scripture with the authority of Christ. Brunner believed that the Scriptures themselves are not the authority, but Christ, who is the Truth and who meets the reader in the pages of Scripture, is the authority.[35] The Bible supposedly contains the element before which the theologian bows. Such a position is a denial of the formal principle of Protestantism, *sola scriptura*, and makes Scripture merely an instrumental authority.

Karl Barth also took an instrumental approach to the Bible's authority. He taught that the Bible only becomes the Word of God when God condescends to reveal himself in Scripture. And he held that God freely reveals himself personally through this witness.[36] In the 1950s, American evangelicals produced a number of defenses of biblical authority.[37]

---

33. They also decreed the immaculate conception of Mary in 1854, as well as Mary's bodily assumption in 1950.

34. See Bradley N. Seeman, "The 'Old Princetonians' on Biblical Authority," in *The Enduring Authority of the Christian Scriptures*, ed. D. A. Carson (Grand Rapids: Eerdmans, 2016), 195–237.

35. Emil Brunner, *The Christian Doctrine of God*, vol. 1, *Dogmatics* (London: Lutterworth, 1955), 110: "The authority of Scripture is not formal but material: Christ, the revelation. Even subjectively, however, this authority is not based upon the Scriptures as such, but upon the encounter of faith with the Christ of Scripture" (as cited by Allison, *Historical Theology*, 95).

36. David Gibson, "The Answering Speech of Men: Karl Barth on Holy Scripture," in *The Enduring Authority of the Christian Scriptures*, ed. D. A. Carson (Grand Rapids: Eerdmans, 2016), 266–91.

37. J. I. Packer wrote *Fundamentalism and the Word of God* in 1958; D. Martin Lloyd-Jones wrote *Authority* in 1958; Edward J. Carnell wrote *The Case for Orthodox Theology* in 1959.

Inerrancy.[38] Jean LeClerc (1657–1736) was an Amsterdam Remonstrant who proposed in his 1684 *Entretiens* that reason is an infallible guide. He held that Mosaic authorship of the Pentateuch should be rejected and that within Scripture there is a need to distinguish between that which was inspired, such as Christ's words, and that which was not inspired, such as portions of human research. And he dismissed the notion of full inspiration and inerrancy.

Anthony Collins (1676–1729) argued in *Discourse on Freethinking* that anything that is not in harmony with reason cannot be revelation. In *Discourse on the Grounds and Reason of the Christian Religion*, he denied that there are valid proofs for the validity of Christianity.[39]

Johann Salomo Semler (1725–1791) distinguished between the Bible and the Word of God. He believed that the Word of God contains moral truths and that the Bible is God's accommodation to teach humanity through miracles and prophecies. Semler taught that God condescended to the erroneous views of biblical times.[40]

The movement called the OT "documentary hypothesis" developed in Germany over a one-hundred-year period. It began with Jean Astruc (1753) and continued through Johann Gottfried Eichorn (1780–1783), Willhelm DeWette (1805), Herman Hupfeld (1853), Karl Heinrich Graf, and Abraham Kuenen (1869). In 1878, Julius Wellhausen ably defended the theory that there were four different authors of the Pentateuch and designated them as J, E, D, and P.[41]

This hypothesis caught fire in England and was promoted by William Robertson Smith (1875), who was dismissed from his teaching position because of his views. The theory began to seep into the thinking of the United States as well. Crawford H. Toy, a professor at the Southern Baptist Theological Seminary, taught that Genesis 1 and 2 are conflicting accounts of creation. Also, he did not hold to a literal, six-day view of creation. He resigned in 1876.[42]

In the twentieth century, Karl Barth said that it was important to admit and affirm that the Bible contains errors, for it was written by

38. For an excellent definition of inerrant veracity, see Joel R. Beeke and Paul M. Smalley, *Reformed Systematic Theology*, vol. 1, *Revelation and God* (Wheaton IL: Crossway, 2019), 373.
39. Allison, *Historical Theology*, 113–14.
40. Ibid., 113.
41. For more information on this erroneous hypothesis, see *WCG* 1:374–77.
42. Allison, *Historical Theology*, 114.

men who sin and make mistakes.[43] Under the weight of this pressure to redefine one's view of Scripture, evangelicals began to differentiate between *infallibility* and *inerrancy*. Many began to say that the Bible is infallible in faith and practice but contains historical and scientific errors. To continue holding to inerrancy while believing that there are errors in the Bible, they redefined the term. The Bible is without error if an error is defined as willful deception on the part of the biblical writers—and no one would say that the biblical authors willfully deceived. Fuller Theological Seminary in California became a place of turmoil in this area.[44]

Clarity or Perspicuity. Some have traced the development of modern philosophical hermeneutics back to Lorenzo Valla, who determined the Donation of Constantine to be a forgery. By the time of the Enlightenment, scholars began to use the Bible as a secular text. The nineteenth century saw development in the science of hermeneutics, which pertained to all literature, not just the Bible. Religious hermeneutics were separated from philosophical hermeneutics.

Schleiermacher used both grammatical and psychological tools to analyze texts of Scripture. Modern philosophical hermeneutics said that hermeneutics is the art of avoiding misunderstanding. *Understanding* involved not just the exact words of a text but also the writer's distinctive point of view. Schleiermacher, however, continued to detract from Scripture's clarity. He argued that non-Christian religions have within them an inner fire, which is the true essence of religion.[45]

These hermeneutical trends, along with biblical criticism, proved detrimental to understanding the clarity of Scripture. Critics continued to search for and prove more and more contradictions within Scripture, and they attempted to determine a canon within a canon. Certainty of faith deteriorates when the Bible's clarity and sufficiency are invalidated.[46] Scholars now began to search for the existential or experiential core of the divine sacred fire in any religious canon. These teachings set the stage in the twentieth century for John Hick's notion

43. Ibid., 117.
44. Ibid., 116–17.
45. Friedrich Schleiermacher, *On Religion: Speeches to Its Cultured Despisers*, rev. ed. (Philadelphia: Westminster John Knox Press, 1974), as cited by Beeke and Smalley, *Reformed Systematic Theology*, 1:300.
46. Allison, *Historical Theology*, 139.

of religious pluralism, which was the human search for an ultimate, transcendent reality.[47]

Necessity and Sufficiency. Charles Hodge argued against the Roman Catholic Church's teaching that the Scriptures are incomplete. Roman Catholics maintain that there are doctrines that are incompletely revealed in Scripture, including: the canon, inspiration of the biblical writers, the doctrine of the Trinity, the personality and divinity of the Holy Spirit, infant baptism, Sunday as the Christian Sabbath, the threefold order of ministry, church government by bishops, the perpetuity of the apostolic office, the grace of orders, the Eucharist as sacrifice, the seven sacraments, and purgatory. Thus for them, tradition is not only the interpreter but the actual completion of Scripture.[48]

While Protestants rightly reject the Roman Catholic overemphasis on tradition, tradition should play a role in Protestant faith. Protestants affirm what is referred to as "the analogy of faith," which recognizes that Scripture repeats and advances truth through progressive revelation. In addition, there is the common faith of the church, which cannot be rejected. There are several good reasons to affirm this common faith. First, that which competent readers of a plain book understand to be the book's meaning is its meaning. Second, the Holy Spirit guides believers; so what those believers agree on under the Spirit's teaching must be true. But this teaching is different from an infallible church tradition as a necessary supplement to Scripture.[49]

The Wesleyan tradition asserted what they referred to as a *quadrilateral*, which embraced four sources of theology: Scripture, tradition, experience, and reason. Yet among these four, they still held Scripture to be supreme.[50]

Pentecostal/charismatic theology plainly challenged classic Protestant teaching. The charismatic movement is often analyzed in three

47. See John Hick, *An Interpretation of Religion* (New Haven: Yale University Press, 1989), cited by Beeke and Smalley (*Reformed Systematic Theology*, 1:301), who offer six massive criticisms of pluralism (see ibid., 304–5). They also connect pluralism through Barth, Brunner, and Kierkegaard and brilliantly critique them all (ibid., 307–9).

48. Charles Hodge, *Systematic Theology*, 3 vols. (London: Clarke, 1960), 1:106, cited in Allison, *Historical Theology*, 159.

49. Hodge, *Systematic Theology*, 1:113–14, in Allison, *Historical Theology*, 159–60.

50. See *Methodist Articles of Religion 1784*, cited in Allison, *Historical Theology*, 160.

stages. The first wave of this movement was Pentecostalism, which began with the Azusa Street Revivals of 1906–1915 led by William Seymour. The second wave was the charismatic movement, which emerged in the 1960s and infiltrated mainline congregations.[51] These first two waves affirmed the continuing, direct guidance of the Holy Spirit in believers' lives and the continuation of the prophetic gifts and words of knowledge.

The so-called "third-wave evangelicalism" began in the 1980s and affirmed Pentecostal and charismatic theology's teaching that the gifts of prophecy, speaking in tongues, and healing continued in the life of the modern church. But this third wave affirmed that baptism with the Holy Spirit occurs at baptism or conversion and is not a subsequent gift. Most Pentecostals hold to the doctrine of what is called *subsequence*.[52] Wayne Grudem is the foremost theologian of this movement. He supposedly affirms the sufficiency of Scripture while also believing in the continuation of the spiritual gifts. Grudem teaches that everything that God wants humans to know about doctrine or practice is revealed in Scripture, that God does not want humans to believe anything about him or redemption that is not found in Scripture, that sinful acts are defined in Scripture explicitly or implicitly, and that nothing is required of humans beyond explicit or implicit scriptural commands.[53]

Interpretation. Spinoza rejected that the church, specifically the Roman Catholic Church, could be the sole interpreter of Scripture. He taught that instead people had the right to judge freely for themselves. Spinoza believed that no one could proscribe or interpret another's religion. Thus modern theology began to be defined largely by the principle of subjectivism in interpretation.[54]

In the middle of the nineteenth century, biblical criticism taught that the Bible should be read and interpreted with the same rules as

51. See Ed Stetzer, "The Third Wave: The Continualist Movement Continues," in *Christianity Today*, October 23, 2013.

52. The term comes from C. Peter Wagner (1930–2016) of Fuller Seminary in *The Third Wave of the Holy Spirit*, 4th ed. (Ann Arbor, MI: Vine Books, 1988). John Wimber of Fuller was also a prominent part of the third wave. For more information, see Wayne Grudem, ed., *Are Miraculous Gifts for Today? Four Views* (Grand Rapids: Zondervan, 2011).

53. Allison, *Historical Theology*, 161.

54. Ibid., 180.

any other piece of literature. Professors such as William Robertson Smith taught that the OT revealed a gradual development of Judaism from a simple to a mature religious system. They taught that the more barbaric parts of this system, such as the sacrifices, had no connection to true Christianity.[55]

Nineteenth-century evangelical interpretation rejected Spinoza's highly subjective approach and embraced what it referred to as a *scientific* approach to biblical interpretation. This movement was influenced by Sir Francis Bacon's book *New Method*, which appeared in 1620 and was intended to replace Aristotle's methodology in the *Organon*. In his work, Bacon both developed scientific method and rejected Aristotelianism.

Chapter 20 demonstrated that old Princeton Seminary combined this scientific approach with Scottish common-sense realism. Old Princeton understood the facts of history, the arguments of reason, and even objective science all to validate the truthfulness of Scripture. The Dutch, however, did not agree with Princeton's approach.[56] The Dutch held to an antithesis between believing and unbelieving thought.[57]

Liberal scholarship continued to develop and revise the critical approach. New Testament studies focused on source, form, and redaction criticism.[58] Thus for evangelicals, the dominant question was no longer "What does this passage mean?"—it had deteriorated to "Is this passage true?" There were two dominant evangelical responses to biblical criticism. One response was to abandon inerrancy altogether, and the other was to disregard criticism as irrelevant. Neither option is best.

This time also saw advances in literary criticism, or hermeneutic theory. The dominant question was whether the meaning of a text is determined by authorial intent. Many argued that the meaning of a

---

55. Ibid., 179.

56. Mark A. Noll, *The Princeton Theology, 1812–1921: Scripture, Science, and Theological Method from Archibald Alexander to Benjamin Breckinridge Warfield* (Grand Rapids: Baker, 1983), 41: "Warfield held that history, reason, and objective science could demonstrate the validity of Scripture as divine revelation. Individuals convinced by such demonstration could then rely on Scripture to construct theology. Kuyper and Bavinck, to the contrary, placed very little store by Warfield's kind of evidentialist apologetics."

57. There were similarities and differences between "Old Amsterdam" and "Old Princeton." See Richard B. Gaffin, "Old Amsterdam and Inerrancy?," *WTJ* 45, no. 2 (Fall 1983): 219–72.

58. For more information on source, form, and redaction criticism, see *WCG* 2:117–19, 424.

text is not what the author had intended. But this position only invites chaos and subjectivity into interpretation.[59]

Rudolf Bultmann attempted to hold in balance a skeptical attitude toward the factual or historical content of the Gospel narratives while still believing in the overall message of the NT. The purpose of digging beneath the myth is not to search for a historical substratum. According to Bultmann, the entire message is a myth, and thus the Christian task is to liberate Christianity from myth and present it in its unshackled form. The restatement is called *demythologizing.*

Bultmann desired to translate the Bible from mythical language into an understandable text. He defined *demythologizing* as a method of interpretation and exegesis. He believed that the NT text must be made meaningful for human existence. In his endeavor to demythologize the text, Bultmann was indebted to the Marburg philosopher Martin Heidegger. Heidegger helped him use an existential interpretation to gain an analysis of human existence. Bultmann did much to make the NT meaningful to the contemporary reader with his existential interpretation.

Nevertheless, Bultmann failed to provide sufficient answers to the fundamental hermeneutical question. He was simply unable to resolve the problem of the historical Jesus. Part of the hermeneutical problem lies in the issue of the nature of history itself. Bultmann saw a need to redefine the very concept of *history.*

Nonevangelical thinking on biblical interpretation advanced beyond Bultmann. Macquarrie saw value in Bultmann's attempt to extract insight from the supposed myths or restate the meanings those myths have attempted to express. Bultmann interpreted some of the biblical myths into existentially meaningful communication.[60] But Bultmann did not account for what Macquarrie termed the *ontological element* in myth. Proper analysis requires a more careful examination of the relationship between myth and symbol. The problem of symbols confronts readers when they analyze supposedly mythical communication.[61]

59. E. D. Hirsch delineated the difference between the meaning of a text or authorial intent and the significance of a text in *Validity in Interpretation* (New Haven: Yale University Press, 1967).

60. John Macquarrie, *Principles of Christian Theology* (New York: Scribner's Sons, 1966), 122.

61. Ibid.

Macquarrie maintained that all language has a symbolic character. Yet symbolic language—understood in the narrow sense, in which words are understood as indirect references that bounce off that to which they properly refer—may be differentiated from literal language. In symbolic language of this type, that which serves as the intermediary between the language and its highest referent can also be a symbol.[62] He noted that Tillich had already distinguished between a sign and a symbol, yet Macquarrie referred to a sign as a *conventional symbol* and a symbol as an *intrinsic symbol*. An intrinsic symbol has, in itself, a kinship with that which it symbolizes, while a conventional symbol does not. Only important religious symbols, such as the NT notion of light, meet the requirement for being true symbols.[63]

Macquarrie addressed how religious symbols connect to the language of being and how theologians can correlate individual being and Being. First, in opposition to Barth, Being and the beings cannot be separated from each other. There could be no beings without the Being that lets them be. Yet apart from the beings, Being would become indistinguishable from nothing; therefore, Being and the beings cannot be separated. Macquarrie's analogy of being followed a twofold line, from Being to the beings and beings in the light of Being.

Analyzing the movement from beings toward Being, Macquarrie postulated the existential response, which stated that things, persons, and qualities arouse readers to various psychological states, and in these states readers find Being disclosing itself to them.[64] Second is analysis of the similarity of relation—an analogy of proportionality between a relation of beings and a relation of Being to a being. Examples of similarity of relation are analogies of God as king, shepherd, and judge. Third, Macquarrie posited that God is the prior enabling condition of any existent entity—that is, God is the prior enabling condition of any good whatsoever.[65]

---

62. Ibid., 123.

63. Macquarrie criticizes Tillich's terminology, or at least the examples that Tillich used to elucidate his terms. The flag was mentioned as a symbol in Tillichian terminology, yet the flag does not meet Tillich's own requirements for being a symbol. He adds that there are no private or universal symbols; for a symbol only applies to a specific community with shared historical and cultural presuppositions. Also, one group of symbols serves to illuminate another group (ibid.).

64. Ibid., 127.

65. Ibid., 129.

Turning to an analysis of Being's disclosing itself symbolically in beings, Macquarrie mentions the presence and manifestation of Being in the beings. This presence and manifestation means that beings express Being and participation in Being. There is also a range of participation in Being that belongs to the entity that is to serve as a symbol. Symbols drawn from personal life, therefore, have the highest range of participation, for man has the most vast range of being. Second, there is a hierarchy of beings, exemplified, for instance, in a worm relative to a man. Finally, there is a paradoxicality of symbols in that they both stand for what they symbolize and fall short of it at the same time.[66] Certainly the nonevangelical modern world wallowed in the mire of confusion when it came to biblical interpretation.

HUMANITY

Machen's Analysis. Just after the death of J. Gresham Machen in 1937, his final work was published: *The Christian View of Man*, a book of sweeping theological breadth. In this work, before addressing the origin of humanity, he covered in a clear and simple fashion the living and true God, God's decrees, God's decrees and man's freedom, predestination, creation and providence, and miracles.

In his chapter on creation, Machen critiqued the prevalent evolutionary views of his day. He began his argument by asserting that God created man in a supernatural act. At this point in the book, he had already defined *miracle* as an event in which God enters the normal course of nature. He held that the existence of miracles is the real matter to address in regard to evolution.[67] An evolutionist would claim that modern science has demonstrated that man has come from evolution. Though in no way claiming to be a scientist, Machen objected to such a claim. He held that the question is not about the facts themselves but the relevance of the facts to the matter in question. The facts are merely that the information surrounding the origin of the first man is obscure. Specifically, there are significant historical gaps in the evo-

66. Ibid., 132.
67. J. Gresham Machen, *The Christian View of Man* (London: Banner of Truth, 1965), 114–18.

lutionist's claims about lower animals and men. Since that history is rather obscure, he suggests examining a place and era for which there is a large amount of historical information. He proposes the time and place of the birth of Jesus Christ.[68]

While Jesus of Nazareth would have looked like any other man in his time, the Bible claims that he was not generated in the normal fashion of men. In his virgin birth, there is historical record of special creation. Machen proposed that there is adequate testimony to believe in the virgin birth. In the case of Jesus of Nazareth's supernatural birth, the scientific expert has no greater knowledge than does the common man. Thus, if there is evidence that God miraculously intervened in history two thousand years ago, why, argues Machen, is it not possible that God miraculously intervened in the appearance of the first man?[69] So evolution's real question is whether or not there is a God who can creatively enter his world. If the answer is no, then one is naturally inclined to hold to the evolutionary view. But if one holds a different presupposition—namely, that God exists—then it is not a stretch to believe that God created man.[70]

Machen wrestled with the existence and significance of a soul in his chapter on how God created man. The Christian believes in a soul, which is different from the teaching of Greek philosophy, though it too argues for a soul. Materialism, however, denies the soul's existence. Materialism claims that all actions can be explained simply by physiological connections. While materialism is a simple system, its simplicity is its great weakness. Materialism is unable to account for human thought or consciousness. It cannot distinguish between the mind and the brain. A materialist would likely retort that it is of no benefit to humans to burden themselves with the imponderable questions of consciousness and the mind. Machen pushed back against this assertion; he argued that just because materialists do not want to address a problem does not in any way eliminate it. He urged his readers to deal with the facts that are given, and the existence of human consciousness is a fact.[71]

68. Ibid., 118–20.
69. Ibid., 120–22.
70. Ibid., 122–24.
71. Ibid., 124–31.

At times, argued idealist thinkers, it seems that the mind is more self-evident than the external world. Machen agreed that idealism is more appealing than materialism but said that philosophical idealism as a system is also false. The idealist philosopher takes issue with statements such as "The book is blue." He argues that the color *blue* is only a mental category, not a property of the book itself. The idealist philosopher doubts even that there is an external world that is independent of the mind. But such philosophical idealism is contradicted by the simple wince from one's stubbing a toe on the frame of a bed. The bed is most certainly not merely in the mind! But idealist philosophers are not so easily stumped. They would argue that the sense of touch is just as unreliable as the sense of sight. If there were in fact an external world, idealist philosophers press, how could humans know for certain that it exists—or know anything about it, for that matter? Many idealists would answer this question by pointing to the reality of other minds, and theistic idealists would point to the mind of God, thus proving an external reality. But Machen correctly argues that when idealists admit that there are minds other than their own, they are admitting that there is a reality outside their own brains, and this admission topples idealism.[72]

God created man to have both a soul and a body. Machen thought that psychologists studied human behavior without reference to the soul. A methodological question that Machen asked—a question that still bears relevance today—is whether or not believers can take the scholarship of unbelievers and use their research within the limited sphere of psychology. Machen, in a presuppositional manner, answered that tight separation cannot be maintained between departments of knowledge. Humans' views of God and of the soul color their view of human behavior.[73]

Granting that humanity consists of a body and a soul, Machen emphasized the union of the soul and the mind. Each person is a unity of the two, and his consciousness is truly his. Furthermore, Machen acknowledged that the individual soul can, at times, feel isolated. There is a loneliness of the soul, sometimes referred to as the "cry of the human heart," that is directly connected to the soul's

72. Ibid., 131–36.
73. Ibid., 137–38.

indivisibility. This loneliness of the soul makes people human, and sin does not destroy it but changes it into "an unspeakable horror and curse."[74]

Machen also addressed trichotomy—the belief that humans are comprised of body, soul, and spirit.[75] In this area, theologians have created undue subtleties that have muddied the simplicity of the Bible. Machen believed that the trichotomist position is exegetically invalid.[76] He understood this position to tend toward an "empty-room anthropology," which leads to the assumption that humans are essentially fine, but they have a part, an empty room, that lies dormant until it is regenerated. With that regeneration, the so-called "spiritual man" is then supposedly given the prominence that it deserves. But Scripture is clear: no part of man was left untouched by the fall.[77]

Machen then addressed humanity as created in God's image. He wrote that because God is a spirit, the human soul is created in the image of God. Humanity is made of the dust of the ground and possesses personal freedom as well as personal companionship with the infinite and eternal God. Some have contended that here lies the full extent that man bears of the image of God and that humans share no moral likeness to God. They argue that prior to the fall, Adam was neutral relative to good and evil and was given a choice. Proponents of this view would claim that the image of God in man is personal freedom, not goodness.[78] But this view is misguided. A person makes choices, and there has not been even one morally neutral person, not even Adam.

Deterioration by Synergism. The modern age continued its deterioration from classic biblical teaching by mixing biblical teaching with human wisdom. Though stumbling in this area is expected of nonevangelical theologians, even evangelicals began to face increasingly complex issues of relating biblical teaching to current philosophical and scientific advances.

74. Ibid., 139.

75. For more information on trichotomy, see *WCG* 1:244–49.

76. Having examined 1 Corinthians 2:14–15 and 1 Thessalonians 5:23, Machen said, "We ought to reject very firmly, therefore, the view that the nature of man is divided by the Bible into body, soul and spirit . . . a rather serious error" (ibid., 143).

77. Ibid., 143–44.

78. Ibid., 145.

William Newton Clarke (1841–1912), who taught at Johns Hopkins, Harvard, and Yale, is an early twentieth-century example of classic capitulation to contemporary science—a classic bridge builder. The Bible teaches that humans are a combination of body and spirit, but Clarke argued that an understanding of human composition should not come from the Bible's teaching alone but also from self-knowledge. Psychology as an abstract science has confirmed this inherent teaching on humanity. In methodological continuity, Clarke argued that theologians should listen to science relative to human origins. While acknowledging that humanity comes from God, he developed a theistic evolution.[79]

In addition, contemporary philosophy often plays a prominent role in shaping mainstream theological constructs of humanity. Karl Barth began his treatment of God's image in humanity by dismissing the account of Adam and Eve as a saga. Thus Kant argued that classic formulations of the image of God as something that humanity is or does should be rejected.[80] Instead, a supposedly better model provided by the philosopher Martin Buber is that humanity is to be comprehended as persons who are in relationship. God is in relationship with himself, man is in relationship with God, and humanity is in relationship with other humans. The Genesis account focuses on humanity as male and female, thus reflecting the plurality of persons in the Trinity. Barth's view of God's image in humanity is relationality.[81]

Emil Brunner (1889–1966), a Swiss theologian at Zurich, was influenced by existentialist philosophy to such an extent that he argued that the defining characteristic of humanity is the need to make authentic decisions. He held that to be created in God's image is to be created for a loving relationship with God; thus all humans must make a responsible decision for God. Brunner also distinguished between a formal and a material sense of God's image. The formal aspect of the divine image is freedom, reason, conscience, and language. He believed that these aspects of humanity could not be lost even by the most sinful of people. He did, however, argue that sinful people have lost the

---

79. Allison, *Historical Theology*, 335.

80. Saga for Barth was "an intuitive and poetic picture of a prehistorical reality of history which is enacted once and for all confines of time and space." Barth noted that while classic Christian teaching emphasized the image in willing and thinking, the Genesis account of creation does not mention those aspects (ibid., 336).

81. Ibid., 336–37.

material element, which consists particularly in love. God is repulsive to such people, and they are perverted in his sight.[82]

The Dutch evangelical G. C. Berkouwer (1903–1996) advanced the discussion of human nature. While opposing the propositions of Barth and Brunner, Berkouwer sought to broaden analysis of the image of God beyond the classic Christian notions of reason, free will, and the activity of exercising dominion over creation. He proposed what he considered to be a holistic approach that emphasized all the various parts of humanity—the whole person. Thus Berkouwer believed that it was illegitimate to talk about human nature as having a higher part that is more holy and a lower part that is further from God.[83]

Post-Fall Image of God. John Wesley affirmed Adam's representation of all humanity. Wesley taught that after Adam's fall, humanity became mortal, souls died, sinful natures infected humans' compositions, and people became children of wrath. Even infants are included in this original sin. But Wesley believed that no one will be damned exclusively for Adam's sin, for God needs more than inherited corruption for him to punish justly. Humans' inherited corrupted nature, however, gives birth to actual sins. Wesley taught that it is only for actual sins that people are liable to punishment. But he believed that God, in his goodness, grants prevenient grace to all to remove the disabilities that are rooted in their corrupted nature. Wesley argued that prevenient grace overcomes the effects of original sin and enables all people to pursue salvation.[84] He taught that Christians could be perfect if *perfection* is defined as not willfully breaking any known law of God. In contrast to Wesley, Jonathan Edwards's *Freedom of the Will* is the best example of articulating how the will functions and defining the nature of human freedom relative to willing.

As liberalism continued to advance, the notion of sin grew less significant and was even reformulated according to contemporary philosophy. Immanuel Kant offered an a priori argument for the existence of universal sin beginning with the original predisposition to good

---

82. Emil Brunner, *The Christian Doctrine of Creation and Redemption,* trans. Olive Wyon (Philadelphia: Westminster Press, 1953), 56–57; and *Man in Revolt: A Christian Anthropology* (Philadelphia: Westminster Press, 1947), 85–87, as cited by Allison, *Historical Theology,* 337–38.

83. G. C. Berkouwer, *Man: The Image of God* (Grand Rapids: Eerdmans, 1962), 33–36, 70–73, 77, 98, as cited by Allison, *Historical Theology,* 338.

84. Allison, *Historical Theology,* 358–59.

in human nature. Schleiermacher reconfigured the doctrine of sin so that sin was defined as the opposite of a tender God-consciousness. Søren Kierkegaard again reformulated the notion of sin as individual despair. Paul Tillich recast the doctrine of sin according to existentialist philosophy.[85]

The Social Gospel also provided a distinct perspective on sin. Walter Rauschenbusch understood sin to be more of a social than an individual phenomenon. Thus he believed that repentance should focus more on collective sins than individual sins. Proponents of the Social Gospel claimed that it corrected the theological overemphasis on the fall by returning the focus to Jesus's teaching against selfish behavior. The Social Gospel held that sin is connected to selfishness and antisocial behavior.[86] But in its redefinition and shifting of emphasis, this movement has not actually corrected a theological mistake.[87]

Transitioning now to contemporary theologians, Millard J. Erickson distances himself from the biblical position on original sin. Though he affirms that all humans possess a corrupt nature and are condemned in Adam, he yet sees a parallel between the necessity in forensic justification for people to make a decision to accept Christ, and for people to accept or approve of their corrupt nature in Adam. Until people make this choice about their reprehensible sin, there is only a conditional imputation of Adamic guilt. Erickson believed that before God, people are guilty of Adam's sin when they acquiesce in that nature. This is a conditional imputation of Adam's guilt.[88]

Moving to a Reformed interpretation, Neil Plantinga of Calvin Theological Seminary is an excellent writer who has developed evangelical doctrine with creative metaphors for sin. In the opening of his book *Not*

85. Ibid., 359.
86. Ibid., 360.
87. Adam had both a natural and a federal headship. Realism, that all are germinally present in Adam, underlines humanity's physical oneness in sin, but realism alone is an insufficient foundation for unity with Adam. He was also a federal head. For more information on Adam's fall, see *WCG* 1:187–217.
88. Millard J. Erickson, *Christian Theology*, 2nd ed. (Grand Rapids: Baker, 1998), 656, as cited by Allison, *Historical Theology*, 361. More radical is David L. Smith (*With Willful Intent: A Theology of Sin* [Wheaton, IL: Victor Books, 1994]), who said that God does not impute Adam's sin to his posterity. Every person is guilty because of actual sins and is condemned only because of them. This position, of course, denies the classic biblical doctrine. Allison, *Historical Theology*, 361.

the Way It's Supposed to Be: A Breviary of Sin, he reminds readers that all humans deal with annoyances, regrets, the pains of aging, outright miseries, boredom, and fear. These realities remind humans that things in life are not as they ought to be. Yet for all these longings and troubles, Plantinga argues, none matter so much as sin. Sin lies at the root of all miseries, and its veins interlace with all that is troubling in life.[89] Plantinga defines sin as a culpable and personal affront to a personal God. But for him sin is still more—it is also the breaking of universal flourishing, wholeness, and delight, which he refers to as *shalom*.[90]

SOTERIOLOGY

Predestination, Election, and Reprobation. John Wesley wrote against Calvinism in his *Predestination Calmly Considered*. He affirmed unconditional election in the sense that certain men are predetermined to do certain tasks; he cites the apostle Paul as an example of such a man. But Wesley believed that there is only conditional election relative to human salvation. For he knew that if he were to affirm unconditional election, unconditional reprobation would be implied, and he was entirely unwilling to subscribe to this implication. Thus he articulated that a believer's election is conditioned on his faith, and an unbeliever's reprobation is conditioned on his perpetual unbelief. Wesley's system included universal grace, unlimited atonement, conditional election, and conditional reprobation.[91] In *Free Grace*, Wesley argued that if predestination were true, then the gospel would be superfluous, holiness would be left unpursued, the Scriptures would be unnecessary and therefore false, and God would be more cruel than Satan.[92]

Karl Barth believed that to understand election, Jesus Christ must be known as the electing God and elected man. Christ, as electing God, elects all humanity in himself. Yet as the passive elected man, he

---

89. Cornelius Plantinga Jr., *Not the Way It's Supposed to Be: A Breviary of Sin* (Grand Rapids: Eerdmans, 1995), 1–6. Plantinga was a colleague at Calvin Seminary and eventually became president of the institution.

90. He spoke of sin as a parasite, masquerade, folly, addiction, attack, and flight (ibid., 13, 87–88, 98, 147, 153, 197).

91. Allison, *Historical Theology*, 469–70.

92. Ibid., 470–71.

stands above humanity as the Elect. He is elected to suffering, which ultimately accomplishes salvation. But as elected man, he is also electing God. Thus the condemnation and wrath under which humanity is liable is transferred to Christ, whom God loves and elects, who is elected as humanity's head.[93] Thus election is a communal, not just an individual, act.

For Barth there are many who are sinful, godless, and unrighteous. Nevertheless, even when people reject Christ, their rebellious rejection will be reversed by the divine election of grace. God has seen all humanity in his Son Jesus; thus the wicked person's rejection of Christ is divinely rejected, and divine election is consummated.[94] He wrongly believes that each person will be saved.

Regeneration, Conversion, and Calling.[95] John Wesley taught that for all humans there is universal prevenient grace—a grace that overcomes the effects of original sin and removes the need for an effective call.[96] Wesley believed that anyone who cooperates with prevenient grace is enabled to repent of sin and believe in Christ.[97]

Jonathan Edwards acknowledged common grace and special grace, and he believed that salvation is only found in the latter. He used the words *conversion, regeneration,* and *calling* interchangeably. He taught that conversion is done at once. Edwards also defended the authenticity of the revivals of the 1740s.[98]

Samuel Hopkins (1721–1803) was the founder of the New Divinity or New School theology and played a prominent role in the Second Great Awakening. He viewed regeneration as a divine act but conversion as a human act.[99] Hopkins taught that it is regeneration that

93. Ibid., 471–72.

94. Karl Barth, *Church Dogmatics,* vol. 2, *The Doctrine of God* (New York: Scribner's Sons, 1956), 2.2, 316–17, 322, as cited by Allison, *Historical Theology,* 472–73.

95. Reformed systematic theology defines regeneration as a direct, unmediated divine work while conversion takes place through the human response of faith and repentance. Regeneration is the cause of conversion. Believers repent and believe because they have been regenerated. The effective call has logical but not temporal priority in the order of salvation. See *WCG* 1:219–20, 248–49; 2:610–33.

96. John Wesley, *Methodist Article of Religion,* 8, as cited by Philip Schaff, *History of the Christian Church,* 8 vols. (Grand Rapids: Eerdmans, 1979), 3:809.

97. Allison, *Historical Theology,* 489–90.

98. Ibid., 491.

99. Historians mark three Great Awakenings: the first was that of Edwards in the 1700s; the second began in 1800 in south-central Kentucky; the third is connected to D. L. Moody's

causes the conversion. He believed that the mind is unaffected by sin, thus regeneration is a divine change of will.[100]

Though a Presbyterian minister, Charles Finney (1792–1875) stood against Old School Presbyterianism and Calvinism in general. He also opposed the making of a distinction between regeneration and conversion because he thought that such a distinction caused sinners to await regeneration before turning to God.[101] He thought of revival as the proper use of God-given means, not as a God-given miracle. He suggested a set of means for revival: anxious meetings, extended meetings, and the anxious seat. These measures shifted the paradigm within the Protestant community. In his revivals, Finney made aggressive calls for conversion and invited attenders to come forward at the anxious bench. The anxious bench developed over time into the altar call.[102]

Justification, Adoption, and Assurance. John Wesley modified standard Protestant teaching on the issue of justification. While he agreed with classic formulations of justification as it relates to regeneration and sanctification, he tied justification more tightly with regeneration and sanctification. Wesley rejected the notion that in justification God simply reckons sinners to be righteous. Instead, Wesley taught that God views a person as righteous because that person actually is righteous.[103]

In Scotland, debates on this issue were called the Marrow Controversy, which began in 1717. The key theologian in the debate was Thomas Boston (1676–1732). Boston had read and was influenced by Edward Fisher's *The Marrow of Modern Divinity*, first published in 1645.[104] The Scottish General Assembly was so vehemently against Fisher's book that in 1720 they prohibited ministers from so much as saying a positive word about it. But there was a group of twelve men who did not agree with the General Assembly, and they published a protest.[105] (Later, in 1726, Boston would publish a commentary on *The*

---

preaching (ibid., 494–95).

100. Ibid., 492.

101. Charles G. Finney, *Finney's Systematic Theology: New Expanded Edition*, ed. Dennis Carroll, Bill Nicely, and L. G. Parkhurst Jr. (Minneapolis: Bethany, 1994).

102. Allison, *Historical Theology*, 494.

103. Ibid., 514–15.

104. Republished by James Hog of Carnock, one of the Marrow Men, in 1718.

105. Those men, besides Boston, included Ralph and Ebenezer Erskine. See Sinclair B. Ferguson, *The Whole Christ: Legalism, Antinomianism, and Gospel Assurance—Why the Marrow Controversy Still Matters* (Wheaton, IL: Crossway, 2016), 26–34.

Marrow.) The controversy was a protest against alleged antinomianism, on the one side, and a reaction against neonomianism, on the other. The controversy resulted in the split of the Scottish church.[106]

One of the points stressed by the twelve men who disagreed with the General Assembly (and who were referred to as the Marrow Men) was that Christ is to be offered to all men.[107] There is both freedom and fullness of grace for all who will come to Christ.[108] The Marrow Men wanted to hold Christ together with his benefits to protect against the thought that the benefits of Christ are somehow possessed by sinners beforehand.[109] The Marrow Men's position accorded with Calvin's earlier teaching.[110] The issue, at least in part, was the warrant for faith. The Marrow Men were rightly convinced that the warrant is exclusively Christ's work, not a secret knowledge of election nor some type of universal redemption.[111]

The eighteenth-century Scottish church had developed a preparationism that separated Christ and his benefits. This preparation for receiving the gospel often made the Holy Spirit's work in the believer, after regeneration, a condition for first coming to Christ.[112] People were expected to repent of their sins as a ground on which Christ was offered.[113]

At this time, there were competing models of salvation. Both William Perkins (1558–1602) and John Bunyan (1628–1688) had produced pictorial charts of salvation. While the same elements were present in each chart, Perkins's chart had a central spine of Christ, thus revealing Calvin's influence.[114] In his chart, Bunyan had the three

---

106. James Buchanan, *The Doctrine of Justification: An Outline of Its History in the Church and of Its Exposition from Scripture* (Edinburgh: Banner of Truth, 1991), 182.

107. Ferguson, *Whole Christ*, 39.

108. Ibid., 42.

109. Ibid., 45: "Without this perspective it is highly likely that we will have a tendency to separate Christ from his benefits and abstract those benefits from him (in whom alone they are to be found) *as though we possessed them in ourselves*"; and 46: "while we can distinguish Christ's person and his work in analytical theological categories, they are inseparable from each other."

110. Ibid., 47: "This is perfectly in keeping with Calvin's emphasis that salvation becomes ours *in* Christ and not merely *through* Christ."

111. Ibid., 51.

112. Ibid., 57.

113. Ibid., 58: "Repentance, turning from sin, and degrees of conviction of sin do not constitute the grounds on which Christ is offered to us."

114. Ibid., 60n7: "Some scholars have taken the opposite view, namely, that Perkins's theology is one of the major influences on a later federal theology that moved away from Calvin

persons of the Trinity as the fountainhead of salvation, and the aspects were related to the three persons, not to Christ. These charts reveal two ways of understanding how the gospel functions.[115] A better understanding of this controversy necessitates an examination of the *ordo salutis* ("order of salvation") and union with Christ.[116]

In Perkins's understanding of the gospel, union with Christ was central, and every spiritual blessing was tied to Christ. But in Bunyan's chart, the blessings were separated. Bunyan's method of thinking about the *ordo salutis* may drift into steps of salvation "in which a quasi-chronological order of experience precedes actual faith," says Ferguson.[117] Bunyan's order should be contrasted to the model that Peter provided on the day of Pentecost. Peter made no condition for the offer of Christ to the crowds. They did not first have to experience deep conviction of sin.[118] Trouble begins when the preacher moves away from Perkins's model, and once this understanding of the gospel has been abandoned, it is difficult to return. The Bunyan model tends to shift a Protestant *ordo salutis* back toward a more medieval form "in which what was accomplished in the individual 'by grace' then became the ground for further operations of grace and ultimately actual justification."[119] The Marrow Men knew that the offer of grace in Christ is solely dependent on Christ.[120] Boston offered Christ to people who were dead in their sin, not only to those who had repented.[121]

While the doctrine of justification was not the formal topic of debate, since both groups claimed adherence to the Westminster Confession of Faith, at issue was whether assurance is of the essence of the faith—a view that the Marrow Men were charged with affirming and a position that was charged as being contrary to the WCF.[122]

---

and to that extent was less Christ centered. But the high Calvinism of Perkins's chart should not blind us to the central role of Christ in it."

115. Ibid., 61.

116. For more information, see the whole of chapter 15 of WCG2.

117. Ferguson, *Whole Christ*, 62.

118. Ibid.: "Christ himself is the warrant for faith, and so his sermon is profoundly Christocentric."

119. Ibid., 64n14.

120. Ibid., 64: They "saw that to make the offer of grace dependent upon anything, not least upon graces, was to distort the nature of grace."

121. Ibid., 65.

122. Buchanan, *Justification*, 184.

The Marrow Men argued that assurance is founded on the divine truth of the promises of salvation. Faith has full assurance of the truthfulness of those promises. Thus, since God has revealed these promises, believers must rest in them with full confidence.[123] Buchanan said that in his own day, the nineteeenth century, many complained of a lack of assurance and the message of the Marrow Men should be heeded.[124]

The Marrow Men were falsely accused of teaching universal salvation and of insisting that every believer should be able to say that Christ died individually for him or her. The Marrow Men found their warrant not from the eternal decree but from Scripture and the public proclamation of grace.[125] The theological issue in the controversy was the nature of God the Father's love and the order of salvation. Boston held that the foundation for salvation is the Father's love, not the Father's love as conditioned by the Son's suffering and by the believer's repentance.[126] Scottish ministry had become rooted in conditional grace, which produced "orthodoxy without love for sinners and a conditional and conditioned love for the righteous."[127] The Scottish church also believed that growth in holiness strengthens justification. While growth may confirm justification, it cannot strengthen it.

In other words, repentance cannot be given a chronological priority to faith.[128] Boston endeavored to emphasize the distinction between faith and repentance. The believer first grasps Christ's mercy by faith, and then a new life of repentance flows as its fruit.[129] Chronologically, faith and repentance cannot be divided, but when presenting

---

123. Ibid., 185.

124. Ibid., 186: "For there is reason to fear that the want of assurance, of which many complain, often arises from a latent doubt in regard to some of the truths of the Gospel,—that they have never thoroughly believed Jesus to be the Christ, the divinely anointed Saviour of sinners,—that they have never actually received and rested upon Him for salvation,—that they have never realized to themselves the fact, that they are individually warranted, and even commanded to embrace Him as God's ordinance for their salvation,—and that, consequently, they have not yet commenced that direct exercise of faith on Christ, in the absence of which there can be no spiritual experience, and no inward evidence, to confirm their hope."

125. Ibid., 187.

126. Ferguson, *Whole Christ*, 71.

127. Ibid., 72.

128. Ibid., 97: "Thomas Boston was particularly burdened by the way in which repentance was being given not only a logical but a chronological priority over faith in the *ordo salutis*."

129. Ibid., 101.

the gospel repentance cannot precede faith.[130] Rutherford had argued that the offer of Christ to sinners cannot be dependent on something within man.[131]

The Marrow Controversy also involved wrestling with legalism.[132] A covenant is different from a contract, and believers should not view God's law simply as a contract that must be fulfilled. A covenant is a gracious, unconditional promise in which God announces that he will be a people's God. Covenant is an indicative—a statement of fact. It is God's promising, "I will be your God." From this promise, the implication is that "You will be my people." A contract would say, "If you live as becomes my people, then I will be your God." The connection of a covenant is not with the word if but rather with the word *therefore*: "I will be your God, therefore you will be my people."[133]

Boston understood the law to be "the covenant of grace, but in it the substance of the covenant of works was repeated for particular subservient ends."[134] Law can never be abstracted from the lawgiver.[135] This truth is why the WCF distinguishes between the law as a covenant of works and as a rule for life. There is grace in the law.[136]

From the complexities of the Marrow Controversy, this chapter now transitions to Charles Finney (1792–1875), who drastically changed Reformational teaching. Finney thought it absurd to believe sinners to be forensically pronounced as just. For Finney, justification was not a forensic or judicial proceeding. He also rejected the imputation of Christ's righteousness. He fought against what he wrongly thought of as antinomianism. He also opposed the notion that a justified believer is always justified, no matter what he does.[137]

---

130. Ibid., 104.

131. Samuel Rutherford, *Christ Dying and Drawing Sinners to Himselfe* (London: Andrew Crooke, 1647), 442: "Reprobates have as fair a warrant to believe in Christ as the elect have" (as cited by Ferguson, *Whole Christ*, 110).

132. Ferguson, *Whole Christ*, 131.

133. Ibid., 115–16.

134. *The Marrow* held that the Mosaic covenant was a republication of the covenant of works. Boston rightly disagreed at this point (see ibid., 118).

135. Boston, along with Samuel Rutherford, Stephen Charnock, Anthony Burgess, and John Owen, saw the Adamic covenant as gracious. It was gracious that God condescended to have a relationship with Adam, but that grace should not be confused with saving grace. See Thomas Boston, *Human Nature in Its Fourfold State*; Ferguson, *Whole Christ*, 119n45.

136. Ferguson, *Whole Christ*, 120.

137. Allison, *Historical Theology*, 515–16.

Moving back to Scotland, James Buchanan (1804–1870) began ministry in 1828 in North Leith near Edinburgh. In 1845, he became professor of apologetics at the Free Church's New College, and two years later he moved to the chair of systematic theology. He retired in 1868.[138] In Buchanan's day, there was a rise of the Scottish Anglican church. In addition, John Henry Newman led a movement from Anglicanism back into Roman Catholicism.[139]

Buchanan wrote a magnificent work on justification. In some ways a microcosm for *The Whole Counsel of God*, Buchanan's analysis began with the OT, moved to the NT, then to the ancient church and scholastics, proceeded to the Reformation, then addressed the Roman Catholic Church after the Reformation, and, finally, developed the doctrine to his own day.[140] Buchanan tied justification to a biblical view of the nature of divine law and righteousness. It focused on the prelapsarian covenant with Adam as the federal head of all humanity. That covenant provided Buchanan with the structure to comprehend Christ's sacrifice as federal head.[141]

Buchanan judged *adoption* to be a biblical concept with a purely forensic character derived from Roman law. He explained that adoption is a change of relation, not a change in character. There is a difference between the privilege of adoption and its spirit. In a court system, one can legally be a son yet neither feel nor act like a son. Buchanan held that such was not the case with Christian adoption. So Buchanan distinguished between adoption—a change of relation—and the spirit of adoption, which implies a character change.[142]

The world of nineteenth- and twentieth-century liberalism was vastly different. For Schleiermacher, justification was not an objec-

138. J. I. Packer, introduction to *The Doctrine of Justification: An Outline of Its History in the Church and of Its Exposition from Scripture*, by James Buchanan (Edinburgh: Banner of Truth, 1991), xiv.

139. For information on Buchanan's historical context, see Carl R. Trueman, "A Tract for the Times: James Buchanan's *The Doctrine of Justification in Historical and Theological Context*," in *The Faith Once Delivered*, ed. Anthony Selvagio (Phillipsburg, NJ: P&R Publishing, 2007), 33–42; 62: "Current controversies on justification are reminiscent . . . of the issues raised relative to this doctrine through the centuries, not least by the Tractarians of the nineteenth century." As I write these words, a recent seminary graduate and my former teaching assistant has just announced that he is leaving the Presbyterian church for the Anglican church.

140. Buchanan, *Justification*, 1–174.

141. Trueman, "Buchanan," 44–45.

142. Buchanan, *Justification*, 261–62.

tive reality but the subjective consciousness of absolute dependence on God.[143] Paul Tillich looked around at the world and saw doubt and despair everywhere he looked, and he believed that justification is the divine response to this human predicament. Rudolf Bultmann understood justification to be a divine offer to turn from inauthentic existence to authentic existence through faith.[144]

Sanctification. In regard to sanctification, John Wesley broke with the Protestant tradition in a view sometimes referred to as *sinless perfection*, a label that even Wesley did not appreciate. Regardless, in this view Christians are supposedly able to live as free from wrong thoughts or tempers and without anything in them contrary to love, with the result that all the believer's thoughts and actions are governed by pure love. Wesley granted that Christians in this state could still made mistakes and suffer from ignorance, but he asserted that they could be free from outward transgressions of God's law. Wesley was convinced that it is the privilege of every Christian to be perfect so as not to commit sin. God's children subject all their desires to the obedience of Christ and their will to God and set their whole affection on him.[145]

In 1875, the Keswick movement began with a convention in Keswick, England, and other locations that followed up on Wesley's proposal. The Keswick movement taught that the normal Christian life is one of sustained victory over sin. They reasoned that believers are presented with no temptation without a way of escape, and thus believers are offered sustained victory over sin. This movement did not think that believers should live in constant defeat and grinding bondage. For Christ's provision of victory, freedom, and rest is through surrender to God and the indwelling of the Holy Spirit. So Christians should experience abounding life, which is fullness of life in Christ through the indwelling of the Spirit.

The Keswick movement had a seven-step process, which included: (1) abandonment of all known sins, (2) surrender to Christ not only

---

143. Allison, *Historical Theology*, 516.

144. Ibid.

145. Wesley, *Thoughts on Christian Perfection*, answer to question 26: "He experiences a total death to sin and an entire renewal in the love and image of God, so as to rejoice always, to pray without ceasing and in everything to give thanks" (as cited by Allison, *Historical Theology*, 538). Charles Finney followed this theology too.

as Savior but also as Lord, (3) appropriation of the promises of God, (4) mortification, (5) transformation of the inner man, (6) separation to God for holiness, and (7) service and empowerment through the Holy Spirit.[146]

Atonement Theory. The nineteenth-century German theologian Friedrich Schleiermacher changed much of classical Christianity. The god that Schleiermacher proposed was not a personal transcendent being but resembled a Buddha or a postmodern notion of an infinite spiritual reality that flows through all that exists. For Schleiermacher, the main issue of Christianity was the human heart—learning to nurture an awareness of being dependent on this world-spirit. In a universe that lacks a powerful and personal holy God, a world where sin against this God is minimized—in other words Schleiermacher's world—there is in fact not much need for atonement theory; rather, Jesus the Redeemer simply absorbs Christians into his own mighty God-consciousness, and in this absorption lies his redemptive activity.[147]

More than a century after Schleiermacher's death, John Macquarrie also offered a novel interpretation of Christ's atoning work. Macquarrie said that as believers consider Christ's sacrificial death and atonement, they must transcend elements of both subjectivity and objectivity. By *objective atonement*, Macquarrie meant when a person recognizes an atonement that is both outside and independent of man. And subjectivity is the human response to the love manifested in Christ. Both attitudes by themselves are inadequate, for objective views erase the existential dimension, while the subjective view fails to account for the dimension of grace that works in the being of man. Macquarrie substitutes instead a new view of the traditional threefold offices of Christ as prophet, priest, and king. In Christ there is a transcending of the older views. The antiquated, subjective view is embraced in his prophetic role, or his moral influence. The objective view is seen in Christ's priestly role, as sacrificing. And the enveloping view of king overcomes the distinction between the subjective and objective views while still embracing the two.[148] Christ's work of atonement is not tied to the historic time period of its actual, physical occurrence—it

146. Allison, *Historical Theology*, 539–40.
147. Schleiermacher, *The Christian Faith*, 425, in Allison, *Historical Theology*, 407.
148. Macquarrie, *Principles of Christian Theology*, 285.

occurs (though not literally) every time a person incorporates Christ's atonement into his or her own personal history.[149]

ECCLESIOLOGY

Ecumenical Movement. The modern age witnessed great extension and expansion in the membership of the church, from the Methodists, who ordained bishops in America and broke with the Anglican church in 1784, to William Carey and his mission to India. During this time, hundreds of foreign mission societies arose.

A vast ecumenical movement also arose in the twentieth century, from the World Missionary Conference in Edinburgh in 1920 to the establishment of the World Council of Churches in 1948. At first, nearly all mainline Protestant churches participated, with Russian Orthodox and Roman Catholic theologians serving as observers. Most evangelical denominations did not join.[150] But in 1942 the National Association of Evangelicals was born with a focus on evangelism and missions.

The Roman Catholic Church also underwent changes during this era. It held the First Vatican Council in 1870. It was at this council that the Catholic Church developed the dogma of papal infallibility. In the twentieth century it held the Second Vatican Council, which included Protestant observers.

Government. Augustus Hopkins (A. H.) Strong (1836–1921) was the theologian of American Baptist congregationalism.[151] He argued that church government does not require a plurality of elders. According to him, each church was to have a sole pastor, usually a board of deacons, and as many assistant pastors as needed. His notion of congregational government with a single pastor exercised significant influence throughout the United States.[152]

American Presbyterianism also developed theories of church government. While agreeing on general Presbyterian principles, the large Presbyterian church, which split at the time of the American Civil

---

149. Ibid., 290–91.
150. Allison, *Historical Theology*, 583.
151. His three-volume *Systematic Theology* appeared in 1912.
152. Allison, *Historical Theology*, 607.

War, was not monolithic in its views on the office of ruling elder, the role of deacons, and how denominational church boards should function. Relative to the offices of ruling elder and deacon, debates raged over a two- or three-office view. The two-office view holds to a parity between ruling elders and teaching elders; there is one office of elder but two functions within it. The three-office view maintains that the teaching elder is unique and that he holds the exclusive right to preach. Debates on the office of deacon included whether deacons functioned with authority, and thus had the right to attend the session or consistory meeting, or simply served with no ruling function.

Further, Dutch Reformed Church polity should not be confused with Presbyterianism. For example, the great systematician Louis Berkhof taught that Christ is the head of the church and the source of all its authority and that he exercises this authority through his Word. Christ has endowed the church with power and provided for the specific exercise of this authority through representative structures. Thus the authority of the church resides in the local congregation. The original source is the consistory, known as *session* in Presbyterianism, and is then transferred to the larger, not higher, assemblies of classis and synod.[153] This thinking is not the same as Presbyterian polity, which acknowledges the presbytery to be the locus or most important source of authority in the church.

In the nineteenth century, several denominations began to ordain women to gospel ministry. In the twentieth century, Pentecostal churches began to ordain women, such as Aimee Semple McPherson of the International Foursquare Gospel Church in 1927. In the middle of the twentieth century, mainline Methodist and Presbyterian denominations also began to ordain women. These denominations were soon followed by the Southern Baptists and American Episcopalians.

In general, larger American churches began to transition to a business or corporate model in the late 1960s. Churches essentially became businesses, with the goal of the pastor being to manage a large staff, who made the decisions and ran various ministries. The vision was to implement business efficiency and marketing strategy to foster what is, essentially, customer growth.

153. Louis Berkhof, *Systematic Theology*, rev. ed. (Grand Rapids: Eerdmans, 1996), 580–84.

Baptism. Wesley viewed baptism as an initiatory sacrament that washes away the guilt of original sin. In the case of infants, he equated baptism with the new birth. But every infant grows up, rejects God's grace, and sins. Wesley taught that because of their personal sin, these regenerated infants lose the gift of eternal life that was given to them in baptism. Thus they must be converted again as adults. Wesley strongly warned those who had been baptized as infants that they needed to be converted again to Christ.[154]

ESCHATOLOGY

Individual. Christians have always believed in the immortality of the soul. Yet Kant attacked every proof for the soul's immortality; he stated that if the soul is actually immortal, then it is so only as a postulate of practical reason. Many were persuaded by Kant's arguments.[155] But some theologians still valued the proofs that Kant had attacked.

The nineteenth century saw a revival of annihilationism disguised under the title *conditional immortality*. Proponents of conditional immortality pointed to scientific arguments that denied any notion of immortality, as well as some of the language used by fathers of the early church.[156] Some nineteenth-century theologians embraced an intermediate state of further probation for those who do not accept Christ while on earth.[157]

Sadly, annihilationism began to appear in the broadly evangelical church in the twentieth century. John Stott, for example, felt that the notion of eternal conscious punishment is simply intolerable. He thought that the tradition of such torment must now give way to a more biblical understanding. Stott argued that eternal torment in hell

154. Karl Barth, even though a Reformed pastor, denied the Reformational theology of infant baptism (see Allison, *Historical Theology*, 631–33).

155. Herman Bavinck, *Reformed Dogmatics*, ed. John Bolt (Grand Rapids: Baker Academic, 2003) (*RD*), 4:593: "They have totally abandoned the immortality of the soul or at most assert its possibility and merely speak of a hope of immortality."

156. Berkhof, *Systematic Theology*, 690: This view was "taught by Arnobius and the early Socinians, and by the philosophers Locke and Hobbes . . . which seems to imply at least that only believers receive the gift of immortality." Allison (*Historical Theology*, 716) said that romantic writers, such as Alfred Lord Tennyson, also yearned for universal salvation.

157. Berkhof, *Systematic Theology*, 681.

is cruel, unjust, and difficult to align with Scripture's teaching that God will have ultimate victory over evil. He concluded that "the ultimate annihilation of the wicked should at least be accepted as a legitimate, biblically founded alternative to the eternal conscious torment."[158]

John Wenham (1913–1996) of Oxford, whose NT Greek text is popular and who affirmed inerrancy, also found the notion of eternal punishment in hell unpalatable. He argued for conditional immortality. He reasoned that God alone is immortal, but when believers are regenerated, they then begin to partake in the nature of God, which includes his immortality. He held that the notion of the immortality of humans was birthed in Greek philosophy, not the Bible. Thus, he argued, when unbelievers die, they are consumed in God's fiery judgment and merely cease to exist.[159] Of course, all arguments in favor of annihilationism are inconclusive and contradicted by Scripture.[160]

Friedrich Schleiermacher stood against the classic articulations of final judgment and eternal punishment. He denied a divine separation between Christians and the reprobate. As he analyzed the purpose of divine punishment, he rejected that it could be ordained as reformative or retributive. He held that divine punishment can only deter. It restrains humans from giving in to dominant, sensuous tendencies. Thus, though Schleiermacher rejected the notion of a last judgment altogether, since it had been universally accepted in Christendom, Schleiermacher attempted merely to offer a reinterpretation. He held that the last judgment meant freedom from evil and hope that all would experience absolute divine dependence. He denied any biblical warrant for the doctrine of eternal damnation and believed in the universal restoration of all.[161]

158. David L. Edwards, with a response from John Stott, *Evangelical Essentials: A Liberal-Evangelical Dialogue* (Downers Grove, IL: InterVarsity Press, 1989), 320, as cited by Allison, *Historical Theology*, 721.

159. John Wenham, "The Case for Conditional Immortality," in *Universalism and the Doctrine of Hell*, by Nigel M. de S. Cameron, 162, as cited by Allison, *Historical Theology*, 721. Late in the twentieth century, Edward Fudge's book, with a preface by British evangelical F. F. Bruce, also gave an extensive biblical argument for annihilationism.

160. Berkhof, *Systematic Theology*, 691.

161. Schleiermacher, *The Christian Faith*, 351–52, 714–22, as cited by Allison, *Historical Theology*, 715–16. After Schleiermacher, Frederick Farrar (1831–1903) in his book *Eternal Hope* (1878) did not support universalism or conditional immortality, yet he yearned for some type of broader salvation than was held by orthodox churches. His position was opposed in

In the twentieth century, William Newton Clarke's *Outline of Christian Theology* taught that final judgment had human destiny in view, not any vindication for God in Christ. This position opposed the classic biblical teaching of the final judgment. Clarke argued that God has power to vindicate himself, has no need to involve people in that vindication, and a divine vindication before men actually made humanity God's judge. In conjunction with this view of final judgment, there was no need, from Clarke's perspective, for a visible return of Christ. He held that the last judgment was not a cataclysmic event but a private evaluation of every human.[162]

By the middle of the century, British theologian John A. T. Robinson fully embraced universalism in his book *In the End, God*. Cognizant that earlier expressions of universalism were rejected by the church, Robinson explained that God's divine mercy would transcend anyone's expectations and merits and be spread to all humanity. He argued that the Bible teaches the reality of human freedom and the seriousness of hell. And he held that God's infinite love does not abrogate human freedom. He also acknowledged that each person feels an existential urge to choose between heaven and hell. But while this is a serious existential choice, according to Robinson, God supposedly knows that hell is not real.[163]

Karl Barth also taught universal salvation and based it on God's grace. He believed that such gracious salvation from sin is certainly unexpected but should, paradoxically, be expected.[164]

The notion of a second probation also became popular in the nineteenth century. This view proposes that some people who are in the intermediate state will have an opportunity to embrace Christ as their Savior though they did not do so during their earthly lives. The notion is that only those who resist Christ's offer of grace even in the intermediate state are eternally damned. Proponents of this view point

---

1880 by Edward Pusey, who wrote *What Is of Faith, as to Everlasting Punishment* in 1880. See Allison (*Historical Theology*, 716), who has an incorrect title to Pusey's work.

162. Allison, *Historical Theology*, 717.

163. Ibid., 717–18.

164. Karl Barth, *The Humanity of God*, trans. John N. Thomas and Thomas Wieser (Atlanta: John Knox Press, 1960), 61–62; Oliver Crisp, *Deviant Calvinism: Broadening Reformed Theology* (Minneapolis: Fortress, 2014), 155. Some Barth scholars, however, deny that Barth was a universalist.

to God's love and justice while attempting to make Christ's saving work as extensive and inclusive as possible. The Bible clearly teaches, however, that unbelievers after death are in an eternally fixed state.[165]

General. Seventeenth-century British theologians such as John Cotton and John Owen started to develop postmillennialism. They taught a doctrine of a latter glory in which God's kingdom would come in power and people would flock to Christ. In this view, magistrates would support the church, and the church would attain purity in theology and worship. The gospel would bear great fruit, the Jews would enter the Holy Land, then a thousand-year golden age would bring peace and blessing. Finally, after that kingdom arrived, Christ would return.[166]

This development makes sense in the light of these men's cultural context. John Owen was chaplain to Lord Protector Oliver Cromwell. Catholicism, the great beast, had been defeated in the British Isles. Soldiers huddled to study their Bibles before heading into combat in the English Civil War. From Owen's perspective, the church was now expanding by bringing toleration for the Independents hand in hand with the Presbyterians. Of course it seemed that a golden age was approaching on the horizon!

In the eighteenth century, Jonathan Edwards thought that the Reformation began a movement that would see the demise of the Antichrist, the papacy. Edwards believed in both a literal millennium and that the Jews would be saved and restored to a nation. The Holy Spirit was working mightily in the Great Awakening of the 1740s, and expectation was that the millennium might be rapidly approaching. The cultural milieu of the later American Revolution also encouraged postmillennialism.

The Second Great Awakening came in the nineteenth century, and along with it a resurgence in postmillennialism. The prosperity of the time led Charles Finney and others to this view. Postmillennialism also fueled social causes, such as ending slavery, prohibition, and women's suffrage.[167]

---

165. Berkhof, *Systematic Theology*, 692–93.
166. Allison, *Historical Theology*, 693.
167. Allison, *Historical Theology*, 693–94. Also, Charles Hodge and William G. T. Shedd opposed premillennialism.

Baptist minister A. H. Strong was a strong defender of postmillennialism. His multivolume *Systematic Theology* provided a classic postmillennial interpretation of Revelation 20. But postmillennialism declined in the twentieth century, particularly after the disheartening World War I.

Amillennialism as a term is of recent origin. Gaffin argues that until the twentieth century there were essentially only two eschatological positions: premillennialism and postmillennialism.[168] The amillennialist view was basically included within postmillennialism, since both views hold that Christ will return after the millennium.[169] But amillennialism is distinct from postmillennialism because it holds that the entire interadventual period is the millennium, not just an era toward its close. Nevertheless, Gaffin argues that, in at least one sense, all amillennials are postmillennial.[170]

Postmillennial is not a monolithic term. This view is characterized by an emphasis on the kingship of the ascended Christ. But this postmillennial vision of the millennium includes a future golden age before Christ's return.[171] Nevertheless, Gaffin argued that "the NT will not tolerate such a construction."[172] The postmillennial vision does not have the proper view of the eschatological victory of the ascended Christ. God has already placed all things under his feet! There will be a change in Christ's kingship, but that change will come precisely when he returns in glory, not at some intermediate point prior to his return. Christ's kingship began at his resurrection and continues undiminished in the eschatological power of the Holy Spirit. Believers are now in the golden age of the church. To push the golden age into the future is to deny the eschatological quality of the church's present existence. There should be no separation between the eschatological and victory. If there is a future golden era, then by implication Christ

---

168. WCG 2:329–36, 668–69, speaks about judgment and premillennialism.

169. See WCG 2:210.

170. Richard B. Gaffin, "Theonomy and Eschatology: Reflections on Postmillennialism," in *Theonomy: A Reformed Critique*, ed. William S. Barker and Robert Godfrey (Grand Rapids: Zondervan, 1990), 198–201. For example, Geerhardus Vos classifies himself as postmillennial while he is clearly amillennial. Gaffin also argues that B. B. Warfield was amillennial in his exegesis, as was John Murray.

171. Gaffin, "Theonomy," 202: "Postmils misperceive the basic structure of New Testament Eschatology and so, in a fundamental way, devalue Christian life in the present."

172. Ibid., 203.

is not now reigning in eschatological victory. There is no room for different stages of his eschatological glory while believers anticipate the second coming.[173]

The question to be answered is whether millennial victory is over the entire interadventual period or remains a future expectation. Amillennials contend that millennial victory triumphs over the entire period, and postmillennials believe it to be a future expectation. Post-millennials describe the present state of the church as indecisive and not yet victorious, but they anticipate the coming of a better time. The present, however, cannot be de-eschatologized in a search for a future victory.[174]

Yet neither have amillennials always had perfect eschatology. At times they have tended to de-eschatologize the entire interadventual period. But the church must be confident of the victory it has in the exalted Christ. True NT eschatology is decidedly optimistic.[175]

Gaffin painted the picture of the church's present eschatological life with broad strokes of suffering. He argued that suffering is a characteristic aspect of the life of the church, even that it is missiological. Union with Christ is manifested in the believer's sufferings.[176] Sharing in suffering manifests resurrection power.[177] The nature of those sufferings includes not only persecution and martyrdom but also mundane, earthly frustrations and annoyances. Until Christ's coming, this frustration, suffering, and decay will saturate believers' lives.

The notion that this futility will be reduced at some time in the interadventual period is foreign to NT eschatology. The church will remain in humiliation until the time of her exaltation at Christ's return. The very meaning of the kingdom is suffering service.[178]

The notion that there will be no suffering for the church, characteristic of a postmillennial golden age, is at odds with both Jesus's and Paul's teaching. Such a view confuses the church's identity. There are

173. So what happened with the fall of Jerusalem was simply a secondary aftershock of the beginning of the destruction when the veil of the temple was torn in two (see Gaffin, "Theonomy," 204–5).

174. Ibid., 206–8.

175. Ibid., 208–10.

176. See *WCG* 2:250–73.

177. Gaffin, "Theonomy," 210–13.

178. Ibid., 214–15.

critical hermeneutical issues involved in this discussion. The question is whether the NT interprets OT prophecies or whether those OT prophecies are read in isolation. The postmillennial view distorts the church's understanding of its mission in the world.[179]

Gaffin is opposed to understanding Romans 11:11 as predicting a future mass conversion of the Jewish people. Paul saw the triumph of the gospel that was spread throughout the whole world already fulfilled in his day, with his own ministry to the Gentiles already bringing about the fullness of the Jews. Jews who convert are not simply added to the remnant but are a part of the inaugural fullness, which will continue through the interadventral period.[180] Thus Christ could return at any time. He could have returned immediately after the apostolic foundations, for all the demands of prophecy had been met. What is happening since the apostles is the church's filling up what is lacking in Christ's afflictions—a missiological reality. The NT calls the church to an eager longing for Christ's return.[181] This position is also that of the book of Hebrews. The church should view herself as an alien and a stranger on the earth. There will be no dominion period when the church is outside wilderness sufferings. When absent from Christ's body, the church suffers, but when in his bodily presence she enters God's final rest.[182]

Eternal Punishment and Eternal State. Following the pattern that it had for most of the other theological loci, liberalism discarded the doctrine of eternal punishment. Schleiermacher refused to believe that God would eternally punish sinners either out of vengeance or in an attempt to bring about reform in sinners' lives. Schleiermacher also dismissed eternal damnation because he believed that it had insufficient support. He believed that redemption's power was strong enough to restore every soul.[183] Schleiermacher also abandoned the idea of a new heaven and a new earth.

In contrast, biblically faithful nineteenth-century teaching held to a new heaven and a new earth. Charles Hodge helped with the

---

179. Ibid., 215–17.
180. Ibid., 218.
181. Ibid., 218–20.
182. Ibid., 222–24.
183. Allison, *Historical Theology*, 714–15.

articulation of this doctrine. He argued against the annihilation of the existing universe. Hodge limited the renovation to the earth—he did not extend it to the entire universe.[184]

Twentieth-century evangelical debate did not focus on the renovation or annihilation of the heavens and earth but on the nature of heaven itself. The question of this time was whether heaven is a place or a state. Some sought to emphasize the physical nature of heaven, while others stressed the spiritual reality of life with God in Christ. A balanced presentation affirms the physical reality of heaven without drawing attention to its physical attractions at the expense of the unfathomable spiritual benefits of direct access to the presence of God.[185]

THEOLOGICAL METHOD

Calvin to Kant. The errors of modern theology began many years ago. In some ways, contemporary troubles can be traced back to the French philosopher Descartes and his famous dictum, "I think, therefore I am." With these words he wrongly asserted that he had unearthed epistemological certainty. It may be true that he and others existed as a thinking thing, yet on closer inspection that poor thing was tossed about on the waves of chance.

Descartes, and Calvin before him, began with man, not God's existence. Descartes, however, began with man as intelligible to himself and the source through which both God and the world are intelligible. But Calvin viewed man as not intelligible on his own; instead, Calvin saw man as a creature who comprehends himself and God's world through the Creator's gracious revelation.

184. Hodge, *Systematic Theology* (London: Clarke, 1960), 3:851–54, as cited by Allison, *Historical Theology*, 730–31. Archibald Alexander Hodge (in *Evangelical Theology*) gave a moving description of heaven as adapted to human capacity. Allison, continuing a sad pattern of incorrect historical placement, analyzed the son's theology before his father's.

185. Donald Guthrie (in *New Testament Theology* [Leicester/Downers Grove, IL: Inter-Varsity Press, 1981], 875, 880) underlined the spiritual reality to the point of saying that "we shall not expect . . . to find a description of a place, so much as the presence of a person." Millard Erickson (in *Christian Theology*) defined heaven specifically as the state of God's presence rather than a place. On the other hand, Gordon Lewis and Bruce Demarest, Wayne Grudem, and Randy Alcorn want to emphasize heaven both as a state as well as a place. See Allison, *Historical Theology*, 731–33.

This difference in approach is the major theological theme of modern theology. Modern theologians who have not submitted to the Word of God cannot conclude that they know who and what they are or the nature of reality around them. Such knowledge is available only when humans turn to divine revelation for answers.

It has already been observed earlier in this book how seventeenth-century European philosophy separated itself from Christianity. Instead of relying on God's Word, this movement turned to human reason. It attempted to free itself from the binding authority of the Word of God and make men into autonomous creatures. For the rationalists, the word *reason* meant that which was opposed to sensory experience. For the empiricists, reason was based on sensory experience. By the end of the eighteenth century, philosophical thought had significantly influenced theological reflection. Sadly, theologians reconstructed their theology to agree with the assumptions of philosophy. Theologians began to read their Bibles as an errant but wise human document. They believed the Bible is errant particularly where it recounts miracles. Thus they rejected both the Bible's authority and its supernatural content. Those writers who reject the Bible's inerrancy and affirm the philosophical presuppositions of intellectual autonomy, yet maintain that there is a legitimate Christian theology, can be termed *liberals*.

By the end of the eighteenth century, there was a philosophical battle for the mind—a battle between empiricism and rationalism. In many ways the debate was over facts. The question was whether facts were established on the basis of sensory experience or logic. Both movements frantically sought to avoid skepticism. But Christians do not need to take either side of this debate. The Bible offers an alternative: both facts and the surrounding world exist, and humans can know those facts and themselves when they begin to see themselves as creatures made by a Creator who desires them to comprehend not only themselves but also him.

Kant, however, did not affirm Jesus's miracles, deity, or even historical existence. For him, Jesus was a moral archetype—a mere symbol of humans' ability to overcome evil and draw nearer to moral perfection. Kant wrote to German citizens who could have practical faith in Jesus, a confidence that Jesus as a moral archetype points people in the right direction. Kant completely rejected divine revelation. He taught

904

that any supposed divine revelation must be subjected to autonomous rationality; enlightened men and women judge such claims by their reason. Thus, according to Kant, no morality, religion, or faith can be based on revelation. Religion for Kant was works-based righteousness.

Kant believed that scientific knowledge is discovered in the realm of phenomena. This phenomenal world is subordinate to the realm of the spirit, known as the *noumenal* world. Kant held that it is impossible to have knowledge of any world beyond that of space and time—that is, the noumenal world. The world beyond cannot be grasped by human concepts.

Thus thinkers can aim at, or something may point toward, the idea of an absolute Being. Yet humans cannot know anything about such a Being. There is dualism between being able to know and being able to believe. One knows truth from philosophy and science. This system was a subtle rejection of the Bible's method of knowing. The Bible reveals that thinking people can only know themselves and the world around them by knowing that God created them and has revealed himself in his Word.

As time pushed forward, philosophy and science allied themselves against any belief in God. The scientific world claimed an ability to explain everything naturally and mechanistically, including the very origin of the universe. The union of these two bore its most rotten fruit in the nineteenth century, when biology joined this godless alliance.

Optimistic Humanism and the Death of God. Kant claimed that God exists in the noumenal world, entirely unable to communicate with the phenomenal. Thus Kant attempted to remove the benefit of special revelation from the Christian faith. Nevertheless, with his philosophy he believed that all human knowledge is now available. There were even suggestions by nineteenth-century intellectual elites that a new religion, the "religion of humanity," should replace Christianity. Sadly, many in the church simply ignored or dismissed these bold external challenges. Some have called this anti-Christian, nineteenth-century mindset "optimistic humanism."

The theological challenge of optimistic humanism could have been met by the church, but was simply left unaddressed. For whatever reason, the church was caught off guard when she should not have been. Perhaps the failure relates to the church's adopting mid-Victorian self-satisfaction. Part of the aim of this volume is to detail ways in which theology deteriorated or wandered in the past so that the modern church may avoid these past errors.

This movement is also called by the name Death of God. It entered a world in which Christian values could supposedly exist, but not an atoning Christ or a transcendent God. There are clear ties between the Death of God movement and the rise of political totalitarianism, as can be observed in both Friedrich Nietzsche and Fyodor Dostoevsky (1821–1881). Some have even argued for the inevitability of totalitarianism with the Death of God movement.

The optimistic humanists or Death of God thinkers lost their intellectual basis or center. They forfeited all absolutes, and when they were intellectually honest, such as were the twentieth-century existentialists, they recognized this loss for what it was. Such thinkers, when fully self-conscious, know that they are simply accidents, and to avoid massive depression they amuse themselves. People caught in this intricate and destructive web will necessarily remain frustrated.

Kierkegaard to Tillich. Kierkegaard's Christianity demonstrates a complete absorption of biblical thinking into philosophical culture. He taught that Christianity is absolute paradox, or contradiction, and that truth is subjective. For Kierkegaard, there was no historical objectivity by itself; history offered only probability. So he also had issues with objective revelation. He held that individuals enter into a relationship with God by believing that which is beyond understanding and thus are transformed. This transformation means living a life of fellowship with Christ. And in this life of fellowship, sin is no longer mere guilt but a matter of breaking fellowship. Kierkegaard did not think that God revealed himself directly or provided personal instruction. In fact, Kierkegaard argued that the belief that God is directly related to man is the thinking of paganism, not Christianity. Kierkegaard stressed that faith cannot be founded on doctrine, for he believed that if faith could be so founded, then it would be a purely intellectual activity. Neither did he believe that Christianity could or should be rationally defended. He considered any defense of the faith to be a shameful and insidious betrayal. Similarly, Ritschl rejected what he considered speculative philosophic theology as simply valueless. He rejected metaphysics as an aid to Christian truth.

As a trained historian, Adolf von Harnack reflected on the nature of theological method. Inherent in the work of theology and discernable as early as the writings of Origen was what he considered to be a necessary secular element that wrapped up or enveloped all human intellectual investigation. This secular element was the supposedly needed science, structure, or organizing principle of biblical and theological interpretation. By this time it was a given that theology needed to combine with some form of nonbiblical philosophical framework to complete its task.

While Schleiermacher had focused on God's immanence—that is, God in humanity's experience—Barth focused his theological method on God's transcendence. Barth argued that Schleiermacher started from the wrong epistemological certainty of self-consciousness and only then asked about knowing God.

Tillich, however, rejected Barth's thinking, as well as any notion of a literalistic supernaturalism. He perceived a need for a new theological structure—one that could synthesize human wisdom and experience with biblical religion. Some have called his method *correlation*. This theological method is the same one seen in his theological predecessors.

The Hodges and Bavinck. Charles Hodge was keenly aware of the importance of theological method. He commented on it in his critical review of Charles Finney's *Lectures on Systematic Theology*. According to Hodge, Finney was driven by philosophical presuppositions, rather than exegesis and sound doctrine, in his stance on the liberty of the human will.[186]

Archibald Alexander Hodge's inaugural lecture at Western Seminary in Pittsburgh provided valuable insight into how the Princetonians viewed the nature of systematic theology. His method was to begin with the broadest principles, then narrow his focus. He began defining religion in general and then narrowed to theology as the science

---

186. Charles Hodge, *Biblical Repertory*, 1846: "The scriptures are throughout recognized as a mere subordinate authority. . . . 'The true and Christian method is to begin with the doctrines,' Hodge countered, 'and let them determine our philosophy, and not to begin with philosophy and allow it to give law to the doctrines'" (as cited by David B. Calhoun, *Princeton Seminary* [Edinburgh: Banner of Truth, 1994], 1:306). On the other hand, Kevin J. Vanhoozer, whom we will examine in chapter 25, criticizes Hodge for an overemphasis on content at the expense of language and experience in dogmatic construction. See Kevin J. Vanhoozer, "Analytics, Poetics, and the Mission of Dogmatic Discourse," in *The Task of Dogmatics*, ed. Oliver D. Crisp and Fred Sanders (Grand Rapids: Zondervan, 2017), 25.

of religion. He narrowed even further to presentations of the notions of natural theology and revealed theology. Protestantism is the fruit of revealed theology, and the great formal principle of Protestantism is that the Scriptures are the only authoritative source and standard of truth. The formal principle of Protestantism led him into his broad definition of theology:

> Theology is that science which embraces the literature of this inspired book, its accurate interpretation, the systematic construction and exhibition of its doctrinal contents and the deduction therefrom of practical principles and rules. It, therefore, includes the entire curriculum of studies taught in a theological Seminary to theological students.[187]

From this definition, Hodge transitioned to theology's tasks. These tasks included apologetics, both positive evidences and defense, the determination of the authenticity and genuineness of the canon, biblical criticism, hermeneutics, exegetical theology, systematic theology, ecclesiology, and church history.

The responsibility of systematic theology, he believed, is to take the results of exegesis and demonstrate the implicitly contained symmetrical system in the Bible, including definitions of the doctrines and their relationships to one another. It is also the task of systematics to refute error and to compare the results with church history and the creeds. Hodge held that systematic theology relies on the results furnished by scientific exegesis, and the two—systematics and exegesis—may never be separated.

But Hodge believed there is more to systematic theology than working with the text of Scripture. Systematic theology satisfies human longings for the order and unity of knowledge and answers questions concerning the relationship between God's special revelation and the natural world in which humans find themselves. Hodge, however, realized that theology is the work of limited human minds and therefore requires time to grow and mature. Thus he said that historical theology

187. "Addresses at the inauguration of Rev. Archibald A. Hodge: as professor of didactic, polemic and historical theology in the Western Theological Seminary." ed. James M. Platt (Pittsburgh: Western Theological Seminary, 1864), printed by James McMillin, p. 25.

and polemics must work in conjunction with systematics. In sum, Hodge said that systematic theology is the presentation of all that is taught in Scripture, which includes demonstrating its development over time and defending biblical teaching against those who would oppose it.[188]

Herman Bavinck knew that all human thought must be taken captive to Christ. Bavinck's theological method was to show the exegetical and then historical development of doctrine. He was sensitive to the patristic, medieval, and Reformation eras. He was also very careful and cautious in his statements. He was free of the inordinate need to answer all minute and abstruse questions.

Bavinck defined dogmatics (that is, systematic theology) as the scientific system of the knowledge of God, concerning both himself and creation as related to himself, as revealed in his Word to his church.[189] The study of ethics is also based on dogmatics. A sound dogmatics must reckon with the development of the doctrine in the church, the author's personal convictions, and the confessional deliverances of the church. While Scripture is principal, nevertheless the author's own dogmatic tradition is indispensable. He divided his *Reformed Dogmatics* between general and special revelation. The general established the *why*, and the special the what of belief.

God is the essential principle of theology, and his self-communication is the principle of that which is known. Bavinck divided this knowledge from the Scriptures into interior and exterior knowledge. He rejected innate ideas and insisted that outward experience is indispensable, yet there are still a priori truths that the mind knows through the process of acquiring external knowledge.

Religion is objectively identical to God's revelation and consists in the covenant, while subjectively it consists in absolute dependence on God. Creaturely dependence is the foundation of all religion. Religion embraces the whole man, while science, morality, and art belong to separate faculties, such as feeling, will, or intellect.

Bavinck defined revelation as every activity from God that places and keeps humanity in relationship to himself, which is called *religion*.

---

188. See also *WCG* 1:94–95 for an analysis of A. A. Hodge's theological method.

189. For more on how Bavinck defines dogmatics, see Scott R. Swain, "Dogmatics as Systematic Theology," in *The Task of Dogmatics*, ed. Oliver D. Crisp and Fred Sanders (Grand Rapids: Zondervan, 2017), 49–50, 61, 65, 68.

One of Bavinck's theological weaknesses is that he considers general and special revelation as parallel. In fact, Bavinck wrestled with the nature of inspiration as a source of the Scriptures and found it to be a vexing problem.[190]

In his later work, *The Philosophy of Revelation*, he argued for a qualitative difference between general and special revelation. In general revelation, God demonstrates the beauty of his mind. Yet in special revelation, because the apex of creation—humanity—needs it so desperately, God manifests the beauty of his loving heart. In special revelation, which is necessarily connected to God's being and character, that revelation gives content from God but also explains its own origin.

In Bavinck's later volume, he wrestled with revelation that was found in conflict with other truth claims. Even a century later this question is still difficult! With the development of modern science, many abandoned the religious roots of human identity and culture. Turning to God's explanation of life was no longer considered a respectable option. Nevertheless, some desired to retain some type of supernatural revelation and thus found a type of limiting concept in some smaller part of special revelation. Bavinck argued that such a choice denies the character of special revelation itself, which cannot, and will not, be so limited. For true answers to any truth claim, humanity must turn to the whole Word of God, which is foundational to all knowledge.

In conclusion, the theological method of the three-volume *The Whole Counsel of God* has been modeled in many ways after Vos's vision set forth in *Biblical Theology*. He rightly argued that the best way to understand God's self-revelation is to view it the way in which God himself unfolded it: historically. That historical presentation was the goal of volumes 1 and 2. Heeding the wisdom of the Hodges and Bavinck, this third volume intends to put on display how the Holy Spirit has been working in the history of the church to help her better realize the pearl of great price found in Scripture.

Conclusion to Part 6. This sixth part has unveiled an ongoing struggle between the church and the world.[191] Unlike the first part,

---

190. B. B. Warfield wrestled with this area as well. See the analysis of Warfield in chapter 21.

191. Even though it has taken many pages to develop an analysis of modern theology, experts in the field will, correctly, find the evaluation to be incomplete in many places. Such is the tension found in a one-volume summary of the development of doctrine.

which examined the church's battling the pagan state for survival, the modern Western church has to battle not only the world but also the more subtle temptations for the church to accommodate herself to the surrounding world. In this battle, God raised up many faithful theological voices that were true to his Word. Yet God also permitted so-called *theologians* who systematically worked to destroy the beauty of God's inerrant Word. Examining those ongoing, massive battles will continue into the next and final section on the postmodern world.

KEY TERMS

process philosophy
open theism
kenotic Christology
creation theories
documentary hypothesis

STUDY QUESTIONS

1. Now that the church has been wrestling with the creation narrative for many decades and debating the age of the earth, how will you guide a Bible study or sermon series on this difficult topic?
2. Christianity teaches that all humans have undying souls. What approach would you take to defend that teaching against a materialist who says that when we die, that is it?
3. Can you explain the relationship between union with Christ, justification, and assurance?
4. What model of church government have you adopted: congregational, Presbyterian, or episcopal? Can you provide reasons for your decision?

RESOURCES FOR FURTHER STUDY

There are a number of primary texts suggested at the ends of chapters 19, 20, 21, and 22, including works by Jonathan Edwards, Abraham Kuyper, Herman Bavinck, Hodge father and son, J. W. Alexander, Geerhardus Vos, Oscar Cullmann, Cornelius Van Til, and John Murray.

Hoffecker, W. Andrew, ed. *Revolutions in Worldview: Understanding the Flow of Western Thought*. Phillipsburg, NJ: P&R Publishing, 2007. For excellent summary and analysis, see the chapters titled "The Age of Intellecutal Iconoclasm: Revolt against Theism," by Richard Lints, and "Philosophy among the Ruins: The Twentieth Century and Beyond," by Michael Payne.

PART 7

The Postmodern World

24

Postmodernism

AFTER A LECTURE ON Adam and Eve's prelapsarian state, as well as the nature of divorce in the OT, an African student wanted to ask a question about America's high divorce rate. In his culture, divorce is not a very big issue; however, polygamy is a true problem! What the African student could not understand was why divorce is so widespread in America—even in the so-called "evangelical church."

The answer to his very practical question, besides the obvious fact of human sin, in some ways gets to the heart of the issue of postmodernism. It may at first appear strange to link divorce with postmodernism. But postmodernism's philosophy has helped produce such widespread divorce in American culture. Postmodernism has also helped make divorce acceptable—even within parts of the American evangelical church. Of course, the scandal of divorce antedates postmodernism, but its prevalence is one of the many fruits of a culture that has been swept away by this current philosophy. To respond to postmodernism's challenges, it is necessary to comprehend the nature of that culture.

DEVELOPMENT AND IMPORTANCE OF POSTMODERNISM

Shifts in Western Culture. Social and intellectual historians divide European history into sections or periods. Scholars have noted certain cultural shifts that demarcate the various historical eras.[1] Although

1. Gene Edward Veith Jr., *Postmodern Times: A Christian Guide to Contemporary Thought and Culture* (Wheaton, IL: Crossway, 1994), 18–19.

these shifts are not always datable to a specific year, there are comprehensible distinctions between the ages of history.

For example, the vast cultural shifts from medieval to early modern Europe, and then from early modern to modern western Europe, were clear. With each new era there were advances in science, changes in technology, and new thoughts and variations in religion, all of which helped produce the succeeding era. Specifically, the Reformation era is termed "early modern European history"—and modern European history follows quickly after the Reformation.

Historians of philosophy assert that after the time of the seventeenth-century French philosopher René Descartes, philosophy becomes modern. The two disciplines of philosophy and history agree that modern history began somewhere in the seventeenth century. Thus modern European history spanned almost three hundred years, that is, from the seventeenth century until the twentieth. Like the previous historical shifts, the movement from modern European history and philosophy to our own postmodern times has not been climactic. But unlike the previous shifts, the change to postmodernism has been comparatively very rapid. So the first task is to determine how this rapid change came about.

Rise of Postmodernism. The beginning of postmodernism has been dated as early as 1968 and as late as 1989, that is, within a short, twenty-one year span.[2] Whenever exactly it started, postmodernism has nineteenth-century, anti-Christian historical and philosophical roots. The roots of postmodernism lie dormant in modernism itself.[3] In various parts of nineteenth-century Europe, a movement aimed against Christianity became stronger and stronger. Some would assert that the high point of that anti-Christian movement was exhibited in the writings of the German Swiss philosopher Friedrich Nietzsche.[4] A second candidate for the king of nineteenth-century anti-Christian

2. Thomas Oden dates postmodernism to the fall of the Berlin Wall in 1989. Charles Jencks dates it at 1972. See Veith, *Postmodern Times*, 27, 39–40.

3. The problem lies with Kant and locating truth in the phenomenal. See the following reaction section.

4. I am not arguing that it came suddenly in the nineteenth century. Like all historical epochs, it had earlier roots. Nietzsche and Arthur Schopenhauer were examined in chapter 20. Schopenhauer was a pessimist who taught that this world was the worst of all possible worlds. Schopenhauer was a romantic; he sometimes took the intellect as superficial and tried to find refuge in some deeper form of life. For him, the major aspect of humanity was the will. The

thought is Karl Marx and the rise of his radical dialectical materialism.[5] Both men are good candidates for initiating the movement toward postmodernism. Marx and Nietzsche attacked the practice of religion in general and Christianity in particular. But Nietzsche attacked not only Christianity—he also attacked the existence of truth itself.[6]

World War I and its massive destruction also seems to be an important contributor to the rise of postmodernism. Some argue, however, that instead of growing out of German soil, postmodernism was born in France and was based on the literary philosophical movement called *existentialism*, which was a twentieth-century phenomenon. Scholars still debate the precise beginnings and high point of this anti-Christian movement, but it is clear that postmodernism began slowly to replace the supposed Judeo-Christian or modern culture of Europe around the end of World War I.[7] When that anti-Christian movement began, the centuries-old Christian and modern-European culture was ripped away from Europe. The destruction came not from foreign invasion but from within Europe itself—it was not forced on the thinkers from the outside.

It seems simple to conclude that the background of postmodernism, besides the nineteenth-century anti-Christian movement, as well as the disaster of World War I and rise of French existentialism, is as a negative reaction to modernism.[8] Postmodernism is an overreaction to the claims of, and false elements within, modernism.[9] The movement called

---

human will was neither rational nor moral; nature was blind and purposeless, and human life had no goal. Nietzsche represents the apex of the movement, not its inauguration.

5. Marx and Marxism also influenced Christianity. This influence is observed most clearly in liberation theology, which is treated in the next chapter.

6. Friedrich Nietzsche, "On Truth and Lie in an Extra-Moral Sense," in *The Portable Nietzsche*, ed. Walter Kaufmann (New York: Viking Press, 1954), 46. See also, "What Is Truth? A Mobile Army of Metaphors, Metonyms and Anthropomorphisms." He later said that there are no facts: "Truths are illusions about which one has forgotten that this is what they are; metaphors which are worn out and without sensuous power; coins which have lost their pictures and now matter only as metal, no longer as coins" (ibid., 47).

7. Veith, *Postmodern Times*, 42. Existentialism was investigated in chapter 21. See Arthur P. Mendel, *The Twentieth Century 1914–1964* (New York: Free Press, 1965), 4–6. World War I, with its trench warfare and mustard gas, destroyed many postmillennial hopes for culture's/society's getting "better and better."

8. Stanley J. Grenz and Roger Olson, *20th Century Theology: God and the World in a Transitional Age* (Downers Grove, IL: InterVarsity Press, 1992).

9. Douglas Groothuis, *Truth Decay: Defending Christianity against the Challenges of Postmodernism* (Downers Grove, IL: InterVarsity Press, 2000), 41. See Veith, *Postmodern Times*,

the Enlightenment, foundational to modernism, boasted of technical mastery and universal knowledge.[10] Modernism exalted natural law and scientific knowledge based on the observation of nature. Truth was found in nature—and not outside it. Thus morality, since it cannot be weighed or measured, became simply a concept. There was no objective referent to many morally based ideas.[11]

The postmodern response was that the contemporary social context makes a unified worldview nonviable. Religious diversity makes one exclusive religion look out of the question. Personal identity in terms of the one best way of life looks impossible. Language is viewed as a creation of human beings—written texts do not have one knowable determinate meaning. The bottom line is the notion that truth is really a quest for power.[12] Postmodernists hold that moral values are relative—they are constructed by cultures and certainly not somehow ordained by God.[13]

Sadly, closer examination demonstrates that postmodernism was actually aided by the institutional church. While strong roots were found in the anti-Christian world of Nietzsche, so-called Christian theologians have played an important role in the birth of postmodernism.[14] A modern Christian thinker that helped further postmodernism was Reinhold Niebuhr (1892–1971). Niebuhr served as the pastor of a Presbyterian church in Detroit, Michigan. His practical ministry among assembly-line workers profoundly influenced him. The harsh reality of urban life caused him to reject his own theological heritage of social liberalism, with its concomitant hope for a cultural utopia. He left his

---

42, 80; and David Harvey, *The Condition of Postmodernity* (Cambridge: Blackwell, 1989), 38.

10. Groothuis, *Truth Decay*, 40–41. Modernism falsely taught an objective human reason.

11. Ibid., 41.

12. Ibid., 26–31.

13. Ibid., 38, 40–41.

14. Some would claim that the apex of nineteenth-century anti-Christian thinking was actually found in the theologian David Friedrich Strauss. Strauss was the first radical who wrote mostly religious material. Perhaps his assault on the NT can be explained as a safe attack on Prussian politics. In his *Leben Jesu, kritisch bearbeitet* (1835–1836) Strauss aimed to complete Christianity's destruction, which the earlier theologian Schleiermacher and the philosopher Hegel had so timidly begun. While Strauss admitted that there is truth in Christianity, as well as in all other religions, nevertheless the truths are not expressed in a strict philosophical form. The question for him was whether it is worthwhile to work on the truth concepts to bring them up to a "proper" philosophical level. He concluded that, in effect, the supposedly historical facts of Christianity are instead only products of mythologizing. Karl Barth wrote on him in *Protestant Thought in the 19th Century* (London: SCM Press, 1972), 356.

Detroit pastorate to become professor at Union Theological Seminary in New York City.[15] For Niebuhr, theology's task was to respond to the strong force of blind economic power. He had an accurate vision of humanity's fallenness and proposed social justice as the answer to that problem.[16] But detrimental to what could be known as the *Christian culture* found in America, Niebuhr asserted that both individual Christians and churches or denominations were both manipulative and self-serving. In the face of overwhelming urban economic/social problems, Niebuhr saw the church as actually a big part of the world's problems and lacking answers to those problems.

Importance and Influence. However we interpret the rise of post-modernism, Christians must be interested in understanding post-modernism itself. It has affected all levels of contemporary American society—the way people do business, the methods and thinking of science and scientists, theories of art, and even contemporary architecture.[17]

We can demonstrate how postmodernism has influenced education. For example, schoolteachers in America used to stand in their classrooms, and oftentimes in their communities, as authority figures who had truth.[18] Their task as teachers was to communicate that truth to their students. With the rise of postmodernism and the transformation of American culture, that vision of the classroom has changed.

---

15. One of his earliest and most important works was *Moral Man and Immoral Society: A Study in Ethics and Politics* (New York: Scribner's Sons, 1932). For more information, see Richard Harries, ed., *Reinhold Niebuhr and the Issues of Our Time* (London/Oxford: Mowbray, 1986); Kenneth Durkin, *Reinhold Niebuhr* (London: Chapman, 1989); and Richard W. Fox, *Reinhold Niebuhr: A Biography* (New York: Pantheon, 1985). After Niebuhr published *Does Civilization Need Religion?* (New York: Macmillan, 1927), some of his other works included *The Nature and Destiny of Man*, 2 vols. (New York: Scribner's Sons, 1941–1943), and *Children of Light and Children of Darkness: A Vindication of Democracy and a Critique of Its Traditional Defense* (New York: Scribner's Sons, 1944).

16. See Anthony Thiselton, *Interpreting God and the Postmodern Self: On Meaning, Manipulation, and Promise* (Grand Rapids: Eerdmans, 1995), 139.

17. Veith, *Postmodern Times*, 177–78. Business is set up with less hierarchy and more empowering of employees. There are now quality control groups; the medical profession has HMOs (ibid., 181–82). There is a distrust of some medical technology and a desire for alternative medicine. Chaos theory and string theory question an orderly universe. See Nancy R. Pearcey and Charles B. Thaxton, *The Soul of Science* (Wheaton, IL: Crossway, 1994). In architecture is the example of the Pompideau Center in Paris, which features the "guts" of the building on the outside, not hidden inside (Veith, *Postmodern Times*, 111–20).

18. See the movies *Dead Poets Society* and *The Emperor's Club*.

Non-Christian students now often think of their teachers as those who stand against them. Their teachers are viewed as powerful manipulators who use rhetoric, also known as their teaching, to control and manipulate the powerless students. The public school classroom has also changed. Instead of focusing on individual achievement, students now work in groups and receive group grades.[19] Sometimes there is no grade but simply an outcomes-based education. Postmodernism has influenced not only public school teachers in the great urban centers of America but even Sunday school teachers in the rural areas.[20] It should easily be granted that postmodernism has a great impact in contemporary culture.

Postmodernism has also influenced academic theology. Contemporary postmodern theologians argue that the biblical writers themselves held to a postmodern view of truth.[21] That is, the evangelical notion of the Bible as speaking timeless truth is supposedly derived from Greek philosophy and is not biblical.[22]

This section will introduce the names of some of the people connected to the movement and their lines of thought, as well as briefly answer some questions connected to postmodernism. For having learned something of the rise of postmodernism, its character, and its importance, we should now understand some of the players in the postmodern game.[23]

19. Veith, *Postmodern Times*, 183.

20. Anthony Thiselton, *Interpreting God*, 9: "If the challenge of postmodernism invites the transposition of issues of truth and argument into questions of power and rhetoric, this becomes a fundamental issue for theology."

21. For example, relative to the NT's having timeless truths, Anthony Thiselton (*The Two Horizons: New Testament Hermeneutics and Philosophical Description with Special Reference to Heidegger, Bultmann, Gadamer, and Wittgenstein* [1980; repr., Grand Rapids: Eerdmans, 1993], 95) asserts: "If this is what is meant by claiming that the Bible conveys 'timeless' truth, quite clearly this would not be the view of the biblical writers themselves. Such a view of truth can be described as theological only if Christianity is built on Platonist metaphysics"; and further (ibid., 97): "It is doubtful whether the word 'timeless' is being used in exactly the same way in each statement. However, it is the responsibility of those who appeal to the timeless nature of the NT truth as an argument against the necessity for hermeneutics to show both in what sense they use the term, and how this sense substantiates their argument. I am not aware of a carefully argued attempt to achieve this, let alone of one that is successful."

22. Ibid., 95–96.

23. An important figure not analyzed is Jürgen Habermas, whose works include *The Theory of Communicative Action*, Engl., 2 vols. (Cambridge: Polity Press, 1984); *The Philosophical Discourse of Modernity*, Engl. (New York: Polity Press, 1988); and *Die Zukunft der menschlichen Natur: Auf dem Weg zu einer liberalen Eugenik* , 5 Aufl. (Frankfurt: Suhrkamp

Postmodernism can be analyzed by grouping thinkers into schools. Gadamer and Ricœur, a German and a Frenchman, represent the first school of postmodernism. They are not actually a school, but they embody a less radical or milder form of postmodernism. The second school groups thinkers together simply for ease of presentation.

FIRST SCHOOL OF POSTMODERNISM

Hans-Georg Gadamer (A.D. 1900–2002).[24] While Gadamer is not classified as one of the two or three most important thinkers of the twentieth century, he is nevertheless highly important for hermeneutic theory, and he directly influenced the German theologians Wolfhart Pannenberg and Jürgen Moltmann.[25] Gadamer's doctoral dissertation was written at Marburg on the Greek philosopher Plato.[26] His studies in Marburg brought him into what is called the Marburg neo-Kantian school.[27] His *Habilitation* writing, or second dissertation, also focused on Plato and was done under the guidance of Martin Heidegger. Gadamer began teaching at Marburg, and was thus a student and colleague of Rudolf Bultmann, but also taught at Leipzig and Frankfurt before finishing his career in Heidelberg by succeeding the well-known Karl Jaspers from 1949 to 1968.[28] His best-known work is *Truth and Method*, published in 1960.

Verlag, 2001). See Richard J. Bernstein, ed., *Habermas and Modernity* (Cambridge: Polity Press, 1985).

24. See Jean Grondin, *Hans-Georg Gadamer: A Biography* (New Haven: Yale University Press, 2004). Gadamer's memoir is titled *Philosophical Apprenticeships* (Cambridge: MIT Press, 1985).

25. Thiselton, *Two Horizons*, 16: "For understanding to take place there must also occur what he calls a 'fusion of horizons.'"

26. He wrote it in 1922 at Marburg under the Plato scholar Paul Natorp (1854–1924), author of *Religion Innerhalb der Grenzen die Humanität* (Leipzig, 1894). He was a founder of neo-Kantianism. See Thiselton, *Two Horizons*, 208.

27. The neo-Kantian thinkers took Kant as their point of departure but wanted, still consistently with him, to move beyond him. They judged that Kant had not thought through all the implications of his own philosophy. The *object* or thing in itself is not simply a *given* but is formed by individual consciousness (Thiselton, *Two Horizons*, 208–10).

28. He lectured in Marburg through the early 1930s, in Leipzig in 1946, then in Frankfurt. Some of his other writings include: *The Idea of the Good in Platonic-Aristotelian Philosophy* (Cambridge: MIT Press, 1983); *Reason in the Age of Science*; *Philosophical Hermeneutics* (Berkeley: University of California Press, 1977); *Beginning of Knowledge*; *Beginning of Philosophy*; and *Hermeneutics, Religion and Ethics* (New Haven: Yale University Press, 2000); *Dialogue*

Gadamer's idea of truth was crafted in knowing opposition to Nietzsche's analysis. Gadamer saw Plato not as the beginner of the demise of Western civilization but just the opposite. For Gadamer, Plato's dialectic, or what we term the *Socratic method* of questioning, was the savior of truth. Thus according to Gadamer, truth both exists and is ascertainable. For him, conversation was the only method from which people can obtain this truth and even obtain self-consciousness.[29] Only through discussion is it possible for humans to take something to themselves as true. The result of his position is a necessity for Western thinkers to work in community. People can only understand themselves, and any text, when they understand it in dialogue or conversation with others.[30]

A second teaching concerned how truth is ascertained. On one side of the German academic curriculum was the humanities and on the other side the natural sciences. In the academic strife between the two fields, the humanities tried to model themselves on the natural sciences—a move that Gadamer considered to be a grave mistake.[31] Furthermore, the humanities as a discipline made another critical error. Following Wilhelm Dilthey's lead, the correct way to interpret a text, or to ascertain its meaning, was supposedly to recover the author's original intention. But the meaning of a text, according to Gadamer, is not what was in the original author's mind.[32] Thus truth and method were sometimes at odds with each other, and the resolution to that problem led to the title of his book.[33]

---

and Dialectic: Eight Hermeneutical Studies on Plato (New Haven: Yale University Press, 1983); *Praise of Theory: Speeches and Essays* (New Haven: Yale University Press, 1999).

29. See Stanley Obitts, "The Meaning and Use of Religious Language," in *Tensions in Contemporary Theology*, 2nd ed., ed. Stanley N. Gundry and Alan F. Johnson (Grand Rapids: Baker, 1976), 110.

30. Hans-Georg Gadamer, *Wahrheit und Methode: Grundzüge einer philosophische Herme-neutik* (Tübingen: Mohr Siebeck, 1960; 4th ed., 1975); ET, *Truth and Method* (New York: Sea-bury, 1975), 158: "Dialectic or conversation constitutes the only non-manipulative original mode of apprehending truth which does not predetermine what counts as true in advance." Richard Rorty (*From Modernism to Postmodernism: An Anthology*, ed. Lawrence E. Cahoone [Oxford: Blackwell, 1996], 581 says that Gadamer developed "a 'hermeneutic' theory of knowledge as interpretation, inspired by Heidegger's work." See also Thiselton, *Interpreting God*, 55, 70–71.

31. Thiselton, *Two Horizons*, 294.

32. Ibid., 20.

33. The perceived tension flows perhaps from his biography. His father was a chemist, and Gadamer wanted to go into the humanities.

Gadamer's work has expanded to how to interpret a text to embrace the nature of communication and the philosophy of language.[34] In his writings, Gadamer picked up the ball from Heidegger and proposed corrections that follow these lines.[35] The reader of a text has a historically effected consciousness. That is, the reader is placed in a particular time and culture which may be vastly different from the original author's. So when someone reads a text, there is a fusion of horizons between the text and the reader, for no matter how hard the diligent reader tries to understand the text from within the text's own historical era, he cannot escape his own era.[36] The reader makes a connection between the ancient text's history and his own history and background—and the result is the meaning of the text. The meaning of a text always goes beyond the original author. The reader truly comprehends the text when there occurs this fusion between the past, found in the text, and the present, the interpreter.[37]

Making these connections is called *hermeneutics*. Hermeneutics revolves around the reader's own experience—including his presuppositions concerning reality and his own traditions. Each reader has his or her own presuppositions.[38] The reader always comes to the ancient text with presuppositions—no one comes to an ancient text without them. There is no presupposition-free exegesis.[39] The reader must recognize the fact of his presuppositions and then be open to the influences of the ancient text.[40]

Gadamer's theory concerning the text and reader was not thought of as some type of new hermeneutic but simply a description of what is actually done, even if done unselfconsciously.[41] The notion that the

34. John M. Frame, *Systematic Theology: An Introduction to Christian Belief* (Phillipsburg, NJ: P&R Publishing, 2013), 659.

35. Thiselton, *Two Horizons*, 301.

36. Ibid., 306.

37. Ibid., 307.

38. Ibid., 442–43.

39. Ibid., 313.

40. Ibid., 304–5.

41. Gadamer, as cited in ibid., 28: "Fundamentally, I am not proposing a method, but I am describing what is the case (*ich beschreibe, was ist*). That it is as I describe it cannot, I think, be seriously questioned. . . . I consider the only scientific thing is to recognize what it is (*anzuerkennen, was ist*), instead of starting from what ought to be or could be." In opposition, clearly the meaning of a biblical text can go beyond the author's intent; take, for example, Noah's prophecy about his sons. See Richard C. Gamble, *The Whole Counsel of God*, vol. 1,

reader has a tradition is not a negative term for Gadamer.[42] There is not a clear antithesis between historical knowledge and tradition. The reader's presuppositions and traditions determine who he or she is.[43]

Also, with influence from Heidegger and Wittgenstein, for Gadamer the meaning of the text lay in its application, at least in the fields of law and theology.[44] Gadamer acknowledged that he was influenced by Heidegger but thought of his own project as more descriptive than speculative. He was not concerned with theoretical thought but with the ways by which truth is communicated.[45]

Gadamer could best illustrate his philosophy through the analysis of art, thought, and reality. Both language and the fine arts, such as music and drama, transcend a person's own conscious awareness. In language and art, it is what Gadamer called the *game* itself, not the person's reflections on the game, that determines the game's reality.[46] Music and drama consist in their performance, not when a musician reads the score or script privately. Furthermore, a performance on a given day transcends what has happened simply in the mind of the composer. As a musician plays a particular piece, the music produced is more than an interpretation of the composer's notes—it is an actual creative event in its own right.[47]

Encountering literature is not simply a matter of intellectual concepts but relates to experience. There is a difference between experience and cognitive concepts. Think of a parable, for example, which opens up a new world that can deeply affect the listener. The words of a Protestant sermon or the words and actions of a Catholic Mass can, he argued, newly open reality with each separate and repeated occurrence of them. The truth or being disclosed in the discourse is only possible when the hearer willingly enters into the world created by the words being spoken.[48]

God's Mighty Acts in the Old Testament (Phillipsburg, NJ: P&R Publishing, 2009) (*WCG1*), 301–3. But Gadamer says that it must go beyond the author's intent. Such a position leaves readers with nothing but existential subjectivism.

42. Thiselton, *Two Horizons*, 306.
43. Ibid., 305.
44. Ibid., 5, 308.
45. Ibid., 293.
46. Ibid., 297.
47. Ibid., 298.
48. Ibid., 298–99.

This experience relates to the visual arts as well. Gadamer believed that when people observe a magnificent piece of artwork, they enter that work's world and experience, which become their own world and experience. This analysis has moved aesthetic theory way beyond the old Cartesian perspective, which judges that the person as active subject simply scrutinizes those passive objects of art. Gadamer was convinced that his philosophical theory moved thinkers from the emptiness of subjectivized aesthetics.[49]

To understand something requires the use of language. It is through language that a person understands an object, and it is through language that this person explains the object. The words used will remain the person's own words. When an interpreter describes something, he must necessarily use his own concepts. He cannot put aside his own manner of thinking and completely adopt the ways of thinking embedded in the ancient text. The interpreter cannot understand what he is describing unless he puts what he understands into his own words and concepts.[50]

Gadamer criticized past thinkers such as Hegel as he moved toward creating his own vision of the nature of truth itself. Hermeneutics, thought Gadamer, is more than a pedantic theory of reading but relates to a metaphysical theory of truth itself. Understanding the truth requires comprehending the general relationship of humanity to the world. That relationship is a dialectical one by which the subject speaks only in his own language. Thus the Kantian thing in itself can come into being only through language.[51] Moving to art and truth, Gadamer offered a fundamental critique of how they had been comprehended in the past. If truth is simply a property of concepts, as it was in the old Kantian way of thinking, then what does one do with the visual arts?[52] He was convinced that there needs to be a different way of understanding truth.

In conclusion, Gadamer underlined what he termed the "importance of the question." As a reader approaches a text, he has certain questions that he wants or expects the text to answer. But that reader's comprehension of the text is bound by the questions that he has concerning

49. Ibid., 299.
50. Ibid., 310.
51. Ibid., 313.
52. Ibid., 296: "The objective does not become, as in knowing, an image and an idea, but an element in the life process itself."

the text. Contemporary readers, however, will never have exactly the same questions that the original author had. So understanding any text will always be a creative process, never a simple reproduction.[53] While Gadamer has brilliant insights into hermeneutical theory, his analysis would apply only to human documents, not the divinely preserved Word of God. Let us move now to the second thinker in this school of postmodernism.

Paul Ricœur (A.D. 1913–2005).[54] Ricœur is particularly important to evangelical readers because he is known as a Christian philosopher.[55] He was a Protestant but had a friendly relationship with the pope. He was orphaned, trained in France, and happily married in 1935. Drafted by the French army during World War II, he was almost immediately captured and spent five years as a prisoner of war in Germany. Ricœur taught philosophy for about ten years at Strasbourg, then took a chair at Paris in 1957.

In 1960 Ricœur's *Symbolism of Evil* initiated his writings on hermeneutics. His thesis was that men and women are not so much the creators of symbols as their creatures. Philosophy's very limited task is to discern the symbols' multiple meanings—not really intending to gain knowledge but simply to think of the world in the light of the depth of human ignorance. Ricœur's popularity in the United States began around 1970, when he began teaching at the University of Chicago as well as at Paris. By that time he had already published quite a number of volumes in French.[56]

Although a hermeneutical theory called *structuralism* was very popular in France at the time, Ricœur was not a structuralist.[57] Of his

53. Ibid., 309.

54. Some of Paul Ricœur's other writings include *Fallible Man*, trans. Charles Kelbley (Chicago: Henry Regnery, 1965); and *Hermeneutics and the Human Sciences* (Cambridge: Cambridge University Press, 1981). At least twelve volumes of analysis were written on Ricœur in English during the thirty-year period between 1971 and 2001.

55. The title of an obituary in Britain's *The Guardian* (May 23, 2005) reads: "Paul Ricœur: Radical Christian Philosopher Struggling with the Dilemmas of Existence."

56. Some of those works include: *Freedom and Nature*, ET 1966; *Husserl*, ET 1966; *The Symbolism of Evil* (1960), ET 1967; *Freud and Philosophy* (1965), ET 1970; *Tragic Wisdom and Beyond*, ET 1973; and *The Conflict of Interpretations: Essays in Hermeneutics* (Evanston, IL: Northwestern University Press, 1974), ET 1976.

57. Structuralism developed particularly in France beginning with the Swiss Ferdinand de Saussure (1857–1913) on linguistics. He noted that different languages use different words to refer to the same concept. Thus the relationship between a signifier and its concept is arbitrary.

more than twenty books, his most widely read, in chronological order of their publication, are: *The Rule of Metaphor*,[58] *Time and Narrative*,[59] *From Text to Action*,[60] and *Oneself as Another*.[61] His last-published major work is *Memory, History and Forgetting*, which came out in French in 2000 and in English four years later.

Moving to his thought, we can see that Ricœur judged the study of the self or human subjectivity as important. He argued that the self is spatially and historically locatable. Thus his work is sometimes called *philosophical anthropology*. He desired to replace the notion of the ego as master of itself with the self as being a disciple of the text. Ricœur said that the self is "a narrative text that embodies a narrative plot."[62] By that phrase he meant that each person is situated in a specific physical, historical, and social world. Also, there is no meta-physical entity that can be called the *self*, but only *selfhood*. Selfhood for Ricœur is neither purely abstract nor an animal self-awareness.[63]

Ricœur moved to the important issue of self-knowledge. He made it clear that he stood against the French philosopher Descartes's modern notion of *cogito ergo sum* as foundational to self-knowledge.[64] In an earlier chapter we learned that Descartes asked the question, "What does the human being really know?"[65] Descartes asserted that a person,

---

Claude Lévi-Strauss (1908–2009) worked in structuralist anthropology and determined that there is no human freedom because behavior is determined by various structures. Ricœur considered structuralism philosophically dogmatic. He criticized the structuralists in a kind way. As an aside, apparently Ricœur was a candidate for a chair at the Collège de France but lost the position to Michel Foucault in the 1960s.

58. Paul Ricœur, *The Rule of Metaphor* (1975; ET, London: Routledge/Kegan Paul, 1978).

59. Paul Ricœur, *Time and Narrative*, 3 vols. (1983–1985; ET, Chicago: University of Chicago Press, 1984–1988).

60. Paul Ricœur, *From Text to Action* (Evanston, IL: Northwestern University Press, 1991).

61. *Oneself as Another* comprises the Gifford Lectures of 1986.

62. Paul Ricœur, *Oneself as Another* (Chicago: University of Chicago Press, 1992), 23–25. Ricœur is not always recognized as a postmodern by many postmoderns. He is not very antagonistic to Christianity, and he talks about personal agency and even future accountability. See Thiselton, *Interpreting God*, 60.

63. See Ricœur, *Oneself as Another*, 34–35.

64. Ricœur's early research was on Sigmund Freud, and Ricœur found that he and Freud had some similar interests. They both struggled with the notions of *desire* and *language*. See Paul Ricœur, *Freud and Philosophy: An Essay on Interpretation* (New Haven: Yale University Press, 1970), 5; and Thiselton, *Interpreting God*, 68.

65. Descartes's answer was that people can only know what the human mind fully understands. The human mind is presented with many objects of ideas. These objects of ideas are interrelated. The objects of ideas must therefore be separated and analyzed individually to be truly understood. He found the beginning of knowledge to be in questioning or doubting; from

from knowing that he exists, can use reason to deduce everything, thus giving him supposed epistemological certainty of undoubted first principles. For Descartes, self-consciousness was the key.

But three important theorists about modern humanity—Sigmund Freud, Friedrich Nietzsche, and Karl Marx—all opposed the notion of self-consciousness. They doubted their self-consciousness and found victory over that dark doubt via an exegesis of meaning. According to Ricœur, for the first time philosophers realized that human self-comprehension is hermeneutics.[66] Thus Ricœur thought that Descartes actually got the nature of self-knowledge backwards. In contrast to Descartes, a person does not know of his personal existence via solitary thinking but rather by being in relationship or community. Thus for self-understanding, the self needs to be in relationship. This being in relationship as foundational for self-understanding relates to Ricœur's view of the self as embodied subjectivity.

Presupposed in his idea of embodied subjectivity is that selfhood has a double nature. There are both voluntary and involuntary parts to the self. For example, sometimes our bodies are in a state that forces involuntary actions upon us, such as when we are sick; but the self can also experience, even in those moments, voluntary freedom of the will. By *embodied subjectivity*, Ricœur means that the human self is found in a body. The self is inseparable from the self's body, thus the technical term *embodied subjectivity*. Such embodied subjectivity may at times even force the self to be an other to itself.[67] At times, thinking human beings have deep inner tension. A person becomes who he is through relationship with the other—either one's own body or another's body.[68] In conclusion, human subjectivity is always in the human body and the material world.

From this background information it seems apparent that Ricœur's philosophical method flowed out of his own biography and view of

---

there, he thought, a solid epistemological foundation could be built. That foundation was that *cogito ergo sum*. Descartes, therefore, had one supposedly certain principle that could not be doubted: *cogito ergo sum*. The implication from the process is that reason is the basis for all knowledge, and whether something is reasonable became the critical measure for everything.

66. Thiselton, *Two Horizons*, 113–14.

67. Ricoueur acknowledged that this thought was seen earlier in the existentialist Gabriel Marcel's *Being and Having: An Existentialist Diary* (New York: Harper & Row, 1965).

68. For more information on the self and one's own body see Ricœur, *Oneself as Another*, 319–29.

selfhood. His life was one of tensions and ambiguities, beginning with the stresses he experienced as a prisoner of war in Nazi Germany. His body was captured and chained, but his mind was very free. That inescapable reality produced deep tensions. He extrapolated from his experience that all lives are in tension and that tension is basic to and inherent in life itself.

Since all lives are in tension, humans view themselves from different theoretical approaches, frameworks, and angles in their attempt to understand themselves and to have a unified view of selfhood. It was from the self that Ricœur extrapolated to other philosophical disciplines. For him, the different theoretical frameworks implemented within diverse academic subjects, such as those of philosophy and science, existed as a fruit of the inherent anxieties of life, not necessarily because of philosophical ignorance or from plays for power.[69] Thus Ricœur's philosophical method intentionally weaved together diverse concepts—an approach that reflected his view of the vast pressures of life as the self struggles to hold all the diverse parts together.[70]

Those tensions, which produced different theoretical frameworks, were called *fault lines*. Those fault lines give meaning to the various states of our lives. Sometimes our lives are stable, and frankly, sometimes they are not. Stability is based on a host of tensions—from within our own bodies in sickness, from others, and from external powers and institutions.

Ricœur offers epistemological certainty from what he calls his *narrative theory*—a path to a unified, meaningful life. Since life has inherent tensions, one can hold it together via poetics, which he called *exemplified narrative*, by means of structures, called *synthetic strategies*. Doing so can supposedly bring a coherent sense of both human selfhood and life.

In his next-to-last work, Ricœur continued to wrestle with the nature of the self who is in history.[71] Part of each self includes that

69. In other words, they reflect reality as it is, not as a foreign influence.
70. In *From Text to Action*'s chapter titled "Explanation and Understanding," Ricœur sees the tensions in human behavior as between the concepts of material causation and the language of action and motive. In *What Makes Us Think* (Princeton/Oxford: Princeton University Press, 2000), he sees a person's mental life as a tension between neurobiological conceptions of mind and phenomenological concepts.
71. He had already written *History and Truth* (Evanston, IL: Northwestern University Press, 1965), as well as *Time and Narrative*.

self's—that person's—memories.[72] An important question for the post-modern thinker is whether memory is primordially personal or collective; the academic consensus is that it is collective.[73]

Ricœur then moved from the anthropology of memory to fundamental issues, such as the nature of historical knowing, and suggested that there is a tension between memory and history.[74] History intends to explain something, to answer the question, Why? The answer to the question is, Because. Historians attempt to correlate the temporal dimensions of social action, to give a because and usually provide interpretation at three levels of historical discourse: documentary, explanation/understanding, and literary representation of the past.[75] It is in the notion of representation, the necessary split between privileged object of explanation and the historiographical operation, that will remain in confrontation.[76] Through the entire process of historiographical operation there is interpretation.[77] Thus Ricœur wants to move the discussion from the earlier impasse of the notion of history as narrative to what he terms *critical hermeneutics* and *ontological hermeneutics*.[78] He is convinced that there is a quality-of-life issue for individuals, peoples, and cultures concerning the need for history or for viewing human existence as historical.[79] There are traces of the

72. Ricœur first took his readers back in time to analyze the Greek philosophical thinking of Plato and Aristotle. See Paul Ricœur, *Memory, History, Forgetting*, trans. Kathleen Blamey and David Pellauer (Chicago: University of Chicago Press, 2004), 6–57.

73. Ibid., 95: "For sociology at the turn of the twentieth century, collective consciousness is thus one of those realities whose ontological status is not in question. . . . Individual memory and collective memory are placed in a position of rivalry. . . . The task of philosophy concerned with understanding how historiography articulates its discourse in terms of that of the phenomenology of memory is, first, to discern the reason for this radical misunderstanding through an examination of the internal functioning of the discourses proffered on either side."

74. Ibid., 126–44, 145: "The suspicion would have to be exorcised that history remains a hindrance to memory, just like the *pharmakon* of the myth, where in the end we do not know whether it is a remedy or a poison, or both at once. We shall have to allow this unavoidable suspicion to express itself again more than one time."

75. Ibid., 182: "To explain, generally speaking, is to answer the question 'Why?' through a variety of uses of the connector 'because.'"

76. Ibid., 182–88.

77. Ibid., 200–35.

78. Ibid., 284: "The insurmountable historical condition of that being . . . [is] the necessity of the twofold passage from historical knowledge to critical hermeneutics and from the latter to ontological hermeneutics. . . . Up to the end, the presumed connection will remain a working hypothesis."

79. Ibid., 290.

past that are lost, that are beyond memory, and there are traces of the past that are intentionally forgotten through censorship or for other reasons. Ricœur concludes with an incomplete epilogue on the guilt of historical forgetting and the possibility of forgiveness for that guilt.

In conclusion, although Gadamer and Ricœur did not work together, their writings can be combined for analysis. For both men, hermeneutical questions were foundational for truth. Hermeneutical questions, they thought, protect the truth. "Language is the universal medium in which understanding itself occurs," said Gadamer.[80] Gadamer and Ricœur saw hermeneutics as an encounter with Being through language.[81]

But some postmoderns disagree with Gadamer and Ricœur on the nature of human subjectivity—they view it as nothing more than an effect of language, and they have a much more narrow view of selfhood than does Ricœur in particular. For Ricœur, language was a kind of second-order articulation; for the following thinkers, it is primary.[82] They represent a second school of postmodernism.[83]

SECOND SCHOOL OF POSTMODERNISM

Michel Foucault (A.D. 1926–1984), the first member of this school, is also a Frenchman. His father was a surgeon. He studied philosophy with Maurice Merleau-Ponty (1908–1961) in Paris and received degrees in philosophy and psychology.[84] He taught French language

80. Gadamer, *Wahrheit und Methode*, 366.

81. Obitts, "Religious Language," 110; Thiselton, *Interpreting God*, 41.

82. Ricœur, for example, is not found in Richard Rorty's *Philosophy and the Mirror of Nature* index.

83. Jean-Francois Lyotard (1926–1998) should also be included in this group. Lyotard is considered by many as the one who has defined postmodernism. His conclusion is that the old modern notions of philosophical justification, of system, of proofs, and of the unity of science no longer hold. Lyotard has written *The Postmodern Condition: A Report on Knowledge* (Minneapolis: University of Minnesota Press, 1984); and *Toward the Postmodern*, ed. Robert Harvey and Mark S. Roberts (*Atlantic Highlands*, NJ/London: Humanities Press International, 1993). Lawrence E. Cahoone, ed., *From Modernism to Postmodernism: An Anthology* (Oxford: Blackwell, 1996), 481–83, contains excerpts from *The Postmodern Condition*.

84. Other works by Foucault include: *Adventures of the Dialectic*, trans. Joseph Bien (Evanston, IL: Northwestern University Press, 1973); *The Essential Writings of Merleau-Ponty*, ed. Alden L. Fisher (New York: Harcourt, Brace, & World, 1969); *Humanism and Terror: An Essay on the Communist Problem*, trans. John O'Neill (Boston: Beacon, 1969); *Phenomenol-*

in Sweden and returned to France in 1960 to teach philosophy. In the same year, he published *Madness and Civilization* and met his lover Daniel Defert.[85] Six years later he produced *The Order of Things*. In that book, Foucault studied the areas of economics, sociology, politics, linguistics, and history. In 1975 he published *Discipline and Punishment: The Origin of the Prison*, which is considered his most influential book. The first volume of his *History of Sexuality* saw the light of day in 1976, followed by the second and third volumes right before his death in 1984.

Foucault's view of the nature of truth is very different from that of an evangelical. There is no truth if by the word *truth* one means true things in contrast to false things. There are only games of truth that are the rules according to which a subject may say certain things that depend on the question of true and false. Truth and falsehood are simply the "forms according to which discourses capable of being declared true or false are articulated concerning a domain of things."[86]

Also, the notions of *truth* and *humanity* are related. The most important question is how the subject, the human self, interprets himself or becomes an object of knowledge. Here is the history of subjectivity, and the issue is the way in which the subject experiences himself in the so-called "game of truth," in which he somehow relates to himself.

Of primary importance in Foucault's philosophical method was a systematic skepticism toward all anthropological universals, such as Descartes's notion of *cogito ergo sum*. He rejected universals, such as *madness* and *delinquency*, as well as *sexuality*. He said that there are no universals; rather, there are what he considered to be historical constructs. In his thinking there can be no universal that is not

---

ogy of Perception, trans. Colin Smith (London: Routledge/Kegan Paul, 1962); *The Primacy of Perception, and Other Essays on Phenomenology, Psychology, the Philosophy of Art, History and Politics*, ed. James M. Edie (Evanston, IL: Northwestern University Press, 1964); *Prose of the World*, trans. John O'Neill (Evanston, IL: Northwestern University Press, 1969); *Sense and Nonsense*, trans. H. L. Dreyfus and P. A. Dreyfus (Evanston, IL: Northwestern University Press, 1964); *Signs*, trans. Richard C. McCleary (Evanston, IL: Northwestern University Press, 1964); *The Structure of Behaviour*, trans. Alden L. Fischer (London: Methuen, 1965); and *The Visible and the Invisible*, trans. Alphonso Lingis (Evanston, IL: Northwestern University Press, 1968).

85. In *Madness and Civilization*, he claims that the differences between sanity and madness are mere inventions of the age of reason.

86. "Foucault," *Dictionnaire des philosophes*, ed. Denis Huisman (Paris: Presses Universitaires de France, 1984), 942–44.

anthropological. A secondary emphasis of Foucault's was that the thinking subject is constituted within a domain of concrete practices; thus there is interaction between subject and object. Neither the thinking subject nor the object exists in itself. The two constantly modify each other. A third emphasis was analyzing the way things were done or managed in the past to elicit what people thought about the reality of what they were handling.

In conclusion, Foucault addressed truth, power, and humanity. Agreeing with Friedrich Nietzsche, Foucault held that the most important issue of life is power. He asserted that truth is not outside power or lacking in power. Truth is a thing of this world: it is produced only by virtue of multiple forms of constraint.[87] In his studies of madness, criminality, and sexuality, he determined that something external to the subject acted to shape, direct, and modify the subject. This method is also how people are governed.[88] Thus the concept of *liberty* is simply an invention of the controlling ruling class.[89] Sadly, at the end of *The Order of Things*, Foucault predicted that man is nearing his end. He said that man "would be erased, like a face drawn in the sand at the edge of the sea."[90] Nietzsche was certain that God is dead. Foucault is equally certain that man is dead.

Jacques Derrida (A.D. 1930–2004). Born of Jewish parents in Algeria, Jacques Derrida studied at Paris, then taught there from 1965 to 1984 and was also a professor at the University of California, Irvine. In 1967 he became well known in the United States when he gave special lectures at Johns Hopkins University. Derrida was a brilliant scholar with honorary doctorates from multiple preeminent universities. His academic work began with analysis of the German philosopher Edmund Husserl (1859–1938), who founded what is called *phenomenology*.[91]

87. Michel Foucault, "Truth and Power," reprinted in Cahoone, *From Modernism to Postmodernism*, 379–81.

88. Frances Bridget Eleanor Healy, "Foucault's Ethic of Power" (PhD diss., University of Tasmania, 2013), https://eprints.utas.edu.au/17510/1/Whole-Healy-_thesis.pdf downloaded 8/12/2020, 52.

89. Cited by Veith, *Postmodern Times*, 77.

90. Michel Foucault, *The Order of Things: An Archaeology of the Human Sciences* (New York: Pantheon Books, 1971), 422.

91. Phenomenology is a reaction against the antihuman scientific naturalism of his times. Husserl in turn influenced Heidegger. See Husserl's *The Crisis of European Sciences and Transcendental Phenomenology* (Evanston, IL: Northwestern University Press, 1970).

Derrida called attention to problems implicit in Husserl's fundamental distinctions. The problems relate to the written word.

Derrida addressed questions of the nature of meaning and language. In his work titled *Of Grammatology*, he asserted that much of philosophy is the attempt to grasp the origin of meaning.[92] But he claimed that the meaning of the written word is ungraspable![93] He was convinced that the spoken word is better than the written word. The spoken word connects each hearer to the human speaker, whereas the written word is marked by mediation and uncertainty of meaning.[94]

Ricœur, Foucault, and Derrida are all united in that they opposed structuralism and are considered philosophical post-structuralists. While still adopting some of the presuppositions of structuralism, Derrida reacted against it by proposing an alternative called *deconstruction*. He assumed that the meaning of the relationship between signs, or words, emanates from the contrast between the signs, not from a given word's being an unmediated expression of something nonlinguistic.[95] Thus the meaning of a sign is found in relationship to other signs. A concept is comprehended in the context of its opposite. Among these opposites there is a powerful hierarchy. Deconstruction first detects these oppositions within a text. There is, according to Derrida, an arbitrary violence intrinsic to all texts.[96] He is not satisfied, however, with simply marking the oppositions in a work. The goal is certainly not smoothing out the oppositions—which is never possible to achieve; rather, thinkers are to create new terms that are necessary for analysis.[97] Thus for Derrida, language does not reveal meaning but instead constructs meaning. For deconstructionists,

92. Judith Butler, introduction to Jacques Derrida, *Of Grammatology* (Baltimore: Johns Hopkins University Press, 1974), xlii–lxxiv.

93. Ibid., 292: "The morrow of the festival inevitably resembles the eve of the festival and the point of the dance is only the ungraspable limit of their difference."

94. Ibid., 11, 33, 71, 184.

95. This idea stands in contrast to nearly all earlier philosophical thinking, which assumed that a word expresses some type of concrete, nondeferred meaning.

96. Ibid., 40: "Deconstructing this tradition will therefore not consist of reversing it, of making writing innocent. Rather of showing why the violence of writing does not *befall* an innocent language"; and 115: it is not "that digression about the violence that does not supervene from without upon an innocent language in order to surprise it, a language that suffers the aggression of writing as the accident of its disease, its defeat and its fall; but the ordinary violence of a language which is always already a writing."

97. Ibid., xvi, xxxiv.

meaning is a social construct. This type of thinking is a massively complex relativism.

Richard Rorty (A.D. 1931–2007).[98] Born in New York City, Rorty graduated from the University of Chicago at age eighteen and obtained his doctorate from Yale by the age of twenty-five. He first taught at Princeton, then moved to the University of Virginia until his retirement. After retirement, he taught at Stanford University.[99] By the year 2000, he had received five honorary doctorates. Between 1990 and 2002 there were ten full books written on Rorty. His thought is a massive challenge to modernity, and even though Christianity itself has issues with some of the presuppositions of modernity, Rorty's thinking fully intends also to destroy Christianity.

Rorty's purpose is to attack the very foundation of modern philosophical thinking.[100] Specifically, he denies the traditional philosophical pursuit of some type of ultimate, transcendent, foundational knowledge as either a valid or a desirable enterprise.[101] This section will focus on his 1979 *Philosophy and the Mirror of Nature*, which presented a very deep critique of modern Western philosophy.

His attack begins with the modern notion of epistemology and truth—both of which he intends to question and destroy. For him, epistemology, or how a person knows, is not the essence of philosophy.[102]

98. Two of Richard Rorty's works are *Consequences of Pragmatism: Essays 1972–1980* (Minneapolis: University of Minnesota Press, 1982) and *Contingency, Irony, and Solidarity* (New York: Cambridge University Press, 1989).

99. He was at Wellesley College (1958–1961); professor of philosophy at Princeton University (1961–1982); University Professor of the Humanities, University of Virginia (1982–1998); and professor of comparative literature, Stanford University (1998–2007).

100. Richard Rorty, *Philosophy and the Mirror of Nature* (1979; repr., Princeton: Princeton University Press, 1980), 7: "The aim . . . is to undermine the reader's confidence in 'the mind' as something about which one should have a 'philosophical' view, in knowledge as something about which there ought to be a theory and which has foundation and in philosophy as it has been conceived since Kant." He hopes that philosophers will no longer take seriously the notion that they provide foundations or justifications for the rest of culture or that they provide the (Kantian) *quaestiones juris* about other domains. The "philosopher's moral concern should be with continuing the conversation of the West, rather than with insisting upon a place for the traditional problems of modern philosophy within that conversation" (ibid., 394).

101. Richard Rorty, "Solidarity or Objectivity?," in *Objectivity, Relativism and Truth*, by Richard Rorty (Cambridge: Cambridge University Press, 1991), 21–34, reprinted in Cahoone, *From Modernism to Postmodernism*, 573–86.

102. Rorty, *Philosophy and the Mirror*, 392: that epistemology is at philosophy's center "is a reflection of the fact that the professional philosopher's self image depends upon his professional preoccupation with the image of the Mirror of Nature. Without the Kantian assumption

He deeply disparages the modern notion of epistemology and argues that it is simply a desire for constraint, something sadly to cling to.[103] He focused on whether people can make a real claim of knowledge at all and whether classical philosophical reflection itself is even possible. Modern notions of truth are meant to touch on the nature of reality—for example, to say that the present weather in Pittsburgh is beautiful on this August afternoon connects with reality. But truth for Rorty has nothing to do with connecting to reality. Truth is simply what is best for us to believe at the moment.[104]

Rorty terms the modern, wrong way of thinking *representationalist epistemology*, and the wrong philosophy is called *neo-Kantianism*.[105] The antiquated representationalist epistemology, according to which a mind supposedly works from empirical content to produce notions such as thoughts or representations that may mirror reality, must be rejected.

The philosophical background to Rorty's thinking is located in the philosophies of Dewey, Heidegger, and Wittgenstein, who helped Rorty see the bankruptcy of post-Kantian modern thought.[106] In its place, he

that the philosopher can decide *questiones juris* concerning the claims of the rest of culture, this self-image collapses." Rorty rejects the assumption that there is "understanding the essence of knowledge." He rejects "the philosopher as knowing something about knowing which nobody else knows so well."

103. Ibid., 315: "The demise of foundational epistemology is often felt to leave a vacuum which needs to be filled."

104. Ibid., 10: "'Accurate representation' is simply an automatic and empty compliment which we pay to those beliefs which are successful in helping us do what we want to do." Rorty's thinking is a terrible horizontalization of ethics. For example the Nazi or White racist would claim that it is best to believe that Jews and Blacks are subhuman, though we know that belief to be undeniably false.

105. Ibid., 168: Philosophical problems are nothing "other than transient tensions in the dynamics of evolving, contingent vocabularies"; further, 3: "we owe the notion of a 'theory of knowledge' based on an understanding of 'mental processes' to the seventeenth century, and especially to Locke"; and 4: "Nineteenth century neo-Kantians viewed philosophy as a foundational discipline which grounds knowledge-claims." Philosophy became a substitute for religion for the intellectuals. Problems arose at the beginning of the twentieth century with the rise of the men of letters who exercised leadership and challenged the philosophers for intellectual leadership; 134–35: The neo-Kantians had epistemology and metaphysics as the center of philosophy. From them came the terms *Erkenntnislehre* and *Erkenntnistheorie*; 149: Neo-Kantians conceive distinctly philosophical thought as "the relation between universals and particulars"; 393: the neo-Kantians see philosophy as a profession involved with the mind or language mirroring nature. Perhaps we are at an end of an era.

106. Ibid., 6: They said that knowledge as an accurate representation made possible by special mental processes and intelligible through a general theory of representation needs to be abandoned. Epistemology and metaphysics must be abandoned as disciplines. Post-Kantian culture sets aside any discipline that claims to legitimate or ground the others; and 166: they

proposes what some have called the "social justification of belief," or "pragmatic theory." Rorty's view of knowledge has sometimes been termed "epistemological behaviorism" or the "conversationalist view of truth and knowledge."[107] In this new way of thinking, knowledge is the social justification of belief or conversation and social practice, and questions as to whether those thoughts represent reality are actually unimportant.[108] Philosophy's task is to continue what he terms the *conversation of culture.*[109] His new way is to consider contemporary philosophical issues as events in a stage of conversation.[110]

His next project was to expand the pragmatic theory of truth.[111] The pragmatic theory stands against the Platonic tradition, which in his opinion has simply outlived its usefulness. Pragmatists are saying that the best hope for philosophy is not to practice philosophy. Rorty divided the history of philosophy into two schools. The one, called *transcendental philosophy*, was initiated by Plato and is supposedly otherworldly. It asserts that humans have respect because they have one foot beyond space and time. This school thinks that natural science is not the last word and that there is more truth to be found. Rorty's other school is *empirical philosophy*. For these thinkers, space and time make up the only reality, and truth is correspondence to that reality. They see facts, especially those of natural science, as the sum total of truth. But this group is still doing philosophy. They separate truth into a lower and an upper story, or opinion and genuine knowledge; for example, "It rained yesterday" is from the lower story, while "Men should be just in their dealings" is from the upper story. Those two

"were provoked to radical criticisms of 'truth as correspondence' and 'knowledge as accuracy of representation' thus threatening the entire Kantian notion of philosophy as metacriticism of the special disciplines."

107. Ibid., 176: "The idea of truth as objective must be abandoned with the demise of modernism, which is regarded as the misguided attempt of the Enlightenment to attain objective certitude on matters of philosophical, scientific and moral concern." See Stephen Louthan, "On Religion: A Discussion with Richard Rorty, Alvin Plantinga and Nicholas Wolterstorff," *Christian Scholars Review* 26, no. 2 (1996): 177–83, and Groothuis, *Truth Decay*, 20.

108. Rorty, *Philosophy and the Mirror*, 170–71.

109. Rorty, "Solidarity or Objectivity?," 21–34, reprinted in Cahoone, *From Modernism to Postmodernism*, 573–75.

110. Rorty, *Philosophy and the Mirror*, 391: the conversation is one "which once knew nothing of these issues and may know nothing of them again." In agreement with Foucault, he sees philosophical questions simply as the "results of historical accidents."

111. See Rorty's introduction to *Consequences of Pragmatism*.

schools fought it out in the nineteenth century. But the problem with both philosophical schools was that they actually had the same basic presupposition, namely, that truth exists.

Then the positivist philosophers came along, from Hobbes to Carnap. They said that the lower-story sentence "It rained yesterday" was the paradigm of what truth looked like. The higher-story sentence was perhaps an expression of emotion. So what the transcendental philosophers saw as the spiritual, the empirical philosophers saw as the emotional. The empirical philosophers saw natural science as discovering the nature of reality, while the transcendental philosophers saw such discovery as irrelevant to truth. Pragmatic theory fundamentally questions both schools' common presupposition that there is a distinction between kinds of truth. The issue of a true sentence for pragmatist theory is not correspondence with reality.[112]

The anti-Platonists have insisted on the ubiquity of language. But more recent philosophy has tried to get behind language to something that may ground it. The reason they have insisted on the ubiquity of language is because all other natural starting points, such as sensory data or clear innate ideas, have failed.[113] While Rorty believed that the best philosophy is the end of philosophy, he did actually make positive suggestions.

Rorty suggested a postmodern type of false religion. He called it *spiritual development*,[114] and he connected it to the sense of exaltation that one gets by reading certain novels—for him, those written by Proust and James.[115] He compared that sense of exaltation to what a

112. Ibid., 4–6.

113. Ibid., 8, 96–100.

114. Richard Rorty, "Redemption from Egotism: James and Proust as Spiritual Exercises," *Telos* 3, no. 3 (2001): 243–63: "The term 'spiritual development' is usually used only in reference to the attempt to get in touch with the divine. But it is occasionally used in a broader sense, one in which it covers any attempt to transform oneself into a better sort of person by changing one's sense of what matters most. In this broader sense of the term, I would urge that the novels of Proust and James help us achieve spiritual growth, and thereby help many of us do what devotional reading helped our ancestors to do."

115. Ibid.: "Using the term 'spiritual' in this sense has the advantage of avoiding both 'aesthetic' and 'moral' when explaining why Proust and James seem so important to so many. The question of whether these men's novels are 'beautiful' does not strike members of their cults as having much point. But to say that the novels are morally rather than, or as well as, aesthetically important seems to leave something out. What it leaves out, I have suggested, is the sense of exaltation that readers of these novels share with religious people who come away from reading devotional literature with a sense of having visited a better world."

religious person gets from reading devotional literature. It is as though he had visited a better world. But what he is looking for is not to be found in a beautiful literary couplet or a parallel antithetical argument, rather, in the whole of the literary piece. Rorty actually compares this sense of exaltation to following the entire journey of the character Christian in Bunyan's *Pilgrim's Progress*. By following those stories, the reader supposedly obtains hope that he, too, might overcome the confusion and incoherence of his life.[116] In contrast to the religious person, who seeks union with God and another world, the seeker for spiritual development hopes that someday he will see his life in this world as a work of art or as having some sort of pattern. Sadly, for Rorty the hope is futile.

One main reason for his position is his denial of the philosophical notion of objectivity relative to spheres of analysis.[117] Denying objectivity is part of his overall metaphilosophical critique. With bitterness he says, "so-called [philosophical] methods are simply descriptions of the activities engaged in by the enthusiastic imitators of one or another original mind."[118]

Conclusion. In conclusion, the first school of postmodernism affirms that truth exists, but it is only found in community. Hermeneutical questions, therefore, are all that these thinkers have. The second postmodern school says that there simply is no truth—or if there is truth, it can only come by means of personal manipulation.

FRUIT OF POSTMODERNISM

While the battles rage in the ivory towers of academia, the movement of postmodernism is not relegated to them. So far, we have particularly observed postmodernism's impact on the nature of truth, language, belief, and the self. It would be good to examine more deeply how postmodernism has influenced how people view themselves.

116. Ibid.: "Following such careers lifts up the heart by letting the reader hope that she herself might eventually overcome the immaturity, the confusion, and the incoherence of her days."

117. Rorty, "Solidarity or Objectivity?," 21–34, reprinted in Cahoone, *From Modernism to Postmodernism*, 573–86.

118. Richard Rorty, *Truth and Progress*, Philosophical Papers 3 (Cambridge: Cambridge University Press, 1998), 10.

The postmodern person sees him- or herself as only a product.[119] What he does, he does not as a self-actuated person but only as a small ship floating on a large ocean. The postmodern self is decentered. He is not an active agent. Roles are forced on him by society and by his own inner drives. He is not a moral agent but a decentered product of social and psycholinguistic forces.[120] He suffers loss, which manifests itself in accusation and conflict. The loss is blamed on the manipulative power-interests of competing groups.[121] This problem of the self in America is vividly manifested in high school shootings and the recent massive riots relative to racial tensions. Unfortunately, because of postmodernism's devaluation of rational or reasonable dialogue into rhetoric, it has brought, and will continue to bring, destruction.[122] The postmodern person has lost confidence in civil justice, and that loss escalates to crime against the society. "It's them against me," he complains. Often, the postmodern person succumbs to despair. There is another interesting twist concerning the nature of the self or person.

Moving away from the United States, Germany as a nation and culture through the modern era defined itself as an organized, punctual people. Their trains ran on time, and German automobiles, clocks, and scientific equipment have been highly valued for decades. Postmodernism is now affecting how Germans view themselves. The German author Martin S. Lambeck has written about the relationship between human freedom and European culture. While modern German culture had defined itself by its excellent work habits, that old view has come into serious critique. With cultural values now considered relative and flexible, German intellectual and political leaders are questioning why quality work is in any sense a better definition for a people and society than is more abundant free time for recreation. As a postmodern, Lambeck argues that it is not right for Germans to define themselves by their work; rather, they should define the self through the availability of high quality leisure.[123] For this postmodern

119. Veith, *Postmodern Times*, 73, 79.
120. Thiselton, *Interpreting God*, 4, 70, 121–22.
121. Ibid., 131.
122. Ibid., 135: "For where reasoning and appeal to decency fails, resort to pressure takes its place."
123. Martin S. Lambeck, *Die Zeit*, February 21, 2001.

German author, since there is no truth, one cannot say that it is better to work than simply to have fun. The postmodern view of the self has affected all levels of secular thought.

But postmodernism has also influenced the view of the self as it relates to theology and life in the church. First, it has to be granted that postmodern culture has infected every American Christian under the age of thirty. Some sections of the United States seem to be more affected by it than others.[124] These changing notions of the human self, from the postmodern vantagepoint, have also affected the way in which pastoral theology is approached. Many Christian counselors now talk about "our story," or even "our text," when they actually mean to refer to the human self. Humans, as the individual human text, "demand a hearing on its own merit," says one prominent counseling theorist.[125] Instead of confronting sin and seeking changes in patterns of life, the task in pastoral counseling, it is asserted, is dialogue and dialectic. Directing life changes, where the Bible speaks against certain sinful behaviors, is replaced by discussion.[126]

A REFORMED RESPONSE TO THE CHALLENGE OF POSTMODERN CULTURE

Given the challenges that postmodernism presents to the church, it is imperative to come to a Reformed response to postmodernism. When Christian leaders in the United States first realized the threats of postmodern culture some time ago, they felt overwhelmed by the

124. Already more than two decades ago I had heated discussions with a bright seminary student who went on to do doctoral work. The student was used to getting all A grades in his Christian college classes; but on his first midterm exam in seminary, he did not get a very good grade. It is not abnormal for a good college student not to do well on a first exam in graduate school; there is often a big transition between college and seminary requirements. Yet as we discussed the exam, this student did not admit that he had received the grade that he deserved; rather, he said that I, the professor, had "a will to power" over him. I was surprised by his answer. What was particularly interesting was that the student did not think that his comment was inappropriate. The young man was an earnest Christian and was raised in a Christian home, and he had unknowingly accepted the presuppositions of postmodern culture.

125. Charles V. Gerkin, *The Living Human Document: Re-visioning Pastoral Counseling in a Hermeneutical Mode* (Nashville: Abingdon Press, 1984), 38; Thiselton, *Interpreting God*, 54, 75.

126. Donald Capps, *Pastoral Care and Hermeneutics* (Philadelphia: Fortress, 1984), 15–36. See Gerkin, *Pastoral Care*, 39–46.

test. Time has moderated that anxiety, but postmodernism is indeed not a slight challenge.

In fact, the trials of postmodern culture are an opportunity for communicating the gospel, not a hindrance to doing so.[127] A full response to postmodernism should have at least four foci: (1) answering difficult philosophical questions; (2) rebutting theologians who have capitulated to postmodernism; (3) reexamining the work of evangelism in the light of postmodernism; and (4) emphasizing the importance of propositional truth within the Christian community. A full response would only extend this already large volume.[128] The rest of this chapter can provide a partial answer, focusing on addressing difficult philosophical questions and reexamining evangelism.

Philosophical Problem: Mind and Reality Blur. Postmodern thinkers usually blur distinctions between the human mind and external reality. For many postmoderns, the mind and external reality are conflated—it is claimed that truth is not established by anything outside the mind or the culture that shapes beliefs.[129] Postmodern thinkers like Rorty sometimes deny that the mind is an immaterial, metaphysical entity that exists apart from the brain. For them, ideas are produced by biological and cultural forces. The mind cannot transcend itself and discover some type of truth about some reality that exists beyond human sensory perception.[130] Also, of course, postmodernism denies the reality of a divine mind.

Believers must response to the mind/reality blur.[131] The Christian knows that the human mind, or the thinking subject, exists.[132] The Christian also knows that the world, external reality, exists.[133] The

127. Veith, *Postmodern Times*, 28.

128. Postmodernism is dealt with in part in Richard C. Gamble, *The Whole Counsel of God*, vol. 2, *The Full Revelation of God* (Phillipsburg, NJ: P&R Publishing, 2018) (*WCG2*), 10–11, 24, 954. Postmodern theologians are discussed in the following chapter.

129. Groothuis, *Truth Decay*, 93.

130. Ibid., 42.

131. *WCG* 2:965n96: "For postmodernism, distinctions between mind, belief, and reality are blurred. They are conflated, and postmoderns claim that truth is established by the mind or the culture that shapes belief."

132. For more information on the subject/object problem, see ibid., 2:23–25, but especially 2:616 on the subject/object relationship relative to human knowledge.

133. Ibid., 2:963–64: "Recognize that there is a correspondence between what we see here on this earth and true reality. That is, there is a connection between the tree that I see with my eyes on this earth and the same tree that God sees. That tree (an object) is real; I am not imagin-

world is real and was created by God.[134] The Christian also knows that truth is something established from outside the human mind. God established truth in the garden of Eden and it continues through history to today.

Concerning language and reality, we agree with postmodernism that language is very important and that it has gaps, limits, and slippage.[135] Nevertheless, already centuries ago Aristotle defined the nature of true and false propositions, or language, in his *The Metaphysics*.[136] So understanding the nature of language and logic is not a new science. A proposition makes a truth claim. It is what a declarative sentence states or means. Questions and other locutions are not propositions but may still be true. Thus the words *snow is white* comprise a proposition that is also true. It is a fact.

Modern thought contained the notion that a sign could refer to some type of depth of meaning. A sign could at least in some sense be exchanged for meaning. Ultimately, the guarantee of the exchange was none other than God. But what if God were himself only a sign? In that case, there would be only an uninterrupted circuit.[137] Since, for the postmodern, there is no God, there is no connection between signifier and signified. Postmoderns hold to a disjunction between the signifier, or language, and the signified, or reality.[138] Furthermore, postmoderns assert that semantics, or the meanings of words, and syntax, the words in their grammatical structure of language, are contingent and are thus ultimately arbitrary.[139]

To comprehend postmodern thinking better, we will analyze the rather silly phrase, "Unicorns are real."[140] First, when it comes to lan-

---

ing something. Knowing this reality helps in facing postmodern attack"; and see 2:963–71 for the section on the believer's response to the reality of these worlds.

134. Furthermore, it is our triune God who gives the ultimate reference in human thinking. See ibid., 2:353–55.

135. For more information on the problem of language, see ibid., 2:72–75, 80–82, 98–100, and especially 343–49. See also Veith, *Postmodern Times*, 67.

136. Douglas Groothuis, *Truth Decay*, 87–88.

137. Jean Baudrillard, "The Map Precedes the Territory," in *The Truth about the Truth: De-confusing and Re-constructing the Postmodern World*, ed. Walter Truett Anderson (New York: Putnam, 1995), 80–81, as cited by Groothuis, *Truth Decay*, 42.

138. Groothuis, *Truth Decay*, 41.

139. Ibid., 94.

140. John Searle (*The Construction of Social Reality* [New York: Free Press, 1995], as cited by Groothuis, *Truth Decay*, 94) refutes this thinking.

guage and reality, we must admit that minds may be either knowing or ignorant of a subject.[141] My mind is ignorant concerning calculus, for example, while yours may be quite knowing. This is the state of affairs with academic as well as practical subjects. It is possible that my mind is much less knowing about unicorns than yours is.

Second, someone can make a statement, a proposition about something, which may be either true or false. The statement "Unicorns are like white horses with one horn" is true. Thus the statement "Unicorns have one horn" is true—but does that statement have a reference to reality?

We acknowledge that reality concerns objects or states of affairs that are either real or imaginary. Since no unicorns actually exist on this earth or in heaven, unicorns as objects are imaginary. The laptop in front of me is not imaginary but real. Thus some objects are real, while other objects or states of affairs are imaginary. It is possible to offer a preliminary response to the statement "Unicorns are real." Unicorns may be real if and only if there is a disconnect between that which is imaginary and that which is real.[142] Someone can say that it is a fact that unicorns are white horses with one horn. But such a fact is not very meaningful. Proper analysis, therefore, requires a third section—one on the nature of truth.[143] Language relates to both reality and to truth.

But reflecting on the nature of truth, postmoderns say that truth is simply a function of relationships of power.[144] For them, truth is a sociological issue. They reject the referential theory of truth, in other words, that there is a coherent correspondence between the meaning of a word in the object it describes and that there is objective truth or truthful propositions.[145] So the question still stands as to whether or not unicorns are real.

141. Groothuis, *Truth Decay*, 89.

142. This disconnect is made by the postmodern when someone such as Foucault asserts that bestiality, a sexual perversity, may be good in his world. Such a world must needs be an imaginary world. But he would question why I call that world *imaginary*.

143. "Facts don't need statements in order to exist, but statements need facts in order to be true" (Searle, *Construction of Reality*, as cited by Groothuis, *Truth Decay*, 90).

144. Groothuis, *Truth Decay*, 98–99; see also Veith, *Postmodern Times*, 63–64.

145. See *WCG* 2:81n185. Thiselton, *Two Horizons*, 123: "First of all, Wittgenstein notes that the problem of communication or intelligibility cannot be solved by referential theories. . . . The second problem about both theories of reference and ostensive definition is that they

Responses to Postmodern *Truth*. There are at least two possible responses to the claim of the relativity of truth: a passionate one and an impassionate one. The impassionate response is suggested by Richard Rorty, who simply uses language manipulation—in other words, adapting the way that you speak to accomplish your goals. Language manipulation is also called *propaganda*. Propaganda has been most effectively used by Nazis, racists, and varieties of fascists. The question believers need to pose to postmoderns is whether using propaganda is the way a person wants self-consciously to communicate.

There is also a passionate response to the problem of relativism. Perhaps God has given believers a tool for answering the threat of postmodernism relative to truth. Sadly, that answer can be offered in the light of the terrible bombing of the World Trade Center. In a *New York Times* editorial from September 2001, in the light of the terrorists' great destruction, the author faced up to some fundamental flaws of postmodernism.[146] The author was convinced that the attack on the World Trade Center challenges the ideas of postmodernism. He reminded his readers that "in general postmodernists challenge assertions that truth and ethical judgment have any objective validity." Later, he again noted, "postmodernism is partly an attempt to question the fundamental philosophical and political promises of the West. It argues that many of the concepts we take for granted—including truth, morality and objectivity—are culturally 'constructed.'"

Yet the editor confessed that the destruction of the World Trade Center "seems to cry out for a transcendent ethical perspective. An even milder relativism seems troubling in contrast." And he concluded, correctly, "one can only hope that finally, the Western relativism of postmodernism will be widely seen as ethically perverse."[147] Sadly, now twenty years later that hope has turned into nothing more than warm mist.

---

only work when we are thinking of certain types of words." Rorty's view is dialectical, uses new words (called *neologistic jargon*), and uses old words in new senses, so that the opponent is persuaded by the manipulation of language. See Rorty, "Contingency, Irony, and Solidarity," 78, as cited by Groothuis, 104–5.

146. *The New York Times*, September 22, 2001.

147. The editorial continued: "The great ironic twist is that the values latent in postmodernism and in postcolonialism—an insistence that differing perspectives be accounted for and that the other be comprehended—are consequences of the very ideas of the Western Enlightenment—reason and universality—that they work to undo" (ibid.).

In conclusion, postmodernism as a philosophical system perversely rejects the God of the Bible. Yet it is sophisticated and, in many ways, true—given its own presuppositions! For there is no escape without Christ. Our task as Christians is to demonstrate that only in Jesus Christ do we have a worldview that can answer the ultimate questions of humankind. In Christ, there is truth.[148]

Evangelism. There are a number of evangelistic approaches to postmodernism. The first approach is to remind postmoderns that they must listen to our story relative to Christ and what he has done. They reject the notion of refuting other theories as objectively false. To refute an opponent's theory as false would require assuming the correspondence view of truth. So in encounters with postmoderns, our story cannot, for them, be false.[149] They must listen.

On the other hand, we have to listen to their story. One way to address an opponent's arguments is through internal consistency. A good story will be internally consistent. That consistency is the beauty of long and great literary works—their stories are consistent all the way through.[150] But it is not difficult to demonstrate that postmodern thinkers are inconsistent.[151] The postmodern thinker may reply in defense that internal consistency is not necessary for truth. They can reply by asserting that truth is relative.

All postmoderns assume the notion of the relativity of truth. In the United States, at times the response to a gospel presentation is: "Christianity may be true for you but it is not necessarily true for me." Even worse is a hostile response—an accusation that our attempts are to manipulate. The key to evangelism with postmodern people is getting to know each other as persons. The individuals to whom you are talking must know that you are interested in them as real persons. This interest

---

148. See Veith, *Postmodern Times*, 68, 228. The Christ of Psalm 2 sits enthroned on high. He calls princes of the earth, rulers, and judges to bow to him. In the battle for the human heart and mind, we must do the same. Rebellious thinkers need to kiss the Son before he dashes them to pieces with a rod of iron.

149. Groothuis, *Truth Decay*, 104–5.

150. Rorty likes long stories.

151. For example, as a naturalist Rorty relies on Darwin's theory of evolution for his account of the beginning of life. Darwin's theory for him is true. But Rorty is also critical of Darwin. Darwinism asserts that humanity, unlike all other creatures, is oriented toward truth. Rorty says that this part of the theory cannot be true. Thus Darwinism is true except for the part of it that asserts that humans search for truth; that part is untrue. We need to ask a person like Rorty, therefore, "Where does truth come from?" Ibid., 42.

cannot be faked. Once a genuine relationship is established, there is a sense of interpersonal community, which is of prime importance to the postmodern. We can thus learn to do evangelism in a way that can be effective with those who live in a postmodern culture. The answer to the challenges of postmodern culture is to address non-Christians influenced by that philosophy from the standpoint of being in community.

This answer may require changing some of our evangelistic methods. One of the older ways of evangelism—simply handing out tracts on the streets—will be less effective, because the recipient will lack a personal connection to the message contained in the tract. Cold, door-to-door evangelism may also be less effective. Likewise, old-style street preaching should be rethought. We must find ways to communicate the gospel as individuals to individuals. We must find points of personal connection with others. Those points of connection could be through schools, social organizations, sports, or perhaps musical activities. It seems that from this vantage point—that of the postmodern person's having some type of trust in the Christian as another person—we will be able to communicate the gospel of Jesus Christ effectively.[152] Expanding beyond postmodernism, the final section of this chapter will address the church and the world.

THE CHURCH IN A BATTLE

The church of Christ is in a battle. Sadly, the church often forgets that there is a battle over every single person. Yet Satan does exist, and he hates the church passionately.

When the Church Forgets. When the church forgets, she accommodates to the world. Some time ago, Francis Schaeffer correctly observed that there were, at his time, only two values for Western culture: personal peace, and affluence. He was correct but probably not comprehensive. There would appear to be a third massive value: selfish individualism.[153] It seems to many that modern culture runs on envy, greed, and lust.

---

152. Veith, *Postmodern Times*, 227. See also Rosaria Butterfield, *The Gospel Comes with a Housekey* (Wheaton, IL: Crossway, 2018).

153. Richard L. Ganz and William J. Edgar, *Sold Out* (Ottawa, ON: Onward Press, 1990), 86.

When the church forgets that she is in a battle, she will adopt pagan ways. Many evangelical believers in the United States have very similar goals as the pagans around them have. Believers are oftentimes intimidated and defeatist and will not give a counterattack. In addition, if the church continues only to coexist with society, it will necessarily die.[154] In the family, we know that selfishness ruins marriages. Yet it can be argued that the church has adopted the world's selfish individualism, for even in the home and with the family many Christians act like the world. For example, in the family Christian parents ask their children the wrong types of questions. Instead of asking, "What do you believe to be God's plan for your life?" we ask "What do you want to do?" The young person's greatest fear, beyond mistakes and hardship, is unhappiness.[155]

When the church forgets the battle, there will be a contradiction between her words and actions. For example, on the one hand believers may outwardly articulate that every day of their life belongs to God. But if someone insists on Sabbath observance, then that person is labeled a legalist. Believers may also say that all that we have is the Lord's but then fail to give the Lord his tithe. It appears that the focus of the battle between the church and world is in the areas of worship, time, and money.[156]

When the church forgets, she will participate in a postmodern blurring of the distinction between good and evil. The church is afraid to make sacrifices, and to avoid making sacrifices we blur distinctions. This forgetting can be demonstrated in the divorce rate in the evangelical church.[157]

Battle against the Church. Battle will be brought against the church. There is biblical precedent in which we can see the battle brought by the culture against Christ's bride. The OT people of God provide a precedent: When there was ignorance of the truth, when God's people

154. Veith, *Postmodern Times*, 211; Ganz and Edgar, *Sold Out*, 88.

155. Ganz and Edgar, *Sold Out*, 87.

156. Ibid., 95–96, 107.

157. Veith, *Postmodern Times*, 211; Ganz and Edgar, *Sold Out*, 96–97. They cite Solzhenitsyn, in a 1976 BBC interview, who said that enlightened people consider these concepts old-fashioned and laughable. Nevertheless, without them we are left with the philosopher Bertrand Russell's expression "Better red than dead." Russell's statement is horrible and shows an absence of all moral criteria.

worshipped idols, then came foreign persecution. Yet there is also NT precedent for such a battle against the church. Luke 13:1–3 records Jesus's comment on Pilate's slaughter of the Galileans, which reminds the church that the cultural or political rulers of this world can and will battle against the church.[158]

There is also historical precedent for this battle. Roman culture was supposedly pluralistic—except toward the Christians![159] The church has suffered persecution and will continue to be persecuted. There is already some persecution of Christians in North America, as can be observed in the entertainment industry and in education, as well as in the courts.[160] The public schools are supposedly religion-free zones.[161] The social and political problems seen in Germany, Russia, and China can make their way also to North America. Secular humanists will attack Sunday morning worship, Bible studies, and church property.[162] How should the church respond?

Church Battles Back. While we maintain our rear-guard defenses, we must go on offense in schools, education, and the press.[163] To do so, we as individual believers and the institutional church must resolve to acknowledge and obey Christ in everything.[164] We must begin to claim as much for Christ and his kingdom as the Muslims and humanists do for their leaders. The other groups have a vision of conquest and the courage to implement it, while believers have had a defeatist vision and have been lazy.[165]

To speak plainly, we need a public religion.[166] We must teach that it is the Christian's duty to obey Christ and his law in civic and pub-

158. "There were some present at that very time who told him about the Galileans whose blood Pilate had mingled with their sacrifices. And he answered them, 'Do you think that these Galileans were worse sinners than all the other Galileans, because they suffered in this way? No, I tell you; but unless you repent, you will all likewise perish'" (Luke 13:1–3). See Ganz and Edgar, *Sold Out*, 108.
159. Veith, *Postmodern Times*, 229; Stephen Benko, *Pagan Rome and the Early Christians* (Bloomington, IN: Indiana University Press, 1984), 58–59.
160. Ganz and Edgar, *Sold Out*, 89. And see *WORLD Magazine* articles on Harvard Law School, April 30, 2005.
161. Ganz and Edgar, *Sold Out*, 107.
162. Ibid., 94, 107.
163. Ibid., 97; see Veith, *Postmodern Times*, 210.
164. Ganz and Edgar, *Sold Out*, 98.
165. Ibid., 97.
166. Contra some Christian scholars who insist that Christians can formulate private views on public issues on biblical grounds but then need common ground with unbelievers for public

lic affairs if we really want society in toto to come under the rule of Christ's law. We must reject the notion of maintaining private piety and public accommodation.[167] We need a new message that includes a kingdom vision combined with a fighting spirit.[168] We need to act morally, that is, vigorously work to have our nation and the world echo Christ's teachings.[169]

To accomplish this goal, we need courageous preachers and other church leaders. The preacher's task is to declare God's Word even if the people do not want to hear it.[170] Preachers must realize that judgment begins with God's household.[171] They must awaken the church, because the church falsely thinks that she will be left unscathed on the day of God's judgment.[172] As in the days of the prophet Joel, preachers must alarm the people.[173]

Also, the church must repent.[174] And the church needs to demonstrate her repentance. One of the ways to do so is in giving more money and repenting of adopting the world's economic value system. Christians need to repent of simply guarding their own souls and not caring about their friends and neighbors.[175] They need to watch less television, including the great American sacrament of football.[176] We cannot afford silence any longer. There is no longer room for compromise.[177] Church members need to reject secularism and careerism. We can no longer make fun of large families or of stay-at-home wives.

The church must repent of her accommodated worship.[178] In worship, the church has become like the Pharisees by preferring our

---

defense. This approach is surely dishonoring to Christ.

167. Ibid., 98.

168. Ibid., 112.

169. Ibid., 113.

170. Ibid., 103; Veith, *Postmodern Times*, 213. Abandon doctrine and moral authority and we head on a pilgrimage to postmodernism.

171. Ganz and Edgar, *Sold Out*, 104: "Would God be so strict with a bunch of slaves out of Egypt who had only a few books of His Law, yet be ambivalent towards the disobedience and complacency of we who have His entire revealed Word?"

172. Ibid., 106.

173. Ibid., 108–9.

174. Ibid., 110–11.

175. Ibid., 111.

176. Ibid., 113.

177. Ibid., 112.

178. Ibid., 118.

own traditions to God's commandments.[179] The church's worship has become careless.[180] We must repent of the yardstick of how we feel and what we experience as the barometer and basis for the corporate worship of God.[181]

Individuals as well as the church need to demonstrate repentance. Our identity as the church underlines the importance of worship. True worship must obey God and his commands.[182] At least two changes should be implemented in today's worship services: singing God's Word back to him, and giving increased importance to the Word of God.[183]

The church needs to see and embrace her identity.[184] That people have different identities is normal. Each one of us is a son or daughter of someone, a citizen of a certain nation, and a member of a certain social class.[185] The Christian's primary identity is linked to Jesus Christ, because we are part of God's kingdom. The church is a people possessed by God who, in the light of that possession, give up all selfish ambition[186] and instead pursue a life of glorifying God and denying self.[187]

KEY TERMS

postmodernism
embodied subjectivity
post-structuralism

STUDY QUESTIONS

1. Is the meaning of a text what was in the original author's mind?
2. What are some of the strengths and weaknesses of modernism? Are you postmodern in your thinking?

179. Ibid., 120.
180. Ibid., 121.
181. Ibid., 123–24.
182. Ibid., 117–18.
183. A good question for evaluating worship is to measure the amount of time spent reading portions of Scripture compared to time spent on announcements.
184. For union with Christ and the believer's new identity, see WCG 2:907–41.
185. Ganz and Edgar, *Sold Out*, 115.
186. Ibid., 116.
187. Ibid., 117.

3. In what ways have the issues of postmodernism affected your particular congregation?

RESOURCES FOR FURTHER STUDY

Erickson, Millard J. *Truth or Consequences: The Promise and Perils of Post-modernism.* Downers Grove, IL: InterVarsity Press, 2001. Defines terms, provides historical introductions, and shows strengths and weaknesses of postmodernism.

Kapic, Kelly M., and Bruce L. McCormack, eds. *Mapping Modern Theology: A Thematic and Historical Introduction.* Grand Rapids: Baker Academic, 2012. A collection of chapters arranged by classic theological loci. Authors include the two editors as well as Michael Horton and Richard Lints, among others. This book intends to paint the story of modern theology—the theology that no longer tries to defend orthodoxy but intends to ask how theological values in those old orthodoxies may be given newer expression.

Trueman, Carl R. *The Rise and Triumph of the Modern Self: Cultural Amnesia, Expressive Individualism, and the Road to Sexual Revolution.* Wheaton, IL: Crossway, 2020. A deep, fascinating, and penetrating analysis of the modern self by a trusted cultural analyst.

25

Later Twentieth-Century and Contemporary Theology

THIS CHAPTER WILL NOT attempt to cover the myriad of prominent contemporary thinkers but will be content to analyze only two German and two British theologians.

JÜRGEN MOLTMANN (A.D. 1926–)

The movement of Jürgen Moltmann, an influential contemporary theologian, is at the fore of European intellectual trends, with adherents even from within the United States. His theology has one great end: to call the Christian community back to the pure religion of the Bible. The thinking of Moltmann is a theological tidal wave that, in all likelihood, will continue to rise for some time yet.

Biography. Raised in a proudly secular home, Moltmann served in the German army during World War II. He became disillusioned by the evil deeds done by his own nation. During the war, he was captured by the British and spent three years as a prisoner of war. While a prisoner in England, he encountered students of theology. Even at an early age, he longed to build a theology that would speak to the tragedy of his own generation. He received his doctorate from the University of Göttingen in 1952, pastored until 1957, began teaching in Wuppertal, then joined the theological faculty at Bonn in 1963. In 1967 he transferred to Tübingen, where he remained until his retirement.

History, Humanity, and the Resurrection. Moltmann presents original ideas regarding the nature of history, of revelation, of eschatology, and the character of Christian hope—all of which are foundational for his notion of Christ's resurrection.

Moltmann's unique conception of history is foundational to a proper understanding of his theology of hope. He argues that history must be rediscovered and understood through a new lens. His approach to history is unique in two ways. First, he defines *history* differently from the way it has been defined since the time of Immanuel Kant. Second, he considers the nature of promise within the overall concept of history.[1]

Moltmann opposes the modern notion of history that has been the norm since Kant. In this "outdated" schema, conditions of possible experience were usually viewed in a transcendental sense—that is, as though time were or could be held at a standstill.[2] The post-Enlightenment understanding of history has had a distinctly anthropocentric character founded on man's ability to calculate and make for himself. This notion of history, according to Moltmann, makes the resurrection of Christ by the power of God simply impossible.[3]

Moltmann argues that this modern view of history does not account for the reality that history, as a concept, is fluid. To explain history's fluidity, he defines history as "forms assumed in history by the spirit in the course of an eschatological process which is kept in hope and in motion by the promise grounded in the cross and resurrection of Christ."[4] Stated another way, he explains that history is that "which is experienced from the eschatological future of the truth as the category of time."[5] In other words, the meaning of every event of history is left open to the interpretation of the future, thus leaving no events static. With his new view of history, Moltmann claims to open the door to a meaningful discussion of the possibility of the resurrection.

Moltmann's conception of history is connected to his understanding of the biblical notion of *promise*. He believes that history is fashioned by promise and that events are experienced by humans as anticipated promises. When events are experienced as expected promises, they are

---

1. This idea is similar to Cullmann's earlier notion of prophecy and history.

2. Moltmann criticizes Cullmann's notion of *Heilsgeschichte* here.

3. Jürgen Moltmann, *Theology of Hope: On the Ground and the Implications of a Christian Eschatology* (London: SCM Press, 1967), 174–85.

4. Moltmann, *Hope*, 50.

5. Ibid.

"experienced as truly 'historic' events."[6] Thus history is in the process of becoming, to employ a theological term not used by Moltmann. But the promise character of all events that have occurred in the past, and the promise's referring to events yet to happen, necessitates a fluid concept of meaning when applied to these historic events.

The following is an example that Moltmann has not used but that will hopefully be helpful. In a hypothetical, tragic series of events, a seminary student is in a car accident and loses sight in one eye. There is no immediate or obvious "good" to be found in this needless suffering and loss. But motivated by this traumatic experience, the student might form a ministry to sight-impaired people. Or he might leverage his suffering in any number of other ways to minister to others who suffer. If he were to do so, then years after the accident this partially blind former student would likely interpret this "needless suffering" differently in the light of the opportunities his impairment afforded him to minister to other hurting people. Moltmann would argue that the meaning of this car accident traveled beyond the experience of the first moments, days, weeks, and months of suffering and disorientation. He would claim that the future contributed fresh meaning to this one event, meaning that was nowhere to be found in that first dark day.

For Moltmann, a fact of history is never complete in itself. Facts do not manifest their own truth; rather, the facts of history are stages on a road—they are in process.[7] Thus Moltmann asserts that theologians ought not to use the word *fact* (or words like it) to express what Israel experienced in her history. Words such as *fact*, understood with an absoluteness or finality, cannot be integrated with the promise aspect inherent in all reality. This promise aspect embraces both past and future.

Introducing the promise aspect of history opens new horizons that have important theoretical and practical implications for Christianity

---

6. Ibid., 107.

7. It is easy to see the influence of Hegel's philosophy here. John M. Frame, *A History of Western Philosophy and Theology* (Phillipsburg, NJ: P&R Publishing, 2015) (*HWPT*), 416: Moltmann "became acquainted with the Marxist philosopher Ernst Bloch (1885–1977), author of *The Principle of Hope*"; and 417: "As the existentialists denied that human beings have a fixed essence or nature, Bloch said the same about history. . . . So there are no normative, fixed categories that human thought must observe."

in Moltmann's system. According to Moltmann, promise announces the coming of a not-yet-existing reality from the future of the truth. Ultimately, this promise aspect, which attaches all biblical and nonbiblical events as well as past and present events, related to the promise of God's resurrecting Christ from the dead.

Just as the Lord made promises to his people, Israel, so Christ's resurrection extends promises to the people of God today. Thus Moltmann argues that every so-called *fact* of the past and present remains pregnant with meaning, as both the past and the present await future completion. The notion of promise forces the theologian to analyze every past and present moment in the light of the future.[8] Moltmann views other theories of history as inferior, for he believes that these other theories do violence both to the biblical data and to entire sections of the Christian faith.

The promise aspect of history has significant implications for Christianity at large—and more specifically, for the resurrection of Christ. If someone were to deny Moltmann's view, Moltmann would contend that, at worst, this person has made the resurrection of Christ impossible, and, at best, he has made it uninteresting. Moltmann believes that the modern scientific view of history, given its presuppositions, has made the resurrection impossible and thus entirely meaningless; therefore, "neither the historian nor the theologian can allow methods based on the principle that what must not, cannot be."[9]

Moltmann also disregards the approach of modern Bultmanian form criticism in combination with existentialism as unviable: "That the resurrection actually took place is not thereby denied, but does not lie within the field of interest."[10]

These claims are strong and, if proven, also significant. Earlier theologians discussed the historical method and its relationship to eschatology. Moltmann maintains, however, that at least two of those theologians—Albert Schweitzer and Rudolf Bultmann—were misguided in their analysis of the relationship between history and eschatology. "It

---

8. See Richard C. Gamble, *The Whole Counsel of God*, vol. 2, *The Full Revelation of God* (Phillipsburg, NJ: P&R Publishing, 2018) (*WCG2*).

9. Moltmann, *Hope*, 174.

10. Ibid., 185. Moltmann has a valuable analysis of the development of form critical research making for a deadly combination with existentialism (see ibid., 184–86).

is neither that history swallows up eschatology (Albert Schweitzer) nor does eschatology swallow up history (Rudolf Bultmann)."[11]

In the word of the *eschaton*, a promise is made that is "not yet." It is the promise of the eschaton that is the driving force of history; therefore, there can be no swallowing of one by the other.

The theology of hope depends on and coincides with a specific eschatological view.[12] Moltmann emphasizes Christian relevance; so when certain events are relegated to the last days, he considers those events to be vacated of significance, as they no longer have relevance for life here on earth, in history.[13]

Moltmann provides a number of definitions of *eschatology* throughout his works. Eschatology can basically be understood as "the doctrine of the Christian hope, which embraces both the object hoped for and also the hope inspired by it."[14] In other words, Christianity and eschatology are inextricably linked. According to Moltmann, eschatology must no longer function simply as a locus of theology but actually as the key to or medium of the Christian faith itself.[15]

Moltmann is convinced that any properly constructed theology must be arranged in the light of its future goal.[16] This assertion means that eschatology begins Christian doctrine but does not finish it. He believes that eschatology is to be the very medium of theological thinking. For him, eschatology begins within a definite reality in history.

When Moltmann's conception of history is combined with the event of the resurrection, the resurrection can be referred to as *historic*. Moltmann understands the resurrection to be more than an isolated event, namely, as the beginning of a general resurrection. To him the

11. Ibid., 165.
12. *HWPT*, 418: "The Ritschlians . . . simply suppressed the eschatological element in order to regard Jesus as primarily a moral teacher. . . . Barth sought to make use of it, hence his *crisis theology*. . . . Barth's *Eschaton* is . . . an intersection of time and eternity, and so not locatable in calendar time and geographic space. So it is not much like the eschatological expectation of the NT."
13. Ibid., 419: "Moltmann intends to formulate . . . a *realistic* eschatology: not epiphany, but apocalypse; not *logos*, but promise."
14. Moltmann, *Hope*, 16.
15. Ibid.
16. Frame (*HWPT*, 422) rightly criticizes: "If the future is as 'open' as Moltmann claims, then why should we think our actions can affect it? . . . Why should we think the future will be better rather than worse? . . . He renounces absolute ethical norms and embraces a form of ethical utilitarianism. . . . How do we know what constitutes oppression or liberation?"

resurrection is not an accident in a static, unchanging world but the beginning of a process, initiated by God, that will result in the transformation of the entire world. Christ's resurrection is the beginning of the end of history in the midst of history.

To Moltmann, the resurrection was not anthropocentric—it did not announce anthropological hopes or world-historical tendencies.[17] The resurrection was instead the kernel of a new righteousness in a world in desperate need of righteousness.

Moltmann's misguided understanding of the benefits of resurrection is due, at least in part, to his false understanding of sin. He rejects Paul's notion that the wages of sin is death. Death, for Moltmann, is not a consequence of sin or a divine punishment but, following Origen, an aspect of creation. He believes that sin carries with it its own misery and thus requires no further punishment.[18]

Criticisms. The first criticism of Moltmann is in regard to his doctrine of revelation. Biblical facts that occurred in history supposedly receive their truth only from the goal that has been promised by God and is to be expected from him.[19] Moltmann's view of the Bible leads him to understand theology as something that must be organized according to its future goals.[20]

There are also serious problems with his doctrine of God. Perhaps in the light of the German holocaust, Moltmann rejects the traditional notion of God's impassibility because he is convinced that God suffers with the oppressed. He believes that arguments for the impassibility of God were unduly influenced by Greek philosophy. Moltmann then reduces all God's attributes to the singular suffering love.[21] But denial of

17. Ibid., 421.

18. Jürgen Moltmann, *The Trinity and the Kingdom*, trans. Margaret Kohl (Philadelphia: Fortress, 1993), 50, as cited by Michael Horton, *The Christian Faith: A Systematic Theology for Pilgrims on the Way* (Grand Rapids: Zondervan, 2011), 427.

19. Moltmann, *Hope*, 107–8. There can be no authoritative Word of God for Moltmann. *HWPT*, 420: "Revelation, then, has the character of *promise*. . . . It is apocalyptic, not epiphany. . . . Since the future is open . . . revelation does not give us propositional information about the future. . . . So there can be no 'static' norms for thought or life, nor any certainty about historical events. . . . For Moltmann, there is no transcendent sphere of reality in the present in which God may be found"; and 420n15: "There he makes a case for *social Trinitarianism*, which emphasizes the distinctness of the Trinitarian persons from one another at the expense of the unity of the Godhead."

20. This theme is also heard earlier in Cullmann.

21. Horton, *Christian Faith*, 244–45.

the equal ultimacy of all the divine attributes is a serious flaw. Moltmann also mistakenly holds to a social Trinitarianism. Perhaps in reaction to Barth, Moltmann sees a weakness within classical Christian reflection on monotheism because of monarchical thinking.[22] He proposes a divine, internal community as foundational for Trinitarian reflection. First and foremost, he believes that God should be comprehended as a Trinity, as three persons. Unity within this social relationship is embraced exclusively through the *perichoresis* of the three persons.[23] This speculation is also fundamentally flawed. God is one in essence and three in persons, but Moltmann describes the Trinity as three persons in one social community. *Perichoresis* is a proper theological concept, but it is proper only within the biblical presupposition of God as united in essence, a view that Moltmann rejects.

Not only is his Trinitarian thinking mistaken, but also his Christology does not fit with Scripture. For Moltmann, Jesus of Nazareth is the powerless kenotic Christ with a vague deity who suffers for humanity.[24] Finally, in Moltmann's theology creatures are not dependent on a creator. There is, for him, no supreme power.[25]

EBERHARD JÜNGEL (A.D. 1934–)

Biography. Born in East Germany, Eberhard Jüngel was trained at a seminary in East Berlin and then studied for two years in Switzerland with Barth and Brunner. He finished his doctorate in East Berlin and began teaching there in 1962. After four years, he moved to teach at Zurich. In 1969 he moved again to Tübingen, where he remained until his retirement in 2003. Jüngel's *Gott als Geheimnis der Welt* appeared in 1983 as *God as the Mystery of the World*. This text intends to address three problems: (1) that modern man does not need God and cannot understand traditional metaphysical conceptions about God;

---

22. Monarchical thinking began with Aristotle. It encompassed political thinking (that there should be one emperor) and even the entire cosmos (that there should be one God). See ibid., 296.

23. *Perichoresis* is the mutual indwelling relationship of love, equality, and fellowship among the three persons of the Trinity. See *WCG* 2:362.

24. *HWPT*, 421: "His deity is that he embodies the future of man. His resurrection is not a past event, but the beginning of the future. Therefore, it is not 'in' history, but is rather the *basis* of history and hope."

25. Ibid., 420–21.

(2) that there is a worldly nonnecessity of God; and (3) that there is a Death of God movement.

Rejection of the Traditional Metaphysical Conception of God. Jüngel says that the problem of contemporary Christianity is that there is no need for God in science. God has no place in our world, in our thoughts, or even in our language.

The traditional metaphysical conception of God came from Aquinas and Anselm. Anselm defined God as that which nothing greater can be thought. But such a definition of God is beyond contemporary European thinking. If God is such an idea, then he simply does not exist. Jüngel argues that the person of faith must resist this ancient path and proceed toward a new way to think about God.[26]

This problem of a metaphysical conception of God was compounded by Descartes's thinking. Descartes's notion of *cogito ergo sum* made God's existence secured through the human self. Thus the modern concepts of *being* and *reality* were established on the human self. Jüngel rightly critiques such a foundation because it is locked into a basically anthropological orientation.[27] Since humanity understands itself in terms of itself, instead of in terms of God, people automatically raise the question of the necessity of God. It became an assumption of the modern age that God had to prove that he is God in and through man. Theology had to confront the question of God's necessity. The modern world is a place in which man newly discovers himself to be the focal point for all that exists. In such a world it is not easy to have meaningful talk about God.[28]

God's Nonnecessity. Jüngel perceptively argues that it is good for theologians to face the question of God's worldly nonnecessity.[29] Theologians can improperly resent the situation or fight it.[30] Jüngel wants theology to recognize the genuinely theological character of the truth of God's worldly nonnecessity. This truth speaks not only about the world and about man but also about God himself.[31] Wrestling with

---

26. Eberhard Jüngel, *God as the Mystery of the World* (Grand Rapids: Eerdmans, 1983), 9.
27. Ibid., 16.
28. Ibid., 14.
29. There is a problem with his formulation: Even if God is more than necessary, is he not at least necessary to the world's existence? Jüngel appears to be engaging in verbal sleight of hand.
30. Ibid., 18.
31. Ibid., 19.

this question is theology's fundamental task.[32] Jüngel demonstrates that the concept of *necessary being* itself is inherently problematic.

How then should believers talk about God? European Christianity has consistently talked about God in his being without thinking at the same time of God as the Crucified One. This type of thinking should no longer be the case even if the habit is hard to break. Even the Bible supposedly presents Jesus's death and God as relating in antithesis.[33] In addition, European theology has failed to wrestle with the major problem of God's absoluteness. It is the problem of simple contradiction between God's life and the death of Jesus. The death of Jesus should have more consequence for the doctrine of God. Theologians should see the problem and reject the axiom of God's absoluteness. Contemporary humanity is allergic to this type of absoluteness.[34] It is supposedly the axiom of absoluteness and its uncertainty that led to the Death of God movement.[35]

Death of God Movement. Jüngel is convinced that theology must reject the metaphysical tradition of God's being over or beyond man, because then he is nowhere. Terms such as the *death of God* are difficult to define, but Jüngel is convinced that responsible modern theology must wrestle with the issue. Atheism can only be rejected by overcoming the constructions of traditional theism. The first question to answer in reformulating traditional theism is whether God can be over mankind.[36] If one maintains that he can be, then he is both everywhere and nowhere! The problem lies in the relationship between Christianity and metaphysics. Christianity must leave behind the metaphysical tradition.[37]

32. Ibid., 23: "It is the fundamental task of theology to probe the question about what it means for the relationship of God to man and for man's corresponding relationship to God if God is not necessary in the world."

33. See ibid., 39, where Jüngel struggles to harmonize Christ's crucifixion with God's absolute nature. For example, Jesus is presented as crucified in human weakness, which is directly opposed to God's absoluteness. But he maintains that the antithesis is not absolute and that careful exegesis can demonstrate that the apparent antithesis is deceptive.

34. It is as though Jungel said, "God should not be thought of absolutely. Man does not want an absolute God; therefore, if there were no absolute God, then man would love God."

35. Ibid., 41. The absoluteness axiom probably remained in Luther because of his nominalistic background.

36. The metaphysical problem of God's being over us reaches back to Anselm's *Monologium*. Anselm discussed the highest of all existing beings.

37. Jüngel does not hold that Christians can eliminate metaphysics. Nevertheless, the tradition must be used critically. He views theology as being in confrontation with metaphysics. The relationship is at best ambivalent (ibid., 54).

To get the answer to this question, Jüngel turns to what he considers to be the penetrating analysis of Hegel and Bonhoeffer.[38] They answer the question "Where is God?" with the notion of the death of God. Beginning with Bonhoeffer, Jüngel declares that God is the one who permits himself to be pushed out of the world. Understanding God in this way enables Jüngel to define God's omnipotence in a new fashion: he is omnipresent precisely in his presence on the cross and in his death. Jüngel concludes that the concept of *God* can be defined in terms of the eternal divinity's suffering both finitude and death so that God's being may become real. It is in Christ's death that God enters history, and in that death there is a transformation of the meaning of the terms *subject* and *substance.*[39] In that transformation, the death of God is to be understood positively.

There are limitations to human thinking, which does not have the ability to contemplate that which is inherently beyond itself. Since human thought cannot conceive of that which is beyond all other beyonds, it is impossible to contemplate a divine essence. Because that essence is unthinkable, discussion of the topic is ridiculous.[40] "The unthinkability of the essence of God leads to the proclamation of the death of God as the greatest event of modern history."[41]

It is in this context that Jüngel fleshes out his belief that the metaphysical tradition's notion of God's being over mankind leads to his being nowhere. If that belief is true, then God is both everywhere and nowhere![42] If God is conceived in traditional theological terms—as

38. Dietrich Bonhoeffer (1906–1945) was a young Lutheran pastor and theologian who had many contacts with the United States and was executed by the Nazis. He wrote *Christ the Center* (San Francisco: Harper & Row, 1978) and *Ethics* (London: SCM Press, 1955).

39. This transformation is philosophically important for Jüngel. Commenting on Hegel's proposition, "the substance made itself subject," Jüngel asserts that the two words were originally interchangeable. The meaning of both was that which was foundational and already present. It is the source for all that arises out of something. It lies behind or beneath all other things and is that on which other things are able to exist. That which has nothing more beneath it or behind it bears its essence or nature in itself. It has its own grounding and is self-dependent.

40. Jüngel, *God as Mystery*, 101. He fully elaborates Nietzsche's theories as they relate to contemporary theism/atheism. It is Nietzsche who asserted the impossibility of thinking the essence of God.

41. Ibid.

42. An analogy not offered by Jüngel from politics is that when it is "everyone's business" to fight racism, it becomes "nobody's business."

the omnipotent one or the one beyond—then one is forced to ask the question, "Where is God?"[43]

Jüngel rejects the distinction between God's essence and existence. The problem began once again with Descartes. Since modern thought is grounded in Descartes's *cogito*, that very grounding initiates the destruction of a metaphysically based certainty of God. The reason is that in Descartes's approach, God is necessary for the human *res cognitans*, or "thinking thing."[44] God, in Descartes's system, needed to be secured for the purpose of providing assurance for the human ego.[45] This epistemological move resulted in God's becoming a predicate of perfection as well as in requiring a fundamental distinction between the certainty of God's essence and existence. These results meant that God is proven to exist only as God is present with man.[46] Yet Jüngel rightly argues that God is also superior to the human ego. So as God confers man's "self" on him, so man appropriates God, and as man appropriates and enters into relationship with God, man becomes in a sense responsible for God. Yet after discovering this problem, Descartes concealed the problem that he himself had raised.

Descartes's contradiction did not continue in darkness. The contradiction leads to the disintegration of God's being, because his being is divided into an essence over humans, on the one hand, and an existence through and with humans, on the other hand. This thinking establishes God as being both over and coterminously with the human ego.[47] This antithetical definition will necessarily lead to Nietzsche's question, "Where has God gone?"

To avoid this abyss, Christianity must follow a different pathway. No longer can thought about God be grounded on the bankrupt metaphysical notion of Descartes's "I think."[48] Believers must also reject

43. His thinking is certainly subject to critique. His question can only be answered, "Nowhere," because Jüngel holds to an autonomy of human thought that is incapable of contemplating omnipotence. Since human thought cannot conceive of this divine essence, it must not exist!

44. Ibid., 119.

45. Ibid., 122.

46. Ibid., 124.

47. Ibid., 126: "To conceive in a new way the bringing together of God's essence and existence in this antithesis became the task in which modern metaphysics failed and had to fail."

48. Ibid., 128–29. Jüngel traces the line of thinking from Descartes to Nietzsche through the philosophical systems of Kant, Fichte, and Feuerbach. Basically, the problem is that Kant presupposed in his synthetic unity of transcendental apperception the Cartesian self-grounding

Anselm's metaphysical notion of God as that than which nothing greater can be conceived. To keep that notion leads to the frustration that comes from demanding from the thinking man to think higher and further beyond himself than he is able to do.[49] God becomes factually inconceivable, and atheism becomes a foregone conclusion.[50]

Return to Classic Liberalism. With the inherent problems in earlier formulations, Jüngel turned back to Schleiermacher to understand God. He argues that there is a certain experience that is characteristic of the Christian faith.[51] The experience is made possible by the word of the cross. This experience is seen before the backdrop of the possibility of nonbeing, and it is the event on the cross that makes human nonbeing impossible. By neglecting the question of why there is anything at all rather than nothing, theologians sometimes think of nothing at all when they speak about God.

While many hold that only that which is necessary is essential, Jüngel denies that this statement applies to God. To assert that God is necessary is both unworthy of God and inherently problematic.[52] The problem goes back in the history of philosophy. Aristotle defined necessity as that which cannot be otherwise. But with that definition of necessity, Jüngel questions who is able to make such a determination relative to God.[53] Jüngel determined that the word or concept of *necessity* requires dependence or grounding on something else.[54] *Necessity* is a relational concept.[55] Any concept of necessity that rejects the relational aspect will be rejected.[56]

---

of thought in the "I think." It developed in Fichte, who fought against the thinkability of God because of his metaphysically understood conception of God's glory, as well as in Feuerbach, whose conception of humanity necessitated God—because of the metaphysical identity between man and God. Nietzsche recognized the consequences of the previous thinkers' findings, particularly those of Feuerbach and Hegel.

49. Ibid., 149.

50. Ibid., 151–52.

51. Ibid., ix: It is the experience that "allows one to think and to tell of God as the mystery of the world."

52. Ibid., 25. The proposition is "not worthy of God."

53. Ibid. In Aristotle's *Metaphysica*, necessity is "that which cannot be otherwise."

54. Ibid., 24.

55. Ibid., 25–27. Jüngel follows Nicolai Hartman's meaning for the term *necessity* in Hartman's *Möglichkeit und Wirklichkeit*. Jüngel then adds another definition of necessity, one that he labels *hermeneutical necessity*.

56. He discussed Kant and Hegel's differences regarding the nature of an absolute necessity that eliminates a relational necessity. For Hegel, absolute necessity is pure being. But for Jüngel,

In contrast, God as necessary being is more than necessary. To explain his meaning, Leibniz formulated the proposition of adequate cause or adequate reason.[57] Thus in using the phrase "more than necessary," Jüngel does not mean that God is necessary and then somehow adds to that necessity a more than necessity; rather, God is necessary being because he is more than necessary.[58]

Jüngel finds that in questioning the ground of the non-nonbeing of that which exists, nonbeing now appears to man as a possibility, which opens up the experience with experience.[59] This experience with experience can produce either anxiety or gratitude as the experience is experienced. From Schelling to Heidegger, the experience with experience resulted in anxiety. Yet when it is experienced as an affirmation of being, then a "miracle" takes place. This miracle is possible only as the result of an event called the "revelation of God." Given this context, it is not necessary to arrive at talk about God in the experience of one's own being, for God is, in this sense, not necessary.[60] The important point is that God does not come from the context of the world but rather from God himself.[61] This worldly groundlessness of God is to be understood against the metaphysical tradition. And this analysis drives Jüngel to his conclusion or solution.

Hegel's definition is inherently problematic. There can be no adequate treatment of necessary existence without relationship (ibid., 27–28). Yet Jüngel has been rightly criticized for this statement. Jan Rohls ("Ist Gott notwendig?—Zu einer These von E. Jüngels," *Neue Zeitschrift für Systematische Theologie und Religionsphilosophie* 22 [1980]: 288) takes this thesis as the springboard for discussing whether or not one can assert God's necessity. He faults Jüngel for being too dependent on Kant in his rejection of any absolute necessity.

57. Jüngel, *God as Mystery*, 29. The proposition of adequate cause or proposition of adequate reason is that nothing takes place without sufficient reason, or there is no effect without a cause. From this analysis, Jüngel denies the ontological proof for God's existence (ibid., 25n17). The proposition makes God the necessary being or the final reason of things. This proposition of adequate reason was also dealt with by Kant, as well as by Heidegger, Jaspers, and Tillich. In their wrestling with the concept, it developed into the basic wrestling with being and the possibility of nonbeing. It is this questioning that will lead to the experience with experience.

58. Ibid., 24n15. Schelling had already addressed this question and, as he debated God's necessary existence, he argued that if God were simply necessary being, then God would be a dead God. A living God must be more than necessary—God transforms necessary being into self-established being.

59. Ibid., 32.

60. Thus he differs with the Cartesian starting point. All that this means is that no one is compelled to believe.

61. Ibid., 34.

Solution. Jüngel's goal is to think and talk about God.[62] To accomplish that goal necessitates expositing the statement from 1 John that God is love. God as love, as the mystery of love, moves humanity into the freedom to be able to be. This view helps provide the foundation for Jüngel's doctrine of God, which is formally the identification of God and love, and materially the doctrine of the Trinity—all of which is based on the identification of God with the crucified Jesus.

Second, Jüngel also believes that God is freedom and Christianity is a religion of freedom.[63] Humanity is destined to freedom and is related to God both in humanity's lack of freedom but especially in his freedom. Believers speak about God in connection with Jesus, the crucified man. This Jesus speaks of God and announces God. So when believers think of God, they must think of him as the one who communicates and expresses himself in the person Jesus. Thus the real definition of God must be the Crucified One.[64]

According to Jüngel, there is a basic theological uncertainty to Christian talk about God. The proper expression of the nonnecessity of God in a worldly sense is simply that God comes from God. This phrase means that God is self-determination taking place.[65] This self-determination is ontologically expressed as freedom. God's freedom must be carefully conceptualized. Christ's cross must be united with any conception of God's freedom because God is only determined by himself.[66] But God determines himself to be God not without humanity. Nevertheless, God is not ontologically necessary for humanity, for the two are in a relationship of love, which surpasses the concept of *necessity*. God's love surpasses necessity.[67]

Theology must rethink God, and such thinking requires an understanding of what is meant by the term *faith*. Faith is not subordinate to

---

62. Ibid., vii: His goal is "to illumine the possibility of talk about God based on the experience of the humanity of God, and to learn to think God again on the basis of unambiguous talk about God."

63. Ibid., xi.

64. Ibid., 13.

65. Ibid., 36.

66. Ibid., 37.

67. Ibid., 37–38. Jüngel says that there can be no separation of God's humanity and his divinity. God is more than necessary for man, for God "does not desire to come to himself without man. . . . Thus, God's humanity belongs to his divinity. This is what theology must finally begin to learn."

thought or any type of knowing.[68] Also, faith cannot replace thought. Faith is a form of human behavior that provides self-definition for man—but not human self-grounding. There is no self-grounding, because faith involves the ego as being taken along by God.[69] Also, God cannot be understood without faith. This point is fundamental to an evangelical theology.[70] The believer can then begin to think God, for in thinking God, thought is "taken along in that it thinks faith and what faith believes in."[71] This reasoning means that when thought, which is normally reflective, thinks faith, that reflective character is transformed into a nonreflective one. Such thinking, instead of returning to itself, stays with the object of faith, which is belief. This faith is an experience unlike other experiences, for it is an experience that is ready to have new experiences with experience itself, as previewed in Jüngel's earlier notion of experience with experience.[72]

Jüngel's concept of *God* is both complex and postmodern. He rejects classic notions of God's being and attributes. For him, God can speak through a notion of the crucified Christ.[73] This chapter will now turn to examine how he comprehends classic Christian teaching on justification.

Justification. As earlier twentieth-century theologians attempted to answer the question of how the Bible can make sense to modern man, Jüngel asked whether the bulwark Protestant notion of justification by faith alone is still meaningful to the postmodern German. The German Protestant's first problem, says Jüngel, is to define his theological identity in present-day Germany. The best answer to the difficulty is to turn back in time to Luther's foundational notion of justification by faith alone. But translating Luther's concept into simple contemporary German is apparently not an easy task! The gospel, says Jüngel, is both simple and revolutionary. It is a message of joy and a word from the cross. He expresses his notion in these powerful words:

68. Ibid., 163. It is not a lower form of knowing.

69. Ibid., 164. For more information, see Gerhard Ebeling, *Introduction to the Theological Theory of Language* (Philadelphia: Fortress, 1973).

70. Jüngel, *God as Mystery*, 154. Jungel defines evangelical theology as "talk about God which expresses the identity of God with the crucified Jesus as the gospel. As evangelical theology, it is catholic."

71. Ibid., 167.

72. Ibid., 168. The notion was introduced as early as page 18.

73. Jüngel wrote that "the crucified is, as it were, the material definition of what is meant by 'God'" (ibid., 13).

God for the godless! Life for those threatened and destroyed by death! Salvation for a humanity caught in personal and corporate guilt! Liberating truth for men and women who suppress the truth in unrighteousness (Rom. 1:18) and who bind themselves and others in the destructive lies of life.[74]

These words convey, according to Jüngel, Paul the apostle's notion of the justification of the unrighteous. The roots of Paul's thinking were established in the OT, particularly in the fratricide of Abel by Cain. Cain represents, in his hideous crime, all humans. God's dealing with Cain is the first *verbum iustificationis*, or "word of justification," as well as the first sign of justification: a mark from God that continues for Cain's earthly life. Jüngel is convinced that Cain was fully justified by God's actions. The ground for that belief is that the antisocial murderer has the privilege of establishing a city, a community of life. Cain is actually improved in this process; that is, the antisocial one is enveloped into healthy social and political life.

God's actions are the opposite of those of humanity, which took God's good creation and turned it into evil. God's actions are good, and God, as social Trinity, is good. God's goodness is, for Jüngel, observable in his being as social being. Thus social being on earth is good because God, as social being, is good. Cain, the epitome of evil because he is antisocial, becomes saved as a social being. Authentic human existence is being with God.

Postmodern influence is very pronounced here. The passive, postmodern self is, through the transforming work of the Holy Spirit, moved from one who lusts for power to one who has love for others and for God.

ANTHONY THISELTON (A.D. 1937–)

Biography. Thiselton was trained in London and received his doctorate from the University of Sheffield. He taught at the University of Durham and retired from the University of Nottingham in 2001. In

---

74. Eberhard Jüngel, *Das Evangelium von der Rechtfertigung des Gottlosen als Zentrum des christlichen Glaubens. Eine theologische Studie in oekumenischer Absicht*, 2. Aufl. (Tübingen: Mohr Siebeck, 1999), 1 (my translation).

his 1980 work *The Two Horizons*, Thiselton argues that there ought to be no more naive readings of historical texts.

Cultural Context or Horizon. An ancient text should be understood within the original readers' own cultural context. There are then two horizons: that of the readers of the ancient original text, and that of the contemporary reader of the text.[75] This principle also applies to the NT. The original authors had their own cultural horizon, that is, they had a cultural/theological agenda, and that agenda was communicated in their writings.[76] The NT writers understood there to be a hermeneutical gap between their own era and the more ancient (even to them) world of the OT. They wrote with an understanding of the tension between the two eras. Thus the hermeneutical problem is not unique to the nineteenth century.[77] The author of any ancient text had his own conditioning, just as the modern interpreter of the text does.[78]

Preunderstanding. The term *preunderstanding* refers to the modern reader's context.[79] Based on this concept of preunderstanding, Thiselton asks, "Does that knowledge of preunderstanding force contemporary readers to approach the NT with certain presuppositions?"[80]

Thiselton uses philosophical insights to elucidate this task. He is convinced that both Heidegger and Wittgenstein have made valuable contributions.[81] But NT scholars have thus far failed to be helped by

75. Anthony Thiselton, *The Two Horizons* (Grand Rapids: Eerdmans, 1980), 17: "Everything becomes dominated . . . by the interpreter's own pre-understanding and the ancient text becomes merely a projection of his own ideas or preconceptions."

76. Ibid., 18–19: "They begin with a pre-understanding."

77. Ibid., 19: "Two horizons are brought together in the hermeneutical process. . . . The conclusions . . . demonstrate that the two-sided nature of the underlying problem of hermeneutics is more than a novel creation of Bultmann, Gadamer, and the exponents of the new hermeneutic. In this sense, they serve to confirm that the problem which we have outlined is a genuine one."

78. Ibid., 22.

79. Ibid., 22–23.

80. Ibid., 23: "If the New Testament writers approached the Old Testament in the light of a pre-understanding that was theologically informed . . . does this not mean that in order to be true to the tradition of the New Testament itself the interpreter will consciously approach the text from a particular theological angle?"

81. Ibid., 24. He regrets that linguistic philosophers have simply ignored Heidegger's approach. While many contemporary philosophers would disagree, he is convinced that there are important relationships among the supposedly dissimilar Gadamer, Heidegger, and Wittgenstein. Ibid., 33: "Wittgenstein's notion of 'language-game' has striking parallels with Heidegger's understanding of 'world' and even with Gadamer's notion of the interpreter's horizons. . . . Many British philosophers would regard Wittgenstein and Heidegger as representing two totally incompatible traditions of philosophical thought and method, and that from this point of

Wittgenstein to understand the NT.[82] For example, using Wittgenstein's understanding, Luther's famous phrase for describing the believer, *simul iustus et peccator* (at the same time righteous and a sinner), is no longer contradictory but "two evaluations made from within different language-games."[83] The issue is the importance of philosophical description, that is, the givenness of the world or tradition of the investigator.[84] Thiselton desires to use these new philosophical categories in the service of understanding the NT.[85] His use of philosophical description gives tools both for the hermeneutical task and to the meaning of certain NT texts.[86]

He helps his readers understand terms such as *timeless truths*, thus supposedly improving on earlier analysis.[87] He stands against those who, even in some modified fashion, believe scholars can still speak about timeless truths.[88] He is convinced that to speak of NT timeless truths would be unfaithful to the NT writers themselves.[89] He recognizes that the NT writers had a hermeneutic and interpretation and that contemporary readers also approach the NT with a hermeneutic and interpretation.[90]

The advantage to knowing the importance of preunderstanding is that contemporary NT scholars are no longer forced to adopt either Heidegger's existentialism or classic liberalism's philosophy.[91] He judges

---

view some would doubtless argue that their questions and contexts of thought are so radically different as to be incapable of fruitful comparison." Wittgenstein provides many philosophical categories, such as *prejudice*, *world*, and *time distance*, that are helpful by playing a fruitful role in understanding past texts. Ibid., 32–33: "He takes up all these categories . . . and shows how they may perform a fruitful role in facilitating understanding, especially the interpreter's understanding of texts written in the past."

82. Ibid., 45.

83. Ibid., 44.

84. Ibid., 30.

85. Ibid., 46–47.

86. He asks his readers to suspend judgment if his method appears peculiar and different from others (ibid., 46–47). He contrasts his method with that of Nels F. S. Ferré and Georges Van Riet.

87. Ibid., 96–97. He claims to improve on the analysis offered by Helm, Tillich, and Thielicke. Ibid., 98: "In point of fact, the more closely we examine claims about 'timeless truth,' the clearer it becomes that the biblical material itself points in the other direction. . . . If an effort is made in this direction there arises the false notion of perennial theology characterized by an abstract conceptual system. Scholasticism and seventeenth-century orthodoxy are classical examples."

88. Ibid., 98.

89. Ibid., 99.

90. Ibid., 100.

91. Ibid., 112–13, 114: "[Freud's, Nietzsche's, and Marx's] view of 'meaning' is inseparable from their own pre-understanding. . . . 'Understanding' dawns in the interaction between pre-

that Pannenberg is the best contemporary thinker when it comes to these hermeneutical matters.[92] To solidify his point on preunderstanding, Thiselton is required to destroy the notion of *objectification*, which is to say that a person can examine something objectively.[93] Kant had already warned against objectivism, but later thinkers such as Hegel and Dilthey could not overcome the problem.[94] His conclusion is that old-style objectivism is dead.[95]

Thiselton used the example of the visual arts to demonstrate that final knowledge is impossible, for a great piece of art can never be fully comprehended.[96] Similarly, there is no one who understands an ancient text without having a dogmatic guideline.[97] In this way, hermeneutics is more an art than it is a science.[98] For example, some OT prophets spoke words that they themselves did not fully understand.[99]

Thiselton has been building up to his next point and hinted at it when he said that this question relates to the manner in which one does a systematic theology of the NT. He asks what philosophical grids are appropriate to the task.[100] Another important issue is the relationship between exegesis and systematic theology.[101]

Language itself represents worldview. Language is not simply a philological issue but also a philosophical one, because language presupposes a worldview. It carries the very possibilities of being.[102] Without language, there would be no worldview. The prejudgments of each

---

understanding and meaning. . . . The problems posed by this phenomenon cannot be avoided."

92. Ibid., 99.

93. Ibid., 211.

94. Ibid., 302.

95. Ibid., 303.

96. Ibid., 296–97.

97. Ibid.: "A creative act in which truth is hidden in the text is brought to light."

98. Ibid., 302.

99. Ibid.: "'The historical scholar is likely to deny any such possibility . . . and yet it must be recognized that the Biblical records, because they have to do with God . . . constantly point to realities that are far beyond the conscious grasp of any human being."

100. Ibid., 23: "The question which is never far in the background is to what extent, if at all, philosophical description can help us to find answers to these and to other similar questions."

101. Ibid., 306–7: "Systematic theology might be said to represent the end-process, to date, of that long growth of tradition in which the Christian community has struggled to arrive at an interpretation of the biblical texts which both does justice to its own present place in tradition and seeks to discard those false pre-judgments which have proved unfruitful."

102. Ibid., 311: "As it is, language and the possibilities of thought are bound so closely together that we cannot think of some abstract 're-given system of possibilities of being.'"

person are derived from his or her language. An understanding of both the self and its surrounding world is rooted in language, and these two "prior" concepts inform humans' view of their cultural context and traditions.[103] The earlier linguistic world must be first understood before stepping into hermeneutics. Humans cannot transcend their linguistic worlds. When the scholar is self-conscious about the presuppositions of his linguistic world, then reflects critically on those presuppositions, there emerges something that supposedly transcends both.[104]

Thought and Language. Human thought cannot be separated from language.[105] Language is an enormous compilation of interdependent terms.[106] Thinking is done by a body that speaks.[107] Meaning does not come simply from a word.[108] Thiselton is convinced that Wittgenstein was correct when he argued that language is grounded in the individual's life.[109]

The relationship between preunderstanding and exegesis, while difficult, need not terminate in cynicism.[110] That the NT writers themselves were not naive about the significance of precritical understanding is demonstrated in their approach to the OT. Humans are simply unable to step outside their times and traditions.[111]

At the end of his book, Thiselton returns to his main theme: the destruction of those who hold to timeless truths. Anyone who uses

---

103. Ibid., 312: "A language-world carries with it attitudes or pre-judgments which are prior to the individual cognition and theoretical distancing."

104. Ibid., 312–13.

105. Ibid., 314.

106. Ibid., 428.

107. Ibid., 429.

108. Ibid. There are different understandings of that relationship, for example, between Structuralists and Wittgenstein. "In structuralism, however, we have a different type of contrast, between 'message' and 'code.' But here the difficulty is that different structuralists discover different types of codes behind or beneath each message. . . . All three versions of the code have found their way into biblical studies."

109. Ibid., 430: "But if the code is divorced from historic human life, how is it still related to language as a *human* activity? Wittgenstein rightly insists as his most central axiom that language is grounded in life. . . . This is not to deny Saussure's insight that the connection between the signifier and the signified is 'arbitrary,' or based on convention. . . . How does the structuralist code relate to the 'meaning' of the text in any acceptable sense of the word 'meaning'? . . . This is precisely what marks the most crucial point of difference between the *Tractatus* and the *Investigations*, and between linguistics and hermeneutics."

110. Ibid., 439: "It raised positive and fruitful questions about the relations between exegesis and systematic theology as expressing the ongoing tradition of the Christian community."

111. Ibid., 439–40.

words such as *faith* or *timeless truth* needs to use them with extreme precision. There is a critical need for a proper hermeneutical theory because language and thought are entirely interrelated.[112] When a person is already committed to a theological tradition and then does exegesis, he needs to remember the importance of distancing. But the great flaw of nineteenth-century theology was the ideal of finding a type of pure distancing. Pure distancing does not exist. Systematic theology and exegesis are mutually interdependent and never final.[113] Thiselton's monumental work, written more than forty years ago, stands as a pillar for comprehending contemporary views of hermeneutics, exegesis, and theological method.

N. T. WRIGHT (A.D. 1948–)

Biography. Nicholas Thomas (N. T.) Wright was trained in classics at Exeter College, Oxford, from 1968 to 1971. From 1971 to 1975, he studied theology at Exeter and Wycliffe Hall. He then served as a teaching fellow at Oxford and Cambridge until 1981, when he received a doctorate from Merton College, Oxford. He then traveled to Canada to teach NT at McGill University in Montreal. He remained in this position for five years before returning to England. In all, Wright has led a varied career by holding positions such as dean of Lichfield Cathedral, canon theologian of Westminster Abbey, bishop of Durham, professor of NT at St Andrews University in Scotland, and most recently senior research fellow at Oxford. Wright is currently the most prominent NT scholar working in the English language.

Saint Paul.[114] In 1997 Wright, well-credentialed to speak to Pauline theology,[115] published *What Saint Paul Really Said*. Wright explains

---

112. Ibid., 440.

113. Ibid., 443.

114. Earlier works by N. T. Wright, such as *The New Testament and the People of God* (Minneapolis: Fortress, 1992) and *Jesus and the Victory of God* (Minneapolis: Fortress, 1996), are cited in WCG2. N. T. Wright, *What Saint Paul Really Said* (Grand Rapids: Eerdmans, 1997), 7.

115. Ibid.: He wrote his "doctoral dissertation on the letter to the Romans, a commentary on the letters to the Colossians and to Philemon, and a monograph on Paul's view of Christ and the law," and his "large volume is still in preparation." See Wright, *Victory of God*.

that this book was in no way intended to be a complete study but instead a focus on Paul's proclamation and its implications.[116]

He set his thesis within the overall Pauline interpretation of the twentieth century.[117] Paul was a Jewish thinker, but scholars have debated Paul's relationship to contemporary Judaism.[118] They have also struggled to determine whether or not there was a center to Pauline thought.[119] Contemporary researchers are largely baffled as to how to interpret Paul.[120] This inability on the part of contemporary researchers is part of a larger, three-fold problem: (1) nontheologians study Paul; (2) exegetes produce massive tomes of detail rather than theology; and (3) expositors are unable to apply Paul's teaching to modern life.[121] Paul wrote to the paganism of his own time, and his teaching has something to say to his readers today.[122]

Saul was a Shammaite Pharisee raised in a world of theological and political debate and party loyalty. The goal of the Pharisee was to be left alone to study the Torah in peace. Some thought that the Torah itself demanded that Israel be free from a Gentile yoke. Paul described himself as being zealous for the traditions in Scripture, and part of what it meant to be a Shammaite was to be involved in revolutionary activity. The Shammaites were in political ascendency. They were zealous for the long-awaited kingdom of God and would do anything to draw it nearer. Paul could not have been a Hillelite, for Gamaliel would never have approved of the stoning of Stephen. As Israelites, the Shammaites believed themselves to be God's covenant people, those who would undo the effects of Adam's sin. There were three cardinal points to Judaism: monotheism, election, and eschatology. The Pharisees believed that observing Torah would hasten the fulfillment of God's promises, which included the defeat of evil and the Jews being vindicated as God's one true people.[123]

116. Wright uses the undisputed Pauline writings: Romans, Corinthians, Galatians, Philippians, Colossians, and probably Ephesians (Wright, *Saint Paul*, 8).
117. Wright, *Saint Paul*, 12.
118. Ibid., 20.
119. Ibid.
120. Ibid., 22. See *WCG* 2:156.
121. Wright, *Saint Paul*, 21.
122. Ibid., 22. Wright stands against what he calls "an old-style 'preaching of the gospel' in which the basic problem is human sin and pride and the basic answer is the cross of Christ."
123. Ibid., 26–31. See *WCG* 2:157.

After his conversion, Paul continued to be loyal to Israel's God, who gave the Law and spoke through the prophets.[124] Within the modern church, there is great misunderstanding regarding the nature of the gospel. Thus it is essential to understand what Paul, in his own historical context, meant by the word *gospel*. Wright argues that often what modern believers mean by the word is different, though not wrong, from what Paul intended. For Paul, the word *gospel* did not refer to the *ordo salutis*.[125] The background to Paul's use of the term was both Greek and Jewish; these notions were not antithetical but were harmonized in Paul.[126] The Jewish usage derived from Paul's interpretation of Isaiah.[127] The prophets spoke of a return from exile, which had yet to occur.[128] More specifically, Isaiah's message was that God's enthronement meant the defeat of pagan gods and rulers.[129] God's enthronement meant that all other claims to lordship were false.[130] The Greek meaning of the concept of *gospel* was equally plain—it announced a great victory or the rise of a new emperor.[131]

This understanding takes Paul to the nature of the gospel concerning Jesus. The gospel is of mediatorial kingship—that is, of Jesus Christ as King of the entire world.[132] To Paul, the gospel was not simply the presentation of a system of how to get saved[133] but a message of the crucified Christ, with the cross at its center. In the cross, God won victory over the world's enslaving powers. The gospel was a declaration of reversal.[134] To announce the coming of the Messiah was to declare to

124. Wright, *Saint Paul*, 39.

125. Ibid., 40–41.

126. Ibid., 41–43. See *WCG* 2:191.

127. Wright, *Saint Paul*, 42. See *WCG* 2:176.

128. Wright, *Saint Paul*, 43. See *WCG* 2:192.

129. Wright, *Saint Paul*, 44: "The 'secular' claims of the imperial cult were in fact profoundly 'religious.' . . . If and when YHWH set up his own king as the true ruler, his true earthly representative, all other kingdoms would be confronted with their rightful overlord."

130. Ibid.: "The all-embracing royal and religious claims of Caesar . . . were directly challenged by the equally all-embracing claim of Israel's God. To announce that YHWH was king was to announce that Caesar is not."

131. Ibid., 40, 43.

132. Ibid., 45: "Isaiah's message was about Israel's God becoming king—king of all the world, not just of Israel," and 46: "he was thereby installed as Lord of the world."

133. Ibid., 45: "But 'the gospel' itself, strictly speaking, is the narrative proclamation of King Jesus. . . . When the herald makes a royal proclamation, he says, 'Nero' (or whomever) has become emperor."

134. Ibid., 47.

present rulers and powers and principalities that their reign had come to an end.[135] But the victory was not exclusively political—it was the fulfillment of God's promises of victory over sin and death as well.[136]

Jesus's death was God's fulfillment of his covenantal promises to Abraham, and as such, the gospel proclaimed victory—through Jewish history and traditions[137]—to the pagan world. That the Messiah died for sins according to the Scriptures was not a reality created by creatively weaving together passages that predicted the crucifixion; rather, it was the very starting point of the gospel.[138]

Jesus's resurrection was fundamental to the message of the gospel. Without it, there was no gospel and there was no salvation.[139] The resurrection also meant that the age to come was arriving in two stages. Paul's modified Jewish apocalyptic included that the age had already happened in Jesus's resurrection and was still to happen when all his people are raised.[140]

The resurrected Jesus is King Jesus. Wright begins with the statement, "'Christ' is not a name. It is a title." The Messiah, or anointed one, meant the coming King. Paul's gospel was the good news of the coming King.[141] In Romans, Paul's gospel concerned the son of David, a well-attested theme of the Messiah.[142] This son of David is King not only of Israel but also of the entire world. Paul also taught this theology in Galatians 3:1–4:11, where the true seed of Abraham points back to the promises of Genesis 49:10. This royal theology must be viewed messianically.[143] In Galatians 4, Paul argues that the pagan nations are brought under submission to the coming King.[144]

Paul had a clear understanding of Jesus as Lord. That which was true of the true Davidic King was verifiable of Jesus. The true Davidic

---

135. Ibid.: "'The gospel' is indeed the announcement of a royal victory."

136. Ibid., 48. See WCG 2:194.

137. Wright, *Saint Paul*, 48: "Neither Paul nor any of his Jewish contemporaries had expected their God to act in anything like this way. . . . The power of his 'gospel' came precisely from the fact that it addressed the pagan world with the full weight of Jewish history and tradition behind it."

138. Ibid., 49.

139. Ibid., 49–50.

140. Ibid., 51. See WCG 2:445.

141. Wright, *Saint Paul*, 52. See WCG 2:513–14.

142. Wright, *Saint Paul*, 53. See WCG 2:509–10.

143. Wright, *Saint Paul*, 54. See WCG 2:182.

144. Wright, *Saint Paul*, 55.

King was to reign over all the earth; thus the gospel is a royal announcement.[145] Paul often used the term *lord*, which carried both a Jewish and a Greek meaning. For the Greek or Roman, *lord* was a form of address—whether it be polite, to a superior, or to the very emperor. There was only one emperor, one ultimate lord. Now there is another King—Jesus, who subverts all the claims of Caesar.[146]

Though Paul's gospel had its roots in Judaism, his message was aimed at the powers of Rome, beginning with Caesar.[147] The kingdom of the Messiah was to be established all over the world. The gospel is that God fulfilled the long-foretold prophecies, sent his Son to redeem his people from the elements of this world, and thus confronts the power of spurious gods.[148]

As is likely apparent, Paul's gospel had a number of aspects.[149] First, in the cross Christ obtained victory over the power of evil, including sin and death. Second, the resurrection inaugurated the new age—one of the fulfillment of prophecy, the return of Israel from exile, and the Creator's addressing the world. Third, Jesus is Israel's Messiah, her representative King. Finally, as Lord, Jesus is the true King of the world. At his name every knee will bow. These four conclusions of the gospel are predicated on the reality that Israel's God is the one true God and that God is made known through the person of Jesus.

Paul's proclamation of the gospel, however, was more than a mere transmission of information concerning Christ's kingship. The gospel summons allegiance. Embedded in this proclamation was the very power of God for salvation. In the summons of the gospel, people were formed into a community of love, liberated from pagan captivity, and made truly human. To embrace this authoritative message meant to reject all other loyalties.[150] The next question is the relationship between King Jesus as God and the God of Israel.

Pauline thought accorded with Jewish monotheism, and he thus believed Jesus to be divine. The first-century Jewish community held that their God was true, that worshipping idols was sinful, and that

145. Ibid.
146. Ibid., 56.
147. Ibid., 57.
148. Ibid., 58–59.
149. Ibid., 60.
150. Ibid., 61. See *WCG* 2:199, 396.

their God would vindicate Israel as his people. They believed that their God, though transcendent, acted in this world.[151] Thus the Jewish community rejected the dualistic notion that the world is evil and that their goal was to escape from it. Instead, they understood the kingdom to be one that was coming into this world.[152] They believed that those who died prior to the coming of this kingdom would be physically raised to life. This belief stood squarely against emperor worship. Israel's rebellion was a clash of worldviews.[153]

Jesus fit within Paul's Jewish monotheistic understanding. Paul reinterpreted the *Shema*[154] in a revolutionary fashion. His interpretation is consonant with wisdom literature.[155] In Philippians 2:5–11, Paul quoted an OT text in his explanation that Jesus was equal with God, but that divine equality was not "something to exploit." To be equal with God, Jesus became human, obeyed the Father, and died.[156] This message is good news for the pagans. Pauline thought fits into a Jewish matrix, but the precise details of the Jewish matrix and how Paul's thought fit into it are still under debate.[157] Paul's message was good news to the pagans, but it was news that undermined their worldview.[158]

To determine Paul's theological method, scholars must extrapolate from his letters to find what lies beneath them. This extrapolation is necessary for those who do not want to be left with competing theologies. Wright does not want to look for an abstract theological framework. The history-of-religions method does not help. What is necessary is to examine polemical engagement, then critique it from within.[159]

---

151. Wright, *Saint Paul*, 64.

152. Ibid., 63–64.

153. Ibid., 65.

154. The *Shema* (from the first Hebrew word in the biblical confession found at Deuteronomy 6:4) says, "the Lord our God is one" (see Richard C. Gamble, *The Whole Counsel of God*, vol. 1, *God's Mighty Acts in the Old Testament* [Phillipsburg, NJ: P&R Publishing, 2009] [*WCG1*], 17, 653; *WCG* 2:47).

155. Ibid., 66– 67: "God's 'wisdom' is the one through whom the world was made. Similarly, in the passages where Paul speaks of God 'sending' his Son, this too is the language of wisdom, sent by and from the creator to dwell among humans, specifically among Israel."

156. Ibid., 68. Paul says that Jesus offered the true interpretation of what it meant to be equal with God: he became human and died under the weight of the sin of the world in obedience to the divine saving plan.

157. Ibid., 77.

158. Ibid., 78.

159. Ibid., 80.

Here we have the beginning of the Gentile mission. It was not some type of displacement or Paul's attempt to bolster his own tired spirit, transform Judaism, or produce the eschatological event. In Christ, the promises of Israel's restoration were fulfilled. The new age had come, and the Gentiles were welcomed in. The positive misson's polemical engagement was central. Paul did not have to transform the message in order for pagans to understand it. It was a Jewish message for a pagan world, contra the history-of- religions notion.[160] But Paul's engagement with paganism also carried with it an internal critique of Judaism.[161] The internal critique was that Paul was similar to a prophet—he stood in continuity with Saul. Saul had opposed the surrounding paganism and was zealous for Torah observance. But Paul's zeal was now according to knowledge.[162]

Wright arrives at six conclusions. First, Paul believed God to have created heaven and earth.[163] Second, Paul addressed the cultic challenge of pagan gods being involved in everything.[164] Third, there was a challenge of power.[165] Fourth, the way to be truly human differed from the self-destructive tendencies of paganism. Paul's gospel was a counter-empire movement. It is no wonder people thought him "dangerous."[166] Fifth, the gospel opposed pagan mythology because it presented reality with a purpose.[167] It took a linear view of history, with the new age inaugurated and to be consummated. God owns and is reclaiming his world. God does not affirm the world as it is now;[168] rather, as Paul taught in Romans 8, the world longs for exodus. The gospel is a triple exodus, in which Israel is redeemed, humankind is redeemed, and creation itself is redeemed.[169] Finally, Paul's gospel is a challenge to pagan philosophy.[170]

160. Ibid., 82.
161. Ibid., 83.
162. Ibid., 85.
163. Ibid., 86.
164. Ibid., 87.
165. Ibid., 88.
166. Ibid., 89.
167. Ibid.
168. Ibid., 90.
169. Ibid., 91.
170. Ibid.

Wright concludes that the zeal of Saul the Pharisee was replaced with a new zeal. Saul/Paul understood the God of Israel to be opposed to paganism. Thus Saul/Paul strongly opposed Israel's disloyalty. He believed Scripture's prophecies were true; those prophecies show Israel as God's people and that the pagans were wrong and must now bow the knee. Paul believed the great act had occurred.[171]

To this point, Wright's research and analysis have been excellent. But it is here that his thinking becomes less helpful.

Resurrection. One of his next writing projects was on Christ's resurrection. Anyone who has read even just several pages of N. T. Wright's work acknowledges his undeniable sophistication as a writer. As such, in his opening pages Wright acknowledges the significance of words and definitions on such a topic as this one. One of Wright's main questions is whether or not early Christians intended for the word *resurrection* to refer to a concrete state of affairs.[172] Wright seeks to understand what early Christians believed really happened to Jesus—and how plausible their beliefs were.[173]

Wright admits that, over the years, scholars have traversed down many a wrong avenue in their attempts to understand the resurrection. In particular, nineteenth- and twentieth-century writers have read much of their own thought into first-century worldviews.[174] But Wright reminds scholars that early Christians learned about resurrection from Second Temple Judaism.[175] In Wright's investigation of Israel's hope, he noted that the OT was not particularly concerned with life after death, let alone resurrection.[176] But Israel knew that God was their own inheritance and that he was a loving God. Since his love was so strong, "there was no ultimate bar to seeing death itself as a beaten foe."[177]

171. Ibid., 93.

172. N. T. Wright, *The Resurrection of the Son of God*, vol. 3, of *Christian Origins and the Question of God* (Minneapolis: Fortress, 2003), xix: "The terms 'literal' and 'metaphorical' refer, properly, to *the ways words refer to things*, not to the things to which the words refer. . . . One of the main questions of this book is whether the early Christians, who were in so many ways cheerful and eager innovators, used the language of resurrection like that as well."

173. Ibid., 6, 28.

174. Ibid., 20. Pannenberg is underscored as having gone too far in making a direct link between resurrection and incarnational Christology (see ibid., 24).

175. Ibid., 85.

176. Ibid., 87–99, 103.

177. Ibid., 108.

Wright examines the literature produced up to the life of Jesus and concludes that resurrection was a revolutionary doctrine. But as Wright presents it, the resurrection is concerned with the present world and its renewal.[178] Nevertheless, the OT-era texts demonstrate the existence of belief in a bodily resurrection.[179]

When Wright transitions to an analysis of the NT, he again emphasizes how much perceived misunderstanding there is regarding resurrection.[180] While granting the complexity of Pauline thought on the resurrection, Wright notes three main themes: (1) Jesus was bodily resurrected by God; (2) there will be a bodily resurrection for those who are Christ's; and (3) in the present life believers are to anticipate their own bodily resurrection.[181] Paul's understanding of the resurrection also influenced his view of justification by faith, which was based on Christ's accomplished work and anticipated his future judgment.[182]

Paul's understanding of the resurrection was rooted in Judaism but did not remain static.[183] The Messiah's resurrection body laid the

178. Ibid., 138: "Resurrection is precisely concerned with the present world and its renewal, not with escaping the present world and going somewhere else; and, in its early Jewish forms [right rough] to its developed Christian forms, it was always concerned with divine judgment, with the creator god acting within history to put right that which is wrong. . . . Only if we misunderstand what resurrection actually involved can we line it up with the kind of 'pie in the sky' promises which earned the scorn of many twentieth-century social reformers."

179. Ibid., 148.

180. Ibid., 213: "This investigation is more urgent in that . . . a serious misreading of Paul on the crucial point has become so widespread in secondary and indeed popular discussions as to be almost taken for granted."

181. Ibid., 271–72: "And all is set within a larger picture, articulated most fully in Romans 8, of the entire new world that God is going to make, and of how this will be accomplished." Wright also notes that Paul had been convinced in his early writings that he would be alive for the Messianic return but later thought that he might die before it happened. Ibid., 273: "Paul developed new linguistic tools to articulate the fresh position to which he had come. His crucial distinction between 'flesh' (*sarx*) and 'body' (*soma*) enabled him to establish both continuity and discontinuity between the present embodied existence and the future embodied existence."

182. Ibid., 274: "The two-stage resurrection is thus, especially in Romans, the framework for Paul's central doctrine of justification by faith, based on the accomplishment of Jesus and anticipating the verdict of the last day."

183. Ibid., 275: "Paul's worldview thus shows at every point *both* that he remained rooted in Judaism, drawing his basic inspiration and categories from that rich stock, *and* that he consistently developed them, specifically around and because of the resurrection of Jesus and the conclusions he drew from that event"; and 372: "He believed that Israel's God, being both the creator of the world and the God of justice, would accomplish this resurrection by his Spirit, who was already at work in the Messiah's people. . . . Second, he believed, and articulated in considerable detail, that the resurrection would not only be bodily (the idea of a non-bodily resurrection would have been as much an oxymoron to him as it would to both Jews and pa-

foundation for Paul's view of the resurrection body.[184] He understood resurrection to be God's gift of new bodily life.[185] This resurrection had been promised by the prophets and had occurred in the resurrection of Jesus.[186]

At the center of the theology of the book of Acts sits the resurrection of Jesus.[187] The author's view of the resurrection included a change in Christ's physical body to one of incorruption.[188] Likewise, the author of Hebrews viewed the resurrection in line with first-century Judaism as well as Paul.[189] Through the resurrection, Christ defeated death.[190]

The entire NT teaches that through his resurrection from the dead, Jesus is Lord over angels, powers, and authorities. Resurrection is a central tenet of the entire NT except for the book of Hebrews.[191] The resurrection is divided into two aspects: (1) the resurrection of Jesus, and (2) the resurrection of his people. His people will have bodies incapable of dying; their bodies are transphysical. While such a story may be difficult to comprehend, Wright claims that it is what the early Christians believed.[192]

The early followers of Jesus did not simply hold these beliefs—they lived them. They behaved as though the old covenant had been renewed and as though the kingdom was already in the here and now, though also still anticipated. When challenged by opponents, Christians replied that Jesus had triumphed over death.[193] They moved their day of worship to celebrate all that occurred on the day of Christ's

---

gans of his day; whether you believed in resurrection or not, the word meant bodies), but that it would also involve *transformation*."

184. Ibid., 374: "Nor is there any explanation for why Paul developed his view of the future resurrection body in the way he did, except for the one that would have been obvious to him: that the Messiah's own resurrection body was certainly the same and curiously different, alive with a new kind of life."

185. Ibid., 448.

186. Ibid., 452.

187. Ibid., 453, 456.

188. Ibid., 455.

189. Ibid., 458.

190. Ibid., 460.

191. Ibid., 469–77.

192. Ibid., 478n72: "Küng 1976, 350f. stresses the unimaginability of the resurrection as part of his argument that 'the resurrection of Jesus was not an event in space and time.'"

193. Ibid., 578–79.

resurrection.[194] The announcement of Christ's resurrection meant that his lordship made claims even on Caesar. Jesus was the one to whom every knee should bow.

The NT authors did not write so as to make it appear that Jesus's resurrection occurred—they were convinced that Jesus really did rise from the dead. The resurrection was an actual event.[195] Paul and the other NT authors did not spend their time defending the resurrection; rather, they spoke of it as a given. Despite volumes of liberal literature that have attempted to erase or cast doubt on the reliability of the resurrection, Wright concludes that the NT authors consistently present the centrality of the resurrection, the resurrection of Christ's people in his resurrection, and bodily transformation in resurrection.[196]

Critique of Doctrine of Scripture and Resurrection. In *WCG2* I briefly outlined the decline of the biblically faithful view of Scripture in the modern period.[197] The linguistic turn arose from an interest in language as a hoped-for solution to perceived failures in traditional philosophy. Then came the later Wittgenstein and ordinary language analysis, which gave up on a notion of correlation between an object and naming that object. Now the goal was simply to describe, not to explain.[198] These movements have influenced the thinking of N. T. Wright.[199]

A proper doctrine of Scripture comes from the Word of God alone, not the Word plus information from the world surrounding the Bible. It is important to comprehend the language and culture of the Bible, but the humanness and cultural context of the Bible do not comprise

194. Ibid., 581–82: "The first Christians . . . were thereby committed to living and working *within history*. . . . Because it was assumed by many scholars that nothing much had happened in the world of space-time events—because . . . it was taken for granted that the bodily resurrection did not happen—all the weight was put at another point, the imminent 'second coming.' In fact . . . they rested the weight of their theology on the event which, they firmly believed, had already happened."

195. Ibid., 630–46; 680: "The basic stories themselves, of the empty tomb and the appearances of Jesus, show no signs of having been generated at a later stage. . . . The main conclusion that emerges from these four studies of the canonical evangelists is that each of them, in their very different ways, believed that they were writing about events that actually took place."

196. Ibid., 681–706.

197. See *WCG* 2:97.

198. See *WCG* 2:98.

199. *WCG* 2:11n58: "Wright, *People of God*, 5, dismisses evangelicalism, or what he terms 'fundamentalism,' as simply being caught up in Enlightenment thought. His wrongheaded 'project' (26) is to combine premodern, modern, and postmodern philosophies."

Scripture's nature.[200] Wright's view is directly based on a contemporary epistemological philosophy called *critical realism* (see below). He does not hide his philosophical background, which I have analyzed elsewhere in a short article.[201] It is Wright's incorrect view of how humans know that pushes him askew when it comes to a proper view of Scripture. And it is his improper view of Scripture that gives him an improper view of the resurrection.

Wright should be praised for his many penetrating critiques of liberalism's view of the resurrection. For liberals, Christ's resurrection is merely a theological interpretation of events by NT authors. Wright brilliantly demonstrates that the theological emperors of liberalism have no clothes. It is also true that a quick read of his book on the resurrection makes him sound as though he is evangelical.[202] That, however, is not the case.

Wright's view of Scripture, and thus the resurrection, is driven by his philosophy of history.[203] His critical realism forces any historical knowledge, including Scripture, into a set of fallible interpretations. To understand the resurrection, he believes, a scholar must comprehend it within Second Temple Judaism. In other words, fallible human interpretations of events become the norm—not God's overriding control of the divine inspiration of Scripture. For Wright, to know something of history is to know its "story."[204] Similar to Thiselton's view, this story is a dialogue or conversation between horizons. The conversation includes the observer and his perspective, or worldview, which is informed by his community of assumptions and traditions. Thus all knowledge of

200. See *WCG* 2:107.

201. See Richard C. Gamble "Critical Realism and the New Perspective," *RPTJ* 1, no. 2 (Spring 2015): 2–12.

202. The German systematic theologian Michael Welker in fact derogatorily labels him a "fundamentalist." The scholar and pastor John Piper acknowledges that Wright may be confusing—but would not say that his views are false. Furthermore, author and pastor Tim Keller said in an interview that Wright takes a "nice old-fashioned approach" to the resurrection and that reading his book "was a wonderful experience. It was both an intellectual and emotional experience" (Anthony Sacramone, "An Interview with Tim Keller," *First Things* [February 2008], https://www.firstthings.com/web-exclusives/2008/02/an-interview-with-timothy-kell). Accessed January 12, 2015.

203. Thanks to colleague Dr. Jeffrey Stivason for some of the following insights.

204. Wright, *People of God*, 35: "[the] process of 'knowing' . . . acknowledges the *reality of the thing known, as something other than the knower* . . . while also fully acknowledging that the only access we have to this reality lies along the spiralling path of *appropriate dialogue or conversation between the knower and the thing known*."

fact is embedded in continuing perceptions and reflections.[205] That assertion means that all statements are provisional in nature. Once again, there are no timeless historical truths. What exists in the Bible relative to the resurrection is someone's reflection or interpretation of the actual event.[206] In contrast, a vibrant Christianity needs a true bodily resurrection of Christ that is based on the sure witness of no less than God himself, who sets his *imprimatur* on the Scriptures.

Justification. Wright addresses the nature, scope, and means of salvation, as well as the meaning of *justification*. He argues that Paul's doctrine of justification is about the work of Jesus, Israel's Messiah.[207] Paul's doctrine of justification is about the covenant and the divine law court, and is bound up with eschatology. Paul argues for both a present and a final justification.[208]

Wright is motivated to write because he believes that scholars have yet to address the entirety of Pauline teaching.[209] He claims that most scholars miss either Paul's use of the OT[210] or Paul's understanding of Israel's story.[211]

Paul taught that God had a single plan or narrative to rescue the world and the human race—a plan centered on Israel's call, which came to function in Israel's representative, the Messiah. Wright explains that Paul's teaching was misunderstood after the Reformation, through the Enlightenment, the Romantic era, Pietism, and existentialism.[212] "The voice of the apostle," he laments, "has become all but unrecognizable."[213]

After establishing the problem, Wright turns to exegesis. Scripture answers the questions that it seeks to address, not the questions that

205. Ibid., 83: "In reality what we call 'facts' always belong in a context of response, perception, and interaction—a process which is both complex and continuing."

206. Ibid., 83–84: "If we say 'Christ died for our sins,' it is not too difficult to see an obvious element of interpretation. . . . But even if we say 'Christ died,' we have not escaped interpretation. . . . Our apparently bare historical remark is the product of a multi-faceted interpretive decision. Nor is this unusual. It is typical of all history."

207. N. T. Wright, *Justification, God's Plan & Paul's Vision* (Downers Grove, IL: IVP Academic, 2009), 9–11. In contrast, for Piper Israel's story seems more likely to be a backdrop.

208. Ibid., 12.

209. Wright (*Justification*, 28, 31–32) claims that he invented the term *New Perspective on Paul* in 1978.

210. Ibid., 33. The exception is Richard Hays.

211. Ibid., 34.

212. Ibid., 36–37.

213. Ibid., 37

are imposed on it.[214] Necessary exegetical procedure consists in marking the text's flow, context, and specific arguments.[215]

One of the main problems in hermeneutics is that conservatives have turned to their traditions, not to Scripture. Wright believes that there needs to be what he terms a *hermeneutics of doctrine*.[216] He writes of this hermeneutic that it is "when our tradition presses us to regard as central something which is seldom if even actually said by Paul himself."[217]

Wright is convinced that scholars need to read the NT within its first-century context.[218] All terms must be located within their historical context—a task that requires a level of historical research.[219] He claims that there is no neutral, ordinary reading of a text, and he calls for the testing of long-held theological traditions.[220] Wright then turns to first-century Judaism and Josephus's making clear that first-century Jews were not concerned with going to heaven; instead, they longed for earthly deliverance.[221] The theme of exile, and the anticipation of deliverance, was a controlling and continuing motif.[222] Even though they had returned from Babylon, Israel was still in exile.[223]

Concerning God's righteousness and the covenant, the covenant of Daniel 9:4–14 points back to Deuteronomy 27–30. *God's righteousness* means that Israel has broken her covenantal promises, but God has not and will not do so. Israel's hope is that God will return the people from exile and thus fulfill righteousness.[224] Wright addressed some of

214. Ibid., 40. Wright says that he stands opposed to Edmund P. Clowney, "The Biblical Doctrine of Justification by Faith," in *Right with God: Justification in the Bible and the World*, ed. D. A. Carson (Grand Rapids: Baker, 1992), 44.

215. Ibid., 41. Ephesians and Colossians were written by Paul, and the entire book of Ephesians is an argument for the new perspective. "No wonder Lutheran scholars have been so suspicious of it" (ibid., 43–44).

216. Ibid., 45.

217. Ibid., 46.

218. Ibid., 46–47.

219. Ibid., 48.

220. Ibid., 50. This goes contra the NIV's translation (see ibid., 51–53).

221. Ibid., 55–57.

222. Ibid., 59.

223. Ibid., 60–61. That exile is a continuing theme is neglected by both Dunn and Sanders.

224. Ibid., 63. Wright addressed Piper's criticisms. Piper ignores the huge mass of scholarly literature, has an idiosyncratic definition of God's righteousness, does not grapple with the context of Romans 3–4, and fails in his attempt to downplay the law court metaphor, and his notion of God's righteousness is going in the wrong direction (Wright, *Justification*, 64–71).

his critics on this issue. It is here that theological traditions can play an important but misguided role. Lutheranism condemned the folly of self-righteous law keeping and judged first-century Judaism to be the wrong religion. Wright speculates that if the Reformed rather than the Lutheran view of the Law would have won in the battle for Pauline interpretation, a new perspective on Paul would have been unnecessary. In a reaction to Lutheranism, NT scholar E. P. Sanders offered a way out by viewing the Torah as the covenantal charter. He proposed *covenantal nomism*—in essence, "now that you are in the covenant, here is the law to keep."[225] The theological issue is the relationship between God and man relative to obedience. Wright challenges the older interpretation of the Sermon on the Mount on the divine-human relationship of moral effort.[226]

Wright's conclusion is that the focus of Scripture is not individual salvation but God's purpose for Israel and the world. God was about to bring in the age to come. In that age, the Israel who has kept the Torah will be vindicated. Thus Torah has both a covenantal and an eschatological framework. The keeping of the Torah connects back to Deuteronomy 30, which Paul cites in Romans 10.[227]

Transitioning to the doctrine of justification, Wright maintains that the concept of justification should be distinguished from the doctrine of justification. And the doctrine of justification is not the same as Paul's doctrine.[228]

Sadly, the formal doctrine of justification has distorted the church's understanding of Pauline thought. Paul's concept of justification is distinct from Augustine's great doctrine.[229] The doctrine of justification is made up of many angles and components, as opposed to Paul's view, which was singular.[230]

225. Ibid., 72–74. Wright interprets Sanders and covenantal nomism as Calvinism. D. A. Carson (in *Justification and Variegated Nomism*, vol. 1, *The Complexities of Second Temple Judaism*, ed. D. A. Carson, Peter T. O'Brien, and Mark Siefrid [Grand Rapids: Baker, 2001]) responded against Sanders, but Wright claims that research has supposedly supported Sanders.

226. Wright, *Justification*, 75.

227. Ibid., 75–77.

228. Ibid., 79–84. We are all in a hermeneutical spiral. Later theology has screened out the earlier overtones from the history of Israel and covenant. Wrede and Schweitzer anticipated the new perspective.

229. Ibid., 85.

230. Ibid., 86–87.

There are two English words involved in a discussion of law—the words *just* and *righteous*.[231] Righteousness "denotes the status that someone has when the court has found in their favor."[232] The court of law has nothing to do with the moral character or behavior of an individual.[233] Justification is not an action that transforms but a declaration that grants status.[234] The doctrine of justification has to be understood as connected to the covenant. God called Abraham in order that God could rescue the world through his family.[235] God's simple purpose came into function with Jesus Christ.[236] The notion of covenant meant how God's people understood themselves; their very being in covenant with Abraham.[237] Paul retrieved the story and included Jesus the Messiah.[238] Pauline theology can be summarized in the term *covenant*.[239]

But eschatology also plays a part in this doctrine. Eschatological impact means that God's plan is headed toward a specific goal that is launched in Jesus Christ, thus ushering in the inauguration of a new age.[240] Wright combines covenant, law court, and eschatology: God's promises to Abraham have been fulfilled, Jesus has been vindicated, and a new world has been inaugurated. There remains only the final goal.[241]

Christology also plays an important role in justification. Paul's use of the terms *Jesus*, *Christ*, *Son of God*, and *Lord* means that Jesus is "the reality of which all earthly emperors are mere parodies."[242] The Messiah sums up God's people; what is true of him is true of them. The Messiah offered the obedience that Israel failed to offer.[243] The Messiah represents his people and absorbs the death that they deserve.[244]

231. Ibid., 88.
232. Ibid., 90.
233. Ibid.
234. Ibid., 91. In contrast, Piper says it grants a moral righteousness from Christ (ibid., 92).
235. Ibid., 94.
236. Ibid., 94–95.
237. Ibid., 95.
238. Ibid., 96.
239. Ibid., 99.
240. Ibid., 101.
241. Ibid.
242. Ibid., 103.
243. Ibid., 104.
244. Ibid., 105.

The Messiah's resurrection is the beginning of the new creation, and the Spirit makes his people children.[245] On the last day, Jesus, as the Messiah, will be the judge.[246]

In the book of Galatians, Paul brings together the themes of *law court, covenant, eschatology, Christology,* and the *meaning of justification.*[247] The pressing issues addressed in Galatians are whether or not Jews and Gentiles should be seated at the same table[248] plus other practices connected with ethnic identity.[249] The first statement of justification by faith is that people are not justified by the Jewish law, known as Torah. But what does it mean to be justified? It does not equate with the offering of forgiveness or the reckoning of a right relationship with God. To be justified means to be a member of the family and thus permitted table fellowship.[250] Justification is God's declaration of membership in his family.

Justification is not by works of the Law but by the faithfulness of Jesus. The faithfulness of Jesus Christ to God's long, single purpose is the instrument of justification. People appropriate this justification by faith.[251] The Law was flawed, however, in two ways: (1) it created division between Jew and Gentile, and (2) no one could keep it.[252] The people of God are reconstituted from the rule of Torah, and righteousness denotes a status, not a moral quality.[253]

Ecclesiology and soteriology are not opposed to each other, or even as disconnected as many might suppose. In fact, they are in an intimate relationship. Membership in God's people (ecclesiology) means being saved on the last day (soteriology). Saul had membership in the covenant by grace. Justification by works of Torah was not intended to earn covenantal membership or add merit to grace. For Saul, it was a

245. Ibid., 106.
246. Ibid., 107.
247. Ibid., 111.
248. Ibid., 114.
249. Ibid., 115.
250. Ibid., 116.
251. Ibid., 117.
252. Ibid., 118–20. Galatians 2:17–18 should not be answered by saying that we are justified in Christ but are still sinners who commit actual sin. Galatians 2:19–20 teaches that Paul and the Jews both died to the old identity of Torah righteousness that separated them from the Gentiles.
253. Ibid., 121.

sign in the present that he would participate in future vindication or justification.[254] Philippians 3:7–11 undermines justification by works.

The last day has now come in the Messiah. One of the primary forces for Paul's identification of God's people was *inaugurated eschatology*.[255] Paul's status in Christ includes: the court's finding in favor of him despite his unworthiness; covenantal membership; advanced eschatological judgment, that is, hearing in the present the future verdict; and the verdict that Jesus is truly God's Son in the resurrection.[256]

There is a great exchange taught in 1 Corinthians 1:18–2:5 that is summarized in 1:30. The theme is status; the boast is in the crucified Christ, not worldly status.[257] The treasure includes wisdom,[258] righteousness, sanctification, and redemption. According to Wright, 1 Corinthians 1:30 is not intended to be a precise theological statement or to imply imputation; for wisdom, sanctification, and redemption are not imputed to the believer.[259]

Righteousness refers to the believer's status in Jesus, since God vindicated him as his Son, the Israel-in-person. Sanctification is believers' status, in part, as God's holy people, but more particularly it refers to their life of holiness.[260] Redemption is neither a status nor an element of life but "the accomplishment of God on their behalf, the great new exodus through which they have been set free from the slavery of sin."[261] In conclusion, Wright's treatment is not a ringing endorsement of the theological notion of imputed righteousness.[262] Instead, God's righteousness refers to God's personal righteousness as God's covenantal faithfulness to his promises.[263]

Wright's positive message is that Christians are the true people of God and the pagan gods were defeated in Christ's resurrection.

254. Ibid., 147–49.
255. Ibid., 148.
256. Ibid., 150.
257. The text has a quotation from Isaiah 29; the theme is well known in Romans and glimpsed at in Galatians 6:14 (Wright, ibid., 155).
258. All the wisdom ideas of Judaism are relocated in Jesus, and believers are to see him as the personal presence of the divine wisdom (Wright, ibid., 155–56).
259. Ibid., 156–57.
260. As God has put to death all that is fleshly in Jesus, raised him, and given him a new body, so believers can put sin to death (Wright, ibid., 157).
261. Ibid., 156.
262. Ibid., 158.
263. Ibid., 164.

Wright's new perspective is that the message of Christ's resurrection does not establish a new soteriology—that of faith in Christ versus attempts at attaining righteousness through works of law—but, more simply, reconfigures God's people.[264] It is the promise that God will rescue his people.

Critique of Justification and New Perspective. The second volume of *The Whole Counsel of God* (*WGC2*) included a brief critique of the New Perspective on Paul. That critique began with an examination of interpretations of Paul spanning from the 1960s to the 1990s.[265] The critique then centered on the understandings held by a number of authors (other than N. T. Wright) on Paul's presentation of justification.[266] Subsequently, the section on the new perspective began with an analysis of Krister Stendahl, E. P. Sanders, and J. G. Dunn, as well as Wright. Proponents of the New Perspective on Paul contend that prior interpretations of Paul have fallen short because they have viewed Pauline thought, particularly as found in Galatians or Romans, to be concerned with grace over against the pursuit of righteousness (works). Those older scholars fundamentally misinterpreted Judaism. Paul's intent was not to create an artificial systematic theological soteriology but to emphasize the lordship of Christ.[267] Then *WCG2* transitioned to a preliminary critique of the new perspective that focused on scholars other than Wright. The further information and critique promised for the third (or present) volume follows.[268]

Wright has a false view of justification.[269] A proper view of justification requires a biblical understanding of God's holiness or righ-

---

264. Wright, *People of God*, 369–70, as cited by Guy Prentiss Waters, *Justification and the New Perspectives on Paul: A Review and Response* (Phillipsburg, NJ: P&R Publishing, 2004), 123.

265. WCG 2:214–16.

266. Focus was on the countermovement against Käsemann led by Martyn and de Boer as well as Hays. See *WCG* 2:216–20.

267. Ibid., 2:220–21.

268. That critique included an analysis of Martyn's completely false view of salvation in the OT and his equally false view that Paul doubted that there were any elect in Israel. Hays came into criticism with his false view of the nature of historical texts, as well as his false presupposition that Paul doubted that he was a writer of Scripture. Enns came under critique for believing that Paul adopted Jewish lore into Scripture (see ibid., 2:221–23).

269. Wright's idea is a caricature of contemporary evangelicalism. Historic evangelicalism has never held that believing in justification by faith is the whole of the gospel. Connected is Wright's critique of Reformation theology, which equated the Judaizers with medieval salvation without grace. See Sinclair B. Ferguson, introduction to *Justified in Christ: God's Plan for Us in Justification*, ed. K. Scott Oliphint (Fearn, Scotland: Mentor, 2007), xx.

teousness, of his law, and of human sin. But no matter his prestigious education and intellectual dexterity, Wright has failed to grasp these central truths. For example, he teaches that in Romans the righteousness of God is his decisive covenantal faithfulness, which delivers his people from sin and ushers in the inaugurated new covenant. The justified are those who are included in Jesus's death and resurrection. Their circumcision is not by race but by Jesus, hence by faith.[270] Wright also believes that God's righteousness has three backgrounds: covenant, law court, and eschatology.[271] In contrast to Wright, Paul opened Romans by identifying the gospel as the message of God's righteousness, which includes God's absolute holiness and condemnation for anything less than perfect conformity to his law.[272]

Because of his inadequate view of God's holiness and righteousness, Wright necessarily has an inadequate view of sin and evil—which he views in terms of injustice. He believes that God is restoring things to how they should be and that covenantal faithfulness is "cosmic restorative justice."[273] But these mistaken notions have led him wrongly to deny that there is an imputation of Christ's righteousness to believers. The reason he gives is that one of God's attributes is righteousness and, by definition, an attribute cannot be imputed. This assertion is a fundamental theological mistake.[274] Also, Wright wrongly denies the notion of penal substitutionary atonement.[275] Instead, he substitutes the notion that salvation is Christ's victory over principalities and powers.[276]

270. Wright, *People of God*, 458.

271. The LXX teaches "God's own faithfulness to his promises, to the covenant." In Isaiah 40–55, righteousness is God's character, displayed in his saving Israel despite her unworthiness. "God's righteousness is thus cognate with his trustworthiness on the one hand, and Israel's salvation on the other" (Wright, *What Paul Really Said*, 96, as cited by Waters, *Justification*, 124).

272. See WCG 2:159 and the section at WCG 2:191–99 outlining the gospel of God in Romans 1:1–7.

273. N. T. Wright, *Romans*, in *Acts, Introduction to Epistolary Literature, Romans, 1 Corinthians*, by Robert W. Wall, J. Paul Sampley, and N. T. Wright, vol. 10, *The New Interpreter's Bible* (Nashville: Abingdon Press, 2002), 399–400, as cited by Waters, *Justification*, 125.

274. A question is whether attributes can be imputed. Ferguson (*Justified in Christ*, xix) correctly asks whether sin can be attributed if righteousness cannot be imputed.

275. There is "no specific reference to the atonement, far less an explicit confession of Christ's death as penal and substitutionary" (ibid.). Ferguson argues that it is not openly denied and can be argued that it is present in Jesus's lordship.

276. This notion is taken from the writings of Swedish theologian Gustav Aulen, who deemphasizes or repudiates penal substitution (ibid.)

Further, Paul's conversion was more than simply recognizing Jesus as Lord and Messiah, though Paul's doing so was certainly an important part of his conversion.[277] Wright has misunderstood Paul's gospel itself, beginning with the OT.[278] While he spends many pages on defining the gospel, he makes sure that his readers know what it is not—and according to Wright, the gospel is not about getting saved.[279]

Conclusion. This chapter marks the end of our historical analysis of the development of doctrine. As mentioned in the introduction and throughout the text, the purpose of this analysis has been to show forth the beauty of the Holy Spirit of God's guiding the church into a greater understanding of the luster of the pearl of great price, Scripture. All this information should help strengthen biblical preaching. Yet this chapter has also demonstrated that there are, and have been, many who include themselves in Christ's church who would attempt to cover the pearl's luster with their own foolishness. Part of the aim of *The Whole Counsel of God* is to protect and defend Christ's church against such attacks. The next chapter will take the lessons from all three volumes and focus on the Christian's obligation to defend the faith.

KEY TERMS

social Trinitarianism
two horizons

277. Ibid., xxi.

278. The new perspective also misinterprets Second Temple Judaism's understanding of grace. The OT teaches that fellowship with God is by grace, but in rabbinical literature that grace is because they have suffered—a condition. God is gracious, but his graciousness is conditioned (ibid., xx).

279. WCG 2:513n391: "Wright, *Saint Paul*, 45. While Wright supposedly rejects what he calls either-or thinking (for example at 43: 'The antithesis between the two is a false one, based on the spurious either-or that has misleadingly divided NT studies for many years'), he falls victim to his own trap in his definition of 'gospel.' Granted that Wright is very cautious, nevertheless he tries to prove too much when he says that Paul's gospel is not 'a system of how people get saved.' While, according to Wright, the gospel results in salvation, '"the gospel" itself, strictly speaking, is the narrative proclamation of King Jesus.' Why is it not possible for the 'narrative proclamation of Christ' the great mediatorial King to include a call to rebellious men and women to come to himself in the same way that a king summons his servants? Certainly that was the message of Ps. 2, that the Son is King but that all men and women, including earthly kings, are to come and 'kiss' this Son. Clearly, this call to faith and repentance was also part of Paul's technical teaching of 'the gospel.'"

preunderstanding
New Perspective on Paul

STUDY QUESTIONS

1. How do some modern theologians understand the word *historic* when it is applied to events such as the resurrection?
2. Is God's character changing in any way?
3. In what ways can we say that God is love? Is his love his most important attribute?
4. Do you see ways in which postmodernism is influencing theology?

RESOURCES FOR FURTHER STUDY

A number of topics were omitted from this chapter for considerations of space, the first topic being liberation theology. Important primary texts for that area are:

Miguez Bonino, José. *Doing Theology in a Revolutionary Situation.* Minneapolis: Fortress, 2009.
Gutierrez, Gustavo. *A Theology of Liberation.* Maryknoll, NY: Orbis, 1973
Cone, James H. *A Black Theology of Liberation.* Maryknoll, NY: Orbis, 1970.

A powerful analysis and critique of their thinking consists in:

Conn, Harvie M. "Theologies of Liberation: An Overview" and "Theologies of Liberation: Toward a Common View." In *Tensions in Contemporary Theology*, ed. Stanley N. Gundry and Alan F. Johnson, 327–94 and 395–436. Grand Rapids: Baker, 1976.

A number of prominent German theologians have not been analyzed in this chapter. For information on an important book by German theologian Michael Welker titled *God the Revealed: Christology* (trans. Douglas W. Stott; Grand Rapids/Cambridge: Eerdmans, 2013), see:

Gamble, Richard C. Review of *God the Revealed: Christology*, by Michael Welker. *Westminster Theological Journal* 77, no. 1 (Spring 2015): 165–67.

The three most important theologians working in the English language at this time are John M. Frame (b. 1939), Vern Poythress (b. 1946), and Sinclair Ferguson (b. 1948). They have been extensively cited in all three volumes of *WCG*. Proper analysis of their lives and writings would extend this already thick book. It has been one of my life's greatest privileges to be a colleague of each of these godly and brilliant men, and Dr. Ferguson did me the distinct honor of writing the foreword to *WCG2* as well as to this volume.

26

God's People Respond to God's Mighty Acts: Answering Questions

THIS NEARLY FINAL CHAPTER is based on the information that we have learned thus far and will present a way to defend Christianity against unbelieving thought. The method used to make that defense will be to answer the questions that unbelievers entertain. Thinking people must ask questions about themselves and the world around them. Granted, there are many humans who, sadly, do not ask these types of questions—unfortunately, for them, there is not much that believers can say to or do for them except pray.[1] God has given them over to the hardness of their own hearts.

People face perplexing questions through every stage of human life. Some of those questions are considered classic, such as, "Why do bad things happen to good people?" Another example is, "Why do loved ones have to die?" The best way to proceed is to analyze these various types of fundamental human questions.

ORDERING PEOPLE'S QUESTIONS INTO CATEGORIES AND DETERMINING THEIR RELATIONSHIPS

Definitions of Types of Questions. Looking at life as a big picture, some questions are posed by children and are therefore childish. For example, every parent has heard the mournful, "How much longer will

---

1. This is the type of person who is simply satisfied with a good job, house, and family and is not concerned with any deeper questions of life.

this trip last?" Yet other supposedly childish questions are genuinely profound, such as, "What is the meaning of life?" In between those two childish sample questions are hosts of others. Many of those questions have embedded within them various degrees of internal complexity; thus the questions that people ask can be organized under different subject headings.

Some of these questions can be categorized as *How?* questions, others as *scientific* questions, some as *Why?* questions, and some as *ought* questions. Questions about who we are are classified as *anthropological*. Questions about what we know are *epistemological*. Questions about how we are to behave are termed *ethical*. There are complicated interrelationships between all the various questions, and sometimes an inquiry will fall between multiple categories. Furthermore, different philosophers classify diverse questions differently.

First are the *How?* questions. Examples of this sort of inquiry include, "How do we know that there is a law of gravity?" This category of question, and the field related to it, is called *epistemology*. Associated questions are: "Are there limits to our knowledge?" "How can we know if our knowledge is valid?" and "What is the origin of our knowledge?" A subcategory within the How? or epistemological questions are inquiries about concepts. For example, "What is the relationship between words and ultimate reality?" This subcategory includes questions about philosophical method, including the problem of the one and the many.[2] Finally, there is the issue of the ability of the human subject to know anything.

Second are scientific questions. Examples of this type include, "What is the relationship between liquid gasoline and the running engine of a car?" and "Why does a pencil appear to bend when it is inserted into a

2. See Richard C. Gamble, *The Whole Counsel of God*, vol. 1, *God's Mighty Acts in the Old Testament* (Phillipsburg, NJ: P&R Publishing, 2009) (*WCG1*), 87; Richard C. Gamble, *The Whole Counsel of God*, vol. 2, *The Full Revelation of God* (Phillipsburg, NJ: P&R Publishing, 2018) (*WCG2*), 967, 1018: "'one and many' problem: A problem that addresses how thinkers can relate their experiences of various phenomena with an overarching unifying phenomenon. For example, it addresses the differences between cultures relative to notions of beauty. Is there an abstract notion of Beauty (one) that unites various cultural differences relative to beauty (many)? Christianity answers the problem of the one and many. God defines the universals in his Word. God unites the particulars of our everyday experience into one beautiful, connected whole. In God as Trinity, believers can understand how there can be an equal ultimacy of the one (the universal) and the many (the particulars)."

clear glass of water?" A not very serious question is "Why do the scales change when we get older even though we are not putting on weight?"

Then there are *Why?* questions. Examples of this type are "Why are people cruel?" "Why do we love someone?" and "Why do we like music and art?" This category of question, and the field related to it, is often called *aesthetics.*

A why question that moves into the next field is, "Why do we make the choices that we do?" These kinds of questions are classified as *value* questions, and asking value questions is termed *axiology.* "Why do we consider diamonds to be valuable but dirt almost worthless?" What is meant by the qualitative nature of value? Is value perceived intuitively? What is something worthwhile, fundamental, and enduring? How do we know whether something is of minor value versus ultimate value?[3] Values are judged by their power to increase or decrease happiness. "Regret is freedom's looking back on an irretrievably lost opportunity," said one Christian philosopher.[4]

Another category could be questions of metaphysics, that is, questions about that which is beyond sensory experience. An example is, "Why are people afraid of death?"[5]

Ought questions deal with the field of ethics. Examples of this type include, "Why ought we come to class?" Other examples could relate to culture or to politics, which areas also include issues of ought, or that which is judged as good or bad. This group includes questions of the individual and his rights versus the collective and collective rights. This topic is sometimes also referred to as *morality.*[6]

Mature Christians must face and answer many of these questions for themselves—and they will find the answers in the Bible. Granted that these questions are profound, how can someone not united to Christ approach answering them?[7] One way is to assert that men and women simply have no choice in anything. Life's questions can be

3. Edward J. Carnell, *A Philosophy of the Christian Religion* (Grand Rapids: Eerdmans, 1954), 16, 20, 23–25.
4. Ibid., 21.
5. Edward J. Carnell, *An Introduction to Christian Apologetics* (Grand Rapids: Eerdmans, 1948), 122.
6. A subcategory is the "is-ought" question, sometimes known as *Hume's law.*
7. Carnell, *Philosophy,* 18: "The individual is the totality of his value commitments, for without interest there is no life. To live is to strive, to hope, and to die for the worth-while."

answered only with despondency. In the light of this desperate situation, one may choose death, but most people do not do so because they fear that death may in fact be worse than life.[8]

Preliminary Definitions: Terms Used to Classify Questions. Some of the example questions open up huge areas for debate. We do not all see eye to eye on the questions! Thus there are what have been termed *foundational questions* that must be addressed before someone is even able to ask intelligent questions! To prove the point with an example, does even asking a question necessarily have any meaning? It may seem to be a strange point, but under normal circumstances it is not meaningful for me to ask a deaf person his opinion of a poem that someone just read out loud, with no interpreter's signing its translation.

Also, I used the adjective *intelligent* to describe the questions asked. Who determines whether or not a given question is intelligent? To continue further analysis, there is a need to define terms. An important issue is the relationship between correspondence and meaning. The word *meaning* has various shades of meaning! The basic questions that are posed on the topic involve whether or not there is a correspondence between what I see or observe and what you see or observe.

Furthermore, is there any correspondence between the words that I speak, the conception of those words in my own mind, and the conception that comes into your mind from your hearing of the same words that I just uttered?[9] Only when meaning is agreed on—only when it is agreed that there is some type of correspondence between my words and what your mind conceives from them—can the questioner move forward.[10]

To continue requires us to address the question of the one and the many. Having determined that language between two thinking human beings can be meaningful, that is, we can communicate with each other, we can advance to the next set of questions. A next basic question concerns the relationship between our experience of something and some type of broadly universal experience of it. To choose what should

---

8. Ibid., 19.

9. Carnell, *Apologetics*, 30–31. There is a problem of what is termed *significant speech*, and the problem is resolved "by dividing the particulars in reality (the many) into teleologically related class-concepts (the one)." See also John M. Frame, *Cornelius Van Til: An Analysis of His Thought* (Phillipsburg, NJ: Presbyterian and Reformed, 1995) (*CVT*), 91.

10. L. Kalsbeek, *Contours of a Christian Philosophy* (Toronto: Wedge, 1975), 60.

be an easy example, is my experience of gravity (the one) the same as all people's experience of gravity at all times (the many)? Certainly my experience is different from the experience of a weightless astronaut. Also, my experience of gravity if I were floating in the Dead Sea, a body of water filled with salt, would be different from my experience of gravity when standing before you. Likewise, when I begin a hike with a pack on my back, the pack, of course, "becomes" heavier as I ascend the hill. But you may not feel the weight of the same pack as much as I do if you are forty years younger than I am.

To continue, is my experience of justice (the one) the same as everyone else's experience (universal)? What about my notion of *father* compared with the notion of *father* held by a woman who was abused by her father when she was a child? Finally, is there an overall coherence to all of the diversity of life?

We must turn to the person who is asking questions. We can call this person the *thinking self* or the *ego*.[11] Complex questions, philosophical thinking, cannot be abstracted from the actual thinking self. I as a person living in the here and now ask these particular questions. It is not easy to keep the questions separated into pure categories or types, and it is impossible to abstract the questions from the thinking self. We will need to expand the analysis of the thinking self later.

SOME QUESTIONS BEHIND THE QUESTIONS

To analyze the nature of these important human questions is the work of philosophy. To succeed in that effort we need to have more tools. The first task is to separate various subjects.

Divisions of the One and the Many. The first, and largest, division could be called *spheres* or termed *creation structures*. All of us experience great big spheres in life. In general, we talk about the spheres of the family, the church, and the state. The concept of *creation structure* or *sphere* is one of the notions thinkers use to get a handle on the question of the one and many. In other words, there are thousands of individual families, yet we can talk about the family as a universal or as a unit. While different cultures have different family structures, such

11. See WCG 2:95.

as nuclear families or extended families, each person has experienced some type of family structure. Furthermore, the state is made up of many communities, yet it too is seen as a unit. Another example is the church. There are thousands of individual churches, yet believers can talk about the church as a single unit.

The next division of the problem looks at smaller units. One can look at the question of the one and the many from various special disciplines.[12] Some examples are the larger branches of learning called the *mathematical*, the *spatial*, and the *natural* sciences. But these large disciplines have subcategories; for example, biology is a subcategory of the natural sciences. Some special disciplines are more complex than those mentioned. For example, is human faith a product of chemical reactions and thus a natural science, or is it a sociological issue and thus a social science—or is belief its own type of special discipline?

Within the various special disciplines, an object may have functions both as a subject and as an object. In plumbing, the plumber is the subject and the pipe is the object. In botany, a tree may be an object of a scientist's investigation, while if you believe that all living things have a spirit, the tree is a subject to itself.

More on the *Thinking Self*. Nearly all philosophers have said that it is important for us to know ourselves.[13] The thinking self always functions or plays a role within the various special disciplines.[14] That statement does not mean that each and every thinking individual is, or must be, involved in all the many disciplines. But there are no special disciplines that exist independently of the researcher, scientist, or philosopher who analyzes that particular discipline. While there may be many plants, there is no discipline of botany without an active botanist.

Furthermore, the scientist or philosopher, as a thinking self, finds the thinking self to be the concentration point of all his or her activities. This case is certainly true in the sciences; therefore, the thinking self is foundational to the abstract concept of *philosophical thought*.[15] Since

---

12. These special disciplines can have a number of names, such as *modalities* or *modal aspects*.

13. Kalsbeek, *Contours*, 58. Kalsbeek lamented Descartes's thinking, as it demonstrated a lack of true self-knowledge.

14. My use of the term *special discipline* is equivalent to Herman Dooyeweerd's *modal aspects*.

15. Herman Dooyeweerd, *A New Critique of Theoretical Thought*, vol. 1, *The Necessary Presuppositions of Philosophy*, trans. David Freeman and William Young (Philadelphia: Presbyterian and Reformed, 1953), 5.

the thinking self is foundational to the special discipline, it can be said that the thinking self is transcendent with respect to the complexities of all the diverse special disciplines, including philosophy.[16] In other words, for there to be any knowledge of any special discipline, there must be a person, a thinking self, who has that knowledge. Stated differently, there is no such thing as abstract pure thinking, because all thinking must be connected to a specific thinking ego, a self. The self "expresses itself in all special modal aspects of our existence."[17]

The thinking self begins philosophical reflection and needs content to his or her thought. The content deals with words and their meanings. Also, the thinking self needs a direction, a method, or a way, to think. Thus the thinking self chooses a place from among the myriad one and many possibilities from which to start or stand—and then to begin his or her thinking.[18] The most important question relative to defending the whole counsel of God is, "From where do thinking selves choose their standpoint or starting place?"

On the one hand, children do not reflect on this starting place or standpoint. They simply imitate the words and actions they see around them. But when the time for college comes, a thinking self must reflect on him- or herself and determine the direction of his or her studies—and choose a major. Here, at least, is a beginning point of reflection. The student must find for him- or herself a place to stand, a place to survey possibilities, a tower from which to look out on the vast field of special disciplines. That important tower, the place where he or she stands to observe and make judgments about the world—simply put, a college major—can be called the "ultimate reference."[19]

The Ultimate Reference.[20] All philosophical thinking needs a fixed point of reference to begin an analysis of thought in particular or the world in general.[21] That ultimate reference is the center or core of the person's philosophical thinking. The philosopher recognizes that

16. Ibid., 1:16.
17. Ibid., 1:15.
18. Ibid., 1:8.
19. If it is a helpful analogy, that place to stand can be compared to the twin towers of J. R. R. Tolkein's imaginary world.
20. I use *ultimate reference* as an equivalent to Dooyeweerd's *archimedean point*. Kalsbeek, *Contours*, 347: It is "a sure place to stand; a vantage point from which everything can in principle be seen in true perspective."
21. Ibid., 56–57.

ultimate reference point as the center of both truth and reality, and it is a fixed place from which thinking people form the idea of the totality of meaning.[22] In other words, philosophy's first task is to find a proper starting point for the investigation of all reality. From that place, philosophy reflects on the totality of the world. To make that reflection requires a fixed point from which to view the world.[23]

In general, an ultimate reference cannot be found from within the philosophical disciplines themselves. The ultimate reference cannot remain as purely theoretical thought or act. Thus any approach to abstract philosophical thought that seeks its ultimate reference from within theoretical thought will end up in futility. The following section will demonstrate that it is necessary to find the ultimate reference somewhere outside any of the pure philosophical domains.[24]

The first inherent problem in attempting to find the ultimate reference from within any of the numerous meaning aspects is the difficulty of determining which one of those many aspects should be absolutized to take that primary place. For example, there is no compelling reason to choose mathematics over biology as central. In fact, none of the many individual spheres can provide the necessary vista from which to view the entire universe.[25]

Second, no type of abstract particularity—for example, the notion of a pure law, say of physics or math—or some type of uninterpreted brute fact—such as gravity—can provide an adequate ultimate reference, because there are no pure laws without particular laws, and vice versa. Any example of an overall law is part of particular laws. Likewise, an overall fact is an aspect of a host of particular facts.

Third, it is not possible to separate the investigating person, the object that is being studied, and the method of that person's study. The person and the object are always in an interdependent relationship.[26]

Finally, philosophical self-reflection, which is necessary for an ultimate reference, directs its thought toward itself. It must then tran-

22. Dooyeweerd, *New Critique*, 1:8.
23. Ronald H. Nash, *Dooyeweerd and the Amsterdam Philosophy* (Grand Rapids: Zondervan, 1962), 25, 80.
24. Dooyeweerd, *New Critique*, 1:21; Kalsbeek, *Contours*, 57.
25. Nash, *Dooyeweerd*, 76.
26. Frame, *Van Til*, 172.

scend the limits of philosophical thought to reach self-reflection. The issue is the thinking self accounting for itself.[27]

It would be good now to define the *ultimate reference*. For it to function as its name indicates, three conditions must be satisfied.[28] First, it must be connected to the thinking self.[29] Second, it must be connected to the law of the thinking self's existence. Third, it must transcend the diversities of the special disciplines and somehow be found in the unity of that diversity.[30] Concerning the third condition, the ultimate reference must transcend even an ultimate coherence within the vast assortment of special disciplines.[31] The necessity for such an ultimate reference underlies many of the mistakes that are made by non-Christian thinkers. Thus the only true ultimate reference point recognizes that because humans are created beings, we are utterly and entirely dependent on God. What is vital to defending the faith is to realize, therefore, that there can be no legitimate ultimate reference point outside God and his beautiful revelation of himself.[32]

In the history of thought, there have been a number of major, but nevertheless inadequate, so-called "ultimate references." They were incorrect particularly because they did not satisfy the third requirement for such references, that is, they did not transcend any of the special disciplines.[33] We can do a quick survey of wrong ultimate references. It is here that is the payoff for reading the earlier chapters on the history of Western thought. This chapter and the pages that follow comprise the reason for my wanting you to wade through analysis in the first chapter on early Greek thinking to the critique of postmodernism. Any philosophical ultimate reference not built on the rock of Christ cannot stand against the raging storms of life.

The first mistaken approach is what could be classified under the general title of *immanence philosophy*.[34] This category is a broad one

27. Dooyeweerd, *New Critique*, 1:7, 21.

28. See Nash, *Dooyeweerd*, 71, 79.

29. Dooyeweerd, *New Critique*, 1:8. The thinking self must participate in this totality of meaning.

30. Ibid., 1:12.

31. Ibid., 1:16.

32. Kalsbeek, *Contours*, 57. Here I strongly disagree with Dooyeweerd, who has the ultimate reference in the heart.

33. See Dallas Willard, *The Divine Conspiracy: Rediscovering Our Hidden Life in God* (London: William Collins, 2014).

34. Nash, *Dooyeweerd*, 74.

because immanence philosophies are diverse; they traverse metaphysical rationalism to logical positivism and the irrationalist philosophy of life.[35] In general, immanence philosophy refers to the belief that one can find a valid ultimate reference within the boundaries of philosophical thinking itself. Unfortunately, in immanence philosophy the self is hidden.[36]

By finding such an ultimate reference, immanence philosophers believe that they remain free from any religious or transcendent influences in their philosophy. They are convicted that their position concerning an ultimate reference, and theirs alone, maintains philosophy's so-called *scientific*, and therefore superior, character.[37] One example of that type of immanence thinking, coming from the beginning of the modern era, is found in the French thinker René Descartes.[38] He had as an ultimate reference the notion of *cogito ergo sum*, or abstract thought not necessarily connected to an individual. But his thinking introduces a complicating factor: the use of logic. One of the tasks that a thinking self does is use logic as a special discipline. A statement like Descartes made with an *ergo*, or "therefore," in it is a logical statement. Logic, like all the special disciplines, does not exist independently of the thinking self. Stated more philosophically, for the thinking self the ultimate reference is not found exclusively in the logical sphere, since logic is simply one function of many possible spheres.[39] Descartes's ultimate reference was doomed to failure because it was rationalistic.

There is another critique of Descartes that also applies to twentieth-century existentialism. Existentialism has an ultimate reference in existential thought and is doomed because each of us as thinking selves actually lives for more than existential thought.[40] Both of these past positions are mistaken because, for one, they have not dealt with the true nature of the thinking self. Descartes did not understand that there is something that must posit *cogito* ("I think"). That something could be called Descartes's own *thinking self* or *ego*. But Descartes's

35. Dooyeweerd, *New Critique*, 1:13.

36. Ibid., 1:11, 21. Cornelius Van Til, *A Christian Theory of Knowledge* (Nutley, NJ: Presbyterian and Reformed, 1969), 50.

37. Dooyeweerd, *New Critique*, 1:14.

38. Kalsbeek, *Contours*, 57. For Descartes, see chapter 16.

39. Dooyeweerd, *New Critique*, 1:17.

40. Ibid., 1:12.

thinking self was not exactly *cogito*, nor did his notion of *cogito* exhaust the fullness of the whole of the thinking self that was Descartes. In other words, Descartes, as thinking self, was a lot more than a simple "I think."[41]

The second wrong ultimate reference can be termed *transcendental consciousness*. The German philosopher Immanuel Kant had a false ultimate reference called the *transcendental cogito*, or the *transcendental unity of apperception*, or the *transcendental logical ego*.[42] Kant wrongly believed that there are "things in themselves" that exist outside human consciousness and that we can know nothing about. What men and women can know are the forms or categories of the human mind and the forms of intuition. In other words, abstract notions such as *space* and *time* are only constructs of the human mind. These constructs are immanent within the human consciousness.[43] Thus he mistakenly thought that a good ultimate reference would be reason.[44]

Immanence philosophy's standpoint is impossible unless it transcends the limits of philosophical thought.[45] The ultimate reference must transcend the modal diversity of meaning. It must also transcend the coherence of modal diversity. The bottom line is that a philosopher cannot have an ultimate reference within philosophical thought.[46] Stated again, since creation is dependent on God, thinking men and women can have no other ultimate reference outside God.

To summarize, we know that all thinkers need to find an ultimate reference. A true ultimate reference must transcend all the special disciplines or modal aspects of meaning. Philosophical thought alone cannot provide a true ultimate reference, for it does not transcend the special disciplines.[47] The only possibility for transcendence, and thus a true ultimate reference, is in what some would call the *religious roots* of human life.[48]

41. Kalsbeek, *Contours*, 57.
42. Dooyeweerd, *New Critique*, 1:16; Kalsbeek, *Contours*, 60. For Kant, see chapter 19.
43. Kalsbeek, *Contours*, 60–61.
44. Dooyeweerd, *New Critique*, 1:19. Dooyeweerd says that Kant's transcendental logicism identifies cosmic diversity of meaning with diversity in a logical or an analytical sense.
45. Ibid., 1:15.
46. Ibid., 1:19.
47. Van Til, *Christian Theory of Knowledge*, 50.
48. John R. Muether, *Cornelius Van Til: Reformed Apologist and Churchman* (Phillipsburg, NJ: P&R Publishing, 2008), 54. When Van Til finished his Princeton doctorate on the problem

The analysis put forward in the last few pages is complex, and a clear presentation of it is of high importance as we defend the whole counsel of God against unbelief. A simpler, more accessible though less philosophically precise approach follows here.

We know that humanity's ultimate concern is for personal happiness. Yet before a person can attain that goal, there are conditions that have to be met, as will make sense to any unbeliever. First, personal happiness is elusive because humanity is gripped by the fear of death. This fear can be seen in medieval paintings and perceived by reading existentialist novels. The unbeliever must find hope for immortality, and that hope must have a satisfying intellectual framework. That satisfying intellectual framework has requirements. It necessitates the existence and knowability of some type of truth.[49] Of course, the notion of truth has been attacked in postmodern times, but the statement that there is no truth is, in fact, a statement of truth. The intellectual framework, another way of looking at ultimate questions, requires not only that truth can and must be found but also that a rational universe must be plotted, and truth and a rational universe must be related in a way that there is a basis to hold to personal immortality.[50] These fundamental requirements for ultimate reference lead to the next section.

EPISTEMOLOGICAL QUESTIONS

The study that describes how and whether humans know anything is termed *epistemology*.[51] As it was necessary to define terms relative to the nature of questions, likewise, discussing epistemological issues intelligently requires consideration of basic terms. Human beings can, of course, know many things.[52]

---

of human freedom, he determined that covenant theology avoided all the philosophical pitfalls. A transcendental realism provided the philosophical basis for covenant theology.

49. Carnell, *Apologetics*, 45.

50. Ibid., 89.

51. Greg L. Bahnsen, *Van Til's Apologetic: Readings & Analysis* (Phillipsburg, NJ: P&R Publishing, 1998), 4n8. On epistemology, see *WCG* 1:17–18, 59, 82–84; 2:993: "By the word epistemology I mean all the sticky strands of a person's whole web of beliefs. This web includes the nature of reality and how someone is to live in that reality. A person chooses an epistemological method based on what that person thinks reflects the actual state of affairs."

52. Muether, *Van Til*, 55.

Conflicting Truth Claims. The ultimate question relative to episte-mology is how humans know anything at all. How thinking men and women validate any knowledge claims is a big question to answer. For example, what is a true statement, and why is it true?[53] Every philosophy, every life- or worldview has its own unique theory of knowledge and truth. That theory is dictated by how the given person sees or understands the entire world in which she or he lives. If one's epistemology is determined by his or her understanding of the world, then there are large apologetic implications.

Specifically, a Christian makes certain truth claims, and his unbe-lieving neighbor does the same. The next question is, "Who is right?" What is more, how is the correctness of the conflicting claims to be determined? We cannot hide the fact that these competing claims necessarily involve confrontation. This opposition of conflicting truth claims involves a participant's theory of knowledge or epistemology.

Myth of Religious Neutrality.[54] A person may claim that he will look at a truth issue neutrally, then determine which competing system is the best system. But that person has established criteria to determine which of the systems is best. The tester has already presupposed that he or she knows the nature of bestness as it relates to truth. Instead of quality, or bestness, another way to test competing systems is to determine which one of them has the most truth. Similarly, the person must already have some idea of what the truth is! In one sense this question is one of quality or quantity.

Everyone has a worldview, and every worldview has its own dis-tinctive epistemological method that is based on the core beliefs of that worldview.[55] There is an interconnectedness of ideas, and each one of the parts of our life- and worldview influences the other parts. The many diverse ideas are intertwined. This intertwining is clear not only in complex philosophy but also in popular culture.[56] Since that

53. Carnell, *Apologetics*, 45–47.

54. See Roy A. Clouser, *The Myth of Religious Neutrality* (Notre Dame: University of Notre Dame Press, 1991).

55. See Herman Bavinck (*Reformed Dogmatics*, ed. John Bolt [Grand Rapids: Baker Aca-demic, 2003] [*RD*], 1:298–99), who demonstrates that humanity cannot decide on morality and justice—let alone religion. He also demonstrates that to judge which type of revelation is the best requires a criterion for revelation.

56. For example, in the movie *The Last Samurai*, the Westerners call the Samurai *savages*, and the Westerners are termed *barbarians* by the Japanese. Based on these core beliefs, the two

is the case, and the basic epistemological parts touch a core set, or are attached like the spokes of a wheel, there can be no section of one's worldview that is not colored by the core parts. Thus there can be no neutral view of the various aspects of life that somehow sees things without some type of bias or without being affected by the other parts of the given person's complex worldview.[57] All humans reason according to their distinctive worldview, and there is some level of consistency to an individual's overall thought about the world. To speak plainly, we begin with our philosophical biases, and we never depart from them.

Since neutrality relative to judging truth is not possible, the Christian needs to remain honest. Neutrality is impossible when judging conflicting truth claims, because the intertwined nature of ideas destroys the possibility of neutrality; therefore, neutrality at face value is a false claim. In apologetic encounters (see below), some unbelievers may want Christians to assume an attitude of neutrality—to pretend that the best approach is a neutral one. But assuming neutrality robs the believer of God's treasure house of knowledge, is immoral, and is ultimately impossible.[58] The believer knows that he is not neutral relative to worldview. He takes Scripture, God's revelational authority, as the controlling factor for his starting point in all his thought and reasoning—even the most complex philosophy. He recognizes that in Colossians 2:8, Paul asserts that fools despise wisdom—the same teaching that we find in the OT.[59] The unbeliever's wisdom is nothing but vain deception. For Paul, true wisdom is found in Christ.[60] All hearts must be captive to Christ![61]

Asking a Christian to pretend to be neutral relative to God is like asking someone to pretend to be a bank robber, like asking a Christian

groups expect the other competing group to think and behave in a certain fashion.

57. We examined postmodernism in chapter 24. This popular philosophical flavor in America actually aids the presentation of Christianity at a few places. Postmodern people, in contrast to people in the earlier modern era, understand the philosophical problem of supposed objectivity.

58. Greg L. Bahnsen, *Always Ready* (Nacogdoches, TX: Covenant Media Press, 2004), 4–11, 15.

59. Psalm 36:9—it is in God's light that we can see the light; Ps. 119:105—our paths are lighted by God's Word. See *WCG* 1:680–82; 2:949–1004.

60. Colossians 2:3.

61. Unbelievers' hearts are not captive to Christ. At Ephesians 4:17–18, Paul says that their minds are vain and their understanding is darkened. See Ephesians 5:6, "Let no one deceive you with empty words." See also Colossians 1:16–18.

to put on a mask, hold a plastic gun, and pretend, while in a bank, that he is a robber. That suggestion is foolish. Nevertheless, acknowledging Scripture's authority does not mean that Christians are always consistent in their thinking.

Consistent Reasoning and Objectivity. Like all rational humans, Christians necessarily think in what may be termed a *consistent* or a *coherent* fashion. This type of thinking should generally be characterized as *consistency*.[62] There is a consistency to the entire Christian system, from its beginning to its end.[63] Another way to express that a system is well-thought-through is to call it a *spiral argument*.[64]

Since all human thought begins with beginning core beliefs, and a person's thinking remains more or less consistent to him or to her, in some sense human reasoning is ultimately circular.[65] To some extent, circularity is unavoidable in epistemology. Intertwining ideas produces circularity or consistency. Even if this type of argumentation is considered by some to be problematic, the Christian cannot avoid the method.

This consistent or spiral thinking is not the same as a circular argument. A circular argument is a logical fallacy and is one in which the conclusion of the argument is simply a restatement, in one form or another, of one of its premises.[66] There are different kinds of consistent thinking that are used in different contexts. Circular arguments are different from spiral or consistent arguments in two ways. First, spiral thinking does not preclude the possibility of learning something new, and second, it still allows for real communication with the unbeliever.[67]

---

62. I do not define *consistency* as obedience to the law of contradiction. See Charles M. Horne, "Van Til and Carnell, Part II," *Jerusalem and Athens: Critical Discussions on the Theology and Apologetics of Cornelius Van Til*, ed. E. R. Geehan (Nutley, NJ: P&R Publishing, 1971), 370n10.

63. But here I do not mean the technical systematic consistency of the philosophy of Boston personalism. See Frame, *Van Til*, 290, on Carnell.

64. Used by Van Til; cited in ibid., 303–5.

65. Cornelius Van Til, *The Defense of the Faith* (Philadelphia: Presbyterian and Reformed, 1955), 118.

66. Van Til was not always clear, or consistent, in his statements concerning circularity. As Bahnsen (*Van Til*, 516n122) says, he "sometimes repudiated and sometimes tolerated the notion that his apologetics was circular—which has undoubtedly been confusing to his readers and students." Bahnsen also cites Van Til at the latter's *A Survey of Christian Epistemology*: "His fundamental and determining fact is the fact of God's existence. That is his final conclusion. But that must also be his starting point" (see ibid., 170). For examples of circular arguments, see Frame, *Van Til*, 302–4.

67. Frame, *Van Til*, 305–7.

A visual example of it is a spider's web, with all its interconnecting threads, rather than a circle.

This chapter is intended as an aid to what we can call an apologetic encounter, when we as believers defend Christianity against someone who opposes our position. As we engage in an apologetic encounter, we undertake a particular type of thinking and arguing. Apologetic encounters between believers and unbelievers touch on the issue of the apex of a person's values. For the believer, God is rightly the highest value, and we explore the unbeliever's values, which are always off the mark. While an apologetic encounter uses reasoning, in this case reasoning is necessarily connected to deep religious commitments or values.[68]

Comprehending how both believers and unbelievers think is directly connected to how believers present the claims of Christ to unbelievers. Technically stated, in an apologetic encounter you and your antagonist must establish tests for truth. You know that it is true that Christ is Lord, but your apologetic opponent says that he knows that Christ is not Lord.

You must ask the existentially important question, "How does the unbeliever know that his judgments correspond to the mind of God—which is ultimate truth?"[69] The history of philosophy has provided various tests for determining truth. They include, but are not limited to, instinct, custom, tradition, the consent of the nations, feeling, sensory perception, intuition, correspondence, pragmatism, and systematic consistency.[70] But in an apologetic encounter, all these well-established truth tests will fall short of the mark.

A proper apologetic method relates to how one knows many truths of Christianity. Believers must know important truths that present intellectual challenges. They must know that the Bible is the Word of God, that Christ is fully human as well as fully divine, that Christ has risen from the dead, that he died for their sins, and a host of related questions.

When a person comes to faith, he or she has adopted a certain worldview—one that acknowledges that a holy Triune God exists and speaks authoritatively in the Bible. This Word of God confronts men

68. Ibid., 409–10.
69. Carnell, *Apologetics*, 47.
70. Ibid., 47–62.

and women with their sin and provides the answer to the problem of their sin—the answer in Jesus Christ. There is necessarily a relationship between the Christian life- and worldview, the importance of Scripture to that view, and apologetic method.[71]

Relative to God's existence, the unbeliever hopes to search for God with some type of neutral or supposedly objective criterion. In other words, he or she attempts to move somehow from neutrality to truth. But by using a linear, noncircular method of reasoning, it is not possible for a person to learn that he must change his way of thinking and modify his philosophical thought to the truths of Christianity.[72]

Two analogies summarize this section. Since thinking is consistent, it is similar to a train running on tracks. The locomotive will begin at point A, stay on the tracks, and finally arrive at point Z. It cannot go to a point that is not found on the tracks. The train will consistently stay on the tracks as it travels great distances. In an apologetic encounter, both the believer's and the unbeliever's train are running on tracks. You can travel side by side for hundreds of miles but cannot and will not leave your own tracks. The unbeliever cannot claim, objectively, that his train's tracks are better than yours. He is just as committed to traveling on the rails of his system as you are committed to traveling on yours.

Presupposition. Christians and non-Christians both assume many things in life. Understanding these basic assumptions in life and thinking are very important for the study of apologetics. Technically, the assumptions are called *presuppositions*.[73] There are large and small presuppositions. If you sit somewhere to read this book, you assume that the chair you choose will not float up and into heaven but, rather, that the chair will support your weight. That example demonstrates a common, and small, presupposition. A presupposition is not simply an assumption in a sophisticated argument. Presuppositions can go beyond arguments or thoughts to personal commitments. Presuppositions are located at the most basic human level of thought and action. They are the starting points from which we make evaluations. Furthermore, they are held preciously.[74]

71. One of the most compelling presentations is Carnell's notion of perfect systematic consistency; ibid., 62–64.

72. Frame, *Van Til*, 410–11.

73. See *WCG* 2:999–1002.

74. Bahnsen, *Van Til*, 2n4.

There are also large presuppositions. All humans entertain certain core beliefs or presuppositions about the nature of the world and its political and economic systems and about the universe and its creation. Clearly, if Christians hold presuppositions, so do unbelievers. It seems that all thinking beings begin with their presuppositions. Stated another way, all humans reason according to their distinctive worldview, and there is a consistency to their overall thought about the world. To speak plainly, we begin with our philosophical biases, and we never depart from them. Having briefly examined consistent reasoning and the importance of presuppositions, we can turn to a more detailed analysis of truth.

Truth. When Jesus was about to be crucified, Pilate asked the question, "What is truth?" While there are different technical definitions of truth, two prominent notions are the *coherence* and *correspondence* theories of truth.[75] Coherence thinkers equate truth with simple logical consistency. Thus, if a set of propositions is logically consistent, then that statement is true. If all the statements cohere, then the statement presents truth. Likewise if the propositions are not consistent, then the statement is not true. These thinkers reject correspondence with reality as the highest measure for truth.[76]

According to the correspondence theory, true statements are those that accurately represent reality.[77] The issue for this theory of truth is not how well known or even important the statement is but whether it corresponds with reality and is thus true. If the statement is profound, it will be more significant to someone, but the statement's profundity does not make it more true.[78] Also, this definition of truth relates to logic. The laws of logic are true because they correspond to all reality.[79]

There are thoughtful critiques of both of these truth theories. The coherence theory is rightly criticized by asserting that a worldview

---

75. I define *truth* as correspondence with the mind of God. God's thoughts and words are true. God's revelation in Scripture is the ultimate standard of truth. I defined the coherence view of truth as that which requires individual elements to fit within the whole system and the correspondence view as truth that is determined by how it accurately describes the world. See WCG 2:992n46.

76. Douglas Groothuis, *Truth Decay: Defending Christianity against the Challenges of Postmodernism* (Downers Grove, IL: InterVarsity Press, 2000), 92–96, 97.

77. Ibid., 84–88.

78. Ibid., 89.

79. Ibid., 92.

may be logically consistent but not correspond with external reality. For example, when someone enters the world of Tolkien found in *The Lord of the Rings*, that person is in the midst of a very consistent, even logically consistent, world. But that fascinating world simply does not correspond to any known reality! The critique is that coherence, logical consistency, is one necessary but not sufficient test for truth.[80] Also, postmodern thinkers are very critical of those who hold to the coherency theory. Some go so far as to say that logical coherence is simply another sad example of modernist logocentrism.[81]

On the other hand, philosophers also critique the correspondence theory. The issue that must be resolved is how anyone knows that his view of reality actually corresponds to the external world. When we are sleeping, the world of our dreams certainly seems real and may appear to be real the first few seconds after we wake up—but the dream does not correspond to reality. Only Christianity provides a theory of truth that satisfies the demands of both coherence and correspondence. Believers know the truth.[82] Believers think in a coherent fashion and know that their view of reality corresponds to reality.[83] When it comes to arguments, we can, and at times must, differentiate between those that are true, are valid, are persuasive, and are sound. An argument is sound, in contrast to valid, when the premises are accepted as true.[84]

Persuasion plays an important role in apologetic encounters. Paul clearly tried to persuade his hearers. A persuasive argument will, when possible, use the opponent's own beliefs to its advantage. It will argue in a manner that will make the opponent think the other person's

---

80. Ibid., 98.

81. Ibid., 97.

82. Gordon Clark wrongly charged that Van Til was influenced by neoorthodoxy and thus taught that believers could not know the truth. See Muether, *Van Til*, 109; Gordon H. Clark, "The Bible as Truth," *Bibliotheca Sacra* 114, no. 454 (April 1957): 163.

83. Believers know the truth because truth is found in God. For debate on whether that truth requires univocal knowledge between God and man, and for refutation of the false charge that Van Til's thought leads to skepticism and ignorance, see the insightful critiques by Muether, *Van Til*, 109–11. If there is not one-to-one correspondence, then there is analogy. God's incomprehensibility is supplemented with God's communicability. Ibid., 111: "The communicability of God rescued Van Til's thought from skepticism." See also R. Scott Clark, "Janus, the Well-Meant Offer of the Gospel, and Westminster Theology," in *The Pattern of Sound Doctrine: Systematic Theology at the Westminster Seminaries*, ed. David VanDrunen (Phillipsburg, NJ: P&R Publishing, 2004), 157–60.

84. Oliphint, *Battle*, 149–50.

argument to be the more likely one. Nevertheless, no matter how appealing our arguments, we confess that it is the Holy Spirit alone who can persuade one of the truths of Christianity.[85]

Words, Meaning, and Truth. These three great concepts are intimately related. To speak truth to a person is to use words. Words are combined to make propositions. A proposition has a subject and a predicate. The words *the paper is white* is a proposition. The subject in the proposition is *the paper*. In the predicate, the object of the subject, we give the property of *whiteness* to the subject, the paper.

Words are signs that we use with the intention of conveying meaning.[86] In the simple statement about the paper, we predicate something that we term *whiteness*. This predication, or ascribing an abstract property to something, is an act of the mind.[87] Some thinkers assert that predication is perhaps the greatest philosophical problem.[88] Whether or not it is so, it is certainly not a simple problem.

When the mind understands and affirms the proposition, it then becomes a judgment.[89] These propositions that become judgments, these true or false statements, are always perceived by a thinking individual. It is I who see, hear, and understand the truth. The statement is true for me.[90] A person affirms words gathered into propositions to be true when those words are related in a way that is comprehensible to the person within his or her entire range of experiences in life.[91] In other words, a true statement corresponds to reality as the person comprehends it. If the statement does not connect to reality in any sense, the person judges that the statement cannot be true. Thus truth can be defined as a person's judgment about a statement that that statement is consistent with the person's experiences or expectations. It is a judgment that comports with reality as the person understands it.[92]

Since truth must be consistent with a person's experiences and expectations, for a proposition to be true for him or her, it will not be

---

85. Ibid., 151–52.
86. Carnell, *Apologetics*, 62.
87. For more information on predication, see *WCG* 2:351n31, 992–95.
88. Carnell, *Apologetics*, 34.
89. Ibid., 30.
90. Dooyeweerd, *New Critique*, 1:4.
91. Carnell, *Apologetics*, 64.
92. Ibid., 45–46.

able to diverge from that person's experiences of reality. Thus truth cannot be different from what the person expects—it cannot conform to reality one day and not conform the next day. Said another way, truth cannot be changing. If truth changes, then the proposition that is being judged cannot be judged as true or false, because it has no meaning. Also, if truth is exclusively subjective, then there is only skepticism.[93] Moving toward a complex notion, the connecting links between the one and the many must be personally meaningful. The connections must also correspond to our understanding of reality;[94] therefore, when all these factors do so, the statement will be true.[95]

By now it is clear that the existence of the abstract notion of *meaning* is relative to a host of factors. For a proposition to be meaningful, the words that we speak or read are gathered into propositions, and predication is attributed to some of those words. For the proposition to be meaningful to someone, it will agree with that person's view of reality. Given the complexity of meaning, it would make sense that there must be something that is prior to it, something on which meaning itself depends, something that is bigger than the abstract philosophical concept of *meaning*.

If that is the case, then the meaning of a statement relates to what can be called the *prior origin* of the abstract notion of meaning.[96] This philosophically prior origin cannot be relative or changing, because it grounds meaning for a person and is connected to the person. The origin must be an absolute.[97] In other words, the origin of meaning must be transcendent.[98] Now that we have examined the nature of truth and the relationship between truth and meaning, the next topic we must tackle is the nature of philosophy as it relates to proper theology or apologetics.[99]

Philosophy and Apologetics. There exists a need to determine the working relationship between theology and philosophy.[100] And there is

---

93. Ibid., 36–37.
94. Dooyeweerd, *New Critique*, 1:4.
95. Ibid., 1:16.
96. The concept of *meaning* is not philosophically self-sufficient. See ibid., 1:9, 11.
97. Ibid., 1:10.
98. Ibid., 1:16.
99. Carnell, *Apologetics*, 33.
100. See Peter J. Steen, *The Structure of Herman Dooyeweerd's Thought* (Toronto: Wedge, 1983), 10–14.

an assortment of good working definitions of *philosophy*. The first one, proposed by a number of Christian philosophers, is that philosophy is deciding the total nature of reality; or stated differently, philosophy is theoretical thought on the totality of meaning and reality.[101] This definition is helpful because each person must decide what is the overall nature of reality, and when they make this determination they are acting as philosophers.[102] Other Christian philosophers have said that technical philosophy began with the reduction of multiplicity to unity. Reducing the many to a unified whole is a good definition as well, because all thinking people have to perform that task to understand their world. It is also necessary to realize that philosophy is not possible without critical self-reflection.[103]

Putting all of the parts together, philosophy can be defined as a thinking person's reflection about the total meaning and structure of reality, which includes his own thinking in that reality, thinking in time, and determining how all the various parts fit together into a harmonious whole.[104] Given that definition, almost all human beings are at one time or another philosophers—either consciously or unconsciously. Since philosophy is a thinking person's reflection about the total meaning and structure of reality and determining how all the various parts fit together into a harmonious whole, philosophical activity is something concrete.

It must be granted that even the most learned professional philosopher is not supposed to know all the details of everything in the whole world. Even a professional has to specialize in one or another part of the vast field of philosophy. The general philosophical subjects that are highly important for apologetics are the topics of cosmology (how the world came into being), epistemology (how we know), teleology (where the world is headed), and metaphysics (understanding the world beyond sensory experience).[105]

---

101. Dooyeweerd, *New Critique*, 1:4, 7.
102. Carnell, *Apologetics*, 97.
103. Dooyeweerd, *New Critique*, 1:5.
104. Since the philosopher cannot actually remove himself from temporal reality, all philosophy has this basic temporal or time-bound starting point. See Steen, *Structure*, 9; Carnell, *Apologetics*, 124.
105. Gordon H. Clark, *Thales to Dewey* (Boston: Houghton Mifflin, 1957), 4.

Sometimes these enormous philosophical subjects cannot be separated.[106] While there is luxury in technical specialization, nevertheless the competent philosopher must study all the fields of human interest and find places where the many specialized subjects and sciences relate to each other. In general, the philosopher helps people understand how the many parts of their lives relate to some larger whole; in other words, he helps them to create a unified worldview.[107] A unified worldview must knit together a series of hypotheses to create a coherent pattern of meaning that explains the origin, purpose, and final end of all reality.

Later, we will carefully define the formal discipline of apologetics and critique different apologetic approaches. A working definition of apologetics is "presenting and defending Christ to those who stand in rebellion against him."[108] The disciplines of apologetics and philosophy belong together. Since most thinking persons are philosophers, and since believers are commanded to present Jesus Christ to all persons, knowing philosophy is essential to presenting Christ to all people. So philosophy and apologetics can never be separated—along with theology, they are parts of the whole counsel of God.

Also, understanding complex issues connects philosophy and apologetics. For example, many humans think that their world is wrapped up in a secure job, home, and food. But we know that those same people's ultimate reference is that they actually think of themselves as God. This ultimate reference, whether it is hidden or open to the unbeliever, can be called the *spiritual antithesis*. The Bible says that the basis for all human decisions actually comes from the heart, for "the fool says in his heart, 'There is no God'" (Ps. 14:1). The word *heart* here does not mean the organ that pumps blood but the person's spirit or soul. This heart is either in loving fellowship with God or it is not. Every philosopher's ultimate reference or philosophical emphasis comes from his heart. This center or core of our being is not simply our thinking, our *cogito*, because selfhood transcends our own thinking. The self is, in fact, religious in nature. Realizing the important connections between philosophy and apologetics, we need next to examine some details.

106. Carnell, *Apologetics*, 34.
107. Ibid., 89, 93.
108. Muether, *Van Til*, 70.

A problem that must be addressed is the long-standing philosophical issue of individuality. Plato had trouble finding the relationship between the forms and the particulars. Aristotle saw matter as the basis for individuality.[109] Christian thinkers must also determine the basis for individuality.[110] Necessary to proper philosophical thinking is knowing that there is an individual subject; more specifically, one must know the nature of that thinking subject.

There is also an important relationship between the subject and the object. There are objects that are studied by the subject. The philosopher determines the nature of that subject-object relationship and must connect the two. Assuming that there is a relationship between the subject and the object, and that there is a philosophical need to explain the nature of the relationship, the nature of the relationship can be described as the *analytical function*. If philosophy cannot explain how knowledge is derived from the object by the subject (the analytical function), then there is no place for the special disciplines, the various fields of intellectual pursuits.[111] Here is the basic problem of epistemology: specifically, finding a synthesis between what is called the *analytical function* and the *nonanalytical function* of the object.[112]

Let us come to some preliminary conclusions concerning genuine philosophical thought. First, genuine philosophical thought, whether done by a Christian or a non-Christian, will be directed toward the origin of the whole cosmos, or temporal reality.[113] Second, it will also include reflection on the thinking self's own origin.[114] Third, genuine philosophical thought will presuppose some type of ultimate reference. The ultimate reference is the person's tower, his place of deep and solid security. Finally, genuine philosophical thought also takes a position relative to the origin of the ultimate reference. The origin of the ultimate reference transcends all meaning and is the location in which the thinker's deepest self comes to rest in the process of philosophical thought.[115]

109. Nash, *Dooyeweerd*, 61–62.
110. Ibid., 65–66.
111. Ibid., 74.
112. Ibid., 74–75.
113. Dooyeweerd, *New Critique*, 1:9, 11.
114. Ibid., 1:11.
115. Ibid.

Of highest importance for apologetics is the fact that philosophical thought itself does not offer an ultimate reference. Theoretical or philosophical thought is not self-sufficient in philosophy proper.[116] Since genuine philosophical thought cannot come from itself, it must come from somewhere else. It will come from the religious root of humanity. Having laid the groundwork, we are now ready to make our defense of Christianity to the thoughtful unbeliever.

BASIC APOLOGETIC APPROACHES

Definition of Apologetics.[117] There are a number of questions that arise in connection with the nature and study of the field of apologetics, and answers to the questions will determine its definition. Volume 2 of *The Whole Cousel of God* addressed some of those questions.[118]

That volume also dealt with some incomplete definitions of apologetics.[119] Both volume 2 and this one want to underline that it is wrong to isolate the defense of the faith from the definition of the faith or to separate the gospel from apologetics.[120] Paul's defense of Christianity,

116. Ibid., 1:21.

117. The word *apologetics* is a transliteration of a Greek word that in the NT occurs as a verb (*apologeomai*) ten times and as a noun eight times. In its usage in the NT, there is an obvious emphasis on defense. It isignifies answering specific charges. Luke uses the word in ten of the word's eighteen occurrences (see Luke 12:11; 21:14; Acts 19:33; 21:10; 22:1; 25:8, 16; 26:1, 2, 24).

118. For example, is the object of apologetics simply the defense of the gospel? Another question is how believers can and ought to argue with unbelievers. Still others include: Is the study of apologetics separate from the discipline of systematic theology? Is apologetics an organic part of doctrine and thus belongs in the theology division of a seminary, or since it aims to confront the wicked and defend the faith, should it be part of practical theology? See *WCG* 2:983.

119. Apologetics has been defined as the branch of Christian theology that answers the question, "Is Christianity rationally defensible?" This definition is a good beginning but not wholly adequate. Most Christian apologists answer this question affirmatively. Of what is this apologetics a defense? Is it a defense simply of the truthfulness of the Christian religion, or of Christianity as a whole? Some say that the discipline of apologetics is a defense of only the truthfulness of Christianity and is thus fundamentally different from the task and purpose of systematic theology. Yet isolation of the discipline of apologetics (as simply the defense of Christianity) from theology (as that which provides the definitions of theology) does not seem warranted from the biblical material. See ibid.

120. Clark Pinnock argues that apologetics is a defense of the truthfulness of the Christian religion. Yet he argues that the concept of the "defense of Christianity" is defense in isolation from theology itself. Pinnock's argument runs thus: There is an important difference between the task of theology and the task of apologetics. The theologian's task is to define the content of revealed

even his self-defense, was always couched in a positive presentation of Christ or the gospel. In the NT, Christianity's defense has a strong confessional element to it. Apologists should not divorce the content of their defense from the concept.[121]

Apologetics should be defined as a *vindication* of the Christian philosophy of life against the various forms of the non-Christian philosophy of life.[122] A philosophy of life is the same as a worldview, which is an interpretation of all the facts in the world. To continue our analysis, it seems necessary to begin discussing basic apologetic approaches—how believing theologians have actually done apologetics.[123]

Fideists. There are some Christians who do not think that Christianity is rationally defensible. Those persons answer the question of whether Christianity is defensible by saying "No, Christianity is not rationally defensible." Christian faith is supposedly of the heart, it is argued, and not of the mind. Since it is of the heart, not the mind, Christianity is not rational or logical but personal. For example, the doctrine of the Trinity is supposedly not logical, so although it is an essential doctrine, there is no need for, nor is Christianity capable of, defending it rationally.[124]

Most theologians rightly reject this fideistic position because it asserts unsubstantiated beliefs. Any absurdity can be believed without its substantiation. As a system of unjustified beliefs, fideism cannot lay claims to truth. In addition, it acknowledges mutually exclusive beliefs. Third, on fideistic grounds alone, all views have an equal claim to truth, for anything believable can be claimed to be true. But since

---

truth. The apologist's task is to defend its validity. Clark Pinnock, *Set Forth Your Case: Studies in Christian Apologetics* (Chicago: Moody Press, 1971), 3: "Theology and apologetics are twin members of a common family. In our spiritual warfare, one is defensive, the other offensive."

121. This method fails to deal with important questions concerning knowing and rational defense. First, how do humans know anything, and second, what do the words *rationally defensible* mean? Can a rational defense be made for the existence of either unicorns or dragons? The first definition, therefore, has proven not very helpful. WCG 2:983.

122. WCG 2:984.

123. Steven B. Cowan (introduction to *Five Views on Apologetics* [Grand Rapids: Zondervan, 2000], 9–20) provides a very helpful taxonomy of apologetic methods. In 1961 Bernard Ramm organized various apologetic approaches according to three relationships between faith and reason. In 1976 Gordon Lewis organized them according to their religious epistemologies. Cowan found both approaches wanting and organized his book according to argumentative strategy.

124. WCG 2:991.

there are many believable views that are contradictory, not all of them can be true. Actually, on fideistic grounds, even mutually exclusive views have an equal claim alone to be true. Furthermore, fideism does not even make a truth claim; rather, it is psychological expression. Since there are conflicting truth claims, anything that makes a claim to truth must offer some justification for the claim.[125]

Classical or Evidentialist Apologetics. Recent examples of important theologians who hold or have held to classical or evidentialist apologetics are J. Oliver Buswell, John Gerstner, R. C. Sproul, and Gary Habermas. In contrast to fideists, evidentialist apologists say that Christianity is most certainly defensible. They say that Christianity accords with the facts of the case and is highly probable but not necessarily certain.[126] Christianity is reasonable, and it can be presented in a way that is persuasive.

The evidentialist method is built on two presuppositions. First, it assumes that all people, in every culture, use what is called the "law of contradiction." That law states that proposition A cannot be both A and non-A at the same time. Second, it assumes that all humans understand and use the complex philosophical notion of *probability*. A person can, through the use of reason, see that the evidence in favor of Christianity presents an overwhelming probability of its veracity.

For the evidentialist, the starting point of apologetics is to lay the foundation for the discipline of systematic theology.[127] This method uses the traditional theistic arguments and evidences for God's existence—the cosmological, ontological, and teleological arguments for the veracity of Christianity.[128] The third presupposition of four is that sensory data is the best or most logical starting point for such arguments. Here is found common ground with unbelievers, namely, that sensory data are reliable.

An evidentialist argues that there are three places, related to the first three presuppositions, where believers and unbelievers have the

125. Norman L. Geisler, "Syllabus on Christian Apologetics" (Mundelein, IL: n.p., 1976), 3.
126. J. O. Buswell, "We may not have intellectually 100% demonstrative arguments . . . The Christian Gospel might be true"; and Carnell, *Apologetics*, 113: "Let us establish securely the fact that proof for the Christian faith cannot rise above rational probability" (as cited by Bahnsen, *Van Til*, 71n69).
127. Bahnsen, *Van Til*, 47.
128. Those arguments are found in chapter 9.

same or at least similar experience. Their experience of sensory data, of the law of contradiction, and of probability correspond. Both groups of people have the ability to approach that data with an open mind, or what could be called *objectivity*. Thus for the evidentialist, the facts of sensory data are self-interpreting. Evidentialist thinking includes a presupposition that is assumed by Christians and non-Christians: self-consciousness.[129] The criteria of truth or claims of truth are tested by their correspondence with relevant observations. Reason is used critically to test truth claims. Belief or faith requires high probability, not total certainty.

But from a worldview definition of apologetics, the facts that men and women find all around them are not self-interpreting. Neither do they establish truth. Furthermore, the same facts can be interpreted in ways so as to be used in competing worldviews. Particularly in the light of postmodernism, everyone knows that the same facts are capable of differing interpretations. Hence facts as such do not establish the truth of a worldview.[130] For example, consider a puppy who feels the need to perform a very natural function. But whenever he performs that function in the house, it seems that his master hits him with a newspaper. Eventually the puppy notes the relationship between that natural function and the bad newspaper. So he learns to bark and head for the door when he feels pressure on his bladder. The fact of his experience fits into his worldview.

Presuppositionalism. Presuppositionalists also affirm that Christianity is rationally defensible. Contrary to some popular notions, they actually agree with the classical approach that Christianity is logical and rational. This approach is named *presuppositionalism* because it begins with at least one, but perhaps a number of, presuppositions. The Christian will always presuppose the truth of God's Word from first point to last point.[131] While a radically biblical method, it is not an easy one. It will be epistemologically self-conscious. It will present

129. R. C. Sproul, "The Case for Inerrancy: A Methodological Analysis," in *God's Inerrant Word: An International Symposium on the Trustworthiness of Scripture*, ed. John Warwick Montgomery (Minneapolis: Bethany Fellowship, 1974), 247. See also R. C. Sproul, John Gerstner, and Arthur Lindsley, *Classical Apologetics: A Rational Defense of the Christian Faith and a Critique of Presuppositional Apologetics* (Grand Rapids: Academie Books, 1984).

130. Geisler, "Syllabus," 4.

131. See Sproul, "Case for Inerrancy," 245–46.

the strongest intellectual challenge to non-Christian thought. It will not merely assert that the Word of God is the best foundation but will be aggressive and say that it is the only philosophically sound foundation for human thought. It will recognize that God is always wiser than men. It will show that not only is there no hope for eternal life apart from Christ but neither is there any intellectual hope apart from Christ. The presuppositional method will argue that only based on a Christian worldview will the areas of logic, science, or morality have any meaning.[132] It will hold its ground and not give in to the pressure of saying that the non-Christian has merely an incomplete worldview. It will not say that the non-Christian has a correct worldview, the natural, and only needs the other half of the apple, the supernatural.[133]

A presuppositional apologetic will be epistemologically self-conscious.[134] A Reformed theology has epistemological implications for that theology. Reformed theology rightly asserts that God created the heavens and the earth. To think rightly about the world means that one must view that world as God's creation. The doctrine of creation has an impact on the ancient philosophical problem of the subject-object relationship. That doctrine of creation means that God, as Lord of creation, has committed himself to creation for eternity. He will not destroy the world but keep it for himself. God, as Lord of creation, is not on equal terms with his creation. As God relates to humanity, he must condescend to that creation by taking on human language and maintaining a covenant.[135]

In a similar fashion, while humanity is created in God's image, still humanity is of the dust of the earth and inextricably linked to creation. Yet Adam, having had the breath of God breathed into his nostrils, was the apex of that creation. Thus, as made in the image of God, Adam was bound both to God and to creation. As God is the Lord over creation, so Adam and Eve were meant to rule over creation. God linked Adam to creation in a way that was to reflect God's

132. Bahnsen, *Van Til*, 4–5.

133. This assertion stands in contrast to the position of Francis Schaeffer, who (in *Death in the City* [Wheaton, IL: Crossway, 1969], 130–31) argues this way, according to Bahnsen, *Van Til*, 52.

134. *WCG* 2:991.

135. K. Scott Oliphint, "The Old-New Reformed Epistemology," in *Revelation and Reason*, ed. K. Scott Oliphint and Lane G. Tipton (Phillipsburg, NJ: P&R Publishing, 2007), 207–9, 211.

character. God initiated and has sustained humanity's connection with the world—which is the key to proper epistemology.[136]

When Adam and Eve fell into sin, the image of God became a source of shame. The postlapsarian human reaction to being an image bearer is to hide and suppress that image. In Adam and Eve's wicked act, because man fell, creation also fell. Creation fell because it was in a covenantal bond with Adam, a bond that cannot be broken. The implications of the fall and the pervasive effects of sin must be placed front and center when discussing human cognitive faculties. Originally, Adam was created to do everything to God's glory, not only his labor but also his thinking and knowing. Now ensnared and enslaved by sin, humanity does everything for its own vain glory. But when sin entered the world, it was not as though God fled from his creation. He still manifests himself both in the creatures made in his image and in creation itself.[137] Thus a presuppositional apologetic method will know that what it knows is true because humanity is made in God's image and lives in God's world.

This method will not make a distinction in kind between apologetics and theology but a difference in degree. There is interdependency between them. Evangelism applies the Word of God, but so do theology and apologetics.[138] Apologetics cannot be isolated from evangelism—it is not pre-evangelism.[139] Stated another way, "the apologist defends what the theologian has learned, with the tools and insights refined by the philosopher, for the evangelistic purpose of seeing the unbeliever's heart and mind changed."[140]

Since at Proverbs 1:7 the Bible teaches that "the fear of the LORD is the beginning of knowledge," that fear of God will be the starting point of apologetics.[141] The starting point is not sensory data. The starting point is the assumption of God as revealed in Scripture. The common ground with unbelievers, based on Paul's teaching at Romans 1:17, is that the unbeliever knows in his heart that God exists.

---

136. Ibid., 211.
137. Ibid., 211–13.
138. Bahnsen, *Van Til*, 43.
139. Francis Schaeffer does so in *The God Who Is There* (Downers Grove, IL: InterVarsity Press, 1968), 137, 143, as cited by Bahnsen, *Van Til*, 52.
140. Bahnsen, *Van Til*, 44.
141. Ibid., 3.

In Romans 1:16–18, Paul established that all people know God's righteousness—it is universal in scope. Those who are in Christ and know this righteousness are a new humanity and have entered into an eschatological righteousness that was inaugurated in Christ's resurrection and will be fully revealed in the eschaton. On the other hand are those who are not in Christ but stand in divine wrath. This wrath is also universal and eschatological. Thus there is a parallel: righteousness revealed, and wrath revealed. Each person stands in one or the other relationship relative to God, as covenant keepers or covenant breakers.[142]

There is a reason why God's wrath is revealed. Romans 1:19 teaches that those in the first Adam have been suppressing the truth. That suppressed truth concerns God. That truth is evident to them. It is evident to them because God has made it evident to unbelievers—it is not some knowledge that humans can produce in themselves.[143] Furthermore, that truth has specific content about God. Romans 1:20 says that it is about God's eternal power and deity, which are invisible. Competent commentators rightly argue that such a description by Paul would include all of God's divine perfections.[144]

There are further specifics about this knowledge. It is not abstract; rather, it is relational and personal. Romans 1:32 addresses this quality by saying that the unbeliever knows God's ordinances. Knowing them means knowing something of God's requirements for humanity. Breaking those divine ordinances makes one worthy of death. This knowledge of God demands obedience to God.[145] Second, this knowledge is clear, concrete, and in no way hidden.

The unbeliever takes this knowledge and suppresses it—which is the actual cause of and impetus behind his sinful irrationality. There is an exegetical basis for arguing that unbelief is irrational, but it is difficult to define *rationality*. Rationality is usually defined as a corresponding relationship between the way things really are and

---

142. K. Scott Oliphint, "The Irrationality of Unbelief: An Exegetical Study," in *Revelation and Reason*, ed. K. Scott Oliphint and Lane G. Tipton (Phillipsburg, NJ: P&R Publishing, 2007), 60–63.

143. Ibid., 63–66.

144. More specifically, the truth is of God's existence, infinity, eternality, immutablility, glory, and wisdom (ibid., 66).

145. Ibid., 66–67.

what someone knows and believes about that reality.[146] It is irrational to know something, in this case God, and to pretend that God is not there. The unbeliever exchanges that known information and transforms it into some type of idolatry to which he or she bows down. Thus idolatry is not from ignorance but always from perverting the truth and irrationally twisting reality.[147]

So sin is irrational.[148] It is irrational to make a disjunction between the world as it really is, created by God, and to live in idolatry as though God does not exist and is not a righteous judge. There is a pattern to this stubborn, unbelieving irrationality revealed in Romans 1:18–28. In illustrating the unbeliever's suppression of the truth and exchanging that truth for a lie, Paul uses the example of homosexuality, whereby God gives the unbeliever over to his own deep sinfulness. The apex of Adamic life is earnestly to seek to deny the obvious and to create an unreal imaginary world. No one could call such a lifestyle *rational*.[149]

With this exegetical background, it could be argued that apologetics acts as a reminder to the unbeliever. Believers inform unbelievers of what unbelievers already know. They know that they have rejected the obvious. They stand without excuse. The believer confronts their suppression and shares with them the glorious gospel of Christ.[150]

The criterion of truth is found in the ultimate source of truth, who is God. Reason is used to interpret and make deductions from Scripture, but reason is not superior to Scripture. The basis of faith is not found in sensory perception or in probability but in the self-authentication of the assumption.[151] This school holds that there are two types of people—believers and unbelievers. Both groups have fully developed and quite diverse philosophies.[152]

In conclusion, the whole counsel of God requires mature believers to be able to defend Christ's lordship over every part of life. The unbeliever's ultimate reference is simple reliance on sinking sand—

146. Oliphint, "Irrationality," 59–60.
147. Ibid., 67–69.
148. See *WCG* 1:187–89.
149. Oliphint, "Irrationality," 69–72.
150. Ibid., 72–73.
151. See *WCG* 2:991–1002.
152. Jim S. Halsey, *For a Time Such as This* (Nutley, NJ: Presbyterian and Reformed, 1976), 3. See Greg L. Bahnsen, "The Crucial Concept of Self-Deception in Presuppositional Apologetics," *WTJ* 57, no. 1 (Spring 1995): 1–31.

which ends in destruction. While one's apologetic method is of high importance—of greatest importance is that we are always ready to give an account for the hope that is within us.

KEY TERMS

epistemology
thinking self
special discipline
ultimate reference
presupposition
fideists
evidentialism
presuppositionalism

STUDY QUESTIONS

1. How can you use asking questions of an unbeliever to help defend Christianity?
2. Does an unbeliever have a consistent view of the nature of reality?
3. How can you determine an unbeliever's ultimate reference?

RESOURCES FOR FURTHER STUDY

There are a number of wonderful aids for students of apologetics.

Frame, John M. *Apologetics to the Glory of God*. Phillipsburg, NJ: P&R Publishing, 2012. Highly recommended.
Oliphint, K. Scott. *The Battle Belongs to the Lord: The Power of Scripture for Defending Our Faith*. Phillipsburg, NJ: P&R Publishing, 2003. This is the best book on apologetics at this time.

27

Contemporary
Theological Debates

THIS FINAL CHAPTER WILL not outline historical theology or present apologetics but instead present an analysis of pressing theological issues that the church is facing today. Like all the other chapters, this one is selective in the issues that it examines. Here we will examine only two areas of controversy: the doctrine of God, and soteriology.

DOCTRINE OF GOD[1]

Introduction. As mentioned briefly in the previous volumes of *The Whole Counsel of God*, there are difficulties in comprehending the doctrine of God.[2] The unity and diversity of the Trinity is a true mystery. There is a plethora of possible approaches, such as a historical analysis of Augustine's *On the Trinity* or an exegetical analysis of John 17.

The topic is addressed well through an analysis of the Athanasian Creed, which says "the Father is not," and so on. This section will not be an exposition of the content of the creed but rather an analysis of the theological and philosophical assumptions and presuppositions necessary for understanding the creed's content.

---

1. For a more extensive presentation of some of these ideas, see Richard C. Gamble, "Comprehending the Eternal Union of God," *RPTJ* 2, no. 1 (Fall 2015): 4–13.
2. See Richard C. Gamble, *The Whole Counsel of God*, vol. 1, *God's Mighty Acts in the Old Testament* (Phillipsburg, NJ: P&R Publishing, 2009) (*WCG1*), 177, 650; Richard C. Gamble, *The Whole Counsel of God*, vol. 2, *The Full Revelation of God* (Phillipsburg, NJ: P&R Publishing, 2018) (*WCG2*), 343–51.

There are problems inherent to the word *comprehend* relative to the doctrine of God. The factors that are necessary for peoples' comprehension of complex biblical truth must be addressed. The first task is to analyze the nature of the language that is used to speak of this divine phenomenon.

The place to begin this discussion is the medium of discussion itself: language. There are at least three types of language used in the Bible and in common life. While a number of possible words may be used to describe those three types, they are, generally: *ordinary* language, *scientific* language, and *poetic* language.[3] Among these three types, ordinary language is foundational to the other two. But for the discussion of the doctrine of God, poetic language must receive attention. Poetry is not merely a stimulant of emotion but a real and significant medium of information. Poetic language is best at describing some type of experience that the author understands but that the reader has not had. So describing that which someone experiences, including religious experience, is best expressed in poetic language.

Each language type has its strengths and weaknesses. Poetic language's strength is in its ability to communicate experience, thus making it superior to scientific language, which cannot communicate experience. But the reader must trust what the biblical author is saying. Christians believe what the biblical author is saying and desire to understand.

Thus it is apparent how important poetic language is to an analysis of the doctrine of God.[4] The Bible communicates ancient information by people personally unknown to modern believers. Believers must

---

3. WCG 2:344: "To make the different types clear, here are some biblical examples, all of which concern wheat. An example of ordinary language comes from Genesis 30:14, 'In the days of wheat harvest Reuben went and found mandrakes in the field.' A example of the scientific use comes from Ezra 7:21–22, 'And I, Artaxerxes the king, make a decree to all the treasurers in the province beyond the river: Whatever Ezra the priest, the scribe of the Law of the God of heaven, requires of you, let it be done with all diligence, up to 100 talents of silver, 100 cors of wheat.' Here King Artaxerxes made an order for a specific amount of wheat that was able to be weighed and measured. The unit of measure (a cor) was about six bushels. This description of wheat has scientific precision. The final example, from the Song of Solomon 7:2, is poetic: 'Your navel is a rounded bowl that never lacks mixed wine. Your belly is a heap of wheat, encircled with lilies.' In this verse the author was describing a woman's body part. If we read this description with scientific precision or even ordinary language, the woman would either be insulted or be some type of monster, which would be the opposite of the poetic author's purpose."

4. See ibid., 2:343–47.

listen to this information sympathetically and try to translate in a meaningful way the experiences being communicated. Believers trust and believe the God who speaks, and they try to comprehend his message. Poetic language can only properly communicate when the reader trusts the speaker and wants to comprehend whatever it is that the author is communicating. Recognizing the need for unique language when it comes to the doctrine of God, the matter of its unique content must now be addressed.

Communicating content is difficult. Finding the right words to describe the beauty of a mountain or the loveliness of a spouse is not easy. Thus, understandably, learning content about the Creator of the heavens and the earth is extremely difficult. Before creation, God existed entirely outside space and time. But humans live only within space and time and cannot comprehend that which is outside geographical and chronological limits. When creatures think about God, they must remember that for God to teach them about himself in a way that they can understand, he must enter into space and time. God speaks to his people in covenantal language.[5]

Given that reality, all human thinking about God, or knowledge of God, is properly termed *ectypal* in contrast to that which is archetypal.[6] Christians, therefore, should think concretely about God. They should be nearly overwhelmed by the challenge of how to describe God's unity, as both the doctrine and the content are unique and rich.

Christians must also affirm that God's being and attributes are identical. They are not, and cannot be, in some type of economic or functional relationship, because the two are identical. So when a theologian tries to insert either economic (functional) or ontological (being) hierarchies into his analysis of God's attributes, his own method produces unnecessary difficulties. Analysis of God's being and attributes requires a methodological balance. A proper approach will analyze God's attributes or perfections as he himself has revealed them in the historical unfolding of his special revelation.[7]

5. See ibid., 2:347–49.
6. Ibid., 2:349: "God is self-contained, and he is the archetype. He is the original. Humans are created analogues of him, and man's being is analogical of God's being. Thus, our thinking is ectypal."
7. Ibid., 2:350–51. For an analysis of God's aseity and simplicity, see ibid., 2:351–53.

All discussions of God must also be Trinitarian. Concerning the relations among the persons of the Trinity, there must be an equality in their being and works.[8] The three persons are in intimate communion with one another.[9] With this very basic information introduced, this chapter will now transition to contemporary discussions and debates.

Van Til and Frame on the Trinity.[10] In 2002, a colleague from another seminary was to be invited to join the faculty where I was then teaching. That colleague was a supporter of Dr. Van Til's position on the Trinity. Before his arrival, the seminary's president asked me to defend the invited colleague before the faculty against the charge that he and Van Til were both guilty of "a radically new heresy."[11] Such a charge is both preposterous and emotive. The word *heresy* means that the heretic is condemned to hell. That death verdict should only be pronounced by a church court. There are sufficient grounds to deny such a charge.[12]

But the issue is as follows. Cornelius Van Til, speaking on the doctrine of God, said: "Yet this is not the whole truth of the matter. We do assert that God, that is, the whole Godhead, is one person." This expression is undoubtedly peculiar. The question is whether the statement is a radically new heresy. Van Til and Frame were charged by a faculty colleague with rejecting the doctrine of the Trinity as taught in the Athanasian Creed and the Westminster Confession of Faith.

Van Til's position is still under discussion and critique. A decade later, R. Scott Clark noted that Van Til's statement is highly controversial. In the sixteenth and seventeenth centuries, to have said that God is one person would have been rejected as heretical. Only the medieval theologian Abelard ever spoke so, and he was condemned twice. There is nothing like this statement in any of the Reformed confessions. Clark warned that every sensible Christian should be profoundly wary of such language.[13]

8. See ibid., 2:353–60.
9. See ibid., 2:360–63.
10. For more information, see Gamble, "Comprehending," 4–13.
11. See John W. Robbins, *Cornelius Van Til: The Man and the Myth* (Dallas: Trinity Foundation, 1986), 20, as cited by John M. Frame, *Cornelius Van Til: An Analysis of His Thought* (Phillipsburg, NJ: P&R Publishing, 1995) (*CVT*), 66.
12. The following pages are the actual words used for that faculty debate in 2002, intentionally not updated.
13. R. Scott Clark, Heidelblog, March 6, 2013, https://heidelblog.net/2013/03/van-til-yet-this-is-not-the-whole-truth/. Accessed January 13, 2019.

Here is how I described Dr. Van Til's position at that faculty meeting nearly twenty years ago. The first ground is that Van Til does not say that the doctrine of the Trinity is a contradiction. In fact, he explicitly denies that it is a contradiction. He says that it is an error to say that the mystery of the Trinity is irrational.[14] His favorite phrase to describe this threeness and oneness in God is that it is "super-rational."[15]

Nevertheless, even a young student will admit that Van Til's formulation, "God is one person and God is three persons," is contradictory at face value.[16] Does this sentence mean that while his words specifically deny that the doctrine is contradictory, his articulation of the doctrine is itself still contradictory? The answer must be No. On the topic of the Trinity, or the philosophical one and many, it would be methodologically illegitimate not to permit complexities in nuance.

John Frame rightly counters that when Van Til said this is "not the whole truth," his statement is not the same as a rejection of the doctrine. "Only the Bible contains the whole truth of God's revelation," said Frame, "and even the Bible does not necessarily answer every question that we may wish to ask about the Trinity."[17] Frame correctly defends Van Til's position when he refers to the Augustinian notion of the *circumincession* in the Trinity.[18] The concept is also called the *perichoresis* of the Trinity and is well-defined by Heinrich Heppe.[19]

14. Cornelius Van Til, *Introduction to Systematic Theology*, 2nd ed. (Phillipsburg, NJ: P&R Publishing, 2007) (*IST*), 229. See *CVT*, 66–67, citing Cornelius Van Til, *Common Grace and the Gospel* (Nutley, NJ: Presbyterian and Reformed, 1972), 9: We "shun the really contradictory, embrace the idea of the apparently contradictory."

15. *IST*, 230.

16. Ibid., 229–30. Gordon H. Clark (*The Trinity* [Jefferson, MD: Trinity Foundation, 2010], 86) is wrong when he says that Van Til holds "that the Godhead is three and one in precisely the same sense." If Clark were correct, that Van Til held that God is three in the same sense in which he is said to be one, then it is a contradiction.

17. *CVT*, 65–66.

18. "God can clearly be both one person and not-one person, if the meaning of 'person' changes somewhat between the two uses" (ibid., 69).

19. Heinrich Heppe, *Reformed Dogmatics* (Eugene, OR: Wipf & Stock, 1977), 113–14: "The Persons of the Trinity are one essence; and singular and sole numerically." "They are *tota in singulis personis*. The consubstantiality of the divine persons is that whereby the three persons are of one and the same substance or essence but numerically singular and sole (*unicae*). The *perichoresis* in the divine persons is the completely close union, whereby one person is in another, because of the numerically one and same essence, the whole of which the separate persons possess." While Frame is correct in his defense of Van Til, Van Til's sentence should have been ignored. The sentence itself is not at all helpful. Gordon Clark is truly excited by the statement. It is a heresy unfounded in the history of heresies. Not even Sabellius was so bad

The second ground is that Van Til does not deny the creedal view that God is one in one respect and three in another.[20] He does stand guilty as charged of asserting that the creeds do not present the "whole truth of the matter." He joins with John Calvin, who refused to sign the Athanasian Creed and was thus charged with Arianism. Yet Calvin was not heretical![21] Neither is Van Til. A senior scholar on the faculty who made the charge, aware of the seriousness of his statement, would not make it lightly. Certainly, his concerns can be explained.

There are at least two possible underlying reasons for the debate. The first reason is that there are inherent ambiguities in the original Latin and Greek terms. Frame's historical arguments for their ambiguity are accurate.[22] The second reason is that Gordon Clark and John Frame implement differing/opposing theological models. I have isolated at least three of those differences.

The first difference is that they use distinct Trinitarian models. More than one hundred and twenty years ago, Charles Hodge held to an antithesis between the unity in God and the unity in men. "It is clearly taught in Scripture and universally believed in the Church," he said, "that the persons of the Trinity are one God in an infinitely higher sense than that in which all men are one man."[23] Louis Berkhof agreed with Hodge,[24] as did Van Til. Gordon Clark, on the other hand,

---

(Clark, *Trinity*, 87)! Clark catches himself and qualifies, "this is not to suggest that Van Til is a Sabellian" (ibid., 88).

20. *IST*, 230: "Within the being of the one person we are permitted and compelled by Scripture to make the distinction between a specific or generic type of being and three personal subsistences."

21. Calvin would not sign because he believed that the creed was insufficient. Should Van Til be condemned for saying the same thing?

22. *CVT*, 69: "The Greek term *ousia*, which was used to designate God's essence, was not, in the Greek language, precisely differentiated from *hypostasis*, the term used for the three persons. . . . But there was nothing about either term that uniquely fitted it for its particular task, over against the other"; further, 69–70: "Indeed, the church fathers might have reversed them ('one *hypostasis*, three *ousiai*') without loss"; and 70: "On that account, we can see that in effect the Greeks spoke of God as 'three substances' and the Latins of 'one substance.' Doubtless these choices of terms caused some misunderstanding. But, from our vantage point, we cannot regard either formulation as unorthodox."

23. Charles Hodge, *Systematic Theology*, 3 vols. (London: Clarke, 1960), 2:58.

24. Berkhof, *Systematic Theology* (Carlisle, PA: Banner of Truth, 1972), 88: "The divine nature is distinguished from the human nature in that it can subsist wholly and indivisibly in more than one person. . . . Human nature or essence may be regarded as a species, of which each man has an individual part, so that there is a specific (from species) unity; but the divine nature is indivisible and therefore identical in the persons of the Godhead."

thought that more could be said on this relationship. Clark employed what could be called a *realistic* model for the Trinity.[25]

The second difference is the use of philosophical abstraction in systematic theology. Van Til followed the traditional Dutch position of Bavinck and others, which rejected what they called such abstraction. This presupposition caused them to reject Clark's realistic notion of the Trinity out of hand. Frame, following Van Til, argues that Clark's model of the persons of the Trinity as the individuals, and the divine essence (God) as the unity, is an illegitimate abstraction.

Van Til's antipathy for abstraction caused him not to embrace the traditional expression.[26] There is an important reason why abstractions should be avoided. They should be avoided because they are not personal. God is personal reality. Van Til said, "Each of the persons of the Godhead is coterminous with the being of the Godhead."[27] This assertion is a standard Reformed statement on God. In his explanation, Van Til said that to be "coterminous" means to exhaust the divine essence. Since God is personal, his essence must also be personal. Since God is an absolute person and is one (simplicity), in some sense God must also be one person. Thus God's acts are personal and involve all three persons acting in unity.[28]

"But of course," argues Frame, "this model is entirely inadequate for the Trinity, God is not an abstraction."[29] On the other hand, Robert Reymond questions this presupposition: "Simply to assert that the divine unity is different from the specific unity of three men is not suf-

25. "Unless we know how the Persons [of the Godhead] are one and how men are one, we cannot tell whether the unity is the same or different" (Clark, as cited by Robert L. Reymond, *A New Systematic Theology of the Christian Faith* [Nashville: Thomas Nelson, 1998], 323).

26. *CVT*, 67: "He is one 'being,' not three; the three partake of one 'essence.'" Van Til could argue that Fritz, Pudge, and Maitli are three individual canines with a common essence, that of *dogness* or *doghood*—but that doghood is an abstraction. You can take Fritz out for a walk, but you cannot put doghood on a leash.

27. *IST*, 229.

28. *CVT*, 68: "God is not an abstraction. . . . God is a concrete, personal reality. . . . If the three persons (individually and collectively) exhaust the divine essence (are 'coterminous' with it), then the divine essence itself must be personal. And if God is an absolute person, and he is one, there must be a sense in which he is one person. . . . Therefore, every act of God is a personal act involving all three persons acting in unity. . . . I do believe that when Van Til's argument is seriously considered, his formulation will not sound so outlandish. Indeed, I believe that the argument is cogent and that the formulation is true. It is also traditional, for it is clearly implied by the doctrine that the divine persons each contain the fullness of God."

29. *IST*, 67–68.

ficient. One must spell out the nature of each unity if one is to insist that they are different."[30]

The third difference is the use of metaphor and linguistic ambiguity in theology. Frame argues that there are useful master metaphors or theological models in Scripture. An example is "the use of *substance* and *person* in the doctrine of the Trinity (a model derived from philosophy)."[31] Frame is comfortable with linguistic ambiguity in theology; Clark was not.

In conclusion, if Frame's doctrine of God is judged to be inadequate by people like Clark and his disciples, I asked the faculty, then who could we hire instead? How about Charles Hodge? "Charles Hodge," said Clark, "because of inadequate philosophical training, makes utterly unintelligible assertions" concerning the knowledge of God.[32] Perhaps crossing the ocean to find Bavinck is better. "Bavinck, because of his faulty philosophy, distorts the doctrine of the Trinity."[33] Well then, do we want a Dutch-American like Berkhof? Louis Berkhof is "clearly mistaken" in his analysis of the church fathers on God and "extends the [Scripture] beyond its stated limits" in trying to defend his view of God's incomprehensibility. As a matter of fact, Clark maintained, Berkhof is "extremely confused" on the matter, and his theology is "destructive of the simplicity of the divine nature."[34] Furthermore, Berkhof makes statements "inconsistent with God's eternity."[35] I concluded with this: "Gentlemen, I submit to you that if Frame falls short on the doctrine of God, he finds himself with some pretty tall companions."

This brief presentation is not meant to offer a detailed analysis of a complex debate but to reveal the fact that within the Reformed theological community, there is continuing healthy discussion of important topics relative to the doctrine of God.

---

30. Reymond, *New Systematic Theology*, 322. Given the presuppositions of the Clark/Reymond realistic model of the Trinity, and using Clark's example from dice, Van Til's statement would sound like this: God is one die and three dice.

31. John M. Frame, *The Doctrine of the Knowledge of God* (Phillipsburg, NJ: Presbyterian and Reformed, 1987), 227. CVT, 69n20: Scripture does not "give us a precise or comprehensive account of the eternal relations between Father, Son, Holy Spirit, and the divine essence."

32. Clark, *Trinity*, 73.

33. Ibid., 84.

34. Ibid., 74–76.

35. Ibid., 78–79.

K. Scott Oliphint on Bavinck's Realism. It is granted that there is Trinitarian debate within Reformed theology, and some of that debate relates to incorporating philosophical realism. K. Scott Oliphint wants to determine, given comments by Vos, Van Til, and recently by John Bolt, whether Herman Bavinck's epistemological realism was consistent with the theology of *Reformed Dogmatics* and whether Bavinck was consistent in suggesting that the Logos is the subjective and objective ground of knowledge.[36]

To answer his question, Oliphint needed first to define epistemological realism in general, Bavinck's epistemological realism in particular, and then what it means to assert that the Logos is the subjective and objective ground of knowledge. Oliphint began by arguing that Bavinck, following Aquinas and many other Reformed thinkers, was an epistemological realist.[37] This realism rejected both empiricism and rationalism, but it took valuable parts from both and combined them. Bavinck's realism was founded on the Triune God.[38] For background information, Oliphint presented Aquinas's realism and metaphysics. For Aquinas, being was pure act or actuality; pure act or actuality was different from essence, which was potential existence or potency. Thus an object's existence was ontologically superior to that object's essence.[39]

It was a given for Bavinck, as a Reformed theologian, that Scripture governed dogmatics and that other scholarly analytical tools

36. K. Scott Oliphint, "Bavinck's Realism, the Logos Principle and Sola Scriptura," *WTJ* 72, no. 2 (2010): 359–60. Vos asserted that Bavinck's realism was grounded in Scottish common sense (Princetonian) principles, while Van Til thought that his realism was grounded in some principle different from the principium of the God of the Bible.
37. Oliphint, "Bavinck's Realism," 363, 365: "On Being and Essence, [Aquinas] adopts what has come to be called a 'moderate realism.' Unlike Plato, the realist, who affirmed the actual existence of all universals, or Roscelin (and, following him and Aquinas, Ockham), who saw the universals as having no real foundation in reality, Aquinas sought to show that the universals did indeed exist in the mind. Unlike the nominalist conception, these universals had their foundation in the existence of the particulars. All of this Bavinck thus far affirms."
38. Ibid., 364: "Realism, then, differs from rationalism in that it has a special view of the intellect, and from empiricism in that it recognizes that it must abstract from the things perceived the 'logical element naturally inherent in those things. . . . Hence the starting point of all human knowledge is perception.'"
39. Ibid., 366: "It has been called an 'existential' in distinction from an 'essentialistic' metaphysic (the latter of which would be more in line with Aristotle). . . . Because we can conceptualize . . . a unicorn without asserting its actual existence, there must be a distinction between a thing's essence, in this case a unicorn, and its existence."

were subordinate to it.[40] So when it comes to dogmatics proper, a revelational epistemology should be, and was in Bavinck, explicitly articulated. But Van Til noted that Bavinck seemed to waver on his commitment to revelation when it came to other fields, such as science.[41] Oliphint went a step further and concluded that Bavinck's embrace of realism undermined a commitment to revelation in fields other than dogmatics.[42]

Oliphint is convinced that a Logos principle is critical to comprehending the internal foundation of knowledge.[43] He concludes that the Logos principle should be both the subjective and objective ground for knowledge. Bavinck embraced the subjective side but did not hold to the objective. In conclusion, even one of the most stalwart Reformed theologians can rightly be criticized. Debate continues in the Reformed community concerning how to construct a doctrine of God properly.

Theistic Mutualism.[44] When it comes to criticism, a recent book has placed a number of Reformed and evangelical theologians under the glaring light of critique. A group of theologians labeled *theistic mutualists* supposedly rejects classical Christian theism. "No less than true religion is at stake in the contest between theistic mutualism and classical Christian theism," writes the author.[45] The important and popular *Tabletalk Magazine* has endorsed this book's findings.[46]

40. Ibid., 361.
41. Ibid., 362: "His analysis of scientific foundations, [could] be interpreted as an argument for a generic, universally recognized epistemological foundation"; further, 364: John Bolt says that Bavinck rejects *sola scriptura* as an epistemology; and 365: Bolt says that the biblical-theological approach is insufficient.
42. Ibid., 387: "If we couple this truth [from John's prologue] with Paul's similar affirmations in Rom 1:18–32, we can begin to see why an epistemology of realism, even if a Christianized version of realism, is insufficient as an application of the Logos principle in epistemology."
43. Ibid., 362: Bavinck said, "The Logos who shines in the world must also let his light shine in our consciousness. That is the light of reason, the intellect, which, itself originating in the Logos, discovers and recognizes the Logos in things. It is the internal foundation of knowledge (*principium cognoscendi internum*)."
44. For more precise and expanded analysis, see Richard C. Gamble, "Reflections on Theological Method and the Doctrine of God: A Review of James Dolezal's *All That Is in God*," *RPTJ* 5, no. 2 (Spring 2019): 14–25.
45. James Dolezal, *All That Is in God* (Grand Rapids: Reformation Heritage, 2017), 104. He opened the book with the statement, "Two distinctly different models of Christian theism are presently vying for the heart and mind of evangelical Christianity" (ibid., 1).
46. Keith A. Mathison, "Unlatched Theism: An Examination of John Frame's Response to *All That Is in God*," *Tabletalk Magazine*, November 30, 2017.

Both John Frame and K. Scott Oliphint find themselves caught in the author's harsh light.[47]

A theistic mutualist insists that God is involved in a genuine relationship with his creatures and is committed to a way of thinking about God and his relationship to the world in the same way that humans do, even if on a much grander scale.[48] They "allow for a measure of ontological becoming and process in God."[49] Theistic mutualism relativizes God's being.[50] Adherents of it advance "an idolatrous form of theism" because they locate God's being within the order of finite beings.[51] Theistic mutualists have failed to grasp a proper view of God's self-sufficiency, immutability, and aseity.[52]

The heart of theistic mutualism is supposedly a correlative relationality between God and his people. Such a position affirms that God is subject to alteration in his being and thus is becoming in at least some respect. Supposedly, this thinking is the prevailing position among many evangelical and Reformed theologians.[53] Some Reformed

47. In addition are Covenant and Knox Seminary's Robert Reymond, Regent Seminary's J. I. Packer, and Trinity Seminary's D. A. Carson. Richard A. Muller, the most prominent church historian of our day, claims in his foreword to *All That Is in God* that Dolezal's opponents have replaced traditional understandings of God with notions of a changing, temporal deity whose oneness is merely social (Dolezal, *All in God*, ix). These theistic mutualists, with their "aberrant argumentation," argue that God "takes new attributes to his nature," or "a series of new 'properties'" (ibid., x). Their theistic mutualism leads to the conclusion "that God is passible, composed of parts, and temporally bound." Furthermore, theistic mutualists argue that the three persons of the Trinity are "three discrete beings" (ibid., xi). His scathing conclusion is that "the modern aberration of theistic mutualism invents new divine attributes and has a somewhat mutable deity altered by relationality. It is a 'confused mess of misleading theologians put forth today under the guise of new and relevant reconstructions of the evangelical and Reformed faith'" (ibid., xii).

48. Dolezal, *All in God*, 2–3: Theistic mutualism is "the belief that any meaningful relationship between God and man must involve God in a transaction wherein he receives some determination of being from his creatures."

49. A theistic mutualist holds that in some sense God derives some part of his being in relationship to the creation. Ibid., 6–7: They have "embraced a rudimentary form of process theism to the extent that they allow some measure of ontological becoming and dependency in God."

50. Ibid., 8.

51. Ibid., 7: "Their God is inevitably mutable and finite and as such is unworthy of worship."

52. This divine self-sufficiency entails that God is purely actual in his being. God cannot become more than he is or other than he is. Ibid., 4; 15: "One of the better known arguments for God's pure actuality appears in Thomas Aquinas's"; further, 16: "Pure actuality is understood by Thomists"; 31n.49: "God . . . is pure act."; 33n.52: "As purely actual . . . God"; 56: "He must be purely actual in all that he is"; and finally, 58: "divine pure actuality—constitutes a baseline, a controlling grammar for all of our thoughts and beliefs about God."

53. Ibid., 27–28.

theistic mutualists grant that God undergoes changes but insist that he goes through changes because he wills to change. In other words, God is in control of those changes, so they are acceptable. This position can be summarized as divinely self-controlled mutability.[54]

Some theistic mutualists oppose or deny divine simplicity. There are a number of reasons for their denial. Some say that it is nonsensical to argue that all God's properties are identical with all the others. It seems self-evident that God's power, love, and knowledge are clearly not identical properties. Others have said that divine simplicity is not warranted by Scripture. They argue that the Bible presents God as composite in some sense.[55] The third approach is to recover simplicity in a way that distorts its teaching. Some revisionists do not believe that the divine essence itself is simple but instead has genuine complexities. They argue that there is universal language about God that makes God's attributes real and distinguishable characteristics of his divine being.[56]

Some Reformed theistic mutualists insist that God's eternality is in fact an endless succession of moments. For them, God is "everlasting" rather than eternal.[57] Other theistic mutualists hold that God existed before time and creation but that when God created the world, he entered into time. God is thus timeless without the universe but temporal with the universe.[58] Yet others underline that God takes on new attributes to his essence to relate to his creatures, in time, after creation.[59]

A prominent Reformed theologian argues that since time and history change, God, who exists in time, also changes. Nevertheless, God

54. Theistic mutualism is the view that a righteous man can produce divine pleasure that he would otherwise lack, and God has chosen to do so for himself (see ibid., 31–35).

55. Theologians who come under scrutiny here are Ronald H. Nash, *The Concept of God: An Exploration of Contemporary Difficulties with the Attributes of God* (Grand Rapids: Zondervan, 1983); Alvin Plantinga, *Does God Have a Nature?* (Milwaukee: Marquette University Press, 1980); and John S. Feinberg, *No One Like Him: The Doctrine of God* (Wheaton, IL: Crossway, 2001). See Dolezal, *All in God*, 67–69.

56. Theologians who fall into this category include Charles Hodge, R. L. Dabney, Robert Reymond, John Frame, and Kevin Vanhoozer.

57. Nicholas Wolterstorff ("God Everlasting," in *Philosophy of Religion: A Guide and Anthology*, ed. Brian Davies [Oxford: Oxford University Press, 2000], 485–504) comes into view here. See Dolezal, *All in God*, 90.

58. William Lane Craig ("Timelessness and Omnitemporality," in *God and Time: Four Views*, ed. Gregory E. Ganssel [Downers Grove, IL: IVP Academic, 2001], 129–60), apparently argues in this fashion. See Dolezal, *All in God*, 91.

59. This reference is to Rob Lister, *God Is Impassible and Impassioned: Toward a Theology of Divine Emotion* (Wheaton, IL: Crossway, 2012). See Dolezal, *All in God*, 92.

is unchangeable in his supratemporal existence. Still, his changing existence in time is no less real than his atemporal existence. God assumed this new manner of being at the creation.[60]

Since evangelical theistic mutualists disregard divine simplicity, they are faced with the three persons of the godhead as either three parts of God or three discrete beings who compose the social unit called *God*.[61] Theistic mutualists often explain Trinitarian unity by using the notion of *perichoresis* (mutual indwelling) to account for God's unity.

Theistic mutualists offer composition models of Trinitarianism. Social Trinitarianism is their favorite model. Evangelical theologians J. P. Moreland and William Lane Craig are apparently social Trinitarians who assent to the one divine nature as being an aggregate of the three persons—each with distinct centers of consciousness. For them, it is the Trinity as a whole that is properly God. The three persons are parts of the one God. Also, Cornelius Plantinga favors a social Trinitarianism and rejects the Augustinian tradition's notion that God has a singular mind and will. He asserts that the three persons have distinct centers of knowledge, with a harmony of knowledge rather than an identity of knowledge. For Plantinga, the Trinity is a complex thing of persons, essences, and relations.[62] But there are some evangelicals who apparently hold to modified forms of social Trinitarianism.[63] Others argue for functional subordination within the godhead.[64]

60. The referent (Dolezal, *All in God*, 92–94) is John M. Frame in *The Doctrine of God* (Phillipsburg, NJ: P&R Publishing, 2002).

61. Dolezal, *All in God*, 105–6.

62. The literature in the section includes Jürgen Moltmann, *The Trinity and the Kingdom*, trans. Margaret Kohl (Philadelphia: Fortress, 1993); J. P. Moreland and William Lane Craig, *Philosophical Foundations for a Christian Worldview* (Downer's Grove, IL: IVP Academic, 2003); and Cornelius Plantinga, "Social Trinity and Tritheism," in *A Reader in Contemporary Philosophical Theology*, ed. Oliver D. Crisp (London: T&T Clark, 2009), 67–89. See Dolezal, *All in God*, 123–27.

63. In *No One Like Him*, John Feinberg argues that for the Trinity to have true fellowship, the three persons cannot always be thinking of everything they know. But if Feinberg is correct, then the three persons have discrete acts of will; divine knowing and willing are distinguished from the divine essence; and to say that God knows something is the result of different acts of knowing that coalesce. See Dolezal, *All in God*, 130–32.

64. For them, the Father exercises authority over the Son not just as incarnate but from eternity. Each person exercises a power of will that is distinct. Such a view means that God's will and power comprise a collective aggregation of acts. Bruce A. Ware, *Father, Son, and Holy Spirit: Relationships, Roles, and Relevance* (Wheaton, IL: Crossway, 2005); Wayne Grudem, *Systematic Theology* (Grand Rapids: Zondervan, 1994). See Dolezal, *All in God*, 132–34.

To analyze the dilemma, it would be beneficial to consider Charles Hodge's analysis of the issues and briefly examine his analysis of the divine attributes. Hodge began by asserting that the divine essence is unchangeable and contains certain perfections.[65] Those perfections are revealed, he argued, both in the constitution of human nature as well as in Scripture.[66] The perfections are called *attributes*, which are essential to God's being and are necessarily involved in the believer's idea of God. God's attributes are distinguished from predicates that refer to him, from the properties or distinguishing characteristics of the three persons of the Trinity, and from accidents or qualities that may or may not belong to a substance.[67]

Hodge's analysis of the historical development of the attributes indicated that there were paths that he thought believing theologians should not follow. Those paths were nominalism and realism. The medieval realist notion viewed God as a composite being comprising different elements. Those realists believed that general terms did not express mere thought or conceptions in the mind but substantive existence.[68] While Hodge advised against walking down that path, the route looks familiar because it has at least similarities to the road advocated by the univocists. If that is the case, then it could perhaps be suggested that the univocist's position is not solely the child of Enlightenment thinking but may actually have a much longer theological pedigree.[69]

65. Dolezal, *All in God*, 73. In earlier analysis of A. A. Hodge's thinking, Dolezal laments, 64: "just how much the mechanistic Enlightenment thinking has impacted Christian theology."

66. Hodge made very strong univocist claims (using Dolezal's term) when he asserted: "The Scriptural view of this subject, which distinguishes the attributes in God as distinct, and assumes that knowledge in Him, in its essential nature, is what knowledge is in us, does not conflict with the unity and simplicity of God as a spiritual being." He continued by asserting "that knowledge in God is knowledge, and not power or eternity; that it is what knowledge is in us, not indeed in its modes and objects, but in its essential nature. We must remove from our conceptions of the divine attributes all the limitations and imperfections which belong to the corresponding attributes in us; but we are not to destroy their nature. . . . God, therefore, does and can know in the ordinary and proper sense of that word" (Charles Hodge, *Systematic Theology*, 3 vols. [London: Clarke, 1960], 1:396).

67. Ibid., 1:368.

68. Ibid., 1:369: They comprehended "the divine attributes as differing from each other *realiter*, as one *res* or thing differs from another."

69. The other dead-end street for Hodge was the way of nominalism. Nominalists argue that general terms are words that answer to mental abstractions. Nominalists "confound the attributes, making them all mean the same thing, which is equivalent to denying them all together," and in referring to the different attributes, they "only use different words for one and the same thing" (ibid.).

Another objectionable way to describe the relationship between God's attributes and essence would be to follow Aquinas and some Lutherans who argue that God is pure act. This representation is false, according to Hodge, and should be corrected. To say that the divine attributes differ only in name, or are simply divine accommodations, is "to destroy all true knowledge of God."[70] This view makes God a simple force that can be known only by its effects. Theologians are left with either abandoning attempts to determine the divine attributes or renouncing knowledge of God, as well as faith in the revelation that he has graciously given of himself. Viewing God as such a force means that he is not a person and has no will, and such a view "is essentially pantheistic."[71] Furthermore, if God is *actus purus* ("pure act"), then he cannot have knowledge. If omniscience is only a different name for omnipotence, it ceases to be a distinct attribute of God. Furthermore, Hodge was strongly against confounding knowledge and power in God. To say that they are identical in the divine being is to affirm "that as God knows from eternity He creates from eternity. . . . We are thus led, by these speculations, into pantheistical views of the nature of God and of his relation to the world."[72] To be clear on his strong rejection of this medieval notion, Hodge lamented: "It is deeply to be regretted that . . . the Lutheran and Reformed theologians, after renouncing the authority of the schoolmen, almost immediately yielded themselves to their speculations."[73]

Hodge argued that the best way to represent God's attributes and essence would be, from a historical perspective, to follow Francis Turretin and others. Turretin taught that the attributes had a real foundation in the divine nature, and Hodge believed that there should be a real distinction between the divine attributes. God's attributes,

70. Ibid., 1:371.

71. Hodge cited with approval an author who said that this teaching is "the denial of God as He is revealed in the Scriptures" and that "there can be no difference between the actual and the possible, for the one as well as the other is always present to the divine mind. It would also follow that the creation must be infinite, or God finite." Aquinas's teaching "is derogatory to God." Positively citing Hans Lassen Martensen (*Die christliche Dogmatik* [Charleston, SC: Nabu Press, 2011], 113): "It is the denial of the very essence of faith, if it is only in our thoughts that God is holy and righteous, and not in his own nature; if it is we who so address Him, and not He who so reveals Himself" (Hodge, *Systematic Theology*, 1:372).

72. Hodge, *Systematic Theology*, 1:395.

73. Ibid., 1:394.

as revealed in Scripture, are objectively true and are grounded in the divine essence. Theologians should reject the "extreme view of the simplicity of his essence," said Hodge, "which requires us to assume that the divine attributes differ only in our conceptions."[74] The ground for that rejection is that the divine attributes differ not only in human thinking, but there is a reason also in God why theologians think of him as possessing these diverse perfections. In other words, "the divine perfections are really what the Bible declares them to be."[75] He summarized the problem when he lamented,

> Instead of determining the nature of the divine attributes from the representations of Scripture and from the constitution of man as the image of God, and from the necessities of our moral and religious nature, they allowed themselves to be controlled by *a priori* speculations as to the nature of the infinite and absolute.[76]

In terms of method, argued Hodge, theologians must be controlled by Scripture and the laws of humanity's nature, not by speculative medieval thinking.[77]

The great northern Presbyterian theologian Charles Hodge held to a notion of a complex divine essence.[78] Those contemporary American Reformed theologians who come under sharp critique can certainly claim an honored American pedigree. Despite their being able to claim a long American heritage, however, the warnings against some contemporary evangelical theological expressions are correct.[79]

74. Theologians then distinguish between the reason as determining and the reason as determined (*ratio rationantis*/*ratio rationatae*) relative to the attributes. Hodge expressed himself precisely: "The divine attributes differ neither *realiter*, nor *nominaliter* but *virtualiter*" (ibid., 1:373).

75. Ibid.

76. Ibid., 1:394.

77. Ibid., 1:396: "And in determining what is, and what is not, consistent with the nature of God as an infinitely perfect being, we are to be controlled by the teaching of the Scriptures, and by the necessities (or laws) of our moral and religious nature, and not by our speculative notions of the Infinite and Absolute." For more information on Hodge's theological method, see *WCG* 1:73–75.

78. Dolezal notes that the prominent southern Presbyterian theologian Robert Lewis Dabney was also a univocist who asserted that if someone claims that the divine attributes differ only in name, then "they are unmeaning" (Dolezal, *All in God*, 73).

79. Believing theologians must combat any denial of fundamental biblical teaching regarding God's attributes, and Dolezal has done a great service in bringing this important teaching to his readers' attention.

This theological debate involves theological method. The question concerns the relationship between the doctrine of God proper, and thus all other doctrines, and theological method.[80] To choose a theological method is also to select a way of looking at and thinking about the world from a specific cultural viewpoint.[81] Theistic mutualists are charged with being intellectually trapped within a post-Kantian world and with formulating their doctrine of God, specifically their equivocist thinking, according to that worldview. That charge may or may not be true. But contemporary systematic theology should not be confined to pre-Enlightenment, neo-Thomist thought patterns either.[82] A better alternative would be for the faithful systematic theologian to theologize, as far as possible, within a radically biblical framework rather than self-consciously utilizing either past or contemporary cultural or philosophical grids.[83] Debate on this topic will probably continue. Another area of controversy concerns the nature of salvation.

SOTERIOLOGICAL STRIFE

Incorrect Views. A proper atonement theory is essential. Within the evangelical world, there are a number of authors who improperly deny the penal substitutionary atonement of Christ.[84] But there are

80. For more information on how humans are to speak and know about God, see *WCG* 1:85–90.

81. For information on culture and the philosophy of Aristotle in theological method, see ibid., 1:46–47; for cultural influences, see ibid., 1:79–80; for epistemological foundations, see ibid., 1:82–84. For information on John Owen's rejection of Aristotle's method in theology, see ibid., 1:92; for a note comparing Aquinas, Calvin, and Turretin, see ibid., 1:53n107.

82. The doctrine of divine simplicity supposedly reached its summit in Aquinas. See Dolezal, *All in God*, 55: "Several factors enabled Thomas . . . perhaps most important of which was the recovery of Aristotle's metaphysical framework. . . . The conceptual framework did not alter the essential claims of the doctrine, though it did enable Thomas to explicate it in more precisely existential terms"; and 61: "early modern mechanism displaced the older, predominantly Aristotelian, natural philosophy"; further, 61–62: "mechanism took over the field of natural philosophy"; 62: The philosophical change brought "a restricted understanding of the meaning and significance of divine simplicity"; and finally, 63: For those elaborate denials to make sense, "one would need to presuppose the basic accuracy of Aristotelian metaphysics."

83. For more information on a radical biblical theological method, see *WCG* 1:5–8, 10, 17–18, 23–24, 27–31, 41–48, 56–72, 76–77, and 94–99.

84. For example, Bruce Demarest, *The Cross and Salvation* (Wheaton, IL: Crossway, 2006), 191: "We conclude that in terms of the atonement's provision, Christ died not merely for the elect but for all sinners in all times and places. . . . Christ, in other words, provided

also unbelievers who know that God exists, and at times they create grotesque imitations of biblical atonement theory.[85] Sadly, some scholars who term themselves *Christian* present perverted notions of biblical atonement theory.

Two examples will demonstrate the point.[86] The first is Miroslav Volf's proposal for the human embrace of others as reflecting God's embrace of hostile humanity.[87] Volf is searching for justice and an end to violence. He finds that goal's being met in what he terms "God the crucified Messiah." This receptive God, who yearns to be with humanity, empties himself on the cross. Seeing this divine example gives humanity an example by which men and women can forgive those who sin against them. Such a proposal fails in its analysis of human nature and sin as well as God's nature and the free grace offered in Christ.[88]

A second example is Serene Jones's feminist theology of atonement. She is convinced that the classic formulations of the atonement have been harmful to women.[89] She thinks Luther's proper notion of justification, as though it takes place in a courtroom where God is the judge, tacitly excludes women. She counters that it is men who need divine confrontation for their aggressive pride. Western women already have fragmented lives and presently feel their guilt. The solution to the problem, as she envisions it, is to reverse the theological loci by putting sanctification prior to justification. Putting sanctification first supposedly provides

---

salvation for more people than those to whom he purposed to apply its saving benefits." There seems to be a double intention: God has a purpose regarding the provision of the atonement that is different from the application. Christ's death is universal in intention but particular in application. There were replies by evangelicals, and particularly good was that by Charles E. Hill and Frank A. James III, eds., *The Glory of the Atonement: Biblical, Historical, and Practical Perspectives* (Downers Grove, IL: InterVarsity Press, 2004). This criticism would apply to the New Perspective on Paul as well. See the analysis in chapter 25.

85. For compelling analysis of perverted atonement theories, see William Edgar, "Justification and Violence: Reflections on Atonement and Contemporary Apologetics," in *Justified in Christ: God's Plan for Us in Justification*, ed. K. Scott Oliphint (Fearn, Scotland: Mentor, 2007), 132–38. Edgar analyzes the French Revolution, American lynchings, and the Holocaust.

86. Other mistaken notions, in which ethics is the initial focus of justification, are found in Moltmann, Pannenberg, and Jüngel. See Mark C. Mattas, *The Role of Justification in Contemporary Theology* (Grand Rapids: Eerdmans, 2004), as cited by Edgar, "Reflections on Atonement," 147n34.

87. Miroslav Volf, *Exclusion and Embrace: A Theological Exploration of Identity, Otherness and Reconciliation* (Nashville: Abingdon Press, 1996).

88. Edgar, "Reflections on Atonement," 138–43.

89. Serene Jones, *Feminist Theory and Christian Theology: Cartographies of Grace* (Minneapolis: Fortress, 2000).

women with divine liberation and empowerment. Justification follows and is further liberation, this time as freedom from the cultural and societal constructions that bind women. In this way women can have their own status before God rather than subordinate status through men. Here Jones fails to deal both with the depth of human sin, female as well as male, and with the righteous requirements of a holy God.[90]

Chronological Unfolding. While evangelical errors and anti-Christian caricatures of atonement theory are interesting, this final section will focus on conflict from within the specifically evangelical Reformed community. In 1974 Norman Shepherd, professor of systematic theology and successor to John Murray, submitted several documents to the faculty of Westminster Seminary concerning his reflections on the doctrine of justification. Discussion and debate continued within the faculty, then moved to the board of trustees, and in 1977 went to the Orthodox Presbyterian Church's Presbytery of Philadelphia.[91] The process ended with Professor Shepherd's dismissal from the faculty in 1982 and his leaving Philadelphia to pastor in the Christian Reformed Church.[92]

While there was relative quiet on the topic for a while, in 2000 Shepherd published *The Call of Grace: How the Covenant Illuminates Salvation and Evangelism*. That publication eroded the support Shepherd had with his former faculty colleagues and resulted in numerous negative reviews. More appeared from his pen in 2004 and 2007.[93]

90. Edgar, "Reflections on Atonement," 143–47.
91. OPC website, accessed July 3, 2019: "In November 1978, Prof. Shepherd presented to the Presbytery of Philadelphia *Thirty-four Theses on Justification in Relation to Faith, Repentance, and Good Works*. The presbytery held ten special meetings in the next year to study the theses, many of which were approved. However, at its January 1980 meeting, the Presbytery first defeated a motion to reject the theses. Then by a tie vote (34–34) it defeated a recommendation to approve the theses."
92. There are a number of accounts of the process of Shepherd's removal. From a perspective critical of Shepherd, see W. Robert Godfrey, "Westminster, Justification, and the Reformed Confessions," in *The Pattern of Sound Doctrine*, ed. David VanDrunen (Philippsburg NJ: P&R Publishing, 2004), 136–40; A. Donald MacLeod, *W. Stanford Reid: An Evangelical Calvinist in the Academy* (Montreal: McGill-Queen's University Press, 2004), 257–79. From a perspective sympathetic to Professor Shepherd, see Ian Hewitson, *Trust and Obey: Norman Shepherd and the Justification Controversy at Westminster Theological Seminary* (Minneapolis: NextStep Resources, 2011). See also P. Andrew Sandlin and John Barak, eds., *Obedient Faith: a Festschrift for Norman Shepherd* (Mount Hermon, CA.: Kerygma Press, 2012).
93. Norman Shepherd, *The Call of Grace: How the Covenant Illuminates Salvation and Evangelism* (Phillipsburg, NJ: P&R Publishing, 2000); P. Andrew Sandlin, ed., *Backbone of the*

John V. Fesko, now of Reformed Theological Seminary, recently summarized Shepherd's teaching under three headings. He said that Shepherd was accused, but he did not go so far as to say that the charges were established. He said that "critics suspected," but he did not say that those suspicions were proven. "Like Piscator, Shepherd denied the imputed active obedience of Christ and claimed Calvin and Ursinus as patriarchs of his view."[94] This section will investigate this debate in greater detail.

Debate between the Two Westminster Seminaries. In 2007, three different books appeared from Westminster Seminary faculty on the topic of soteriology. One book was by Michael S. Horton: *Covenant and Salvation: Union with Christ* (Westminster/John Knox, 2007). A second book was offered by a number of members of the Westminster faculty and edited by K. Scott Oliphint: *Justified in Christ: God's Plan for Us in Justification.* The third book was submitted by the faculty of Westminster Seminary California (WS–C) and edited by R. Scott Clark: *Covenant, Justification, and Pastoral Ministry.*[95] This section will examine only one chapter from *Justified in Christ.*

Drawing his readers back to Luther and Calvin, Peter Lillback begins by asserting that while Wittenberg and Geneva mutually attacked Rome and had many common elements, Luther and Calvin had distinctive approaches to justification.[96] Differences between Luther and the Swiss Reformed antedated Calvin and his *Institutes.*[97] Calvin

---

Bible: *Covenant in Contempory Perspective* (Nacogdoches, TX: Covenant Media Press, 2004).

94. John V. Fesko, "The Ground of Religion: Justification according to the Reformed Tradition," in *The Doctrine on which the Church Stands or Falls: Justification in Biblical, Theological, Historical, and Pastoral Perspective*, ed. Matthew Barrett (Wheaton, IL: Crossway, 2019), 736.

95. Michael S. Horton, *Covenant and Salvation: Union with Christ* (Philadelphia: Westminster John Knox Press, 2007); K. Scott Oliphint, ed., *Justified in Christ: God's Plan for Us in Justification* (Fearn, Scotland: Mentor, 2007); R. Scott Clark, ed., *Covenant, Justification, and Pastoral Ministry* (Phillipsburg, NJ: P&R Publishing, 2007).

96. Peter A. Lillback, "Calvin's Development of the Doctrine of Forensic Justification: Calvin and the Early Lutherans on the Relationship of Justification and Renewal," in *Justified in Christ: God's Plan for Us in Justification*, ed. K. Scott Oliphint (Fearn, Scotland: Mentor, 2007), 51–52, 55. The union against Rome was important and included not merging justification with sanctification and renewal.

97. Lillback mentions disagreement on the doctrine of the sacraments (1529) and Luther's 1531 *Commentary on Galatians*, in which the German reformer attacked the Zwinglian tradition (ibid., 53). See Lillback's massive work on Calvin's doctrine of the covenant and justification: *Binding of God: Calvin's Role in the Development of Covenant Theology* (Grand Rapids: Baker Academic, 2001).

and the Lutherans gradually developed distinctive understandings of justification.

First, there was early Lutheran teaching. Lillback carefully analyzed Luther's doctrine of justification.[98] Luther viewed renewal as an aspect of justification.[99] Lillback charged "that Calvin came to view the merging of forensic justification with renewal, as found in the early Lutheran theologians, as a generally non-biblical way of describing the doctrine." The views of Luther, Melanchthon, and Chemnitz were judged "as largely inconsistent with the forensic nature of justification."[100] Later Lutheran theology became clearer than the earlier attempts.[101]

Second, there was also development in Calvin's thinking. The first edition of the *Institutes* did not even discuss justification, but in the second edition it was defined in terms of someone "who is both reckoned righteous in God's judgment and has been accepted on account of his righteousness."[102] In the third edition, four years later, Calvin defined the concept more carefully still.[103] At times it appeared that Calvin was working out loud in trying carefully to define the nature of justification and its relationship to renewal.[104] Calvin knew about early debate on whether it was legitimate to include regeneration within justification.[105] He opted to distinguish regeneration from justification.[106]

---

98. See Richard C. Gamble, "The Very Gate of Paradise to Me: The Development of Protestantism's Teaching on Justification by Faith," *RPTJ* 4, no. 1 (Fall 2017): 28–29.

99. Lillback ("Calvin's Development," 66–71) analyzed Melanchthon's views and (ibid., 71–78) Luther's thinking.

100. Ibid., 53; 59: "Melanchthon's *Apology of the Augsburg Confession* (1531) is cited as an example . . . of the Lutheran teachers who have used non-forensic synonyms for justification."

101. Lillback (ibid., 57–60) analyzed Chemnitz's thinking in the latter's 1566–1575 *Examination of the Council of Trent.*

102. John Calvin, *Institutes of the Christian Religion*, ed. John T. McNeill, trans. Ford Lewis Battles (Philadelphia: Westminster Press, 1960) (*Institutes*), 3.11.2, in Lillback, "Calvin's Development," 60.

103. *Institutes*, 3.11.2, in Lillback, "Calvin's Development," 61: "Therefore, we explain justification simply as the acceptance with which God receives us into his favor as righteous men. And we say that it consists in the remission of sins and the imputation of Christ's righteousness." Lillback frames the change in the light of Calvin's 1539 commentary on Romans as well as interaction with Melanchthon's thinking.

104. Lillback ("Calvin's Development," 62–64) mentions comments on Calvin's commentary to Titus at 3:7, from 1549, where he admits the possibility of regeneration as being a part of justification. Calvin is convinced this is what Paul is doing in this passage. Yet such a position had been opposed by Calvin two years earlier in his refutation of the German interim.

105. Ibid., 64.

106. Ibid., 62.

As Calvin developed, he differed from early Lutheranism on the order of salvation. He wanted to underline justification in terms of forensic justification and imputation. Significantly for contemporary discussion, Calvin wanted *duplex gratia*, the "double grace" of justification and sanctification, to be comprehended within the notion of union with Christ.[107] Lillback contributed to the discussion by demonstrating a line of thought from Geerhardus Vos to Louis Berkhof. Lutherans, according to Vos, hold that mystical union occurs by the act of justification.[108]

In the same year, the faculty of WS–C published their collection in great part to respond to incorrect teaching connected to Federal Vision.[109] To underline the need for such a volume, J. Ligon Duncan III, provost of Reformed Theological Seminary, said: "The historic Reformational understanding of justification, imputation, active obedience, and covenant theology is under assault even from within sectors of the Reformed community." The WS–C book generated an expected counter volume from those specifically identified as the source of the problems on justification.[110]

But debate on the WS–C collection of essays erupted from what would appear to be an unexpected source as well. Mark Garcia's review in an OPC publication was critical of the overall perspective on justification propounded by the WS–C faculty.[111]

That negative review produced an acidic response by two representatives of WS–C.[112] The two professors who replied argued that any *ordo salutis* that denies that justification has a certain priority

107. *Institutes*, 3.11.10, as cited by Richard B. Gaffin, "Biblical Theology and the Westminster Standards," in *The Practical Calvinist: An Introduction to the Presbyterian and Reformed Heritage*, ed. Peter A. Lillback (Fearn, Scotland: Mentor, 2002), 39. See Lillback, "Calvin's Development," 65.

108. Lillback, "Calvin's Development," 65–66n34. Geerhardus Vos, "Doctrine of the Covenant in Reformed Theology," in *Redemptive History and Biblical Interpretation: The Shorter Writings of Geerhardus Vos*, ed. Richard B. Gaffin (P&R Publishing, 2001), 256.

109. Four theologians met at a PCA in Louisiana in 2002 to address the topic of what was called Reformed Covenantalism or the Reformed Vision. A number of others have agreed with the original four, signing "A Joint Federal Vision Profession." Many have rightly written against this movement. See WCG 2:376

110. P. Andrew Sandlin, *A Faith That Is Never Alone: A Response to Westminster Seminary in California* (Mount Hermon, CA: Kerygma Press, 2008).

111. See Mark A. Garcia, "Review Article: No Reformed Theology of Justification?," *Ordained Servant*, October 2007, https://opc.org/os.html?article_id=66. Accessed January 14, 2019.

112. W. Robert Godfrey and David VanDrunen, *Ordained Servant*, December 2007.

to sanctification "is fundamentally flawed, neither being historically Reformed nor accounting for key biblical teaching."[113]

David VanDrunen and W. Robert Godfrey argue that they affirm the standard systematic-textbook relationship between those two parts of salvation. They believe that if a theologian denies a priority to justification, then sanctification itself is transformed. They contend that the very character and identity of the Christian life are at stake in the debate. The reason a believer pursues sanctification is that he has already been made right with God. A proper theology of union with Christ will be compatible with this doctrine, they argue. It is the doctrines of justification and sanctification that inform the believer's understanding of union with Christ, not vice versa.[114]

Debate continued in 2008 with the appearance of three other controversial works. Mark Garcia produced a study on the topic of union with Christ in the works of Calvin; Fesko published a book on justification; and Richard Gaffin penned a chapter on justification and union with Christ in Calvin.[115] In the following year, Fesko reviewed Garcia's *Life in Christ.*

Fesko claimed that Garcia was wrong when he argued that Calvin's soteriology is different from that of Lutheranism. The issue is the relationship between justification and sanctification. Justification, for Calvin, apparently does not have a logical or temporal priority over

113. Ibid.: "[There are] exegetical, theological, and moral reasons for affirming that justification has a priority to sanctification in the *ordo salutis.*" It seems apparent that the key to understanding sanctification for these authors is that they are assuming progressive sanctification.

114. Ibid.: "If anything, WLC 69 warns us against starting with an abstract doctrine of union from which we deduce the relationship (or lack thereof) between justification and sanctification. The WLC points us precisely to justification, adoption, and sanctification as those blessings that manifest our union. If we want to understand union, then, we must look to our justification, adoption, and sanctification. These blessings show us what our union with Christ is. . . . A sound biblical and Reformed understanding of union with Christ must include and support the idea that justification is prior to sanctification in the *ordo salutis* in a very important sense. . . . We all believe in union with Christ, but what makes the difference for how one understands the basics of salvation and the gospel message is the concrete content by which one defines what this union is."

115. Mark A. Garcia, *Life in Christ: Union with Christ and Twofold Grace in Calvin's Theology*— Studies in Christian History and Thought (Milton Keynes/Waynesboro, GA: Paternoster, 2008); John V. Fesko, *Justification: Understanding the Classic Reformed Doctrine* (Phillipsburg, NJ: P&R Publishing, 2008); and Richard B. Gaffin, "Justification and Union with Christ (3.11–18)," in *A Theological Guide to Calvin's Institutes: Essays and Analysis*, ed. David W. Hall and Peter A. Lillback (Phillipsburg, NJ: P&R Publishing, 2008), 248–69.

sanctification, as it does in Lutheranism. For Calvin, union with Christ was more fundamental than either justification or sanctification.[116] Garcia understands Calvin's soteriology as the redeemed's receiving justification and sanctification inseparably and simultaneously in their union with Christ. According to Garcia, Calvin is here simply following Paul at Romans 8:29–30.[117]

Fesko argues that Garcia's view of Calvin's doctrine of salvation is not actually based on his reading of Calvin but instead is established in the theology of Richard Gaffin. It is Gaffin's thesis that Paul does not understand the *ordo salutis* as a sequence of events but as a single act of union with Christ.[118] Sometime after making this discovery, Gaffin apparently became convinced that this understanding was Calvin's *ordo salutis* as well.[119]

116. In his review of Garcia's *Life in Christ*, John Fesko (*Ordained Servant*, 2009), wrote: "His argument is that Calvin provides a unique answer to this question, one that is distinctly set apart from his Lutheran counterparts. In fact, showing how different Calvin's soteriology (especially with respect to the relationship between justification and sanctification) is from his Lutheran counterparts, is something of a leitmotif of Garcia's work (xv, 3, 7, 75–77, 241, 251–52, 260). The crux of Garcia's argument is contra popular expressions that sanctification is grounded in justification, or that justification is the cause of sanctification. Calvin, according to Garcia, believes that there is something more fundamental to both justification and sanctification, namely union with Christ (3, 264, 267 n.7). In this regard, one finds that Garcia differs from Billings in his appraisal of the place of union with Christ in Calvin's theology."

117. Fesko, *Ordained Servant*, 2009: Garcia argues "that justification does not have any sort of priority, logical or temporal, as Garcia understands the Lutheran tradition to argue, but on the other side of the coin, neither does sanctification have any sort of logical or temporal priority, as say legalists of various stripes might try to maintain. Rather, Garcia's reading of Calvin has the Reformer arguing that the *duplex gratia* of justification and sanctification are received inseparably and simultaneously, but at the same time should not be confused. . . . In other words, union with Christ is controlling and singularly determinative (133, 162–63, 235, 248, 250). Garcia further argues that Calvin's own understanding of the *unio Christi-duplex gratia* (3) merely reflects the Pauline *ordo* of Rom 8:29–30: 'Theologically, this *ordo* reflects the union believers have with Christ by the Spirit through faith' (253)."

118. Ibid.: "This [Gaffin's influence] raises a legitimate question pertinent to the present review, one that provides a possible answer to the divergent readings of Billings and Garcia. Gaffin published his doctoral dissertation in 1977 in which he called for a restructuring of the *ordo salutis* along Pauline lines, namely ensuring that the *ordo* reflected the centrality of union with Christ. Gaffin writes, 'Everywhere Paul speaks of the believer's justification, adoption, sanctification, glorification . . . there the more basic underlying consideration is resurrection with Christ, that is, (existential) union with Christ as resurrected.'"

119. Ibid.: "But it appears that Gaffin's own personal understanding of the union priority antedates his discovery of the same pattern in Calvin. For example, it is not until 2002 that Gaffin writes: 'This, in a nutshell, is Calvin's *ordo salutis*: union with Christ by (Spirit-worked) faith.' As a matter of historiography, it appears that proponents of this school also find the very same features in Calvin's doctrine of union with Christ. However, this also poses another

Gaffin's reading of Calvin is also found in former students besides Garcia.[120] Thus Fesko identifies a "Gaffin school" of comprehending union with Christ that is supposedly rooted in Paul, then expressed historically in Calvin. This distinctive school rejects any logical or theological priority of justification to sanctification.

Fesko says that he is not charging Garcia or Gaffin with irresponsible eisegesis. Garcia might have brought assumptions and presuppositions into his historical research, and those presuppositions simply must be squared with the evidence. Contra Garcia, Fesko believes that Calvin assigns priority to justification over sanctification.[121] Furthermore, he does not think that union with Christ is an architectonic principle of Calvin's soteriology but simply a significant theme.[122]

Then Fesko begins his assault against the so-called "Gaffin school."[123] First, it is hypothetically possible that the Gaffin reading of Calvin presented by Garcia is correct. If it is so, then more research is necessary to establish that reading. Second, if the Gaffin school is correct, then many within the Reformed community need to reconsider the relationship between justification and sanctification. Third, the debate between Westminster in California and Westminster in

---

question. What came first, the chicken or the egg? Was Gaffin influenced by Calvin or did he later find his own understanding of the Pauline *ordo* in Calvin?"

120. Ibid.: "For example, in an essay by Craig Carpenter that both Garcia and Gaffin cite as part of their case for the centrality of union in Calvin, one finds the following: 'As important as justification by imputed righteousness is for him, it is not justification by faith but union with Christ that is the controlling principle of the Reformer's doctrine of applied soteriology.' Or there is the following similar statement, 'It appears that Calvin's *ordo salutis* does not require the logical or temporal priority of a forensic act to a renovative act. Although he does speak of one's progressive sanctification following in time one's justification, the legal and the transformative blessings of salvation are given together in the Spirit's act of uniting the sinner to Christ."

121. Ibid.: "Calvin . . . even uses language of causality to do so. In this regard, it seems crucial that one note that when Calvin explains the *duplex gratia*, the first grace is justification and the second is sanctification. If there is no priority of justification, as Garcia maintains, does one ever find Calvin reversing the order of the *duplex gratia*? It would seem that the answer to this question is a definite no, though Garcia in one place does reverse them (96–97). If one turns to Calvin's sermons, there is further evidence to consider."

122. Ibid.: "The small bits of gathered evidence seem to point away from Garcia's conclusions."

123. Ibid.: "Another question is, How widespread is this particular reading of Calvin? Can one find it prior to 1977 and the publication of Gaffin's doctoral dissertation? Is there a Gaffin-school reading of Calvin, one driven by Gaffin's reading of Paul? These questions are important on several levels."

Philadelphia on this topic has broader ecclesiological implications.[124] Finally, time will tell whether the Gaffin school will be proven correct, but Fesko believes that contemporary scholarly research is leaning against it.[125]

The sparks did not fly from Escondido only. Gaffin reviewed Michael Horton's *Covenant and Salvation* in 2009. In the first part of the volume, Gaffin conveys that Horton rightly holds to a bicovenantal structure in the OT—one of works and grace. Nevertheless, Gaffin was not persuaded by some of the details of Horton's presentation.[126] It is the second half of Horton's book about which Gaffin is concerned. First, Horton has established a covenantal ontology that includes justification as a creating and effective forensicism. This viewpoint seems unclear to Gaffin and reminds him of Karl Barth's position.[127]

Second, Gaffin charges that Horton has not made clear the relationship between justification and union with Christ.[128] Gaffin's own position is

124. Ibid.: "The difference of opinion has for the most part been cordial, but at times there have been pointed exchanges."

125. Ibid.: "It can sometimes take a generation or more to establish a historical-theological corrective reading. . . . It does appear, however, that Billings's reading of Calvin is a more accurate portrait. Others have arrived at similar conclusions. Cornelius Venema writes: 'In my judgment, Garcia and Carpenter overstate the extent to which union with Christ "coordinates" its two benefits of justification and sanctification, and do not do justice to the careful way Calvin also maintains the (theological, not temporal) "order" of justification in relation to sanctification' [16]."

126. Richard B. Gaffin, "Covenant and Salvation: A Review Article," *Ordained Servant*, March 2009 (reprinted in The Aquila Report, 2011): "Under the Mosaic economy the judicial role of the law in the life of God's people functioned, at the typological level, for inheritance by works (as the covenant of works reintroduced) in antithesis to grace." Also, "the reason Israel went into exile was not failure as a nation to maintain a requisite level of formal obedience to the law in all its details. Rather, Israel lost the land for the deeper reason of *unbelief*, because of the *idolatry* that was at the root of and focused the unbelieving nonremnant's disobedience of God and his law."

127. Gaffin (ibid.) is disturbed by Horton's positive references to Bruce McCormack's treatment—since McCormack has a Barthian reading of justification [Michael Horton, *Covenant and Salvation: Union with Christ* (Louisville/London: Westminster John Knox, 2007)]: "I wish Horton had more clearly distanced himself from McCormack's position in the article Horton utilizes positively. . . . That position . . . necessarily entails doing away with the distinction between the once-for-all accomplishment of redemption and its ongoing application (as well as the historical before and after of Christ's states of humiliation and exaltation). The result is an understanding of the constitutive or effective nature of justification and of its relationship to sanctification that differs radically from confessional Reformed orthodoxy."

128. Gaffin (ibid.) notes that "in discussing Reformation views of union, he [Horton] says, 'Regardless of whether union temporally preceded justification, Calvin is clear that the latter is

to see union with Christ by faith as what is antecedently 'constitutive' in our salvation, issuing in both justification and sanctification, the forensic and the nonforensic/renovative, each with its own constitutive or effective moment, distinct yet inseparable from the other."

Third, Horton overlooks differences between Lutheran and Reformed positions regarding the application of redemption. Fourth, Horton is critical of the Reformed handling of the doctrine of regeneration. He does not like the idea that regeneration produces habitual change, or a new *habitus*. Horton proposes the counter notion of regeneration as effectual calling, with which Gaffin is not satisfied.[129] Gaffin rightly argues that regeneration is distinct from effectual calling—the two are not identical.

Fesko's review of Garcia's book invited a response—not by Garcia, as one would expect, but by Gaffin. Gaffin was perplexed as to Fesko's statements but did not take into account Gaffin's most recent writing.[130] Gaffin answered Fesko's question as to whether Gaffin came to his understanding of soteriology before reading Calvin. He said that it came prior to reading Calvin. Gaffin realizes that it is anachronistic to argue about Calvin's *ordo salutis*, since those theological discussions came after Calvin. Gaffin rebuffs the charge that he thinks that, for Calvin, sanctification precedes salvation.[131] Fesko charges that Gaffin has confused Calvin's *ordo docendi* (or "order of teaching") with his *ordo salutis*, a charge Gaffin also denies.

The issue of contention is whether Calvin held to the priority of justification to sanctification. Gaffin is firm that in Calvin, as well as in Gaffin and Garcia, there is priority of justification to progressive

---

the basis for the former' (as far as I can see, the Calvin citation in the following sentence does not support this statement and the quote from *Institutes*, 3.16.1 on the previous page in fact tells against it); and on page 147: 'While a great deal more than justification is included as a result of being in Christ, Reformed theology has emphasized with Lutheran doctrine that justification is the judicial ground of it all.'"

129. Gaffin (ibid.): "'Regeneration *as* Effectual Calling' as a corrective . . . seems to involve a kind of actualism."

130. Richard B. Gaffin, "Reply to Fesko," *Ordained Servant*, March 2009. The writing that Gaffin has in mind is Gaffin's chapter in *Theological Guide to Calvin's Institutes*. Fesko apparently footnoted it but did not incorporate it.

131. Ibid.: "It was the farthest thing from my mind even to suggest that because in Book 3 of the *Institutes* Calvin discusses the life of ongoing sanctification before justification that therefore the former precedes the latter in the actual application of redemption."

sanctification.[132] Thus forensic justification is a necessary prerequisite to a life of sanctification. Justification is both a logical and a temporal priority over progressive sanctification.

Gaffin understands Calvin's soteriology, which he says concurs with Paul's, as following these lines: the believer is united to Christ and, in that union, experiences justification and definitive sanctification. Union with Christ is antecedent to justification. Believers receive justification and sanctification by their union with Christ. Being united to Christ by faith effects both justification and sanctification.[133] Relative to the relationship between justification and sanctification, Calvin again opposes the priority of justification.[134]

For Calvin, union with Christ is antecedent to the twofold grace. He does not hold to settled justification, then subsequent sanctification. Coincident with justification is a disposition to holiness. One cannot say that for Calvin justification causes or is the cause of sanctification. Nevertheless, justification is the indispensable precondition of progressive sanctification. While Fesko gives a citation for the causal priority of justification, Gaffin counters that both the translation and the meaning are ambiguous.[135] Gaffin concludes that he hopes the institutional differences between the two Westminster seminaries will prove to be nonexistent.[136]

132. Note the adjective "progressive." Ibid.: "justification is prior to sanctification in the sense that the latter, as a life-long and imperfect process, follows the former as complete and perfect from the inception of the Christian life."

133. Ibid.: "Without union, the benefits that flow from it, including my justification, are nonexistent."

134. Ibid.: "Calvin knows nothing of a justification that is first settled and then only subsequently is followed by sanctification. Rather, coincident with this settled and irreversible justification, at the moment it takes place and given with it, is a disposition to godliness and holy living, no matter how undoubtedly weak and sin-plagued that disposition and how imperfectly manifested subsequently."

135. He also concludes that there is no Gaffin school. His views follow *WCF*; see WLC 69 and, similarly, WSC 29–32.

136. In the same year, D. G. Hart and John Muether wrote a blog article on this topic. While the original article is no longer available, many online journals carried those authors' apology for what they wrote about Dr. Gaffin. It is truly sad when mature ruling elders and established scholars misquote other elders in print. See https://www.reformation21.org/an _apology (accessed July 5, 2019): "With reference to the article 'Priorities' in the last *Nicotine Theological Journal* (Winter 2009), the editors unreservedly apologize for implying that there is any tension between the position of Carl Trueman and Richard Gaffin on the matter of justification regarding the bounds of confessional orthodoxy; we also apologize for the fact that Dr. Gaffin was quoted out of context in the article in a manner that distorted his views, and we

While these debates are both important and complex, they are far from over. In the following year, William B. Evans wrote on the soteriological controversy.[137] His article also provoked a response with a counter reply. Evans argued that Reformed theology in America has not been monolithic. Calvin's position, which included union with Christ, was not fully developed and explained. Calvin's approach, however, was eclipsed by federal theology.

Federal theology speaks of an extrinsic legal union, forensic salvation by faith, and a vital or spiritual union whereby the Christian experiences divine transformation. This theology developed an *ordo salutis* in which the forensic, including justification and adoption, not only logically but also temporally preceded the transformatory—sanctification and glorification. Justification was separated from the life of obedience. The unity of these two parts was found in the divine decree rather than in Christ.

In the nineteenth century, the Hodges taught that justification preceded sanctification both chronologically and logically. Their teaching was continued by stalwarts B. B. Warfield, Robert Lewis Dabney, and Louis Berkhof.[138]

Evans provided a taxonomy of the debate. There is a biblical-theological trajectory begun in Vos and continued through Murray and Gaffin. While this group was committed to the Westminster Standards, Vos's *Pauline Eschatology* was groundbreaking. It opened new avenues to study, and in 1976 Gaffin said that it was time to reexplore the relationship between systematic theology and biblical theology. Evans contended that biblical-theological analysis corrects some of the federal theological mistakes. The biblical-theological trajectory

---

affirm that his recent response to John Fesko in *Ordained Servant* (March, 2009) represents a satisfactory clarification of the comment we misquoted; we further apologize for implying that Dr. Gaffin's views are contrary to the Protestant confessional consensus on justification and for writing that they constitute 'a new perspective on Paul,' which uses eschatology to overturn the consensus of the Reformers and the Reformed creeds; and we acknowledge that the biblical notion of union with Christ does not contradict or contravene, directly or impliedly, anything taught in the Westminster Standards."

137. William B. Evans, "Déjà Vu All Over Again? The Contemporary Reformed Soteriological Controversy in Historical Perspective," *WTJ* 72, no. 1 (Spring 2010): 138–41. Also see William B. Evans, *Imputation and Importation: Union with Christ in American Reformed Theology* (Milton Keynes: Paternoster, 2008).

138. Evans, "Déjà Vu," 135–37.

emphasized union with Christ. *Union* was the central soteriological concept. *Union with Christ* is an umbrella category for all soteriological aspects. Gaffin said that the forensic functions within the participatory. Instead of a bifurcated union, those functions speak of one union with different aspects. Such a union preserves from both legalism and antinomianism. Evans said this trajectory teaches both forensic and synthetic justification.[139]

While Evans added more fuel to the fire of debate from a different angle, Rob Edwards addressed Fesko's criticisms of Gaffin. His article opens with setting the stage of debate between the two Westminster seminaries on a proper *ordo salutis*. Edwards nuances well why both sides are zealous for their positions. He specifically addresses many of the challenges presented by Horton and Fesko to the Westminster Seminary interpretation. Specifically, one challenge is that if the Westminster position is correct, then there should be further historical corroboration. It is this corroboration that Edwards provides beautifully. John Flavel was well known and respected in his own day and has been cherished by many Reformed theologians to the present day. Flavel, as presented by Edwards, held exactly to the position as presented by Gaffin.[140]

Besides Flavel, Edwards also treats William Ames's *Marrow of Theology*, which is cited by both Horton and Fesko as supporting their view. Fesko argues that for Ames, justification is the cause of sanctification. Edwards demonstrates that those scholars have overlooked Ames's larger framework or broader structure. For Ames, justification and sanctification, as distinct, both flow out of union with Christ.[141]

Flavel's emphasis is on the person of Christ and not the benefit of justification. In fact, Flavel's theology speaks to the current controversy in three ways. First, there is the possibility of confusing the distinction between redemption accomplished and applied.[142] Second, faith seems to be reduced to its function in justification for those who hold

139. Ibid., 141.

140. Rob Edwards, "John Flavel [1627–1691] on the Priority of Union with Christ: Further Historical Perspective on the Structure of Reformed Soteriology," *WTJ* 74, no. 1 (Spring 2012): 33–53.

141. Ibid., 54–55.

142. Ibid., 56. For example, Fesko (in his article "William Perkins on Union with Christ and Justification," *Mid America Journal of Theology* 21 [2010], 32) argues that "justification secures salvation," which, as Edwards views it, fails to underline that it is Christ who secures salvation.

to the priority of justification. The object of faith is not Christ but the benefit received through him. Flavel stressed that faith first receives his person, then his privileges.[143] Third, the emphasis in Flavel is to the person of Christ, whom believers receive—that is, union with Christ is to his person. Communion in benefits presupposes union with his person, whereas Godfrey and Fesko describe union with Christ as simply synonymous with the *ordo salutis*, the various benefits of salvation. Christ's benefits are not primary—it is Christ who is primary.[144]

With this extended controversy as a backdrop, a few years later Richard Gaffin was again able to investigate the work of Christ in his state of exaltation. Gaffin presented the differences between the *ordo* and *historia salutis* ("history of salvation") and argued against Karl Barth's rejection of a difference between salvation accomplished and applied. He examined the *ordo salutis* and sin, then moved to Christ's exaltation and the application of his work, while noting that "nothing is more essential and central in the activity of the exalted Christ in applying salvation than his ongoing intercession."[145]

The heart of Gaffin's teaching focuses on union with Christ. He is rightly convinced that this union is central to the application of Christ's work and is the foremost reality of salvation. For Gaffin, union with Christ has a number of dimensions. It reaches back in the past to encompass election, has a present or existential sense, and also embraces the future. There is only one union, but it has different aspects or phases. Proper theology neither denies any of the aspects nor blurs the distinctions between those aspects.[146]

Present union with Christ includes four interrelated aspects. Mystical union is the mystery of how believers are now revealed to be in Christ while having been hidden in God's eternal purpose. It is also the mystery of sinful believers' being united to the exalted

143. Edwards, "Flavel," 56–57.

144. Ibid., 57. In addition to these historical studies, there were other publications adding further fuel to this rather hot fire. Horton (*The Christian Faith*, 594n11) commented negatively on Garcia's work. Ralph Cunningham opposes Fesko's notion that definitive sanctification muddies the waters of the *duplex gratia* in "Definitive Sanctification: A Response to John Fesko," *Evangelical Quarterly* 84, no. 3 (2012): 235–40.

145. Richard B. Gaffin, "The Work of Christ Applied," in *Christian Dogmatics: Reformed Theology for the Church Catholic*, ed. Michael Allen and Scott R. Swain (Grand Rapids: Baker Academic, 2016), 279.

146. Ibid., 280–81.

Christm.[147] Union with Christ can also be characterized as spiritual in that it has a reciprocal character. Not only are believers in Christ, but he is also in them. This union is the work of Christ and the Holy Spirit. As the Spirit indwells believers, so it is the indwelling of Christ. This union is also vital, or life-giving. Believers are alive in Christ, and for them to live is Christ. Last, it is an indissoluble union rooted in God's immutable decree of election.

Gaffin is very much indebted to Calvin's theology for his analysis of union with Christ and twofold grace.[148] That grace is both judicial and recreative—that is, justification that is judicial and settled, and sanctification that is definitive and progressive. The judicial and recreative are distinct and inseparable. First, this union is not partial; rather, it is whole and complete. Believers receive the whole Christ, in whom they receive both justification and sanctification. Second, that present or existential union with Christ comes through the Holy Spirit's working faith in the sinner. Union with Christ is through Spirit-wrought faith. Gaffin is convinced that Calvin taught that union with Christ is the source of justification and sanctification. So discussion of the work of Christ applied should be neither justification-centered nor sanctification-centered but centered on both, because it is Christ-centered.[149] Gaffin also argues that this theology is not limited to Calvin's thinking but is also clearly articulated by the Westminster Standards.[150]

Moving to union with Christ and imputation, Gaffin argues that the ground for the believer's union with Christ must be Christ's own righteousness. It must be in Christ, as distinct from the believer. It is in Christ, in contrast to the renovating work of the Spirit in the believer.[151] This teaching was also that of Calvin.[152]

147. The operative passages are Ephesians 5:32 and John 17:20–23, along with other relational analogies for this union. As a union wrought by the Holy Spirit, it is not ontological, hypostatic, psychosomatic, somatic, or merely intellectual and moral (ibid., 281–82).

148. Ibid., 283, again underlined the centrality of union for Calvin: "This union is so central, so pivotal, that without it the saving work of Christ, the once-for-all redemption he has accomplished, 'remains useless and of no value.' Union is the all-or-nothing reality on which everything depends in the application of salvation. . . . Without union, the benefits that flow from it are otherwise nonexistent or irrelevant."

149. Ibid., 284–85.

150. For example, WSC 30, 32–33; WLC 69. See Gaffin, "Work of Christ Applied," 285.

151. Gaffin, "Work of Christ Applied," 287: "Christ's sacrifice for me, not the Spirit's work in me, is the basis of my being forgiven, fully and perfectly."

152. See *Institutes*, 3.11.10–11.

Gaffin concludes with an analysis of Romans 8:29–30, a classic proof text for the *ordo salutis*. He argues that the purpose of being foreknown and predestined is to be conformed to the image of Christ. The overall or ultimate goal is for the believer to bear Christ's image, and, to that end, justification is essential. Believers are in Christ so that they can be conformed to Christ. There is an adoption in view that will be realized in a still-future bodily resurrection. Furthermore, there are cosmic dimensions to this union as the whole creation awaits deliverance from decay and futility. Yet all these aspects are penultimate to Christ's preeminent exaltation glory.[153]

David Garner, professor of systematic theology and academic dean at Westminster Seminary, added further fuel to the justification fire in his *Sons of the Son*. While the more precise topic of his book is adoption, nevertheless Garner analyzes some of the broad sweeps of discussion concerning the *ordo salutis* itself.[154]

One faulty approach he terms *forensic fixation*. This position is the one that is clearly articulated in the Augsburg Confession and can rightly be classified as the standard Lutheran teaching on the topic.[155] There are positive reasons for structuring salvation as not focusing on justification. First, for Garner, it is difficult to see how justification is ultimately more important than sanctification/glorification. Christ's work to forgive sin is not more important than his power over its master.[156] Also, the Scriptures clearly teach that Christ's work, which actually makes the sinner righteous, is equal to forensic justification. This transformation is fundamental to the gospel, and that transformation will be manifested in the eschaton. Purity and holiness are not afterthoughts of Christ's work.[157] When examining sin's forgiveness to

153. Gaffin, "Work of Christ Applied," 288–90.

154. His intentions are massive. David B. Garner, *Sons in the Son* (Phillipsburg, NJ: P&R Publishing, 2016), 286: "The vast scope of adoption's significance in covenant and redemptive history, its Christological solidarity, and its eschatological dynamic require a thorough reconsideration of adoption's place in systematic theology and the *ordo salutis* in particular."

155. Robert Letham wrote on this theme in *Union with Christ in Scripture, History, and Theology* (Phillipsburg, NJ: P&R Publishing, 2011), 82, when he argued that the Reformed notion of union with Christ differs from the Lutheran notion of a purely external justification.

156. Garner, *Sons in the Son*, 274.

157. Ibid., 274: "Truly the door of biblical soteriology swings on the hinge of justification. But that soteriological door requires a second hinge, which bears the weight of an equally critical feature of gospel grace—that is, the efficacy of Christ's life, death, and resurrection to make sinners righteous. This transforming power of Christ's work is also a sine qua non of the

its fullest extent, one must also have in view the sinner's purification. While purification cannot occur without forgiveness, that forgiveness does not cause purification. "Without this sanctification," Garner argues, "the gospel is no longer the gospel."[158]

Garner opposes the Lutheran, or forensic-fixation, way of structuring justification on a number of grounds. When justification is primary over sanctification and glorification, justification becomes both the gift and giver, and it is Christ alone who is the great Benefactor.[159] When justification is primary, while it does not deny other features of Christ's work, it unavoidably mutes them. So making those other features subordinate reduces their soteriological clarity. Also, forensic fixation can actually push toward the theology of Rome.[160] Forensic fixation buries proper NT filial Christology. In addition, it is improper to resort to speech-act theory to attempt to rescue forensic fixation.[161] In conclusion, forensic fixation "emasculates the consummate covenantal victory of the Son of God and distorts biblical soteriology as a whole!"[162]

Garner is convinced that his view of the *ordo salutis* fits precisely with classic Reformed and Presbyterian standards. His view of Calvin and the WCF is supported by Garcia and opposed by Fesko. Garner concludes: "It is my strong contention that Garcia faithfully represents Calvin and the historic Reformed approach to insisting on the priority of union with Christ for justification, rather than any alternative."[163]

Garner charges that recent scholarship has wrongly argued that the Lutheran or forensic-fixation and Reformed concepts of justification are essentially indistinguishable.[164] In fact, the Reformed concept is different from the Lutheran concept, and the differences between them are not

gospel. The sons of God declared are the sons of God changed. . . . To wit, the grand finale of the gospel entails more than a declaration of justification or of legal sonship; it is a manifestation of the sons *transformed* into the image of their Elder Brother."

158. Ibid., 275.

159. Ibid., 226: "Such paradigms suffer soteriological and Christological derailment."

160. Ibid., 227: "The irony here is patent."

161. Ibid., 245n74: "Speech-act theory has provided a novel tool for turning forensic declaration into the transformative sphere, in which the forensic locution allegedly bears transformative illocutionary force." See Michael S. Horton, *Covenant and Eschatology: The Divine Drama* (Louisville: Westminster John Knox Press, 2002), 126–31, 145–46.

162. Garner, *Sons in the Son*, 274–75.

163. Ibid., 288n3.

164. Ibid., 225.

merely semantic.[165] Garner charges that Horton, in his contribution to *Justification: Five Views*, as well as in his 2011 *The Christian Faith*, presents a Reformed view that is the same as the Lutheran view.[166] James Beilby and Paul Eddy comment on Horton's contribution to their volume: "Horton's traditional Reformed view is functionally identical in all the significant theological aspects to the traditional Lutheran view."[167]

Garner proposes his own understanding of salvation: Following Calvin, believers are bonded by the Spirit of adoption to Christ with the simultaneous distinct benefits of the forensic and renovative. Such a salvation embraces the already established relationship to God as well as the eschatological hope. Still following Calvin, adoption is the gospel itself.[168] Archibald Alexander Hodge apparently built on this foundation, united the forensic and moral/regenerative in adoption, and moved away from Turretin's forensic fixation. He moved beyond the WCF, but in a compatible fashion. He placed adoption so that it embraced the grace of justification and sanctification. Adoption extends beyond a single benefit and aligns closely to union with Christ.[169]

Garner presents four ways that Reformed theology has structured an order of salvation, complete with illustrative charts. The first way is the highly displeasing forensic fixation. In this model, justification is the source of the other soteriological benefits, including union with Christ.[170] The second *ordo* model is adoption as justification. Here, adoption is purely forensic.[171] The third model focuses on union with Christ, with adoption as a distinctive part. The WCF has adoption, justification, and sanctification as separate benefits flowing from union with Christ. But having adoption, justification, and sanctification in direct parallel appears to misalign adoption.[172] A fourth model, having adoption in its own proper orbit, is the preferred model.

165. Ibid., 226n25.
166. Ibid., 225.
167. James K. Beilby and Paul R. Eddy, eds., *Justification: Five Views*, Spectrum Multiview Books (Downers Grove, IL: IVP Academic, 2011), 10, as cited by Garner, *Sons in the Son*, 225n21.
168. Garner, *Sons in the Son*, 294–95.
169. Ibid., 297: "Forensic and transformative benefits flow from union with Christ, and adoption in some way ties these benefits to one another."
170. Ibid., 301.
171. Ibid., 302. His classification has two divisions, one more Lutheran and one more Reformed.
172. Ibid., 303.

There are tremendous benefits to the model of adoption in Christ.[173] In a proper model, justification needs to retain its forensic purity, and sanctification must retain its unique transformative force.[174] Keeping justification and sanctification in their respective purity will be maintained only when the force of adoption frames the redemptive benefits. Thus union with Christ is embraced by adoption. Adoption qualifies all the other benefits of salvation, unites them to Christ's resurrection, and frames union with Christ according to its eschatological character. *Adoption* is the most comprehensive soteriological concept. It is the unique benefit of union with Christ, with justification and sanctification functioning as core subsets. These benefits are not logically or chronologically sequential but eschatologically vital.[175] In a proper model, union with Christ is adoption in Christ.[176] Union with Christ cannot be viewed as a series of events, for the graces come punctiliarly in the moment of saving faith, when the redeemed receive Christ by the work of the Spirit of adoption. Soteriological graces are shaped by that faith union.[177] Adoption is the supreme benefit to believers because of its christological substance. In fact, all benefits, including justification and sanctification, manifest themselves in the fellowship of believers. Thus adoption "draws the soteriological into the ecclesiological."[178]

Christians draw the benefits of redemption from Christ's actual biography—his incarnation, perfect obedience, death, and triumphant resurrection. There is a vital connection between Christ and his experiences and the benefits that flow to believers. A model that fails

---

173. Ibid., 305–6: "By the Spirit of adoption, believers enjoy vindication/justification . . . consecration/sanctification unto full conformity with the Son of God in their own bodily resurrection. . . . the believer currently enjoys the full measure of the resurrected Son in his inner man, and anticipates the complete realization of the Son's benefits upon bodily resurrection. . . . What coalesced for Christ at his resurrection will coalesce in the believer's experience as well. . . . Paul qualifies his entire soteriological paradigm by the filial because he qualifies Christology by the filial."

174. Ibid., 306: "Neither drives or eclipses the other; neither distorts the other by infringing on its distinctive nature."

175. Ibid., 307.

176. Ibid., 308n44, argues that most would place the WCF in his model 10.4 but the improved model 10.5 is consistent with the standards.

177. Ibid., 309.

178. Ibid., 310. In fact, adoption expansively informs many Pauline themes, including the image of God, eschatological glory, God's kingdom, ecclesiology and sacraments, and ethics. See also ibid., 313–14.

to preserve this connection "elicits theological abstraction, diluting Christ's work and fictionalizing redemption applied."[179]

There have been various critical reviews of Garner's *Sons in the Son* that focus on the issue of justification and the *ordo salutis*.[180] Ryan McGraw argues that the situation is not so simple as choosing between either the forensic-fixation view or Garner's alternative, in which there are no logical priorities between justification, adoption, and sanctification in that they all evidence union with Christ. Instead, the classic Reformed *ordo salutis*, McGraw argues, has justification, adoption, and sanctification flowing from union with Christ but still within a logical order in relationship to each other.[181] Recently, Tim Trumper, formerly a professor at Westminster, reviewed Garner's work in the *Journal of the Evangelical Theological Society*. Here is the critical question on which Trumper ends his review: he wonders whether Garner's view, which denies the logical sequence of justification-adoption, is consistent with the Westminster Standards. He appears to hint that there may be problems with smoothing out the wrinkles of a redemptive-historical approach to the doctrine of adoption.[182] It would appear that debate on adoption and the *ordo salutis* will continue.

In 2018, Michael Horton provided a massive two-volume work on justification. In it, he briefly criticized Evans, Garcia, and others for maintaining that justification has no relation to sanctification, but both are gifts of union with Christ.[183] There was little criticism of Gaffin throughout the work, and Horton distanced himself from

179. Ibid., 314: "The redeemed are sons—justified and sanctified, because we are, by the life-giving Spirit of adoption, gloriously and permanently adopted sons in the Son."

180. One reviewer commented that the debates between WS-C and Westminster Theological Seminary on *ordo salutis* were a bit parochial (Dane Ortlund, "Reflections on Handling the Old Testament as Jesus Would Have Us: Psalm 15 as a Case Study," *Themelios* 42, no. 1 [2017]: 166; https://www.thegospelcoalition.org/themelios/article/reflections-on-handling-the-old-testament-as-jesus-would-have-us-psalm-15/). Accessed January 14, 2019.

181. Ryan McGraw, "Review: *Sons in the Son* by David B. Garner," *Ordained Servant*, 2017, https://opc.org/os.html?article_id=607, Accessed July 1, 2019.

182. Tim Trumper, *Journal of the Evangelical Theological Society* 62, no. 1 (2019): 204–9: "Is Garner's denial of the logical sequence of justification-adoption consistent with the Westminster Standards? If not, his methodological divergence from the Westminster Standards confirms that the new wine of the redemptive-historical approach to adoption calls for new wine skins (the methodological and attitudinal renewal of Puritan/Presbyterian systematics). Garner disavows this constructive form of Calvinism, yet his volume, to a degree, presents the case for it, and supplies a springboard from which adoption may be recovered and Westminster Calvinism renewed."

183. Michael Horton, *Justification*, 2 vols. (Grand Rapids: Zondervan, 2018), 2:469.

Gaffin's expressed fear of viewing justification itself, instead of union with Christ, as legal and transformative.[184]

There was another large study produced on the doctrine of justification in 2019. David VanDrunen's "A Contested Union: Union with Christ and the Justification Debate" is a continuation and elaboration of the debate held in *Ordained Servant* a decade earlier. What bothers VanDrunen is that the Gaffin school challenges the traditional Reformed doctrine of the *ordo salutis*. The specific problem focuses on justification's established relationship to the other soteriological blessings. He centers on the particular issue that Gaffin does not seem to affirm that justification is a cause of sanctification. Furthermore, VanDrunen does not think that Murray's notion of definitive sanctification is at all helpful. Thus he views sanctification as a process. He is convinced that reflection on a person's justification is a cause of his sanctification.[185]

In the same volume, John Fesko argues that Reformed theologians embraced Luther's teaching on justification.[186] Calvin rejected the Council of Trent's twofold justification, the first in baptism and the second in final judgment. He taught a *duplex gratia* of justification and sanctification that are united but nevertheless distinct. Calvin, in *Institutes* 3.11.5, also opposed Osiander, who argued that believers in union with Christ receive Christ's essential righteousness rather than imputed righteousness. Calvin still held justification together with union with Christ. Here, he thinks, is a shift in Protestant address.[187] After examination of the Heidelberg Catechism, he turned to early orthodoxy.

Johannes Piscator (1546–1625) said that justification is merely the forgiveness of sins, and he denied Christ's imputed righteousness in justification. Piscator claimed to follow Calvin. David Pareus (1548–1622) defended him and argued for the imputation of Christ's passive obedi-

---

184. Ibid., 2:450: "And union with Christ, I suggest, is the wider rubric of 'salvation' in its application. Along the same lines Richard Gaffin observes"; and 2:471: "In short, whereas Luther and Calvin see *union with Christ* involving both legal and transformative elements, Bates and numerous others see *justification* itself as legal and transformative.

185. David VanDrunen, "A Contested Union," in *The Doctrine on Which the Church Stands or Falls*, ed. Matthew Barrett (Wheaton, IL: Crossway, 2019), 497.

186. Fesko, "Ground of Religion," in Barrett, *Doctrine*, 702–6. He evaluated Luther, Zwingli, Bullinger, Juan de Valdes, and Peter Martyr Vermigli. Vermigli's mature teaching was "that justification was not by works but by faith alone and that it brings the forgiveness of sins and the imputation of Christ's righteousness; it is not a process but a divine act" (ibid., 706).

187. Ibid., 707–9.

ence, a single imputation. Thus there was a distinction between Christ's active and passive obedience, and Piscator's rejection of the imputation of Christ's active obedience produced pushback.[188] Of course, the Synod of Dordt rejected Arminius's denial of faith as the instrumental cause of justification.[189] The WCF fits into the period of high orthodoxy. The divines debated the imputation of Christ's active obedience. Van Dixhoorn says that at WCF 11.1, they omitted the phrase "whole obedience" to accommodate the anti–active obedience party. Fesko says that this purpose is plausible but that the evidence demonstrates that they codified the imputation of Christ's active obedience.[190] Richard Baxter (1615–1691) and John Owen (1616–1683) sparred, and Owen wrote his *The Doctrine of Justification* against Baxter.[191]

Late orthodoxy (1700–1790) saw the Marrow Controversy. Fesko argues that Jonathan Edwards had a faulty view of justification because he conflated faith and its evidences. He had what Fesko termed a *twofold justification* that is not compatible with the WCF.[192]

It appears that Gaffin's good hope that debate on this topic between the two seminaries might subside—a hope expressed more than a decade ago—did not pan out in reality.[193] But healthy theological debate on important topics serves to further the whole counsel of God.

Conclusion to Part 7. This final section briefly examined the postmodern world. Comprehending that world helps the faithful Christian know how unbelievers think, and it helps enable one to critique his or her own thoughts about the nature of life and life in the church against the backdrop of Scripture. The church as church, as well as individuals within that church, can never forget that they are in a battle. This section also analyzed supposedly Christian theology that has, to a greater or lesser extent, imbibed from the poisonous cup of postmodern thinking.

188. Ibid., 711–13.
189. Ibid., 714–17.
190. Ibid., 720–21.
191. Ibid., 721.
192. Ibid., 729–31. Fesko also examined A. A. Alexander, Buchanan, Machen, and Norman Shepherd. Shepherd was wrong: "Like Piscator, Shepherd denied the imputed active obedience of Christ and claimed Calvin and Ursinus as patriarchs of his view" (ibid., 735–36).
193. With Fesko's move to Reformed Theological Seminary in Jackson, Mississippi, yet another seminary is involved.

Methodologically consonant with the first two volumes of *The Whole Counsel of God*, we also briefly examined apologetic implications of living in a postmodern world. That chapter focused on addressing questions that unbelievers have about the nature of reality and using those questions to defend the faith.

The section ended by exploring contemporary theological debates on the doctrine of God and soteriology. Debates can be very heated at times, but as long as we observe the ninth commandment and protect and preserve our neighbor's good name, those debates can be helpful and advance theological discussion.

Conclusion to Volume 3. *The Whole Counsel of God* is founded on the pearl of great price, God's Holy Word. Volume 1 presented a biblical-theological analysis of the OT, and volume 2 followed the same method with the NT. This third volume has presented a glimpse of the life of the church as she developed and handled that pearl over the centuries. The goal of this volume was to present both historical and theological development couched within the church's cultural context. It is my hope that by first understanding God's Word, then analyzing how theologians developed that teaching, current students can take this rich heritage and apply it to their own cultural and historical contexts, while always being ready to give an account of the hope that is within them.

KEY TERMS

theistic mutualists
philosophical abstraction

STUDY QUESTIONS

1. Since comprehending the Trinity is impossible, should the church simply give up trying to do so?
2. Justification is by faith alone. Does faith play a role in our continuing sanctification?
3. Is it important to know the relationship between justification, sanctification, and union with Christ?

Resources for Further Study

Vern S. Poythress has recently produced a number of volumes related to the doctrine of God. They include the first three titles listed below.

Poythress, Vern S. *Theophany: A Biblical Theology of God's Appearing*. Wheaton, IL: Crossway, 2018.

———. *Knowing and the Trinity: How Perspectives in Human Knowledge Imitate the Trinity*. Phillipsburg, NJ: P&R Publishing, 2018.

———. *The Mystery of the Trinity: A Trinitarian Approach to the Attributes of God*. Phillipsburg, NJ: P&R Publishing, 2020.

Letham, Robert. *The Holy Trinity: In Scripture, History, Theology, and Worship*. Rev. and exp. ed. Phillipsburg, NJ: P&R Publishing, 2019.

Glossary

adoptionism (3). The notion that Jesus of Nazareth was not eternally the Son of God but at some point in time was adopted into that position by God the Father.

Alexandrian exegesis (3). An exegetical method that uses allegory and is associated with the city of Alexandria and the theologians Clement and Origen.

amillennialism (22). One of three eschatological views that holds that the millennium began with Christ's resurrection and will last longer than one thousand years. See *premillennialism.*

analytic judgment (19). A judgment is a knowledge claim. In an analytic judgment, the predicate is logically necessarily present in the subject. The simplest analytic judgments are definitions. See *synthetic judgment.*

antinomianism (17). The general teaching that because Christ has fulfilled the whole of God's law for the believer, the believer has no obligation to follow God's law in his or her Christian walk.

Antiochene Christology (7). Embraced by theologians who want to press a distinction between Christ's human and divine natures.

Antiochene exegesis (3). A grammatical-historical method of exegesis associated with the Cappadocian fathers.

apologists (2) Early Christian theologians who defended Christianity during the time of persecution.

Apostles' Creed (4). A grandchild of what is called the Old Roman Creed. Its Latin source was produced in A.D. 404.

apostolic fathers (2). The earliest Christian writers after the time of the New Testament.

a posteriori **argument** (10). An argument that is based on human experience and proceeds from particular instances to a general principle based on observation.

a priori **argument** (10). An argument that is prior to human experience or without appealing to experience.

Arius's theology (4). Asserts that God's unity prohibits any distinctions within the divine nature; that there can be no divine contact with the world, so the transcendent God is ultimately unknowable; that God's being is hidden to all, including even the Son; and that the Son is a creation.

Arminianism (17). Named after the seventeenth-century Dutch theologian Jacob Arminius and holding that there is no unconditional election; rather, people are free to choose or reject Christ.

atomists (1). Pre-Socratic thinkers who expanded beyond those who held to one fundamental element of the universe. They thought the universe consists of countless numbers of atoms that are indivisible and are constantly moving yet are not the cause of motion.

Auburn Affirmation (21). A 1924 document signed by Presbyterian ministers who said that there are alternative interpretations to the five fundamentals. See *fundamentalism*.

Augsburg Confession (12). The defining Lutheran statement of faith originally written in 1530 and containing twenty-eight articles.

beatific vision (10). A supposed vision of God given by grace in which the intellect can understand God's essence by God's uniting himself to it. Proponents argue that a beatific vision is the most perfect way to understand God.

beginning principle (1). The philosophical principle that was to provide an explanation of the efficient cause of all things and from which principle the notion of *time* could begin. It was to help determine what is fundamental to reality.

Benedictine rules (6). Rules for how monks should live in the monastery established by Benedict of Nursa. He established twelve monasteries, and his guidelines spread through many of the early church and medieval monasteries.

brute fact (22). Van Til's notion that there are no facts that are not in a relationship to other facts that contribute to the meaning of that fact. There are no bare facts that stand alone.

Cappadocian fathers (4). Greek-speaking fourth-century fathers named Basil of Caesarea, Gregory of Nyssa, and Gregory of Nazianzus.

Chalcedonian Creed (7). A counsel and creed from Chalcedon in A.D. 451 that proclaimed that Christ is truly God and truly man.

circumincession (5). The internal unity of the three persons of the godhead.

communism (21). An approach to solve the problem of poverty by abolishing private ownership. Communists think there should be public ownership of capital.

concupiscence (5). An inordinate power of sensuous desire.

Constantinopolitan Creed (4). A counsel and creed from Constantinople in A.D. 381 that was a truly universal creed, affirmed in the West and East from A.D. 451 onward. It states that in the incarnation, there was no conversion of God into man. On the other hand, there was no conversion of man into God.

consubstantiation (15). Luther's view of the Lord's Supper: Christ is physically in, with, and around the bread and wine.

Council of Trent (12). A council called by the Roman Catholic Church to counteract Protestant theology. The council determined that the Protestant definition of justification was anathema.

creation theories (23). Rejecting the traditional six-day creation, some have proposed a gap theory, which argues for vast geological ages before Genesis 1:3; or the day-age theory, interpreting the days of Genesis as geological ages; or the framework hypothesis, which argues that the week of creation is an artistic arrangement not to be understood literally.

Crusades (8). Medieval armed conflicts with the general purpose of regaining from Islamic possession what Christians sometimes call *the Holy Land*.

dialectical method (20). Hegel's notion that truth is always developing from thesis to antithesis and synthesis.

deism (16). The belief that there are common religious notions imprinted on humans by God independently of the Bible. Those common notions are the foundation for all true religion. Deists reject certain fundamental biblical notions because they seem unreasonable.

documentary hypothesis (23). The false idea that there were at least four different authors of the Pentateuch instead of Moses.

Donation of Constantine (8). A forged document giving power to the pope over the other bishops and temporal rule over Italy and the Western provinces supposedly granted by the Emperor Constantine.

Donatists (5). Schismatics who taught that the clergy must be perfect to have an effective ministry. See *Novatianists*.

embodied subjectivity (24). Ricœur's notion that Descartes had it backwards—a person does not know of his existence by solitary thinking but by being in relationship.

empiricism (16). A way of viewing the world that sees the foundation for knowing as being in sensory experience: what you can see is what you know. Knowledge is gained by means of empirical inquiry.

1073

Enlightenment (16). A movement in which religious and church life began to become less important to people. It offered a new world and life view—a transformed worldview that included the embracing of science combined with a concomitant rejection of religion.

episcopacy (14). The notion that some ordained offices are ontologically higher than others, specifically that the offices of bishop and archbishop are higher than that of local pastor or priest.

epistemology (26). The study of how we know.

eternal generation (5). The Son's relationship to the Father. The relationship does not imply subordination or change in God.

Eucharist (6). The most important medieval sacrament, in which the bread and wine are supposedly transformed into the body and blood of Christ. Some Protestants use the term *Eucharist* to define the Lord's Supper.

Eutyches (7). A monk who denied Christ's consubstantiability with God the Father as well as with men in an overresponse to Nestorius's error.

evidentialism (26). A method Christians use to defend the faith based on the reliability of sensory experience and the law of contradiction.

existentialism (21). A movement in which the individual feels himself in a hostile world. It is a protest against modern society.

existential interpretation (22). A term used by Bultmann and his followers to differentiate the truth of what the Bible says relative to historical facts from the meaning of those facts for the reader. For Bultmann, what is true is what it means existentially—what it means for me, which may have no relationship to what the text actually means.

feudal system (8). The medieval economic system in which very powerful nobles owned and controlled lands and most means of production. The serfs in that system had very limited rights and barely survived economically.

fideists (26). Those Christians who deny in one way or another that Christianity is capable of rational defense.

filioque (10). A Latin term meaning "and the Son" and that describes the procession of the Holy Spirit from the Father and the Son.

forerunners of the Reformation (11). A number of Germanic theologians who in some aspects wrote on themes that predate the Reformation.

form and matter (1). Aristotle's notion, against Plato's two worlds, that all substances in the universe have within them two separate qualities, *form* and *matter*.

fundamentalism (21). Summarized around five articles of the faith: the Bible's inspiration, Christ's virgin birth, Christ's substitutionary atonement, Christ's bodily resurrection, and the reality of miracles, including Christ's second advent.

Gnosticism (1). A movement that claimed to mediate a *gnosis* or "knowledge" that would bring salvation. It affirmed an antithesis of spirit and matter.

Heidelberg Catechism (15). The 1563 catechism written by German Reformed theologians to instruct in the faith and request that their views be tolerated in Germany.

Heilsgeschichte (22). A German word that means "salvation history."

Holy Roman Empire (8). After the destruction of the Roman Empire, Charlemagne united the West with a new empire under this new name. It continued in various iterations for centuries.

hylozoism (1). The idea that somehow all matter is alive. The Milesians began a scientific rather than religious attitude toward nature and explained natural phenomena by avoiding supernatural causes.

hypostatic union (7). Christ's fully divine and fully human nature in one person. This teaching was hammered out in the *Chalcedonian Creed* in 451.

idealist philosophy (21). Asserts that each fact stands in relationship to other facts—otherwise a fact means nothing. Bare or singular facts are in themselves unintelligible. Thus idealism is a counter philosophy to *empiricism*.

imputation (17). Its main idea is the imputation of the guilt of Adam's sin to all human beings and the imputation of Christ's righteousness to believers.

Independents (18). A group at the Westminster Assembly who were neither Episcopalian nor *Presbyterian*. For them, the local congregation was the seat of authority in the church.

indulgence (13). The sales made by the Roman Catholic Church that were the immediate catalyst for the German Reformation.

Islam (8). The religion established by *Muhammad*. Its holy book is the Qur'an. Followers of Islam, or *Muslims*, believe in one god, called Allah, and they deny the Trinity and the deity of Christ.

jus divinum (18). A Latin term that is translated "divine law." The term was used to defend different views of church government. The argument was that *episcopacy*, or independency, or *Presbyterianism* is the form of government taught by divine law and thus the only authorized view.

kenotic Christology (23). The false teaching that the Son of God could not have maintained his full divinity in the incarnation.

law of contradiction (1). States that the same attribute cannot attach to the same thing in the same respect; put otherwise, contrary attributes cannot belong to the same subject at the same time.

line of despair (22). Schaeffer's notion that at a certain time in both Europe and America intellectual leaders doubted or outright rejected the notion that the world and its events have a true explanation.

Manichaeans (5). Followers of Mani who were dualistic, viewing the world as a massive struggle between good and evil.

mechanical theory of inspiration (10). Proposed first in the ancient church, Wycliffe taught that the prophets and authors of the Bible spoke the pure word of God with no human input.

mercenary service (13). When men sell their service as soldiers to foreign governments and institutions. Such service was important to the Swiss and a point of conflict at the time of the Reformation.

metaphysics (8). The study of that reality which lies behind the universe's natural phenomena.

Milesian thinking (1). The earliest Greek philosophers who attempted to find an underlying unity amid the great diversity of life.

monad (16). Leibniz's principle that all reality is made up of living particles that are small, indivisible, and infinite in number and can think.

Monarchianism (3). The mistaken notion that God can be only one being, with the result that the second and third persons of the Trinity are deeply subordinate. See *Sabellianism*.

monophysites (7). Theologians who after the Council of Constantinople conceded that after the incarnation Christ had a composite nature, not two distinct natures.

Muhammad (8). Founder of the Islamic religion who considered himself a prophet and composed a book called the Qur'an.

myth (22). This word has shades of meaning and nuances but is generally used by nonevangelicals to describe some aspect of biblical history.

Nestorius (7). Rejected Mary's being the mother of God and Christ's hypostatic union of the divine and human natures.

Nicene Creed (4). Theologians met in A.D. 325 at Nicaea and creedally established Christ's eternal preexistence in the godhead. The formulation excluded Arianism, and Jesus was declared to be "of one substance" with the Father.

negative theology (8). Assumes that God cannot be reached by human thinking, that he is incomprehensible, so the theologian can only say what God is not. Sometimes known as the *via negativa*.

new monarchy (11). Marks a transition from the feudal system. Lesser nobles were subjected to the sovereign, who had a permanent mercenary army, instead of relying on the nobles' own army. Royal taxation was also regularized.

New Perspective on Paul (25). A school of Pauline interpretation begun in the late 1970s that argues that previous interpretations of Paul's notion of justification, particularly the Lutheran view, are incorrect.

noumenal realm (19). Kant's world of free personality—a spiritual world that is beyond and that cannot be grasped by any of our concepts. See *phenomenal realm.*

Novatianists (3). Schismatics who taught that the church must consist of the spiritually perfect. See *Donatists.*

open theism (23). An erroneous view that posits that God has omniscience but not exhaustive foreknowledge.

Peasants' War (12). A movement in Germany during the time of the Reformation. The peasants were oppressed by the nobles and demanded further rights. Luther opposed the movement.

Pelagians (5). A heretical view of human free will which was so extreme that it denied original sin.

perichoresis (7). The mutual indwelling of the three persons of the Trinity. The three are united by their identity of essence and power.

phenomenal realm (19). Kant's description of the world in which we live. It is where we can taste and smell and the place of scientific knowledge. See *noumenal realm.*

philosophical abstraction (27). This term touches on how far and in what ways philosophical terminology can be taken into systematic theological discussion.

Pietism (17). A Protestant movement seen in the Lutheran and Reformed churches. In its best manifestation it underlines the importance of personal piety and a close relationship to Christ and his church.

postmodernism (24). Our current philosophical/historical era and a reaction against the thinking of modernism, which began in the 1960s.

post-structuralism (24). An anthropology that denies human freedom on the basis that behavior is determined by structures. Ricœur, Foucault, and Derrida opposed structuralism.

premillennialism (3). One of three eschatological views that asserts that Jesus will return to the earth before a thousand-year reign of peace. See *amillennialism.*

Presbyterianism (14). A geographically locatable meeting of elders who are both ruling and teaching. They regard the highest source of church authority as not located in the congregation or in the synod or General Assembly but in the presbytery.

presupposition (26). An assumption that a person makes based on experiences that he or she has had.

presuppositionalism (26). A method of defending the faith that is based on the truth that all humans know that God exists and that the believer should build on that truth in making a defense.

preunderstanding (25). A hermeneutical tool that recognizes that the reader of a text comes to that text with certain ideas of the nature of reality.

prevenient grace (7). A term introduced in the Pelagian debate. It is grace that prepares for justification. God first offers grace to the unregenerate, who then cooperate with it. The Council of Trent affirmed its necessity, and it was supported by Arminius and the Wesleys.

process philosophy (23). Emphasizes the significance of becoming—a process—over being or stability.

public disputation (13). A means used by the Swiss reformers to further biblical reforms in the various cities.

purgatory (10). A notion developed by Aquinas as the place for souls that needed cleansing from venial or forgivable sins—a place of temporal punishment.

Pythagoreans (1). Dualists, not monists, who were scientific but also had religious interests. The technical term *philosophy*, as a longing for wisdom, seems to have been first used by this group.

Qur'an (8). The holy book of *Islam*. Composition began at the time of *Muhammad* but was codified later. It was written in Arabic and is official only in that language.

ransom to Satan (9). A mistaken atonement theory in the ancient church that held that Christ's work of salvation was to pay a ransom for souls rightly held by Satan instead of focusing on God's righteous judgment against sin.

rationalism (16). Asserts that the mind has innate principles that help it to order the way humans know. It emphasizes not sensory experience but reason.

recapitulation Christology (3). Irenaeus's notion that Christ redeemed the whole of life, so he needed to live to be more than forty years of age.

religious feeling (20). Schleiermacher's notion that religion is a person's inborn sense of that which is true and eternal and that finds its source in something deeper than mere metaphysical philosophy and officially sanctioned theological systems.

Renaissance (11). A major movement at the end of the Middle Ages to recapture the sources of Western civilization. The Italian Renaissance was slightly different from the Germanic. The Renaissance was instrumental for beginning the Reformation.

romanticism (20). Romantic thinkers say that the point of contact with reality is not with or through the intellect but with intuition or perhaps mystical intuition. So God, or reality, is not equated with the intellect or understanding but instead with feeling.

Sabellianism (3). The erroneous teaching that the Father, Son, and Holy Spirit are three different aspects or modes of God rather than three persons. See *Monarchianism*.

sacrament (8). The medieval church determined that there were seven sacraments. For them, a sacrament was not a memorial but actually conveyed a specific spiritual benefit.

satisfaction theory of atonement (10). Anselm's notion that God is like a feudal lord who has to be paid back what has been taken. God must be satisfied, and Christ is the only one capable of paying that debt.

Schleitheim Confession (12). A 1527 confession of early Anabaptists that defined the movement under seven points of doctrine.

semi-Pelagianism (7). A view developed during the Pelagius–Augustine debate associated with the name John Cassian. It asserts that God offers grace, and the human will is good enough to cooperate with that grace.

Social Gospel (21). The notion that the gospel is embodied in a kingdom of God where people are socialized and sinful social structures are addressed.

social Trinitarianism (25). A mistaken Trinitarian view that sees God as three persons in one social community.

Solemn League and Covenant (18). An agreement in 1643 between Scotland and England whereby Scotland came to England's aid during the First English Civil War. The condition was that England would reform religion in England and Ireland and reject Roman Catholicism as well as *episcopacy*.

sophists (1). Emerged during a period of Greek thinking when philosophers were no longer solely concerned with the structure of the natural world but turned their attention to human nature and society. Sophists instructed in a *new virtue* that stressed social effectiveness and an integrated personality.

special disciplines (26). All the specialized academic subjects, from anthropology to zoology, that one can study in the world.

subordinationism (2). Christological thinking begun in the ancient church and according to which Christ is placed under the Father not only in terms of the economic Trinity but also the ontological Trinity.

synthetic judgment (19). A judgment is an assertion about a subject. A synthetic judgment is when the predicate is not found in the subject. See *analytic judgment*.

theistic mutualists (27). Dolezal's notion that some evangelical theologians see God and the creation in a mutual relationship.

thinking self (26). The critically self-conscious person doing theological and/ or philosophical reflection.

Thirty-Nine Articles (14). The foundational theological statements of the Church of England.

transubstantiation (6). That the bread and wine in the Eucharist are substantially changed into Christ's body and blood—the church's official teaching at the Fourth Lateran Council in 1215.

trichotomy (3). The mistaken notion that humanity is composed of body, soul, and spirit as three independent parts.

two horizons (25). The hermeneutical notion that includes the cultural and historical backgrounds of the ancient author as well as the backgrounds of the reader.

typology (2). Reading the OT in such a way that it becomes an immediate witness for Christian truth. It searches out types of Christ particularly.

ultimate reference (26). The most basic thoughts and beliefs that a person holds dearly.

universals (8). A method to relate intellectual concepts to each other.

unmoved mover (1). Aristotle's *pure form*. It is an impersonal pure reason or prime mover. The unmoved mover engages in eternal thoughts and is pure thought thinking only about itself.

via negativa (10). Following the negative way of describing God and rejecting all positive assertions about his being.

will to power (20). Nietzsche's notion that power is good and weakness is bad. Christianity is a bad system, and each person should be a god to himself.

world of forms (1). Also known as the *world of ideas*. It is not the sensory world but one of higher value contemplated by the mind.

Bibliography

Abelard. *Ethical Writings*. Translated by Paul Vincent Spade. Cambridge: Hackett, 1995.

á Brakel, Wilhelmus. *The Christian's Reasonable Service*. Translated by Bartel Elshout. 4 vols. Grand Rapids: Reformation Heritage Books, 1995.

Adam, Alfred. *Lehrbuch der Dogmengeschichte*. Vol. 1, *Die Zeit der alten Kirche*. Gütersloh: Mohn, 1965.

Adler, Mortimer Jerome. *The Difference of Man and the Difference It Makes*. New York: World Publishing, 1971.

Alan, E. L. *Existentialism from Within*. London: Routledge/Kegan Paul, 1953.

Allen, George Cantrell. *The Didache: Or, The Teaching of the Twelve Apostles*. London: Astolat Press, 1903.

Allen, Michael. "Divine Attributes." In *Christian Dogmatics: Reformed Theology for the Church Catholic*, edited by Michael Allen and Scott R. Swain, 57–77. Grand Rapids: Baker Academic, 2016.

———. "Knowledge of God." In *Christian Dogmatics: Reformed Theology for the Church Catholic*, edited by Michael Allen and Scott R. Swain, 7–29. Grand Rapids: Baker Academic, 2016.

Allen, P. S., H. M. Allen, and H. W. Garrod, eds. *Erasmi Epistolae*. 12 vols. Oxford: Oxford University Press, 1906–1958.

Allen, Reginald E., ed. *Greek Philosophy: Thales to Aristotle*. New York: Free Press, 1991.

Alexander, J. W. *The Life of Archibald Alexander*. New York: Scribner's Sons, 1854.

———. *Thoughts on Family Worship*. Grand Rapids: Reformation Heritage Books, 1998.

———. *Thoughts on Preaching*. Reprint, Edinburgh: Banner of Truth, 1988.

Alexander, Samuel. "Turretin." *The Biblical Repertory and Princeton Review* 20 (1848): 452–63.

Allison, Greg R. *Historical Theology: An Introduction to Christian Doctrine—A Companion to Wayne Grudem's Systematic Theology*. Grand Rapids: Zondervan, 2011.

Altaner, Berthold, and Alfred Stuiber. *Patrologie: Leben, Schriften und Lehre der Kirchenväter*. Freiburg: Herder, 1978.

Ames, William. *The Marrow of Theology*. Translated by John Dykstra Eusden. Durham, NC: Labyrinth, 1983.

Anderson, John M. Introduction to *Discourse on Thinking*, by Martin Heidegger, 11–40. New York: Harper & Row, 1966.

Anderson, Marvin. *Peter Martyr: A Reformer in Exile (1542–1562)*. Leiden: Brill, 1975.

Anderson, Walter Truett. *Reality Isn't What It Used to Be: Theatrical Politics, Ready-to-Wear Religion, Global Myths, Primitive Chic, and Other Wonders of the Postmodern World*. San Francisco: Harper & Row, 1990.

Anonymous. *Lives of Alexander Henderson and James Guthrie: With Specimens of Their Writings*. Edinburgh: John Greig, 1846.

Anselm. *Proslogion*. In *Christian Apologetics Past and Present: A Primary Source Reader*, by William Edgar and K. Scott Oliphint, 365–83. Wheaton, IL: Crossway, 2009.

———. *Why God Became Man*. Library of Christian Classics 10. Edited and translated by Eugene R. Fairweather. London, SCM Press: 1956.

Aquinas, Thomas. *Summa Theologiae: A Concise Translation*. Edited by Timothy McDermott. Notre Dame: Christian Classics, 1989.

Arminius, James. *The Writings of James Arminius*. Translated by James Nichols. Grand Rapids: Baker, 1956.

Armstrong, A. H., ed. *The Cambridge History of Later Greek and Early Medieval Philosophy*. Cambridge: Cambridge University Press, 1970.

Armstrong, Brian. *Calvin and the Amyraut Heresy: Protestant Scholasticism and Humanism in France*. Madison: University of Wisconsin Press, 1969.

Arnold, Mathieu. *Oscar Cullmann: Un docteur de l'Eglise*. Lyon: Olivétan éditiones, 2019.

Augustine. *Confessions*. Rev. ed. Oxford: Oxford University Press, 2009.

———. *De trinitate*. 4th ed. Hyde Park, NY: New City Press, 2002.

Austin, J. L. *Philosophical Papers*. Oxford: Oxford University Press, 1961.

Bahnsen, Greg L. *Always Ready: Directions for Defending the Faith*. Nacogdoches, TX: Covenant Media Press, 2004.

———. "The Crucial Concept of Self-Deception in Presuppositional Apologetics." *Westminster Theological Journal* 57, no. 1 (Spring 1995): 1–31.

———. "Socrates or Christ: The Reformation of Christian Apologetics." In *Foundations of Christian Scholarship*, edited by Gary North, 191–239. Vallecito, CA: Ross House, 1979.

———. *Van Til's Apologetic: Readings & Analysis*. Phillipsburg, NJ: P&R Publishing, 1998.

Bainton, Roland. *Erasmus of Christendom*. Peabody, MA: Hendrickson Publishers, 2016.

———. *Women in the Reformation*. Minneapolis: Fortress, 1971.

Baker, J. Wayne. *Heinrich Bullinger and the Covenant: The Reformed Tradition*. Athens, OH: Ohio University Press, 1980.

Baker, J. Wayne, and Ernst Koch. *Die Theologie der Confessio Helvetica Posterior*. Beiträge zur Geschichte und Lehre der Reformierten Kirche. Neukirchen-Vluyn: Neukirchener Verlag, 1968.

Balke, Willem. *Calvin and the Anabaptist Radicals*. Grand Rapids: Eerdmans, 1981.

Bangs, Carl. *Arminius: A Study in the Dutch Reformation*. Nashville: Abingdon Press, 1971.

Bannerman, John. *The Church of Christ*. 2 vols. Carlisle, PA: Banner of Truth, 2015.

Barker, William S. "The Historical Context of the *Institutes* as a Work in Theology." In *A Theological Guide to Calvin's Institutes*, edited by David W. Hall and Peter A. Lillback, 1–15. Phillipsburg, NJ: P&R Publishing, 2008.

Barrett, Matthew, ed. *The Doctrine on Which the Church Stands or Falls*. Wheaton, IL: Crossway, 2019.

Barth, Karl. *Die Christliche Dogmatik im Entwurf*. Munich: Kaiser, 1927.

———. *Church Dogmatics*. Vol. 1, *The Doctrine of the Word of God*. New York, Scribner's Sons, 1956.

———. *Church Dogmatics*. Vol. 2, *The Doctrine of God*. New York, Scribner's Sons, 1956.

———. *Church Dogmatics*. Vol. 4, *The Doctrine of Reconciliation*. New York: Scribner's Sons, 1956.

———. *Evangelical Theology: An Introduction*. New York: Holt, Rinehart & Winston, 1963.

———. *The Humanity of God.* Translated by John N. Thomas and Thomas Wieser. Atlanta: John Knox Press, 1960.

———. *Protestant Theology in the 19th Century.* London: SCM Press, 1972.

———. *Protestant Thought.* New York: Harper, 1959.

———. *Die Theologie und die Kirche.* Munich: Kaiser, 1928.

———. *The Theology of Schleiermacher.* Grand Rapids: Eerdmans, 1982.

Battenhouse, Roy W. *A Companion to the Study of St. Augustine.* New York: Oxford University Press, 1955.

Battles, Ford Lewis. *Boethius.* Pittsburgh: Pittsburgh Theological Seminary, 1968.

———. "Introduction to *Confession of Faith of 1538*." N.p, 1972.

———. Introduction to *Institutes of the Christian Religion, 1536 Edition.* Translated and annotated by Ford Lewis Battles. Grand Rapids: Meeter Center/Eerdmans, 1986.

———. *The Piety of Calvin.* Phillipsburg, NJ: P&R Publishing, 2018.

———. Preface to *Calvin's Catechism (1538)*, i–xii. Pittsburgh: Pittsburgh Theological Seminary, 1974.

———. "The Sources." In *Interpreting John Calvin*, edited by Robert Benedetto, 86–88. Grand Rapids: Baker, 1996.

Baudrillard, Jean. "The Map Precedes the Territory." In *The Truth about the Truth: De-confusing and Re-constructing the Postmodern World*, edited by Walter Truett Anderson, 79–85. New York: Putnam, 1995.

———. *The Perfect Crime.* New York: Verso, 1996.

Baur, Chrysostomus. *John Chrysostom and His Time.* Translated by M. Gonzaga. Westminster, MD: Newman Press, 1959.

Baur, Ferdinand Christian. *Lehrbuch der christlichen Dogmengeschichte.* Tübingen: Verlag und Druck von L. Fr. Fues, 1858.

Bavinck, Herman. *The Doctrine of God.* Carlisle, PA: Banner of Truth, 1977.

———. *Gereformeerde Dogmatiek.* Kampen: Kok, 1911.

———. *The Last Things: Hope for This World and the Next.* Grand Rapids: Baker, 1996.

———. *The Philosophy of Revelation.* Grand Rapids: Eerdmans, 1953.

———. *Reformed Dogmatics.* Edited by John Bolt. Grand Rapids: Baker Academic, 2003.

Beardslee, John W. "Theological Development at Geneva under Francis and Jean-Alphonse Turretin (1648–1737)." PhD diss., Yale University, 1956.

———, trans. Reformed Dogmatics: J. Wollebius, G. Voetius, and F. Turretin. New York: Oxford University Press, 1965.

Beeke, Joel R. *Debated Issues in Sovereign Predestination: Early Lutheran Predestination, Calvinian Reprobation and Variations in Geneva Lapsarianism.* Göttingen: Vandenhoeck & Ruprecht, 2017.

———. "Toward a Reformed Marriage of Knowledge and Piety: The Contribution of Gisbertus Voetius." *Reformation and Revival* 10, no. 1 (Winter 2001): 125–42.

Beeke, Joel R., and Randall J. Pederson. *Meet the Puritans.* Grand Rapids: Reformation Heritage Books, 2006.

Beeke, J. R., and Paul Smalley. *Reformed Systematic Theology.* Vol. 1, *Revelation and God.* Wheaton, IL: Crossway, 2019.

Beilby, James K., and Paul R. Eddy, eds. *Justification: Five Views.* Spectrum Multiview Books. Downers Grove, IL: IVP Academic, 2011.

Bene, Charles. *Erasme et Saint Augustin.* Geneva: Droz, 1969.

Benedict. *The Rule of Saint Benedict.* Edited and translated by Bruce L. Venarde. Dumbarton Oaks Medieval Library 6. Cambridge: Harvard University Press, 2011.

Benko, Stephen. *Pagan Rome and the Early Christians.* Bloomington, IN: Indiana University Press, 1984.

Bennett, John C. "A Non-Barthian's Gratitude to Karl Barth." *Union Seminary Quarterly Review* 28, no. 1 (Fall 1972): 99–108.

Berkhof, Louis. *The History of Christian Doctrines.* Carlisle, PA: Banner of Truth, 1969.

———. *Systematic Theology.* Grand Rapids: Eerdmans, 1972.

Berkouwer, G. C. *Holy Scripture.* Edited and translated by Jack B. Rogers. Grand Rapids: Eerdmans, 1975.

———. *Man: The Image of God.* Grand Rapids: Eerdmans, 1962.

Bernard of Clairvaux. "On the Love of God." In *Late Medieval Mysticism,* edited by Ray C. Petry. London: SCM Press, 1957.

———. "Of the Three Ways in Which We Love God." In *Late Medieval Mysticism,* edited by Ray C. Petry. London: SCM Press, 1957.

Bernstein, Richard J., ed. *Habermas and Modernity.* Cambridge: Polity Press, 1985.

Bigg, Charles. *The Christian Platonists of Alexandria: Eight Lectures Preached before the University of Oxford in the Year 1886.* Oxford: Clarendon, 1913.

Blomberg, Craig. *Jesus and the Gospels*. Nashville: B&H, 2009.

Boice, James Montgomery. *Mind Renewal in a Mindless Age: Preparing to Think and Act Biblically*. Grand Rapids: Baker, 1993.

———. *Whatever Happened to the Gospel of Grace?* Wheaton, IL: Crossway, 2001.

Bolt, John. *Bavinck on the Christian Life*. Wheaton, IL: Crossway, 2015.

Boethius. "A Treatise against Eutyches and Nestorius." In *The Theological Tractates*, edited by G. P. Goold and translated by H. F. Stewart, E. K. Rand, and S. J. Tester, 72–129. Cambridge: Harvard University Press, 1973.

Bonhoeffer, Dietrich. *Christ the Center*. San Francisco: Harper & Row, 1978.

———. *Ethics*. London: SCM Press, 1955.

Bonino, José Miguez. *Doing Theology in a Revolutionary Situation*. Minneapolis: Fortress, 2009.

Borchardt, C. F. A. *Hilary of Poitiers' Role in the Arian Struggle*. The Hague: Nijhoff, 1966.

Bornkamm, Heinrich. *Luther und das Alte Testament*. Tübingen: Mohr Siebeck, 1948.

Boston, Thomas. *Human Nature in Its Fourfold State: of Primitive Integrity, Entire Depravation, Begun Recovery, and Consummate Happiness or Misery*. 1720; repr., London: Banner of Truth Trust 1964.

Bougerol, Jacques-Guy. "The Church Fathers and *Auctoritates* in Scholastic Theology to Bonaventure." In *The Reception of the Church Fathers in the West: From the Carolingians to the Maurists*, edited by Irena Dorota Backus, 289–336. Leiden: Brill, 1997.

Bower, John R. *The Confession of Faith: A Critical Text and Introduction*. Grand Rapids: Reformation Heritage Books, 2020.

Brändle, Rudolf. *John Chrysostom: Bishop, Reformer, Martyr*. Translated by John Cawte and Silke Trzcionka. Strathfield, Australia: St Pauls Publications, 2004.

Bratt, James, ed. *Abraham Kuyper*. Grand Rapids: Eerdmans, 1998.

Brauer, Siegfried, and Manfred Kobuch, eds. *Thomas Müntzer Briefwechsel*. Leipzig: Evangelischen Verlagsanstalt, 2010.

Bray, Gerald. *Biblical Interpretation: Past and Present*. Downers Grove, IL: InterVarsity Press, 1996.

Bremmer, R. H. *Herman Bavinck als Dogmaticus*. Kampen: Kok, 1961.

Bretall, Robert, ed. *A Kierkegaard Anthology*. New York: Random House, 1946.

Bromiley, Geoffrey W. *Historical Theology: An Introduction*. Grand Rapids: Eerdmans, 1978.

Brown, Colin. *Philosophy & the Christian Faith: A Historical Sketch from the Middle Ages to the Present Day*. Downers Grove, IL: InterVarsity Press, 1968.

Brown, Peter. *Augustine of Hippo: A Biography*. Rev. ed. Berkeley/Los Angeles: University of California Press, 2000.

Bruce, F. F. *The Growing Day: The Progress of Christianity from the Fall of Jerusalem to the Accession of Constantine*. Grand Rapids: Eerdmans, 1953.

Brunner, Emil. *The Christian Doctrine of Creation and Redemption*. Translated by Olive Wyon. Philadelphia: Westminster Press, 1953.

———. *The Christian Doctrine of God*. Vol. 1, *Dogmatics*. London: Lutterworth, 1955.

———. *Man in Revolt: A Christian Anthropology*. Philadelphia: Westminster Press, 1947.

Bucer, Martin. *De regno Christi*. In *Melanchton and Bucer*, edited by Wilhelm Pauck, 174–394. Philadelphia: Westminster John Knox Press, 1969.

Buchanan, James. *The Doctrine of Justification: An Outline of Its History in the Church and of Its Exposition from Scripture*. 1984. Reprint, Edinburgh: Banner of Truth, 1991.

Bultmann, Rudolf. *Commentary on John*. Philadelphia: Westminster John Knox Press, 1971.

———. *Essays: Philosophical and Theological*. New York/London: Macmillan/SCM Press, 1955.

———. *Existence and Faith*. London: Fontana, 1964.

———. *Faith and Understanding: Collected Essays*. Translated by L. P. Smith. Library of Philosophy and Theology. New York/London: Harper & Row/SCM Press, 1969.

———. "Heilsgeschichte und Geschichte. Über O. Cullmanns *Christus und die Zeit*." *Theologische Literaturzeitung* 73(1948): 659–66.

———. *History and Eschatology: The Presence of Eternity*. New York: Harper & Row, 1957.

———. *The History of the Synoptic Tradition*. Translated by John Marsh. New York: Harper & Row, 1963.

———. *Jesus Christ and Mythology*. New York: Scribner's Sons, 1958.

———. *Jesus and the Word*. New York: Scribner's Sons, 1934.

———. *The Johannine Epistles: A Commentary*. Minneapolis: Augsburg Fortress, 1973.

———. *Kerygma and Myth*. New York: Harper, 1961.

———. *New Testament and Mythology and Other Basic Writings*. Edited by Schubert M. Ogden. Minneapolis: Augsburg Fortress, 1984.

———. *Primitive Christology in Its Contemporary Setting*. Minneapolis: Augsburg Fortress, 1975.

———. *Second Letter to the Corinthians*. Minneapolis: Augsburg Fortress, 1985.

———. *Theologie des Neuen Testaments*. 5 Aufl. Tübingen: Mohr Siebeck, 1965.

———. *The Theology of the New Testament*. Translated by K. Grobel. 2 vols. New York: Scribner's Sons, 1951, 1955.

———. *What Is Theology?* Fortress Texts in Modern Theology. Minneapolis: Augsburg Fortress, 1997.

Bultmann, Rudolf, and Karl Kundsin. *Form Criticism: Two Essays on New Testament Research*. Translated by Frederick C. Grant. New York: Harper & Row, 1962.

Burleigh, J. H. S. *A Church History of Scotland*. Edinburgh: Hope Trust, 1988.

Butler, Judith. Introduction to *Of Grammatology*, by Jacques Derrida, xlii–lxxiv. Baltimore: Johns Hopkins University Press, 1974.

Butterfield, Rosaria. *The Gospel Comes with a Housekey*. Wheaton, IL: Crossway, 2018.

Cadiou, René. *Origen: His Life at Alexandria*. Translated by J. A. Southwell. London: Herder, 1944.

Cahoone, Lawrence E., ed. *From Modernism to Postmodernism: An Anthology*. Oxford: Blackwell, 1996.

Calhoun, David B. *Princeton Seminary*. Edinburgh: Banner of Truth, 1994.

Calvin, John. *Commentary on the Epistles of Paul the Apostle to the Philippians, Colossians and Thessalonians*. Edited and Translated by John Pringle. Edinburgh: Calvin Translation Society, 1849. Reprinted in *Calvin's Commentaries* vol. 21. Grand Rapids: Baker Book House, 2003.

———. *Commentary on Seneca's De Clementia*. Translated and edited by Ford Lewis Battles and André Hugo. Leiden: Brill, 1969.

———. *Institutes of the Christian Religion*. Edited by John T. McNeill. Translated by Ford Lewis Battles. Philadelphia: Westminster Press, 1960.

———. *Institutes of the Christian Religion, 1536 Edition*. Translated and annotated by Ford Lewis Battles. Grand Rapids: Meeter Center/Eerdmans, 1986.

———. *Necessity of Reform*. In *Selected Works of John Calvin: Tracts and Letters*. Vol. 1, *Tracts*. Edited and translated by Henry Beveridge. Grand Rapids: Baker, 1983.

———. *Treatises against the Anabaptists and Against the Libertines*. Edited and translated by Benjamin Wirt Farley. Grand Rapids: Baker, 1982.

Cam, Helen. *England before Elizabeth*. New York: Harper & Row, 1960.

Cameron, J. K., ed. *Letters of John Johnston and Robert Howie*. Edinburgh: Oliver & Boyd, 1963.

Campbell, Marion. *Alexander III: King of Scots*. Argyll, Scotland: House of Lochar, 1999.

Capps, Donald. *Pastoral Care and Hermeneutics*. Philadelphia: Fortress, 1984.

Carnell, Edward J. *An Introduction to Christian Apologetics*. Grand Rapids: Eerdmans, 1948.

———. *A Philosophy of the Christian Religion*. Grand Rapids: Eerdmans, 1954.

Carrington, Philip. *The Early Christian Church*. Vol. 2, *The Second Christian Century*. Cambridge: Cambridge University Press, 1957.

Carson, D. A., Peter T. O'Brien, and Mark Seifrid, eds. *Justification and Variegated Nomism*. Vol. 1, *The Complexities of Second Temple Judaism*. Grand Rapids: Baker, 2001.

Casalis, Georges. *Portrait of Karl Barth*. New York: Doubleday, 1963.

Chadwick, Henry. *The Early Church*. Grand Rapids: Eerdmans, 1967.

———. "Philo and the Beginnings of Christian Thought." In *The Cambridge History of Later Greek and Early Medieval Philosophy*, edited by A. H. Armstrong, 137–94. Cambridge: Cambridge University Press, 1970.

Chadwick, Owen. *The Reformation*. New York: Penguin Books, 1990.

Changeux, Jean-Pierre, and Paul Ricœur. *What Makes Us Think? A Neuroscientist and a Philosopher Argue about Ethics, Human Nature, and the Brain*. Translated by M. B. DeBevoise. Princeton: Princeton University Press, 2000.

Chaucer, Geoffrey. *The Canterbury Tales*. Rev. ed. New York: Penguin Classics, 2003.

Childs, Brevard S. *Introduction to the Old Testament as Scripture*. Philadelphia: Fortress, 1979.

———. *The New Testament as Canon: An Introduction* (Valley Forge, PA: Trinity Press International, 1994

Christ, Felix, ed. *Oikonimia: Heilsgeschichte als Thema der Theologie*. Hamburg: Reich, 1967.

Clark, Gordon H. "The Bible as Truth." *Bibliotheca Sacra* 114, no. 454 (April 1957): 157–70.

———. *Religion, Reason and Revelation*. Jefferson, MD: Trinity Foundation, 1986.

———. *Thales to Dewey: A History of Philosophy*. Boston: Houghton Mifflin, 1957.

———. *The Trinity*. Jefferson, MD: Trinity Foundation, 2010.

Clark, Malcolm. *Logic and System: A Study of the Transition from Vorstellung to Thought in the Philosophy of Hegel*. The Hague: Nijhoff, 1971.

Clark, R. Scott. Heidelblog, March 6, 2013. https://heidelblog.net/2013/03/van-til-yet-this-is-not-the-whole-truth/. Accessed January 13, 2019.

———. "Janus, the Well-Meant Offer of the Gospel, and Westminster Theology." In *The Pattern of Sound Doctrine: Systematic Theology at the Westminster Seminaries*, edited by David VanDrunen, 149–79. Phillipsburg, NJ: P&R Publishing, 2004.

———, ed. *Covenant, Justification, and Pastoral Ministry*. Phillipsburg, NJ: P&R Publishing, 2007.

Clement of Rome. *The First Epistle of Clement to the Corinthians*. Aeterna Press, 2016.

Cloud, Henry, and John Townsend. *How People Grow*. Grand Rapids: Zondervan, 2001.

Clouser, Roy A. *The Myth of Religious Neutrality*. Notre Dame: University of Notre Dame Press, 1991.

Clowney, Edmund P. *The Church*. Leicester: InterVarsity Press, 1995.

———. "The Biblical Doctrine of Justification by Faith." In *Right with God: Justification in the Bible and the World*, edited by D. A. Carson, 17–50. Grand Rapids: Baker, 1992.

Cobb, John B., Jr., and David Ray Griffin. *Process Theology: An Introductory Exposition*. Philadelphia: Westminster Press, 1976.

Cochrane, Arthur C. *Reformed Confessions of the 16th Century*. Philadelphia: Westminster Press, 1966.

Coffey, John. *Politics, Religion and the British Revolutions: The Mind of Samuel Rutherford*. Cambridge: Cambridge University Press, 1997.

Colish, Marcia L. *Studies in Scholasticism*. Aldershot, England: Ashgate, 2006.

Cone, James H. *A Black Theology of Liberation*. Maryknoll, NY: Orbis, 1970.

Conn, Harvie M., ed. *Inerrancy and Hermeneutic: A Tradition, a Challenge, a Debate*. Grand Rapids: Baker, 1988.

————. "Theologies of Liberation: An Overview." In *Tensions in Contemporary Theology*, edited by Stanley N. Gundry and Alan F. Johnson, 327–94. Grand Rapids: Baker, 1976.

————. "Theologies of Liberation: Toward a Common View." In *Tensions in Contemporary Theology*, edited by Stanley N. Gundry and Alan F. Johnson, 395–436. Grand Rapids: Baker, 1976.

Copenhaver, Brian P., Calvin G. Normore, and Terence Parsons. *Peter of Spain: Summaries of Logic: Text, Translation, and Introduction*. New York: Oxford University Press, 2014.

Copleston, Frederick C. *Contemporary Philosophy: Studies of Logical Positivism and Existentialism*. London: Burns & Oates, 1963.

————. *Friedrich Nietzsche: Philosopher of Culture*. London: Search Press, 1975.

————. *A History of Philosophy*, vol. 1, *Medieval Philosophy*. Garden City, NY: Image Books, 1952.

Cottret, Bernard. *Calvin: A Biography*. Grand Rapids: Eerdmans, 2000.

Cowan, Steven B. Introduction to *Five Views on Apologetics*, edited by Steven B. Cowan, 7–20. Grand Rapids: Zondervan, 2000.

Coxe, A. Cleveland, ed. *The Ante-Nicene Fathers*. Vol. 1, *The Apostolic Fathers, Justin Martyr, Irenaeus*. Grand Rapids: Eerdmans, 1988.

————. *The Ante-Nicene Fathers*. Vol. 2, *Fathers of the Second Century: Hermas, Tatian, Athenagoras, Theophilus, and Clement of Alexandria*. Grand Rapids: Eerdmans, 1988.

————. *The Ante-Nicene Fathers*. Vol. 3, *Latin Christianity: Its Founder, Tertullian I. Apologetic; II. Anti-Marcion; III. Ethical*. Grand Rapids: Eerdmans, 1988.

————. *The Ante-Nicene Fathers*. Vol. 6, *Gregory Thaumaturgus, Dionysius the Great, Julius Africanus, Anatolius and Minor Writers, Methodius, Arnobius*. Grand Rapids: Eerdmans, 1988.

————. *The Ante-Nicene Fathers*. Vol. 10, *The Writings of the Fathers down to A.D. 325*. Grand Rapids: Eerdmans, 1988.

Craig, William Lane. "Timelessness and Omnitemporality." In *God and Time: Four Views*, edited by Gregory E. Ganssel, 129–60. Downers Grove, IL: IVP Academic, 2001.

1091

Crisp, Oliver D. *Deviant Calvinism: Broadening Reformed Theology.* Minneapolis: Fortress, 2014.

Crisp, Oliver D., and Fred Sanders, eds. *The Task of Dogmatics: Explorations in Theological Method.* Grand Rapids: Zondervan, 2017.

Cullmann, Oscar. *Baptism in the New Testament.* Studies in Biblical Theology 1. Naperville, IL: Allenson, 1950.

———. *Christus und die Zeit.* Zurich: Evangelischer Verlag, 1945.

———. *Christ and Time.* Translated by Floyd Filson. Philadelphia: Westminster Press, 1950.

———. *The Christology of the New Testament.* Philadelphia: Westminster Press, 1959.

———. *The Earliest Christian Confessions.* Translated by J. K. S. Reid. London: Lutterworth, 1949.

———. *Early Christian Worship.* Naperville, IL: Allenson, 1953.

———. *The Early Church.* Philadelphia: Westminster Press, 1956.

———. "Eschatologie und Mission im Neuen Testament," *Evangelisches Missionszeitung* 85 (July 1941): 98–108.

———. *Heil als Geschichte.* 2. durchgesehene Aufl.Tübingen: J. C. B. Mohr, 1967.

———. "Formation de la Tradition Evangelique." *Revue d'histoire et de Philosophie Religieuses* 5 (1925): 564–79.

———. *Immortality of the Soul or Resurrection of the Dead?* New York: Macmillan, 1958.

———. *The Johannine Circle.* Translated by John Bowden. Philadelphia: Westminster Press, 1975.

———. "The Kingship of Christ and the Church in the New Testament." In *The Early Church*, edited by A. J. B. Higgins, 105–40. London: SCM Press, 1956.

———. *Königsherrschaft Christi und Kirche im Neuen Testament.* Zollikon/Zürich: Evangelischer Verlag, 1941.

———. *Peter.* Philadelphia: Westminster Press, 1962.

———. *Les premieres confessions de foi chrétiennes.* Paris: Presses Universitaires de France, 1943.

———. *Le problème littéraire et historique du Roman pseudo-Clémentin.* Paris: Librarie Félix Alcan, 1930.

———. "Les récentes études sur la formation de la tradition évangélique." *Revue d'histoire et de philosophie Religieuse* 5 (1925): 564–79.

————. *Salvation in History*. New York: Harper & Row, 1967.

————. *The State in the New Testament*. London: SCM Press, 1957.

————. *Die Tauflehre des Neuen Testaments—Erwachsenen und Kindertaufe*. Zurich: Zwingli-Verlag, 1948.

Cunningham, Ralph. "Definitive Sanctification: A Response to John Fesko." *Evangelical Quarterly* 84, no. 3 (2012): 235–40.

Cunningham, William. *Discussions on Church Principles*. Edinburgh: T&T Clark, 1863.

————. *Historical Theology*. Vol. 1. Edinburgh: Banner of Truth, 1979.

Cushman, Robert E. *Therapeia: Plato's Conception of Philosophy*. Chapel Hill: University of North Carolina Press, 1958.

Dabney, Robert Lewis. *Discussions of Robert Lewis Dabney*. Edinburgh: Banner of Truth, 1991.

————. *Systematic Theology*. Edinburgh: Banner of Truth, 1985.

Daniélou, Jean. *Gospel Message and Hellenistic Culture*. Philadelphia: Westminster Press, 1980.

————. *A History of Early Christian Doctrine before the Council of Nicaea*. Vol. 3, *The Origins of Latin Christianity*. Philadelphia: Westminster Press, 1980.

Davies, J. G. *The Early Christian Church: A History of Its First Five Centuries*. Grand Rapids: Baker, 1980.

Davis, Kenneth R. "Erasmus as Progenitor of Anabaptist Theology and Piety." *Mennonite Quarterly* 47 (1973): 163–68.

De Greef, W. *The Writings of John Calvin*. Translated by Lyle D. Bierma. Grand Rapids: Baker, 1993.

De Jong, Peter Y. *Crisis in the Reformed Churches: Essays in Commemoration of the Synod of Dort (1618–1619)*. Grand Rapids: Reformed Fellowship, 1968.

De Labriolle, Pierre. *History and Literature of Christianity from Tertullian to Boethius*. New York: Barnes and Noble Books, 1968.

Dekker, Eef. "Duns Scotus over absolute en geordineerde macht." In *Aktueel Filosoferen*, edited by W. van Dooren and T. Hoof, 119–23. Delft, Netherlands: 1993.

Demarest, Bruce. *The Cross and Salvation*. Wheaton, IL: Crossway, 2006.

Denck, Hans. "Divine Order." In *Early Anabaptist Spirituality: Selected Writings*, edited by Daniel Liechty, 121–36. New York: Paulist Press, 1994.

Dennis, Lane T. *Letters of Francis A. Schaeffer*. Westchester, IL: Crossway, 1987.

Dennison, James T., Jr. *The Letters of Geerhardus Vos*. Phillipsburg, NJ: P&R Publishing, 2005.

Dennison, William. "Reason, History, and Revelation: Biblical Theology and the Enlightenment." *Kerux: The Journal of Northwest Theological Seminary* 18, no. 1 (May 2003): 3–25.

DeRusha, Michelle. *Katharina & Martin Luther: The Radical Marriage of a Runaway Nun and a Renegade Monk*. Grand Rapids: Baker, 2017.

Descartes, René. *Discourse on Method* and *Meditations*. Translated by Laurence J. Lafleur. Indianapolis/New York: Bobbs-Merrill, 1960.

DeWitt, J. R. *Jus Divinum: The Westminster Assembly and the Divine Right of Church Government*. Kampen: Kok, 1969.

Dinneen, Francis P. *Language in Dispute: An English Translation of Peter of Spain's Tractatus*. Amsterdam/Philadelphia: Benjamin's, 1990.

Dobson, James. *Dare to Discipline*. Carol Stream, IL: Tyndale House, 1977.

———. *Parenting Isn't for Cowards*. Carol Stream, IL: Tyndale Momentum, 2007.

———. *The Strong-Willed Child*. Carol Stream, IL: Tyndale House, 2014.

Dolezal, James. *All That Is in God*. Grand Rapids: Reformation Heritage, 2017.

Donnelly, J. P. *Calvinism and Scholasticism in Vermigli's Doctrine of Man and Grace*. Leiden: Brill, 1976.

Dooyeweerd, Herman. *A New Critique of Theoretical Thought*. Vol. 1, *The Necessary Presuppositions of Philosophy*. Translated by David Freeman and William Young. Philadelphia: Presbyterian and Reformed, 1953.

Dorman, Theodore Martin. *The Hermeneutics of Oscar Cullmann*. San Francisco: Mellen, 1991.

Dosker, H. E. B. "Herman Bavinck." *Princeton Theological Review* 20 (1922): 448–64.

Douglas, J. D. *Light in the North*. Grand Rapids: Eerdmans, 1964.

Du Bois, W. E. B. *Dark Water: Voices from within the Veil*. Mineola, NY: Dover, 1999.

Duchesne, Louis. *Early History of the Christian Church: From Its Foundation to the End of the Fifth Century*. London: Murray, 1965.

Dudden, Frederick Homes. *The Life and Times of Saint Ambrose*. Oxford: Clarendon, 1935.

Durkin, Kenneth. *Reinhold Niebuhr*. London: Chapman, 1989.

Easton, Stewart C. *The Western Heritage*. New York: Holt, Rinehart & Winston, 1961.

Ebeling, Gerhard. *Introduction to the Theological Theory of Language*. Philadelphia: Fortress, 1973.

Edgar, William. "Geerhardus Vos and Culture." In *Resurrection and Eschatology*, edited by Lane G. Tipton and Jeffrey C. Waddington, 383–95. Phillipsburg, NJ: P&R Publishing, 2008.

———. "Justification and Violence: Reflections on Atonement and Contemporary Apologetics." In *Justified in Christ: God's Plan for Us in Justification*, edited by K. Scott Oliphint, 131–52. Fearn, Scotland: Mentor, 2007.

Edgar, William, and K. Scott Oliphint. *Christian Apologetics Past and Present: A Primary Source Reader*. Wheaton, IL: Crossway, 2009.

Edwards, Charles Eugene. "Turretin's Theology." *Princeton Theological Review* 26 (1928): 142–49.

Edwards, David L., with a response from John Stott. *Evangelical Essentials: A Liberal-Evangelical Dialogue*. Downers Grove, IL: InterVarsity Press, 1989.

Edwards, Jonathan. *Freedom of the Will*. Edited by Paul Ramsey. New Haven: Yale University Press, 1957.

———. *The Works of Jonathan Edwards*. Vol. 22, *Sermons and Discourses, 1739–42*. Edited by Harry S. Stout and Nathan O. Hatch. New Haven: Yale University Press, 2003.

Edwards, Rob. "John Flavel [1627–1691] on the Priority of Union with Christ: Further Historical Perspective on the Structure of Reformed Soteriology." *Westminster Theological Journal* 74, no. 1 (Spring 2012): 33–56.

Eells, Hastings. *Martin Bucer*. New York: Russell and Russell, 1971.

Eglinton, James. *Bavinck: A Critical Biography*. Grand Rapids: Baker Academic, 2020.

Eliot, Charles W. *English Philosophers: The Harvard Classics*. New York: Collier, 1910.

Elliott, Mark W. "Spiritual Theology in Bruce, Howie, Johnston, Boyd, and Leighton." In *The History of Scottish Theology*, vol. 1, *Celtic Origins to Reformed Orthodoxy*, edited by David Fergusson and Mark W. Elliott, chapter 15. Oxford: Oxford University Press, 2019.

Elton, Geoffrey R. *Reformation Europe: 1517–1559*. New York: Harper & Row, 1963.

Erasmus. *The Adages of Erasmus*. Compiled by William Barker. Toronto: University of Toronto Press, 2001.

————. "Letter to Richard Pace (July 5, 1521)." In *Voices of the Reformation: Contemporary Accounts of Daily Life*, edited by John A. Wagner, 27–32. Santa Barbara, CA: Greenwood Press, 2015.

Erickson, Millard J. *Christian Theology*. 2nd ed. Grand Rapids: Baker, 1998.

————. *Truth or Consequences: The Promise and Perils of Postmodernism*. Downers Grove, IL: InterVarsity Press, 2001.

Eusden, John Dykstra. Foreword, preface, and introduction to *The Marrow of Theology*, by William Ames, translated by John Dykstra Eusden, vii–65. Durham, NC: Labyrinth, 1983.

Eusebius. *The History of the Church from Christ to Constantine*. Translated by G. A. Williamson. New York: Dorset, 1965.

Evans, William B. "Déjà Vu All Over Again? The Contemporary Reformed Soteriological Controversy in Historical Perspective." *Westminster Theological Journal* 72, no. 1 (Spring 2010): 135–51.

————. *Imputation and Importation: Union with Christ in American Reformed Theology*. Milton Keynes: Paternoster, 2008.

Falckenberg, Richard. *Geschichte der neueren philosophie von Nikolaus von Kues bis zur Gegenwart*. Leipzig: Veit, 1927.

Faludy, George. *Erasmus of Rotterdam*. New York: Stein and Day, 1970.

Farrar, Frederic W. *History of Interpretation*. Grand Rapids: Baker, 1961.

Fast, Heinhold. *Heinrich Bullinger und die Täufer: Ein Beitrag zur Historiographie und Theologie im 16. Jahrhundert*. Weierhof: Mennonitischer Geschichtsverein, 1959.

Faulenbach, Heiner. *Weg und Ziel der Erkenntnis Christi: Eine Untersuchung zur Theologie des Johannes Coccejus*. Beiträge zur Geschichte und Lehre der reformierten Kirche 26. Neukirchen-Vluyn: Neukirchener Verlag, 1973.

Feinberg, John S. *No One Like Him: The Doctrine of God*. Wheaton, IL: Crossway, 2001.

Ferguson, Robert. *The Vikings: A History*. New York: Viking Penguin, 2009.

Ferguson, Sinclair B. Introduction to *Justified in Christ: God's Plan for Us in Justification*, edited by K. Scott Oliphint, vii–xxiv. Fearn, Scotland: Mentor, 2007.

————. *John Owen on the Christian Life*. Edinburgh: Banner of Truth, 1987.

————. *The Whole Christ: Legalism, Antinomianism, and Gospel Assurance— Why the Marrow Controversy Still Matters*. Wheaton, IL: Crossway, 2016.

Fesko, John V. "The Ground of Religion: Justification according to the Reformed Tradition." In *The Doctrine on which the Church Stands or*

Falls: Justification in Biblical, Theological, Historical, and Pastoral Perspective, edited by Matthew Barrett, 701–39. Wheaton, IL: Crossway, 2019.

———. *Justification: Understanding the Classic Reformed Doctrine.* Phillipsburg, NJ: P&R Publishing, 2008

———. "William Perkins on Union with Christ and Justification." *Mid America Journal of Theology* 21 (2010): 21–34.

Finlayson, Sandy. "Machen and Scholarship." In *Christianity and Liberalism*, by J. Gresham Machen, 221–24. Legacy ed. Philadelphia: Westminster Seminary Press, 2019.

Finney, Charles G. *Finney's Systematic Theology: New Expanded Edition.* Edited by Dennis Carroll, Bill Nicely, and L. G. Parkhurst Jr. Minneapolis: Bethany, 1994.

Fletcher, Richard. *The Cross and the Crescent: Christianity and Islam from Muhammad to the Reformation.* New York: Penguin Books, 2003.

Foster, A. Durwood. "Albrecht Ritschl." In *A Handbook of Christian Theologians*, edited by Martin E. Marty and Dean G. Peerman, 55–68. Nashville: Abingdon Press, 1985.

Foucault, Michel. *Adventures of the Dialectic.* Translated by Joseph Bien. Evanston, IL: Northwestern University Press, 1973.

———. *The Essential Writings of Merleau-Ponty.* Edited by Alden L. Fisher. New York: Harcourt, Brace, & World, 1969.

———. *Humanism and Terror: An Essay on the Communist Problem.* Translated by John O'Neill. Boston: Beacon, 1969.

———. *The Order of Things: An Archaeology of the Human Sciences.* New York: Pantheon, 1971.

———. *Phenomenology of Perception.* Translated by Colin Smith. London: Routledge/Kegan Paul, 1962.

———. *Primacy of Perception, and Other Essays on Phenomenology, Psychology, the Philosophy of Art, History and Politics.* Edited by James M. Edie. Evanston, IL: Northwestern University Press, 1964.

———. *Prose of the World.* Translated by John O'Neill. Evanston, IL: Northwestern University Press, 1969.

———. *Sense and Nonsense.* Translated by H. L. Dreyfus and P. A. Dreyfus. Evanston, IL: Northwestern University Press, 1964.

———. *Signs.* Translated by Richard C. McCleary. Evanston, IL: Northwestern University Press, 1964.

———. *The Structure of Behaviour.*Translated by Alden L. Fischer. London: Methuen, 1965.

———. "Truth and Power." In *From Modernism to Postmodernism: An Anthology*, edited by Lawrence E. Cahoone, 379–81. Oxford: Blackwell, 1996.

———. *The Visible and the Invisible.* Translated by Alphonso Lingis. Evanston, IL: Northwestern University Press, 1968.

Fox, Richard W. *Reinhold Niebuhr: A Biography.* New York: Pantheon, 1985.

Frame, John M. *Apologetics to the Glory of God.* Phillipsburg, NJ: P&R Publishing, 2012.

———. *Cornelius Van Til: An Analysis of His Thought.* Phillipsburg, NJ: P&R Publishing, 1995.

———. "Divine Aseity and Apologetics." In *Revelation and Reason: New Essays in Reformed Apologetics*, edited by K. Scott Oliphint and Lane G. Tipton, 115–30. Phillipsburg, NJ: P&R Publishing, 2007.

———. *The Doctrine of God.* Phillipsburg, NJ: P&R Publishing, 2002.

———. *The Doctrine of the Knowledge of God.* Phillipsburg, NJ: Presbyterian and Reformed, 1987.

———. "Greeks Bearing Gifts." In *Revolutions in Worldview: Understanding the Flow of Western Thought*, edited by W. Andrew Hoffecker, 1–36. Phillipsburg, NJ: P&R Publishing, 2007.

———. *A History of Western Philosophy and Theology.* Phillipsburg, NJ: P&R Publishing, 2015.

———. *Modern Theology and General Culture.* Phillipsburg, NJ: Presbyterian and Reformed, 1987.

———. *No Other God: A Response to Open Theism.* Phillipsburg, NJ: P&R Publishing, 2001.

———. "Scripture Speaks for Itself." In *God's Inerrant Word: An International Symposium on the Trustworthiness of Scripture*, edited by John Warwick Montgomery, 178–200. Minneapolis: Bethany Fellowship, 1974.

———. *Systematic Theology: An Introduction to Christian Belief.* Phillipsburg, NJ: P&R Publishing, 2013.

Franke, John R. *The Character of Theology: A Postconservative Evangelical Approach: An Introduction to Its Nature, Task, and Purpose.* Grand Rapids: Baker, 2005.

Fraser, Antonia. *Mary Queen of Scots.* New York: Greenwish House, 1969.

Frend, W. H. C. *Martyrdom and Persecution in the Early Church*. Grand Rapids: Baker, 1981.

Frey, Jörg. *Die Johanneische Eschatologie I*. Wissenschaftliche Untersuchungen zum Neuen Testament 96. Tübingen: Mohr Siebeck, 1997.

Friesen, Abraham. *Thomas Müntzer: A Destroyer of the Godless*. Berkeley: University of California Press, 1990.

Fuller, Daniel. "Biblical Theology and the Analogy of Faith." In *Unity and Diversity in New Testament Theology: Essays in Honor of George E. Ladd*, edited by R. A. Guelich, 195–213. Grand Rapids: Eerdmans, 1978.

Gäbler, Ulrich. *Huldrych Zwingli: His Life and Work*. Philadelphia: Fortress, 1986.

Gadamer, Hans-Georg. *The Beginning of Knowledge*. New Haven: Yale University Press, 2000.

———. *The Beginning of Philosophy*. New Haven: Yale University Press, 2000.

———. *Dialogue and Dialectic: Eight Hermeneutical Studies on Plato*. New Haven: Yale University Press, 1983.

———. *Hermeneutics, Religion and Ethics*. New Haven: Yale University Press, 2000.

———. *The Idea of the Good in Platonic-Aristotelian Philosophy*. Cambridge: MIT Press, 1983.

———. *Philosophical Apprenticeships*. Cambridge: MIT Press, 1985.

———. *Praise of Theory: Speeches and Essays*. New Haven: Yale University Press, 1999.

———. *Reason in the Age of Science; Philosophical Hermeneutics*. Berkeley: University of California Press, 1977.

———. *Truth and Method*. New York: Seabury Press, 1975.

———. *Wahrheit und Methode: Grundzuge einer philosophische hermeneutik*. Tübingen: Mohr Siebeck, 1960.

Gaffin, Richard B. "Biblical Theology and the Westminster Standards." In *The Practical Calvinist: An Introduction to the Presbyterian and Reformed Heritage*, edited by Peter A. Lillback, 425–42. Fearn, Scotland: Mentor, 2002.

———. "Covenant and Salvation: A Review Article." *Ordained Servant*, March 2009. https://opc.org/os.html?article_id=141. Accessed January 15, 2019.

———. *By Faith, Not by Sight: Paul and the Order of Salvation*. Waynesboro, GA: Paternoster, 2006.

———. "Justification and Union with Christ (3.11–18)." In *A Theological Guide to Calvin's Institutes: Essays and Analysis*, 248–69. Phillipsburg, NJ: P&R Publishing, 2008.

———. "Old Amsterdam and Inerrancy?" *Westminster Theological Journal* 45, no. 2 (Fall 1983): 219–72.

———. "A Response to John Fesko's Review." *Ordained Servant*, March 2009. https://opc.org/os.html?article_id=140. Accessed January 16, 2019.

———. "Theonomy and Eschatology: Reflections on Postmillennialism." In *Theonomy: A Reformed Critique*, edited by William S. Barker and Robert Godfrey, 197–226. Grand Rapids: Zondervan, 1990.

———. "The Work of Christ Applied." In *Christian Dogmatics: Reformed Theology for the Church Catholic*, edited by Michael Allen and Scott R. Swain, 268–90. Grand Rapids: Baker Academic, 2016.

Gamble, Richard C. *Articles on Calvin and Calvinism*. Vol. 1, *The Biography of Calvin*. New York/London: Garland, 1992.

———. *Articles on Calvin and Calvinism*. Vol. 2, *Calvin's Early Writings and Ministry*. New York/London: Garland, 1992.

———. *Articles on Calvin and Calvinism*. Vol. 3, *Calvin's Work in Geneva*. New York/London: Garland, 1992.

———. *Articles on Calvin and Calvinism*. Vol. 6, *Calvin and Hermeneutics*. New York/London: Garland, 1992.

———. *Articles on Calvin and Calvinism*. Vol. 10, *Calvin's Ecclesiology; Sacraments and Deacons*. New York/London: Garland, 1992.

———. *Articles on Calvin and Calvinism*. Vol. 14, *Calvinism in France, Netherlands, Scotland, and England*. New York/London: Garland, 1992.

———. *Augustinus contra Maximinum: An Analysis of Augustine's Anti-Arian Writings*. Ann Arbor, MI: McNaughton and Gunn, 1985.

———. "*Brevitas et Facilitas*: Toward an Understanding of Calvin's Hermeneutic." *Westminster Theological Journal* 47, no. 1 (Spring 1985): 1–17.

———. "Calvin on Irresistible Grace." *Reformed Theological Journal* 25 (2009): 14–21.

———. "Calvin and Sixteenth-century Spirituality: Comparison with the Anabaptists." *Calvin Theological Journal* 31, no. 2 (1996); 335–58.

———. "Calvin as Theologian and Exegete: Is There Anything New?" *Calvin Theological Journal* 23, no. 2 (1988): 178–94.

———. "Calvin's Controversies." In *The Cambridge Companion to John Calvin*, edited by Donald K. McKim, 188–206. Cambridge: Cambridge University Press, 2004.

———. "Calvin's Spirituality." *Reformed Theological Journal* 25 (2009): 5–13.

———. "Calvin's Theological Method: The Case of Caroli." In *Calvin Erbe und Auftrag: Festschrift für Wilhelm Neuser*, edited by Willem Van't Spijker, 130–38. Leuven: Peeters, 1991.

———. "Calvin's Theological Method: Word and Spirit—A Case Study," 63–75." In *Calviniana: Ideas and Influences of Jean Calvin*, edited by Robert Schnucker. Sixteenth Century Essays and Studies 10. Kirksville, MO: Sixteenth Century, 1988.

———. "The Christian and the Tyrant: Beza and Knox on Political Resistance Theory." *Westminster Theological Journal* 46, no. 1 (Spring 1984): 125–29.

———. "Christianity from the Early Fathers to Charlemagne." In *Revolutions in Worldview: Understanding the Flow of Western Thought*, edited by W. Andrew Hoffecker, 100–139. Phillipsburg, NJ: P&R Publishing, 2007.

———. "The Clash of King and Kirk." In *The Practical Calvinist: An Introduction to the Presbyterian and Reformed Heritage*, edited by Peter A. Lillback, 215–32. Fearn, Scotland: Mentor, 2002.

———. "Comprehending the Eternal Union of God." *Reformed Presbyterian Theological Journal* 2, no. 1 (Fall 2015): 4–13.

———. "Critical Realism and the New Perspective." *Reformed Presbyterian Theological Journal* 1, no. 2 (Spring 2015): 4–12.

———. "The Doctrine of the Atonement from the Westminster Assembly to the Twentieth Century." In *The Faith Once Delivered*, edited by Anthony T. Selvaggio, 247–73. Phillipsburg, NJ: P&R Publishing, 2007.

———. "Exposition and Method in Calvin." *Westminster Theological Journal* 49, no. 1 (Spring 1987): 153–65.

———. "He Is Not Lord over Evil Is He?" *Reformed Presbyterian Theological Journal* 3, no. 1 (Fall 2016): 27–38.

———. "Medieval Monasticism." *Tabletalk Magazine*, January 1, 1995, 14–15, 53.

———. "Not One Iota." *Tabletalk Magazine*, August 1, 2004, 11–14.

———. "Presbyterianism and the Ancient Church." In *Pressing toward the Mark: Essays Commemorating Fifty Years of the Orthodox Presbyterian Church*, edited by Charles G. Dennison and Richard C. Gamble, 53–62.

Philadelphia: Committee for the Historian of the Orthodox Presbyterian Church, 1986.

———. "Reflections on Theological Method and the Doctrine of God: A Review of James Dolezal's *All That Is in God*." *Reformed Presbyterian Theological Journal* 5, no. 2 (Spring 2019): 14–25.

———. Review of *Christus Exemplum: Studien zur Christologie und Christusverkundigung Augustins*, by Wilhelm Geerlings. *Theologische Zeitschrift* 35, no. 6 (Nov/Dez 1979): 374–75.

———. Review of *God the Revealed: Christology*, by Michael Welker. *Westminster Theological Journal* 77, no. 1 (Spring 2015): 165–67.

———. Review of *Statesman and Saint: Cardinal Wolsey, Sir Thomas More and the Politics of Henry VIII*, by Jasper Ridley. *Westminster Theological Journal* 45, no. 2 (Fall 1983): 455–56.

———. "Sacramental Continuity among Reformed Refugees: Peter Martyr Vermigli and John Calvin." In *Peter Martyr Vermigli and the European Reformations: Semper Reformanda*, edited by Frank A. James III, 97–114. Leiden: Brill, 2004.

———. "The Second Use of the Law in Scottish Context." *Reformed Presbyterian Theological Journal* 1, no. 1 (Fall 2014): 18–27.

———. "The Sources of Calvin's Genesis Commentary: A Preliminary Report." *Archiv für Reformationsgeschichte* 84 (1993): 206–21.

———. "Switzerland: Triumph and Decline." In *John Calvin: His Influence in the Western World*, edited by W. Stanford Reid, 55–75. Grand Rapids: Zondervan, 1981.

———. "The Very Gate of Paradise to Me: The Development of Protestantism's Teaching on Justification by Faith." *RPTJ* 4, no. 1 (Fall 2017): 8–42.

———. *The Whole Counsel of God*. Vol. 1, *God's Mighty Acts in the Old Testament*. Phillipsburg, NJ: P&R Publishing, 2009.

———. *The Whole Counsel of God*. Vol. 2, *The Full Revelation of God*. Phillipsburg, NJ: P&R Publishing, 2018.

Gamble, Whitney G. *Christ and the Law: Antinomianism at the Westminster Assembly*. Grand Rapids: Reformation Heritage Books, 2018.

———. "John Owen on Justification by Faith." In *Handbook of John Owen*, edited by John Tweeddale and Crawford Gribben. Edinburgh: T&T Clark, forthcoming.

———. "Missing the Point?" Review of *Antinomianism: Reformed Theology's Unwelcome Guest?* by Mark Jones. *European Journal of Theology* 21, no. 2 (2014): 192–93.

———. "The Significance of English Antinomianism for Anna Trapnel." *Reformation & Renaissance Review* 17, no. 2 (2015): 155–66.

———. "The Theology of the Westminster Confession of Faith in Its Context." In *The History of Scottish Theology*, vol. 1, edited by David Fergusson and Mark W. Elliott, 265–78. Oxford: Oxford University Press, 2019.

Gamwell, Franklin. "On the Theology of Schubert M. Ogden." *Religious Studies Review* 23, no. 4 (October 1997): 333–37.

Ganoczy, Alexander. *The Young Calvin.* Translated by David Foxgrover and Wade Provo. Philadelphia: Westminster Press, 1987.

Ganoczy, Alexander, and Stefan Scheld. *Die Hermeneutik Calvins: Geistesgeschichtliche Voraussetzungen und Grundzüge.* Wiesbaden: Steiner, 1983.

Ganz, Richard L. *You Shall Be Free Indeed! The Statutes of Liberty for Godly Living.* Nepean, ON: GSG, 1989.

Ganz, Richard L., and William J. Edgar. *Sold Out.* Ottawa, ON: Onward Press, 1990.

Garcia, Mark A. *Life in Christ: Union with Christ and Twofold Grace in Calvin's Theology—Studies in Christian History and Thought.* Milton Keynes/Waynesboro, GA: Paternoster, 2008.

Garner, David B. *Sons in the Son.* Phillipsburg, NJ: P&R Publishing, 2016.

Garrity, John A., ed. *Columbia History of the World.* New York: Harper & Row, 1988.

Gaustad, Edwin S. *Faith of Our Fathers: Religion and the New Nation.* San Francisco: Harper & Row, 1987.

Geerlings, Wilhelm. *Christus Exemplum: Studien zur Christologie und Christusverkündigung Augustins.* Tübinger Theologische Studien Bd 13. Mainz: Matthias Grünewald Verlag, 1978.

Geisler, Norman L. "Syllabus on Christian Apologetics." Mundelein, IL: n.p., 1976.

Geisler, Norman L., and Abdul Saleeb. *Answering Islam: The Crescent in Light of the Cross.* Ada, MI: Baker, 2002.

George, A. Chacko. "Martin Luther's Doctrine of Sanctification with Special Reference to the Formula 'Simul iustus et peccator': A Study in Luther's Lectures on Romans and Galatians." ThD diss., Westminster Theological Seminary, 1982.

George, Timothy. *Theology of the Reformers.* Nashville: Broadman, 1988.

Gerkin, Charles V. *The Living Human Document: Re-visioning Pastoral Counseling in a Hermeneutical Mode.* Nashville: Abingdon Press, 1984.

Gibson, David. "The Answering Speech of Men: Karl Barth on Holy Scripture." In *The Enduring Authority of the Christian Scriptures*, edited by D. A. Carson, 266–91. Grand Rapids: Eerdmans, 2016.

Gill, Jerry H. *The Tacit Mode: Michael Polanyi's Postmodern Philosophy.* New York: State University of New York Press, 1999.

Gleason, Ron. *Herman Bavinck: Pastor, Churchman, Statesman, Theologian.* Phillipsburg, NJ: P&R Publishing, 2010.

Godfrey, W. Robert. "Calvin and Calvinism in the Netherlands." In *John Calvin: His Influence in the Western World*, edited by W. Stanford Reid, 95–122. Grand Rapids: Zondervan, 1982.

————. "The Synod of Dordt." *Tabletalk Magazine* 42, no. 6 (June 2018): 72–75

————. "Westminster, Justification, and the Reformed Confessions." In *The Pattern of Sound Doctrine: Systematic Theology at the Westminster Seminaries*, edited by David VanDrunen, 127–48. Phillipsburg, NJ: P&R Publishing, 2004.

Goertz, Hans-Jürgen. *Thomas Müntzer: Apocalyptic, Mystic and Revolutionary.* Edinburgh: T&T Clark, 1993.

Gonzalez, Justo L. *A History of Christian Thought.* Nashville: Abingdon Press, 1975.

Gooding-Williams, Robert. "W. E. B. Du Bois." In *The Stanford Encyclopedia of Philosophy*, edited by Edward N. Zalta, Spring 2020. https://plato.stanford.edu/archives/spr2020/entries/dubois/. Accessed April 15, 2020.

Gordon, Bruce. *Clerical Discipline and the Rural Reformation: The Synod in Zurich, 1532–1580.* Bern: Lang, 1992.

Gordon, F. Bruce. *Calvin.* New Haven: Yale University Press, 2009.

Gorman, Michael J. *Abortion and the Early Church.* Eugene, OR: Wipf & Stock, 1998.

Grant, Robert M. *Gnosticism and Early Christianity.* New York: Columbia University Press, 1959.

Green, V. H. H. *John Wesley.* London: Thomas Nelson, 1970.

Greene, Marjorie. Introduction to *Knowing and Being*, by Michael Polyani, ix–I. Chicago: University of Chicago Press, 1969.

Greene, Theodore Meyer. *Kant Selections.* New York: Scribner's Sons, 1929.

Greer, Thomas H. *A Brief History of the Western World.* 4th ed. New York: Harcourt Brace Jovanovich, 1982.

Gregg, Robert C., and Dennis E. Groh. *Early Arianism: A View of Salvation.* London: SCM Press, 1981.

Grenz, Stanley J., and Roger Olson. *20th Century Theology: God and the World in a Transitional Age.* Downers Grove, IL: InterVarsity Press, 1992.

Gribben, Crawford. *John Owen and English Puritanism: Experiences of Defeat.* Oxford: Oxford University Press, 2017.

Grillmeier, Aloys. *Christ in Christian Tradition.* Vol. 1, *From the Apostolic Age to Chalcedon (451).* Translated by John Bowden. Atlanta: John Knox Press, 1975.

Grondin, Jean. *Hans-Georg Gadamer: A Biography.* New Haven: Yale University Press, 2004.

Groothius, Douglas. *Truth Decay: Defending Christianity against the Challenges of Postmodernism.* Downers Grove, IL: InterVarsity Press, 2000.

Grounds, Vernon C. "Pacesetters for the Radical Theologians of the Sixties and Seventies." In *Tensions in Contemporary Theology*, edited by Stanley N. Gundry and Alan F. Johnson, 45–104. 2nd ed. Grand Rapids: Baker, 1986.

Grudem, Wayne, ed. *Are Miraculous Gifts for Today? Four Views.* Grand Rapids: Zondervan, 2011.

———. *Systematic Theology.* Grand Rapids: Zondervan, 1994.

Guinness, Os. *The Dust of Death.* Downers Grove, IL: InterVarsity Press, 1973.

Gundry, Stanley N., and Alan F. Johnson, eds. *Tensions in Contemporary Theology.* Chicago: Moody, 1976.

Guthrie, Donald. *New Testament Theology* . Leicester/Downers Grove, IL: InterVarsity Press, 1981.

Guthrie, S. C., Jr. "Oscar Cullmann." In *A Handbook of Christian Theologians*, edited by Martin E. Marty and Dean G. Peerman, 338–54. Nashville: Abingdon Press, 1985.

Guthrie, W. K. C. *The Greek Philosophers from Thales to Aristotle.* New York: Harper & Row, 1975.

Gutierrez, Gustavo. *A Theology of Liberation.* Maryknoll, NY: Orbis, 1973.

Gwatkin, H. M. *The Arian Controversy.* London: Longmans, Green, 1889.

Habermas, Jürgen. *The Philosophical Discourse of Modernity.* New York: Polity Press, 1988. English.

———. *The Theory of Communicative Action.* 2 vols. Cambridge: Polity Press, 1984. English.

——. *Die Zukunft der menschlichen Natur: Auf dem Weg zu einer liberalen Eugenik*. 5 Aufl. Frankfurt: Suhrkamp Verlag, 2001.

Hadot, Pierre. "L'image de la Trinité dans l'âme chez Victorinus et chez saint Augustin." In *Studia Patristica: Papers Presented to the Third International Conference on Patristic Studies Held at Christ Church, Oxford, 1959*, vol. 6, edited by Frank L. Cross, 409–42. Berlin: Akademie, 1962.

——. *Marius Victorinus: Recherches sur sa vie et ses oeuvres*. Paris: Études Augustiniennes, 1971.

Hagemann, Hermann. *Die Romische Kirche und ihr Einfluß auf Disciplin und Dogma in den ersten drei Jahrhunderten: Nach den Qullen auf's Neue untersucht*. Freiburg im Breisgau: Herder, 1864.

Hahn, Fritz. "Faber Stapulensis und Luther." *Zeitschrift für Kirchengeschichte* 57 (1938): 356–432.

——. "Zur Hermeneutik Gersons." *Zeitschrift für Theologie und Kirche* 51 (1954): 34–50.

Hall, David W. *Calvin in the Public Square: Liberal Democracies, Rights, and Civil Liberties*. Phillipsburg, NJ: P&R Publishing, 2009.

Halsey, Jim S. *For a Time Such as This*. Nutley, NJ: Presbyterian and Reformed, 1976.

Hanko, Herman. "Johann Agricola and Antinomianism (1)." *The Standard Bearer* 78, no. 16 (May 15, 2002): 373–756.

——. "Johann Agricola and Antinomianism (2)." *The Standardbearer* 78, no. 18 (July 1, 2002): 424–46.

Hanson, R. P. C. *Allegory and Event: A Study of the Sources and Significance of Origen's Interpretation of Scripture*. Richmond, VA: John Knox Press, 1959.

——, ed. *Hermias: Satire des Philosophes Païens*. Sources Chrétiennes 388. Paris: Les Éditions du Cerf, 1993.

Harinck, George. "The Poetry of Theologian Geerhardus Vos." In *Dutch-American Arts and Letters in Historical Perspective*, edited by Robert P. Swierenga, Jacob E. Nyenhuis, and Nella Kennedy, 69–80. Holland, MI: Van Raalte Press, 2008.

Harries, Richard, ed. *Reinhold Niebuhr and the Issues of Our Time*. London/Oxford: Mowbray, 1986.

Harris, E. D. *Nature, Mind and Modern Science*. London: Allen and Unwin, 1954.

Harris, Horton. *The Tübingen School*. Oxford: Clarendon, 1975.

Hart, D. G. *Defending the Faith: J. Gresham Machen and the Crisis of Conservative Protestantism in Modern America.* Phillipsburg, NJ: P&R Publishing, 2003.

———, ed. *J. Gresham Machen: Selected Shorter Writings.* Phillipsburg, NJ: P&R Publishing, 2004.

Hartman, Nicolai. *Möglichkeit und Wirklichkeit.* Berlin: de Gruyter, 1966.

Harvey, David. *The Condition of Postmodernity.* Cambridge: Blackwell, 1989.

Hazlett, Ian. "A New Version of the Scots Confession, 1560." *Theology in Scotland* 17, no. 2 (2010): 35.

Healy, Frances Bridget Eleanor. "Foucault's Ethic of Power." PhD diss., University of Tasmania, 2013. https://eprints.utas.edu.au/17510/1/Whole -Healy-_thesis.pdf downloaded 8/12/2020.

Hefele, Charles Joseph. *A History of the Christian Councils.* Edinburgh: T&T Clark, 1862.

Heidegger, Martin. *Being and Time.* New York: Harper & Row, 1962. Reprint, New York: Harper Perennial Modern Classics, 2008.

———. *Discourse on Thinking.* New York: Harper & Row, 1966.

———. *Gelassenheit.* Stuttgart: Pfullingen, 1959.

———. *Introduction to Metaphysics.* New Haven: Yale University Press, 1959.

———. *Unterwegs zur Sprache.* Stuttgart: Pfullingen, 1959.

———. *Vom Wesen Des Grundes. The Essence of Reasons: A Bilingual Edition, Incorporating the German Text.* Translated by Terence Malick. Evanston, IL: Northwestern University Press, 1969.

Heinecken, Martin J. "Søren Kierkegaard." In *A Handbook of Christian Theologians,* edited by Martin E. Marty and Dean G. Peerman, 125–43. Nashville: Abingdon Press, 1985.

Held, Wieland, and Siegfried Hoyer, eds. *Quellen zu Thomas Müntzer.* Leipzig: Evangelischen Verlagsanstalt, 2004.

Henry, Paul. "The 'Adversus Arium' of Marius Victorinus: The First Systematic Exposition of the Trinity." *Journal of Theological Studies* 1 (April 1950): 42–55.

Hepp, V. *Dr. Herman Bavinck.* Amsterdam: W. ten Have, 1921.

Heppe, Heinrich. *Reformed Dogmatics.* Eugene, OR: Wipf & Stock, 1977.

Herminjard, Aimé Louis. *Correspondance des Réformateurs dans les Pays de Langue Française.* Nieuwkoop: De Graaf, 1965.

Herrmann, Wilhelm. *Schriften zur Grundlegung der Theologie.* Teil I. Munich: Kaiser, 1966.

Heussi, Karl. *Kompendium der Kirchengeschichte*. Tübingen: Mohr Siebeck, 1971.

Hewitson, Ian. *Trust and Obey: Norman Shepherd and the Justification Controversy at Westminster Theological Seminary*. Minneapolis: NextStep Resources, 2011.

Hick, John. *An Interpretation of Religion*. New Haven: Yale University Press, 1989.

———. *The Philosophy of Religion*. Englewood Cliffs, NJ: Prentice Hall, 1970.

Hilary of Poitiers. *De trinitate*. In *Patrologiae Cursus Completus: Series Latina*, edited by J. P. Migne, 10:130–404. Paris: Garnier Fratres, 1857.

Hill, Charles E. "The Truth above All Demonstration." In *The Enduring Authority of the Christian Scriptures*, edited by D. A. Carson, 43–88. Grand Rapids: Eerdmans, 2016.

Hill, Charles E., and Frank A. James III, eds. *The Glory of the Atonement: Biblical, Historical, and Practical Perspectives*. Downers Grove, IL: InterVarsity Press, 2004.

Hillerbrand, H., ed. *Erasmus and His Age: Selected Letters*. New York: Harper & Row, 1970.

Himmelfarb, Gertrude. *The De-Moralization of Society: From Victorian Virtues to Modern Values*. New York: Knopf, 1995.

Hindson, Edward, ed. *Introduction to Puritan Theology*. Grand Rapids: Baker, 1976.

Hirsch, E. D. *Validity in Interpretation*. New Haven: Yale University Press, 1967.

Hobbes, Thomas. *Leviathan*. New York: Atria, 2008.

Hodge, Archibald Alexander. *The Atonement*. Philadelphia: Presbyterian Board of Education, 1867.

———. *A Commentary on the Westminster Confession of Faith*. Carlisle, PA: Banner of Truth, 1958.

———. *The Confession of Faith*. Edinburgh: Banner of Truth, 1978.

———. *The Life of Charles Hodge*. New York: Scribner's Sons, 1880.

———. *Outline of Theology*. Reprint, Edinburgh: Banner of Truth, 1991.

Hodge, Charles. "Memoir of Archibald Alexander." *Biblical Repertory and Princeton Review* 27 (January 1855): 133–59.

———. *Romans*. Grand Rapids: Eerdmans, 1993.

———. *Systematic Theology*. 3 vols. London: Clarke, 1960.

———. *What Is Darwinism?* New York: Scribner, Armstrong, and Co., 1874.

Hodges, Zane C. *Absolutely Free!* Grand Rapids: Zondervan, 1989.

———. *Dead Faith: What Is It?* Dallas: Redención Viva, 1987.

———. *The Gospel under Siege: Faith and Works in Tension.* Dallas: Redención Viva, 1992.

Hoffecker, W. Andrew. *Charles Hodge: The Pride of Princeton.* Phillipsburg, NJ: P&R Publishing, 2011.

———. *Piety and the Princeton Theologians.* Phillipsburg, NJ: Presbyterian and Reformed, 1981.

———. *Revolutions in Worldview: Understanding the Flow of Western Thought.* Phillipsburg, NJ: P&R Publishing, 2007.

Hoffman, Manfred. *Rhetoric and Theology: The Hermeneutic of Erasmus.* Toronto: University of Toronto Press, 1993.

Hoepfl, Harro. *The Christian Polity of John Calvin.* New York: Cambridge University Press, 1982.

Hofstadter, Richard. *The American Political Tradition.* New York: Vintage, 1957.

Holland, David Larrimore. "Die Synode von Antiochien (324/25) und ihre Bedeutung für Eusebius von Caesarea und das Konzil von Nizäa." *Zeitschrift für Kirchengeschichte* 81 (1970): 163–81.

Höpfl, Harro. *The Christian Polity of John Calvin.* New York: Cambridge University Press, 1982.

Hopkins, Jasper. *A Companion to the Study of St. Anselm.* Minneapolis: University of Minnesota Press, 1972.

Horne, Charles M. "Van Til and Carnell, Part II." In *Jerusalem and Athens: Critical Discussions on the Theology and Apologetics of Cornelius Van Til,* edited by E. R. Geehan, 367–79. Nutley, NJ: P&R Publishing, 1971.

Horsch, John. *Mennonites in Europe.* Scottdale, PA: Mennonite Publishing House, 1950.

Horton, Michael S. *The Christian Faith: A Systematic Theology for Pilgrims on the Way.* Grand Rapids: Zondervan, 2011.

———. *Covenant and Eschatology: The Divine Drama.* Louisville: Westminster John Knox, 2002.

———. *Covenant and Salvation: Union with Christ.* Philadelphia: Westminster John Knox Press, 2007.

———. *Justification.* 2 vols. Grand Rapids: Zondervan, 2018.

House, Paul. *Old Testament Theology.* Downers Grove, IL: InterVarsity Press, 1998.

Hugh of Saint Victor. *Selected Spiritual Writings*. Edited by Aelred Squire. New York: Harper & Row, 1962.

Hughes, Philip Edgcumbe. *Lefèvre: Pioneer of Ecclesiastical Renewal in France*. Grand Rapids: Eerdmans, 1985.

——. *The Register of the Company of Pastors of Geneva in the Time of Calvin*. Grand Rapids: Eerdmans, 1966.

——. *Theology of the English Reformers*. Grand Rapids: Eerdmans, 1966.

Huijgen, Arnold, and Karin Maag. *Calvinus frater in Domino*. Göttingen: Vandenhoeck & Ruprecht, 2020.

Huisman, Denis, ed. "Foucault." In *Dictionnaire des philosophes*, 942–44. Paris: Presses Universitaires de France, 1984.

Huizinga, Johan. *Erasmus and the Age of the Reformation*. New York: Harper & Row, 1957.

Hume, David. *Enquiry Concerning Human Understanding*. Chicago: Encyclopedia Britannica, 1955.

Hurtado, Larry W. *Lord Jesus Christ: Devotion to Jesus in Earliest Christianity*. Grand Rapids: Eerdmans, 2005.

Husserl, E. *The Crisis of European Sciences and Transcendental Phenomenology*. Evanston, IL: Northwestern University Press, 1970.

Inge, William Ralph. *Christian Mysticism: Considered in Eight Lectures Delivered before the University of Oxford*. London: Methuen, 1899.

——. *Mysticism in Religion*. Chicago: University of Chicago Press, 1948.

——. *Origen*. London: Cumberlege, 1946.

Irenaeus. *Adversus haereses: Ante-Nicene Fathers*. Vol. 1. Edinburgh: T&T Clark, 1884.

Issacson, Walter. *Benjamin Franklin*. New York: Simon & Schuster, 2003.

James, Frank A., III. *Peter Martyr Vermigli and Predestination*. Oxford: Clarendon, 1998.

James, George Payne R. *A History of the Life of Richard Coeur-de-lion, King of England*. London: Bohn, 1854.

James, John Angell. *The Christian Father's Present*. Morgan, PA: Soli Deo Gloria, 1995.

Janz, Denis R. *A Reformation Reader*. Minneapolis: Fortress, 2008.

Jefford, Clayton N. *The Epistle to Diognetus (with the Fragment of Quadratus): Introduction, Text and Commentary*. Oxford: Oxford University Press, 2013.

Jenkins, Daniel. "Karl Barth." In *A Handbook of Christian Theologians*, edited by Martin E. Marty and Dean G. Peerman, 396–409. Nashville: Abingdon Press, 1985.

Johnson, William, and John H. Leith, eds. *Reformed Reader: A Sourcebook in Christian Theology*. Philadelphia: Westminster John Knox Press, 1993.

Jonas, Hans. *The Gnostic Religion: The Message of the Alien God and the Beginnings of Christianity*. 2nd rev. ed. Boston: Beacon, 1963.

Jones, Mark. *Antinomianism: Reformed Theology's Unwelcome Guest?* Phillipsburg, NJ: P&R Publishing, 2013.

Jones, Serene. *Feminist Theory and Christian Theology: Cartographies of Grace*. Minneapolis: Fortress, 2000.

Jongeneel, J. A. B. "The Missiology of Gisbertus Voetius: The First Comprehensive Protestant Theology of Missions." *Calvin Theological Journal* 26, no. 1 (1991): 47–79.

Jüngel, Eberhard. *Das Evangelium von der Rechtfertigung des Gottlosen als Zentrum des christlichen Glaubens*. 2 Aufl. Tübingen: Mohr Siebeck, 1999.

———. *God as the Mystery of the World*. Grand Rapids: Eerdmans, 1983.

Kähler, Martin. *The So-Called Historical Jesus and the Historic, Biblical Christ*. Translated by Carl Braaten. Philadelphia: Fortress, 1964.

Kalsbeek, L. *Contours of Christian Philosophy*. Toronto: Wedge, 1975.

Kant, Immanuel. "Beantwortung der Frage: Was ist Aufklarung?" In *Berlinische Monatsschrift* 2 (1784): 481–94.

———. *Critique of Pure Reason*. Translated by Paul Guyer and Allen W. Wood. Cambridge: Cambridge University Press, 1998.

———. *Gesammelte Schriften*. Berlin: Reimer, 1900.

———. *Kritik der reinen Vernunft*. Rev. ed. Edited by Erich Adickes. Berlin: Reimer, 1889.

Kapic, Kelly M., and Randall C. Gleason. *The Devoted Life: An Invitation to the Puritan Classics*. Downers Grove, IL: InterVarsity Press, 2004.

Kapic, Kelly M., and Bruce L. McCormack, eds. *Mapping Modern Theology: A Thematic and Historical Introduction*. Grand Rapids: Baker Academic, 2012.

Käsemann, Ernst. *Exegetische Versuche und Besinnungen*. Göttingen: Vandenhoeck & Ruprecht, 1954.

Kaufmann, Walter, ed. *Existentialism from Dostoevsky to Sartre*. Cleveland: Meridian, 1956.

Kelly, Douglas F. *Systematic Theology*. Vol. 1, *Grounded in Holy Scripture and Understood in the Light of the Church*. Fearn, Scotland: Mentor, 2008.

———. *Systematic Theology*. Vol. 2, *The Beauty of Christ—A Trinitarian Vision*. Fearn, Scotland: Mentor, 2014.

———. "The Westminster Shorter Catechism." In *To Glorify and Enjoy God: A Commemoration of the 350th Anniversary of the Westminster Assembly*, edited by John L. Carlson and David W. Hall, 101–26. Edinburgh: Banner of Truth, 1994.

Kelly, J. N. D. *Early Christian Creeds*. London: Longman, 1972.

———. *Early Christian Doctrines*. Rev. ed. London: Black, 1977.

Kepple, Robert. "An Analysis of Antiochene Exegesis of Galatians 4:24–26." *Westminster Theological Journal* 39, no. 2 (Spring 1977): 239–49.

Kickel, Walter. *Vernunft und Offenbarung bei Theodor Beza: Zum Problem der Verhältnisses von Theologie, Philosophie und Staat*. Neukirchen-Vluyn: Neukirchener Verlag, 1967.

Kidd, B. J. *A History of the Christian Church to* A.D. *461*. Oxford: Oxford University Press, 1922.

Kierkegaard, Søren. *Concluding Unscientific Postscript*. Princeton: Princeton University Press, 1992.

———. *Papers and Journals: A Selection*. New York: Penguin Books, 1996.

Kingdon, Robert M. *The Political Thought of Peter Martyr Vermigli*. Paris: Droz, 1980.

———, ed. *Registers of the Consistory of Geneva in the Time of Calvin: Volume 1, 1542–44*. Grand Rapids: Eerdmans, 2000.

Kirk, G. S., and J. E. Raven. *The Presocratic Philosophers*. Cambridge: Cambridge University Press, 1963.

Klapwijk, Jacob. Einleitung zu *Glaubenslehre*, von Ernst Troeltsch, v–xxvi. Aalen: Scientia Verlag, 1981.

Klauber, Martin I. "Francis Turretin on Biblical Accommodation: Loyal Calvinist or Reformed Scholastic?" *Westminster Theological Journal* 55, no. 1 (Spring 1993): 73–86.

Klooster, Fred H. *The Incomprehensibility of God in the Orthodox Presbyterian Confict*. Franeker, Netherlands: Wever, 1951.

Klotsche, E. H. *The History of Christian Doctrine*. Rev. ed. Grand Rapids: Baker, 1979.

Kneale, William, and Mary Kneale. *The Development of Logic*. Oxford: Clarendon, 1962.

Knowles, David. "The Middle Ages 604–1350." In *A History of Christian Doctrine*, edited by Hubert Cunliffe-Jones, 227–86. 1978. Reprint, New York: T&T Clark, 2006.

Knowles, M. D. *Geschichte der Kirche.* Band II, *Früh und Hochmittelalter.* Zurich: Benziger, 1971.

Knudson, Albert C. *The Doctrine of God.* New York: Abingdon Press, 1930.

Kohls, Ernst W. *Die Theologie des Erasmus.* 2 vols. Basel: Reinhardt, 1966.

Kohnle, Armin, and Elke Wolgast. *Schriften, Manuskripte un Notizen.* Leipzig: Evangelischen Verlagsanstalt, 2017.

Kolb, Robert. "The Bible in the Reformation and Protestant Orthodoxy." In *The Enduring Authority of the Christian Scriptures*, edited by D. A. Carson, 90–98. Grand Rapids: Eerdmans, 2016.

Kretschmar, Georg. *Studien zur frühchristlichen Trinitätstheologie.* Tübingen: Mohr Siebeck, 1956.

Kristeller, Paul Oskar. *The Classics and Renaissance Thought.* Cambridge: Harvard University Press, 1955.

Küng, Hans. *On Being a Christian.* Translated by Edward Quinn. Garden City, NY: Doubleday, 1976.

Kuschke, Arthur W. Introduction to *Selected Shorter Writings of Benjamin B. Warfield*, edited by John Meeter, 1:xiii–xv. 2 vols. Phillipsburg, NJ: Presbyterian and Reformed, 1979.

Kuyper, Abraham. *E Voto Dordraceno: Toelichting op den Heidelbergschen Catechismus.* 4 vols. Amsterdam: J. A. Wormser, 1892–95.

Kuyper, Catherine M. E. "Abraham Kuyper: His Early Life and Conversion." *International Reformed Bulletin* 3 (April 1960): 19–25.

Lambeck, Martin S. *Die Zeit*, February 21, 2001.

Lampe, G. W. H. "Christian Theology in the Patristic Period." In *A History of Christian Doctrine*, edited by Hubert Cunliffe-Jones, 21–180. 1978. Reprint, New York: T&T Clark, 2006.

Langford, T. A. *Practical Divinity: Theology in the Wesleyan Tradition.* Nashville: Abingdon Press, 1984.

Langford, Thomas A., and William H. Poteat, eds. *Intellect and Hope: Essays in the Thought of Michael Polanyi.* Durham, NC: Duke University Press, 1968.

Latourette, Kenneth Scott. *A History of Christianity.* 2 vols. Peabody, MA: Prince, 2005.

Le Goff, Jacques. *Medieval Civilization 400–1500.* Translated by Julia Barrow. Oxford: Blackwell, 1988.

Lee, Francis Nigel. *A Christian Introduction to the History of Philosophy*. Nutley, NJ: Craig Press, 1969.

Leith, John H. *Assembly at Westminster: Reformed Theology in the Making*. Richmond, VA: John Knox Press, 1973.

———. Foreword to *John Calvin: Instruction in Faith (1537)*, edited and translated Paul T. Fuhrmann, 9–13. Louisville: John Knox Press, 1992.

Leithart, Peter. *Against Christianity*. Moscow, ID: Canon, 2003.

Letham, Robert. *The Holy Trinity: In Scripture, History, Theology, and Worship*. Rev. and exp. ed. Phillipsburg, NJ: P&R Publishing, 2019.

———. *Systematic Theology*. Wheaton, IL: Crossway, 2019.

———. *Union with Christ in Scripture, History, and Theology*. Phillipsburg, NJ: P&R Publishing, 2011.

———. *The Westminster Assembly: Reading Its Theology in Historical Context*. Phillipsburg, NJ: P&R Publishing, 2009.

Levin, Dan. *Spinoza: The Young Thinker Who Destroyed the Past*. New York: Weybright and Talley, 1970.

Lewis, C. S. *The Problem of Pain*. New York: Macmillan, 1944.

Lewis, Gordon R. *Testing Christianity's Truth Claims: Approaches to Apologetics*. Lanham, MD: University Press of America, 1990.

Liebeschutz, H. "Western Thought from Boethius to Anselm." In *The Cambridge History of Later Greek and Early Medieval Philosophy*, edited by A. H. Armstrong, 538–642. Cambridge: Cambridge University Press, 1970.

Liechty, Daniel. *Early Anabaptist Spirituality*. New York: Paulist Press, 1994.

Lietzmann, Hans. *Geschichte der alten Kirche*. Berlin: de Gruyter, 1932.

Lillback, Peter A. *The Binding of God: Calvin's Role in the Development of Covenant Theology*. Grand Rapids: Baker Academic, 2001.

———. "Calvin's Development of the Doctrine of Forensic Justification." In *Justified in Christ: God's Plan for Us in Justification*, edited by K. Scott Oliphint, 51–80. Fearn, Scotland: Mentor, 2007.

———. *George Washington's Sacred Fire*. King of Prussia, PA: Providence Forum Press, 2006.

———. "J. Gresham Machen, Fundamentalism, and Westminster Seminary." In *Christianity and Liberalism*, by J. Gresham Machen, 191–97. Legacy ed. Philadelphia: Westminster Seminary Press, 2019.

———. *Wall of Misconception*. King of Prussia, PA: Providence Forum Press, 2007.

Lindberg, Carter. *The European Reformations*. 2nd ed. Malden, MA: Wiley-Blackwell, 2010.

Lindsay, Thomas M. *History of the Reformation*. 2 vols. Edinburgh: T&T Clark, 1963.

Lints, Richard. "The Age of Intellectual Iconoclasm: The Nineteenth-Century Revolt against Theism." In *Revolutions in Worldview: Understanding the Flow of Western Thought*, edited by W. Andrew Hoffecker, 281–317. Phillipsburg, NJ: P&R Publishing, 2007.

Lister, Rob. *God Is Impassible and Impassioned: Toward a Theology of Divine Emotion*. Wheaton, IL: Crossway, 2012.

Lloyd-Jones, Martyn. "Ecclesiola in Ecclesia." In *Puritan Papers*, edited by J. I. Packer, 4:75–97. 5 vols. Phillipsburg, NJ: P&R Publishing, 2004.

Locher, Gottfried W. *Die Zwinglishche Reformation im Rahmen der europäischen Kirchengeschichte*. Göttingen: Vandenhoeck & Ruprecht, 1979.

———. *Die Theologie Huldrych Zwinglis*. Zurich: Zwingli-Verlag, 1952.

Locke, John. *A Commonplace-Book to the Holy Bible on the Scripture's Sufficiency Practically Demonstrated*. 5th ed. New York: American Tract Society, 1858.

Loetscher, Lefferts A. *Facing the Enlightenment and Pietism: Archibald Alexander and the Founding of Princeton Theological Seminary*. Westport, CT: Greenwood, 1983.

Loewith, Karl. *From Hegel to Nietzsche: The Revolution in Nineteenth-Century Thought*. London: Constable, 1965.

Lombard, Peter. *The Sentences, Books 1–4*. Translated by Giulio Silano. 4 vols. Toronto: Pontifical Institute of Mediaeval Studies, 2007–2010.

Loofs, Friedrich. *Leitfaden zum Studium der Dogmengeshichte*. Berlin: de Gruyter, 1959.

Louthan, Stephen. "On Religion: A Discussion with Richard Rorty, Alvin Plantinga and Nicholas Wolterstorff." *Christian Scholars Review* 26, no. 2 (1996): 177–83.

Lowrie, Donald A. *Rebellious Prophet: A Life of Nicolai Berdyaev*. New York: Harper, 1960.

Lowrie, Walter. *Søren Kierkegaard*. 2 vols. New York: Harper, 1962.

Lubac, Henri de. *Geist aus der Geschichte: Das Schriftverständnis des Origines*. Translated by Hans Urs von Balthasar. Einsiedeln: Johannes Verlag, 1968.

———. *Medieval Exegesis: The Four Senses of Scripture*. Grand Rapids: Eerdmans, 1998.

Luther, Martin. *The Bondage of the Will.* Translated by James I. Packer and O. R. Johnston. Old Tappan, NJ: Revel, 1957.

———. *Luther's Works.* Edited by Jaroslav Pelikan and Helmut T. Lehmann. 56 vols. St. Louis: Concordia, 1968.

———. *What Luther Says.* Edited by Ewald M. Plass. 3 vols. St. Louis: Concordia, 1959.

Lyotard, Jean-Francois. *The Postmodern Condition: A Report on Knowledge.* Minneapolis: University of Minnesota Press, 1984.

———. *Toward the Postmodern.* Edited by Robert Harvey and Mark S. Roberts. *Atlantic Highlands,* NJ/London: Humanities Press International, 1993.

MacArthur, John. *The Gospel According to Jesus.* Grand Rapids: Zondervan, 1994.

MacCulloch, Diarmaid. *Christianity: The First Three Thousand Years.* New York: Viking, 2010.

Machen, J. Gresham. *The Christian View of Man.* London: Banner of Truth, 1965.

———. *Christianity and Liberalism.* New York: Macmillan, 1923. Reprint, Grand Rapids: Eerdmans, 2009.

———. "Essentials for Prosperity." *The Annals of the American Academy of Political and Social Science* 165 (January 1933): 2–9.

Machen, J. Gresham, and Charles P. Fagnani. "Does Fundamentalism Obstruct Social Progress?" *The Survey Graphic* 5 (1924): 388–92, 425–27.

Mackintosh, Hugh Ross. *Types of Modern Theology: Schleiermacher to Barth.* London: Nisbet, 1956.

MacLeod, A. Donald. *W. Stanford Reid: An Evangelical Calvinist in the Academy.* Montreal: McGill-Queen's University Press, 2004.

Macleod, John. *Scottish Theology.* Edinburgh: Banner of Truth, 2015.

Macmillan, Donald. *John Knox: A Biography.* London: Andrew Melrose, 1905.

Macquarrie, John. *An Existentialist Theology: A Comparison of Heidegger and Bultmann.* New York and Evanston: Harper & Row, 1965.

———. *Principles of Christian Theology.* New York: Scribner's Sons, 1966.

———. "Rudolf Bultmann." In *A Handbook of Christian Theologians,* edited by Martin E. Marty and Dean G. Peerman. Nashville: Abingdon Press, 1985.

———. *The Scope of Demythologizing: Bultmann and His Critics.* New York: Harper & Row, 1961.

———. *Studies in Christian Existentialism.* Montreal: McGill-Queen's University Press, 1965.

Marcel, Gabriel. *Being and Having: An Existentialist Diary*. New York: Harper & Row, 1965.

Marenbon, John. *The Philosophy of Peter Abelard*. Cambridge: Cambridge University Press, 1997.

Markus, Robert A. "Marius Victorinus and Augustine." In *The Cambridge History of Later Greek and Early Medieval Philosophy*, edited by A. H. Armstrong, 331–424. Cambridge: Cambridge University Press, 1970.

———. "Trinitarian Theology and the Economy." *Journal of Theological Studies* 9, no. 1 (April 1958): 89–102.

Marsden, George M. *Evangelicalism and Modern America*. Grand Rapids: Eerdmans, 1984.

———. *Fundamentalism and American Culture: The Shaping of Twentieth-Century Evangelicalism, 1870–1925*. New York: Oxford University Press, 1980.

———. *Jonathan Edwards*. New Haven: Yale University Press, 2003.

Martensen, Hans Lassen. *Die christliche Dogmatik*. Charleston, SC: Nabu Press, 2011.

Martin, Seymour G. *A History of Philosophy*. New York: Appleton-Century-Crofts, 1941.

Marty, Martin E., and Dean G. Peerman, eds. *A Handbook of Christian Theologians*. Nashville: Abingdon Press, 1985.

Masselink, William. *General Revelation and Common Grace: A Defense of the Historic Reformed Faith over and against the Theology and Philosophy of the So-Called "Reconstructionist" Movement*. Grand Rapids: Eerdmans, 1953.

Matheson, Peter. *The Collected Works of Thomas Müntzer*. Edinburgh: T&T Clark, 1988.

Mathison, Keith A. "Unlatched Theism, An Examination of John Frame's Response to *All That Is in God*," *Tabletalk Magazine*, November 30, 2017.

Mattas, Mark C. *The Role of Justification in Contemporary Theology*. Grand Rapids: Eerdmans, 2004.

Mayer, Hans Eberhard. "Die Kanzlei Richards I von England auf dem Dritten Kreuzzug." *Kreuzzüge lateinischer Osten* 9. 1977. Reprint, London: Variorum Collected Studies, 1983.

MacArthur, John. *The Gospel According to Jesus*. Grand Rapids: Zondervan, 1994.

McCoy, Charles S. "Johannes Cocceius: Federal Theologian." *Scottish Journal of Theology* 16, no. 4 (1963): 352–70.

McCoy, F. N. *Robert Baillie and the Second Scots Reformation.* Los Angeles: University of California Press, 1974.

McCallum, James Ramsay. *Abelard's Christian Theology.* New York: Richwood Publishing, 1976.

McCullough, David M. *John Adams.* New York: Simon & Schuster, 2001.

McGiffert, Arthur Cushman. *A History of Christian Thought.* New York: Scribner's Sons, 1953.

McGoldrick, James Edward. *God's Renaissance Man: The Life and Work of Abraham Kuyper.* Auburn, MA: Evangelical Press, 2000.

McGrath, Alister E. "Forerunners of the Reformation? A Critical Examination of the Evidence for Precursors of the Reformation Doctrines of Justification." *Harvard Theological Review* 75, no. 1 (1982): 219–42.

McGraw, Ryan M. "Review: *Sons in the Son* by David B. Garner." *Ordained Servant*, February 2017. https://opc.org/os.html?article_id=607. Accessed July 1, 2019.

McKay, W. D. J. An Ecclesiastical Republic: Church Government in the Writings of George Gillespie. Edinburgh: Rutherford House, 1997.

———. "George Gillespie and the Westminster Assembly: The Defence of Presbyterianism." *Scottish Bulletin of Evangelical Theology* 13, no. 1 (1995): 51–71.

McKelway, Alexander T. "Magister Dialecticae et Optimarium Partium: Recollections of Karl Barth as Teacher." *Union Seminary Quarterly Review* 28, no. 1 (Fall 1972): 99–108.

McLelland, John C. *The Visible Words of God: An Exposition of the Sacramental Theology of Peter Martyr Vermigli.* Grand Rapids: Eerdmans, 1957.

———, ed. *Peter Martyr Vermigli and Italian Reform.* Waterloo, ON: Wilfrid Laurier University Press, 1980.

McLelland, John C., and G. E. Duffield, eds. *The Life, Early Letters and Eucharistic Writings of Peter Martyr.* Oxford: Sutton Courtenay Press, 1989.

McMillan, William. *The Worship of the Scottish Reformed Church, 1550–1638.* London: Clark, 1931.

Meagher, Robert E. *An Introduction to Augustine.* New York: New York University Press, 1978.

Medel, Arthur P. *The Twentieth Century, 1914–1964*. New York: Free Press, 1965.

Meijering, E. P. *Hilary of Poitiers on the Trinity*. Leiden: Brill, 1982.

Menand, Louis. *The Metaphysical Club: A Story of Ideas in America*. New York: Farrar Straus Giroux, 2001.

Mendel, Arthur P. *The Twentieth Century 1914–1964*. New York: Free Press, 1965.

Merlan, P. "Greek Philosophy from Plato to Plotinus." In *The Cambridge History of Later Greek and Early Medieval Philosophy*, edited by A. H. Armstrong, 14–136. Cambridge: Cambridge University Press, 1970.

Meyer, C. S. *Luther's and Zwingli's Propositions for Debate*. Leiden: Brill, 1963.

Migne, Jean-Paul. *Patrologiae Cursus Completus: Series Graeca*. Paris: Garnier Fratres, 1857.

———. *Patrologiae Cursus Completus: Series Latina*. Paris: Garnier Fratres, 1857.

Miller, Samuel. *An Essay on the Warrant, Nature and Duties of the Office of the Ruling Elder in the Presbyterian Church*. Jackson, MS: Presbyterian Heritage Publications, 1987.

Milne, Bruce. *Know the Truth*. Downers Grove, IL: InterVarsity Press, 1999.

Milton, Anthony. *The British Delegation and the Synod of Dort (1618–1619)*. Church of England Record Society 13. Suffolk: Boydell Press, 2005.

Minutes of the Thirty-fifth General Assembly, May 14–17, 1968. Philadelphia: The Orthodox Presbyterian Church, 1968.

Moessner, David P. *Lord of the Banquet: The Literary and Theological Significance of the Lukan Travel Narrative*. Minneapolis: Fortress, 1989.

Moltmann, Jürgen. *Hope and the Crucified God*. Minneapolis: Augsburg Fortress, 2015.

———. *Theology of Hope: On the Ground and the Implications of a Christian Eschatology*. London: SCM Press, 1967.

———. *The Trinity and the Kingdom*. Translated by Margaret Kohl. Philadelphia: Fortress, 1993.

Monter, William. *Calvin's Geneva*. New York: Wiley & Sons, 1967.

Montgomery, John Warwick, ed. *God's Inerrant Word: An International Symposium on the Trustworthiness of Scripture*. Minneapolis: Bethany Fellowship, 1974.

Moore, Edwin Nisbet. *Our Covenanter Heritage*. Fearn, Scotland: Christian Focus, 2000.

Moreland, J. P., and William Lane Craig. *Philosophical Foundations for a Christian Worldview*. Downer's Grove, IL: IVP Academic, 2003.

Morris, Thomas V. *Francis Schaeffer's Apologetic: A Critique*. Chicago: Moody Press, 1976.

Moss, Henry St. Lawrence Beaufort. *The Birth of the Middle Ages: 395–814*. Oxford: Clarendon, 1935.

Mounce, Robert H. *Romans*. Nashville: Broadman & Holman, 1995.

Mountain, W. J. *Sancti Aurelii Augustini. De Trinitiate Libri XV. Corpus Christianorum: Series Latina*. Turnholti: Typography Brepolis Editores Pontificii, 1968.

Muether, John R. *Cornelius Van Til: Reformed Apologist and Churchman*. Phillipsburg, NJ: P&R Publishing, 2008.

Muller, Richard A. Foreword to *All That Is in God*, by James Dolezal, ix–xii. Grand Rapids: Reformation Heritage, 2017.

———. *God, Creation, and Providence in the Thought of Jacob Arminius*. Grand Rapids: Baker, 1991.

———. "Aquinas Reconsidered." *Reformation21*, February 19, 2018, https://www.reformation21.org/articles/aquinas-reconsidered.php. Accessed January 20, 2019.

———. "Aquinas Reconsidered (Part 3)." *Reformation21*, March 5, 2018, https://www.reformation21.org/blogs/aquinas-reconsidered-part-3.php. Accessed January 20, 2019.

———. *Calvin and the Reformed Tradition*. Grand Rapids: Baker, 2012.

———. *Post-Reformation Reformed Dogmatics*. Vol. 1, *Prolegomena to Theology*. Grand Rapids: Baker, 1987.

Mundy, John Hine. *Europe in the High Middle Ages, 1150–1300*. London: Longman, 1973.

Murray, Iain H. *Evangelicalism Divided: A Record of Crucial Change in the Years 1952–2000*. Edinburgh: Banner of Truth, 2000.

———. *Jonathan Edwards: A New Biography*. Edinburgh: Banner of Truth, 1987.

Murray, John. *Baptism*. Phillipsburg, NJ: Presbyterian and Reformed, 1991.

———. *Calvin on Scripture and Divine Sovereignty*. Grand Rapids: Baker, 1960.

———. *Collected Writings of John Murray*. Edited by Iain Murray. 4 vols. Edinburgh: Banner of Truth, 1976–1982.

———. *The Covenant of Grace: a Biblico-Theological Study.* London: Tyndale Press, 1954.

———. *The Epistle to the Romans: The English Text, with Introduction, Exposition and Notes.* London: Marshall, Morgan & Scott, 1960.

———. *The Imputation of Adam's Sin.* 1959. Reprint, Nutley, NJ: Presbyterian and Reformed, 1977.

———. *O Death, Where is Thy Sting?* Philadelphia: Westminster Seminary Press, 2017.

———. *Principles of Conduct: Aspects of Biblical Ethics.* London: Tyndale Press, 1951.

———. *Redemption Accomplished and Applied.* Grand Rapids: Eerdmans, 1955.

———. "The Relation of Church and State." In *Collected Writings of John Murray*, edited by Iain Murray, 1:253–59 . Edinburgh: Banner of Truth, 1982.

———. "The Theology of the Westminster Confession." In *Scripture and Confession*, edited by John Skilton, 125–48. Nutley, NJ: Presbyterian and Reformed, 1973.

Murray, Thomas. *The Life of Samuel Rutherford.* Edinburgh: Oliphant, 1828.

Nagle, Thomas. *The Last Word.* New York: Oxford University Press, 1997.

Nash, Ronald H. *The Concept of God: An Exploration of Contemporary Difficulties with the Attributes of God.* Grand Rapids: Zondervan, 1983.

———. *Dooyeweerd and the Amsterdam Philosophy.* Grand Rapids: Zondervan, 1962.

———. *The Light of the Mind: St Augustine's Theory of Knowledge.* Lexington: The University Press of Kentucky, 1969.

Needham, Nicholas R. *2,000 Years of Christ's Power.* Vol. 1, *The Age of the Early Church Fathers.* London: Grace Publications, 1997.

———. *2,000 Years of Christ's Power.* Vol. 2, *The Middle Ages.* 2000. Reprint, London: Grace Publications, 2004.

———. *2,000 Years of Christ's Power.* Vol. 3, *Renaissance and Reformation.* London: Grace Publications, 2005.

Neele, Adriaan. "Life and Work." In *Theoretical-Practical Theology*, vol. 1, *Prolegomena*, by Petrus van Mastricht, edited by Joel R. Beeke, translated by Todd M. Rester, 1:xxv–lxiii. Grand Rapids: Reformation Heritage Books, 2018.

Nelson, John Oliver. "The Rise of the Princeton Theology: A Genetic Study of American Presbyterianism until 1830." PhD diss., Yale University, 1935.

Neuser, Wilhelm H. *Die reformatorische Wende bei Zwingli*. Neukirchen-Vluyn: Neukirchener Verlag, 1984.

Newton, John Thomas. "The Importance of Augustine's Use of the Neoplatonic Doctrine of Hypostatic Union for the Development of Christology." *Augustinian Studies* 2 (1971): 1–17.

Niebuhr, Reinhold. *Children of Light and Children of Darkness: A Vindication of Democracy and a Critique of Its Traditional Defense*. New York: Scribner's Sons, 1944.

———. *Does Civilization Need Religion?* New York: Macmillan, 1927.

———. *Moral Man and Immoral Society: A Study in Ethics and Politics*. New York: Scribner's Sons, 1932.

———. *The Nature and Destiny of Man*. 2 vols. New York: Scribner's Sons, 1941–1943.

Niebuhr, Richard R. "Friedrich Schleiermacher." In *A Handbook of Christian Theologians*, edited by Martin E. Marty and Dean G. Peerman, 17–35. Nashville: Abingdon Press, 1985.

———. *Schleiermacher on Christ and Religion*. New York: Scribner's Sons, 1964.

Niesel, W. *The Theology of Calvin*. Translated by H. Knight. Grand Rapids: Baker, 1980.

Nietzsche, Friedrich. *The Complete Works*. 18 vols. London: Allen & Unwin, 1909–1913.

———. "On Truth and Lie in an Extra-Moral Sense." In *The Portable Nietzsche*, edited and translated by Walter Kaufmann, 42–46. New York: Viking Press, 1954.

———. *The Portable Nietzsche*. Edited and translated by Walter Kaufmann. New York: Viking Press, 1954.

Nixon, LeRoy. *John Calvin: Expository Preacher*. Grand Rapids: Eerdmans, 1950.

Noll, Mark A. "The Innocence of Billy Graham." *First Things* 79 (January 1998): 34–40.

———. *The Princeton Theology, 1812–1921: Scripture, Science, and Theological Method from Archibald Alexander to Benjamin Breckinridge Warfield*. Grand Rapids: Baker, 1983.

———. *The Scandal of the Evangelical Mind*. Grand Rapids: Eerdmans, 2008.

———. "The Spirit of Old Princeton and the Spirit of the OPC." In *Pressing Toward the Mark: Essays Commemorating Fifty Years of the Orthodox Presbyterian Church*, edited by Charles G. Dennison and Richard C. Gamble, 235–46. Philadelphia: Committee for the Historian of the Orthodox Presbyterian Church, 1986.

Nugent, Donald. *Ecumenism in the Age of the Reformation*. Cambridge: Harvard University Press, 1974.

Oakley, Francis. *Omnipotence, Covenant, and Order: An Excursion in the History of Ideas from Abelard to Leibniz*. Ithaca, NY: Cornell University Press, 1984.

Oberman, Heiko Augustinus. *The Dawn of the Reformation: Essays in Late Medieval and Early Reformation Thought*. Edinburgh: T&T Clark, 1986.

———. *Forerunners of the Reformation*. Philadelphia: Fortress, 1981.

———. *The Harvest of Medieval Theology: Gabriel Biel and Late Medieval Nominalism*. Cambridge: Harvard University Press, 1963.

———. "*Quo Vadis, Petre?* Tradition from Irenaeus to Humani Generis." In *The Dawn of the Reformation: Essays in Late Medieval and Early Reformation Thought*, by Heiko Augustinus Oberman, 259–96. Edinburgh: T&T Clark, 1986.

Obitts, Stanley. "The Meaning and Use of Religious Language." In *Tensions in Contemporary Theology*, edited by Stanley N. Gundry and Alan F. Johnson, 105–56. Grand Rapids: Baker, 1976.

Ogden, Schubert M. *The Reality of God and Other Essays*. New York: Harper & Row, 1966.

Ogden, Schubert M., and Charles Hartshorne. *Theology in Crisis: A Colloquium on the Credibility of God*. New Concord, OH: Muskingum College, 1967.

O'Lachlan, Thomas. *The Didache: A Window on the Earliest Christians*. London: SPCK, 2011.

Olasky, Marvin. *The American Leadership Tradition*. Wheaton, IL: Crossway, 1999.

Old, Hughes Oliphint. *The Patristic Roots of Reformed Worship (American Edition)*. Black Mountain, NC: Worship Press, 2004.

Olinger, Danny E. *Geerhardus Vos: Reformed Biblical Theologian, Confessional Presbyterian*. Philadelphia: Reformed Forum 2018.

Oliphint, K. Scott. *The Battle Belongs to the Lord: The Power of Scripture for Defending Our Faith*. Phillipsburg, NJ: P&R Publishing, 2003.

———. "Bavinck's Realism, the Logos Principle and Sola Scriptura." *Westminster Theological Journal* 72, no. 2 (2010): 359–90.

———. "The Consistency of Van Til's Methodology." *Westminster Theologial Journal* 52, no. 1 (Spring 1990): 27–49.

———. "Cornelius Van Til and the Reformation of Christian Apologetics." In *Revelation and Reason*, edited by K. Scott Oliphint and Lane G. Tipton, 279–303. Phillipsburg, NJ: P&R Publishing, 2007.

———. *Covenantal Apologetics: Principles and Practice in Defense of Our Faith*. Wheaton, IL: Crossway, 2013.

———. Forward and preface to *Christian Theistic Evidences*, by Cornelius Van Til, ix–xxxv. Phillipsburg, NJ: P&R Publishing, 2016.

———. "The Irrationality of Unbelief: An Exegetical Study." In *Revelation and Reason*, edited by K. Scott Oliphint and Lane G. Tipton, 59–73. Phillipsburg, NJ: P&R Publishing, 2007.

———. "Machen and Philosophy." In *Christianity and Liberalism*, by J. Gresham Machen, 203–6. Legacy ed. Philadelphia: Westminster Seminary Press, 2019.

———. "The Old-New Reformed Epistemology." In *Revelation and Reason*, edited by K. Scott Oliphint and Lane G. Tipton, 207–19. Phillipsburg, NJ: P&R Publishing, 2007.

———. *Thomas Aquinas*. Phillipsburg, NJ: P&R Publishing, 2017.

———, ed. *Justified in Christ: God's Plan for Us in Justification*. Fearn, Scotland: Mentor, 2007.

Oliphint, K. Scott, and Lane G. Tipton, eds. *Revelation and Reason*. Phillipsburg, NJ: P&R Publishing, 2007.

Oliver, Herbert C. *No Flesh Shall Glory*. Philadelphia: Presbyterian and Reformed, 1959.

Ong, Walter J. *Ramus, Method, and the Decay of Dialogue: From the Art of Discourse to the Art of Reason*. Cambridge: Harvard University Press, 1958.

Orr, James. *The Progress of Dogma*. New York: Armstrong, 1908.

Orr, Robert Low. *Alexander Henderson: Churchman and Statesman*. London: Hodder & Stoughton, 1919.

Ortlund, Dane. "Reflections on Handling the Old Testament as Jesus Would Have Us: Psalm 15 as a Case Study." *Themelios* 42, no. 1 (2017): 74–88. https://www.thegospelcoalition.org/themelios/article/reflections-on

-handling-the-old-testament-as-jesus-would-have-us-psalm-15/. Accessed January 20, 2019.

Owen, John. *Biblical Theology*. Morgan, PA: Soli Deo Gloria, 1996.

———. *The Works of John Owen*. Edited by William H. Goold. 16 vols. Edinburgh: Banner of Truth, 1965.

Owens, Joseph. *The Doctrine of Being in the Aristotelian Metaphysics: A Study in the Background of Medieval Thought*. Toronto: Pontifical Institute of Medieval Studies, 1963.

Ozment, Steven. *The Age of Reform, 1250–1550*. New Haven: Yale University Press, 1980.

Packer, J. I. Foreword to *Biblical Theology*, by John Owen, xi–xiii. Morgan, PA: Soli Deo Gloria, 1996.

———. "Introduction: On Covenant Theology." In *The Economy of the Covenants*, by Herman Witsius, 1:1–18. Escondido, CA: The den Dulk Foundation/Presbyterian and Reformed, 1990.

———. Introduction to *The Doctrine of Justification: An Outline of Its History in the Church and of Its Exposition from Scripture*, by James Buchanan, vii–xv. Edinburgh: Banner of Truth, 1991.

Palmer, B. M. *Theology of Prayer*. Hinton, VA: Sprinkle Publications, 1980.

Parker, T. H. L. *John Calvin: A Biography*. Philadelphia: Westminster Press, 1975.

———. *The Oracles of God: An Introduction to the Preaching of John Calvin*. London: Lutterworth, 1947.

Pauck, Wilhelm. "Adolf von Harnack." In *A Handbook of Christian Theologians*, edited by Martin E. Marty and Dean G. Peerman, 86–111. Nashville: Abingdon Press, 1985.

———. "A Brief Criticism of Barth's Dogmatics." In *From Luther to Tillich: The Reformers and Their Heirs*, 146–51. New York: Harper & Row, 1984.

———. *From Luther to Tillich: The Reformers and Their Heirs*. Edited by Marion Pauck. New York: Harper & Row, 1984.

———, ed. *Luther: Lectures on Romans*. Philadelphia: Westminster John Knox Press, 1961.

Paul, Robert S. *The Assembly of the Lord: Politics and Religion in the Westminster Assembly and the 'Grand Debate.'* Edinburgh: T&T Clark, 1985.

Pearcey, Nancy R., and Charles B. Thaxton. *The Soul of Science*. Wheaton, IL: Crossway, 1994.

Perkins, William. *The Calling of the Ministry*. Edited by Sinclair Ferguson. Edinburgh: Banner of Truth, 1996.

Petersen, William L. *Tatian's Diatessaron: Its Creation, Dissemination, Significance, and History in Scholarship*. Leiden: Brill, 1994.

Petry, Ray C., ed. *Late Medieval Mysticism*. London: SCM Press, 1957.

Pinnock, Clark. *Set Forth Your Case: Studies in Christian Apologetics*. Chicago: Moody Press, 1971.

Plantinga, Alvin. *Does God Have a Nature?* Milwaukee: Marquette University Press, 1980.

———, ed. *The Ontological Argument from St. Anselm to Contemporary Philosophers*. Garden City, NY: Anchor Books, 1965.

Plantinga, Cornelius, Jr. *Not the Way It's Supposed to Be: A Breviary of Sin*. Grand Rapids: Eerdmans, 1995.

———. "Social Trinity and Tritheism." In *A Reader in Contemporary Philosophical Theology*, edited by Oliver D. Crisp, 67–89. London: T&T Clark, 2009.

Plato. *The Trial and Death of Socrates: Being the Euthyphron, Apology, Crito, and Phaedo of Plato*. Translated by F. J. Church. London: Macmillan, 1927.

Polanyi, Michael. "Beyond Nihilism (1960)." In *Knowing and Being*, by Michael Polanyi, 3–23. Chicago: University of Chicago Press, 1969.

———. "Faith and Reason." *Journal of Religion* 41, no. 4 (1961): 237–47.

———. *Knowing and Being*. Edited by Marjorie Greene. London: Routledge/Kegan Paul, 1961.

———. *The Logic of Liberty*. London: Routledge/Kegan Paul, 1951.

———. *Personal Knowledge: Towards a Post-Critical Philosophy*. 1958. Reprint, Chicago: University of Chicago Press, 1962.

———. *Science, Faith, and Society*. 1945. Reprint, Chicago/London: University of Chicago Press, 1964.

———. *The Study of Man*. 1951. Reprint, Chicago/London: University of Chicago Press, 1959.

———. *The Tacit Dimension*. Chicago/London: University of Chicago Press, 1966.

———. "The Two Cultures (1959)." In *Knowing and Being*, by Michael Polanyi, 40–48. Chicago: University of Chicago Press, 1969.

Polman, A. D. R. *Barth*. An International Library of Philosophy and Theology. Philadelphia: Presbyterian and Reformed, 1960.

Postman, Neil. *Amusing Ourselves to Death: Public Discourse in the Age of Show Business*. New York: Penguin Books, 1986.

Potter, G. R. *Zwingli*. Cambridge: Cambridge University Press, 1976.

Poythress, Diane. *Reformer of Basel: The Life, Thought, and Influence of Johannes Oecolampadius*. Grand Rapids: Reformation Heritage Books, 2011.

Poythress, Vern S. "Christianity and Liberalism and Hermeneutical Presuppositions." In *Christianity and Liberalism*, by J. Gresham Machen, 263–65, legacy ed. Philadelphia: Westminster Seminary Press, 2019.

Praamsma, L. *Let Christ Be King: Reflections on the Life and Times of Abraham Kuyper*. Thorold, ON: Paideia Press, 1985.

Prestige, George Leonard. *Fathers and Heretics*. London: SPCK, 1940.

———. *God in Patristic Thought*. London: SPCK, 1952.

Quasten, Johannes. *Patrology*. 3 vols. Utrecht: Spectrum, 1975.

Quistorp, Heinrich. *Calvin's Doctrine of the Last Things*. Louisville: John Knox Press, 1955.

Rabil, Albert. *Erasmus and the New Testament: The Mind of a Christian Humanist*. San Antonio, TX: Trinity University Press, 1972.

Rae, C. E. "The Political Thought of Samuel Rutherford." MA thesis, University of Guelph, 1991.

Ramsey, Ian. "Polanyi and J. L. Austin." In *Intellect and Hope: Essays in the Thought of Michael Polanyi*, edited by A. Langford and W. Poteat, 169–97. Durham: Duke University Press, 1968.

Ramsey, Paul. Introduction to *Freedom of the Will*, by Jonathan Edwards, edited by Paul Ramsey, 1:1–127. New Haven: Yale University Press, 1957.

Rauschenbusch, Walter. *Christianity and the Social Crisis in the 21st Century*, edited by Paul Rauschenbush. New York: HarperOne, 2007.

Read, Piers Paul. *The Templars*. Cambridge, MA: Da Capo Press, 1999.

Reed, Kevin. "Biographical Sketch of Samuel Miller." In *Holding Fast the Faithful Word: Sermons and Addresses by Samuel Miller*, ix–xxxii. Grand Rapids: Reformation Heritage Books, 2018.

Rehnman, U. S. G. "Theologia Traditia: A Study in the Prolegomenous Discourse of John Owen (1616–1683)." PhD diss., University of Oxford, 1997.

Reichley, James. *Religion in American Public Life*. Washington, DC: Brookings Institute, 1985.

Reicke, Bo. *The Disobedient Spirits and Christian Baptism*. New York: AMS Press, 1984.

Reid, James. *Memoirs of the Lives and Writings of Those Eminent Divines Who Convened in the Famous Assembly at Westminster in the Seventeenth Century.* Paisley, Scotland: Young, 1815.

Rendell, K. G. *Samuel Rutherford: The Man and His Ministry.* Fearn, Scotland: Christian Focus, 2003.

Reymond, Robert L. *Introductory Studies in Contemporary Theology.* Philadelphia: Presbyterian and Reformed, 1968.

———. *The Justification of Knowledge: An Introductory Study in Christian Apologetic Methodology.* Nutley, NJ: Presbyterian and Reformed, 1976.

———. *A New Systematic Theology of the Christian Faith.* Nashville: Thomas Nelson, 1998.

Rice, Eugene F. *The Foundations of Early Modern Europe 1460–1559.* New York: Norton, 1970.

Richardson, Cyril C. "The Enigma of the Trinity." In *A Companion to the Study of St. Augustine,* edited by Roy W. Battenhouse, 235–56. New York: Oxford University Press, 1956.

Ricœur, Paul. *The Conflict of Interpretations: Essays in Hermeneutics.* Evanston, IL: Northwestern University Press, 1974.

———. *Fallible Man.* Translated by Charles Kelbley. Chicago: Henry Regnery, 1965.

———. *Freud and Philosophy: An Essay on Interpretation.* New Haven: Yale University Press, 1970.

———. *Hermeneutics and the Human Sciences.* Cambridge: Cambridge University Press, 1981.

———. *History and Truth* (Evanston, IL: Northwestern University Press, 1965.

———. *Memory, History, Forgetting.* Translated by Kathleen Blamey and David Pellauer. Chicago: University of Chicago Press, 2004.

———. *Oneself as Another.* Chicago: University of Chicago Press, 1992.

———. *The Rule of Metaphor.* 1975. ET, London: Routledge/Kegan Paul, 1978.

———. *From Text to Action.* Evanston, IL: Northwestern University Press, 1991.

———. *Time and Narrative.* 3 vols. 1983–1985. ET, Chicago: University of Chicago Press, 1984–1988.

Ridderbos, Herman. *The Authority of the New Testament Scriptures.* Grand Rapids: Baker, 1963.

———. *Paul: An Outline of His Theology*. Grand Rapids: Eerdmans, 1997.

Riddlebarger, Kim. *The Lion of Princeton: B. B. Warfield as Apologist and Theologian*. Bellingham, WA: Lexham Press, 2015.

Ridley, Jasper. *Statesman and Saint: Cardinal Wolsey, Sir Thomas More and the Politics of Henry VIII*. New York: Viking Press, 1983.

———. *John Knox*. Oxford: Clarendon, 1968.

Ritschl, Dietrich. *Athanasius: Versuch einer Interpretation*. Zürich: Theologische Studien, 1964.

Robbins, John W. *Cornelius Van Til: The Man and the Myth*. Dallas: Trinity Foundation, 1986.

Robinson, James M., and John B. Cobb Jr. *New Frontiers in Theology: Discussions among Continental and American Theologians*. New York: Harper & Row, 1963.

Rodgers, R. E. L. *The Incarnation of the Antithesis: An Introduction to the Educational Thought and Practice of Abraham Kuyper*. Edinburgh: Pentland Press, 1992.

Rogers, Jack B., and Donald K. McKim. *The Authority and Interpretation of the Bible*. San Francisco: Harper & Row, 1979.

Rogerson, Barnaby. *The Heirs of Muhammad: Islam's First Century and the Origins of the Sunni-Shia Split*. New York: Overlook Press, 2006.

Rohls, Jan. "Ist Gott notwendig?—Zu einer These von E. Jüngels." *Neue Zeitschrift für Systematische Theologie und Religionsphilosophie* 22 (1980): 282–96.

Rorty, Richard. *Consequences of Pragmatism: Essays 1972–1980*. Minneapolis: University of Minnesota Press, 1982.

———. *Contingency, Irony, and Solidarity*. New York: Cambridge University Press, 1989.

———. *Philosophy and the Mirror of Nature*. 1979. Reprint, Princeton: Princeton University Press, 1980.

———. "Redemption from Egotism: James and Proust as Spiritual Exercises." *Telos* 3, no. 3 (2001): 243–63.

———. "Solidarity or Objectivity?" In *Objectivity, Relativism and Truth*, by Richard Rorty, 21–34. Cambridge: Cambridge University Press, 1991.

———. *Truth and Progress*. Philosophical Papers 3. Cambridge: Cambridge University Press, 1998.

Ross, J. M. "Samuel Rutherford." *The Month* 236 (1975): 207–11.

Ross, Sir David. *Aristotle*. New York: Routledge, 2004.

——. *Plato's Theory of Ideas*. Oxford: Clarendon, 1951.

Rousseau, Jean-Jacques. *A Discourse on the Moral Effects of the Arts and Sciences*. London: Dent, 1961.

——. *The Social Contract*. Translated by G. D. H. Cole. London: Dent, 1961.

Ruegsegger, Ronald W., ed. *Reflections on Francis Schaeffer*. Grand Rapids: Zondervan, 1986.

Rupp, E. Gordon. "Christian Doctrine from 1350 to the Eve of the Reformation." In *A History of Christian Doctrine*, edited by Hubert Cunliffe-Jones, 287–304. 1978. Reprint, New York: T&T Clark, 2006.

——. *Luther and Erasmus*. Library of Christian Classics. Philadelphia: Westminster John Knox Press, 1969.

——. *Patterns of Reformation*. London: Epworth, 1969.

Russell, C. Allyn. *Voices of Fundamentalism: Seven Biographical Studies*. Philadelphia: Westminster Press, 1976.

Russell, Bertrand. *A History of Western Philosophy*. New York: Simon & Schuster, 1945.

Rutherford, Samuel. *Christ Dying and Drawing Sinners to Himselfe*. London: Andrew Crooke, 1647.

——. *The Letters of Samuel Rutherford*. Edinburgh: Banner of Truth, 1984.

——. *Loveliness of Christ*. Edinburgh: Banner of Truth, 2007.

——. *Rutherford's Catechism*. Edinburgh, Scotland: Blue Banner, 1998.

——. *The Trial and Triumph of Faith*. Edinburgh: Banner of Truth, 2001.

Sacramone, Anthony. "An Interview with Tim Keller." *First Things*, February 2008. https://www.firstthings.com/web-exclusives/2008/02/an-interview -with-timothy-kell. Accessed January 12, 2015.

Sammons, Peter. *Reprobation: From Augustine to the Synod of Dort—The Historical Development of the Reformed Doctrine of Reprobation*. Göttingen: Vandenhoeck & Ruprecht, 2020.

Sanders, E. P. *Paul and Palestinian Judaism*. Philadelphia: Fortress, 1977.

Sanders, John. *The God Who Risks: A Theology of Providence*. Downers Grove, IL: InterVarsity Press, 1998.

Sandlin, P. Andrew. *A Faith That Is Never Alone: A Response to Westminster Seminary in California*. Mount Hermon, CA: Kerygma Press, 2008.

——, ed. *Backbone of the Bible: Covenant in Contempory Perspective*. Nacogdoches, TX: Covenant Media Press, 2004.

Sandlin, P. Andrew, and John Barak, eds. *Obedient Faith: A Festschrift for Norman Shepherd*. Mount Hermon, CA.: Kerygma Press, 2012.

Sartre, Jean-Paul. *Being and Nothingness*. Secaucus, NJ: Citadel, 1977.

——. *Existentialism Is a Humanism*. New Haven: Yale University Press, 2007.

Scarisbrick, J. J. *Henry VIII*. Berkeley: University of California Press, 1968.

Schaeffer, Francis A. *The Church at the End of the 20th Century*. Downers Grove, IL: InterVarsity Press, 1970.

——. *Death in the City*. Wheaton, IL: Crossway, 1969.

——. *Escape from Reason*. Chicago: InterVarsity Press, 1968.

——. *The God Who Is There*. Downers Grove, IL: InterVarsity Press, 1968.

——. *How Should We Then Live?* Westchester, IL: Crossway, 1983.

Schaff, Philip. *The Creeds of Christendom*. Grand Rapids: Baker, 1984.

——. *History of the Christian Church*. 8 vols. Grand Rapids: Eerdmans, 1979.

Schleiermacher, Friedrich. *The Christian Faith*. Edited by H. R. Mackintosh and J. S. Stewart. 1928. Reprint, New York: Harper, 1963. Reprint, Edinburgh: T&T Clark, 1989.

——. *On Religion: Speeches to Its Cultured Despisers*. Rev. ed. Philadelphia: Westminster John Knox Press, 1974.

Schmidt, Kurt D. *Grundriss der Kirchengeschichte*. Göttingen: Vandenhoek & Ruprecht, 1963.

Schmidt, Reinhold. *Marius Victorinus Rhetor und seine Beziehungen zu Augustin*. Kiel: Uebermuth, 1985.

Schmitt, Charles B. *Aristotle and the Renaissance*. Cambridge: Harvard University Press, 1983.

Schneemelcher, Wilhelm, and R. M. Wilson. *New Testament Apocrypha: Writings Related to the Apostles*. Louisville: Westminster John Knox Press, 1992.

Schoenwald, Richard L. *Nineteenth-Century Thought: The Discovery of Change*. Englewood Cliffs, NJ: Prentice Hall, 1965.

Schrenk, Gottlob. *Gottesreich und Bund im altern Protestantismus vornehmlich bei Johannes Coccejus*. 1923. Reprint, Giessen: Brunnen, 1985.

Schweitzer, Albert. *The Quest of the Historical Jesus: A Critical Study of Its Progress from Reimarus to Wrede*. Translated by W. Montgomery. London: Black, 1910.

Scott, Drusilla. *Everyman Revived*. Grand Rapids: Eerdmans, 1985.

Scott, Thomas. *Thomas Muntzer: Theology and Revolution in the German Reformation*. New York: St. Martin's Press, 1989.

Searle, John. *The Construction of Social Reality*. New York: Free Press, 1995.

———. *Mind, Language, and Society: Philosophy in the Real World*. New York: Free Press, 1995.

Seeburg, R. *Text-Book of the History of Doctrines*. Grand Rapids: Baker, 1977.

Seeman, Bradley N. "The 'Old Princetonians' on Biblical Authority." In *The Enduring Authority of the Christian Scriptures*, edited by D. A. Carson, 195–237. Grand Rapids: Eerdmans, 2016.

Selderhuis, Herman J. *Calvinus Pastor Ecclesiae*. Göttingen: Vandenhoeck & Ruprecht, 2016.

Sell, Alan P. F. *John Locke and the Eighteenth-century Divines*. Cardiff: University of Wales Press, 1997.

Sellers, R. V. *The Council of Chalcedon: A Historical and Doctrinal Survey*. London: SPCK, 1953.

Seutonius. *Lives of the Twelve Caesars*. Charles River Editors, 2018. Atla Epub.

Shedd, William G. T. *A History of Christian Doctrine*. 2 vols. Minneapolis: Klock & Klock, 1978.

Sheldon-Williams, I. P. "Greek Christian Platonist Tradition." In *The Cambridge History of Later Greek and Early Medieval Philosophy*, edited by A. H. Armstrong, 425–537. Cambridge: Cambridge University Press, 1970.

Shepherd, Norman. *The Call of Grace: How the Covenant Illuminates Salvation and Evangelism*. Phillipsburg, NJ: P&R Publishing, 2000.

Shestov, Lev. *Athens and Jerusalem*. New York: Simon & Shuster, 1966.

Simonetti, Manlio. "S. Agostino e gli Ariani." *Revue d'Études Augustiniennes et Patristiques* 13 (1967): 55–84.

Simons, Menno. *The Complete Writings of Menno Simons*. Edited by J. C. Wenger. Translated by Leonard Verduin. Scottdale, PA: Herald Press, 1984.

Simonson, Harold. *Jonathan Edwards: Theologian of the Heart*. Grand Rapids: Eerdmans, 1974.

Singer, E. A., Jr. *Experience and Reflection*. Philadelphia: University of Pennsylvania Press, 1959.

Singer, C. Gregg. *A Theological Interpretation of American History*. Phillipsburg, NJ: Presbyterian and Reformed, 1981.

Smith, David L. *With Willful Intent: A Theology of Sin*. Wheaton, IL: Victor Books, 1994.

Smith, Margaret. *Introduction to the History of Mysticism*. London: SPCK, 1930.

Southern, R. W. *The Making of the Middle Ages*. New Haven: Yale University Press, 1992.

———. *Western Society and the Church in the Middle Ages*. The Pelican History of the Church 2. Middlesex, England: Pelican Books, 1976.

Spear, Wayne R. *Covenanted Uniformity in Religion: The Influence of the Scottish Commissioners upon the Ecclesiology of the Westminster Assembly*. Grand Rapids: Reformation Heritage Books, 2013.

———. *Faith of Our Fathers: A Commentary on the Westminster Confession of Faith*. Pittsburgh: Crown & Covenant, 2013.

Spinka, Matthew. *The Beginning and the End*. New York: Harper & Brothers, 1952.

———. *Nicolas Berdyaev, Captive of Freedom*. Philadelphia: Westminster Press, 1950.

———. *Truth and Revelation*. New York: Scribner's Sons, 1953.

Spitz, Lewis W. *The Renaissance and Reformation Movements*. St. Louis: Concordia, 1971.

Springer, Keith L. *The Learned Dr. William Ames*. Urbana, IL: University of Illinois Press, 1972.

Sproul, R. C. "The Case for Inerrancy: A Methodological Analysis." In *God's Inerrant Word: An International Symposium on the Trustworthiness of Scripture*, edited by John Warwick Montgomery, 248–49, 59. Minneapolis: Bethany Fellowship, 1974.

———. "TULIP and Reformed Theology: Limited Atonement," *Ligonier Ministries*, April 8, 2017. https://www.ligonier.org/blog/tulip-and-reformed-theology-limited-atonement/. Accessed June 12, 2017.

Sproul, R. C., John Gerstner, and Arthur Lindsley. *Classical Apologetics: A Rational Defense of the Christian Faith and a Critique of Presuppositional Apologetics*. Grand Rapids: Academie Books, 1984.

Staehelin, Ernst. *Die Verkündigung des Reiches Gottes in der Kirche Jesu Christi*. Vol. 1, *Von der Zeit der Apostel bis zur Auflösung des Römischen Reiches*. Basel: Reinhardt, 1951.

Stark, Rodney. *God's Battalions: The Case for the Crusades*. San Francisco: HarperOne, 2009.

Stadtland, Tjarko. *Rechtfertigung und Heiligung bei Calvin*. Neukirchen-Vluyn: Neukirchener Verlag, 1972.

Steen, Peter J. *The Structure of Herman Dooyeweerd's Thought*. Toronto: Wedge, 1983.

Stephens, W. P. *The Theology of Huldrych Zwingli*. Oxford: Clarendon, 1986.

Stetzer, Ed. "The Third Wave: The Continualist Movement Continues." *Christianity Today*, October 23, 2013. https://www.christianitytoday .com/edstetzer/2013/october/third-wave.html. Accessed January 15, 2019.

Stivason, Jeffrey A. *From Inscrutability to Concursus: Benjamin B. Warfield's Theological Construction of Revelation's Mode from 1880 to 1915*. Phillipsburg, NJ: P&R Publishing, 2017.

Stoeffler, F. E. *German Pietism during the Eighteenth Century*. Leiden: Brill, 1973.

———. *The Rise of Evangelical Pietism*. Leiden: Brill, 1965.

Stonehouse, Ned B. *J. Gresham Machen: A Biographical Memoir*. Grand Rapids: Eerdmans, 1954.

Strickland, D. "Union with Christ in the Theology of Samuel Rutherford: An Examination of His Doctrine of the Holy Spirit." PhD diss., University of Edinburgh, 1972.

Strimple, Robert B. *The Modern Search for the Real Jesus: An Introductory Survey of the Historical Roots of Gospel Criticism*. Phillipsburg, NJ: P&R Publishing, 1995.

Stroll, Avrum. *Epistemology: New Essays in the Theory of Knowledge*. San Francisco: Harper & Row, 1967.

Swain, Scott R. "Divine Trinity." In *Christian Dogmatics: Reformed Theology for the Church Catholic*, edited by Michael Allen and Scott R. Swain, 78–106. Grand Rapids: Baker Academic, 2016.

———. "Dogmatics as Systematic Theology." In *The Task of Dogmatics: Explorations in Theological Method*, edited by Oliver D. Crisp and Fred Sanders, 49–69. Grand Rapids: Zondervan, 2017.

Symington, William. *Messiah the Prince*. Pittsburgh: Crown and Covenant, 2012.

Tacitus, Cornelius. *The Annals of Imperial Rome*. Translated and introduction by Michael Grant. Baltimore: Penguin Books, 1959.

Tangelder, Johan D. "Dr. Herman Bavinck, 1854–1921: Theologian of the Word." *Christian Renewal*, January 29, 2001, 14–15.

Taylor, A. E. *Plato, The Man and His Work*. London: Methuen, 1955.

Taylor, Mark. "The Boundless Love of God and the Bounds of Critical Reflection: Schubert Ogden's Contribution to a Theology of Liberation." *Journal of the American Academy of Religion* 57, no. 1 (Spring 1989): 103–47.

Temple, William. *Christianity and Social Order*. New York: Hammondsworth, 1942.

Tertullian. *Adversus Praxean*. Corpus Scriptorum Ecclesiasticorum Latinorum. Leipzig: Freytag, 1096.

Thiselton, Anthony. *Interpreting God and the Postmodern Self: On Meaning, Manipulation and Promise*. Grand Rapids: Eerdmans, 1995.

———. *The Two Horizons: New Testament Hermeneutics and Philosophical Description with Special Reference to Heidegger, Bultmann, Gadamer, and Wittgenstein*. 1980. Reprint, Grand Rapids: Eerdmans, 1993.

Thomson, Andrew. *John Owen: Prince of Puritans*. Reprint, Fearn, Scotland: Christian Focus 2004.

Tillich, Paul. *Biblical Religion and the Search for Ultimate Reality*. Chicago: University of Chicago Press, 1955.

———. *A Complete History of Christian Thought*. New York: Harper & Row, 1968.

———. *The Courage to Be*. New Haven: Yale University Press, 1952.

———. *The Eternal Now*. New York: Scribner's Sons, 1963.

———. *Morality and Beyond*. New York: Harper & Row, 1963.

———. *The Religious Situation*. Translated by H. Richard Niebuhr. New York: H. Holt and Co., 1932.

Tjernagel, Neelak. *Henry VIII and the Lutherans*. St. Louis: Concordia, 1965.

Toon, Peter. *God's Statesman: The Life and Work of John Owen—Pastor, Educator, Theologian*. Exeter: Paternoster, 1971.

Torrance, Thomas F. *The Hermeneutics of John Calvin*. Edited by A. I. C. Heron and Iain R. Torrance. Edinburgh: Scottish Academic Press, 1988.

Tracy, J. D. *Erasmus: The Growth of a Mind*. Geneva: Droz, 1972.

Treier, Daniel J. "Incarnation." In *Christian Dogmatics: Reformed Theology for the Church Catholic*, edited by Michael Allen and Scott R. Swain, 216–42. Grand Rapids: Baker Academic, 2016.

Troeltsch, Ernst. *Glaubenslehre*. Aalen, England: Scientia, 1981.

Trueman, Carl R. "The Impending Evangelical Crisis." *Evangelicals Now* (February 1998): https://www.e-n.org.uk/1998/02/features/the-impending-evangelical-crisis/. Accessed April 12, 2019.

———. *John Owen, Reformed Catholic*. Aldershot, England: Routledge, 2007.

———. "John Owen's Dissertation on Divine Justice: An Exercise in Christocentric Scholasticism." *Calvin Theological Journal* 33, no. 1 (1998): 87–103.

———. *Luther on the Christian Life*. Wheaton, IL: Crossway, 2015.

———. *The Rise and Triumph of the Modern Self: Cultural Amnesia, Expressive Individualism, and the Road to Sexual Revolution*. Wheaton, IL: Crossway, 2020.

———. "A Tract for the Times: James Buchanan's *The Doctrine of Justification in Historical and Theological Context*." In *The Faith Once Delivered*, edited by Anthony Selvagio, 33–42. Phillipsburg, NJ: P&R Publishing, 2007.

Trumper, Tim J. R.. "Review of David B. Garner, *Sons in the Son*," *Journal of the Evangelical Theological Society* 62, no. 1 (2019): 204–9.

Tucker, Robert C. *Philosophy & Myth in Karl Marx*. Cambridge: Cambridge University Press, 1961.

Tucker, Ruth A. *Katie Luther: First Lady of the Reformation*. Grand Rapids: Zondervan, 2017.

Tuckett, Christopher, ed. *2 Clement: Introduction, Text, and Commentary*. Oxford: Oxford University Press, 2012.

Turretin, Francis. *Institutes of Elenctic Theology*. Edited by James T. Dennison. Translated by George M. Giger. 3 vols. Phillipsburg, NJ: P&R Publishing, 1992–1997.

Underhill, Evelyn. *Mysticism: A Study in the Nature and Development of Man's Spiritual Consciousness*. Cleveland: Meridian Books, 1955.

Van den Brink, Gert. "Impetration and Application in John Owen's Theology." In *The Ashgate Research Companion to John Owen's Theology*, edited by Kelly M. Kapic and Mark Jones, 85–96. Farnham, England: Ashgate, 2012.

Van der Meer, Frederic. *Augustine the Bishop: The Life and Work of a Father of the Church*. Translated by B. Battershaw and G. R. Lamb. London: Sheed and Ward, 1978.

Van Dixhoorn, Chad. *Confessing the Faith: A Reader's Guide to the Westminster Confession of Faith*. Edinburgh: Banner of Truth, 2014.

———. *God's Ambassadors: The Westminster Assembly and the Reformation of the English Pulpit, 1643–53*. Grand Rapids: Reformation Heritage Books, 2017.

———. *The Minutes and Papers of the Westminster Assembly, 1643–53*. Oxford: Oxford University Press, 2012.

———. "Presbyterian Ecclesiologies at the Westminster Assembly." In *Church Polity and Politics in the British Atlantic World, 1635–66*, edited by H. Powell and E. Vernon, 104–29. Manchester: University of Manchester Press, 2020.

Van Gelder, Craig. "Postmodernism as an Emerging Worldview." *Calvin Theological Journal* 26, no. 2 (1991): 412–17.

Van Genderen, J., and W. H. Velema. *Concise Reformed Dogmatics.* Translated by Gerrit Bilkes and Ed M. van der Maas. Phillipsburg, NJ: P&R Publishing, 2008.

Van Mastricht, Petrus. *Theoretical-Practical Theology.* Translated by Todd M. Rester. Edited by Joel R. Beeke. Grand Rapids: Reformation Heritage Books, 2018.

Van Til, Cornelius. *Bavinck the Theologian.* Philadelphia: Westminster Theological Seminary, 1961.

———. *Christian Theistic Evidences.* Edited by K. Scott Oliphint. Phillipsburg, NJ: Presbyterian and Reformed, 2016.

———. *A Christian Theory of Knowledge.* Nutley, NJ: Presbyterian and Reformed, 1969.

———. *Christianity and Barthianism.* Philadelphia: Presbyterian and Reformed, 1962. Reprint, Phillipsburg, NJ: P&R Publishing, 2004.

———. *Common Grace and the Gospel.* Nutley, NJ: Presbyterian and Reformed, 1972.

———. *The Defense of the Faith.* Philadelphia: Presbyterian and Reformed, 1955.

———. *The Great Debate Today.* Nutley, NJ: Presbyterian and Reformed, 1971.

———. *Introduction to Systematic Theology.* 2nd ed. Phillipsburg, NJ: P&R Publishing, 2007.

———. "My Credo." In *Jerusalem and Athens: Critical Discussions on the Theology and Apologetics of Cornelius Van Til,* edited by E. R. Geehan, 1–22. Nutley, NJ: Presbyterian and Reformed, 1971.

———. *The New Hermeneutic.* Nutley, NJ: Presbyterian and Reformed, 1974.

———. *The New Modernism.* Louisville: Presbyterian Publishing Co., 1946.

———. *A Survey of Christian Epistemology.* Nutley, NJ: Presbyterian and Reformed, 1977.

———. *Toward a Reformed Apologetics.* Philadelphia: privately printed, 1972.

———. "What Shall We Feed Our Children? A Plea for Christian Education." *Presbyterian Guardian,* October 24, 1936, 23–24.

———. *Who Do You Say That I Am?* Nutley, NJ: Presbyterian and Reformed, 1975.

Van Unnik, W. C., ed. *Neotestamentica et Patristica*. Leiden: Brill, 1962.

Vandenberg, Frank. *Abraham Kuyper*. Grand Rapids: Eerdmans, 1960.

VanDrunen, David. "A Contested Union." In *The Doctrine on which the Church Stands or Falls*, edited by Matthew Barrett, 469–504. Wheaton, IL: Crossway, 2019.

Vanhoozer, Kevin J. "Analytics, Poetics, and the Mission of Dogmatic Discourse." In *The Task of Dogmatics: Explorations in Theological Method*, edited by Oliver D. Crisp and Fred Sanders, 23–48. Grand Rapids: Zondervan, 2017.

———. *The Drama of Doctrine: A Canonical-Linguistic Approach to Christian Theology*. Louisville: Westminster John Knox Press, 2005.

———. *Remythologizing Theology: Divine Action, Passion, and Authorship*. Cambridge: Cambridge University Press, 2010.

———, ed. *The Cambridge Companion to Postmodern Philosophy*. Cambridge: Cambridge University Press, 2003.

Van't Spijker, Willem. "Bucer's Influence on Calvin: Church and Community." In *Martin Bucer: Reforming Church and Community*, edited by David F. Wright, 32–44. Cambridge: Cambridge University Press, 1994.

Veith, Gene Edward, Jr. *Postmodern Times: A Christian Guide to Contemporary Thought and Culture*. Wheaton, IL: Crossway, 1994.

———. *Reading between the Lines: A Christian Guide to Literature*. Wheaton, IL: Crossway, 2013.

Venema, Cornelis. *Chosen in Christ: Revisiting the Contours of Predestination*. Fearn, Scotland: Christian Focus, 2019.

Volf, Miroslav. *Exclusion and Embrace: A Theological Exploration of Identity, Otherness and Reconciliation*. Nashville: Abingdon Press, 1996.

Von Campenhausen, Hans Freiherr. *Griechische Kirchenväter*. Stuttgart: Kohlhammer, 1977.

von Harnack, Adolf. *History of Dogma*. Translated by Neil Buchanan. Boston: Little, Brown, 1902.

———. *Thoughts on the Present Position of Protestantism*. Translated by Thomas Saunders. London: Black, 1899.

Von Hase, Karl. *Kirchengeschichte: Lehrbuch, zunächst für academische Vorlesungen*. Leipzig: Breitkopf & Härtel, 1836.

Von Mosheim. J. L. *Institutionum historiae ecclesticae antiquae et recentoris libri quatuor*. Helmstedt, 1755.

von Schelling, Friedrich Wilhelm Joseph. *Lectures on the Method of Academic Studies*. Translated by E. E. Harris and P. Heath. Cambridge: Cambridge University Press, 1988.

Von Schubert, Hans. *Geschichte der christlichen Kirche im Frühmittelalter*. Tübingen: Mohr Siebeck, 1921.

von Wright, Georg Henrik. "Ludwig Wittgenstein: A Biographical Sketch." *The Philosophical Review* 64, no. 4 (October 1955): 527–45.

———. *Ludwig Wittgenstein: A Memoir, with a Biographical Sketch*. Oxford: Oxford University Press, 1962.

Vos, Geerhardus. *Biblical Theology*. 3rd ed. Edinburgh: Banner of Truth, 2014.

———. "Doctrine of the Covenant in Reformed Theology." In *Redemptive History and Biblical Interpretation: The Shorter Writings of Geerhardus Vos*, edited by Richard B. Gaffin, 234–70. Phillipsburg, NJ: P&R Publishing, 2001.

———. *Grace and Glory*. Rev. ed. Edinburgh: Banner of Truth, 2020.

———. *Pauline Eschatology*. Princeton: Princeton University Press, 1930.

———. *Redemptive History and Biblical Interpretation: Shorter Writings of Geerhardus Vos*. Edited by Richard B. Gaffin. Phillipsburg, NJ: P&R Publishing, 2001.

———. *Reformed Dogmatics*. 5 vols. Bellingham, WA: Lexham Press, 2012–2016.

———. *The Self Disclosure of Jesus*. New York: George H. Doran, 1926.

———. *The Teaching of the Epistle to the Hebrews*. Nutley, NJ: Presbyterian and Reformed, 1977.

———. *The Teaching of Jesus Concerning the Kingdom of God and the Church*. New York: American Tract Society, 1903.

Vos, Johannes G. *The Scottish Covenanters*. Pittsburgh: Crown & Covenant, 1995.

———. *The Westminster Larger Catechism: A Commentary*. Phillipsburg, NJ: P&R Publishing, 2002.

Wagner, C. Peter. *The Third Wave of the Holy Spirit*. 4th ed. Ann Arbor, MI: Vine Books, 1988.

Walchenbach, John R. "John Calvin as Biblical Commentator." PhD diss., University of Pittsburgh, 1974.

Walker, Williston. *A History of the Christian Church*. New York: Scribner's Sons, 1959.

———. *John Calvin: The Organizer of Reformed Protestantism*. New York: Putnam, 1906.

Walker, Williston, Richard A. Norris, David W. Lotz, and Robert T. Handy. *A History of the Christian Church*. 4th ed. New York: Scribner's Sons, 1985.

Wallace, Ronald S. *Calvin, Geneva & the Reformation: A Study of Calvin as Social Reformer, Churchman, Pastor and Theologian*. Grand Rapids: Baker, 1988.

———. *Calvin's Doctrine of the Christian Life*. Edinburgh: Oliver & Boyd, 1959.

———. *Calvin's Doctrine of the Word and Sacrament*. Eugene, OR: Wipf & Stock, 1997.

Ward, Rowland S. *God and Adam: Reformed Theology and the Creation Covenant*. Melbourne: New Melbourne Press, 2003.

Ware, Bruce A. *Father, Son, and Holy Spirit: Relationships, Roles, and Relevance*. Wheaton, IL: Crossway, 2005.

Warfield, Benjamin B. "A Brief and Non-Technical Statement of the Reformed Faith." In *Selected Shorter Writings of Benjamin B. Warfield*, edited by John E. Meeter, 1:407–10. 2 vols. Phillipsburg, NJ: P&R Publishing, 1970.

———. *Calvin and Augustine*. Philadelphia: Presbyterian and Reformed, 1956.

———. *Calvin and Calvinism*. New York: Oxford University Press, 1931.

———. "Christian Supernaturalism." In *Studies in Theology* , by Benjamin B. Warfield, 25–48. New York: Oxford University Press, 1932.

———. "The Literary History of Calvin's Institutes." *The Presbyterian and Reformed Review* 10 (April 1899): 193–219.

———. *The Person and Work of Christ*. Phillipsburg, NJ: Presbyterian and Reformed, 1989.

———. *Studies in Tertullian and Augustine*. Whitefish, MT: Kessinger, 2010.

———. *The Westminster Assembly and Its Work*. New York: Oxford University Press, 1931.

Warraq, Ibn. *Why I Am Not a Muslim*. Amherst, NY: Prometheus Books, 1994.

Waters, Guy Prentiss. *Justification and the New Perspectives on Paul: A Review and Response*. Phillipsburg, NJ: P&R Publishing, 2004.

Webb, Eugene. *Philosophers of Consciousness*. Seattle: University of Washington Press, 1988.

Webb, O. K. "The Political Thought of Samuel Rutherford." PhD diss., Duke University, 1964.

Weber, Hans Emil. *Reformation, Orthodoxie und Rationalismus.* 2 vols. Leipzig: Gutersloh, 1937–1951.

Weiß, J. *Das Urchristentum.* Göttingen: Vandenhoeck & Ruprecht, 1917.

Welch, Edward T., and Gary Shogren. *Addictive Behavior.* Grand Rapids: Baker, 1995.

Wells, David F. *No Place for Truth.* Grand Rapids: Eerdmans, 1993.

————. "On Being Framed." *Westminster Theological Journal* 59, no. 2 (Fall 1997): 293–300.

Wendel, François. *Calvin: The Origins and Development of His Religious Thought.* London: Collins, 1974.

————. "Le Commentaire sur le De Clementia de Seneque." In *Calvin et l'humanisme,* 37–62. Paris: Presses Universitaires de France, 1976.

Werner, M. *Die Entstehung des christlichen Dogmas.* Bern/Leipzig: Haupt, 1941. 2. Aufl., 1953.

Wessel, Leonhard P. *G. E. Lessing's Theology: A Reinterpretation.* The Hague: Mouton, 1977.

Westerholm, Stephen. *Perspectives Old and New on Paul: The "Lutheran" Paul and His Critics.* Grand Rapids: Eerdmans, 2004.

Whitehead, Alfred North. *Adventures of Ideas.* New York: New American, 1933.

————. *The Aims of Education and Other Essays.* New York: Macmillan, 1929.

————. *The Concept of Nature.* Cambridge: Cambridge University Press, 1920.

————. *Essays in Science and Philosophy.* New York: Philosophical Library, 1947.

————. *The Function of Reason.* Princeton: Princeton University Press, 1929.

————. *Modes of Thought.* New York: Macmillan, 1938.

————. *Nature and Life.* Chicago: University of Chicago Press, 1934.

————. *The Principle of Relativity with Applications to Physical Science.* Cambridge: Cambridge University Press, 1922.

————. *Process and Reality: An Essay in Cosmology.* New York: Macmillan, 1929.

————. *Religion in the Making.* New York: Macmillan, 1926.

————. *Science and the Modern World.* Rev. ed. Cambridge: Cambridge University Press, 1932.

———. *Symbolism, Its Meaning and Effect*. New York: Macmillan, 1927.

———. *A Treatise on Universal Algebra*. Cambridge: Cambridge University Press, 1898.

Whitla, David G. *Archibald Johnston of Warriston, the National Covenant, and the Formation of British Puritanism (1611–38)*. St Andrews Studies in Reformation History. Leiden: Brill Academic, forthcoming.

———. "Lord of History." *RPTJ* 6, no. 2 (Spring 2020): 4–9.

Wiles, Maurice, and Mark Santer, eds. *Documents in Early Christian Thought*. Cambridge: Cambridge University Press, 1975.

Willard, Dallas. *The Divine Conspiracy: Rediscovering Our Hidden Life in God*. London: William Collins, 2014.

Williams, George Hunston. *The Radical Reformation*. Philadelphia: Westminster Press, 1962.

Williams, Stephen. "Observations on the Future of System." In *Always Reforming: Explorations in Systematic Theology*, edited by A. T. B. McGowan, 41–66. Leicester, England: Apollos, 2006.

Willis, E. David. "The Social Context of the 1536 Edition of Calvin's *Institutes*." In *In Honor of John Calvin, 1509–64, Papers from the 1986 International Calvin Symposium, McGill University*, edited by E. J. Furcha, 133–53. Montreal: McGill University Press, 1987.

Wilson, Edward O. *Consilience: The Unity of Knowledge*. New York: Knopf, 1998.

Windisch, Hans. *Handbuch zum Neuen Testament, Ergänzungsband Die Apostolischen Väter*. Vol. 3, Der Barnabasbrief. Tübingen: Mohr Siebeck, 1920.

Witsius, Hermann. *The Economy of the Covenants*. 2 vols. Escondido, CA: The den Dulk Christian Foundation, 1990.

———. *Sacred Dissertations on the Apostles' Creed*. 2 vols. Grand Rapids: Reformation Heritage Books, 2012.

Wittgenstein, Ludwig. *Tractatus Logico-Philosophicus*. New York: Harcourt, Brace & Company, 1922. Reprint, New York: Cosimo Classics, 2010.

Wolfe, Hans Heinrich. *Die Einheit des Bundes: Das Verhältnis von Alten und Neuen Testament bei Calvin*. Neukirchen-Vluyn: Neukirchener Verlag, 1958.

Wolfson, H. A. *The Philosophy of the Church Fathers*. Cambridge: Harvard University Press, 1956.

Wolterstorff, Nicholas. "God Everlasting." In *Philosophy of Religion: A Guide and Anthology*, edited by Brian Davies, 485–504. Oxford: Oxford University Press, 2000.

———. *Reason within the Bounds of Religion*. Grand Rapids: Eerdmans, 1976.

Woo, B. Hoon. "The Understanding of Gisbertus Voetius and René Descartes on the Relationship of Faith and Reason, and Theology and Philosophy." *Westminster Theological Journal* 75, no. 1 (Spring 2013): 45–63.

Woodbridge, John D. *Biblical Authority: A Critique of the Rogers/McKim Proposal*. Grand Rapids: Zondervan, 1982.

Woodbridge, John D., and Frank A. James III. *Church History*. Grand Rapids: Zondervan, 2013.

Woollcombe, K. J. "The Biblical Origins and Patristic Development of Theology." In *Essays on Typology*, edited by K. J. Woollcombe and G. W. H. Lampe, 39–75. Studies in Biblical Theology 22. Naperville, IL: Allenson, 1957.

Woolley, Paul. *The Significance of J. Gresham Machen Today*. Nutley, NJ: Presbyterian and Reformed, 1977.

———. "What Is a Creed For? Some Answers from History." In *Scripture and Confession*, edited by John Skilton, 95–124. Nutley, NJ: Presbyterian and Reformed, 1973.

Wright, David F., ed. *Essays in Evangelical Social Ethics*. Exeter: Paternoster, 1979.

———. *Martin Bucer: Reforming Church and Community*. Cambridge: Cambridge University Press, 1994.

Wright, N. T. *Jesus and the Victory of God*. Minneapolis: Fortress, 1996.

———. *Justification, God's Plan & Paul's Vision*. Downers Grove, IL: IVP Academic, 2009.

———. *The New Testament and the People of God*. Minneapolis: Fortress, 1992.

———. *Paul: In Fresh Perspective*. Minneapolis: Fortress, 2005.

———. *The Resurrection of the Son of God*. Vol. 3, *Christian Origins and the Question of God*. Minneapolis: Fortress, 2003.

———. *Romans*. In *Acts, Introduction to Epistolary Literature, Romans, 1 Corinthians*, by Robert W. Wall, J. Paul Sampley, and N. T. Wright. Vol. 10, *The New Interpreter's Bible*. Nashville: Abingdon Press, 2002.

———. *What Saint Paul Really Said*. Grand Rapids: Eerdmans, 1997.

Young, Edward J. *An Introduction to the Old Testament*. Grand Rapids: Eerdmans, 1964.

Young, Frances. *Biblical Exegesis and the Formation of Christian Culture*. Peabody, MA: Hendrickson Publishers, 2002.

———. *From Nicaea to Chalcedon*. Philadelphia: Fortress, 1983.

Young, Warren C. *A Christian Approach to Philosophy*. Grand Rapids: Baker, 1969.

Zaka, Anees, and Diane Coleman. *The Truth about Islam*. Phillipsburg, NJ: P&R Publishing, 2004.

Zaspel, Fred. *The Theology of B. B. Warfield: A Systematic Summary*. Wheaton, IL: Crossway, 2010.

Zeller, Eduard. *Outlines of the History of Greek Philosophy*. 13th ed. New York: Meridian Books, 1960.

Zwingli, Ulrich. "Of the Clarity and Certainty of the Word of God." In *Zwingli and Bullinger*, translated by G. W. Bromiley, 49–95. Philadelphia: Westminster Press, 1953.

———. *Commentary on True and False Religion*. Reprint, New York: Labyrinth Press, 1981.

———. *Huldreich Zwinglis Sämtliche Werke*. Hg. Emil Egli und Georg Finsler. *Corpus Reformatorum* 88–89. Berlin/Leipzig/Zurich: M. Heinsius Nachfolger, 1904.

———. *Ulrich Zwingli: Early Writings*. Edited by Samuel Macauley Jackson. 1912. Reprint, London: Labyrinth Press, 1987.

———. *On Providence and Other Essays*. Reprint, London: Labyrinth Press, 1983.

Index of Scripture

Index of Subjects and Names

P&R Academic

Reliable. Relevant. Reformed.

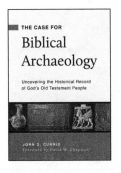

"I strongly recommend this."
—H. Wayne House

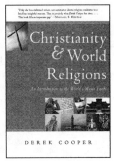

"Fills an important gap."
—Michael Horton

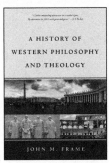

"[An] outstanding achievement."
—J. I. Packer

"Refreshingly insightful,
profoundly biblical."
—Wayne Grudem

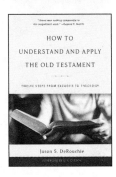

"[A] magnificent work."
—Eugene H. Merrill

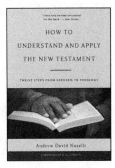

"Accessible and user-friendly."
—Timothy Keller